# Interactive Financial Calculators

**Regular IRA Calculator**

How can contributing to a regular IRA help you in your retirement?

**Amortizing Loan Calculator**

Enter your desired payment and let us calculate your loan amount, or enter in the loan amount and we will calculate your monthly payment!

**Enhanced Loan Calculator**

Use the slider controls to instantly change your monthly payment, loan amount, interest rate, or term.

**Credit Card Payoff**

Use this calculator to see what it will take to pay off your credit card balance and what you can change to meet your repayment goals.

**Rolldown Your Credit Card Debt!**

The Credit Card Rolldown Calculator applies two simple principles to paying off your credit card debt.

**Auto Loans**

Find out how much automobile you can buy based on your monthly payment, or find out your loan payment based on your purchase price!

**Auto Loan vs. Home Equity Loan**

Lower interest rates and a tax deduction are good reasons to take a look at a home equity loan to finance your next automobile purchase.

**Lease vs. Buy**

Should you lease your next automobile or finance it? Find out with this calculator!

**Mortgage Calculator**

Use this calculator to determine your monthly payment and amortization schedule.

**Bi-weekly Payment Calculator**

Using bi-weekly payments can accelerate your mortgage payoff and save you thousands in interest. Use this calculator to compare a typical monthly payment schedule to an accelerated bi-weekly payment.

**Refinance Breakeven**

Should you refinance your mortgage? Use this calculator to find out!

**Rent vs. Buy**

Are you better off buying your home, or should you continue to rent?

**Life Insurance Calculator**

How much life insurance do you really need? Find out here!

*Students will need their access code packaged with the Personal Finance Workbook.*

# Personal Finance

## Turning Money into Wealth

### Third Edition

# PRENTICE HALL FINANCE SERIES

**Personal Finance**
**Keown,** *Personal Finance: Turning Money into Wealth*
**Trivoli,** *Personal Portfolio Management: Fundamentals and Strategies*
**Winger/Frasca,** *Personal Finance, An Integrated Planning Approach*

**Investments**
**Alexander/Sharpe/Bailey,** *Fundamentals of Investments*
**Fabozzi,** *Investment Management*
**Fischer/Jordan,** *Security Analysis and Portfolio Management*
**Haugen,** *Modern Investment Theory*
**Haugen,** *The New Finance*
**Haugen,** *The Beast on Wall Street*
**Haugen,** *The Inefficient Stock Market*
**Sharpe/Alexander/Bailey,** *Investments*
**Taggart,** *Quantitative Analysis for Investment Management*
**Winger/Frasca,** *Investments*

**Portfolio Analysis**
**Alexander/Sharpe/Bailey,** *Fundamentals of Investments*
**Fischer/Jordan,** *Security Analysis and Portfolio Management*
**Haugen,** *Modern Investment Theory*
**Sharpe/Alexander/Bailey,** *Investments*

**Options/Futures/Derivatives**
**Hull,** *Introduction to Futures and Options Markets*
**Hull,** *Options, Futures, and Other Derivatives*

**Risk Management/Financial Engineering**
**Hull,** *Financial Engineering and Risk Management*
**Mason/Merton/Perold/Tufano,** *Cases in Financial Engineering*

**Fixed Income Securities**
**Van Horne,** *Financial Market, Rates and Flows*
**Handa,** *FinCoach: Fixed Income* (software)

**Bond Markets**
**Fabozzi,** *Bond Markets, Analysis and Strategies*
**Van Horne,** *Financial Market, Rates and Flows*

**Capital Markets**
**Fabozzi/Modigliani,** *Capital Markets: Institutions and Instruments*
**Van Horne,** *Financial Market, Rates and Flows*

**Corporate Finance, Survey of Finance, & Financial Economics**
**Bodie/Merton,** *Finance*
**Emery/Finnerty/Stowe,** *Principles of Financial Management*
**Emery/Finnerty,** *Corporate Financial Management*
**Gallagher/Andrew,** *Financial Management: Principles and Practices*
**Haugen,** *The New Finance: The Case Against Efficient Markets*
**Keown/Martin/Petty/Scott,** *Basic Financial Management*
**Keown/Martin/Petty/Scott,** *Foundations of Finance: The Logic and Practice of Financial Management*

**Shapiro/Balbirer, Modern Corporate Finance:** *A Multidisciplinary Approach to Value Creation*
**Van Horne,** *Financial Management and Policy*
**Van Horne/Wachowicz,** *Fundamentals of Financial Management*

**International Finance**
**Baker,** *International Finance: Management Markets, and Institutions*
**Grabbe,** *International Financial Markets*
**Rivera-Batiz/Rivera-Batiz,** *International Finance and Open Economy Macroeconomics*

**Capital Budgeting**
**Aggarwal,** *Capital Budgeting Under Uncertainty*
**Bierman/Smidt,** *The Capital Budgeting Decision*

**Mergers/Acquisitions/Takeovers**
**Hill/Sartoris,** *Short Term Financial Management*
**Weston/Chung/Siu,** *Takeovers, Restructuring and Corporate Governance*

**Short-Term Finance**
**Hill/Sartoris,** *Short Term Financial Management*

**Taxes**
**Scholes/Wolfson,** *Taxes and Business Strategy: A Global Planning Approach*

**Insurance**
**Black/Skipper,** *Life and Health Insurance*
**Dorfman,** *Introduction to Risk Management and Insurance*
**Rejda,** *Social Insurance and Economic Security*

**Financial Markets and Institutions**
**Arshadi/Karels,** *Modern Financial Intermediaries and Markets*
**Dietrich,** *Financial Services and Financial Institutions*
**Fabozzi//Modigliani/Ferri/Jones,** *Foundations of Financial Markets and Institutions*
**Kaufman,** *The U.S. Financial Systems*
**Van Horne,** *Financial Market Rates and Flows*

**Commercial Banking**
**Arshadi/Karels,** *Modern Financial Intermediaries and Markets*
**Dietrich,** *Financial Services and Financial Institutions*
**Sinkey,** *Commercial Bank Financial Management*

**Entrepreneurial Finance**
**Adelman/Marks,** *Entrepreneurial Finance*
**Vaughn,** *Financial Planning for the Entrepreneur*

**Cases in Finance**
**May/May/Andrew,** *Effective Writing: A Handbook for Finance People*

**Financial Statement Analysis**
**Fraser/Ormiston,** *Understanding Financial Statements*

**Finance Center**
*For downloadable supplements and much more . . . visit us at*
**www.prenhall.com/financecenter**

# Personal Finance

## Turning Money into Wealth

### Third Edition

## Arthur J. Keown

*Virginia Polytechnic Institute
and State University
R.B. Pamplin Professor of Finance*

Prentice Hall
*Upper Saddle River, New Jersey 07458*

Library of Congress Cataloging-in-Publication Data

Keown, Arthur J.
    Personal finance: turning money into wealth / Arthur J. Keown.—3rd ed.
        p. cm.—(Prentice Hall finance series)
    Includes bibliographical references and index.
    ISBN 0-13-100608-8
    1. Finance, Personal. 2. Investments. I. Title. II. Series.

HG179 .K47 2003
332.024--dc21

2002193010

AVP/Executive Editor: *Mickey Cox*
Editor-in-Chief: *P.J. Boardman*
Managing Editor (Editorial): *Gladys Soto*
Assistant Editor: *Beth Romph*
Editorial Assistant: *Francesca Calogero*
Media Project Manager: *Victoria Anderson*
AVP/Executive Marketing Manager: *Kathleen Mclellan*
Marketing Assistant: *Christopher Bath*
Managing Editor (Production): *Cynthia Regan*
Production Editor: *Carol Samet*
Production Assistant: *Joe DeProspero*
Permissions Coordinator: *Suzanne Grappi*
Associate Director, Manufacturing: *Vincent Scelta*
Production Manager: *Arnold Vila*

Manufacturing Buyer: *Arnold Vila*
Design Manager: *Maria Lange*
Art Director: *Janet Slowik*
Interior Design: *Jill Little*
Cover Design: *Jill Little*
Cover Illustrator: *William Duke*
Cover Photo: *Kevin Fleming/Corbis*
Illustrator (Interior): *Accurate Art*
Manager, Multimedia Production: *Christy Mahon*
Composition: *Progressive Information Technologies*
Full-Service Project Management: *Progressive Publishing Alternatives*
Printer/Binder: *RR Donnelley*

Photo credits: Page 1, Getty Images Inc.–Hulton Archive Photos; page 29, Steven Sands/Corbis/Sygma; page 59, New Line Cinema/courtesy K. Wright/The Neal Peters Collection; page 89, Fox/courtesy The Neal Peters Collection; page 137, Henry Diltz/Corbis; page 167, Rafael Macia/Photo Researchers, Inc.; page 195, Corbis; page 225, Hollywood Pictures/courtesy Suzanne Tenner/The Neal Peters Collection; page 273, AP/Wide World Photos; page 321, Bob Riha/Getty Images, Inc.–Liaison; page 349, Jamie Squire/Getty Images, Inc.–Allsport Photography; page 383, Chabruken/Getty Images, Inc.–Taxi; page 415, AP/Wide World Photos; page 447, Movie Still Archives; page 479, Lisa Rose/Globe Photos, Inc.; page 513, AP/Wide World Photos; page 547, AP/Wide World Photos; page 575, Globe Photos, Inc.

Pearson Education LTD.
Pearson Education Australia PTY, Limited
Pearson Education Singapore, Pte. Ltd
Pearson Education North Asia Ltd
Pearson Education, Canada, Ltd
Pearson Educación de Mexico, S.A. de C.V.
Pearson Education—Japan
Pearson Education Malaysia, Pte. Ltd.

10 9 8 7 6 5 4 3 2 1
ISBN 0-13-100608-8

*To Barb, my partner and my love—*
*for showing me happiness that money can't buy*

# About the Author

Arthur J. Keown is the R. B. Pamplin Professor of Finance at Virginia Polytechnic Institute and State University. He received his bachelor's degree from Ohio Wesleyan University, his M.B.A. from the University of Michigan, and his doctorate from Indiana University. An award-winning teacher, he is a member of the Academy of Teaching Excellence at Virginia Tech, has received five Certificates of Teaching Excellence, the W. E. Wine Award for Teaching Excellence, and the Alumni Teaching Excellence Award, and in 1999 received the Outstanding Faculty Award from the State of Virginia. Professor Keown is widely published in academic journals. His work has appeared in *The Journal of Finance*, the *Journal of Financial Economics*, the *Journal of Financial and Quantitative Analysis*, *The Journal of Financial Research*, the *Journal of Banking and Finance*, *Financial Management*, the *Journal of Portfolio Management*, and many others. Two of his books are widely used in college finance classes all over the country—*Financial Management* and *Foundations of Finance: The Logic and Practice of Financial Management*. Professor Keown is Fellow of the Decision Sciences Institute and former head of the finance department. In addition, he has served as the co-editor of *The Journal of Financial Research*, and is presently the co-editor of the Financial Management Association's Survey and Synthesis Series. He was recently inducted into Ohio Wesleyan's Athletic Hall of Fame and lives with his wife and two children in Blacksburg, Virginia, where he collects original art from *Mad Magazine*.

# Brief Contents

# Contents

## Part 3 ▮ Protecting Yourself with Insurance

## Part 4 ▌ Managing Your Investments

# Preface

The response to the second edition of *Personal Finance: Turning Money into Wealth* was overwhelming. With its success comes an even greater responsibility to deliver the finest possible text and supplementary package in the third edition. To do this, we have taken a two-pronged approach: refinements based upon users' comments and focus groups, and value-added innovations to maintain our leadership in the field.

*Personal Finance: Turning Money into Wealth* introduces the student to the concepts, tools, and applications of personal finance and investments. It assumes little or no prior knowledge of the subject matter and focuses on helping the student understand the process of financial planning and the logic that drives it. The writing style is as accessible to students as possible: it is deliberately colloquial, interesting, and fluid so that students will want to read the book. But an accessible writing style does not mean any compromise with terminology: all technical terms are fully defined at introduction.

For many students, this course is their initial and only exposure to personal finance, so the material must be presented in a way that leaves a lasting impression. Tools, techniques, and equations are easily forgotten, but the logic and fundamental principles that drive their use, once understood, will stay. These principles become part of students' "financial personality" and are available to help them deal effectively with an ever-changing financial environment. For this reason, the presentation is centered around 15 fundamental principles of personal finance that are introduced in Chapter 1 and then reappear in every chapter throughout the book.

Tying the topics of personal finance together through the use of basic principles is a radical change from the present generation of personal finance texts. Other texts tend to be descriptive in nature, emphasizing lists and procedures. The Chapters appear to be bound together only by the book's binding. The purpose of this text is to educate the student in the discipline of personal finance, not just the procedures, because it is only through an understanding of the principles that students can successfully make and carry out a plan for their financial future.

## New to the Third Edition

**Chapter 18: Fitting the Pieces Together**  This chapter has been re-crafted so that the student can easily walk away from this course with the ability to create their own financial plan. In addition, this edition places increased emphasis on the Internet, with exercises and problems on the book's Web page that lead the student to some of the best and most useful sites around. These exercises and problems are placed on the Web rather than in the book to allow their addresses to be continuously updated. In addition, this edition introduces 25 Web-based calculators covering a wide range of personal finance issues dedicated to this edition.

## Continuing Features

**Principles**   The 15 principles have been revised to make them more intuitive and easier to grasp. They are introduced in Chapter 1 and appear throughout the text, with a distinctive icon in the margin at the point of mention.

**Chapter Opening Vignettes**   To make the book as interesting as possible, opening vignettes feature the likes of Elvis, Homer Simpson, Meatloaf, Elton John, Tina Turner, Denzel Washington, Sarah Jessica Parker, Kevin Bacon, Johnny Depp, and Dr. Evil from the Austin Powers movies.

**Learning Objectives**   Each chapter opens with a set of action-oriented learning objectives. As these objectives are covered in the text, an identifying icon appears in the margin.

**Margin Glossary**   Key terms are boldfaced in the text and defined in the margin when they first appear, allowing students to find and understand technical terms as they go along.

**23 "In the News" Boxes featuring Jonathan Clements**   The "In The News" boxes with excerpts from *Kiplinger's Personal Finance Magazine* and *The Wall Street Journal* continue, but in this edition there are 23 boxes featuring the work of Jonathan Clements, the famous *Wall Street Journal* reporter.

**Integrated Coverage of the Economic Growth and Tax Relief Reconciliation Act of 2001 (commonly called the Tax Relief Act of 2001)**   The impact of the Tax Relief Act of 2001 has been totally integrated throughout the text.

**Totally Updated Content**   The content has been totally updated to reflect all that has happened in the economy and in personal finance. For example, the dramatic drop in technology stocks, the impact of the tragedy of September 11th on personal finance, and the scandal dealing with analysts' reports and stock market advice are covered.

**Web-Based Calculators**   With this edition, we have included 25 Web-based calculators aimed at bringing the material alive in a way that today's student can easily relate to. Many of these calculators include interactive slider controls allowing you to instantly see the impact of a change in one of the variables. These Web-based calculators include:

| | |
|---|---|
| **Home Budget Analyzer!** | Analyze your budget, see where your money goes, and find out where you can improve! |
| **Checkbook Balancer** | Balance your checkbook with this quick and easy calculator. |
| **Savings Calculator** | Find out how consistent investments over a number of years can be an effective strategy to accumulate wealth. |
| **Compound Interest** | This calculator demonstrates how compounding can affect your savings. |
| **Benefit of Spending Less** | Reducing your spending can be worth more than you might think. Use this calculator to see just how much your budget reductions may be worth. |
| **Lunch Savings Calculator** | Use this calculator to see how a simple change such as bringing a bagged lunch to work can really add up. |

| | |
|---|---|
| **Net Worth Calculator** | This calculator helps you determine your net worth. It also estimates how your net worth could grow (or shrink!) over the next ten years. |
| **Retirement Planner** | Quickly determine if your retirement plan is on track—and learn how to keep it there. |
| **Retirement Shortfall Calculator** | This calculator helps you determine your projected short fall or surplus at retirement. If your results project a short fall, you might need to save more, earn a better rate of return, or possibly delay your retirement. |
| **401(k) Savings** | A 401(k) can be one of your best tools for creating a secure retirement. |
| **Calculator** | Use this calculator to see why this is a retirement savings plan you can not afford to pass up. |
| **Roth vs. Traditional IRA** | Which is better: a Roth IRA or a traditional IRA? |
| **Roth IRA Calculator** | Use this calculator to compare the Roth IRA to an ordinary taxable investment. |
| **Regular IRA Calculator** | How can contributing to a regular IRA help you in your retirement? |
| **Amortizing Loan Calculator** | Enter your desired payment—and let us calculate your loan amount or enter in the loan amount and we will calculate your monthly payment! |
| **Enhanced Loan Calculator** | Use the slider controls to instantly change your monthly payment, loan amount, interest rate, or term. |
| **Credit Card Payoff** | Use this calculator to see what it will take to pay off your credit card balance, and what you can change to meet your repayment goals. |
| **Rolldown Your Credit Card Debt!** | The Credit Card Rolldown Calculator applies two simple principles to paying off your credit card debt. |
| **Auto Loans** | Find out how much automobile you can buy based on your monthly payment, or find out your loan payment based on your purchase price! |
| **Auto Loan vs. Home Equity Loan** | Lower interest rates and a tax deduction are good reasons to take a look at a home equity loan to finance your next automobile purchase. |
| **Lease vs. Buy** | Should you lease your next automobile or finance it? Find out with this calculator! |
| **Mortgage Calculator** | Use this calculator to determine your monthly payment and amortization schedule. |
| **Bi-weekly Payment Calculator** | Using bi-weekly payments can accelerate your mortgage payoff and save you thousands in interest. Use this calculator to compare a typical monthly payment schedule to an accelerated bi-weekly payment. |

| Refinance Breakeven | Should you refinance your mortgage? Use this calculator to find out! |
| Rent vs. Buy | Are you better off buying your home, or should you continue to rent? |
| Life Insurance Calculator | How much life insurance do you really need? Find out here! |

**Checklists**   This edition has proactive checklists that provide the student with easy to follow advice. This feature is also intended as a learning tool: checklists identify areas of concern and questions to be asked when buying a car, getting insurance, investing in mutual funds, and performing other personal finance tasks.

**Personal Finance Workbook**   A separate workbook containing worksheets that accompany the text is included free of charge with each new copy of the book. The worksheets provide a step-by-step analysis of many of the personal finance decisions examined in the book. They can be used for homework assignments or to guide students through actual decisions. The workbook includes a section on how to use a financial calculator. Text references to the worksheets appear in the margin at the appropriate point.

**Downloadable Excel Versions of Personal Finance Worksheets**   Many of the personal finance worksheets are also downloadable in Excel from the *Personal Finance Navigator* site. Students just enter basic information, and the calculations are done for them directly on the spreadsheet.

**Stop and Think**   These short boxes provide the student with insights as to what the material actually means—implications and the big picture.

**Finance Matters (previously called Just Do It!)**   Boxes at the end of each chapter written by Marcy Furney, CFP, provide checklists of things to do—in effect, free advice from a certified financial planner.

**Mini Cases**   Each chapter closes with a set of two mini cases that provide students with real-life problems that tie together the chapter topics and need a practical financial decision.

**Continuing Case—Cory and Tisha Dumont**   At the end of each part in the book, a continuing case provides an opportunity to synthesize and integrate the many different financial concepts presented in the book. It gives the student a chance to construct financial statements, analyze a changing financial situation, calculate taxes, measure risk exposure, and develop a financial plan.

**Personal Finance Navigator Web Site**   (www.prenhall.com/keown) Developed specifically for this text, this activity-based site guides students to the most current financial information. The activities and source data are organized to follow the chapter sequence. Listings of links to other sites, articles, and exercises are all aimed at getting the student financially organized and are continuously monitored by the author to ensure that they are both current and accurate. Click onto Internet sites and articles of interest to help plan college finance requirements, make a lease versus purchase decision on a new car, get job hunting and investment information, understand tax changes, find out where to get the best loan deal, and much more.

**Expanded Internet Exercises for Student Assignments**   One feature of the first edition that was extremely popular were the Internet Exercises provided on the

Personal Finance Navigator site. These exercises have been revised and expanded for this edition. The assignments introduce the students to some of the more valuable personal finance sites on the Internet and allow them to see not only how the sites work, but also how helpful the information can be. All the student needs is a connection to the Internet and the ability to point and click and follow instructions.

## Content Update

In response to continuing developments in personal finance and reviewer comments, the text has been revised and updated. Some of these changes include:

**Chapter 1**   This chapter was updated and revised reflecting the tech stock implosion and the growing importance of the Internet in personal finance decisions. In addition, the impact of 911 on personal finance was also explored.

**Chapter 2**   Chapter 2 includes a new introduction featuring the contrast between Sarah Jessica Parker's character Carrie Bradshaw in HBO's *Sex in the City*, and Sarah's approach to financial planning in real life. In addition, this chapter has been updated reflecting the growing importance of the Internet on personal finance decisions.

**Chapter 3**   The time value of money chapter has been simplified and streamlined so that it is accessible to any student regardless of his or her math skills. The emphasis is on understanding the power of compounding and the importance of starting a saving program early in life.

**Chapter 4**   This chapter was thoroughly updated to reflect the changes resulting from the passage of the Economic Growth and Tax Relief Reconciliation Act of 2001 (commonly called the Tax Relief Act of 2001). In addition, a new introduction featuring the Simpson's has been added. Finally, a new section on E-filing is now included.

**Chapter 5**   Includes a new introduction based on Kevin Bacon and the "Six Degrees of Kevin Bacon" game as featured in the recent Visa Checkcard TV ads. In addition, the effect of the Internet on cash management has been integrated throughout this chapter.

**Chapter 6**   The coverage of credit cards has been updated and revised, with increased attention given to the problems students can get into using credit cards.

**Chapter 7**   Opens up with a new introduction featuring the consumer debt problems recently faced by Elton John, demonstrating that it is not how much you make that determines whether or not you will have consumer debt problems, but how you manage your spending habits and debt management. The chapter also includes an updated discussion of payday loans.

**Chapter 8**   This chapter has been thoroughly revised and updated, with an emphasis on using the Internet to help in making more knowledgeable major financial decisions.

**Chapter 9**   Opens up with a new introduction featuring Denzel Washington in *John Q*, focusing on the health care insurance problems facing many Americans. The use of the Internet in purchasing insurance has also been added.

**Chapter 10**   This chapter has been totally updated and revised to reflect changes in property and liability insurance.

**Chapter 11** This chapter has been updated to reflecting the dramatic changes in the stock market, particularly the implosion of Tech and dot.com stocks, through the end of 2001. In addition, two new Jonathan Clements' "In the News" boxes have been added, titled, "Investors' Worst Enemy: Themselves" and "Five Reasons Diversification Works."

**Chapter 12** This chapter has been updated to reflect changes in the stock market through the end of 2001. In addition, two new Jonathan Clements' "In the News" boxes titled, "How the Stock Drop Has Schooled Me" and "Don't Be Shy: Emerging Markets are OK" have been added.

**Chapter 13** Again, this chapter has been updated to include the impact of the implosion of Tech and dot.com stocks. In addition, two new "In the News" boxes have been added, one by Jonathan Clements, titled, "Don't Ignore Luck's Role in Stock Picks" and "Analysts' Reports: Don't Believe the Hype." The latter deals with the growing scandal on Wall Street involving the worth of analyst's reports.

**Chapter 14** Along with updating the bond chapter, two new "In the News" boxes by Jonathan Clements were added, one titled, "Need a Lift? Inflation Bonds Are Handy," and the other titled, "Bond Fans: Try a New Chicken Dance," which deals with the need for diversification in bond investing.

**Chapter 15** In addition to updating the chapter and adding additional material dealing with mutual fund information available on the Internet, two new "In the News" boxes by Jonathan Clements were added—the first titled, "Why Indexing Is a Winning Strategy" and the second titled, "Why Investors Cling to Managed Funds."

**Chapter 16** The retirement planning chapter has been updated and revised to reflect the recent tax changes. In addition, a new section has been added dealing with saving for college. This chapter also includes two "In the News" boxes by Jonathan Clements, titled, "A Must-Do Checklist for Retirement" and "Golden Years Carry a Hefty Pricetag."

**Chapter 17** The estate planning chapter now opens with a new introduction featuring George Harrison. This chapter has been completely revised and updated to reflect the tax changes resulting from the Tax Relief Act of 2001. In addition, two new "In the News" boxes by Jonathan Clements titled, "Ways to Leave a Good Impression" and "Estate-Planning Pitfalls to Avoid" have been added.

**Chapter 18** This chapter has been recrafted to tie together many of the topics introduced earlier in the book and to provide the student with an action plan for immediate action. In so doing, two new "In the News" boxes by Jonathan Clements titled, "Four Ways to Get Your Finances in Shape" and "Some Insights to Keep You Afloat" have been added.

## Supplements

The following supplements are available with *Personal Finance: Turning Money into Wealth,* third edition:

**For the Instructor**

**Instructor's Manual** The Instructor's Manual was written by Ruth Lytton of Virginia Tech and Derek Klock of Virginia Tech. This manual provides chapter summaries along with solutions to the questions, problems, and cases that appear in each chapter.

**Test Item File**   The test item file was prepared by Frederick H. Mull of Fort Lewis College. This Test Item File is made up of approximately twenty-five true/false questions, thirty-five multiple-choice questions, and ten short answer/essay questions per chapter. The questions vary in degree of difficulty while covering all pertinent topics.

**Prentice Hall Test Manager**   The test bank is designed for use with the Prentice Hall Test Manager, a computerized package that allows instructors to custom design, save, and generate classroom tests.

**For the Student**   **Personal Finance Navigator** *(www.prenhall.com/keown)*, is an activity-based Web site that offers students numerous exercises and activities for personal analysis and financial planning. This companion site for the book links students to the most current financial information around. The Navigator is accessed using the pass code included with each copy of *Personal Finance, Third Edition*, and includes the following features:

- ✓ Companion Web site **Practice Quizzes** offer students another opportunity to sharpen their problem-solving skills and to assess their understanding of the text material. Completely revised and updated by Ruth Lytton, this online study guide contains true/false, multiple-choice, and short answer quizzes for each chapter, all with a built-in grading feature and coaching comments for incorrect answers.

- ✓ **Internet Exercises** by Frederick Mull of Fort Lewis College. From the Bureau of Economic Statistics to the Wills on the Web page, these comprehensive exercises and activities expose students to the most current and relevant information on the Internet while challenging them to engage in intelligent personal financial planning.

- ✓ **Case Problems** created by Ruth Lytton. These calculator-based problems are tied directly to the two Discussion Cases at the end of each chapter and are in addition to the case problems supplied. Many of the Case Problems allow the student to utilize the Web-based Personal Finance Calculators available on the Navigator site.

- ✓ **Interactive Financial Calculators.** With this edition, we have included 25 Web-based financial calculators aimed at bringing the material alive in a way that today's student can easily relate to. Many of these calculators include interactive slider controls allowing you to instantly see the impact of a change in one of the variables. These calculators are incorporated into the Internet Exercises as well as the Case Problems. (See inside cover for a complete list of Calculators.)

- ✓ **Worksheets** These Financial planning worksheets provide students the opportunity to develop and implement a personal financial plan. Each Worksheet can be personalized by the student. The Worksheets feed into our new Personal Financial Planner Software.

- ✓ **Personal Financial Planner Software**  The interactive software available on the book Web site provides users with a fundamental financial plan as well as a list of steps necessary to implement the plan. The software developers have attempted to make the program as flexible and adaptable as possible for use across various stages of the financial life cycle. It also may be used to suit differing curriculum and schedule requirements. The software is equally applicable to the typical college student as well as the nontraditional student by providing suggestions to begin a sound financial plan or to bolster an existing plan.

This software individualizes results by allowing users to incorporate their own goals and financial data into the action plan. A series of questions and financial calculators used in conjunction with several worksheets, checklists, and external research options, guides users through the building of an individualized action plan. Areas of emphasis include: budgeting and goal identification, cash and credit management, major purchase management, insurance management, investment management, and retirement and estate planning. This program also helps users understand their risk tolerance and its effect on financial decision-making by integrating a risk tolerance questionnaire. This important software application, as well as the worksheets and calculators, are available to you from the text's Navigator Web site, www.prenhall.com/keown. You will need to use the Access Code in your Workbook to activate your 6-month subscription.

**PowerPoint Lectures**   Created by Derek Klock, a set of PowerPoint slides with lecture notes corresponding to each chapter of the text is available for download on the text's Companion Web site, www.prenhall.com/keown.

## Acknowledgments

I gratefully acknowledge the assistance, support, and encouragement of those individuals who have contributed to *Personal Finance: Turning Money into Wealth.* Specifically, I wish to recognize the very helpful insights provided by many of my colleagues. For their careful comments and helpful reviews of the text, I am indebted to:

Mike Barry, Boston College

Karin Bonding, University of Virginia

Lynda S. Clark, Maple Woods Community College

Bobbie D. Corbett, Northern Virginia Community College

Charles P. Corcoran, University of Wisconsin-River Falls

Kathy J. Daruty, Los Angeles Pierce College

Richard A. Deus, Sacramento City College

Ramon Griffin, Metropolitan State College of Denver

Jack Griggs, Abilene Christian University

Carolyn M. Hair, Wake Tech. Community College

Marilynn E. Hood, Texas A&M University

Joe Howell, Salt Lake Community College

Robert Jensen, Metropolitan Community Colleges

Ernest W. King, University of Southern Mississippi

Edward Krohn, Miami-Dade Community College

Karen Lahey, University of Akron

K.T. Magnusson, Salt Lake Community College

James E. Mallett, Stetson University

Dianne R. Morrison, University of Wisconsin-LaCrosse

Frederick H. Mull, Fort Lewis College

David W. Murphy, Madisonville Community College

David Overbye, Keller School of Management

Ted Pilger, Southern Illinois University

Robert Rencher, Liberty University

Irving E. Richards, Cuyahoga Community College

Pat Rudolph, American University

Nick Sarantakes, Austin Community College

Daniel L. Schneid, Central Michigan University

Thomas M. Springer, Florida Atlantic University

Shafi Ullah, Broward Community College

Martha A. Zenns, Jamestown Community College

I would like to thank a wonderful group of people at Prentice Hall. My Executive Editor, Mickey Cox, has been a joy to work with. With her guidance, I believe we have produced the finest possible textbook and supplements package. She is truly creative and insightful, along with being a wonderful person. I must also thank Gladys Soto who served as the Managing Editor on this revision. In a perfect world, every author would get a chance to work with Gladys. She continuously offered insights and direction, often serving as a sounding board for revisions and new ideas—it is simply impossible to say enough good things about Gladys. Even more, she is a great person and true friend. I also want to thank Torie Anderson, the Media Project Manager, for her tireless efforts in providing and maintaining great media products. She went well beyond the call of duty to make sure this project's media supplements stay cuttting edge. For her marketing prowess, I owe Kathleen Mclellan, my marketing manager, a debt of gratitude: she has an amazing under-standing of the market, coupled with an intuitive understanding of what the market is looking for. To Carol Samet, the production editor, I express a very special thank you for seeing the book through a complex production process and keeping it all on schedule while maintaining extremely high quality. This is the second edition of this text that Carol has worked on and it continues to be a joy to work with her.

I must also express my gratitude to Rick Mull who teaches at Fort Lewis College. Rick is a master at making material from the Internet both interesting and relevant. He has done a great job putting together the best set of Web exercises in the personal finance area anywhere—Rick, many thanks! Finally, I should also thank Paul Donnelly and David Cohen. Paul is a past editor and good friend, without whom this project would never have been started. Dave served as the developmental editor and helped mold this book into a text that is fun to read.

My appreciation to the people at Prentice Hall would be incomplete without mention of the highly professional Prentice Hall field sales staff and their managers. In my opinion, they are the best in the business, and I am honored to work with them. In particular I must single out Bill Beville, the regional acquisitions editor. He is one of the most dogged and delightful people I have ever met. Bill pursued me relentlessly until I agreed to do this book. I will always owe Bill a debt of gratitude. Bill, I'm glad you're on my side.

My most sincere thanks, along with a profound debt of gratitude goes to Ruth Lytton, for her outstanding work on cases and end-of-chapter material. She is always professional and perfectionist, and as a result, her efforts result in a pedagogy that works. If credit were given as it is deserved, Ruth Lytton's name would appear as a co-author. She is the consummate teacher, and also a perfectionist in reviewing chapters and writing problems and cases. In working with Ruth, I was constantly in awe of her effortless grasp of the many aspects of personal finance and of her ability to make complex concepts accessible to any student: she is truly one of the "gifted ones." Her suggestions and insights made a profound impact on the book, from start to finish, and greatly added to its value. In short, this is our book.

I also owe a huge debt of gratitude to John Grable of Kansas State. John worked on the outstanding cases and problems in the first two editions, and contributed far more than I had ever anticipated. Indeed, Kansas State is extremely lucky to have John. A salute goes also to Marcy Furney for her exceptional work on the "Money Matters" boxes. She also read and reviewed the manuscript, and provided insights and comments that materially improved the book. I also thank Glenn Furney formerly at Texas Instruments for his help in bringing to life the use of calculators in the teaching of personal finance. Given the contributions of Marcy, Ruth, John, and Derek, I think it is only fitting to provide a short biography of each. I thank you all.

**Marcy Furney,** Chartered Financial Consultant and Certified Financial Planner,™ is a Registered Representative of Allmerica investments, Inc., and a Financial Planner with Allmerica Investment Management Company, Inc. She lives in Dallas, where she has been affiliated with Gekiere and Associates since 1990. With 18 years in the financial services industry, she has worked extensively in insurance, executive deferred compensation plans, retirement programs, small business benefits, and personal financial needs. Marcy graduated summa cum laude with a Bachelor of Arts degree from Texas Tech University and attended graduate school at the University of Texas.

**John E. Grable** received his undergraduate degree in economics and business from the University of Nevada, an MBA from Clarkson University, and a Ph.D. from Virginia Tech. He is the Certified Financial Planner™ Program Director at Kansas State University. He is also the Director of the Institute of Personal Financial Planning in the School of Family Studies and Human Services at Kansas State University. His research interests include financial risk-tolerance assessment, financial planning help-seeking behavior, and financial wellness assessment. He serves on the Board of Directors of the International Association of Registered Financial Consultants as an academic advisor.

**Ruth H. Lytton** is Associate Professor of Financial Resource Management and the director for the Certified Financial Planner™ Board of Standards, Inc. registered program at Virginia Tech. She has been recognized for her teaching, research, and service. Her personal finance course is a popular elective for students throughout the campus. She received the 1994–95 College of Human Resources Certificate of Teaching Excellence and in 1995 was recognized by the Association for Financial Counseling and Planning Education (AFCPE) as the Mary Ellen Edmondson Educator of the Year. She was co-recipient of the 1999 best conference paper award, also presented by the AFCPE. During 2001, she was recognized by the College of Human Resources and Education with the Excellence in Undergraduate Student Advising Award and by Virginia Tech with the Award for Excellence in Career Advising.

Ruth also worked on the Instructor's Manual, which includes the solutions to all the end of chapter material in the text, completely revised and updated the Companion Website internet quizzes for each chapter, and created all new Internet Case Problems for the Personal Finance Navigator text site.

**Derek Klock**, a graduate from the family financial management program at Virginia Polytechnic Institute and State University works in bank management and brokerage. Mr Klock has completed his National Association of Securities Dealers (NASD) General Securities Representative—Series 7 and Uniform Securities Agent State Law Exam— Series 63 as well as his state life and health insurance license. Mr. Klock's real-world client experience and a long history of tracking and analyzing investments enables him to bring a unique perspective to the cases and problems developed for this text.

Together, Ruth and Derek bring a blend of talent that capitalizes on classroom experience and an understanding of students with professional experience and an understanding of real-world client situations.

As a final word, I express my sincere thanks to those using *Personal Finance: Turning Money into Wealth* in the classroom. I thank you for making me a part of your team.

Arthur J. Keown

# 1 Financial Planning: The Ties That Bind

## Learning Objectives

**Explain** the role of personal financial planning.

**Describe** the five basic steps of personal financial planning.

**Set** your financial goals.

**Describe** the different stages of the financial life cycle.

**Explain** why career management and education are the key factors in determining your income level.

When he graduated from high school in June 1953, he took a job at the Precision Tool Company and later drove a truck for Crown Electric. His career goal at that time was to become a truck driver, but all that changed when he met Sam Phillips, who owned Sun Records. From there it didn't take long for Elvis Presley to make his name as a rock 'n' roll star. For the rest of his life he continued to be a musical force, and he made millions and millions of dollars. Yet by the time he was in his early forties, he faced financial ruin. How did this happen? The answer is that he ignored the financial planning side of his life. He used his father, a former truck driver who had once served an 8-month prison sentence for passing bad checks, as his business advisor. He naively allowed his business manager to earn almost 50-percent commission as opposed to the industry standard of 10 percent. He opposed tax shelters on principle, and he impulsively gave away cash and expensive gifts. Moreover, it took over half a million dollars a year just to maintain Graceland (Elvis's estate).

Being financially secure involves more than just making money—it involves balancing what you make with what you spend. Basically, you must live within your means, regardless of what you make. Elvis certainly made plenty of money, but he managed to spend even more. After Elvis died in 1977, Priscilla Presley took over the management of the estate, which was valued at only $5 million. With the help of some serious personal financial planning, Priscilla was able to turn the Presley financial affairs around, and today the estate is worth well over $100 million.

What's the point? Life is better with a bit of personal financial planning. It's always easier to spend than to save. It was true for Elvis, and it's no doubt true for you. If that weren't the case, there wouldn't be much need for this or the hundreds of other personal finance books that fill bookstore shelves. Unfortunately, financial planning is not something that comes naturally to most people, and as a result many people work themselves into a financial corner that is much easier to avoid than it is to get out of. This text provides you with the know-how to avoid financial pitfalls and to achieve all your financial goals. In fact, with good financial planning, you can get that car you've always wanted or that vacation home by the beach, or you could retire early.

In addition to providing the necessary tools and techniques for managing your personal finances, this text also explains the basic logic behind them. That way you can understand why the tools and techniques work and how to apply them outside of this text. To make life a little easier, we've sorted the underlying logic behind all of financial planning into 15 basic principles that are used to guide you through the book. If you can understand these principles, you're well on your way to successful financial planning. And you'll be doing even better than Elvis.

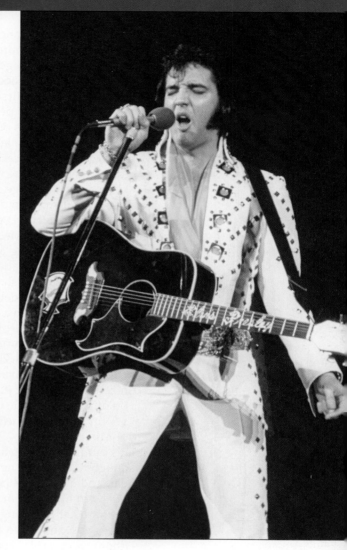

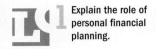

Explain the role of personal financial planning.

## Why Personal Financial Planning?

How big are the financial challenges you face? They're very big indeed. You are no doubt gaining an appreciation for the incredible cost of college. At many small private schools a college education can cost $1,000 a week. Once you've got the diploma, there's a good chance you've also got a student loan. Paying off that loan may be one of your first financial challenges. College tuition at a private school averages around $17,100 per year; at a public school, the average is $3,750 per year. Add to this housing costs of $3,000 per year, $2,000 for food, a computer and printer for $1,600, and the essentials—a minirefrigerator, a parking permit, lots of change for the laundry, a bit more cash to cover library fines, and late-night pizza money. How do most students finance it? The answer is, by borrowing.

Today, the average student graduates with over $13,000 in debts, and many students are far more in debt than that. Take, for example, Sheri Springs-Phillips, who was recently written up in the *Wall Street Journal*. She's a neurology resident at Loyola University Medical Center. On her 11-year journey from the South Side of Chicago to becoming a doctor, she piled up $102,000 in debt. Although her friends think she's got it made, she worries about the $2,500 monthly loan payments that begin when she finishes her residency. Fortunately, Sheri is an exception, but even the average level of debt is daunting. However, it becomes a real problem only without financial planning.

Why do people *need* to make a financial plan? Because it's always easier to spend than to save. Certainly that was the case for Elvis. It's also the case for most Americans. In fact, in 2001 over half of all Americans had no retirement savings at all. Why not? Because there always seems to be something better to spend your money on instead of saving it. Remember, though, that without a financial plan for saving, you might not be able to afford to retire!

Why should you *want* to make a financial plan? Because it can help you achieve all your financial goals. "Achieving financial goals" may seem a little abstract to you, so let's put it in context. Say you really want to be able to buy a Jeep with a stereo loud enough to wake the neighbors (and the dead) when you graduate. That's a financial goal, and a good financial plan will help you achieve it. A good plan may also help you get to Europe some day or have your own place instead of having a roommate.

Financial planning may not help you earn more, but it can help you use the money you do earn to achieve the goals you really want to achieve. In the real world, either you control your finances, or they control you—it's your choice.

Managing your finances isn't a skill you're born with. In fact, there really aren't too many skills that you're born with. Most people have to be taught the skills they are to use in life. For example, if you're planning on becoming a teacher, you've probably taken a course or two on teaching; if your career choice is engineering, you've no doubt taken a number of courses in engineering.

Unfortunately, personal finance courses aren't the norm in high school, and in many families money is not something to talk about—only to disagree on. In fact, financial problems can be a major cause of marital problems. Disagreements and fights about money can instill a "fear of finance" at an early age, and a lack of financial education just makes matters worse. As a result, most people grow up feeling very uncomfortable about money.

In addition, the details of finance itself don't soothe anybody's fears. At first glance, there seems to be an almost unending number of investment, insurance, and estate planning choices. In addition, poor advice and unethical characters abound. Even more confusing is the fact that investments and personal finance have a language of their own. How can you make choices when you don't speak the language? Well, you can't. That's why you're reading this text and taking this course—to allow you to navigate in the world of money.

The bottom line is that personal financial planning works—it certainly worked for Priscilla Presley—and ignoring personal financial planning can have painful results, regardless of how much you make—that's the lesson of Elvis.

Specifically, we hope that this text and this course will allow you to accomplish the following:

- **Manage the unplanned:** It may seem odd to plan to deal with the unexpected or unplanned. Hey, stuff happens. Unfortunately, no matter how well you plan, much of life is unexpected. A sound financial plan will allow you to bounce back from a few hard knocks instead of going down for the count.

- **Accumulate wealth for special expenses:** College for your children, a summer home, and travel are all special expenses that will probably be impossible to carry if you don't plan ahead for them. Financial planning helps you map out a strategy to pay for that house by the beach.

- **Save for retirement:** You may not think much about it now, but you don't want to be penniless when you're 65. A strong financial plan will help you look at the costs of retirement and develop a plan that allows you to live a life of retirement ease.

- **"Cover your assets":** A financial plan is no good if it doesn't protect what you've got. A complete financial plan will include adequate insurance at as low a cost as possible.

- **Invest intelligently:** When it comes to investing savings, the uninformed don't do it very well. Quite frankly, there are too many shady investment advisors and dirty deals out there. Before making a financial plan, arm yourself with an understanding of the basic principles of investment.

- **Minimize your payments to Uncle Sam:** Why earn money for the government when you can instead earn it for yourself? Part of financial planning is to help you legally reduce the amount of tax you have to pay on your earnings.

## The Personal Financial Planning Process

**L(2** Describe the five basic steps of personal financial planning.

The benefits of a solid financial plan certainly seem to be valuable. The question now is how to put them in place. Financial planning is an ongoing process that changes as your financial situation and position in life change. However, there are five basic steps to personal financial planning that need to be examined before we move on.

### Step 1: Evaluate Your Financial Health

A financial plan begins with an examination of your current financial situation. How wealthy are you? How much money do you make? How much are you spending, and what are you spending it on? To survive financially, you have to step back and see your whole financial picture. Of course,

**STOP & THINK** A recent survey showed that typical Americans think they need $1.5 million in order to feel rich. Unfortunately, that's a goal few reach. In fact, 59 percent of those over 65 have saved less than $100,000. Even worse, almost 45 percent of Americans over 65 have annual incomes of less than $15,000, and only 30 percent have annual incomes over $25,000, and this includes Social Security benefits! That's one reason why financial planning is so important. As Carl Sandburg once wrote, "Nothing happens unless first a dream."

seeing your whole financial picture and evaluating your current situation are going to require a lot of careful record keeping, especially when it comes to spending.

Keeping track of what you spend may simply be a matter of taking a few minutes each evening to enter all of the day's expenses into a little budget book. Is this record keeping dull and tedious? Sure, but it will also be revealing, and it's a first step to taking control of your financial well-being. In Chapter 2 we take a closer look at this process.

## Step 2: Define Your Financial Goals

You can't get what you want if you don't know what you want. The second step of the financial planning process is defining your goals: accumulating wealth for retirement, providing funds for a child's college education, or buying a new pickup truck. In a later section we look in detail at possible goals and financial concerns you might want to provide for in your financial plan. You'll notice that, as you age, your goals change. Keep in mind, though, that your goals aren't elusive and ever changing. Rather, as events happen and goals are achieved, they give way to other goals. Goals are like stepping-stones: Without a sound financial plan as a solid footing, it's easy to lose your step.

## Step 3: Develop a Plan of Action

The third step of the process involves developing a plan of action to achieve your goals. Although everyone's plan is a bit different (owing to the wide range of goals we all have), some common concerns should guide all financial plans: flexibility, liquidity, protection, and minimization of taxes.

Developing a game plan for your financial future may seem overwhelming, so you may be tempted to turn to investment advisors or professional financial planners for help. Before you do so, you should develop an understanding of personal finance for your own protection. Planners and advisors can help you; in fact, for many individuals they are their financial salvation. However, in the end, you're still the one who must decide on your own plan.

**Flexibility**   Remember when we mentioned planning for the unplanned? That's what flexibility is all about. Your financial plan must be flexible enough to respond to changes in your life and unexpected events (like wrapping your Honda around a telephone pole). An investment plan that doesn't give you any access to your money until you retire doesn't do you much good when you suddenly get fired for using your office computer to play Doom or The Sims.

**Liquidity**   Dealing with the unplanned requires more than just flexibility. Sometimes it requires cold, hard cash, and it requires it immediately. **Liquidity** involves having access to your money when you need it. No one likes to think about things like illness, losing a job, or even wrecking your car. But if something happens, you want to make sure you have access to enough money to make it through.

**Protection**   What happens if the unexpected turns out to be catastrophic? Liquidity will get you through the repair bill for an unexpected fender bender, but what happens if the accident is a lot worse and you wind up seriously injured? What if the cost of an unexpected event is a lot more than you've got? Liquidity allows you to carry on during an unexpected event, but insurance shields you from events that might threaten your financial security. Insurance offers protection against the worst, and costliest, unexpected events, such as flood, fire, major illness, and death. However, insurance isn't free. A good financial plan

**Liquidity**
The relative ease and speed with which you can convert noncash assets into cash. In effect, it involves having access to your money when you need it.

includes enough insurance to prevent financial ruin, either from catastrophe or from paying too much for your insurance.

**Minimization of Taxes**  Finally, your financial plan should take taxes into account. Keep in mind that a chunk of your earnings goes to the government, so if you need to earn $1,000 from an investment, make sure it yields $1,000 *after taxes*. It's always good to pay as little in taxes as possible, but it's even better to understand in advance that taxes will lessen your earnings and to plan accordingly. In effect, your goal is not necessarily to minimize taxes but to maximize the cash that is available to you after taxes have been paid.

Besides considering these four factors, a plan of action should take into account all your goals. For example, it should involve creating an informed and controlled budget; determining your investment strategy; planning for big-ticket items, such as a house or a car; debt planning; insurance planning; funding for raising children or sending them to college; planning for retirement; and providing for your loved ones after you pass on.

## Step 4: Implement Your Plan

Although it's important to carefully and thoughtfully develop a financial plan, it is even more important to actually stick to that plan. For most people, sticking to the plan also means using common sense and moderation—you don't want to become a slave to your financial plan. If you force yourself to write down every penny spent and track every expenditure, your efforts will probably stop in no time.

Keep in mind that your financial plan is not the goal; it is the tool you use to achieve your goals. In effect, think of your financial plan not as punishment but as a road map. Your destination may change, and you may get lost or even go down a few dead ends, but if your map is good enough, you'll always find your way again. Remember to add in new roads as they are built, and be prepared to pave a few yourself to get to where you want to go. Always keep your goals in mind and keep driving toward them.

## Step 5: Review Your Progress, Reevaluate, and Revise Your Plan

What happens if you want to go to Seattle but all you have is a road map of Philadelphia? It's time to get a new road map! Periodically you must review your progress and reexamine your financial plan. If necessary, you must be prepared to start all over again and formulate a different plan. In other words, the last step in financial planning often returns to the first. No plan is fixed for life. Still, this doesn't in any way detract from the importance of setting up a personal financial plan and using it. Goals are fantasy without a plan.

Figure 1.1 summarizes these five basic steps to financial planning.

## Defining Your Goals

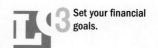
Set your financial goals.

You've already seen that the second step of the financial planning process is setting goals. Defining your goals involves writing down or formalizing your financial goals, attaching costs to them, and determining when the money to accomplish those goals will be needed. Unfortunately, establishing personal financial goals is something most people never actually do. Although not a difficult task, it's an easy one to put off. But if you never set goals, you'll never reach them either.

## Figure 1.1 The Budgeting and Planning Process

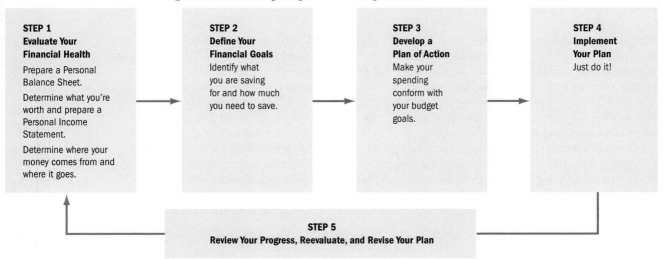

**STEP 1**
**Evaluate Your Financial Health**
Prepare a Personal Balance Sheet.
Determine what you're worth and prepare a Personal Income Statement.
Determine where your money comes from and where it goes.

**STEP 2**
**Define Your Financial Goals**
Identify what you are saving for and how much you need to save.

**STEP 3**
**Develop a Plan of Action**
Make your spending conform with your budget goals.

**STEP 4**
**Implement Your Plan**
Just do it!

**STEP 5**
**Review Your Progress, Reevaluate, and Revise Your Plan**

Actually, goal setting is nothing new to most people. You may have a target grade point average you're shooting for at graduation, or perhaps you have a goal of getting an "A" in this course. Goals are second nature to most people. However, in the financial arena, many people don't set goals because they have absolutely no idea how to go about achieving them. That's what this course and this text are all about—giving you the tools and understanding to be financially literate.

Everyone knows that saving and planning are necessary to achieve the good life. In spite of this, although most people have time for television, the movies, gardening, and all types of activities, they don't seem to have time to plan their financial future. Why? Often the reason is that they have never set financial goals. Without setting formal goals, you don't have to think about the long run—what's going to happen in 10, 20, or 30 years. Many others don't set financial goals so they can avoid thinking about finances. However, only when you set goals—and analyze them and decide if you're willing to make the financial commitment necessary to achieve them—can you achieve them.

Financial goals cover three time horizons: (1) short term, (2) intermediate term, and (3) long term. Short-term goals, such as buying a television or taking a vacation, can be accomplished within a 1-year period. An intermediate-term goal may take from 1 year to 10 years to accomplish. Examples might include paying for college for an older child or accumulating enough money for a down payment on a new house. A long-term goal is one for which it takes more than 10 years to accumulate the money. Retirement is a common example of a long-term financial goal.

Figure 1.2 is a worksheet that lists a number of possible short-, intermediate-, and long-term goals. The purpose of this worksheet is to provide you with a handy tool for determining your own specific goals. In defining your goals, it is important to be as specific as possible. Rather than list "saving money" as a goal, state the purpose of your saving efforts, such as buying a car, and exactly how much you want saved by what time. Also, it's important to be realistic. That is, your goals should reflect your financial and life situations. It's a bit unrealistic to plan for a million-dollar home on an income of $15,000 a year.

Once you've set up a list of goals, you need to rank them. At this point you may need to reevaluate and refine your goals. You may realize that your goals are simply unrealistic. However, once you have your final goals in place, they become the

**WORKSHEET**

Figure 1.2 Personal Financial Goals Worksheet

| Goal | Short-Term Goals (less than 1 year) | | |
|---|---|---|---|
| | Priority Level | Desired Achievement Date | Anticipated Cost |
| Accumulate Emergency Funds Equal to 3 Months' Living Expenses | _____ | _____ | _____ |
| Pay Off Outstanding Bills | _____ | _____ | _____ |
| Pay Off Outstanding Credit Cards | _____ | _____ | _____ |
| Purchase Adequate Property, Health, Disability, and Liability Insurance | _____ | _____ | _____ |
| Purchase a Major Item | _____ | _____ | _____ |
| Finance a Vacation or Some Other Entertainment Item | _____ | _____ | _____ |
| Other Short-Term Goals (Specify) | _____ | _____ | _____ |
| | **Intermediate-Term Goals (1 to 10 years)** | | |
| Save Funds for College for an Older Child | _____ | _____ | _____ |
| Save for a Major Home Improvement | _____ | _____ | _____ |
| Save for a Down Payment on a House | _____ | _____ | _____ |
| Pay Off Outstanding Major Debt | _____ | _____ | _____ |
| Finance Very Large Items (Weddings) | _____ | _____ | _____ |
| Purchase a Vacation Home or Time-Share Unit | _____ | _____ | _____ |
| Finance a Major Vacation (Overseas) | _____ | _____ | _____ |
| Other Intermediate-Term Goals (Specify) | _____ | _____ | _____ |
| | **Long-Term Goals (greater than 10 years)** | | |
| Save Funds for College for a Young Child | _____ | _____ | _____ |
| Purchase a Second Home for Retirement | _____ | _____ | _____ |
| Create a Retirement Fund Large Enough to Supplement Your Pension so That You Can Live at Your Current Standard | _____ | _____ | _____ |
| Take Care of Your Parents After They Retire | _____ | _____ | _____ |
| Start Your Own Business | _____ | _____ | _____ |
| Other Long-Term Goals (Specify) | _____ | _____ | _____ |

cornerstone of your personal financial plan, serving as a guide to action and a benchmark for evaluating the effectiveness of the plan. The process of setting goals and determining an appropriate personal financial plan is ongoing. After Elvis died, Priscilla would have lost everything without goals, a realistic financial plan, and discipline. Instead, today she has over 100 million reasons for believing in personal financial planning.

## The Life Cycle of Financial Planning

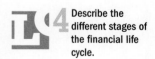

Describe the different stages of the financial life cycle.

As we said earlier, people's goals change throughout their lives. Although many of these changes are due to unexpected events, the majority are based on a general financial life cycle pattern that applies to most people, even you. Figure 1.3 illustrates the financial life cycle of a typical individual. What's the significance of this financial life cycle? Well, it allows you to better understand the timing and areas of financial concern that you'll probably experience. It allows you to focus on those concerns earlier and to plan ahead to avoid future problems. Look at retirement. If you're a typical student, retirement is probably the furthest thing from your mind—in fact, you probably don't even have a job now. However, if you understand the financial life cycle, you'll realize that you need to make retirement funding one of your first goals after graduation.

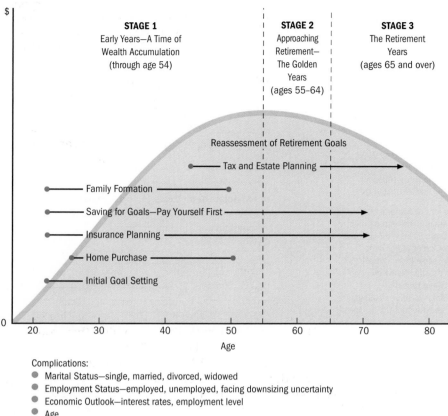

Figure 1.3 A Typical Individual's Financial Life Cycle

Complications:
- Marital Status—single, married, divorced, widowed
- Employment Status—employed, unemployed, facing downsizing uncertainty
- Economic Outlook—interest rates, employment level
- Age
- Number of Dependents—children, parents
- Family Money—inheritance

The first 18 to 20 years of an individual's life tend to involve negative income (and you thought it was only you). You can think of this as the "prenatal" stage of your financial life cycle. During this period most people are in school and still depend on their parents to pay the bills. Once your education is completed, your financial life cycle should begin in earnest.

The first stage involves a long period that centers on the accumulation of wealth. For most people that period continues through their mid-50s. During this time, goal setting, insurance, home buying, and family formation get the spotlight in terms of planning.

The second stage involves a shorter period approaching retirement. Financial goals shift to the preservation and continued growth of the wealth you have already accumulated. This second stage is generally the period during which most people begin the process of **estate planning**, that is, planning for the passage of their wealth to their heirs.

For most people, the third and final stage, retirement, begins in their mid-60s. During retirement you are no longer saving; you are spending. However, you must still allow for some growth in your savings simply to keep **inflation** from eating it away. Safety, income, and estate planning take on increased importance.

You can probably understand the general life cycle if you look at it in terms of a family life cycle. Many people marry in their 20s and 30s, have kids shortly thereafter, spend the next 18 or 20 years raising the kids, putting the kids through

**Estate Planning**
Planning for your eventual death and the passage of your wealth to your heirs.

**Inflation**
An economic condition in which rising prices reduce the purchasing power of money.

college, and settling down as a couple again when and if the kids move out to form their own families. Obviously, a typical individual's experiences don't fit everyone perfectly. Today, with more single-parent families and more young people postponing marriage, it simply isn't reasonable to refer to any family experience as typical. However, regardless of how unusual your life is, you'll be surprised at how much it has in common with a typical financial life cycle.

The financial life cycle has also usually been seen as a career life cycle. Today, though, career changes are becoming more the norm. As a result, it becomes more difficult to generalize about a typical career experience. However, for most people retirement occurs at approximately the same time, which gives you a target date for having your financial house in order. Again, although experiences may vary, the life cycle approach provides you with a framework you can modify to fit your goals and career cycle.

We now examine the three stages of the financial life cycle in a little more detail.

## The Early Years—A Time of Wealth Accumulation

In general, the biggest investment of your lifetime, purchasing a home, occurs during these early years. With a house comes a long-term borrowing commitment and your introduction to debt planning. Although this event may seem to dominate your financial life during this period, you can't lose track of the rest of your plan.

You must develop a regular pattern of saving. The importance of making saving a habit cannot be overstressed. Once you make a commitment to save, then you need to ask the following questions: (1) How much can be saved? (2) Is that enough? (3) Where should those savings dollars be invested? Your savings will hopefully go beyond merely helping to fund the down payment on your home, with some being directed toward your children's education, the establishment of an emergency fund, and your retirement. You'll also wind up funding the government, so don't forget to keep an eye on the tax implications of your savings.

To say the least, the early years aren't the same for everyone. Decisions that may not seem financial will have a major impact on your financial situation. Take, for example, something as routine as raising a child. Although having children isn't considered a financial decision, it certainly has enormous financial implications, as Table 1.1 illustrates. As you can see, kids cost a lot. In fact, for a middle-income family,

## Table 1.1 The Cost of Raising a Child

*These calculations are for the second child in a two-child family. For families with only one child, the costs of raising that child are more and can be determined by multiplying the totals by 1.26. For families with two or more children, the costs of an additional child can be determined by multiplying the totals by 0.78.*

| Annual Income | Annual Spending First 3 Years | All Expenses | Total Spent Over 18 Years For | | | | | | |
|---|---|---|---|---|---|---|---|---|---|
| | | | Housing | Food | Transportation | Clothing | Health Care | Child Care and Education | Other[a] |
| Less than $38,000 | $ 6,280 | $121,230 | $39,900 | $23,820 | $17,550 | $ 9,120 | $ 8,970 | $ 9,480 | $12,390 |
| $38,000–$64,000 | 8,740 | 165,630 | 55,170 | 28,650 | 24,420 | 10,680 | 11,640 | 16,560 | 18,510 |
| More than $64,000 | 13,000 | 241,770 | 89,580 | 35,670 | 32,760 | 13,770 | 13,380 | 26,520 | 30,090 |

[a]Other expenses include personal-care items, entertainment, and reading material.

Source: Expenditure on Children by Families, 2000 Annual Report, U.S. Department of Agriculture, Agricultural Research Service.

the total cost of raising a child from birth to age 18 is $165,630. As you might expect, the more you make, the more you spend on raising children. Those with annual incomes of more than $64,000 spend about twice that of those with annual incomes less than $38,000. The major differences occur in housing, child care, and education.

As you look at these figures, keep in mind that they cover only the costs of a child from birth to age 18—they don't include the costs of college. Considering the $6,000 to $13,000 a year it costs to raise a child, saving to finance that child's college education may seem like a real challenge. Without a sound financial plan, you might not be up to that challenge.

You must also begin using insurance to protect your assets. Initially you may require only medical, disability, and liability insurance, but as your family grows, the needs of your dependents come into play, and you will need to provide for them in the event of a tragedy. For families with young children, adequate life insurance is essential. Similarly, you may need home, auto, and property insurance.

Just as you begin retirement planning early on, you should also begin estate planning. If you have children, preparing a will is extremely important. Your will should not only oversee the disposition of your estate but also preselect a guardian for your children in the event that both you and your spouse die.

By the end of this first stage many of your financial goals have been accomplished and the ground is prepared for the rest of them. After all, this is the stage on which everything else rests. Short-term goals such as buying a car and getting insurance are met, intermediate-term goals such as buying a house and saving for college for your eldest are begun and met, and long-term goals such as retirement saving are begun.

## Approaching Retirement—The Golden Years

Stage 2 involves a transition from your earning years, when you will earn more than you spend, to your retirement years, when you will spend more than you earn. Much of this stage involves fine-tuning. Retirement goals become the center of your attention. As you approach retirement, you must continuously review your financial decisions, including insurance protection and estate planning.

Very few financial decisions are not modified over time. Moreover, unplanned events, such as being a victim of corporate downsizing, a divorce, or the death of a spouse, may have dramatic effects on your goals. The point is that personal financial planning is an extremely dynamic process—one that must be attended to on a regular basis.

## The Retirement Years

During your retirement years, you'll be living off your savings. Certainly, the decision of when to retire will reflect how well you have saved. Once you retire, your financial focus deals with ensuring your continued wealth, despite not having an income.

**STOP &THINK** Forty-five percent of those aged 65 are dependent on relatives, and another 30 percent live on charity. If you're like most young people, fresh out of college, you probably will have an urge to spend all that cash that you may be seeing for the first time in your life. You need to be reminded to set aside enough to pay off your student loan and to accumulate some savings. Feel free to spend, as long as you manage to save for your goals, and *make sure you begin planning for your financial future now.*

Once again, the management of savings and assets must be continuously reviewed and monitored. Your investment strategy will probably become less risky as you move toward preserving rather than creating wealth. In addition, your insurance planning must be continuously reviewed. Now your insurance concerns may include such items as protection against the costs of

an extended nursing home stay.

Finally, estate planning decisions become paramount. You should move to trim estate tax bills at this time. Wills, living wills, health proxies, power of attorney, and record keeping should all be in place to help protect you along with your assets for your heirs.

How well you live during retirement largely depends on how well you planned and saved during your early years. The key is to start the personal financial planning process early in life and make saving a habit.

## Picking a Career and Getting a Job

L5 Explain why career management and education are the key factors in determining your income level.

Just as you are responsible for managing your finances, you are responsible for managing your career. Because your career should last you the rest of your life, it should involve work you find enjoyable and satisfying. It should also provide the necessary financial support to allow you to lead the kind of life you want. In general, your first job isn't the one you'll spend the rest of your life at. Most careers involve a series of positions that allow you the opportunity to display your skills and lead to a job that you find satisfying and allows you the proper balance between work and personal life. Career planning is the process of identifying a job that you feel is important and that will lead to the lifestyle you want. Figure 1.4 is a Job Search Worksheet that will help you manage your career.

WORKSHEET

### Deciding on a Career

The first step in career planning involves self-assessment, that is, developing an understanding of what you want. Specifically, it involves a self-evaluation of your interests, skills, values, personal traits, and desired lifestyle. You begin by looking at your educational record. What courses did you like the most and the least? Which courses did you do the best in? What activities do you enjoy? How do you like to spend your time? What other skills do you have that might be of value in a career? From there, take a look at your work experience. Make a list of all the jobs you've had, whether you found them satisfying, what you liked or didn't like about the job, and why you left.

As you are probably realizing, conducting an effective self-assessment is not an easy task. You have to examine your entire life's activities, and you have to examine them honestly. That means you'll probably need help from family, and from counselors and teachers, along with a serious reflective effort on your part. Fortunately, there is quite a bit of help on the Internet in the form of online self-assessment tests.

Once you have completed your self-assessment, you should have an idea of your skills and interests. It is now time to research academic and career alternatives and identify jobs where those skills are valued. This involves identifying specific college majors that fit your interests, skills, values, and desired lifestyle. In doing this you'll want to be sure to look at the negative aspects of these potential jobs. Do they require travel? Do they offer the status and earning potential you are looking for? Are they cyclical? To do all this you're going to need the help of your school counselor to find out more about specific college majors and how those majors relate to different occupations. Then take this information and test it against the job market by talking to individuals in those occupations and finding out exactly what they do and what they like and dislike about their jobs.

Once you've done this, you're ready to make a decision and put it into action. First, you decide on a career field that fits your interests and that is realistically achievable, taking into account your limitations. From there you identify the coursework needed to achieve your goal.

**Figure 1.4** Job Search Worksheet

|  | Notes |
|---|---|
| **The Search** (Complete items 1 to 3 on this checklist before starting your job search.) | |

**1. Identify Occupations**
- Make a background and experience list.
- Review information on jobs.
- Identify jobs that use your talents.

_____

**2. Identify Employers**
- Ask relatives and friends to help you look for job openings.
- Go to your State Employment Service Office for assistance.
- Contact employers to get company and job information.

_____

**3. Prepare Materials**
- Write résumés (if needed). Use job announcements to "fit" your skills with job requirements.
- Write cover letters or letters of application.

_____

**The Daily Effort**

**4. Contact Employers**
- Call employers directly (even if they're not advertising openings). Talk to the person who would supervise you if you were hired. Make note of names.
- Go to companies to fill out applications.
- Contact your friends and relatives to see if they know about any openings.

_____

**The Interview** (Complete items 5 to 8 when you have interviews.)

**5. Prepare for Interviews**
- Learn about the company you're interviewing with.
- Review job announcements to determine how your skills will help you do the job.
- Assemble résumés, application forms, etc. (make sure everything is neat).

_____

**6. Go to Interviews**
- Dress right for the interview.
- Go alone.
- Be clean, concise, and positive.
- Thank the interviewer.

_____

**7. Evaluate Interviews**
- Send a thank-you note to the interviewer within 24 hours of the interview.
- Think about how you could improve the interview.

_____

**8. Take Tests**
- Find out about the test(s) you're taking.
- Brush up on job skills.
- Relax and be confident.

_____

**9. Accept the Job!**
- Get an understanding of job duties and expectations, work hours, salary, benefits, and so on.
- Be flexible when discussing salary (but don't sell yourself short).
- _Congratulations!_

_____

If you're still lost, you might want to try the Internet as a source of career advice. The first place to stop is the Personal Finance Navigator, which accompanies this book. It's organized by chapters and loaded with links to other sites and articles of interest. In addition, it's maintained by the author of this text and kept up-to-date. Another source of good advice is the *Career Guide to Industries,* which is published by the U.S. Department of Labor at **www.bls.gov/oco/cg**. This guide provides information on available careers by industry, including the nature of the industry, working conditions, employment, occupations in the industry, training and advancement, earnings and benefits, and employment outlook along with lists of organizations that can provide additional information. It's pretty comprehensive, too; in fact, it discusses over 42 industries, accounting for over 7 out of every 10 wage and salary jobs. You also might want to check out the FTCareerPoint Web site of the *Financial Times* at **ftcareerpoint.ft.com/ftcareerpoint**, which has some great tools and self-tests for understanding your personal values, sharpening your interviewing skills, and revising your résumé.

## Getting a Job

Very few things are more stressful than hunting for your first career job. That's because you probably don't have any career job hunting experience and there aren't any specific guidelines that can guarantee success. You have to view your first job as that of getting a job. You also have to start early. Remember what Woody Allen once said, "Eighty-five percent of success is simply showing up." That means that if you're graduating in May, you have to begin your job search the summer before your senior year.

Why start that early? There are three reasons. First, you will find that if you wait until the fall to write up a résumé, it will probably get delayed by a month or two. The beginning of the fall semester is generally hectic. Beginning in the summer guarantees you'll be prepared to start your job search in the fall. Second, starting early sends a message that you are both serious and organized—two traits employers love. Third, for many companies, the fall is the beginning of their recruiting cycle.

When you arrive on campus in the fall, your first stop should be at the career development office. You should show up with a résumé in hand. If the career development office doesn't provide help in putting together your résumé, look to the Web, where a number of sites provide guidelines and tips. Checklist 1.1 lists some things to keep in mind while putting your résumé and cover letter together.

Once you've made it through the initial screening process, it's time to begin preparing for the interview. Because the interview may determine whether or not

# Checklist 1.1 ■ Résumé and Cover Letter Tips

| | |
|---|---|
| Make your résumé look professional—print it on a high-quality printer.<br>Use high-quality white or off-white paper.<br>Avoid styles that are hard to read.<br>Use typical job descriptions. Many first-pass evaluations are done by computers that look for matches in work history, goals, education, and experience. This also means you should use a common font that is easily scannable.<br>Proofread, proofread, and proofread one more time. Don't make it an automatic rejection.<br>If you send your résumé out, make sure a cover letter goes with it. | Tailor each cover letter to the particular company.<br>In your cover letter, cite why you are a good candidate. Indicate your strengths and how they would help the company.<br>Tell them why you are interested in the company. Make it as specific as possible.<br>Never send anything addressed to "To Whom It May Concern." You may have to do some phone calling, but that's part of the price of getting a job.<br>Just as with your résumé, proofread, proofread, and proofread one more time. |

you get the job, once again, the key is to be prepared. That means going through several practice interviews. One way to do this is to use career days on campus along with family, friends, and career counselors to practice your interviewing. Many college career development offices provide courses or help in developing the interpersonal skills that are necessary for a good interview.

For your interview to be successful, one of your first stops should be the library or the Internet to search for information on the company you're interviewing with. You should have a good understanding of the company, how it makes its money, its history, its financial status, and any new developments. You need a good night's rest if you intend to make a good first impression. You'll also want to dress appropriately. Plan to arrive about 30 minutes before your interview to guard against the unexpected, and display strong body language—a strong handshake, good eye contact, good posture. Try to relax. Once you finish, make sure you thank the interviewer for his or her time and for giving you the opportunity to talk. Finally, when you get home, send a follow-up letter, thanking the interviewer.

## Making It a Successful Career

Just one job isn't a career. Never has this been so true. In fact, it is likely that if you are just starting out, you'll probably work for at least three or four different companies and have over 10 different jobs. Your job switching may be the result of great opportunities or it may be the result of downsizing. The point is that job security is a thing of the past. The way to protect yourself is to have a marketable skill, and the way to

# In The News

San Francisco Examiner May 15, 1999

### How the Stock Market Affects the Job Market

Money isn't a fashionable thing for a lot of career counselors to talk about. You should have a career you love, they say, and then the money will take care of itself. What they overlook, though, is that having money gives you more career options, such as starting your own business, working part time, or doing something you love that doesn't pay much.

Here are some things to think about regarding the stock market and your career:

*The Internet has changed everything.* It used to be hard for small investors to keep up with the news about individual stocks. Now there are tons of Internet sites with news and statistics.

At work, it's the same thing. Job hunters need to realize that if they don't know much about a company or what their salary should be, they haven't done their homework. Internet sites like jobsmart.org have salary comparisons, and most companies have Web sites.

*This cannot be said loudly enough: If you're an investor or a job hunter and you don't use the Internet, you're operating under a severe handicap.* (☛A)

Understand all the risks. People are intimidated because stocks have bad days or months or even years, and that sounds too risky for them. What they overlook is that having plain old savings accounts also carries a risk: Inflation and taxes can wipe out any interest they receive.

*Changing jobs or careers and even quitting a job out-right all are risky. But staying in the same job for 20 or 30 years also carries a risk: If you're laid off, finding another job can be almost impossible because you don't have the variety of experience that employers are looking for.* (☛B)

## THE BOTTOM LINE . . .

**A** According to Robert Reich, the former Secretary of Labor, the first rule for new graduates to help them find work and keep up with the workplace of the future is to remember that you are "born to be wired." That is, whether you work in an office or manage the crew that cleans it, you've got to be computer literate. Even truck driving and factory work require some computer skills. If you don't have them, get them. Now.

**B** Another of Reich's rules is to "ditch the ladder, catch the web. Think of a career less as a ladder and more like a web— webs have a center but no top, and a lot of paths that connect. Forget the climb— smart workers move along webs, earning more from skills they have gained, not seniority. Unlike ladders, webs often dissolve when their purpose is fulfilled."

Source: Murphy, Dave. "How the Stock Market Affects the Job Market." *San Francisco Examiner*, 15 May 1999. Used by permission.

do that is through education and by keeping up with changing technology. Other ways to make sure your career goes in the right direction include the following tips:

- Do good work.
- Project the right image—an image aligned with the organization's values and wants.
- Gain an understanding of the power structure so that you can work within it.
- Gain visibility. Make those with power aware of your contributions.
- Take new assignments. Gain experience and an understanding of the various operations of the organization.
- Be loyal and supportive of your boss. Remember, your boss controls your immediate future.
- Never stop acquiring new skills, in particular, skills that are not easy to duplicate.
- Develop a strong network of friends, colleagues, neighbors, customers, and other contacts in case you ever need to look for a new job for whatever reason.

The bottom line is that managing your career is an ongoing process that will end only when you finally retire.

## Your Income: What Determines It

Your financial plan needs to be realistic, and to be realistic, it needs to be based on your income level. What you earn does not determine how happy you are, but it does determine the standard of living you can afford. However, there is great variation in what different people earn at the same job with different companies, Table 1.2 provides a listing of typical salaries at the entry level, average, and high end for a number of different jobs. One thing that sticks out in these salary averages is that the more special skills and training a job requires, the higher paying it tends to be.

If you look at the financial profile of the middle class versus the wealthy you find that the key differentiating factor is how well educated you are. If we define a middle-class household as one with annual income between $25,000 and $100,000, and a wealthy household as one with annual income greater than $100,000, whereas only 29 percent of the middle-class householders finished college, 70 percent of the wealthy householders finished college. Moreover, the percentage of wealthy householders with a postgraduate degree was almost four times that of the middle class. Right now, you may be making the best single investment you will ever make—your education. Interestingly, being married is also a trait of the wealthy. Whereas a married couple heads 70 percent of the middle class households, that number climbs to 85 percent for wealthy households.

### Impact of the Tragedies of September 11, 2001, on Personal Finance

Beyond the immeasurable suffering and loss of human life, the cowardly and horrific attacks of September 11, 2001, also had major impact on the financial system. Aimed at the heart of the U.S. economic and financial system, the attack on the World Trade Center was an unsuccessful attempt to destroy our economy and the capitalistic system.

We learned a lot about our country and about our financial system during the time that followed. First, we united as a country, sharing the sorrow of those who lost family members and loved ones as if every loss was a family member. Second, we

## Table 1.2  Average Salary Ranges

| Profession | Initial Pay | Industry Average | Typical Top Pay |
|---|---|---|---|
| *Accounting and finance* | | | |
| Public accountant | $ 33,180 | $  47,713 | $   76,150 |
| Management consulting | 36,100 | 55,908 | 88,290 |
| *Advertising* | | | |
| Advertising copywriter | 34,100 | 54,200 | 103,800 |
| Account executive | 31,950 | 61,770 | 370,000 |
| *Education* | | | |
| University professor | 45,100 | 53,448 | 74,469 |
| K–12 teacher | 26,640 | 40,964 | 56,764 |
| *Financial services* | | | |
| Financial planner | 31,100 | 57,500 | 210,000 |
| Portfolio manager | 45,800 | 145,050 | 210,000 |
| Actuary | 29,258 | 42,553 | 67,386 |
| Life insurance underwriter | 27,050 | 43,302 | 60,592 |
| *Health care* | | | |
| Family practice physician | | | |
| Private | 99,050 | 142,400 | 180,410 |
| HMO | 111,400 | 142,177 | 181,050 |
| Neurosurgeon | 159,000 | 279,000 | 479,300 |
| Nurse practitioner | 39,000 | 63,056 | 93,491 |
| *Law* | | | |
| Private practice | | | |
| Associate | 67,950 | 85,625 | 119,280 |
| Partner | 131,600 | 211,290 | 347,600 |
| Public prosecutor | 26,500 | 34,620 | 43,770 |
| Corporate lawyer | 71,350 | 91,377 | 128,750 |
| *Manufacturing* | | | |
| Foreman | 37,150 | 46,430 | 55,700 |
| Purchasing agent | 48,670 | 60,814 | 72,950 |
| *Marketing* | | | |
| Marketing assistant | 21,750 | 27,700 | 34,500 |
| Marketing research manager | 48,750 | 77,425 | 117,000 |
| *Media* | | | |
| Newspaper reporter | 25,130 | 27,800 | 43,771 |
| Book editor | 24,175 | 50,800 | 84,130 |
| TV news reporter | 19,060 | 35,030 | 106,000 |
| TV news anchor | 29,280 | 75,879 | 285,000 |
| Movie producer | 400,000 | 1,000,000 | 5,000,000 |
| *Sales* | | | |
| Sales trainee | 22,800 | 33,500 | 38,500 |
| Sales representative | 44,800 | 55,700 | 69,000 |
| Sales manager | 64,325 | 75,290 | 95,000 |
| *Wall Street* | | | |
| Investment banker | 101,000 | 450,000 | 1,250,000 |
| Trader | 63,900 | 310,000 | 1,000,000 |

Sources:   U.S. Department of Labor, Bureau of Labor Statistics. *Occupational Outlook Handbook.* Washington, DC (various editions); JobStar Salary Survey, *Wall Street Journal Careers, Salaries and Profiles;* and Martin, Justin. "How Does Your Pay Really Stack Up?" *Fortune,* 24 June 1996: 79–86. Author's extrapolations to January 2003.

learned that our financial system is stronger and more amazing than we might have thought. When the New York Stock Exchange opened on September 17, we saw an almost instant 700-point decline followed by a feeble rally attempt and ominous calm. The next two days brought successive 300-plus point declines, during which there were intraday swings of over 700 points and times at which it seemed stocks were in free fall. The week closed with a 140.40-point decline bringing the Dow Jones Industrial Average to 8235.81, and the Nasdaq to 1423.19, in effect, wiping out three years of stock market gains. Thus, although any financial losses suffered by the American people seem trivial when compared with the loss of life, personal suffering, and pain that our country experienced, the loss of wealth was still enormous.

Throughout all this chaos, the financial markets remained intact, did not panic, and continued to function smoothly and without interruption. The American people were determined not to let the terrorists achieve their goal of destroying our financial system. As the next six months passed, we saw the economy rebound led on by strong consumer spending, and six months later the Dow Jones Industrial Average was back around 10,500, climbing over 25 percent in six months.

Although the events of September 11, 2001, were horrific, they demonstrated the strength of our country, our people, and our financial system. As you study finance this year, you will see **Principle 5: The Curse of Competitive Markets** (which will be introduced later in this chapter) play out as the markets took all the available information and reacted immediately to it. You will see that the valuation models we will introduce in Part 4 of this text, "Managing Your Investments," worked with precision, continuously revaluing stocks and bonds, as more information on risk and future returns became known. In short, you will see the impact of this tragic event throughout this text. You will also see an amazing financial system—capitalism—one that has provided us with economic benefits and a quality of life that many of us take for granted. It is this system, not the government or "good luck," that has created all this prosperity, quality of life, and opportunities to move up the economic ladder, and it has done it without violence. In "Capitalism: The Unknown Ideal" the famous philosopher Ayn Rand wrote: "It is a system where men deal with one another, not as victims and executioners, nor as masters and slaves, but as traders, by free, voluntary exchange to mutual benefit. It is a system where no man may obtain any values from others by resorting to physical force, and no man may initiate the use of physical force against others." Enjoy your introduction to personal finance, and be amazed—it is truly a wondrous system.

## The 15 Principles That Form the Foundations of Personal Finance

To the first-time student of personal finance, this text may seem like a collection of tools and techniques held together solely by the binding on the book. Not so! In fact, the techniques and tools are all based on some very straightforward logic, which we've summed up in 15 simple principles. *Although it's not necessary to understand personal finance in order to understand these principles, it's necessary to understand these principles in order to understand personal finance.*

These principles are used throughout the text to unify and relate the topics being presented. They also allow you to focus on the conceptual underpinnings of personal finance and thereby not lose sight of the concepts as you are introduced to the techniques. Let's face it, your situation and the personal finance challenges you'll face won't fit into a simple formula. You have to understand the logic behind the material in the book in order to apply it to your life.

The following sections identify and define the 15 principles that form the foundations of personal finance and of this book. They are as much statements of common sense as they are theoretical statements. If all you can remember from this course are these principles, you'll still have an excellent grasp of personal finance and, thus, a better chance of attaining wealth and achieving your financial goals.

## Principle 1: The Risk–Return Trade-Off

At some point just about everyone has saved up some money. Why? The answer is simple: to buy goods or services in the future—in economic terms, to delay consumption. You generally invest your savings to make it earn interest and grow, so you can buy even more in the future. You are able to earn a return on your savings dollars because some individuals, businesses, and governments are willing to pay you for the use of your money. In effect, you are lending them your savings and earning a fee for doing so. Assuming there are a lot of different borrowers out there that would like to have use of your savings, what determines how much return you get on your money?

Actually, the answer is quite simple, and it provides the logic behind much of what is done in finance. Investors demand a minimum return for delaying consumption. This return must be greater than the anticipated level of inflation. Why? If the return isn't enough to cover the loss of purchasing power due to inflation, then the investor has, in effect, lost money. There's no sense in making an investment that loses money.

Now that you know what the minimum return is, how do you decide among all the various alternatives? Obviously, some investments are safer than others. Why should investors put their money in a risky investment when there are safer alternatives? Basically, investors won't unless they are compensated for taking that additional risk. In other words, investors demand additional expected return for taking on added risk. Notice that we refer to "expected" return rather than "actual" return. You may have expectations and even assurances of what the returns from investing will be, but because risk exists, you never know what those returns are actually going to be.

If investors could see into the future, no one would have invested money in Enron on November 27, 2001, the day before its stock dropped 85 percent. That's why Apple Computer bonds pay more interest than do U.S. Treasury bonds of the same **maturity date.** The government will be around to pay off its borrowing, but Apple may not be. It's that added incentive of additional interest that convinces some investors to take on the added risk of an Apple Computer bond rather than a U.S. Treasury bond. The more risk an investment has, the higher its expected return should be. This relationship between risk and expected return is shown graphically in Figure 1.5.

**Maturity Date**
The date upon which a borrower is to repay a debt.

Figure 1.5 The Risk–Return Trade-Off

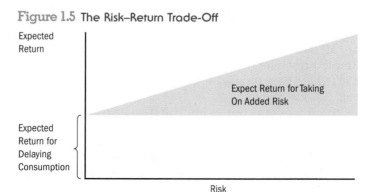

Needless to say, Figure 1.5 shows a simple relationship that makes a good deal of sense: Investors demand a return for delaying consumption and an additional return for taking on added risk. We'll get into risk measurement later in this course when we discuss valuing such investments as stocks and bonds.

## Principle 2: The Time Value of Money

Perhaps the most important concept in personal finance is that money has a time value associated with it. Simply stated, because you can earn interest on any money you receive, money received today is worth more than money received in, say, a year. Although this idea is not a major surprise to most people, they simply don't grasp its importance. The importance of the time value of money is twofold. First, it allows us to understand how investments grow over time. Second, it allows us to compare dollar amounts in different time periods.

In this text, we focus on the creation and preservation of wealth. To create wealth, we invest savings and allow it to grow over time. This growth is an illustration of the time value of money. In fact, much of personal finance involves efforts to move money through time. Early in your financial life cycle you may borrow money to buy a house. In taking out that home mortgage, you are really spending money today and paying later. In saving for retirement, you are saving money today with the intention of spending it later. In each case money is moved through time. You either spend in today's dollars and pay back in tomorrow's dollars, or save in today's dollars and later spend in tomorrow's dollars. Without recognizing the existence of the time value of money, it is impossible to understand **compound interest**, which allows investments to grow over time.

> **Compound Interest**
> Interest paid on interest. This occurs when interest paid on an investment is reinvested and added to the principal, thus allowing you to earn interest on the interest, as well as on the principal.

## Principle 3: Diversification Reduces Risk

Principle 1 introduced us to risk. The concept of **diversification** enters the picture by allowing you to reduce or "diversify away" some of your risk without affecting your expected return. The concept of diversification is one you probably already know. There is an old saying that goes, "Don't put all your eggs in one basket." When you diversify, you are spreading your money in several investments instead of putting all your money in one. Then, when one of those investments goes bust, another goes boom to make up for the loss. In effect, diversification allows you to iron out the ups and downs of investing. You don't experience the great returns, but you don't experience great losses either—instead you receive the average return.

> **Diversification**
> Acquisition of a variety of different investments instead of just one to reduce risk.

Perhaps the easiest way to understand diversification is to look at it graphically. Consider what happens when you combine two stocks, as depicted in Figure 1.6. In this case, the returns from these stocks move in opposite directions, and when they are combined, their highs and lows cancel each other out. Notice that the average return has not changed—both stocks and their combined returns average 10 percent. For most investments, some risk, but not all, can be eliminated through random diversification. Some risk cannot.

## Principle 4: All Risk Is Not Equal

Principle 3 shows that the process of diversification allows for much of an investment's risk or variability to be eliminated or "diversified away." The degree to which the total risk is reduced is a function of how two investments' returns move together. For example, if two stocks move in an exactly opposite manner, combining them can

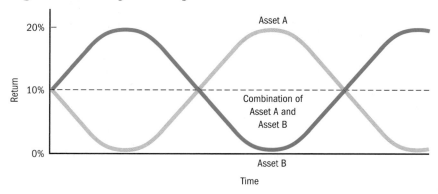

**Figure 1.6** Reducing Risk Through Diversification

result in the elimination of all variability for the combination. However, because most stocks move together—climbing during market upswings and declining during market downswings—not all of their variability can be diversified away when they are combined. *The bottom line is that all risk is not equal. We are going to be very concerned with risk that we cannot remove through diversification.*

## Principle 5: The Curse of Competitive Investment Markets

Your goal as an investor is to create wealth for yourself. Therefore, you need to understand what different investments, such as stocks, bonds, and real estate, are really worth. As you will see, it's very difficult finding investments that are exceptionally profitable, that is, ones that outperform similar investments. To understand why, it is necessary to have an understanding of the concept of **efficient markets**.

**Efficient Markets**

A situation in which investment prices instantly reflect all publicly available information and, as a result, the price of any investment accurately reflects the best estimate of its value.

In an efficient market, information such as new earnings figures or the announcement of a new product is reflected in investment prices with such speed that there are no opportunities for investors to earn higher than expected profits from publicly available information. In other words, all investments return what Principle 1 says they should return—the more risk they have, the higher their expected return.

This situation comes about because in an efficient market a large number of profit-driven investors act independently of one another. Each looks for investments with whopping returns. In effect, investors buy investments they feel are underpriced—pushing them upward—and sell investments they feel are overpriced—pushing them downward—until equilibrium is reached. In short, investors' hunger for profits ensures that different investments earn what Principle 1 says they should.

What are the implications of the concept of efficient markets for us? It means that, in general, it is very difficult to "beat the market," that is, to find that investment with a whoppingly high return. It means that you should look carefully at "hot tips" and recommendations before acting on them. The point is that, in competitive investment markets, "bargains" don't remain "bargains" for very long.

## Principle 6: Taxes Affect Personal Finance Decisions

Because they help determine the realized return of an investment, taxes play an important role in personal finance. In fact, hardly any decision can be made without considering the impact of taxes. All you should be concerned with is the results of your investment or planning strategy *after taxes.*

Your goal will not necessarily be to minimize taxes but to maximize the after-tax income available to you. Thus, you must look at all your alternatives on an after-tax basis. Taxes aren't the same on all investments, so you will find that effective personal financial planning requires you to have an understanding of the tax laws and how they affect investment decisions.

## Principle 7: Stuff Happens, or the Importance of Liquidity

Although much of the focus of personal financial planning is on long-term investing for lifetime goals, you must also plan for the unexpected. If liquid funds are not available, an unexpected need, such as job loss or injury, may force you to liquidate a longer-term investment. The unexpected forces us to act immediately, which might entail selling real estate when prices are low or selling common stock and, as a result, taking on an unwanted tax liability. Such actions might ruin your plans and cause you to miss opportunities. If an emergency forced you to sell a rental house you owned, you might receive only a fraction of what you could have sold the property for if you had had 2 or 3 months to sell it.

What if you don't have something to sell? The answer is that you'll have to borrow money fast. That kind of borrowing will probably bring along with it a high interest rate and payments you aren't ready for. Unfortunately, once you take on unplanned borrowing, it's generally pretty tough to pay it off. We can't emphasize enough the importance of having adequate liquid funds available.

## Principle 8: Nothing Happens Without a Plan

Most people spend more time planning their summer vacation than they do planning their financial future. It's incredibly easy to avoid thinking about retirement, to avoid thinking about how you're going to pay for your children's education, and to avoid thinking—at least when it comes to tightening your financial belt and saving money. We began this book with the statement that it is easier to spend than to save. We can go beyond even that and say it is easier to think about how you're going to spend your money than it is to think about how you're going to save your money.

If you're like most people, you can probably spend money without thinking about it, but you can't save money without thinking about it. That's the problem. Saving isn't a natural event: It must be planned. Unfortunately, planning isn't natural either. Start off with a modest, uncomplicated financial plan. Once the discipline of saving becomes second nature, or at least accepted behavior, modify and expand your plan. The bottom line is that a financial plan cannot be postponed. The longer you put it off, the more difficult accomplishing goals becomes. When goals look insurmountable, you may not even attempt to reach them.

## Principle 9: The Best Protection Is Knowledge

Although a professional financial planner can many times do wonders in helping set up and establish a lifetime financial plan, you simply must take responsibility for your own affairs. Knowledge is your best friend for the following four major reasons.

1. Without an understanding of personal financial planning, you are a prime target for the unethical, the incompetent, and the unscrupulous. Any time the primary resource being dealt with is money, an entire cast of dubious characters will most certainly be lurking around, waiting to take more than their share.

2. An appreciation of personal finance and valuation will provide you with an understanding of the importance of planning for your future.

3. Without an understanding of personal finance, and valuation in particular, you will not have the ability to take advantage of changes in the economy and interest rates.

4. Because financial problems in real life seldom perfectly reflect textbook problems and solutions, you must be able to abstract from what you learn in order to apply it. The only way you can effectively abstract something is to understand it. To invest intelligently, you must understand the process of valuation and the risk–return relationship from Principle 1. As with most else in life, it's much easier to do it right if you understand what you're doing.

## Principle 10: Protect Yourself Against Major Catastrophes

The worst time to find out that you don't have the right amount or right kind of insurance is just after a tragedy occurs. As you'll see, insurance is an unusual item to purchase. In fact, most people don't "buy" insurance, they're "sold" insurance. It's generally the insurance salesperson who initiates the sale and leads the client through the process of determining what to purchase.

What makes this process a problem is that it is extremely difficult to compare policies, because of the many subtle differences they contain. Moreover, most individuals have insurance but have never read their policies. To avoid the consequences of a major tragedy, you need to buy the kind of insurance that's right for you and to know what your insurance policy really says.

The focus of insurance should be on major catastrophes—those events that, although remote, can be financially devastating. Hurricanes, floods, earthquakes, and fires are examples. These are the events you can't afford, and these are the events insurance should protect you against.

## Principle 11: The Time Dimension of Investing

In general, if you intend to hold an investment for a long period, you can afford to take on a riskier investment. Take stocks, for example. Over the past 73 years, large-company stock prices have risen an average of 11.2 percent per year. However, it has not been a smooth ride. The problem with stocks is that "on average" may not be what you actually get. You may, for whatever reason, put your money in the stock market during the wrong period. If you need your money for your child's college education, which begins next year, the stock market is not the right place to invest it. You do not want to stake your child's college education on the hope that this will be a good year—or, more important, that this will not be a bad year.

If you are in your twenties and saving for your retirement, investing in the stock market makes sense. Although you can almost guarantee that there will be some down times, there will also be some good times. Over a long time horizon, the exceptionally good and exceptionally bad times will probably cancel each other out. That doesn't mean there isn't a lot of variability with respect to how much you have when you retire. It does mean that if you invest in stocks, you'll most likely end up with a lot more than you would if you had invested in a less risky alternative like bonds or kept your money in the bank.

## Principle 12: The Agency Problem—Beware of the Sales Pitch

The **agency problem** in personal finance is the result of the fact that those who act as your agents—insurance salespeople, personal financial advisors, and stockbrokers—may actually be acting in *their own* interests rather than in *your* best interest. For example, an insurance salesperson, motivated by the commission, may try to sell you insurance you don't need. A personal financial advisor may try to sell you financial products, such as insurance policies or mutual funds, that are more expensive than similar products because he or she receives a hefty commission on them.

The agency problem doesn't mean that you should avoid insurance salespeople or financial planners but that you should choose them carefully. Pick a financial planner just as you pick a competent and trustworthy doctor. If you trust your doctor—or financial planner—you have to believe they have your best interests at heart. Just keep your eyes open. Of course, you must be aware of ulterior motives in making financial decisions.

This brings us back to **Principle 9: The Best Protection Is Knowledge.** Without an understanding of the world of investments, you may be forced to rely on agents who are less concerned with your financial well-being and more concerned with taking your money. If you need professional help, we suggest that you look very carefully before you choose an advisor, and never choose at random. Try to find an advisor who fits your needs and has a proven record of ethical and effective assistance to clients.

## Principle 13: Pay Yourself First

It's much easier to save than to spend, right? No, just checking—you know the opposite is true. For most people, savings are a residual. That means that you spend what you like and save what is left, and the amount you save is simply what you earn minus what you spend. When you pay yourself first, what you spend becomes the residual. That is, you first set aside your savings, and what is left becomes the amount you can spend.

By paying yourself first, you acknowledge the fact that your long-term goals are of paramount importance. "Buying into" these goals is the first expenditure you make, which ensures that these goals actually get funded. In short, this axiom dictates a behavior pattern in which saving for long-term goals becomes automatic, and excuses for why this month's savings can be passed up no longer work.

## Principle 14: Money Isn't Everything

The purpose of personal financial planning is to allow you to extend your financial plans beyond the present—to allow you to achieve goals that are well off in the future. In effect, personal financial planning allows you to be realistic about your finances—to act your wage. Unfortunately, for some people financial goals become all consuming. They see nothing but dollar signs and lose a healthy perspective on what is actually important in life. In the movie *Arthur* there is an exchange between Dudley Moore and Liza Minelli in which Moore, who plays Arthur Bach, says: "Money has screwed me up my whole life. I've always been rich, and I've never been happy." To this Minelli, who plays Linda Marolla (Arthur's girlfriend), replies: "Well, I've always been poor, and I've usually been happy." Arthur's mother then steps in and responds, "I've always been rich, and I've always been happy!" Money doesn't necessarily bring on happiness; however, facing college expenses or retirement without the necessary funding certainly brings on anxiety.

### Principle 15: Just Do It!

Making the commitment to actually get started may be the most difficult step in the entire personal financial planning process. However, the positive reinforcement associated with making progress toward your goals and taking control of your financial affairs generally means that, once you take the first step, the following steps become much easier.

One of your investment allies is stronger now than it ever will be. That ally is time. Because of **Principle 2: The Time Value of Money,** taking investment action now—just doing it—becomes even more critical. If you are 20 right now and you are saving your money at 12 percent for retirement at age 67, a dollar saved today is worth about $11 saved at age 40, and is worth about the same as $40 saved at age 50. Table 1.3 provides a listing of the level of monthly saving necessary to accumulate $1 million by age 67. As you can see, it's a lot easier if you start early. The bottom line is that there simply is no good reason to postpone investing and financial planning. Just do it!

**Table 1.3**   **Importance of Starting Early—Just Do It!— to Accumulate $1 Million at Age 67 Investing Your Money at 12%**

| Making Your Last Payment on Your 67th Birthday and Your First When You Turn | Your Monthly Payment Would Have to Be |
|---|---|
| 20 | $    33 |
| 21 | 37 |
| 22 | 42 |
| 23 | 47 |
| 24 | 53 |
| 25 | 60 |
| 26 | 67 |
| 27 | 76 |
| 28 | 85 |
| 29 | 96 |
| 30 | 109 |
| 31 | 123 |
| 32 | 138 |
| 33 | 156 |
| 34 | 176 |
| 35 | 199 |
| 40 | 366 |
| 50 | 1,319 |
| 60 | 6,253 |

## SUMMARY

Personal financial planning will allow you to (1) manage the unplanned, (2) accumulate wealth for special expenses, (3) realistically save for retirement, (4) "cover your assets," (5) invest intelligently, and (6) minimize your payments to Uncle Sam.

There are five basic steps to personal financial planning:

1. Evaluate your financial health
2. Define your financial goals
3. Develop a plan of action
4. Implement your plan
5. Review, reevaluate, and revise your plan

In fact, the last step in financial planning is often the first, because no plan is fixed for life.

To reach your financial goals you must first set them. This process involves writing down your financial goals and attaching costs to them, along with when the money to accomplish those goals will be needed. Once you have set your goals, they will become the cornerstone of your personal financial plan, a guide to action, and a benchmark for evaluating the effectiveness of the plan.

A general financial life cycle pattern applies to most people, even you. There are three stages in the financial life cycle: (1) the early years—a time of wealth accumulation, (2) approaching retirement—the golden years, and (3) the retirement years.

In general, the more educated you are, the more you will earn. This is because the more special skills and training needed for the job, the higher the pay tends to be.

The chapter closes with an examination of the 15 principles on which personal financial planning is built and that motivate the techniques and tools introduced in this text.

## REVIEW QUESTIONS

1. Why does everyone need to develop an adaptable financial plan? Why should they want to?
2. Explain why it is difficult to manage your finances.
3. What five steps make up the financial planning process?
4. Procrastination, or postponing the development and implementation of a financial plan, is a common problem. Why?
5. List and explain the four common concerns that should guide all financial plans.
6. What eight fundamental financial goals should everyone consider as a foundation for developing a financial plan of action?
7. Explain the time horizon for short-term, intermediate-term, and long-term goals. Give an example of each.
8. Why are financial goals the cornerstone of your financial plan?
9. List and characterize the stages of the life cycle. For each stage note a complication that might affect the plan.
10. Define career planning. How is it related to financial planning?
11. What is the relationship among income/earnings potential, education, and standard of living or lifestyle? How do these characteristics differ between middle-class and wealthy households?
12. List three reasons why college seniors returning to campus should have a résumé already prepared.
13. What are the two reasons investors demand compensation when making an investment? Why might investors who ignore these principles lose money? Explain how Principles 1, 2, and 11 impact the investors' choice to delay consumption.
14. Define the terms "maturity date," "diversification," and "liquidity." Give an example to illustrate each concept.
15. Risk is a central concept in Principles 1, 3, 4, and 11. Explain the importance of risk in the context of each.

## PROBLEMS AND ACTIVITIES

1. What financial strategies should you develop as a result of studying personal financial planning? What financial problems might you avoid?
2. List the five steps in the financial planning process. For each, list an activity, or financial task, that you should be accomplishing.
3. Financial goals should be specific, realistic, prioritized, and anchored in time. Using these characteristics, identify five financial goals for yourself.

4. As the cornerstone of your financial plan, goals should reflect your lifestyle, serve as a guide to action, and act as a benchmark for evaluating the effectiveness of your plan. For one of the goals identified previously, explain this statement.

5. The goal of financing the cost of education is obviously important in your present stage of the financial life cycle. Explain how this goal might continue to be important in future stages.

## SUGGESTED PROJECTS

1. Interview three financial managers, each from a household representing a different stage of the life cycle or socioeconomic status. Inquire about their financial planning process and their strategies to identify and save for short-term, intermediate-term, and long-term goals. Share your findings with the class.

2. A financial plan can be thought of a "financial road map to guide you through life." Develop a visual display that illustrates this principle and the five steps of the financial planning process. Try to incorporate examples that illustrate how the "new roads" on the map may change over the life cycle.

3. Visit your campus career counseling office to learn about the services available to help with your career search and your job search. What career management services, if any, are available after you graduate?

6. Three major steps are recommended when deciding on a career. List those steps.

7. Explain how **Principle 7: Stuff Happens, or the Importance of Liquidity** and **Principle 10: Protect Yourself Against Major Catastrophes** may be related. What are you currently doing to protect yourself, and your financial future, from "stuff and other major catastrophes"?

4. Talk with your academic advisor and a professional employed in your career field. What educational requirements are necessary for entry and advancement in the field? List four examples of how the advice "born to be wired" and "ditch the ladder, catch the Web" apply to your career.

5. As a group project, have each member of the group visit a financial professional (e.g., benefits officer, stockbroker, insurance salesperson, loan officer, banker, financial planner, etc.). Present the list of 15 principles that form the foundations of personal finance. Ask the professional to pick the three to five principles that he or she considers to be most important to personal financial success. Share the results in your group and prepare an essay or oral report of your findings. Which principles appear to be *most* important? Rate each professional using Principle 12.

## Discussion Case 1

Jimmy, an accountant, and Bethany just returned from their honeymoon in the Bahamas. They celebrated their marriage and the completion of Bethany's M.B.A. program. They have been encouraged by their parents to establish some personal and financial goals for their future. However, they do not know how to set or achieve these goals. They know that they would like to own their home and have children, but those are the only goals they have considered. Jimmy knows of a financial advisor who might be able to help with their predicament, but they don't think they can afford professional help.

### Questions

1. If you were serving as the couple's financial advisor, how would you explain the five steps in financial planning and their importance to future financial success?

2. What financial goals (short term, intermediate, and long term) would you determine to be the most important or least important to Jimmy and Bethany considering their current life cycle stage? Support your answer. *Hint:* See Figure 1.2.

3. What four principles should guide the development of their financial plan? How do these relate to Principles 6, 7, and 10?

4. List five tips for Bethany to keep in mind during her job search.

5. Identify three important strategies for young professionals like Jimmy and Bethany to remember to ensure success in their chosen careers.

# Money Matters

## THE ABC'S OF FINDING AN ADVISOR

*Analyze your needs.* Are you a "do-it-yourselfer" who needs just a basic plan to follow, or do you need assistance in implementing any recommendations? Are you just starting out, or do you have a family and estate planning needs? Perhaps you have both personal and business concerns, such as a professional practice or your own firm.

*Decide what type of advisor you want.* Are you set on a "fee only" planner? Do you like the idea of a general practitioner, or does your situation dictate the need for a highly specialized individual, such as an estate attorney? Once you've figured out what type of advisor you want, attend seminars, or better yet, ask for referrals from friends and family.

*Visit with one or more advisors before you make a decision.* Most offer a complementary initial consultation. Caution: Don't feel you have to keep shopping if you're fortunate to find the right person on the first try.

*Investigate your candidates.* Ask for an explanation of services or a sample plan. Check for complaints and resolutions through the Better Business

Bureau or regulatory bodies such as the CFP Board of Standards. Find out how long the firm has been in business. (Will they be there when you need them?) How is the advisor compensated?

*Set a deadline for selecting your advisor and stick to it.* I have met people who admit to spending 5 or more years searching for the "perfect planner."

*Open your mind!* Gray hair and wrinkles don't always mean wisdom, and peach fuzz is not synonymous with fresh ideas. If the candidates are relatively new in practice, make sure they have, or are pursuing a professional designation and that they have associates who can take over for them if they don't continue in the practice.

*Rely on your knowledge and instincts.* If you're not comfortable enough with the person to reveal all your financial details, run, don't walk, away. Annoying "faults" and suspicions become major roadblocks with time. Select someone you like, trust, and respect—someone you think could be your lifetime financial advisor. As Mom always said, "Don't date 'em if you wouldn't marry 'em."

## Discussion Case 2

Doug and Marita Jones, from Rochester, New York, are the proud new parents of twin baby girls. This was quite a shock to them and 2-year-old Jarred. They were not prepared for twins and this has left their financial plans in ruins. They had been planning to pay for education costs, but now they are unsure whether they will be able to afford expenses for three children in college at the same time. They also have a dream to retire early and travel. They want to start over with their objectives and establish a long-term plan that incorporates all of the new goals. Marita has told Doug that she wants to attend a personal finance seminar given at a local conference center, but Doug thinks they should seek assistance from a financial planner. As Doug points out, *now* they have a pile of medical bills and their day care costs are tripling, but they both have good jobs with the potential for rapid advancement and salary increases.

### Questions

**1.** In your own words explain to Doug and Marita why personal

financial planning is crucial to their future. Why are Principles 9 and 12 important if they choose to seek professional advice?

**2.** Using the information in Table 1.1, estimate the cost of raising the twins from birth to age 18 if the Joneses' current annual income is approximately $75,000 and both parents plan to continue working full-time.

**3.** In addition to funding the children's education, name seven other goals the Joneses should consider as they begin to establish a plan of action.

**4.** Given the eight general goals identified earlier, categorize each as a short-term, intermediate-term, or long-term goal. Which of these goals will be particularly important during the retirement years?

**5.** With three children to consider, how might Principles 7, 10, and 11 pertain to the Joneses' situation?

Visit our Web site for additional case problems, interactive exercises, and practice quizzes for this chapter— **www.prenhall.com/keown**.

# 2 Measuring Your Financial Health and Making a Plan

**Learning Objectives**

**Calculate** your level of net worth or wealth using a balance sheet.

**Analyze** where your money comes from and where it goes using an income statement.

**Use** ratios to identify your financial strengths and weaknesses.

**Set up** a record-keeping system to track your income and expenditures.

**Implement** a financial plan or budget that will provide for the level of savings needed to achieve your goals.

**Decide** if a professional financial planner will play a role in your financial affairs.

An episode of HBO's *Sex in the City* finds Carrie Bradshaw taking a break from the pressures of trying to come up with a down payment to buy her apartment by doing what she does best, shoe shopping with her friend Miranda.

"Where did all my money go? I know I made some . . ."

Holding up a pair of Manolo Blahnik shoes, Miranda replies, "At 400 bucks a pop how many of these do you have? 50? 100?"

"Would that be wrong?"

"One hundred times four hundred, that's your down payment," Miranda replies.

"Well, that's only . . . 4,000."

"No, that's 40,000," corrects Miranda.

"I spent $40,000 on shoes and have no place to live!"

Sure, *Sex in the City* is only a TV show, but TV tends to reflect society, and this was one of those shows that left many viewers saying to themselves, "That could happen to me—I know I make money, I just don't know where it goes."

Fortunately, that's not the case for Sarah Jessica Parker who plays Carrie Bradshaw. Today, she and her husband Matthew Broderick, who starred in such classic movies as *Ferris Bueller's Day Off* and *The Freshman* and then moved to

Broadway to star in *The Producers*, lead a relatively frugal life and have financial security well in hand. However, that hasn't always been the case for Sarah. "I remember being poor. There was no great way to hide it. We didn't have electricity sometimes. We didn't have Christmases sometimes, or we didn't have birthdays sometimes, or the bill collectors came, or the phone company would call and say, 'We're shutting your phones off.' And we were all old enough to either get the calls, or watch my mother's reactions or watch my parents shuffling the money around."

Actually, it doesn't matter how much or how little you make, the key to financial success is control. Although Sarah and Matthew are doing well, there are plenty of other celebrities who have proven that making money doesn't guarantee financial success unless there is a plan. For example, M. C. Hammer, who earned $33 million in 1990 singing "Too Legit to Quit," declared bankruptcy in 1996 with $13.7 million in debts. In the 1990s bankruptcy also bit film stars Kim Basinger and Burt Reynolds, as well as Shannen Doherty of *Beverly Hills, 90210* fame, among others. Then in 2002 New Orleans Saints cornerback Dale Carter filed for bankruptcy the same month he signed a $28 million contract, and just three years after signing a four-year, $22.8 million contract with the Denver Broncos that included a $7.8 million signing bonus.

How does this all relate to you? There aren't many of us who will get a starring role on HBO and the money that goes with it. But we can all get ourselves into trouble, regardless of how much or how little we have. You don't have to be rich to lose control of your money; you just have to forget about financial planning.

**Principle**
**P 8** Nothing Happens Without a Plan

It would be incredibly easy to avoid thinking about our financial future—dealing with the present is difficult enough. However, don't forget **Principle 8: Nothing Happens Without a Plan.** If you're like most people, you can probably spend money without thinking about it, but you can't save money without thinking about it. For Carrie Bradshaw, that certainly was the case. Saving isn't a natural event. It must be planned.

Planning and budgeting require control—they don't come naturally. For Carrie, that means looking into the future, facing financial reality and the sacrifices that go with it, and taking action. But without the ability to measure her financial health and develop a plan and budget to achieve her goals, those goals will never be achieved. Showing financial restraint isn't as much fun as spending with reckless abandon, but it's a lot more fun than winding up broke and homeless. Making and sticking with a plan isn't necessarily easy, and it often involves what some people would consider sacrifices, such as getting a job over spring break instead of going down to Panama City to be on MTV's *Spring Break*, or just skipping that daily designer coffee. The fact is, though, that the rewards of taking financial control are worth any small sacrifices and more. After all, you don't want to share Carrie's fate, "I will literally be the old woman who lived in her shoes."

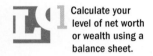

1 Calculate your level of net worth or wealth using a balance sheet.

**Personal Balance Sheet**
A statement of your financial position on a given date. It includes the assets you own, the debt or liabilities you have incurred, and your level of wealth, which is referred to as net worth.

**Assets**
What you own.

**Liabilities**
Something that is owed or the borrowing of money.

**Net Worth or Equity**
A measure of the level of your wealth. It is determined by subtracting the level of your debt or borrowing from the value of your assets.

**Fair Market Value**
What an asset could be sold for rather than what it cost or what it will be worth sometime in the future.

## Using a Balance Sheet to Measure Your Wealth

Before you can decide how much you need to save to reach your goals, you have to measure your financial condition—what you own and what you owe. Corporations use a balance sheet for this purpose, and so can you. A **personal balance sheet** is a statement of your financial position on a given date—a snapshot of your financial status at a particular point in time. It lists the **assets** you own, the debt or **liabilities** you've incurred, and your general level of wealth, which is your **net worth or equity**. Assets represent what you own. Liabilities represent your debt or what you owe. To determine your level of wealth or net worth, you subtract your level of debt or borrowing from the value of your assets.

Figure 2.1 shows the relationship of these three main balance sheet elements. As you can see, a balance sheet gets its name from the fact that the two sides have to balance, or be equal. The first major section of your balance sheet represents all your assets. All your possessions are considered assets whether or not you still owe money on them. From the value of your assets, subtract the amount of debt you owe. This total, your assets minus your borrowing, equals your net worth. This means that your net worth or wealth is actually how much you have after all borrowing has been paid off. Figure 2.2 provides a sample balance sheet worksheet.

### Assets: What You Own

When you estimate the value of all your assets, list them using their **fair market value,** not what they cost or what they will be worth a year from now. The fair market value can be more or less than the price you paid for a given asset, depending on

## Figure 2.1 Net Worth

| Value of Your Assets | − | Amount of Debt or Borrowing | = | Net Worth or Wealth |

what others are willing to pay for that asset now. Remember, a balance sheet is a snapshot in time, so all values must be current.

There are a number of different types of assets. A monetary asset is basically a liquid asset—one that is either cash or can easily be turned into cash with little or no loss in value. Monetary assets include the cash you hold, your checking and savings account balances, and your money market funds. These are the cash and cash equivalents you use for everyday life. They also provide the necessary liquidity in case of an emergency.

The second major category of assets, investments, involves such financial assets as common stocks, mutual funds, or bonds. In general, the purpose of these assets is to accumulate wealth to satisfy a goal like buying a house or having sufficient savings for college or retirement. You can usually determine the value of your investments by reading the financial quotes in the *Wall Street Journal.*

Your insurance policy may also be an investment asset if it has a savings element that accumulates over time, because its purpose is to generate wealth. For example, with permanent or cash value life insurance, which accounts for more than half of all life insurance policies sold in the United States, the policy can be terminated

WORKSHEET

## Figure 2.2 Personal Balance Sheet

### Assets (What You Own)

| | | |
|---|---|---|
| A. Monetary Assets (bank account, etc.) | | _____ |
| B. Investments | + | _____ |
| C. Retirement Plans | + | _____ |
| D. Housing (market value) | + | _____ |
| E. Automobiles | + | _____ |
| F. Personal Property | + | _____ |
| G. Other Assets | + | _____ |
| H. Your Total Assets (add lines A–G) | = | _____ |

### Liabilities or Debt (What You Owe)

**Current Debt**

| | | |
|---|---|---|
| I. Current Bills | | _____ |
| J. Credit Card Debt | + | _____ |

**Long-Term Debt**

| | | |
|---|---|---|
| K. Housing | | _____ |
| L. Automobile Loans | + | _____ |
| M. Other Debt | + | _____ |
| N. Your Total Debt (add lines I–M) | = | _____ |

### Your Net Worth

| | | |
|---|---|---|
| H. Total Assets | | _____ |
| N. Less: Total Debt | − | _____ |
| O. Equals: Your Net Worth | = | _____ |

before the insured's death, at which time the policyholder will receive the cash value of the policy.

If you have an insurance policy with a cash surrender value (the dollar amount that you would receive if you cashed in the policy today), then that value should be included as part of your investment assets. If you have an annuity—a contract written by an insurance company that provides the contract holder with a constant income, generally for the remainder of the holder's life—the cash value of this annuity should also be included as one of your investment assets. Finally, any real estate purchased for investment purposes should also appear as an asset. The common thread among all these assets is that they are not meant for use, as you would use a car or a house. Instead, they have been purchased for the purpose of generating wealth.

The next category of assets is retirement plans. These include investments made by you or your employer aimed directly at achieving your goal of saving for retirement. Retirement plans are usually in the form of IRAs, 401(k) or 403(b) plans, Keogh plans, SEP-IRA plans, and company pension plans. IRAs are individual retirement accounts to which individuals, depending upon their income level, can make a tax-deductible contribution of up to $3,000 in years 2002 through 2004, $4,000 in years 2005 through 2007, and $5,000 in 2008.

The 401(k) and 403(b) plans allow employees to place a portion of their salary into a tax-deferred investment account. Keogh and SEP-IRA plans are tax-deductible retirement plans for self-employed individuals. The current value of your stake in your company's pension plan should also be included as a retirement plan asset. If you work for a company that offers a pension plan, the easiest way to value your stake in the plan is to call up your benefits office and ask them how much it's worth.

Your house comprises another asset category. Although a house is an asset that you use—a **tangible asset**—it usually holds the majority of your savings. The value of your house recorded on the balance sheet should be its fair market value, even though at that price it may take several months for it to sell. You might consult with a real estate agent for help in valuing your home. Keep in mind that even if you owe money on your home, it's still yours.

Your car, truck, motorcycle, or other vehicle also gets its own asset category. Like your home, your vehicle is a tangible asset—one you probably use daily. However, unlike your home, your vehicle is likely to be worth less than you paid for it. The fair market value for vehicles almost always goes down, often starting right after you take it home from the showroom. You can find the fair market value for most vehicles in an automotive **Blue Book**. Do not include any cars you lease as assets. If the car is leased, you don't hold title to it and thus don't actually own it. Likewise, a company car that you get to use but don't own wouldn't count as an asset.

Personal property is another category of assets. Personal property consists of tangible assets. Basically, personal property is all your possessions—furniture, appliances, jewelry, TVs, and so forth. In general, although you may have spent a good deal of money on these items, their fair market value will be only a fraction of the purchase amount.

The "other" category includes anything that has not yet been accounted for. For example, you might have an ownership share in a business, you might own a massive collection of semivaluable (or so you think) Pez dispensers, or you might be owed money by a deadbeat friend. All of these count as assets and must appear at their fair market value on your balance sheet. Of course, if your friend *is* a deadbeat, the amount owed shouldn't appear as an asset—you'll never see it!

Summed up, these asset categories represent the total value of everything you own. You might be surprised to find out you are worth much more than you originally thought.

**Tangible Asset**
A physical asset, such as a house or a car, as opposed to an investment.

**Blue Book**
A listing of used-car prices, giving the average price a particular year and model sells for and what you might expect to receive for it as a trade-in.

## Liabilities: What You Own

A liability may refer to such debts as your unpaid credit card balance or your unpaid student loan. In any case, it's a debt that you have taken on and that you must repay in the future. Most financial planners classify liabilities as current or long-term. Current liabilities are those that must be paid off within the next year, and long-term liabilities come due beyond a year's time. In listing your liabilities, be sure to include only the unpaid balances on those liabilities. Remember, you owe only the unpaid portion of any loan.

In general, your unpaid bills and credit card debt will be the only sources of current liabilities. Unpaid utility bills, past due rent, cable TV bills, insurance premiums that you owe, and so forth all involve money you currently owe and should be included as liabilities. In fact, even if you have not yet received a bill for a purchase you made on credit, the amount you owe on this purchase should be included as a liability. The unpaid balance on your credit cards represents a current liability because it's a debt that you should pay off within a year.

Long-term debt tends to consist of debt on larger assets, such as your home or car, although your biggest source of long-term debt right now is probably your student loan. Because of the nature of the assets it finances, long-term debt almost always involves larger amounts than does current debt. If you think about it, the very reason long-term debt covers the long term is that it involves sums too large for the average individual to be able to pay off within 1 year. The largest debt you ever take on, and thus the longest-term debt you ever take on, will probably be the mortgage on your home.

Car loans are another major category of long-term debt. Just as a leased car is not considered an asset, the remaining lease obligation should not be considered a liability, or something that you owe. In effect, you are "renting" your car when you lease it. Actually, it's a very fine line between a debt obligation and a lease contract. Some leases simply can't be broken so they may be considered debt. The point to keep in mind is that things such as future lease payments, future insurance payments, and future rent payments are something you may owe in the future, but they are not something you owe right now.

Finally, any other loans that you have outstanding should be included. For example, student loans, loans on your life insurance policy, bank loans, and installment loans are liabilities. Together, long-term debt and current liabilities represent what you owe.

## Net Worth: A Measure of Your Wealth

Your net worth represents the level of wealth you or your family have accumulated. To calculate your net worth, simply subtract your liabilities from the value of your assets. If your liabilities are greater than the value of your assets, then your net worth has a negative value, and you're considered **insolvent**. Insolvency results from consuming more than you take in financially, and in some instances it can lead to bankruptcy.

What is a "good" level of net worth? That depends upon your goals and your place in the financial life cycle. You would expect a 25-year-old to have a considerably lower net worth than a 45-year-old. Likewise, a 45-year-old who has saved for college for three children may have a higher net worth than a 45-year-old with no children. Which one is in better financial shape? The answer doesn't necessarily rest on who has the larger net worth, but on who has done a better job of achieving financial goals. Just to give you an idea of where most people stand,

**Insolvent**
The condition in which you owe more money than your assets are worth.

## Table 2.1   How Do You Compare?

| | |
|---|---|
| Average annual salary: | |
| High school graduate | $26,312 |
| College graduate | $43,316 |
| Median net worth | $71,600 |
| Median home equity | $38,000 |
| If your family income is at least . . . | then you're in the top . . . |
| $355,000 | 1% |
| 130,000 | 5 |
| 93,800 | 10 |
| 60,800 | 25 |
| 33,400 | 50 |
| Average annual amount spent by full-time college students on beer and pizza . . . | $1,750 |
| Average annual cost of tuition and room at a private U.S. university . . . | $24,946 |
| Projected cost in 18 years . . . | $60,120 |

Source:   Melynda Dovel Wilcox, "Are You Above Average?" *Kiplinger's Personal Finance*, January 2001: 86. Judy Feldman, "Price Points," *Money Magazine*, October 2001: 30. Farnoosh Torab, "Price Points," *Money Magazine*, September 2001: 26.

Table 2.1 presents the average annual salary and net worth for individuals along with some other financial data.

Your goal in financial planning is to manage your net worth or wealth in such a way that your goals are met in a timely fashion. You use the balance sheet to measure your progress toward these goals, to monitor your financial well-being. You use the balance sheet to detect changes in your financial well-being that might otherwise go unnoticed and correct them early on. In effect, you use the balance sheet to monitor your financial health in the same way a doctor would use a medical instrument to monitor your physical health.

## Sample Balance Sheet for Larry and Louise Tate

WORKSHEET

To illustrate the construction and use of a balance sheet, we have a sample from Larry and Louise Tate in Figure 2.3. Remember, a balance sheet provides a snapshot of an individual's or family's financial worth at a given point in time. As investment values fluctuate daily with the movements in the stock market, so does net worth. The balance sheet in Figure 2.3 was constructed on December 31, 2003, and reflects the value of the Tates' assets, liabilities, and net worth on that specific date.

To gain an understanding of what their balance sheet means, let's look at the Tates' background. The Tates are both 35 years old, have been married for 10 years, and have 2 children, ages 4 and 2. Larry is a production supervisor for a large home builder in the Denver, Colorado, area. He's been working there for 13 years, ever since his graduation from college with a degree in building construction. Over that time he has progressed steadily in his job, moving up the corporate ladder to a position where he now has over 200 employees working for him. For Larry, the future looks bright. After college, Louise worked for 9 years as a laboratory technician in a blood bank. When the children arrived, she quit her job and took a part-time job as a

**Figure 2.3** A Balance Sheet for Louise and Larry Tate, December 31, 2003

## Assets (What You Own)

| | | | |
|---|---|---|---:|
| Cash | | | 340 |
| Checking | | + | 250 |
| Savings/CDs | | + | 1,500 |
| Money Market Funds | | + | 1,500 |
| **A. Monetary Assets** | **A.** | **=** | **3,590** |
| Mutual Funds | | | 5,600 |
| Stocks | | + | 8,500 |
| Bonds | | + | 1,000 |
| Life Insurance (cash value) | | + | 0 |
| Cash Value of Annuities | | + | 0 |
| Investment Real Estate (REITs, partnerships) | | + | 0 |
| **B. Investments** | **B.** | **=** | **15,100** |
| 401(k) and 403(b) | | | 0 |
| Company Pension | | + | 8,000 |
| Keogh | | + | 2,500 |
| IRA | | + | 8,000 |
| **C. Retirement Plans** | **C.** | **=** | **18,500** |
| Primary Residence | | | 170,000 |
| Second Home | | + | 0 |
| Time-Shares/Condominiums | | + | 70,000 |
| **D. Housing (market value)** | **D.** | **=** | **240,000** |
| Automobile 1 | | | 9,000 |
| Automobile 2 | | + | 3,000 |
| **E. Automobiles** | **E.** | **=** | **12,000** |
| Collectibles | | | 3,000 |
| Boats | | + | 0 |
| Furniture | | + | 8,000 |
| **F. Personal Property** | **F.** | **=** | **11,000** |
| Money Owed You | | | 0 |
| Market Value of Your Business | | + | 0 |
| Other | | + | 0 |
| **G. Other Assets** | **G.** | **=** | **0** |
| **H. Total Assets (add lines A–G)** | **H.** | **=** | **$300,190** |

## Liabilities or Debt (What You Owe)

| | | | |
|---|---|---|---:|
| **I.  Current Bills (unpaid balance)** | **I.** | **=** | **350** |
| Visa | | | 1,150 |
| MasterCard | | + | 0 |
| Other Credit Cards | | + | 0 |
| **J.  Credit Card Debt** | **J.** | **=** | **1,150** |
| First Mortgage | | | 105,000 |
| Second Home Mortgage | | + | 52,000 |
| Home Equity Loan | | + | 9,000 |
| **K. Housing** | **K.** | **=** | **166,000** |
| Automobile 1 | | | 3,000 |
| Automobile 2 | | + | 0 |
| **L.  Automobile Loans** | **L.** | **=** | **3,000** |
| College Loans | | | 4,000 |
| Loans on Life Insurance Policies | | + | 0 |
| Bank Loans | | + | 0 |
| Installment Loans | | + | 1,000 |
| Other | | + | 0 |
| **M. Other Debt** | **M.** | **=** | **5,000** |
| **N. Total Debt (add lines I–M)** | **N.** | **=** | **$175,500** |

## Your Net Worth

| | | | |
|---|---|---|---:|
| **H. Total Assets** | **H.** | **+** | **$300,190** |
| **N. Less: Total Debt** | **N.** | **–** | **$175,500** |
| **O. Equals: Net Worth** | **O.** | **=** | **$124,690** |

medical supplies salesperson, which allowed her to spend most of her time at home raising her children.

The Tates live just outside Boulder in an older house they purchased 7 years ago. Since that time they have put an addition on the house and remodeled the kitchen and bathrooms. They love skiing and hiking in the mountains and have already started taking their kids along. In fact, 6 years ago they purchased a condominium in Vail, and they try to visit it at least twice a month. On the financial front, they don't seem to have serious concerns regarding the future; however, they have begun to save for their children's college education.

**Calculating What the Tates Own: Their Total Assets**  The Tates' primary investments are their home and their vacation condominium in Vail, which have market values of $170,000 and $70,000, respectively. They have total monetary assets of $3,590 spread among cash, checking and savings accounts, certificates of deposit, and money market mutual funds. These assets are aimed at both paying off bills and debts that are coming due and providing the Tates with a cash buffer against any unexpected emergencies.

Their long-term savings, aimed at providing college funds for their children and building a retirement nest egg for themselves, total $15,100 and are primarily invested in common stock and mutual funds. They also have $18,500 in retirement plans. Their final assets are two cars valued at $12,000, personal property of $8,000, which is mostly furniture, and collectibles valued at $3,000, which include Larry's collection of Three Stooges memorabilia, the highlight of which is a set of letters between Moe and his mother. Thus, the Tates own or have total assets of $300,190.

**Calculating What the Tates Owe: Their Total Liabilities**  Just as the Tates' homes make up their primary assets, their mortgages on these homes make up their primary liabilities. Their mortgage loans total $166,000, which includes a home equity loan of $9,000 taken out 2 years ago to remodel the bathrooms and kitchen area of their primary residence. The Tates have a relatively low level of current liabilities, with only $350 in unpaid bills and an unpaid credit card balance of $1,150. Their other liabilities include an outstanding car loan of $3,000, an education loan of $4,000, and an installment loan of $1,000, associated with the purchase of a big-screen television earlier this year. Thus, the Tates' total liabilities, or what they owe, equals $175,500.

**Calculating the Tates' Wealth: Their Net Worth**  By subtracting the Tates' total liabilities from their total assets, you can determine the Tates' net worth to be $124,690. This sum represents the amount of wealth the Tates have accumulated as of December 31, 2003. This wealth could have resulted either from the Tates saving money (spending less than they earn) or from the appreciation in value of some of their assets, such as stocks, mutual funds, or their homes. If the Tates sold all their assets and paid off all their debts, they would have $124,690 in cash.

Because the Tates won't be selling off their assets in the near future, what does this net worth figure really mean? Actually, it's a measure by which the Tates will gauge their financial progress. If in future balance sheets their net worth figure is higher, the Tates will know that they're accumulating more wealth. If their net worth goes down, they'll know that they need to be more careful protecting the wealth they have. Still, the balance sheet alone does not give a complete picture of financial status. You also need a personal income statement.

# Using an Income Statement to Trace Your Money

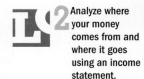

**L** 2 Analyze where your money comes from and where it goes using an income statement.

A balance sheet is like a financial snapshot: It tells you how much wealth you have accumulated as of a *certain date*. An **income statement** is more like a financial motion picture: It tells you where your money has come from and where it has gone over some *period of time*. Actually, although it's generally called an income statement, it's really an income and expenditure, or net income statement, because it looks at both what you take in and what you spend.

**Income Statement**
A statement that tells you where your money has come from and where it has gone over some *period of time*.

An income statement can help you stay solvent by telling you whether or not you're earning more than you spend. If you're spending too much, your income statement shows exactly where your money is going so that you can spot problem areas quickly. Of course, if you don't have a spending problem, your income statement tells you how much of your income is available for savings and for meeting financial goals. With a good income statement, you'll never end another month wondering where all of your money went.

Personal income statements are prepared on a cash basis, meaning they're based entirely on actual cash flows. You record income only when you actually receive money, and you record expenditures only when you actually pay money out. Giving someone an IOU wouldn't appear on an income statement, but receiving a paycheck would. Buying a stereo on credit wouldn't appear on your income statement, but making a payment to the credit card company would. As a result, a personal income statement truly reflects the pattern of cash flows that the individual or family experiences.

To construct an income statement, you need only record your income for the given time period and subtract from it the expenses you incurred during that period. The result tells you your contribution to savings. Figure 2.4 shows a general outline for an income statement.

**7** WORKSHEET

## Income: Where Your Money Comes From

For your income statement, income, or cash inflows, will include such items as wages, salary, bonuses, tips, royalties, and commissions, in addition to any other sources of income you may have. Additional sources of income might include family income, payments from the government (e.g., veterans' benefits or welfare income),

**Figure 2.4** A Simplified Income Statement

**Your Take-Home Pay**

| | |
|---|---|
| A. Total Income | A. _____ |
| B. Total Income Taxes | − B. _____ |
| C. After-Tax Income Available for Living Expenditures or Take-Home Pay (line A minus line B) | = C. _____ |

**Your Living Expenses**

| | | |
|---|---|---|
| D. Total Housing Expenditures | D. _____ | |
| E. Total Food Expenditures | + E. _____ | |
| F. Total Clothing and Personal Care Expenditures | + F. _____ | |
| G. Total Transportation Expenditures | + G. _____ | |
| H. Total Recreation Expenditures | + H. _____ | |
| I. Total Medical Expenditures | + I. _____ | |
| J. Total Insurance Expenditures | + J. _____ | |
| K. Total Other Expenditures | + K. _____ | |
| L. Total Living Expenditures (add lines D–K) | | = L. _____ |
| M. Income Available for Savings and Investment (line C minus line L) | | = M. _____ |

retirement income, investment income, and those yearly checks you get from Ed McMahon for winning the Publishers' Clearinghouse Sweepstakes. In short, any funds that you actually receive would be considered income.

Some of your income may not ever reach your pocketbook. Instead, it may be automatically invested in a voluntary retirement plan, pay for insurance you buy through work, or sent to the government to cover taxes. For example, if your total earnings are $50,000 and you automatically have $10,000 deducted for taxes, then your income would be $50,000 even though your take-home pay is only $40,000. You must make sure to record the full amount of what you earned—your full earnings and taxes paid, not just the dollar value of your paycheck. The key point here is that any money you receive, even if you automatically spend it (even for taxes), is considered income at the point in time when it is received.

## Expenditures: Where Your Money Goes

Although income is usually very easy to calculate, expenditures usually are not. Why? Because many expenditures are cash transactions and do not leave a paper trail. It's hard to keep track of all the little things you spend your money on. If you don't keep careful track of your expenses, though, you'll never figure out where your money goes.

One way to make tracking expenditures a bit less formidable is to categorize them as in Figure 2.4. The two general categories you use are take-home pay and living expenses. Income taxes include both federal and state income taxes in addition to Social Security taxes. This is income taken out of your paycheck before you receive it. If you take your total income and subtract from that your total income taxes, you arrive at after-tax income available for living expenditures, or take-home pay. This amount gives you an understanding of what level of cash flow you have for living expenditures. Once living expenses have been subtracted, the remainder contributes to savings and investments, as shown in Figure 2.4.

**WORKSHEET**

| Net Income or Contribution to Savings = Income on a Cash Basis – Taxes on a Cash Basis – Living Expenses on a Cash Basis |
|---|

Some financial planners also classify living expenses as **variable** or **fixed expenditures**, depending on whether you have control over the expenditure. These classifications are appealing, but not all expenses fit neatly into them. For example, it's difficult to categorize car or home repairs as being either variable (you have a choice in spending this money) or fixed (you have no choice in spending this money). They may be postponable but probably not for too long.

**Variable Expenditure**
An expenditure over which you have control. That is, you are not obligated to make that expenditure, and it may vary from month to month.

**Fixed Expenditure**
An expenditure over which you have no control. You are obligated to make this expenditure, and it is generally at a constant level each month.

What does the average American household spend its money on? That depends on how much it earns. The more it earns, the more it spends on such things as education and entertainment. Figure 2.5 provides a breakdown of spending for the average U.S. household using the number of days worked as a yardstick. Interestingly, in 2002, the average U.S. household worked 117 days to pay for taxes—more time than it takes to pay for food and housing combined. Most of this time, 80 days, is spent to pay off the federal tax bill. The remainder, 37 days, is spent working to pay state and local taxes. After taxes, the big expenses are food, housing, and medical care.

You should keep in mind that the amounts in Figure 2.5 are spending averages, and they tend to vary across the country. For example, people living in San Francisco spend quite a bit more on food because they tend to eat out more often than those who live elsewhere (better restaurants, I guess). In addition, keep in mind that when you buy something, it actually costs more than you may think—at least in terms of

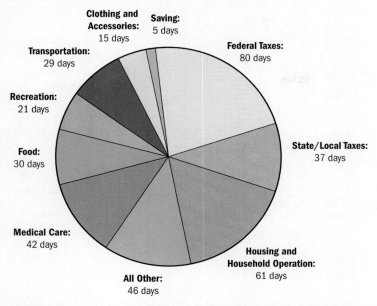

Figure 2.5 How Americans Spent Their Money in 2002

Clothing and Accessories: 15 days

Saving: 5 days

Federal Taxes: 80 days

Transportation: 29 days

Recreation: 21 days

State/Local Taxes: 37 days

Food: 30 days

Medical Care: 42 days

Housing and Household Operation: 61 days

All Other: 46 days

Source: "America Celebrates Tax Freedom Day." Washington DC: The Tax Foundation, 2002.

how much money you must earn to buy it. For example, if you are in the 28 percent tax bracket and you buy a new stereo for $720, you had to earn $1,000 to pay for it. The first $280 of your $1,000 earnings went to Uncle Sam, leaving you $720 for your stereo.

## Preparing an Income Statement: Louise and Larry Tate

To get a better understanding of the preparation of an income statement, take a look at the one for Louise and Larry Tate in Figure 2.6. Last year Larry earned $57,500 at his management job in building construction, and Louise earned $12,000 at her part-time sales job. In addition, they received $720 in interest and dividends. Approximately 19.5 percent of their income went toward income taxes. As a result, for every dollar the Tates earned, only about 79.5¢ was available after taxes for living expenses. The largest item in their living expenses was housing, which totaled $30,776, or approximately 44 percent of income. The Tates' housing expenditures are this large because they own both a house and a vacation condominium. Other expenditures are given in Figure 2.6.

WORKSHEET

Some of the expenditures in Figure 2.6 may look low to you. How can the Tates get along on only $670 per year for movies, theater, and sporting events? The answer is that you've got to live within your means, and you've got to make some sacrifices. In fact, you may find some of your necessities are actually luxuries, and expensive ones at that. For example, a $50 a month cable bill is $600 per year! That doesn't mean you've got to drop *Spongebob Squarepants* and *Road Rules* from your life, but you do have to make choices, and before you do that you've got to understand the trade-offs. That's what a cash budget will do for you.

Once their total living expenditures (line L) have been subtracted from the after-tax income available for living expenditures (line C), the Tates arrive at their cash flow, or income available for savings and investment. As you can see, the Tates have

Figure 2.6 Louise and Larry Tate's Personal Income Statement

## Income

| | | |
|---|---|---|
| Wages and Salaries | | |
|   Wage Earner 1 | $57,500 | |
|   + Wage Earner 2 | 12,000 | |
| = Total Wages and Salaries | | 69,500 |
| + Interest and Dividends | | 720 |
| + Royalties, Commissions, and Rents | | 0 |
| + Other Income | | 0 |
| **= A. Total Income** | | **$70,220** |

## Taxes

| | |
|---|---|
| Federal Income and Social Security | 11,830 |
| + State Income | 1,880 |
| **= B. Total Income Taxes** | **$13,710** |
| **C. After-Tax Income Available for Living Expenditures or Take-Home Pay (line A minus line B)** | **$56,510** |

## Living Expenses

**Housing**

| | |
|---|---|
| Rent | 0 |
| + Mortgage Payments | 19,656 |
| + Utilities | 2,420 |
| + Maintenance | 1,500 |
| + Real Estate and Property Taxes | 4,800 |
| + Fixed Assets—furniture, appliances, televisions, etc. | 1,700 |
| + Other Living Expenses _____ | 400 |
| **= D. Total Housing Expenditures** | **$30,476** |

**Food**

| | |
|---|---|
| Food and Supplies | 5,800 |
| + Restaurant Expenses | 1,400 |
| **= E. Total Food Expenditures** | **$ 7,200** |

**Clothing and Personal Care**

| | |
|---|---|
| New Clothes | 2,100 |
| + Cleaning | 190 |
| + Tailoring | 0 |
| + Personal Care—hair care | 200 |
| + Other Clothing and Personal Care Expenses _____ | 100 |
| **= F. Total Clothing and Personal Care Expenditures** | **$ 2,590** |

**Transportation**

| | |
|---|---|
| Automobile Purchase | 0 |
| + Payments | 2,588 |
| + Gas, Tolls, Parking | 840 |
| + Automobile Registration/Tags/Stickers | 110 |
| + Repairs | 600 |
| + Other Transportation Expenses _____ | 0 |
| **= G. Total Transportation Expenditures** | **$ 4,138** |

**Recreation**

| | |
|---|---|
| Movies, Theater, Sporting Events | 670 |
| + Club Memberships | 240 |
| + Vacations | 2,000 |
| + Hobbies | 150 |
| + Sporting Goods | 100 |
| + Gifts | 180 |
| + Reading Materials (books, newspapers, magazines) | 130 |
| + Other Recreation Expenses (big screen TV payments) | 230 |
| **= H. Total Recreation Expenditures** | **$ 3,700** |

(figure continues)

(figure continued)

| | |
|---|---|
| **Medical Expenditures** | |
| Doctor | 180 |
| + Dental | 70 |
| + Prescription Drugs and Medicines | 160 |
| = I. **Total Medical Expenditures** | **$ 410** |
| **Insurance Expenditures** | |
| Health | 0 |
| + Life | 420 |
| + Automobile | 1,260 |
| + Disability | 260 |
| + Liability | 0 |
| + Other Insurance Expenses _____ | 0 |
| = J. **Total Insurance Expenditures** | **$ 1,940** |
| **Other Expenditures** | |
| Educational Expenditures (college loan payments) | 1,600 |
| + Child Care | 180 |
| + Other Expenses _____ | 0 |
| = K. **Total Other Expenditures** | **$ 1,780** |
| L. **Total Living Expenditures (add lines D–K)** | **$52,234** |
| = M. **Income Available for Savings and Investment (line C minus line L)** | **$ 4,276** |

$4,276 they can use to pay off debt or to invest in new assets. Note that this $4,276 increases the Tates' net worth. If they were to prepare a balance sheet at the beginning and end of the period covered by the income statement in Figure 2.6, the amount of their net worth would increase by exactly $4,276.

The income statement and balance sheet, then, can and should be used together. The balance sheet lets you judge your financial standing by showing your net worth, and the income statement tells you exactly how your spending and saving habits affect that net worth. If your balance sheet shows you that you're not building your net worth as much as or as quickly as you'd like, or if you're overspending and actually decreasing your net worth, your income statement can help.

By reviewing all your expenses and spending patterns, you can set specific goals to cut back on purchases and increase savings. This process of setting spending goals for the upcoming month or year is referred to as setting a **budget**. As you will see later in this chapter, a smart budget includes estimates of all future expenses and helps you manage your money to meet specific financial goals.

But before you can design and implement a budget plan, you first need to analyze your balance sheet and income statement using ratios to better understand any financial shortcomings or deficiencies you discover.

**Budget**
A plan for controlling cash inflows and cash outflows. Based on your goals and financial obligations, a budget limits spending in different categories.

## Using Ratios: A Financial Thermometer

By themselves the numbers in your balance sheet and income statement are helpful and informative, but they don't tell you everything you need to know about your financial well-being. Instead, you need a tool to help you pick out all the meaning you can from these numbers. That tool is ratios.

Financial ratios allow you to analyze the raw data in your balance sheet and income statement and to compare them with a preset target or your own previous performance. In general, your purpose in using ratios is to gain a better

Use ratios to identify your financial strengths and weaknesses.

# In The News

**Wall Street Journal June 26, 2001**

## *"I Plan to Save Like Crazy—Someday"*

We all agree that it is smart to save diligently, spend prudently, and invest intelligently. No doubt about it, these are entirely worthy long-term goals. There's just one drawback: They sure don't seem very appealing right now.

For instance, if your spouse suggested saving money by eating out less in the future, you might readily agree. But if your spouse proposed canceling tonight's restaurant reservation, you would likely balk.

It's no great surprise that we seek to postpone pain, financial or otherwise. But what's interesting is how much more amenable we become if we can delay the cost for just a short while. Often we happily agree to unpleasant tasks that are months away, only to regret it when the time rolls around. Indeed, at that juncture, we may try to weasel out of our commitment.

*What explains this odd behavior? At issue is our lack of self-control. But that seems to be exacerbated by two behavioral phenomena.* (☛A)

Postponing costs, of course, eventually catches up with us. "Often, you can save a lot of money by buying energy-efficient appliances," says Meir Statman, a finance

professor at Santa Clara University in California. "But people will gravitate toward the cheaper appliance," even though it is less energy efficient and, thus, may cost more in the long run.

It is not just that we discount future pain and pleasure at a surprisingly steep rate. There is a second related notion of "time inconsistency."

*How can we overcome these behavioral tendencies and thereby become better investors? "To the extent that you can make the benefits [of saving] loom large and the costs seem small, you are more likely to do the right thing," Mr. Statman says.* (☛B)

Mr. Statman suggests not only setting a firm goal for the money but also making a point of telling others about your plans. "If you make a public announcement to friends and family that this is the money for your child's education, it makes it more costly emotionally to spend that money," he says. "You'll feel very guilty."

## THE BOTTOM LINE . . .

**A** The end result is that we constantly defer key financial decisions, even though we know they are in our

long-term interest. As you will see, procrastination may be the biggest challenge you face in personal finance. Remember **Principle 8: Nothing Happens Without a Plan.**

**B** Also, don't just look at what you're spending today—look at what it will be in the future if you pass on spending today and save the money. For example, as you'll see (and be able to calculate) when we look at the time value of money, if instead of spending $1,000 today, you invest it for 25 years at 10 percent, you'd end up with $10,835! That will make it seem as if you are blowing some serious money if you spend it.

Source: Jonathan Clements, "I Plan to Save Like Crazy—Someday," *Wall Street Journal,* 26 June 2001: C1. Copyright (c) 2001, Dow Jones & Company, Inc. Reproduced with permission of DOW JONES & CO INC in the format Textbook via Copyright Clearance Center.

understanding of how you're managing your financial resources. Specifically, you try to answer the following questions:

1. Do I have adequate liquidity to meet emergencies?
2. Do I have the ability to meet my debt obligations?
3. Am I saving as much as I think I am?

## Question 1: Do I Have Adequate Liquidity to Meet Emergencies?

If your TV died in the middle of the playoffs or that miniseries you've been watching, would you have enough cash on hand to buy another one immediately? To judge your liquidity, you need to compare the amount of your cash and other liquid assets with the amount of debt you have currently coming due. In other words, you need to look at your balance sheet and divide your monetary assets by your current liabilities. The resultant measure of your liquidity is called the **current ratio**:

**Current Ratio**
A ratio aimed at determining if you have adequate liquidity to meet emergencies, defined as monetary assets divided by current liabilities.

$$\text{current ratio} = \frac{\text{monetary assets}}{\text{current liabilities}}$$

We can see from Larry and Louise Tates' balance sheet that their monetary assets total $3,590 and their current liabilities (current bills and credit card debt) total $1,500. Thus, the Tates' current ratio is:

$$\text{current ratio} = \frac{\$3,590}{\$1,500} = 2.39$$

Although there's no set rule for how large the current ratio should be, it certainly should be greater than 1.0. Most financial advisors look for a current ratio above 2.0. More important than the level of the current ratio is its trend—is it going up, or more important, is it going down? If it is going down, you have to try to find the cause. To do this you have to see what changes have caused the ratio to decrease.

One problem with the current ratio is that people generally have a number of monthly expenses that are not considered current liabilities. For example, long-term debt payments such as mortgage payments, auto loan payments, and so forth may not be considered current liabilities but still must be paid on a monthly basis. Therefore, it's also helpful to calculate the ratio of monetary assets to monthly living expenses, called the **month's living expenses covered ratio.**

$$\text{month's living expenses covered ratio} = \frac{\text{monetary assets}}{\text{annual living expenditures}/12}$$

**Month's Living Expenses Covered Ratio**
A ratio aimed at determining if you have adequate liquidity to meet emergencies, defined as monetary assets divided by annual living expenditures divided by 12.

As the name suggests, this ratio tells you how many months of living expenditures you can cover with your present level of monetary assets. Again, the numerator is the level of monetary assets, and the denominator is the annual living expenditures (as on line L of the income statement in Fig. 2.6) divided by 12. For the Tates, this ratio would be:

$$\frac{\$3,590}{\$52,234/12} = \frac{\$3,590}{\$4,353} = 0.825 \text{ months}$$

This means the Tates currently have enough cash and liquid assets on hand to cover 0.825 months of expenditures.

The traditional rule of thumb in personal finance is that an individual or family should have enough liquid assets to cover 3 to 6 months of expenditures. The Tates fall well short of this amount. However, as with all rules of thumb, you must use some caution in applying them. This rule was set up long before credit cards and home equity lines of credit. The logic behind it is that you need to set money aside in case of the untimely death of a television, a major car repair, or some other unexpected event.

When you have emergency funds, you don't need to tap into money for long-term goals. If you have sufficient credit from your credit cards or a home equity line of credit to cover emergency expenses, you also won't have to disturb this money. Of course, you may have to pay high interest on any credit you use, but the return you get from having to keep less in emergency funds may be enough to compensate.

Most emergency funds earn very little return, because as you gain liquidity you give up expected return. That all comes from **Principle 1: The Risk–Return Trade-Off.** Liquid investments are low risk and low return because the money is always safe and readily available.

The bottom line is that the Tates, and most people, may be better off investing most of their emergency funds in higher yielding, less liquid investments. For

Principle

The Risk–Return Trade-Off

example, if the Tates invest their emergency funds in a money market fund paying 3 percent, those funds will grow 34 percent over the next 10 years. If they invested them in a stock fund that grew at an annual rate of 9 percent, their investment would have grown 137 percent over that same period. Thus, given enough credit and insurance protection to provide income in the face of an emergency, you can safely reduce the number of months of living expenses you keep in your emergency fund to 3 or below.

Regardless of what you do with your emergency funds, the months living expenses covered ratio still provides a good, easy-to-understand indication of the relative level of cash on hand. It's a better personal liquidity measure than the current ratio. You would want to track it over time to make sure that it does not drop unexpectedly.

## Question 2: Do I Have the Ability to Meet My Debt Obligations?

**Debt Ratio**
A ratio aimed at determining if you have the ability to meet your debt obligations, defined as total debt or liabilities divided by total assets.

A second question you can answer using ratios is, Have I taken on too much debt, or do I have the ability to meet my debt obligations? In other words, you saw it, you borrowed money and bought it, now can you pay for it? To answer this question you need to look at the debt ratio and the debt coverage ratio. The **debt ratio** answers the question dealing with what percentage of your assets has been financed by borrowing. This ratio can be expressed as follows:

$$\text{debt ratio} = \frac{\text{total debt or liabilities}}{\text{total assets}}$$

Looking at the Tates' balance sheet, we see that the level of their total debt or liabilities is $175,500, while their total assets or what they own is $300,190. Thus, their debt ratio becomes $175,500/$300,190 = 0.5846. This ratio figure means that just over half of their assets are financed with borrowing. This ratio should go down as you get older.

**Long-Term Debt Coverage Ratio**
A ratio aimed at determining if you have the ability to meet your debt obligations, defined as total income available for living expenses divided by total long-term debt payments.

The **long-term debt coverage ratio** relates the amount of funds available for debt repayment to the size of the debt payments. In effect, this ratio is the number of times you could make your debt payments with your current income. It focuses on long-term obligations such as home mortgage payments, auto loan payments, and any other long-term credit obligations. If credit card debt has gotten large enough, it too represents a long-term obligation. The denominator of this ratio represents your total outstanding long-term debt payments (excluding short-term borrowing such as credit cards and bills coming due). The numerator represents the funds available to make these payments.

$$\text{long-term debt coverage ratio} = \frac{\text{total income available for living expenses}}{\text{total long-term debt payments}}$$

For the Tates, total income available for living expenses is found on line C of their income statement and is $56,510. The only long-term debt obligations they have are their mortgage payments of $19,656, their automobile loan payments of $2,588, college loan payments of $1,600, and an installment loan on a TV of $230. Thus, their debt coverage ratio is [$56,510/($19,656 + $2,588 + $1,600 + $230)] = 2.35 times. In general, a debt coverage ratio of less than approximately 2.5 should raise a caution flag.

You should also keep track of your long-term debt coverage ratio to make sure it does not creep downward. The Tates are at their limit in terms of the level of debt that they can manage comfortably. Such a low debt coverage ratio, though, is not surprising, because most of their assets are tied up in housing.

Another way of looking at the debt coverage ratio is to take its inverse; that is, divide the total debt payments by the total income available for living expenses. In this case, the inverse of the Tates' debt coverage ratio is 0.43, or 43 percent, indicating that 43 percent of the Tates' total income available for living expenses goes to cover debt payments.

## Question 3: Am I Saving as Much as I Think I Am?

The final question you can answer using ratios is how much of your income are you really saving. In effect, are you really saving as much as you think you are? To answer this question you need to look at the **savings ratio,** which is simply the ratio of income available for savings and investment (line M of Fig. 2.6) to income available for living expenses (line C of Fig. 2.6). This ratio tells you what proportion of your after-tax income is being saved.

**Savings Ratio**
A ratio aimed at determining how much you are saving, defined as income available for saving and investments divided by income available for living expenses.

$$\text{savings ratio} = \frac{\text{income available for savings and investment}}{\text{income available for living expenses}}$$

For the Tates, this ratio is ($4,276/$56,510) = .076 or 7.6 percent. This figure is in the range of what is typical in this country. Actually, for families saving for their first house it tends to be higher, and for families that have just purchased their first house and now are experiencing large mortgage payments, it tends to be lower. Again, as with the other ratios, this ratio should be compared with past savings ratios and target savings ratios to determine whether or not the Tates' savings efforts are enough.

If you're not presently saving, then you're living above your means. The only effective way to make saving work is to put to work **Principle 13: Pay Yourself First.** That is, you first set aside your savings, and what is left becomes the amount you can spend. As a result, saving for long-term goals becomes automatic. By paying yourself first, you acknowledge the fact that your long-term goals are paramount.

Principle

13 Pay Yourself First

## Record Keeping

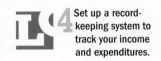

4 Set up a record-keeping system to track your income and expenditures.

Most people keep records of the important things in their lives. They keep them stuffed in a drawer, or in a file folder, or somewhere in the house, and say, "If you'll just give me a day or two, I'm sure I'll find them." One of the keys to good personal financial planning is organizing and maintaining these records. Keeping accurate, detailed records is important for three reasons. First, without adequate records it's extremely difficult to prepare taxes. Second, a strong record-keeping system allows you to track expenses and know exactly how much you're spending and where you're spending it. In short, if you don't know where and how much you're spending, you don't have control of your finances. Third, organized record keeping makes it easier for someone else to step in during an emergency and understand your financial situation.

Record keeping really involves two steps: tracking your personal financial dealings, and filing and storing your financial records in such a way that they are readily accessible. Very simply, if you don't know where financial records are, you won't feel in control of your affairs. Record keeping should also involve the safekeeping of documents and records such as birth certificates and passports.

# Checklist 2.1 ∎ Storing Financial Files

**Long-Term or Permanent Storage**
**(keep at home in a file cabinet or safe spot):**

→ **Tax Records (may be discarded after 6 years)**

Tax returns
Paychecks
W-2 forms
1099 forms
Charitable contributions
Alimony payments
Medical bills
Property taxes
Any other documentation

→ **Investment Records**

Bank records and non-tax-related checks less than a year old
Safety deposit box information
Stock, bond, and mutual fund transactions
Brokerage statements
Dividend records
Any additional investment documentation

→ **Retirement and Estate Planning**

Copy of will
Pension plan documentation
IRA documentation
Keogh plan transactions
Social Security information
Any additional retirement documentation

→ **Personal Planning**

Personal balance sheet
Personal income statement
Personal budget
Insurance policies and documentation
Warranties
Receipts for major purchases
Credit card information (account numbers and telephone numbers)

Birth certificates
Rental agreement if renting a dwelling
Automobile registration
Powers of attorney
Any additional personal planning documentation

**Safety Deposit Box Storage**

→ **Investment Records**

Certificates of deposit
Listing of bank accounts
Stock and bond certificates
Collectibles

→ **Retirement and Estate Planning**

Copy of will
Nondeductible IRA records

→ **Personal Planning**

Copy of will
Deed for home
Mortgage
Title insurance policy
Personal papers (birth and death certificates, alimony, adoption/custody, divorce, military, immigration, etc.)
Documentation of valuables (videotape or photos)
Home repair/improvement receipts
Auto title
Listing of insurance policies
Credit card information (account numbers and telephone numbers)

→ **Throw Out**

Non-tax-related checks over a year old
Records from cars and boats you no longer own
Expired insurance polices on which there will be no future claims
Expired warranties
Non-tax-related credit card slips over a year old

---

In determining how best to track your personal financial dealings, you must keep in mind that the best system is one that you will use. This may sound silly, but because of the tedious nature of record keeping, anything too complex just won't be used. Do yourself a favor and keep your system simple.

In general, credit card and check expenditures are easy to track because they leave an obvious paper trail. It's the cash expenditures that cause the most concern. Cash expenditures must be tracked as they occur; if not, they will be lost and forgotten. The simplest way to keep track of all cash expenditures is by recording them in a notebook or your checkbook register as they occur and then using these records, in addition to check and credit card transactions, to generate a monthly income statement. You would then compare this monthly income statement with your annual and target income statements to determine whether or not you have any problems. Sure, the process may be tedious, but it's necessary. Remember, your budget is your best friend, because the key to controlling expenditures is to keep track of them.

Once you've tracked your expenditures, you need to record them in an organized way. How should you do this? A relatively easy way is to set up a budget book similar to the income statement shown in Figure 2.4 and manually enter your expenditures. Alternatively, a number of personal finance computer programs can track your monthly and yearly expenses and your financial position once you've entered your daily expenditures. This approach is ideal. However, for those without a PC, the money for such a software program, or the time to set up such a system, the manual approach works just as well. The two most popular personal financial management programs for the PC are Intuit's Quicken and Microsoft's Money.

When recording your transactions, you should have a section in your **ledger** for each month broken down by the major types of expenditures. In addition, each month should be broken down by day. The more detailed your records are, the easier it is to track your money. For example, when you spend $200 on new clothes, you should enter the expense in the new clothes subsection of the clothes and personal care section of the proper month on the day on which the expenditure occurred (it sounds more complicated than it is). At the end of the month you should add up your expenditures and compile your monthly income statement.

After you've been keeping records for a while, you'll notice that they really start to pile up. How long do you have to hang on to these records? This, of course, depends upon the item. In general, items dealing with taxes must be kept for at least 6 years after the transaction takes place; some items should be kept for life. Checklist 2.1 provides a summary of where and for how long financial records should be kept.

**Ledger**
A book or notebook set aside to record expenditures.

WORKSHEET

## Putting It All Together: Budgeting

Implement a financial plan or budget that will provide level of savings needed to achieve your goals.

Chapter 1 introduced the planning cycle as a five-step process (see Fig. 1.1 on p. 6). Now that you have a better understanding of the tools involved in that process, how about a little review? Let's see how the balance sheet and income statement fit into the planning process.

The planning process begins by evaluating your financial health, which is exactly what the balance sheet and income statement are all about. Your balance sheet sums up everything you own or owe and lets you know your net worth, the basic element of financial health. Your income statement furthers your understanding by showing you where your money comes from, where it goes, and your spending patterns. Once you understand how much you have coming in and how you tend to spend your money, you can figure out how much you can realistically afford to save. If you don't know how much you can actually save, you can't come up with realistic financial goals, the second step of the planning process.

By providing you with information on how far you need to go to achieve a certain level of wealth and how you might realistically balance spending and saving to get

# In The News

Wall Street Journal January 7, 2001

## Pinch Your Pennies and Prosper

### by Jonathan Clements

Great investment portfolios begin with a few coupons clipped, some nights on the town forgone, and a couple of spending sprees avoided.

Everybody loves to chat about hot stocks and superstar mutual funds. Nobody ever mentions saving the cash to buy these investments. Yet, if you want to invest, you have to save.

Indeed, a healthy savings habit is probably the greatest investment virtue. Consider:

- Saving money is the surest path to a fatter portfolio. When you buy a stock, you can't be sure you have yourself a winner. But if you save an extra $100 a month, your portfolio will definitely grow faster.
- Saving regularly lets you profit from the struggling stock market. If you sock away money every month, market declines become opportunities, because your monthly investments buy shares at cheaper prices.

*Despite the compelling arguments for salting away money, many folks save pitifully little. What to do? A vague commitment to save won't get you anywhere. Instead, you need to lay down clear-cut rules about saving and spending and then force yourself to follow them. (☛A)*

If you boost your savings, you will be compelled to trim your spending. But where will you cut back? To get a handle on your spending, write down all your expenditures over the next week or two.

To keep spending under control, I am a big fan of leaving the credit cards at home and sticking strictly with cash and debit cards. But if you like the convenience of credit cards, consider following the example of Suzy Hoffman, a 37-year-old computer consultant in Milwaukee.

*"I deduct each credit-card transaction from my checking account, just as I would a check or cash-machine withdrawal," she says. "Then, when the credit-card statement arrives, I simply write a check to the credit-card company for the*

*total. Meanwhile, any rebates or frequent-flier miles from the card are mine." (☛B)*

## THE BOTTOM LINE . . .

**A** The easiest way to start saving is to set up some rules. For example, you might commit to saving all windfalls, such as bonuses, money from second jobs, or tax refunds. In addition, put your savings account, certificates of deposit, and other investments off limits. Also, remember **Principle 13: Pay Yourself First**

**B** As you consider each dollar spent, you will instinctively tighten your belt. In effect, saving will become contagious— nothing is more inspiring than success. The more you save, the more you will look for savings.

Source: Jonathan Clements, "Pinch Your Pennies and Prosper," *Wall Street Journal*, 7 January 2001:3. Copyright (c) 2001, Dow Jones & Company, Inc. Reproduced with permission of DOW JONES & CO., INC. in the format Textbook via Copyright Clearance Center.

there, your balance sheet and income statement not only help you set goals, but also they help you achieve them. Developing a plan of action to achieve your goals is the third step in the planning process, and here your income statement is the key.

Your income statement helps you set up a cash budget (which we examine in more detail in the next section) that allows you to manage your saving while considering flexibility, liquidity, protection, and minimization of taxes. Once your plan is in place, you'll need to monitor your progress. Because this last step is really the same as the first, you're right back to using your balance sheet and income statement again. As you can see, without these documents, the planning process isn't nearly as effective.

**STOP & THINK** What happens if it doesn't look like you're going to be able to reach your financial goals? You need to change either your goals or your saving pattern. Fortunately, a small change in your financial lifestyle can produce large benefits down the road. For example, if you are 22 now and you save $10 per month— that works out to about 33¢ per day—at 12 percent, by age 67 when you retire, it will have grown to over $240,000. Small changes can pay off.

## Developing a Cash Budget

A budget is really nothing more than a plan for controlling cash inflows and outflows. The purpose of the cash budget is to keep income in line with expenditures plus savings. Your cash budget should allocate certain dollar amounts for different spending categories, based on your goals and financial obligations.

To prepare a cash budget, you begin with your most recent annual personal income statement. First, examine last year's total income, making any adjustments to it you expect for the coming year. Perhaps you have received a raise, taken a second job, or anticipate an increase in royalty payments. Based on your income level, estimate what your taxes will be. This figure provides you with an estimate of your anticipated after-tax income available for living expenditures, which is commonly called take-home pay.

Just as your estimate of anticipated take-home pay flows from your most recent annual personal income statement, so does your estimate of living expenses. Using last year's personal income statement, identify expenditures over which you have no control—fixed expenditures. Then determine your variable expenses. These are the expenses over which you have complete control, and you can increase or decrease them as you see fit.

This is the category in which you have to start looking for ways to reduce your spending and increase your saving. For example, you can generate savings just by reducing the amount you spend on food—substitute bean dip for those exotic fresh fruits as your evening snack (of course, any savings there will probably be offset in an increase in exercise equipment this year). You must also keep in mind that when you buy on credit, you obligate yourself to future expenditures to pay off your debt. When you borrow you are spending your future income, which limits your ability to save.

Finally, subtract your anticipated living expenditures from your anticipated take-home pay to determine income available for savings and investment. Then compare your anticipated monthly savings with your target savings level, which is, as we mentioned earlier, based on a quantification of your goals. If it doesn't look as if you'll be able to fund all your goals, then you must earn more, spend less, or downsize your goals. The choice is, of course, personal; however, you should keep in mind that regardless of your level of income, an awful lot of people live on less than what you're earning.

How do Louise and Larry Tate develop a cash budget? First, assume that the only change in income they expect for the coming year is a $5,000 increase in wages and salaries from $69,500 to $74,500. Last year, the Tates paid approximately 20 percent in federal and state income taxes. If they pay the same percentage this year, their $5,000 raise will result in an increase in take-home pay of $4,000, with 20 percent of the raise, or $1,000, going to pay increased taxes.

The Tates' personal income statement is given in Figure 2.6. They're planning minor changes in several expenditure categories. Interestingly, some of the anticipated changes involve increases in planned spending. A cash budget, then, does not necessarily curb spending in all areas. Instead it allows you to decide ahead of time how much to spend where.

Assume that the Tates' target level of savings for the entire year is $6,400. If the Tates stick to this cash budget, they will exceed their target. Were this not the case, they would have been forced to adjust their budget so that it covered their target savings. To make your annual cash budget easier to control, you should break it down into monthly budgets by simply dividing by 12.

A key point to remember when budgeting is that no budget is set in stone. As **Principle 7** says, **Stuff Happens.** A TV, a car, a washer—unexpected expenditures seem to appear out of nowhere. Conversely, you may be pleasantly surprised that you wound up spending far less than you planned. Then again, you may change your goals—you don't want that house, your apartment's fine for the moment, but you do want to be able to buy a yak farm in Peru. Basically, the budgeting process is a dynamic one: You must continuously monitor the financial impact of change on your spending and saving habits.

## Implementing the Cash Budget

**WORKSHEET**

Now that you have your plan, how do you make it work? Essentially, you just put it in place and try to make a go of it for a month. At the end of the month, compare your actual expenditures in each category with your budgeted amounts. If you spent more than you budgeted, you may want to pay closer attention to expenditures in that category or you may want to change the budgeted amount. If you do need to increase one budgeted amount, you might try to reduce spending in another area. Keep in mind that responsibility for sticking to the budget remains with you, but by examining deviations from desired spending patterns on a monthly basis, you can focus on where you need to exert additional self-control. If you need help, see Worksheet 4, which is downloadable from the textbook's Web site. As shown in Figure 2.7, this is a budget tracker in the form of an Excel spreadsheet. It not only does the calculations for you, but also allows you to track how close you came to your budgeted amount in each category.

**STOP & THINK** Most people spend what they earn, regardless of how much that is. It comes in and goes out. To save, you've got to change your attitude and follow **Principle 13: Pay Yourself First.** That means you won't be able to buy everything you want, and something is going to have to go. The first place to look is the *small stuff*—latte, magazines, CDs. Pop—within a day or two most of that stuff is worthless or gone. In other words, sweat the small stuff.

If sticking to a desired budget remains a problem, one possible control method is using what's generally called the envelope system. At the beginning of each month the dollar amount of each major expenditure category is put into an envelope. To spend money in that area, simply take it out of the envelope. When the envelope is empty, you're done spending in that area.

If you are having trouble controlling spending only in certain areas, envelopes could be used just for those areas. For example, if you budgeted $120 per month for

**Figure 2.7** Budget Tracker

The Budget Tracker is downloadable from the textbook's Web site.

| Budget Tracker: Personal Income Statement Worksheet | | | |
|---|---|---|---|
| **Directions:** *Fill in the gold cells with your data. Be careful not to modify the red cells.* | | | |
| **Income** | **Month Budget Income** | **Actual Income** | **Difference** |
| Wages and salaries | | | |
| Wage Earner 1 | | | 0 |
| Wage Earner 2 | | | 0 |
| =Total Wages and salaries | 0 | 0 | 0 |
| + Interest and Dividends | | | 0 |
| + Royalties, Commissions and Rents | | | 0 |
| +Other Income | | | 0 |
| =A. Total Income | 0 | 0 | 0 |
| **Taxes** | | | |
| Federal Income and Social Security | | | 0 |
| +State Income | | | 0 |
| =B. Total Income Taxes | 0 | 0 | 0 |
| **C. After-Tax Income Available for Living Expenditures or Take-Home Pay (line A minus line B)** | 0 | 0 | 0 |
| **Living Expenses** | **Budget Amount** | **Actual Spending** | **Difference** |
| Housing | | | 0 |
| Rent | | | 0 |
| +Mortgage Payments | | | 0 |
| +Utilities | | | 0 |
| +Maintainance | | | 0 |
| +Reas Eastate and Property Taxes | | | 0 |
| +Fixed Assets-furniture, appliances, televisions, etc. | | | 0 |
| +Other Living Expenses | | | 0 |
| =D. Total Housing Expenditures | 0 | 0 | 0 |
| **Food** | | | |

restaurant expenditures, put $120 in an envelope each month. When it is exhausted, trips to the restaurant are over for the month. This includes pizza home delivery, so no cheating!

## Hiring a Professional

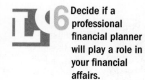

Decide if a professional financial planner will play a role in your financial affairs.

The goal of this course and text is to give you the understanding, tools, and motivation to manage your own financial affairs. Sometimes, though, good management involves knowing when to ask for help. When it comes to personal financial management, there's good help to be found. Actually, you have three options available regarding working with professionals: (1) Go it alone, make your own plan, and have it checked by a professional; (2) work with a professional to come up with a plan; or (3) leave it all in the hands of a pro (though preferably not one with a bad toupee, leisure suit, and beat-up Ford Pinto). Although this is a question that should not be answered until you have finished this course and have a better grasp of the process and alternatives available to you and of your ability to set your own plan of action, let's take a moment to look further at the options.

### What Planners Do

For relatively simple personal financial matters, computerized financial planning programs provide basic budgeting tools and advice. However, as with most standardized advice, they simply may not fit your particular situation. The more unique your situation, the greater the need for professional help.

A professional financial planner might be used to validate the financial plan you've developed yourself. If you design your own home, it would be a good idea to pass the plans by an architect before building, just to make sure there are no flaws in the design. Similarly, you might hire a professional financial planner to look over your plan and point out any flaws, in addition to suggesting improvements, based on your goals, values, and interests.

You can also work directly with a professional financial planner to develop your plan, because the planner can help on complex tax and legal issues. This option is the most logical way to use financial planners—as a reference tool. However, for this approach to work, you must have a solid understanding of personal finance, the logic that drives it, plus the time and willingness to give it the attention required.

Finally, you could hire a professional to put your plan together for you, from start to finish. In this case, you provide the planner with information on your goals, values, and lifestyle, and the planner crafts a plan that addresses those goals. Depending upon your net worth or income, the planner's reputation, and whether or not the planner also collects commissions on investments you make in addition to a fee, this service could cost between $500 and $10,000.

A downside to this approach is that without enough knowledge to understand the planner's proposal, you can't judge its merits. This makes it extremely important that you find someone who is competent and trustworthy. If something goes wrong, you bear the consequences. For that reason, you must understand the basics of personal financial planning in order to monitor your game plan. Using a financial planner to put together the entire plan is reasonable only if you realize that you are merely receiving advice and that you bear the ultimate responsibility.

Although the overwhelming majority of financial planners are dedicated, responsible, and competent, that doesn't guarantee you won't pick one of the incompetent or unethical ones. There are regulations in place meant to protect consumers, but

Principle **12** The Agency Problem— Beware of the Sales Pitch

Principle **9** The Best Protection Is Knowledge

these regulations don't mean that all planners are equally qualified. Remember **Principle 12: The Agency Problem—Beware of the Sales Pitch.** For example, financial planners may try to sell you products that are more expensive because they receive a commission on them. Be wary of those who promise you quick riches, and walk away from anyone using high-pressure tactics. Building wealth takes time and constant attention.

Still, your best protection is knowledge, bringing you back to **Principle 9: The Best Protection Is Knowledge.** Without an understanding of the world of investments, you can't determine whether the planner's recommendations make sense for you, and you may end up relying on someone who may, in turn, be working in his or her best interests rather than in yours.

## Paying Your Financial Planner

Financial planners or advisors come in all shapes and sizes. One way of differentiating them is by the services they offer: Some are full-service advisors, and some specialize in such areas as estate planning or investments. Another way of differentiating them is by how they're compensated. These classifications can have a big effect on how much advice will cost you.

Fee-only planners earn income only through the fees they charge and thus may charge more for a plan than the person just starting out may want to pay. There are fewer of this type of planner than any other, and they tend to work with bigger, more involved, and specialized situations. The plus of using this kind of planner is that you personally will have total control of the products purchased to complete your plan, and therefore you control commission costs. However, you have to sort through a sometimes overwhelming array of options and deal with several different vendors. Whether the planner charges an hourly rate, operates with a schedule of services and prices, or has some other pricing structure, make sure you sign a fee agreement before you begin.

Some planners who charge fees also collect commissions on products they recommend. The upside of this is that fees may be less if you do choose to use some of their commissioned products. The downside is that if you're dealing with a less than ethical person, you could be directed toward higher-commission products. The key to making a decision on this type of advisor is, again, to be aware of what you're paying for.

Finally, there are commission-based advisors. This is by far the most available type of advisor. They can provide an analysis of your personal financial situation, offer solutions to problems, and assist you in implementing the plan. Except for some noncommission investments, most financial products pay a commission to someone. Some commission-based planners represent only one or two companies, while others work with a wide range of companies. You want to make sure your planner has a wide range of choices available to you.

## Choosing a Professional Planner

There are an awful lot of excellent financial planners out there, but unfortunately, there are enough bad ones that you should use care in picking someone. One approach is to limit your search to those who have received accreditation from a professional organization. For example, a personal financial specialist (PFS) is a certified public accountant. To receive this designation, an individual must pass certification tests in personal financial planning administered by the American Institute of Certified Public Accountants, in addition to having 3 years of personal financial

# Checklist 2.2 ■ What to Ask a Financial Planner

You should ask the following questions about a financial planner's background:

How long have they been a financial planner?

What are their credentials and professional designations?

Do they actively participate in continuing education to keep pace with changes in financial planning?

How do they keep up with the latest financial changes?

Would they provide you with references?

Could you see a copy of a financial plan they made for someone with a somewhat similar financial situation with, of course, names removed to preserve confidentiality?

Who will work with you on a regular basis, and will the creation of the plan be done by a junior staffer or using a computer program?

How many companies do they represent?

How will they be paid—by fee or commission? What will it be, and how will that fee be calculated?

Would they provide you with a written estimate of the services you can expect and the cost of those services?

---

planning experience. Another certification, certified financial planner (CFP), requires the satisfactory completion of a 10-hour, 2-day exam and a minimum of 3 years of experience in the field. There are also chartered financial consultants, or ChFCs. The requirements for a ChFC designation, which is administered by the American College, includes coursework and 10 exams.

Regardless of the credentials of the planner, you should be concerned with the person's experience. In addition, you should feel comfortable that the advice you're receiving is tailored to your specific circumstance rather than preprogrammed or canned. You should also look to referrals—do you have friends or relatives who have had good experiences with financial planners in the past?

Make sure you interview several financial planners thoroughly before you decide to use their services or sign any agreements. Keep in mind that the title "financial planner" is not legally defined—it just means that the individual offers comprehensive financial planning services and says nothing about competence. See Checklist 2.2 for some questions to ask.

If you have trouble getting recommendations, try calling the Financial Planning Association at 800-282-7526 or the CFP Board of Standards at 303-830-7543 for help. Remember, you bear all the consequences of bad decisions, so you must take responsibility for doing it right.

## SUMMARY

A personal balance sheet is a statement of your financial position on a given date. It includes the assets you own; the debt, or liabilities, you have incurred; and your level of wealth. The difference between the value of your assets (what you own) and your liabilities (what you owe) is your net worth, the level of wealth that you or your family has accumulated.

Whereas a balance sheet tells you how much wealth you have accumulated as of a *certain date,* an income statement tells you where your money has come from and where it has gone over some *period of time.* Actually, an income statement is really an income and expenditure or net income statement, because it looks at both cash inflows and outflows. Once you understand where your money comes from and where it goes, you'll be able to determine whether you're saving enough to meet your goals and how you might change your expenditure patterns to meet your goals. Then you'll be able to construct a budget.

Financial ratios help you in identifying your financial standing. These ratios are analyzed over time to determine trends and are also compared with standards or target ratios. The purpose of using ratios is to gain a better understanding of how you are managing your financial resources.

To keep track of your income and expenditures and to calculate your net worth, you need a sound system of record keeping. Such a system not only helps with tax preparation, but also allows you to identify how much you are spending and where you are spending it.

Developing a plan of action involves setting up a cash budget. The starting point for the cash budget, which is the center point of the plan of action, flows directly from the personal income statement. By comparing the income available for savings and investments with the level of savings needed to achieve your goals, you can determine whether your current spending patterns need to be altered and by how much. Once you have established a plan, it's your responsibility to stick to your budget.

If you need help in financial planning, there are professional planners out there who can provide such help. Professional planners can be used simply to validate the plan you have developed, or they can be hired to put the entire plan together, from start to finish.

## REVIEW QUESTIONS

1. Developing a balance sheet is the first step in measuring your financial health. Why? What is the purpose of a balance sheet?

2. What is a financial liability? How do current liabilities differ from long-term liabilities? Give examples of each.

3. What information needs to be gathered to develop an accurate balance sheet? How do you determine the current value of your assets? How do you determine the amount owed on current and long-term liabilities?

4. Define and give examples of the seven categories of assets.

5. Calculating an income statement is the second step in measuring your financial health. Why? What is the purpose of an income statement?

6. What information needs to be gathered to calculate an accurate income statement?

7. Explain the practical difference between a fixed and a variable expense. Over which type of expense does the debtor have greater control? Why might the use of one type of expense over the other be preferable?

8. Why are financial ratios important to someone trying to determine financial well-being?

9. If Larry and Louise Tate were trying to determine how long they would be able to continue paying their bills if they both lost their jobs, which financial ratio would be most useful?

10. List the three most important reasons for keeping accurate financial records. Failing to keep accurate financial records can result in what kind of problems?

11. Can you remember where you spent *all* the money from your last ATM withdrawal? How could you benefit from a cash budget?

12. Summarize the steps in the process of establishing a cash budget.

13. How could **Principle 13: Pay Yourself First** make budgeting easier?

14. The three financial tools—a balance sheet, an income statement, and a budget or financial plan—represent the time perspectives of past, present, and future. Match the tools and the time represented in each. Explain your answer.

15. What is the major difference between a fee-only planner and a commission-based planner? How might **Principle 9: The Best Protection Is Knowledge** and **Principle 12: The Agency Problem, Beware of the Sales Pitch** affect your choice? Why?

16. Explain why hiring a professional financial planner may not always be necessary. What are your four options for receiving assistance in developing a financial plan?

## PROBLEMS AND ACTIVITIES

1. Mike and Mary Jane McCarthy have a yearly income of $65,000 and own a house worth $90,000, two cars worth a total of $20,000, and furniture worth $10,000. The house has a mortgage of $50,000 and the cars have outstanding loans of $2,000 each. Utility bills, totaling $150 for this month, have not been paid.

Determine their net worth and explain what it means.

2. Using the preceding information, calculate the debt ratio for the McCarthy household.

3. Ed and Marta get paid $3,250 after taxes every month. Monthly expenses include $1,200 on housing and utilities, $550 for auto loans, $300 on food, and an average of $1,000 on clothing and other variable expenses. Calculate and interpret their savings ratio. Hint: Prepare an income statement and then compute the ratio.

4. A recent car accident has Barry and Karen concerned about their preparation for meeting financial emergencies. Help them calculate their current ratio given the following assets and liabilities:

| | |
|---|---|
| Checking Account | $2,000 |
| Savings Account | $4,000 |
| Stocks | $8,000 |
| Utility Bills | $500 |
| Credit Card Bills | $1,000 |
| Auto Loan | $2,600 |

5. Faith Brooks, a 28-year-old college graduate, never took a personal finance class. She pays her bills on time, has managed to save a little in a mutual fund, and with the help of an inheritance managed a down payment on a condominium. But Faith worries about her financial situation. Given the following information, prepare an income statement, balance sheet, and calculate the current ratio, savings ratio, monthly living expenses covered ratio, debt ratio, and long-term debt coverage ratio. Interpret these financial statements and ratios for Faith. In addition to the following list, Faith offers these explanations:

▪ All short-term and long-term liabilities are unpaid.

▪ "Other expenses, monthly" represents cash spent without a record.

She charges all incidentals on her credit cards and pays the balances off monthly. The balances given represent her average monthly balances.

| | |
|---|---|
| Visa bill | $355 |
| Stocks | $5,500 |
| MasterCard bill | $245 |
| Monthly paycheck, net | $2,400 |
| Annual medical expenses | $264 |
| Mortgage payment, monthly | $530 |
| Temple Mutual Fund | $2,100 |
| 401(k) retirement account | $4,500 |
| Car payment, monthly | $265 |
| Total monthly utilities | $275 |
| Savings account | $2,300 |
| Clothing expense, monthly | $45 |
| Checking account | $825 |
| Quarterly auto insurance (not due) | $450 |
| Inherited coin collection | $3,250 |
| Condominium | $65,000 |
| Food, monthly | $225 |
| Auto | $9,000 |
| Furnishings | $5,500 |
| Mortgage outstanding | $50,000 |
| Auto loan outstanding | $4,225 |
| Other personal property | $8,000 |
| Other expenses, monthly | $150 |

6. Your friend Charles heard about your personal finance class and asked for your help planning his finances. Explain to Charles why he should establish a budget and what information he needs.

7. If the Potinsky household spends $39,000 annually on all living expenses and long-term debt, calculate the amount recommended for an emergency fund. How might household circumstances (e.g., earners in the household, available credit, type and stability of employment) affect this decision?

## SUGGESTED PROJECTS

1. Talk to your parents about their finances. Determine their monthly bills as well as their long-term debt. Prepare an income statement and categorize all liabilities as either fixed or variable. Taxes need not be calculated; however, include as much information as possible. Finally, calculate your parents' savings ratio and discuss with them if they are saving this amount.

2. Prepare a one-month spending record and compile an accurate income and expense statement. Analyze your income and expense statement to

determine your spending patterns. Prepare a budget based on the modified spending analysis. See how long you can follow the budget. Should you consider an envelope system?

3. Talk to someone about his or her efforts to monitor his or her financial health. How often does he or she calculate a balance sheet? An income and expense statement? Does he or she have a budget or spending plan for expenses? Does he or she consult a professional for advice? Share your findings as an oral or written report.

4. Locate at least three different Web sites with net worth calculators (e.g., **money.cnn.com/**). Compare and contrast the listings of assets and liabilities. Do any of the calculators offer guidelines for interpreting results? Comment on the ease of use. Share your findings in an oral or written report.

5. The phrase *GIGO*—"garbage in, garbage out"— is commonly associated with computer-automated analysis. How does GIGO apply to the calculation of a balance sheet or income and expense statement? Explain how an individual preparing these documents guards against GIGO?

6. Determine an item that you want to purchase (over $200) and, instead of buying it on credit,

save a little each month toward the purchase price. Determine when the item will be purchased and how much you need to save each month to reach your goal.

7. Call a certified financial planner (CFP) and tell her that you are a student doing research for a class. Ask the CFP to explain why someone would benefit from her service. Keep the phone call brief, but get as much information as possible. Summarize your findings in a written report.

8. Interview five people who use a computer software program to track their finances or do budgeting. List the different types of software they use and the capabilities of each. Which one of these software programs would best suit your needs? Why?

9. Find as many of your financial records as you can, including bank and credit card statements. Now calculate how much money you spent in the past 12 months. Was this amount more or less than you anticipated? List and explain five ways that you could spend less in the coming 12 months.

10. Write a one-page essay that explains at least four reasons why you believe that people do not budget. Hint: Consider each of the six chapter objectives in your response.

## Discussion Case 1

Sami, 34, and Ronald, 31, want to buy their first home. Their current combined net income is $45,000 and they have two auto loans totaling $32,000. They have saved approximately $12,000 for the purchase of the home and have total assets worth $55,000, which are mostly savings for retirement. Ronald has always been cautious about spending large amounts of money, but Sami really likes the idea of owning their own home, especially with their first child on the way. They do not have a budget but they do keep track of their expenses, which amounted to $35,000 last year. They pay off all credit card bills on a monthly basis and do not have any other debt or loans outstanding. Other than that, they do not spend a great deal of time tracking their finances.

### Questions

1. What financial statements should Sami and Ronald prepare to begin realizing their home purchase goal? What records should they use to compile these statements?

2. Calculate their net worth and income surplus.

3. Calculate and interpret their month's living expenses covered ratio and their debt ratio.

4. What other information would be necessary or helpful in developing more complete statements? Give as much detail as possible.

5. What six- to eight-step process should Sami and Ronald undertake to develop a budget?

6. Would you suggest that they see a financial planner? What might the planner tell them to do? Hint: Consider Principle 12.

## Discussion Case 2

Tim and Jill Taylor are preparing for retirement. Tim has worked for the electric company his entire life and has participated in all of the retirement savings opportunities that the company

offered. As a result, the Taylors have a very large retirement portfolio that is currently being handled by an investment broker. Jill has scrimped and saved every penny for 35 years and would like

*Tips from Marcy Furney, ChFC, Certified Financial Planner™*

# Money Matters
## FOR THE RECORD

Starting a budget and don't know what the utilities cost last summer? Having a battle with Visa regarding a credit that hasn't shown up on the bill? Even if you already use bookkeeping software, a good system for maintaining paper records could be your salvation.

**Set up a place in your home for record storage.** *Keep everything in one location—a desk, a file cabinet, or even an extra kitchen drawer.*

**Create file folders for each type of monthly bill.** *Also make one for major purchase receipts and warranties, pay stubs, benefit and insurance documents, investment reports, bank statements, car and/or home records, and IRS-related items.*

**Mark on each bill the date you paid it and the number of the check used to pay it.** *Then file each in the appropriate folder.*

**Put your charge receipts in the designated charge card folder and then use them to reconcile your monthly statement.** *When you pay the bill, staple the receipts to your section of the statement, and file it. Keep any credit slips to make sure the charge is reversed. Make notations on your statement regarding problems, phone calls to the credit card company, or deductibility of any charges for your next tax return.*

**When you call the company regarding a bill,** *note the date, time, with whom you spoke, and the resolution on your copy.*

**Don't throw away bills or receipts until you purge your files.** *When you file your tax return for the year, put supporting documents with your return and keep it in a separate envelope. There are many opinions regarding how long to keep tax returns; 5 to 7 years seems sufficient for most. However, those that report the purchase or sale of a home, deductions that can carry forward, or other unusual tax situations are best kept for much longer periods.*

**When you purge folders,** *remove the material that wasn't used as tax support from the spending and pay stub files. Bundle it up and store it for 1 more year. After that you should be able to throw away most of it. Use your judgment if you think something needs to be kept longer. Keep receipts for major purchases, warranties, titles, deeds, and year-end investment statements until you no longer own the item.*

---

to live "the good life" for a while, but she is concerned about overspending their resources. Tim, however, figures, "I earned it, I'll spend it." Nevertheless, Tim and Jill agree on two things. First, they want to be able to leave money to help pay for the grandchildren's educations. Second, they are committed to taking control of their financial life.

## Questions

1. The Taylors just received a statement from their broker outlining the total value of their investment portfolio. How can they use this information?

2. Why might it be important for the Taylors to establish the market value of their investments?

3. How might an expense statement ensure that they will have the desired amount to leave for their grandchildren?

4. If both their income and expenses change, how would you suggest to them that they not "go overboard in living the good life" during retirement?

5. Should they try and manage the funds themselves or should they leave the funds in the care of the financial advisor? Why?

6. Do the Taylors need to track their expenses more or less closely now that Tim has retired? Why?

---

 Visit our Web site for additional case problems, interactive exercises, and practice quizzes for this chapter—**www.prenhall.com/keown**.

# 3 Understanding the Time Value of Money

*"Let's just do what we always do—hijack some nuclear weapons and hold the world ransom."*

## Learning Objectives

**Explain** the mechanics of compounding.

**Use** a financial calculator to determine the time value of money.

**Understand** the power of time in compounding.

**Explain** the importance of the interest rate in determining how an investment grows.

**Calculate** the present value of money to be received in the future.

**Define** an annuity and calculate its compound or future value.

Those are the words of Dr. Evil, played by Mike Myers, in the movie *Austin Powers, International Man of Mystery.* Frozen, along with his cat, Mr. Bigglesworth, in 1967 after escaping from the Electric Psychedelic Pussycat Swinger's Club in London in a giant Big Boy rocket ship, Dr. Evil is finally thawed out in 1997 and immediately resumes his evil ways.

Dr. Evil continues with his plan: "Gentlemen, it has come to my attention that a breakaway Russian Republic Ripblackastan is about to transfer a nuclear warhead to the United Nations in a few days. Here's the plan. We get the warhead, and we hold the world ransom for . . . $1 million!"

Silence, followed by, "Umm, umm, umm" from Dr. Evil's Number 2 man, played by Robert Wagner: "Don't you think we should ask for more than a million dollars? A million dollars is not exactly a lot of money these days."

"OK, then we hold the world ransom for $100 billion."

A million dollars in 1967 isn't the same as a million dollars in 1997, or today, for that matter. If Dr. Evil or Austin Danger Powers, who was also frozen for 30 years, had taken a million dollars in 1967 and put it in the stock market, it would have accumulated to over $30.7 million when they were thawed out in 1997. Unfortunately, it wouldn't have the same purchasing power it did in 1967. In fact, given the rate of inflation over that period, it would only purchase about one-fifth of what it would have in 1967.

Thirty years is a long time. In fact, when Dr. Evil and Austin Powers were frozen, one of the top-rated TV shows was *Bewitched*, *The Monkees* won an Emmy Award for the best comedy series, and the Green Bay Packers won Super Bowl I. Thirty years later Dr. Evil and Austin Powers woke up to those same sitcoms showing on "Nick at Night" and the Green Bay Packers winning Super Bowl XXXI. Still, times had changed—just look at personal computers, compact disks, MP3s, and all the different channels available on cable TV. Now look to the future: For most of you, it will be well over 30 years before you retire. When you're trying to figure out how much you need, coming up with a number in today's dollars just doesn't make much sense. Why is that?

As we saw in **Principle 2: The Time Value of Money**, a dollar received today is worth more than a dollar received in the future. Obviously, a dollar received and invested today starts earning interest sooner than a dollar received and invested some time in the future. However, the **time value of money** means that we can't compare amounts of money from two different periods without adjusting for this difference in value. It means that money you invest today will grow to fund your goals tomorrow. In short, it means that if you want a firm grasp on personal finance, you'd better understand the time value of money.

Just how powerful is the time value of money? Well, if we were to invest $1,000 at only 8 percent interest for 400 years, we'd end up with $23 quadrillion—approximately $5 million per person on earth. Of course, your investments

Principle 2
**The Time Value of Money**

**Time Value of Money**
The concept that a dollar received today is worth more than a dollar received in the future and, therefore, comparisons between sums in different time periods cannot be made without adjustments to their values.

won't span 400 years—it's doubtful that you'll be cryogenically frozen like Dr. Evil and Austin Powers—but your investments will rely on the time value of money. If you manage properly, time can be the ace up your sleeve—the one that lets you rake in more than you would have otherwise imagined possible.

Remember that in personal finance, the time value of money is just as widespread as it is powerful. We're always comparing money from different periods—for example, buying a bond today and receiving interest payments in the future, borrowing money to buy a house today and paying it back over the next 30 years, or determining exactly how much to save annually to achieve a certain goal. In fact, there's very little in personal finance that doesn't have some thread of the time value of money woven through it.

**Explain the mechanics of compounding.**

**Compound Interest**
The effect of earning interest on interest, resulting from the reinvestment of interest paid on an investment's principal.

**Principal**
The face value of the deposit or debt instrument.

**Future Value (FV)**
The value of an investment at some future point in time.

**Present Value (PV)**
The current value, that is, the value in today's dollars of a future sum of money.

## Compound Interest and Future Values

How does the time value of money turn small sums of money into extremely large sums of money? Through compound interest. **Compound interest** is basically interest paid on interest. If you take the interest you earn on an investment and reinvest it, you then start earning interest on the **principal** and the reinvested interest. In this way, the amount of interest you earn grows, or compounds.

### How Compound Interest Works

Anyone who has ever had a savings account has received compound interest. For example, suppose you place $100 in a savings account that pays 6 percent interest annually. How will your savings grow? At the end of the first year you'll have earned 6 percent, or $6 on your initial deposit of $100, giving you a total of $106 in your savings account. That $106 is the **future value (FV)** of your investment, that is, the value of your investment at some future point in time. The mathematical formula illustrating the payment of interest is

$$\text{future value} = \text{present value or beginning amount} + \text{interest earned}$$
$$FV_1 = PV + PV(i) = PV(1 + i) \tag{3.1}$$

where

$FV_1$ = the future value of the investment at the end of 1 year

$i$ = the annual interest rate; the interest earned is based on the balance at the beginning of the year and is paid at the end of the year. In this case $i = 6\%$ or, expressed in decimal form, 0.06.

$PV$ = the **present value**, or the current value; that is, the value in today's dollars of a sum of money

In our example

$$\begin{aligned} FV_1 &= PV + PV(i) \\ &= PV(1 + i) \\ &= \$100(1 + .06) \\ &= \$100(1.06) \\ &= \$106 \end{aligned} \tag{3.1}$$

Assuming you leave the $6 interest payment in your savings account, known as **reinvesting**, what will your savings look like at the end of the second year? The future value of $106 at the end of the first year, $FV_1$, becomes the present value at the beginning of the second year. Inserting this number into equation (3.1), we get

**Reinvesting**
Taking money that you have earned on an investment and plowing it back into that investment.

$$FV_2 = FV_1(1 + i) \qquad (3.2)$$

which, for the example, gives

$$FV_2 = \$106(1.06)$$
$$= \$112.36$$

What will your savings look like at the end of 3 years? 5 years? 10 years? Figure 3.1 illustrates how an investment of $100 would continue to grow for the first 10 years at a compound interest rate of 6 percent. Notice how the amount of interest earned annually increases each year because of compounding.

Why do you earn more interest during the second year than you did during the first? Simply because you now earn interest on the sum of the original principal, or present value, *and* the interest you earned in the first year. In effect, you are now earning interest on interest, which is the concept of compound interest.

**Figure 3.1** Compound Interest at 6% over Time

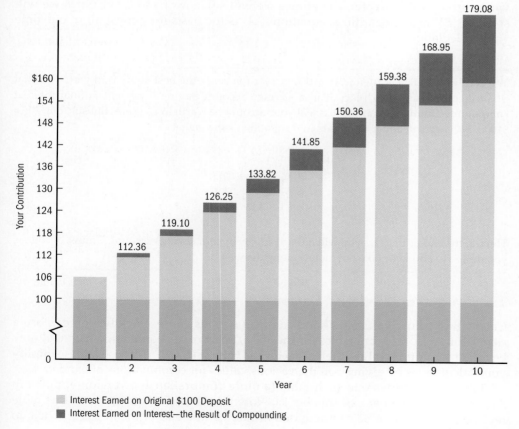

Year

☐ Interest Earned on Original $100 Deposit
■ Interest Earned on Interest—the Result of Compounding

How did we determine all the future values of your investment in Figure 3.1? We started with equations (3.1) and (3.2). Because those two equations share a common element, $FV_1$, we combine them to get

$$FV_2 = FV_1(1 + i) \tag{3.2}$$
$$= PV(1 + i)(1 + i)$$
$$= PV(1 + i)^2 \tag{3.3}$$

To find what we had at the end of year 2, we just took the amount we had at the end of year 1 and multiplied it by $(1 + i)$.

We can generalize equation (3.3) to illustrate the value of your investment for any number of years by using the following equation:

$$FV_n = PV(1 + i)^n \tag{3.4}$$

where

$FV_n$ = the future value of the investment at the end of $n$ years

$n$ = the number of years during which the compounding occurs

$i$ = the annual interest rate

$PV$ = the present value, or the current value; that is, the value of a sum of money in today's dollars

Equation (3.4) *is* the time value of money formula, and it will work for any investment that pays a fixed amount of interest, $i$, for the life of the investment. As we work through this chapter, sometimes we will solve for $i$ and other times we will solve for $PV$ or $n$. Regardless, equation (3.4) is the basis for almost all of our time value calculations.

→ **Example**

**Compounded Annually**
With annual compounding the interest is received at the end of each year and then reinvested back into the investment. Then, at the end of the second year, interest is earned on this new sum.

You receive a $1,000 academic award this year for being the best student in your personal finance course, and you place it in a savings account paying 5 percent annual interest **compounded annually**. How much will your account be worth in 10 years? Substituting $PV = \$1000$, $i = 5$ percent, and $n = 10$ years into equation (3.4), you get

$$FV_n = PV(1 + i)^n$$
$$= \$1,000(1 + 0.05)^{10}$$
$$= \$1,000(1.62889)$$
$$= \$1,628.89 \tag{3.4}$$

Thus, at the end of 10 years you will have $1,628.89 in your savings account. Unless, of course, you decide to add in or take out money along the way.

## The Future-Value Interest Factor

**Future-Value Interest Factor ($FVIF_{i,\,n}$)**
The value of $(1 + i)^n$ used as a multiplier to calculate an amount's future value.

Calculating future values by hand can be a serious chore. Luckily, you can use a calculator. Also, there are tables for the $(1 + i)^n$ part of the equation, which will now be called the **future-value interest factor** for $i$ and $n$ ($FVIF_{i,\,n}$). These tables simplify your calculations by giving you the various values for combinations of $i$ and $n$.

Table 3.1 provides one such table (a more comprehensive version appears in Appendix A at the back of this book). Note that the amounts given in this table represent the value of $1 compounded at rate $i$ at the end of the $n$th year. Thus, to

## Table 3.1    $FVIF_{i,n}$, or the Compound Sum of $1

*Instructions: Each future-value interest factor ($FVIF_{i\%, \, n \, years}$) corresponds to a specific time period and interest rate. For example, to find the future-value interest factor for 5 percent and 10 years ($FVIF_{5\%, \, 10 \, yr}$), simply move down the $i = 5\%$ column until you reach its intersection with the $n = 10$ years row: 1.629. The future value is then calculated as follows:*

$$future \; value \; = \; present \; value \times future\text{-}value \; interest \; factor$$
$$or \; FV_n \; = \; PV(FVIF_{i\%, \, n \, years})$$

| n | 1% | 2% | 3% | 4% | 5% | 6% | 7% | 8% | 9% | 10% |
|---|----|----|----|----|----|----|----|----|----|-----|
| 1 | 1.010 | 1.020 | 1.030 | 1.040 | 1.050 | 1.060 | 1.070 | 1.080 | 1.090 | 1.100 |
| 2 | 1.020 | 1.040 | 1.061 | 1.082 | 1.102 | 1.124 | 1.145 | 1.166 | 1.188 | 1.210 |
| 3 | 1.030 | 1.061 | 1.093 | 1.125 | 1.158 | 1.191 | 1.225 | 1.260 | 1.295 | 1.331 |
| 4 | 1.041 | 1.082 | 1.126 | 1.170 | 1.216 | 1.262 | 1.311 | 1.360 | 1.412 | 1.464 |
| 5 | 1.051 | 1.104 | 1.159 | 1.217 | 1.276 | 1.338 | 1.403 | 1.469 | 1.539 | 1.611 |
| 6 | 1.062 | 1.126 | 1.194 | 1.265 | 1.340 | 1.419 | 1.501 | 1.587 | 1.677 | 1.772 |
| 7 | 1.072 | 1.149 | 1.230 | 1.316 | 1.407 | 1.504 | 1.606 | 1.714 | 1.828 | 1.949 |
| 8 | 1.083 | 1.172 | 1.267 | 1.369 | 1.477 | 1.594 | 1.718 | 1.851 | 1.993 | 2.144 |
| 9 | 1.094 | 1.195 | 1.305 | 1.423 | 1.551 | 1.689 | 1.838 | 1.999 | 2.172 | 2.358 |
| 10 | 1.105 | 1.219 | 1.344 | 1.480 | 1.629 | 1.791 | 1.967 | 2.159 | 2.367 | 2.594 |
| 11 | 1.116 | 1.243 | 1.384 | 1.539 | 1.710 | 1.898 | 2.105 | 2.332 | 2.580 | 2.853 |
| 12 | 1.127 | 1.268 | 1.426 | 1.601 | 1.796 | 2.012 | 2.252 | 2.518 | 2.813 | 3.138 |
| 13 | 1.138 | 1.294 | 1.469 | 1.665 | 1.886 | 2.133 | 2.410 | 2.720 | 3.066 | 3.452 |
| 14 | 1.149 | 1.319 | 1.513 | 1.732 | 1.980 | 2.261 | 2.579 | 2.937 | 3.342 | 3.797 |
| 15 | 1.161 | 1.346 | 1.558 | 1.801 | 2.079 | 2.397 | 2.759 | 3.172 | 3.642 | 4.177 |

calculate the future value of an initial investment, you need only determine the $FVIF_{i, \, n}$ using a calculator or a table and multiply this amount by the initial investment. In effect, you can rewrite equation (3.4) as follows:

$$future \; value \; = \; present \; value \times future\text{-}value \; interest \; factor$$
$$or \; FV_n \; = \; PV(FVIF_{i, \, n}) \tag{3.4a}$$

Let's look back at the previous example of investing $1,000 at 5 percent compounded annually for 10 years. In Table 3.1 at the intersection of the $n = 10$ row and the 5% column, we find a value for $FVIF_{5\%, \, 10 \, yr} = 1.629$. Thus,

$$FV_{10} = \$1,000 \, (1.629)$$
$$= \$1,629$$

This is the same answer we got before. You can also use this equation to solve for $n$ and $i$.

---

**Example ←**

The average cost of a wedding in 2002 was approximately $20,000. What will that wedding cost in 30 years, assuming a 4-percent annual rate of inflation? We know that $FV_n = PV(FVIF_{i\%, \, n \, years})$. To find the future value of a wedding in 30 years we need only multiply the present value ($PV$) of a wedding ($20,000) times the future-value interest factor for 4% and 30 years ($FVIF_{4\%, \, 30 \, yr}$). To find the future-value interest factor for 4% and 30 years, go to the $FVIF$ table (see Appendix A) and simply move down the $i = 4\%$ column until you reach its intersection with the $n = 30$ years row: 3.243. Thus, the future value of a wedding in 30 years is:

$$\text{future value} = \text{present value} \times \text{future-value interest factor}$$
$$FV = PV(FVIF_{i\%,\ n\ \text{years}})$$
$$FV = \$20,000(3.243)$$
$$= \$64,860$$

Today's average wedding will cost $64,860 30 years from now!

---

Now let's assume that the DaimlerChrysler Corporation has guaranteed that the price of a new Jeep will always be $20,000. You'd like to buy one, but currently you have only $7,752. How many years will it take for your initial investment of $7,752 to grow to $20,000 if it is invested at 9 percent compounded annually? We can use equation (3.4a) to solve for this problem as well. Substituting the known values in equation (3.4a), you find

$$FV_n = PV(FVIF_{i,\ n})$$
$$\$20,000 = \$7,752(FVIF_{i\%,\ n\ \text{yr}})$$
$$\$20,000\,/\,\$7,752 = \$7,752(FVIF_{9\%,\ n\ \text{yr}})\,/\,\$7,752$$
$$2.58 = FVIF_{9\%,\ n\ \text{yr}} \tag{3.4a}$$

Thus, you're looking for a value of 2.58 in the $FVIF_{i,\ n}$ tables, and you know it must be in the 9% column. To finish solving the problem, look down the 9-percent column for the value closest to 2.58. You'll find that it occurs in the $n = 11$ row. Thus, it will take 11 years for an initial investment of $7,752 to grow to $20,000 if it is invested at 9 percent compounded annually.

Now let's solve for the compound annual growth rate, and let's go back to that Jeep that always costs $20,000. In 10 years you'd really like to have $20,000 to buy a new Jeep, but you have only $11,167. At what rate must your $11,167 be compounded annually for it to grow to $20,000 in 10 years? Substituting the known variables into equation (3.4a), you get

$$FV_n = PV(FVIF_{i,\ n})$$
$$\$20,000 = \$11,167(FVIF_{i,\ 10\ \text{yr}})$$
$$\frac{\$20,000}{\$11,167} = \frac{\$11,167(FVIF_{i,\ 10\ \text{yr}})}{\$11,167}$$
$$1.791 = FVIF_{i,\ 10\ \text{yr}} \tag{3.4a}$$

You know to look in the $n = 10$ row of the $FVIF_{i,\ n}$ tables for a value of 1.791, and you find this in the $i = 6\%$ column. Thus, if you want your initial investment of $11,167 to grow to $20,000 in 10 years, you must invest it at 6 percent.

## The Rule of 72

Now you know how to determine the future value of any investment. What if all you want to know is how long it will take to double your money in that investment? One simple way to approximate how long it will take for a given sum to double in value is called the **Rule of 72**. This "rule" states that you can determine how many years it will take for a given sum to double by dividing the investment's annual growth or interest rate into 72. For example, if an investment grows at an annual rate of 9 percent per year, according to the Rule of 72 it should take $72/9 = 8$ years for that sum to double.

**Rule of 72**
A helpful investment rule that states you can determine how many years it will take for a sum to double by dividing the annual growth rate into 72.

Keep in mind that this is not a hard and fast rule, just an approximation, but it's a pretty good approximation at that. For example, the future-value interest factor from Table 3.1 for 8 years at 9 percent is 1.993, which is pretty close to the Rule of 72's approximation of 2.0.

---

**Example** ←

Using the "Rule of 72," how long will it take to double your money if you invest it at 12 percent compounded annually?

$$\text{number of years to double} = \frac{72}{\text{annual compound growth rate}}$$
$$= \frac{72}{12}$$
$$= 6 \text{ years}$$

---

## Compound Interest with Nonannual Periods

Until now we've assumed that the compounding period is always annual. Sometimes, though, financial institutions compound interest on a quarterly, daily, or even continuous basis. What happens to your investment when your compounding period is nonannual? You earn more money faster. The sooner your interest is paid, the sooner you start earning interest on it, and the sooner you experience the benefits of compound interest.

The bottom line is that your money grows faster as the compounding period becomes shorter—for example, from annual compounding to monthly compounding. That's because interest is earned on interest more frequently as the length of the compounding period declines.

## Using a Financial Calculator

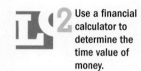

Use a financial calculator to determine the time value of money.

Time value of money calculations can be made simple with the aid of a financial calculator. Before you try to whoop it up solving time value of money problems on your financial calculator, you might want to take note of a few keys that will prove helpful (necessary, actually).

*Key Description*

| N | Stores (or calculates) the total number of payments or compounding periods. |

| I/Y | Stores (or calculates) the interest or discount rate. |

| PV | Stores (or calculates) the present value. |

| FV | Stores (or calculates) the future value. |

| PMT | Stores (or calculates) the dollar amount of each annuity payment. (We talk about these later in the chapter, but an annuity is a series of equal dollar payments for a specified number of time periods.) |

| CPT | This is the compute key on the Texas Instruments BAII Plus calculator, the calculator we use in examples in this text. If you want to compute the present value, you enter the known variables and press CPT PV. |

Something to keep in mind when using a financial calculator is that each problem will have two cash flows, and one will be a positive number and one a negative number. The idea is that you deposit money in the bank at some point in time (a negative number, because it "leaves your hands"), and at some other point in time you take money out of the bank (a positive number, because it "returns to your hands"). Also, every calculator operates a bit differently with respect to entering variables. It is a good idea to familiarize yourself with exactly how your calculator functions.

To solve a time value of money problem using a financial calculator, all you need to do is enter the appropriate numbers for three of the four variables and then press the key of the final variable to calculate its value.

Now let's solve the previous example using a financial calculator. We were trying to find at what rate $11,167 must be compounded annually for it to grow to $20,000 in 10 years.

**STEP 1:** Input Values of Known Variables

| Data Input | Function Key | Description |
|---|---|---|
| 10 | N | Stores $N = 10$ years |
| –11,167 | PV | Stores $PV = -\$11{,}167$ |
| 20,000 | FV | Stores $FV = \$20{,}000$ |
| 0 | PMT | Clears PMT to $= 0$ because that variable is not included in this problem |

**STEP 2:** Calculate the Value of the Unknown Variable

| Function Key | Answer | Description |
|---|---|---|
| CPT I/Y | 6.00% | Calculates $I/Y = 6.00\%$ |

Any of the problems in this chapter can easily be solved using a financial calculator. If you are using the TI BAII Plus, make sure you have selected both the "one payment per year" ($P/Y = 1$) and "END MODE." This sets the payment conditions to a maximum of one payment per period occurring at the end of the period. One final point: You will notice that solutions using the present value tables versus solutions using a calculator may vary slightly. Don't worry—this discrepancy is just a result of rounding errors in the tables.

Understand the power of time in compounding.

## Compounding and the Power of Time

Manhattan Island was purchased by Peter Minuit from Native Americans in 1624 for $24 in "knickknacks" and jewelry. If at the end of 1624 the Native Americans had invested their $24 at 8 percent compounded annually, it would be worth over $111.6 trillion today (by the end of 2003, 379 years later). That's certainly enough to buy back all of Manhattan. In fact, with $111.6 trillion in the bank, the $80 billion to $90 billion you'd have to pay to buy back all of Manhattan would seem like pocket change. The story illustrates the incredible power of time in compounding. There simply is no substitute for it.

**Figure 3.2** The Power of Time in Compounding

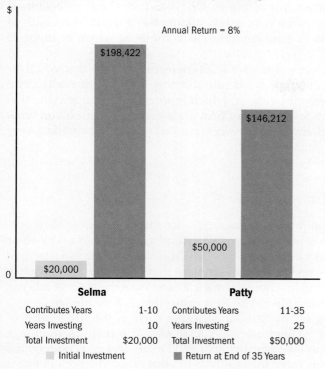

Annual Return = 8%

|  | Selma |  | Patty |  |
|---|---|---|---|---|
| Contributes Years | 1-10 | Contributes Years | 11-35 |
| Years Investing | 10 | Years Investing | 25 |
| Total Investment | $20,000 | Total Investment | $50,000 |

☐ Initial Investment　　■ Return at End of 35 Years

## The Power of Time

Why should you care about compounding? Well, the sooner you start saving for retirement and other long-term goals, the less painful the process of saving will be. Consider the tale of twin sisters who work at the Springfield DMV. Selma and Patty Bouvier decide to save for retirement, which is 35 years away. They'll both receive an 8-percent annual return on their investment over the next 35 years.

Selma invests $2,000 per year at the end of each year *only* for the first 10 years of the 35-year period—for a total of $20,000 saved. Patty doesn't start saving for 10 years and then saves $2,000 per year at the end of each year for the remaining 25 years—for a total of $50,000 saved. When they retire, Selma will have accumulated just under $200,000, while Patty will have accumulated just under $150,000, despite the fact that Selma saved for only 10 years while Patty saved for 25 years. Figure 3.2 presents their results and illustrates the power of time in compounding.

Let's look at another example to see what this really means to you. The compound growth rate in the stock market over the period 1926–2001 was approximately 10.7 percent.[1] Although the rate of return on stocks has been far from constant over this period, assume for the moment that you could earn a constant annual return of 11.2 percent compounded annually on an investment in stocks. If you invested $500 in stocks at the beginning of 1926 and earned 10.7 percent compounded annually, your investment would have grown to $1,388,304 by the end of 2003 (78 years). That would make you one wealthy senior citizen.

---

[1]See Ibbotson Associates, *Stocks, Bonds, Bills, & Inflation 2002 Yearbook*™ (Chicago, 2002).

The power of compounding is truly amazing. Say you're 22 and intend to retire at age 65—43 years from now. If you place $10,411 in stocks and they earn 11.2 percent compounded annually over those 43 years, you'd have accumulated $1 million by retirement—all in just 15,695 days!

One final example illustrates the danger in just looking at the bottom-line numbers without considering the time value of money. One of today's "hot" collectibles is the Schwinn Deluxe Tornado boys' bicycle, which sold for $49.95 in 1959. In 2003, 44 years later, a Schwinn Tornado in mint condition sells for $650, which is about 13 times its original cost.

At first glance you might view this as a 1,300-percent return—but you'd be ignoring the time value of money. At what rate did this investment really compound? The answer is 6.00 percent per year, which ignores any storage costs that might have been incurred. The Schwinn may provide a great ride, but given what you just saw common stocks doing over the same period, it doesn't provide a very good return.

**4** Explain the importance of the interest rate in determining how an investment grows.

Principle

**9** The Best Protection Is Knowledge

## The Importance of the Interest Rate

It's not just time that makes money grow in value, it's also the interest rate. Most people understand that a higher interest rate earns you more money—that's why some people are willing to buy a risky bond issued by MGM Grand that pays 11 percent rather than a very safe bond issued by the government that pays only 5.0 percent—but most people don't understand just how dramatic a difference the interest rate can make. This brings us back to **Principle 9: The Best Protection Is Knowledge**.

Without an understanding of investment concepts such as the time value of money, you're a prime target for bad advice. You're also at a real disadvantage because you might not be able to take advantage of good deals and even understand basic financial principles, such as those that apply to interest rates. The bottom line is it's much easier to do things correctly if you understand what you're doing. Let's take a closer look at interest rates.

Obviously, the choice of interest rate plays a critical role in how much an investment grows. But do small changes in the interest rate have much of an impact on future values? To answer this question, let's look back to Peter Minuit's purchase of Manhattan. If the Native Americans had invested their $24 at 10 percent rather than 8 percent compounded annually at the end of 1624, they would have over $117.0 quadrillion by the end of 2003 (379 years). That's 117.0 moved over 15 decimal places, or $117,000,000,000,000,000. Actually, that's enough to buy back not only Manhattan Island, but the entire world and still have plenty left over!

Now let's assume a lower interest rate, say 6 percent. In that case the $24 would have grown to a mere $93.6 billion—one thousandth of what it grew to at 8 percent, and only one millionth of what it would have grown to at 10 percent. With today's real estate prices, you might be able to buy Manhattan, but you probably couldn't pay your taxes!

Now let's take another look at some historical returns and see what you might have earned from 1926 through 2001. Recall that the compound growth rate on stocks over that period was approximately 10.7 percent. The average return on long-term corporate bonds over that same period was only 5.8 percent compounded annually. If you'd invested $500 in bonds rather than stocks at the beginning of 1926 and earned 5.8 percent compounded annually, your investment would have grown to $34,308 by the end of 2003 (78 years). This amount is well below the $40,630 you would have ended up with if your money had been invested in the stock market, which grew at 10.7 percent.

To illustrate the power of a high interest rate in compounding, let's look at a "daily double." A "daily double" simply means that your money doubles each day. In effect, it assumes an interest rate of 100 percent compounded on a daily basis. Let's

## Table 3.2 The Daily Double

| Day | "Daily double": 1¢ at 100% Compounded Daily Would Become |
|-----|----------------------------------------------------------|
| Day 1 | $.01 |
| Day 2 | .02 |
| Day 3 | .04 |
| Day 4 | .08 |
| Day 5 | .16 |
| Day 6 | .32 |
| Day 7 | .64 |
| Day 8 | 1.28 |
| Day 15 | 163.84 |
| Day 20 | 5,242.88 |
| Day 25 | 167,772.16 |
| Day 30 | 5,368,709.12 |
| Day 31 | 10,737,418.24 |

see what can happen to a penny over a month's worth of daily doubles, assuming that the month has 31 days in it. The first day begins with 1¢, the second day it compounds to 2¢, the third day it becomes 4¢, the fourth day 8¢, the fifth day 16¢, and so forth. As shown in Table 3.2, by day 20 it would have grown to $5,242.88, and by the day 31 it would have grown to over $10 million. Going from 1¢ to $10 million in 31 days is a bigger rush than going from 0 to 60 mph in 6 seconds!

**STOP & THINK** If you receive an inheritance of $25,000 and invest it at 6 percent (ignoring taxes) for 40 years, it will accumulate to $257,125. If you invest it at 12 percent (again ignoring taxes) over this same period, it would accumulate to $2,326,225! Almost 10 times more!

These examples explain why Albert Einstein once marveled that "Compound interest is the eighth wonder of the world."

## Present Value

**L5** Calculate the present value of money to be received in the future.

Up until this point we've been moving money forward in time; that is, we know how much we have to begin with and are trying to determine how much that sum will grow in a certain number of years when compounded at a specific rate. We're now going to look at the reverse question: What's the value in today's dollars of a sum of money to be received in the future? That is, what's the present value?

Why is present value important to us? It lets us strip away the effects of inflation and see what future cash flows are worth in today's dollars. It also lets us compare dollar values from different periods. In later chapters we'll use the present value to determine how much to pay for stocks and bonds.

In finding the present value of a future sum, we're moving future money back to the present. What we're doing is, in fact, nothing other than inverse compounding. In compounding we talked about the compound interest rate and the initial investment; in determining the present value we will talk about the **discount rate** and present value.

When we use the term "discount rate," we mean the interest rate used to bring future money back to present, that is, the interest rate used to "discount" that future money back to present. For example, if we expected to receive a sum of money in 10 years and wanted to know what it would buy in today's dollars, we would discount that future sum of money back to present at the anticipated inflation rate. Other than

**Discount Rate**
The interest rate used to bring future dollars back to the present.

that, the technique and the terminology remain the same, and the mathematics are simply reversed.

Let's return to equation (3.4), the time value of money equation. We now want to solve for present value instead of future value, so we divide both sides of the equation by $(1 + i)^n$ to get

$$FV_n = PV(1 + i)^n \tag{3.4}$$

$$\frac{FV_n}{(1 + i)^n} = \frac{PV(1 + i)^n}{(1 + i)^n}$$

$$FV_n\left(\frac{1}{(1 + i)^n}\right) = PV$$

$$\text{or } PV = FV_n\left(\frac{1}{(1 + i)^n}\right) \tag{3.5}$$

where

$FV_n$ = the future value of the investment at the end of $n$ years
$n$ = the number of years until the payment will be received
$i$ = the annual discount (or interest) rate
$PV$ = the present value of the future sum of money

**Present-Value Interest Factor ($PVIF_{i, n}$)**
The value $[1/(1 + i)^n]$ used as a multiplier to calculate an amount's present value.

Because the mathematical procedure for determining the present value is exactly the inverse of determining the future value, the relationships among $n$, $i$, and $PV$ are just the opposite of those we observed in future value. The present value of a future sum of money is inversely related to both the number of years until the payment will be received and the discount rate. Figure 3.3 shows this relationship graphically.

To aid in the computation of present values, we once again have some handy tables. This time they calculate the $[1/(1 + i)^n]$ part of the equation, which we call the **present-value interest factor** for $i$ and $n$, or $PVIF_{i, n}$. These tables simplify the math by

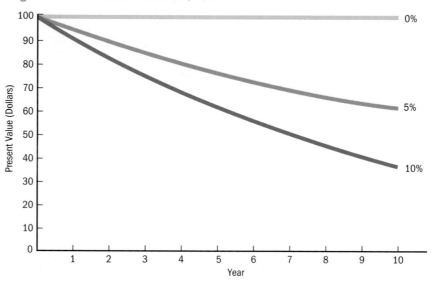

Figure 3.3 The Present Value of $100

# Table 3.3  $PVIF_{i, n}$, or the Present Value of $1

*Instructions: Each present-value interest factor ($PVIF_{i\%, \text{ n years}}$) corresponds to a specific time period and interest rate. To find the present-value interest factor for 6 percent and 10 years ($PVIF_{6\%, \text{ 10 yr}}$), simply move down the i = 6% column until you reach its intersection with the n = 10 years row: 0.558. The present value is then calculated as follows:*

$$\text{present value} = \text{future value} \times \text{present - value interest factor}$$
$$\text{or } PV = FV_n(PVIF_{i\%, \text{ n years}})$$

| n | 1% | 2% | 3% | 4% | 5% | 6% | 7% | 8% | 9% | 10% |
|---|----|----|----|----|----|----|----|----|----|-----|
| 1 | .990 | .980 | .971 | .962 | .952 | .943 | .935 | .926 | .917 | .909 |
| 2 | .980 | .961 | .943 | .925 | .907 | .890 | .873 | .857 | .842 | .826 |
| 3 | .971 | .942 | .915 | .889 | .864 | .840 | .816 | .794 | .772 | .751 |
| 4 | .961 | .924 | .888 | .855 | .823 | .792 | .763 | .735 | .708 | .683 |
| 5 | .951 | .906 | .863 | .822 | .784 | .747 | .713 | .681 | .650 | .621 |
| 6 | .942 | .888 | .837 | .790 | .746 | .705 | .666 | .630 | .596 | .564 |
| 7 | .933 | .871 | .813 | .760 | .711 | .655 | .623 | .583 | .547 | .513 |
| 8 | .923 | .853 | .789 | .731 | .677 | .627 | .582 | .540 | .502 | .467 |
| 9 | .914 | .837 | .766 | .703 | .645 | .592 | .544 | .500 | .460 | .424 |
| 10 | .905 | .820 | .744 | .676 | .614 | .558 | .508 | .463 | .422 | .386 |
| 11 | .896 | .804 | .722 | .650 | .585 | .527 | .475 | .429 | .388 | .350 |
| 12 | .887 | .789 | .701 | .625 | .557 | .497 | .444 | .397 | .356 | .319 |
| 13 | .879 | .773 | .681 | .601 | .530 | .469 | .415 | .368 | .326 | .290 |
| 14 | .870 | .758 | .661 | .577 | .505 | .442 | .388 | .340 | .299 | .263 |
| 15 | .861 | .743 | .642 | .555 | .481 | .417 | .362 | .315 | .275 | .239 |

giving us the various values for combinations of $i$ and $n$ defined as $[1/(1 + i)^n]$. Appendix B at the back of this book presents fairly complete versions of these tables, and an abbreviated version appears in Table 3.3.

A close examination of Table 3.3 shows that the values in these tables are the inverse of the tables found in Appendix A and Table 3.1. Of course, this inversion makes sense because the values in Appendix A are $(1 + i)^n$ and those in Appendix B are $[1/(1 + i)^n]$. To determine the present value of a sum of money to be received at some future date, you need only determine the value of the appropriate $PVIF_{i, n}$, by using a calculator or consulting the tables, and multiply it by the future value. In effect, you can use the new notation and rewrite equation (3.5) as follows:

$$\text{present value} = \text{future value} \times \text{present-value interest factor}$$

or

$$PV = FV_n(PVIF_{i, n}) \tag{3.5a}$$

**Example ←**

You're on vacation in a rather remote part of Florida and see an advertisement stating that if you take a sales tour of some condominiums, "you will be given $100 just for taking the tour." However, the $100 that you get is in the form of a savings bond that will not pay you the $100 for 10 years. What is the present value of $100 to be received 10 years from today if your discount rate is 6 percent? By looking at the $n = 10$ row and $i = 6\%$ column of Table 3.3, you find the $PVIF_{6\%, 10 \text{ yr}}$ is 0.558. Substituting $FV_{10} = \$100$ and $PVIF_{6\%, 10 \text{ yr}} = 0.558$ into equation (3.5a), you find

$$
\begin{aligned}
PV &= \$100(PVIF_{6\%, 10 \text{ yr}}) \\
&= \$100(0.558) \\
&= \$55.80
\end{aligned}
$$

Thus, the value in today's dollars of that $100 savings bond is only $55.80. That's not a bad take for touring some condominiums, but it's not $100.

→ **Example**

Let's consider the "prodigal son" who wants his estate NOW! His father has promised him $500,000 in 40 years. Assuming the appropriate discount rate (i.e., the interest rate used to bring future money back to the present) is 6 percent, what is the present value of the $500,000? We know that $PV = FV_n(PVIF_{i\%, n \text{ years}})$. To find the present value of the estate we need only multiply the future value ($FV_n$), which is $500,000 times the present-value interest factor for 6% and 40 years ($PVIF_{6\%, 40 \text{ yr}}$). To find the present-value interest factor for 6% and 40 years, go to the $PVIF$ table (see Appendix B) and simply move down the $i = 6\%$ column until you reach its intersection with the $n = 40$ years row: 0.097. Thus, the present value of the estate is:

$$
\begin{aligned}
PV &= FV_n(PVIF_{i\%, n \text{ years}}) \\
PV &= \$500,000(0.097) \\
&= \$48,500
\end{aligned}
$$

That $500,000 the son is to receive in 40 years is worth only $48,500 in today's dollars. Another way of looking at this problem is that if you deposit $48,500 in the bank today earning 6 percent annually, in 40 years you'd have $500,000.

→ **Example**

You own a $1,000 savings bond that will mature at the end of 10 years. Because of an economic report you just heard, you assume that between now and then, inflation will be at an annual rate of 5 percent. You've been doing a little financial planning, and want to know how helpful your savings bond will be in achieving your future goals. The only problem is that all of your best estimates are based on today's dollars, not the inflated dollars of 10 years from now.

You need to adjust the value of your savings bond for inflation. What is the value of this $1,000 to be received 10 years from now in today's dollars? By looking at the $n = 10$ row and $i = 5\%$ column of Table 3.3, you find the $PVIF_{5\%, 10 \text{ yr}}$ is 0.614. Substituting this value into equation (3.5a), you find

$$
\begin{aligned}
PV &= \$1000(0.614) \\
&= \$614.00
\end{aligned}
$$

Thus, the present value of this $1,000 payment is $614.00. That means that if the inflation rate is 5 percent over the next 10 years, the purchasing power of the $1,000 that you receive at that time will be worth only $614.00 in today's dollars. It looks like it's best not to plan on using that bond to buy anything that currently costs more than $614.

Keep in mind that there is really only one time value of money equation. That is, equations (3.4) and (3.5) are actually identical—they simply solve for different variables. One solves for future value, the other for present value. The logic behind both equations is the same: To adjust for the time value of money, we must compare dollar values, present and future, in the same time period. Because all present values are comparable (they are all measured in dollars of the same time period), you can add and subtract the present value of inflows and outflows to determine the present value of an investment.

**STOP & THINK** Why should you be interested in stripping away the effects of inflation from money you receive in the future? Because the dollar value of future money is not as important as that money's purchasing power. For example, you might be excited if you were told you would receive $1 million in 20 years. However, if you then found out that in 20 years a new car will cost $800,000, your average monthly food bill will be $15,000, and a typical month's rent on your apartment will be $30,000, you would have a different view of the $1 million. Using the time value of money to strip away the effects of inflation allows you to calculate the value of a future amount in terms of the purchasing power of today's dollars.

**Example ←**

What is the present value of an investment that yields both $500 to be received in 5 years and $1,000 to be received in 10 years if the discount rate is 4 percent? Substituting the values of $n = 5$, $i = 4\%$, and $FV_5 = \$500$; and $n = 10$, $i = 4\%$, and $FV_{10} = \$1,000$ into equation (3.5a) and adding these values together, we find

$$PV = \$500(PVIF_{4\%, \, 5 \, yr}) + \$1,000(PVIF_{4\%, \, 10 \, yr})$$
$$= \$500(0.822) + \$1,000(0.676)$$
$$= \$411 + \$676$$
$$= \$1,087$$

Present values are comparable and can be added together because they are measured in the same time period's dollars.

## Annuities

Define an annuity and calculate its compound or future value.

To this point, we've been examining single deposits—moving them back and forth in time. Now we're going to examine annuities. Most people deal with a great number of annuities. Pension funds, insurance obligations, and interest received from bonds all involve annuities. An **annuity** is a series of equal dollar payments coming at the end of each time period for a specified number of time periods (years, months, etc.). Because annuities occur frequently in finance—for example, as bond interest payments and mortgage payments—they are treated specially. Although compounding and determining the present value of an annuity can be done using equations (3.4) and (3.5), these calculations can be time-consuming, especially for larger annuities. Thus, we have modified the formulas to deal directly with annuities.

**Annuity**
A series of equal dollar payments coming at the end of each time period for a specified number of time periods.

### Compound Annuities

A **compound annuity** involves depositing or investing an equal sum of money at the end of each year (or time period) for a certain number of years (or time periods, e.g., months) and allowing it to grow. Perhaps you are saving money for education, a new car, or a vacation home. In each case you'll want to know how much your savings will have grown by some point in the future.

**Compound Annuity**
An investment that involves depositing an equal sum of money at the end of each year for a certain number of years and allowing it to grow.

Actually, you can find the answer by using equation (3.4) and compounding each of the individual deposits to its future value. For example, if to provide for a college education you are going to deposit $500 at the end of each year for the next 5 years in a bank where it will earn 6 percent interest, how much will you have at the end of 5 years? Compounding each of these values using equation (3.4), you find that you will have $2,818.50 at the end of 5 years.

$$
\begin{aligned}
FV_5 &= \$500(1 + 0.06)^4 + \$500(1 + 0.06)^3 + \$500(1 + 0.06)^2 + \$500(1 + 0.06) + \$500 \\
&= \$500(1.262) + \$500(1.191) + \$500(1.124) + \$500(1.060) + \$500 \\
&= \$631.00 + \$595.50 + \$562.00 + \$530.00 + \$500.00 \\
&= \$2,818.50
\end{aligned}
$$

As Table 3.4 shows, all we're really doing in the preceding calculation is summing up a number of consecutive future-value interest factors. To simplify this process once again, there are tables providing the **future-value interest factor for an annuity** for $i$ and $n$ ($FVIFA_{i, n}$). Appendix C provides a fairly complete version of these tables, and Table 3.5 presents an abbreviated version. Using this new factor, we can calculate the future value of an annuity as follows:

> future value of an annuity = annual payment
> $\times$ future-value interest factor of an annuity

or

$$
FV_n = PMT(FVIFA_{i, n}) \tag{3.6}
$$

Using the future-value interest factor for an annuity ($FVIFA$) to solve our previous example involving 5 years of deposits of $500, invested at 6 percent interest, we would look in the $i = 6\%$ column and $n = 5$ row and find the value of the $FVIFA_{6\%, 5\ yr}$ to be 5.637. Substituting this value into equation (3.6), we get

$$
\begin{aligned}
FV_5 &= \$500(FVIFA_{6\%,\ 5\ yr}) \\
FV_5 &= \$500(5.637) \\
&= \$2,818.50
\end{aligned}
$$

This is the same answer we obtained earlier. (If it weren't, I'd need to get a new job!)

**Future-Value Interest Factor for an Annuity ($FVIFA_{i,\ n}$)**
A multiplier used to determine the future value of an annuity. The future-value interest factors for an annuity are found in Appendix C.

## Table 3.4    Illustration of a 5-Year $500 Annuity Compounded at 6%

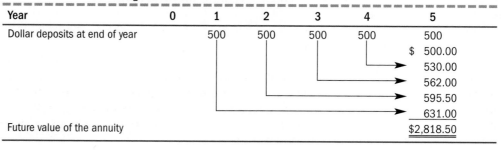

| Year | 0 | 1 | 2 | 3 | 4 | 5 |
|---|---|---|---|---|---|---|
| Dollar deposits at end of year | | 500 | 500 | 500 | 500 | 500 |
| | | | | | | $ 500.00 |
| | | | | | | 530.00 |
| | | | | | | 562.00 |
| | | | | | | 595.50 |
| | | | | | | 631.00 |
| Future value of the annuity | | | | | | $2,818.50 |

# Table 3.5 $FVIFA_{i,\,n}$, or the Sum of an Annuity of $1 for $n$ Years

*Instructions: Each future-value interest factor for an annuity ($FVIFA_{i\%,\;n\,years}$) corresponds to a specific time period (number of years) and interest rate. For example, to find the future-value interest factor of an annuity for 6 percent and 5 years ($FVIFA_{6\%,\;5\,yr}$), simply move down the i = 6% column until you reach its intersection with the n = 5 years row: 5.637. The future value is calculated as follows:*

future value = annual payment × future-value interest factor for an annuity

or $FV_n = PMT(FVIFA_{i\%,\;n\,years})$

| n | 1% | 2% | 3% | 4% | 5% | 6% | 7% | 8% | 9% | 10% |
|---|----|----|----|----|----|----|----|----|----|-----|
| 1 | 1.000 | 1.000 | 1.000 | 1.000 | 1.000 | 1.000 | 1.000 | 1.000 | 1.000 | 1.000 |
| 2 | 2.010 | 2.020 | 2.030 | 2.040 | 2.050 | 2.060 | 2.070 | 2.080 | 2.090 | 2.100 |
| 3 | 3.030 | 3.060 | 3.091 | 3.122 | 3.152 | 3.184 | 3.215 | 3.246 | 3.278 | 3.310 |
| 4 | 4.060 | 4.122 | 4.184 | 4.246 | 4.310 | 4.375 | 4.440 | 4.506 | 4.573 | 4.641 |
| 5 | 5.101 | 5.204 | 5.309 | 5.416 | 5.526 | 5.637 | 5.751 | 5.867 | 5.985 | 6.105 |
| 6 | 6.152 | 6.308 | 6.468 | 6.633 | 6.802 | 6.975 | 7.153 | 7.336 | 7.523 | 7.716 |
| 7 | 7.214 | 7.434 | 7.662 | 7.898 | 8.142 | 8.394 | 8.654 | 8.923 | 9.200 | 9.487 |
| 8 | 8.286 | 8.583 | 8.892 | 9.214 | 9.549 | 9.897 | 10.260 | 10.637 | 11.028 | 11.436 |
| 9 | 9.368 | 9.755 | 10.159 | 10.583 | 11.027 | 11.491 | 11.978 | 12.488 | 13.021 | 13.579 |
| 10 | 10.462 | 10.950 | 11.464 | 12.006 | 12.578 | 13.181 | 13.816 | 14.487 | 15.193 | 15.937 |
| 11 | 11.567 | 12.169 | 12.808 | 13.486 | 14.207 | 14.972 | 15.784 | 16.645 | 17.560 | 18.531 |
| 12 | 12.682 | 13.412 | 14.192 | 15.026 | 15.917 | 16.870 | 17.888 | 18.977 | 20.141 | 21.384 |
| 13 | 13.809 | 14.680 | 15.618 | 16.627 | 17.713 | 18.882 | 20.141 | 21.495 | 22.953 | 24.523 |
| 14 | 14.947 | 15.974 | 17.086 | 18.292 | 19.598 | 21.015 | 22.550 | 24.215 | 26.019 | 27.975 |
| 15 | 16.097 | 17.293 | 18.599 | 20.023 | 21.578 | 23.276 | 25.129 | 27.152 | 29.361 | 31.772 |

Rather than ask how much you'll accumulate if you deposit an equal sum in a savings account each year, a more common question is, how much must you deposit each year to accumulate a certain amount of savings? This question often arises when saving for large expenditures, such as retirement or a down payment on a home.

For example, you may know that you'll need $10,000 for education in 8 years. How much must you put away at the end of each year at 6 percent interest to have the college money ready? In this case, you know the values of $n$, $i$, and $FV_n$ in equation (3.6), but you don't know the value of *PMT*. Substituting these example values in equation (3.6), you find

$$\$10{,}000 = PMT(FVIFA_{6\%,\;8\,yr})$$
$$\$10{,}000 = PMT(9.897)$$
$$\$10{,}000\,/\,9.897 = PMT$$
$$PMT = \$1{,}010.41$$

Thus, you must invest $1,010.41 at the end of each year at 6 percent interest to accumulate $10,000 at the end of 8 years.

For a moment let's use the future value of an annuity and think back to the discussion of the power of time. There's no question of the power of time. One way to illustrate this power is to look at how much you'd have to save each month to reach some far-off goal. For example, you'd like to save up $50,000 by the time you turn 60 to use to go see a Rolling Stones concert. (There's a good chance they'll still be on tour and that concert tickets will cost that much.)

If you can invest your money at 12 percent and start saving when you turn 21, making your last payment on your sixtieth birthday, you'll need to put aside only $4.25 per month. If you started at age 31, that figure would be $14.31 per month. However, if you waited until age 51, it would rise to $217.35 per month. When it comes to compounding, time is on your side.

**STOP &THINK** If a couple goes out to dinner and a movie four times a month at $75 an outing and cuts this down to two times per month, they will save $1,800 per year. If they take this saved money and invest it at the end of each year, earning 10 percent compounded annually (ignoring taxes), in 30 years they would accumulate $296,089!

→ **Example**

If you deposit $2,000 in an individual retirement account (IRA) at the end of each year and it grows at a rate of 10 percent per year, how much will you have at the end of 40 years? We know that $FV_n = PMT(FVIFA_{i\%,\ n\ \text{years}})$. To find what your $2,000 annual deposit will have grown to after 40 years ($FV_{40}$), we need only multiply the annual payment ($PMT$), which is $2,000, times the future-value interest factor for an annuity at 10% and 40 years ($FVIFA_{10\%,\ 40\ \text{yr}}$).

To find the future-value interest factor for an annuity at 10% and 40 years, go to the *FVIFA* table (see Appendix C) and simply move down the $i = 10\%$ column until you reach its intersection with the $n = 40$ years row: 442.58. Thus, the future value after 40 years of an annual deposit of $2,000 per year is:

$$\text{future value} = \text{annual payment} \times \text{future-value interest factor of an annuity}$$
$$\text{or } FV_n = PMT(FVIFA_{i\%,\ n\ \text{years}})$$
$$FV_n = \$2{,}000(442.58)$$
$$= \$885{,}160$$

You'll have $885,160 in 40 years!

→ **Example**

You'd like to take a world cruise in 10 years and you know that the cost of the cruise at that time will be $5,000. How much must you deposit in an 8-percent savings account at the end of each year to accumulate $5,000 at the end of 10 years? Substituting the values $FV_{10} = \$5{,}000$, $n = 10$, and $i = 8\%$ into equation (3.6), we find

$$\$5{,}000 = PMT(FVIFA_{8\%,\ 10\ \text{yr}})$$
$$\$5{,}000 = PMT(14.487)$$
$$\frac{\$5{,}000}{14.487} = PMT$$
$$PMT = \$345.14$$

You must deposit $345.14 per year for 10 years at 8 percent to accumulate $5,000.

→ **Example**

Let's take one more look at the power of compounding. Assume you empty the change out of your pocket each day—averaging a dollar a day—and set it aside. Then, at the end of each year, invest it at 12 percent. If you began doing this at age 18, 50 years later you would have accumulated $876,007. If you waited until you were 33 to begin your pocket-emptying ritual, you'd accumulate only $157,557. Keep in mind that between the time you were 18 and when you turned 33 you invested only a total of $5,475. Remember **Principle 15: Just Do It**. There is no substitute for time in the world of investing.

Principle

**15** Just Do It!

## Present Value of an Annuity

In planning your finances, you need to examine the relative value of all your annuities. To compare them, you need to know the present value of each. Although you can find the present value of an annuity by using the present value table in Appendix B, this process can be tedious, particularly when the annuity lasts for several years. If you wish to know what $500 received at the end of the next 5 years is worth to you given the appropriate discount rate of 6 percent, you can simply substitute the appropriate values into equation (3.6), such that

$$
\begin{aligned}
PV &= \$500(PVIF_{6\%,\ 1\ yr}) + \$500(PVIF_{6\%,\ 2\ yr}) + \$500(PVIF_{6\%,\ 3\ yr}) \\
&\quad + \$500(PVIF_{6\%,\ 4\ yr}) + \$500(PVIF_{6\%,\ 5\ yr}) \\
&= \$500(0.943) + \$500(0.890) + \$500(0.840) + \$500(0.792) + \$500(0.747) \\
&= \$2,106
\end{aligned}
$$

Thus, the present value of this annuity is $2,106.00. As Table 3.6 shows, all we're really doing in this calculation is adding up *PVIF*s. Because annuities occur so frequently in personal finance, the process of determining the present value of an annuity has been simplified by defining the **present-value interest factor for an annuity** for $i$ and $n$ ($PVIFA_{i,\ n}$). The $PVIFA_{i,\ n}$ is simply the sum of the *PVIF*s for years 1 to $n$. Tables for values of $PVIFA_{i,\ n}$ have once again been compiled for various combinations of $i$ and $n$. Appendix D provides a fairly complete version of these tables, and Table 3.7 provides an abbreviated version.

> **Present-Value Interest Factor for an Annuity ($PVIFA_{i,\ n}$)**
> A multiplier used to determine the present value of an annuity. The present-value interest factors are found in Appendix D.

Using this new factor, we can determine the present value of an annuity as follows:

present value of an annuity = annual payment
$\qquad\qquad\qquad$ × present-value interest factor of an annuity

or

$$
PV = PMT(PVIFA_{i,\ n}) \tag{3.7}
$$

Using the *PVIFA* to solve our previous example involving $500 received annually and discounted back to the present at 6 percent, we would look in the $i = 6\%$ column and the $n = 5$ row and find the $PVIFA_{6\%,\ 5\ yr}$ to be 4.212. Substituting the appropriate values into equation (3.7), we find

$$
\begin{aligned}
PV &= PMT(PVIFA_{i,\ n}) \\
PV &= \$500(PVIFA_{6\%,\ 5\ yr}) \\
&= \$500(4.212) \\
&= \$2,106
\end{aligned}
$$

Again, we get the same answer we previously did. (We're on a roll now!) We didn't get the same answer just because we're smart. Actually, we got the same answer both times because the *PVIFA* tables are calculated by adding up the values in the *PVIF* table. That is, the *PVIFA* table value found in Table 3.7 for an $n$-year annuity for any discount rate $i$ is merely the sum of the first $n$ *PVIF* values in Table 3.3.

You can see this by comparing the value in the *PVIFA* table (Table 3.7) for $i = 8\%$ and $n = 6$ years, which is 4.623, with the sum of the values in the $i = 8\%$ column and $n = 1, \ldots, 6$ rows of the present value table (Table 3.3), which is equal to 4.623, as shown in Table 3.8.

## Table 3.6 Illustration of a 5-Year $500 Annuity Discounted Back to the Present at 6%

| Year | 0 | 1 | 2 | 3 | 4 | 5 |
|------|---|---|---|---|---|---|
| Dollars received at end of year | | 500 | 500 | 500 | 500 | 500 |
| | $ 471.50 ◄ | | | | | |
| | 445.00 ◄ | | | | | |
| | 420.00 ◄ | | | | | |
| | 396.00 ◄ | | | | | |
| | 373.50 ◄ | | | | | |
| Present value of the annuity | $2,106.00 | | | | | |

## Table 3.7 $PVIFA_{i, n}$, or the Present Value of an Annuity of $1

*Instructions: Each present-value interest factor for an annuity ($PVIFA_{i\%, n\ years}$) corresponds to a specific time period (number of years) and interest rate. For example, to find the present-value interest factor of an annuity for 6 percent and 5 years ($FVIFA_{6\%, 5\ yr}$), simply move down the i = 6% column until you reach its intersection with the n = 5 years row: 4.212. The future value is then calculated as follows:*

$$present\ value = annual\ payment \times present\text{-}value\ interest\ factor\ for\ an\ annuity$$
$$or\ PV = PMT(FVIFA_{i\%, n\ years})$$

| n | 1% | 2% | 3% | 4% | 5% | 6% | 7% | 8% | 9% | 10% |
|---|----|----|----|----|----|----|----|----|----|-----|
| 1 | 0.990 | 0.980 | 0.971 | 0.962 | 0.952 | 0.943 | 0.935 | 0.926 | 0.917 | 0.909 |
| 2 | 1.970 | 1.942 | 1.913 | 1.886 | 1.859 | 1.833 | 1.808 | 1.783 | 1.759 | 1.736 |
| 3 | 2.941 | 2.884 | 2.829 | 2.775 | 2.723 | 2.673 | 2.624 | 2.577 | 2.531 | 2.487 |
| 4 | 3.902 | 3.808 | 3.717 | 3.630 | 3.546 | 3.465 | 3.387 | 3.312 | 3.240 | 3.170 |
| 5 | 4.853 | 4.713 | 4.580 | 4.452 | 4.329 | 4.212 | 4.100 | 3.993 | 3.890 | 3.791 |
| 6 | 5.795 | 5.601 | 5.417 | 5.242 | 5.076 | 4.917 | 4.767 | 4.623 | 4.486 | 4.355 |
| 7 | 6.728 | 6.472 | 6.230 | 6.002 | 5.786 | 5.582 | 5.389 | 5.206 | 5.033 | 4.868 |
| 8 | 7.652 | 7.326 | 7.020 | 6.733 | 6.463 | 6.210 | 5.971 | 5.747 | 5.535 | 5.335 |
| 9 | 8.566 | 8.162 | 7.786 | 7.435 | 7.108 | 6.802 | 6.515 | 6.247 | 5.995 | 5.759 |
| 10 | 9.471 | 8.983 | 8.530 | 8.111 | 7.722 | 7.360 | 7.024 | 6.710 | 6.418 | 6.145 |
| 11 | 10.368 | 9.787 | 9.253 | 8.760 | 8.306 | 7.887 | 7.499 | 7.139 | 6.805 | 6.495 |
| 12 | 11.255 | 10.575 | 9.954 | 9.385 | 8.863 | 8.384 | 7.943 | 7.536 | 7.161 | 6.814 |
| 13 | 12.134 | 11.348 | 10.635 | 9.986 | 9.394 | 8.853 | 8.358 | 7.904 | 7.487 | 7.103 |
| 14 | 13.004 | 12.106 | 11.296 | 10.563 | 9.899 | 9.295 | 8.746 | 8.244 | 7.786 | 7.367 |
| 15 | 13.865 | 12.849 | 11.938 | 11.118 | 10.380 | 9.712 | 9.108 | 8.560 | 8.061 | 7.606 |

## Table 3.8 Present Value of a 6-Year Annuity Discounted at 8% (the Present Value of Each $1 Is Taken from Table 3.3)

| $1 Received at End of Year | 0 | 1 | 2 | 3 | 4 | 5 | 6 |
|---|---|---|---|---|---|---|---|
| Present value | | | | | | | |
| | .926 ◄ | | | | | | |
| | .857 ◄ | | | | | | |
| | .794 ◄ | | | | | | |
| | .735 ◄ | | | | | | |
| | .681 ◄ | | | | | | |
| | .630 ◄ | | | | | | |
| Present value of annuity | 4.623 | | | | | | |

# In The News

Wall Street Journal, April 22, 1994

## Make a Child (or Yourself) a Millionaire, Just Take Your Time

Thanks a million.

Even if you haven't got a lot of money, you can easily give $1 million or more to your children, grandchildren, or favorite charity. All it takes is a small initial investment and a lot of time.

Suppose your 16-year-old daughter plans to take a summer job, which will pay her at least $2,000. Because she has earned income, she can open an individual retirement account. If you would like to help fund her retirement, Kenneth Klegon, a financial planner in Lansing, Michigan, suggests giving her $2,000 to set up the IRA. He then advises doing the same in each of the next 5 years, so that your daughter stashes away a total of $12,000.

*Result? If the money is invested in stocks, and stocks deliver their historical average annual return of 10 percent, your daughter will have more than $1 million by the time she turns 65. (☛A)*

*Because of the corrosive effect of inflation, that $1 million will only buy a quarter of what $1 million buys today, presuming the cost of living rises at 3 percent a year. Nonetheless, your $12,000 gift will go a long*

*way toward paying your daughter's retirement. The huge gain is possible because of the way stock market compounding works, with money earned each year not only on your initial investment but also on the gains accumulated from earlier years. (☛B)*

### THE BOTTOM LINE . . .

A Using the principles and techniques set out in this chapter, we can easily see how big this IRA investment will grow. We can first take the $2,000 6-year annuity and determine its future value (i.e., its value when your daughter is 21 and the last payment takes place) as follows:

$$FV = PMT(FVIFA_{10\%,\ 6\ yr})$$
$$= \$2,000(FVIFA_{10\%,\ 6\ yr})$$
$$= \$15,431.22$$

We could take this amount that your daughter has when she is 21 and compound it out 44 years to when she is 65 as follows:

$$FV = PV(FVIF_{10\%,\ 44\ yr})$$
$$= \$15,431.22(FVIF_{10\%,\ 44\ yr})$$
$$= \$1,022,535.54$$

Thus, your daughter's IRA would have accumulated to $1,022,535.54 by age 65 if it grew at 10 percent compounded annually.

B To determine how much this amount is worth in today's dollars, we calculate the present value of $1,022,535.54 to be received in 49 years given a discount rate of 3 percent:

$$PV = FV(PVIF_{3\%,\ 49\ yr})$$
$$= \$1,022,235.54(PVIF_{3\%,\ 49\ yr})$$
$$= \$240,245.02$$

You can change the growth and inflation rates and come up with all kinds of numbers, but one thing holds—there is incredible power in compounding!

---

**Example ←**

What is the present value of a 10-year $1,000 annuity discounted back to the present at 5%? Substituting $n = 10$ years, $i = 5\%$, and $PMT = \$1,000$ into equation (3.7), you find

$$PV = \$1,000(PVIFA_{5\%,\ 10\ yr})$$

Determining the value for the $PVIFA_{5\%,\ 10\ yr}$ from Table 3.7, row $n = 10$, column $i = 5\%$, and substituting it into our equation, we get

$$PV = \$1,000(7.722)$$
$$PV = \$7,722$$

Thus, the present value of this annuity is $7,722.

---

**Example ←**

Let's consider the example of the soon-to-be ex-spouse who has been offered a settlement that includes annual payments (occurring at the end of each year) of $50,000 per year for 25 years. The spouse wants the money now. Assuming a 5-percent discount rate, what is the present value of this stream of future payments? We know that $PV = PMT(PVIFA_{1\%,\ n\ years})$. To find the present value of the proposed settlement we need only multiply the annual payment ($PMT$), which is $50,000 times the present-value interest factor of an annuity for 5% and 25 years ($PVIFA_{5\%,\ 25\ yr}$). To find the present-value interest factor of an annuity for 5% and 25 years, go to the $PVIFA$ table (see Appendix D) and simply move down the $i = 5\%$ column until you reach its intersection with the $n = 25$ years row: 14.094.

$$\text{present value} = \text{annual payment}$$
$$\times \text{present-value interest factor of an annuity}$$
$$\text{or } PV = PMT(PVIFA_{i\%,\ n\ \text{years}})$$
$$PV = \$50,000(14.094)$$
$$= \$704,700$$

Thus, the present value of the 25-year $50,000 annuity is $704,700.

---

As with the other problems involving compounding and present-value tables, given any three of the four unknowns in equation (3.7), we can solve for the fourth. In the case of the $PVIFA$ table, we may be interested in solving for $PMT$, if we know $i$, $n$, and $PV$. The financial interpretation of this action would be: How much can be withdrawn, perhaps as a pension or to make loan payments, from an account that earns $i$ percent compounded annually for each of the next $n$ years if you wish to have nothing left at the end of $n$ years?

Say you have saved $1 million in an account earning 8 percent interest for your retirement. The day you turn 60 years old and retire, how large an annuity can you draw out at the end of each year if you want nothing left at the end of 40 years? (You plan on living to be 100—after all, George Burns made it to 100 and he smoked an average of 5,475 cigars per year.) In this case the present value, $PV$, of the annuity is $1,000,000, $n = 40$ years, $i = 8\%$, and $PMT$ is unknown. Substituting this into equation (3.7), you find

$$PV = PMT(PVIFA_{8\%,\ 40\ yr})$$
$$\$1,000,000 = PMT(11.925)$$
$$\frac{\$1,000,000}{11.925} = \frac{PMT(11.925)}{11.925}$$
$$\$83,857.44 = PMT$$

Thus, this account will fall to zero at the end of 40 years if you withdraw $83,857.44 at the end of each year. With that kind of money you could afford Cuban cigars.

## Amortized Loans

**Amortized Loan**
A loan paid off in equal installments.

Don't think you're always on the receiving end of an annuity. More often, your annuity will involve paying off a loan in equal installments over time. Loans that are paid off this way, in equal periodic payments, are called **amortized loans**. Examples of amortized loans include car loans and mortgages.

Suppose you borrowed $6,000 at 15-percent interest to buy a car and wish to repay it in four equal payments at the end of each of the next 4 years. We can use equation (3.7) to determine what the annual payments will be and solve for the value of $PMT$, the annual annuity. Again, you know three of the four values in that equation, $PV$, $i$, and $n$. $PV$, the present value of the future annuity, is $6,000; $i$, the annual interest rate, is 15 percent; and $n$, the number of years for which the annuity will last, is 4 years. $PMT$, the annuity payment received (by the lender and paid

**Figure 3.4** Loan Amortization Schedule Involving a $6,000 Loan at 15% to Be Repaid in 4 Years

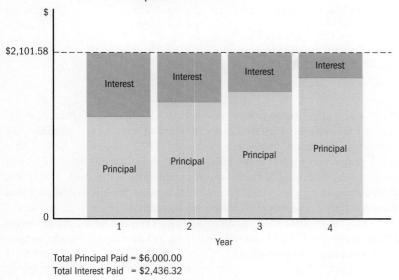

Total Principal Paid = $6,000.00
Total Interest Paid  = $2,436.32

by you) at the end of each year, is unknown. Substituting these values into equation (3.7) you find

$$PV = PMT(PVIFA_{i\%, \, n \, \text{yr}})$$
$$\$6,000 = PMT(PVIFA_{15\%, \, 4 \, \text{yr}})$$
$$\$6,000 = PMT(2.855)$$
$$\$6,000/2.855 = PMT(2.855)/2.855$$
$$\$2,101.58 = PMT$$

To repay the principal and interest on the outstanding loan in 4 years, the annual payments would be $2,101.58. The breakdown of interest and principal payments is given in the loan amortization schedule in Figure 3.4. As you can see, the interest payment declines each year as the loan outstanding declines.

**Example ←**

The Virginia State Lottery runs like most other state lotteries: You must select 6 out of 44 numbers correctly to win the jackpot. If you come close there are some significantly lesser prizes — we will ignore them for now. For each million dollars in the lottery jackpot, you receive $50,000 per year for 20 years, and your chance of winning is 1 in 7.1 million. One of the recent advertisements for the Virginia State Lottery went as follows: "Okay, you got two kinds of people. You've got the kind who play Lotto all the time, and the kind who play Lotto some of the time. You know, like only on a Saturday when they stop in at the store on the corner for some peanut butter cups and diet soda and the jackpot happens to be really big. I mean, my friend Ned? He's like, 'Hey, it's only two million dollars this week.' Well, hellloooo, anybody home? I mean, I don't know about you, but I wouldn't mind having a measly two mill coming my way. . . ."

What is the present value of these payments? The answer to this question depends on what assumption you make as to the time value of money — in this case, let's assume that your required rate of return on an investment with this level of risk is 10 percent. Keep in mind that the Lotto is an annuity—that is, on a $2 million lottery you would get $100,000 per year for 20 years.[2] Thus, the present value of this 20-year annuity discounted back to the present at 10 percent becomes

$$
\begin{aligned}
PV &= PMT(PVIFA_{i\%,\ n\,\text{yr}}) \\
&= \$100{,}000(PVIFA_{10\%,\ 20\,\text{yr}}) \\
&= \$100{,}000(8.514) \\
&= \$851{,}400
\end{aligned}
$$

The present value of a $2 million Lotto jackpot is less than $1 million if 10 percent is the appropriate discount rate. Moreover, because the chance of winning is only 1 in 7.1 million, the expected value of each dollar "invested" in the lottery is only (1/7.1 million) × ($851,400) = 11.99¢. That is, for every dollar you spend on the lottery when the jackpot is $2 million, you should expect to get, *on average*, about 12¢ back—not a particularly good deal. While this ignores the minor prizes for coming close, it also ignores taxes and the prize splitting that takes place if more than one person guesses all six numbers correctly.

In this case, it looks like "my friend Ned" is doing the right thing. Obviously, the main value of the lottery is entertainment. Unfortunately, without an understanding of the time value of money, it can sound like a good investment.

## Perpetuities

A **perpetuity** is an annuity that continues forever. That is, every year from its establishment, this investment pays the same dollar amount and never stops paying. Determining the present value of a perpetuity is delightfully simple: You merely need to divide the payment amount by the discount rate. For example, the present value of a perpetuity that pays a constant dividend of $10 per share forever if the appropriate discount rate is 5 percent is $10/0.05 = $200. Thus, the equation representing the present value of a perpetuity is

$$
PV = PP/i \tag{3.8}
$$

where

$PV$ = the present value of the perpetuity
$PP$ = the annual dollar amount provided by the perpetuity
$i$ = the annual interest (or discount) rate

## SUMMARY

Almost every decision in personal finance involves the techniques of compounding and time value of money—putting aside money now to achieve some future goal. The cornerstone of the time value of money is the concept of compound interest, which is interest paid on interest.

With the time value of money, you can determine how much an investment will grow over time using the following formula:

$$
FV_n = PV(1 + i)^n \tag{3.4}
$$

To simplify these calculations, there are tables for the $(1 + i)^n$ part of the equation (the future-value

---

[2]Actually, we've simplified things a bit here. With the Virginia State Lottery you get your first $100,000 immediately and then at the end of each of the next 19 years you get another $100,000. Remember, we assume that cash flows occur at the end of each year with annuities. We've also ignored taxes.

interest factor for $i$ and $n$, or $FVIF_{i, n}$). In effect, you can rewrite equation (3.4) as follows:

$$\text{future value} = \text{present value} \times \text{future-value interest factor}$$

or

$$FV_n = PV(FVIF_{i, n}) \qquad (3.4a)$$

It is also important to understand the role of the interest rate in determining how large an investment grows. Together, time and the interest rate determine how much you will need to save in order to achieve your goals. You can also use the Rule of 72 to determine how long it will take to double your invested money. This "rule" is only an approximation:

$$\text{number of years to double} = 72/\text{annual compound growth rate}$$

Many times we also want to solve for present value instead of future value. We use the following formula to do this:

$$PV = FV_n[1/(1 + i)^n] \qquad (3.5)$$

$$PV = FV_n(PVIF_{i, n}) \qquad (3.5a)$$

An annuity is a series of equal annual dollar payments coming at the end of each year for a specified number of years. Because annuities occur frequently in finance—for example, as bond interest payments and mortgage payments—they are treated specially. A compound annuity involves depositing or investing an equal sum of money at the end of each year for a certain number of years and allowing it to grow.

$$\text{future value of an annuity} = \text{annual payment} \times \text{future-value interest factor of an annuity}$$

or

$$FV_n = PMT(FVIFA_{i, n}) \qquad (3.6)$$

To find the present value of an annuity, we use the following formula:

$$\text{present value} = \text{annual payment} \times \text{present-value interest factor of an annuity}$$

or

$$PV = PMT(PVIFA_{i, n})$$

Many times annuities involve paying off a loan in equal installments over time. Loans that are paid off this way, in equal periodic payments, are called amortized loans. Examples of amortized loans include car loans and mortgages.

## REVIEW QUESTIONS

1. What is compound interest? How is compound interest related to the time value of money?
2. Describe how the Rule of 72 can be used to make financial planning decisions.
3. What four variables are needed to solve a time value of money problem with a compound interest table or financial calculator?
4. Explain the concept of the time value of money. Explain two ways this concept is relevant in financial planning.
5. What two factors most affect how much people need to save to achieve their financial goals?
6. Why do you think that Albert Einstein once called compound interest the "eighth wonder of the world"?
7. Why do investors require a greater expected return for an investment of longer maturity although the required return to reach a goal, with an equal initial investment, decreases with the longer time horizon?
8. What is the most commonly used discount rate when calculating present value?
9. Why is the interest rate in a time value of money calculation sometimes referred to as the discount rate? Why is it also called "inverse compounding"?
10. What is a perpetuity? Name an example of a perpetuity (payments or receipt of income) in personal finance.
11. Define an amortized loan and give two common examples.
12. What is "future value" and why is it important to calculate?
13. Explain in terms of the future value interest factor why, given a certain goal, that as the period of

time to invest increases the required periodic investment decreases.

14. What is the primary difference between an annuity and a compound annuity?

15. What is the relationship between present-value and future-value interest factors and present and future interest factors for annuities?

## PROBLEMS AND ACTIVITIES

1. Your mother just won $250,000 for splitting a Nobel Prize with three coworkers. If she invests her prize money in a diversified portfolio earning 8 percent interest, approximately how long will it take her to become a millionaire?  18 years

2. Linda Baer has saved $5,000 for a previously owned vehicle. She hopes she will only need $7,500. Ignoring taxes and assuming her savings is earning 5 percent in a CD, how long will it take to buy the car? (Hint: The answer is between 6 and 10 years.)  9 years

3. Paul Ramos just graduated from college and landed his first "real" job, which pays $23,000 a year. In 10 years, what will he need to earn to maintain the same purchasing power if inflation averages 3.5 percent?  32,476

4. Anthony and Michelle Mitchell just got married and received $30,000 in cash gifts for their wedding. If they place half of this money in a health sciences sector mutual fund earning 12 percent, how much will they have on their tenth, twenty-fifth, and fiftieth anniversaries?  46,590  255,000  4,334,940

5. Calculate the future value of $5,000 earning 10 percent assuming an annual compounding period. Calculate the future value of $5,000 earning 10 percent assuming simple interest (the interest earned does not earn future interest). How much interest did the interest earn?  33,637  5,000

6. Ahmed Mustafa just turned 22 and wants to have $10,000 saved by his thirtieth birthday. Assuming no additional deposits, if he currently has $6,000 in an intermediate-term bond fund earning a 5 percent yield, will he reach his goal? If not, what rate of return is required to meet his goal?  No  7%

7. Assuming a 4 percent inflation rate, if the remake of the movie *Austin Powers, International Man of Mystery*, is released in 2007, determine the equivalent ransom to Dr. Evil's 1967 $1 million demand? Assuming 3 percent inflation?  3,262,000  4,801,020

8. When a small child, Derek's grandfather established a trust fund for him to receive $20,000 on his thirty-fifth birthday. (Any earnings beyond $20,000 reverted to his grandfather.) Derek just turned 23. What is the value of his trust today if the trust fund earns 7 percent interest? What is the present value if he had to wait until age 40 to receive the money?

9. You and 11 coworkers just won $12 million from the state lottery. Assuming you each receive your share over 20 years and that the state lottery earns a 5.5 percent return on its funds, what is the present value of your prize before taxes if you request the "up-front cash" option?  594,300

10. Richard Gorman is 65 years old and about to retire. He has $500,000 saved to supplement his pension and Social Security and would like to withdraw it in equal annual dollar amounts so that nothing is left after 15 years. How much does he have to withdraw each year if he earns 7 percent on his money?  54,896

11. Assume you are 25 and earn $35,000 per year, never expect to receive a raise, and plan to retire at age 55. If you invest 5 percent of your salary in a 401(k) plan returning 10 percent annually and the company provides a $0.50 per $1.00 match on your contributions up to 3 percent of salary, what is your estimated future value? How much can you withdraw monthly if you want to deplete your account over 30 years?  374,217

12. Four years ago, you began contributing to an employer 401(k) plan that is now worth $5,000. If you deposit $3,000 a year and your employer matches 50 percent of your contribution for the next 15 years, how much will the account be worth assuming an 8 percent average annual return?  138,044

13. Joe Eiss, 22, just started working full-time and plans to deposit $3,000 annually into an IRA earning 6 percent interest. How much would he have in 20 years? 30 years? 40 years? If he increased his investment return to 9 percent, how much would he have after the same three time periods? Comment on the differences over time.

12 = 6,840   17 = 6,331

# SUGGESTED PROJECTS

1. Ask older friends and relatives about the cost of specific items (e.g., a gallon of gas, cup of coffee, etc.) during their youth. Also inquire about average wages in the past. Compare these figures to current expenses and incomes. Explain your findings using time value of money concepts.

2. Calculate what an individual retirement arrangement (IRA) would be worth if you begin contributing $3,000 annually following graduation. Define your own retirement age and make any other assumptions needed. Explain the key factors that will influence the amount of money saved at retirement.

3. Develop and solve a future value, a present value, a future value of an annuity, and a present value of an annuity problem. Establish the three known variables in each problem and solve for the fourth. Do not always solve for the same variable. Explain the results.

4. Using a financial calculator, determine the difference in total return of $5,000 invested at 7 percent for 15 years with annual, semiannual, and monthly compounding.

5. Research the cost of five products or services that were advertised in newspapers or magazines published more than 20 years ago. Then find the current cost of these items. Calculate the rate of inflation for each item between the two points in time.

6. Visit a local financial institution and record the interest rates and minimum balance requirements for the various financial products offered.

Using the information gathered, determine how much interest would be earned if you deposited $2,500 in each account. For each, calculate your total return subtracting any applicable service charges.

7. Visit or call a local bank and inquire about the auto and unsecured loan rates of different maturities. Using the information, develop a sample amortized loan chart noting the amounts borrowed, the interest rates, and the terms of the loans. Calculate the annual payment required for each loan. What did you notice about the rate charged as the length of the loan increased? Explain this relationship.

8. Assume you can save $4,000 a year (about $80 per week) after graduation. Set a financial goal for yourself; specify the time frame and cost. Calculate the interest rate required to achieve the goal. Is it possible to achieve your goal, with moderate risk, in today's financial market? If not, describe changes that could be made to bring the goal closer to reality.

9. Investigate a specific financial planning issue or decision that involves the use of time value of money concepts. Describe why it is necessary to make a time value of money calculation.

   *Examples:* determining how much retirement income to withdraw per year over your life expectancy, calculating loan payments, calculating present pension plan contributions needed to fund future benefits, calculating future value of an IRA or 401(k), calculating present value (purchasing power) of money to be received in the future.

# Discussion Case 1

Jenny Smith, 28, just received a promotion at work. Her salary has increased to $30,000 and she is now eligible to participate in her employer's 401(k) plan. The employer matches workers' contributions up to 6 percent of their salary. Jenny wants to buy a new car in 2 years. The model car she wants to buy currently costs $18,000. She wants to save enough to make a $5,000 down payment and plans to finance the balance. At age 30, Jenny will be eligible to receive a $50,000 inheritance left by her late grandfather. Her trust fund is invested in zero coupon bonds that pay 7 percent interest. Also in her plans is a wedding. Jenny and her boyfriend, Paul, have set a wedding date 2 years in the future, after he finishes medical school. Paul will have $80,000 of student loans to repay after graduation. Both Jenny and Paul want to buy a home of their own as soon as possible.

## Questions

1. Justify Jenny's participation in her employer's 401(k) plan using time value of money concepts.

2. Calculate the amount that Jenny needs to save each year for the down payment on a new car, assuming she can earn 6 percent on her savings.

3. How much of her down payment will come from interest earned assuming a 7 percent annual rate of return? 10 percent?

## *Tips from Marcy Furney, ChFC, Certified Financial Planner™*

# Money Matters

## A MILLION DOLLARS IS A MILLION DOLLARS

In my previous life, I helped enroll executives in special deferred compensation plans. They had to agree not to take a part of their pay each year in exchange for a large lump payment at retirement. One day, a 30-year-old man sat across from me to review the plan agreement. After a few minutes together he told me, "I don't need to try to support my family on any less income. My retirement plan will be worth a million dollars at 65." When I asked if he thought that would be enough, he replied, "A million dollars is a million dollars!" I was too tired from a long flight to argue. He was determined not to participate, so away he went. Later I calculated that his million dollars at 4 percent inflation would be worth only about $250,000 in current buying power. I wonder if he'll realize in a few years that sometimes a million dollars isn't a million dollars.

The moral of the story may be

**When accumulating money for a long-range goal such as retirement or a child's education,** *you must always include the impact of inflation. Establish your goal in today's dollars, then calculate the future amount needed using a reasonable inflation rate assumption.*

**Now that you've learned the magic of compounding, start saving.** *Even a small monthly investment at an early age will grow into a respectable sum at retirement. Just as compounding grows your money, inflation erodes it.*

**As soon as the opportunity presents itself,** *get into an employer sponsored savings plan such as a 401(k) or SIMPLE. If your company makes a matching contribution of 50 cents for each dollar you put in, it's like a 50-percent rate of return in the first year. Where else can you make that kind of investment?*

**Save your raises.** *When you get a raise at work, increase your savings to include that amount. You're already used to living on your current take-home pay.*

**Calculate the real cost of that new CD player** *if paid out over a year or two on a credit card. You may find it's worth waiting until you've saved the funds.*

**When purchasing a big-ticket item like a car,** *take the initiative to do your own time value of money calculations to make sure the interest rate, number of payments, or total price is not being "adjusted" to produce an attractive payment.*

**If a financial calculator isn't one of your wardrobe accessories,** *always remember the Rule of 72. You'll be surprised the ways it comes in handy when making investment, savings, or borrowing decisions.*

4. What will be the value of Jenny's trust fund at age 60, assuming she takes possession of the money at age 30, uses half for a house down payment, and leaves half of the money untouched where it is currently invested?

5. If Paul wants to repay his student loans in full within 10 years and pays a 7.75 percent interest rate, what will be his annual payment?

6. List at least three actions that Jenny and Paul could take to make the time value of money work in their favor.

## Discussion Case 2

Doug Klock, 56, just retired after 31 years of teaching. He is a husband and father of three, two of whom are still dependent. He received a $150,000 lump-sum retirement bonus and will receive $2,800 per month from his retirement annuity. He has saved $150,000 in a 403b retirement plan and another $100,000 in other accounts. His 403b plan is invested in mutual funds, but most of his other investments are in bank accounts earning 2 or 3 percent annually. Doug has asked your advice in deciding where to invest his lump-sum settlement and other accounts now that he has retired. He also wants to know how much he can withdraw per month considering he has two children in college and a nonworking spouse. Because Kevin and Adam are still in college, his current monthly expenses total $5,800. He is not eligible for Social Security until age 62, when he will draw approximately $1,200 per month; however, he would rather defer until age 67 to increase his monthly amount to $1,550. He has grown accustomed to some risk but wants most of his money in FDIC-insured accounts.

## Questions

1. Assume Doug has another account set aside for emergencies. How much of his other assets can he withdraw monthly to supplement his retirement annuity, assuming his investments average a 5 percent return and he assumes a life expectancy of 30 years?

2. Ignoring his Social Security benefit, is the amount determined in question 1 sufficient to meet his current monthly expenses? If not, how long will his retirement last if his current expenses remain the same? If his expenses are reduced to $4,500 per month?

3. Considering the information obtained in question 2, should he wait until age 67 for his Social Security benefits? If he waits until age 67, how will his Social Security benefit change the answers to question 2? (Hint: Calculate his portfolio value as of age 67 and then recalculate the future value formula reflecting the increased current income.)

4. If inflation averages 3.5 percent during Doug's retirement, will prices double if he lives until age 80? If so, how old will he be when this happens?

Visit our Web site for additional case problems, interactive exercises, and practice quizzes for this chapter—**www.prenhall.com/keown**.

# 4  Tax Planning and Strategies

**Learning Objectives**

**Describe** how the present U.S. income tax system came into being.

**Identify** and understand the major tax features that affect all taxpayers.

**Describe** other non-income-based taxes that you must pay.

**Understand** what is taxable income and how taxes are determined.

**Choose** the tax form that's right for you.

**Calculate** your income taxes.

"The Trouble with Trillions" episode of the *Simpsons* begins with the family watching the 11 o'clock news.

"This is Kent Brockman at the Springfield Post Office on Tax Day. It's literally the 11th hour, 10 P.M., and tardy taxpayers are scrambling to mail their returns by midnight."

"Will you look at those morons? I paid my taxes over a year ago," Homer chimes in.

"Dad! That was last year's taxes. You have to pay again this year," Lisa replies.

"No, because you see I went ahead and . . . year-wise, I was counting forward from the last previous . . . d-oh!" Frantically putting together his tax return Homer shouts out, "Marge, how many kids do we have, no time to count, I'll just estimate 9. OK (looking at Marge) if anyone asks you need 24-hour nursing care, Lisa is a clergyman, Maggie is 7 people, and Bart was wounded in Vietnam."

"Cool!" replies Bart. Needless to say, things went from bad to worse with Homer's tax return accidentally falling into the "severe audit bin" at the IRS. Homer is then nabbed by the government and forced to go undercover on a mission to retrieve a trillion-dollar bill stolen by his greedy boss Mr. Burns.

But it isn't only cartoon characters that have trouble with the IRS—just look at Willie Nelson. He has made millions of dollars and spent millions of dollars, and for quite some time he ignored his taxes entirely. That lack of attention finally caught up with him in 1990, when the IRS sent him a bill for $32 million. Yikes! But as Willie said, "Thirty-two million ain't much if you say it fast." How did Willie manage to run up such a tax bill? On bad advice, he got involved in a number of tax shelters (investments aimed at lowering your taxes) that were disallowed by the IRS because they were such blatant tax-avoidance schemes. Eventually, Willie and the IRS settled on a $9 million payment, and Willie sued the accounting firm of Price Waterhouse, claiming it had mismanaged his finances. By 1995, Willie had paid back the government, but to do it he had to auction off nearly all of his possessions—leaving him with his long hair and beard, headband, worn blue jeans, guitar, and little else.

Most people cringe at the thought of tax planning and the mention of the IRS because taxes are unavoidable, too high, and determined by a tax code that is close to incomprehensible. People just don't like taxes—everyone knows that. However, like them or not, taxes are a fact of life, and they have a dramatic impact on many aspects of your finances, in particular your investment choices.

In fact, most of the decisions that you make are affected in one way or another by taxes—that's **Principle 6: Taxes Affect Personal Finance Decisions**. Given that the average American pays over $10,000 annually in taxes, limiting Uncle Sam's cut of your income is important. Remember, what you pay in April each year is based on income, expenses, and tax-planning decisions from the previous year. If you don't

MATT GROENING

Principle **6** Taxes Affect Personal Finance Decisions

understand the tax system, you're probably paying more than you have to. The purpose of this chapter is not to teach you all the ins and outs of filing your own return but rather to help you understand how taxes are imposed, what strategies can be used to reduce them, and the role of tax planning in personal financial planning. With proper tax planning you will be able to avoid wasting money in tax payments, invest those funds to achieve your financial goals, and avoid looking at your tax bill and saying "D-oh!"

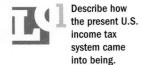

Describe how the present U.S. income tax system came into being.

## How It All Began

Our present income tax system first appeared in 1913, when the Sixteenth Amendment gave Congress authorization to impose such a tax. That was the year zippers were invented and Cracker Jacks first put toys in its boxes. Back then the rate was only 1 percent on income greater than $3,000 for an individual, or $4,000 for a married couple. Although a break on the first $3,000 to $4,000 may not sound like much now, back in 1913 it was quite a bit.

Only about 1 percent of the population had to pay income taxes. The first tax was also *progressive,* or graduated, meaning that the tax rose as income rose above $20,000. The tax rose from an additional 1 percent on income between $20,000 and $50,000 all the way to an additional 6 percent on income greater than $300,000. It was also a simple, easy-to-understand code with a conspicuous lack of loopholes.

Since that time, continuous tinkering to fund the government, influence the economy, promote socially desirable actions, and simply satisfy powerful special interest groups has produced a 2,000-page tax code with countless forms. These changes have generally been made in a piecemeal fashion—changing one aspect of the tax code one year and another aspect another year. The end result is that the logic of the tax code has been overpowered by its complexity. In the minds of many, fairness has fallen through the countless loopholes.

The current U.S. tax system dictates the single largest annual expenditure for most families—taxes. Regardless of what you think of the system, it's one that you have no choice but to face. Many people's initial reaction is that tax planning is for the wealthy. Yes, wealthy people probably have the most to gain from effective tax planning. And the wealthy, in general, do a good job of tax planning. Unfortunately, those who don't fall into the wealthy range—that is, those who need the tax savings the most—don't do a very good job of planning. In fact, most people view tax planning as a problem. Well, what's more of a problem, doing a few hours' worth of planning, or paying Uncle Sam a few thousand dollars more than you really need to?

Everyone works too hard to earn money to pay more than is necessary in taxes. In fact, the Tax Foundation, a private research group, each year determines the Tax Freedom Day as a means of showing how hard everyone works to pay taxes. The Tax Freedom Day is the day by which the average American has earned enough to pay total federal, state, and local taxes for the year.

As Table 4.1 shows, in 1950 the average American had earned enough to pay the annual tax bill by March 29; in 2002, the Tax Freedom Day had crept all the way to April 27. In other words, all the money the average American earned before April 27 went to pay taxes. Given the fact that the average American spends over a third of each year earning money just to pay taxes, it's important to make sure that you don't overpay. The longer you work to pay taxes, the less time you can work to pay yourself.

## Table 4.1  Tax Freedom Day

The day the average American has earned enough to pay for federal, state, and local taxes.

| Year | Day | Year | Day |
|------|-----|------|-----|
| 1950 | March 29 | 1995 | April 23 |
| 1955 | April 01 | 1996 | April 24 |
| 1960 | April 08 | 1997 | April 26 |
| 1965 | April 05 | 1998 | April 27 |
| 1970 | April 16 | 1999 | April 29 |
| 1975 | April 14 | 2000 | May 01 |
| 1980 | April 19 | 2001 | April 29 |
| 1985 | April 10 | 2002 | April 27 |
| 1990 | April 20 | | |

Note:   Leap day is omitted to make days comparable over time.

Source:   Tax Foundation, Washington, DC, 2002.

## Federal Income Tax Structure

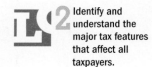

Identify and understand the major tax features that affect all taxpayers.

**Progressive or Graduated Tax**
A tax system in which tax rates increase for higher incomes.

The starting point for tax planning is understanding what the tax rates actually are. Because the U.S. tax code is so complicated, we need to learn about the overall structure of the income tax before we examine actual tax rates. Our present tax structure is a **progressive or graduated tax**, meaning that increased income is taxed at increasing rates. This system is based on the idea that those who earn more can afford to have a higher percentage of their income taken away in taxes. In fact, according to the Congressional Joint Committee on Taxation in 2000, taxpayers in the highest 10 percent of income distribution, which includes families making more than about $100,000, pay 66.4 percent of all federal income taxes paid. In addition, taxpayers earning $50,000 or more paid 92.5 percent of all federal income taxes in 2000. That doesn't mean that if you're not making over $50,000 you shouldn't do any tax planning. It just means that the tax code with all its loopholes is still progressive.

### The Economic Growth and Tax Relief Reconciliation Act of 2001 (commonly called The Tax Relief Act of 2001)

In June 2001, President Bush signed into law the Economic Growth and Tax Relief Reconciliation Act of 2001, the largest tax cut in 20 years. This $1.35 trillion tax cut provided for rebate checks of $300 to $600 mailed during the second half of 2001 to almost every income taxpayer. The centerpiece of this act was the reduction in the income tax rates coupled with an eventual repeal of estate taxes. This act has a number of implications for financial planning, with many of these changes slated to be implemented over the 10 years following its passage. However, the most interesting fact about the law is that much of it expires on December 31, 2010—a sunset provision put in because of Congressional rules governing spending more than a decade in the future.

You'll see the effect of this act appearing in a number of places throughout this chapter, but the centerpiece of the new tax law was an across-the-board cut in income taxes. Prior to the new law, rates ranged from 15 to 39.6 percent. The Tax Relief Act of 2001 made three major changes to the tax-rate system:

- It created a new 10 percent tax bracket.
- It gradually lowered the top tax rate to 35 percent.
- It cut most other tax rates by three percentage points.

First, let's take a look at the new 10 percent tax bracket.

**The New 10 Percent Tax Bracket**   The act not only lowered all the tax brackets (with the exception of the 15 percent tax bracket) but it also introduced a new 10 percent bracket. This new 10 percent tax rate bracket, which became effective beginning in 2001, benefits all taxpayers with taxable income. The 10 percent tax rate applies to the first

- $6,000 of taxable income for single persons
- $10,000 of taxable income for heads of households
- $12,000 of taxable income for married couples

Beginning in 2008, the 10 percent tax rate bracket is expanded to apply to the first:

- $7,000 of taxable income for single persons
- $10,000 of taxable income for heads of households
- $14,000 of taxable income for married couples

Not only was there a tax cut but also most taxpayers received a tax rebate check from the IRS in the summer or fall of 2001 representing the difference between the 15 percent rate and the 10 percent rate. In effect, for tax year 2001, a portion of the 15 percent rate bracket was reduced to 10 percent and the taxpayers got a check in the mail from the IRS that covered this tax reduction.

**Phase-In of Individual Income Tax Rate Reductions**   Along with the introduction of the new 10 percent tax bracket, with the exception of the 15 percent tax bracket, all rates are reduced. This reduction of the various tax brackets is phased in as follows:

| Calendar Year | Portion of 15% Rate Reduced to* | 28% Rate Reduced to | 31% Rate Reduced to | 36% Rate Reduced to | 39.6% Rate Reduced to |
|---|---|---|---|---|---|
| 2001 | 10% | 27.5% | 30.5% | 35.5% | 39.1% |
| 2002 | 10% | 27% | 30% | 35% | 38.6% |
| 2003 | 10% | 27% | 30% | 35% | 38.6% |
| 2004 | 10% | 26% | 29% | 34% | 37.6% |
| 2005 | 10% | 26% | 29% | 34% | 37.6% |
| 2006 | 10% | 25% | 28% | 33% | 35% |

* The other portion of the 15% bracket will remain as under current law.

What does this all mean to you? First, it means that between now and 2006 rates will fall. To take advantage, you should consider deferring income and accelerating deductions. For example, if you have a bonus coming in, consider delaying it until the next year if taxes are set to drop that year. Also consider making annual charitable contributions for the following year in December.

**The Tax Rebates of 2001—The Check's in the Mail**   The Economic Growth and Tax Relief Reconciliation Act of 2001 directed the Treasury to send tax rebate checks to most income taxpayers in the summer and fall of 2001. These tax rebate checks were actually an advance payment of a 2001 tax credit. This was a one-time event and will not happen again. As a result, in order to keep from adding more confusion to the presentation of taxes than is necessary (Congress has done an outstanding job of putting more than enough confusion into the IRS tax code), we are going to assume away these tax rebate checks when we look at the calculation of taxes for 2001. That way, you'll get a better feel for the different tax brackets and the marginal and average tax rates. However, before we do this let's take a quick look at these tax rebate checks to gain an understanding of where they came from.

The tax rebate checks resulted from the creation of the new 10 percent rate bracket. Under the new law the 15 percent rate bracket was reduced to 10 percent as the tax rate for the first $12,000 of taxable income on a joint return ($6,000 for singles and $10,000 for heads of household). To reflect the rate cut, Congress decided to order the Treasury to send taxpayers a lump-sum check. Sending the rebate was deemed a quicker way to deliver money into the pockets of Americans—and stimulate the economy—than through an adjustment to the withholding tables.

The rebate was in lieu of getting the benefit of the 10 percent rate on 2001 tax returns. (If you do the math, you'll find the rebate was the same as the savings reaped from having the rate reduced. For example, a couple having the first $12,000 of income taxed at 10 percent, instead of 15 percent, would realize tax savings of $600—the same as the maximum rebate for married couples.)

The Treasury based the rebate amount on information reported on your 2000 income tax returns. If you received less of a rebate than you're due based on your 2001 income (perhaps because you didn't earn enough income in 2000 to qualify for the full rebate), you were able to claim a special "rate reduction credit" on your 2001 income tax return.

On the other hand, if you received more than you were due (perhaps because you paid tax in 2000 but owed no tax for 2001), you were not required to repay that amount to the Treasury.

## Taxable Income and Tax Rates

However, just knowing the **tax brackets** is not enough, because not all income is taxed. Some income is tax free because of **personal exemptions**, and other income is shielded by **itemized** or **standard deductions**. Your **taxable income** is a function of three numbers—adjusted gross income, deductions, and exemptions. From there, the tax rates determine how much of the difference between income and deductions will be taken away in taxes. Table 4.2 provides the 2001 federal income tax rates for four different classifications of taxpayers.

To better understand what the rates in Table 4.2 actually mean, see what you might pay in taxes in 2001 if you were married with three children, had a combined income of $70,000, and were filing a joint return. That $70,000 would be your gross income, and from that you would then subtract out certain adjustments allowed by law to arrive at your adjusted gross income. For example, you can subtract your deductible IRA contributions along with any interest you might have paid on student loans from your gross income. Once you've subtracted those out, you then have your adjusted gross income. As you can see, $70,000 falls between $45,200 and $109,250, which for the tax year 2001 puts you into the 27.5-percent tax bracket. Remember, however, that your total income of $70,000 isn't taxed; *only the difference between your income and your deductions is taxed.*

**Tax Brackets**
Income ranges in which the same marginal tax rates apply. For example, an individual might fall into the 15-percent or 27.5-percent marginal tax bracket.

**Personal Exemptions**
An IRS-allowed reduction in your income before you compute your taxes. You are given one exemption for yourself, one for your spouse, and one for each dependent.

**Deductions**
Expenses that reduce taxable income.

**Itemized Deductions**
Deductions calculated using Schedule A. The allowable deductions are added up and then subtracted from taxable income.

**Standard Deduction**
A set deduction allowed by the IRS regardless of what taxpayers' expenses actually were.

**Taxable Income**
Income subject to taxes.

**STOP & THINK** It was the Massachusetts Bay Colony that first imposed income taxes in the New World in 1643. Taxes have been around forever, but that doesn't mean you pay more than your fair share. In 1934 Judge Learned Hand of the U.S. Court of Appeals said, "Anyone may so arrange his affairs that his taxes shall be as low as possible; he is not bound to choose that pattern which will best pay the treasury; there is not even a patriotic duty to increase one's taxes."

## Table 4.2   2001 Tax Rates and Brackets

**Single**

| If Taxable Income Is Over | But Not Over | The Tax Is | Of the Amount Over |
|---|---|---|---|
| $0 | $6,000 | 10.0% | $0 |
| 6,000 | 27,050 | $600 + 15.0% | 6,000 |
| 27,050 | 65,550 | 3,757.50 + 27.5% | 27,050 |
| 65,550 | 136,750 | 14,345.00 + 30.5% | 65,550 |
| 136,750 | 297,350 | 36,061.00 + 35.5% | 136,750 |
| 297,350 | | 93,074.00 + 39.1% | 297,350 |

**Head of Household**

| If Taxable Income Is Over | But Not Over | The Tax Is | Of the Amount Over |
|---|---|---|---|
| $0 | $10,000 | 10.0% | $0 |
| 10,000 | 36,250 | $1,000.00 + 15.0% | 10,000 |
| 36,250 | 93,650 | 4,937.50 + 27.5% | 36,250 |
| 93,650 | 151,650 | 20,722.50 + 30.5% | 93,650 |
| 151,650 | 297,350 | 38,412.50 + 35.5% | 151,650 |
| 297,350 | | 90,136.00 + 39.1% | 297,350 |

**Married Filing Jointly or Qualifying Widow(er)**

| If Taxable Income Is Over | But Not Over | The Tax Is | Of the Amount Over |
|---|---|---|---|
| $0 | $12,000 | 10.0% | $0 |
| 12,000 | 45,200 | $1,200.00 + 15.0% | 12,000 |
| 45,200 | 109,250 | 6,180.00 + 27.5% | 45,200 |
| 109,250 | 166,500 | 23,793.75 + 30.5% | 109,250 |
| 166,500 | 297,350 | 41,255.00 + 35.5% | 166,500 |
| 297,350 | | 87,706.75 + 39.1% | 297,350 |

**Married Filing Separately**

| If Taxable Income Is Over | But Not Over | The Tax Is | Of the Amount Over |
|---|---|---|---|
| $0 | $6,000 | 10.0% | $0 |
| 6,000 | 22,600 | $600.00 + 15.0% | 6,000 |
| 22,600 | 54,625 | 3,090.00 + 27.5% | 22,600 |
| 54,625 | 83,250 | 11,896.88 + 30.5% | 54,625 |
| 83,250 | 148,675 | 20,627.50 + 35.5% | 83,250 |
| 148,675 | | 43,853.38 + 39.1% | 148,675 |

To determine how much you would pay, you must first subtract personal exemptions and deductions. To begin with, you receive one exemption for each family member you claim on your tax return—one for you and your spouse and each of your three children. Each exemption allows you to subtract $2,900 from your income, resulting in a total reduction of $14,500. Next, you need to subtract your deduction, either standard or itemized. Let's assume you use the standard deduction because it's higher than your itemized deduction would be. For the 2001 tax year, that would give you a deduction of $7,600. The minimum level of deductions that you have is $14,500 + $7,600 = $22,100. Subtracting these from your income of $70,000 leaves taxable income of $47,900.

Even after your deductions, you're still in the 27.5-percent tax bracket. Do you then have to pay 27.5 percent of your taxable income of $47,900 in taxes? No. It means that the last dollars you earned are taxed at 27.5 percent. As Table 4.2 shows, the first $12,000 of taxable income is taxed at 10 percent, the next $33,200 (income from $12,000 to $45,200) is taxed at 15 percent; then the next $2,700, that is, your income from $45,200 to $47,900, is taxed at 27.5 percent, resulting in a total tax bill before tax credits of $6,922.50.[1]

| Taxable Income | × | Tax Rate | = | Taxes Paid |
|---|---|---|---|---|
| $0 to $12,000 ($12,000) | × | 10% | = | $1,200.00 |
| $12,000 to $45,200 ($33,200) | × | 15% | = | $4,980.00 |
| $45,200 to $47,900 ($2,700) | × | 27.5% | = | $ 742.50 |
| | | Total taxes before credits | = | $6,922.50 |

## Marginal Versus Average Rates

Let's take a different look at the amount of taxes you paid in the previous example. You paid taxes of $6,922.50 on taxable income of $47,900, so your average tax rate on *taxable income* was $\frac{\$6,922.50}{\$47,900.00}$, or about 14.5 percent. Your average tax rate on your *overall* income of $70,000 was $6,922.50/$70,000, or about 9.9 percent The term *average tax rate* refers to this latter figure—the average amount of your total income taken away in taxes.

Although your goal is to keep your average tax rate as low as possible, you'll need to focus more on your marginal tax rate. Your **marginal tax rate** or **marginal tax bracket** refers to the percentage of the last dollar you made that goes to taxes. In effect, it is the tax bracket that your taxable income falls into. If your taxable income is $47,900, and $47,900 falls in the 27.5-percent tax bracket, then 27.5 percent is your marginal tax rate. If you get a $5,000 raise, it is your marginal tax rate that determines how much of that raise you have left to spend.

**Marginal Tax Rate or Marginal Tax Bracket**
The percentage of the last dollar you earn that goes toward taxes.

In addition, if you are in the 27.5-percent marginal tax bracket and have a choice of investing in tax-free bonds that earn 7 percent or taxable bonds that earn 9 percent, your marginal tax rate can help you determine which is the better investment. Even though your average tax rate may be only 13 percent, this additional income is taxed at your marginal tax rate, which, in this example, is 27.5 percent. To make a fair comparison, you must look at your after-tax returns. The tax-free bond would still return 7 percent after taxes, but the 9-percent bond would have 27.5 percent of its returns confiscated for taxes, resulting in a return of 9% × (1 − .275) = 6.525%.

Your marginal tax rate also becomes important when you're considering investing in a **tax-deferred** retirement plan. The government allows tax deductions for any funds you contribute to the retirement plan. So, if you are in the 27.5-percent marginal tax bracket and you contribute $1,000 to a tax-deferred retirement plan, you would lower your taxes by $275 (0.275 × $1,000). This reduction allows you to invest the entire $1,000 rather than only $725, that is, $1,000 less $275 in taxes.

**Tax-Deferred**
Income on which the payment of taxes is postponed until some future date.

---

[1]As we will see shortly, this amount drops even more because of the child tax credit, which in 2001 provides qualifying families with a tax credit of $600 for each child under age 17 at of the close of each year. This tax credit offsets taxes owed on a dollar-for-dollar basis. That is, if you owe $5,000 in taxes and have a $600 tax credit, you only need to write the IRS a check for $4,400. The child tax credit will gradually increase to $1,000 in 2010.

As you can see from Table 4.2, once you earn enough to pay taxes—have income beyond the personal exemption and standard deduction levels—there are six different marginal tax rates, and as we saw earlier, they are going down in the future as a result of the Taxpayers Relief Act of 2001, which is being phased in through 2006. However, even these rate changes are not set in stone. Whenever Congress wishes, it can change the tax rates and the tax code. In fact, in 1964 the top marginal rate was 91 percent, and in 1981 it was still at 70 percent. Needless to say, changes in the marginal tax rates have a major impact on investment strategies, so you need to keep a close eye on tax law changes.[2]

## Effective Marginal Tax Rate

Although most people think federal income taxes are far more than enough, these are not the only income-based taxes you pay. Many states impose state income taxes, there are also Social Security taxes, and in some cases city income taxes. For example, New York City imposes an income tax. As a result of all these taxes, your effective marginal tax rate is greater than the marginal tax rate on your federal income taxes.

To determine your effective marginal tax rate, you need to add up the rates of the different taxes you pay on income. Let's assume you have a marginal federal tax rate of 27 percent, a state income tax rate of 4.75 percent, and a city income tax rate of 2 percent. The tax on Social Security is 7.65 percent, so your total effective marginal tax rate would be 41.40 percent (27% + 4.75% + 2% + 7.65%).

## Capital Gains Taxes and the Taxpayer Relief Act of 1997

**Capital Asset**
An asset you own, except for certain business assets, including stocks, bonds, real estate, or collectibles.

**Capital Gain/Capital Loss**
The amount by which the selling price of a capital asset differs from its purchase price. If the selling price is higher than the purchase price, a capital gain results; if the purchase price is higher than the selling price, a capital loss results.

**Capital Gains Tax**
The tax you pay on your capital gains.

The income you make on your investments is taxed somewhat differently from other income. Almost any asset you own, except for certain business assets, is called a **capital asset**. A **capital gain** is what you make if you sell a capital asset for a profit, and a **capital loss** is what you lose when you sell a capital asset for a loss. Capital losses can be used to offset capital gains.

If the losses exceed the gains, you may deduct the excess from up to $3,000 of other income. For example, if you purchase 100 shares of GM stock for $50 per share and sell them 2 years later for $70 per share, your capital gain would be 100 shares times ($70 – $50) = $2,000. The tax you pay on your capital gains is called, appropriately, the **capital gains tax**. Exactly how much you pay in capital gains taxes depends on how long you've held your investments (short term or long term).

The Taxpayer Relief Act of 1997 both redefined a long-term capital gain and cut the long-term capital gains tax rate. An asset must be held for 12 months to qualify as long term, and the maximum tax rate paid on net long-term capital gains on any

---

[2]Actually, although the listed rates seem to be quite straightforward, the IRS also phases out deductions and exemptions for those in the higher income brackets. For example, for the tax year 2001 for those filing as single, the phase-out for deductions and exemptions affects those with AGI greater than $132,950. This level is adjusted annually for inflation. As a result, the marginal tax bracket for those in the highest brackets can actually be 1 to 5 percent higher than it appears, depending on income level and number of exemptions. That's because as you earn more, you lose deductions and exemptions. As a result of the Tax Relief Act of 2001 these phase-outs will be repealed. The repeal will be phased in, beginning in 2006, over a five-year period.

trades is 20 percent. For those in the 15-percent tax bracket, the net long-term capital gains tax rate dropped to 10 percent.

Then, beginning in the year 2001, a new top rate of 18 percent on long-term capital gains on assets purchased *in* or *after* the year 2001 and held for at least 5 years goes into effect. As a result, no one will benefit from this 18-percent rate until 2006.[3] For investors in the 15-percent tax bracket who sell assets held for at least 5 years, the rate drops to 8 percent.

Although the new long-term capital gains tax applies to profits from the sale of stocks, bonds, and most other investments, it doesn't apply to gains from the sale of collectibles. In addition, real estate investments don't necessarily receive the full benefit of the cut.

How much do capital gains save you? That depends on your tax bracket. If you're in the 38.6-percent tax bracket and have long-term capital gains income of $50,000, you would pay only $10,000 in taxes, and when the 18-percent tax bracket comes into place, only $9,000. If this $50,000 of income had been from wages or dividends, you would have paid $19,800, about twice what you paid on long-term capital gains.

Just as valuable as the tax break on capital gains income is the fact that you do not have to claim it—and, therefore, pay taxes on it—until you sell the asset. That is, you can decide when you want to claim your capital gains. For example, at the end of 1994 you may have invested $20,000 in Berkshire Hathaway stock, only to see it grow in value, reaching $73,000 by 2002. Although you've "made" $53,000 on your investment, you don't have to pay any taxes on this gain. You pay taxes only when you sell the stock and realize the gain. In effect, you can postpone your capital gains taxes.

As long as you can earn interest on money you don't pay out in taxes, it's better to postpone paying taxes for as long as possible—that's what we learned in **Principle 2: The Time Value of Money**. Because the maximum tax rate on long-term capital gains is lower than the ordinary tax rate and you have the ability to postpone its tax liability, capital gains income is preferable to ordinary income.

Principle
2 The Time Value of Money

**What Does This Mean to You?**    The effect of the cut in the long-term capital gains tax rate is that it's even more important to avoid frequent trading. That means holding on to your investment for at least 12 months before selling and, if purchased in or after 2001, for at least 5 years. If you invest in mutual funds, you should look for funds that do a minimum of trading—that is, tax-managed mutual funds. This capital gains tax cut also puts a premium on stocks that pay small dividends or none at all. That's because dividends are taxed as ordinary income while capital gains are taxed at lower rates. Given all this, your strategy should be to:

▌ **Head for low-turnover, "tax-managed" mutual funds.** The typical mutual fund has a turnover ratio of about 90 percent, meaning, on average, any stock in that fund is only held for about 13 months. To benefit from the new capital gains law, you need to put your money in a mutual fund that is tax managed—that is, it trades in such a way that your profits are taxed at the capital gains rate rather than the ordinary rate. Most indexed funds work much like tax-managed funds because they have very little trading; however, they generally have more income from dividends than do tax-managed funds.

---

[3]For assets purchased before January 1, 2001, you can elect to treat them as if you sold them on January 1 or 2 of 2001 in order to start your holding period over.

▌ **Buy individual stocks and make your own mutual fund.** One way to make sure all trading profits qualify as long-term capital gains is to put your money into stocks so you can control the trades and focus on stocks that pay little in dividends. The only problem here is that you need enough money to diversify sufficiently, while making sure you invest enough in each individual stock position to avoid excessive brokerage costs. This probably means that you'd need to invest at least $100,000, with about $5,000 in each of 20 stocks. This would allow sufficient diversification, in addition to letting you buy 100 shares of each stock to help keep brokerage fees down. Unfortunately, $100,000 is more than most people have to invest, so investing in tax-managed mutual funds should work almost as well.

**Long-Term Capital Gains on Homes**   For most homeowners, the Taxpayer Relief Act of 1997 effectively eliminates capital gains taxes on the sale of their homes. It does this by exempting from taxation gains of up to $500,000 for couples filing jointly or $250,000 for those filing single on the sale of a principal residence. To be eligible for the complete exemption, the home must be your principal residence and you must have occupied it for at least 2 years during the 5 years before the sale. This is not a one-time exemption. In fact, you are eligible for this exemption once every 2 years. Under the old law, you paid no tax on profits from the sale of your house if the gain was "rolled over" by buying another home worth at least as much as the one that you sold.

## Filing Status

Table 4.2, 2001 tax rates, shows that filing status plays a major role in determining what you pay in the way of taxes. But you may not have much of a choice in deciding your filing status. Filing status is somewhat akin to marital status. But, as is always the case with taxes, it's not that simple. Let's look at the different classifications.

*Single.*   You are single at the end of the year and do not have any dependent children.

*Married Filing Jointly and Surviving Spouses.*   You file a joint return with your spouse, combining incomes and deductions into a single return. If your spouse dies, you can still qualify for this status for up to 2 years after the year in which your spouse died if you have a dependent child living with you, you pay more than half the cost of keeping up your home, and you are not remarried. Of course, if you remarry, you can file a joint return with your new spouse.

*Married Filing Separately.*   Married couples also have the choice of filing separately. For most couples this filing status makes little financial sense—in effect, the rates are set to encourage them to file a joint return. This status is most often used when a couple is separated or in the process of getting a divorce.

*Head of Household.*   Head of household status applies to someone who is unmarried and has at least one child or relative living with him or her. The advantage of this status is that your tax rate will be lower and your standard deduction higher than if you had filed with single status. To qualify for head of household status, you must be unmarried on the last day of the tax year, have paid more than half the cost of keeping up your home, and had a child or dependent live with you for at least half of the year.

## Cost of Living Increases in Tax Brackets, Exemptions, and Deductions

Since 1985, tax brackets have changed annually to reflect increases in the cost of living (inflation). For example, if the 27.5-percent tax bracket presently begins at $45,200 and the cost of living rises by 2.434 percent, this tax bracket will shift upward by 2.434 percent and begin at $45,200 × 1.02434 = $46,300. In addition, the standard deductions and personal exemptions are also increased to reflect the increased cost of living.

The purpose of these adjustments is to make sure your tax payments don't go up as your wages increase to keep pace with inflation. In the past, taxpayers' incomes rose during periods of high inflation, but their purchasing power didn't. As a result, rising incomes that only kept pace with inflation nudged taxpayers into higher tax brackets. In effect, taxpayers paid more taxes while the real value of their wages remained constant.

The tax increase caused by inflation is referred to as **bracket creep**. For those whose earnings remain the same each year, the inflation adjustment of tax brackets actually results in lower taxes. Of course, if your earnings don't increase to keep pace with inflation, you're worse off with each passing year and probably deserve a reduced tax bill!

**Bracket Creep**
The movement into higher tax brackets as a result of inflation increasing wages.

## Paying Your Income Taxes

Taxes are collected on a pay-as-you-go basis through withholding or by sending in estimated tax payments as you earn money. Most taxes are withheld from wages. In fact, about 70 percent of individual income taxes are collected through withholding. The idea behind withholding is to collect taxes gradually so that when your taxes are due in the spring, you won't feel the pain of paying in one lump sum. Also, without withholding, too many people would spend the money they should be saving for taxes. These withholdings also cover Social Security and state and local taxes. Other ways in which taxes are collected include quarterly estimated taxes sent to the IRS, payments with the tax return, and withholding from stock dividends, retirement funds, and prizes or gambling winnings.

You do have some control over how much is deducted for taxes from your wages. Your withholdings are determined by your income level and by the information you provide on your W-4 form. The W-4 form shows marital status, the number of exemptions you wish to claim, and any additional withholding you would like. Most people fill out their W-4 when they begin employment and never think about it or change it again. However, if your tax level doesn't match your withholdings, revising your W-4 to make appropriate adjustments might not be a bad idea.

## Other Taxes

### Other Income-Based Taxes

**Social Security or FICA**   **Social Security** is really a mandatory insurance program, administered by the government, which provides for you and your family in the event of death, disability, health problems, or retirement. To pay for these benefits, both you and your employer pay into the system. Each pays 7.65 percent of your gross salary. This deduction appears on your pay slip as "FICA," which stands for the Federal Insurance Contributions Act. These funds actually go to both Social Security and **Medicare**, which is a government health care insurance program.

**Social Security**
A federal program that provides disability and retirement benefits based on years worked, amount paid into the plan, and retirement age.

**Medicare**
The federal government's insurance program to provide medical benefits to those over 65.

The FICA tax is deducted from your salary at a rate of 7.65 percent (6.20 percent for Social Security and 1.45 percent for Medicare) until your salary reaches a certain cap ($80,400 in 2001), at which point your remaining salary is no longer taxed. Medicare, however, keeps on taxing after the Social Security cap has been reached, taking an additional 1.45 percent of your total salary from both you and your employer. Thus, if your salary is $85,000 in 2001 your FICA contribution would be [$80,400 × 7.65% + ($85,000 − $80,400) × 1.45%] = ($6,150.60 + $66.70) = $6,217.30.

If you are self-employed, you have to pay both the employer and employee portion of FICA for a total rate of 15.3 percent, up to the 2001 limit of $80,400, paying a total of ($80,400 × 15.3%) = $12,301.20. However, if you're self-employed, half of your contribution is tax deductible. Also, if you're self-employed and you earned more than $80,400 in 2001, you continue to pay both the employer (1.45%) and employee (1.45%) portions of the Medicare tax—a total of 2.9 percent—on any income above $80,400, again with half of this contribution being tax deductible.

Unfortunately, the Social Security system is feeling financial strains. As a result, it's impossible to forecast what will happen to Social Security taxes over the next 20 years. The problem facing Social Security is that there are more people receiving benefits than ever before. Forty years ago 16 workers contributed for every Social Security recipient. Today, the ratio is down to 3 workers for every recipient, and in another 40 years it will be down to 2 workers for every recipient. As a result, the system can't continue in its present form.

**State and Local Income Taxes**  In addition to Social Security and federal income taxes, most individuals also face state and, in some cases, local income taxes. Most states impose some type of income tax, though the level varies greatly from state to state. Local income taxes are relatively uncommon and are generally confined to large cities; New York City, for example, imposes an income tax.

## Non-Income-Based Taxes

Describe other non-income-based taxes that you must pay.

In addition to paying federal income taxes, Social Security taxes, and state and local taxes, you also face excise taxes, sales taxes, property taxes, and gift and estate taxes.

Excise taxes are taxes imposed on specific purchases, such as alcoholic beverages, cigarettes, gasoline, telephone service, jewelry, and air travel. Often such taxes are aimed at reducing consumption of the items being taxed. For example, liquor and tobacco taxes are referred to as "sin taxes."

Most local taxes take the form of property taxes on real estate and personal property, such as automobiles and boats. The level of property taxes is based on the assessed value of real estate or other property.

Some states and localities also impose sales taxes on certain purchases. These taxes can range up to around 8 percent (in New York) and in general cover most sales, with the exception of food and drugs. These taxes tend to be quite regressive, with lower-income individuals paying a higher percentage of their income in sales taxes. Unfortunately, these taxes are quite difficult to avoid.

Gift and estate taxes are imposed when you transfer wealth to another person, either when you die, in the case of estate taxes, or while you're alive, in the case of gift taxes (remember, gifts of $11,000 or less aren't taxed). For 2002 and 2003, the tax

"Isn't this exciting! I earned this. I wiped tables for it, I steamed milk for it, and it's—[*opening her paycheck*]—not worth it! Who's FICA? Why is he getting my money?" This is the response of Rachel Green on the TV show *Friends* upon seeing her first Central Perk paycheck on the episode "The One with George Stephanopoulos." Your first paycheck is a real shock. Federal, state, and local taxes, in addition to FICA, a contribution to your firm's hospitalization plan, and retirement savings take a real bite out of your paycheck. Financial planning is all the more important if you're to make the best use of what's left.

code allows for an estate valued at up to $1.0 million to be transferred tax free to any heir. In 2002 and 2003, this rises to $1.5 million. In 2006, 2007, and 2008 it climbs to $2 million, and in 2009 it climbs to $3.5 million. Unfortunately, once this tax-free threshold has been reached, taxes begin at an effective rate of 41 percent, which quickly climbs to 50 percent. Finally, in 2010 the maximum gift tax will be 35 percent—the top individual income tax rate. As the law is written, the estate tax repeal is scheduled to be very short-lived. After 2010, the estate tax goes back to the way it was before the legislation was enacted; however, if this tax law goes the way of others in the past, it will experience a number of changes and modifications before 2010.

The U.S. tax code allows for an unlimited marital deduction for gift and estate tax purposes. This means that when a husband or wife dies, the estate, regardless of size, can be transferred to the survivor totally tax free.

## Calculating Your Taxes

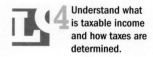

**Understand what is taxable income and how taxes are determined.**

As we mentioned earlier, once you've determined your income and your deductions, calculating your taxes is mainly just a matter of using the U.S. tax rates. Although this sounds quite simple, the IRS has a way of complicating things. To begin with, not all income is the same. For tax purposes, the IRS defines three different types of income—**active income** (from wages or a business), **portfolio** or **investment income** (from securities), and **passive income** (from activities in which the taxpayer does not actively participate). With some minor exceptions, it limits the deductions from each of these sources to the amount of income derived from that source. That is, your passive income deductions are limited to the level of passive income you received, your active income deductions are limited to the level of active income received, and so on. Think this classification is complicated? Just wait.

**Active Income**
Income that comes from wages or a business.

**Portfolio or Investment Income**
Income that comes from securities.

**Passive Income**
Income that comes from activities in which the taxpayer does not actively participate.

### Who Has to File a Return?

The first step to take before calculating your taxes is determining whether you need to file a tax return. If you don't think you need to file, you still might want to calculate your taxes, because if you don't file, you won't get a refund. According to 2001 regulations, if your income is more than $15,200, you need to file a return. If it's less than this amount, you may not need to file, depending on your filing status, age, and whether you can be claimed as a **dependent** on someone else's tax return. Figure 4.1 lists the rules for who must file a return.

The only exception to these rules deals with dependents. The income threshold for filing a tax return is generally lower for anyone who may be claimed as a dependent. Dependents with income generally include children who have a job or earn investment income or elderly parents who have some investment income. If you are considered a dependent on someone else's tax return, you'll want to check carefully to make sure that you don't have to file a return even if your income is below the levels in Figure 4.1. For example, if you're a dependent child in 2001 and have income of more than $4,550 from a job, you must file a return. If your income is "unearned," that is, from investments, an income level of only $750 means you must file a return.

**Dependent**
Person you take financial care of.

### Determining Gross or Total Income

If you do need to file, the first step in calculating your taxes is determining your total income. **Total** or **gross income** is simply the sum of all taxable income from all sources. It includes wages, salaries, and tips, in addition to any taxable interest income and dividends. Generally, your wages are reported to you on a W-2 form,

**Total or Gross Income**
The sum of all your taxable income from all sources.

## Figure 4.1 Who Has to File*

If your gross income is equal to or greater than the amount listed below, you must, in general, file a return.

What if you're a dependent? If another taxpayer can claim you as a dependent on his or her tax return, the filing thresholds are usually much lower.

If you are single and under 65 (and you are not blind), you must file if any of the following apply:

- Your unearned income was more than $750.
- Your earned income was more than $4,550.
- Your gross income was more than the greater of $750 or your earned income (up to $4,300) plus $250.

| FILING STATUS | |
| --- | --- |
| Age | Gross Income |
| **SINGLE** | |
| ● Under 65 | $ 7,450 |
| ● 65 or older | $ 8,550 |
| **MARRIED FILING JOINTLY** | |
| ● Both under 65 | $13,400 |
| ● One 65 or older | $14,300 |
| ● Both 65 or older | $15,200 |
| **MARRIED FILING SEPARATELY** | |
| ● Under 65 | $ 2,900 |
| ● 65 or older | $ 2,900 |
| **HEAD OF HOUSEHOLD** | |
| ● Under 65 | $ 9,550 |
| ● 65 or older | $10,650 |
| **SURVIVING SPOUSE** | |
| ● Under 65 | $10,500 |
| ● 65 or older | $11,400 |

Gross income is your total income before exclusions and deductions. Gross income includes such common forms of income as wages, interest, dividends, and business income. It does not include tax-exempt income.

*Based on tax year 2001 laws.

while interest and dividends are reported on a Form 1099. Total income also includes alimony, business income, capital gains, taxable IRA distributions, pensions and annuities, rental income, royalties, farm income, unemployment compensation, taxable Social Security benefits, and any other income. In short, whatever you receive in taxable income is summed to make up your total or gross income:

Gross Income = Sum of Income from All Sources

Although this calculation appears simple and relatively straightforward, it's harder than it looks because of the IRS and its lovely little rules.

Remember that not all income is taxable, and so not all income is included in total income. The main source of tax-exempt income is interest on state and local debt. Other sources include gifts, inheritances, earnings on your IRA, federal income tax refunds, child support payments, and welfare benefits.

### Calculating Adjusted Gross Income

**Adjusted Gross Income (AGI)**
Total income less allowable deductions.

**Adjusted gross income (AGI)** is simply total income less allowable deductions. Adjustments to total income center on payments set aside for retirement and also include moving and alimony payments. In effect, the IRS allows you to reduce your taxable income when you incur specific expenses or when you contribute to certain retirement plans. The advantage of these deductions is that they lower your taxes,

# In The News

Kiplinger's Personal Finance Magazine April 1999

## Timely Tips for Last-Minute Filers

The inevitable April 15 tax deadline is about to neatly divide millions of eleventh-hour taxpayers into two camps: those who owe more and those who don't. Whichever direction your bottom line points—you last-minute filer, you—make the most of the situation.

### When the IRS Owes Y.O.U.

Huzzah! You're getting money back. You should probably be kicking yourself in the rear rather than patting yourself on the back, but we'll discuss that later. First, maximize your good fortune. *If you use a computer to do your return, file electronically. Not only will your refund come back more quickly (even during the deadline crunch you should have your money within three weeks), but the chance of a processing error ensnaring an electronic return is much lower than with the paper variety.* (☛A)

As pleased as you are to be getting a refund, don't kid yourself: It's neither a gift nor a badge of honor. Rather, it's evidence that you allowed the government to withhold too much of your pay last year.

This year's refunds are expected to average even more than last year's record $1,365. Your goal is to be below average in this category next year. File a new W-4 form with your employer to reduce withholding. If you find the form daunting, order a copy of Publication 919, *Is My Withholding Correct for 1999?*, by calling 800-829-3676, or download it from the IRS Web site.

### Paying the Piper

Did you win the lottery or cash out your shares of Yahoo!? Or perhaps you converted a traditional IRA to a Roth at the cost of paying tax sooner rather than later. Well, sooner has arrived. *If you didn't pay estimated taxes or adjust your withholding to cover the extra bite, it's time to pay the piper.* (☛B)

You might even owe an underpayment penalty. If you're in the hole for at least $1,000 more than either 90 percent of your 1998 tax bill or 100 percent of what you owed in 1997, you're liable. You can figure the damage on Form 2210, but why waste your time? The IRS will be happy to compute the penalty and send you a bill.

Since the clock stops running on the penalty when you pay your tax with your return, let the IRS do the ciphering: You'll not only save time and aggravation, but you'll hold on to your money for a while longer.

### THE BOTTOM LINE . . .

A Regardless of whether you file electronically, you should request that you receive your refund by direct deposit. You can do this by putting your bank account information on line 66 of Form 1040. This speed ups the time it takes to get your refund and ensures that your refund is not lost in the mail.

B You now have the option of paying by credit card. Don't even consider it. The costs are enormous; in fact, you'll end up paying a "convenience fee" of $25 if you owe $700, for example, and $218 if you charge $9,000.

Source: "Timely Tips for Last-Minute Filers." *Kiplinger's Personal Finance Magazine*, April 1999: 151.

allowing you to invest or spend (hopefully, invest) money that you would otherwise send to Uncle Sam.

If neither you nor your spouse is covered by a retirement plan at work, you can annually deduct a contribution up to $2,000 on a tax-deferred basis to your IRA in 2001. This maximum contribution to an IRA climbs to $3,000 annually from 2002 through 2004, $4,000 annually from 2005 through 2007, and in 2008 up to $5,000 (thereafter the maximum contribution is adjusted for inflation in $500 increments). In addition, individuals age 50 and over are permitted to make additional annual contributions of $500 in 2002 through 2005 and $1,000 in 2006 thereafter. There is also a break for married couples with only one "working spouse." A married couple with only one spouse working outside the home can contribute up to the maximum annual amount to both the husband's and wife's IRA as long as the working spouse had that much in the way of earned income.

If you are covered by a pension plan at work there are limits on the size of your deductible contribution. The Tax Relief Act of 1997 expanded the ability of individuals to make tax-deductible contributions to **Individual Retirement Arrangements (IRAs)** by increasing the income limits for those who can make contributions. Deductible contributions for nonworking spouses of individuals who are in an employer-sponsored retirement plan are also permitted. The deduction is phased out for taxpayers with AGIs between $150,000 and $160,000.

**IRA**
An individual retirement arrangement which is a tax-deferred retirement savings account allowed by the government.

In addition, the Tax Relief Act of 1997 created new tax-favored accounts, called Roth IRAs, to which after-tax dollars are contributed and allowed to grow tax free and be withdrawn for retirement without taxes after a reasonable holding period.

Other adjustments to income include moving expenses associated with taking a job at a new location that is at least 50 miles farther from your home than your previous job. Self-employed tax filers are allowed to deduct half of the Social Security and Medicare taxes that they pay as well as up to 60 percent of the cost of their family's health insurance through 2001. This deductible percentage of health insurance expenses rises to 70 percent in 2002 and 100 percent in 2003 and later years. Alimony payments, provided certain requirements are met, are also deductible, because the person receiving the payments must pay taxes on them.

Because adjustments to income reduce your taxes, it's important to understand these adjustments and take advantage of them. After adding up all your adjustments to income, you subtract this amount from total income to arrive at your AGI:

> Gross Income = Sum of Income from All Sources

Less

> Adjustments to Gross Income: Tax-Deductible Expenses and Retirement Contributions (traditional IRA, Keogh contributions, moving expenses, and so on)

Equals

> Adjusted Gross Income (AGI)

**An Adjustment for (Almost) Everyone: Interest on Student Loans**   You can deduct interest payments on student loans up to $2,500 as an adjustment to gross income regardless of whether you itemize. This deduction begins phasing out at $60,000 for those filing as couples and is eliminated for couples with modified AGIs above $75,000. Singles making less than $40,000 receive the full deduction, while those making between $40,000 and $55,000 receive a partial deduction.

In addition, this deduction is limited to the first 5 years of the loan. For existing loans, interest payments can be deducted provided the loan isn't more than 5 years old. Remember, this deduction is even available to those who don't itemize; it is subtracted right off on line 24 of Form 1040. Beginning in tax year 2002, things get better as a result of the Tax Relief Act of 2001. First, the "60-month limit" that disallowed the deduction of student loan interest beyond the first 60 months in which interest payments are required was eliminated along with the restriction that voluntary payments of interest are not deductible. In addition, effective in 2002, the income level at which eligibility for the deduction begins to phase out rises from $50,000 to $65,000 for single filers and from $100,000 to $130,000 for joint filers.

## Subtracting Deductions

Once you know your AGI, the next step is to subtract your deductions. You have your choice of the standard deduction or itemizing, whichever benefits you the most. Obviously, taking the largest possible deduction is important. In fact, if you're in the 30 percent marginal tax bracket and you're able to take an additional $5,000 in deductions, you've actually reduced your tax bill by $5,000 × 0.30 = $1,500. That's $1,500 that you can spend on Domino's pizza or invest for retirement—whichever seems more important.

What's the difference between standardized and itemized deductions? On the simplest level, one is calculated for you and the other you have to calculate yourself. Of course, the answer's really more complicated than that. Let's start by taking a look at the deduction you have to calculate yourself—the itemized deduction.

**Itemizing Deductions**   We should note that taxpayers in higher income brackets don't get credit for all their itemized deductions. These limits don't affect many taxpayers. The 2001 tax year limits don't come into play unless your AGI is greater than $132,950 for those filing as single, joint, or head of household status.

The IRS has decided that you shouldn't be taxed on income that's used to pay for certain expenses. These are considered deductible expenses. Itemizing is simply listing all the deductions you're allowed to take. Of course, it's your responsibility to determine and document these deductible expenses.

Which expenses count as deductible? Let's take a look at the most common ones.

▮ **Medical and Dental Expenses.** Medical and dental expenses are deductible only to the extent that they exceed 7.5 percent of your AGI. For an individual with an AGI of $60,000, only those medical and dental expenses in excess of $4,500 would be deductible. The definition of what's considered a medical or dental expense is quite broad and includes medical treatment, hospital care, prescription drugs, and health insurance.

▮ **Tax Expenses.** Some, but not all, tax expenses are deductible. Although the biggest chunk of taxes you pay—federal, Social Security, and all sales taxes—are not tax deductible, state and local income taxes, along with real estate taxes, are deductible. State income taxes are deductible in the year in which they are paid. In addition, any county or city income taxes are tax deductible. Some states impose a personal property tax—generally a tax on automobiles—which is also tax deductible.

▮ **Home Mortgage and Investment Interest Payments.** Several types of interest are tax deductible. Interest that you pay on your home mortgage is deductible. Interest on **home equity loans** is also deductible on home equity debt up to $100,000.

**Home Equity Loan**
A loan that uses your home as collateral, that is, a loan that is secured by your home. If you default, the lender can take possession of your home to recapture money lost on the loan.

The last type of tax-deductible interest is investment interest, or interest on money borrowed to invest. The maximum deduction on investment interest is limited to the amount of investment income that you earn. Why does the IRS let you deduct these interest payments? Because it wants to make it easier for you to buy a house and make investments to help the overall economy. By making home interest payments tax deductible, the government is in effect subsidizing your purchase of a home.

Once you buy a home, you're generally better off itemizing deductions because of the home mortgage interest payments. Home mortgage interest payments push you over the threshold so you have enough deductible expenses to make itemizing worthwhile. As a result, expenses that previously had no value, such as personal property taxes, charitable contributions, and the cost of a safety deposit box, may now be deductible and, thus, result in tax savings.

- **Gifts to Charity.** Charitable gifts to qualified organizations are tax deductible. If you're in the 27-percent tax bracket and you give $1,000 to a charitable organization, it really only costs you $730, because you've given away $1,000 and as a result lowered your taxes by $270 ($0.27 \times \$1,000$). In effect, Congress is encouraging you to make charitable gifts. The only requirement for this deduction is that the gift go to a qualified organization and that if you make a single gift of more than $250, you show a receipt for that gift (a canceled check won't do). Of course, regardless of the size of the gift, you must make sure that you maintain good records. If you can't keep track of your donations, how can you deduct them?
- **Casualty and Theft Loss.** Although you're able to deduct casualty and theft losses, this deduction is rather limited and is of value only to those who suffer huge losses or have very low earnings. The reason for its limited usefulness is that (1) for tax purposes, the first $100 of losses is excluded and (2) you can deduct losses only to the extent that the remaining losses exceed 10 percent of your AGI.
- **Miscellaneous Deductibles.** These deductions include unreimbursed job-related expenses, tax preparation expenses, and investment-related expenses. The problem with these expenses is that they are only deductible to the extent that they are in excess of 2 percent of your AGI. In general, this percentage is a tough hurdle to pass, and, as a result, most taxpayers are not able to benefit from miscellaneous deductions.

Earlier we mentioned that once your income gets above a certain level, you begin losing a percentage of your itemized deductions. For those filing as married filing separately, the threshold is $64,475 (for those filing joint returns the threshold is $132,950) in 2001. In effect, once your AGI reached the phase-out threshold level, the more your AGI went up, the more your itemized deductions were reduced. Actually, the phase-out of itemized deductions (and personal exemptions that we will look at in a moment) served to raise the marginal tax rate once individuals reached the phase-out thresholds. At present, after taxpayers reach a phase-out threshold, their itemized deductions are reduced. The Tax Relief Act of 2001 eliminates the phase-out of itemized deductions for all taxpayers starting in 2010. Prior to the act, itemized deductions are reduced by 3 percent of a taxpayer's AGI once the phase-out threshold has been reached. The repeal is being phased in beginning in 2006.

This erosion of the value of itemized deductions is relatively complicated and doesn't affect all deductions equally. However, if your AGI is greater than this threshold level, you should have a clear understanding of how the reduction affects you.

**The Standard Deduction**   The alternative to itemizing deductions is to take the standard deduction. Basically, the standard deduction is the government's best estimate of what the average person would be able to deduct by itemizing. In other words, with the standard deduction, the government has done it for you already. You don't need to figure out your expenses and provide receipts or justification. Unlike itemized deductions, which are limited for higher AGI levels, the standard deduction remains the same regardless of income level. In fact, the level of the standard deduction increases every year to keep up with inflation. Figure 4.2 provides the standard deductions for 2000 through 2002. Note that additional standard deductions are given to the elderly and the blind.

**The Choice: Itemizing or Taking the Standard Deduction**   The decision between taking the standard deduction or itemizing may not be particularly difficult if one provides a greater deduction than the other. The choice becomes much more difficult, and also more interesting, when they are close in value. In that case, it may

**Figure 4.2** Standard Deduction Amounts

| Filing Status | 2000 | 2001 | 2002 |
|---|---|---|---|
| Single | $4,400 | $4,550 | $4,700 |
| Married Filing Jointly or Surviving Spouse | $7,350 | $7,600 | $7,850 |
| Head of Household | $6,450 | $6,650 | $6,900 |
| Married Filing Separately | $3,675 | $3,800 | $3,920 |

*Additional Standard Deductions for Elderly and Blind:* For a taxpayer (and spouse) who is elderly (age 65 or over) or blind, there is an additional deduction allowed.

be best to bunch your deductions and alternate each year between taking the standard deduction and itemizing.

In effect, you try to avoid incurring deductible expenses in years that you don't itemize. If possible, you postpone them to years when you do itemize and, therefore, get credit for them. There's no question that taking the standard deduction is easier than itemizing, but don't choose to take the standard deduction just because it's simpler—you don't want laziness to cost you money.

## Claiming Your Exemptions

Once you've subtracted the deductions from the AGI, you're ready to subtract the exemptions. An **exemption** is a deduction that you can make on your return for each person supported by the income on your tax return. The government provides these exemptions so that everyone will have a little bit of untaxed money to spend on necessities. In effect, each exemption allows you to lower your taxable income by $2,900 for the 2001 tax year and $3,000 for the 2002 tax year.[4] Thus, if you're in the 30.5-percent marginal tax bracket, each exemption you take in 2001 will lower your taxes by $884.50.

There are two types of exemptions—personal and dependency. You receive a personal exemption for yourself regardless of your filing status, or yourself and your spouse if filing a joint return, no questions asked. However, qualifying for a dependency exemption is more difficult. First, dependents must pass a relationship or household member test. If they're related to you as children, grandchildren, stepchildren, siblings, parents, grandparents, stepparents, uncles, aunts, nieces, nephews, in-laws, and so forth, they're considered to have a qualifying relationship. In fact, almost any relationship short of being a cousin qualifies under the IRS. If they're not related to you, then they must have lived with you over the entire tax year.

Second, the individual being claimed as a dependent generally can't earn more than the exemption amount. However, this income test does not apply to your children under the age of 19 or to children under the age of 24 who are full-time students. Third, you must provide more than half of the dependent's support. In addition, the dependent must be a U.S. citizen, resident or national, or a resident of either Mexico or Canada.

Just as with itemized deductions, once your AGI reaches a certain level, the value of your exemptions is reduced. For those filing joint returns, once their AGI reaches the threshold level of $199,450 (for tax year 2001), all exemption amounts claimed on

**Exemption**
A deduction you can take on your return for each person supported by the income listed on your tax return.

[4]Exemptions, like standard deductions, are raised each year to match inflation rates. You can claim anyone as an exemption, even if you're not related, if you provide more than half of that person's support. However, if you claim someone as a dependent on your return, that individual can't appear as an exemption on anyone else's return—even the dependent's own.

## Figure 4.3 Calculation of Taxable Income

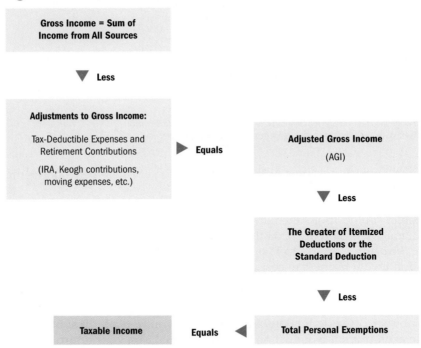

## Table 4.3    Phase-out of Exemptions

*Exemption claims are reduced by 2% for each $2,500 of AGI in excess of the appropriate threshold amount, with the threshold amounts annually adjusted for inflation.*

| | 2001 | |
|---|---|---|
| Filing Status | Phase-out Begins When AGI Exceeds | Phase-out Completed When AGI Exceeds |
| Single | $132,950 | $255,450 |
| Married Filing Jointly or Surviving Spouse | 199,450 | 321,950 |
| Head of Household | 166,200 | 288,700 |
| Married Filing Separately | 99,750 | 160,975 |

the return are reduced by 2 percent for each $2,500 of AGI in excess of the threshold amount.[5] Naturally, the higher your AGI, the lower your exemption until your exemption is phased out altogether.

Table 4.3 presents the thresholds at which phase-outs begin and the points at which the phase-out of exemptions is completed. These threshold points are adjusted annually for inflation. Essentially, if your AGI is above the threshold point, your marginal tax rate is effectively increased because as you earn more, you lose a percentage of your exemptions. The more exemptions you have, the more important this phase-out becomes. For example, if in 2001 you had 12 exemptions and an AGI level above the phase-out threshold, for each additional $2,500 of AGI you received, your

---

[5]This threshold level is raised each year to match inflation.

exemptions would be reduced by $696, which is 2 percent of the value of your total exemptions (12 exemptions × $2,900 × 0.02 = $696).

## Calculating Your Base Income Tax

Now that you've subtracted your deductions and your exemptions from your AGI, you know your taxable income, which is the amount your taxes are based on. Figure 4.3 shows these calculations. For most taxpayers, once you've determined your taxable income, your income tax can be determined directly using the tax tables found in the middle of your federal income tax instructions booklet. The intersection of your taxable income and your filing status determines your taxes due, as shown in Figure 4.4.

If your taxable income is greater than $100,000, you must determine your taxes using the rate schedules because the tax tables don't go that high. The tax rate schedules are found at the end of your federal income tax instructions booklet and were provided earlier in Table 4.2.

**Figure 4.4** Determining Your Taxes Using the 2001 Tax Tables

Assuming you are married filing jointly with taxable income of $37,301, your taxes would be $4,999

| If taxable income is — | | And you are — | | | |
|---|---|---|---|---|---|
| At least | But less than | Single | Married filing jointly | Married filing sepa- rately | Head of a house- hold |
| | | | Your tax is — | | |
| **37,000** | | | | | |
| 37,000 | 37,050 | 6,501 | 4,954 | 7,057 | 5,151 |
| 37,050 | 37,100 | 6,514 | 4,961 | 7,071 | 5,164 |
| 37,100 | 37,150 | 6,528 | 4,969 | 7,084 | 5,178 |
| 37,150 | 37,200 | 6,542 | 4,976 | 7,098 | 5,192 |
| 37,200 | 37,250 | 6,556 | 4,984 | 7,112 | 5,206 |
| 37,250 | 37,300 | 6,569 | 4,991 | 7,126 | 5,219 |
| 37,300 | 37,350 | 6,583 | 4,999 | 7,139 | 5,233 |
| 37,350 | 37,400 | 6,597 | 5,006 | 7,153 | 5,247 |
| 37,400 | 37,450 | 6,611 | 5,014 | 7,167 | 5,261 |
| 37,450 | 37,500 | 6,624 | 5,021 | 7,181 | 5,274 |
| 37,500 | 37,550 | 6,638 | 5,029 | 7,194 | 5,288 |
| 37,550 | 37,600 | 6,652 | 5,036 | 7,208 | 5,302 |
| 37,600 | 37,650 | 6,666 | 5,044 | 7,222 | 5,316 |
| 37,650 | 37,700 | 6,679 | 5,051 | 7,236 | 5,329 |
| 37,700 | 37,750 | 6,693 | 5,059 | 7,249 | 5,343 |
| 37,750 | 37,800 | 6,707 | 5,066 | 7,263 | 5,357 |
| 37,800 | 37,850 | 6,721 | 5,074 | 7,277 | 5,371 |
| 37,850 | 37,900 | 6,734 | 5,081 | 7,291 | 5,384 |
| 37,900 | 37,950 | 6,748 | 5,089 | 7,304 | 5,398 |
| 37,950 | 38,000 | 6,762 | 5,096 | 7,318 | 5,412 |

Each year the amount of taxable income within each bracket is adjusted to reflect inflation.

The taxable income is $37,301. Thus, they look in this row to determine their taxes.

The filing status is married filing jointly. Thus, they look in this column to calculate their taxes.

There's also an alternative minimum tax that's aimed at preventing the very wealthy from using tax breaks to the extent that they pay little or nothing. For most people this tax isn't a concern, but for the very wealthy, it must be dealt with. It applies different rules in calculating taxable income and then applies a 26-percent and a 28-percent tax rate to all income. It's really Congress's method of ensuring that everyone pays taxes.

## Determining Your Credits

Tax credits offset your taxes in a direct dollar-for-dollar manner. That is, they don't merely reduce your taxable income, they offset taxes.

**Child Credit** In 2001 there was a $600 child tax credit for each child under 17. The Tax Relief Act of 2001 doubles the child tax credit from its 2000 level of $500 to $1,000 by the year 2010, rising to $600 for years 2001 to 2004, $700 for years 2005 to 2007, $800 in year 2009, and $1,000 in year 2010 and later. A qualifying child is an individual for whom the taxpayer can claim a dependency exemption, and is the child, grandchild, stepchild, or eligible foster child of the taxpayer. This child tax credit comes on top of the personal exemption for each child. Again, this is a tax credit, which means it cuts your tax bill dollar for dollar. Thus, a family with three children under 17 saved $1,800 in taxes in 2001.

This tax credit can even become a tax refund for low-income families who don't pay taxes. At the high end of the income scale, this child tax credit begins being phased out after a single parent's income reaches $75,000 or a couple's income reaches $110,000 regardless of the number of children they have. Once the phase-out begins, the credit is reduced by $50 for every $1,000 the single parent earns over $75,000.

**The Hope Scholarship Tax Credit and the Lifetime Learning Credit** For most parents, thinking about how much they need to save for their children's education results in paralyzing horror and guilt. As a result, the Taxpayer Relief Act of 1997 tried to make college funding a bit easier (not painless, just easier). Under this legislation, parents get a 100-percent tax credit for the first $1,000 of college expenses during each of the first two years of college. On top of that they also get a 50-percent tax credit on the next $1,000 of expenses for a total tax credit of up to $1,500 a year for the first 2 years of college. This tax credit is called the **Hope Scholarship tax credit**. Qualifying expenses include tuition and books but not room and board. To qualify, the student must be enrolled on at least a part-time basis in an accredited vocational school, college, or university.

There are, of course, a number of restrictions on the use of the Hope Scholarship tax credit. To qualify, you must both pay the student's tuition and list the student as a dependent on your tax return. The size of the tax credit can also be affected by the amount of financial aid and scholarship funds that are received.

As with most other tax breaks, the Hope Scholarship tax credit gets phased out for single individuals with incomes greater than $40,000 and for families filing joint returns with incomes greater than $80,000. It is eliminated for single filers with modified AGIs above $50,000 and for joint filers with AGI above $100,000. These phase-out levels will be inflation adjusted beginning in 2002.

During the third and fourth years of college or for graduate students, the **Lifetime Learning tax credit** applies. It also applies to working adults taking classes

**Hope Scholarship Tax Credit**
A tax credit of up to $1,500 per year for the first 2 years of college.

**Lifetime Learning Tax Credit**
A tax credit for the third and fourth years of college or graduate students. It also applies to working adults taking classes to improve their work skills.

---

**STOP &THINK** The Hope Scholarship is set up to help everyone get at least a 2-year degree at a community college. In fact, the $1,500 credit is about $300 above the national average community college tuition rate. That means a community college education is "tuition free" for all those who qualify, which is about two-thirds of all community college students.

---

to improve their work skills. This tax credit amounts to 20 percent of the first $5,000 through 2002 for tuition and related expenses for *all* eligible students in the family, rising to 20 percent of the first $10,000 in 2003. The $1,000 limit applies regardless of the number of eligible students for whom you pay education expenses. In effect, the maximum Lifetime Learning credit you may claim in 2001 is $1,000 and it rises to $2,000 in 2003. Just as with the Hope Scholarship, the Lifetime Learning tax credit gets phased out for those in the higher income brackets.

This tax credit is fully available for those filing single returns with incomes less than $40,000 and for families filing joint returns with incomes less than $80,000. Partial credits are available for single filers with modified AGIs between $40,000 and $50,000 and for joint filers with modified AGIs between $80,000 and $100,000 with these phase-out levels being adjusted for inflation beginning in 2002.

Again, as with the Hope Scholarship, if you're taking money out of an education IRA to pay expenses, you can't claim the Lifetime Learning credit. In addition, parents must be paying their child's tuition and claiming the child as a dependent in order to qualify for the credit.

**Other Tax Credits**  Another common tax credit is the **child and dependent care credit**. The logic behind this credit is that child care is an expense of having a job; that is, you have to spend money on child care to earn a living. With the increased number of single-parent and dual-income families, the child and dependent care credit is used quite often. The credit applies both to dependent children under the age of 13 and to disabled dependents or a disabled spouse, regardless of age. To qualify, you must have earned income—that is, noninvestment income—and if you file a joint return, both spouses must have earned income.

**Child and Dependent Care Credit**
A tax credit that offsets your taxes in a direct dollar-for-dollar manner for child and dependent care expenses.

The maximum amount of child and dependent care expenses that qualified for the credit in 2001 was $2,400 for one child/dependent and $4,800 for two or more, and you receive only a percentage of that amount as a tax credit. The size of the credit you actually receive depends upon how much you spent on child/dependent care and your AGI. For example, those with an AGI of less than $10,000 receive 30 percent of their child/dependent care expenses up to $2,400 or $4,800 as a tax credit; those earning over $28,000 only receive 20 percent of their child/dependent care expenses up to $2,400 or $4,800 as a tax credit.

If your AGI was $35,000 and you had two children in child care at a total cost of $5,000, your child care credit would be $960. Why? Because only the first $4,800 of your child care expenses qualifies for the credit, and because your AGI is over $28,000, you receive a credit of only 20 percent of your qualified expenses (0.20 × $4,800 = $960). Of course, you can't get a credit for more than you owe in taxes.

Many of the features of the Tax Relief Act of 2001 were aimed at married couples and families with children. With this in mind, the dependent care tax credit was expanded. Effective in 2003:

- The maximum dependent care credit is increased to 35 percent of qualified care expenses (the credit was 30 percent of expenses).
- The point at which the credit percentage begins to decrease is increased to $15,000 of adjusted gross income (previously, the credit percentage began to decrease once adjusted gross income reached $10,000).
- The credit percentage is reduced to 20 percent for taxpayers with adjusted gross incomes over $43,000 (previously, it was reduced to 20 percent for taxpayers with adjusted gross incomes over $28,000).

There's also an **earned income credit** available to low-income taxpayers, which effectively serves as a negative income tax. With the child and dependent care credit,

**Earned Income Credit**
A tax credit available to low-income taxpayers, which effectively serves as a negative income tax.

you couldn't get a credit for more than you owed in taxes, but with the earned income credit you could actually get a credit for more than you paid in taxes. In other words, you could pay no taxes and get money back from the IRS.

Of all the credits, this one is perhaps the most complicated with respect to determining exactly what you qualify for. For those with no children, the maximum credit is $364, with the credit disappearing entirely when AGI or earned income exceeds $10,710.[6] The maximum credit is $2,428 for those with one qualifying child and is totally phased out when AGI or earned income rises above $28,281. For those with more than one child, the maximum credit is $4,008 and is totally phased out once earned income or your AGI reaches $32,121.[7]

The Tax Relief Act of 2001 also increases the earned income credit, which provides a refundable tax credit for lower-income wage earners by raising the earned income phase-out levels. Beginning in 2002, the act increases the beginning and ending points of the phase-out range for the earned income credit for joint filers by $1,000 for 2002, 2003, and 2004; $2,000 for 2005, 2006, and 2007; and $3,000 for 2008. After 2008 annual adjustments for these phase-out ranges will be adjusted annually for inflation.

**Adoption Credit**
A tax credit of up to $5,000 available for qualifying costs of adopting a child.

Another important credit for some taxpayers is the **adoption credit.** It allows for a tax credit of up to $5,000 for the qualifying cost of adopting a child under the age of 18, or someone who is physically or mentally incapable of self-care.[8] This credit is phased out for those with an AGI (after certain adjustments) between $75,000 and $115,000.[9] As a result of the Tax Relief Act of 2001, effective in 2002, the maximum credit is increased to $10,000 per eligible child, for both special needs children and other children. In addition, the income phase-out range applicable to the credit and the exclusion is increased to modified adjusted gross incomes between $150,000 and $190,000.

Some taxpayers are eligible for additional tax credits, as outlined in the following list:

▪ Totally disabled taxpayers and those over 65 with low incomes
▪ Taxpayers who pay income tax to another country
▪ Taxpayers who purchase gasoline for nonhighway vehicles used in a business can receive tax credits on federal gasoline taxes
▪ Those who overpay Social Security taxes because they work more than one job

Although there are not nearly the number of tax credits that there once were, it behooves you to be aware of what qualifies for a tax credit and to take advantage of any credit you qualify for. Once again, *tax credits are subtracted directly from taxes due on a dollar-for-dollar basis.* Your total income tax becomes your base income tax less your tax credits:

Base Income Tax (from tax tables or tax rate calculations)

Less

Tax Credits

Equals

Total Income Tax Due

---

[6]Based on tax year 2001 laws.
[7]Based on tax year 2001 laws.
[8]Based on tax year 2001 laws.
[9]Based on tax year 2001 laws.

# Checklist 4.1 ■ You Might be Able to Use Form 1040EZ if...

Your filing status is either single or married filing jointly.
You don't itemize deductions.
Your taxable income is less than $50,000.
Your taxable interest income is less than $400.
You have no dependents.
You aren't making a deductible contribution to an IRA or a deduction for student loan interest.
You don't have alimony, taxable pension benefits, or Social Security benefits to report.

## Other Filing Considerations

Before you file you'll have to pick a form and decide if you want to file electronically or not. You'll also want to know how to file an amended return, what to do if you can't make the tax deadline, and where to get help. Fortunately, April 15 only comes once a year.

### Choosing a Tax Form

A key to calculating your taxes is deciding which 1040 form to use: 1040EZ, 1040A, or 1040. If the IRS has sent you material, it's already made a guess at what form you'll need and has included it. Still, you have the option of choosing a different form if you like.

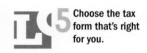 Choose the tax form that's right for you.

Form 1040EZ is aimed at those with no dependents, and with taxable income less than $50,000 per year, who don't itemize. Presently, it's used by about 20 million taxpayers. As its name implies, it is an "easy" form to fill out. Form 1040EZ consists of only 12 lines of information, and the instructions fit on the back of the form. In fact, it can even be filled out over the telephone. Checklist 4.1 provides some of the basic requirements you must meet in order to use Form 1040EZ.

Slightly less "EZ" than Form 1040EZ, but still not too complicated, is Form 1040A, the original easy form. It loosens up the requirements for use quite a bit from those associated with Form 1040EZ. It is used by about 25 million taxpayers. Although it still limits total taxable income to $50,000, this income can come from interest, dividends, Social Security benefits, pensions and annuities, scholarships, IRA distributions, and unemployment compensation. In effect, it allows for a much broader range of income sources than is allowed on Form 1040EZ. Form 1040A also allows for dependents and deductible contributions to an IRA. Checklist 4.2 provides some of the basic requirements that must be met in order to use Form 1040A.

 WORKSHEET

# Checklist 4.2 ■ You Might be Able to Use Form 1040A if...

You don't itemize deductions.
Your taxable income is less than $50,000.
The only adjustment you make to income is an IRA contribution or the student loan interest deduction.
You don't have alimony or capital gains to report.
You don't have alimony, taxable pension benefits, or Social Security benefits to report.

## Table 4.4    Schedules Included with Form 1040

| | |
|---|---|
| Schedule A: Itemized Deductions | Schedule EIC: Earned Income Credit |
| Schedule B: Interest and Dividend Income | Schedule F: Profit or Loss from Farming |
| Schedule C: Profit or Loss from Business | Schedule H: Household Employment Taxes |
| Schedule D: Capital Gains and Losses | Schedule R: Credit for the Elderly or the Disabled |
| Schedule E: Supplemental Income and Loss | Schedule SE: Self-Employment Tax |

Form 1040, which is also called the "1040 long form," is used by everyone else—about 75 million taxpayers—and throws "easy" right out the door. It's longer because it allows for the many complications that can make filing taxes a frustrating experience. On the bright side, though, the 1040 long form allows for the opportunity to avoid paying more in the way of taxes than is legally required. That is, it allows for itemized deductions and adjustments to income that can result in lower taxes. Obviously, your choice of a tax form should not be based on what's easiest to fill out. It should be based on what's financially advantageous to you.

**Schedules**
Attachments to Form 1040 on which you provide additional information.

Along with Form 1040, you also get a number of **schedules**. A schedule is an attachment to Form 1040 on which you provide information regarding income and expenses that flow through to Form 1040. Some of the more common schedules are listed in Table 4.4. If you need a form or schedule, they're easy to get. In fact, each year the IRS sends out about 8 billion pages of forms, requiring around 300,000 trees to make the paper. If you still need an IRS schedule or form, the easiest way to get it is simply to download it off the IRS Web site at **www.irs.gov** or to call 800-TAX-FORM. The IRS will send it directly to you just as soon as it's done chopping down more trees.

### Electronic Filing

While you may not have a choice on paying your taxes, you do have a choice on how to pay them. You can also file your return electronically. For tax year 2001, of the more than 130 million individual tax returns that were filed, more than 40 million were filed via IRS e-file. That's a 13.6 percent increase over tax year 2000 filing. The IRS expects more than 46 million e-filers in 2002 and hopes to have 80 million filing electronically by 2007, as more and more taxpayers look for these benefits:

- Faster refunds: Direct deposit can speed refunds to e-filers in as few as 10 days. Most e-file refunds are issued and mailed within three weeks.
- More accurate returns: IRS computers quickly and automatically check for errors or other missing information, making e-filed returns more accurate and reducing the chance of getting an error letter from the IRS.
- Quick electronic confirmation: Computer e-filers receive an acknowledgment that the IRS has received their returns. Callers using TeleFile receive a confirmation number while they're still on the phone, letting them know that the TeleFile system has accepted their return.
- Delete the paperwork with electronic signatures: There is nothing to mail to the IRS.
- Easy payment options: E-filers with a balance due can schedule an electronic funds withdrawal from their bank account or pay with a credit card.
- Federal/state e-filing: Taxpayers in 37 states and the District of Columbia can e-file their federal and state tax returns in one transmission to the IRS. The IRS forwards the state data to the appropriate state tax agency.

There are several e-file options available to you. The most popular is computer filing through an authorized provider, accounting for 28.9 million returns in 2001. Using this method, tax professionals send clients' returns electronically to the IRS. Some prepare their clients' returns and send them. Others take returns prepared by their clients, enter the data, and then send them to the IRS.

Taxpayers with a computer, a modem, or Internet access and tax preparation software can also e-file their tax returns from home any time, day or night. To do so, a taxpayer sends a completed electronic tax return to a transmitter. The transmitter converts the file to an IRS-approved format and then sends the converted return file to the IRS. Within 48 hours, the IRS notifies the taxpayer through the transmitter whether or not the return is accepted. This approach was used by more than 6.8 million taxpayers in 2001. If you're interested in this method, the IRS Web site at **www.irs.gov** has a list of companies offering online filing software, as well as direct links to firms with low- or no-cost e-filing options.

For those who are eligible, TeleFile, the IRS file-by-phone system, is the easiest way to file a return. In 2001, 4.4 million people used TeleFile instead of filling out Form 1040EZ.

## Filing Late and Amended Returns

Although most returns are filed by April 15, sometimes taxpayers simply can't make the deadline. In addition, if you discover an error in a prior year's returns, you can file an amended return.

**Filing Late**   If you're unable to file by April 15, you can request a filing extension from the IRS. All you need to do is file Form 4868, Application for Automatic Extension of Time to File U.S. Individual Income Tax Return, and the extension is automatic—no questions asked. This extension gives you an additional 4 months to file your return.

As you might expect, a filing extension is a fairly popular request, with over 5 million taxpayers asking for one each year. However, the IRS isn't about to let you off the hook that easily. In addition to filling out the extension request form, you're asked to enclose a check for any estimated taxes you owe. If you don't enclose a check, you'll be charged interest on the taxes. Moreover, if the amount due is more than 10 percent of your tax bill, you'll also be charged a late penalty of 1/2 percent per month.

**Amending Returns**   It's not unusual for someone to make a mistake on a tax return or to realize later that a deduction was omitted. To amend your return use Form 1040X, Amended U.S. Individual Income Tax Return. In fact, you can even amend an amended tax return. Occasionally, an amended return can be prompted by a retroactive change the IRS may make. For example, in 1994 the IRS changed the deductibility of a fee associated with taking out a home mortgage and made this change retroactive to 3 years.

There are some limitations on the use of an amended return. For example, there is a limit on how far back you can go: You can't file an amended return more than 3 years after the original tax due date that you filed. Finally, if you file an amended federal return, make sure you also amend your state and local returns.

## Being Audited

Each year the IRS audits the returns of more than 1 million taxpayers, which accounts for just under 1 percent of all tax returns filed. What might bring on an **audit**?

**Audit**
An examination of your tax return by the IRS.

Unfortunately, you may just have bad luck—the IRS randomly selects a large number of returns each year. You may also be audited because you were audited in the past, particularly if the IRS found some error in your return. In this case, the IRS is merely checking to make sure the error doesn't occur again. You may have been selected because you earn a lot of money. You're over five times more likely to be audited if your income is over $100,000 than if your income is between $25,000 and $50,000.

From the IRS point of view, the more income you have, the more likely you are to fake a questionable deduction. In fact, if your itemized deductions are more than 44 percent of your income, your odds of being audited rise even further. In addition, your odds of being audited go up significantly if your return contains a Schedule C for self-employment income. If your expenses on Schedule C amount to more than one-third of your Schedule C income, the odds of an audit rise again.

No one wants to be audited, but unless you've been cheating on your taxes, it's nothing to worry about. Audits come in different forms. Some only ask for additional information and can be handled through the mail. Others require you to meet face-to-face with an IRS representative. In either case, you're given several weeks to prepare your response.

The first step in preparing for an audit is to reexamine the areas in which the IRS has questions. You should gather all supporting data—canceled checks, receipts, records—you have, then try to anticipate any questions the IRS might have and formulate responses to them. The key to winning an audit is good records. If you need help, you can hire a tax accountant or attorney. In fact, this agent can go to the audit in your place, provided you sign a power of attorney form.

If you're not satisfied with the outcome of the audit, you have the right to appeal. The first step is to see the auditor. Present your argument and see if you can win the appeal with additional information. If you are still not satisfied with the results, you turn to your auditor's manager. If you are still not satisfied, you can file a formal appeal and even go to tax court if necessary.

Unfortunately, an appeal does not guarantee satisfaction, but you do have a right to appeal if you wish. The important point is that you have the right to receive credit for any and all legal deductions, and you should not let fear of being audited interfere with paying the minimum amount of income taxes, provided you do it legally.

## Help in Preparing Taxes

Sometimes preparing your taxes is more than you can handle by yourself. The first place to look for help is the IRS. While that may seem akin to consorting with the enemy, the IRS is a good place to start. Information from the IRS is knowledgeable and cheap—in fact, it's free. In addition to the instructions provided with your income tax form, the IRS also has a number of booklets, many of which are free, that can be extremely helpful. One of the more informative is IRS Publication 17, *Your Federal Income Tax*, which gives detailed step-by-step instructions to aid you in filing your taxes.

The IRS also provides a phone service, a toll-free "hot line" for tax questions. Although the IRS won't accept any liability for incorrect advice, representatives are generally correct. Moreover, using the IRS hot line as a reference can save you both time and money in getting that answer. The major problem with using the hot line is that it's often busy. The closer you get to April 15, the more difficult it is to connect. The IRS also provides a walk-in service in most areas, where you can meet directly with an IRS employee. Once again, the closer it is to April 15, the harder it is to make an appointment.

In addition to publications from the IRS, there are a number of excellent self-help tax publications, including J. K. Lasser's and Ernst & Young's income tax guides.

These tax guides tend to point out areas in which legitimate deductions, which might otherwise be overlooked, can be found. For those with access to a computer and some degree of computer literacy, there are a number of outstanding computer programs for tax preparation, including Intuit's TurboTax and MacInTax and TaxCut by HR Block Financial.

These programs all work essentially the same way. They lead you through a number of questions that help you construct your tax return. If you have access to a computer and are computer literate, these programs are generally both reliable and easy to use.

Your final option in preparing your taxes is to hire a tax specialist. Although going to a specialist sounds safe, remember that tax specialists are not licensed or tested—anyone can declare himself or herself to be a tax specialist. There are some rules governing tax specialists, but there's no penalty imposed on your advisor if you pay too much taxes.

Tax specialists can be divided into those with a national affiliation, such as H&R Block, and independent tax specialists. One advantage of the national affiliation is that employees generally get standardized training, keeping them current with the latest IRS changes and rulings. With independent tax specialists, there's much more variability in terms of training and in the quality of work they do.

If you decide to use a tax specialist, you should make sure you avoid the April rush. Because of the volume of tax work that's done at the last minute, last-minute returns may not get the attention they deserve. In addition, make sure you get references and inquire about the specialist's background and experience. If your tax specialist does not begin with an extensive interview in which your financial affairs are fully probed, you probably won't get your money's worth.

## Model Taxpayers: The Taylors File Their 2001 Return

**L6** Calculate your income taxes.

Let's take a look at the various steps in calculating taxes for Form 1040. We'll use the Taylors as an example. Chuck and Dianne Taylor have two children: Lindsey, who's 4, and Kathleen, who's 6. Chuck is a computer analyst for Burlington Industries, where he earned $31,450 in 2001, and Dianne works part-time at a coffee shop, where she earned $6,250 in 2001. On Chuck and Dianne's wages and salaries there was a total of $5,095 in federal tax withheld.

In addition, Chuck has a consulting business where he does computer programming, and in 2001 this business provided additional net income of $7,450. Because no taxes were taken out of Chuck's consulting income, he made estimated tax payments of $200. In 2001 the Taylors also received interest income of $760, dividends of $580, $755 in capital gains on stock held for less than 12 months and then sold,[10] and a gift of $10,000 from Chuck's parents. Chuck also contributed $1,000 to his **Keogh plan**, which is a tax-deferred retirement plan for self-employed individuals.

**Keogh Plan**
A tax-deferred retirement plan for the self-employed.

The Taylors had another more interesting source of income: They were winners on *The Price Is Right*. Dianne won a 2001 Ford Focus just by telling Bob Barker the third number in its price. A stunned Dianne Taylor stood on the stage of the CBS studio in Burbank, California, hearing the announcer say: "That's right, Dianne, this brand-new Ford Focus comes fully equipped with air, AM/FM cassette, automatic windows, and California emission controls. You'll enjoy making heads turn as you drive down the street in this, *your new car!*" What she didn't hear is that she would have to pay taxes on her prize. What she's taxed on is the fair market price of the car,

---

[10]Since the capital gains were realized on stock held for less than 12 months, the entire gain is taxable as ordinary income.

which is interpreted as what she could realize on an immediate resale. In this case that amount is $12,500, and it becomes part of their taxable income.

Because the Taylors have total taxable income greater than $50,000, they have no choice but to use the 1040 long form. The first step is to get organized, which means gathering together a copy of last year's return along with all of this year's tax-related information: salary, taxes withheld, mortgage payments, the market price of the car

Figure 4.5 2001 Federal Income Tax Return for the Taylors, Using Form 1040

Take the time to set up a good tax record-keeping system. Once it's set up, use it!

Married people generally file as Married Filing Jointly (in general, it saves money over filing separately), but for those with widely divergent levels of income and deductions, it might be better to use the Married Filing Separately status.

If you work for yourself, your income gets reported on Schedule C.

If you put money into an IRA or tax-deferred retirement plan and you haven't yet paid taxes on that money, you will have to pay taxes on it when you withdraw it at retirement.

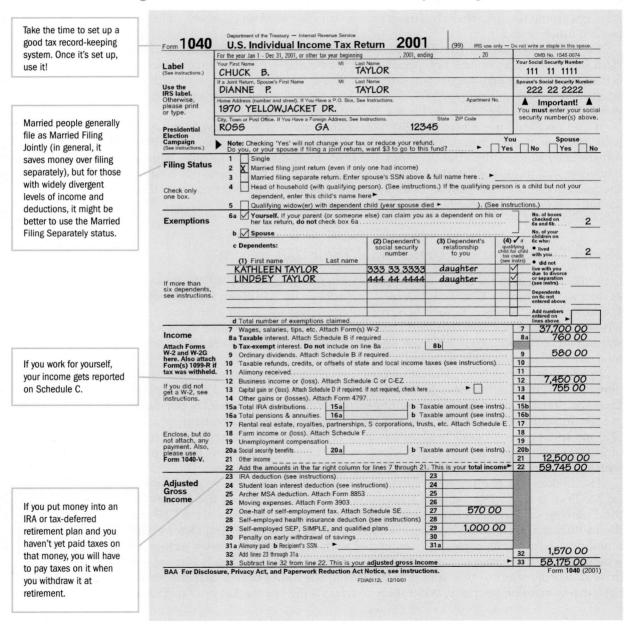

(figure continues)

Dianne won, medical expenses, and so on. Fortunately, over the past year the Taylors set aside all their tax-related materials in a folder in Dianne's desk.

One of the first questions asked on Form 1040 is filing status. For the Taylors, filing a joint return makes the most sense. Remember, the rates are set up to encourage you to file a joint return if you are married. The total exemptions claimed by the Taylors were four—one each for Chuck, Dianne, Kathleen, and Lindsey. Figure 4.5 shows the Taylors' 2001 Form 1040. We'll use this figure as a reference as we examine how the Taylors calculated their taxes. All line references correspond to the numbered lines shown on Form 1040.

(figure continued)

Before sitting down to do your taxes, gather up everything you will need, including any tax-related business expenses from the previous year.

If you pay for child or dependent care while you are working, you may be entitled to a tax credit.

| Form 1040 (2001) | | | | Page 2 |
|---|---|---|---|---|
| **Tax and Credits** | 34 | Amount from line 33 (adjusted gross income) | 34 | 58,175 00 |
| | 35a | Check if: ☐ You were 65 or older, ☐ Blind; ☐ Spouse was 65 or older, ☐ Blind. Add the number of boxes checked above and enter the total here ▶ 35a | | |
| Standard Deduction for— | b | If you are married filing separately and your spouse itemizes deductions, or you were a dual-status alien, see page 31 and check here ▶ 35b ☐ | | |
| People who checked any box on line 35a or 35b or who can be claimed as a dependent, see page 31. | 36 | Itemized deductions (from Schedule A) or your standard deduction (see left margin) | 36 | 9,274 00 |
| | 37 | Subtract line 36 from line 34 | 37 | 48,901 00 |
| | 38 | If line 34 is $99,725 or less, multiply $2,900 by the total number of exemptions claimed on line 6d. If line 34 is over $99,725, see the worksheet on page 32 | 38 | 11,600 00 |
| All others: | 39 | Taxable income. Subtract line 38 from line 37. If line 38 is more than line 37, enter -0- | 39 | 37,301 00 |
| Single, $4,550 | 40 | Tax (see page 33). Check if any tax is from a ☐ Form(s) 8814 b ☐ Form 4972 | 40 | 4,999 00 |
| Head of household, $6,650 | 41 | Alternative minimum tax (see page 34). Attach Form 6251 | 41 | |
| | 42 | Add lines 40 and 41 | 42 | 4,999 00 |
| Married filing jointly or Qualifying widow(er), $7,600 | 43 | Foreign tax credit. Attach Form 1116 if required | 43 | |
| | 44 | Credit for child and dependent care expenses. Attach Form 2441 | 44 | |
| | 45 | Credit for the elderly or the disabled. Attach Schedule R | 45 | |
| Married filing separately, $3,800 | 46 | Education credits. Attach Form 8863 | 46 | |
| | 47 | Rate reduction credit. See the worksheet on page 36 | 47 | |
| | 48 | Child tax credit (see page 37) | 48 | 1,200 00 |
| | 49 | Adoption credit. Attach Form 8839 | 49 | |
| | 50 | Other credits from: a ☐ Form 3800 b ☐ Form 8396 c ☐ Form 8801 d ☐ Form (specify) | 50 | |
| | 51 | Add lines 43 through 50. These are your total credits | 51 | 1,200 00 |
| | 52 | Subtract line 51 from line 42. If line 51 is more than line 42, enter -0- | 52 | 3,799 00 |
| **Other Taxes** | 53 | Self-employment tax. Attach Schedule SE | 53 | 1,140 00 |
| | 54 | Social security and Medicare tax on tip income not reported to employer. Attach Form 4137 | 54 | |
| | 55 | Tax on qualified plans, including IRAs, and other tax-favored accounts. Attach Form 5329 if required | 55 | |
| | 56 | Advance earned income credit payments from Form(s) W-2 | 56 | |
| | 57 | Household employment taxes. Attach Schedule H | 57 | |
| | 58 | Add lines 52 through 57. This is your total tax | 58 | 4,939 00 |
| **Payments** | 59 | Federal income tax withheld from Forms W-2 and 1099 | 59 5,095 00 | |
| | 60 | 2001 estimated tax payments and amount applied from 2000 return | 60 200 00 | |
| If you have a qualifying child, attach Schedule EIC. | 61a | Earned income credit (EIC) | 61a | |
| | b | Nontaxable earned income 61b | | |
| | 62 | Excess social security and RRTA tax withheld (see page 51) | 62 | |
| | 63 | Additional child tax credit. Attach Form 8812 | 63 | |
| | 64 | Amount paid with request for extension to file (see page 51) | 64 | |
| | 65 | Other payments. Check if from a ☐ Form 2439 b ☐ Form 4136 | 65 | |
| | 66 | Add lines 59, 60, 61a, and 62 through 65. These are your total payments | 66 | 5,295 00 |
| **Refund** Direct deposit? See page 51 and fill in 68b, 68c, and 68d. | 67 | If line 66 is more than line 58, subtract line 58 from line 66. This is the amount you overpaid | 67 | 356 00 |
| | 68a | Amount of line 67 you want refunded to you | 68a | 356 00 |
| | b | Routing number | | |
| | | c Type: ☐ Checking ☐ Savings | | |
| | d | Account number | | |
| | 69 | Amount of line 67 you want applied to your 2002 estimated tax | 69 | |
| **Amount You Owe** | 70 | Amount you owe. Subtract line 66 from line 58. For details on how to pay, see page 52 | 70 | |
| | 71 | Estimated tax penalty. Also include on line 70 | 71 | |
| **Third Party Designee** | | Do you want to allow another person to discuss this return with the IRS (see page 53)? ☐ Yes. Complete the following. ☐ No | | |
| | | Designee's name | Phone no. ( ) | Personal identification number (PIN) |
| **Sign Here** Joint return? See page 19. Keep a copy for your records. | | Under penalties of perjury, I declare that I have examined this return and accompanying schedules and statements, and to the best of my knowledge and belief, they are true, correct, and complete. Declaration of preparer (other than taxpayer) is based on all information of which preparer has any knowledge. | | |
| | | Your signature *Chuck B. Taylor* Date 3/19/02 | Your occupation Computer Analyst | Daytime phone number ( ) |
| | | Spouse's signature. If a joint return, both must sign. *Dianne P. Taylor* Date 3/19/02 | Spouse's occupation Part-Time Sales Person | |
| **Paid Preparer's Use Only** | | Preparer's signature | Date Check if self-employed ☐ | Preparer's SSN or PTIN |
| | | Firm's name (or yours if self-employed), address, and ZIP code | | EIN Phone no. ( ) |
| | | | | Form **1040** (2001) |

### Determining Gross or Total Income (line 22)

Gross or total income is simply the sum of all your taxable income from all sources. For the Taylors it includes Chuck and Dianne's wages and salaries of $31,450 + $6,250 = $37,700 (line 7). It also includes taxable interest income of $760 (line 8a), $580 in dividends (line 9), and $755 in capital gains (line 13). In addition Chuck's consulting income of $7,450 appears on line 12 as business income. Line 21, other income, includes $12,500, the fair market value of the car Dianne won on *The Price Is Right*. Finally, all this taxable income is summed to make up total income (line 22).

| | |
|---|---:|
| Chuck and Dianne's salary and wages (line 7) | $37,700 |
| Taxable interest income (line 8a) | 760 |
| Dividend income (line 9) | 580 |
| Business income (line 12) | 7,450 |
| Capital gains (line 13) | 755 |
| Other income (line 21) | 12,500 |
| Total income (line 22) | $59,745 |

Notice that a $10,000 gift the Taylors received from Chuck's parents does not appear as income. This is because gifts are not considered taxable income. Other common sources of income that would not be taxed include interest on state and local debt.

### Subtracting Adjustments to Gross or Total Income and Calculating Adjusted Gross Income (line 33)

For the Taylors, the only adjustments to total income are the deduction of Chuck's contribution of $1,000 to his self-employed retirement or Keogh plan (line 29) and the deduction of half of the self-employment tax associated with Chuck's consulting. Recall that in addition to income tax, self-employment income is subject to Social Security tax at a rate of 15.3 percent until earned income from all sources reaches $80,400. Thus, Chuck's self-employment tax on his business income of $7,450 is $7,450 × 0.153 = $1,140 (line 53). Half of this amount ($570) is then tax deductible as an adjustment to income on line 27. Thus, total adjustments are $1,000 + $570 = $1,570 (line 32). Subtracting these adjustments from total income gives the Taylors an AGI of $58,175 (line 33).

### Subtracting Deductions (line 36)

The Taylors have their choice of taking the standard deduction, which for 2001 was $7,600, or itemizing their deductions. The Taylors' itemized deductions amounted to $9,274, primarily as a result of interest paid on their home mortgage. Figure 4.6 shows the Taylors' deductions. In addition to home mortgage interest payments of $7,079, they paid $1,543 in state and local income taxes and real estate taxes, and made $652 in tax-deductible charitable contributions for a total of $9,274 in deductions. The Taylors were unable to deduct any medical or miscellaneous expenses because neither of these exceeded the AGI limitations set by the IRS. Because the level of the itemized deductions exceeded the standard deduction, they chose to itemize. The itemized

Figure 4.6 Schedule A from the Taylors' 2001 Federal Income Tax Return

Only those medical expenses that exceed 7.5% of your adjusted gross income are tax deductible.

The state, local, personal property, real estate, and foreign income taxes you paid are tax deductible.

Charitable contributions are deductible. However, if you make noncash contributions of clothing, goods, or property, they must be listed on Form 8283 if they exceed $500.

Only if total job-related and other expenses exceed 2% of your adjusted gross income are they tax deductible.

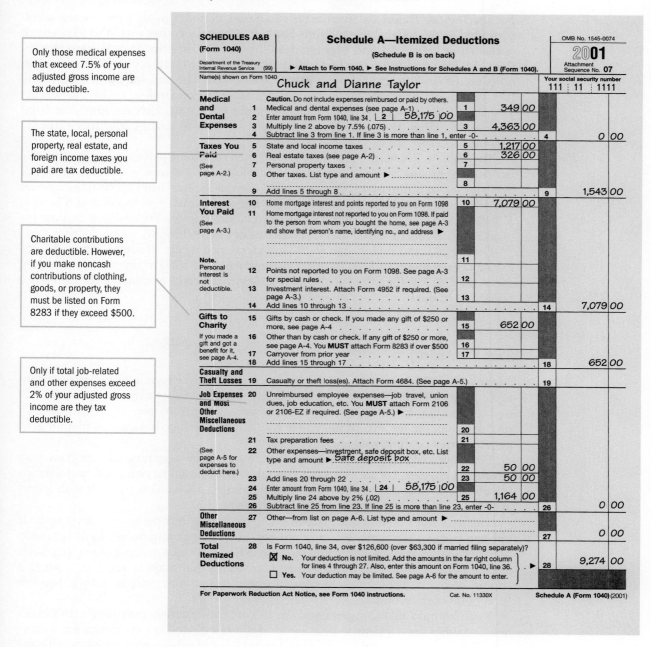

deduction of $9,274 is entered in line 36 on Form 1040. Subtracting this amount from their AGI reduces their taxable income to $48,901 (line 37).

## Claiming Exemptions (line 38)

The Taylors qualify for four exemptions, with the 2001 exemption amount being $2,900. Thus, the level of total exemptions entered on line 38 is 4 × 2,900 = $11,600. Subtracting this amount further reduces their taxable income to $48,901 − $11,600 = $37,301 (line 39).

## Calculating Total Tax (line 58)

For the Taylors, their base income tax can be calculated directly from the tax tables provided in the federal instructions booklet. Their tax comes out to $4,999, which is shown in Figure 4.4 and is entered on line 40. Because the Taylors have dependent children under the age of 17, they qualify for the child tax credit. Remember, a tax credit is subtracted directly from taxes owed. The child tax credit currently (tax year 2001) provides for a tax credit of $600 per dependent child. For the tax year 2001, the Taylors received $1,200 in child tax credit. This amount is entered on line 48. Thus, the total credits entered on line 51 are $1,200, then, line 52 becomes $3,799.

The only "other taxes" that the Taylors owe is a self-employment tax on Chuck's consulting business. Once again, self-employment income is subject to Social Security tax at a rate of 15.3 percent until earned income from all sources reaches $80,400. Thus, Chuck's self-employment tax on his business income of $7,450 is $7,450 × 0.153 = $1,140 (line 53). This amount is added to the Taylors' base income tax of $3,799 (line 52), resulting in total taxes due of $4,939 (line 58).

During 2001 the Taylors had $5,095 in federal income tax withheld and made estimated tax payments of $200 for total tax payments of $5,295 in line 66. Because they owed ($4,939) less than they paid ($5,295), they will receive a refund of the difference of $356 from the IRS.

## Tax Planning

So far we've looked only at preparing your taxes. We now turn to the very important topic of tax planning strategies. Although a tax specialist can help you identify deductions you might otherwise miss, once you begin to prepare your taxes it's probably too late for any strategy that will result in reduced taxes. Tax planning, in general, must be done well ahead of time.

Few people do their tax planning alone. Instead they consult a CPA or even a tax attorney. However, before you see a specialist, you should have a good understanding of how the tax code works. This understanding allows you to work with a specialist to map out a strategy that suits your needs.

The basic idea behind the planning is to minimize unnecessary tax payments. If you can keep your payments to a minimum, you'll have more money to use in meeting your financial goals. Unfortunately, the IRS has closed a number of tax loopholes in recent years, but there still are many strategies that make sense. Tax strategies should be methods of supplementing a sound investment strategy rather than the focal point of investing.

Keep in mind that Congress and the IRS are continuously tinkering with the tax laws, so what may appear to be a wonderful loophole today may disappear tomorrow. Your strategy should be to supplement a solid investment strategy with tax considerations.

There are five general tax strategies you can use. They include the following:

- Maximize deductions.
- Look to capital gains income.
- Shift income to family members in lower tax brackets.
- Receive tax-exempt income.
- Defer taxes to the future.

Each of these strategies is aimed at avoiding unnecessary taxes, not evading taxes, that is, overstating deductions or not reporting all your income. It's certainly illegal and unwise to evade taxes, but it's foolish to pay more than your fair share.

## Maximize Deductions

Strategies for maximizing deductions center on three different tactics: (1) using tax-deferred retire-

**STOP &THINK**  It's hard to overstress how valuable tax-deferred retirement plans actually are. Not only do they reduce taxable income but also the contributions grow tax deferred, and many companies match part of your contribution, putting in 50 cents for each dollar that you contribute.

ment programs to reduce taxes, (2) using your home as a tax shelter, and (3) shifting and bunching deductions. Each of these three tactics has the same goal: to reduce taxable income to its minimum level.

**Using Tax-Deferred Retirement Programs**  To encourage retirement savings, the government allows several different types of tax-deferred retirement programs. The advantage of these plans is that you (1) don't pay taxes on the money you invest and (2) don't pay interest on the earnings from your retirement account. Let's look at the difference that results from putting your savings in a tax-deferred retirement plan instead of in a normal savings account, both earning a 10-percent return. Let's also assume that you are in the 27-percent marginal tax bracket.

If you took $1,000 of your taxable earnings and decided to invest without using a tax-deferred retirement plan, you would first pay $270 in taxes, leaving you with only $730 to invest. During the first year you would earn $73 in interest and pay $19.71 in taxes, leaving you with $53.29 of interest after taxes. At the end of the year you would have $783.29 saved. If you let this amount grow at 10 percent before taxes for 25 years, it would accumulate to a total of $4,249.

Now let's look at what would happen if you put your money in a tax-deferred account, also earning 10 percent. First, you wouldn't pay taxes on the $1,000, because taxes aren't assessed until you withdraw the money from this account. Thus, you would earn 10 percent interest on $1,000 for a total of $100 interest. In addition, because this is a tax-deferred account, you wouldn't pay taxes on any of this interest, giving you a total of $1,100 after the year. If you left this amount in the tax-deferred account for 25 years, you would have accumulated $10,834.

Of course, you eventually would have to pay taxes on this amount, but even after taking 27-percent taxes on $10,834 you still have about $7,909. Why is the difference between the investments so great? Because you've been able to earn interest on money that would have otherwise already been collected by the IRS.

**Using Your Home as a Tax Shelter**  The tax benefits associated with owning a home are twofold. First, mortgage interest payments are tax deductible and, as such, reduce your taxes. Second, when you eventually sell your house, you are exempt from paying taxes on gains of up to $500,000 for couples filing jointly and $250,000 for those filing single on the sale of a principal residence.

Just how valuable is the deductibility of your home mortgage interest payments? That depends on several factors. For those in the highest tax brackets, the tax deductibility is much more valuable than it is for those in the lowest bracket. Although if you earn too much, this deduction begins to lose value because of the phase-out of itemized deductions discussed earlier. In addition, if you do not itemize deductions, the tax deductibility of mortgage interest payments is of no value. Moreover, if you would have taken the standard deduction without them, and now

# In The News

Wall Street Journal September 9, 2001

## "Why the Roth Wins in the Long Run"

### by Jonathan Clements

It's a battle of investment heavyweights.

In the early going, the edge belongs to the tax-deductible individual retirement account, while the Roth IRA offers no immediate tax savings. Still, the Roth may be a better bet to go the distance.

Once retired, Roth investors don't owe anything to Uncle Sam, while regular IRA investors must pay income taxes on their withdrawals. And the Roth's advantages don't stop there. Consider:

Suppose a husband and wife both invested $2,000, each buying the same stock. The wife buys her shares in a Roth, while the husband invests through a tax-deductible IRA. Because the couple is in the 28 percent tax bracket, the husband's $2,000 contribution garners a $560 tax deduction.

*To have any hope of keeping up with his wife, the husband must invest the $560, which he uses to buy the same stock in a taxable account. Over the next 20 years, the stock pays no dividends, but it climbs 400 percent. The wife now has $10,000 in her Roth IRA, while* the husband has $10,000 in his IRA and *another $2,800 in a taxable account.* (☛**A**)

Both husband and wife empty their IRAs. She owes no taxes, so she pockets $10,000. Because the couple still pays taxes at 28 percent, he owes $2,800 on his $10,000 IRA withdrawal. As it happens, he has this sum in his taxable account.

All even? Not quite. When he sells the $2,800 of stock, he triggers taxes on the $2,240 of appreciation. If he pays capital gains taxes at 20 percent, the sale will net $2,352. Result? After taxes, the husband has $448 less than his wife.

*Sound appealing? In the years ahead, you will be able to sock away even more. As with regular IRAs, the annual amount you can stash in a Roth is scheduled to increase, hitting $5,000 in 2008.* (☛**B**)

## THE BOTTOM LINE . . .

**A** You've seen the incredible power of compounding in the previous chapter. With the Roth IRA you get the opportunity to take advantage of your two biggest investment advantages— the fact that you have a long investment time horizon, perhaps over 40 years until retirement, and the fact that you are probably in a relatively low tax bracket at present. The only problem is coming up with the money to invest. If you can overcome that, you've got a wonderful investment alternative right in front of you. It also has its roots in **Principle 6: Taxes Affect Personal Finance Decisions.**

**B** Another great feature of the Roth IRA is that, at any time, you can pull out an amount up to your original contribution without getting hit with a tax penalty.

itemize with them, they reduce your taxable income only by the difference between the standard deduction and your itemized deductions.

The amount that this reduction in taxable income reduces your taxes is their value. In effect, the tax deductibility of mortgage interest payments reduces the cost of your mortgage by (1 − marginal tax rate). Thus, the after-tax cost of a home mortgage can be determined as follows:

$$\text{after-tax cost of mortgage interest} =$$
$$\text{before-tax cost of mortgage interest} \times (1 - \text{marginal tax rate})$$

**STOP & THINK** As we'll see in coming chapters, home equity debt, because of the tax deductibility of the interest payments, is the cheapest source of borrowing. Often it is a good idea to use the money from a home equity loan to consolidate and pay off more costly debt.

In short, the value of the tax deductibility of mortgage interest payments depends on your marginal tax bracket and whether or not you itemize deductions.

In addition, using your home as collateral, you can take out a home equity loan and deduct your interest payments. This deduction lowers the cost of borrowing. For example, you might consider a home equity loan to finance buying a car. In early 2002 the average cost of a 36-month car loan was about 7.1 percent, and the average cost of a home equity loan was about 7.8 percent. However, the interest on the home equity is generally tax deductible, whereas the interest on the car loan is not.

Recalculating the cost of a home equity loan for an individual in the 27-percent tax bracket on an after-tax basis, it becomes 7.8 (1 − marginal tax rate) or 7.8 (1 − 0.27) = 5.69 percent. Thus, in many cases the cheapest way to borrow money is with a home equity loan.

**Shifting and Bunching Deductions**   When we discussed itemizing versus taking the standard deduction, we presented the concept of shifting and bunching deductions. The decision between taking the standard deduction or itemizing becomes difficult when they are close in value. The concept of shifting and bunching deductions involves trying to avoid incurring deductible expenses in years that you don't itemize. Instead, you postpone them to years when you do itemize and, therefore, get credit for them. For example, you may wish to make 13 mortgage payments and double up your charitable contributions during years that you itemize.

## Look to Capital Gains Income

Recall from our earlier discussion that capital gains refers to the amount by which the selling price of a capital asset—that is, an asset being kept for investment purposes such as stocks, bonds, or real estate—exceeds its purchase price. The example we used was the purchase of 100 shares of GM stock for $50 per share and the sale 2 years later of those same shares of GM stock for $70 per share. In this case, your capital gains would be 100 shares × ($70 − $50) = $2,000.

If you hold an asset for a year or more, the gain is taxed at a maximum rate of 20 percent or only 10 percent if you are in the 15-percent bracket. Thus, if you were in the 38.6-percent marginal tax bracket, you'd pay just over at half your ordinary tax rate.

This rate even drops further for lower-bracket taxpayers if the asset is held for 5 years or more. Under a tax law change that became effective in 2001, individuals in the 15 percent tax bracket will pay capital gains tax at a rate of 8 percent, instead of 10 percent, on profits from the sale of investments held more than 5 years.

A similar rate reduction will eventually apply to higher-income investors. If you're in a tax bracket higher than 15 percent, you'll be eligible for an 18 percent capital gains rate, rather than 20 percent, for investments acquired on or after January 1, 2001, and then held more than 5 years.

The other benefit from capital gains is the fact that you don't have to claim it—and, therefore, pay taxes on it—until you sell the asset. In effect, you can postpone paying taxes by not selling the asset. Without question, if you have to pay taxes, it's better to pay 10 years from now than today.

## Shift Income to Family Members in Lower Tax Brackets

Income shifting involves transferring income from family members in high tax brackets to those in lower tax brackets. Although the concept is relatively simple, it can be a complex process involving lawyers and the establishment of **trusts**. A less complicated kind of income shifting involves a relatively simple idea—gifts. You're allowed to give $11,000 per year tax-free to as many different people as you like.[11] One of the nice things about annual gifts of under $11,000 is that the person receiving

**Trust**
A fiduciary agreement in which one individual holds property for the benefit of another person.

---

[11]Based on tax year 2002.

the gift doesn't pay any taxes either. On annual gifts of $11,000 or less, neither the person who gives nor the person who receives pays any taxes. Best of all, every year you get another gift exclusion that allows you to give $11,000 tax-free to as many different people as you like.

If you're planning on passing your estate on to your children when you die, you might be wise to give some of it away now. That way you can pass on both income and taxes. For example, if Heshie Rothbaum is in the 35-percent tax bracket, he might be better off giving his son Izzy, who is in the 10-percent tax bracket, a $11,000 gift rather than keeping the $11K for himself. If Heshie gives it as a gift, he doesn't pay taxes on it, and because Izzy is in a lower tax bracket, taxes paid on any future earning on this $11,000 are calculated at a lower rate. As a result, the money grows more than it would otherwise.

### Receive Tax-Exempt Income

Interest paid on state and local government debt is tax exempt for federal income tax purposes. That means if you buy a bond issued by a state or city (a municipal bond), you can collect the interest and not have to pay any taxes on it. For example, in 2002 the city of Atlanta, Georgia, issued over $100 million in bonds set to mature in 2041. The equivalent taxable yield on a municipal bond is calculated as follows:

$$\text{equivalent taxable yield} = \frac{\text{tax-free yield on the municipal}}{(1 - \text{investor's marginal tax bracket})}$$

Thus, if you're in the 30-percent marginal tax bracket, the equivalent taxable yield on a 6-percent municipal bond would be 6%/(1 − 0.30) = 8.57 percent. In effect, that means that on an after-tax basis, a taxable bond yielding 8.57 percent and a municipal bond yielding 6 percent are equivalent. The higher your marginal tax bracket, the more beneficial tax-free income is.

### Defer Taxes to the Future

**401(k) Plan**
A tax-deferred retirement plan.

As we've already seen, tax-deferred retirement programs such as traditional IRAs, self-employed retirement or Keogh plans, and **401(k) plans** allow you to defer taxes to the future rather than pay those taxes today. Roth IRAs allow taxes to be paid on the contribution and never again. The idea is to allow you to earn interest on money that would have otherwise already been collected by the IRS.

This concept also applies to capital gains, because you can postpone capital gains taxes until you sell the asset. If you don't recognize all these terms, don't worry. We'll discuss them in depth later in the book. For now, the important point is that saving on a tax-deferred basis has real benefits.

## SUMMARY

The U.S. tax code is a patchwork system that has grown to over 2,000 pages today, with its complexity at times overshadowing its logic. The rate structure for the U.S. tax code is progressive, with six different marginal tax rates. These rates are going down in the future as a result of the Tax Relief Act of 2001, phasing in through 2006. Of special importance is the marginal tax rate, because this is the rate you pay on your next dollar of income.

A capital gain refers to the amount by which the selling price of a capital asset—that is, an asset being kept for investment purposes such as stocks or bonds—exceeds its purchase price. Net long-term capital gains less any net short-term capital losses are taxed at a lower maximum rate than ordinary income (short-term gains are treated as ordinary income).

To calculate your taxes, you must first determine your total income by summing up your income from all sources. From this amount, adjustments that center on tax-deductible expenses and retirement contributions are subtracted, with the result being adjusted gross income (AGI). From AGI, the deductions, the greater of either the itemized deductions or the standard deduction, and the exemptions are subtracted, with the end result being taxable income.

We also looked at who must file tax returns, when they must file, what forms to use, electronic filing and what information is needed to prepare a tax return.

If you're unable to file by April 15, you can request a filing extension from the IRS. In addition, if you discover an error in a prior year's returns, you can file an amended return.

Audits can happen to anyone, but are more likely to happen to those with higher incomes or those who are self-employed. The first step in preparing for an audit is to reexamine the areas in which the IRS has questions. If you are not satisfied with the outcome of the audit, you have the right to appeal.

If you need help in filing your return, the first place to look is the IRS. There are several good tax books you can use to help prepare your taxes. For those with access to a computer and some degree of computer literacy, a number of outstanding computer programs are available. The final option in preparing your taxes is to hire a tax specialist.

Five general tax strategies can be used to keep your tax bill to a minimum:

- Maximize deductions.
- Look to capital gains income.
- Shift income to family members in lower tax brackets.
- Receive tax-exempt income.
- Defer taxes to the future.

In addition to paying federal income taxes, Social Security taxes, and state and local taxes, you also pay excise taxes, sales taxes, property taxes, and gift and estate taxes.

## REVIEW QUESTIONS

1. Although the Tax Relief Act of 2001 provided for a decade of tax law changes, what were the two major outcomes of the legislation? Specifically, how will the tax rate system change?

2. Why is the advice to "defer income and accelerate deductions" a good tax planning strategy over the next few years?

3. What factors affect taxable income, or the difference between gross and taxable income?

4. If someone is in the 30 percent marginal tax bracket, is that person's entire income taxed at 30 percent? Why or why not?

5. It can be said that capital gains are better than investment income because of taxes and timing. Why?

6. What is meant by "bracket creep"? What method is employed by the IRS to control "bracket creep"?

7. Describe the method used for collecting income tax and explain why it is done in this manner.

8. In addition to federal income tax, what other income-based taxes does the federal government collect? What percentage of income does the IRS collect, and are these progressive or regressive taxes?

9. List and describe four non-income-based taxes.

10. What are the three main types of income included in gross income?

11. What is taxable income and what is the formula for determining taxable income?

12. What are the major categories of adjustments to gross income?

13. List the six most common itemized deductions and describe the limits set on each.

14. What are the eligibility requirements for the Hope Scholarship tax credit? For the Lifetime Learning credit? Name two other credits a household might claim.

15. What is the maximum allowable taxable income for filing a 1040A or 1040EZ income tax form?

16. Whereas paying income taxes with a credit card may be problematic, electronic filing of tax returns offers distinct advantages. What are they?

17. What federal income tax form is used when filing a late or amended return, and what's the procedure that must be followed?

18. What are the four most common "signals" the IRS looks for when selecting people for audits?

19. What are the three main types of assistance available to the general public for completing their tax forms?

20. What are the five general tax reduction strategies? Give a brief synopsis of each.

## PROBLEMS AND ACTIVITIES

1. The Jacksons' 2001 gross annual income is $68,000 and their taxable income is $50,000. Determine their marginal and average tax rates assuming their filing status is married filing jointly.

2. Consider two hypothetical investors who each want cash to fund a goal. Both have investments they have held for more than three years. Investor A has $1,500 in annual dividend income. Investor B decides to sell $1,500 of mutual fund shares. Assuming no commissions or sales charges and a 29 percent marginal tax bracket, which investment will yield the greater return after taxes? In other words, are the taxes the same on the $1,500 received by both investors?

3. Sukeeta is a young mother trying to figure out her income taxes. Her husband, who was killed last year in an accident, always handled the tax filing. Assuming 2001 standard deduction amounts, which filing status should she use? Why? Does she have a choice of status?

4. A couple with four children has an annual adjusted gross income of $200,000. Calculate the total dollar amount of personal exemptions that can be claimed for the 2001 tax year.

5. Jack and Jill have $51,500 in gross income and enough allowable deductions to itemize. Determine the best income tax form for them to use if filing jointly. Explain why they wouldn't use the other forms.

6. Calculate the total 2001 tax liability for a single parent of one child with gross income of $46,250, taking the standard deduction.

7. Using the married filing jointly status and their income and expense statement, calculate the 1998 tax liability for Shameka and Curtis Williams. First use the standard deduction, and then use the following itemized deductions.

| Income | |
|---|---|
| Earned income | $43,000 |
| Interest income | 2,100 |
| Expenses | |
| Home mortgage interest | 6,200 |
| Real estate and state income taxes | 4,200 |
| Miscellaneous deductions | 800 |

Write a paragraph explaining to the Williamses which method they should use and why.

8. Using Figure 4.1, determine if a couple, ages 73 and 75, must file a return. Calculate their gross taxable income from the following information.

| Taxable pension benefits | $9,200 |
|---|---|
| Inheritance | $8,000 |
| Quilt sales income | $12,500 |

If they do not have to file a 2001 return, should they anyway? Why or why not?

9. Calculate the Lifetime Learning tax credit available to a single filer earning $35,000 per year if she spent $7,000 on qualified expenses during 2001.

10. Calculate the 2001 total tax for Gordon Geist, a single taxpayer without dependents. He has active income of $36,000, investment income of $6,000 from the sale of stock, and $4,000 of passive income. He does not itemize deductions.

11. Otto Marx is a self-employed mason with a 2001 taxable annual income of $75,000 after exemptions and deductions. Calculate his total 2001 income tax liability, including federal, state (4.75 percent), and FICA.

12. Mrs. Hubbard, a mother of two, has been selected for an audit. Advise her on what to do to prepare for the audit and what to do if the audit does not turn out favorably.

13. Harry and Harriet Porter are in their golden years. Discuss the best tax reduction method for them to use in reducing their estate taxes.

# SUGGESTED PROJECTS

1. The 2001 tax rebate checks were planned to (1) implement the rate reduction with the 10 percent bracket and (2) stimulate the economy. What other examples of social or economic policy are evident in the tax code?

2. Talk with several people or families in different socioeconomic groups or stages in the life cycle about their tax record-keeping methods. Question them about how their methods have evolved as their situations have changed.

3. Write a one-page paper discussing why taxes are withheld directly from your pay rather than collected on an annual basis. Also explain how the amount of taxes withheld is determined.

4. Calculate your income tax liability using two approaches. First, assume that your parents claim you as a dependent. What is your tax liability? Second, assume that you are independent and claim yourself as a dependent. What is your tax liability? Explain the difference.

5. Estimate your non-income-based tax expenditures for the last six months. Consider sales tax, excise taxes, and personal property taxes.

   Hints: To estimate your *personal property taxes* consult your tax statements or talk with your parents about the taxes on your vehicle (if applicable).

   To estimate your *sales tax* call the applicable state Department of Commerce to determine the tax rates and on what items the taxes are collected.

   To estimate your *excise taxes* call the state Department of Commerce to establish the tax rates on items such as tobacco, gasoline, and alcohol. Excise taxes are also collected on phone usage; to get this figure consult your phone bill.

6. Using the information in this chapter, determine which tax form you should use and outline the specific points of information that helped you make this determination.

7. Prepare yourself for an audit by collecting all relevant tax records from the last year. Include all pay stubs that verify deductions, credit card bills and their matching receipts that verify tax-deductible expenditures, and all bank account statements. Now grade yourself on how well you are prepared for an audit.

8. Call a certified public accountant (CPA) and explain that you are a student currently studying taxes. Ask the accountant to explain three of the most commonly recommended tax saving strategies and three of the most commonly audited tax return sections. Prepare a report on your findings.

9. Talk to your parents about their taxes. Do they follow any of the five tax reduction strategies presented in this chapter? Talk to them about the benefit of following one or more of these strategies. Summarize your discussion in a report.

## Discussion Case 1

Holly and Zachary Neal, from Dublin, Virginia, are preparing to file their 2001 income taxes. Their children are grown; however, Holly's mother, Martha, has moved in with them so Holly is no longer working. She is dependent on their income for support except for her $491 monthly Social Security benefit.

Zachary works for a software company and earns enough to keep their heads above water; however, he had to discontinue participation in his retirement plan so they could pay the bills. Holly is taking this opportunity to work toward her master's degree. They know they will file jointly but need your help preparing their tax return. They have gathered all of the appropriate records, as follows:

| | |
|---|---|
| 1099-DIV, Capital Gains, short-term | $600 |
| Zachary's W-2, Wage and Tax Statement | $48,000 |

| | |
|---|---|
| Gambling winnings | $500 |
| Inheritance | $50,000 |
| Holly's traditional IRA contribution | $2,000 |
| Martha's unreimbursed medical expenses | $5,100 |
| The Neals' unreimbursed medical expenses | $1,700 |
| Martha's total living expenses, excluding medical | $13,000 |
| State taxes withheld | $2,280 |
| Mortgage interest expense | $6,000 |
| Holly's student loan interest payments | $90 |
| Holly's education expense | $1,150 |

# Money Matters

## DO NOT GO GENTLY INTO THAT TAX RETURN

I take one folder with a few forms, 1099s, my Quicken reports, and one spreadsheet to my CPA in February. My best friend takes three bulging shoe boxes of paper in about April 14. Guess who pays the lower tax preparation fee, and probably saves taxes by having good records of deductions? Organization, as strange as it may sound, is a partial cure for the tax-filing blues.

***If you itemize deductions and don't use accounting software,*** *circle any deductible items in your check register. At the end of the year, check off each circled item as you list it, and make sure you have receipts where needed. A list with supporting evidence is a tax preparer's dream and may prevent overlooking deductions. It's also a lifesaver if you get that dreaded audit letter.*

***Keep a record of all income sources and check each one off as the W-2 or 1099 comes in.*** *It's a bit painful to get your 1040 done and then receive a W-2 from that part-time painting job you had 1 month last summer. Also, the IRS doesn't accept the "I didn't get a 1099" excuse for excluding interests or dividends. Call any company that hasn't sent you the required forms by the end of January.*

***Try completing a tax preparer's checklist*** *before beginning your return or heading off to the CPA.*

***Procrastination can be costly.*** *If you got a refund last year, set a deadline to change your W-4. About the worst investment, besides burying your money in the backyard, is giving the U.S. government an interest-free loan for the year. Also, prepare your return early. If you're expecting a refund, the sooner you get the money back, the sooner it can go to work for you.*

***One of the biggest time consumers in tax preparation is determining the cost basis of investments that were liquidated during the year.*** *If you don't have records of the original purchase and intervening transactions, you are at the mercy of a brokerage house or investment company to provide the documentation. Prepare a folder when you first set up stock or a mutual fund account and keep every statement. Just a little organization can save time and ensure that the proper amount of tax is paid.*

## Questions

1. Is Martha's unreimbursed medical expense deductible on the Neals' tax return? Why?
2. Is Martha required to file a tax return? Why or why not?
3. What tax advantage(s), attributable to Holly's education expenses, can be included on the Neals' return?
4. Can the Neals' IRA contributions be deducted on their tax return? If so, to what extent?
5. Would the Neals benefit from itemizing their deductions? Why?
6. Calculate the Neals' total 2001 tax liability using the method most advantageous to them.

## Discussion Case 2

Austin and Anya Gould are a middle-aged couple with two children, Rusty age 13 and Sam age 11, whom they adopted this year. They also bought a new home in the area to give the children a yard in which to play. The Goulds also have an extensive retirement portfolio invested primarily in growth-oriented mutual funds. Their annual investment income is only $500, none of which is attributable to capital gains. Austin works in the banking industry and receives an annual income of $32,500. Anya, who owns the only travel agency in town, makes about $40,000 a year.

The Goulds give extensively to charities. They also have tax deductions from their mortgage interest expense, business expenses, tax expenses, and unreimbursed medical expenses, as follows:

| | |
|---|---|
| Health insurance (provided by Anya) | $2,200 |
| Rusty's braces | $1,500 |
| Mortgage interest expense | $7,200 |
| Real estate taxes | $900 |
| Investment and tax planning expenses | $1,450 |
| Other medical expenses | $3,600 |
| Charitable contributions | $3,500 |
| Moving expenses | $3,000 |
| Austin's unreimbursed business expenses | $2,300 |
| Qualified adoption expenses | $6,700 |
| State taxes withheld | $4,000 |

Remember that Anya has some special tax expense deductions because she is self-employed. Be sure to include them when completing their 2001 tax form.

## Questions

1. Calculate Anya's Social Security and Medicare taxes. Calculate how much of the taxes are deductible.
2. Are the moving expenses deductible? Why or why not?
3. Will the Goulds take the standard deduction or will they itemize? What is the amount of their deduction?
4. What tax form will the Goulds use? Why?
5. What credits might the Goulds use to reduce their tax liability?

 Visit our Web site for additional case problems, interactive exercises, and practice quizzes for this chapter—**www.prenhall.com/keown**.

# CONTINUING CASE: Cory and Tisha Dumont

The objective of the continuing case study is to help you synthesize and integrate the many and varied financial planning concepts you have been learning. The case will help you apply your knowledge of constructing financial statements, assessing financial data and resources, calculating taxes, measuring risk exposures, creating specific financial plans for accumulating assets, and analyzing strengths and weaknesses in financial situations.

At the end of each section in this book you will be asked to help Cory and Tisha Dumont answer personal finance questions. By the end of the book you'll know more about Cory and Tisha than you ever thought you would need to know. Who knows, maybe you will encounter the same issues that face the Dumonts. Hopefully, after helping the Dumonts answer their questions you will be better able to achieve your own financial objectives.

## BACKGROUND

Cory and Tisha Dumont recently read an article on personal financial planning in *Newsweek*. The article discussed common financial dilemmas that families face throughout the life cycle. After reading the article, Cory and Tisha realized they need to learn more about personal finance concepts, applications, and strategies. They are considering enrolling in a personal finance course at their local university next semester, but they think they need more urgent help right now. Based on record-keeping suggestions in the *Newsweek* article, Cory and Tisha have put together the following information for your use in helping them answer their personal finance questions.

1. *Family:* Cory and Tisha met in college when they were in their early twenties. They continued to date after graduation, and 6 years ago got married. Cory is 35 years old. Tisha is 33 years old. Their son Chad just turned 4 years old and their daughter, Haley, is 2 years old. They also have a cat named Freddie.

2. *Employment:* Cory works as a store manager and makes $35,000 a year. Tisha works as an accountant and earns $38,000 a year.

3. *Housing:* The Dumonts currently rent a three-bedroom town home for $900 per month, but they hope to buy a house. Tisha indicated that she would like to purchase a home within the

next 2 to 3 years. The Dumonts are well on their way to achieving their goal. When they were married they opted for a small wedding and applied all gifts and contributions to a market index mutual fund for their "dream" house. When they last checked, the fund account had a balance of $13,000.

## FINANCIAL CONCERNS

1. *Taxes:* Cory and Tisha have been surprised at the amount of federal, state, Social Security, and Medicare taxes withheld from their pay. They aren't sure if the tax calculations are correct.

2. *Insurance:* They are also unsure about the amount of automobile, home, health, and life insurance they should have. Up until this point, they have always opted for the lowest premiums without much regard to coverage. They were a little amazed to learn recently that the cash value of Tisha's life insurance policy is only $1,800 although they have paid annual premiums of $720 for several years.

3. *Credit and cash management:* Cory and Tisha are also curious about the use of credit. It seems as though they receive two to three offers per week for a new credit card that promises a low interest rate and lots of bonuses. They aren't sure if they should be taking these offers or keeping their current credit cards. They are often surprised by the amount charged on their monthly credit card statements, and although they pay $100 each month towards credit card debt, their combined account balances always seem to hover around $1,300. It is common for them to withdraw money from bank ATMs to cover daily expenses, and they usually carry about $100 in cash between them. Even so, it still seems as if they often rely on their credit cards to make ends meet.

4. *Savings:* Cory and Tisha were intrigued by the following recommendation made in the *Newsweek* article: "Pay yourself first." In fact, it was this statement that prompted the Dumonts to undertake a review of their personal finances. They like the concept, but are unsure of how to go about implementing such a goal. They currently have a savings account balance of

$2,500 that earns 3 percent in annual interest. The bank where they have their checking account requires them to keep a minimum balance of $1,000 in order to earn annual interest of 1.75 percent. Their current checking account balance is $1,800.

5. *College savings:* After talking with Tisha's mother about personal finances, it occurred to Cory and Tisha that they should start thinking about college expenses for Chad and Haley.

6. *Retirement savings:* Cory and Tisha both know that they participate in a "qualified retirement plan" at work, but they don't know exactly what that means. They do not currently have an individual retirement arrangement (IRA) or access to profit-sharing plans. A recent statement from Cory's former employer indicated a value of $2,500 in pension funds he left with that company.

7. *Risk:* Cory is quick to point out that he doesn't like financial surprises. Tisha, on the other hand, indicated that she is willing to take financial risks when she thinks the returns are worthwhile.

8. *Estate planning issues:* They do not have a will nor do they have any type of trust.

9. *Recreation and health:* Cory and Tisha enjoy bicycling and hiking with Chad and Haley. They also enjoy playing golf and have considered joining a golf club that charges a $250 monthly fee. The Dumonts are in good health, although they think that Chad will need eyeglasses and braces for his teeth in the next few years.

## ADDITIONAL INFORMATION

### Other Estimated Annual Expenditures:

| | |
|---|---|
| Food (at home and dining out) | $ 6,200 |
| Clothing | $ 3,100 |
| Auto insurance | $ 2,100 |
| Transportation (use, maintenance, licensing) | $ 1,900 |
| Dental and health care | $ 750 |
| Life insurance for Tisha | $ 720 |
| Medical insurance | $ 2,200 |
| Renters insurance | $ 150 |
| Utilities | $ 3,300 |
| Entertainment | $ 2,500 |

| | |
|---|---|
| Taxes (federal, state, Social Security, Medicare) | $15,000 |
| Property taxes (auto) | $ 695 |
| Charity donations | $ 1,200 |
| Day care | $ 9,700 |
| Savings | $ 1,000 |
| Miscellaneous | $ 1,330 |

### Other Assets:

▌ Automobile No. 1

2-year-old, midsize station wagon with a fair market value (FMV) of $14,800

Amount owed: $9,800 (30 months remaining on the loan)

Monthly payment: $490

▌ Automobile No. 2

4-year-old, 2-door coupe with a FMV of $7,800

Amount owed: $0

▌ Household furniture, electronics, and other personal property worth approximately $12,000

▌ Antique jewelry

Tisha received this as an inheritance from her grandmother and has indicated that she would never part with the jewelry. The jewelry has an estimated value of $19,700.

▌ When Tisha turned 21 her father gave her 100 shares of the Great Basin Balanced Mutual Fund worth $1,000. Today the fund is worth $2,300.

### Other Consumer Debt:

▌ Credit card debt (Visa, MasterCard, Discover, American Express, and several store cards) with a revolving outstanding balance of $1,300.

Minimum monthly payments: $32

Actual monthly payment: $100

▌ Student loan debt (in Cory's name)

$8,200 balance

$100 monthly payment

▌ Furniture company loan

$5,300 balance

$175 monthly payment (30 months remaining on the loan)

# PART I: FINANCIAL PLANNING

## Questions

1. Identify which stage of the life cycle best describes Cory and Tisha today. What important financial planning issues characterize this stage?

2. Based on the issues identified above, help Cory and Tisha determine their short-term, intermediate-term, and long-term financial goals.

3. Create an income and expense statement for the Dumonts. (*Hint:* Data for the income and expense statement are presented both as background material and as listed annual expenses.)

4. Develop a balance sheet for the Dumonts. Do they have a positive or negative net worth?

5. Using information from the income and expense statement and the balance sheet, calculate the following ratios:
   a. Current ratio
   b. Monthly living expense covered ratio
   c. Debt ratio
   d. Long-term debt coverage ratio
   e. Savings ratio

6. Use the information provided by the ratio analysis to assess the Dumonts' financial health. (*Hint:* Use the recommended ratio limits provided in the text as guidelines for measuring the Dumonts' financial flexibility and liquidity.) What recommendations would you make to improve their financial health?

7. Do the Dumonts have an emergency fund? Should they? How much would you recommend that they have in an emergency fund?

8. According to the *Newsweek* article Cory and Tisha read, they can expect to pay as much as $100,000 in tuition and related college expenses when Chad enters college and even more when Haley is ready for college. In the case of Chad, the Dumonts hope that he will receive academic scholarships that will reduce their total college costs to about $40,000. Assuming that the Dumonts started a college-savings program today and managed to earn 9 percent a year, ignoring taxes, until Chad was 18, how much would they need to save at the end of each year? How much will the Dumonts need to save each year if Chad does not receive scholarships?

9. How much will the Dumonts need to save at the beginning of each year to accumulate $40,000 for Haley to attend college if they can earn 11 percent on their savings? Assuming that the Dumonts need to accumulate $110,000 to fund all of Haley's college expenses, how much do they need to save at the beginning of each year? If, instead, they saved money at the end of each year, how much will they need to put away every year to meet the $110,000 goal if they can earn 11 percent compounded annually starting today?

10. How much will Tisha's Great Basin Balanced Mutual Fund shares (currently valued at $2,300) be worth when Chad enters college, assuming the fund returns 9 percent after taxes on an annualized basis? How much will the funds be worth when Haley turns 18 years old? What will be the value of the shares when Tisha retires at age 67, assuming a 9 percent after-tax return and no deductions from the account? What has been the actual annualized rate of return for the fund since Tisha received it as a gift?

11. Recall that the Dumonts set up a house savings fund for a future down payment with gifts and contributions from their marriage. How much will this house savings fund be worth in 3, 5, and 7 years if they can earn a current rate of return of 8 percent? How much will the fund be worth in 3, 5, and 7 years if they could obtain a 12-percent rate of return?

12. Assuming an 8-percent return for the current year from their market index fund, and a 27.5-percent federal marginal tax rate, how much will the Dumonts pay in taxes on their investment, either from their savings or current income, this year? By how much, after taxes, will their account grow this year?

13. Assuming that Cory does nothing with his pension from his former employer, and the account grows at a rate of 5 percent annually, how much will Cory have when he retires at 67? If, instead, Cory took control of the money and invested it in a tax-deferred account earning 11 percent annually, how much would he have at age 67?

14. Calculate the amount of Social Security and Medicare taxes withheld from Cory's and Tisha's pay based on their current income.

15. Explain the tax ramifications of Cory's student loan as a result of the Taxpayer Relief Act of 1997. How does your answer change if you learned

that Cory actually finished college 2 years ago? (*Hint:* Review income limitations related to deductibility.)

16. Using the income and expense estimates provided by Tisha, calculate their taxable income using the 2001 tax information provided in the text. Do the Dumonts have enough tax-deductible expenses to itemize deductions?

17. Calculate the Dumonts' total federal income tax liability.

18. Calculate the child tax and child and dependent care credits. What is the Dumonts' final tax liability?

19. Assume the Dumonts' marginal state income tax rate is 5.75 percent calculated on the basis of the federal taxable income. Calculate their state tax liability.

20. Based on the total Social Security tax, Medicare tax, federal income tax, and state income tax liabilities calculated above, how close did Tisha come in estimating their total tax liability for the year? How does the difference between Tisha's estimated tax liability and their actual tax liability change their financial situation? What recommendations would you make?

# 5 Cash or Liquid Asset Management

## Learning Objectives

1 **Manage** your cash and understand why you need liquid assets.

2 **Automate** your savings.

3 **Choose** from among the different types of financial institutions that provide cash management services.

4 **Compare** the various cash management alternatives.

5 **Compare** rates on the different liquid investment alternatives.

6 **Establish** and use a checking account.

7 **Transfer** funds electronically and understand how electronic funds transfers (EFTs) work.

What do Bob Dole and Daffy Duck have in common? Before you start commenting on the uncanny physical similarities, you should realize that Deion Sanders and James Bond, along with Kevin Bacon, also have this in common with Bob and Daffy. Sure, Daffy and Dole might have played a little football in their time, but they never had a license to kill. Give up? Well, they've all been hassled in recent years when trying to pay a bill with a check. At least, they have on the commercials for Visa's check card.

The commercials all happen just about the same way. Each "celebrity" is immediately recognized and fawned over by the store clerk or other store patrons, but when he goes to pay for a purchase with a check (Sanders is buying some posters of himself in a sports memorabilia store; Daffy is buying tons of merchandise at a Warner Brothers store—where his face is on about every other item; Dole is just trying to buy a meal at a small diner in his hometown of Russell, Kansas; and the Steelers' Stadium sound crew is trying to buy a copy of "Who Let the Dogs Out" to play at the game), he's asked for a million different forms of ID, none of which he has. Dole, playing off his loss in the 1996 presidential election, claims he can't win; Daffy—as is his trademark—complains that the store clerk is dittttth-picable; poor Sanders is too shell-shocked to speak; and Bond can pass through security clearances—fingerprints,

PART 2: MANAGING YOUR MONEY

voice recognition, and cornea identification—but can't cash a check. "We just need some ID . . . you know . . . driver's license, license to kill, that sort of thing."

As for Kevin Bacon, he's also forgotten his ID. Playing off the game "six degrees of Kevin Bacon," he runs around and finds some people and manages to link himself to the store clerk through a priest, a doctor, the clerk's ex-girlfriend, and two others. "See, we're almost brothers!"[1]

What saves the day for our beleaguered heroes? The Visa check card. Instead of having to produce ID to pay with a check, our heroes could simply pay with the Visa check card, which works much like a credit card except that it takes the funds for the purchase right out of their checking account. It's better living through plastic.

Needless to say, Sanders's, Daffy's, Dole's, 007's, and Kevin's experiences weren't ideal—or so Visa would like us to believe. Hey, at least they actually had checking accounts with, we assume, enough funds to cover their purchases. What about people who don't have checking accounts? What about people who are unfortunate enough to have major expenses just pop up out of nowhere—like the guy who didn't just run a red light but actually ran his

---

[1]This game is based on the concept of "six degrees of separation," which is based on the premise that if you took everyone you know, and then added everyone they knew, and so on, that within six steps you would have included all the 6 billion people on the face of the earth. In the game "six degrees of Kevin Bacon" you try to link actors through the movies they've starred in to Kevin Bacon. Here you're given the name of an actor and you must think of a movie that this actor was in with Kevin Bacon, or work through a list of other movies to provide a chain of costars that eventually leads to Kevin Bacon. There's even a Web site that will provide the chain for you at **www.cs.virginia.edu/oracle/**. For example, Elvis Presley was in *Speedway* (1968) with Courtney Brown; and Courtney Brown was in *My Dog Skip* (2000) with Kevin Bacon—two degrees of separation for the King and Kevin.

Harley-Davidson *into* the red light? As **Principle 7** reminds us, **Stuff Happens,** so don't forget to expect the unexpected.

Unless you're a psychic, you can't predict the unexpected (it wouldn't be unexpected then, would it?), but you can prepare for it. How? By keeping some liquid funds available. Or, in the case of Sanders, Daffy, Dole, 007, and Kevin, you could at least carry some ID.

Without liquid funds to cover the unexpected and even everyday expenses like a meal in a restaurant, you might have to compromise your long-term investments. For example, you might have to sell your stocks and incur unwanted taxes just to cover your bills. Why ruin your financial plan over some pocket change or an unforeseen expense? Liquid funds are a necessity of personal financial management, and in this chapter we discuss how to manage liquid funds effectively.

Manage your cash and understand why you need liquid assets.

**Cash Management**
The management of cash and near cash (liquid) assets.

## Managing Liquid Assets

Thirty years ago, **cash management** meant depositing your cash in a checking or savings account at a local bank. You could shop around as much as you liked, but all banks pretty much looked the same and the services were limited. It's different today: Sparked by less regulation and increased competition, banks and other financial institutions offer what seems like an endless array of accounts and investments.

Recent changes in the financial system have redefined what a bank is and what it can do. Banks are now providing services that don't look "banklike," and other financial institutions are competing directly with banks by looking more and more banklike. As a result, cash management is much more complex than it was in the past. To understand cash management you must also understand the institutions. The purpose here is not just to show you the underlying logic behind modern cash management, but to teach you how to manage your **liquid assets**.

**Liquid Assets**
Cash and investments that can easily be converted into cash, such as checking accounts, money market funds, and certificates of deposit (CDs).

Cash management begins and ends with liquid assets. It deals with choosing from all the alternatives out there, and it deals with maintaining and managing the results of those choices. In effect, cash management is deciding how much to keep in liquid assets and where to keep it. Why do you need to keep some of your money in liquid assets? So you can pay your bills and your other normal living expenses without having to dip into your long-term investments—that is, so you aren't forced to sell stocks or real estate when you don't want to.

One way to think of liquid assets is as a reservoir, with money moving in as wages are received and moving out as living expenditures and savings aimed at long-term goals. In effect, money moves in and out, and an adequate level of liquid assets keeps this well from running dry. Hey, you don't want your liquid assets to evaporate!

**Principle**

**1** The Risk–Return Trade-Off

Just as with everything else in personal finance, there are risk–return trade-offs associated with keeping money in the form of liquid assets—it's **Principle 1: The Risk–Return Trade-Off** in action. Because liquid assets can be turned into cash quickly and with no loss, they have little risk associated with them. However, because they have little risk, they don't provide a high return. Simply put, liquid assets are characterized by low risk and low expected return. It's really the low risk that's important in cash management.

The funds you keep in liquid assets are funds that you expect to use in the near future. For that reason, you want to make sure that you're not taking any chances with these funds, that they're invested in safe assets. Given the low return on liquid assets, though, you don't want to tie up too much of your money in them. Keep in mind that it's the balancing of the risk of not having enough in the way of liquid assets against return that drives the logic behind cash management.

There's another type of risk associated with keeping liquid assets: The more cash you have, the more you're tempted to spend. Remember your cash budget from Chapter 2? Well, the easiest way to blow your budget is by walking around a mall with your checkbook or a pocketful of cash. Don't worry, though—even if you have no self-restraint, cash management can help. You see, cash management doesn't just involve deciding where and in what to keep your cash, it involves managing your money and staying on your budget.

## Automating Savings: Pay Yourself First

You can easily use cash management alternatives to automate your savings—it all boils down to **Principle 13: Pay Yourself First**. The key here is to start saving early and to make saving a part of your everyday life. As **Principle 15: Just Do It!** points out, the earlier you start saving, the better off you are. Automating your savings is a great way to make saving less of a chore, and what you don't see you can't spend. If you have some of your income automatically deducted from your paycheck and placed in savings, you learn to live at your take-home salary level. Therefore, it's a good idea to have some of your salary automatically deposited in savings.

Moreover, as you know from **Principle 2: The Time Value of Money**, the earlier you start, the easier it is to achieve your goals. Don't put off financial discipline until you're "making more money"—start it today.

Several of the various cash management alternatives lend themselves well to an automated deposit program. Money market mutual funds, asset management accounts, and Series EE savings bonds all work nicely with automated payroll deduction systems. The advantage of the automated payroll deduction plan is that not only is the money withdrawn from your pay before you get a chance to think about spending it, but it's immediately deposited in an account to earn interest. Thus, your money is immediately put to work.

## Financial Institutions

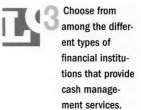

Before we examine the different types of liquid assets, let's take a look at the financial institutions that offer them. In recent years the difference between what you might think of as a bank and other types of financial institutions has blurred dramatically. The changes started with the passage of the Depositary Institutions Deregulation and Monetary Control Act of 1980, which allowed increased competition between banks and other financial institutions. The result of the act has been increased competition and the introduction of a wide range of financial products for cash management.

Although it's become more and more difficult to differentiate between types of financial institutions, they can be categorized as **deposit-type financial institutions**, which are commonly referred to as "banks," or **nondeposit-type financial institutions**, such as mutual funds and brokerage firms. As you'll see, the distinction between these institutions can seem a bit arbitrary.

**Deposit-Type Financial Institutions**
Financial institutions that provide traditional checking and savings accounts. Commonly referred to as "banks."

**Nondeposit-Type Financial Institutions**
Financial institutions such as mutual funds and stock brokerage firms, which don't provide checking and savings accounts.

# "Banks" or Deposit-Type Financial Institutions

Financial institutions that provide traditional checking and savings accounts are commonly called "banks" or deposit-type financial institutions. Technically, many of these institutions aren't actually banks but are, in fact, other types of financial institutions that act very similarly to banks.

**Commercial Banks**   What most people think of when they hear the word "bank" is a commercial bank. Citibank, NationsBank, First Union—these are all commercial banks. Commercial banks traditionally offer the widest variety of financial services, including checking and savings accounts, credit cards, safety deposit boxes, financial consulting, and all types of lending services.

They also have more branch offices or locations than any other type of financial institution. Approximately 15,000 commercial banks have around 65,000 main and branch locations. In addition, they dominate in terms of the dollar value of the assets they hold. The neighborhood locations of commercial bank branches allow depositors to build personal relationships with their bankers, and the size of the overall banking organization ensures that each branch will offer most of the financial and cash management services you might need. It is the convenience of their physical locations and the comfort or security associated with knowing with whom you are dealing that draws many people to commercial banks.

For those who would rather stay home there is online banking, which allows you to do your banking without leaving your home, 24 hours a day. **Online banking** is simply access to your bank and your account through your personal computer. You can gain access by using a standard Web browser (Netscape Navigator or Microsoft's Explorer), through your personal finance software (Quicken or Microsoft Money), or through the bank's software.

There's no question that online banking is a service of the future. In fact, it is estimated that 60 percent of the adults in the United States will have access to online banking services. The question is: Should you take advantage of it? Not only will online banking allow you to transfer funds from one account to another and make credit card and loan payments on-line, but it will also allow you to check your automated teller machine (ATM) transactions, download transactions information directly into your personal finance software, and monitor your accounts so you can avoid overdrafts. The only downside is that it costs something—on average from $4 to $6 per month.

**Savings and Loan Associations**   **Savings and loan associations (S&Ls)**, or **"thrifts,"** were originally established to provide mortgage loans to depositors. The depositors' money was pooled and then lent out to other depositors to use in paying for homes. There are two types of S&L ownership structures: **mutual** and **corporate**. In a mutual S&L the depositors are really the owners of the S&L. They receive dividends rather than interest on savings. With a corporate S&L, depositors receive interest rather than dividends, just like in a commercial bank. This is really a technical difference, with dividends from mutual S&Ls treated as if they were really interest payments, and it shouldn't play any part in your personal finance decisions.

Since deregulation, the services offered by S&Ls and commercial banks have become very similar, with both offering almost identical savings alternatives. Savings accounts at S&Ls many times earn one-quarter percent more than savings accounts at competing commercial banks. However, the rates vary from location to

**Online Banking**
The ability to perform banking operations through your personal computer.

**Savings and Loan Associations (S&Ls), or "Thrifts"**
Financial institutions similar to banks that borrow money from depositors and primarily lend this money out in the form of home mortgages.

**Mutual S&L**
A savings and loan association in which the depositors are really the owners of the S&L and, thus, earn dividends, not interest, on their savings accounts.

**Corporate S&L**
A savings and loan association with an ownership setup similar to a commercial bank and in which the depositors receive interest rather than dividends on their savings accounts.

# In The News

## "Online Banking Beats Standing in Bank Lines"

Now that banks have shifted from expensive software-based programs to the Internet, it's possible—even preferable, perhaps—to do all your banking without ever setting foot inside a branch office. In addition to the usual online-banking tasks, such as checking account balances and paying bills, you can order checks, verify that a check's been cashed, apply for a mortgage or other loan—even buy CDs and investment products.

By 2003, 60 percent of adults in the United States are expected to have access to online services. And "the more they shop on-line, the more they will want to bank on-line," says Thomas Miller, vice president of Cyber Dialogue, a research and consulting firm.

*Banks will do battle on a whole new playing field. In cyberspace, small banks look just like big ones. A fierce fight is brewing between "Net only" banks and bricks-and-mortar institutions. With their lower costs, the pure Internet banks can pay better rates on deposits. For example, First Internet Bank pays 5.2 percent on six-month CDs, compared with the national average of 4.1 percent. As long as you keep a $5,000 balance, the bank will give you a rebate of $10 worth of ATM surcharges a month.* (☞A)

*Traditional banks will counter with their own Net-only accounts. You'll get better rates, but your only access to the bank will be via the Internet, the phone center and ATMs, and you'll be charged for visiting a branch, says Lauri Giesen, editor of Financial Services Online magazine, "Banks recognize that customers who don't use branches don't cost as much." Salem Five Cents already gives Internet customers slightly higher rates on CDs and money-market accounts.* (☞B)

### THE BOTTOM LINE . . .

**A** In fact, the Salem Five Cents Savings Bank, a small bank in Massachusetts, has the fourth-ranked online bank site in the nation based on 50 criteria including ease of use, cost, consumer confidence, and on-site resources.

**B** All this means that if you're ready for online banking, you've got the opportunity to earn a little more on your savings dollars. You also may end up doing your banking with a bank across the country.

Source: "Online Banking Beats Standing in Bank Lines." *Kiplinger's Personal Finance Magazine,* June 1999: 21.

location, so be sure to shop around. The other distinguishing feature of S&Ls is that they still play an important role in funding home mortgage loans. Laws require that at least 70 percent of the loans of federally chartered S&Ls go toward home mortgages. Commercial banks invest the money they gather from depositors in many different ways.

S&Ls also operate on a smaller scale than commercial banks. There are approximately 5,000 S&Ls nationwide, with only around 25,000 main and branch offices. However, from the depositor's point of view, there's very little difference between a commercial bank and a savings and loan association.

**Savings Banks**  A savings bank is a close cousin to a savings and loan association, especially a mutual S&L, and is generally found in the northeastern United States. Most savings banks are depositor owned, basically making them *mutual* savings banks. Like mutual S&Ls, they pay dividends rather than interest to their depositor/owners. Also like S&Ls, their primary purpose historically has been to provide mortgage funding to their depositors.

In fact, in recent years many S&Ls have changed their charter and name and become savings banks. This change is purely cosmetic and is generally done just to allow the use of the word "bank" in their name. This name change by many S&Ls is a further sign of a continued blurring of the differences between the different deposit-type financial institutions.

**Credit Unions**  Credit unions are another type of depositor-owned financial institution. In this case, it's a not-for-profit cooperative made up of members with some type of common bond. A member might be anything from a Baptist, to an employee at General Electric, to a student at a major college. Usually, this membership requirement is the biggest drawback to credit unions. In fact, only about half of all Americans are eligible to join them.

Aside from the organizational differences, credit unions are quite similar to commercial banks and S&Ls, and offer a wide range of competitive financial services. They do have one advantage over other financial institutions, and that's cost. Because of their tax-exempt status as not-for-profit organizations and their generally more efficient, smaller scale, they often pay more than depositors would otherwise earn at a commercial bank.

In addition, they tend to have lower fees and minimum balances associated with their accounts. Their loans also tend to be at favorable rates, again owing to their tax-exempt status. Another advantage of credit unions is their convenience—they're often located right at the members' place of work. For example, a branch of the Virginia Tech credit union is located right in the student union.

## Nondeposit-Type Financial Institutions

Willing to go almost anywhere to make money, mutual funds, stockbrokerage firms, insurance companies, and some other firms have moved into what used to be banking territory and have begun offering services that look an awful lot like those offered by banks. Today, it's possible to have a checking account with Merrill Lynch, a consumer loan with General Motors, and a home mortgage with General Electric. Actually, this banking competition from outside the normal banking industry is a relatively recent occurrence, with its roots in the deregulation of the 1980s. However, the competition has been a two-way street, with brokerage firms offering traditional banking services and banks offering stockbrokerage services.

**Mutual Fund**
An investment fund that raises funds from investors, pools the money, and invests it in stocks, bonds, and other investments. Investors own shares proportionate to the amount of their investment level.

**Mutual Funds** In a **mutual fund**, investors pool their money and give it to a professional investment manager hired by the investment company that operates the mutual fund, and the professional invests those funds for them. Although there are many different types of mutual funds, *money market mutual funds,* which invest in short-term (generally with an average maturity of 90 days or less) notes of very high denomination, provide effective competition for banks. Because these mutual funds are of such short maturity, they're generally regarded as practically risk free, despite the fact that they're not insured.

**Stockbrokerage Firms** Stockbrokerage firms have traditionally dealt only with investments, such as stocks (hence, their name). To compete with traditional banks, though, many brokerage firms have recently introduced a wide variety of cash management tools, including financial counseling, credit cards, and their own money market mutual funds. In effect, they've entered into direct competition with traditional banks.

## What to Look for in a Financial Institution

So how do you choose among all these alternatives? Well, there are three obvious questions you need to keep in mind. First, which financial institution offers the kind of services you want and need? Of course, this requires knowing what you need, but if you do and an institution won't give it to you, why deal with it? Second, is your investment safe? What guarantee do you have that money you deposit today won't vanish tomorrow? Third, what are all the costs and returns associated with the services you want? Are there minimum deposit requirements or hidden fees? Remember that costs and returns vary not only among different services, but also between the same services at different financial institutions. Of course, you always want to have the lowest costs and highest returns.

Once you've answered these obvious questions, you should look at the personal service offered. You want a financial institution that will work for you—one where you can talk to and get to know the manager. The more personal the relationship you have with your financial institution, the more you'll be able to adapt its services to your needs, and the better you'll feel about your investment. Also consider convenience. You want an institution with a convenient location and convenient hours.

Finally, there's no reason why you should limit yourself to one institution. In fact, financial institutions have different strengths and offer different services at different costs. Feel free to mix and match to take advantage of their different strengths and rates and to get the best and most appropriate services you can.

## Cash Management Alternatives

Compare the various cash management alternatives.

Now that we know what kinds of financial institutions exist, let's take a look at the cash management alternatives they all offer.

### Checking Accounts

Many people use checking accounts as a convenient way of paying bills. In choosing between the available checking accounts, it may seem as though there are countless choices, but there are really just two basic types: interest-bearing and non-interest-bearing. A non-interest-bearing checking account is actually a **demand deposit** and can be offered only by a commercial bank. The ability to offer demand deposit accounts is one thing that distinguishes commercial banks from other financial institutions.

**Demand Deposit**
A type of checking account on which no interest is paid.

At one time, the ability to offer demand deposits provided commercial banks with a big competitive edge. Today, with other financial institutions offering interest-paying checking accounts, this distinction lacks real importance. Usually with a demand deposit account, the customer pays for the checking privilege by maintaining a minimum balance or being charged per check.

As you can guess from the name, an interest-bearing checking account pays interest. Another name for an interest-bearing checking account is a **NOW (negotiable order of withdrawal) account**. These NOW accounts are simply checking accounts on which you earn interest on your balance. Although S&Ls can't offer demand deposits, they can offer checking accounts, but these accounts must pay interest.

**Negotiable Order of Withdrawal (NOW) Account**
A checking account on which you earn interest on your balance.

Everyone knows that an account that pays interest is more desirable from a financial standpoint than an account that doesn't pay interest, right? Not necessarily. Although you receive interest on your balance in a NOW account, you generally must maintain a high minimum balance in addition to paying a monthly fee. The monthly fee, of course, represents a cost, but so does the minimum balance. The cost of a minimum balance is really an opportunity cost.

Even though an interest-bearing checking account pays interest, it generally pays less than other cash management alternatives. Because the minimum balance forces you to hold more money in your checking account than you otherwise would (this is called the forced balance), that checking account has an opportunity cost associated with it. Given these costs, an interest-bearing checking account is not always preferable.

To determine which type of account is better for you, compare the interest you earn on the interest-bearing checking account against any monthly fees that you incur plus any lost interest resulting from holding more money in your checking account than you otherwise would. Figure 5.1 provides a comparison between an interest-bearing and a non-interest-bearing checking account.

Because a checking account is one of the most important liquid assets you'll ever have, we take a much closer look at the mechanics of opening one later in this chapter.

## Savings Accounts

**Savings Account**
A deposit account that pays interest.

A **savings account**, which is also called a time deposit, is one step removed from a checking account in terms of risk–return trade-off. With a savings account you deposit your money in the bank and are guaranteed a fixed return on your deposit. When you want to withdraw your money, you must go to the bank to do so. A savings account is less liquid and therefore more risky than a checking account in that you must go to the bank to withdraw your funds, and, technically, the bank could require a grace period before relinquishing those funds to you.

In the past, withdrawals and other transactions would have been registered in a

**Figure 5.1** An Interest-Bearing and a Non-Interest-Bearing Checking Account

| Statement—Non-Interest Checking | |
| --- | --- |
| Service Fee | $2.00 per month |
| 1. Total Cost per Year | $24.00 |
| Minimum Balance | $200.00 |
| Interest Earned on | |
| 2. Checking Account | $0.00 |
| Forced Balance* | $0.00 |
| 3. Opportunity Cost of Forced Balance† | $0.00 |
| Interest Minus Costs‡ | –$24.00 |

| Statement—Interest Checking (4% rate) | |
| --- | --- |
| Service Fee | $3.00 per month |
| 1. Total Cost per Year | $36.00 |
| Minimum Balance | $1,000.00 |
| Interest Earned on | |
| 2. Checking Account | $40.00 |
| Forced Balance* | $800.00 |
| 3. Opportunity Cost of Forced Balance† | $48.00 |
| Interest Minus Costs‡ | –$44.00 |

**Assume that in the absence of minimum balances you maintain a balance of $200 in your checking account. In this case it is less costly to maintain a non-interest-bearing checking account because of the relatively low return on the forced balance.**

*The minimum balance forces you to hold more money in your checking account than you otherwise would. This additional money held in your checking account is called your forced balance. In this case, you must maintain $1,000 in your account, whereas the non-interest-bearing checking account only requires $200.

†Assume that your alternative investment for the forced balance is a money market mutual fund that earns 6%. Thus, the opportunity cost on the forced balance is $800.00 × 0.06 = $48.00.

‡Line 2 minus lines 1 and 3.

passbook, which is why many savings accounts used to be called "passbook" accounts. Today, although passbook accounts still exist, statement accounts—where the customer receives a monthly statement of the balance—are replacing passbook accounts as the dominant type of savings account. Figure 5.2 provides a sample savings account statement.

Because savings accounts are extremely liquid, they don't have a high yield. In fact, up until 1982 the interest on savings accounts was limited by law to 5.25 percent for commercial banks and 5.5 percent for savings banks. The advantages of a savings account are really in the accessibility you have to your money and the ease with which you can set up and maintain the account. The disadvantages revolve around the low rate of interest relative to other liquid investments. Keep in mind that your

**Figure 5.2** A Savings Account Statement

Some savings accounts allow withdrawals to be made with something that closely resembles a credit card.

This savings account allows automatic transfers to be made to your checking account whenever your account doesn't contain enough cash to cover the checks you've written.

# 1ˢᵗ National Bank

## Personal Savings

**Personal Savings**                              1/01/03 thru 3/31/03

**Account number:**        000000007
**Account holder(s):**     Zachary Cohen
                           8142 Jerome St
                           Garcia, CA 41111

**Account Summary**

| | |
|---|---|
| **Opening balance 1/01** | $1,043.84 |
| **Deposits and other credits** | 100.00 + |
| **Interest paid** | 6.45 + |
| **Withdrawals** | 200.00 – |
| **Closing balance 3/31** | $950.29 |

**Deposits and Other Credits**

| Date | Amount | Withdrawn |
|------|--------|-----------|
| 1/06 | 100.00 | Deposit |
| 1/31 | 2.19 | Interest from 01/01/2003 through 01/31/2003 |
| 2/28 | 2.02 | Interest from 02/01/2003 through 02/29/2003 |
| 3/31 | 2.24 | Interest from 03/01/2003 through 03/31/2003 |
| **Total** | **$106.45** | |

**Interest**

| | |
|---|---|
| Number of days this statement period | 90 |
| Annual percentage yield earned | 2.32% |
| Interest earned this statement period | $6.45 |
| Interest paid this statement period | $6.45 |
| Interest paid this year | $6.45 |

This savings account earned only 2.32% interest.

**Withdrawals**

| Date | Amount | Withdrawn |
|------|--------|-----------|
| 3/31 | $200.00 | Transfer to Checking |
| **Total** | **$200.00** | |

*RECEIVE 5 FREE ACCOUNT INQUIRIES/MONTH USING OUR AUTOMATED TOUCH-TONE SYSTEM. AFTER 5 FREE, THE CHARGE WILL BE $.50 PER INQUIRY. AFTER 2 FREE INQUIRIES/MONTH TO A CUSTOMER SERVICE REP, THE CHARGE WILL BE $2.00 PER INQUIRY. FEE IS NOT CHARGED ON CAP AND EXPRESS ACCOUNTS OR ACCOUNTS MAINTAINING MINIMUM MONTHLY BALANCES*

This savings account provides statements on a quarterly basis. If you want to make telephone account inquiries, it provides 5 free per month. After that a fee is charged.

return on a savings account may be reduced even further by the requirement of a minimum balance or a service charge.

## Money Market Deposit Account

A **money market deposit account (MMDA)** is an alternative to the savings account offered by commercial banks. It works about the same way a savings account works—you deposit your money in a bank and have to return to the bank when you want to withdraw it. But rather than a guaranteed fixed rate, with the MMDA you receive a rate of interest that varies with the current market rate of interest. The primary advantage of an MMDA over a savings account is that although this rate fluctuates on a weekly basis, it is, in general, higher than the fixed rate paid on savings accounts. In addition, some MMDAs also offer limited check-writing service of three checks per month.

The only disadvantage of an MMDA relative to a savings account is that it generally requires a high minimum balance, many times of up to $1,000, and imposes penalties if your balance drops below this level. The disadvantages relative to other investment alternatives stem from its relative return in addition to the minimum balance required. In general, MMDA pays less interest than do some of the other cash management alternatives we look at. Therefore, in making a decision to invest funds in an MMDA, you should determine whether this type of account meets your needs. You should then compare all the associated costs with the return. As with other choices, it's not simply what this investment returns, but what the alternative investments return that determines whether this is a desirable alternative.

**STOP & THINK** You shouldn't be enticed to put your savings in an MMDA just because it pays a bit more than a normal savings account. You must also look carefully at the minimum required balance. Many times this minimum balance forces you to keep more in the MMDA than you would otherwise.

## Certificates of Deposit

A **certificate of deposit (CD)** is a savings alternative that pays a fixed rate of interest while keeping your funds on deposit for a set period of time, which can range from 30 days to several years. The longer the time period for which the funds are tied up, the higher the interest rate paid on the CD. Because the interest rate is generally fixed, if interest rates drop you still receive the promised rate. If interest rates rise, the interest you receive on your CD stays fixed at its lower rate. In addition, the rate your CD earns depends on its size. Generally, the higher the deposit on the CD, the higher the interest rates. One downside of investing in a CD is that if you need your money before the CD matures or comes due, you may face an early withdrawal penalty.

With a CD, then, the trade-off is loss of liquidity versus higher return. CDs are for money that you have in hand now and want to keep safe, and are generally considered liquid assets because the time periods involved are fairly short. Maybe you have money now from your summer job with College Pro Painters that you'll want to use in a year for tuition or the down payment on a new car. A CD will hold that money out of temptation's way and return more than will a general savings account.

The rate you can earn on a CD varies from bank to bank and between banks and other institutions that offer them, such as brokerage firms. Interestingly, banks use CDs as a marketing tool to lure new customers by offering high interest rates. If you look around, you can usually find a great interest rate. Sometimes, though, you need to look a little further than just your neighborhood. The interest rate offered on CDs can vary dramatically from region to region—in fact, differences of 2 percent or more are possible. The bottom line is that if you're considering investing in a CD, search nationally. Purchasing a CD from a bank in another geographic region merely involves wiring or mailing your funds to the target bank.

## Money Market Mutual Funds

**Money market mutual funds (MMMFs)** provide an interesting alternative to traditional liquid investments offered by financial institutions. Investors in MMMFs receive interest on a pool of investments less an administrative fee, which is usually less than 1 percent of the total investment. An MMMF draws together the savings of many individuals and invests those funds in very large, creditworthy notes issued by the government or by large corporations.

The advantage of MMMFs is that by pooling investments, they can purchase higher-priced investments and, thus, earn a higher rate of return than investors could get individually. As a result, they almost always have a higher yield than do bank money market deposit accounts.

The interest rate earned on an MMMF varies daily as interest rates change. In fact, the yield on these funds is extremely sensitive to changes in the short-term market interest rates, with MMMF rates varying between 2 percent and 17 percent. Exactly how much more than MMDAs they yield, of course, depends on the level of interest rates. When rates are low, the difference can drop to less than one-half percent. When rates are high, it can be several percentage points.

When you invest in an MMMF, you purchase shares at the price of $1 per share. You then earn interest, less administrative costs, on your shares on a daily basis, although interest is posted to your account monthly. For most MMMFs there's a minimum initial investment of between $500 and $2,000, after which there may be a minimum level for subsequent deposits.

One nice feature of MMMFs is that they allow limited check-writing privileges, although there's generally a minimum amount for which the check must be written. However, in an attempt to lure funds away from bank checking accounts, a number of MMMFs have lifted limits on both the number of checks written and check amounts. In fact, by 2003 more than 50 funds offered unlimited checking. However, these funds generally don't provide canceled checks for record keeping.

Although MMMFs are not perfect substitutes for checking accounts, they do provide an attractive place to put excess funds awaiting more permanent investment. They also compare very favorably with savings accounts, the only difference being that money is deposited by mail and withdrawn by writing a check. They also generally pay more than traditional savings accounts.

## Asset Management Account

An **asset management account** is a comprehensive financial services package offered by a brokerage firm. It can include a checking account; a credit card; an MMMF; loans; automatic payment of any fixed debt such as mortgages; brokerage services (buying and selling stock or bonds); and a system for the direct payment of interest, dividends, and proceeds from security sales into the MMMF. The parent brokerage firm provides the customer with a monthly statement summarizing all financial activities. These all-purpose accounts were established by brokerage firms primarily to bring new accounts to the firm, but as a result of their comprehensive nature they provide investors with a number of advantages over other cash management alternatives.

**Money Market Mutual Funds (MMMFs)**
Mutual funds that invest in short-term (generally with a maturity of less than 90 days) notes of very high denomination.

**Asset Management Accounts**
Comprehensive financial services packages offered by a brokerage firm, which can include a checking account; credit and debit cards; an MMMF; loans; automatic payment of fixed payments such as mortgages; brokerage services (buying and selling stocks or bonds); and a system for the direct payment of interest, dividends, and proceeds from security sales into the MMMF.

The major advantage of an asset management account is that it automatically coordinates the flow of funds into and out of your MMMF. The parent brokerage firm does this with a computer program that "sweeps" funds into and out of the MMMF. For example, interest and dividends received from securities owned are automatically "swept" into the MMMF. If you write a check for an amount greater than what is held in your MMMF, securities from the investment portion of your asset management account are automatically sold and the proceeds "swept" into the money market fund to cover the check. Similarly, a deposit into the MMMF automatically goes toward reducing any loans outstanding and thereafter automatically goes into the MMMF.

Although many different variations of the asset management account are offered by different brokers, they really don't involve any management of assets. The only automatic management of assets occurs when stocks are sold to cover checks that exceed the MMMF. For those with numerous security holdings and somewhat complicated financial dealings, an asset management account may be of value. One advantage is that it provides the customer with a single consolidated monthly financial statement for tax purposes.

In addition to an annual service charge of $50 to $125, there is generally a rather large minimum balance required, ranging upward of $5,000 in stocks and cash. Also, brokerage firms charge commissions on any stock transactions they perform. So, although the benefits of an asset management account may be great, they come with a fairly steep price. The commissions paid on the sale of stocks associated with an asset management account may be much higher than you might have paid if there had been the opportunity to shop around and sell the stock through the least expensive broker.

In short, although these accounts are an interesting alternative cash management tool, you must weigh the service charge, the high minimum balance, and the relatively high commissions on any stock sales against their returns in making your decision. You've also got to do some research and find the lowest cost alternative. The costs associated with asset management accounts vary a lot. If you're willing to do your own research and execute your own trades online, you may be able to cut your costs significantly. As with everything else, a bit of research can save you a lot of money.

## U.S. Treasury Bills, or T-Bills

**U.S. Treasury bills**, or **T-bills**, are short-term notes of debt issued by the federal government, with maturities ranging from 3 months to 12 months. The minimum **denomination** or face value is $1,000. When you purchase a T-bill you don't receive any interest payment. Instead, your interest comes in the form of appreciation. That is, you pay less than its face value, and when the T-bill matures you receive its full face value.

T-bills are extremely liquid investments. When you need cash, all you need do is sell the T-bill through a broker, which is quite easy. They are also extremely safe, having been issued by the federal government. In terms of returns, the interest rate carried on T-bills is similar to that on MMMFs. In addition, your return, although subject to federal taxes, isn't subject to state or local taxes.

## U.S. Series EE Bonds

In recent years government savings **bonds** have become attractive investment alternatives for short-term funds. U.S. Series EE bonds are issued by the Treasury

---

**U.S. Treasury Bills, or T-Bills**
Short-term notes of debt issued by the federal government, with maturities ranging from 3 months to 12 months.

**Denomination**
The face value or amount that's returned to the bondholder at maturity. It's also referred to as the bond's par value.

**Bond**
A type of security that's actually a loan on which you receive interest, generally every 6 months for the life of the bond. When the bond matures, or comes due, you get back your investment, or "loan." What you get back at maturity is usually the face value of the loan, although the amount you get could be more or less than what you paid for the bond originally.

with low denominations and variable interest rates. They can be purchased for as little as $25 each. When a Series EE bond is purchased, its price is one-half its face value, with face values from $50 to $10,000. Interest accrues on these bonds until they are worth their face value at the time of their maturity. In other words, you buy a bond, wait a specified amount of time, and get double your money back.

Series EE bonds are liquid in the sense that they can be cashed at any time, although cashing them before they mature may result in a reduced yield. In addition, they're safe because they're backed by the government. Making them more attractive is that the interest rate earned on EE bonds is set at 90 percent of the average 5-year treasury security rate over the prior 6 months. Thus, the actual rate earned on Series EE bonds, which varies with the market interest rate, is currently quite competitive. If you'd like to get the current rate on Series EE bonds, you can call 800-US-BONDS or check the Web site at **www.savingsbond.gov**.

One of the major advantages of Series EE bonds is that, because they're issued by the federal government, they aren't taxed at the state or local level. Taxes on their interest can be reported annually or deferred until they are redeemed. Another tax advantage of Series EE bonds is associated with accumulating funds for college. Depending on your tax level, they can be exempt from federal taxes if cashed to pay for college tuition and fees. Another advantage of Series EE bonds is their convenience—that is, they can be purchased through a payroll deduction plan or directly from a bank with no fees or commissions involved.

How do they stack up against the other cash management alternatives? Returnwise, not bad; but in terms of liquidity, not that good. Remember, if you cash them before maturity, you

> **STOP & THINK** One of the mistakes many people make is keeping too much in very liquid assets. They view investments in CDs and MMMFs as "safe." In reality, they're not "safe" in the sense that they'll have a difficult time keeping pace with inflation, let alone growing in terms of purchasing power. In short, too little in liquid assets is dangerous and can be costly when an emergency occurs. Too much in liquid assets is dangerous in that you may tie up too much of your savings in low-return investments. As a result, you may not be able to achieve your future spending goals.

may receive a reduced return. Moreover, if you're using them to save money for college, they really aren't liquid at all. After all, the money is for college, not for emergencies.

## Comparing Cash Management Alternatives

Now that you know what cash management alternatives are available to you, how do you compare them to determine what's best for you? We've already compared them in terms of advantages and disadvantages (Table 5.1 provides a summary comparison of the different types of cash management alternatives). But how do you choose the best of what's available? Once we've examined service and convenience, to decide between them we need to (1) examine returns using comparable interest rates, (2) take into account their tax status, and (3) consider their safety or risk.

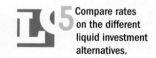

Compare rates on the different liquid investment alternatives.

### Comparable Interest Rates

To make intelligent decisions on where to invest your money, you need to compare interest rates. Unfortunately, comparing interest rates is difficult because some rates are quoted as compounded annually, and others are quoted as compounded

# Table 5.1  Different Cash Management Alternatives

| Cash Management Technique | Advantages | Disadvantages |
|---|---|---|
| **Checking or Demand Deposit Account** | Convenience<br>Easy to use<br>Low minimum balance<br>Insured | No interest or low relative interest<br>Minimum requirements can be costly |
| **Savings or Time Deposit Account** | Higher return than on a checking account<br>Insured | Low return relative to alternatives<br>Not as liquid as a checking account |
| **Money Market Deposit Account** | Relatively attractive rate that varies with the current market rate of interest<br>Limited checking privileges<br>Insured | High minimum balance<br>Pays less than some other short-term investments such as CDs and money market mutual funds |
| **Certificate of Deposit (CD)** | High interest rate<br>Fixed rate—if interest rates fall you still get your guaranteed return<br>Insured<br>Lends itself well to an automated payroll deduction plan | Limited liquidity—penalties for early withdrawal<br>If interest rates rise, your rate is locked in<br>Minimum deposit required |
| **Money Market Mutual Fund** | High interest rate<br>Some checking privileges<br>Limited risk due to short maturity of investments<br>Lends itself well to an automated payroll deduction plan | Minimum initial balance between $500 and $1,000<br>Not federally insured<br>Minimum check size |
| **Asset Management Account** | High return<br>Automatic coordination of money management<br>Lends itself well to an automated payroll deduction plan | Costly—monthly fees range from $25 to $200<br>Not insured<br>Large minimum balance upward of $5,000 |
| **U.S. Treasury Bills, or T-Bills** | Attractive interest rates<br>Exempt from state and local taxes<br>Guaranteed by the federal government<br>Taxes vary with current rates | Low liquidity—less convenient to liquidate than other cash management alternatives |
| **U.S. Series EE Bonds** | Attractive interest rate that varies with current rates<br>Low denominations<br>Can be purchased through payroll deduction or at most banks<br>Exempt from state and local taxes<br>Can be redeemed at any bank<br>Guaranteed by the federal government<br>No sales commissions or fees<br>Lends itself well to an automated payroll deduction plan<br>Can be exempt from federal taxes if used for college | Low liquidity—penalty for redemption before 5 years<br>Long maturity<br>Must wait at least 6 months before redemption unless there is an emergency<br>Interest accrues only twice per year |

quarterly or even daily. As we already know from Chapter 3, it's not fair to compare interest rates with different compounding periods. The only way interest rates can logically be compared is to convert them to some common compounding period. That's what the **annual percentage yield (APY)** is all about.

The Truth in Savings Act of 1993 requires financial institutions to report the rate of interest using the APY so that it's easier for the consumer to make comparisons. The APY converts interest rates compounded for different periods into comparable annual rates, allowing you to compare interest rates easily. However, make sure that you're comparing APYs and not "quoted rates," which may assume different compounding periods.

Once you understand differences in rates, make sure you understand the method used to determine the account balance on which interest will be paid. Is it your actual balance, your lowest monthly balance, or what? The method that's the best for you, the saver, and is the most fair bases interest on your money from the day you deposit it until the day you withdraw it. Fortunately, this is the method most institutions use, but it's still good to make sure.

## Tax Considerations

As we saw in Chapter 4, taxes can affect the real rate of return on investments. In comparing the returns on cash management investment alternatives, you must also make sure that the rates you compare are all on the same tax basis—that is, they are all either before- or after-tax calculations. On some investments part of the return is taxable and part is tax exempt, making these calculations a bit tricky.

As you recall from Chapter 4, calculation of the after-tax return begins with a determination of your marginal tax bracket, that is, the tax rate at which any additional income you receive will be taxed. This marginal tax rate combines the federal and state tax rates that you pay on the investment that you're considering. The **after-tax return** can then be determined as follows:

after-tax return = taxable return (1 − marginal tax rate) + nontaxable return

Here's an example: Assume you're considering two MMMFs. Fund A is tax exempt and pays 5 percent, and fund B is taxable and pays 6.5 percent. Further assume that your top tax bracket is 27 percent and you live in a state that doesn't impose income taxes. Which of these two alternatives is better? To compare them, you must put both on an after-tax basis:

$$\text{fund A's after-tax return} = 5\%$$
(Remember, it's a tax-exempt fund, so it's all nontaxable.)
$$\text{fund B's after-tax return} = 6.5\% \times (1 - 0.27) = 4.745\%$$

Thus, given your marginal tax bracket, fund A, which provides a tax-exempt return of 5 percent, is the better of the two alternatives.

Keep in mind that although fund A may be the better alternative for you, it's not the best alternative for everyone. For example, the after-tax return on fund B for a person with a marginal tax rate of 10 percent is:

$$\text{fund B's after-tax return given a 10\% marginal tax bracket}$$
$$= 6.5\% \times (1 - 0.10) = 5.85\%$$

Thus, the higher your marginal tax bracket, the more you benefit from a tax-exempt investment.

In calculating the after-tax return, you must keep in mind that you are interested in the return after *both* federal and state taxes. When calculating the after-tax return on a Treasury bond, which is taxed at the federal but not the state level, you must adjust for federal taxes. Likewise, when calculating the after-tax return on a municipal bond that is tax exempt at the federal but not the state level, you must adjust for state taxes.

## Safety

You might think that any deposit in any financial institution is safe. Not so. Some banks and S&Ls take more risk than they should. Sometimes that risk catches up with them, and it's your money that's lost. However, some deposits at financial institutions are insured, and some cash management alternatives are safer than others. To understand how safe your investments are, it's necessary to understand how federal insurance works and how MMMFs operate.

**Federal Deposit Insurance** Although most liquid investments are quite safe, federal deposit insurance should eliminate any questions and worries you might have about safety. The **Federal Deposit Insurance Corporation (FDIC)** insures deposits at commercial banks and S&Ls, and the **National Credit Union Association** insures credit unions. These are federal agencies established to protect you against failures involving financial institutions.

**Federal Deposit Insurance Corporation (FDIC)**
The federal agency that insures deposits at commercial banks.

**National Credit Union Association**
The federal agency that insures accounts at credit unions.

Today if your account is with a federally insured institution, it's insured for up to $100,000 per depositor (not per account). For example, you may have $90,000 in a savings account and $80,000 in a checking account, both in your name at the same institution. Your combined money ($170,000) will be insured for only $100,000. However, if these accounts were held with one in your name and one in your spouse's name, both would be fully insured. If you would like more coverage, you can simply spread your accounts among different federally insured banks, and each account at each separate bank receives the $100,000 insurance. This insurance guarantees that you'll get back your money, up to the insured limit, if the financial institution goes bust.

**Money Market Mutual Funds** Although funds in MMMFs aren't insured, they're invested in a diversified portfolio of government bonds guaranteed by the government and short-term corporate bonds that are virtually risk-free. The safety of an investment in an MMMF comes from the fact that it is well diversified and that investments are limited to very short-term government and corporate debt. Because it takes time for a corporation's problems to become so severe that it defaults on its debt, it's relatively easy to predict whether debt is risky if it has only a 90-day maturity.

**STOP &THINK** The idea behind cash management is to keep some money, but not too much, set aside in case there is an emergency. The more you keep set aside, the safer you are, but the money you set aside will be lucky to keep pace with inflation. For example, if you can earn 5 percent on an MMMF, but you are in the 30-percent marginal tax bracket, your after-tax return would be 5% (1 − 0.30) = 3.5%. If inflation were 4 percent, your real return would be −0.5%.

So MMMFs are essentially risk free. The only risk they might have would be associated with possible criminal activity on the part of the fund managers. This risk is eliminated through effective monitoring of the fund's activities, which occurs in the larger funds. Investing in a large, high-quality MMMF is pretty much risk free.

## Establishing and Using a Checking Account

L6 Establish and use a checking account.

There are a lot of alternatives available for cash management, but it would be almost impossible to function in today's economy without a checking account. Most people write checks to cover the purchase of groceries, textbooks, tuition, rent, and pizza. Carrying cash to cover purchases would be too dangerous—checks are convenient and simple. In fact, each year approximately 60 billion checks are written.

We now show you how to open and maintain a checking account. Keep in mind that checking accounts can be set up at all types of financial institutions, not just commercial banks.

### Choosing a Financial Institution

The first step in opening a checking account is choosing a financial institution. In deciding where to open a checking account, you should consider the three Cs—cost, convenience, and consideration—in addition to the safety of the financial institution. Checklist 5.1 provides a summary of these concerns. Remember, in picking a checking account you're also picking a financial institution with which you'll have a financial relationship. Thus, you should consider not only cost, but also convenience and how comfortable you are with the manager and employees.

W11 WORKSHEET

### The Cost Factor

The cost of the account is probably the basic factor in determining what type of account to open and where to open. If you meet a minimum balance level, some financial institutions provide you with free checking privileges. Unfortunately, this minimum balance is usually in the $500 to $1,000 range. If the minimum isn't met, one of a number of alternative fee structures will be imposed. Let's take a moment to examine the fee arrangements for checking accounts.

**Monthly Fee**   With a monthly fee arrangement, you pay a set fee regardless of your average balance and how many checks you write.

**Minimum Balance**   Under a minimum balance arrangement, your monthly fee depends upon how much cash you maintain in your account. If your average balance exceeds a set level, the monthly fee is waived; if not, you pay the monthly

## Checklist 5.1 ■ The Three Cs of Choosing a Financial Institution

| | |
|---|---|
| **Cost**<br>Fees<br>Rates<br>Minimum balances<br>Per check charges | Availability of overdraft protection<br>Availability of all banking services<br>    you desire |
| **Convenience**<br>Location<br>Access to ATMs<br>Availability of safety-deposit boxes<br>Availability of direct-deposit services | **Consideration**<br>Personal attention provided<br>Financial advice that you are comfortable<br>    accessing<br>A banking staff that is out to serve you<br><br>**Safety—The Final Consideration**<br>Federal deposit insurance |

fee. Even if the fee is waived, you still pay the opportunity cost of having your funds tied up in the minimum balance, where they either do not earn interest or earn a very low rate.

**Charge Per Check**   At some financial institutions, in addition to paying a small fixed monthly fee, there's also a charge per check. The trade-off here is that if you don't use many checks, the total cost of this type of account may be considerably less than an account with a higher monthly fee and no per check charge.

**Balance-Dependent Scaled Fees**   Under balance-dependent scaled fees, the fee declines depending on the average balance held. That is, for accounts with small average balances, there is a relatively high monthly fee. However, for accounts with larger average balances, the monthly fee declines and is eventually eliminated for accounts with very large average balances.

When opening a NOW account, which you recall is simply a checking account on which you earn interest, remember that any interest you earn helps offset fees and minimum balance requirements.

## Convenience Factor

In addition to low cost, your financial institution should offer services that make it easy to use. Obviously, you want an institution located near your home—the closer you are to the bank, the easier it is to make financial transactions. However, there are other dimensions to convenience. For example, having access to a cash or automated teller machine, not only at the financial institution's location but also all across the nation, makes it easier for you to access your account. In addition, safety-deposit boxes, **direct deposit** services, and overdraft protection are other conveniences.

**Direct Deposit**
The depositing of payments, such as payroll checks, directly into your checking account. This is done electronically.

**Safety-Deposit Boxes**   **Safety-deposit boxes** serve as important storage places for financial documents and valuables. Smaller safety-deposit boxes can cost as little as $25 to $50 per year, with the costs varying by location and increasing as the size of the box increases. There are two keys to every safety-deposit box. You're given one key, and the financial institution retains the second key. Both keys are needed to open the box. Given the importance of access, it's worthwhile to have your safety-deposit box located in a financial institution close to your home.

**Safety-Deposit Box**
A storage unit at a bank or other financial institution in which valuables and important documents are stored for safekeeping.

**Overdraft Protection**   **Overdraft protection** is an automatic loan made to your checking account whenever your account doesn't contain enough cash to cover the checks that you've written against it. Checks drawn against a checking account with overdraft protection will not bounce. Given the charges for bounced checks, and the hassle of dealing with them, overdraft protection is certainly a good feature. Overdraft loans generally come in $100 increments, so if your checking account is $5 overdrawn, you receive an automatic loan of $100 and now have a checking account balance of $95. The downside is that the interest rate charged on the overdraft loan may be quite high. Although overdraft protection is desirable, it's still a convenience that should be viewed as a safety net against errors you may make, not as a device to rely on regularly.

**Overdraft Protection**
Provision of an automatic loan to your checking account whenever sufficient funds are not available to cover checks that have been written against the account.

Another convenience is the ability to give a **stop payment** on a check. If you want to cancel a check you've already written, you can call your financial institution and ask that payment on this check be stopped. You'll generally have to follow up with a written authorization, and the service involves a cost of between $5 and $20. The

**Stop Payment**
An order you can give your financial institution to stop payment on a check you've written.

stop payment remains in effect for a limited time period, but can be extended at an additional cost. If the check slips through and gets paid while the stop payment is in effect, the financial institution bears the responsibility for the payment.

## Consideration Factor

In choosing a financial institution, you want one that gives personal attention. If you have a problem, you want to feel comfortable in approaching a manager or employee and having that person deal with it. If you need financial advice, is there a knowledgeable person who's easily approachable? Although ATMs are extremely convenient, they don't answer questions, correct whatever's wrong, or work with you when you need a loan.

If you're not satisfied with the personal attention you get, move your account. A smaller institution and a small branch location are good places to look. Because of their smaller size, it's often easier for them to provide the personal attention you need.

## Balancing Your Checking Account

Anyone who's ever tried to build anything with blocks knows that unbalanced objects tend to fall over. Checking accounts can be the same way. If the records you keep in your check register produce the same numbers that appear in your statement, your checking account is balanced. If not, well, you'd better hope that you have overdraft protection. Although it's not essential that your checking account be perfectly balanced at all times, you're a lot less likely to accidentally bounce a check if your account is balanced.

The basics of balancing a checkbook are relatively simple. First, you've got to keep track of every transaction—every check you write, every deposit, every ATM transaction—and enter it in your check register. Obviously, if you don't keep track of the checks you've written and the ATM withdrawals you've made, you can't balance your checkbook. Then, when your monthly statement arrives, check it against your check register to make sure that no mistakes have been made. If you've received interest on your account or had any bad check charges, enter them. Then, try to reconcile what you think your balance is with what the bank says your balance is.

By reconciling your balance with the monthly statement you receive from the bank, you can locate any errors you or the bank might have made. Figures 5.3 and 5.4 show you how to balance a checking account. Many banks provide a reconciliation form on the back of the monthly statement. To determine your balance, begin with the ending statement balance shown on your monthly statement. To this you add any deposits or credits you've made since the statement date. Then subtract any outstanding checks or debits issued by you but not yet paid as of the date of the statement. The difference should be the ending balance on your current statement. If this number doesn't agree with the account register balance, check your math and make sure that all transactions are correct and entered into your register.

## Other Types of Checks

If the purchase amount is very large or you are buying abroad, a personal check isn't an acceptable form of payment. After all, what guarantee do sellers have that you've got enough money in your account to cover the check? In that case, you can guarantee payment through the use of a cashier's check, a certified check, a money order, or a traveler's check.

**Figure 5.3** Worksheet for Balancing Your Checking Account

1. Record in your check register all items that appear on the monthly statement received from the bank that have not previously been entered, for example, cash withdrawals from an ATM, automatic transfers, service charges, and any other transactions.
2. In your checking account register, check off any deposits or credits and checks or debits shown on the monthly statement.
3. In the Deposits and Credits section below (section A), list any deposits that have been made since the date of the statement.

**Section A: Deposits and Credits**

| Date | Amount |
|---|---|
| 1. | |
| 2. | |
| 3. | |
| 4. | |
| 5. | |
| 6. | |
| **Total Amount:** | _____ |

4. In the Outstanding Checks and Debits section below (section B), list any checks and debits issued by you that have not yet been reported on your account statement.

**Section B: Outstanding Checks and Debits**

| Check Number | Amount |
|---|---|
| 1. | |
| 2. | |
| 3. | |
| 4. | |
| 5. | |
| 6. | |
| 7. | |
| **Total Amount:** | _____ |

5. Write in the Ending Statement Balance provided in the monthly statement that you received from your bank. ................................................................. _____
6. Write in the total amount of the Deposits and Credits you have made since the statement date (total of section A above). .................................................. + _____
7. Total the amounts in lines 5 and 6. ................................................................. = _____
8. Write in the total amounts of Outstanding Checks and Debits (total of section B above). ................................................................. − _____
9. Subtract the amount in line 8 from the amount in line 7. This is your **Adjusted Statement Balance.** ................................................................. = _____

If your Adjusted Statement Balance as calculated above does not agree with your Account Register Balance:

A. Review last month's statement to reconcilement to make sure any differences were corrected.
B. Check to make sure that all deposits, interest earned, and service charges shown on the monthly statement from your bank are included in your account register.
C. Check your addition and subtraction in both your account register and in this month's checking account balance reconcilement above.

**Cashier's Check**

A check drawn on a bank or financial institution's account.

**Cashier's Check**   A **cashier's check** is a check drawn on the bank or financial institution's account. These checks can be used by people with no checking account. Because it's really a check from a bank, it can bounce only if the bank doesn't have funds to cover it—which isn't too likely. A cashier's check usually costs you a fee of around $10, as well as the amount of the check. The bank then writes a check from its own account to a specific payee.

**Certified Check**

A personal check that's been certified as being good by the financial institution on which it's drawn.

**Certified Check**   A **certified check** is a personal check that has been certified as being good by the financial institution on which it's drawn. To certify a check, the bank first makes sure there are sufficient funds in the individual's account to cover the check. Funds equal to the amount of the check are then immediately frozen, and the check is certified. The cost for this service generally runs around $10 per certified check.

## Figure 5.4 Balancing Your Checking Account

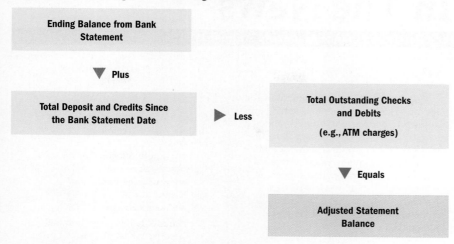

**Ending Balance from Bank Statement**

▼ **Plus**

**Total Deposit and Credits Since the Bank Statement Date**

▶ **Less**

**Total Outstanding Checks and Debits**

(e.g., ATM charges)

▼ **Equals**

**Adjusted Statement Balance**

**This should equal the balance on your checking account register. If it doesn't:**

- Check last month's statement to be sure it was balanced.
- Make sure all deposits and withdrawals, interest earned, and service charges are included on your account register.
- Check your math.

**Money Order** A **money order** is a variation of the cashier's check, except that it's generally issued by the U.S. Postal Service or some other nonbanking institution. For example, money orders can be purchased at many 7-Eleven stores. The fee associated with a money order generally varies, depending on the size of the money order.

**Traveler's Checks** **Traveler's checks** are similar to cashier's checks except that they don't specify a specific payee, and they come in specific denominations ($20, $50, and $100). They're issued by large financial institutions, such as Citibank, Visa, and American Express, and are sold through local banking institutions. The advantage of traveler's checks is that they're accepted almost anywhere in the world because they are viewed as riskless checks. Also, if lost or stolen, they're generally replaced quickly, without charge. The cost to purchase traveler's checks is generally 1 percent. Thus, $500 worth of traveler's checks would involve a $5 purchase fee.

## Electronic Funds Transfers

The area of cash management that's changing the fastest today centers on **electronic funds transfer (EFT)**, which refers to any financial transaction that takes place electronically. With an EFT, funds move between accounts instantly and without paper. Examples of EFTs are paying for groceries with a debit card, withdrawing cash from an automated teller machine, or having your paycheck directly deposited at your bank.

The advantages of EFTs are that the transactions take place immediately, and the consumer doesn't have to carry cash or write a check. They're great for things like paying bills such as insurance premiums, mortgage payments, phone, and utilities. EFTs can tighten up your cash management habits by ensuring that you never carry cash. It's ironic, but you might be better able to manage your cash by not using cash.

**Money Order**
A check similar to a cashier's check except that it is generally issued by the U.S. Postal Service or some other nonbanking institution.

**Traveler's Checks**
Checks issued by large financial institutions, such as Citibank, Visa, and American Express, that are sold through local banking institutions and are similar to cashier's checks except that they don't specify a specific payee and they come in specific denominations ($20, $50, and $100).

Transfer funds electronically and understand how these electronic funds transfers (EFTs) work.

**Electronic Funds Transfer (EFT)**
Any financial transaction that takes place electronically.

# In The News

Kiplinger's Personal Finance Magazine August 1999

## "The Best Banks You'll Never See"

Internet banking can deliver supercheap checking and robust CD yields.

Hardly ever set foot in your bank? Maybe you're ready to take a bold step into the frontier of Internet-only banking. Your reward for leaving the neighborhood branch behind can be supercheap checking and robust yields on CDs.

*Of the six banks that do business exclusively over the Internet, CompuBank of Houston offers the best checking account deal: free checking with no minimum balance and a minimum opening deposit of just $100. CompuBank charges no ATM fees and reimburses you for other banks' ATM surcharges—up to four per month at $1.50 each. Electronic bill paying is free, too, along with your first order of checks. (☞A)*

Because online-only banks have no ATMs of their own, those that reimburse you for the cost of using other banks' machines are the best bet for most consumers. Telebank also reimburses you for four $1.50 surcharges a month if you apply for your account through Yahoo!

Virtual banks can also pass along the benefit of lower overhead expenses in the form of higher interest rates. NetBank's offerings, for instance, often appear on our monthly list of top-yielding CDs. Recently, the bank paid 5.75 percent on a 30-month CD and 5.35 percent on a 6-month CD.

*What's at risk when you bank online? Not a lot. All the banks named here are FDIC insured. Online transactions are encrypted, and under federal law the banks bear the burden of any computer fraud. You can usually access your account 24 hours a day, and telephone customer-service hours tend to be substantially longer than traditional banking hours. You typically receive your statement online rather than on paper—but you can always print it out. (☞B)*

### THE BOTTOM LINE . . .

**A** Check out these online banks; you'll find they have great rates:
Netbank:
   **www.netbank.com/**
USA Access Bank of Louisville:
   **www.usaccessbank.com/**
RBC Centura:
   **www.centura.com**

**B** The real problem you run into with online banks is that there isn't a physical location to go to in the event that you have a problem. In addition, you can't develop that personal relationship with an online banker that you can with your neighborhood banker—in effect, the consideration factor is missing. In addition, you may still need a local financial institution to gain access to a safety deposit box.

Source: "The Best Banks You'll Never See." *Kiplinger's Personal Finance Magazine*, August 1999: 51.

---

To give you a better understanding of EFT and how it affects you, we discuss ATMs, debit cards, and smart cards in the following sections. You'll notice that there's no mention of credit cards here. Why? Because credit cards don't involve the electronic transfer of money—they involve the electronic *borrowing* of money. Don't worry, we deal with them in detail in the next chapter.

## Automated Teller Machines

**Automated Teller Machine (ATM) or Cash Machine**
Machines found at most financial institutions that can be used to make withdrawals, deposits, transfers, and account inquiries.

An **automated teller machine (ATM)** or **cash machine** provides cash instantly and can be accessed through a credit or debit card. If you use a credit card to access the ATM, then the cash is "borrowed" from the line of credit you have with the financial institution that issued your credit card. Because these funds are borrowed, you begin paying usually very high interest on them immediately. The ATM can also be used to access funds held in an account—for example, funds can be withdrawn from your checking account using a debit card.

The obvious appeal of ATMs is their convenience. ATMs never close and are available around the world. To use an ATM, you must insert your card and punch in your **personal identification number**, or **PIN**, which is a four- to seven-digit number assigned to your account. However, as with everything else in finance, there's a cost to convenience. In the case of ATMs, most banks charge an access fee for any transaction. If you're using an ATM not owned by the bank that issued your card, this charge can range up to $3 per transaction. The bank that owns the ATM can also charge you up to $2 for using its machine. At a grand total of up to $5 per transaction, using an ATM can be quite expensive.

**Personal Identification Number (PIN)**
A four- to seven-digit personal identification number assigned to your credit account.

# Checklist 5.2 ■ ATM Security

## Keep Your Card Secure

Treat your ATM card like cash. Always keep your card in a safe place. It's a good idea to store your card in a card sleeve. The sleeve protects the card's magnetic strip and helps ensure that the card functions properly.

Keep your "secret code" a secret. Your ATM card will only work with your personal identification number (PIN). Memorize your code. Never write it on your card or store it with the card. Never tell your code to anyone. And never let someone else enter your code for you.

Do not give out any information over the telephone. No one needs to know your secret code.

Report a lost or stolen card at once. Even though your ATM card cannot be used without your secret code, promptly report a lost or stolen card.

Check your receipts against your monthly statement to guard against ATM fraud.

## Security at Walk-Up ATMs

Always observe your surroundings before conducting an ATM transaction. If you are driving to an ATM, park as close as possible to the terminal. Observe the entire area from the safety of your car before getting out. If you see anyone or anything suspicious, leave the area at once.

If an ATM is obstructed from view or poorly lit, go to another ATM.

Whenever possible, take a companion along when using an ATM—especially at night.

Minimize time spent at the ATM by having your card out and ready to use.

Stand between the ATM and anyone waiting to use the terminal so that others cannot see your secret code or transaction amount.

If you see anyone or anything suspicious while conducting a transaction, cancel your transaction and leave.

If you are followed after making an ATM transaction, go immediately to a heavily populated, well-lighted area and call the police.

## Security at Drive-Up ATMs

Keep your engine running, the doors locked, and the windows up at all times when waiting in line at a drive-up ATM.

When possible, leave enough room between cars to allow for a quick exit should it become necessary.

Before rolling down the windows to use the ATM, check the entire area for anything or anyone suspicious.

Minimize time spent at the ATM by having your card out and ready to use.

If you see anyone or anything suspicious while conducting a transaction, cancel your transaction and leave.

If you are followed after making an ATM transaction, go immediately to a heavily populated, well-lighted area and call the police.

---

The big problem with an ATM transaction is crime. Obviously, most people who walk away from an ATM have money on them. As a result, ATMs tend to attract criminals. This doesn't mean that you shouldn't use them, but you should be careful. Don't use them late at night, don't use them in isolated areas, don't be the only person at the ATM, and don't drive up to an ATM in an unlocked car.

In addition, take care that no one has access to your PIN. Although your liability for unauthorized transactions on an ATM is only $50 provided you notify the bank immediately (it jumps to $500 if a delay of 2 days in reporting occurs and becomes unlimited if the delay exceeds 60 days), you should choose a PIN different from your birthday, Social Security number, street address, or any other number a criminal might logically guess. It simply isn't smart to be anything less than cautious. Checklist 5.2 provides a number of steps to follow to ensure ATM security.

## Debit Cards

A **debit card** is something of a cross between a credit card and a checking account. It's like a credit card in that it's a plastic card you can use instead of cash, but it works more like a checking account. When you write a check, you're spending money that you have in your checking account. Unless you have overdraft protection, you can't

**Debit Card**
A card that allows you to access the money in your accounts electronically.

write a check for more than what's in your account. A debit card is linked to an account, and when you use it, you're spending the money in that account. It's kind of like writing an electronic check, only there's no paper involved, and the check gets "cashed" instantly. When the money in your account runs out, you can't use your debit card again until you make another deposit.

Debit cards, like credit cards, allow you to avoid carrying cash, but unlike credit cards, they also allow you to avoid carrying a big credit card balance. With a debit card, you're spending your own money, as opposed to borrowing money. You probably have a debit card now: Your ATM card is actually a type of debit card. Formal debit cards are gaining more popularity with financial institutions, and some predict that debit cards will soon replace checking accounts.

## Smart Cards

**Smart Cards**
Similar to debit cards, but these cards actually magnetically store their own accounts. Funds are transferred into the cards, which are then used the same way you'd use a debit card. When the funds run out, the card is useless until more funds are magnetically transferred in.

**Smart cards**, sometimes called memory cards or electronic wallets, are a variation on debit cards, but instead of withdrawing funds from a designated account with a bank, you withdraw them from an account that's actually stored magnetically in the smart card. The issuing bank or financial institution transfers funds into the smart card, which you can then use in much the same way you use a credit or debit card. When the funds allocated to your card run out, you have to put more funds into it before you can use it again.

Smart cards perform the same service as credit or debit cards—they can be used at the grocery store to buy groceries or at a restaurant to pay for food. In addition, there are smart cards with issuer-limited usage—they can be used only by the business that issues the cards. For example, Kinko's issues smart cards for copying. You receive a card and "buy" future usage at a Kinko's copying machine. In addition, many universities provide smart cards to students. The student deposits funds in the smart card, and the card can then be used in vending machines on campus, for meals in dining halls, in copy machines in the library, and to buy tickets to university events.

The advantages to the issuing agency are that it receives use of the funds in the smart cards before the transactions are completed and can reduce paperwork considerably. The advantages to the user are that smart cards are convenient and reduce the need to carry cash.

## Fixing Mistakes—Theirs, Not Yours

How can errors occur in EFTs? Sometimes they're human errors—not getting full credit for deposits—and sometimes they're computer errors. Unfortunately, electronic glitches can occur. The first step in dealing with errors is to avoid letting them occur. You may not have much control with computer errors, but you can avoid human errors.

Perhaps the most common human error involves deposits, with most problems stemming from cash deposits made directly in ATMs. To avoid this type of error, never deposit cash in an ATM. If an error occurs and you aren't credited for what you deposited, it's very difficult to prove that you're right.

If an error does occur, report it immediately. Call the bank, and if it's closed, try to leave a message. By law you must write to the bank within 60 days of receiving your statement. If you can't settle the dispute with the bank, write to the Federal Reserve Board's Division of Consumer and Community Affairs, 20th and C Streets NW, Washington, DC 20551.

# SUMMARY

Cash management is the management of your cash and liquid assets. Liquid assets allow you to invest your money while still keeping it available to pay bills or to cover an emergency. Although liquid asset investments are low risk and provide you with emergency funds, they don't provide you with a very good return. The basic idea behind cash management is balancing the risk of not having enough in the way of liquid assets with the potential for greater return on other investments.

The key to meeting long-term goals is to make saving a part of your everyday life. Having some of your income automatically placed in savings forces you to learn to live at your take-home salary level.

In recent years there have been many changes in the field of cash management, and nowhere is this more evident than in financial institutions themselves. Industry changes and increased competition have resulted in a vast reshaping of many institutions. However, we can still divide them into deposit-type institutions (banks) and nondeposit-type institutions. Recently, nondeposit institutions have been offering traditional banking services, resulting in more choices than ever for managing cash.

Given the number of different financial institutions vying for your liquid funds, it's no surprise that there are a variety of different cash management alternatives.

When comparing different liquid investment alternatives, you must look not only at their return but also at how safe they are. In addition, you must remember that the only valid rate comparisons are ones that use similar compounding methods (annual, semiannual, and so on) and have similar tax treatment.

Your checking account is your most essential cash management tool. When deciding where to open a checking account, you should give consideration to the three Cs: cost, convenience, and consideration. You should also keep an eye out for safety—are your funds federally insured?

"Electronic funds transfer" refers to any financial transaction that takes place electronically, for example, paying for dinner with a debit card or having your paycheck deposited directly. The advantage of electronic funds transfer is that the transaction takes place immediately and the consumer does not have to carry cash or write a check.

# REVIEW QUESTIONS

1. What are liquid assets and how do **Principles 1** and **7** relate to this category of asset?
2. Name three characteristics of liquid assets. What are the disadvantages of having too much or too little money held as liquid assets?
3. What factors have affected the alternatives available to consumers for cash management?
4. What is the primary advantage of automating your savings?
5. Give two examples of both deposit-type and nondeposit-type financial institutions. Describe their similarities.
6. Describe and compare the differences among commercial banks, S&Ls, and savings banks.
7. What is a credit union and what are some of its distinguishing features?
8. What is a NOW account? What are its advantages and disadvantages?
9. List three characteristics of certificates of deposit (CDs).
10. Describe and compare a money market deposit account (MMDA) and a money market mutual fund (MMMF).
11. Describe how an asset management account works and what financial services are included. What are the disadvantages associated with this type of account?
12. Describe and compare two common federal government debt instruments: Treasury bills and U.S. EE savings bonds.
13. Explain how a person's marginal tax rate affects his or her real rate of return on investments.
14. What factors should be considered when choosing a financial institution?
15. What are electronic funds transfers (EFTs)? Describe and compare three different types of EFTs.
16. List the features included with online banking, debit cards, and smart cards. For each, identify one disadvantage.

## PROBLEMS AND ACTIVITIES

1. List five examples of financial emergencies that necessitate having liquid assets.

2. Aaron and Ruth Harless earn a combined gross annual income of $42,000 and have $36,000 after taxes. Their monthly expenses total $2,200. How much of an emergency fund should they have?

3. List three short-term goals and/or expenses for which a savings account, money market mutual fund, or other liquid assets vehicle would be the appropriate place for your money.

4. Tony Mercadante has two accounts, one for $60,000 and the other for $75,000, at ABC Bank. What amount of savings is covered by FDIC insurance? If the two accounts were split between ABC Bank ($60,000) and XYZ Bank ($75,000), how much of Tony's savings would be FDIC insured?

5. Your friend Ed has a money market mutual fund account, automatic deposit of his paycheck into an interest-bearing checking account at the company credit union, and a CD from the local branch of a bank that advertises "coast-to-coast" banking. What is the benefit of "mixing and matching" financial institutions and their services?

6. ABC Bank requires a minimum balance of $1,000 to waive the monthly service charge on an interest-bearing checking account. Your monthly expenses total $1,300. What is the annual opportunity cost of the forced balance if the checking account pays 1.5 percent interest and you could earn 4 percent in a money market mutual fund?

7. What is the annual percentage rate (APR) of return on a 3-month Treasury bill if you pay $9,812 to purchase it and receive its full face value at maturity?

8. Calculate the after-tax return of a 8.65 percent corporate bond for an investor in the 15 percent marginal tax bracket. Compare this yield to a 5.5 percent tax-exempt municipal bond and explain which is a better alternative. Repeat the calculations and comparison for a 27 percent tax bracket investor.

9. Calculate the real rate of return to a taxpayer in the 30 percent marginal tax bracket on a $50,000 money market account, assuming a 4.5 percent yield and 3.5 percent inflation. What are the implications of this result for cash management decisions?

10. Describe the features that you have used—or would use in the future—to select a checking account.

11. Ben Chang never seems to have enough change to make copies at the university library. What type of electronic funds transfer (EFT) instrument would help him do his copying with less hassle?

## SUGGESTED PROJECTS

1. Based on your projected monthly expenses (assume 60 percent of your gross projected entry-level salary), how much should you plan to save in an emergency fund? What factors should be considered when determining the actual amount to set aside? Identify the best type of account for this money. Support your choice.

2. Compare your current bank or credit union checking account to at least two others according to the "3 C" criteria. Describe which is the best account for you and why.

3. Consult the Web site **www.ibcdata.com/mfs** for a comparison of current earnings on different money market mutual funds. Visit the Web sites for at least three of the funds to compare features. For example, what is the minimum initial amount required to open an account? The minimum amount required for subsequent deposits? The minimum allowable amount for a check written on the account?

4. Shop for a new liquid asset account appropriate for your needs (e.g., bank account, CD, money market mutual fund). Describe the purchase process (e.g., dollar cost, "paperwork") and your anticipated future use(s) for this money.

5. Interview a stockbroker about the characteristics of liquid assets sold by brokerage firms. Inquire about the fees charged for purchasing these products and the interest rate that can be earned. Request and read available product literature.

6. Review your latest savings account statement. Find the annual percentage yield (APY) paid on your account and compare it to the "quoted rate." What method is used to determine the account balance in which interest is credited? What was your after-tax and real (after inflation) rate of return?

7. Use the formula provided in Figure 5.4 to reconcile the balance in a bank or credit union checking account.

8. Banks were estimated to have made over $5 billion from the fees charged on the more than 450

million "bad checks" in 1998. As a group project, survey several local financial institutions to determine their "bounced check" fee.

9. Describe a past experience using electronic funds transfer (EFT) technology. What were the advantages and disadvantages? What additional ways do you plan to use EFTs in the future?

10. As a group project, develop a chart noting the cost of making a transaction at an ATM machine owned by your bank and at a machine owned by another bank Compare the costs reported by the members of the group. How can these fees be avoided? How do they relate to the "three Cs" criteria for choosing a financial institution.

## Discussion Case 1

Su Chang, 22, has just moved to Denver to begin her first professional job. She is concerned about her finances and, specifically, wants to save for "a rainy day" and a new car purchase in 2 years. Su's new job pays $30,500, of which she keeps $24,000 after taxes. Her monthly expenses total $1,600. Su's new employer offers a 401(k) plan and matches employee contribu-

tions up to 6 percent of their salary. The employer also provides a credit union and U.S. savings bond purchase program. Su also just inherited $5,000.

Su's older brother, Todd, has urged Su to start saving from "day 1" on the job. Todd has lost a job twice in the last five years through company downsizing and now keeps $35,000 in a 4

*Tips from Marcy Furney, ChFC, Certified Financial Planner*™

# Money Matters
## CHECK IT OUT

*Balance your checkbook* **immediately after receiving your statement every month.** *You'll avoid possible charges for letting your balance get too low or bouncing checks. Mark off each canceled check in your register and compare your balance to the balance on the statement. Don't just take the bank's word for it.*

*Enter into your check register any automatic EFTs or bank drafts for next month when you do your reconciliation. This avoids the possibility of overdraft. EFTs are a great time and postage saver for bills like insurance premiums, mortgages, and car payments, but you must keep up with them. A $20 insufficient funds fee for each returned check can cancel out much of the benefit.*

*If you have a computer, consider purchasing personal bookkeeping software. Most programs are very easy to use and are excellent sources of information for budgeting, cash flow analysis, and even tracking debt and investments.*

*If you need to get a handle on your spending or are watching your budget, include in your check register what each check was written for. Many registers provide a shaded line below each check entry for that purpose. If yours doesn't, just record checks on every other line and fill in the*

*reason below each one. At the end of each month, take a few minutes to analyze your outflows. Caution: Entries such as "misc." or "household item" aren't very useful.*

*Examine your bank statement for any charges or maintenance fees and make sure they're actually due. Ideally you should find a bank that charges no monthly fees if the balance is kept at a reasonably low level. Be aware that minimum balances may be calculated in different ways. Some may charge a fee if your balance ever goes below a given amount, while others use an average daily balance calculation.*

*Read the inserts in your monthly bank statement. Even though they may appear to be "junk mail," they're your bank's means of notifying you regarding important procedural and charging changes.*

*Investigate the costs and values of other services the bank may offer in association with your checking account before using them. For example, check printing through a bank is normally higher than through outside companies. Also, investments the bank offers may be limited and carry relatively high loads without giving you the service and level of advice provided by a personal advisor.*

percent money market mutual fund in case it happens again. Todd's annual take-home pay is $46,000.

Su has started shopping around for accounts to hold her liquid assets. She'd like to earn the highest rate possible and avoid paying fees for falling below a specified minimum balance. She plans to open two accounts: one for paying monthly bills and another for short-term savings.

## Questions

**1.** Name three ways that Su could automate her savings.

**2.** What major factors should Su consider when selecting a checking and/or savings account?

**3.** Why does Su need an emergency fund? How much emergency savings should she try to set aside? What type of account would you recommend for her emergency fund?

**4.** Comment on Todd's use of liquid assets.

**5.** Which liquid asset vehicle(s) would you recommend for paying Su's monthly expenses and for her savings for the car down payment? She has narrowed her choices to a standard checking account paying 1.5 percent, a money market deposit account paying 3 percent, and a money market mutual fund earning 3.75 percent.

**6.** Su has heard that some local auto dealerships may require a cashier's check for the down payment. Why is a cashier's check preferable to a certified check?

# Discussion Case 2

Jarod Douglas Jones is a young professional just getting started in the world. He has been having some difficulty getting his checkbook to match his bank statement. Last month all he had to do was to subtract the service charge from his checkbook register and the amounts matched. This month is different. He

would like your help reconciling the problem. Help him find his mistake(s) and learn the procedures for balancing his checkbook each month.

*Hint:* Use Figure 5.4 or Worksheet 12.

**Big USA Bank**

### Summary

| Beginning balance | 6/27 | $3,060.84 |
|---|---|---|
| Total deposits | | $2,508.60 |
| Total withdrawals | | $2,889.24 |
| Service charges | | $4.50 |
| Ending balance | 7/29 | $2,675.70 |

### Deposits

| Automatic payroll | 6/30 | $614.71 |
|---|---|---|
| Automatic payroll | 7/15 | $318.89 |
| Branch deposit | 7/23 | $1,575.00 |

### Withdrawals

| ATM | 7/10 | $30.00 |
|---|---|---|
| ATM | 7/21 | $50.00 |

### Checkcard Purchases

| Big Al's-U-Care-To-Eat | 7/27 | $39.00 |
|---|---|---|

### Checks

| 1071 | $30.00 | 7/01 |
|---|---|---|
| 1072 | $50.00 | 7/03 |
| 1073 | $100.00 | 7/08 |
| 1074 | $45.20 | 7/06 |
| 1075 | $147.11 | 7/09 |
| 1076 | $69.75 | 7/16 |
| 1077 | $27.81 | 7/10 |
| 1078 | $302.20 | 7/12 |
| 1080* | $350.00 | 7/20 |
| 1081 | $20.50 | 7/21 |
| 1082 | $1,599.11 | 7/22 |
| 1084* | $28.56 | 7/23 |

*Break in Sequence

| Date | Number | Payee/Description | Credit | Debit | Balance |
|------|--------|-------------------|--------|-------|---------|
| | | | | | $3,102.65 |
| 24-Jun | 1070 | Dinner out | | $41.81 | ($41.81) |
| | | | | | $3,060.84 |
| 26-Jun | 1071 | Cash | | $30.00 | ($30.00) |
| | | | | | $3,030.84 |
| 29-Jun | 1072 | Video game | | $50.00 | ($50.00) |
| | | | | | $2,980.84 |
| 30-Jun | | Payroll | $614.71 | | $614.71 |
| | | | | | $3,595.55 |
| 1-Jul | 1073 | Cash | | $100.00 | ($100.00) |
| | | | | | $3,495.55 |
| 3-Jul | 1074 | Visa | | $45.20 | ($45.20) |
| | | | | | $3,450.35 |
| 3-Jul | 1075 | Store card | | $147.11 | ($147.11) |
| | | | | | $3,303.24 |
| 8-Jul | 1076 | Gas card | | $69.75 | ($69.75) |
| | | | | | $3,243.49 |
| 8-Jul | 1077 | Cell phone | | $27.81 | ($27.81) |
| | | | | | $3,215.68 |
| 9-Jul | 1078 | Owed to parents | | $302.20 | ($320.20) |
| | | | | | $2,895.48 |
| 12-Jul | 1079 | Dinner out | | $37.87 | ($37.87) |
| | | | | | $2,857.61 |
| 15-Jul | | Payroll | $318.89 | | $318.89 |
| | | | | | $3,176.50 |
| 15-Jul | 1080 | Auto payment | | $350.00 | ($350.00) |
| | | | | | $2,826.50 |
| 15-Jul | 1081 | MasterCard | | $20.50 | ($20.50) |
| | | | | | $2,806.00 |
| 18-Jul | 1082 | Discover Card | | $1,599.11 | ($1,599.11) |
| | | | | | $1,206.89 |
| 18-Jul | 1083 | Cash | | $125.00 | ($125.00) |
| | | | | | $1,081.89 |
| 23-Jul | 1084 | Cell phone | | $28.56 | ($28.56) |
| | | | | | $1,053.33 |
| 23-Jul | | Gift | $1,575.00 | | $1,575.00 |
| | | | | | $2,628.33 |
| 21-Jul | | ATM withdrawal | | $50.00 | ($50.00) |
| | | | | | $2,578.33 |
| 28-Jul | 1085 | Cheap Food Store | | $47.25 | ($47.25) |
| | | | | | $2,531.08 |
| 29-Jul | 1086 | Sears | | $9.16 | ($9.16) |
| | | | | | $2,521.92 |

Visit our Web site for additional case problems, interactive exercises,
and practice quizzes for this chapter—**www.prenhall.com/keown**.

# 6 Using Credit Cards: The Role of Open Credit

**Learning Objectives**

1. **Know** how credit cards work.

2. **Understand** the costs involved.

3. **Describe** the different types of credit cards.

4. **Know** what determines your credit card worthiness and how to secure a credit card.

5. **Manage** your credit cards and open credit.

As any parent knows, when you need Harry Potter or Lord of the Rings "stuff," the place to go is Toys "R" Us, and, as any parent knows, you can spend a lot of money there. As a result, Toys "R" Us issues a lot of credit cards, but not to Lawrence B. Lindsey. Lindsey has a clean credit record, earns $123,100 a year, is a member of the Federal Reserve Board in Washington, DC, *and* was refused a Toys "R" Us, Inc., credit card from the Bank of New York.

Lindsey had two major strikes against him: eight companies had checked his credit history in the last 6 months, and he didn't have a savings account. These "strikes" usually indicate a bad credit risk, but not in Lindsey's case. The credit checks were due to refinancing a mortgage and a change in an equity line account. The lack of a savings account is actually considered by some as the sign of a wise investor. Not only is he a wise investor, but he's a member of the Federal Reserve Board, the agency that manages our economy, sets interest rates, and regulates banks. Hey, if a member of the Federal Reserve Board can't get a credit card, who can?

Eventually, Lindsey was offered a Toys "R" Us credit card—and an apology. You might be wondering what happened to the poor bozo who turned down Lindsey's credit application. The answer is, not much. That "poor bozo" was a computer, perhaps the same computer that's making credit decisions about you.

If you've ever had to make hotel reservations or buy concert tickets over the phone, you understand the importance of having a credit card. In today's economy, where so much is bought and sold over the phone or the Internet, you really need to have a credit card. And almost everyone has one. In fact, Americans hold more than 1.2 billion credit cards of all types—that's over 4 cards for each man, woman, and child—not to mention all the charge accounts they have. There's just no denying that having and using credit cards have become part of our financial culture.

You can't beat them for convenience, but if you're not careful, you can't beat them for cost either. Credit cards can be deceptively expensive. Some even charge over 20 percent interest on unpaid balances. Most people don't consider these interest charges when they're buying whatever it is they've just got to have at that moment. As a result, the total sum of outstanding balances on credit cards in the United States is estimated to be over $500 billion. If the interest rate on this sum were 20 percent, that would mean America is paying $100 billion each year in credit card charges. Unless you want to pay out your share of that $100 billion, you need to manage your credit cards wisely.

**1** Know how credit cards work.

**Credit**
Receiving cash, goods, or services with an obligation to pay later.

**Open Credit or Revolving Credit**
A line of credit that you can use and then pay back at whatever pace you like so long as you pay a minimum balance each month, paying interest on the unpaid balance.

**Annual Percentage Rate (APR)**
The true simple interest rate paid over the life of the loan. It's a reasonable approximation for the true cost of borrowing, and the Truth in Lending Act requires that all consumer loan agreements disclose the APR in bold print.

# Credit Cards and Open Credit: An Introduction

**Credit** involves receiving cash, goods, or services with an obligation to pay later. In shopper's language, "Charge it," "Put it on my account," and "I'll pay for it with plastic," are all opening lines to the use of credit. Credit purchases made for personal needs other than for home mortgages are referred to collectively as consumer credit.

**Open credit** or **revolving credit** refers to a line of consumer credit extended before you make a purchase. Once you use open credit, you can pay back your debt at whatever pace you like so long as you pay a specified minimum balance each month. Today, most consumer credit comes in the form of credit card purchases, but consumer credit involves more than just credit cards. It's actually any type of charge or credit account, all the way from the charge account you have at a local hardware store, to an Exxon charge card, to a credit account you have with your broker, and back to your Austin Power's Titanium Visa card. However, credit cards dominate, which isn't that surprising, given that there are around 7,000 different kinds of Visas, MasterCards, and other cards to choose from. Because of the predominance of credit cards, most of our discussion focuses on them, but the same basic principles apply to all credit accounts.

When buying on credit, you can charge whatever you want, as long as you stay under the credit limit. Each month you'll receive a statement that shows both the outstanding balance on your account and the minimum payment due. You can then pay anywhere between the minimum payment and the balance. Any unpaid balance plus interest on that unpaid balance carries over and becomes part of next month's outstanding balance. As long as you pay the minimum balance every month, the credit issuer will continue to extend you a line of credit.

As you probably already know, the higher the balance you maintain on your credit lines, the higher your costs will be. A number of factors determine your costs. The following sections discuss the basic factors that affect the costs of credit cards and other forms of open credit, including the interest rate, the balance calculation method, the cost of cash advances, the grace period, the annual fee, and other additional or penalty fees.

## Interest Rates

The main factor that determines the cost of a line of open credit is the **annual percentage rate (APR)**, which is the true simple interest rate paid over the life of the loan. It takes all costs into account, including interest on the balance, the cost of credit reports, the cost of all possible fees, and so forth. The importance of the APR is that it's calculated the same way by all lenders, and the federal Truth in Lending Act requires that all consumer loan agreements disclose the APR in bold print. As a result, it's a good place to start in comparing competing lines of credit.

In addition, some credit cards have fixed rates and some have variable rates. With a variable-rate credit card, the rate you pay is tied to another interest rate—for example, it may be tied to the prime rate of interest, which is the rate banks charge their best customers. For example, you may pay the prime rate plus 6 percent. On the other hand, you may have a fixed-rate card and think that the rate you pay can't change. Not so—all the credit card company needs to do is to inform you in writing at least 15 days before changing its rates.

The APR can vary dramatically from one credit account to another. In terms of credit cards, in early 2002 when the national average APR on standard fixed-rate credit cards was 14.10 percent, whereas the variable rate on standard credit cards was 13.39 percent, one bank offered credit cards with rates as low as 4.75 percent.

Rates can vary not only from one account to another, but also over time on the same card. Some rates stay fixed, but others can and will change based on market factors.

Some credit cards also offer low introductory rates called "teaser rates." These initial rates, which last 3 months to a year, can run as low as 0.0 percent, but they typically jump to 17 to 18 percent after the introductory period is over. About two-thirds of the credit card offers sent out in the mail each year have some type of teaser rate.

Also keep in mind that most credit accounts compound interest—that is, you end up paying interest on interest. So, if your credit card compounds interest on a monthly basis and you carry a balance, you could end up paying a rate of 21.7 percent on a credit card with a 19.8-percent OPR.

## Calculating the Balance Owed

Once you know your APR, it's easy to calculate the cost of your credit account. You simply multiply your APR by your outstanding balance. That's easy enough, right? Wrong. The **method of determining the balance** (or **balance calculation method**) can also vary from one credit account to another. The best way to keep the average balance calculation from confusing the process of selecting the best credit account is to pay off the outstanding balance each month. In that case there is no unpaid balance and therefore no interest charge.

The three primary methods used to determine interest charges on an unpaid credit balance are (1) the average daily balance method, (2) the previous balance method, and (3) the adjusted balance method.

The most commonly used method for calculating interest payments is the **average daily balance method**. This method adds up your daily balances for each day during the billing period and then divides this sum by the number of days in the billing period to calculate your average balance. Your interest payments are then based on this balance.

An alternative to this method is the **previous balance method**, in which interest payments are charged against what you owed at the end of the previous billing period, with no credit given for this month's payments. This method is relatively simple, but it's also expensive.

A third method used by lenders is the **adjusted balance method**, which is a favorable variation of the previous balance method. Under this method, interest is charged against the previous month's balance only after any payments have been subtracted. Because interest isn't charged on payments, this method results in lower interest charges than the previous balance method. An example of interest calculations using these three methods is given in Figure 6.1.

There are numerous variations to these three methods. For example, some lenders calculate the average daily balance *including* new purchases; others *exclude* them. There's been a recent trend toward using a two-cycle average daily balance. Interest is calculated over the past two billing periods whenever the entire balance isn't completely paid off. Actually, the interest payments are the same under the two-cycle and one-cycle average daily balance methods for anyone who pays off the balance each month or who carries a balance from month to month.

The big losers under a two-cycle average daily balance method are those who periodically pay off their entire balance. A study by the Bankcard Holders of America showed that a cardholder with a 19.8-percent interest rate who charged $1,000 per month, paid only the minimum payment except for every third month when the entire balance was paid, and continued this pattern for the entire year, would pay $132 in finance charges under the one-cycle method and over $196 under the two-cycle method.

**Method of Determining the Balance (or Balance Calculation Method)**
The method by which a credit card balance is determined. The finance charges are then based on the level of this balance.

**Average Daily Balance Method**
A method of calculating the balance on which interest is paid by summing the outstanding balances owed each day during the billing period and dividing by the number of days in the period.

**Previous Balance Method**
A method of calculating interest payments on outstanding credit using the balance at the end of the previous billing period.

**Adjusted Balance Method**
A method of calculating interest payments on outstanding credit in which interest payments are charged against the balance at the end of the previous billing period less any payments and returns made.

**STOP &THINK** In 1999, the number of credit card solicitations flooding mailboxes increased to approximately 3.45 billion. That's about 22 solicitations for every American aged 18 to 64.

## Figure 6.1 Calculation of Interest on Outstanding Balances

Example: Your credit card interest rate is 18 percent and you begin the month with a previous balance of $1,000. In addition, your payments against your credit card balance this month are $900, which are made on the 15th of the month. You make no additional purchases during the month.

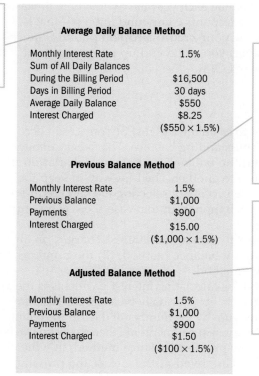

Calculate your average daily balance by summing the daily balances and dividing by the number of days in the period.

**Average Daily Balance Method**

| | |
|---|---|
| Monthly Interest Rate | 1.5% |
| Sum of All Daily Balances During the Billing Period | $16,500 |
| Days in Billing Period | 30 days |
| Average Daily Balance | $550 |
| Interest Charged | $8.25 |
| | ($550 × 1.5%) |

Under the previous balance method, interest payments are charged against the balance at the end of the previous billing period. In effect, interest is charged on the entire closing balance regardless of whether or not payments and returns are made. Thus, regardless of the size of any partial credit repayment during the month, you will still pay interest on the total unpaid balance you had at the end of the previous billing period.

**Previous Balance Method**

| | |
|---|---|
| Monthly Interest Rate | 1.5% |
| Previous Balance | $1,000 |
| Payments | $900 |
| Interest Charged | $15.00 |
| | ($1,000 × 1.5%) |

The adjusted balance method is a favorable variation of the previous balance method in which interest payments are charged against the balance at the end of the previous billing period less any payments and returns made. Because interest is not charged on payments, this method results in lower interest charges than does the previous balance method.

**Adjusted Balance Method**

| | |
|---|---|
| Monthly Interest Rate | 1.5% |
| Previous Balance | $1,000 |
| Payments | $900 |
| Interest Charged | $1.50 |
| | ($100 × 1.5%) |

To say the least, calculating the charges on your balance is extremely confusing. There's one surefire way around this problem: Pay off your balance every month.

### Buying Money: The Cash Advance

Many credit cards allow you to get cash advances at automated teller machines (ATMs). In effect, you're taking out a loan when you get a cash advance—and it's an extremely expensive way to borrow money. In addition, when you withdraw cash from an ATM using your credit card, you begin paying interest *immediately*. Not only do you begin paying interest immediately, but many credit cards charge a higher rate on cash advances than they do on normal purchases.

Cash advances also generally carry an up-front fee of 2 to 4 percent of the amount advanced. Finally, many cards require you to pay down the balances for purchase before you pay down the higher interest rate cash advance balance. Keep in mind that although you can give yourself a big, fat, immediate cash loan using your credit card, that loan comes with some big, fat, immediate charges.

**Grace Period**
The length of time given to make a payment before interest is charged against the outstanding balance on a credit card.

### Grace Period

Typically, the lender allows you a **grace period** before charging interest on an outstanding balance. For most credit cards, there's a 20- to 25-day grace period from the date of the bill. Once the grace period has passed, you're charged the APR on the balance as determined by the credit card issuer. As a result of the grace period, finance charges might not be assessed against credit card purchases for almost 2 months.

For example, if the credit card issuer mails out bills on the first of the month, a purchase made on the second of the month would not appear until the next month's bill and not have to be paid until the end of the grace period—22 to 25 days after that—a total of almost 2 months. Although most credit cards allow a grace period on normal purchases, it's a general rule that with cash advances there is no grace period, meaning that finance charges are assessed against the cash advance from the date it is received.

About one-quarter of all credit cards don't have a grace period—that is, you start paying interest when you make the purchase. If your credit card doesn't provide for a grace period, then each month you not only pay for what you've charged against your card, but you also pay a finance charge on those purchases.

Perhaps the greatest confusion with respect to grace periods comes from the fact that, with most credit cards, if you don't completely pay off all your previous month's borrowing, then the grace period doesn't apply. In fact, the size of your unpaid balance doesn't matter—it could be only one penny. The result is the same: On most credit cards the grace period is canceled if you carry an unpaid balance from the previous month.

## Annual Fee

Some credit card issuers also impose an **annual fee** for the privilege of using their card. The charge usually ranges from $10 to $100, but American Express charges $300 annually for its Platinum card. Although these fees can start to add up and seem like a lot to you if you have a lot of cards, rest assured that the credit card companies aren't getting rich off your annual fee. In fact, over 70 percent of the 25 biggest credit card issuers don't charge a fee at all, and others don't charge one as long as you use their card at least once per year.

How, then, do these card issuers make money? Well, there's the huge rate of interest they charge on outstanding balances. In addition, they charge a fee to the merchants that accept their card. Typically, when you charge a purchase against your credit card, the merchant pays a percentage of the sale, called the **merchant's discount fee**, to the credit card issuer. This fee typically ranges from 1.5 to 5 percent (and in some cases up to 10 percent) of the amount charged.

**Annual Fee**
A fixed annual charge imposed by a credit card.

**Merchant's Discount Fee**
The percentage of the sale that the merchant pays to the credit card issuer.

## Additional Fees

If credit card issuers make money from merchant discount fees every time you use their cards, you'd think that paying your annual fee and the exorbitant interest on your balance would be enough to keep them happy. Of course, you'd be wrong. There are still plenty of additional and penalty fees.

First, there's a **cash advance fee**, which is either a fixed amount—for example, $2 per transaction—or a percentage—usually between 2 and 4 percent—of the cash advance. Remember, that's on top of the interest you are charged from the date of the advance. Actually some credit card issuers charge a higher interest rate on cash advances than they do on normal charges to the card. The bottom line is that a small cash advance can wind up being a big financial setback.

Another fee you might get stuck paying is a **late fee**, which results from not paying your credit card bill on time. By "on time," the credit card company may not just mean a specific date, but also a certain time may be specified, say, 1:00 P.M. On top of the late fee, you might also get hit with an **over-the-limit fee** for charging more than

**Cash Advance Fee**
A charge for making a cash advance, paid as either a fixed amount or a percentage of the cash advance.

**Late Fee**
A fee imposed as a result of not paying your credit card bill on time.

**Over-the-Limit Fee**
A fee imposed whenever you go over your credit limit.

**Penalty Rate**
The rate you pay if you don't make your minimum payments on time.

your credit limit allows. According to Bankrate.com, in 2002, these penalty fees averaged $29, and they're on the rise.

Finally, there are **penalty rates**. This is the rate you pay if you don't make your minimum payments on time. For example, the rate you pay on your balance could rise by 10 percent or more if you don't make your minimum payment on time. In addition, you could also be paying a late fee. Needless to say, you'd better make sure you at least make your minimum payments.

Sounds confusing, doesn't it? Well, it is, and it's made worse by the fact that the terms on a credit card can change at any time. You've got to watch closely for changes in policies and rates. These are usually announced via "bill stuffers." Be alert for the words: "Important Notice of Change in Terms." If you don't watch out, you may be facing a higher late fee and a shorter grace period.

**STOP & THINK** If you pay only your minimum balance, you might be paying for a long time. If you have a balance of $3,900 on a card with an 18-percent APR, and you pay only the minimum amount required by some cards each month, paying off your bill would take 35 years. Moreover, you'd end up paying $10,096 in interest in addition to the principal of $3,900.

The bottom line to all this is: Beware! Before you sign up for that N'SyncUltraTitaniumCard with a $100,000 line of credit and an introductory 0.0 percent APR, read the fine print—you might be surprised. Effective October 1, 2002, the fine print, including all the various penalties, including the penalty APR for late payments, and the permanent rate, must be clearly stated (in print size that a normal person can actually read) on the back of the application. This appears in the "Schumer" box, named after Senator Charles Schumer of New York who sponsored the legislation that requires this disclosure.

**2** Understand the costs involved.

## Your Credit Card: When to Use It, When to Avoid It

Now that you know how expensive credit can be, why would you ever want to use it? There are plenty of good answers to that question, both for and against. Let's take a look at the pros and cons.

### Pros of Credit Cards

Without question, it would be difficult to function in society today without some kind of credit card or open credit. Simple tasks like making hotel reservations or purchasing an item through a catalog would be nearly impossible. Credit cards can be used when making motel or hotel reservations almost anywhere in the world. They can be used not only to make the reservations, but also to guarantee late arrival. In addition, credit cards can be used as identification when cashing checks, for video rental memberships, and almost anywhere else multiple pieces of identification are needed.

It's more convenient to purchase items with credit cards. Not only do you receive an itemized billing of exactly how much you spent and where you spent it, but you also reduce the risk of theft associated with carrying around large amounts of cash. You can't make purchases over the phone or the Internet with cash. Using credit extends your shopping opportunities. Open credit also is an easy source of temporary emergency funds. If you have enough open credit to cover emergency expenses, you don't need to keep as much in liquid emergency funds. Credit, then, frees you to put your money in higher-yielding investments.

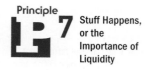

**Principle 7** Stuff Happens, or the Importance of Liquidity

By purchasing an item on credit, you get to use it before you actually pay for it. So, when you buy an Abercrombie & Fitch shirt or a Dixie Chicks CD and charge it, you can wear the shirt or play the CD as much as you like in spite of the fact that you won't really pay for it until you pay your credit card bill. And by using a single credit card to make purchases from a variety of sources, you can consolidate your bills. Many individuals with numerous bills outstanding transfer all these debts to a single credit card in an effort to get better control over their borrowing.

If the price on an item that you intend to purchase is about to go up, buying the item on credit today lets you pay less than you'd have to pay tomorrow. In addition, if you pay your full credit card balance each month, a credit card gives you the use of funds interest-free from the date of the purchase until the payment date.

Many cards offer free extended product warranties and travel insurance. Some give you frequent flier miles on your favorite airline or credit toward the purchase of anything from Shell gasoline and GM cars to *Rolling Stone* magazine or toys at Toys "R" Us. These benefits aren't actually free, because the cards that offer them are more likely to carry an annual fee.

## Cons of Credit Cards

Although credit cards are indispensable in today's economy, they've also caused countless problems for many individuals. Here are a number of reasons why you should be wary of credit cards and open credit. The number of disadvantages are fewer than the number of advantages, but the disadvantages are significant. It is because of them that you must use your credit cards with caution.

# In The News

**Wall Street Journal October 25, 2001**

### Many Consumers Can Cut Cost of Credit

#### by Ruth Simon

Lots of other credit card holders are paying higher rates than they need to. Here are some tips for trimming your credit card costs:

Know how much you owe. There is often a trade-off between the interest rate you pay and a card's annual cost. Bank One Corp.'s First USA credit card division, for instance, currently offers a credit card under the Wachovia name that carries a low 5.5 percent interest rate, albeit with a steep $88 annual fee. That doesn't make sense for someone with a small balance. But for someone with a $4,000 balance, the total charges would be the same as paying 7.7 percent on a card that doesn't levy a fee, the bank says.

Don't be scared to negotiate. If you threaten to move your business elsewhere, your bank will often lower your rate. Mr. McBride of Bankrate.com says you are more likely to get a lower rate "if you're someone who always carries a balance but has always paid on time."

*Arkansas, anybody? Some of the best deals come from Arkansas-based banks. That is because state usury laws limit the rates they can charge to five percentage points above the Federal Reserve's discount rate—or 7 percent at current levels. As a result, Arkansas banks are very choosy about to whom they give cards. But if you can qualify, they are a bargain.* (☞A)

Give teasers a look. Introductory teaser rates—which typically last for three to nine months—can be a good deal for people who expect to pay off their balance quickly.

*Kathy Iwasaka, a stay-at-home mother in Torrance, California, jumped on a 2.99 percent teaser rate offered by J.P. Morgan Chase about eight months ago. Until then, she had been paying about 12.9 percent on her credit card balance of roughly $6,000. "I shopped to find which card would save me the most money while I got it paid off," says Ms. Iwasaka, who had paid off her balance by the time the rate climbed to 12.99 percent nine months later.* (☞B)

### THE BOTTOM LINE . . .

**A** The rates offered by banks located in Arkansas banks began to rise in October 2001 when the Eighth Circuit U.S. Court of Appeals held that state usury laws were overruled by financial services reform legislation enacted by Congress in 1999. Still, Arkansas is the home for some of the best credit card rates around. Does it matter that the bank that issues your credit card is located in Arkansas and you live somewhere else? Not particularly.

**B** If you've got a balance that you can't pay off, you're in trouble. The first thing to do is to set out some rules, then transfer your debt to a lower-costing card. Once you've done that it's time to swear off cards and set up a date for clearing off your balance.

# Checklist 6.1 ■ Why to Use and Why to Avoid Credit Cards

| Reasons to Use Credit Cards | Reasons to Avoid Credit Cards |
|---|---|
| Convenience or ease of shopping. | They make it easy to lose control of spending. |
| Emergency use. | Credit cards are, in general, an expensive way to borrow money. |
| Allows for consumption before the purchase is fully paid for. | Credit card use means you'll have less spendable income in the future. |
| Allows for consolidation of bills. | |
| Can be used in anticipation of price increases. | |
| As a source of interest-free credit. | |
| For making reservations. | |
| For use as identification. | |
| As a source of free benefits. | |

It's simply too easy to spend money with a credit card, because it seems as if you haven't really spent money. Moreover, it's too easy to lose track of exactly how much you've spent. What you've charged doesn't appear until your monthly statement shows up. Once you've overspent, your only recourse may be to pay off your purchases over time. You get stuck paying hefty amounts of interest and spending much more than you'd bargained for.

It's not just that you pay interest on an unpaid credit card balance, but also it's the high rate of interest that you pay that makes credit card borrowing so unappealing. For example, in early 2002 the average 15-year fixed-rate home mortgage charged 5.96 percent, the average home equity line of credit charged 4.62 percent, and the average credit card charged 14.10 percent. At the same time, 1-year CDs paid only 2.74 percent. Banks are effectively borrowing money at 2.74 percent and lending it out at 14.10 percent. That's quite a tidy profit, and it explains why you keep getting credit card applications in the mail.

Any time you use a credit card, you're obligating future income. That is, in the future you'll have less budget flexibility because a portion of your take-home pay will have to be used to pay off credit card expenditures plus any interest on your unpaid balance. If you don't control your spending, you can wind up with some heavy budgetary problems as a larger and larger portion of your income goes toward paying off past debt and interest owed. If this problem sounds familiar, look no further than our national debt. Checklist 6.1 provides a summary of why to use and why to avoid credit cards.

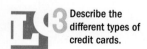
Describe the different types of credit cards.

## Choosing a Source of Open Credit

There are several different types of open credit available today. Almost all of these types of credit involve a card of some sort, and they are remarkably similar to general credit cards. We take a look at these options, after which we discuss how you choose which one is best for your particular needs.

**Bank Credit Card**
A credit card issued by a bank or large corporation, generally as a Visa or MasterCard.

### Bank Credit Cards

Most credit card purchases are made on bank credit cards. A **bank credit card** is simply a credit card issued by a bank or large corporation, generally as a Visa or

MasterCard. Visa and MasterCard don't actually issue cards themselves; rather, they act as franchise organizations that provide credit authorization systems, accounting-statement record keeping, and advertising services, and allow banks and large corporations to issue the cards with the Visa or MasterCard name. Within certain broad limits, banks can establish their own policies with respect to interest, grace periods, fees, and services. As a result, there are dramatic differences among bank credit cards.

Visa and MasterCard are so popular because they provide an efficient system of credit authorization. Being able to check a customer's credit at the time of purchase provides merchants with an assurance that there is no problem with the credit card or line of credit. It has led to the wide acceptance of these bank credit cards both in the United States and abroad. As a result, there are over 7,000 to choose from.

Today many bank cards also offer benefits. These include such perks as rental-car damage coverage, extended warranties, and travel accident insurance, along with frequent flier miles and rebates of all kinds. Generally, when bank cards provide rebates, they're referred to as "co-branded" or "rebate cards." They have a "brand name" listed on the card and provide a rebate such as discounts on long-distance calls from AT&T or GE products, rebates on GM cars, or frequent flier miles from almost any airline.

In general these cards also require an annual fee. For example, in 2002, the British Airways Visa has an annual fee of $50 and a 17.99 percent fixed rate while the Capital One Bank card only has a $19 annual fee and carries a 9.90 percent fixed rate. A good place to check and compare rates is **www.bankrate.com**. Still, if you pay off your balance each month and charge from $5,000 to $8,000 a year, you might want to look closely at these cards. Remember, you have to make sure that whatever benefits you receive are worth more than the card's annual fee.

**STOP &THINK** Even if you're "preapproved" for a card, it doesn't mean that that's the card you'll actually get. After the credit card company reviews your credit history and the facts you disclose in the application, you may be sent a card with less favorable terms. So before you activate your new card, make sure it is what you expected. If you aren't happy, don't activate the card and close down the account.

The one card that is a bit different is the Discover card. Although Visa and MasterCard license their services to the banks that in turn issue the credit cards, the Discover card is issued by a single bank. Not only is the Discover bank card different in that it has a single issuer, it also contains some unusual features: It carries no annual fee and returns to cardholders a small percentage of their annual purchases.

## Bank Card Variations

One popular variation of the traditional bank card is the **premium** or **prestige credit card**. A Visa or MasterCard Gold or Platinum or a Visa Signature card would be examples. Premium or prestige cards are simply bank credit cards that offer credit limits as high as $100,000 or more as well as numerous added perks, including emergency medical and legal services, travel insurance and services, rebates, and warranties on new purchases. MasterCard requires all issuers to provide valuable perks on all its premium cards.

Actually, there are several different card classes from which you can choose. First of all, a card class refers to the credit level of the cardholder. At the low end is the standard with credit limits from $500 to $3,000. Above that are Gold cards, which offer a bigger line of credit, generally $5,000 and up, and provide extra perks or incentives. Finally, as we just noted are the premium cards, generally listed as Platinum cards, which have a higher limit and more perks than Gold. Finally, there are now Titanium cards, which offer even higher limits than Platinum cards.

**Premium or Prestige Card**
A bank or T&E credit card that offers credit limits as high as $100,000 or more in addition to numerous added perks, including emergency medical and legal services, travel services, rebates, and insurance on new purchases.

Many people carry these cards not for the added benefits but for their "prestige." At one time credit cards were available only to a select few and were a status symbol. Today even a lowly college student with no visible means of support can get a credit card. As a result, some people take pleasure in using a card issued only to those meeting rather high annual income requirements.

Another variation of the bank credit card is the **affinity card**, which is a credit card issued in conjunction with a specific charity or organization. Organizations such as the Sierra Club, Mothers Against Drunk Drivers (MADD), the National Rifle Association (NRA), and most colleges and universities have affinity cards. The card bears the sponsoring group's name, logo, and/or picture. These cards send a portion of their annual fee or a percentage of the purchases back to the sponsoring organization.

Although the fees and annual interest rates on affinity cards vary from card to card, in general affinity cards are expensive: They charge an annual fee of $20 or more and a high annual interest rate. Given the fact that, for the consumer, they work just like a traditional credit card and there are less expensive bank credit cards available, what accounts for the popularity of affinity cards? Many individuals see them as an easy, painless way to make donations to their favorite charity or organization. The fact is, it's generally an expensive way to make charitable donations, particularly if you ever maintain an unpaid balance on your credit card. Also, a large part of your charitable donation actually gets "donated" to the issuing bank, and you can't take a tax deduction for the donation!

The final variation on the bank credit card is the **secured credit card**. A secured credit card is a regular bank credit card backed by the pledge of some collateralized asset. If you can't pay what you've charged to your credit card, the issuing bank has a specific asset it can lay claim to. For example, your credit card may be linked to a CD you hold in the issuing bank. In this case, the issuing bank knows exactly where to go if you can't pay off your charges—so long, CD. For the bank, no customer is a bad risk if collateral can be put up. The question then becomes: If you also must hold a CD at the issuing bank, why would you ever want a secured credit card? If you're a bad credit risk, you may not have any alternative.

## Travel and Entertainment Cards

**Travel and entertainment (T&E) cards,** such as the American Express Corporate card, were initially aimed at providing business customers with a means of paying for travel, business entertainment, and other business expenses, while keeping these charges separate from personal expenditures. Over time, however, T&E cards have come to be used like traditional bank credit cards. The major difference between T&E cards and bank credit cards is that T&E cards *do not* offer revolving credit and require full payment of the balance each month. Aside from the prestige they afford holders, their only advantage is their interest-free grace period.

The issuer's only income from these cards is the annual fee, which can run as high as $300 per year, and the merchant's discount fee on each purchase. The three primary issuers of T&E cards are American Express, Diners Club, and Carte Blanche, with American Express dominating this market. There are also T&E premium or prestige cards.

## Single-Purpose Cards

A **single-purpose card** is a credit card that can be used only at a specific company. For example, a Texaco credit card can be used only to charge purchases at a Texaco service station, and an MCI credit card can be used only to make long-distance calls

---

**Affinity Card**
A credit card issued in conjunction with a specific charity or organization. It carries the sponsoring group's name and/or picture on the credit card itself and sends a portion of the annual fee or a percentage of the purchases back to the sponsoring organization.

**Secured Credit Card**
A credit card backed by the pledge of some collateralized asset.

**Travel and Entertainment (T&E) Card**
A credit card initially meant for business customers to allow them to pay for travel and entertainment expenses, keeping them separate from their other expenditures.

**Single-Purpose Card**
A credit card that can be used only at a specific company.

through MCI. These companies issue their own cards and avoid merchant's discount fees. The terms associated with single-purpose cards vary dramatically from card to card: some allow for revolving credit and others do not, but in general, they don't require an annual fee.

If you can use your Visa card at the Texaco station, why do you need a Texaco charge card? The answer is, you don't, and if you're trying to get enough miles for that free flight to San Francisco on your USAir Visa card, you might be better off using it instead. Why then might you want a single-purpose card? Many times these cards are used because they limit credit access to a single company. For example, a parent may want his or her 16-year-old daughter to have a Texaco credit card in case she needs to buy gas but not want her to have a Visa card.

## Traditional Charge Account

A **traditional charge account** is simply a charge account offered by a business. For example, phone and utility companies and even doctors and dentists provide services and bill you later, usually giving you a grace period to pay up. This payment system is a type of open credit account—one in which no cards are involved. After you receive your monthly bill, you're expected to pay it in full. If payment is not received by the due date, an interest penalty is generally tacked on.

**STOP & THINK** There are more than 1.2 billion credit cards issued to Americans alone. To many, these cards are an extension of their personality. That probably explains the popularity of celebrity credit cards. Now if you're a fan of someone, your credit card can say so. You can adorn it with anyone from Elvis and Ol' Blue Eyes to "Hollywood" Hulk Hogan and the dancing Nitro Girls. Unfortunately, these cards generally don't come with an interest rate that you'll be a fan of. Take care in picking a card that fits your financial needs.

The major advantage of a charge account is convenience. Just think how tedious it would be to have to pay for each long-distance phone call, or to pay for your electricity on a daily basis. In addition, there's the benefit of an interest-free grace period and enjoying services before having to pay for them. For the billing company, a traditional charge account is primarily a matter of convenience—it's just an easy and efficient way to collect bills.

## The Choice: It's a Matter of Your Philosophy

In evaluating the many kinds of credit cards available, you'll find that different cards have different strong points. Some cards have low fees and extended grace periods but high interest rates. Although this may be the best combination for some, it may be the worst for others. You have to understand how you're going to use it before you can decide which credit card to choose. Most individuals tend to use credit cards for convenience, for credit, or both.

A *credit user* generally carries an unpaid balance from month to month. Most credit users don't use the grace period, and the annual fee pales relative to the amount of interest they pay annually. If you're a credit user, the most important decision factor is the APR or interest rate on the unpaid balance, because it will be the largest credit expense you face. Because interest rates on credit cards can vary dramatically, shopping around for the lowest-cost card is extremely important for a credit user. For example, in early 2000 when the national average interest rate on various credit cards was 15.88 percent, Pulaski Bank and Trust was offering a credit card with an interest rate of 7.99 percent. Pulaski Bank and Trust is headquartered in Arkansas, but should the issuing bank's location be a concern in choosing a credit card? No: Regardless of where your credit card issuer is located, your card works essentially the same. A credit user should search as far and wide as necessary to get the card with the lowest possible interest rate.

Figure 6.2 What Features Different Types of Credit Card Users Find Important

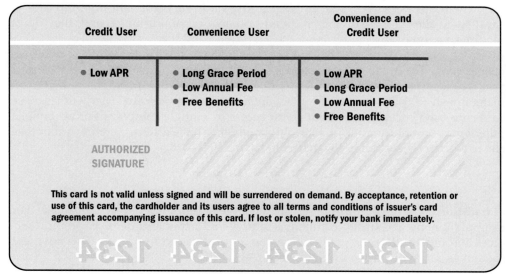

For a *convenience user*—someone who pays off the credit card balance each month—the interest rate is irrelevant. Convenience users should look for a credit card with a low annual fee and an interest-free grace period. The interest-free grace period is especially important because it allows convenience users to pay off their balance each month without incurring any interest payments. Beyond a low annual fee and an interest-free grace period, a convenience user might consider a card that carries free benefits, such as a GM credit card or one that gives frequent flier miles.

A *convenience and credit user* is someone who generally, but not always, pays off all of the balance. For this type of credit user, the ideal card is one with no annual fee, an interest-free grace period, and a low interest rate on the unpaid balance. Unfortunately, finding all of this in one card is next to impossible. Convenience and credit users, therefore, must simply look for the combination of features they think will result in the lowest total cost considering both the interest rate and the annual fee. Figure 6.2 shows what features different types of credit card users find important.

Know what determines your credit card worthiness and how to secure a credit card.

## Getting a Credit Card

For a college student today, getting a credit card is generally not a problem. Credit card issuers see college students as excellent prospects. They may not be earning much now, but their future earning prospects are bright. Also, lenders try to ensure themselves of payment by requiring parents to co-sign on the credit cards or simply assuming that the student's parents will step in if there are problems paying off any debt. Credit card issuers generally set up shop on large campuses by offering free gifts—anything from free or discount flights to free Frisbees—for those who apply.

For a student, getting a credit card is an excellent idea. First, it can be used for emergency funds while away from home. Second, by using a credit card prudently, a student can build up a solid credit history. Is your credit history important? Well, yes, if you ever want to do such things as buy a house, rent an apartment, or get a job.

The first step in obtaining a credit card is applying. The application focuses on factors that determine your creditworthiness, or your ability and willingness to repay any charges incurred. Sometimes the lender may insist on an interview. You've absolutely got to be honest and consistent in the application process. If your answers are inconsistent or don't conform to what the lender has independently found out, your application will be turned down. Let's find out what makes you creditworthy.

## Credit Evaluation: The Five C's of Credit

In determining what makes an individual creditworthy, most lenders refer to the "five C's" of credit: character, capacity, capital, collateral, and conditions. *Character* refers to your sense of responsibility with respect to debt payment. Have you established a record of timely repayment of past debts, such as student loans? Keep in mind that exhibiting good character involves not overextending yourself with respect to credit—not taking on too much debt given your income level. In assessing your character, lenders also look at how long you've lived at one address and how long you've held your current job. In effect, stability often passes for character.

*Capacity* and *capital* work together in determining your ability to repay any credit card charges. In assessing your *capacity*, lenders look to both your current income level and your current level of borrowing—that is, lenders are concerned with your level of nonobligated income. Most financial advisors suggest that your total debt payments, including mortgage payments, should account for less than 36 percent of your gross pay.

*Capital* refers to the size of your financial holdings or investment portfolio. Obviously, the more you have in savings, the more creditworthy you are. The question answered by looking at your capital is, given your financial holdings, is your income sufficient to provide for the debt you've already incurred? The larger your nonobligated annual income (capacity) and the value of your investment portfolio (capital), the more creditworthy you are.

*Collateral* refers to assets or property offered as security to obtain credit. If you were to default, the property, perhaps a car or a piece of land, would be sold, and the proceeds from the sale would go to repay the debt. Obviously, the more the collateral is worth, the more creditworthy you are.

The last of the five C's is *conditions*. Conditions refer to the impact the current economic environment may have on your ability to repay any borrowing. You may appear to be strong in all other aspects, but if you're laid off because of a downswing in the economy, you might not be able to meet your obligations.

## Credit Evaluation: The Credit Bureau

Credit card issuers verify the information you put down on your application and get information about your character and financial situation through a credit report supplied from a credit bureau. A **credit bureau** is a private organization that maintains credit information on individuals, which it allows subscribers to access for a fee. The credit bureau accumulates its credit data from information provided by subscribers, from public court records, and from information the individual has forwarded to the credit bureau. Information is collected by local credit bureaus, which then share it with one of the three national credit bureaus: Experian (formerly TRW), Trans Union, or Equifax Credit Information Services.

Your credit report contains only information regarding your financial situation and dealings. It contains no information about your personal lifestyle. Also, a credit

**Credit Bureau**
A company that gathers information on consumers' financial history, including how quickly they have paid bills and whether they have been delinquent on bills in the past. The company summarizes this information and sells it to customers.

## Table 6.1   Information Contained in Your Credit Report

*Personal Information:*  Age, Social Security number, current address, previous address.

*Employment Record:*  Current and past employers and what you do for a living.

*Your Credit History:*  The number of bank cards and charge cards you have and for how long you've had them, your payment history including the largest amount you've ever owed, the current amount owed, and the number of times payments have been past due.

*Your Public Financial History:*  Bankruptcies (carried for 10 years), liens, criminal convictions, and court action including judgments awarded to creditors.

*Past Inquiries Regarding Your Credit Report:* A record of everyone who has seen your credit report over the past 2 years.

---

**STOP &THINK**  Many credit cards have extremely low annual income requirements—as low as $8,000. Although you may be able to qualify for a credit card at this level of income, if you get one, you should use it with the utmost discretion.

bureau doesn't make credit decisions: It merely supplies data that a bank or S&L uses to make a credit decision. Table 6.1 provides a listing of what's typically contained in a credit report, and Figure 6.3 shows a sample credit report.

### Determining Creditworthiness—Credit Scoring

**Credit Scoring**
The numerical evaluation of credit applicants based on their answers to a simple set of questions.

Once lenders have all your credit information, how do they evaluate it to determine your creditworthiness? Although a few look at each application individually and make a judgment call, it's more common that your credit application will be evaluated using credit scoring. **Credit scoring** involves the numerical evaluation or "scoring" of applicants based on their answers to a simple set of questions. This score is then evaluated according to a predetermined standard. If your score is up to the acceptance standard, you get credit. The major advantage of credit scoring is that it's relatively inexpensive. Once the standards are set, the evaluation can be done automatically by a computer.

The techniques used for constructing credit-scoring indexes range from the simple to the sophisticated. Figure 6.4 provides a sample credit "scorecard." This scorecard is somewhat simplified in that actual credit-scoring systems can involve evaluation of 20 or 30 different factors. The credit card issuer then assigns a minimum cutoff score.

You'll notice in Figure 6.4 that age is used as a discriminating factor in credit scoring. Although the Equal Credit Opportunity Act prohibits lenders from discriminating against borrowers aged 62 or older, anyone younger can be penalized or rewarded depending on age. Also, bankruptcy remains a mark against you for a period of 10 years after it occurs.

Credit scoring is efficient and relatively inexpensive for the lender, but it can also involve a lack of common sense and judgment that hurts the borrower. Remember the opening vignette, when Lawrence B. Lindsey's application for a Toys "R" Us credit card was rejected. Credit scoring doesn't always work perfectly.

Your creditworthiness determines not only whether you qualify for credit, but what interest rate you'll be offered. Many credit card issuers determine what rate to offer credit card holders depending on their riskiness. The more risky customers pay higher rates. In effect, there's a tiered pricing system in credit cards.

**STOP &THINK**  For most people, a bad credit rating is a problem. However, if your inability to control your spending caused your credit-rating problem, then your lack of credit may actually keep you out of further trouble by helping to curb your spending habits. Being without credit may not be enjoyable, but it may be the best thing for you.

# Figure 6.3 A Sample Credit Report

Make sure you are not being confused with someone else with a similar name or Social Security number.

Make sure all information is accurate and let the credit bureau know if there are any errors.

Any adverse information in these accounts is listed >in brackets.<

Any time you dispute an item Trans Union will conduct an investigation and then inform you of its findings. In this case there were four disputed items reported on.

Make sure all damaging information has been removed after a disputed issue has been resolved.

Whenever an inquiry is made concerning your creditworthiness, it appears. In this case two inquiries were made.

---

**TRANS UNION**
PO BOX 123456
WICHITA, KS 12345-1234

YOUR TRANS UNION FILE NUMBER: 97ZZ0093-001
PAGE 1 OF 2 (INTL USE: CC    08IN 01)
DATE THIS REPORT PRINTED: 01/10/97

SOCIAL SECURITY NUMBER: 123-12-1234
BIRTH DATE:         09/61
YOU HAVE BEEN IN OUR FILES SINCE: 07/83

CONSUMER REPORT FOR:

*****
ASTEB, JAMES, ROBERT
2 RR 3 BOX 22
GARY, IN 46162

FORMER ADDRESSES REPORTED:

232 S EMERSON AV, GREENVILLE, IN 46143

INVESTIGATION RESULTS

WE HAVE COMPLETED OUR INVESTIGATION OF THE ITEM(S) YOU DISPUTED. OUR FINDINGS
ARE SUMMARIZED AS FOLLOWS:

| ITEM | DESCRIPTION | RESULTS |
|------|-------------|---------|
| ATT UNIV CRD | # 4324324324324329 | VERIFIED AS ACCURATE |
| STAR BANK | # 4897654020253144 | DELETED |
| FIRST CARD | # 4321321321321 | NEW INFORMATION BELOW |
| DISCOVER CRD | # 32132137281372819 | VERIFIED AS ACCURATE |

ANY CORRECTIONS TO YOUR IDENTIFICATION REQUESTED BY YOU HAVE BEEN MADE AS NOTED
ABOVE. IF OUR INVESTIGATION HAS NOT RESOLVED YOUR DISPUTE, YOU MAY ADD A 100
WORD CONSUMER STATEMENT TO YOUR REPORT. YOUR UPDATED CREDIT INFORMATION
FOLLOWS:

YOUR CREDIT INFORMATION

THE FOLLOWING ACCOUNTS CONTAIN INFORMATION WHICH SOME CREDITORS MAY CONSIDER TO
BE ADVERSE.  THE ADVERSE INFORMATION IN THESE ACCOUNTS HAS BEEN PRINTED IN
>BRACKETS< FOR YOUR CONVENIENCE, TO HELP YOU UNDERSTAND YOUR REPORT.  THEY ARE
NOT BRACKETED THIS WAY FOR CREDITORS. (NOTE: THE ACCOUNT # MAY BE SCRAMBLED BY
THE CREDITOR FOR YOUR PROTECTION).

ATT UNIV CRD - # 4324324324324329          REVOLVING ACCOUNT
>PROFIT AND LOSS WRITEOFF<                  CREDIT CARD
    VERIF'D  12/96   BALANCE:      $556     INDIVIDUAL ACCOUNT
    OPENED   08/90   MOST OWED:   $2200     CREDIT LIMIT:     $2200
    CLOSED   10/93   PAST DUE:     $556<
    >STATUS AS OF 10/93: CHARGED OFF AS BAD DEBT<

REPORT ON ASTEB, JAMES, ROBERT                             PAGE 2 OF 2
SOCIAL SECURITY NUMBER: 123-12-1234      TRANS UNION FILE NUMBER: 97ZZ0093-001

FIRST CARD   - # 4321321321321            REVOLVING ACCOUNT
>CANCELLED BY CREDIT GRANTOR<              CREDIT CARD
    VERIF'D  01/97   BALANCE:     $3721    INDIVIDUAL ACCOUNT
    OPENED   04/91   MOST OWED:   $4999    PAY TERMS:  MONTHLY $77
    CLOSED   09/93                         CREDIT LIMIT:    $5000
    >IN PRIOR 14 MONTHS FROM DATE CLOSED  1 TIME 60 DAYS LATE<
    STATUS AS OF 09/93: PAID AS AGREED

DISCOVER CRD - # 32132137281372819        REVOLVING ACCOUNT
>CANCELLED BY CREDIT GRANTOR<              CREDIT CARD
    VERIF'D  12/96   BALANCE:     $1413    INDIVIDUAL ACCOUNT
    OPENED   10/89   MOST OWED:   $2065    PAY TERMS:  MINIMUM $40
    CLOSED   09/92                         CREDIT LIMIT:    $2500
    >IN PRIOR 24 MONTHS FROM DATE CLOSED  2 TIMES 60 DAYS LATE<
    STATUS AS OF 09/92: PAID AS AGREED

THE FOLLOWING ACCOUNTS ARE REPORTED WITH NO ADVERSE INFORMATION

AMERICAN EXP - # 3213212121300            OPEN ACCOUNT
ACCOUNT CLOSED                            CREDIT CARD
    UPDATED  12/96   BALANCE:      $67     INDIVIDUAL ACCOUNT
    OPENED   03/91   MOST OWED:     $67
    CLOSED   03/95
    IN PRIOR 48 MONTHS FROM DATE CLOSED NEVER LATE
    STATUS AS OF 03/95: PAID AS AGREED

L S AYRES    - # 321321321                REVOLVING ACCOUNT
    UPDATED  04/92   BALANCE:       $0     JOINT ACCOUNT
    OPENED   07/83   MOST OWED:      $0
    IN PRIOR 25 MONTHS FROM LAST UPDATE NEVER LATE
    STATUS AS OF 04/92: NO RATING

THE FOLLOWING COMPANIES HAVE RECEIVED YOUR CREDIT REPORT.  THEIR INQUIRIES
REMAIN ON YOUR CREDIT REPORT FOR TWO YEARS.  (NOTE: "CONSUM DISCL" REFERS TO
TRANS UNION CONSUMER RELATIONS AND ARE NOT VIEWED BY CREDITORS).

              INQUIRY TYPE                           INQUIRY TYPE
CONSUM DISCL 12/17/96  INDIVIDUAL       CONS ACPT    09/23/96  INDIVIDUAL
CONSUM DISCL 09/10/96  INDIVIDUAL       AM STAR FNCL 07/12/96  INDIVIDUAL

THE FOLLOWING COMPANIES DID NOT GET YOUR FULL REPORT, BUT INSTEAD RECEIVED ONLY
YOUR NAME AND ADDRESS INFORMATION FOR THE PURPOSE OF MAKING YOU A CREDIT OFFER,
OR TO REVIEW YOUR ACCOUNT. THEIR INQUIRIES ARE NOT SEEN BY CREDITORS.

CHASE NA    08/96    FIRST CARD   08/96    FIRST CARD    09/96

IF YOU BELIEVE ANY OF THE INFORMATION IN YOUR CREDIT REPORT IS INCORRECT,
PLEASE LET US KNOW.  PLEASE ADDRESS ALL CORRESPONDENCE REGARDING YOUR CREDIT
REPORT TO:

TRANS UNION CONSUMER RELATIONS
PO BOX 123456
WICHITA, KS 12345-1234
1-800-123-1234

Source: Trans Union Corporation, Chicago, Illinois, 1997. Used by permission.

## Figure 6.4 Sample Credit "Scorecard"

| 1. Annual Income | POINTS |
|---|---|
| Less than $15,000 | 2 |
| $15,001-$25,000 | 5 |
| $25,001-$35,000 | 10 |
| $35,001-$45,000 | 16 |
| $45,001-$60,000 | 21 |
| Over $60,000 | 24 |

| 2. Length of Residence | |
|---|---|
| Less than 1 year | 0 |
| 1-2 years | 3 |
| 3-5 years | 9 |
| 6-10 years | 13 |
| Over 10 years | 17 |

| 3. Length of Time on Current Job | |
|---|---|
| Less than 6 months | 0 |
| 6 months to 2 years | 3 |
| 2-5 years | 10 |
| More than 5 years | 18 |

| 4. Housing | |
|---|---|
| Rent | 1 |
| Home with mortgage | 12 |
| Own home | 18 |
| Other | 0 |

| 5. Employment | |
|---|---|
| Self-employed | -5 |
| Unskilled manual | 0 |
| Skilled manual | 3 |
| Clerical | 6 |
| Managerial | 12 |
| Professional | 18 |

| 6. Age | POINTS |
|---|---|
| Under 20 | -5 |
| 20-21 | -1 |
| 22-24 | 3 |
| 25-30 | 7 |
| 31-40 | 10 |
| 41-50 | 14 |
| Over 50 | 12 |

| 7. Bank Accounts | |
|---|---|
| None | -8 |
| 1 | 0 |
| 2 | 6 |
| More than 2 | 8 |

| 8. Number of Credit Cards | |
|---|---|
| None | -4 |
| 1-4 | 10 |
| Over 4 | -4 |

| 9. Telephone | |
|---|---|
| Yes | 5 |
| No | -3 |

| 10. Credit History | |
|---|---|
| No history | -4 |
| Bankruptcy | -15 |
| Excellent | 20 |

## Consumer Credit Rights

As you might expect, there are a number of federal laws aimed at protecting you if you have a complaint about credit. Of course, the easiest way to resolve a credit complaint is to take it directly to the creditor. If that doesn't work, these laws set up a framework for resolving complaints.

### The Credit Bureau and Your Rights

Because your credit report is so important, Congress passed the Fair Credit Reporting Act (FCRA) in 1971 and subsequently amended it to help ensure that consumers' credit reports are accurate. Under the FCRA you have the right to view your credit report. It's a good idea to do this every 2 to 3 years. In fact, approximately 70 percent of all Americans have at least one negative remark in their credit reports. Moreover, almost half of all credit reports contain inaccurate, misleading, or obsolete material.

**Table 6.2** National Credit Bureaus

| Equifax Credit Information Services www.equifax.com | Experian (formerly TRW) www.experian.com | Trans Union www.tuc.com |
|---|---|---|
| Report Fraud | Report Fraud | Report Fraud |
| 800-525-6285 | Experian Consumer Assistance P.O. Box 949 Allen, Texas 75013-0949 888-397-3742 | 800-916-8800 |
| Get a Copy of Your Report | Get a Copy of Your Report | Get a Copy of Your Report |
| P.O. Box 740241 Atlanta, GA 30374-0241 800-685-1111 | P.O. Box 949 Allen, Texas 75013-0949 888-397-3742 | P.O. Box 390 Springfield, PA 19064-0390 800-916-8800 |
| Dispute Something in Your Report | Dispute Something in Your Report | Dispute Something in Your Report |
| P.O. Box 740256 Atlanta, GA 30374-0256 800-216-1035 800-685-5000 | P.O. Box 949 Allen, Texas 75013-0949 888-397-3742 | P.O. Box 34012 Fullerton, CA 92634 800-916-8800 |

If you're turned down for credit, it's a good idea to review your report to make sure all the information contained in it is accurate. Your local bank or the institution that turned you down should be able to supply you with the address and phone number of your local credit bureau. To get a copy of your credit report, you can contact your local credit bureau or one of the three national credit bureaus listed in Table 6.2. For a small fee, generally around $8 to $10, you'll be sent a copy of your report. If you've been denied credit based on a credit report, the report is free.

If the information in your file isn't accurate or complete, the credit bureau must investigate any errors you point out and make corrections. For example, your file may inadvertently contain information about someone with a name very similar to yours, or it may contain incorrect or incomplete credit information, perhaps listing accounts that are closed or that you never had. If there are any mistakes, you should notify your credit bureau so it can investigate and make the corrections.

If the credit bureau investigates and determines that the information in your report is accurate, you have the right to have in your file a statement presenting your view of the issue. This statement gives you the chance to dispute the accuracy of information in your file. In any case, if you do find inaccuracies, they should be pointed out immediately.

The FCRA also limits the length of time damaging information can remain in your file. Bankruptcy information can remain in your file for only 10 years, and other negative information must be removed from your file after 7 years.

The FCRA also limits access to your credit file to those who have a legitimate right to view it, such as a financial institution considering extending you credit, an employer, or a company doing business with you. You also have the right to know who has seen your credit report.

## If Your Credit Card Application Is Rejected

If your credit card application is rejected, you have two choices. First, apply for a card with another financial institution. Getting rejected at one bank doesn't necessarily mean you'll get rejected at another. Second, find out why you've been rejected. Set up an appointment with the credit card manager and find out what caused your rejection. Once you know the reason, correct the problem. You might have to correct inaccurate information on your credit report, or you might have to start doing some things differently. In either case, the place to begin is by finding out why you've been rejected.

## Resolving Billing Errors

Your statement may contain a math error, it may include billing for an item you never received, it may include double billing for an item you purchased—the possible errors are many. Fortunately, the Fair Credit Billing Act (FCBA) provides a procedure for correcting billing errors. Under the FCBA you're allowed to withhold payment for the item in question while you petition the card issuer to investigate the matter. Table 6.3 provides a summary of the major laws governing consumer credit.

To begin an investigation of a billing problem, the FCBA requires that you notify your card issuer *in writing within 60 days* of the statement date. In your inquiry you must include your name, address, and account number in addition to a description of the error, including its date, the dollar amount of the billing error, and the reason you feel it's in error. You should also note in your letter that you're making this billing inquiry under the FCBA.

This letter should then be sent to the "billing inquiry" or "billing error" address given on your credit card bill. Because most bill payments are handled automatically, including your complaint with your payment will likely ensure that it'll be lost forever. Moreover, the FCBA requires that an address to which billing questions should be directed be included on your statement. Make sure you keep a copy of your letter for future reference.

Within 30 days you should receive notice that an investigation of your complaint has been initiated. The card issuer has 90 days or two billing cycles to complete the

## Table 6.3 Major Provisions of Consumer Credit Laws

**Truth in Lending Act of 1968:** Requires lenders to disclose the true cost of consumer credit, explaining all charges, terms, and conditions involved. It requires that the consumer be provided with the total finance charge and annual percentage rate on the loan.

**Truth in Lending Act (amended 1971):** Prohibits lenders from sending unauthorized credit cards and limits cardholders' liability to $50 for unauthorized use.

**Fair Credit Billing Act of 1975:** Sets procedures for correcting billing errors on open credit accounts. It also allows consumers to withhold payment for defective goods purchased with a credit card. In addition, it sets limits on the time some information can be kept in your credit file.

**Equal Credit Opportunity Act of 1975:** Prohibits credit discrimination on the basis of sex and marital status. It also requires lenders to provide a written statement explaining any adverse action taken.

**Equal Credit Opportunity Act (amended 1977):** Prohibits credit discrimination based on race, national origin, religion, age, or receipt of public assistance.

**Fair Debt Collection Practices Act of 1978:** Prohibits unfair, abusive, and deceptive practices by debt collectors, and establishes procedures for debt collection.

**Truth in Lending Act (amended 1982):** Requires installment credit contracts to be written in plain English.

**Fair Credit Reporting Reform Act of 1996 (updated version of the Fair Credit Reporting Act of 1971):** Requires that consumers be provided with the name of any credit agency supplying a credit report that leads to the denial of credit. It gives consumers the right to know what is in their credit reports and challenge incorrect information. It also requires that employers get written permission from current or prospective employees before reviewing their credit files. In addition, it allows consumers to sue creditors if reporting errors are not corrected.

investigation. On completion of the investigation, either your account will be credited the disputed amount or you'll receive an explanation from the card issuer as to why it feels your complaint isn't legitimate.

You can continue to dispute your billing charges by notifying the card issuer within your grace period, but the process of correcting it becomes more complicated. If you don't pay, you can be reported delinquent to your credit agency, and you risk the chance of being sued by the card issuer and having your credit rating go down the tubes. Still, if you feel the bank isn't handling your inquiry in an appropriate manner, contact the regulatory agency that oversees the card. Alternatively, you could contact an attorney or consider filing a claim in small claims court.

## Controlling and Managing Your Credit Cards and Open Credit

Manage your credit cards and open credit.

The first step in managing your credit is knowing what you have charged. It's far too easy to charge a pizza here, a gas fill-up there, and so forth until all control is lost. Remember, a lot of personal finance is about control. If you don't keep track of what you've spent, it's hard to know what kind of financial shape you're in.

### Reducing Your Balance

In addition to knowing exactly what the interest charge is on your credit card, you should understand how long it takes to pay off debt if you don't make meaningful payments—that is, payments well above the required minimum monthly payment. First, you should realize that most credit cards require that you pay only between 2 and 3 percent of your outstanding balance monthly. As a result, if you're paying 18 percent interest on that balance, you're getting almost nowhere. In other words, if you don't pay more than the minimum, you're almost assured of owing on your credit cards for life.

To get an idea of how long it takes to get rid of credit card debt, let's look at how many months it would take to get rid of your debt if you paid off a set percentage of your initial balance. If your initial balance is $3,000 and you pay off 2 percent each month, you'd be paying off $60 a month. In addition to the amount you pay off each month, your credit card interest rate also plays a role in determining how long it takes to eliminate your debt. Table 6.4 shows you how to calculate how long it would take to pay off your balance. Simply find the intersection of the percentage of your initial balance that you are paying off and the interest rate on your credit card.

WORKSHEET

If you pay off only 2 percent of your initial balance per month, and the credit card interest rate is 15 percent, it would take 79 months or over 6 1/2 years before your credit card debt is paid. Keep in mind that this time frame assumes you don't charge anything more on your card. If you have a substantial balance and keep charging, you may never get out of debt.

### Protecting Against Fraud

What happens if your credit card is stolen? That depends on how quickly you report the loss. If you report the loss before any fraudulent charges occur, you owe nothing. Even if your card has been used, your liability is limited to $50 per card, which makes credit card insurance unnecessary. Still, the inconvenience associated with the loss of your credit card makes it imperative that you guard against fraud.

Most steps to guard against credit card fraud are obvious. First, save all your credit card receipts and compare them against your credit card bill. After you've compared them with your billings, you should destroy these receipts, because they contain your credit card number.

## Table 6.4 How Long It Can Take to Eliminate Credit Card Debt

| Each Month Pay This Percentage of the Initial Outstanding Balance | Annual Credit Card Interest Rate | | | |
|---|---|---|---|---|
| | 9% | 12% | 15% | 18% |
| 2% | 63 months | 70 months | 79 months | 93 months |
| 3% | 39 months | 41 months | 43 months | 47 months |
| 5% | 22 months | 22 months | 23 months | 24 months |
| 10% | 10 months | 11 months | 11 months | 11 months |
| 15% | 7 months | 7 months | 7 months | 7 months |

**Step 1:** Find the row that corresponds to the percentage of your initial balance that you intend to pay off each month. If you have an initial outstanding balance of $5,000 and you intend to pay off $150 each month, you would be paying off $150/$5,000 = 3% each month. Thus, you should look in the 3% row.

**Step 2:** Find the column that corresponds to the annual percentage that you pay on your credit card. If your credit card charges 15%, look in the 15% column.

**Step 3:** The intersection of the payments row and the credit card interest column shows how many months it would take to pay off your initial balance. If you pay off 3% of your initial balance each month and the card charges 15%, it would take 43 months to pay off your initial balance.

# In The News

Wall Street Journal Sunday April 29, 2001

### How to Form Good Financial Habits

by Jonathan Clements

We're all on the financial treadmill. But only some of us are going forward. As we manage our money, there are cycles of virtue and vice. Good financial habits beget further gains, while bad habits tend to snowball. As Charles Dickens put it so succinctly in *David Copperfield*: "Annual income twenty pounds, annual expenditure nineteen six, result happiness. Annual income twenty pounds, annual expenditure twenty pounds ought and six, result misery."

*This is where the cycles of virtue and vice begin. If your spending outstrips your income, the debts start mounting. But if you spend less than you earn, you have money to save. And the younger you start saving, the better off you will be.* (☞A)

Most folks, of course, don't set out to amass credit card debt. Instead, they slip slowly into hock. Making summer vacation plans? You could buy the airline tickets now, stick them on your debit card, and get the cost out of the way before you climb on the plane. Once on vacation, you could use your debit card for the hotel bills, while paying cash for your meals.

*But the credit card balance never gets paid off, because by then there are Christmas gifts to buy. Suddenly, debt is getting piled on top of debt. "There's nothing more miserable than having the tan gone but the hotel bill continue," quips Minneapolis financial planner Ross Levin. "People don't stop to think that it (compound interest) works the other way when they're charging on their credit cards," Mr. Levin adds. "People think they're buying something on sale, so they're saving money. But they put it on their credit card, and they end up paying more for it," thanks to the 17 percent or 18 percent interest rate that the credit card charges.* (☞B)

As those interest charges are added to the original credit card balance, it makes it even more difficult to get out of debt. Suddenly, a little scrimping and saving isn't enough. Instead, to get back on track, you have to take an ax to your spending.

## THE BOTTOM LINE . . .

**A** The problem is that it's just too easy to spend money with credit cards—it just doesn't feel like you've spent anything. In addition, it's just too easy to lose track of exactly how much you've spent.

**B** Keep in mind, that any time you use a credit card you're spending some of your future income. That means when you make money in the future, some of that money is already spent. To try and keep control over what you spend, subtract any credit card charges you make from your check register. Then when you get your credit card bill, you know you'll have enough to pay it off.

Use care in giving your credit card number over the phone unless you're purchasing an item and you initiated the sale. Even if you're initiating the sale, never give your credit card number out over a public phone—you never know who's listening. Finally, never leave a store without your card. One way of ensuring you never leave your card behind is to hold your wallet in your hand until you receive your credit card back.

## Trouble Signs in Credit Card Spending

The next step in controlling credit card borrowing is to examine your credit card habits and determine whether you have a problem. Although there's no simple formula for highlighting problems, many financial planners use a credit card habits quiz that forces you to look at your habits and recognize any weaknesses you might have.

Checklist 6.2 provides sample questions that might be used in a credit card habits quiz. There's no cutoff for wrong answers. In fact, the questions are really intended to make you think about and reevaluate your credit card habits. However, if you answer yes to any question, you should know that you might have a problem. If you have problems with any of these questions, you should seriously reevaluate your credit card habits.

## Controlling Spending

The first steps to control your credit card spending are to set goals and develop a budget to achieve these goals—this is the point of **Principle 8: Nothing Happens Without a Plan**. The next step in controlling credit card spending is to track it. The best way is to keep a running tab on how much you've charged. Every time you use your credit card, write down the date and amount charged.

Your checkbook register is an ideal place to do this. In fact, Citibank will provide you with a free "Credit Minder" credit card register if you don't have a spare check register (800-669-2635). Subtract the amount of each charge from what you have in your checking account. When your credit card bill comes in, you'll have enough in

Principle

8 Nothing Happens Without a Plan

# Checklist 6.2 ∎ The Credit Card Habits Quiz

**If you answer yes to any of these questions, you have some credit card problems.**

Do you only make the minimum payment on your credit card each month?

Have you reached your spending limit on one or more credit cards?

When out to dinner with a group of friends, do you pay the entire bill with your credit card and have them reimburse you for their share with cash?

Do you wait for your monthly bill to determine how much you have charged on your credit card rather than keep track of all your credit card spending as it occurs?

Do you get cash advances because you do not have enough in your checking account?

Have you been turned down for credit or had one of your credit cards canceled?

Have you used some of your savings to pay off credit card bills?

Do you know how much of your credit card bills is from interest?

Does your stomach start churning when you get your credit card bill?

your checking account to pay it off completely. Once you understand how your credit card has gotten you into trouble, it's much easier to control its use.

### If You Can't Pay Your Credit Card Bills

Once you've gotten into trouble through the overuse of credit cards, getting out is a real hassle. The first step is, of course, putting in place a budget that brings in more money than you spend. This involves self-control—making sure you act your wage. Along with this remedy there are other options you might consider. First, you should make sure you have the least expensive credit card possible, given your habits. You should have a credit card that fits your usage habits.

A second option is using savings to pay off current credit card debt. Don't make dipping into your savings a habit. If it has to happen at all, it should happen only once—when you are reevaluating and changing your spending and credit card use patterns in a permanent manner. Keep in mind that the interest rate on the unpaid balance on an average credit card is approximately 16 percent. If you're only earning 4 percent after taxes on your savings, then by using savings to pay off credit card borrowing, you'll save 12 percent. As Ben Franklin might have said, 12 percent saved is 12 percent earned. There may be no easier way of earning 12 percent risk free than using savings that earn a low rate to pay off borrowing that costs a high rate.

Again, your credit card use should be controlled in such a way that it doesn't get out of hand and doesn't warrant this remedy on a regular basis. There's purpose to your savings, and to blow it in this way defeats the purpose of planning. In effect, using your savings is an emergency measure to be taken only in the extreme situation.

Another alternative that you might consider to lower the cost of your outstanding debt is to use a secured loan or a home equity loan to pay off your high-cost credit card debt. We'll look at consumer loans and debt of this type in Chapter 7.

## SUMMARY

Open credit is a running line of credit that you can use to make charges up to a certain point as long as you pay off a minimum amount of your debt each month. The main form of open credit is the credit card, which has become an essential part of our personal finances.

Four basic factors that affect the cost of open credit are the interest rate, the balance calculation method, the grace period, the annual fee, and other additional or penalty fees including the over-the-limit fee and penalty rates. The advantages of using credit cards or open credit include (1) convenience or ease of shopping, (2) emergency use, (3) the ability to consume before you pay, (4) consolidation of bills, (5) buying in anticipation of price increases, (6) as a source of interest-free credit, (7) to make reservations, (8) as identification, and (9) as a source of free benefits.

The reasons you should be wary of credit cards and open credit are that it's possible to lose control of spending, they are expensive, and you'll have less spendable income in the future.

There are many choices of open credit lines, including different types of credit cards, as well as charge accounts. There are three basic types of credit cards: bank credit cards, travel and entertainment cards, and single-purpose cards.

In determining what makes an individual creditworthy, most lenders refer to the "five C's" of credit—character, capacity, capital, collateral, and conditions.

A credit card issuer verifies the information you put down on your application against your credit report from a credit bureau. A credit bureau is a private organization that maintains credit information on individuals. The three national credit bureaus are Experian, Trans Union, and Equifax Credit

Information Services. Under the Fair Credit Reporting Act (FCRA) passed by Congress in 1971 (and subsequently amended to help ensure that credit reports are accurate), you have the right to view your credit report.

Different credit cards charge different annual percentage rates (APRs), and they also calculate the finance charges imposed in different ways. It is important to know how the unpaid balance is calculated.

To control credit card use, focus on controlling credit card spending and look for signs of trouble.

## REVIEW QUESTIONS

1. Define the term *credit*. How is credit different from open credit? What is revolving credit?

2. Paying a $30 annual fee for the privilege of using a credit card can be thought of as adding $2.50 to your monthly bill. List examples of other factors that determine the cost of credit.

3. Describe how a lender calculates the annual percentage rate (APR) when issuing credit. Why is the APR such an important tool when shopping for credit?

4. Explain the differences in the three balance calculation methods used by credit card issuers. Given similar account activity, which will result in the lowest monthly interest charge and the highest monthly interest charge?

5. What is a grace period? Why would a grace period be canceled or eliminated?

6. List and briefly describe the most common fees and penalties imposed by credit card issuers. What is the Schumer box?

7. List five benefits, or advantages, associated with credit card or open credit use. What is the major disadvantage?

8. Explain the differences in a bank credit card, a premium or prestige credit card, an affinity credit card, and a secured credit card. What are credit card classes?

9. Although they are called "credit cards," T&E cards and single-purpose cards are uniquely different from bank credit cards. What are the differences? What do they have in common with a traditional charge account?

10. What is (are) the most important decision factor(s) in choosing a credit card for a credit user, a convenience user, and convenience and credit user?

11. Explain the five C's of credit and how they relate to individual creditworthiness.

12. Define the term *credit scoring*. What is the role of the credit bureau in the calculation of a person's score?

13. Describe the steps involved when attempting to resolve a billing error.

14. List four ways to avoid credit card fraud.

15. Develop a list of five to eight warning signs that indicate that someone may be having trouble with credit or be a credit card abuser.

## PROBLEMS AND ACTIVITIES

1. Ted and Tiffany are meeting Mitch and Amber at the Blue Oyster Swing Dance Club later in the evening. Ted figures that tonight might get expensive, so he pulls into a nearby bank, pulls out his favorite credit card, and gets a hefty cash advance. When the two couples meet up for dinner, Tiffany tells Amber that she is going to splurge and get lobster because Ted is rolling in cash. Mitch overhears this and begins to laugh. Mitch looks at Ted and exclaims that getting a cash advance is "way bad." Ted whips back that Mitch is blind to the conveniences offered by credit card cash advances and the ease of "one-stop shopping for cash." Tiffany and Amber ask you to determine who is right. Thoroughly defend your answer to settle the argument.

2. Assume the following: Maggie carried an average daily balance of $550 this month. Her previous balance last month was $1,000, compared to a balance of $900 this month. There are 30 days in this billing cycle and Maggie always makes a payment on the 15th of the month. Based on this information, calculate the monthly interest charges for credit card accounts charging 14 percent, 16 percent, and 18 percent interest. Complete the following chart. Since the average daily balance is the most commonly used balance calculation method, is shopping for a lower interest rate really that important?

|  | 14% | 16% | 18% |
|---|---|---|---|
| Average Daily Balance | $6.42 | | |
| Previous Balance | | $13.33 | |
| Adjusted Balance | | | $1.50 |

3. Last month a community college instructor and her husband, an airline attendant, received 15 credit card offers in the mail, which, if they took them all, would have totaled over $125,000 in available credit. In light of this information, explain the three reasons why consumers should be wary of credit cards. Aside from interest charges, annual fees, and other penalty fees, what is the "cost" of credit?

4. Credit card issuers often use credit bureau data to "preselect" consumers who will be sent marketing materials and application forms. Describe the profile of a consumer who might be sent an application for a bank credit card, a premium or prestige credit card, an affinity credit card, and a secured credit card.

5. Some companies offer the same service or product at a cash price and a credit price. In most cases, the cash price is lower than the credit price. What is the rationale for charging one price to cash customers and another price to credit customers?

6. Using the sample credit scorecard in Figure 6.4, relate each question to one of the five C's of credit. Are all five considered? Why or why not?

7. It is commonly recommended that you should check your credit report every two to three years as well as before applying for credit, after being denied credit, and before applying for a job. Why? Should you add a statement to your report each time? How long can your statement be? Will you have to pay each time?

8. With only a part-time job and the need for a professional wardrobe, Rachel quickly maxed out her credit card the summer after graduation. With her first full-time paycheck in August, she vowed not to use the card and to pay $240 each month toward paying down her $8,000 outstanding balance. The card has an annual interest rate of 18 percent. How long will it take Rachel to pay for her wardrobe? Should she shop for a new card? Why or why not?

9. Consumer credit laws have been implemented over the years to protect consumers against creditor abuses. Match the following consumer credit issues with the appropriate consumer credit law:
   - controls debt collection procedures and practices
   - prohibits credit discrimination because of race or age
   - established the APR and required disclosure of all credit-related costs
   - limits the time information can be reported in a consumer credit report
   - limits marketing of credit cards to the mailing of application packets and prohibits the mailing of unrequested credit cards
   - payment for defective goods purchased with a credit card can legally be withheld
   - limits fraudulent card use to $50 payment by the cardholder
   - ensured that divorced individuals could receive credit

10. A leading financial publication recently reported that the average baby boomer credit user will pay approximately $1,200 in interest annually. If, instead of paying interest, this amount was saved every year, how much would one of these credit users accumulate in a tax-deferred account earning 12 percent in 10, 15, 20, and 30 years?

## SUGGESTED PROJECTS

1. Working in a small group, collect credit card marketing information or the summary of account information sent to cardholders for three to five different cards. Using these materials, complete one or more of the following activities.

   a. Summarize the card information into a chart showing purchase balance calculation method, annual percentage rate (APR) of interest for purchases, grace period, annual fee, and minimum finance charge. Compare the results.

   b. Summarize the card information pertaining to cash advances into a chart showing grace period, interest rate, and transaction fee for cash advances. Compare the results.

   c. Summarize the card information pertaining to additional or penalty fees into a chart.

Consider the penalty APR as well as fees for late payment, exceeding the credit limit, or a bounced check. Compare the results.

   d. Summarize the additional benefits, or "perks," that are available, such as insurance programs, car rental discounts, traveler assistance, and so on. Compare the results.

   e. Select the card that would be most appropriate for a credit user. Justify your choice.

   f. Select the card that would be most appropriate for a convenience user. Justify your choice.

   g. Review the information requested on the application. Explain how the information relates to the "five C's of credit."

2. Share the list of pros and cons of credit cards shown in Figure 6.2 with 15 to 20 other college students. From the list, ask each to identify the top three reasons they use credit cards *and* the primary reason they avoid, or limit, credit card use. Summarize your results in an oral or written report. In general, do the practices of these students suggest a sound financial plan or the potential for developing credit card problems?

3. Some credit card issuers are beginning to assess fees and other charges on convenience users. Ask your friends and peers if they think a convenience credit card user (*note*: you may need to define this term for them) should be charged for the privilege of using a credit card. Note their specific responses and group responses into categories. Use this information to create a short report for class.

4. Interview individuals representing the three stages of the financial life cycle regarding their credit card usage. How many cards do they have? What kind or class of cards (rebate, premium, affinity, T&E, or single purpose) do they have? How often are cards used and typically for what purchases? What is their available line of credit? Classify them as convenience users, credit users, or convenience and credit users. Summarize your findings in an oral or written report noting differences in credit card use across the financial life cycle.

5. Break into two or three groups to discuss the use of affinity cards. Why do group members have an affinity card and how often do they use it? Discuss the benefits offered by an affinity card to the issuer, the sponsor, and the user. What disadvantages are associated with affinity cards? In general, does the group think that the possession and use of an affinity card makes a personality statement about the user?

6. Ask 10 to 20 classmates or friends what they think should be considered by a credit card issuer prior to issuing a card. Make a list of specific factors, and compare the list to the credit scorecard in Figure 6.4. Did your classmates identify the same factors on which credit scoring is based, or were they significantly different? Do you think your list would be different if you asked other friends, relatives, or strangers? Why or why not?

7. Contact the local credit bureau to determine how to check your credit report. Be sure to ask (a) what information should be included in the letter, (b) if a copy of documentation showing your current address should be included, and (c) the cost and method of payment. For additional information check the Web site for Equifax at **www.equifax.com** or Experian at **www.experian.com.** Report your findings. Request and review your credit report.

8. Some students are strongly opposed to having a credit card. Sometimes this opposition is based on family values and sometimes on fear. Other students argue that in today's world it is almost impossible to live without a credit card and that credit is often better than cash. Ask a group of students their opinions on the use of credit. What percentage of the students fall into the credit avoidance category, and what percentage think credit is essential? What is your opinion on this issue? Use this information as the basis for a short class discussion and debate.

9. Research the background and passage of one of the consumer credit laws shown in Table 6.3. Explain why this protection was needed, and describe what practices prompted the passage of this legislation. What changes resulted?

10. Consumer credit legislation offers consumers a variety of protections when securing credit, using credit, or repaying credit. How are consumers kept abreast of these laws? Identify as many sources of information and education as possible. Begin your search with (a) credit contracts and bills, (b) local, state, and federal offices of consumer affairs, (c) the extension service of a land-grant university, or (d) the World Wide Web. Share your results in a report, including examples of brochures, bills, or other materials collected.

# Money Matters
## CREDIT LINES

One of my clients told me she finally got control of her impulse purchasing on credit by putting her cards in a zipper bag and freezing them in a bucket of water. That way she has some time to think things through while she waits for them to thaw. If this sounds too bizarre to you, or your freezer is too full of TV dinners and ice cream, here are some more ideas.

**Carry one credit card and use it only for convenience.** *That means you can use it only if there's money in the bank to cover the amount of the charge.*

**Subtract the charge from your check register when you make it.** *Negative balance? Then no charging!*

**Pay your entire balance each month.**

**If you have large balances on high-interest cards,** *look for one with lower interest and transfer the debt. Don't use that card for any new charges. Set a date for clearing the balance, calculate how much you have to pay each month to meet the deadline, and pay it off. Most cards offer the lower rate for only a year or so and some charge higher interest on new charges than the published rate for the transferred amount.*

**Protect yourself from fraud and temptation** *by shredding those "you have already been approved" credit card applications and the "convenience checks" sent by your credit card company. Though you can't do much about stopping the applications, you can request that your current credit providers discontinue sending the*

*checks. Normally they are part of planned marketing campaigns, and it takes 2 to 3 months for the mailings to stop.*

**If you are in too deep but have an excellent payment record,** *call the credit card company to discuss lowering your interest rate. Some won't consider such a request if you have current charges on that card. Check into a home equity loan to pay off the debt. Be aware, though, that you must have your spending under control and be willing to pay off that loan quickly, or you jeopardize the roof over your head.*

**Don't even consider investing money if you have consumer debt.** *No investment can guarantee you a return equal to the 18- to 21-percent cost of credit.*

**If you're paying off a large balance,** *make that payment a fixed expense in your budget. Never pay just the minimum amount on your statement. You may have to forgo entertainment or "brown bag" your lunch for a while.*

**Take control.** *An excellent credit history is a true asset, and a large line of credit could be very important in case of emergency.*

## Discussion Case 1

Maria will be a college sophomore next year and she is determined to have her own credit card. She will not be employed during the school year but is convinced that she can qualify for a card based on her summer earnings. Maria's parents have read a number of articles about the problems of credit cards and college students, including examples of students leaving school after a downward spiral of credit cards, overspending, working to pay bills, worrying about bills, working more hours to pay bills, and eventually withdrawing from school. When Maria showed up with a handful of applications including Visa, a Gold MasterCard, Discover, a Visa sponsored by her university, an American Express, a secured MasterCard, and a gas company

card her parents were overwhelmed. Maria admitted she didn't want them *all*. "I'm not stupid," she declared. Since Maria obviously needed to learn about credit cards, her parents agreed to cosign her application on one condition. She had to approach her choice just like a class project and research the following questions.

### Questions

1. Assuming Maria does not really care about her parents' approval and ignores their assignment, will she be able to apply for a credit card without their help? *Hint:* Consider the application process and the five C's of credit. How impor-

tant are Maria's summer earnings in determining whether or not she is issued a card?

2. Why would an unemployed college student possibly need a credit card? What are the advantages to having a credit card? What are the disadvantages?

3. Should Maria have more than one card? What is the recommended number of credit cards for the average consumer?

4. Shopping for credit can be compared to shopping for any other consumer product—consider the product cost, features, advantages, and disadvantages. In other words, does the product meet the user's needs? Help Maria compare her credit choices given the applications she has collected.

5. Based on the analysis in question 4, what credit card class(es), if any, should Maria seriously consider? For what other "products," if any, might she consider applications?

6. List and summarize the basic factors that affect credit card costs. Rank these factors in terms of importance and relevance based on Maria's situation.

7. While comparing the applications she had collected, Maria was thrilled to receive a "preapproved" offer for a standard card. What precautions should Maria be alert to with this offer?

8. In order to convince her parents that she can be responsible when using a credit card, Maria volunteered to use a credit tracking system. How should she explain this method to her parents?

9. To avoid problems, what might be considered the most important rule for Maria to follow when using a credit card?

10. How might Maria's credit card use impact her future job search? What should she do to avoid any problems?

11. What steps, such as purchasing credit card insurance, should Maria take to protect herself against fraud?

## Discussion Case 2

Garth was amazed to hear that his friend Lindsey always pays off her credit card at the end of each month. Garth just assumed that everyone used credit cards the same way—buy now, pay later. He buys almost everything he needs or wants, including clothes, food, and entertainment with his card. When Lindsey asked him about the APR for his card, he didn't have a clue. He also didn't know the length of grace period or how his minimum monthly payment was calculated. When Lindsey asked about this, Garth replied that it didn't really matter because he never paid off his balance like she did. Garth reasoned that his credit card made purchases easier by allowing him to buy expensive items—that he couldn't otherwise afford—by paying minimum monthly payments. Over all Garth thinks that he is a responsible credit user, but he admits that over the past two or three years he has been late making a few monthly payments and, once or twice, has gone over his limit. He also uses his card regularly to obtain cash advances. After hearing all of this, Lindsey is worried about her friend. She has come to you for help in answering the following questions.

### Questions

1. What type of credit user is Garth? Based on your answer, what is the number-one factor that should influence Garth's choice of a credit card?

2. Garth recently received a credit card offer from the KPF Bank. This credit card features a two-cycle daily balance method of calculating interest, a no annual fee option, and a six-month introductory APR of 9.9 percent that eventually goes up to 18 percent. What other information should Garth review in the Schumer box? Should Garth take this credit card offer? Why or why not?

3. JoJo Smith, Garth's second cousin, suggested that Garth should obtain a secured credit card, or better yet a Titanium card. Do you agree with JoJo? Why or why not?

4. Based on what you know about Garth, what kind of additional fees and penalties is he most likely to encounter? What is the impact of these fees and penalties on Garth?

5. Explain the differences in credit card interest rates when described as a fixed, variable, teaser, or penalty rate. How do these different rates affect the cost of using a credit card?

6. What factors should Garth consider if he decides to transfer his current card balance to another card?

7. Much to his surprise, Garth was recently rejected on his latest credit card application. What actions, if any, should he take?

8. How long will it take Garth to pay off the outstanding balance on his card ($3,000) if he pays $150 per month with an APR of 18 percent and does not make any additional purchases?

9. Is Garth correct in thinking that one advantage of using credit is that it allows him to make expensive purchases today and pay for them tomorrow? If you agree, what is the opposite side of the argument?

10. What advice would you give Garth if he has trouble paying his credit card bill in the future?

Visit our Web site for additional case problems, interactive exercises, and practice quizzes for this chapter—**www.prenhall.com/keown**.

# 7 Using Consumer Loans: The Role of Planned Borrowing

### Learning Objectives

**Understand** the various consumer loans.

**Calculate** the cost of a consumer loan.

**Pick** an appropriate source for your loan.

**Get** the most favorable interest rate possible on a loan.

**Know** when to borrow.

**Control** your debt.

D ebt and credit aren't necessarily bad things, but like everything else, moderation and control are important.

It's all too easy to end up with more debt than you can comfortably handle, and just how much debt that is depends on your financial status. In 1999, Elton John took borrowing to his limit when he had to secure a $40 million loan from a London bank to consolidate and pay off the debts he had racked up while ringing up as much as $400,000 a week in credit card bills . . . that's a lot of boas. He was blowing through money like a candle in the wind. Along the way, he had become God's gift to the spectacle and sunglasses industry, accumulating over 3,000 pairs of glasses. And his wardrobe made Imelda Marco's look like it had been bought at the Salvation Army. He simply had the gift to spend . . . and, as his spending peaked, he had the need to borrow.

Sure, Elton John could spend a $1 million in a day, but he could also write a song in 15 minutes that would make him another million. Most of us, thank goodness, don't have much in common with Elton John's spending habits, but one thing we do have in common with Elton is the ability to let debt and borrowing get out of control. It's easy to think that going from the poor life as a student to the ranks of the employed is an automatic setup for the good life. It probably is, at least as long as you maintain control of your finances and don't use debt to live beyond your means. As they say, "Credit buying is much like being drunk. The buzz happens immediately and gives you a lift. . . . The hangover comes the day after."

Chapter 6 examined credit cards and other sources of open credit. We now turn our attention to **consumer loans**. You can think of consumer loans as the next step up in debt. They're stricter and more formal than credit cards and other open credit. Instead of giving you a limited, borrow-when-you-want open line of credit, they involve formal contracts detailing exactly how much you're borrowing and exactly when and how you're going to pay it back. Open credit is for making convenience purchases—tonight's dinner or a new pair of Reeboks. Consumer loans are usually used for bigger purchases. With consumer loans, you can borrow more and pay it back at a slower pace than you can with open credit, but you have to lock yourself into a set repayment schedule. Because it forces you to plan your purchase and your repayment, consumer loans tend to be called "planned borrowing."

It would be ideal to be able to buy everything you need or want with your savings. Hey, no one likes owing someone else money. However, sometimes purchases are too big or the timing is such that you have to borrow money to finance a particular goal and pay for it later. Consumer loans allow you to do just that. However, consumer loans are a double-edged sword. On one hand, they let you consume more now. On the other hand, they create a financial obligation that can be a burden later. Control and living within your financial plans and your means is the key—without that even the Rocketman, with all his wealth, couldn't stay in flight.

**Consumer Loan**
A loan involving a formal contract detailing exactly how much you're borrowing and when and how you're going to pay it back.

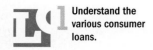

# Characteristics of Consumer Loans

Not all consumer loans look the same. They can range from single-payment, unsecured fixed-rate loans to secured, variable-rate installment loans. What does all that mean? Let's take a look at the characteristics and associated terminology of consumer loans.

## Single-Payment Versus Installment Loans

**Single-Payment or Balloon Loan**
A loan that is paid back in a single lump-sum payment at maturity, or the due date of the loan, which is usually specified in the loan contract. At that date you pay back the amount you borrowed plus all interest charges.

**Bridge or Interim Loan**
A short-term loan that provides funding until a longer-term source can be secured or until additional financing is found.

**Installment Loan**
A loan that calls for repayment of both the interest and the principal at regular intervals, with the payment levels set in such a way that the loan expires at a preset date.

**Loan Amortization**
The repayment of a loan using equal monthly payments that cover a portion of the principal and the interest on the declining balance. The amount of the monthly payment going toward interest payment starts off large and steadily declines, while the amount going toward the principal starts off small and steadily increases.

**Secured Loan**
A loan that's guaranteed by a specific asset.

**Unsecured Loan**
A loan that's not guaranteed by a specific asset.

**Fixed Interest Rate Loan**
A loan with an interest rate that stays fixed for the entire duration of the loan.

Consumer loans can be either single-payment loans or installment loans. A **single-payment** or **balloon loan** is simply a loan that's paid back in a single lump-sum payment at maturity, or the due date of the loan, which is usually specified in the loan contract. At that date you pay back the amount you borrowed plus all interest charges. Single-payment loans generally have a relatively short maturity of less than 1 year. Needless to say, paying off a loan of this kind is generally quite difficult if you don't have access to a large amount of money when it matures. As a result, they're generally used as **bridge** or **interim loans** to provide short-term funding until longer-term or additional financing is found. A bridge loan might be used in financing the building of a house, with the mortgage loan being used to pay off the bridge loan and provide more permanent funding.

An **installment loan** calls for repayment of both interest and principal at regular intervals, with the payment levels set so that the loan expires at a preset date. The amount of the monthly payment going toward interest starts off large and steadily decreases, while the amount going toward the principal starts off small and steadily increases. In effect, as you pay off more of the loan each month, your interest expenses decline, and your principal payment increases. This process is commonly referred to as **loan amortization**. Installment loans are very common and are used to finance cars, appliances, and other big-ticket items.

## Secured Versus Unsecured Loans

Consumer loans are either secured or unsecured. A **secured loan** is guaranteed by a specific asset. If you can't meet the loan payments, that asset can be seized and sold to cover the amount due. Many times the asset purchased with the funds from the loan is used for security. For example, if you borrow money to buy a car, that car is generally used as collateral for the loan. If you don't make your car payment, your car may be repossessed.

Repossessed collateral, though, may or may not cover what you owe. That is, after the collateral is repossessed, you could still owe money. For example, if you owed $10,000 on your car, but the bank could only get $9,000 for it, you'd still owe another $1,000. That means you'd have your car repossessed and still owe money on it! Other assets commonly used as security for a loan are certificates of deposit (CDs), stocks, jewelry, land, and bank accounts. Securities reduce lender risk, so lenders charge a lower rate on a secured loan than they would on a comparable unsecured loan.

An **unsecured loan** requires no collateral. In general, larger unsecured loans are given only to borrowers with excellent credit histories, because the only security the lender has is the individual's promise to pay. The big disadvantage of unsecured loans is that they're quite expensive.

## Variable-Rate Versus Fixed-Rate Loans

The interest payments associated with a consumer loan can either be fixed or variable. A **fixed interest rate loan** isn't tied to market interest rates and maintains a single interest rate for the entire duration of the loan. Regardless of whether market interest rates swing up or down, the interest rate you pay remains fixed. The vast majority of consumer loans have fixed rates.

A **variable** or **adjustable interest rate loan** is tied to a market interest rate, such as the prime rate or the 6-month Treasury bill rate. The interest rate you pay varies as that market rate changes. The **prime rate** is the interest rate banks charge to their most creditworthy customers. Most consumer loans are set above the prime rate or the Treasury bill rate. For example, your loan might be set at 4 percent over prime. In this case, if the prime rate is 9 percent at the moment, the rate you pay on your variable-rate loan would be 13 percent. If the prime rate drops to 8 percent, your rate would change to 12 percent.

Not all variable-rate loans are the same. For example, rates may be adjusted at different, but fixed, intervals. Some loans adjust every month, others every year. The less frequently the loan adjusts, the less you have to worry about rate changes. Another question you should address before taking on a variable-rate loan is, how volatile is the interest rate to which the loan is pegged? In general, short-term market rates tend to change more than long-term market rates. Therefore, variable-rate loans tied to the 6-month Treasury bill rate expose you to more risk of rate changes than do loans tied to, say, the 20-year Treasury bond rate.

Of course, variable-rate loans usually have rate caps that prevent interest rates from varying too much. The periodic cap limits the maximum the interest rate can jump during one adjustment. The lifetime cap limits the amount that the interest rate can jump over the life of the loan. The larger the fluctuations allowed by the caps, the greater the risk. The bottom line on a variable interest rate loan is that if interest rates drop, you win, and if interest rates rise, you lose.

So which is better, a fixed-rate loan or a variable-rate loan? Neither one necessarily. The choice between a variable- or fixed-rate loan is another example of **Principle 1: The Risk–Return Trade-Off**. With a variable-rate loan, you bear the risk that interest rates will go up and the payments will increase accordingly. You might get stuck with interest payments you can no longer afford. With a fixed-rate loan, the lender bears the risk that rates will go up, causing a loss of potential interest income on an already fixed rate. Because the lender bears more risk, fixed-rate loans generally cost more than variable-rate loans.

An alternative to a fixed- or variable-rate loan is a convertible loan. A **convertible loan** is a variable-rate loan that can be converted into a fixed-rate loan at the borrower's option at specified dates in the future. Although convertible loans are much less common than variable- or fixed-rate loans, they do offer the advantage of the lower cost of a variable-rate loan while still being able to lock into the savings of a fixed-rate loan.

## The Loan Contract

The loan contract spells out all the conditions of the loan in exhaustive detail. If the item being purchased is to be used as collateral for the loan, then the contract will contain a **security agreement** saying so. The security agreement identifies whether the lender or borrower retains control over the item being purchased. The formal agreement stating the payment schedule and the rights of both lender and borrower in the case of **default** are outlined in the **note**.

The note is standard on all loans, and the security agreement is standard on secured loans. Other clauses are sometimes included in a loan contract, including an insurance agreement clause, an acceleration clause, a deficiency payment

**Variable or Adjustable Interest Rate Loan**
A loan in which the interest rate does not stay fixed but varies based on the market interest rate.

**Prime Rate**
The interest rate banks charge to their most creditworthy, or "prime," customers.

**Principle 1** The Risk–Return Trade-Off

**Convertible Loan**
A variable-rate loan that can be converted into a fixed-rate loan at the borrower's option at specified dates in the future.

**Security Agreement**
An agreement that identifies whether the lender or borrower retains control over the item being purchased.

**Default**
The failure of a borrower to make a scheduled interest or principal payment.

**Note**
The formal document that outlines the legal obligations of both the lender and the borrower.

clause, and a recourse clause. An example of an installment purchase contract is given in Figure 7.1.

## Insurance Agreement Clause

With an **insurance agreement clause** you're required to purchase credit life insurance to pay off the loan in the event of your death. For you, credit life insurance adds nothing to the loan other than cost. It's really the lender who benefits. If an insurance agreement clause is included, its cost should justifiably be included as a cost of the loan.

## Acceleration Clause

An **acceleration clause** states that if you miss one payment, the entire loan comes due immediately. If at that time you can't pay off the entire loan, the collateral will be repossessed and sold to pay off the balance due. Acceleration clauses are standard in most loans. However, lenders usually won't immediately invoke the

**Figure 7.1** An Installment Purchase Contract

Keep in mind when taking out an installment purchase contract that, just like a product such as a television or an automobile, the loan you are taking out is also a product. You should make sure it's something you can afford and that you understand what you're signing.

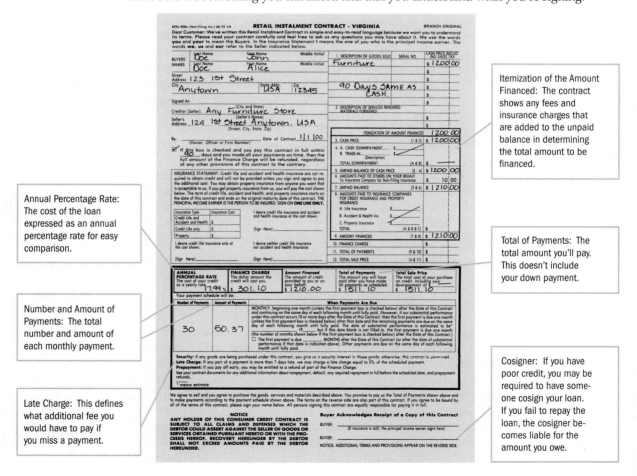

Itemization of the Amount Financed: The contract shows any fees and insurance charges that are added to the unpaid balance in determining the total amount to be financed.

Annual Percentage Rate: The cost of the loan expressed as an annual percentage rate for easy comparison.

Total of Payments: The total amount you'll pay. This doesn't include your down payment.

Number and Amount of Payments: The total number and amount of each monthly payment.

Cosigner: If you have poor credit, you may be required to have someone cosign your loan. If you fail to repay the loan, the cosigner becomes liable for the amount you owe.

Late Charge: This defines what additional fee you would have to pay if you miss a payment.

acceleration clause but instead will allow you a chance to make good on the overdue payments.

## Deficiency Payments Clause

A **deficiency payments clause** states that if you default on a secured loan, not only can the lender repossess whatever is secured, but also if the sale of that asset doesn't cover what you owe, you can be billed for the difference.

To make sense out of this clause, let's say you missed some car payments and had your car repossessed. If you owed a balance of $10,000, and the car was sold at auction by the lender for only $9,000, you'd still owe $1,000. In addition, under the deficiency payments clause you would also be responsible for collection costs, say $150, selling costs, perhaps another $150, and attorney fees of, say, $100. As a result, you'd not only lose your car, but would also be billed for $1,400 ($1,000 + $150 + $150 + $100).

## Recourse Clause

A **recourse clause** defines what actions a lender can take to claim money from you in case you default. The recourse clause may allow the lender to attach your wages, which means that a certain portion of your salary would go directly to the lender to pay off your debt.

## Special Types of Consumer Loans

Although consumer loans are used for almost anything, several special-purpose consumer loans deserve close attention. It's important to look at these loans not only because they are extremely common, but also because they include unique advantages and disadvantages you should be aware of.

## Home Equity Loans

A **home equity loan** or **second mortgage** is a loan that uses the built-up equity in your home as collateral against the loan. A home equity loan is merely a special type of secured loan. Generally, you can borrow from 50 to 85 percent of your equity—that is, your home value minus your first mortgage balance. For example, if you own a home with a market value of $200,000 and have an outstanding balance on your first mortgage of $80,000, your home equity would be $120,000. With this much equity, you would be able to get a home equity loan of between $60,000 and $102,000 (0.50 × $120,000, and 0.85 × $120,000, respectively). In this case, your home is security on a loan that can be used for any purpose (it needn't be home related).

**Advantages of Home Equity Loans** The primary advantage of a home equity loan over an alternative loan is cost. The first cost advantage arises because the interest on a home equity loan is generally tax deductible up to a maximum of $100,000, provided the loan doesn't exceed your home's market value. So, for every dollar of interest you pay on your home equity loan, your taxable income is lowered by $1. It's another example of if you're in a 30-percent marginal tax bracket, paying $1 of interest on a home equity loan will save you 30¢ in taxes. The after-tax cost of paying

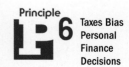

Principle
**6** Taxes Bias Personal Finance Decisions

$1 of interest on this home equity loan would be only 70¢, or $1 (1 − 0.30). Hey, don't scoff at a 30¢ savings. That change adds up: If you're in a 30-percent marginal tax bracket and you borrow $27,778 at 12 percent, you'll save $1,000 a year if the interest is tax-deductible.

You can also calculate the after-tax cost of the home equity loan by taking the before-tax cost of the home equity loan and multiplying it by [1 − (marginal tax rate)]:

$$\text{after-tax cost of a home equity loan} = \text{before-tax cost} (1 - \text{margin tax rate})$$

As you recall from Chapter 4, you have to determine your marginal tax bracket before you can calculate the after-tax cost. This marginal tax rate is the rate at which any additional income you receive will be taxed, and it combines the federal and state tax rates that you pay on the investment you're considering. If the before-tax interest rate on the home equity loan is 9 percent and you're in the 30-percent marginal tax bracket, then the after-tax cost of the loan would be 6.3 percent, calculated as follows:

$$6.3\% = 9\% (1 - 0.30)$$

Thus, you might pay 9 percent on this loan, but the cost to you, after taking into account the fact that interest on this loan lowers your taxes, is only 6.3 percent.

The second cost advantage of home equity loans comes from the fact that they generally carry a lower interest rate than do other consumer loans. Because home equity loans are secured loans, lenders consider them less risky and charge a lower interest rate on them.

**Disadvantages of a Home Equity Loan**   The major disadvantage of a home equity loan is that it puts your home at risk. Now, don't think that a home equity loan is by definition a bad idea. You should just use caution and make sure that you aren't taking on more debt that you can support.

The use of a home equity loan also limits future financing flexibility. Although it's an excellent source of emergency funding, you can have only one home equity loan outstanding at a time. And don't forget that any borrowing places an obligation on future earnings and reduces future disposable income.

## Student Loans

**Student loans** are simply loans with low, federally subsidized interest rates given, based on financial need, to students making satisfactory progress in their degree program. You may already know more about this subject than you'd care to. There are a number of different student loans available, with the two most popular being the Federal Direct/Stafford Loans and the PLUS Direct/PLUS Loans. The only difference between them is that under the Direct Loan Programs the federal government makes loans directly to the students (Federal Direct Loans) and parents (PLUS Direct Loans) through the school's financial aid office, whereas under the Stafford and PLUS Loan Programs, the loans are made by private lenders such as banks and credit unions. The Federal Direct and Stafford Loans are extremely popular: Close to one-fifth of all undergraduates nationally receive them.

Under a Federal Direct or Stafford loan, students borrow the money themselves. For students who are dependents, the borrowing limits are set at $2,625 the first year,

$3,500 the second, and $5,500 the third and fourth year (and also the fifth year if needed) and $8,500 per year for graduate school. These borrowing limits are set even higher for independent students. In addition, the rates on Stafford loans are capped at 8.25 percent and tend to vary below that ceiling. These loans are so appealing because the interest on them is deferred while you are in school. In effect, the government pays your interest while you are a student, and you don't begin making payments until 6 months after graduation. For more information on Stafford loans check out their Web site at **www.staffordloan.com**.

While Federal Direct and Stafford loans are for students, PLUS Direct and PLUS loans are for parents. With PLUS loans the maximum amount you can borrow is based on the total budgeted cost of education minus any other financial aid that is received (in addition to the parents' creditworthiness). That means you may be able to borrow more with a PLUS loan. The interest rate on PLUS loans is set at 3.1 percent above the 52-week Treasury note rate and is capped at 9 percent over the life of the loan. That's the good news. The bad news is that with the PLUS loans you have to start repaying the loan immediately. There is also a PLUS loans Web site at **www.PLUSloans.net**.

The process of applying for one of these loans begins at the financial aid office of your school. You fill out the financial aid form, and your school helps you find a lender. One nice thing about student loans is that, as was noted in Chapter 4, you can deduct up to $2,500 regardless of whether you itemize or not. Under the new tax law, effective for the 2002 tax year, the deduction of student loan interest is allowed beyond the first 60 months in which interest payments are required. In addition, effective in 2002, the income level at which eligibility for the deduction begins to phase out would occur from $50,000 to $65,000 for single filers, and from $100,000 to $130,000 for joint filers.

Obviously, an education is an excellent investment in your future, one worth going into debt over. The student loan program offers a way to borrow at a below-market rate, regardless of your credit situation. Still, you must keep in mind that in taking out a student loan, you're sacrificing future financing flexibility. The increased income you get as a result of completing your education should more than offset this cost. Of course, nothing may offset the hassle of dealing with student loan officers, but that's just life.

## Automobile Loans

An **automobile loan** is simply a secured loan made specifically for the purchase of an automobile, with the automobile being purchased used as the collateral. These loans are generally short term, often for only 24, 36, or 48 months, although they can be as long as 5 or 6 years. In recent years automobile loans have been used as a marketing tool to sell cars. Very low cost loans of 3 percent or less are used to lure customers, or the low rates are used to sell slow-moving models. The rate on auto loans is also quite low because lenders know that if you don't pay, they'll repossess your car and sell it to someone else to pay off the loan.

**Automobile Loan**
A loan made specifically for the purchase of an automobile, which uses the automobile as collateral against the loan.

**STOP & THINK** For some people, it's a race between running out of money versus running out of month. Everything you do in personal finance finds its roots in your budget. While there is a place in your budget for consumer debt, it should be planned rather than result from "running out of money." The key, of course, is to spend less than you bring in—that means living below your means. That's pretty obvious but not always done.

Auto companies also use low-cost auto loan rates to push cars when they produce more than they can sell or when they're trying to get rid of last year's models because new ones are coming out soon. As a result, in early 2002, the national average auto loan rate at 7.30 percent was barely above the average home equity loan rate of 7.06 percent.

# In The News

Collegiate Times September 23, 1999

## Debt Lurking for College Students

Many college students are faced with debt, but few are told how to manage and avoid it. Students incur debt primarily through credit cards and loans.

More than 10,000 Tech students are granted loans each year through the Federal Financial Aid Program, said Barry Simmons, director of Virginia Tech's Office of Scholarships and Financial Aid. By graduation, this debt can add up. Tech students had an average balance of $14,530 Simmons said. The national average debt was somewhat higher, at $18,000 in the 1997–1998 year, said Carolyn Shanley of the Nellie Mae Corp. (☞A)

Fifty-nine percent of last year's graduating class received Direct Stafford Loans from the financial aid program. These loans become a part of the individual's credit history. "All loans (including financial aid loans) are reported to credit bureaus," Simmons said.

Tech offers counseling to students who need loans to pay for their education. Students eligible for loans must complete an entrance counseling session before funds are allocated, Simmons said. The entrance interview gives first time borrowers quite a bit of information

about the loan, and students must sign a form before money is awarded. This signature indicates the students understand what they are undertaking. The loans disbursed in the financial aid program are to be used for "educationally related expenditures," Simmons said. (☞B)

Such expenditures include everything from tuition to rent and books. "Students must know the difference between wants and needs," Simmons said. "Many students have a level of living above their needs." He said students need to budget, and they can get help with this in the Office of Scholarships and Financial Aid before taking loans. "(You must) cut fat off the budget," he said. (☞C)

### THE BOTTOM LINE . . .

A For students, borrowing is a way of life. Over the past 10 years, student-loan volume has more than doubled with almost 6 million students borrowing close to $38 billion.

B When you take out a student loan, make sure you know your options for repaying the loan and what might

happen if you don't meet your obligations. Not only can the government go after your tax refund, the government can snag a percentage of your wages to pay the loan. In fact, it's been said that it's easier to get out of paying child support than it is to get out of paying off a student loan. The key here is to include your student loan payments in your budget—it's a must.

C Many students are surprised by how much they owe because they borrowed small amounts several times. When it's put all together, it can be quite a bit. The end result is that every year tens of thousands of recent graduates fall behind on student-loan payments and then default on the loans altogether. The student-loan default rate has reached 9.6 percent. Delinquent borrowers who get hauled into court may get charged for the government's legal fees, which can add another 20 to 30 percent to the amount owed.

Source: Cousins, Carrie. "Debt Lurking for College Students." *Collegiate Times*, 23 September 1999: 1.

---

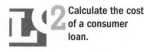

**Calculate the cost of a consumer loan.**

## Cost and Early Payment of Consumer Loans

Before deciding whether to borrow money, you should know exactly what the loan costs and what flexibility you have in terms of paying it off early. Fortunately, this information should be readily available. In fact, under the Truth in Lending Act, you must be informed in writing of the total finance charges and the APR of the loan before you sign a loan agreement.

The finance charges include all the costs associated with the loan—for example, interest payments, loan-processing fees, fees for a credit check, and any required insurance fees. The **APR**, or **annual percentage rate**, is the simple percentage cost of all finance charges over the life of the loan on an annual basis. Keep in mind that this includes noninterest finance charges.

As noted earlier, consumer loans fall into two categories: (1) single-payment or balloon loans, and (2) installment loans.

### Payday Loans

Be wary of "payday loans." Payday loans, generally given by check cashing companies, are aimed at people with jobs and checking accounts, but who need some

**APR, or Annual Percentage Rate**
The true simple interest rate paid over the life of a loan. It's a reasonable approximation for the true cost of borrowing, and the Truth in Lending Act requires that all consumer loan agreements disclose the APR in bold print.

money (usually $100 to $500) to tide them over until their next paycheck (they usually last for only 1 or 2 weeks). Lately, these loans have even surfaced on college campuses where the "clients" may not even have a job, just an "allowance" from home. The cost on these loans comes in the form of a "fee," which generally runs from $15 to $30 for the 1 or 2 week loan.

The loans work like this: You need $100 to cover you until your next paycheck or money from home. So you go to a payday lender and borrow $100. The payday lender gets a check from you for $115 drawn on your empty bank account. Then 2 weeks later, when you get paid, or you get that check from home, the lender either cashes the check or lets you pay another fee to renew the loan for another 2 weeks. If you annualized the interest rate, you'd find that you're borrowing at an interest rate of close to 400 percent. Even worse, if your fee was $30 (that is, you borrowed $100 and gave the payday lender a check for $130 to cover your $100 loan), you'd have paid close to 800 percent interest.

For some, this becomes a treadmill of debt, with a trip to the payday lender every 2 weeks. Once they pay off the payday lender, they have to go back to make it through the next 2 weeks. Think of it: you could borrow $100, pay a $15 fee and another $15 fee every 2 weeks, and never have the loan paid off. That would mean you've paid $390 in fees and still owe the $100! How do you avoid getting trapped in this cycle? Well, if you know what you're paying, you'll probably stay away from them altogether. That all goes back to **Principle 9: The Best Protection Is Knowledge**, along with the old saying, "A fool and his money are soon parted."

Principle 9 · The Best Protection Is Knowledge

Currently, 19 states have exempted payday lenders from laws that limit interest rates, with two other states in the process of joining in. Some states have consumer credit laws that ban payday lenders, and others simply do not have any laws that address the practice. Some of the more important consumer credit laws are presented in Table 6.3 in Chapter 6.

## Cost of Single-Payment Loans

The Truth in Lending Act requires lenders to provide you with the finance charges and APR associated with a loan, but it's a good idea to be familiar with the two different ways loans are made—one that removes interest at the beginning (the discount method) and one that doesn't (the simple interest method). The APR and finance charges are given to you in the form of a **loan disclosure statement** similar to the one provided in Figure 7.2.

**Loan Disclosure Statement**
A statement that provides the APR and interest charges associated with a loan.

**Simple Interest Method**  The calculation of interest under the simple interest loan method is as follows:

$$\text{interest} = \text{principal} \times \text{interest rate} \times \text{time}$$

The principal is the amount borrowed, the interest rate is exactly what you think it is, and the time is the period over which the funds are borrowed. For example, if $10,000 were borrowed for 6 months at an annual rate of 12 percent, the interest charges would be calculated as $600, as follows:

$$\$600 = \$10,000 \times 0.12 \times \tfrac{1}{2}$$

Note that the value for time is $\tfrac{1}{2}$ because the money is borrowed for half of a year. If we're talking about single-payment loans, both the interest and the principal are

## Figure 7.2 A Loan Disclosure Statement

A loan disclosure statement is required by the Truth in Lending Act and provides the APR, the finance charge, and the total of payments associated with the loan.

Annual Percentage Rate: The APR, or annual percentage rate, is the true simple interest rate paid over the life of the loan. It is calculated by dividing the average annual finance charge by the average loan balance outstanding.

Finance Charge: The finance charge includes all the costs associated with the loan, for example, interest payments, loan processing fees, fees for a credit check, and any required insurance fees.

Amount Financed: This is the amount you are borrowing, or the principal.

Total of Payments: This is the sum of your finance charge and the amount that you are borrowing.

| ANNUAL PERCENTAGE RATE The cost of my credit as a yearly rate. | FINANCE CHARGE The dollar amount the credit will cost me. | Amount Financed. The amount of credit provided to me or on my behalf. | Total of Payments. The amount I will have paid after I have made all payments as scheduled. |
| --- | --- | --- | --- |

I have the right to receive at this time an itemization of the Amount Financed: (_____) I want an itemization. (_____) I do not want an itemization.
(Initials)    (Initials)

**My payment schedule will be:**

| No. of Payments | Payment Amount | Frequency | Due Date | No. of Payments | Payment Amount | Frequency | Due Date |
| --- | --- | --- | --- | --- | --- | --- | --- |
| | | | | | | | |

**Variable Rate.**
If my loan, as indicated above, has a variable rate, my interest rate may increase during the term of my loan based on movement of the WSJ Prime Rate. My interest rate will not increase more than once each month. If my loan is secured by a principal dwelling for a term greater than one year, disclosures about the variable rate have been provided to me earlier.

____ If indicated, my loan has multiple payments for a term of more than 60 months. Any increase in my interest rate will increase the number of payments and may increase the payment amounts. If my loan were for $10,000 for 144 months at 12% and the interest rate increased to 12.50% in three months, my regular payment would increase by $7.30 beginning with my Sixty-First payment.

____ **MAXIMUM RATE.** If indicated, the maximum interest rate will not exceed:

____ If indicated, my loan has multiple payments for a term of 60 months or less. Any increase in my interest rate will increase the number of payments. If my loan were for $10,000 for 60 months at 12% and the interest rate increased to 12.50% in three months I would have to make one additional payment of $196.56.

____ If indicated, my loan has a single payment. Any increase in my interest rate will increase the amount due at maturity. If my loan were for $10,000 at 12% for 90 days, and my interest rate increased to 12.25% in 20 days, then my final payment would increase by $4.80.

**Security.** I am giving a security interest in:

____ the goods or property being purchased.    ____ other (describe):

Collateral securing other loans with you may also secure this loan, except my principal dwelling or household goods.

**Filing Fees.**    **Prepayment.** If I pay off early, I may have to pay a penalty and I will not be entitled to a refund of part of any prepaid finance charge.

**Late charges.** If you receive any payment 8 days or more after the due date, I agree to pay you a late charge of 5% of my payment.

____ If indicated, this loan is for the purchase of property used as my principal dwelling and someone buying my principal dwelling cannot assume the remainder of my loan on the original terms.

____ If indicated, the Annual Percentage Rate does not take into account my required deposit.

I may see my contract documents for any additional information about nonpayment, default, any required repayment in full before the scheduled due date, and prepayment refunds and penalties.

I understand that credit life and credit disability insurance are not required to get this loan. **You will not provide it unless I sign the NOTICE OF PROPOSED GROUP CREDIT INSURANCE form and agree to pay the cost.** If I want any of these insurance coverages, I must be sure that the insurance coverage I want is indicated, that the amount of the premium is filled in, and that I have signed below. If I request credit life insurance or credit disability insurance, I have the right to rescind the insurance policy or certificate of insurance by giving written notice to the insurance company within 15 days from the date I received the policy or certificate. The term of any insurance I request is for the stated term of this loan unless shown otherwise.

| INSURED #1    #2 | TYPE | PREMIUM |
| --- | --- | --- |
| ____    ____ | Credit Life | |
| ____ | Credit Disability | |

If this loan is secured, I may obtain property insurance from any insurer I choose.

I request coverage(s) checked for the premiums shown above
_____
Signature of Insured #1 (Life only or Life and Disability)

I request coverage(s) checked for the premiums shown above
_____
Signature of Insured #2 (Life only)

due at maturity. Thus, in the loan we've just described, you'd receive $10,000 when you take out the loan, and 6 months later you'd repay $10,600.

For single-payment loans, the stated interest rate and the APR are always the same if there are no noninterest finance charges. The APR can be calculated as follows:

$$\text{APR} = \frac{\text{average annual finance charges}}{\text{average loan balance outstanding}}$$

In this case, it's calculated as follows:

$$\text{APR} = \frac{(\$600/0.5)}{\$10,000} = \frac{\$1,200}{\$10,000} = 0.12, \text{ or } 12.0\%$$

Notice that the annual finance charges are equal to the total finance charges divided by the number of periods the loan continues. In this case, it's a 6-month loan, and because we paid $600 to have the loan for 6 months, we'd have had to pay $1,200 if the loan were outstanding for a full year. Therefore, $1,200 is the annual finance charge. Keep in mind that if there had been noninterest finance charges, they would be included as part of the finance charges.

**Discount Method**   With a discount method single-payment loan, the entire interest charge is subtracted from the loan principal before you receive the money, and at maturity you repay the principal. For example, if you borrow $10,000 for 1 year and the interest rate is 11 percent, your finance charges would be $1,100 ($10,000 × 0.11). Under the discount method, you'd receive only $8,900 ($10,000 less the interest of $1,100), and in 1 year you'd have to repay the entire principal of $10,000. In effect, you'd really have a loan of only $8,900, because the interest is prepaid. The APR for this example is 12.36 percent, calculated as follows:

$$\text{APR} = \frac{\$1,100}{\$8,900} = 0.1236, \text{ or } 12.36\%$$

Again, you'll notice that we have assumed there are no noninterest finance charges. If our earlier example of a $10,000 loan at 12 percent for 6 months had been lent using the discount method, the APR would be calculated to be 13.64 percent, as follows:

$$\text{APR} = \frac{(\$600/0.5)}{\$8,800} = \frac{\$1,200}{\$8,800} = 0.1364, \text{ or } 13.64\%$$

Notice that the APR is larger when money is lent under the discounted method than when it's lent under the simple interest method. Why? Because under the discount method, with the interest taken out before you receive the loan, you actually receive less than the stated principal of the loan.

## Cost of Installment Loans

With an installment loan, repayment of both the interest and the principal occurs at regular intervals, with payment levels set so that the loan expires at a preset date. Installment loans use either the simple interest or the add-on method to determine what the payments will be.

**Simple Interest Method** The simple interest method is the most common method of calculating payments on an installment loan. Recall that the monthly payments on an installment loan remain the same each month, but the portion of your monthly payment that goes toward interest declines each month, while the portion going toward the principal increases. In effect, you pay interest only on the unpaid balance of the loan, which declines as it's gradually paid off.

We can determine your monthly payment on an installment loan using either a financial calculator (using the present value of an annuity calculation to determine PMT, the payment) or financial tables to determine the monthly payment. The trick here is to remember to set your calculator for 12 payments per year and that the payments occur at the end of each period. Let's look at the example of a 12-month installment loan for $5,000 at 14 percent.

**Calculator Solution** To solve on a financial calculator, first make sure the calculator is set to 12 payments per year, then do the following:

| Enter: | 36 | 10 | 15,000 | | 0 |
|---|---|---|---|---|---|
| | N | I/Y | PV | PMT | FV |
| Solve for: | | | | −448.94 | |

The answer in the output row is shown as a negative number. Remember, with a financial calculator, each problem will have two cash flows, and one will be a positive number and one a negative number. The idea is that you borrow money from the bank (a positive number, because "you receive the money"), and at some other point in time you pay the money back to the bank (a negative number, because "you pay it back").

## Table 7.1 Monthly Installment Loan Tables
### ($1,000 loan with interest payments compounded monthly)

| Interest | Loan Maturity (in months) | | | | | | | | | | |
|---|---|---|---|---|---|---|---|---|---|---|---|
| | 6 | 12 | 18 | 24 | 30 | 36 | 48 | 60 | 72 | 84 | 96 |
| 11.50% | 172.30 | 88.62 | 60.75 | 46.84 | 38.51 | 32.98 | 26.09 | 21.99 | 19.29 | 17.39 | 15.98 |
| 11.75% | 172.42 | 88.73 | 60.87 | 46.96 | 38.63 | 33.10 | 26.21 | 22.12 | 19.42 | 17.52 | 16.12 |
| 12.00% | 172.55 | 88.85 | 60.98 | 47.07 | 38.75 | 33.21 | 26.33 | 22.24 | 19.55 | 17.65 | 16.25 |
| 12.25% | 172.67 | 88.97 | 61.10 | 47.19 | 38.87 | 33.33 | 26.46 | 22.37 | 19.68 | 17.79 | 16.39 |
| 12.50% | 172.80 | 89.08 | 61.21 | 47.31 | 38.98 | 33.45 | 26.58 | 22.50 | 19.81 | 17.92 | 16.53 |
| 12.75% | 172.92 | 89.20 | 61.33 | 47.42 | 39.10 | 33.57 | 26.70 | 22.63 | 19.94 | 18.06 | 16.67 |
| 13.00% | 173.04 | 89.32 | 61.45 | 47.54 | 39.22 | 33.69 | 26.83 | 22.75 | 20.07 | 18.19 | 16.81 |
| 13.25% | 173.17 | 89.43 | 61.56 | 47.66 | 39.34 | 33.81 | 26.95 | 22.88 | 20.21 | 18.33 | 16.95 |
| 13.50% | 173.29 | 89.55 | 61.68 | 47.78 | 39.46 | 33.94 | 27.08 | 23.01 | 20.34 | 18.46 | 17.09 |
| 13.75% | 173.41 | 89.67 | 61.80 | 47.89 | 39.58 | 34.06 | 27.20 | 23.14 | 20.47 | 18.60 | 17.23 |
| 14.00% | 173.54 | 89.79 | 61.92 | 48.01 | 39.70 | 34.18 | 27.33 | 23.27 | 20.61 | 18.74 | 17.37 |
| 14.25% | 173.66 | 89.80 | 62.03 | 48.13 | 39.82 | 34.30 | 27.45 | 23.40 | 20.74 | 18.88 | 17.51 |
| 14.50% | 173.79 | 90.02 | 62.15 | 48.25 | 39.94 | 34.42 | 27.58 | 23.53 | 20.87 | 19.02 | 17.66 |
| 14.75% | 173.91 | 90.14 | 62.27 | 48.37 | 40.06 | 34.54 | 27.70 | 23.66 | 21.01 | 19.16 | 17.80 |
| 15.00% | 174.03 | 90.26 | 62.38 | 48.49 | 40.18 | 34.67 | 27.83 | 23.79 | 21.15 | 19.30 | 17.95 |

Example: Determine the monthly payment on a 12-month, 14% installment loan for $5,000.

**Step 1:** Looking at the intersection of the 14% row and the 12-month column, we find that the monthly payment on a similar $1,000 installment loan would be $89.79.

**Step 2:** To determine the monthly payment on a $5,000 loan, we need only multiply $89.79 by 5 because this loan is for $5,000 rather than $1,000.

Thus, a 12-month installment loan of $5,000 at 14 percent would result in monthly payments of $448.94.

We can also determine the monthly payment using installment loan tables, which appear in Appendix E in the back of the book and in an abbreviated form in Table 7.1. Looking in the interest rate equals 14% row and the 12-month column, we find that the monthly payment on a similar $1,000 installment loan would be $89.79. To determine the monthly payment on a $5,000 loan, we need only multiply this amount by 5 because this loan is for $5,000, not $1,000. Thus, using the tables we find that the monthly payment would be $448.95 (the difference between this and what we determined using a calculator, $448.94, is simply a rounding error). Remember, your loan payments remain constant, and as you pay off more of the loan each month, your interest expenses decline. Therefore, your principal payment increases, as shown in Table 7.2.

Because you're paying interest only on the unpaid balance, if there are no nonfinance charges, the stated interest rate is equal to the APR. In effect, there's no trickery here, you just pay interest on what you owe.

**Add-On Method** With an add-on interest installment loan, interest charges are calculated using the original balance. These charges are then added to the loan, and this amount is paid off over the life of the loan. Loans using the add-on method can be quite costly and, in general, should be avoided. Look back at our example of a 12-month, $5,000 loan at 14 percent. You'd first calculate the total interest payments to be $700, as follows:

$$\text{interest} = \text{principal} \times \text{interest rate} \times \text{time}$$
$$\text{interest} = \$5,000 \times 0.14 \times 1 = \$700$$

You'd then add this interest payment to the principal to determine your total repayment amount. To determine your monthly payments, just divide this figure by the number of months over which the loan is to be repaid. In this case, the loan is to be repaid over 12 months; thus, the monthly payments would be $475.

**Table 7.2    Illustration of a 12-Month Installment Loan for $5,000 at 14%**

| Month | Starting Balance | Total Monthly Payment | Interest Monthly Payment | Principal Monthly Payment | Ending Balance |
|---|---|---|---|---|---|
| 1 | $5,000.00 | $ 448.94 | $ 58.33 | $ 390.61 | $4,609.39 |
| 2 | 4,609.39 | 448.94 | 53.78 | 395.16 | 4,214.23 |
| 3 | 4,214.23 | 448.94 | 49.17 | 399.77 | 3,814.46 |
| 4 | 3,814.46 | 448.94 | 44.50 | 404.44 | 3,410.02 |
| 5 | 3,410.02 | 448.94 | 39.78 | 409.16 | 3,000.86 |
| 6 | 3,000.86 | 448.94 | 35.01 | 413.93 | 2,586.93 |
| 7 | 2,586.93 | 448.94 | 30.18 | 418.76 | 2,168.17 |
| 8 | 2,168.17 | 448.94 | 25.30 | 423.64 | 1,744.53 |
| 9 | 1,744.53 | 448.94 | 20.35 | 428.59 | 1,315.94 |
| 10 | 1,315.94 | 448.94 | 15.35 | 433.59 | 882.35 |
| 11 | 882.35 | 448.94 | 10.29 | 438.65 | 443.70 |
| 12 | 443.70 | 448.94 | 5.18 | 443.76 | 0.00* |
| Total | | $5,387.28 | $387.22 | $5,000.06 | |

*Actually, you've overpaid by 6¢.

$$\frac{\$700 + \$5,000}{12} = \$475$$

These calculations result in an APR of close to 25 percent. As you can see, there's a very big difference between the stated interest rate and the APR for installment loans using the add-on method to determine interest payments. In fact, the add-on method generally results in an APR of close to twice the level of the stated interest rate, because you're paying interest on the original principal over the entire life of the loan.

Even though the amount of outstanding principal keeps decreasing as you pay back the loan, you still pay interest on the amount you originally borrowed. That's why there was such a big difference between the advertised rate of 14 percent and the actual APR of close to 25 percent in the example. Fortunately, the Truth in Lending Act requires lenders to disclose the loan's APR, thereby giving you a more accurate read on the cost of the loan regardless of the method used to calculate interest payments.

The calculation of the APR for add-on loans is extremely complicated. However, an approximation can be calculated using the **N-ratio method**. The N-ratio approximation for the APR is calculated as follows:

**N-Ratio Method**
A method of approximating the APR.

$$N\text{-ratio approximation for the APR} = \frac{M(95N + 9)F}{12N(N + 1)(4P + F)}$$

where

$M$ = the number of payments in a year
$N$ = the number of loan payments over the life of the loan
$F$ = the total finance charge
$P$ = the loan principal

In the example, $M = 12$, $N = 12$, $F = \$700$, and $P = \$5,000$. Substituting these numbers into the N-ratio approximation formula, you get

$$
\begin{aligned}
N\text{-ratio approximation for the APR} &= \frac{(12)[(95)(12) + 9](\$700)}{(12)(12)(12 + 1)[(4)(\$5,000) + \$700]} \\
&= \frac{(12)(1,149)(\$700)}{(12)(12)(13)(\$20,700)} \\
&= \frac{\$9,651,600}{\$38,750,400} \\
&= 24.91\%
\end{aligned}
$$

### Early Payment

With an installment loan, if you decide to repay your loan before maturity you must first determine how much principal you still owe. Under the simple interest method, interest is paid only on the remaining principal, so it's relatively easy to determine how much principal remains to be repaid.

Use of the add-on method makes life a little tougher. If you want to repay an add-on interest installment early, some provision should be made in the loan contract for calculating the unpaid

**STOP & THINK** The easiest way to avoid an add-on loan is to look closely at the fine print and the not-so-fine print. In our example, a 14-percent loan with an add-on interest rate actually works out to be a 25-percent loan. Remember to check those APRs!

principal. The most common method for an add-on installment loan is the **rule of 78s** or the **sum of the year's digits**.

The rule of 78s determines what proportion of each payment goes toward paying the principal. Let's use our earlier example of a 12-month $5,000 loan at 14 percent. Under the rule of 78s, the monthly breakdown between interest and principal is determined by using a monthly interest factor.

How do you determine the monthly interest factor? First, sum up all the digits for the number of months in the loan contract. In this case, we have a 12-month contract; thus, the sum of the digits becomes 78 (that is, if you add the numbers from 1 to 12, you'll get 78, hence, the name rule of 78s). For longer loans we can save ourselves some hassles in calculating the sum of the digits by applying the formula given in Figure 7.3. This sum-of-the-digits figure then becomes the denominator for the

**Rule of 78s or Sum of the Year's Digits**
A rule to determine what proportion of each loan payment goes toward paying the interest and what proportion goes toward paying the principal.

Figure 7.3 Using the Rule of 78s

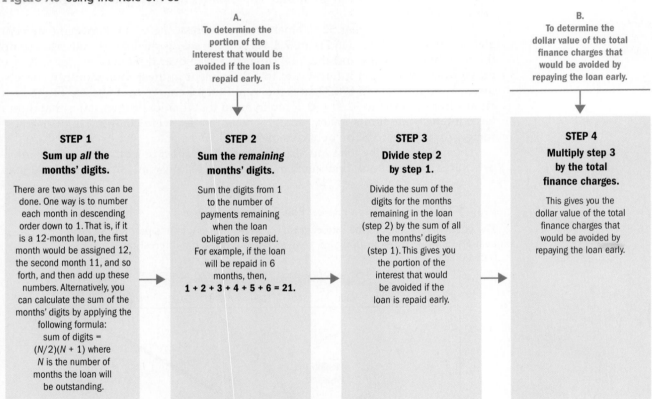

**A.**
To determine the portion of the interest that would be avoided if the loan is repaid early.

**B.**
To determine the dollar value of the total finance charges that would be avoided by repaying the loan early.

**STEP 1**
**Sum up *all* the months' digits.**

There are two ways this can be done. One way is to number each month in descending order down to 1. That is, if it is a 12-month loan, the first month would be assigned 12, the second month 11, and so forth, and then add up these numbers. Alternatively, you can calculate the sum of the months' digits by applying the following formula:
sum of digits = $(N/2)(N + 1)$ where $N$ is the number of months the loan will be outstanding.

**STEP 2**
**Sum the *remaining* months' digits.**

Sum the digits from 1 to the number of payments remaining when the loan obligation is repaid. For example, if the loan will be repaid in 6 months, then,
**$1 + 2 + 3 + 4 + 5 + 6 = 21.$**

**STEP 3**
**Divide step 2 by step 1.**

Divide the sum of the digits for the months remaining in the loan (step 2) by the sum of all the months' digits (step 1). This gives you the portion of the interest that would be avoided if the loan is repaid early.

**STEP 4**
**Multiply step 3 by the total finance charges.**

This gives you the dollar value of the total finance charges that would be avoided by repaying the loan early.

Early Loan Repayment
Let's assume you want to pay off a 12-month loan for $5,000 at 14 percent after only 6 months. The amount needed to repay a loan early is the original principal plus the interest the lender is due over the length of time the loan was outstanding, less any payments that have been made. To calculate the interest that's due over the first 6 months, you use the rule of 78. Thus, over the first 6 months you should be charged $57/78$ of a year's interest (remember 12 + 11 + 10 + 9 + 8 + 7 = 57). In effect, you add the principal to the interest due and subtract out the payments made. For example, if you wanted to repay your loan after 6 months, you'd have to pay

| | |
|---|---|
| Original loan principal | $5,000.00 |
| Plus: interest due lender | |
| ($57/78 \times \$700 = 511.54$) | + 511.54 |
| Total amount due to the lender | $5,511.54 |
| Less payment made (6 × $475 = $2,850) | − $2,850.00 |
| Equals: amount necessary to repay the loan | $2,661.54 |

**14** WORKSHEET

monthly interest factor. The numerator is simply the number of months remaining in the loan. You then multiply this monthly interest factor by the monthly payment to determine what proportion of each payment is considered an interest payment and what proportion is considered a principal payment. If you decide to pay the loan off early you can determine the amount of interest that would be "saved" using the steps that are outlined in Figure 7.3. The bottom line is that add-on loans are very expensive and should be avoided.

## Relationship Between Payment, Interest Rates, and Term of the Loan

Think back to our discussion of the time value of money. You know that a change in interest rate, $i$, or length of time, $n$, causes big changes in the amount of interest paid. Similarly, changes in the interest rate and the length of the loan cause big changes in the amount of interest on an installment loan. Let's take a look at how the duration of your loan and your loan's interest rate affect the size of your payments.

We'll examine a 5-year $2,500 loan whose interest rate varies between 6 percent and 36 percent, as shown in Figure 7.4. As you can see, as the interest rate rises, so do the monthly payments and the total finance charge over the life of the loan. As we move from a 6-percent interest rate to a 36-percent interest rate, monthly charges increase from $48.33 to $90.33, and the total finance charge over the life of the loan climbs from $399.92 to $2,919.80. Keep in mind that in mid-1999, in states that didn't have interest rate limits, many small loan companies were charging high-risk customers up to 36 percent on debt consolidation loans.

The maturity of the loan can also have a major impact on both the monthly interest charge and the total finance charge. Figure 7.5 shows an 18-percent $2,500 loan

**Figure 7.4** Changing Loan Interest Rate

The effect of a change in the interest rate on an installment loan's payments can be best understood by examining a 5-year $2,500 loan with the interest rate varying between 6% and 36%.

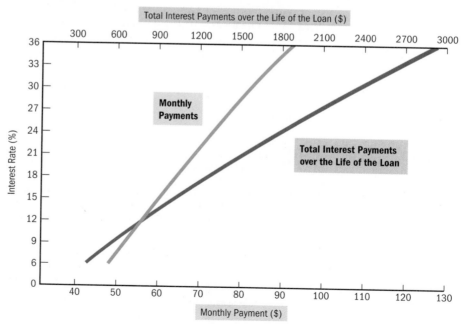

## Figure 7.5 Changing Loan Maturity

A change in the maturity of a loan has an impact on both the monthly interest charge and the total finance charge as shown with a $2,500 installment loan at 18% with maturities varying between 1 year and 8 years.

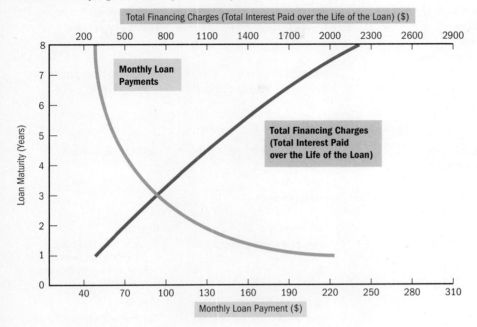

varying in maturity from 12 months or 1 year to 96 months or 8 years. As we change the term of the loan from 12 months to 96 months, the monthly charges decrease from $229.20 to $49.31, and the total finance charge over the life of the loan climbs from $250.40 to $2,233.76.

The trade-offs involved in maturity are lower payments and higher total finance charges versus a quicker elimination of the loan and lower total finance charges. Moreover, lenders generally charge a lower interest rate on shorter-term loans because the shorter the term, the lower the probability that you will experience a financial disaster such as a loss of your job or a medical emergency.

## Sources of Consumer Loans

**3** Pick an appropriate source for your loan.

You should approach applying for a consumer loan in the same way you approach any other consumer purchase. You should shop around for the best deal and be prepared to negotiate. Remember, you're the client or customer purchasing money and agreeing to pay for your purchase in the future.

The question then becomes, Where should you shop for a loan? Well, that depends. There's no one perfect lender for everyone. Not everyone has family members with cash to lend, not everyone belongs to a credit union, and not everyone has a sufficient credit rating to qualify for a bank loan. Just about everyone has a few alternatives, though. Table 7.3 lists a number of possible credit sources along with the types of loans they make and the advantages and limitations of borrowing from those institutions. Let's take a look at some, starting with the least expensive sources.

# Table 7.3    Possible Sources of Credit

| Lenders | Types of Loans | Advantages | Limitations |
|---|---|---|---|
| Commercial Banks | Home mortgage<br>Home improvement<br>Education<br>Personal<br>Auto, mobile home | Widely available<br>Financial counseling may be offered | Generally competitive<br>Do not take credit risks<br>Primarily larger loans |
| Savings and Loans | Home mortgage<br>Home improvement<br>Education*<br>Personal*<br>Auto, mobile home* | Low costs<br>May provide financial counseling | Selective in lending, only lend to good risks |
| Credit Unions | Home mortgage<br>Home improvement<br>Education<br>Personal<br>Auto, mobile home | Easy to arrange for member in good standing<br>Lowest rates<br>Excellent service | Lend to members only |
| Sales Financing Companies (Financing Where You Made the Purchase) | Auto<br>Appliance (major)<br>Boat<br>Mobile home | Very convenient<br>Good terms during special promotions<br>Easy to get<br>Processed quickly | High rates<br>Because loan is secured, defaulting can mean loss of item and payments already made |
| Small Loan Companies (Personal Finance Companies) | Auto<br>Personal | Easy to get<br>Good credit rating not required<br>Processed quickly | High rates<br>Cosigner often required<br>Maximum size limited by law |
| Insurance Companies | General Purpose | Easy to arrange low rates<br>Can borrow up to 95% of policy's surrender value<br>No obligation to repay | Outstanding loan and accumulated interest reduces payment to survivors<br>Policy ownership is required |
| Brokerage Firms | Margin account<br>General-purpose loans, using investments as security | Easy to arrange<br>Little delay in getting money<br>Flexible repayment | Changing value of investments can require payment of additional security<br>Margin requirements can change |

*In some states only.

## Inexpensive Sources

In general, the least expensive source of funds is your family. You don't usually pay the market rate on a family loan; instead you pay what your family would have earned if they had kept this money in a savings account. The obvious downside to a family loan is that if you can't repay it, it's your family that suffers. Also, many people simply feel uncomfortable borrowing money from their families.

Home equity loans and other types of secured loans are also relatively inexpensive because the lending agency has an asset to claim if you can't pay up. The downside of loans of this type is the fact that while assets are tied up as collateral, you can't take out additional first loans on them, so you lose some financing flexibility. Also, if you can't make your payments, you lose your assets. Where do you look for home equity loans? Almost any lending agency, such as banks, S&Ls, and credit unions, offers them.

Insurance companies that lend on the cash value of life insurance policies also offer relatively low rates. Their rates are low because they're really not taking on any risk—you're borrowing against the cash value of an insurance policy you have with them.

## More Expensive Sources

Credit unions, S&Ls, and commercial banks are also good sources of funds. The precise cost of borrowing from each of these institutions depends on the type of loan—secured versus unsecured—the

**STOP & THINK** Actually, when your borrowing isn't tax deductible, which is the case when it's not your mortgage or a home equity loan, the cost of borrowing is actually higher than it appears. If you're in the 30-percent marginal tax bracket, in order to pay $70 of interest you must actually earn $100, with Uncle Sam taking the first $30 out for taxes and leaving you $70 for your interest payment.

length of the loan, and whether it's a variable- or fixed-rate loan. More important is the fact that the same loan may have a significantly different interest rate from one lender to another. Remember, you've got to shop around for your loan. Although these three sources offer loans that are quite similar in nature, credit unions, in general, seem to offer the most favorable terms.

## Most Expensive Sources

In general, financing from retail stores on purchases you make there is quite expensive. Borrowing from a finance company or small loan company is also extremely expensive. Unfortunately, to borrow from other sources, you generally need a solid credit rating. In effect, those who are in the most desperate financial shape generally have to pay the most for credit, which in turn keeps them in desperate financial shape.

## How and When to Borrow

How do you get the most favorable interest rate on a loan? The key to getting a favorable rate, or even qualifying for a loan in the first place, is a strong credit rating. The other keys to securing a favorable rate all involve **Principle 1: The Risk–Return Trade-Off.** To get a low rate, the loan must be relatively risk free to the lender. There are four ways, other than improving your credit rating, that you can use to reduce the lender's risk: (1) use a variable-rate loan, (2) keep the term of the loan as short as possible, (3) provide collateral for the loan, and (4) put a large down payment toward anything being financed.

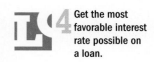
Get the most favorable interest rate possible on a loan.

By accepting a variable-rate loan rather than a fixed-rate loan, you reduce the lender's interest rate risk. You may be borrowing from a bank that's using money from savings deposits to fund your loan. If you had a fixed-rate loan and interest rates rose, the bank could actually end up paying more (in the form of interest on savings deposits) for the funds used to finance your loan than it receives from you in interest.

Principle
The Risk–Return Trade-Off

A variable-rate loan allows a lender to charge you an interest rate that goes up and down with market interest rates, so the lender then gives you a lower interest rate. Of course, instead of the lender doing it, you're now taking on the interest rate risk. If interest rates climb too high, you could end up paying more on the variable interest loan than you would have on a fixed-rate loan.

Interest rates decrease as the length of the loan decreases. As we mentioned earlier, the shorter the term, the lower the probability that you will experience a

WORKSHEET

financial disaster, such as a loss of your job or a medical emergency, and the less risk of default.

Secured loans are less risky because the lender has an asset designated as collateral in the event of default by the borrower.

Finally, the larger your down payment, the less you have to borrow and the larger your ownership stake in the asset being financed. Having a large ownership stake in something is seen as increasing the borrower's desire to pay off the loan.

**Know when to borrow.**

Before looking at the financial aspects of borrowing, let's look at what you accomplish by borrowing. At the start of this chapter, we stated that the decision to borrow should be based on what the funds are to be used for and how the loan fits into your total personal financial planning program. That is, how much debt can you afford? We'll examine this question more closely in the next section, but for now let's assume you haven't borrowed as much or more than you can handle and must decide whether to use cash instead of borrowing, or whether or not to borrow for investment purposes.

In any debt decision, control and planning are the key words. Overriding all your personal finance decisions is the act of setting a budget, living within that budget, and understanding the consequences of your actions.

Unfortunately, debt is, in general, quite expensive. You should pause before you borrow to spend. Actually, you shouldn't just pause, you should come to a complete stop. Not only do you pay more for what you purchase because of the interest on your loans, but making indebtedness a permanent feature in your financial portfolio tends to impair your future financial flexibility.

Don't borrow to spend if you can avoid it. Decide whether or not you really need to buy that new item. Does it fit into your personal financial planning program? If the answer is no, the process stops there. If the answer is yes, the question becomes whether or not to borrow.

In deciding to use cash rather than credit, you must be sure that using cash doesn't materially affect your goal of having sufficient liquidity to carry you through a financial emergency. The answer to this question may leave you with no choice but to borrow. If not, you then have to ask whether the cost of borrowing to purchase the item is greater or less than the after-tax lost return from using savings to purchase the item. That is:

| | | | |
|---|---|---|---|
| Borrow if: | after-tax cost of borrowing to purchase the asset | is less than | after-tax lost return from using savings to purchase the asset |
| Pay cash if: | after-tax cost of borrowing to purchase the asset | is greater than | after-tax lost return from using savings to purchase the asset |

In essence, you're comparing the after-tax cost of borrowing with the lost income from taking money out of savings and using that money to purchase the item instead of earning income. You notice that we talk about the after-tax cost of both using cash and borrowing. Because you must pay taxes on any interest you earn, you must also look at lost income associated with using savings money to purchase the asset on an after-tax basis. Thus, the after-tax opportunity cost of taking money out of savings to purchase the asset would be equal to

after-tax lost return from taking money out of savings to purchase the asset =
before-tax interest on savings × (1 − marginal tax rate)

For example, with your Super Bowl party coming up, it seems like you have no choice—TV City is running a sale on a 50-inch rear-projection TV, and is offering in-store financing at only 5 percent. Should you finance your new TV with a consumer loan at 5 percent from TV City? Or should you take money out of your savings account, which is currently earning 6 percent before taxes? Let's assume your marginal state and federal tax rate is 30 percent. The after-tax lost return from taking money out of savings to purchase the TV would be

$$\text{after-tax lost return from taking money out of savings} \atop \text{to purchase the asset} = 6\%(1 - 0.30) = 4.20\%$$

Thus, because the cost of borrowing from TV City to purchase the TV is greater than the after-tax lost return from using savings to purchase the item, you should tap your savings.

Up to this point we've focused on borrowing to spend rather than on borrowing to invest. When you borrow to invest, you receive an income stream that may more than offset the costs of the borrowed funds. Borrowing to invest is much more in line with our goal of building wealth. When you borrow to invest, the benefits (in this case your earnings from the borrowed money) should be greater than the costs (the cost of the money you borrowed). Perhaps you're considering some investment land or a building to rent. If an investment will return 15 percent and a loan costs you 10 percent, then you'll still make 5-percent profit (15 percent – 10 percent), and you should take on this favorable investment. In short, if the benefits outweigh the costs, borrowing makes sense.

## Controlling Your Use of Debt

Control your debt.

The first step in controlling debt is to determine how much debt you can comfortably handle. Unfortunately, there is no easy formula to determine your level of debt. In fact, as with much else in personal finance, your comfortable debt level changes as you pass through different stages of the financial life cycle. Early on, housing and family demands coupled with a relatively low income level make it natural for individuals to build up debt. In later years, as income rises, debt as a portion of income tends to decline.

The bottom line is that you must use your common sense in analyzing your commitments. However, there are several measures that you can use to control your commitments. They include the debt limit ratio and the debt resolution rule.

### Debt Limit Ratio

The debt limit ratio is simply a measure of the percentage of your take-home pay or income taken up by nonmortgage debt payments.

$$\text{debt limit ratio} = \frac{\text{total monthly nonmortgage debt payments}}{\text{total monthly take-home pay}}$$

An individual's total debt can be divided into consumer debt and mortgage debt. Mortgage payments aren't included in the debt limit ratio because this ratio measures your commitment to consumer credit, which tends to be a more expensive type of debt. In order to maintain a reasonable degree of flexibility, ideally you should strive to keep this ratio below 15 percent. At that debt level, you still have a borrowing reserve for emergencies and the unexpected. That is, because of your low level of debt commitment, you should easily be able to secure additional borrowing without stretching your debt commitment to an uncomfortable level.

Once this ratio reaches 20 percent, most financial planners would advise you to limit the use of any additional consumer debt. One problem when consumer debt payments reach this level is the lack of access to additional debt in an emergency. The importance of maintaining an adequate degree of financial flexibility can't be overemphasized. Obviously, as this ratio increases, your future financial flexibility declines.

Many lenders use what is called the 28/36 rule in evaluating mortgage applicants. That is, if your total projected mortgage payments (including insurance and real estate taxes) fall below 28 percent of your gross monthly income, and your total debt payments including these mortgage payments plus any consumer credit payments fall below 36 percent, you're considered a good credit risk. If you don't meet this minimum standard, you may be required to come up with an additional down payment, or you may simply be rejected.

### Debt Resolution Rule

The debt resolution rule is used by financial planners to help control debt obligations, excluding borrowing associated with education and home financing, by forcing you to repay all your outstanding debt obligations every 4 years. The logic behind this rule is that consumer credit should be short-term in nature. If it lasts over 4 years, it's not short term. Unfortunately, it's all too easy to rely on consumer credit as a long-term source of funding. Given its relative costs, this type of funding should be used sparingly.

### Controlling Consumer Debt

The key to controlling consumer debt is to make sure it fits with the goals you've set and the budget you've developed to achieve these goals. This was the process discussed in Chapter 2. What we're talking about here is control. As you know, control is a major issue in personal finance.

The inspiration for financial discipline must come with an understanding of how costly and potentially painful the alternative is. It's easy to walk out of college with a good deal of consumer debt. However, keep in mind the costs of borrowing and how borrowing limits your future financial flexibility.

## What To Do If You Can't Pay Your Bills

Once you have gotten into trouble through the overuse of credit, getting out becomes a difficult and painful task. The first step is, of course, putting in place a budget that brings in more money than goes out. The second step involves self-control in the use of credit.

What if your problems seem overwhelming? The first place to go may be to the one to whom you owe the money. If you owe money to a bank, go there first. The bank may be willing to restructure the loan. If you're still lost, you might consider seeking help from a **credit counselor**, a trained professional specializing in developing personal budgets and debt repayment programs. A credit counselor can be helpful in organizing your finances and developing a workable plan to pay off your debts.

However, as is always the case in personal finance, you must be careful in choosing a credit counselor. Just because someone advertises doesn't mean his or her

**Credit Counselor**
A trained professional specializing in developing personal budgets and debt repayment programs.

advice will be good or that he or she won't just take your money and do nothing. One good source for a credit counselor is the Consumer Credit Counseling Service (800-388-2227 or on the Web at **www.nfcc.org**), which is a nonprofit agency affiliated with the National Foundation for Consumer Credit. This organization has offices across the nation. If you can't find one in your town, simply phone or write the National Foundation for Consumer Credit, 8701 Georgia Avenue, Suite 507, Silver Spring, MD 20910.

Along with these remedies, there are other options you might consider. First, you should make sure you're borrowing as inexpensively as possible. Small loan companies sometimes charge as much as 40 percent on loans. Avoid them and see if there's a cheaper way to get money.

A second option to consider is using savings to pay off current debt. You shouldn't do so more than once—when you're reevaluating and changing your spending and credit use patterns in a permanent manner. If you are only earning 4 percent after taxes on your savings, then using savings to pay off consumer debt at 10 or 12 percent may be a good idea. However, your borrowing should be controlled in such a way that it doesn't get out of hand and doesn't warrant this remedy on a regular basis. This is an emergency measure to be taken only in the extreme situation.

Another alternative is to use a debt consolidation loan to stretch out your payments and possibly reduce your interest. A **debt consolidation loan** is simply a loan used to pay off all your current debts. The purpose of a loan of this kind is to lower your monthly payment. A debt consolidation loan doesn't eliminate your debt problems, it merely restructures the payments associated with paying off that debt. Again, this isn't the optimum solution. The best solution is to take control of your borrowing from the onset.

A final alternative in the most extreme case of debt is personal **bankruptcy**. This is not a step to be taken lightly. It doesn't wipe out all your obligations—for example, student loans, alimony, and tax liabilities remain—but it relieves some of the financial pressure. Bankruptcy probably happens more than you might think. In fact, in 2001, there were about 1.4 million bankruptcies nationwide, topping the record set in 1998. That's about 1.36 in every 100 U.S. households. One contributing factor to the large number of bankruptcies is the easy availability of credit that leads to living beyond your means. Divorce, job loss, and illness are also major contributors to bankruptcy.

The two most commonly used types of personal bankruptcy are Chapter 13, the wage earner plan, and Chapter 7, straight bankruptcy. Two other types of bankruptcy are also available, but are not commonly used. Chapter 11, although intended for business, accommodates those who exceed Chapter 13 debt limitations or lack regular income. Chapter 12 is a special-purpose personal bankruptcy available only to family farmers. Because Chapter 11 and Chapter 12 bankruptcy are so specialized, we discuss only Chapter 13 and Chapter 7 in detail. Figure 7.6 provides a comparison of the two primary personal bankruptcy options.

**STOP &THINK** Debt consolidation loans are very appealing because they offer hope to those who can't keep up with their current payment schedules. Before taking out a debt consolidation loan, however, keep in mind that you may be paying a higher interest rate on the consolidation loan than you are on your current debt. Moreover if the problems that led you into this dilemma in the first place aren't solved, the solution will only be temporary.

## Chapter 13: The Wage Earner's Plan

To file for Chapter 13 bankruptcy, you must have a regular income, secured debts of less than $807,750, and unsecured debts of less than $269,250. You design a plan

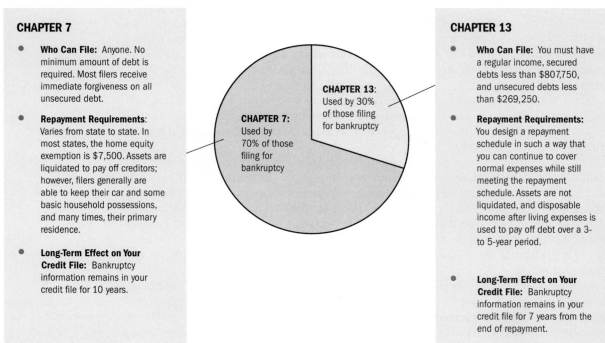

Figure 7.6 Personal Bankruptcy Options

**CHAPTER 7**

- **Who Can File:** Anyone. No minimum amount of debt is required. Most filers receive immediate forgiveness on all unsecured debt.

- **Repayment Requirements:** Varies from state to state. In most states, the home equity exemption is $7,500. Assets are liquidated to pay off creditors; however, filers generally are able to keep their car and some basic household possessions, and many times, their primary residence.

- **Long-Term Effect on Your Credit File:** Bankruptcy information remains in your credit file for 10 years.

**CHAPTER 7:** Used by 70% of those filing for bankruptcy

**CHAPTER 13:** Used by 30% of those filing for bankruptcy

**CHAPTER 13**

- **Who Can File:** You must have a regular income, secured debts less than $807,750, and unsecured debts less than $269,250.

- **Repayment Requirements:** You design a repayment schedule in such a way that you can continue to cover normal expenses while still meeting the repayment schedule. Assets are not liquidated, and disposable income after living expenses is used to pay off debt over a 3- to 5-year period.

- **Long-Term Effect on Your Credit File:** Bankruptcy information remains in your credit file for 7 years from the end of repayment.

that will allow you to repay the majority of your debts. The repayment schedule is designed so that you can continue to cover normal expenses while still meeting the repayment obligation. You maintain title and possession of your assets and, other than the new debt repayment schedule, continue on with life as before. For your creditors, it means a controlled repayment of debt obligations with the court's supervision. For the individual, it may mean relief from the harassment of bill collectors and the pressure of never knowing how future obligations will be met.

If you exceed the debt limitations of Chapter 13 bankruptcy or don't have a regular source of income, you can file under Chapter 11 of the bankruptcy code. This is a relatively uncommon practice because Chapter 11 bankruptcy is really intended for businesses. However, for those who have piled up huge debts and want to restructure their debt, Chapter 11 is an option. The downside of Chapter 11 bankruptcy is that creditors vote on the restructuring plan and can block it.

Bankruptcy happens to all kinds of good people, and it gives them some breathing room to start over when there's no hope. Burt Reynolds, Hollywood's number 1 box office draw from 1978 through 1982, along with Kim Basinger and Toni Braxton, have all filed for bankruptcy. Although Burt Reynolds made a ton of money in movies like *Smokey and the Bandit* and *Cannonball Run,* he also lost around $15 million in Po-Folks restaurants. When he finally filed for bankruptcy he had $11.2 million in debts and assets worth only $6.65 million. Because he exceeded the debt limits of Chapter 13 bankruptcy, he was forced to file under Chapter 11. Among his debts were a loan from CBS of $3.7 million plus interest and $121,797 to his custom wig-maker. Chapter 11 bankruptcy gave him the breathing room to begin again and regain control of his finances.

## Chapter 7: Straight Bankruptcy

Chapter 7 bankruptcy, or straight bankruptcy, is a more severe type of bankruptcy. Under Chapter 7, the individual who doesn't have any possibility of repaying debts is given the opportunity to eliminate them and begin again. Exactly what you can keep varies from state to state. For example, in Maryland none of your equity in your home is exempt, whereas in Florida your entire home equity is exempt in most cases. In most states, the home equity exemption is $7,500, but in Minnesota, the home equity exemption is $250,000.

The bottom line is that while you will not lose everything, you will have to sell a good portion of your assets in order to satisfy Chapter 7 requirements. Most of your debts will be wiped out, but some will remain, like child support, alimony, student loans, and taxes. A trustee arranges to collect and sell all of your nonexempt property, with the proceeds divided among the creditors. In short, the courts confiscate and sell most of your assets to pay off creditors and in return, eliminate most of your debts. Needless to say, Chapter 7 bankruptcy is a drastic step and should be taken only after consultation with a financial advisor and your lawyer.

## SUMMARY

A single-payment loan is simply a loan that's paid back in a single lump-sum payment at maturity. In general, these loans have a stated maturity date. An installment loan calls for repayment of both interest and principal at regular intervals, with the payment levels set in such a way that the loan expires at a pre-set date.

Consumer loans are either secured or unsecured. A secured loan is a loan that is guaranteed by a specific asset. With an unsecured loan, no collateral is required.

With a fixed interest rate loan, the interest rate is fixed for the entire duration of the loan, but with a variable interest rate loan, the interest rate is tied to a market interest rate and periodically adjusts to reflect movements in that market interest rate. A home equity loan, or second mortgage, is a loan that uses a borrower's built-up equity in his or her home as collateral against the loan.

It's important to know exactly what a loan costs. The finance charges include all the costs associated with the loan—interest payments, loan processing fees, fees for a credit check, and any required insurance fees. The APR is the simple percentage cost of the credit paid over the life of the loan on an annual basis.

In general, only the interest on mortgage debt on both your primary and secondary residences is tax-deductible. Thus, when comparing the cost of alternative loans, make sure you're comparing the after-tax costs. This adjustment can be made by taking the before-tax cost of the home equity loan and multiplying it by [1 − (marginal tax rate)].

There are numerous sources of consumer loans, which vary dramatically in terms of cost, including family, insurance companies, credit unions, savings and loan associations, commercial banks, small loan companies, retail stores, and credit cards.

The key to getting a favorable rate on a loan, or even qualifying for a loan in the first place, is a strong credit rating. In addition, there are four other ways that you can reduce the lender's risk and thereby secure a favorable rate: (1) use a variable-rate loan, (2) keep the term of the loan as short as possible, (3) provide collateral for the loan, and (4) put a large down payment toward the item being financed.

Before borrowing, you must make sure that borrowing fits within your financial plan, including living within your budget, and that you understand all the consequences of your actions. You must also determine how much debt you can afford. Not only should you use your common sense in analyzing your debt commitments, but also you should measure the severity of your credit commitments using the ratio of the nonmortgage debt service to take-home pay and the debt resolution rule.

# REVIEW QUESTIONS

1. How does a single-payment or balloon loan differ from an installment loan? What is a bridge loan?

2. What is the fundamental difference between a secured and unsecured loan? Considering **Principle 1: The Risk–Return Trade-Off**, what other differences apply?

3. Describe a fixed interest rate loan, a variable- or adjustable-rate loan, and a convertible loan. Which is best?

4. Credit contracts often include the acceleration clause, the deficiency payments clause, and the recourse clause to give the lender options for collecting the debt. Explain each clause. What is the purpose of the insurance agreement clause?

5. Home equity credit loans and credit lines have become very popular sources of consumer credit. List the advantages and disadvantages of borrowing against home equity. What is the security for this type of loan?

6. Student loan programs are available to students and parents to provide money for college-related expenses. Compare and contrast the programs available to students and parents. How are the interest rates determined?

7. Home equity, student, and auto loans are special-purpose consumer loans. Which ones offer the unique benefit of tax deductibility for interest charges?

8. What is APR?

9. Describe the advantages and disadvantages of payday loans.

10. What methods are used to calculate interest on a single-payment loan? Which method is preferable to the consumer?

11. What methods are used to calculate interest on an installment loan? Which method is preferable to the consumer? What is the most common method of calculating interest on an installment loan?

12. Explain the relationship between payment amount, interest rate, and term of the loan. What rules of thumb apply?

13. Loan costs vary significantly with the lender. Identify at least two inexpensive loan sources, two more expensive loan sources, and two most expensive loan sources.

14. Based on **Principle 1: The Risk–Return Trade-Off**, name five ways you can reduce the risk for the lender thereby reducing the return for the lender and saving yourself money.

15. In any debt decision, control and planning are the key words. Name five factors to consider when deciding to borrow.

16. Borrowing to spend provides immediate benefit from the good or service purchased on credit. What is the benefit when borrowing to invest?

17. As you have learned, your debt limit ratio is affected by the amount you borrow. What other factors affect this ratio?

18. According to the debt resolution rule, what is the time frame for repayment of short-term debt? What types of borrowing are not considered in the debt resolution rule?

19. Remedies for overcoming excessive credit use can impact your present and future financial situation. Name eight remedies to consider when you are having trouble paying your bills. List the advantages and disadvantages of each.

20. According to Figure 7.6, 70 percent of bankruptcy filers choose Chapter 7. What are the advantages of Chapter 7 compared to Chapter 13? What are the disadvantages?

# PROBLEMS AND ACTIVITIES

1. Assuming a period of rapidly rising interest rates, how much could your rate increase over the next four years if you had a 7 percent variable-rate mortgage with a 2 percent annual cap and 6 percent lifetime cap? How would this affect the monthly payment?

2. Rico needs approximately $2,500 to buy a new computer. A 2-year unsecured loan through the credit union is available for 12 percent interest. The current rate on his revolving home equity line is 8.75 percent, although he is reluctant to use it. Rico is in the 27 percent federal tax bracket and the 5.75 percent state tax bracket. Which loan should he choose? Why? Regardless of the loan chosen, Rico wants to pay off the loan in 24 months. Calculate the payments for him, assuming both loans use the simple interest calculation method.

3. Shirley, a recent college graduate, excitedly described the $1,500 sofa, chair, and tables she had found today. In a discussion with her parents, Shirley was surprised to hear that a few

years earlier they had financed furniture with the add-on method of interest calculation. Shirley had not asked about the interest calculation method at the furniture store but knew the bank used the simple interest method for unsecured loans. Calculate the monthly payments and total cost for the bank loan assuming a 1-year repayment period and 14 percent interest. Now assume the store still uses the add-on method on interest calculation. Calculate the monthly payment and total cost with a 1-year repayment period and 12 percent interest. Explain why the bank payment and total cost are lower even though the stated interest rate is higher.

4. Using the information on the two loans described previously, how much interest would have been "saved" or rebated if both Shirley and her parents could have repaid the loans after 6 months?

5. Which is a better deal, borrowing $1,000 to be repaid 12 months later as a single-payment loan or borrowing $1,000 to be repaid as a 12-month installment loan? Assume a simple interest method of calculation at 12 percent interest. Defend your answer.

6. Consumers should comparison shop for credit just like any other consumer good or service. How might stage of the financial life cycle or asset ownership affect the availability of loan sources and the associated cost of the loans offered?

7. Rick wants a new big-screen TV and Dolby® Digital Stereo. He figures the system will cost $4,000. The store will finance up to $3,500 for 2 years at a 10.5 percent interest rate. Assuming Rick accepts the store's financing, how much will he save in total interest if he increases his down payment to $1,000?

8. Antonio would like to replace his golf clubs, actually his father's old set, with a custom measured set. A local sporting goods megastore is advertising custom clubs for $500, including a new bag. In-store financing is available at 5 percent or he can choose not to renew his $500 certificate of deposit (CD), which just matured. Advertised CD renewal rate is 6.5 percent. Antonio knows the in-store financing costs would not affect his taxes, but he knows he'll pay taxes (27 percent federal and 5.75 percent state) on the CD interest earnings. Should he cash the CD or use the in-store financing?

9. Noel and Herman need to replace her car. However, in addition to the furniture and appliance payments, the credit card bills, and the other car payment, they are uncertain if they can afford another payment. The auto-financing representative has asked, "What size payments are you thinking of?" Current payments total $475 of their $2,800 combined monthly take-home pay. Calculate the debt limit ratio to help them decide about the car purchase and answer the question, "What size payments are you thinking of?"

10. Harriet and Alstott Clement have accumulated over $200,000 in unsecured debt. After much discussion, they feel that filing bankruptcy is their only alternative. Under which bankruptcy chapters are they eligible to file? Give a brief synopsis of each alternative.

# SUGGESTED PROJECTS

1. Visit a bank, a credit union, a savings and loan, a consumer finance company, and a retail outlet that offer credit. Ask for a copy of the contract for a consumer installment loan. Compare the contracts for an explanation of the credit terms as well as the various contract clauses identified in this chapter. Prepare a report of your findings.

2. Visit the financial aid office at your school to learn about the different student loans available. What is the application process? Do qualification requirements and repayment plans vary with the different loan programs? What is the "average" monthly payment and repayment period?

3. Visit a bank, a credit union, a savings and loan, and a consumer finance company to learn about their consumer loan options. How do interest rates vary for secured and unsecured loans? Do they offer fixed and adjustable interest rate loans? What method(s) of interest calculation is used? Prepare a report of your findings.

4. Interview the financial manager at an auto dealership to learn about the available financing options. Since the auto purchased will serve as

collateral, and the vehicle trade-in value can be the down payment, how does the interest rate and term of the loan affect, or reduce, the lender's risk? How can the consumer get the best auto financing deal? Discuss the debt resolution rule in light of the increasing number of 5- or 6-year auto loans.

5. Using your anticipated entry-level take-home pay, calculate the maximum nonmortgage debt payment that you can safely handle. What are the implications given your actual or anticipated debt for credit cards, auto loan, or school loans? Can you afford additional borrowing for furniture, appliances, travel, or other needs?

6. Check the Internet or the local phone directory or contact the National Foundation for Consumer Credit to locate a debt counseling service. Determine the services offered to consumers as well as creditors. Ask the counselor to identify factors that commonly contribute to problems in repaying debts. What strategies are used to remedy different situations? Which remedies seem to be the most effective?

7. To learn more about personal bankruptcy, interview a lawyer who often handles bankruptcy proceedings. Question the lawyer about spending trends and household events that appear to contribute to bankruptcy, typical fees for filing bankruptcy, and the effect of filing on the consumer's financial future. Or, if you know someone who has filed bankruptcy, ask him or her similar questions. Report your findings.

8. Talk with a loan officer at a local bank or credit union. Discuss the approval qualifications for unsecured, secured, and home equity loans. Also, discuss the effect, if any, of the debt limit ratio on the interest rate, if the loan is approved. Write a brief synopsis of the information.

## Discussion Case 1

Karou is considering different options for financing the $12,000 balance on her planned new car purchase. The cheapest advertised rate among the local banks is 7 percent for a 48-month car loan. The current rate on her revolving home equity line is 8.5 percent. Karou is in the 27 percent federal tax bracket and the 5.75 percent state tax bracket.

### Questions

1. Determine which loan she should choose. Defend your answer.

2. Calculate the payments for her. Assume both loans have 48-month amortization and use the simple interest method.

3. In a discussion with her father about financing her new car, Karou was surprised to hear that he once financed a car with the add-on method of interest calculation. He planned to repay the $2,000 loan within one year but was able to do so after 9 months because of a bonus he earned at work. The interest rate was 5 percent. Calculate the monthly payments, as well as the final payment to pay off the loan. How much interest was "saved," or rebated, using this method of financing and the rule of 78?

4. Assume Karou's father could finance $2,000 today at 5 percent using the simple interest method of calculation. How much would the payments be? Calculate the final payment to pay off the loan after 9 months. How much interest was "saved"?

5. Considering the information in questions 3 and 4, calculate the difference in finance charges assuming neither loan was paid off early.

6. Assuming Karou did not have access to the home equity credit line, what factors might she consider to reduce the lender's risk and, therefore, "buy" herself a lower-cost loan? (Hint: Consider **Principle 1: The Risk–Return Trade-Off.**)

## Discussion Case 2

You work in the financial aid office and Mary Lou Hennings, a junior, has come to you for some financial advice. She just found out that her father has been laid off from work and she will need to apply for a loan if she wants to return next school year. She already has a part-time job with take-home pay of $375 per month. She expects her annual net earnings to increase to approximately $28,000 after graduation. Her parents have told her she can use their $10,000 home equity line of credit; however, she is not sure she wants to do that. She does not have any debt, except for a $189 auto payment that has 3 years left. She is worried about trying to pay for an additional loan while still in school.

*Tips from Marcy Furney, ChFC, Certified Financial Planner™*

# Money Matters

## AND NOW, A FEW WORDS FROM THE "LOAN RANGER"

When most people apply for a mortgage or other large loan, they often go into the process totally unprepared. This can result in delays, repeated trips, numerous phone calls, and possibly denial of credit if your situation is marginal. Make yourself as creditworthy as possible.

*If you have no credit history,* obtain a credit card or a small loan and make payments on time. You may need a cosigner to obtain a large loan, even if you have an excellent income. Ability to pay isn't the same as demonstrated willingness to pay.

*Pay off all the debt you can before you apply.* A relatively small credit card balance could cause your ratios to be too high to qualify.

*Order your own credit reports and examine them for any errors.* Make sure they're in good order before you proceed. If there's been a payment problem, write out the reason for the problem and the resolution. Also document thoroughly any reports that are being contested.

*List all your investments and cash,* show the name and address of the firm where they're being held, and include account numbers. Make copies of your current statement on each and attach them to the list. Do the same with all debt.

*If you're applying for a mortgage be sure to provide the lenders' names,* their addresses; and your loan numbers for any previous home loans.

*Make copies of your last W-2 and most recent pay stub.* If you're self-employed, take copies of your proof of income, for example, Schedule C and Form 1040 from your most recent tax return.

*Fill out applications neatly and concisely.* Provide copies of all supporting documents. Don't try to hide anything and don't volunteer personal information that isn't requested and isn't directly related to your creditworthiness.

*The more complete and organized the information you provide,* the less the loan processor will have to do. That could give you a slight edge.

*Once you've provided the lender with all the information needed to process the loan,* take the initiative to check on progress periodically.

## Questions

1. What types of student loans are available to her and what lending limits apply?

2. Assume her student loan will have an interest rate of 8 percent and her parents' home equity line has a rate of 9.25 percent. If both loans have a 10-year maturity, what will her monthly payment be on $5,000, ignoring any possible deferments?

3. Considering all available information, which loan would you suggest to Mary Lou? Why?

4. Using her current income, calculate her debt limit ratio for the foregoing loans during school. Using her projected income, calculate her debt limit ratio for the loans after graduation.

5. Explain the tax consequences and advantages of the various options available to Mary Lou and her parents. Are there other options for financing her education expenses?

Visit our Web site for additional case problems, interactive exercises, and practice quizzes for this chapter—**www.prenhall.com/keown**.

# 8 The Home and Automobile Decision

**1** Make good buying decisions.

**2** Choose a vehicle that suits your needs and budget.

**3** Choose housing that meets your needs.

**4** Decide whether to rent or buy housing.

**5** Calculate the costs of buying a home.

**6** Get the most out of your mortgage.

"Home, I have no home. Hunted, despised, living like an animal—the jungle is my home. But I shall show the world that I can be its master. I shall perfect my own race of people. A race of atomic supermen that will conquer the world." These words are spoken by Martin Landau, playing the part of Bela Lugosi in the film *Ed Wood*—a role that won him an Oscar. He made this little speech while Ed Wood, the offbeat director of Lugosi's last movie, *Plan 9 from Outer Space,* watched. In the movie, Ed Wood, who was played by Johnny Depp, adored Lugosi, and in real life Johnny Depp became pretty infatuated with Lugosi also. In fact, Depp was so fascinated that he went after Lugosi's old home.

A beautiful and secluded house, Lugosi's former home and Depp's new one is a gray stone castle with turrets and iron trim. And it's big—7,430 square feet in all, with 28 rooms, including 8 bedrooms and 10 bathrooms—and perhaps a secret vault for spare coffins in the basement. Even for a mega-star like Johnny Depp, the house was a major purchase, costing roughly $2 million. Hey, some people are willing to pay a lot for the perfect house. Of course, Johnny Depp's new place may be perfect for him, but you might cringe at the thought of 10 bathrooms to clean.

What you're looking for in a house generally reflects your lifestyle. Actor Anthony Edwards, who played Dr. Mark Greene on *ER*, the prime-time hospital drama, called an aluminum-skinned Airstream Excella 1000 trailer his home when shooting *ER*.

He had his "silver love sub" parked on the back lot of *ER* and used it as his office and retreat. Decorated in fifties motif, the trailer even sported a pink and silver dinette chair at the kitchen table, where he ate his oatmeal every morning before heading for the set. For him it was perfect. As Edwards proudly said, "The roundness, the curvature of the interior makes a really pleasing environment. It's very womblike."

These homes probably aren't right for you. That's because buying a house isn't just a financial decision, it's also a personal and emotional one. You want a house, and you want the lifestyle that goes with it. What makes the decision to buy a home even more important is the fact that, for most people, buying a home is the single biggest investment they'll ever make. Unfortunately, many first-time homebuyers simply don't understand all the complexities and financial implications of this purchase.

Actually, most people don't understand the financial implications and complexities of any major purchase, including the purchase of a car. Again, for most people, buying a car isn't only a financial decision, it's also a personal one. You don't just want transportation, you want to "look good in your car." Although buying a car isn't considered an investment, it *is* an expenditure, and a huge one at that. In either case—buying a house or a car—you're probably going to need a loan and are thus committing a large portion of your future earnings over a long period of time. Because each purchase has a dramatic impact on your personal finances, you need to look carefully at each one. You don't want to end up "hunted, despised, living like an animal"—on the run from bill collectors because you can't afford the house or car you just purchased.

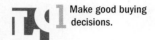

Make good buying decisions.

## Smart Buying

In this chapter, we deal with spending money rather than saving it. Just as you work hard to save money, you should also work hard when spending it. That means you should get the most for your money and make well thought-out spending decisions. Much of our focus is on automobile and housing purchase decisions, but the same basic process applies to all purchases. This is a controlled process, in which your final selection isn't only the best product for the best price, but a product that you need and a purchase that fits your monthly budget. One of the big benefits of this approach is that it eliminates the impulse buying that wreaks havoc on your monthly budget.

### Step 1: Do Your Homework

The first step in smart buying is to separate your wants from your needs. This doesn't mean that you'll never buy anything you simply want but don't need, such as that new DVD player. It does mean you have to recognize that such a purchase is purely a "want" purchase, and that the cost has to fit within your monthly budget. Making a "want" purchase may mean you'll be limited to eating macaroni and cheese for the next 6 months, but that's a trade-off you have to face.

In buying that DVD player, you'll want to make sure your money isn't wasted. You want the best DVD player possible while considering the trade-offs among price, quality, and product attributes. Again, keep in mind that your purchase has to fit within your budget. And you can't figure out what's best for your budget until you know what's actually out there. So take a look at the alternatives.

### Step 2: Make Your Selection

Once you've determined the alternatives, it's time to compare the different products and make trade-offs among quality, different features, and price. Of course, a lot of these trade-offs are based on personal choice, but the personal choice must be within your budget.

You want the best deal you can get for your money, and the only way to get it is through comparison shopping. One way to make this comparison a bit easier is to make a checklist of the different products, along with their prices and features. There are plenty of good sources of information dealing with product quality. Start at your local library with *Consumer Reports;* then look at specialty magazines that rate and compare computers, cameras, cars, and stereos.

There's also a good deal of consumer information available on the Internet. Perhaps the most informative guide on smart buying, the *Consumer's Resource Handbook,* is published by the U.S. Office of Consumer Affairs. It is available free by calling 1-888-878-3256 or is downloadable off the Internet at **www.pueblo.gsa.gov**.

### Step 3: Make Your Purchase

In making most purchases, it may simply be a matter of going to the cheapest source and buying the product. However, with other products, there may be some negotiations involved, especially if you're buying a big-ticket item such as a car, an

# Checklist 8.1 ▌ Before You Buy

Take advantage of sales, but compare prices. Do not assume an item is a bargain just because it is advertised as one.

Don't rush into a large purchase because the "price is only good today."

Be aware of such extra charges as delivery fees, installation charges, service costs, and postage and handling fees. Add them into the total cost.

Ask about the seller's refund or exchange policy.

Don't sign a contract without reading it. Don't sign a contract if there are any blank spaces in it or if you don't understand it. In some states, it is possible to sign away your home to someone else.

Before buying a product or service, contact your consumer protection office to see if there are automatic cancellation periods for the purchase you are making. In some states, there are cancellation periods for dating clubs, health clubs,

and time-share and camp ground memberships. Federal law gives you cancellation rights for certain door-to-door sales.

Walk out or hang up on high-pressure sales tactics. Don't be forced or pressured into buying something.

Don't do business over the telephone with companies you do not know.

Be suspicious of P.O. box addresses. They might be mail drops. If you have a complaint, you might have trouble locating the company.

Do not respond to any prize or gift offer that requires you to pay even a small amount of money.

Don't rely on a salesperson's promises. Get everything in writing.

Source: U.S. Office of Consumer Affairs, *Consumer's Resource Handbook*, 2002.

---

appliance, or some furniture. In this case, you may have to do a good deal of haggling before you arrive at a final price.

The key to negotiating a good price is knowing as much as possible about the markup on the product (the price the dealer adds on above what he or she paid for the product). This gives you an idea of how much room there is for negotiation. You then need to make sure you're dealing with someone with the authority to lower the price. You'll also want to look at the various financing alternatives, not only which is cheapest, but also which is best for you—that is, which fits best into your budget. Checklist 8.1 gives some tips on smart buying.

## Step 4: Maintain Your Purchase

The final step to smart buying is maintaining your purchase. This involves not only maintenance, but also resolving any complaints. If you have a complaint, the first thing to do is contact the seller. Make sure you keep a record of your efforts to resolve the problem. If that doesn't do it, contact the headquarters of the company that made or sold the product. Most large companies have a toll-free 800 number. It's generally on the instructions; if not, you can probably get it through the directory of 800 telephone numbers at your local library or by calling 800-555-1212 (toll-free).

You could write to the company. Make sure to address your letter to the consumer office or the company president. In your correspondence you'll want to describe the problem, what you've done so far to try to resolve it, and what action you'd like taken. Do you want your money back, or do you want the product exchanged? Keep in mind that your problem may not be resolved immediately. When dealing with companies directly, you'll want to keep notes, including the name of the person with whom you spoke, the date, and what was done. Save copies of all letters to and from the company.

If your problem still isn't resolved, it's time to work through such organizations as the Better Business Bureau, along with other local, state, and federal organizations that might provide help. Checklist 8.2 gives some tips on making a complaint, while Figure 8.1 provides a sample complaint letter.

## Figure 8.1 Sample Complaint Letter

Source: U.S. Office of Consumer Affairs, *Consumer's Resource Handbook*, 2002.

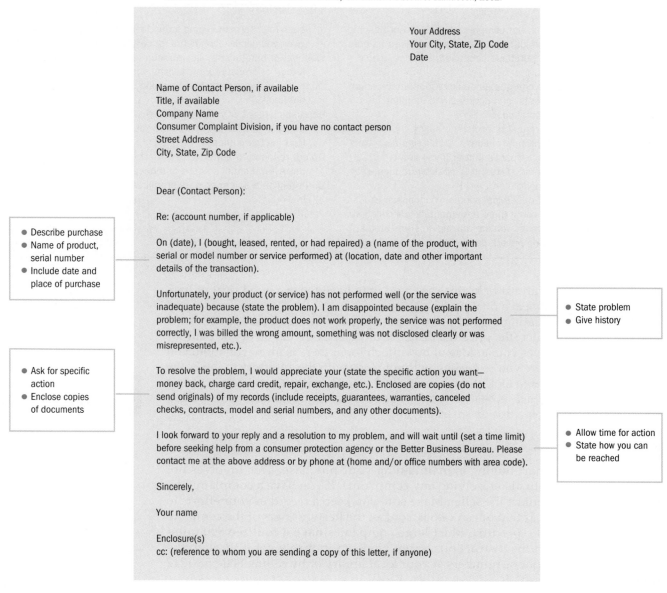

Your Address
Your City, State, Zip Code
Date

Name of Contact Person, if available
Title, if available
Company Name
Consumer Complaint Division, if you have no contact person
Street Address
City, State, Zip Code

Dear (Contact Person):

Re: (account number, if applicable)

- Describe purchase
- Name of product, serial number
- Include date and place of purchase

On (date), I (bought, leased, rented, or had repaired) a (name of the product, with serial or model number or service performed) at (location, date and other important details of the transaction).

- State problem
- Give history

Unfortunately, your product (or service) has not performed well (or the service was inadequate) because (state the problem). I am disappointed because (explain the problem; for example, the product does not work properly, the service was not performed correctly, I was billed the wrong amount, something was not disclosed clearly or was misrepresented, etc.).

- Ask for specific action
- Enclose copies of documents

To resolve the problem, I would appreciate your (state the specific action you want—money back, charge card credit, repair, exchange, etc.). Enclosed are copies (do not send originals) of my records (include receipts, guarantees, warranties, canceled checks, contracts, model and serial numbers, and any other documents).

- Allow time for action
- State how you can be reached

I look forward to your reply and a resolution to my problem, and will wait until (set a time limit) before seeking help from a consumer protection agency or the Better Business Bureau. Please contact me at the above address or by phone at (home and/or office numbers with area code).

Sincerely,

Your name

Enclosure(s)
cc: (reference to whom you are sending a copy of this letter, if anyone)

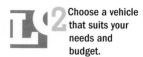

LO2 Choose a vehicle that suits your needs and budget.

## Transportation

Next to buying a house, your vehicle is probably your largest investment. It's also something that most people buy every few years. Although there are major differences—the price, for one thing—between buying a stereo and a car or truck, the process is essentially the same.

Ten years ago, purchasing a vehicle was relatively simple. It involved doing a bit of homework to determine what you needed and what you could afford, figuring out which were lemons and which were good, and negotiating with the dealer. Today, not only do you have to decide which vehicle to purchase, but you also have

# Checklist 8.2 ▌ Making a Complaint

In some instances it will be best to contact the business that sold you the item or performed the service. In other cases, you may wish to go directly to the headquarters of the company or the manufacturer.

Keep a record of your efforts to resolve the problem. When you write to the company, describe the problem, what you have done so far to resolve it, and what solution you want.

Allow time for the person you contacted to resolve your problem. Keep notes of the date, whom you spoke with, what was agreed on, and the next steps to be taken. Save copies of all letters to and from the company. Don't give up if you are not satisfied.

Use the sample consumer complaint letter in Figure 8.1 as a guide. Address letters, faxes, or e-mails to the company consumer affairs department or to the president if there is no consumer affairs office. Keep a copy of your complaint letter and all letters to and from the company.

Make your written or telephone complaint brief. Include the date and place you made the purchase, who performed the service, information about the product (such as the serial or model number, warranty terms, etc.), what went wrong, with whom you have tried to resolve the problem, and what you want done to correct the problem.

Be reasonable, not angry or threatening. Type your letter, if possible, or make sure that your handwriting is neat and easy to read.

Include copies, not originals, of all documents.

You might want to send your complaint letter with a return receipt requested. This will cost more, but it will give you proof that the letter was received and will tell you who signed for it.

If you believe you have given the company enough time to resolve the problem, file a complaint with your state or local consumer protection office, the Better Business Bureau, or the regulatory agency that has jurisdiction over the business.

Source: U.S. Office of Consumer Affairs, *Consumer's Resource Handbook*, 2002.

to decide whether to lease or buy. Making this decision tougher is the fact that leasing has a language of its own.

What has brought on this revolution in vehicle financing? Sticker shock. Today the cost of a new vehicle is beyond the financial means of many Americans. As a result, leasing—which is in effect renting a vehicle for an extended period—with a small or no down payment and low monthly payments has become increasingly popular. To understand the vehicle-buying or vehicle-leasing process, we'll follow the basic smart-buying process, adapting it to fit the vehicle decision.

## Step 1: Narrowing Your Choice

Very few decisions pit needs versus wants as directly as the vehicle decision. A new Dodge Caravan minivan costs about the same as and may satisfy your needs better than a Mazda Miata, but you still may want the Miata. Let's face it—for most people, picking a vehicle is a lifestyle choice. In addition to having different "wants," different people also have different needs. The end result: what's right for one person is a poor choice for someone else. In making this decision, as with any major purchase decision, you should do some research on what alternatives fit your needs, your lifestyle, and your budget.

**Needs and Lifestyle Considerations**  The first question to answer is: What features and qualities do you need and what features do you merely want? You'll find that your lifestyle dictates many of these decisions. If you have young kids, you might want a minivan to haul them around in. If you're single, that Miata may best fit your lifestyle. You may also decide that a new vehicle is just not that important to you, that saving money with a reliable used vehicle is more important. You may also decide you're unwilling to pay extra for a sun roof or antitheft device. In making this list of styles and features, you'll want to keep an eye out for resale and safety.

*Consumer Reports* regularly reports on desirable safety features and the models that maintain strong resale value.

**Fitting Your Car into Your Budget**   What can you realistically afford? Vehicles are expensive. In fact, the typical family spends between 4 and 6 months' worth of its annual income when buying a new vehicle. It makes no sense to purchase a vehicle that will put such financial strain on you that either other goals or your lifestyle must be compromised. In short, your vehicle, as with all purchases, must fit into your budget.

You should first determine the size of the down payment you're willing to make. It's okay to tap into savings to pay for your vehicle, as long as those savings dollars were earmarked for a new vehicle. What you don't want to do is to raid savings that are set aside for your retirement or your children's college education to pay for your vehicle. Once you know how large a down payment you can make, you can then determine how large the monthly payments on the vehicle can be. From that, you can determine how much you can spend.

How can you determine the monthly payment? First, call up your local bank and credit union and ask about auto loan rates. You can then determine what your monthly payment will be by using the same techniques learned in Chapters 3 and 7 when we looked at installment loans.

Basically, auto loans are installment loans for any vehicle. Remember, you can determine your monthly payment on an installment or auto loan using either a financial calculator (using the present value of an annuity calculation to determine PMT, the payment) or the installment loan tables that appear in the back of this book.

Because auto loans require monthly payments, you must make sure your calculator is set for *12 payments per year* and that the payments occur at the end of each period. Let's look at an example of a 36-month installment loan for $15,000 at 10 percent.

**Calculator Solution**   To solve on a financial calculator, first make sure the calculator is set to 12 payments per year, then do the following:

| Enter: | 36 | 10 | 15,000 | | 0 |
|---|---|---|---|---|---|
| | N | I/Y | PV | PMT | FV |
| Solve for: | | | | −484.01 | |

Notice, the answer in the output row is shown as a negative number. Remember, with a financial calculator, each problem has two cash flows—one is a positive number and one is a negative number. The idea is that you borrow money from the bank (a positive number, because "you receive the money"), and at some other point in time you pay the money back to the bank (a negative number, because "you pay it back").

The answer as shown in the output row is −$484.01. Thus, a 36-month installment loan of $15,000 at 10 percent would result in monthly payments of $484.01.

Using the installment loan tables that appear in Appendix E in the back of this book and in an abbreviated form in Table 7.1 is just as easy. Looking in the interest rate equals 10% row and the 36-month column, we find that the monthly payment on a similar $1,000 installment loan would be $32.27. To determine the monthly payment on a $15,000 loan, we need only multiply this amount by 15. Using the tables, we find that the monthly payments would be $484.05.

If you buy a vehicle and finance $15,000 of its price over 36 months, you'll have to come up with $484.05 each month for your payments. How can you come up with this much each month? There's no easy answer—perhaps you can cut down on some of your other expenditures, and perhaps you simply can't do it. It's at this point that you may want to rethink your decision and consider a less expensive vehicle or

# Checklist 8.3 ▌ Buying a Used Vehicle

Check newspaper ads and used-car guides at a local library so you know what's a fair price for the car you want.

Remember, prices are negotiable. You also can look up repair recalls for car models you might be considering.

Call the Auto Safety Hotline at 800-424-9393 to get recall information on a car. Authorized dealers of that make of vehicle must do recall work for free no matter how old the car is.

Shop during daylight hours so that you can thoroughly inspect the car and take a test-drive. Don't forget to check all the lights, air conditioner, heater, and other parts of the electrical system.

Do not agree to buy a car unless you've had it inspected by an independent mechanic of your choice.

Ask questions about the previous ownership and mechanical history of the car. Contact the former owner to find out if the car was in an accident or had any other problems.

Ask the previous owner or the manufacturer for a copy of the original manufacturer's warranty. It still might be in effect and transferable to you.

Don't sign anything that you don't understand. Read all the documents carefully. Negotiate the changes you want and get them written into the contract.

Source: U.S. Office of Consumer Affairs, *Consumer's Resource Handbook*, 2002.

perhaps a used vehicle. In any case, you *must* make sure your vehicle decision fits within your budget. Unfortunately, when it comes to fitting that new dream vehicle into your budget, sometimes, as the movie title says, "reality bites."

Today, with all the formerly leased vehicles coming back on the market as used vehicles, a used vehicle is a reasonable alternative to help you align what you want with what you can afford. In general, a used vehicle costs less and requires less in the way of a down payment. Moreover, a used vehicle tends to decline in value much more slowly than a new vehicle.

The downside of purchasing a used vehicle is that it is more likely to have mechanical problems and may not be under warranty. Checklist 8.3 provides some tips on buying a used vehicle. Buying a used vehicle is a real money saver. In fact, the savings from buying a used vehicle instead of a new vehicle every 3 years have been estimated to be between $1,500 and $2,000 per year.

If you're trying to come up with a few more dollars to buy just what you want, you might consider selling your old vehicle yourself rather than trading it in. Selling your old vehicle yourself generally nets you more money. The question is, do you have the time or the inclination to do it? Another alternative is not to replace your present vehicle, but instead try to keep it running just a little longer.

## Step 2: Picking Your Vehicle

Deciding on which vehicle is best for you centers on comparison shopping—looking at the final choices and trading off the price against product attributes and quality. In making this decision, once again, it's important to realize that buying a vehicle is a personal decision. Every vehicle drives a bit differently, and your choice should fit you physically. As a result, a vehicle should never be purchased without a serious test-drive. Do you feel comfortable driving it? You should never consider purchasing a vehicle without test-driving it—not just a similar model, but the *exact* vehicle under consideration.

Also make sure you consider differences in operating and insurance costs. For example, a used vehicle generally costs more to operate than a new vehicle. You'll also want to consider the vehicle's warranty—the better the warranty, the lower the future costs. In addition, insurance costs on different cars vary dramatically. That Miata is going to have much higher insurance cost than a Taurus station wagon.

### Step 3: Making the Purchase

Once you've decided what's best for you, the next hurdle is getting it for a fair price. You should enter the buying phase only after you know exactly what you want and how much you're willing to spend. With this information in hand, you can avoid making a hasty decision or being pressured into something you don't want. Once you have a fair price, the next step is to determine how to finance the purchase.

**Negotiating the Price**  To determine how much you're willing to spend—that is, what's a fair price—you must first know what the dealer cost or invoice price is. This is a relatively easy number to come by. It can be found in *Edmund's Car Buying Guide,* which is available at most libraries and bookstores; on Edmund's Internet site located at **www.edmund.com**; or on the Internet at AutoSite, at **www.autosite.com/help/allabout.htm**. AutoSite is a massive electronic buyer's guide featuring the manufacturer's suggested retail price, the dealer's invoice, any rebates and financing incentives, projected resale values, and insurance premium information, along with reviews and evaluations.

The factory invoice price is important in determining how much the dealer pays for the car, but it isn't the whole story, because when most cars are sold the dealer receives a **holdback** from the manufacturer. Generally, the holdback amounts to 2 to 3 percent of the price of the vehicle. For example, in 2000 a new Ford Explorer had a sticker price of $24,600. The dealer cost or invoice price was $22,266. So, the markup appears to be 10.5 percent. However, when the dealer sold that Explorer, he or she would receive a 3-percent holdback amounting to $738. Including the holdback, the markup is almost 14 percent. Keep in mind that the average markup on a new vehicle is just over 6 percent.

In addition to the holdback, some cars also have rebates or additional dealer incentives. These holdbacks and dealer incentives are available at the Edmund's Web site.

Now you're ready to approach several dealers and get quotes on the vehicle you want. You want to be prepared when you're ready to negotiate. Checklist 8.4 provides a list of buying tips.

In general, you shouldn't have to pay, after any rebates, more than $100 to $500 over the invoice price on the vehicle if it's an American-made vehicle, and a bit more

**Holdback**
In auto sales, an amount of money, generally in the 2- to 3-percent range, that the manufacturer gives the dealer on the sale of an automobile.

## Checklist 8.4 ■ Tips on Buying a New Vehicle

Evaluate your needs and financial situation. Read consumer magazines and test-drive several models before you make a final choice.

Find out the dealer's invoice price for the car and options. This is what the manufacturer charged the dealer for the car. You can order this information for a small fee from consumer publications you can find at your local library or get it on the Internet.

Find out if the manufacturer is offering rebates that will lower the cost.

Get price quotes from several dealers. Find out if the amounts quoted are the prices before or after the rebates are deducted.

Keep your trade-in negotiations separate from the main deal.

Compare financing from different sources (e.g., banks,

credit unions, and other dealers) before you sign the contract.

Read and understand every document you are asked to sign. Do not sign anything until you have made a final decision to buy.

Think twice about adding expensive extras you probably don't need to your purchase (e.g., credit insurance, service contracts, or rustproofing).

Inspect and test-drive the vehicle you plan to buy, but do not take possession of the car until the whole deal, including financing, is finalized.

Don't buy on impulse or because the salesperson is pressuring you to make a decision.

Source: U.S. Office of Consumer Affairs, *Consumer's Resource Handbook,* 2002.

over this price for a foreign-built vehicle. However, what you'll pay depends on the demand for the car and the size of the holdbacks that the dealer receives from the manufacturer. Getting quotes is the best way to determine what a good price is. If you don't want to negotiate by yourself, the Center for the Study of Services' Car Bargains Service (800-475-7283) will get you a minimum of five competitive bids from dealers in your local area. If you are considering purchasing, the fee is $165 and if you are considering leasing, the fee is $290.

If you're considering a used car, the negotiating process is a bit more complicated. Again, when you find the car you want, you must determine a fair price. Used-car prices can be found in the National Automobile Dealers Association (NADA) Official Used Car Guide and in Edmund's Used Car Prices, both of which are generally available at local libraries or from the Kelley Blue Book, which can be found on the Internet at **www.kbb.com/knight/auto.html**. In addition, you should have the car evaluated by an automobile mechanic. Most independent repair shops are willing to do an evaluation for a fee of between $50 and $80.

**Financing Alternatives** In general, the cheapest way to buy a car is with cash. Unfortunately, with the price of a new car or truck many times going over $20,000, that's not always a realistic alternative. When you're negotiating a price, keep the question of financing out of the negotiations in order to keep the flexibility to borrow money where it's cheapest. You may find it cheaper to borrow from a bank than through the auto dealership, or you may want to consider a home equity loan with its tax advantages. In any case, you should investigate all options.

In Chapter 7, we noted that an auto loan is simply a short-term secured loan made to finance the purchase of a vehicle, with that auto serving as the collateral for the loan. Often, very low-cost loans of 3 percent or less are offered by automakers as a marketing tool, sometimes to sell slow-moving models.

As you might expect, the shorter the term you borrow for, the higher the monthly payments—and the difference can be dramatic. For example, if you were borrowing $15,000 at 9 percent for 24 months, your monthly payment would be $685.27, but if your payments were spread out over 48 months, they would drop to $373.28 per month.

## Step 4: The Lease-Versus-Buy Decision

Leasing appeals to those who are financially stable, like to get a new vehicle every few years, drive less than 15,000 miles annually, and would rather not put up with the hassle of trade-in and maintenance. It's also popular with those who have good credit but don't have the upfront money needed to buy a new vehicle.

Checklist 8.5 provides a brief profile of those who might want to give leasing serious consideration. It covers a lot of people. In fact, almost one-third of all new vehicles are leased instead of bought, and this figure rises to over 50 percent for the more expensive models. However, because leasing is so different from buying, many people don't fully understand the process.

Leasing a vehicle is similar to renting a vehicle for 2 or 3 years. The amount you pay for the lease is determined by how much the value of the vehicle you're leasing is expected to decline while you're leasing it. For example, if you took out a 2-year lease on a vehicle that was worth $25,000 new and was expected to drop in value to $16,000 after 2 years, you'd pay the difference ($25,000 − $16,000 = $9,000) plus finance charges. Thus, it's the amount that the vehicle depreciates or drops in value during the lease that determines the cost of the lease.

There are two basic types of leases: closed-end leases and open-end leases. About 80 percent of all new vehicle leases are **closed-end leases**, or **walk-away leases**, in which

**Closed-End Lease or Walk-Away Lease**
A vehicle lease in which you return the vehicle at the end of the lease and literally walk away from any further responsibilities. You need merely bring the vehicle back in good condition with normal wear and tear, and the vehicle dealer assumes the responsibility for reselling the vehicle.

# Checklist 8.5 ▌ Leasing May Make Sense if ...

The lease under consideration is a closed-end, not an open-end, lease.
You are financially stable.
It is important to you that you have a new car every 2 to 4 years.
You do not drive over 15,000 miles annually.
You take good care of your car and it ages with only normal wear and tear.
You are not bothered by the thought of monthly payments that never end.
You use your vehicle for business travel.
You do not modify your car (e.g., add superchargers or after-market suspension components).
The manufacturer of the vehicle you are interested in is offering very low financing charges.

**Purchase Option**
An automobile lease option that allows you to buy the car at the end of the lease for either its residual value or a fixed price that is specified in the lease.

**Open-End Lease**
An automobile lease stating that when the lease expires, the current market value of the car will be compared to the residual value of the car as specified in the lease. If the car's market value is equal to or greater than its residual value, then you owe nothing, or may even receive a refund.

you return the vehicle at the end of the lease and literally walk away from any further responsibilities. You need merely bring the vehicle back in good condition with normal wear and tear, and the vehicle dealer assumes the responsibility for reselling the vehicle. Many closed-end leases also contain a **purchase option**, which allows you to buy the vehicle at the end of the lease for its residual value or a fixed price specified in the lease.

With an **open-end lease**, when the lease expires, the current market value of the vehicle is compared to what the value of the vehicle was estimated to be as specified in the lease contract. If the vehicle is worth less at the end of the lease than was estimated originally, the open-end lease requires you to pay the difference. That difference can mean an awful lot of money to you; without question, you don't want an open-end lease.

Exactly how is your monthly lease payment determined? Actually, it's made up of two parts. First, there's a monthly depreciation charge that reflects how much the vehicle will decline in value while you're leasing it. For example, if you took out a 2-year lease on a vehicle that was worth $25,000 new and was expected to drop in value to $16,000 after 2 years, you would pay the difference ($25,000 − $16,000 = $9,000) over the life of the lease.

The amount that the vehicle depreciates or drops in value during the lease plays a big part in determining the cost of the lease. In addition to the monthly depreciation charge, there's a rent charge, which is actually the finance charge built into the lease and is like the total interest charged on a loan. Exactly what your monthly lease payment would be then depends on the following criteria:

- The agreed-upon price of the vehicle
- Any other up-front fees, such as taxes, insurance, or service contracts
- Your down payment plus any trade-in allowance or rebate
- The value of the vehicle at the end of the lease
- The rent or finance charges
- The length of the lease

Because of all the difficulties consumers have had in evaluating vehicle leases, the Federal Reserve Board requires dealers and other leasing companies to provide customers with a leasing worksheet explaining the charges. A copy of such a worksheet is provided in Figure 8.2.

One key to getting a good lease is to negotiate a fair agreed-upon value for the car. Just as with buying a car, you can negotiate the "agreed-upon value of the vehicle,"

## Figure 8.2 Federal Consumer Leasing Act Lease Disclosure Form

Be very wary of any "other charges." If there are any, ask about them and check with other dealers to see if they impose similar charges.

The gross capitalized cost is the negotiated "selling price." It should be less than the manufacturer's suggested retail price.

The residual value is the projected market value of the car at the end of the lease. This is negotiated. The difference between this value and the gross capitalized cost (less any down payment, trade-in rebate, or noncash credit) is what you're charged for over the lease period.

While it's difficult to define, normal wear and tear generally refers to normal dings, dents, small scratches, stone chips, and tire wear over the period of the lease. Excessive wear and tear would refer to missing parts, damaged body panels, cuts, tears, and burns in the upholstery, broken glass, and other damage beyond what might be expected. Because it's so difficult to define, you should insist that it be defined in the lease contract.

Date _____

Lessor(s) _____    Lessee(s) _____

| Amount Due at Lease Signing (Itemized below)* | Monthly Payments | Other Charges (not part of your monthly payment) | Total of Payments (The amount you will have paid by the end of the lease) |
|---|---|---|---|
| $ _____ | Your first monthly payment of $ _____ is due on _____, followed by _____ payments of $ _____ due on the _____ of each month. The total of your monthly payments is $ _____. | Disposition fee (if you do not purchase the vehicle)  $ _____ [Annual tax]  _____  Total  $ _____ | $ _____ |

### Itemization of Amount Due at Lease Signing

**Amount Due At Lease Signing:**

| | |
|---|---|
| Capitalized cost reduction | $ _____ |
| First monthly payment | _____ |
| Refundable security deposit | _____ |
| Title fees | _____ |
| Registration fees | _____ |
| _____ | |
| Total | $ _____ |

**How the Amount Due at Lease Signing will be paid:**

| | |
|---|---|
| Net trade-in allowance | $ _____ |
| Rebates and noncash credits | _____ |
| Amount to be paid in cash | _____ |
| Total | $ _____ |

### Your monthly payment is determined as shown below:

**Gross capitalized cost.** The agreed upon value of the vehicle ($ _____ ) and any items you pay over the lease term (such as service contracts, insurance, and any outstanding prior loan or lease balance) ................................................................................. $ _____

If you want an itemization of this amount, please check this box. ☐

**Capitalized cost reduction.** The amount of any net trade-in allowance, rebate, noncash credit, or cash you pay that reduces the gross capitalized cost ....................................................... − _____

**Adjusted capitalized cost.** The amount used in calculating your base monthly payment ......................... = _____

**Residual value.** The value of the vehicle at the end of the lease used in calculating your base monthly payment ............ − _____

**Depreciation and any amortized amounts.** The amount charged for the vehicle's decline in value through normal use and for other items paid over the lease term ...................................... = _____

**Rent charge.** The amount charged in addition to the depreciation and any amortized amounts ................................. + _____

**Total of base monthly payments.** The depreciation and any amortized amounts plus the rent charge ........................ = _____

**Lease term.** The number of months in your lease ................................................................. ÷ _____

**Base monthly payment** ................................................................................................ = _____

**Monthly sales/use tax** ................................................................................................. + _____

**Total monthly payment** ................................................................................................ = $ _____

---

**Early Termination.** You may have to pay a substantial charge if you end this lease early. The charge may be up to several thousand dollars. The actual charge will depend on when the lease is terminated. The earlier you end the lease, the greater this charge is likely to be.

---

**Excessive Wear and Use.** You may be charged for excessive wear based on our standards for normal use [and for mileage in excess of _____ miles per year at the rate of _____ per mile].

**Purchase Option at End of Lease Term.** [You have an option to purchase the vehicle at the end of the lease term for $ _____ [and a purchase option fee of $ _____ ].] [You do not have an option to purchase the vehicle at the end of the lease term.]

**Other Important Terms.** See your lease documents for additional information on early termination, purchase options and maintenance responsibilities, warranties, late and default charges, insurance, and any security interest, if applicable.

---

which is like the selling price, before you sign the lease. In fact, it's a good idea not to announce you're interested in leasing until you negotiate a price for the vehicle. You should also try to keep the down payment to a minimum.

Make sure the warranty covers the entire lease period so that you don't have to pay for major repairs. In addition, make sure that "normal wear and tear" is defined in the contract, and that you understand exactly what the termination fees (fees for ending the lease early) are. Finally, make sure you have insurance protection that would cover any early termination penalty if the car were totaled in an accident.

### Figure 8.3 Worksheet for the Lease-Versus-Purchase Decision

**EXAMPLE** Your decision has come down to purchasing a new Lexus RX-300 SUV at an agreed-upon price of $34,000 or leasing it. If you purchase it, there is a required 20% down payment of $6,800, plus sales taxes, title, and registration.* The monthly payments over the 2 years if it is financed at 8% are $1,230.18. If you didn't buy that car, you could have earned 5% on the money you used for your down payment; thus, the opportunity cost of money is 5%.

In negotiating the lease option, the residual value for the car at the end of

2 years was estimated to be $23,500. If the Lexus is leased with a capitalized cost of $34,000, there would be a down payment or capitalized cost reduction of $2,950. In addition to the down payment is a security deposit of $475, and at signing you must also make the first month's payment plus taxes, title, registration, and other fees similar to those incurred when buying a car outright. Finally, the monthly lease payment is $459.83.

**COST OF PURCHASING**

|  |  | Your Numbers |
|---|---|---|
| a. Agreed-upon purchase price | $34,000 | _____ |
| b. Down payment | $6,800 | _____ |
| c. Total loan payments (monthly loan payment of $1,230.18 × 24 months) | $29,524.32 | _____ |
| d. Opportunity cost on down payment (5% opportunity cost × 2 years × line b) | $680 | _____ |
| e. Less: Expected market value of the car at the end of the loan | −$23,500 | _____ |
| f. **Total cost of purchasing (lines b + c + d − e)** | **$13,504.32** | _____ |

**COST OF LEASING**

|  |  | |
|---|---|---|
| g. Down payment (capitalized cost reduction) of $2,950 plus security deposit of $475 | $3,425 | _____ |
| h. Total lease payments (monthly lease payments of $459.83 × 24 months) | $11,035.92 | _____ |
| i. Opportunity cost of total initial payment (5% opportunity cost × 2 years × line g) | $342.50 | _____ |
| j. Any end-of-lease charges (perhaps for excess miles), if applicable | $0 | _____ |
| k. Less: Refund of security deposit | −$475.00 | _____ |
| l. **Total cost of leasing (lines g + h + i + j − k)** | **$14,328.42** | _____ |

*We ignore taxes, title, and registration in this example because they are generally the same whether you lease or purchase the car.

A second important factor in getting a good lease is to find a vehicle that doesn't depreciate quickly. Remember, the lease payment is based on what the vehicle is worth at the end of the lease. That means that you might pay less on a more expensive car that depreciates slowly.

The last key to getting a good lease is to find one with a low rent or finance charge. Periodically, carmakers offer extremely low lease financing rates that result in very attractive leasing terms. You can find a listing of subsidized leases on the Edmund's Web site.

To determine whether it's better to lease or to buy, you simply need to compare the costs of each over the *same* time frame. That is, you need to compare a 2-year lease with buying and financing a vehicle over 2 years. In addition, as the market for leasing previously leased, 2-year-old vehicles expands, there may be new opportunities, provided you understand the mechanics of leasing.

Figure 8.3 provides a comparative analysis for a lease-versus-purchase decision. In this figure the cost of purchasing is $13,504.32, whereas the cost of leasing is $14,328.42. Thus, it's cheaper to purchase the Lexus in this example than it is to lease it.

## Step 5: Maintaining Your Purchase

Given the size of the investment you make in a vehicle, it only makes sense to keep the vehicle in the best running order possible. The place to start is by reading the owner's manual. You just can't ignore regular maintenance. For example, change your oil and oil filter as specified in your manual. Change the oil and oil filter every 3,000 miles if your driving is mostly stop-and-go or consists of frequent short trips. Also, flush and refill the cooling system about every 24 months, and keep your engine tuned up. A misfiring spark plug can reduce fuel efficiency as much as 30 percent. You'll want to make sure you keep a log of all repairs and service.

If you think about it, you know your car better than anyone else does. You drive it every day and know how it feels and sounds when everything is right. So don't ignore warning signals. Listen for unusual sounds, look for drips, leaks, smoke, warning lights, or gauge readings. Also, watch for any changes in acceleration, engine performance, gas mileage, or fluid levels. These all could be warning signs. And when you take your car in for service, be prepared to describe the symptoms accurately.

You'll also want to start shopping for a repair facility before you need one; you generally make better decisions when you are not rushed or in a panic. Where should you start looking? Ask friends and associates for recommendations. Even in this high-tech era, old-fashioned word-of-mouth reputation is still valuable.

Look for evidence of qualified technicians, such as trade school diplomas, certificates of advanced course work, and ASE certifications—a national standard of technician competence. If the service was not all you expected, don't rush to another shop. Discuss the problem with the manager or owner. Give the business a chance to resolve the problem. Reputable shops value customer feedback and will make a sincere effort to keep your business.

## Step 6: Consumer Protection and Your Car

With a new car purchase, your first line of protection is the warranty, which provides coverage for the basic parts against manufacturer's defects for a set period of time or miles. In addition, corrosion coverage is provided along with coverage of the engine, transmission, and drive train. For most cars this coverage extends through the first 3 years of ownership or 36,000 miles, whichever comes first. However, some cars come with warranties that cover up to 7 years or 70,000 miles.

But what happens if they just can't seem to fix your problems? The answer is *lemon laws*. All states and the District of Columbia provide for a refund if the manufacturer can't seem to fix your problem. Generally these laws require that you make at least four attempts to fix the problem and that your car is out of service for at least 30 days during the first year after purchase or the first 12,000 miles. If that's the case, you're entitled to a refund on your purchase.

## Housing

LO 3 Choose housing that meets your needs.

Owning a home is perhaps the biggest part of the American Dream. In fact, home ownership is often people's primary goal in life. Why, though, is owning your home so important? Sure, your home is your castle, and somehow it just doesn't seem right for the king or queen to rent that castle. However, at least in the United States, many people equate owning your own home with financial success: You've made it, at least in part, if you own your own home. Also it's just kind of neat to own something large enough to walk around in.

### Making a Smart Decision

Buying something as large as a house takes a lot of money. More precisely, for most people, housing costs take up over 26 percent of their after-tax income.[1] Home ownership is also an investment—the biggest investment you're likely to make. Just as you wouldn't normally approach buying another investment—say, a savings

[1]In fact, according to the Tax Foundation, the typical American spent about 61 days earning money to pay for housing in 2001.

bond—as realizing a dream, you shouldn't approach buying a house only as attaining your big dream. If you don't approach it as an investment, your dream could easily become a nightmare.

How do you go about making a smart housing decision? Using the same smart-buying approach we just used for buying a car. First, determine what you need, want, and can afford. After all, buying a home and all the responsibilities that come with it isn't a dream for everyone. The next step is the selection process, where you trade off price against quality and product attributes. In the case of housing, those "product attributes" can be location and neighborhood, nearby schools, square footage, and so forth. After you've honed in on what you want, the process of negotiating price and, if you decide to buy, how best to finance your purchase begins. Finally, there are postpurchase activities, such as maintenance and possibly refinancing. But before we walk through the housing decision step-by-step, let's look at what our housing options are.

## Your Housing Options

For most people, lifestyle is a major player in their housing choice. Kids, schools, pets, privacy, sociability, ability to move around, and other lifestyle concerns tend to point people into one type of housing or another. The needs-versus-wants issue also plays a major role. Most people would prefer to live in a mansion, but that kind of housing just doesn't fit into many monthly budgets. Together, your lifestyle, wants, and needs, constrained by your monthly budget, provide focus on a realistic housing alternative for you.

You know what kind of lifestyle you have, but you might not know what type of housing will best suit it. In fact, you might not even know what various types of housing are available. Let's take a minute to examine the basic choices.

### A House

A house is the most popular choice for most individuals because it offers space and privacy. It also offers greater control over style, decoration, and home improvement. If you want your home to build equity or wealth, buying a house may be a good choice. However, home ownership carries with it more work than do other housing choices. If you own the house, you're responsible for maintenance, repair, and renovations.

----

**STOP & THINK** Don't look at a decision to buy a house without looking at all the different ways it will affect your life. Just filling up your house with furniture, let alone making your mortgage payment, will make a serious dent in your budget. Your home and its neighborhood will also affect your lifestyle.

----

### Cooperatives and Condominiums

**Cooperative or Co-op**
An apartment building or group of apartments owned by a corporation in which the residents of the building are the stockholders.

A **cooperative**, or **co-op**, is an apartment building or group of apartments owned by a corporation in which the residents of the building are the stockholders. The residents buy stock in the corporation, which in turn gives them the right to occupy a unit in the building. Although the residents don't own their units, they do have a right to occupy their units for as long as they own stock in the cooperative.

When you "buy into" a co-op, you buy shares of the corporation that reflect the dollar value of your "space." The larger the size of your space and the more desirable its location, the more shares you have to buy. One problem with co-ops is that you may have a tough time getting a mortgage because many banks and other financial institutions may be uncomfortable using the stock as collateral. In addition to having to purchase stock in the corporation, shareholders also have to pay a monthly **homeowner's fee** to the cooperative corporation, which in turn is responsible for paying taxes and maintaining the building and grounds. There can also be special assessments in addition to the normal maintenance fees to take care of large maintenance items.

Whether or not a co-op is for you depends on your lifestyle. If you're looking for an affordable, low-maintenance situation with a good helping of shared amenities such as swimming pools, tennis courts, health centers, and security guards, a co-op might be for you. However, if you're more interested in privacy and control over style and decoration, a co-op may be a poor choice. In addition, co-ops generally have less potential for capital appreciation than does a house, and they can be difficult to sell.

A **condominium (condo)** is a type of apartment or apartment complex that allows for individual ownership of the dwelling units but joint ownership of the land, common areas, and facilities, including swimming pools, tennis courts, health facilities, parking lots, and grounds. In effect, you pay for and own your apartment, and you have a proportionate share of the land and common areas. As with a co-op, you still have to pay a maintenance fee, which generally covers interest, taxes, groundskeeping, water, and utilities.

The form that condos take can vary greatly—from apartment buildings or townhouses to office buildings or high-rises on the oceanfront. The advantages and disadvantages of living in a condo are similar to those of living in co-ops. However, condos allow for the direct ownership of a specific unit, not just shares in a corporation.

A more recent variation on cooperatives and condominiums are **planned unit developments (PUDs)**. These enjoy most of their popularity on the West Coast. With a Planned Unit Development, you own your own home and the land it sits on, but you share ownership of the development with your neighbors and pay a homeowner's fee for common expenses and maintenance.

## Apartments and Other Rental Housing

Apartments and other rental housing appeal to those who are interested in an affordable, low-maintenance situation with little financial commitment, where it is possible to move with minimum inconvenience. This description often seems to fit the young, single person. As you start out, you simply may not have the funds available to buy a home.

Alternatively, rental housing may simply be a lifestyle decision. You may want limited upkeep and no long-term commitment, or you may be concerned that you might get transferred or change jobs. Regardless of the reason, at some point in time almost all of us live in rental housing. The downside of apartment life generally involves a lack of choice. For example, you may not be allowed to have a pet, or you may have limited ability to remodel the apartment to fit your taste.

## Housing Step 1: Homework

Just as with any other major buying decision, the first step in buying housing is to decide what you're looking for. What fits your housing needs best—are good schools the overriding concern, or is ease of moving, perhaps because of an impending transfer, most important? Look at the alternatives. You also need to examine your budget and determine how much you can spend. You'll need to develop an understanding of the costs associated with owning a home. Finally, you must look at the alternatives of buying versus renting and decide which fits you best.

**Homeowner's Fee**
A monthly fee paid by shareholders to the cooperative corporation for paying property taxes and maintaining the building and grounds.

**Condominium (Condo)**
A type of apartment building or apartment complex that allows for the individual ownership of the apartment units but joint ownership of the apartment land, common areas, and facilities.

**Planned Unit Developments (PUDs)**
A development where you own your own home and the land it sits on, but you share ownership of the development with your neighbors and pay a homeowner's fee.

## Needs Versus Wants

Generally, although apartment and house shopping is exciting, it's also exhausting. Decision making is often both confusing and frustrating. The key to looking is to decide exactly what you're looking for before you begin. After all, how can you search if you don't even know what you're looking for? Before you can decide what to buy, you have to decide what you need and what you want. How many bedrooms do you need? How many bathrooms? Do you need a basement? Do you want a guest room for Aunt Edna? Do you want a playroom? Do you want a walk-in humidor? Are schools a concern? How about closet space? How big should your property be? How about nice little extras such as a tennis court or a pool? These are the kinds of questions you have to answer. You have to decide what qualities you're looking for before you can find housing with those qualities.

Before you search, you also need to consider location. Life in the country is a lot different from life in the suburbs or the city, so choose the location that's going to best suit you. In addition, you should look to the safety of the neighborhood and whether it's conveniently located with respect to your job, shopping, and schools. A desirable location adds to the price of an apartment or home, so expect to pay more for some locations. Fortunately, you can also count on being able to sell for more, too.

In determining your housing needs, you should also allow for future needs, whether they be for additional space as your family grows, or for less space as your children leave home. The housing decision you make should be good enough to last for years.

## Cost of Housing

The biggest concern in choosing a type of housing and especially in choosing whether to buy or rent is money. Where you live is often a result of what you can afford. Do you have enough to buy, or do you have to rent? If you do have enough to buy, can you afford a house, or do you have to settle for a co-op? How do you even know what buying a home costs? Well, at least we can answer the last question.

The costs of home ownership can be divided into (1) one-time, or initial, costs, (2) recurring costs, and (3) maintenance and operating costs. The one-time costs involve the down payment, points, and closing costs paid when you first buy your house. Recurring costs involve mortgage payments, property taxes, and insurance. Maintenance and operating costs vary according to the age, size, and construction of your home. In fact, there may be some years in which the maintenance and operating costs are quite low. Of course, your roof might cave in, leaving a gaping hole through which many squirrels jump so they can gnaw through your carpeting, woodworking, and wiring. That'll be the year your maintenance costs go through the roof.

To make a logical decision as to whether to rent or buy or to determine what you can afford, you need to understand the costs that come with home ownership.

**One-Time Costs** Houses cost a lot of money! As a result, almost no one can afford to pay for a house all at once. For anyone who can, the entire price of the house is a one-time cost. For the rest of us who can't, we take out loans called mortgages. However, mortgages don't cover all the costs associated with a house. Some of the money, which is referred to as the **down payment**, is the up-front money that you must pay at the time of the sale when buying a home.

The down payment is the buyer's equity, or ownership share, in the house, and lenders like to see a large down payment. Why? Because if a borrower stops paying

**Down Payment**
The amount of money outside of or not covered by mortgage funds that the home buyer puts down on a home at the time of sale.

back a loan, he or she loses the title to the house as well as the equity. The more equity—that is, the larger the down payment—the more the borrower stands to lose by not paying, and thus the less likely the borrower is to not pay.

Your down payment will vary according to the type of financing you receive. For traditional mortgage loans, the typical down payment is 20 percent. Thus, for a $150,000 home, a typical down payment is $30,000. Needless to say, that's an awful lot of money. Fortunately, for those who cannot come up with a 20-percent down payment, there are alternatives. For example, you can buy private mortgage insurance, which is insurance that covers the lender if you default. This will allow you to pay as little as 5 percent down.

Although the down payment is a major hurdle for most first-time homebuyers, it's not the only financial hurdle. You'll also have a one-time expense when the ownership title is transferred. This one-time expense is referred to as **closing** or **settlement costs**. Although they vary quite a bit from house to house, depending on the size of the loan, the local costs, and the loan arrangements made, they can easily range anywhere from 3 to 7 percent of the cost of the house.

Several of the more important components of closing costs include the following:

■ **Points** or **discount points**: Points are a one-time additional interest charge by the lender, due at closing—that is, when the sale is final. Each point is equal to 1 percent of the mortgage loan. Thus, if you get a $120,000 loan with two points, the two points would be $2,400, or $1,200 each. Lenders use these points to raise the effective cost of the loan, but points can also be used as a bargaining chip. Many times you'll see trade-offs between interest rates and points—you can get a lower rate with high points or a higher rate with no points.

The longer you plan on staying in a home, the more important a low interest rate is. You pay points only once, at closing, but you pay interest over the life of the loan. If you're planning on staying in your home for a long time, you might be better off taking a few points to get a lower rate. If you don't expect to be there too long, it's important to keep the points you pay to a minimum. The only virtue of points is that they're tax deductible when associated with the financing of the purchase of a home.

■ **Loan origination fee**: A loan origination fee is generally one point, or 1 percent of the loan amount. Its purpose is to compensate the lender for the cost of reviewing and finalizing the loan. Unfortunately, because it's not considered an interest payment, it's not tax deductible.

■ **Loan application fee**: The loan application fee, also paid to the lender, is generally in the $200 to $300 range and covers some of the processing costs associated with the loan.

■ **Appraisal fee**: An appraisal is an estimate of what your home and property are worth. Lenders require an appraisal before a mortgage loan is approved so they can be sure that they aren't lending you more money than the value of the property. Although the costs for an appraisal vary depending on the size and location of the house, an appraisal fee can easily run between $200 and $300.

■ **Other fees and costs**: There are countless other fees and charges you'll need to pay when buying a home. For example, a **title search** fee is paid to an attorney for searching ownership records to make sure the person selling you the property really owns it. Title insurance must be purchased to protect you against challenges to the title, perhaps from a forged deed. There's also an attorney's fee for work on the contract. In addition, there'll be a notary fee, along with a fee for

**Closing or Settlement Costs**
Expenses associated with finalizing the transfer of ownership of the house.

**Points or Discount Points**
Charges used to raise the effective cost of the mortgage loan, which must be paid in full at the time of the sale.

**Loan Origination Fee**
A fee of generally one point, or 1 percent of the loan amount. Its purpose is to compensate the lender for the cost of reviewing and finalizing the loan.

**Loan Application Fee**
A fee, generally in the $200 to $300 range, that is meant to defer some of the processing costs associated with the loan.

**Appraisal Fee**
A fee for an appraisal of the house, which is generally required before a mortgage loan is approved. Although the cost varies depending on the size and location of the house, it can easily run between $200 and $300.

**Title Search**
An investigation of the public records to determine the legal ownership rights to property or a home.

recording the deed at the courthouse. Other charges include the cost of your credit report, along with the cost of termite and radon inspection to make sure the house is in good shape.

Figure 8.4 gives a summary of typical initial costs on a $120,000 mortgage loan—buying a $150,000 house with 20 percent down. You'll notice in the example that initial costs amount to almost 24 percent of the cost of the house. Keep in mind that the law requires that the annual percentage rate (APR) on a mortgage be disclosed to the borrower. Although points must be included in the calculations, fees for taking out the loan application, doing an appraisal, and the credit check are not. In addition, the lender can change the APR by as much as one-eighth of a percent before settlement without notifying the buyer.

**Recurring Costs**   The majority of recurring costs generally consist of monthly mortgage payments, the size of which depends on how much you borrow, at what interest rate, and for how long. Basically, the higher the interest rate on your loan, the higher your monthly payments. In addition, the shorter the maturity, or length, of the mortgage loan, the higher the monthly payments. Obviously, the more you pay each month, the less time it takes to pay off the loan.

Table 8.1 shows the level of monthly payments to repay a $10,000 loan at various combinations of interest rates and maturities. From Table 8.1 you can see that on a 15-year 6.0-percent, $10,000 mortgage, the monthly payments would be $84.39. If you increased the maturity to 30 years, though, the monthly payment drops to $59.96. Thus, if you are considering a $130,000, 15-year mortgage loan at 6.0 percent, the payments would be $1,097.07 ($130,000/$10,000 × $84.39 = 13 × $84.39 = $1,097.07). Similarly, the monthly payments on a $130,000, 30-year mortgage loan at 6.0 percent would be $779.48 ($130,000/$10,000 × $59.96 = 13 × $59.96 = $779.48).

Mortgage payments are the primary recurring cost, but they're actually made up of four costs, generally referred to as **PITI**, which stands for principal, interest, taxes, and insurance. In addition to paying off the loan principal and interest charges, you'll need to pay property taxes and insurance premiums. These monthly property taxes and insurance payments are generally made along with your loan principal and interest payments, and are held for you in a special reserve account, called an **escrow account**. Funds accumulate over time until they are drawn out to pay taxes and insurance.

**PITI**
An acronym standing for the total of your monthly principal, interest, taxes, and insurance.

**Escrow Account**
A reserve account in which funds are deposited, generally on a monthly basis, and accumulate over time until they are drawn out to pay taxes and insurance.

Figure 8.4  Estimated Initial Costs of Buying a Home: The Down Payment, Points, and Closing Costs on the Purchase of a $150,000 House, Borrowing $120,000, with 20% Down at a Rate of 8% with 2 Points

| | |
|---|---|
| Down Payment | $30,000 |
| Points | 2,400 |
| Loan Origination Fee | 1,200 |
| Loan Application Fee | 300 |
| Appraisal Fee | 300 |
| Title Search Fee | 200 |
| Title Insurance | 500 |
| Attorney's Fee | 400 |
| Recording Fee | 20 |
| Credit Report | 50 |
| Termite and Radon Inspection Fee | 150 |
| Notary Fee | 50 |
| **Total Initial Costs** | **$35,570** |

## Table 8.1  Monthly Mortgage Payments Required to Repay a $10,000 Loan with Different Interest Rates and Different Maturities

| Rate of Interest (%) | Loan Maturity | | | | | |
| --- | --- | --- | --- | --- | --- | --- |
| | 10 Years | 15 Years | 20 Years | 25 Years | 30 Years | 40 Years |
| 5.0 | $106.07 | $ 79.08 | $ 66.00 | $ 58.46 | $ 53.68 | $ 48.22 |
| 5.5 | 108.53 | 81.71 | 68.79 | 61.41 | 56.79 | 51.58 |
| 6.0 | 111.02 | 84.39 | 71.64 | 64.43 | 59.96 | 50.22 |
| 6.5 | 113.55 | 87.11 | 74.56 | 67.52 | 63.21 | 58.55 |
| 7.0 | 116.11 | 89.88 | 77.53 | 70.68 | 66.53 | 62.14 |
| 7.5 | 118.71 | 92.71 | 80.56 | 73.90 | 69.93 | 65.81 |
| 8.0 | 121.33 | 95.57 | 83.65 | 77.19 | 73.38 | 69.53 |
| 8.5 | 123.99 | 98.48 | 86.79 | 80.53 | 76.90 | 73.31 |
| 9.0 | 126.68 | 101.43 | 89.98 | 83.92 | 80.47 | 77.14 |
| 9.5 | 129.40 | 104.43 | 93.22 | 87.37 | 84.09 | 81.01 |
| 10.0 | 132.16 | 107.47 | 96.51 | 90.88 | 87.76 | 84.91 |
| 10.5 | 134.94 | 110.54 | 99.84 | 94.42 | 91.48 | 88.86 |
| 11.0 | 137.76 | 113.66 | 103.22 | 98.02 | 95.24 | 92.83 |
| 11.5 | 140.60 | 116.82 | 106.65 | 101.65 | 99.03 | 96.83 |
| 12.0 | 143.48 | 120.02 | 110.11 | 105.33 | 102.86 | 100.85 |
| 12.5 | 146.38 | 123.26 | 113.62 | 109.04 | 106.73 | 104.89 |
| 13.0 | 149.32 | 126.53 | 117.16 | 112.79 | 110.62 | 108.95 |
| 13.5 | 152.27 | 129.83 | 120.74 | 116.56 | 114.54 | 113.03 |
| 14.0 | 155.27 | 133.17 | 124.35 | 120.38 | 118.49 | 117.11 |
| 14.5 | 158.29 | 136.55 | 128.00 | 124.22 | 122.46 | 121.21 |
| 15.0 | 161.33 | 139.96 | 131.68 | 128.08 | 126.44 | 125.32 |

Calculating monthly payments on a loan:

**Step 1:** Divide the amount borrowed by $10,000. For example, for a $100,000 loan, the step 1 value would be $100,000/$10,000 = 10.

**Step 2:** Find the monthly payment for a $10,000 loan at the appropriate interest rate and maturity in the table above. For a 15-year mortgage at 9%, the value would be $101.43.

**Step 3:** Multiply the step 1 value by the step 2 value. In the example, this is 10 × $101.43 = $1,014.30.

The logic behind an escrow account is that paying your insurance and taxes regularly, in small amounts, is less painful than paying them in one large, annual lump sum. Lenders often use the total PITI level to measure an individual's financial capacity. As a rule of thumb, your PITI costs shouldn't exceed 28 percent of your pretax monthly income.

**STOP & THINK**  Remodeling is not as good an investment as purchasing the house in the first place. A recent survey showed that you can expect to recoup 95 percent of the cost of kitchen remodeling, 83 percent of a family room addition, 77 percent of a bathroom remodeling, and 72 percent from the addition of a deck. That means if you remodel your bathroom you'll lose 23 percent—without question, a bad investment.

**Maintenance and Operating Costs**  Whether you buy an old or new, big or small, country or city house, you'll have maintenance and operating costs. For example, you might need to repair a roof, replace a refrigerator, or install a new heating system. The landscaping surrounding your home usually needs some attention. Don't forget to plan for these expenses when buying a home, or your first repair bill will come as a very rude shock.

## Renting Versus Buying

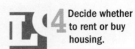
Decide whether to rent or buy housing.

For most people, the rent-versus-buy decision is not a financial decision, it's a personal one—you're making a lifestyle decision. Perhaps you want an apartment because you don't want the responsibilities associated with a house, or you may want to buy a house because you want to live in a particular neighborhood. Still, buying a house is generally the largest single investment that most people ever make. It's also something that many people simply can't fit into their monthly budget without some serious cuts in other budget items. Before making this decision, it's a good idea to understand its financial implications.

For many, the lifestyle choices and financial implications are intertwined—spending more or less on housing can have a big impact on your lifestyle. For example, the first factor you should consider in deciding whether to rent or to buy is how long you intend to live there. If it's for a short period—perhaps you expect to change jobs or get married and relocate in the next 2 or 3 years—then you're almost certainly better off renting. Why? Simply because buying a house is a huge and expensive hassle, as is selling it.

Before examining the advantages of a rent-versus-buy decision from the financial perspective, let's examine Figure 8.5, which provides a listing of a number of advantages to both renting and buying. As you can see, many of the reasons for renting center on flexibility—both financial flexibility, because renting generally involves lower monthly payments, and lifestyle flexibility, because you can avoid the responsibilities associated with ownership. The advantages of buying seem to center on the financial benefits of owning and the personal freedom to remodel and redecorate to suit your taste. The financial benefits come from the tax benefits, from building equity as your mortgage is paid off, and from the possibility of your home appreciating in value over time.

In looking at the rent-versus-buy decision from the financial perspective, we simply compare the costs associated with each alternative. Interestingly, the results that you get often depend mainly on how long you're planning to live in the place. Why? Well, when you buy a house or apartment, you experience a lot of up-front, one-time costs. However, the major financial advantages—price appreciation and the tax benefits—occur gradually over time. As a result, you generally must experience a number of years of price appreciation and tax benefits to offset those initial up-front costs. With renting, you don't have those large, one-time costs—in fact, you generally just have a security deposit that you get back when you move out.

Figure 8.6 presents the financial aspects of the rent-versus-buy decision. In the example, the alternatives being compared are renting an apartment for $900 per

---

Figure 8.5 Renting Versus Buying

| Renting | vs. | Buying |
| --- | --- | --- |
| • Very mobile, can relocate without incurring real estate selling costs | | • Allows you to build up equity over time |
| • No down payment required | | • Possibility of home appreciation |
| • May involve a lower monthly cash flow—you only pay rent; a homeowner pays the mortgage, taxes, insurance, and upkeep | | • Allows for a good deal of personal freedom to remodel, landscape, and redecorate to suit your taste |
| • Avoids the risk of falling housing prices | | • Significant tax advantages, including deduction of interest and property taxes |
| • Many times extensive amenities like swimming pools, tennis courts, and health clubs are provided | | • No chance of rent rising over time |
| • No home repair and maintenance | | • Your home is a potential source of cash in the form of home equity loans |
| • No groundskeeping | | |
| • No property taxes | | |

**Figure 8.6** Worksheet for the Rent-Versus-Buy Decision

**ASSUMPTIONS** Buying option: $20,000 down and an $80,000, 30-year mortgage at 8%. Rental option: $900 per month. Time frames; 1 year and 7 years; 28% marginal tax rate; after-tax rate of return = 5%; house appreciates in value at 3% per year; sales commission is 5% of the price of the house; closing costs = $5,000, which includes 2 points.

## THE COST OF RENTING

| | 1 year | 7 years | Your Numbers |
|---|---|---|---|
| a. Total monthly rent costs (monthly rent $900 × 12 months × no. years) | a.    $10,800 | a.    $75,600 | _____ |
| b. Total renter's insurance (annual renters insurance $250 × no. years) | + b.    $250 | + b.    $1,750 | _____ |
| c. After-tax opportunity cost of interest lost because of having to make a security deposit (security deposit of $1,800 × after-tax rate of return of 5% × no. years) | + c.    $90 | + c.    $630 | _____ |
| d. **Total cost of renting (lines a + b + c)** | = d.    $11,140 | + d.    $77,980 | _____ |

## THE COST OF BUYING

| | 1 year | 7 years | |
|---|---|---|---|
| e. Total mortgage payments (monthly payments $587.01 × 12 months × no. years) | e.  $7,044.12 | e. $49,308.84 | _____ |
| f. Property taxes on the new house (property taxes of $2,200 × no. years) | + f.    $2,200 | + f.    $15,400 | _____ |
| g. Homeowner's insurance (annual homeowner's insurance $600 × no. years) | + g.    $600 | + g.    $4,200 | _____ |
| h. Additional operating costs beyond those of renting. Maintenance, repairs, and any additional utilities and heating costs (additional annual operating costs $500 × no. years) | + h.    $500 | + h.    $3,500 | _____ |
| i. After-tax opportunity cost of interest lost because of having to make a down payment (down payment of $20,000 × after-tax rate of return of 5% × no. years) | + i.    $1,000 | + i.    $7,000 | _____ |
| j. Closing costs, including points (closing costs of $5,000) | + j.    $5,000 | + j.    $5,000 | _____ |
| k. Less savings: Total mortgage payments going toward the loan principal* | − k.    $668.26 | − k.  $6,017.84 | _____ |
| l. Less savings: Estimated appreciation in the value of the home *less* sales commission at the end of the period (current market value of house $100,000 × annual growth in house value of 3% × no. years − sales commission at end of the period of 5% × future value of house) | − l.  ($2,150)† | − l.    $14,950 | _____ |
| m. **Equals: Total cost of buying a home for those who do not itemize (lines e + f + g + h + i + j − k − l)** | = m. $17,825.86 | = m. $63,441.00 | _____ |

**Additional savings to home buyers who itemize**

| | 1 year | 7 years | |
|---|---|---|---|
| n. Less savings: Tax savings from the tax-deductibility of the interest portion of the mortgage payments (total amount of interest payments made × marginal tax rate of 28%) | − n.  $1,785.24 | − n. $12,121.48 | _____ |
| o. Less savings: Tax savings from the tax-deductibility of the property taxes on the new house (property taxes of $2,200 × marginal tax rate of 28% × no. years) | − o.    $616 | − o.    $4,312 | _____ |
| p. Less savings: Tax savings from the tax-deductibility of the points portion of the closing costs (total points paid of $1,600 × marginal tax rate of 28%) | − p.    $448 | − p.    $448 | _____ |
| q. **Total cost of buying a home to homebuyers who itemize (line m minus lines n through p)** | = q. $14,976.62 | = q. $46,559.52 | _____ |

| | 1 year | 7 years | |
|---|---|---|---|
| **Advantage of buying to those who *do not itemize* = Total cost of renting − Total cost of buying for those who *do not itemize*: if negative, rent; if positive, buy (line d − line m)** | −$6,685.86 | $14,539.00 | ═══════ |
| **Advantage of buying to those *who itemize* = Total cost of renting − Total cost of buying for those *who itemize*: if negative, rent; if positive, buy (line d − line q)** | −$3,836.62 | $31,420.48 | ═══════ |

*The total interest and principal payments can be calculated directly or approximated. To approximate the total annual interest payments, multiply the outstanding size of the loan by the interest rate, in this case $80,000 × 0.08 = $6,400, then multiply this by the number of years. In the case of the 1-year time horizon, the approximation method yields $6,400 of total interest while a direct calculation yields $6,375.86. While the approximation method works well for short time horizons, it is less accurate for longer time horizons.

†*Note:* If you only own the home for 1 year, the value here is negative, meaning the sales commission is greater than the appreciation in home value. Thus, this is an additional cost, not a savings, and we are subtracting a negative—in effect, adding the $2,150 to the cost of buying the house.

month versus buying a house for $100,000. The house would be financed by paying 20 percent down and taking a 30-year mortgage at 8 percent, which would include monthly payments of $587.01. (Calculated using a financial calculator. If calculated using Table 8.1, the monthly payment becomes $587.04; the difference is a rounding error.) You'll notice in this example we've ignored the time value of money to simplify the analysis.

The primary cost of renting is the rent itself. The total cost of renting for 7 years is simply seven times the cost of renting for 1 year, although rent will probably increase over those 7 years. Other costs of renting include renter's insurance and the opportunity cost of lost interest due to having funds tied up in the security deposit.

The costs of buying are more complex. Although we have discussed most of the costs associated with owning a home, one cost we haven't looked at yet is the opportunity cost of having money tied up in a down payment. Because the money used for your down payment can no longer be invested to earn a profit, you should consider the after-tax return you'd have earned on this money as a cost of buying. Another cost of ownership comes when you eventually sell—that's the one-time selling cost resulting from the sales commission when the owner moves and sells the house.

Notice that the down payment itself isn't a cost; only the opportunity cost represents a cost. That's because you still have that money; it's still yours. In fact, it's your equity in your house or apartment.

These costs are partially offset by the benefits of ownership, which include the accumulation of equity resulting from a portion of the mortgage payment going toward the loan principal and the appreciation in the value of the home. Further, substantial savings are available to those who itemize. These savings result from the tax deductibility of the interest portion of mortgage payments, property taxes, and any points paid in the closing costs. If you don't itemize your tax deductions, you don't reap the tax benefits from these deductions.

Look at Figure 8.6: you should notice two major points. First, buying a home generally isn't financially desirable if you don't intend to stay in it for more than 2 or 3 years. The longer you stay in the home, the more it appreciates in value, and the more financially advantageous buying (and selling) is. Second, the benefits of buying instead of renting are substantially greater for those who itemize their taxes than for those who don't itemize. In fact, the advantage to buying over renting is more than twice as large for those who itemize ($31,420.48) than for those who don't itemize ($14,539.00) when looking at the 7-year time frame.

Finally, for many people, buying a home is a good means of "forced savings." Because some of your mortgage payment goes toward paying off the loan principal, a mortgage forces you to save in a sense. Although you're really buying something rather than saving, you are buying something that not only doesn't get "used up," but may appreciate in value over time. Moreover, by retirement you should own your home outright and be living "rent free."

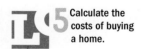

## Determining What's Affordable

The final preshopping homework question to be answered is how much to spend. If you've decided to buy a house, three questions need to be answered: (1) What is the maximum amount that a bank will lend me? (2) Should I borrow up to this maximum? and (3) How big a down payment can I afford? Although a bank may be willing to lend you $150,000, you might not want to borrow that much.

You've got to decide just how much you're interested in borrowing. Don't let a bank tell you how much to borrow. Look at your own financial situation, monthly budget, goals, and lifestyle, and decide for yourself.

Taking on a mortgage involves a large commitment of future earnings. Before you take it on, make sure that it jibes with your goals. Will it keep you from meeting your other goals—in particular, your retirement goals? Moreover, will it put such a strain on your monthly budget that you can no longer maintain the lifestyle that you want? You shouldn't let your mortgage payments, or any other debt payments, control your life.

Regardless of what you think you can afford, banks and other lenders impose a maximum amount that they want to lend you based on your income and current debt levels. Specifically, they look at three things: (1) your financial history, (2) your ability to pay, and (3) the appraised value of the home.

**Financial History**  In evaluating your financial history, lenders generally focus on the steadiness of your income and your credit rating. If you're self-employed, you may have to provide proof that you've maintained steady income for the past several years. Lenders also examine your credit report. You may want to get a copy of your credit report several months before applying for a loan to allow for the correction of any errors that may appear on it. If a lender doesn't like the look of your financial history, you can forget about getting a mortgage.

**Ability to Pay—PITI to Monthly Gross Income**  Lenders generally measure your ability to pay through the use of ratios. In particular, they look at the percentage of your income that goes to housing costs. The ratio lenders generally look at is that of your PITI compared to your monthly gross income. In general, lenders would like to see this ratio at a maximum of 28 percent.

**Ability to Pay—PITI Plus Other Debt Payments to Monthly Gross Income**  Lenders also look at the ratio of your PITI plus any other debt payments that will take over 10 months to pay off, compared to your monthly gross income. This ratio is used to account for the fact that many individuals have a sizable amount of outstanding debt, including student loans, car loans, and credit card debit. In general, lenders would like to see this ratio at a maximum of 36 percent. Note that different lenders may calculate these, or other ratios, a bit differently and have different acceptable maximums.

**Appraised Home Value**  Regardless of your financial history and ability to pay ratios, most lenders limit mortgage loans to 80 percent of the appraised value of the house. This limitation protects lenders by forcing the borrower to put up a substantial down payment. Lenders assume that the larger a borrower's down payment, the less likely he or she will default on the loan.

If a borrower does default, the lender assumes possession of the home, and the 80-percent limitation protects the lender in another way. The lender will sell the home to recoup its losses on the loan, and with the 80-percent rule in effect, the asking price of the home could fall by a full 20 percent—the same amount the borrower initially had to pay out—and the lender would still be able to recover the full amount it loaned out.

**Calculating Your Mortgage Limit**  The maximum loan size you'll qualify for is determined by the financial picture that develops as the lender reviews these three measures of your ability to pay. The lowest amount wins. Figure 8.7 shows the basic methods lenders use to determine how much they'll loan you.

As you can see using the information in Figure 8.7, if lenders limit your monthly housing costs as measured by PITI to 28 percent of your gross monthly income, your maximum mortgage payment will be $1,317 (as calculated in line d of Figure 8.7).

**Figure 8.7** Worksheet for Calculating the Maximum Monthly Mortgage Payment and Mortgage Size for Which You Can Qualify

**ASSUMPTIONS:** Annual gross income = $65,000
Estimated monthly real estate taxes and insurance = $200
Anticipated interest rate on the mortgage loan = 8%
Mortgage maturity = 30 years
Current nonmortgage debt payments on debt that will take over 10 months to pay off = $400
Current monthly child support and alimony payments = $0
Funds available for down payment and closing costs = $56,000
Closing costs are estimated to be $10,000[*]
Minimum acceptable down payment = 20%

**METHOD 1 Determine Your Maximum Monthly Mortgage Payment Using the Ability to Pay, PITI Ratio.**

|  | | Your Numbers |
|---|---|---|
| a. Monthly income (annual income divided by 12) | $5,417 | _____ |
| b. Times 0.28: Percent of PITI (principal, interest, taxes, and insurance) to your monthly gross income that lenders will lend in the form of a mortgage loan (multiply line a by 0.28) | × 0.28 = $1,517 | _____ |
| c. Less: Estimated monthly real estate tax and insurance payments (assumed to be $200 per month) | − $200 | _____ |
| d. Equals: Your maximum monthly mortgage payment using the 28% of PITI ratio | = $1,317 | _____ |
| To Determine the Maximum Mortgage Loan Level Using the Maximum Monthly Mortgage Payments as Determined Using the PITI Ratio (line d): | | |
| STEP 1: Monthly mortgage payment for a $10,000 mortgage with a 30-year maturity and a 8% interest rate (using Table 8.1) | | |
| STEP 2: Maximum mortgage level = maximum monthly mortgage payment (line d) divided by the monthly mortgage payment on a $10,000, 8%, 30-year mortgage | = $73.38 | _____ |
| (step 1 above) times $10,000 = ($1,317/$73.38) × $10,000 | = $179,477 | _____ |

**METHOD 2 Determine Your Maximum Monthly Mortgage Payment Using the Ability to Pay, PITI Plus Other Fixed Monthly Payments, Ratio.**

|  | | Your Numbers |
|---|---|---|
| e. Monthly income (annual income divided by 12) | $5,417 | _____ |
| f. Times 0.36: Percent of PITI + current monthly fixed payments to your monthly gross income that lenders will lend in the form of a mortgage loan (multiply line e by 0.36) | × 0.36 = $1,950 | _____ |
| g. Less: Current nonmortgage debt payments on debt that will take over 10 months to pay off and other monthly legal obligations like child support and alimony payments (assumed to be $400) | − $400 | _____ |
| h. Less: Estimated monthly real estate tax and insurance payments (assumed to be $200 per month) | − $200 | _____ |
| i. Equals: Your maximum monthly mortgage payment using the 36% of PITI + other fixed monthly payments ratio (line f − g − h) | = $1,350 | _____ |
| To Determine the Maximum Mortgage Loan Using the PITI Plus Other Fixed Monthly Payments Ratio (line i): | | |
| STEP 1: Monthly mortgage payment for a $10,000 mortgage with a 30-year maturity and an 8% interest rate (using Table 8.1) | = $73.38 | _____ |
| STEP 2: Maximum mortgage level = maximum monthly mortgage payment (line i) divided by the monthly mortgage payment on a $10,000, 8%, 30-year mortgage (step 1 above) times $10,000 = ($1,350/$73.38) × $10,000 | = $183,974 | _____ |

**METHOD 3 Determine Your Maximum Mortgage Level Using the "80% of the Appraised Value of the House" Rule.**

|  | | Your Numbers |
|---|---|---|
| j. Funds available for down payment and closing costs | $56,000 | _____ |
| k. Less: Closing costs of $10,000 | − $10,000 | _____ |
| l. Equals: Funds available for the down payment | = $46,000 | _____ |
| m. Times 4: Maximum mortgage level using the "80% of the appraised value of the house" rule (the 20% down, line l, times 4 equals the 80% you can borrow) | × 0.36 = $184,000 | _____ |
| ***Conclusion:* Maximum Mortgage Level for Which You Will Qualify (the lower of the amounts using method 1, method 2, or method 3):** | **= $179,477** | _____ |

[*]Closing costs generally vary as a percentage of the amount of the loan; however, to simplify calculations a bit, it is assumed they are estimated to be $10,000.

This payment translates into a mortgage loan of $179,477, given a loan rate of 8 percent and a 30-year term (as calculated in line d, step 2 of Figure 8.7).

Alternatively, when lenders use the 36 percent of total current monthly fixed payments rule as a guide, the maximum monthly mortgage payment you qualify for, given the information in Figure 8.7, is $1,350 (line i of Figure 8.7). This monthly payment translates into a mortgage loan of $183,974, given a loan rate of 8 percent and a 30-year term (as calculated in line i, step 2 of Figure 8.7).

**STOP & THINK** Although $179,477 is the likely limit that'll be imposed on you by the bank, it isn't necessarily the limit that you'll want to impose on yourself. The importance of not letting your mortgage payments, or any other debt payments, control your life and lifestyle can't be overstressed. Before taking on a mortgage, you should make sure that it squares with your goals, and that it won't prohibit you from meeting other goals, especially retirement goals.

Using the rule of lending 80 percent of the appraised value of the house, your maximum mortgage level would be $184,000. In this example, you have $56,000 available for your down payment *and* closing costs. Because closing costs are estimated to be $10,000, you'll have only $46,000 available for a down payment. If your down payment must be at least 20 percent of the value of your home, then you can borrow four times your down payment, or $184,000.

The mortgage level you qualify for is the lowest of these three figures. In this case, the lowest was the first mortgage limit of $179,477. Adding this amount to your down payment of $46,000, you see you can buy a home costing $226,477. However, you should keep in mind that whether these guideline ratios are applied more strictly or with some leniency depends on your financial history.

**Coming Up with the Down Payment**  For many people, especially those buying their first home, the real challenge is getting together a down payment. The most obvious and best way of coming up with a down payment is to save. If owning a home is one of your financial goals, saving for it should have a place in your financial budget.

**STOP & THINK** The most common way of coming up with a down payment for a home purchase is saving. Saving for a down payment may mean that you'll have to cut down on or eliminate traveling or eating out. It may even mean that you need to take on an extra job. For most first-time homebuyers, saving enough for a down payment takes about $2\frac{1}{2}$ years.

In addition to saving, many first-time home-buyers also rely on gifts and funds from parents or relatives. In fact, approximately 30 percent of all first-time homebuyers receive some financial aid from parents or relatives. But for conventional—that is, non-federally-backed loans, at least 5 percent of the closing costs have to come from the homebuyer rather than from gifts. Actually, most lenders require a "gift letter" stating that any funds contributed by relatives don't have to be repaid.

If you're having trouble raising enough money for a down payment, you might consider trying to reduce the size of the down payment you need. Federally backed loans—Federal Housing Administration (FHA), the Department of Veteran Affairs (VA), and the Farmers Home Administration (FmHA) loans—don't require as large a down payment as conventional loans. In fact, the FHA allows a minimum down payment of as little as 5 percent on older homes and 10 percent on new homes.

If all else fails, consider **private mortgage insurance**. This type of insurance protects the lender in the event that the borrower is unable to make the mortgage payments. It is paid for by the borrower and generally runs from 0.3 percent to 2.0 percent of the loan amount, depending on the down payment level. With private mortgage insurance, many lenders will allow you to borrow more than 80 percent of the appraised value of the home.

A final source of funds for your down payment is your IRA. The Taxpayer Relief Act of 1997 allows first-time homebuyers to withdraw up to $10,000 from their IRAs without penalty before age 59 $\frac{1}{2}$. While this is a possible source, it's also one that

**Private Mortgage Insurance**
Insurance that protects the lender in the event that the borrower is unable to make the mortgage payments.

you should try to avoid. Remember, taking money out of your IRA is just trading off one goal (financial security at retirement) for another (homeownership). The problem is that your IRA grows tax free, and once you take the money out, you can't get it back in. Moreover, if it is a traditional (as opposed to Roth) IRA, you will have to pay income tax on the distribution. That means if you are in the 28 percent marginal tax bracket, you'll withdraw $10,000 and pay $2,800 in taxes on the withdrawal, leaving you with $7,200 for your down payment.

**Prequalifying** Although your ability to pay, in addition to the level of funds you have available for a down payment, should give you a realistic idea of how large a mortgage loan you'll qualify for, it's a good idea to have this amount confirmed by seeing a lender and prequalifying for a loan.

The process of prequalifying for a mortgage loan simply involves having a lender determine how large a mortgage it will lend you. Prequalification lessens the uncertainty surrounding what you can and can't spend.

## Housing Step 2: Selection

Just as with any other major purchase, buying a home involves comparison shopping with an eye on price, product attributes (in this case, location, schools, number of rooms, and so forth), and quality (in this case, the quality of the house or apartment). Finding the right house or apartment is both involved and important. In fact, few decisions you make will have as profound an impact on your life. Our discussion of the search process focuses primarily on buying a home, but the same search principles also apply to buying or renting an apartment.

Once you know what you're looking for, it's time to start looking. Most homebuyers enlist the aid of a real estate agent. These agents can provide buyers with a lot of help in searching for homes and deciding on good neighborhoods, but you should note that the traditional real estate agent is really working for the seller: It's the seller who pays the real estate agent's commission. As a result, your best interests and the agent's best interests may be in conflict. Thus, although the agent may be your friend, you should make your own decisions based on a thorough understanding of the alternatives. Differentiating between advice and a sales pitch, and protecting yourself with knowledge, relate to **Principle 12: The Agency Problem in Personal Finance** and **Principle 9: The Best Protection Is Knowledge.** The traditional real estate agent has a bit of a conflict of interest, and it's the buyer's interests that lose out. In addition, real estate agents can sell only listed property—that is, property on which a real estate firm has a contract to sell.

Although this conflict of interest doesn't negate the benefits of using a real estate agent, you should definitely take some precautions. For example, you should never let your agent know your top price. If you tell the agent your top price, you can rest assured that the seller will have that information by the end of the day and your negotiating power will go out the window. You should also say you intend staying within your budget, and that if you don't get a particular house, that's OK, because there will be plenty of others around.

An alternative to the traditional real estate agent is the **independent** or **exclusive buyer-broker**. This type of broker is a real estate agent hired by the prospective buyer, who represents the buyer exclusively and is obligated to get the buyer the best possible deal. In general, the broker is paid by splitting the commission with the seller's agent. Buyer-brokers aren't limited in their search to properties that have been listed through real estate firms. They show both unlisted—that is, homes being sold directly by the owner—and listed homes.

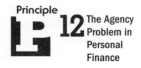

Principle **12** The Agency Problem in Personal Finance

Principle **9** The Best Protection Is Knowledge

**Independent or Exclusive Buyer-Broker**
A real estate agent hired by the prospective homebuyer who exclusively represents the homebuyer. Such brokers are obligated to get the buyer the best possible deal and, in general, are paid by splitting the commission with the seller's agent.

Moreover, because buyer-brokers work for the buyer, they tend to be more objective and critical in examining a house. Although exclusive buyer-brokers have gained popularity, they still aren't that common in many areas of the country. If you're interested in using a buyer-broker and can't find one, you can obtain a referral from Buyers' Resources (800-359-4092) in Englewood, Colorado; Buyers' Agents (800-766-8728) in Memphis, Tennessee; or the National Association of Exclusive Buyer Agents at **www.naeba.org/**. A recent survey showed that individuals who used buyer-brokers saved an average of 9 percent off the home's asking price versus only 3 percent for all buyers.

There is also a wealth of information to help with the search process on the Internet. One of the first places you'll want to explore is msn.Microsoft's HomeAdvisor at **homeadvisor.msn.com/**. It has a section on "Getting Started," which helps you understand the home buying process and how to get started; "Neighborhoods," which helps you find information on schools, crime, and demographics; "Homes," which helps find and compare homes and apartments for sale; "Financing," which provides information and tools to explore your financing options; and "Offer and Closing," which gives information on negotiating, inspecting the house, and closing the deal. Another great source of information on the Web is Homefair.com at **www.homefair.com/**, which provides information on picking the right city, school reports, finding an apartment, finding a home, and organizing your move.

When you find a house you like, you need to get it inspected. The house might be falling apart. Hey, it might even be haunted! A good home should be structurally sound, and its heating, air-conditioning, plumbing, and electrical systems should be free from problems. Unfortunately, very few homebuyers are truly qualified to inspect and judge these areas. If you're not one of the lucky few, you should enlist the aid of a professional building inspector. You should be able to get the name of an inspector from your real estate agent or the local chamber of commerce.

## Housing Step 3: Making the Purchase

Once you've decided which house or apartment you'd like to live in, the next step is making the purchase, or signing the lease. Once again, the process followed here is essentially the same as with any other major purchase: Negotiate a price and evaluate the financing alternatives. Because this step is so different for renting versus buying, we treat them separately.

### Guidelines for Renting

Let's assume you've weighed your options, considered your lifestyle concerns and the costs, and picked out a place to rent. What now? To begin with, when renting an apartment or a house, you're normally required to sign a **lease** or rental agreement. A lease is simply a contract between the renter and the owner of the property that defines the amount of monthly rent, its payment date, penalties for late payment, required deposits, length of the lease, renewal options, and any restrictions (e.g., no pets or children). Before signing a lease, make sure to work through Checklist 8.6.

### Negotiating a Price

Traditionally, negotiating a price for a house or apartment involves a good deal of bargaining. The home is "listed" at a certain selling price by the seller, meaning the seller would like to receive that price. However, all prices are open to negotiation. Many times the buyer will offer a price below what the home is listed at. The offer can also

**Lease**
A contract between the renter and the owner of a property that defines the monthly rent, payment date, penalties for late payment, required deposits, length of the lease, and renewal options, in addition to restrictions (e.g., no pets or children).

# Checklist 8.6 ■ Before You Rent

Determine what you can realistically afford. In general, your monthly costs, including rent, utilities, and insurance, shouldn't exceed 25 percent of your take-home pay.

Examine the location of the apartment closely. If quality schools or accessibility to transportation are important, make sure they're available. Make sure you feel safe with the location of and access to your apartment.

Understand your lease and make sure you are comfortable with it. Look closely at any restrictions and understand beforehand who's responsible for utilities. If you want something specifically included, request that it be added to the lease.

Never agree to verbal promises. Make sure that any changes in the lease are written directly into it.

Try to determine whether the landlord is reliable. Ask current tenants of the apartment building whether the landlord is responsive to complaints and repair requests.

Make sure you have renter's personal property and liability insurance.

---

include conditions or contingencies to be met as part of the contract. For example, you may want certain furniture or draperies to remain in the home, or you may want the mobster who owns the house to remove any dead bodies from the foundation.

The seller will give the buyer a counteroffer or refuse to budge. The counteroffer is carried between the buyer and the seller by the real estate agent—in fact, you may never see the seller face-to-face. In some cases, the haggling can go for some time until a final price is set. In other cases, while the haggling is going on with one potential buyer, another person steps in, offers more, and buys the home.

## Contract

Once the price is agreed upon, an attorney can draw up a contract to buy the home. Real estate contracts are relatively standard, but you should make sure that your contract protects you and provides for your specific needs. Keep in mind that only what's specifically stated in the contract counts—don't rely on verbal agreements. If you want it done, get it in writing in the contract. In addition, the contract should provide for the following:

- The price, method of payment, buyer and seller, date on which the buyer will take possession, and a legal description of the property should all be stated clearly.
- The legal title to the home must be free and clear of all liens and encumbrances. Whether the buyer or the seller pays for the title search should be stated in the contract.
- A house must be certified to be found free of termite or radon problems.
- A contingent on suitable funding clause should be included, stating that if you're unable to secure suitable financing (where you specifically state the amount, rate, and terms), the contract will be voided and you'll receive your deposit back in full.
- Because the home will change ownership during, rather than at the end of, the year, the contract should state what portion of the utilities, insurance, taxes, and interest on mortgage payments will be paid by the buyer and what portion will be paid by the seller.
- The condition the home will be in at the date of transfer should be stated, and a final walk-through should be provided to assure the buyer that the home is in the contracted condition.
- Any other contingencies that have been agreed upon should be included.

If the contract is accepted, the buyer will give the seller some **earnest money**, which is simply a deposit on the purchase assuring the seller that the buyer is serious about buying.

At **closing**, the title is transferred, the seller is paid in full, and the buyer takes possession of the home. At this point, the buyer must pay the balance of the down payment. For example, if you're buying a home for $150,000 with 20 percent down, at closing you must pay $30,000 less any earnest money you paid when the contract was signed.

In addition to the remaining down payment, you'll also have to pay the closing costs with a cashier's or certified check. You don't have to worry about figuring out exactly what you have to pay at closing. The lender will give you a **settlement** or **closing statement** at least one business day before closing. Finally, the legal documents are examined and signed, for which you may want to consult your lawyer, and the keys are passed. You now own a home!

## Financing the Purchase—The Mortgage

Just as a home is the biggest purchase most people ever make, a mortgage is the biggest loan that they ever take on. To say the least, not all mortgages are the same. In fact, whether or not you can afford to buy a house doesn't just depend on how much the house costs, but also on the specifics of the mortgage, such as how long it lasts, whether the interest rate changes over time, and whether it's insured by the government. Lets take a closer look at mortgages, where you get them, and how they work.

## Sources of Mortgages

Savings and loan institutions (S&Ls) and commercial banks are the primary sources of mortgage loans, but they certainly aren't the only sources. Other traditional lenders, such as credit unions and mutual savings banks, offer mortgage loans, in addition to specialized lenders such as mortgage bankers and mortgage brokers.

**Mortgage bankers** originate mortgage loans, sell them to banks, pension funds, and insurance companies, and service or collect the monthly payments. Their only business is making mortgage loans, and, in general, they deal only in fixed-rate mortgage loans. There's really no advantage or disadvantage to using a mortgage banker instead of a traditional source of mortgage loans, such as an S&L. Hey, if the mortgage banker's got the more favorable rate or the better deal, go for it.

**Mortgage brokers** are middlemen whose job is to place mortgage loans with lenders for a fee, but not originate those loans. The advantage of using mortgage brokers is that they do the comparison shopping for you. That is, they work with a number of lenders and choose the best terms and rates available.

## Conventional and Government-Backed Mortgages

Once you find the right lender and get your mortgage, it can be categorized as **conventional** or **government-backed**. Conventional mortgage loans are simply loans from a bank or S&L secured by the property being purchased. If you default on a mortgage loan, the lender seizes the property, sells it, and recovers the funds owed.

With government-backed loans, the traditional lender still makes the loan, but the government insures it. Veteran's Administration (VA) and Federal Housing Administration (FHA) loans are the two primary types of government-backed loans, and together they account for approximately 20 percent of all mortgage

**Earnest Money**
A deposit on the home purchase to assure the seller that the buyer is serious about buying the house.

**Closing**
The time at which the title is transferred and the seller is paid in full for the house. At this time the buyer takes possession of the house.

**Settlement or Closing Statement**
A statement listing the funds required at closing, which should be furnished to the buyer by the real estate broker at least one business day before closing for review.

Get the most out of your mortgage.

**Mortgage Banker**
Someone who originates mortgage loans with funds from other investors, such as pension funds and insurance companies, and services the monthly payments.

**Mortgage Broker**
A middleman who, for a fee, secures mortgage loans for borrowers but doesn't actually make those mortgage loans. Mortgage brokers will find the best loan available for the borrower.

**Conventional Mortgage Loan**
A loan from a bank or S&L that is secured by the property being purchased.

**Government-Backed Mortgage Loan**
A mortgage loan made by a traditional lender, but insured by the government.

loans. Both programs are quite similar, and they both share the same basic advantages and disadvantages. The primary advantages of VA and FHA loans include the following:

▌ An interest rate one-half to 1 percent below that of conventional mortgage loans
▌ A smaller down payment requirement
▌ Less strict financial requirements

The primary disadvantages of VA and FHA loans include the following:

▌ Increased paperwork required to qualify for the loan
▌ Higher closing costs, with FHA loans requiring a 3.8-percent mortgage default insurance fee and VA loans requiring a 1.25-percent VA funding fee
▌ Limits on the amount of funding that can be obtained

Although the FHA guarantees the entire loan, it doesn't assume all the costs for the required mortgage default insurance. In fact, with an FHA loan you're expected to pay for a portion of the cost, which generally runs 3.8 percent of the loan. However, because FHA loans are guaranteed, the interest rate charged on them is generally below the rate charged on conventional loans, so you can still wind up saving money.

VA mortgages are much more limited in access: only veterans and their unmarried surviving spouses are eligible for them. In addition, FHA loans allow for both fixed- and variable-rate loans, but VA loans must be fixed-rate loans with the rate generally being between one-half and one percentage point below that of conventional loans. VA loans don't require anything in the way of a down payment, but they do require a 1.25-percent VA funding fee payable at closing.

## Fixed-Rate Mortgages

Although conventional and government-backed are broad classifications for mortgages, there are also more refined classifications, such as fixed versus variable rate. A fixed-rate mortgage loan is one on which the monthly payment doesn't change, regardless of what happens to market interest rates. That is, no matter how much interest rates fluctuate, your payment remains the same. If mortgage interest rates are low, a fixed-rate mortgage allows you to lock in those low rates for the rest of the loan. The term or length of fixed-rate mortgages is generally either 15 or 30 years, with 30-year fixed-rate mortgage loans being the most popular. Many mortgages also come with assumability and prepayment privileges.

An **assumable loan** is one that can be transferred to a new buyer, who simply assumes or takes over the mortgage obligations. As a result, the new buyer doesn't incur the costs of obtaining a new loan. Moreover, if interest rates have gone up since the original assumable mortgage was taken out, the buyer can assume the mortgage at the lower rate. For example, if the mortgage was originally issued at 7.5 percent and rates have now gone up to 9 percent, the buyer could assume the mortgage at 7.5 percent. These advantages make it easier to sell a home with an assumable mortgage, particularly when interest rates have gone up since the mortgage was issued. The assumability privilege is common to all FHA loans and is also common to many conventional mortgage loans.

The **prepayment privilege** allows the borrower to make early cash payments that are applied toward the principal, thus reducing the amount of interest due. Many

**Assumable Loan**
A mortgage loan that can be transferred to a new buyer, who simply assumes or takes over the mortgage obligations. Such a mortgage saves the new buyer the costs of obtaining a new mortgage loan.

**Prepayment Privilege**
A clause in a mortgage allowing the borrower to make early cash payments that are applied toward the principal.

mortgages restrict prepayment by limiting the amount that can be prepaid or charging a penalty for prepayment. The prepayment privilege is also valuable, particularly if interest rates fall over the life of the mortgage. In that case, you can take out a loan at a lower rate and pay off your higher-rate mortgage loan early.

## Adjustable-Rate Mortgages

With an **adjustable-rate mortgage (ARM)** loan, the interest rate fluctuates according to the level of current market interest rates within limits at specific intervals. From the lender's point of view, ARMs are wonderful because they allow for a matching between the rate the lender pays on savings accounts to fund the loan and the income from the loan. Because lenders like ARMs so much, they generally charge a lower rate of interest on them—that's the appeal of ARMs to borrowers.

Let's look at S&Ls. During the 1980s and then again in the early 2000s, interest rates fluctuated wildly. When interest rates went up, S&Ls had to pay more on their savings accounts, but their income on fixed-rate mortgage loans stayed the same, squeezing profits. However, with ARMs, the income from interest payments on mortgage loans followed the interest rates up, thus allowing S&Ls to continue to make profits on their mortgage loans.

From the borrower's perspective, you're better off with an ARM if interest rates drop, because your interest rate drops accordingly and you won't have to refinance, which costs money. On the other hand, if interest rates rise, you're better off with a fixed-rate loan, because you will have locked in at a low rate.

To understand ARMs you need to understand the terminology that surrounds them, including the initial rate, index, margin, adjustment interval, rate cap, payment cap, and negative amortization.

**Initial Rate**  The **initial rate** is sometimes called the teaser rate. This rate holds only for a short period, generally between 3 and 24 months. In some cases, it's set deceptively low. Once the rate is allowed to move up and down, or float, it generally rises. In evaluating the cost of the ARM, you should focus on the ARM's real rate, that is, what the rate would be today.

**Interest Rate Index**  The rate on ARMs is tied to an interest rate index that's not controlled by the lender. As that interest rate index rises and falls, so does the ARM rate. The following are some of the more common indexes:

▌ The rate on 6- or 12-month U.S. Treasury securities
▌ The Federal Housing Finance Board's National Average Contract Mortgage rate, which is the national average mortgage loan rate
▌ The average cost of funds as measured by either the average rate paid on CDs or the 11th Federal Home Loan Bank District Cost of Funds

Which index is the best is debatable. However, stable indexes are better because they won't produce radical rate shifts. When shopping for an ARM, be sure to ask for some historical data on the index from your lender.

**Margin**  Depending on which index your ARM is tied to, your rate may be set higher than the index at a constant percentage above the index. For example, your ARM may be set at the 6-month U.S. Treasury bill rate plus 2 percent.

**Adjustable-Rate Mortgage (ARM)**
A mortgage loan in which the interest rate charged fluctuates with the level of current interest rates. The loan fluctuates, or is adjusted, at set intervals (say, every 5 years) and only within set limits.

**Initial Rate**
The initial rate charged on an ARM, sometimes called the teaser rate. This rate holds only for a short period, generally between 3 and 24 months, before being adjusted upward.

The amount over the index rate that the rate on the ARM is set at is called the margin. Thus:

$$\text{ARM rate} = \text{index rate} + \text{margin}$$

If the index rate is 5.0 percent and the margin is 2.5 percent, then the ARM rate is 7.5 percent.

**Adjustment Interval**   The adjustment interval defines how frequently the rate on the ARM will be reset. One year is the most common adjustment period, although some ARMs have adjustment intervals as low as 3 months and some as long as 7 years.

An adjustment interval of 1 year means that every year—generally on the anniversary of the loan—the rate on the ARM is reset to the index rate plus the margin. In general, it's better to have a longer adjustment interval, because the shorter the adjustment interval, the more volatile the mortgage payments.

**Rate Cap**   The rate cap limits how much the interest rate on an ARM can change. Most ARMs have both periodic caps and lifetime caps. A *periodic cap* limits the amount by which the interest rate can change during any adjustment. Normally, the ARM rate will go up 3 percent if the index goes up 3 percent. However, if the periodic cap is 2.0 percent and the index rate increases by 3.0 percent, the rate on the ARM would still only increase by 2.0 percent. Most conventional ARM loans have periodic caps of 2 percent. FHA loans have 1 percent periodic caps.

The *lifetime cap* limits the amount by which the interest rate can change during the life of the ARM. Thus, for an ARM with an initial rate of 6.0 percent and a lifetime cap of 5.0 percent, the highest and lowest this ARM could go would be down to 1.0 percent or up to 11.0 percent. Borrowers love lifetime caps because they limit the ARM rate to a specific range. In evaluating a lifetime cap, be sure that you know whether the cap is linked to the initial or the real rate.

**Payment Cap**   A payment cap sets a dollar limit on how much your monthly payment can increase during any adjustment period. A payment cap limits the change in the monthly mortgage payment, but it doesn't limit changes in the interest rate being charged on the borrowed money. If the payments are capped, and the interest rate isn't capped, when interest rates go up, more of your mortgage payment could end up going toward interest and not principal.

In fact, if interest rates keep going up, it's possible that the monthly payment amount will be too small to even cover the interest due. In this case, **negative amortization** occurs. When this happens, the unpaid interest is added to the unpaid balance on the loan. In effect, the size of the mortgage balance can grow over time, and you can end up owing more than the original amount of the loan. You pay interest on your unpaid interest, and the term of the loan can drag out. Because negative amortization is something to avoid, and can only occur when there's a payment cap limit but not an interest rate cap, you should avoid mortgages with payment but not interest rate caps.

**ARM Innovations**   Several variations of the standard ARM have been introduced. They include the convertible ARM, the reduction-option ARM, the two-step ARM, and the price level adjusted mortgage. The convertible ARM is a traditional ARM that allows the borrower to convert the ARM loan to a fixed-rate loan, usually during the second through fifth year. A reduction-option ARM is an ARM with a one-time, optional interest rate adjustment. This allows the borrower

**Negative Amortization**
A situation in which the monthly payments are less than the interest that's due on the loan. As a result, the unpaid interest is added to the principal, and you end up owing more at the end of the month than you did at the beginning of the month.

to adjust the interest rate on the loan to market interest rates one time, generally limited to years 2 through 6.

If interest rates fall, the borrower can exercise his or her option to lower the rates and set the adjustment into motion. If interest rates rise, then the borrower would just leave the rates as they are. With a two-step ARM, the interest rate is adjusted only once, generally at the end of the seventh year. After that, the interest rate remains constant for the remaining life of the loan.

On a price level adjusted mortgage, the initial rate is set very low to make the mortgage more attractive. The monthly payments and interest rate then change with inflation. The idea here is that as inflation increases, so should your salary and ability to make higher and higher mortgage payments. Unfortunately, on a 30-year mortgage, your monthly payments could easily triple over this period.

## Other Mortgage Loan Options

Most of the alternative mortgage loan options serve the same purpose: to keep the initial mortgage payments as low as possible to make buying a house more affordable to first-time and cash-strapped buyers. Unfortunately, keeping the payments down in the early years generally means larger payments in later years, or some other concession.

**Balloon Payment Mortgage Loan**   With a **balloon payment mortgage loan**, you make relatively small monthly payments for several years (generally 5 or 7 years), after which the loan comes due and you must pay it off in one large payment. Exactly how large the initial payments are varies. In some cases, the initial mortgage payments are only large enough to cover the interest on the loan, and in other cases, the payments may be equivalent to the loan's amortized value over 30 years. However, what balloon payment mortgage loans all have in common is that the payments are constant for a few years and then the loan comes due and is paid off with a very large, final payment.

Some traditional lenders don't offer balloon payment mortgages. In fact, most of these mortgages are offered by the sellers themselves, who are anxious to sell the house but don't need the funds from the sale immediately. Watch out for balloon mortgages, because they come with serious potential problems. For many individuals, coming up with the final balloon payment is difficult at best. It generally means they will have to take out a new mortgage just to pay off the old one. If interest rates have risen, the homeowner will be forced to refinance at a higher rate.

In addition, when the balloon payment comes due, the homeowner may have very little in the way of equity in the home if the monthly payments have included only interest. In fact, if the market value of the home has declined, the balloon payment that's due could be greater than the house is worth.

**Balloon Payment Mortgage Loan**
A mortgage with relatively small monthly payments for several years (generally 5 or 7 years), after which the loan must be paid off in one large balloon payment.

**Graduated Payment Mortgages**   With a **graduated payment mortgage**, the payments are set in advance in such a way that they rise steadily for a specified period of time, generally 5 to 10 years, and then level off. The selling point behind graduated payment mortgages is that the initial payments are relatively low, so you'll be able to afford a house sooner. The assumption is that, as your earning power increases over time, you'll be able to afford the rising payments. In effect, you're assuming that your income will grow into the level of future payments. Unfortunately, you might be assuming incorrectly, and you might be putting an obligation on your future income that you can't handle.

**Graduated Payment Mortgage**
A mortgage in which payments are arranged to steadily rise for a specified period of time, generally 5 to 10 years, and then level off.

**Growing Equity Mortgages**   A **growing equity mortgage** is designed to let the homebuyer pay off the mortgage early, which is done by paying a little extra each year. It doesn't really help the cash-strapped buyer. Payments on a growing equity mortgage begin at the same level as on a conventional 30-year fixed-rate mortgage. Each year the payments increase, and this increase goes toward paying off the principal.

With a growing equity mortgage, you know how your payments are going to increase ahead of time. Generally, they increase by between 2 and 9 percent each year. The result is that a 30-year mortgage is paid off in less than 20 years. While a growing equity mortgage forces a disciplined prepayment of your mortgage, there is no advantage, and less flexibility, over a fixed-rate mortgage loan with a prepayment clause.

**Shared Appreciation Mortgages**   With a **shared appreciation mortgage**, the borrower receives a below-market interest rate. In return the lender receives a portion of the future appreciation (usually between 30 and 50 percent) in the value of the home. Thus, if you purchase a $100,000 home with a shared appreciation mortgage that promises the lender 50 percent of any price appreciation and 10 years later sell the home for $180,000, the lender would receive one-half of the $80,000 price appreciation. Generally, mortgages of this type are not issued by traditional mortgage lenders, but by family members or investors.

## Adjustable-Rate Versus Fixed-Rate Mortgages

For the homebuyer, the primary advantage of an adjustable-rate mortgage is that the initial rate charged is lower than that on fixed-rate loans. Initial ARM rates are lower because the borrower assumes the risk that interest rates will rise. Thus, the rate gap between 1-year adjustable-rate mortgages and 30-year fixed-rate mortgages is generally above 1 to 2 percent. For example, in 2002, the rate gap was about 1.47 percent.

One commonly stated advantage of this low initial rate is that you may qualify for a larger loan because your monthly payment, PITI, is lower. However, if interest rates rise, pushing your monthly ARM payment upward, you may find yourself overcommitted.

Don't choose an ARM in the hope that interest rates will fall and your payments will be lower. Predicting future interest rates certainly isn't something you want to gamble your house and financial future on. You can be sure that interest rates will never fall below zero (which would mean that lenders would owe *you* money!), but you can never be sure just how high they'll rise. If you have a lifetime cap on your mortgage, you do know just how high your rates can rise, but this knowledge doesn't help if you're hoping never to have to pay that much. In short, if you can't afford the maximum payment you might have to make on an ARM should interest rates rise, you probably shouldn't take it on.

In general, a fixed-rate mortgage is better than an adjustable-rate mortgage. With a fixed-rate mortgage, you know your payments, and, as a result, can plan for them in advance. Don't forget that the basis of personal financial management is control and planning, and a fixed-rate mortgage allows for both. ARMs allow for neither. If you don't like financial risk and have difficulty handling financial stress, ARMs are dangerous.

Still, if you intend to stay in the house only a few years, or if current interest rates are extremely high, you may want to consider an ARM. Remember, much of the advantage of an ARM comes in the early years when you're guaranteed a low rate.

## Mortgage Decisions: Term of the Loan

Another decision faced by homebuyers is whether to go for a 15- or 30-year maturity on their mortgage. If you can secure a 30-year mortgage with a prepayment privilege, you could easily pay it off in 15 years by making additional payments every month. Why not just take out a 15-year loan if you're planning on paying it off within 15 years anyway?

Well, with a 30-year loan, you wouldn't be locked in to paying the higher monthly rates of a 15-year loan, and you'd have the flexibility of being able to skip making your additional payments and paying a much lower amount per month if an emergency arose. Thus, at first glance, for those with financial discipline, the 30-year mortgage is preferable. However, there is one additional variable that needs to be added into the equation: interest.

In general, the interest rate on 15-year mortgages is lower than the rate on 30-year mortgages. For example, in 2002 the average rate on a 30-year fixed-rate mortgage was 6.43 percent and the average rate on a 15-year fixed-rate mortgage was 5.90 percent. Interest also comes into play when you consider your overall payments. A longer term means you pay interest over a longer period. For example, let's look at a 30-year, 8-percent fixed-rate mortgage for $80,000. The monthly payments on such a mortgage are $587.01.

Figure 8.8 illustrates the portion of each payment that goes toward the principal on a 30-year, 8-percent fixed-rate mortgage. As you can see, initially less than 10 percent of the first monthly payment, only $53.68, goes toward paying off the loan balance. The result is that over the life of a longer-term mortgage, total interest payments are much larger.

Table 8.2 shows the impact of the loan term on total interest paid. Keep in mind that these calculations are for an 8-percent mortgage. If the mortgage rate were higher, the total interest payments for the longer-term loan would be proportionately greater. In effect, as interest rates increase, this relationship becomes even more dramatic. Also, keep in mind that this relationship is amplified by the fact that you would pay a lower interest rate on the shorter-term mortgage.

**Figure 8.8** The Portion of Each Payment That Goes Toward the Principal and Interest on a 30-Year, 8% Fixed-Rate Mortgage for $80,000

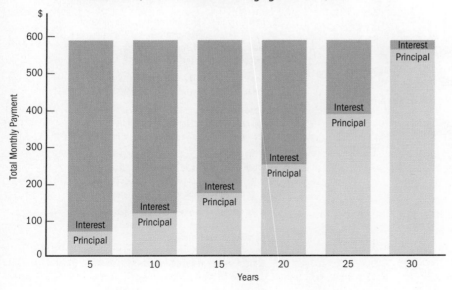

## Table 8.2 Impact of the Loan Term on the Total Interest Paid and Monthly Payment for an $80,000 Fixed-Rate Mortgage at 8%

| Length of Mortgage Loan | Monthly Payment | Total Interest |
|---|---|---|
| 15 years | $764.52 | $ 57,614.13 |
| 20 years | 669.15 | 80,597.38 |
| 25 years | 617.45 | 105,237.47 |
| 30 years | 587.01 | 131,326.30 |

Unfortunately, the total level of interest paid doesn't tell the whole story. There are two other complications: the time value of money and the effect of taxes. Remember, with a longer-term mortgage, your payments are lower but stretched out longer. As a result, you're paying back your loan with future dollars that are worth less because of inflation.

In other words, when you make the smaller, 30-year payment, you can take the difference in payments and invest it until the end of the 30-year period. Of course, with a 15-year mortgage, when the 15-year period ends, you can invest the amount you were paying each month until the end of the 30-year period. Exactly what you have at the end of 30 years depends on what assumptions you make about what you could earn on these investments. Also, don't forget that interest on home mortgages is tax deductible and lowers taxes. As a result, the tax effect favors the longer-term mortgage.

Figure 8.9 provides a listing of some of the advantages of different length mortgages. When deciding on a term length for your mortgage, make sure you weigh all these factors. You've also got to make sure that what you do fits into your grand financial plan. You certainly don't want to be making extra payments to pay off an

Figure 8.9 Comparing a Shorter- Versus Longer-Term Loan

**Advantages to a 15-Year Mortgage**

- Lower interest rate.
- Provides a discipline to force savings.
- Saves quite a bit of interest over the life of the mortgage.
- Equity is built up at a faster pace.
- Increased equity may allow you to trade up to a more expensive house.

**Advantages to a 30-Year Mortgage**

- Lower payments give you more financial flexibility— if a financial emergency arises, the payments are lower and, as such, you have more uncommitted money to address the emergency.
- Provides affordability—you may not be able to buy the house you want with a 15-year mortgage.
- If the mortgage contains a prepayment provision, you can mimic the payment pattern on a 15-year mortgage while maintaining financial flexibility.
- If you are borrowing on credit cards, which are a much more expensive form of debt than mortgages, you would be better off paying off your credit card debt before you took on higher mortgage payments.
- If your investment alternative earns returns well above the mortgage interest rate, and you are a disciplined saver, that along with the tax advantage associated with mortgage debt makes a longer-term mortgage more attractive.

8-percent mortgage while you're borrowing money on your credit card at 18 or 20 percent. Also, don't let repaying your mortgage get in the way of your other financial goals.

## Housing Step 4: Postpurchase Activities

Once you've purchased a home, you're then in charge of upkeep and maintenance. To say the least, owning a home can take up a good deal of time. In addition, you should always keep an eye out toward making sure that you have financed your home in the least expensive way possible. That leads us to a discussion of refinancing your mortgage.

Refinancing is simply taking out a new mortgage, usually at a lower rate, to pay off your old one. Whenever mortgage interest rates drop, people refinance. No one wants to be paying 12 percent on a mortgage when the going rate is now 8 percent. The typical rule of thumb states that you should refinance when mortgage interest rates fall by 2 percent. However, there's more to refinancing than just interest rates.

# In The News

**Wall Street Journal Sunday November 18, 2001**

### "Spreading Your Investment Bets"

by Jonathan Clements

Unusual times call for unusual investments.

Unnerved by the stock market but still hankering for healthy returns? The three strategies that follow are no substitute for a core portfolio of conventional stocks and bonds.

Still, if you are looking to spread your investment bets a little more widely, these strategies all offer an intriguing way to diversify while earning decent returns:

With interest rates so low, homeowners are rushing to refinance their mortgages and lock in the lower rates.

But many folks will find it isn't worth refinancing, because any reduction in their monthly payment doesn't compensate for the hefty refinancing costs.

*Nonetheless, the rush to refinance is a signal that this may be a smart time to make extra principal payments. Think of paying down your mortgage as a substitute for buying bonds.* (☞A)

When you buy bonds, you are lending money, in return for which you receive interest. Currently, the government will pay you 4.75% a year to hold 10-year Treasury notes, while top-rated corporations are forking over 6% to bondholders.

A mortgage also involves borrowed money. But in this case, you are the borrower, so you are the one coughing up interest.

When you pay down principal, it is like buying back some of the bonds you had earlier sold to the mortgage company.

Your extra principal payments reduce the amount of interest due and may allow you to pay off your loan years earlier, thus providing a comforting dose of financial freedom.

*Got a mortgage with a 7% interest rate? That is the effective return you get by paying down principal.* (☞B)

### THE BOTTOM LINE . . .

**A** Many people have an easier time saving money to pay down their mortgage than they do saving money for an investment. That may be because they can see their house and know exactly where the money is going, or it may be because they know they are paying their way out of debt—regardless, if it works, that is, if it helps you spend less than you earn, more power to it.

**B** For example, the monthly payment on a $100,000 30-year mortgage at 7 percent is $655.30. "If you pay an extra $100 a month, you'll pay off your mortgage in about 20 and a half years. It's an easy way to save money.

Source: Jonathan Clements, "Spreading Your Investment Bets," *Wall Street Journal Sunday*, November 18, 2001: 3. Copyright (c) 2001, Dow Jones & Company, Inc. Reproduced with permission of DOW JONES & CO INC in the format Textbook via Copyright Clearance Center.

Figure 8.10 Worksheet for Refinancing Analysis

| Monthly Benefits from Refinancing | Example | Your Numbers |
|---|---|---|
| a. Present monthly mortgage payments | $952.32 | _____ |
| b. Mortgage payments after refinancing | $800.73 | _____ |
| c. Monthly savings, pretax (line a – line b) | $151.59 | _____ |
| d. Additional tax on monthly savings (line c × <u>28%</u> tax rate) | $42.45 | _____ |
| e. Monthly savings on an after-tax basis (line c – line d) | $109.14 | _____ |
| **Cost of Refinancing** | | |
| f. Total after-tax closing costs, including any prepayment penalty incurred | $2,600 | _____ |
| **Number of Months Needed to Break Even** | | |
| g. Months needed for interest saved to equal the refinancing costs incurred as a result of taking out a new mortgage loan (line f ÷ line e) | 23.8 months | _____ |

When you refinance, you again incur most of the closing costs already discussed, including points, the loan application fee, the termite and radon inspection fee, and so on. The refinancing decision really rides on whether or not the lower rate you could get will compensate for these additional costs in a reasonable amount of time.

Let's look at an example: You currently have a 15-year-old, 30-year mortgage at 11 percent and are considering refinancing it with a 15-year mortgage at 8 percent. When you bought your home, you took out a $100,000 mortgage with a monthly payment of $952.32. Today, 15 years later, you still have a balance on your mortgage of $83,789.07. If you refinanced this loan over 15 years at 8 percent, your payments would drop to $800.73.

If you estimate that your total after-tax closing costs would be $2,600, it would take you 23.8 months for the savings from the decrease in monthly payments to cover the closing costs incurred as a result of refinancing, as shown in Figure 8.10. Thus, if you expect to continue in your home for over 2 years, you should consider refinancing at the lower rate. Checklist 8.7 provides a number of reasons why refinancing might be a good idea.

WORKSHEET 25

# Checklist 8.7 ▪ Refinancing Might Be a Good Idea if You ...

Want to get out of a high-interest-rate loan to take advantage of lower rates. This is a good idea only if you intend to stay in the house long enough to make the additional fees worthwhile.

Have an adjustable-rate mortgage (ARM) and want a fixed-rate loan to have the certainty of knowing exactly what the mortgage payment will be for the life of the loan.

Want to convert to an ARM with a lower interest rate or more protective features (such as a better rate and payment caps) than the ARM you currently have.

Want to build up equity more quickly by converting to a loan with a shorter term.

Want to draw on the equity built up in your home to get cash for a major purchase or for your children's education.

Source: *A Consumers Guide to Mortgage Refinancing* (Washington, DC: Federal Reserve Board, 2002).

# SUMMARY

The first step in smart buying is to separate your wants from your needs. Once you've determined the alternatives, it's time to compare the different products and make trade-offs between quality, products' features, and price. The key to success in negotiating is knowing as much as possible about the markup on the product. The final step is the postpurchase process, involving maintenance and resolving any complaints that might arise. This smart buying process works for just about any purchase decision you make.

While your home may be your largest investment, your automobile is your largest frequent expense. Choose a car that fits both your personal and financial needs.

Once you have decided what is best for you, the next hurdle is getting it for a fair price. The place to start here is to find out what the dealer cost or invoice price is. Next, you must make the financing decision. Should you buy or lease? Leasing a car is similar to renting. About 80 percent of all new car leases are closed-end or walk-away leases. With this type of lease you return the car at the end of the lease and literally walk away from any further responsibilities.

No single type of housing is right for everyone. A single-family house is the traditional choice, and it is the most popular choice for most people because it offers more space, privacy, and owner control. A cooperative or co-op is an apartment building or group of apartments owned by a corporation where the residents of the building are the stockholders of the corporation.

There are a number of reasons renting may be preferable to buying. In order to make a logical decision about whether to rent or buy or what is truly affordable, you need to have a basic understanding of the costs that come with home ownership. These include one-time or initial costs such as the down payment, points, and closing costs; recurring costs associated with financing, including mortgage payments, property taxes, and insurance; and recurring costs associated with upkeep and maintenance.

The first step in the housing decision involves preshopping, in which you focus on the rent-versus-buy decision and determine what is affordable. Just as with any other major purchase, the second step involves comparison shopping with an eye on price, product attributes, and the quality of the house or apartment.

Once you decide which house or apartment you'd like to live in, the next step is purchasing the house, or in the case of renting an apartment, signing the lease. Once again, the process is essentially the same as with any other major purchase—negotiate a price and evaluate the financing alternatives. Once you've purchased a home, you're in charge of upkeep and maintenance.

Mortgages can be categorized as conventional or government-backed. Conventional mortgages are simply loans secured by the property being purchased from a bank or S&L. With government-backed loans, the bank or S&L still makes the loan, but the government insures the loan. S&Ls and commercial banks are the primary sources of mortgage loans, but they certainly are not the only sources. Mortgage loans are also available from other traditional lenders like credit unions and mutual savings banks, as well as from specialized lenders: mortgage bankers and mortgage brokers.

Mortgages also come with fixed or adjustable rates. A fixed-rate mortgage loan is one on which the monthly payment does not change regardless of what happens to interest rates. With an adjustable-rate mortgage loan the interest rate fluctuates up and down with the level of current interest rates within limits at specific intervals. If interest rates drop, you may want to refinance your mortgage, which is simply taking out a new mortgage to pay off your old one.

# REVIEW QUESTIONS

1. What is the first question you should answer before making any significant "smart buyer" purchase?
2. Summarize the four-step process for smart buying.
3. Effective complaints do not reflect anger or include threats. List five key points to remember when making an effective complaint.
4. What factors should be considered to determine the vehicle someone should buy?
5. What three factors determine the monthly payment on an automobile loan?
6. What is the holdback on a new car? How are the holdback, rebates, dealer incentive, and markup important when negotiating a new car price?

7. What is the purpose of an auto lease? What are the two types of leases? What is the major difference between the two?

8. Identify the characteristics of a consumer who should seriously consider auto leasing. What are the six factors that determine the monthly lease payment?

9. What is the difference between a condo and a co-op? What are the advantages and disadvantages of each compared to living in a single-family house?

10. What is a Planned Unit Development? How does it differ from a condominium?

11. What three major categories of expenses make up the costs of homeownership? Give two examples of each.

12. What are the initial, or one-time, costs associated with financing a home?

13. What are the advantages and disadvantages of buying versus renting a home?

14. What two primary lifestyle and financial factors should be considered in the buy or rent decision?

15. From a financial point of view, over a seven-year period, why is it better to own than to rent? Consider costs, return, and taxes in your answer. (*Hint:* Use Figure 8.6.)

16. What four separate expenses make up the mortgage payment? What acronym is used to describe a mortgage payment?

17. What three factors determine the maximum amount a bank will finance for a home mortgage?

18. What is the difference between a traditional real estate agent and an independent buyer-broker? Is there an advantage to either for someone buying a home?

19. What factors should be considered before signing a lease or rental agreement?

20. What provisions should be outlined in a real estate contract?

21. What is the difference between mortgage bankers and mortgage brokers? Does either offer prospective homeowners an advantage? If so, what?

22. What are the advantages and disadvantages of government-backed loans, such as VA or FHA loans?

23. What two factors determine the interest rate for an ARM? How might this differ from the initial rate? Why are the factors of rate caps and adjustment intervals important?

24. What mortgages offer the advantage of reduced initial payments for first-time or cash-strapped homebuyers? What are the disadvantages of these mortgage options?

25. List the advantages of a fixed-rate mortgage. In contrast, what are the advantages of an adjustable-rate mortgage, or ARM?

26. How do the time value of money and taxes complicate the decision on mortgage term?

27. What are some factors that determine whether or not a homeowner should refinance?

## PROBLEMS AND ACTIVITIES

1. Consider the following costs of owning a vehicle valued and sold for $15,000. Now calculate the total first-year cost of ownership.

   Auto Loan: Amount—$15,000, Duration—4 years, APR—8.65 percent
   Property Taxes: 2 percent of vehicle value/year
   Sales Taxes: 3 percent of the sales price
   Title and Tags: $40/year
   Maintenance and Usage Costs: $1,500/year
   Insurance: $2,000/year

2. Calculate the monthly payments for a vehicle that costs $27,000 if you financed 80 percent of the price for 5 years at 6.9 percent. Also calculate the payment if you financed the same amount for 3 years at 5.9 percent.

3. Calculate the monthly and total automobile loan payments for each of the following loans.
   a. $24,000, 60 months, 9 percent
   b. $18,000, 36 months, 8 percent
   c. $17,500, 48 months, 7.75 percent
   d. $19,000, 48 months, 5.99 percent
   e. $16,000, 24 months, 9.5 percent
   f. $24,000, 60 months, 7 percent

4. Calculate the monthly payments for a vehicle that costs $15,000 if you financed the entire purchase over 4 years at an annual interest rate of 7 percent. Also calculate the loan payments

assuming rates of 8 percent and 9 percent. Compare the total amount spent on the vehicle under each assumption.

5. Annie's mortgage statement shows a total payment of $699.15 with $604.60 paid toward principal and interest and $94.52 paid for taxes and insurance. Taxes and insurance for 3 months were collected at closing. Now after 6 months of payments, she is curious about the total in her escrow account. Calculate the amount for her and explain the account.

6. Calculate the monthly payments of a 30-year fixed-rate mortgage at 8.25 percent if the amount financed is $100,000. How much interest is paid over the life of the loan? How much interest is saved by increasing the payment to $800 per month?

7. Calculate how much money a prospective homeowner would need for closing costs on a house that costs $100,000. Calculate based on a 20 percent down payment, 2 discount points on the loan, a 1-point origination fee, and $1,400 in miscellaneous other fees.

8. Calculate the monthly payments for a $100,000 mortgage loaned in each of the following ways.

30 year fixed at 8.5 percent
15 year fixed at 7.75 percent
20 year fixed at 8.125 percent

What are the total payments on each loan and which is the best option for a homeowner who can afford payments of $875/month? Explain your answer.

9. Kalid is purchasing a home but expects interest rates to fall, so he is choosing an 8.375 percent adjustable-rate mortgage. During the first 3 years of his mortgage he got lucky and the interest rate fell, but unfortunately his floor rate was 5.5 percent. Calculate his average interest rate for years 1–3 for his 30-year 2/6 ARM assuming the maximum allowable adjustments for the time period.

10. Determine the maximum 30-year fixed-rate mortgage amount for which a couple could qualify if the rate is 9.5 percent. Assume they have other debt payments totaling $500 per month and an annual salary of $45,500. Monthly escrow payments for real estate taxes and homeowner's insurance are estimated to be $125.

## SUGGESTED PROJECTS

1. Your friend recently completed a home addition that included a new laundry room and larger master bath. There appears to be a problem with the plumbing drain. If the master bath commode is flushed while the washer is draining, the commode backs up. So far, it has not overflowed onto the floor. Help your friend write a complaint letter to the construction company.

2. Research several automotive Web sites and write a one-page report on your findings.

3. List your needs (including budget) and your wants for a new automobile. Consult sources such as Web sites, magazines, and dealership literature, and make a financially and personally wise decision about which vehicle to buy. Write your lists and discuss your reasoning in a short report.

4. Go to a dealership and ask to see a copy of the lease agreement. Discuss your option and understanding of the agreement in a one-page

report. (*Note:* If asked, avoid giving your full name. This could lead to an unwanted and unauthorized check of your credit report.)

5. List the pros and cons, from both a financial and personal perspective, of leasing and financing a vehicle.

6. List as many house styles and room names as you can. (*Hint:* A house-planning magazine may help.) Which style and combination of rooms suits you the best? Why?

7. List the pros and cons, from both a financial and personal perspective, on renting and owning a home. Write a one-page summary on your choice, which can be verified by your list.

8. Talk with your parents, another homeowner, or consult your own records to determine the amount of money that was paid in up-front closing costs for the most recent home closing. Write a report outlining the costs.

9. Consult the real estate section in the local paper, real estate listings booklet, or real estate listing

on the Web. Choose a home, regardless of price, that you would like to own. Now choose a house with a price between $100,000 and $150,000 that you would like to own. (If the first house is between $100,000 and $150,000 choose another.) Finally calculate the principal and interest portion of the mortgage payment, the necessary down payment, and estimated closing costs, on each home if you financed 80 percent of the cost over 20 years at a rate of 8.5 percent. Write a report outlining your calculations and the reasoning behind each of your choices. (*Hint:* Use Figure 8.4 to estimate closing costs.)

10. Visit a local bank, mortgage company, and credit union. Speak with a representative about the different mortgages available through their institution. Write a report discussing the features of each and which mortgage you would choose.

11. Assume you are buying a new $130,000 home in the area. Find the mortgage rate information in the local paper and choose a loan from the ones listed. When making your choice consider rate, duration, type, monthly payment, closing costs, and points (if applicable). Calculate the monthly payment based on financing 80 percent and calculate the total amount paid over the life of the loan including up-front costs. Assume that closing costs equal 2.5 percent of the selling price of the house exclusive of down payment and points.

12. Talk with a friend, family member, or banker about either FHA or VA mortgages. Ask them to describe their likes and dislikes with the programs. Would you consider these types of loans if you were eligible? Why or why not?

# Discussion Case 1

Samuel and Grace Paganelli want to replace the 1992 pick-up, which Samuel drives for work. They already own two vehicles, but they need to replace Samuel's pick-up because it has been driven nearly 225,000 miles. The replacement needs to be a vehicle that fits his job as a self-employed electrician.

Samuel knows that he drives a lot on the job and is worried about the high-mileage penalty on many leases, as well as the fees for excessive wear and tear. However, Grace is more concerned about the depreciation expense than the mileage penalty and would rather lease the new vehicle. She also likes the idea of having a new, safer truck every few years without the hassle of resale. Samuel also does not like the fact that, if they lease, they would not own the vehicle he will use for work. Warranty protection to insure the truck remains in service is very important.

They feel that they can afford to spend $550/month over 4 years for a new vehicle, as long as their other associated expenses such as insurance, gas, and maintenance are not too high. The Paganellis also do not know where to start looking for a vehicle without the hassle of negotiating with dealerships.

## Questions

1. Identify seven sources of vehicle buying information and the type of information available in each source.

2. For all the information available, specifically what information about the different makes and models is the most relevant to Samuel and Grace in making their vehicle buying decision?

3. What is the highest price they can pay if they can afford a down payment of $4,000 on the new vehicle? Assume they finance their purchase for 48 months at 7.5 percent.

4. According to the National Automotive Dealer Association guide, are the Paganellis better off to sell their vehicle or use it as a trade-in? Consider both price and time in your answer.

5. Would you recommend leasing or financing? Why?

6. If Samuel purchases a "lemon," what alternatives are available to prevent the truck from "short circuiting" his business?

# Discussion Case 2

With a raise from the investment firm, Seyed Abdallah, 31, is inspired to look for a new home. Buying a home will allow Seyed, who is single and in the 30 percent marginal tax bracket, to itemize taxes. He has come to you for help.

Financially he is fairly secure but is also very risk adverse. His salary is $63,000 a year but he does not know how much he should spend on housing. His current housing expenditures include rent of $900 per month and renter's insurance premiums totaling

*Tips from Marcy Furney, ChFC, Certified Financial Planner™*

# Money Matters
## HOME SWEET HOME

**A home isn't necessarily a money-making invest-
ment.** *Make sure your reasons for purchasing
reach beyond intending to resell at a profit. The
real estate market is intricate, and many factors
are at play in determining resale value.*

**Beware of the "hidden costs" of homeownership.**
*Decorating and landscaping can be major
expenses in a new home. Utilities, maintenance,
and repairs are ongoing budget items. If you're
buying a preowned home, ask to see utility bills
for different seasons.*

**Whenever possible, prequalify for your loan so that
you'll know approximately how much you can
spend.** *You may want to stay below the maximum
you could finance so that you will have some
buffer for other expenses.*

**Make sure the lender locks in the interest rate
quoted you and find out how long it will be guaranteed.** *Be sure to get to closing before that
period runs out or take the initiative to renegoti-
ate the rate.*

**Keep good records of any improvements, not
repairs, you make on your home.** *Include the
cost, what was done, and when. These
improvements can be useful in boosting the
market value of your home when you sell it.*

*On high-dollar houses with potential capital
gains tax, they will also serve to increase your
cost basis.*

**When you shop for your home, be sure to do
detailed investigation of the neighborhood,
schools, pending zoning issues, and so on.**
*Once you have found just the right place,
consider hiring an engineer to check out the
structure itself.*

**If you handle your money responsibly, you may want
to get a loan without an escrow account.** *You
will have to pay your own tax and insurance bills,
but you'll have the flexibility to make some interest on the money you set aside for those
expenses. To some extent, you also time those
payments to fit your cash flow and tax situation.
Different states and lenders have varying
requirements for such a loan.*

**Remember that paying off your mortgage doesn't
mean that you have free housing.** *Besides maintenance, you'll have tax and insurance expenses
forever. People who are retiring now are finding
that their housing costs from these items is
almost equal to the original house payment 30 or
so years ago.*

---

$150 per year. His monthly bills include a $450 per month lease payment for his 2000 Acura RS Coupe and a $150 per month student loan payment. He also paid a security deposit of 2 months' rent from which he could be earning 8 percent after taxes.

Seyed has researched the recurring costs of homeownership. He has found that the real estate tax rate is $0.91 per $100 of assessed value and homeowner's insurance policies cost approximately $275 per year. He is unsure of the maintenance costs but estimates them at $350 per year.

He likes the idea of owning his own home because as the real estate values increase the value of his home will increase instead of his rent payment. Local property values have been increasing at 5 percent per year over the last 7 years and real estate sales commissions equal 6 percent. One concern about buying a home is the immediate cost of the down

payment and closing costs. These closing costs, he has found, include a 1 percent origination fee, 2 discount points on the mortgage, and 3 percent of the home cost in various other fees due at closing. He also knows that he would pay a 20 percent down payment. Another concern is the lost investment income on this money that is currently earning an 8 percent after-tax return.

## Questions

1. Write a short description of the four types of housing generally available for Seyed.
2. List several sources of information applicable to any real estate purchase that might be helpful to Seyed in making a decision.

3. Use the lending guidelines to determine the maximum dollar amount that he could spend per month on his home payment (PITI).

4. Calculate Seyed's monthly PITI payment. To calculate principal and interest (PI) assume he has purchased a home for $140,000 and has an $112,000, 30-year, 7.625 percent fixed-rate mortgage. To calculate the local real estate taxes (T) use the real estate tax rate as given in the case assuming the property has an assessed value of $128,000. Also include Seyed's projected homeowner's insurance (I) cost as given in the case.

5. Complete *Worksheet 22, Worksheet for the Rent Versus Buy Decision* to determine if Seyed should buy or continue renting. To purchase the house considered in question 4, Seyed would pay $6,000 in closing costs including $2,500 in discount points. Consider a 1- and 7-year time horizon.

6. Seyed is considering another home that is selling for $180,000. Estimate the dollar amount Seyed should be ready to pay on the day of closing. Assume an interest rate of 8.625 percent, closing costs of 5 percent of the sales price, and a 20 percent down payment on the house.

7. Assuming the house in question 6 assesses for $180,000 and the information in the case concerning the taxes and insurance holds true, can Seyed afford the home if he finances it for 15 years? 20 years? 30 years? Why or why not?

8. Given his risk tolerance, what type of mortgage would you recommend to Seyed?

---

Visit our Web site for additional case problems, interactive exercises, and practice quizzes for this chapter—**www.prenhall.com/keown**.

# CONTINUING CASE: Cory and Tisha Dumont

Cory and Tisha are back asking for your help, only this time the topics are cash management, credit use, and major purchases. Tempting credit card offers continue to come in the mail. Recall that they have Visa, MasterCard, Discover, and American Express credit cards as well as several other store cards, with a combined average balance of $1,300. Minimum monthly payments equal approximately $32 although they typically pay $100 per month.

Tisha's sister and her husband just bought their first home, making Tisha even more anxious to move from their rented house. Cory wants to wait awhile longer before buying a home and has suggested that they should replace their older high-mileage car. Cory and Tisha realize that funds for another payment are limited, not to mention money for a house payment. Their options are to reduce payments on their credit cards or to reduce other expenses. At any rate, $300 a month seems to be the maximum amount available for an auto loan, not to mention any likely increase in their auto insurance premium associated with the new vehicle. Help them answer the following questions.

## Questions

1. As a result of a recent corporate merger, Tisha is eligible to join a credit union. What are the advantages and disadvantages of doing so?

2. Should they consider online banking? What are the advantages and disadvantages when compared to traditional banking services?

3. The Dumonts' bank was recently taken over by a big, out-of-state bank. Because required minimum balances and bank fees have increased, the Dumonts have decided to look for a new bank for their savings account. What factors should they consider?

4. When considering the previously mentioned account alternatives, what three general factors should the Dumonts review for each? How might debit card services and costs vary with each?

5. Which provides the higher after-tax yield—the Dumonts' 3 percent bank savings account or a federal and state tax-free money market fund yielding 2.25 percent? The Dumonts are in the 27.5-percent federal marginal tax bracket.

6. Because of his concern over "financial surprises," Cory has been on the Web to learn about Treasury bills. Are Treasury bills an appropriate place to put the Dumonts' savings for a house?

7. As he read about Treasury bills, Cory also learned more about EE bonds. How appropriate are EE bonds as a savings vehicle for one or more of the Dumonts' financial goals?

8. The *Newsweek* article recommended, "pay yourself first." Tisha is not sure how to do this but likes the idea of "saving money without having to think about it." Give her some advice about ways to "automate" her savings.

9. The Dumonts' take-home pay (after deductions for taxes and benefits) is approximately $4,325 monthly. Current nonmortgage debt payments equal $865 (i.e., $490 auto, $100 miscellaneous credit, $100 student loan, and $175 furniture). Calculate and interpret their debt limit ratio. Assume they could purchase another auto with a $300 monthly payment. Calculate and interpret their revised debt limit ratio. What advice would you give the Dumonts?

10. Concerned that they might depend on credit too much, Tisha and Cory have asked you about typical warning signs of excessive credit use. List five to eight of those signs. What alternatives should they consider if occasionally they can't pay their bills on time?

11. What is the maximum number of credit cards recommended? Given what you know about the typical characteristics of the cards Cory and Tisha carry, what recommendations would you make about holding the cards they have? Consider the advantages and disadvantages of each type and class of card. Also, what features are important to "credit users" as opposed to "convenience users"?

12. In anticipation of purchasing a home, Cory and Tisha have been advised to check their credit report. Why? What is the role of the credit bureau, and the credit report, in the determination of creditworthiness? How can they get their credit report? What are the Dumonts' alternatives if erroneous information is reported?

13. What are the "five C's" of credit? Define and explain each, based on the information provided about the Dumont household.

14. Cory and Tisha are convinced that "good debt" means "cheap debt." Help them identify one or two sources of credit that would be categorized as inexpensive, more expensive, or most expensive. Where would payday loans fit? Why?

15. Discussions over lunch where Tisha works often turn to "making ends meet." One coworker has been to a credit counselor, while another is currently processing a debt consolidation loan application. Are these alternatives helpful for those who can't pay their bills? What two fundamental strategies are imperative for someone recovering from credit overuse?

16. Help Cory and Tisha apply the four steps of the smart buying process to decide whether or not to replace their car. What sources of consumer information might be useful to them?

17. A recent TV advertisement offered a lease option for $259 a month on a car that both Tisha and Cory like. It fits their budget, but they are unsure of the contract obligations. What criteria should they consider to determine if leasing is their best alternative? What would you caution them about concerning an open-ended lease compared to a close-ended lease?

18. If Cory and Tisha decide to purchase rather than lease another car, what factors must they consider when comparing a new or used car purchase? What factors should they consider in determining whether to sell their car outright or trade it in toward their next purchase?

19. Cory and Tisha found a used car that costs $12,000. They can finance through their bank for 8.75 percent interest for a maximum of 48 months. The rate for new car financing is 7.50 percent for 60 months or 7.35 percent for 48 months. If they could find a comparably priced new vehicle, how much would they save per month in interest charges if they finance the vehicle for 48 months?

20. Considering the information in question 19, how much interest would be saved if the Dumonts financed the vehicle for 36 months, instead of 48 months, if the rate remains the same?

21. In reviewing the sample auto loan contract, Cory questioned Tisha about the term "secured loan." He was also unsure of the terms "default," "repossession," and "deficiency payment clause." Explain these terms. What can they do to avoid repossession?

22. In a few years Tisha and Cory might want to consider a home equity loan to finance a car purchase or to help pay for Chad's or Haley's college costs. What are the advantages and disadvantages of using this credit source as opposed to the typical auto or student loan? Specifically, what are the tax consequences?

23. Tisha and Cory often review the weekly mortgage rate column in their local paper. Last week the interest rate for a 30-year fixed-rate mortgage was 8.5 percent, while the rate for a 7-year balloon payment mortgage was 7.75 percent (payments calculated on the basis of 30-year amortization). A 1-year ARM was available for 6.5 percent (payments calculated on the basis of 30-year amortization). Assuming a loan amount of $120,000, calculate the payment for each mortgage. Aside from the significant differences in the mortgage payment amounts, what other factors should the Dumonts consider when choosing their mortgage?

24. Based on their gross monthly income of $6,083 and monthly debt repayments of $865, what is the maximum mortgage amount for which Cory and Tisha could currently qualify? Monthly real estate tax (T) and homeowners insurance (I) are estimated at $125 per month. Calculate the mortgage amount using both the 28-percent qualification rule and the 36-percent qualification rule. (*Hint:* Refer to Figure 8.7.) Use 8 percent as the current rate of interest and assume a 30-year, fixed-rate mortgage.

25. How has Cory's student loan affected his creditworthiness in applying for a mortgage? What is the relationship between PITI and consumer credit when calculating the 36-percent qualification rule?

26. Compare the Dumonts' monthly mortgage payment for PITI in question 24 with their current monthly rent and renter's insurance cost of $912.50. Should Cory and Tisha consider purchasing a house that would require their maximum qualification mortgage loan amount? Defend your answer.

27. Given the maximum mortgage qualification amount determined in question 24, calculate a 20-percent down payment. If closing costs aver-

age 5 percent of the cost of the house, how much will they need on the day of closing? How does this compare with the $13,000 in the Jimminy Jumpup Index Mutual Fund account for their house down payment?

28. Using the monthly PI payment for the maximum mortgage qualification amount in question 24, calculate the total cost of the Dumonts' home if the mortgage is not paid off early. How much of this cost is interest?

29. Tisha would like to consider a 15-year mortgage so that the house would be paid for before Haley enters college. Explain how the factors of monthly payment, total interest paid, time value of money, and the effect of taxes impact this decision.

# 9 Life and Health Insurance

## Learning Objectives

**1** **Reduce** your financial risk through insurance.

**2** **Determine** your life insurance needs and design a life insurance program.

**3** **Describe** the major types of coverage available and the typical provisions that are included.

**4** **Design** a health care insurance program and understand what provisions are important to you.

**5** **Describe** disability insurance and the choices available to you.

**6** **Explain** the purpose of long-term care insurance and the provisions that might be important to you.

In the movie *John Q,* Denzel Washington plays John Quincy Archibauld, a factory worker who has been cut back to 20 hours a week. Soon after the picture opens, a tow truck is shown hauling away a car from the Archibaulds' modest home. Despite the financial strains, the Archibaulds are a solid family. Then, one Sunday after church, as his parents are cheering him on from the bleachers as he plays baseball, Michael, their grade-school child, suddenly collapses and is rushed to one of Chicago's finest hospitals.

There Michael's life is saved—at least for now. But Michael's heart is three times the size it should be, a condition that was never detected because HMO doctors cut corners on the checkups.

Fortunately, John has major medical coverage—or so he thinks. At the hospital John gets another shock: His employer, having reduced him from full-time to part-time status, has downgraded his insurance. As a result, he has no coverage at all and is informed that the heart transplant needed to save his son's life will cost $250,000 and that he will have to come up with $75,000 as down payment to put Michael on the donor list—unfortunately, the Archibaulds have just $1,000 in the bank.

*John Q* is only a movie, but it works because we all know the "bad guy." After all, although we may not have faced the agony of a dying child, who hasn't had a health claim denied? Worried about losing your health insurance coverage at work? Struggled with red tape just to get reimbursement for a visit to the emergency room? Filled an absurdly high-priced prescription? Or been disappointed by their health care coverage? Now think back to the crack about HMOs that Helen Hunt delivered that connected with so many people in *As Good as It Gets*. There's no question about it—in the public's mind, Insurance and Big Medicine are the bad guys.

An hour before you're about to have life-saving surgery that costs upwards of $200,000 isn't the time to find out that your life insurance won't pay for the procedure. You've got to understand your health insurance before you buy it. Unfortunately, most people don't even want to think about illness or disability, let alone put a lot of effort into insuring against it. In fact, most people hate spending on health insurance. After all, you can't drive it, eat it, or live in it, so what good can it be? Ask that question to someone who's been hit by a bus, is racking up hundreds of thousands of dollars worth of medical bills, and is having them all paid for by insurance. In this chapter, we will tell you what you need to know to make the most of your health insurance. However, we first take a look at life insurance.

Just as with health insurance, you probably don't like thinking about death or life insurance. As a result, when it comes around to getting your first life insurance policy, you probably won't go out and buy it—instead someone will approach you and sell it to you. Because insurance seems to have a language known only to insurance salespeople, most people can't understand the differences between one policy and another, how much to buy, or what options to include.

Life insurance is an odd thing to purchase—it's not meant to benefit you. Hey, you're dead—you no longer have any needs. When you consider your need for life insurance, you must keep in mind its purpose: to protect your dependents in the event of your death. In effect, life insurance is meant to give you peace of mind by ensuring that your dependents have the financial resources to pay off your debts, keep their home, send your children to college, and still have enough income to live comfortably. Most college students, as a rule, don't have a need for life insurance—they tend to be single and have no dependents. That doesn't mean they won't buy life insurance, especially if a persuasive salesperson comes to call.

The goal in this chapter is to give you a basic understanding of life and health insurance, the types of coverage available, and the process of buying insurance so that you can buy the insurance you need.

**1** Reduce your financial risk through insurance.

Principle

**10** Protect Yourself Against Major Catastrophes

## The Logic Behind Insurance: Risk Management

The need for both life and health insurance arises from **Principle 10: Protect Yourself Against Major Catastrophes**. In the case of life insurance, it's not you that's being protected, but your family. If you haven't planned wisely, your death could be a financial catastrophe for your dependents. The key concepts here are *planning* and *control*. After all, this whole book is based on controlling your financial situation through careful planning. If you plan carefully enough, you can control your finances even after your death.

Of course, life insurance planning involves deciding on what and how much insurance to buy. One problem is that the marketing of life insurance is unbelievably confusing. In fact, you're not likely to receive the same recommendation from any two life insurance salespeople. Moreover, not only won't you get the same recommendation, but you probably won't be able to compare the recommended policies because of the incomprehensible jargon that accompanies them.

Keep in mind that an insurance policy is simply a contract with an insurance company that spells out what losses are covered, what the policy costs, and who receives payments if a loss occurs. Whether or not to take out an insurance policy is a matter of risk–return trade-offs. Are you willing to pay for an insurance policy to cover your risks? To start you on the road to understanding life insurance, let's take a look at some of the basic ideas behind it, starting with the relationship of insurance to risk.

The logic behind health insurance is the same as for life insurance, arising from **Principle 10: Protect Yourself Against Major Catastrophes**. But while life insurance provides protection for your family rather than you, health insurance provides protection for you and your family against financially devastating medical bills. There was a time when individuals didn't need health insurance because the cost of medical care simply was not a concern. Today, that is far from the case: Health care costs continue to increase faster than inflation.

One of the major reasons health care is so costly is the lack of incentive to economize. Presently, over 50 percent of Americans receive some government health care entitlements, such as Medicare or Medicaid, and 87 percent of all Americans have medical insurance. As a result, there simply isn't any incentive for patients, doctors, or hospitals to exercise restraint in medical billing. If you aren't paying out of your own pocket, why should you care what your bills are? And if these bills are certain to be paid, why should doctors or hospitals care how much they charge?

In addition, medical care has become extremely sophisticated and costly. For example, it now takes 12 years and costs over $230 million to develop, test, and certify a new drug. You'd better believe the drug companies are passing these costs on to patients. Finally, the cost of litigation from malpractice suits has skyrocketed. It's not uncommon for doctors to pay malpractice insurance premiums of $150,000 or $250,000 per year. These costs are then passed directly on to their patients.

What do these high costs mean for you? First, medical care and medical insurance must become more efficient if we're to continue to be able to afford quality health care. This change may mean that your doctor joins an HMO, or your company's insurance policy no longer covers all your health care expenses. It also means that many companies will try to cut down on their health care costs by providing only limited insurance coverage or hiring temporary workers who don't get a full benefits package.

And what about those workers—and the unemployed—who have no health insurance? They have to pay the huge medical bills out of their own pockets. It's just as bad to be underinsured. Imagine having your insurance policy give you a false sense of security and then leave you in the lurch when the bill arrives. Insurance is serious in the world of personal finance because as medical costs go through the roof, so does your risk of having your financial roof cave in due to health-related problems. They say that one nuclear bomb can ruin your whole day. Well, one simple medical procedure can ruin your whole financial plan.

## Determining Your Life Insurance Needs

Unless medical science comes up with something mighty impressive in the next few years, we all have to die sometime. Life insurance allows you to eliminate or at least substantially reduce the financial consequences of your death for your dependents.

### Pooling Risks

Insurance is based on the concept of **risk pooling**, which simply means that individuals share the financial risks they face. The logic behind risk pooling is drawn from **Principle 3: Diversification Reduces Risk**. Life insurance allows individuals to pool the financial risks associated with death. In effect, everyone pays something into the "pot," and the family of the unlucky loser receives the money, which offsets the lost income due to death. That way, the loser's dependents don't suffer financially from the loser's death.

In the case of insurance, the small amount everyone pays is called a **premium**, and the size of the premium depends on your chance of being the unlucky loser. Basically, the probability of your dying determines your premium. To determine your chance of death, insurance companies employ **actuaries**, statisticians who specialize in estimating the probability of death based on personal characteristics. Insurance companies are able to predict with a good deal of accuracy the number of deaths that will occur in a given population of policyholders and charge each policyholder a fair premium. Smokers stand a much higher risk of dying than do non-smokers, for example, so smokers get charged higher premiums.

**LO2** Determine your life insurance needs and design a life insurance program.

**Principle 3** Diversification Reduces Risk

**Risk Pooling**
Sharing the financial consequences associated with risk.

**Premium**
A life insurance payment.

**Actuaries**
Statisticians who specialize in estimating the probability of death based on personal characteristics.

**Face Amount or Face of Policy**
The amount of insurance provided by the policy at death.

**Insured**
The person whose life is insured by the life insurance policy.

**Policy Owner or Policyholder**
The individual or business that owns the life insurance policy.

**Beneficiary**
The individual designated to receive the insurance policy's proceeds upon the death of the insured.

The amount of insurance provided by the policy at death is called the **face amount** or **face of policy**. The **insured** is the person whose life is insured by the life insurance policy. Sometimes the policy is owned (or "held") by an individual, and other times it's held by a business. In either case, the owner is referred to as the **policyholder** or **policy owner**. The individual designated by the owner of the life insurance policy to receive the insurance policy's proceeds upon the death of the insured is called the **beneficiary**.

Now that we know what insurance is and how it works, we need to figure out whether we really need it. The purpose of life insurance is to provide for your dependents in the event of your death. If you're single and have no dependents, you generally don't need insurance. However, you still might want to buy life insurance if you're at a higher risk of contracting a terminal illness, such as cancer or AIDS, or an uninsurable condition that could prevent later purchases, such as diabetes or heart disease.

Although insurance policies don't pay off until you are dead, if you're terminally ill it's possible to receive a discounted settlement, kind of like borrowing against your policy, or to sell your insurance policy at a discount before you die. For those with a high risk of serious health problems, a life insurance policy can be viewed as a form of health insurance. For anyone else without a spouse or dependents, life insurance simply doesn't make sense.

If you do have a spouse or dependents, then life insurance can help make up for the wages lost as a result of your death. In addition to replacing lost income, it can cover burial expenses, medical and hospital expenses not covered by your health insurance, outstanding bills and loans, and attorney's fees related to estate settlement. Life insurance can also be used to provide funds for housing and for your children's education.

In determining whether or not you need life insurance, think back to what we said about the purpose of life insurance at the opening of this chapter—it's not meant to benefit the insured but those left behind. Table 9.1 provides a listing of who might need life insurance.

**Table 9.1**  Should You Buy Life Insurance?

*Life insurance is* not *necessary if:*

**You're single and don't have any dependents**.

**You're married, a double-income couple, with no children**. Consider life insurance only if you're concerned that your surviving spouse's lifestyle will suffer if you die.

**You're married but aren't employed.** Consider life insurance only if you have young children and your spouse would have financial problems with day care and housekeeping if you die.

**You're retired.** Consider life insurance only if your spouse couldn't live on your savings, including Social Security and your pension, if you die.

*Consider life insurance if:*

**You have children.** You should have coverage for raising and educating your children until they are financially self-sufficient.

**You're married, a single-income couple, with no children.** You should have insurance to allow your surviving spouse to maintain his or her lifestyle until he or she can become self-sufficient.

**You own your own business.** A life insurance policy can allow your family to pay off any business debt if you die.

**The value of your estate is over the estate-tax-free transfer threshold, which was $675,000 per person in 2000 and 2001 and rises annually to $1 million by year 2006.** Life insurance can be an effective tool for passing on an estate without incurring taxes.

# How Much Life Insurance Do You Need?

Let's say you need life insurance. The question then becomes *how much* you need. The first step is deciding what your priorities and goals are. Do you want to provide enough money for your kids to go to college? Do you want enough money for your wife to buy her own home? Do you want to provide your husband with enough money to live on for the next few years while he takes care of the kids? Different people are going to have different philosophies about providing for their survivors, and none of those philosophies is necessarily right or wrong.

The next step in figuring out how much insurance you need involves some numbers. Start with your net worth, because the larger your net worth, the more you have in the way of wealth to support your dependents, and consequently the less life insurance you need. Don't forget to throw in numbers to compensate for inflation and the earnings on possible future investments.

Is the process starting to sound complicated? Luckily, there are two basic approaches you can use to crunch the numbers that will tell you how much life insurance you need: (1) the earnings multiple approach and (2) the needs approach.

**Earnings Multiple Approach**  Some financial planners suggest that you purchase life insurance that covers from 5 to 15 times your annual gross income. The **earnings multiple approach** is used to figure out exactly how much insurance this amounts to. This approach doesn't take into account your individual level of savings or your financial well-being.

The earnings multiple method is based on the notion that you want to replace a stream of annual income that's lost due to the death of a breadwinner. That is, you want to replace one stream of annual income with another. What this approach does is tell you how big a lump-sum settlement you would need to replace that stream of annual income.

Actually, a stream of annual income for a set number of years is just like the annuities we looked at in Chapter 3. The earnings multiple approach works the same way present value of annuity problems work. To determine the lump-sum settlement you need, simply multiply your present annual gross income by the appropriate earnings multiple, where the earnings multiple is simply the appropriate present value interest factor of an annuity ($PVIFA_{i\%,\,n\,yr}$). In this case, you use the $PVIFA_{i\%,\,n\,yr}$, where $i$ is the percentage you assume you can earn both on an after-tax and after-inflation basis in the future on the insurance settlement, and $n$ is the number of years for which you wish to replace the lost earnings.

Table 9.2 uses these $PVIFA$ factors to provide an abbreviated table of earnings multiples. To simplify the presentation (and speed the sale), many insurance agents present the earnings multiple numbers without explaining the logic behind them. You need to keep in mind, then, that the earnings multiple which applies to your situation depends entirely on the number of years you need the lost income stream and the rate of return that you assume you can earn on the insurance settlement. The longer you need to replace the income stream, the greater the multiple. The higher the return you believe you can earn on the settlement, the lower the multiple.

Let's examine how this approach might be applied to Leonard and Nancy Cohen. Leonard's the breadwinner, making a cool $80,000 per year. The Cohens currently have two young children, aged 2 and 4, and they don't plan to have any more. The kids won't be self-supporting for another 20 years, and Leonard and Nancy want to make sure they're provided for if something happens to Leonard. Nancy's a good investor and is sure she could get a 5-percent return, after taxes and inflation, on an invested insurance settlement.

**Earnings Multiple Approach**
A method of determining a rough estimate of how much life insurance you need by using a multiple of your yearly earnings.

## Table 9.2　Earnings Multiples for Life Insurance

| Number of Years You Wish the Lost Earnings Stream Replaced | After-Tax, After-Inflation Return Assumed on the Insurance Settlement | | |
|---|---|---|---|
| | 3% | 4% | 5% |
| 3 years | 2.83 | 2.76 | 2.73 |
| 5 years | 4.58 | 4.45 | 4.33 |
| 7 years | 6.23 | 6.00 | 5.79 |
| 10 years | 8.53 | 8.11 | 7.72 |
| 15 years | 11.94 | 11.12 | 10.38 |
| 20 years | 14.88 | 13.59 | 12.46 |
| 25 years | 17.41 | 15.62 | 14.09 |
| 30 years | 19.06 | 17.29 | 15.37 |
| 40 years | 23.12 | 19.79 | 17.16 |
| 50 years | 25.73 | 21.48 | 18.26 |

How much life insurance do the Cohens need? Rather than simply multiply Leonard's salary times the *PVIFA*, we need to first adjust his salary downward to compensate for the fact that the family's living expenses will drop slightly with Leonard's death. Generally, family living expenses fall by about 30 percent with the loss of an adult family member if there's only one surviving family member.

The larger the size of the surviving family, the less the living expenses drop as a percentage of total family expenses. For example, expenses drop by only 26 percent for a surviving family of two, or 22 percent for a surviving family of three, and they continue to drop another 2 percent for each additional surviving family member. To calculate the Cohens' target replacement salary, we adjust Leonard's present salary downward by multiplying it by a factor of $(1 - 0.22)$, or 0.78. The target replacement salary, thus, becomes $\$80,000 \times 0.78 = \$62,400$.

Now we're ready to use the *PVIFA* value. Remember, we need to measure these amounts in today's dollars. In this case, $n = 20$ years and $i = 5\%$. Looking in the earnings multiples table (Table 9.2), we find a *PVIFA* value of 12.46. Multiplying Leonard's adjusted salary by this factor, we get $777,504. That is, under the earnings multiple method, the level of life insurance needed becomes

$$\begin{aligned} \frac{\text{life insurance}}{\text{needs}} &= \frac{\text{income stream}}{\text{to be replaced}} \times \binom{1 - \text{percentage of family income}}{\text{spent on deceased's needs}} \times PVIFA_{i\%,n\,yr} \\ &= \$80,000 \times (1 - 0.22) \times 12.46 \\ &= \$777,504 \end{aligned}$$

Keep in mind, though, that this method isn't very useful unless it considers the effects of taxes and inflation. Also, remember that this method considers only your income replacement needs, not your need to eliminate debt or save for specific goals. Most important, you've got to remember that your $i$ and $n$ factors are going to change over time. That means that your earnings multiple is going to change over time and that you're going to need to update your insurance coverage from time to time.

**Needs Approach**　A method of determining how much life insurance you need based on funds your family would need to maintain its lifestyle after your death.

**Needs Approach**　The **needs approach** attempts to determine the funds necessary to meet the needs of a family after the death of the primary breadwinner. You can think of the earnings multiple as a "one size fits all" method and the needs approach as a customized method. It is a bit more complicated than the earnings multiplier, but it allows you to account for the fact that your family's needs may be different from average. Let's look at some of those needs:

- **Immediate needs at the time of death:** Sometimes called **cleanup funds**, these include final health costs, burial costs, inheritance taxes, estate taxes, and legal fees.

- **Debt elimination funds:** Funds to cover outstanding debts, including credit card and consumer debt, car loans, and mortgage debt. For example, you may wish to reduce the financial burden on your spouse by paying off half of your outstanding mortgage principal.

- **Immediate transitional funds:** Funds needed to cover expenses such as new job training or a college degree for the surviving spouse and child care during this period. For spouses who are already employed, transitional funds may be used to cover a leave of absence.

- **Dependency expenses:** These are family expenses while children are in school and dependent upon family support. One approach to determine current total household expenses is to use the deceased's income less annual savings as an estimate. Some of this amount may come from the surviving spouse's income as well as Social Security and the deceased's pension from his or her job.

- **Spousal life income:** Supplemental income for the surviving spouse after the children have left home and are self-supporting but before the surviving spouse retires from whatever job he or she has.

- **Educational expenses for the children.**

- **Retirement income:** This would include any additional income stream that might be needed for the surviving spouse after retirement. It would make up for any shortfall after taking into account social security and pension benefits.

To use the needs approach, you must determine the dollar amount that would be needed by your family in each category. Fortunately, most people have assets or some existing insurance that will partially meet their life insurance needs. To calculate additional life insurance needs, you would take the total funds needed and subtract your available assets and insurance.

As you make your calculations, keep in mind that the time value of money is going to come into play if this approach is to have any meaning. For instance, your family will receive the insurance settlement when you die, but some of the uses for that settlement may be far off in the future—perhaps funding your children's college education. Sometimes insurance salespeople simply add up all the needs, regardless of how far off they are, and use that as a target level of life insurance. What that does is overestimate the amount of insurance you need. The easiest way to simplify the calculations and still allow for the time value of money is to download the worksheet from the Personal Financial Navigator Web site (**www.prenhall.com/keown**). Then you only need enter some basic information and investment assumptions and the worksheet will calculate the answer for you.

Once you know how much life insurance you need, it's time to figure out what kind of insurance is available.

## Major Types of Life Insurance

There are two major types of life insurance: term insurance and cash-value insurance. **Term insurance** is pure life insurance. You pay a set premium that's based

**Cleanup Funds**
Funds needed to cover immediate expenses at the time of your death.

 Describe the major types of coverage available and the typical provisions that are included in them.

**Term Insurance**
A type of insurance that pays your beneficiary a specific amount of money if you die while covered by the policy.

on the probability that you'll die—taking into account such factors as age, health, occupation, and whether or not you smoke. For that premium, you receive a set amount of coverage for a set number of years. Term insurance covers only a very specific period, or "term." If you die, your beneficiary receives your death benefits.

**Cash-Value Insurance**
A type of insurance that has two components: life insurance and a savings plan.

**Cash-value insurance** is more than simple life insurance. It has two components: life insurance and a savings plan. Some of your premiums go toward life insurance and some go toward savings. With cash-value insurance, if you die, your beneficiary is paid those savings as part of your death benefit. There's an almost infinite number of variations of cash-value insurance, and there are several different categories of term insurance. Table 9.3 summarizes them all, and we now examine them in detail.

## Term Insurance and Its Features

As we mentioned earlier, term life insurance is pure life insurance that pays the beneficiary the death benefit of the policy if the insured dies during the coverage period. In effect, term insurance has no face value. Its sole purpose is to provide death benefits to the policyholder's beneficiaries.

## Table 9.3   What's What in Life Insurance

| Type of Policy | Coverage Period | Annual Premium | Death Benefit | Cash Value |
|---|---|---|---|---|
| Term Life Insurance | Provides protection for a specified time period, typically 1 to 30 years. | Least expensive form of life insurance. Low initial premium, with the premium increasing as the insured gets older. | Fixed death benefit. | No cash value. |
| Whole Life Insurance | Provides permanent protection. | The premium is fixed. | Fixed death benefit. | The cash value is fixed. The investment portion of the policy grows on a tax-deferred basis while the policy is in force. |
| Universal Life Insurance | Provides permanent protection. | Allows for flexible premium payments so that policy-holders can vary the amount and timing of their payments as their financial needs change. | Death benefits are flexible, although proof of insura-bility may be required if you want to raise them. | The cash value of the policy depends on the level of payments made and the investment results of the insurance company. The investment portion of the policy grows on a tax-deferred basis while the policy is in force. |
| Variable Life Insurance | Provides permanent protection. | Allows for either fixed or flexible premium. | Death benefits are flexible, reflecting the performance of the mutual funds (subaccounts) in the death benefits account. | The cash value of the policy depends on the performance of the mutual funds (subaccounts) in the cash value account. The policyholder controls the investment risk, choosing the investment strategy for the policy. |

The primary advantage of term insurance is its affordability. It's an inexpensive way of protecting your loved ones. The big disadvantage with term insurance is that the cost rises each time your policy is renewed. To counter that complaint, the insurance industry has recently begun to offer 30-year level-term policies. For example in mid-2002, a 25-year-old nonsmoking male could lock in an annual rate of $425 for a policy with a $500,000 death benefit for 30 years from Protective Life.

**Renewable Term Insurance**   The "term" of the term life insurance contract can be 1, 5, 10, 20, or 30 years. Coverage terminates at the end of this period unless it's renewed. In general, most term insurance is **renewable term insurance**, which allows it to be continually renewed for an agreed-upon period or up to a specified age, often 65, 70, or 75 (and in some cases up to 94), regardless of the insured's health. Even if your health declines after you buy the policy you're still able to renew your coverage.

The ability to renew term insurance is critical. After all, if you're basing your family's security on a life insurance policy that you suddenly can't renew, you've got a big problem. You shouldn't consider taking on term insurance that isn't renewable. Each time your contract is renewed, the premium is increased to reflect your increased age and the accompanying increase in the chance of mortality. Without proof of insurability (taking and passing another medical exam), most premiums increase dramatically at the end of the term period. Once an individual reaches the age of 55, the premiums increase rather rapidly, as can be seen in Figure 9.1.

**"Reentry" Term Insurance**   **"Reentry" term insurance** is term insurance that's guaranteed renewable at one of two possible premium levels in the future. This insurance regularly evaluates your health—perhaps every 3 to 5 years—to determine which premium level you qualify for. If you pass a medical exam, you qualify for the lower rate. If you fail the exam, you're stuck with the higher—usually *much* higher—rate.

The appeal of reentry insurance is that if you stay in good shape, you'll be rewarded with lower premiums. The downside of such policies is that it's often unclear exactly what requirements you must meet to pass the medical exam.

**Renewable Term Insurance**
A type of term insurance that can be renewed for an agreed-upon period or up to a specified age (usually 65 or 70) regardless of the insured's health.

**"Reentry" Term Insurance**
Renewable term insurance that increases the premium steeply at each renewal unless you pass a medical exam.

Figure 9.1 The Rising Cost of Yearly Renewable Term Insurance: Annual Premiums for $100,000 Coverage on a 35-Year-Old Nonsmoking Male

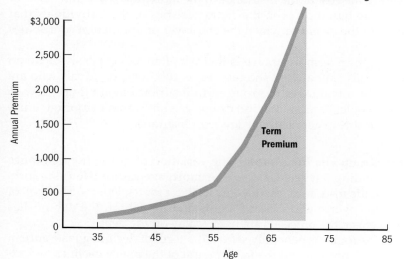

Moreover, if you do have medical problems, as your health breaks down, your premium will go up dramatically. In effect, reentry insurance is a gamble. When evaluating such insurance, you'll want to focus on the premium level if you fail the physical exam.

**Decreasing Term Insurance**   Each time renewable term insurance is renewed, the premium increases. With **decreasing term insurance**, the premiums remain constant, but the face amount of the policy declines. If you purchase decreasing term insurance, you decide on a premium level, and the face amount—the amount of the death benefit to be paid—declines each year to reflect the increased probability that you'll die.

The logic behind decreasing term insurance is that your wealth should increase when your children leave home and become self-sufficient. As a result, you should need less insurance. However, you must make certain your insurance coverage is sufficient at all times. Just because most individuals' insurance needs tend to decline as they get older doesn't mean that'll happen in your case. Moreover, your need for insurance may be greatest as your children approach college age, just when the face value of the declining term insurance drops off.

In addition, not all declining term insurance policies decline the same way. Some decline at a constant, steady rate, and others decline at accelerating rates. What's important here is that you choose a policy that's going to cover your future needs completely.

**Group Term Insurance**   **Group term insurance** refers to the way the insurance is sold rather than to any unusual traits of the policy itself. Group term insurance is term insurance provided, usually without a medical exam, to a specific group of individuals who are associated for some purpose other than to buy insurance. The group may be employees of the same company or members of a common association or professional group. If it's an association or professional group, the members might be required to take a medical exam; most employee term insurance doesn't require an exam.

In some, but certainly not all, cases, an employer may pay all or a portion of the insurance premiums or perform much of the administrative work associated with the plan, thus lowering the cost of the insurance to the individuals. The rate an individual pays is therefore based on both the characteristics of the individuals that make up the group and the extent to which the employer or association contributes to the premiums.

The advantage of group term insurance is that it's often less expensive than an individual policy. But this isn't always the case, especially for individuals who are young and healthy. The advantages of group term insurance many times flow to older or less healthy people. Because medical exams generally aren't required, uninsurable individuals are able to get relatively low-cost insurance.

**Credit or Mortgage Group Life Insurance**   One variation of group life insurance that's promoted by lending agencies is **credit** or **mortgage group life insurance**, which is simply group life insurance provided by a lender for its debtors. The level of coverage is enough to cover the individual's outstanding debt. If the debtor dies while the policy is in effect, the proceeds are used to pay off the debt.

This type of term insurance is generally set up as a form of declining insurance in which the premiums are constant and the face amount of the policy declines, reflecting the declining balance in the debt due. Keep in mind that this type of insurance covers the lender as much as it covers you. After all, it's being sold by the financial institution to which you owe money, and it, not your family, will be designated as the beneficiary. It also may have a noncompetitive rate associated with it.

On one hand, this insurance guarantees that your family won't be saddled with this particular debt if you die. On the other hand, such a policy also ensures the financial institution that it'll get its money back—not to mention the insurance premiums you'll pay!

**Convertible Term Life Insurance**   **Convertible term life insurance** refers to term life insurance that you can convert into cash-value life insurance at your discretion regardless of your medical condition and without a medical exam. Many times this conversion feature is only offered during the first years of the policy. The conversion may be accompanied by a corresponding increase in the premium; however, some convertible term policies are quite reasonably priced. One promoted advantage of convertible term insurance is that it allows an individual a smooth transition from term to cash-value insurance. The question, of course, is whether or not cash-value insurance is the best investment alternative.

There are some real benefits to convertible term insurance. It can allow you to continue insurance coverage when your term insurance expires. For example, when you lose your job, you also tend to lose your group life insurance. To address this problem, most group term insurance plans are also convertible term plans. That is, they contain a conversion privilege that allows anyone leaving the group to convert the term coverage to a cash-value life insurance policy.

> **Convertible Term Life Insurance**
> Term life insurance that can be converted into cash-value life insurance at the insured's discretion regardless of his or her medical condition and without a medical exam.

## Cash-Value Insurance and Its Features

Cash-value insurance is any insurance policy that provides both a death benefit and an opportunity to accumulate cash value. It's a permanent type of insurance—if you make the premium payments, eventually you'll get paid. At some point, you'll have made all the required premium payments (which in the extreme case could last until you're 100), and your cash-value insurance will be completely paid up.

Not all cash-value insurance is the same. In fact, there are tons of different types. However, there are three *basic* types of cash-value insurance: whole life, universal life, and variable life insurance.

**Whole Life Insurance and Its Features**   **Whole life insurance** provides a death benefit when the insured dies, turns 100, or reaches the maximum stated age. The face value of the policy will eventually be paid, provided the premiums have been paid. Another distinguishing feature of whole life insurance is that the premiums are known in advance and in many cases are fixed. Although premiums on term insurance tend to be small during your younger years and dizzyingly high during your later years, whole life insurance premiums, because they are constant over your life, fall somewhere in between. Over all, the payments are higher than they are for term insurance, because the insurance company is guaranteed to eventually make a payout on the policy.

In the early years of the whole life policy, the insurance company deducts amounts for the commission, sales and administrative expenses, cost of death protection, and some profit from the premiums. What's left of the premiums goes into a savings account and is called the **cash value**. This build-up continues over the initial years of the policy, eventually resulting in a large cash value.

> **Whole Life Insurance**
> Cash-value insurance that provides permanent coverage and a death benefit when the insured dies. If the insured turns 100, the policy pays off, even though the insured hasn't died.

> **Cash Value**
> The money that the policyholder is entitled to if the policy is terminated.

As time goes by and the policyholder ages, the premium, which remains constant, is no longer large enough to cover the death claim. Thus, in the later years the cash value is used to supplement the level premiums and provide the desired level of death coverage.

The cash value of the insurance policy is really the policyholder's savings. The policyholder can borrow against the policy's cash value, or, alternatively, the policyholder can gain access to the cash value by terminating the policy. Access is gained by exercising the policyholder's nonforfeiture right. The **nonforfeiture right** gives the policyholder the policy's cash value in exchange for the policyholder giving up his or her right to a death benefit.

If the policyholder doesn't want cash, but instead wants insurance, the cash value can be used to purchase paid-up insurance—that is, insurance that doesn't have any additional payments due—or to buy extended term insurance. Many people see the nonforfeiture right as a major advantage to whole life—at least you get something back when you terminate the policy.

There are a number of different premium payment patterns available to whole life policyholders. *Continuous-, level-,* or *straight-premium whole life* requires the policyholder to pay a constant premium until the insured turns 100 or dies. With a *single-premium* or *-payment whole life* policy, the policyholder makes only one very large initial payment. A hybrid of these two patterns is the *limited-premium whole life* policy, in which large premiums are required for a specified number of years, after which the policy is considered paid up.

For example, you may pay until you are 65, after which the policy is paid up. As with all whole life insurance, it then provides insurance protection for the insured's entire life or until the policy is terminated and the cash value is claimed. The size of the premiums depends, of course, on the number of premiums to be paid and the age of the insured. The popularity of the limited-payment plan stems from the fact that the payments will cease when retirement approaches, and at that point the policy has built up a significant cash value.

As with all else in the life insurance area, there are almost an unlimited number of variations on the whole life theme. One such variation worth noting is *modified whole life*. The premiums begin at a level below comparable whole life and gradually rise in steps until the final premiums are above those of comparable whole life. There are also *combination whole life* policies, which include elements of whole life and decreasing term insurance. The change in coverage is done in such a way that the face amount of the policy remains constant, with the coverage gradually shifting from term to whole life.

What are the primary disadvantages of whole life insurance? First, it doesn't provide nearly the level of death protection that term insurance does for the same price. Second, the yield on the cash value investment portion of the policy generally isn't competitive with yields on alternative investments.

However, whole life insurance does provide for both savings and permanent insurance needs. If you have a need for permanent insurance protection—perhaps you have a child or spouse who'll never be financially independent for whom you must provide—then you should seriously consider whole life insurance.

**Universal Life Insurance and Its Features**  A **universal life** insurance policy is a type of cash-value insurance combining term insurance with a tax-deferred savings feature in a package in which both the premiums and benefits are flexible. Premiums can vary between the insurance company's minimum and the IRS's maximum.

You start out by paying a premium dictated by the insurance company. After the company subtracts expenses and mortality charges to pay for the life insurance protection, the remainder of the premium plus interest is added to the cash value.

**Nonforfeiture Right**
The right of a policyholder to choose to receive the policy's cash value in exchange for the policyholder giving up his or her right to a death benefit.

**Universal Life**
A type of cash value insurance that's much more flexible than whole life. It allows you to vary the premium payments and the level of protection.

**Figure 9.2** Determining the Cash Value on a Universal Life Insurance Policy

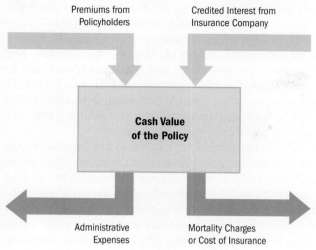

Premium payments may then be increased or decreased by the policyholder, which will increase or decrease the cash value of the policy. You can also increase or decrease the death benefit. In effect, a universal life policy is much like a term insurance policy, with any additional premium going toward savings.

An important feature of universal life insurance is that the funds are broken down into three separate parts: the mortality charge or term insurance, the cash value or savings, and the administrative expenses. This unbundling is what gives the policyholder the flexibility to vary the premium payments. If you skip a payment or don't make one large enough to cover your mortality charge and the administrative expenses, the rest will simply be subtracted from the cash value. If the cash value isn't enough to cover the premium, the policy will lapse!

Although there are limits, if you make a huge payment, the amount greater than that needed to cover the mortality charge and the administrative expenses is credited to your cash value or savings. The relationship that determines the cash value is shown in Figure 9.2.

One of the shortcomings of universal life is that the returns fluctuate dramatically. Moreover, for many policyholders the flexibility to pass on premium payments is just too tempting, and as a result many policies simply lapse. Finally, given fluctuating returns and high expense charges, you may not end up with as much in the way of savings as you had anticipated.

The value of universal life is its flexibility. If you have uneven and fluctuating income and need to be able to skip premium payments, this form of insurance might appeal to you. Still, universal life should be approached with caution. Insurance policies should be purchased mainly for their insurance protection. With universal life, the insurance and administrative portions of the policy are very expensive.

**Variable Life Insurance and Its Features** **Variable life insurance** is aimed at individuals who want to manage their own investments and are willing to take risks. It's a type of whole life in which the cash value and death benefit are tied to and vary according to the performance of a set of investments chosen by the policyholder. The policyholder, rather than the insurance company, takes on the investment risk—that is, you decide how the cash value or savings portion of your policy is invested. If it does well, you benefit; if it bombs, you lose.

**Variable Life**
Insurance that provides permanent insurance coverage as whole life does; however, the policyholder, rather than the insurance company, takes on the investment risk.

There are two basic forms of variable life: (1) straight variable life, which has fixed premiums, and (2) variable universal life, on which the premiums are flexible. The array of investment funds from which the policyholder chooses is quite large, including money market, bond, and stock funds. The returns are earned on a tax-deferred basis just as they are on other cash-value insurance forms. In fact, you can switch between different types of investment funds without suffering any tax consequences.

The cash value of a variable life insurance policy results from fixed premiums minus company expenses and the mortality charges (the cost of the term insurance). There is no guarantee of a minimum cash value, and what happens to the cash value doesn't affect the insurance company. In effect, variable life is similar to buying term insurance and investing money in mutual funds.

To be attracted to variable life insurance, you have to be a risk taker who wants to manage your own investments. However, if you're a risk taker who wants to manage your own investments, you'd be better off putting your money directly into the stock market.

# In The News

**Wall Street Journal Sunday February 10, 2002**

## Insurance Without All the Fancy Stuff

### by Jonathan Clements

Car buyers happily pay up for the latest model. Fashion mavens flock to designer clothes. Tech junkies crave the newest gadget. This sort of behavior hasn't gone unnoticed by insurance companies, which are forever taking perfectly decent products and tacking on bells and whistles, so they can charge fatter fees.

If you want to make sure your children don't suffer financially should you die, you can purchase term insurance, thereby getting heaps of life insurance coverage for a relatively modest sum.

*For instance, if you are a 40-year-old nonsmoker in good health, you shouldn't have any problem finding term insurance that costs less than $150 a year for $100,000 of coverage. Of course, it is hard for the insurance industry to make fat profits off $150 policies. What to do? Insurance agents often cajole folks into buying cash-value life insurance, which—for our nonsmoking 40-year-old—might cost six times as much each year for the same-size death benefit. (☞A)*

Why is cash-value life insurance so much more costly? These policies take the death benefit you get with term insurance and add an investment account. That combination allows these policies to perform a neat trick. As the years pass, the amount of actual insurance you buy gets smaller, because an increasing portion of the policy's death benefit is represented by the investment account's value.

Result: Although cash-value life insurance may be more costly initially, your annual insurance premiums shouldn't climb. By contrast, term insurance can become exorbitantly expensive by the time you reach your late 50s.

*That has prompted insurance agents to tout cash-value policies as "permanent" insurance. Some people do indeed need permanent insurance, which can also help with estate planning and provide valuable tax-deferred investment growth. (☞B)*

But, in all likelihood, you can make do with a cheap term policy. That will provide the necessary financial protection until the kids leave home and the life insurance is no longer needed.

## THE BOTTOM LINE . . .

A It's easy to get online quotes for term insurance, just try:
   **www.instantquote.com**
   **www.iquote.com**
   **www.masterquote.com**
   **www.quotesmith.com**

B Before you try any of the cash-value life insurance alternatives, make sure you've taken full advantage of any tax-advantaged retirement options available to you such as 401(k) plans and IRAs— you may even come out with an employer match.

Source: Jonathan Clements, "Insurance Without All the Fancy Stuff," *Wall Street Journal Sunday*, February 10, 2002: 3. Copyright (c) 2002, Dow Jones & Company, Inc. Reproduced with permission of DOW JONES & CO INC in the format Textbook via Copyright Clearance Center.

## Term Versus Cash-Value Life Insurance

With all these different types of insurance, it can be pretty hard comparing policies and figuring out what you need. You could spend way too much of your waking hours—and even some of your sleeping hours if you're a vivid dreamer—trying to figure out what's best for you. We suggest starting off slowly. The basic question you need to ask yourself is whether you want term insurance or cash-value insurance.

For most individuals, term insurance is the better alternative. It provides for your life insurance needs at a relatively low cost, and that's the real purpose of insurance. It allows for affordable coverage during the years in which you need life insurance most. Also, because the premiums on cash-value insurance are so high, you may be tempted to carry less insurance than you actually need.

The only true advantages of cash-value insurance are tax advantages—the growth of the cash value on a deferred tax basis and the fact that life insurance isn't considered part of your estate. These advantages generally don't make cash-value insurance a good investment in a relative sense—other tax-deferred investment plans are better. You should understand it so that you can make an intelligent life insurance decision.

## Fine-Tuning Your Policy: Contract Clauses and Riders

Although there are hundreds of variations on all the different types of insurance policies, there is some standardization. In fact, there are 10 common features contained in almost all insurance contracts: (1) a beneficiary provision, (2) a grace period, (3) a loan clause, (4) a nonforfeiture clause, (5) a policy reinstatement clause, (6) a change of policy clause, (7) a suicide clause, (8) a payment premium clause, (9) an incontestability clause, and (10) settlement options.

### Beneficiary Provision

The beneficiary provision allows for the naming of a primary and contingent beneficiaries. The primary beneficiary is the person designated to receive the death benefits if the insured dies. This beneficiary can be a person, a business, or a trust. The contingent beneficiary receives the death benefits only if the primary beneficiary dies before the benefits have been distributed.

Many individuals designate their spouse as the primary beneficiary and their children as contingent beneficiaries. This way, if the husband and wife die simultaneously, the benefits will be passed on to the children. The only caution here is that young children cannot be paid life insurance proceeds. If you have young children, you might want to set up an alternative plan to provide income to whoever will raise the children in the event of your death. An irrevocable beneficiary is a beneficiary who can be changed by the policyholder only with the permission of that beneficiary.

### Coverage Grace Period

The **coverage grace period** is an automatic extension for premium payments, which is generally set to 30 or 31 days after the payment is due. During this period payments can be made without penalty, and the policy remains in force. This type of grace period is similar to the grace period involved in credit card payments: They're both periods when payment is due, but no penalties occur.

### Clauses

**Loan Clause**   Cash-value policies include a **loan clause** that allows for loans against the cash value of the policy. The rate paid on the loan is usually quite favorable, generally being fixed at 8 percent or variable and tied to a market interest rate.

**Coverage Grace Period**
The late-payment period for premiums during which time the policy stays in effect and no interest is charged. If payments still aren't made, the policy can be canceled after the grace period.

**Loan Clause**
A clause that provides the right to borrow against the cash value of the policy at a guaranteed interest rate.

In addition to the relatively low rates, other advantages include paying no fees or carrying charges and not having a maturity date. In fact, policy loans don't have to be repaid at all.

However, you should be careful about them. When you take out a policy loan, the death benefits are reduced by a corresponding amount. If the purpose of the policy is to provide basic death protection, the policy loan may conflict with this goal. It would also be prudent to consult a tax advisor to make sure the loan meets the IRS requirements to avoid tax penalties associated with policy withdrawals.

**Nonforfeiture Clause**   The nonforfeiture clause or right gives the policyholder the policy's cash value in exchange for the policyholder giving up his or her right to a death benefit. The nonforfeiture clause defines the choices available to cash-value policyholders who terminate their policies before maturity. These options generally include receiving the policy's cash value, exchanging your policy's cash value for a paid-up policy with a reduced face value, and exchanging your policy's face value for a paid-up term policy.

**Policy Reinstatement Clause**   The **reinstatement clause** deals with the conditions necessary to restore a lapsed policy to its full force and effect. Generally, the reinstatement clause allows you to restore your policy within 3 to 5 years after the policy has expired. Most insurance companies require that the insured pass a physical examination and pay all past-due premiums, any outstanding policy loans, and all accumulated interest.

**Change of Policy Clause**   The **change of policy clause** allows the policyholder to change the form of the policy. For example, you may have a continuous-premium whole life policy and wish to change it to a limited-premium whole life so that the premiums cease. The change of policy clause lets you make this change, although you may have to pass a physical examination first.

**Suicide Clause**   Virtually all insurance contracts include a suicide clause, which states that the insurance policy won't pay off for suicide deaths that occur within 2 years of the purchase of the contract. The 2-year limit is generally imposed by state law.

**Payment Premium Clause**   The payment premium clause simply defines the alternatives available to the policyholder with respect to payment of premiums. These options typically include annual, semiannual, quarterly, or monthly payments. Annual payments are generally the cheapest.

**Incontestability Clause**   The incontestability clause states that the insurance company can't dispute the validity of the contract after it's been in place for a specified number of years, usually 2. In effect, it's like a short statute of limitations. This clause is crucial, and it protects the beneficiary against policy cancellations due to innocent misstatements made by the insured on the original application. Actually, this clause generally protects the beneficiary even if the insured made fraudulent statements when obtaining the insurance, as long as the fraud was not outrageous—for example, if a policy is taken out with the intent to murder the insured.

## Settlement Options

**Settlement options** refer to alternative ways a beneficiary can choose to receive the policy benefits upon the death of the insured. The most common alternatives include

(1) lump-sum settlement, (2) interest-only settlement, (3) installment-payments settlement, and (4) life-annuity settlement. However, before talking about these settlement options, let's discuss settlement and taxes.

**Life Insurance Settlement and Taxes**   In general, life insurance death benefits are income tax free. Thus, if there's a single lump-sum settlement, there are generally no taxes due on the full face value of the contract.

There are situations in which taxes may be levied on a life insurance settlement. For example, if a policy is surrendered for cash value, the excess of the cash value over the total premiums paid will be subject to taxes. However, all death benefit distributions are exempt from federal income tax and, in most cases, from state inheritance taxes.

Keep in mind that although you'll frequently hear that life insurance proceeds are tax free, that isn't always the case. You should make sure you know the tax status of your insurance.

**Lump-Sum Settlement**   Although a lump-sum settlement may not, on the surface, seem to be an overly flexible option, it's actually extremely flexible. By receiving the settlement in a single lump sum, the beneficiary has the freedom to invest those funds in any investment and to withdraw funds from that investment in any pattern desired.

The only drawback is that many people simply don't have the self-control to manage a lump-sum settlement over a long time frame. Forget about a long time frame—many can't resist spending a huge hunk of a big windfall like an insurance settlement. All of a sudden, the funds that were supposed to help put the kids through college are putting them through a trip to Disneyland. A single lump-sum settlement may be appropriate, but you may want to work out a long-run financial plan with a professional financial planner.

**Interest-Only Settlement**   Rather than receive the death benefits immediately, you leave them on deposit with the insurance company for a specified length of time and receive interest on that deposit. Generally, the rate earned is tied to the market interest rate, with a guaranteed minimum rate. There are, of course, many variations associated with this settlement method, including the option of partial or complete withdrawal of the cash value.

**Installment-Payments Settlement**   The cash value, including both interest and principal, is completely distributed over a fixed period or in fixed payments. If you choose the fixed-period option, then the size of the policy settlement, the number of periods for which payments are to be made, and the interest rate credited to the policy settlement work together to determine the size of the payments.

Working out the payment size is simply a matter of solving for the payment size ($PMT$) in the present value of an annuity formula $PV = PMT(PVIFA_{i\%,\, n \text{ periods}})$, where $PV$ is the policy settlement, $i$ is the interest rate credited to the policy settlement, and $n$ is the number of periods over which the payments are to be made.

Instead of choosing a fixed period for the distribution of the settlement, you can actually choose the specific amount of the fixed payments. In this case, the size of the policy settlement, the interest rate credited to the policy settlement, and the desired size of the payments work together to determine the number of periods over which payments will be received.

We're now solving for $n$, the number of periods over which the payments are to be made, in the present value of an annuity formula $PV = PMT(PVIFA_{i\%,\, n \text{ periods}})$, where *PV* is the policy settlement, *PMT* is the desired payment, and *i* is the interest rate credited to the policy settlement.

**Life Annuity Settlement**   Under a life annuity, the beneficiary receives income for life. There are several variations of the life annuity that provide monthly income to the beneficiary for his or her entire life. Under a straight life annuity, beneficiaries receive monthly payments regardless of how long they live. If the beneficiary dies 1 month after the benefits begin, the insurance company's obligations are ended, and the company keeps any remaining cash value.

A young beneficiary will receive much smaller monthly payments than an older beneficiary. Why might people want a life annuity settlement? Because they're worried that they might outlive their available income. With a life annuity settlement, the payments just keep on coming.

An alternative to the straight life annuity is the life income with period certain annuity. Payments are guaranteed for the life of the beneficiary; if the beneficiary dies within a stated period (usually 5, 10, or 20 years), payments are then made to a secondary beneficiary until the stated period ends.

This method guarantees that the insurance company will be making payments over at least the entire stated period. Guaranteed payment is great, but it does come with costs—the payment size is smaller than payments received under the straight life annuity, because these payments continue even if the primary beneficiary dies.

A third choice is the refund annuity. It provides the beneficiary with income for life in addition to returning any remaining death benefit to a secondary beneficiary if the primary beneficiary dies. Again, the insurance company will have to pay out more than it would with a straight annuity. As a result, the monthly annuity payments from a refund annuity are less than they would be under a straight annuity.

The joint life and survivorship annuity means that monthly payments continue as long as one of the two named beneficiaries remains alive. Generally, the two beneficiaries are husband and wife, with the annuity providing them with income as long as one survives. Again, because the insurance company will have to pay out more than it would with a straight life annuity, the monthly annuity payments are less than they would be under a straight life annuity.

## Riders

A **rider** is a special provision that may be added to your policy to provide extra benefits or limit the company's liability under certain conditions. Common riders include (1) waiver of premium for disability, (2) multiple indemnity or accidental death benefit, (3) guaranteed insurability, (4) cost-of-living adjustment (COLA), and (5) living benefits.

**Waiver of Premium for Disability Rider**   A waiver of premium for disability rider allows your insurance protection to stay in place by paying your premiums if you become disabled before you reach a certain age, usually 65. Because your need for insurance certainly doesn't diminish if you become disabled, this is a pretty good rider to have—provided the cost isn't too high. Shop around, and if it's still higher than you'd like, see if you can cover your insurance expenses with a personal disability insurance plan.

**Accidental Death Benefit Rider or Multiple Indemnity**   An accidental death benefit rider or multiple indemnity rider increases the death benefit—doubling it in the case of "double indemnity" and tripling it in the case of "triple indemnity"—if the insured dies in an accident rather than from natural causes. This is usually a relatively inexpensive rider because of the slim chance that the company will have to pay on it.

**Guaranteed Insurability Rider**   A guaranteed insurability rider gives you the right to increase your life insurance protection in the future without a medical examination. You can purchase additional coverage at specified times or after the birth of children. As with other riders, this rider comes with an additional fee.

One way to view the guaranteed insurability rider is as insurance against uninsurability. If you anticipate increased insurance needs in the future, this rider is a relatively inexpensive way to insure the ability to get that coverage.

**Cost-of-Living Adjustment (COLA) Rider**   This rider increases your death benefits at the same rate as inflation without forcing you to pass a medical exam. You pay an annual fee for this protection, but it can be useful if your needs for life insurance change in the same proportion as the change in the cost of living.

**Living Benefits Rider**   Some cash-value policies allow for "living benefits"; that is, they allow for the early payout of a percentage of the anticipated death benefits to the terminally ill insured. Many living benefits riders require a doctor's statement saying you have six months or one year to live. The purpose of this rider is to allow those who are terminally ill to pay their medical bills. A living benefits rider provides you with a portion of the face value of the life insurance policy if you have a terminal disease such as Alzheimer's, cancer, AIDS, or kidney failure.

## Buying Life Insurance

People don't buy insurance, it's sold to them. That is, most individuals don't have an insurance plan in mind when they talk to an insurance salesperson. The marketing of life insurance is about as confusing as it can be. In fact, you're not likely to receive the same recommendation on your life insurance needs from any two salespeople. Moreover, it's extremely difficult to compare policies—almost all policies are one-of-a-kind. As a result, most people rely on the salesperson to tell them what to purchase.

### Buyer Beware

Before you deal with an insurance agent, you should know a bit about how the insurance industry works. First, keep in mind that most insurance is sold on a commission basis. In general, insurance agents make their living through commissions, so they're understandably eager to make a sale. Don't feel obligated to purchase your policy from an agent just because he or she did some research and put together a plan for you—that's the agent's job. If it's term insurance you're looking for, your first step should be the Internet.

If you don't do your homework, you could end up with the policy that pays the highest commission to the agent and provides you with the least protection. Moreover, the legislation governing the industry allows insurance companies to require their commission-based agents to sell specific policies at set prices. The result? Comparison shopping is almost impossible.

Given the fact that shopping for insurance is so difficult, how do you do it? The same way you should do everything else in personal finance—systematically. You've got to do your homework. Figure out your needs. Think about your needs in terms of

**Principle**

**12** The Agency Problem in Personal Finance

**Principle**

**9** The Best Protection Is Knowledge

the basic life insurance products, get a good picture of what kind of policy you need and want, and go get it.

Keep in mind that the salesperson has a lot to gain by selling you life insurance. This all relates back to **Principle 12: The Agency Problem in Personal Finance**. As with everything else in personal finance, the best protection against this is understanding, bringing us back to **Principle 9: The Best Protection Is Knowledge**.

## Selecting an Insurance Company

Without question, not all insurance companies are the same. When you put money in a bank, the government guarantees your account through the FDIC. There are no guarantees with life insurance. Although each state has a guarantee association to protect policyholders if an insurance company goes out of business, generally these state funds have no assets. If an insurance company goes under, the other insurance companies doing business in that state are "taxed" and the funds are used to take care of any claims.[1] As you can imagine, delays and confusion are common.

Select a sound insurance company. If you're considering a cash-value policy, the selection process is even more critical. Keep in mind that cash-value policies generally specify only a minimum return; the efficiency of the insurance company determines your actual return. Therefore, it's essential that you choose an efficiently run life insurance company that'll be around when your policy "matures."

Fortunately, the selection process is made much easier by a number of insurance company rating services. A.M. Best (800-424-2378) (**www.ambest.com**) evaluates an insurance company's financial strength, with A++ being the highest rating. In addition, Standard & Poor's (212-208-1527) (**www.standardandpoors.com**), Moody's (212-553-0377) (**www.moodys.com**), and Duff & Phelps (312-368-3157) (**www.duffllc.com**) all rate the ability of insurance companies to pay off claims. Because you'll be charged a small fee for rating information if you call one of the rating agencies, the simplest way to get ratings is to go to your local library. Table 9.4 provides a listing of the highest and lowest ratings from each service. As you can see, a straight A grade is not necessarily the highest grade that a life insurance company can receive, and a C can be failing.

## Selecting an Agent

Because it's difficult to know all you might like to know about insurance, selecting your agent is extremely important. Your agent should be willing to develop and fine-tune your insurance program rather than develop and fine-tune his or her commission. So how do you find a good agent? Well, it helps to be aware of the agent's

**Table 9.4** Insurance Company Ratings

| Rating Service | Top Four Ratings | Lowest Rating |
|---|---|---|
| A.M. Best | A++, A1, A, A– | F |
| Duff & Phelps | AAA, AA+, AA, AA– | CCC |
| Moody's Investors Service | Aaa, Aa+, Aa2, Aa3 | Ca |
| Standard & Poor's | AAA, AA+, AA, AA– | CCC |

---

[1] In addition, most states impose a limit on the amount of coverage they'll honor. These limits are generally $100,000 for cash value for an individual life-policy, and $300,000 in death benefits, or $300,000 for all claims combined for an individual or family. These limits may be well below your desired coverage level.

professional designation. Is the agent simply licensed to sell insurance, or is he or she a chartered life underwriter (CLU), which is the most rigorous of all life insurance designations? To obtain this title, a life insurance salesperson must master both technical information on insurance and also show mastery in the related areas of finance, accounting, taxation, business law, and economics.

To begin the agent search process, make a list of prospects from good companies. This list can come from friends, colleagues, and relatives in addition to recommendations from bankers, accountants, and lawyers who specialize in personal financial planning. Next, interview the agents to find out which ones you feel comfortable with and whether they're full-time insurance agents with some degree of experience. Once you've selected several agents you feel comfortable with, have them give you a quote on your desired insurance plan.

**27** WORSHEET

**STOP & THINK** It's not unusual for cash-value life insurance policies to have commissions of 80 to 100 percent of the first year's premium. The only way you can find out is to ask. Because this information may help you determine why one policy is being pushed instead of another, the size of the commission is good information to know. All you have to do is ask.

## Comparing Costs

Now it's time to compare the costs of the competing policies. There are several comparison methods you can use, the most common of which are the traditional net cost (TNC) method and the interest-adjusted net cost method (IANC), or surrender cost index.

The **traditional net cost (TNC) method** is calculated by summing the premiums over a stated period (usually 10 or 20 years) and from this subtracting the sum of all dividends over that same period. The policy's cash value at the end of the stated period is then subtracted from this amount. The final result is divided by the number of years in the stated period and presented as total net cost per some level of coverage.

(premiums − dividends − cash value)/number of years = *TNC*

What's important here isn't what's included in the calculations, but what's excluded. The traditional net cost method doesn't take into consideration the time value of money. As a result, it's virtually meaningless. If an agent presents it to you as a reasonable means of analyzing the costs of a policy, you might want to consider another insurance agent.

A more widely accepted means of comparing similar but competing policies is the **interest-adjusted net cost (IANC) method**, which is also called the **surrender cost index**. Although this method has its own shortcomings, it does incorporate the time value of money into its calculations and has gained a good deal of acceptance in the insurance industry.

This method is just like the TNC method except that it recognizes the time value of money. However, this method depends on the choice of the appropriate discount rate and the estimate of the dividends and cash value from the policy. The agent's estimates may be high and not realistic. To be safe, take the results of every comparative analysis method with a hefty grain of salt. Note, though, that there are almost as many methods for comparing insurance costs as there are different types of policies, and they all involve making assumptions.

**Traditional Net Cost (TNC) Method**
A method of comparing insurance costs that sums the premiums over a stated period (usually 10 or 20 years) and subtracts from this the sum of all dividends over that same period.

**Interest-Adjusted Net Cost (IANC) Method or Surrender Cost Index**
A method of comparing insurance costs that incorporates the time value of money into its calculations.

## Alternative Approach: The Net or an Advisor

Once you've decided whether you need life insurance or not, and if so, how much is right for you, the decision becomes term versus cash-value insurance. If you decide on term insurance, consider shopping on the Web. There you can find instant quotes and excellent rates. This is because you can receive instant quotes from over 300 companies, and with that many alternatives, you'll end up with a great rate.

Where do you find this help on the Web? Several instant quote services compile databases of life insurance quotes and provide you with the costs and companies providing the lowest cost policies that fit your needs. QuoteSmith has a continually updated database that contains 375 insurance companies. All you have to do is enter some basic information and you'll get a quote.

Does it pay to shop around? You bet it does! Insurance rates vary dramatically from one company to another. In fact, the annual premiums found on the Internet on a 20-year term policy for $500,000 for a 25-year-old male with preferred rates varied from a low of $260 to a high of $1,465. Take a look at Chapter 9 on the Personal Finance Navigator (**www.prenhall.com/keown**) or try:

| | | |
|---|---|---|
| QuoteSmith | **www.quotesmith.com** | or phone: 800-556-9393 |
| QuickQuote | **www.quickquote.com** | or phone: 800-867-2404 |
| Life Quote | **www.lifequote.com** | or phone: 800-521-7873 |

Once you decide on a policy, the insurance company will, at its expense, send a nurse or technician to your house to give you a basic physical: he or she will ask questions on your medical history, take blood, and give you an EKG. It's just that simple. To make sure you've gotten the best deal, check at least two of the Web quote services and give an independent insurance agent a call.

If you've decided on cash-value insurance, things get a bit more complicated. That's because it's almost impossible to compare different policies, all with different features and different assumptions. Still, you can go to the Web to get quotes on different policies. For example, Ameritas Direct sells low-load cash-value insurance directly to the public, eliminating the agent's commission. When you purchase insurance directly from the company, the premiums are lower. Ameritas Direct can be found at **www.ameritasdirect.com** or can be reached at 800-555-4655. Other companies that deal directly with the public are USAA (800-531-4440) and Wholesale Insurance Network (800-808-5810).

If you're after cash-value insurance and still are confused, another alternative is using a fee-only insurance advisor. The purpose is to get an independent opinion on your insurance needs from an expert who doesn't have a vested interest in selling you something. Unfortunately, fee-only advisors aren't cheap. But when you consider the magnitude of the decision at hand, they aren't outrageously expensive either. Fees range from $100 to $200 per hour. Names of fee-only advisors are provided by the Life Insurance Advisors Association (800-521-4578) and by Fee for Service (800-874-5662).

## Types of Health Insurance Coverage

We live in a world of choices, so of course there are several different types of health insurance coverage available. Hey, if you've got 31 choices when buying such a thing as ice cream, you should at least have a few choices when it comes to buying something as important as health insurance. As with buying ice cream, though, it's easy to get carried away with health insurance and want everything you can get.

Even though there are different types of insurance to cover just about everything down to a common sneeze (bless you), the purpose of insurance isn't to cover all the costs of health care. You're going to have to pay a doctor's bill every now and again, and you'll need to spring for that bottle of Tylenol when you get a headache. Of course, if you've got chronic headaches and go through a bottle of Tylenol every day, you're going to want someone to pick up that cost. Everyone's needs are different, and the key in picking insurance is choosing only the types of coverage you need.

## Basic Health Insurance

Most health insurance includes a combination of hospital, surgical, and physician expense insurance. These three types of insurance are generally sold in a combination called **basic health insurance**. Many policies provide basic health insurance and then allow the policyholder to choose from a long list of policy options. Although each additional option provides additional coverage, it also involves an additional premium.

**Hospital Insurance**   **Hospital insurance** is generally part of every insurance plan. It covers the costs associated with a hospital stay, including room charges, nursing costs, operating room fees, and drugs supplied by the hospital. Depending on the policy, hospital insurance may reimburse the policyholder for specific charges, give the policyholder a set amount of money for each day he or she is hospitalized, or pay the hospital directly for the policyholder's expenses.

   If the policyholder receives a set amount of money per day of hospitalization, the policyholder must make up the difference between what is charged and what is received from the insurance company. Almost all plans, regardless of their type, impose limits on both the daily hospital costs and the number of days covered.

**Surgical Insurance**   **Surgical insurance** covers the cost of surgery. A surgical policy generally lists the specific operations it covers and cites either a maximum dollar amount for each operation, or reimbursement to the surgeon for what's considered reasonable and customary based on typical charges in that region. You'll have to cover any charges above what the policy will cover, and you also might have to pay a deductible. Although surgical insurance may not completely cover surgery charges, it should reduce them to a manageable level.

   One complaint with surgical insurance policies is that many times they don't cover what might be considered "experimental" treatment. Insurance companies have refused to pay for bone marrow transplants to combat cancer and some experimental treatments for AIDS patients. Although the companies look at these coverage limitations as an attempt to keep costs down (experimental surgery tends to be painfully expensive), if you're facing cancer or AIDS you're going to look at things differently. Remember, though, that surgical insurance has its limits. If you're considering a treatment not specified in your policy, you should see a lawyer to help you convince your insurance company ahead of time that the procedure should be covered.

**Physician Expense Insurance**   **Physician expense insurance** covers physicians' fees outside of surgery, including office or home visits, lab fees, and x-ray costs when they're not performed in a hospital.

**Major Medical Expense Insurance**   **Major medical expense insurance** is aimed at covering medical costs beyond those covered by basic health insurance. It's meant to offset all the financial effects of a catastrophic illness. Where basic health insurance leaves off, major medical expense insurance takes over.

   It generally doesn't provide complete coverage, but instead allows for deductibles and coinsurance payments in order to keep costs down. For example, the deductible may require the policyholder to pay for the first two office visits beyond what's covered by the basic insurance policy. It may then cover only 80 percent of the costs, with the policyholder responsible for making up the difference.

**Basic Health Insurance**
A term used to describe most health insurance, which includes a combination of hospital, surgical, and physician expense insurance.

**Hospital Insurance**
Insurance that covers the costs associated with a hospital stay, including room charges, nursing costs, operating room fees, and drugs supplied by the hospital.

**Surgical Insurance**
Insurance that covers the cost of surgery.

**Physician Expense Insurance**
Insurance that covers physicians' fees outside of surgery.

**Major Medical Expense Insurance**
Insurance that covers medical costs beyond those covered by basic health insurance.

It's also not uncommon for such a policy to allow for **stop-loss provision**, which limits the total dollar amount the policyholder is responsible for. When deductibles and coinsurance payments by the policyholder reach a set limit, the insurance company takes full financial responsibility for any additional medical expenses.

Most policies also have a lifetime cap. Most company-provided health care plans have a lifetime cap of $250,000. If that's the case, your health insurance doesn't do what it should—protect against major catastrophes. You should consider a major medical add-on policy that provides protection of up to at least $1 million. With a $25,000 or $50,000 deductible, such a policy isn't particularly expensive.

## Dental and Eye Insurance

As the names imply, dental insurance provides dental coverage and eye insurance provides coverage for eye examinations, glasses, and contact lenses. Although these are certainly nice to have, don't bother buying them if they're not provided by your employer. Remember that you can't afford to offset all the costs of health care, only the catastrophic ones. Dental and eye insurance pay for expenses that are relatively minor and regular—that is, they can be planned for.

## Dread Disease and Accident Insurance

Dread disease and accident insurance are sold to provide additional protection if you're struck by a specific disease or if you're in an accident. An example of dread disease insurance is cancer insurance, which is generally sold on television or through the mail. This insurance provides additional coverage for the costs associated with this one specific disease.

Accident insurance works about the same way. If you're in an accident, an accident insurance policy will provide a specific amount for every day you must stay in the hospital and a certain amount for the loss of any body parts or limbs.

Once again, the idea is to provide protection against major catastrophes while ignoring the small stuff. Because you don't know ahead of time what might bring on this catastrophe, your health insurance must be comprehensive. Avoid the accident and dread disease insurance, and instead make sure your policy is comprehensive.

## Basic Health Care Choices

Before you run out and get yourself some health insurance, you need to understand the basic health care choices that are available. First, who's providing the choices? In other words, where do we go to get health insurance? Well, we can turn to a private insurance company or to the government. In addition, there are two basic types of plans available: (1) traditional fee-for-service plans and (2) managed health care, or prepaid care.

Under a **fee-for-service** or **traditional indemnity plan**, you are reimbursed for all or part of your medical expenditures, and, in general, you have a good deal of freedom to choose your doctor and hospital. Under **managed health care**, most of your expenses are already covered and don't need to be reimbursed, but you're limited to receiving health care from a specified group of participating doctors, hospitals, and clinics.

## Private Health Care Plans

There are more than 800 private insurance companies whose main business comes from selling health insurance policies to individuals and to employers to be offered as part of a benefits package. These companies offer a variety of traditional fee-for-service and managed health care plans. Of note among the private insurance companies is Blue Cross and Blue Shield, which provides coverage to approximately 70 million individuals.

Actually, Blue Cross and Blue Shield provides prepaid health care plans rather than insurance policies. The company contracts with hospitals and doctors to provide specified health care coverage to members for a contracted payment or fee.

Health care insurance is also available from private commercial insurance companies. As you might expect, the benefits vary from plan to plan. Each contract spells out exactly what is covered and to what extent.

**Fee-for-Service or Traditional Indemnity Plans**  With a fee-for-service plan, the doctor or hospital bills you directly for the cost of services, and the insurance company simply reimburses you. Although there may be some restrictions on which doctors and hospitals you can use, these plans provide the greatest degree of health provider choice.

Most fee-for-service plans include a coinsurance provision. A **coinsurance** or **percentage participation provision** defines the percentage of each claim that the insurance company will pay. For example, if there's an 80-percent participation premium on hospital claims up to $2,000 and 100-percent participation thereafter, then you'd pay 20 percent of the first $2,000 of your hospital insurance claim, and the insurance company would pay the remainder.

Most fee-for-service plans also include a co-payment or deductible. A **co-payment** or **deductible** is the amount of your medical expenses that you must pay before the insurance company will reimburse you on a claim. A deductible can be set up in several different ways. For example, there may be a $10 deductible on all prescriptions. The insured pays the first $10 of the prescription, and the insurance company will cover the remainder. There might be an overall deductible of $250 or $500 on all health care. In this case, you'd pay the first $250 or $500 of any medical care costs you might have, and the insurance company will then cover any additional medical care costs up to a certain point.

Overall, fee-for-service plans are very desirable. Their big advantage is complete choice over doctors, hospitals, and clinics. Unfortunately, these plans are relatively expensive and involve a good deal of paperwork. While many employers still provide fee-for-service plans for their workers, they are dropping quickly in terms of popularity in favor of the less expensive managed health care. If you're considering a fee-for-service plan, Checklist 9.1 will lead you through some questions to ask.

**Managed Health Care**  Managed health care plans are offered by health maintenance organizations and allow members access to needed services from specified doctors and hospitals. Managed health care plans both pay for and provide health care services. For example, under a managed health care plan you may receive all your health services at one location. Under some plans you may not be guaranteed that you'll see the same doctor each time, just that you'll get the health care you need at low or no cost. However, most managed care plans provide you with a primary care physician, and many plans allow that physician to be one of your own choosing (for a slight fee).

Just as with the fee-for-service plans, it's quite common for there to be a visit fee or co-payment of around $10. There is also generally a co-payment on prescriptions. The purpose of co-payments is to keep insurance costs down. Not only do they serve as a deductible, forcing the patient to pay the first portion of the health care bill, but they also serve as a disincentive to seek care. As a result, almost all employees have to kick in for their employer-sponsored health care coverage with some of the employee contribution taking the form of co-payments associated with visits to the doctor and prescriptions, and some in the form of monthly premiums.

**Coinsurance or Percentage Participation Provision**
An insurance provision that defines the percentage of each claim that the insurance company will pay.

**Co-Payments or Deductible**
The amount of expenses that the insured must pay before the insurance company will pay any insurance benefits.

# Checklist 9.1 ■ Fee-for-Service Plans

**In Choosing a Fee-for-Service Plan, Ask . . .**

How much is the monthly premium? What will your total cost be each year? There are individual rates and family rates.

What does the policy cover? Does it cover prescription drugs, out-of-hospital care, or home care? Are there limits on the amount or the number of days the company will pay for these services? The best plans cover a broad range of services.

Are you currently being treated for a medical condition that may not be covered under your new plan? Are there limitations or a waiting period involved in the coverage?

What is the deductible? Often, you can lower your monthly health insurance premium by buying a policy with a higher yearly deductible amount.

What is the coinsurance rate? What percent of your bills for allowable services will you have to pay?

What is the maximum you would pay out of pocket per year? How much would it cost you directly before the insurance company would pay everything else?

Is there a lifetime maximum cap the insurer will pay? The cap is an amount after which the insurance company won't pay anymore. This is important to know if you or someone in your family has an illness that requires expensive treatments.

*Source:* Agency for Health Care Policy and Research and the National Council on Patient Information and Education, Rockville, MD, 2002.

---

**Health Maintenance Organization (HMO)**
A prepaid insurance plan that entitles members to the services of participating doctors, hospitals, and clinics.

**Individual Practice Association Plan (IPA)**
An HMO made up of independent doctors, in which the patients visit the doctors and receive their medical treatment in the doctors' regular offices.

**Group Practice Plan**
An insurance plan in which doctors are generally employed directly by an HMO, and members of the HMO must receive their medical treatment from these doctors at a central facility.

**Point-of-Service Plan**
An insurance plan that allows its members to seek medical treatment from both HMO-affiliated doctors and non-HMO-affiliated doctors.

The big advantage of a managed health care plan is its efficiency. Because it offers you health care directly there's considerably less in the way of paperwork and its associated costs. Moreover, because most managed health care plans involve a number of doctors, the entire facility can provide extended office hours, whereas each individual doctor is responsible for staffing the facility for a limited period. In fact, in many managed health care facilities, doctors work at that facility in addition to carrying on a private practice. There are two basic types of managed health care forms: (1) health maintenance organizations, or HMOs, and (2) preferred provider organizations, or PPOs.

**Managed Health Care: HMOs**   The most popular form of managed health care is the **health maintenance organization**, or **HMO**, which is a prepaid insurance plan that entitles members to the services of participating doctors, hospitals, and clinics. Members pay a flat fee for this privilege and then can select a managing physician who is responsible for the care of that member. There may also be a co-payment required with each visit to the doctor or each prescription filled. There are three basic types of HMOs: (1) individual practice association plans, (2) group practice plans, and (3) point-of-service plans.

An **individual practice association plan**, or **IPA**, is an HMO made up of independent doctors. The patients go to the doctors' offices and receive their medical treatment there. In fact, many IPA doctors also maintain a regular practice. With a **group practice plan**, doctors are generally employed directly by the HMO and work out of a central, shared facility. Members of the HMO can receive their medical treatment only from these doctors and only at these central facilities. A **point-of-service plan** allows its members to seek medical treatment from both affiliated and non-affiliated doctors. Coverage by HMO-affiliated doctors tends to be free or at least covered at a very low co-payment rate. Co-payments for non-affiliated doctors tend to be much higher.

Although there are some individual differences, most HMOs have very broad coverage, and include doctor, hospital, laboratory, and emergency costs. Prescription costs are often covered too. Of course, this coverage also requires co-payments.

Most HMOs are associated with an employer's group coverage. That is, the plans are offered through an employer as a part of the employee benefits package. Still, private individuals can join an HMO—and there are plenty to choose from. There are over 600 HMOs operating in the United States. Because each has its own participating doctors and hospitals, each serves a limited geographic area. In order to use health facilities elsewhere, you usually need a referral.

Because members receive comprehensive health care services, HMOs emphasize preventive medicine. Preventing illnesses is an awful lot cheaper than curing them. As a result, many HMOs provide regular physical examinations. In contrast, most fee-for-service plans only cover illness-related health care claims.

Finally, HMOs are efficient, costing as little as 60 percent of what a comparable fee-for-service insurance plan would cost. The preventive care, coupled with minimized paperwork and efficient handling of patients, allows for the cost savings. It's no wonder that employers prefer to offer HMO coverage. If HMOs are cheaper for you, they're also cheaper for your employer, which covers a good deal of your insurance premium each month.

There are, of course, some major drawbacks to HMOs. Service can be too quick or cursory, and waits long. If you need a service not provided by your HMO, receiving a referral, especially one outside of the HMO's geographic area, can be an unbelievable hassle. Many members feel the lack of choice is far too restricting. Having to choose from a small, fixed list of doctors, or not being able to choose at all, makes some people feel as if they're not being allowed to get the kind of care they want. They worry about not being able to build up trust or a personal relationship with a doctor, and they also worry that the available doctors might not be the best or most qualified. More questions about the quality of care stem from some of the incentive systems HMOs use. Doctors often receive bonuses based on the number of patients seen or based on the amount of money saved, leading some to wonder if some doctors don't cut corners to earn bigger bonuses.

If you're choosing an HMO, take a look at Checklist 9.2 for some guidance.

**Managed Health Care: PPOs** A **preferred provider organization (PPO)** is a bit like a cross between a traditional fee-for-service plan and an HMO. Under a PPO, an employer or insurer negotiates with a group of doctors and hospitals to provide health care for its employees or members at reduced rates. Doctors and hospitals that agree to the pricing system become members of the PPO. In fact, a doctor or hospital can be a member of a number of different PPOs. To encourage use of member doctors, PPOs generally have an additional, or penalty, co-payment requirement for service from nonmembers. The big advantage of the PPO is that it allows for health care at a discount, with the negotiating power of the insurer or employer determining how great a discount is achieved.

**Group Versus Individual Health Insurance** **Group health insurance** refers to the way the health insurance is sold rather than to the characteristics of the insurance policy. This insurance is provided to a specific group of individuals who are associated for some purpose other than to buy insurance. Usually this group of individuals all work for the same employer or all belong to a common association or professional group.

Most employee health insurance doesn't require subscribers to pass a medical exam, but group insurance offered through an association or professional group does. In general, the cost of group health insurance is about 15 to 40 percent less than

**Preferred Provider Organization (PPO)**
An insurance plan under which an employer or insurer negotiates with a group of doctors and hospitals to provide health care for its employees or members at reduced rates.

**Group Health Insurance**
Health insurance that's sold, usually without a medical exam, to a specific group of individuals who are associated for some purpose other than to buy insurance.

# Checklist 9.2 ▪ Choosing an HMO

Are there many doctors to choose from? Do you select from a list of contract physicians or from the available staff of a group practice? Which doctors are accepting new patients? How hard is it to change doctors if you decide you want someone else?

How are referrals to specialists handled?

Is it easy to get appointments? How far in advance must routine visits be scheduled? What arrangements does the HMO have for handling emergency care?

Does the HMO offer the services you want? What preventive services are provided? Are there limits on medical tests, surgery, mental health care, home care, or other support offered? What if you need special service not provided by the HMO?

What is the service area of the HMO? Where are the facilities located in your community that serve HMO members? How convenient to your home and workplace are the doctors, hospitals, and emergency care centers that make up the HMO network? What happens if you or a family member are out of town and need medical treatment?

What will the HMO plan cost? What is the yearly total for monthly fees? In addition, are there copayments for office visits, emergency care, prescribed drugs, or other services? How much?

*Source:* Agency for Health Care Policy and Research and the National Council on Patient Information and Education, Rockville, MD, 2002.

---

**Individual Insurance Policy**
An insurance policy that is tailor-made for you, reflecting your age, health (as determined by an examination), and chosen deductible size.

that of a comparable individual health insurance policy. Why? Because an individual simply doesn't have the bargaining power that a group has.

An **individual insurance policy** is one tailor-made for you reflecting your age, health (as determined by an examination), geographic location, and chosen deductible amount. Are there any advantages to individual policies? In general, other than the ability to tailor the policy to meet your specific needs, there are none. Group and individual policies tend to offer the same coverage, so the only major difference between them is cost. Individual policies tend to be more expensive in most, but not all, cases, so you should always try to get group insurance.

**STOP & THINK** If you don't qualify for group coverage, you might want to consider joining a group that has such coverage. Trade groups, alumni, political, and religious organizations are logical places to check out. You'll probably end up saving much more in insurance than you pay in dues.

You may have little choice with respect to your health insurance company. Your employer may have already chosen your insurance company for you. If, however, you don't have insurance through your employer, the choice is yours.

Just as with life insurance companies, it's important to get insurance from a company that's in sound financial condition, that is, one that could absorb higher-than-expected losses and continue to provide coverage. How do you go about selecting such a company? Your insurance company should receive either an A++ or an A+ rating from A. M. Best. Claim service provided by your company should be fast, fair, and courteous. Don't select a company that raises premiums based on claims. Finally, select only a company that's prohibited from canceling policies. You should be able to determine how well a particular company fares in these areas from an interview with your insurance agent.

**Workers' Compensation Laws**
State laws that provide payment for work-related accidents and illness.

## Government-Sponsored Health Care Plans

Government-sponsored plans fall into two categories: (1) state plans, which provide for work-related accidents and illness under state **workers' compensation laws,** and (2) federal plans, such as Medicare and Medicaid.

**Workers' Compensation**   Workers' compensation laws date from the early 1900s, when our economy changed from predominantly agricultural to industrial. At that time workers worked long hours in unsafe conditions, and work-related accidents were all too common. Fueled by the public outcry to Upton Sinclair's 1906 book *The Jungle*, states passed a series of laws aimed at providing work-related accident and illness insurance to workers.

Because these are state laws, each state determines the benefits level for workers. Some states provide broad coverage and others exclude some workers. For example, some states exclude workers for small businesses. Given the variability in coverage from state to state, you should contact your benefits office to see exactly what coverage you have. For workers without enough workers' compensation coverage, or for those with no coverage at all, some private insurance companies offer a type of workers' compensation insurance.

Interestingly, these laws were originally meant to be the final obligation of the employers to their employees. That is, the workers' compensation laws, while allowing for compensation regardless of whose fault the accident was, also initially took away the workers' right to sue. Today it's common for an employee to sue his or her employer for any work-related accident.

**Medicare**   The **Medicare** program was enacted in 1968 to provide medical benefits to the disabled and to persons 65 and older who qualify for Social Security benefits. The cost of this insurance is covered by Social Security, with the individual patient paying an annual deductible. The Medicare program is way too complicated for us to explain here—but we'll try anyway.

> **Medicare**
> A government insurance program enacted in 1968 to provide medical benefits to the disabled and those over 65. It is divided into two parts: Part A, which provides hospital insurance benefits, and Part B, which allows for voluntary supplemental insurance.

Coverage is divided into two parts: Part A, which provides hospital insurance benefits, and Part B, which allows for voluntary supplemental insurance. Participation in Part A is compulsory and covers most hospital costs, including operating room costs, nursing care, a semiprivate room, and prescription drugs furnished by the hospital.

Part B of the Medicare plan is voluntary and provides coverage for doctors' fees and a wide range of medical services and supplies. The medically necessary services of a doctor are covered no matter where you receive them—at home, in the doctor's office, in a clinic, in a nursing home, or in a hospital.

With Part B there's a monthly premium, which was $54.00 in 2002, and a $100 annual deductible, after which Medicare pays 80 percent of the charges for covered medical services. Table 9.5 provides a listing of benefits available through Medicare. A more complete listing of Medicare benefits can be found in *Your Medicare Handbook*, available at any Social Security Administration office or downloadable off the Web at **www.medicare.gov/publications.html**.

Although Medicare has been a very important source of health insurance for many older Americans, there are limitations to its coverage. For example, out-of-hospital prescription drugs are not covered and care in skilled nursing facilities is limited to 100 days per benefit period. In addition, there are deductions and co-payments.

> **Medigap Insurance**
> Insurance sold by private insurance companies aimed at bridging gaps in Medicare coverage.

To bridge this gap in coverage, **Medigap insurance** is sold by private insurance companies. In order to make it easier for the customer to compare policies, in all states except Minnesota, Massachusetts, and Wisconsin, federal law limits the variations of Medigap insurance to 10 standardized contracts. The cost of the coverage, of course, depends on how complete it is. Once you reach 65, you're automatically eligible to buy Medigap insurance, provided you apply within 6 months of enrolling in Medicare Part B. During this 6-month period, you can't be rejected because of illness.

## Table 9.5 Medicare Benefits and Services

| | Medicare Part A: 2002 | | |
| --- | --- | --- | --- |
| Services | Benefit | Medicare Pays | You Pay[a] |
| *Hospitalization* | | | |
| Semiprivate room and board, general nursing, and other hospital services and supplies (payments based on benefit periods) | First 60 days<br>61st to 90th day<br>91st to 150th day[b]<br>Beyond 150 days | All but $812<br>All but $203 a day<br>All but $406 a day<br>Nothing | $812<br>$203 a day<br>$406 a day<br>All costs |
| *Skilled Nursing Facility Care* | | | |
| Semiprivate room and board, skilled nursing and rehabilitative services, and other services and supplies (*payments based on benefit periods*) | First 20 days<br>Additional 80 days<br>Beyond 100 days | 100% of approved amount<br>All but $101.50 a day<br>Nothing | Nothing<br>Up to $101.50 a day<br>All costs |
| *Home Health Care* | | | |
| Part-time or intermittent skilled care, home health aide services, durable medical equipment and supplies, and other services | Unlimited as long as you meet Medicare conditions | 100% of approved amount; 80% of approved amount for durable medical equipment | Nothing for services; 20% of approved amount for durable medical equipment |
| *Hospice Care* | | | |
| Pain relief, symptom management, and support services for the terminally ill | For as long as doctor certifies need | All but limited costs (up to $5) for outpatient drugs and inpatient respite care (up to 5% of the Medicare-approved amount) | Limited costs for outpatient drugs (up to $5) and inpatient respite care (up to 5% of the Medicare-approved amount) |
| *Blood* | | | |
| When furnished by a hospital or skilled nursing facility during a covered stay | Unlimited if medically necessary | All but first 3 pints per calendar year | For first 3 pints[c] |

[a]Either you or your insurance company is responsible for paying the amounts listed in the "You Pay" column.

[b]This 60-reserve-days benefit may be used only once in a lifetime.

[c]Blood paid for or replaced under Part B of Medicare during the calendar year does not have to be paid for or replaced under Part A.

(table continues)

Although these policies are standard from company to company, price tends to vary, so it pays to shop around. Table 9.6 provides a listing of the benefits provided in these 10 Medigap plans.

In reviewing Medicare coverage, keep in mind that you must take responsibility for your own financial well-being. Although Medicare coverage may absolve you of some future financial responsibility, Medicare may not be around in its present form when you need it. Depending on how fast medical costs rise and how long people live, Medicare could face severe financial problems. Be ready to take financial responsibility for your own health care costs in the future by getting good coverage now.

**Medicaid**
A government medical insurance plan for the needy.

**Medicaid** Medicaid was enacted in 1965 and is a medical assistance program aimed at the needy. It's a joint program operated by the federal and state governments, with the benefits varying from state to state. The purpose of Medicaid is to provide medical care for the aged, blind, and disabled as well as to needy families with dependent children. Because some of those covered by Medicaid are also covered by Medicare, Medicaid payments go toward Medicare

(table continued)

**Medicare Part B: 2002**

| Services | Benefit | Medicare Pays | You Pay[a] |
|---|---|---|---|
| *Hospitalization* Doctors' services, inpatient and outpatient medical and surgical services and supplies, physical and speech therapy, diagnostic tests, durable medical equipment, and other services | Unlimited if medically necessary | 80% of approved amount (after $100 deductible) Reduced to 50% for most outpatient mental health services | $100 deductible, plus 20% of approved amount and limited charges above approved amount |
| *Clinical Laboratory Services* Blood tests, urinalyses, and more | Unlimited if medically necessary | Generally 100% of approved amount | Nothing for services |
| *Home Health Care* Part-time or intermittent skilled care, home health aide services, durable medical equipment and supplies, and other services | Unlimited as long as you meet Medicare conditions | 100% of approved amount; 80% of approved amount for durable medical equipment | Nothing for services; 20% of approved amount for durable medical equipment |
| *Outpatient Hospital Treatment* Services for the diagnosis or treatment of illness or injury | Unlimited if medically necessary | Medicare payment to hospital based on hospital cost | 20% of whatever the hospital charges (after $100 deductible) |
| *Blood* | Unlimited if medically necessary | 80% of approved amount (after $100 deductible and starting with 4th pint) | First 3 pints plus 20% of approved amount for additional pints (after $100 deductible)[b] |

[a]Either you or your insurance company is responsible for paying the amounts in the "You Pay" column.

[b]Blood paid for or replaced under Part A of Medicare during the calendar year does not have to be paid for or replaced under Part B.

Source:   Health Care Financing Administration, *Your Medicare Handbook*, 2002.

## Table 9.6   Benefits Provided in 10 Medigap Plans[α]

**Benefits Included in All Plans:**

▪ Hospitalization: Part A coinsurance plus coverage for 365 additional days during your lifetime after Medicare benefits end.

▪ Medical Expenses: Part B coinsurance (generally 20% of Medicare-approved expenses).

▪ Blood: First 3 pints of blood each year.

| Medigap Benefits | A | B | C | D | E | F[b] | G | H | I | J[b] |
|---|---|---|---|---|---|---|---|---|---|---|
| Basic Benefits | ✔ | ✔ | ✔ | ✔ | ✔ | ✔ | ✔ | ✔ | ✔ | ✔ |
| Part A: Inpatient Hospital Deductible | | ✔ | ✔ | ✔ | ✔ | ✔ | ✔ | ✔ | ✔ | ✔ |
| Part A: Skilled-Nursing Facility Coinsurance | | | ✔ | ✔ | ✔ | ✔ | ✔ | ✔ | ✔ | ✔ |
| Part B: Deductible | | | ✔ | | | ✔ | | | | ✔ |
| Foreign Travel Emergency | | | ✔ | ✔ | ✔ | ✔ | ✔ | ✔ | ✔ | ✔ |
| At-Home Recovery | | | | ✔ | | | ✔ | | ✔ | ✔ |
| Part B: Excess Charges | | | | | | 100% | 80% | | 100% | 100% |
| Preventive Care | | | | | ✔ | | | ✔ | | |
| Prescription Drugs | | | | | | | | Basic ✔ coverage | Basic ✔ coverage | Extended ✔ coverage |

[a]Medigap can only be sold in 10 standardized plans. Every company offers Plan A. Companies may have some, all, or none of the other plans. Some plans may not be available in your state.

[b]Plans F and J also have a high deductible option.

Source:   2001 Guide to Health Insurance for People with Medicare, Health Care Financing Administration of the U.S. Department of Health and Human Services, 2002.

premiums, deductibles, and co-payments. Again, this program is very limited in scope, with no guarantee that it will be in its present form at a later point if and when you might need it.

## Controlling Health Care Costs

Without question the first step in controlling health care costs is to stay healthy. Not only is health care insurance cheaper and more accessible if you're healthy, but your out-of-pocket health care expenditures decline, along with lost wages associated with missed work. In fact, a good part of staying healthy doesn't cost anything.

To gain an idea of the benefits of being healthy, let's look at the savings experienced by a "two-pack-a-day" smoker who quits smoking. First, depending on how high your state's cigarette taxes are, the immediate savings could be up to $1,600. If you're in the 30-percent tax bracket, this figure translates to $2,286 of before-tax earnings. Now let's add the savings from not getting lung cancer and not having a baby born with smoking-related illnesses. Of course, you'll have more expenses from living longer than you would if you kept on smoking. In addition to staying healthy, you can also help to control medical costs by using medical reimbursement accounts and, in some cases, opting out of your company's health care plan.

### Medical Reimbursement Accounts

A **medical reimbursement** or **flexible spending account** is a savings plan established by an employer that allows each employee to have pretax earnings deposited into a specially designated account. Employees can withdraw funds from their accounts to offset unreimbursed medical or dental expenses or qualified child care. There's a cap set on the maximum an employee can deposit into this account. In addition, there's a $5,000 ceiling set by the IRS for the child care portion.

The biggest drawback to this plan is that any contributions to the flexible spending account not used by the end of the year are lost. In effect, it's a "use it or lose it" system. Generally, it's a good idea to set aside only 80 percent of anticipated health care expenditures in order to avoid any forfeit of funds at year's end. The advantage of such a plan is that health care expenditures that are otherwise uncovered are made on a before-tax basis. For example, many people use their medical reimbursement accounts to cover the deductible from their insurance plan. Thus, for every $100 set aside into this account, taxable income is reduced by $100.

A flexible spending plan not only provides tax savings on unreimbursed health care expenditures, but also allows for pretax dollars to pay for other medical expenses that many health care plans do not cover, such as eyeglasses and orthodontia expenses. In fact, there is a good deal of flexibility with respect to how funds from a flexible spending plan can be used, as can be seen in Table 9.7.

### COBRA and Changing Jobs

Under COBRA, which stands for the Consolidated Omnibus Budget Reconciliation Act, if you work for a company with 20 employees, you will be given the opportu-

## Table 9.7 The Flexibility of Medical Reimbursement Accounts

*A sampling of what medical reimbursement accounts generally can and can't be used for, based on Internal Revenue Service rules.*

| Can be used for: | Can't be used for: |
|---|---|
| Ambulance service | Baby-sitting and child care (may be reimbursed through flexible spending accounts for dependent care) |
| Acupuncture | |
| Artificial limb | |
| Birth control pills | Cosmetic surgery to improve appearance |
| Braille books and magazines | Diapers |
| Cosmetic surgery (relating to congenital deformity or disfigurement from disease or injury) | Funeral expenses |
| | Health club dues |
| | Housekeeper |
| Dental fees | Insurance premiums |
| Guide dogs | Over-the-counter medical supplies |
| Nursing home care | Maternity clothes |
| Oxygen equipment | Swimming lessons |
| Psychoanalysis | Weight-loss program (for general health) |
| Special school for learning-disabled child | |
| Wheelchairs | |

nity to continue your health insurance coverage for 18 months to 3 years after you leave the company, depending on why you left.

You are, of course, responsible for the cost of this insurance, but it will probably be less expensive than purchasing individual insurance. If you wish to continue your coverage you must notify your employer of your intent to make payment on your insurance within 60 days of leaving the company.

## Choosing No Coverage

As the cost of health care plans has rocketed, many firms have begun to look for ways to reduce health care costs as a means of increasing profitability. More and more firms now offer cash incentives to workers to opt out of the firm's health care plan or to elect not to cover their families. In fact, about half of all companies allow for "opting out," and it's been estimated that up to 20 percent of those who can opt out do, receiving $300 and upward in cash or other benefits for doing so. For example, at Avon Products, Inc., about one-quarter of the 6,700 full-time workers opt out of the health care plan, freeing up $1,450 each in benefit credits. These workers can use these savings to buy other benefits or take the money in cash.

If your spouse also has health care coverage where he or she works, opting out may be reasonable. However, you must first consider what might happen if your spouse lost his or her job or if the company discontinues health care coverage, perhaps in a downsizing move. The question becomes, can you get back in your plan whenever you want?

The answer depends on your company. Some plans require a medical examination or only allow sign-up during an annual reenrollment period. If, however, opting out of your company's health care coverage means being left uncovered, then opting out probably doesn't make any sense at all. It's important not to get lured into trading your financial security for the "easy money" of opting out of coverage. In addition, under the Health Insurance Portability and Accountability Act of 1996, group health plans and health insurance issuers are required to permit certain employees and dependents special enrollment rights. These rights are provided both to employees who were eligible but declined enrollment in the plan when first offered because they were covered under another plan and to individuals upon the marriage, birth, adoption, or placement for adoption of a new dependent. These special enrollment rights permit these individuals to enroll without having to wait until the plan's next regular enrollment period.

Design a health care insurance program and understand what provisions are important to you.

## Finding the Perfect Plan

What should you be looking for in a health insurance policy? First, it should include the full cost of basic services (minus your deductible). As Milton Berle once said, "The problem with a policy is that the big print giveth and the small print taketh away." Second, it should be noncancelable or guaranteed renewable. Don't understand what we just said? That's OK. You'll figure it out as we look at some of the important provisions in health insurance policies.

**Who's Covered?**   Health insurance policies can cover individuals, families, or groups. If you have family coverage, you should have an understanding of (1) the age to which your children are covered and what happens if they're still dependents after this age, (2) what happens if you get divorced, and (3) whether stepchildren are covered. The point here is that you should understand exactly who's covered under your plan.

**Terms of Payment**   The terms of payment define your financial obligation on a health care claim, including any deductibles, coinsurance payments, limits on claims, and stop-loss provisions specified in your policy.

Deductibles or co-payments identify the amount of a claim that the policyholder pays on a claim. The higher the deductible, the lower the premium. It's a good idea to take the highest deductible, because you get more coverage per dollar that way. The insurance coverage is more efficient and you accomplish your goal of providing protection against catastrophes.

**STOP & THINK**   Don't try to save money by buying less health insurance than you actually need—that only defeats the purpose of insurance, which is protection. You should also make sure your policy benefits keep up with inflation and your life circumstances. Review your policy every few years and whenever there's a major change, such as the birth of children, marriage, or divorce.

There may also be limits set on specific claims. For example, there may be a maximum dollar amount the policy will pay for specific operations. Alternatively, the limit may be set at what is customary in a particular geographic area.

In addition, a stop-loss provision may also be included in the policy.

**Preexisting Conditions**   Most policies contain some type of preexisting condition provision, which excludes coverage for a specified length of time or forever for any preexisting illness that the policyholder may have. Obviously, this provision is meant to protect the insurance company and keep individuals from waiting until they identify health problems to sign up for health insurance. For those changing jobs, it's less of a problem. If you have had group health coverage for 2 years and you switch jobs and go to another group coverage plan, the new health plan cannot impose another preexisting condition exclusion period.

Although it probably goes without saying, don't lie on your application—it could make the policy null and void. In addition, make sure you read your entire policy—don't assume the salesperson told you everything. Also, read all the updates that are sent to you—things can change.

**Guaranteed Renewability**   A **guaranteed renewability** provision allows you to renew your health insurance policy regardless of your health until you reach some preset age, generally 65. Although you can't be singled out for a rate increase, your premiums may rise if you are deemed more risky than before. Obviously, you want a health insurance plan you can always renew so that you don't get cut off if you get sick.

> **Guaranteed Renewability**
> A health insurance provision that allows you to renew your policy regardless of your health until you reach some preset age, generally 65.

**Exclusions**   Some policies contain provisions that exclude certain injuries and illnesses. For example, costs associated with self-inflicted injuries, certain dental procedures, mental illness, injuries incurred when the covered individual commits a felony or misdemeanor, and cosmetic surgery are commonly excluded. Maternity expenses are also sometimes excluded, and coverage may not begin for children until they are 14 days old. This last exclusion is amazingly unfair and shouldn't be accepted. The costs associated with having a child and the expenses that can occur during the first 14 days of a child's life are enormous. As a result, some states have outlawed this exclusion, and provide that newborns must be covered immediately. Without maternity coverage and immediate coverage for your children, you could easily wind up spending all your savings and more.

**Emotional and Mental Disorders**   Policies vary greatly with respect to the degree to which they allow for coverage of emotional and mental disorders. Today, stress-related disorders and depression, many times brought on by chemical imbalances in the brain, are extremely common. Although some policies provide full coverage, others don't cover any of these costs, and still others provide only partial or limited coverage for a relatively short time period.

In fact, costs from these disorders have risen so sharply in recent years that most policies require large co-payments or limit the number of annual visits to a psychiatrist or counselor. Given the very high costs that can be associated with emotional and mental disorders, it's a good idea to make sure your health insurance policy provides adequate coverage. Hey, you wouldn't want insurance worries to drive you crazy.

> **STOP & THINK**   The best insurance is living a healthy, safe life. For young adults, this means driving safely. Auto accidents are the number one killer of teenagers. In fact, across the country teens make up 5 percent of the driving population, but account for 14 percent of the country's auto fatalities. Nearly half of all 16- to 19-year-old female deaths occur as a result of automobile accidents. Among boys of the same age, 36 percent of deaths are due to crashes. More than one-quarter of drivers under 21 killed on the roadways have a blood alcohol content of 0.10 or higher. The likelihood of fatal crashes for teenagers is highest between 9 P.M. and 6 A.M.

**What to Look For**   If you don't have health insurance provided by your employer, you'll have to find it on your own. Unfortunately, an individual policy is expensive. That's why you'll want to see if you qualify for any group insurance, or if there are any groups you can join that would allow you to qualify. The first rule in buying health care insurance is not to put the purchase off—you should buy insurance while you're healthy, because you may not be able to get it later. Checklist 9.3 provides a number of suggestions on what you might look for.

It is extremely important that you buy health insurance while you are healthy if you don't have a policy through your place of employment. Once a health catastrophe occurs, it's unlikely that you'll be able to get affordable insurance to cover your health care costs. Health care insurance is too important to be without. Keep in mind that the bottom line is always with you. That is, your health care costs are your responsibility. After you have your health insurance, try to maintain a healthy lifestyle—it's always better not to have the opportunity to use your insurance.

# Checklist 9.3 ■ Health Care Insurance Shopping

The ideal plan is group health insurance through your employer.

Don't put off buying health care insurance—buy it while you're healthy.

Consider only a high-quality insurance company with either an A11 or an A1 rating from A.M. Best. Never consider TV-celebrity-advertised insurance.

Look for group insurance—it's generally cheaper.

Look for companies that provide fast, fair, and courteous claim service.

Avoid policies with major exclusions and limitations.

Get comprehensive health insurance; avoid single disease (like cancer) insurance and accident (as opposed to comprehensive health including illness) insurance.

Only consider insurance that is noncancelable or guaranteed renewable.

Consider Blue Cross and Blue Shield.

Consider joining an HMO or PPO.

Take as high a deductible and coinsurance payments as you can afford. This reduces your premiums greatly.

Consider a policy that covers mental and emotional disorders.

**5** Describe disability insurance and the choices available to you in a disability insurance policy.

**Disability Insurance**
Health insurance that provides payments to the insured in the event that income is interrupted by illness, sickness, or accident.

## Disability Insurance

**Disability insurance** is related to health insurance, but it's more like earning-power insurance. When a disability occurs, life, along with all its expenses, goes on. What stops is your income. Your house payments continue, your children's educational costs continue, food and utility costs continue, and your medical expenses generally rise—all while your income stops.

Who needs disability insurance? Anyone who relies on income from a job. In fact, for individuals between the ages of 35 and 65, your chance of incurring a disability that'd cause you to miss 90 or more days of work is equal to your chance of dying. A 30-year-old has about a 47-percent chance of incurring a 90-day disability before the age of 65. You need disability insurance, even if you're single and without dependents. If you have dependents who rely on your earning power, this insurance is a must. Remember, disability insurance kicks in only if there's a financial catastrophe in the offing. Therefore, it fits in perfectly with our view of necessary insurance.

Given its importance, why are so many people without it? The answer is, the price. Although the price varies greatly depending on age, health, and occupation, in addition to the dollar amount of coverage and how long you're disabled before the policy kicks in, it's easy to spend over $1,000 per year on disability insurance.

Your occupation may have the biggest impact on coverage costs. Insurers generally classify customers into one of five risk classes, depending on occupation. A college professor is generally classified as a class 5 risk, and a construction worker is classified as a class 1 risk. These ratings, in turn, are reflected in the rates charged, with the college professor being given a lower rate than a construction worker because the college professor has a lower probability of becoming disabled.

### Sources of Disability Insurance

Many employers provide some level of disability insurance as part of the benefits package. Employers who don't include it in the benefits package may make group disability insurance available at favorable prices. If you're self-employed, you'll have to find a group plan or purchase an individual policy. Most individuals have some degree of coverage from Social Security or workers' compensation.

Although most workers are covered by some form of workers' compensation, these benefits apply only if the disability is work-related. The degree of coverage is determined by the individual states and, as a result, there's a good deal of variability from state to state. You shouldn't assume that you're covered or that your coverage is comprehensive.

For those covered by Social Security, disability benefits vary according to the number of years you've been in the Social Security system and your salary. However, if you qualify, you don't receive any payments until you've been disabled for 5 months, and then you receive benefits only if your disability is expected to last for at least 1 year or until death. Moreover, in order to qualify for benefits, you must not be able to work at any job, not just what you were trained for.

You can see that Social Security disability benefits, although available, are administered under very strict guidelines. To get an estimate of what these benefits might be, you can call the Social Security Administration at 800-772-1213 for a Personal Earnings and Benefits Estimate Statement.

## How Much Disability Coverage Should You Have?

You should have enough disability insurance to maintain your living standard at an acceptable level if you are no longer able to work. Remember, your investment income won't stop with a disability, it's your income from working that'll stop, and it's the portion of your income from working that you rely on to maintain your current standard of living that must be replaced. If you've accumulated some investments and are earning more than you need to live on—that is, saving a good portion of your earnings—you may need to replace only 30 percent of your after-tax income. However, someone with little savings who's living hand-to-mouth may need disability insurance that covers 80 percent of after-tax income.

Most insurance companies don't write disability policies that cover over 67 to 80 percent of a person's after-tax salary. They figure that if too much of your income is covered, you won't have an incentive to go back to work. Notice that the discussion focuses on the replacement of after-tax income. Although the insurance premiums that you pay on disability income aren't tax deductible, disability income is generally treated as tax-free income. Figure 9.3 provides a worksheet you can use to get an estimate of how much disability insurance coverage you might want or need.

**Figure 9.3** Worksheet for Estimating How Much Disability Insurance Coverage You Need

1. Current monthly after-tax job-related income     _____
2. Existing disability coverage on an *after-tax basis*
   · Social Security benefits     _____
   · Disability insurance from employer     + _____
   · Veterans' benefits and other federal and state
     disability insurance     + _____
   · Other disability coverage in place     + _____

**Total existing coverage**     = _____
3. Added disability coverage needed to maintain current
   level of after-tax job-related income in the event of a
   disability (subtract 2 from 1)     _____

*Note:* We haven't included workers' compensation disability benefits because they accompany only work-related injuries.

## Disability Features That Make Sense

Disability insurance policies vary more from insurance company to company than do health insurance policies. Therefore, you really need to have an idea of what's desirable in a disability plan. The following sections discuss a few key features to look out for.

**Definition of Disability**   What exactly does your policy consider a disability? In general, most policies define people as disabled if they can't perform the duties of their "own occupation" or perform the duties of "any occupation for which reasonably suited." Unfortunately, deciding what occupation for which you are "reasonably suited" may be difficult. It's wise to stick with a policy that defines an individual as disabled if you can't perform your normal job.

An alternative is the combination definition. Under the combination definition, you're covered if you can't perform your "own occupation" for the first 2 years of your disability. Thereafter, you're covered if you can't perform "any occupation for which you're reasonably suited." Defining "disability" in this way promotes retraining during the first 2 years. Policies using this definition tend to be less expensive than those that use only the "own occupation" definition. Given the cost trade-offs, you might want to give serious consideration to policies that use a combination definition.

**Residual or Partial Payments When Returning to Work Part-Time**   Some policies offer partial disability payments that allow workers to return to work on a part-time basis and still receive benefits. These payments make up the difference between what workers would make if working full-time and their part-time earnings. Partial disability payments are a desirable feature, especially for the self-employed.

**Benefit Duration**   Disability policies generally provide benefits for a maximum period, or until the disability ends (or the disabled person reaches 65 or 70 years of age). A **short-term disability (STD)** policy generally provides benefits on disabilities from 6 months to 2 years after a short wait of 8 to 30 days. A **long-term disability (LTD)** policy generally provides benefits until the individual reaches an age specified in the contract, or for the insured's lifetime. Only a long-term disability policy makes any sense, because only a long-term disability policy protects against financial catastrophe.

**Waiting (or Elimination) Period**   The **waiting** or **elimination period** refers to the period after the disability during which no benefits occur. The waiting period is equivalent to a deductible in a health care insurance policy. Most disability policies have waiting periods that range from 1 month to 6 months. Of course, the longer the waiting period, the less expensive the contract. In fact, a contract with a 3-month waiting period might lower costs by almost 30 percent from a contract with a 1-month waiting period.

What disability insurance must protect you against is the loss of income associated with longer-term illnesses. Thus, in light of the cost differences, you should give serious consideration to a 3-month waiting period.

**Waiver of Premium**   In general, it's a good idea to have a **waiver of premium provision**, which waives premium payments if you become disabled. But be sure to look closely at the costs.

---

**Short-Term Disability (STD)**
A disability policy that provides benefits over a given period, generally from 6 months to 2 years.

**Long-Term Disability (LTD)**
A disability policy that provides benefits until the individual reaches an age specified in the contract, generally 65 or 70, or for the insured's lifetime.

**Waiting or Elimination Period**
The period after the disability during which no benefits occur.

**Waiver of Premium Provision**
A disability insurance provision that allows your insurance to stay in force should you become unable to work because of disability or illness.

**Noncancelable**  You should also insist on a policy that's noncancelable. This provision protects you against having your policy canceled if, for whatever reason, your risk of becoming disabled increases, and it guarantees that the policy is renewable. It also protects you against rate increases.

**Rehabilitation Coverage**  A **rehabilitation coverage** provision provides for vocational rehabilitation, allowing the policyholder to be retrained for employment. This coverage generally provides for employment-related educational or job-training programs.

**STOP & THINK**  According to the American Council of Life Insurers, by the time you turn 85, you have a 50 percent chance of needing long-term care, and by 2030, when today's college graduates are turning 50, the cost of nursing homes is expected to run $190,600 a year.

**Rehabilitation Coverage**
A disability insurance provision that allows payments for vocational rehabilitation, allowing the policyholder to be retrained for employment.

## Long-Term Care Insurance

**Long-term care insurance** pays for nursing home expenses as well as home health care. When first introduced some 20 years ago, it was marketed strictly as "nursing home insurance." Now it has evolved to meet the needs of individuals who need care but still can stay in their own home. The insurance is meant to cover the costs associated with long-term care for those who have had strokes, chronic diseases, or Alzheimer's disease, as well as those who can simply no longer manage to live on their own. In effect, it's another form of disability insurance. Its downside is that it's expensive.

It would seem that long-term health care should either be a part of major medical insurance or covered under Medicare. It isn't. This is actually a relatively new area of coverage for insurance. It's been partially inspired by our increasing life expectancies and the resultant increase in the chance that you may eventually need some level of care. The interest in long-term health care coverage has also been inspired by the high cost of such care.

Long-term health care insurance is meant to protect you against the financial consequences of these costs. These policies are generally set up to provide a daily dollar benefit over the time the policyholder requires nursing home care. With most policies, these benefits are not subject to federal taxes.

The payments are generally sent directly to the nursing home to cover charges. They're often not available to individuals under 40 years of age, with the premiums rising for older policyholders.

Unfortunately, many long-term care insurance policies come laden with exceptions and conditions. Moreover, this lack of understanding and uniformity associated with some policies allows them to be sold not as a part of a financial plan, but through the use of fear tactics.

If you're going to purchase long-term health care insurance, make sure you do so while you're healthy. You'll also want to look for good health and marital discounts. In fact, if you're in good health you can save up to 10 percent from John Hancock and up to 20 percent from UNUM. In addition, most companies offer discounts from 10 percent to 20 percent for married couples who purchase two policies. As with other types of health care insurance, it's available only when you don't need it. It should also only be purchased from high-quality insurance companies. Table 9.8 provides a listing

**L⁶**  Explain the purpose of long-term care insurance and the provisions that might be important to you.

**Long-Term Care Insurance**
Insurance that's aimed at covering the costs associated with long-term nursing home care, commonly associated with victims of stroke, chronic illness, or Alzheimer's disease, or those who can simply no longer manage to live on their own.

**STOP & THINK**  According to the AARP, approximately 7 million Americans age 65 or older will need long-term care in 2002 and that number will nearly double to 12 million by 2020. The average annual cost of 1 year in a nursing home reached $4,654 per month in 2002.

WORKSHEET

# In The News

Wall Street Journal January 29, 2002

## Is "Nursing-Home Insurance" Needed?

### by Jonathan Clements

Long-term care insurance has emerged as one of Wall Street's hottest products. Quick, hide your wallet. "Long-term care is the big hustle in the insurance industry," warns Peter Katt, a fee-only insurance advisor in Mattawan, Michigan. "There is a full-court press on to get people to buy."

You may indeed need long-term care insurance, which can help cover nursing-home and home-care costs. But you probably don't need nearly as much coverage as your insurance agent suggests. That is a good thing, because these policies sure aren't cheap.

The cheapest insurance policies, of course, are those you don't need. Who doesn't need long-term care insurance? Those with few assets can take a pass, because they will qualify for Medicaid-financed nursing-home care. Similarly, the rich shouldn't have any problem affording a nursing home.

Instead, long-term care insurance is for folks in the middle, those of moderate wealth who could see their finances devastated by a prolonged nursing-home stay.

The prevailing wisdom is that the earlier you buy long-term care insurance, the better. But it isn't that simple. To understand why, consider some insurance quotes from TIAA-CREF.

*I asked the New York insurer to generate a series of quotes for a policy that paid $150 a day for life. The policy would cover both nursing-home and home-care costs, payments would kick in 90 days after you were deemed eligible, and the daily benefit would rise 5 percent a year to offset inflation.* (☞A)

According to TIAA-CREF, such a policy would cost $2,640 a year if first purchased at age 50, $3,435 if you were 60, and $5,190 if you were 70. Clearly, the longer you wait, the more you will pay each year. But if you buy a policy at age 70 and check into a nursing home soon after, you would have bought coverage for a pittance.

*Waiting, however, also carries a huge risk. Deteriorating health "could make you uninsurable or it could make the size of the premium go up significantly," says Cheryl DeMaio, a second vice president with TIAA-CREF. "You're playing a game of Russian roulette."* (☞B)

## THE BOTTOM LINE...

**A** Make sure you have an inflation adjustment provision. Just keep in mind that if nursing home costs rise by 5 percent a year, they will have doubled in 15 years, and if they rise by 9 percent a year they will double in 8 years.

**B** Another way to keep costs down is to extend the waiting period. Since the purpose of insurance is to protect yourself against major catastrophes (Principle 10), it is really the extended stays that you must protect yourself against—remember **Principle 10: Protect Yourself Against Major Catastrophes**—not everyday expenses.

of some of the provisions you might want to have included in a long-term health care policy.

Those who have a history of long-term disabilities, Alzheimer's, or Parkinson's disease in the family and those who have savings they want to protect should consider long-term health care insurance. If you don't have funds to cover nursing home care, Medicaid, which is aimed at the needy, will cover your costs. If you have money but don't have dependents, you probably don't need long-term health care insurance. If you need nursing home care, pay for it out of your savings. After all, you saved that money to provide for you in retirement.

Most policies require the insured to be unable to perform one or more "activities of daily living" (ADLs) without assistance. These ADLs include such tasks as walking, dressing, and eating. Some plans also allow cognitive impairment, such as the short-term memory loss suffered by Alzheimer's and Parkinson's disease patients, to be sufficient for benefits. You should consider only policies that include coverage for Alzheimer's and Parkinson's disease. The following sections discuss some provisions to consider.

**Type of Care** Policies vary with respect to coverage of home care. Some policies provide only nursing home care, while others provide for adult day care and

# Table 9.8  Long-Term Health Care Provisions

*Necessary*

**Selection of Company.** Consider only high-quality insurance companies with either an A11 or an A1 rating from A. M. Best. Never consider TV-celebrity-advertised insurance.

**Qualifying for Benefits.** The insured is unable to perform at most two "activities of daily living" (ADLs) without assistance.

**Qualifying for Benefits.** Policy includes coverage for Alzheimer's and Parkinson's disease.

**Qualifying for Benefits.** Hospital stay not required for benefits.

**Benefit Period.** A minimum 3- to 6-year benefit period.

**Inflation Adjustment.** The policy should give you the option of purchasing inflation coverage.

**Noncancelability.** The policy should not be cancelable.

*Desirable, but Not Necessary—Cost-Benefit Trade-Offs*

**Waiver of Premium.** While desirable, it may be too expensive to warrant serious consideration.

**Type of Care.** Home care, adult day care, and hospice care for the terminally ill.

**Benefit Period.** Women should consider longer benefit periods.

*Cost-Reducing Provision to Consider*

**Waiting Period.** Consider a waiting period of 100 days or more—if affordable.

*Provisions to Avoid—Not Worth the Cost*

**Nonforfeiture Clause or Provision.** Simply too expensive.

---

hospice care for the terminally ill. In fact, recently a number of long-term care policies have provided for reimbursement for nonlicensed caregivers, including family and friends, rather than requiring care to be provided only by licensed caregivers. It's a good idea to seek a policy with flexible coverage provisions and a home care option.

**Benefit Period**  Benefit periods on long-term health care insurance can range all the way from 1 year to lifetime. Unfortunately, lifetime coverage provisions tend to be very expensive. Because the average stay in a nursing home is under 2 years, you should make sure your coverage has a minimum 3- to 6-year benefit period. In addition, because women tend to spend longer periods in nursing care than men, women should consider a longer benefit period.

**Waiting Period**  Just as with disability insurance, the waiting period on long-term care insurance can be thought of as a deductible—you have to absorb the expense of nursing home care during the waiting period. This waiting period can run anywhere from 0 days up to a full year—but the most common is a waiting period of from 20 to 100 days. As you might expect, the longer the waiting period, the less the cost of the insurance.

For example, at age 65 just by raising the waiting period from 20 days to 100 days you can cut the cost of a long-term care policy to just over 10 percent of what it would cost otherwise. That's a pretty hefty savings, but if you do require care, that difference of 80 days in the waiting period would cost you $12,000 the first year and even more as the level of your protection rises with the inflation protection. For that reason, many financial advisors recommend that you go with a 20-day waiting period.

**Inflation Adjustment**  There's no telling what the cost of nursing home care will be when you need it. If nursing home costs increase by 5 percent per year, they will double in only 15 years. Without some inflation protection, your policy may not be of much help when you need it. Make sure to include an inflation protection provision if you buy long-term health care insurance.

**Waiver of Premium**    A waiver of premium provision allows your insurance to stay in force while you are receiving benefits. This is an area that has under gone a good deal of change recently. Most policies waive premiums once you begin receiving benefits. Recently, many companies have begun to offer dual waiver of premium riders: both spouses' premiums are waived when either one of them meets the waiver of premium conditions. However, you should be careful in selecting this option because the costs associated with it can vary dramatically from policy to policy.

## SUMMARY

The purpose of life insurance is to control the financial effect on your dependents experience when you die. Life insurance can replace the lost income that results from the death of the wage earner. Insurance is based on the concept of risk pooling. With life insurance, everyone pays a premium, determined by the probability of your dying, and no one suffers a big loss.

The first step in determining how much life insurance you need is to review your net worth. The larger your net worth, the more you have in the way of wealth to support your family, and consequently the less life insurance you need. The earnings multiple approach provides a rough estimate of your needs by using a multiple of your yearly income. An alternative method of determining how much insurance you need is the needs approach.

There are two very different categories of life insurance—term and cash-value. Term life insurance is pure life insurance that pays the beneficiary the face value of the policy if the insured individual dies during the coverage period. Cash-value insurance is any policy that provides both a death benefit and an opportunity to accumulate cash value.

One way of fine-tuning your insurance policy is through riders. A rider is a special provision that may be added to your policy. In general, life insurance death benefits are income tax free. Thus, if there's a single lump-sum settlement, there are generally no taxes due on the full face value of the contract.

Once you've determined your needs, the first order of business is selecting an insurance company and an agent. The final step is to compare the costs of the competing policies.

Health insurance serves the same purpose as other forms of insurance—to protect you and your dependents from financial catastrophe. Most health insurance includes a combination of hospital, surgical, and physician expense insurance, which is generally sold in a combination called basic health insurance. Major medical expense insurance is aimed at covering medical costs beyond those covered by basic health insurance.

The choices of health care providers are traditional fee-for-service plans and managed health care or prepaid care. Many times under a fee for service plan, there's a deductible or coinsurance fee. A deductible is the amount the insured must pay before the insurance company will begin paying benefits, and a coinsurance or percentage participation provision defines the percentage of each claim that the insurance company will pay.

Under a managed health care or prepaid care plan, you're entitled to the health care of a specified group of participating doctors, hospitals, and clinics. The most popular form of managed health care is the health maintenance organization, or HMO, which is a prepaid insurance plan that entitles members to the services of participating doctors, hospitals, and clinics. There are three basic types of HMOs: individual practice association plans, group practice plans, and point-of-service plans.

Another alternative is a preferred provider organization (PPO), which is something of a cross between a traditional fee-for-service plan and an HMO. Under the PPO an employer or insurer negotiates with a group of doctors and hospitals to provide health care for employees or members at reduced rates.

There are two basic types of insurance providers: private or government sponsored. Private plans include both individual health insurance policies and group insurance policies.

Government-sponsored plans fall into two categories: state plans, which provide for work-related accidents and illness under state workers' compensation laws, and federal plans, such as Medicare and Medicaid.

A medical reimbursement or flexible spending account allows each employee to have pretax earnings deposited into a specially designated account for the purposes of paying health care bills.

Disability insurance provides income in the event of a disability. Anyone who relies on income from a job for financial support needs disability insurance.

Many employers provide some level of disability insurance as part of their benefits package.

Long-term care insurance is another form of disability insurance that covers the cost of long-term nursing home care.

## REVIEW QUESTIONS

1. Define the following life insurance terms: *beneficiary, face amount, insured, policyholder,* and *policy owner.* How are these terms related?

2. What is the main purpose of life insurance? Describe the types of households that need life insurance and those that do not. Summarize the underlying factors that determine the need for life insurance.

3. Compare and contrast the two basic approaches used to determine the amount of life insurance needed.

4. Briefly describe six common types of term life insurance.

5. Briefly describe the three major categories of cash-value life insurance.

6. Describe the major differences between term and cash-value life insurance. What are the primary advantages and disadvantages associated with each?

7. Define the following life insurance policy features: grace period, incontestability clause, loan clause, nonforfeiture clause, reinstatement clause, and suicide clause.

8. Explain the four life insurance policy settlement options available to the beneficiary.

9. What is a policy rider? Describe five commonly available life insurance policy riders.

10. Explain the systematic process of shopping for life insurance. What factors should you consider when comparing the company, the agent, and the policy? How could an advisor assist you?

11. What is the difference between basic health insurance and major medical insurance?

12. Define the following terms: *coinsurance, percentage participation plan, deductible, co-payment, lifetime cap,* and *stop-loss provision.*

13. Why are dental and eye insurance, dread disease insurance, and accident insurance not recommended?

14. What is the difference between a fee-for-service health care plan and a managed health care?

15. Both an HMO and a PPO health plan are examples of managed health care. Describe the similarities and differences between these two plans.

16. Describe the major differences between group health insurance and individual health insurance. Which is likely to be cheaper?

17. Describe the government-sponsored health care plans of workers' compensation, Medicare, and Medicaid. What criteria are necessary for coverage under each plan?

18. Three strategies are recommended to help control health care costs: live a healthy lifestyle, use a flexible spending account, and opt out of coverage. Summarize the advantages and disadvantages associated with each strategy.

19. Define the following health care policy terms: *guaranteed renewable, noncancelable,* and *preexisting condition.* How are these provisions affected by job changes?

20. What is disability insurance? Why is it important and how much coverage should consumers purchase?

21. Define the following disability insurance terms: *benefit duration, definition of disability, residual (partial) payments,* and *waiting (elimination) period.*

22. Describe long-term care insurance. What policy features should a person considering a long-term care policy look for?

## PROBLEMS AND ACTIVITIES

1. Joetta Hernandez is a single parent with two children and earns $45,000 a year. Her employer group life insurance policy would pay 2.5 times her salary. She also has $60,000 saved in a 401(k) plan, $5,000 in mutual funds, and a $3,000 CD. She wants to purchase term life insurance for 15 years until her youngest child is self-supporting. She is not concerned about her outstanding mortgage, as the children would go live with her

sister in the event of Joetta's death. Assuming she can receive a 3 percent after-tax, after-inflation return on insurance proceeds, use the earnings multiple method to calculate her insurance need. How much more insurance does Joetta need to buy? What other information would you need to know to use the needs approach to calculate Joetta's insurance coverage?

2. Cedric Montyano has a $150,000 whole life insurance policy with $35,000 of cash value. He decides to borrow $20,000 against the policy. If he dies before repaying the remaining $15,000 of the loan, how much would his beneficiary receive? Assuming he and his wife, Jayne, are in the 27 percent marginal tax bracket, how much of the insurance settlement is taxable to Jayne?

3. Lei Wong purchased an insurance policy three years ago and mistakenly checked a box on her application that said she did not have high blood pressure. She does. Yesterday, she died of a heart attack. Will her beneficiary receive the face value of the policy or only the premiums paid to date?

4. Virgil Cronk wants to purchase a life insurance policy where his future coverage can be increased without having to take another medical exam. Virgil's family has a history of cardiac problems. Name at least two policy riders that he should consider adding to his policy. Roy, a friend of Virgil's diagnosed with AIDS, is being treated with a number of experimental drugs. What rider would benefit a terminally ill person like Roy?

5. The Baulding family has a basic health insurance plan that pays 80 percent of out-of-hospital expenses up to $3,000 a year after a deductible of $250 per person. If three family members have doctor and prescription drug expenses of $980, $1840, and $220, respectively,

how much will the Bauldings and the insurance company each pay? How could they benefit from a flexible spending account established through Mr. Baulding's employer? What are the advantages and disadvantages of establishing such an account?

6. Latesha Moore has a choice at work between a traditional health insurance plan that pays 80 percent of the cost of doctor visits after a $250 deductible and an HMO that charges a $10 co-payment per visit plus a $20 monthly premium deduction from her paycheck. Latesha anticipates seeing a doctor once a month for her high blood pressure. The cost of each office visit is $50. She normally sees the doctor an average of three times a year for other health concerns. Comment on the difference in costs between the two health care plans and the advantages and disadvantages of each.

7. Julie Rios has a take-home pay of $3,200 per month and a disability insurance policy that replaces 60 percent of earnings after a 90-day (3-month) waiting period. She has accumulated 80 sick days at work. Julie was involved in an auto accident and was out of work for 4 months. How much income did she lose and how much would be replaced by her disability policy? How else could she replace her lost earnings? If after 4 months Julie could only return to work half-time for an additional 3 months due to continuing physical therapy, how might she benefit from a residual benefits clause? How much will she receive in disability benefits for this period?

8. Bobbi Hilton, 62, is considering the purchase of a 5-year long-term care (LTC) policy. If nursing home costs average $4,000 per month in her area, how much could she have to pay out-of-pocket for 5 years without LTC insurance? What can Bobbi do to reduce the cost of this coverage?

## SUGGESTED PROJECTS

1. Interview at least three people from different stages of the life cycle to determine if they own one or more of the following: life insurance, health insurance, dental or eye care insurance, dread disease insurance, accident insurance, disability insurance, or long-term care insurance. What factors influenced their decision to buy or not buy the insurance coverage? Also inquire about the amount of coverage, type of policy, and premium cost. Prepare a report of your findings.

2. Contact an insurance agent or Internet quote service and obtain life insurance premium quotes for $100,000 of term, whole life, and universal life insurance. Base your request on your own age, gender, and health characteristics (e.g., non-smoker). How would the costs change if your health characteristics changed (e.g., smoker or nonsmoker)? If you waited 10 years? How do your characteristics or the projected changes relate to the concept of risk pooling? Prepare a one-page report of your findings.

3. Interview a friend employed in your career field or interview a benefits representative from a company/agency in your career field. Discuss the benefits that you might expect to receive as an employee (e.g., life, health, dental, eye care, accident, or disability insurance) and the out-of-pocket premium costs. Share your findings within the group; summarize the differences in the benefit packages identified in different industries or sectors of the economy.

4. Read your parents' life insurance policy, or that of a friend or relative, cover to cover. Prepare a one-page report of key policy features including beneficiary designation, policy clauses, settlement options, nonforfeiture options, and riders. Interpret the nonforfeiture options if the policyowner ceased premium payments.

5. Follow the systematic process of shopping for life insurance by comparing information on the company, the agent (if applicable), and the policy for at least two different term policies. Base the purchase on your own personal characteristics and a face amount of $100,000. Be sure to include the guaranteed insurability rider as well as any other riders appropriate to your situation. Document your findings and defend your policy choice.

6. Many college students lose health insurance coverage through their parents' policy on the day of graduation or a specified birthday (e.g., age 23). If you are covered through your parents' policy, determine when your coverage will end. Then determine available options for purchasing health insurance through your parents' group coverage, your university, or other independent or group options. Determine your best alternative; report on the coverage and the premium.

7. Begin or improve an activity associated with maintaining a healthy lifestyle (e.g., diet, exercise). Maintain this activity for at least a month. Report on your experience.

8. Talk to one or more senior citizens about their experiences with Medicare and/or supplemental (Medigap) health insurance. How does this coverage and the processing of claims compare with the coverage available prior to retirement? Report your findings.

9. As a part of a group project, interview a representative from a nursing home, extended care facility, or other retirement home and discuss the methods used by the residents for payment. Are residents using Medicare, Medigap, LTC insurance, or personal funds to pay for the facility services? Be sure to tour the facility and note your impressions. Report your findings to the group and compare the results from different care facilities.

## Discussion Case 1

Adam and Cassie Porterfield were delighted when Adam landed a new job with a promotion and increased salary but disappointed to learn that he would not be eligible for benefits for 90 days. Now, they're not sure 90 days will be enough time to handle all the decisions. The company offers a comprehensive package of health insurance, vision insurance, dental insurance, life insurance (1.5 times salary at no premium charge), and disability insurance. An employee can choose how to spend the employer-provided premium dollars to purchase health or disability insurance or additional life insurance. Fortunately, Cassie has group health insurance with a $1 million lifetime limit per covered individual.

### Questions

1. In the mix of premiums to be spent, how should Adam and Cassie rank Adam's insurance needs? What factors would be important to consider?

2. Should Adam consider purchasing more life insurance than the company-provided free benefit? What two methods could he use to assess his needs relative to his total life insurance coverage?

3. To avoid exclusion of any preexisting conditions by his new employer's health insurance coverage, what should Adam do?

4. Adam has heard that his employer offers an "opt-out" option with a $75 a month payment. Assuming Cassie's employer offers very similar coverage limits, should Adam and Cassie consider the opt-out option? Discuss the pros and cons of "opting out." What premium costs and opt-out payments should they consider in their analysis?

5. Name two or three factors important when purchasing disability insurance. Should Adam first consider short-term or long-term disability?

6. Should the Porterfields consider changing their company-provided insurance benefits if they become parents? Defend your answer.

# Money Matters

## WHAT THEY NEVER TOLD YOU ABOUT LIFE INSURANCE

**Your primary concern should be sufficient death benefit to cover your dependents' needs.** *Accidental death coverage doesn't count in the calculation unless you are 100 percent sure you will die by accident.*

**Take your beneficiary designation seriously.** *It allows money to go to your dependents without the delay of probate. If your beneficiary can't handle money, consider a periodic payment settlement option or designate a trust with a reliable trustee to receive the proceeds. Small children cannot receive life insurance payments directly. To avoid red tape, you should use some type of trust or guardian arrangement.*

**Consider a common disaster clause in your beneficiary designation.** *It will guarantee that your death benefit goes to your contingent beneficiary if the primary beneficiary dies within a stated number of days of your death. Otherwise the proceeds could be tied up in the primary beneficiary's estate and go to someone you wouldn't have chosen.*

**Never count on group life insurance as your total program.** *You could leave your job at a time when your medical condition would prevent obtaining replacement coverage. Although great strides have been made in making group health insurance "portable," the same is not true for group*

*life insurance. Some group life policies are convertible to personal policies, but the rates can be 3 to 10 times higher than the group rate. Also, investigate the rates for group supplemental life programs, which allow you to purchase coverage amounts above what your employer provides. If you are in good health, you may find lower premiums through a personal policy.*

**Put some thought into ownership of your policies.** *Though death benefits are free of income tax, they are normally included in your estate. Certain ownership arrangements can avoid some or all estate taxes. Also, in cases of divorce, it seems best for spouses to own and control each other's policies. This is especially true if there are children relying on potential benefits.*

**Familiarize yourself with riders such as waiver or premium, waiver of charges (on universal policies), and living benefits.** *Know when they pay and under what conditions. Evaluate the cost of riders versus their benefits.*

**Good intentions without complete information could result in tremendous headaches for those you are trying to protect.** *Don't forgo the assistance and knowledge of a competent independent agent for fear of paying higher premiums. Many use the same products with the same prices as Internet and telephone services.*

## Discussion Case 2

Wendy and Frank Kampe, 30 and 35, are considering the purchase of life insurance. Wendy doesn't have any coverage whereas Frank has a $150,000 group policy at work. The Kampes have two young children, ages 3 and 5. Wendy earns $28,000 annually from a part-time, home-based business. Frank's annual salary is $55,000. From their income, they save $7,500 annually. The rest goes for expenses. The couple estimates that the children will be financially dependent for another 20 years.

In preparation for a visit with their insurance agent, the Kampes have estimated the following expenses if Frank were to die:

| | |
|---|---|
| immediate needs at death | $25,000 |
| outstanding debt (including mortgage repayment) | $90,000 |
| transitional funds for Wendy to expand her business to fully support the family | $15,000 |
| college expenses for their two children | $205,000 |

They also anticipate, should Frank die, receiving $8,000 a year in Social Security survivor's benefits until the youngest child turns 18, and $5,000 annually in pension benefits, until

Wendy turns 80. Wendy projects her gross annual income to be $40,000 after her business expansion. Once the children are self-supporting, Wendy wants to plan a spousal life income for 10 more years, from age 50 to age 60, plus retirement income for another 20 years from age 60 to age 80. She anticipates receiving a 5 percent after-tax, after-inflation return on their investments.

To date, the Kampes have accumulated a total of $107,000 of assets, not including $45,000 home equity. Their assets include $10,000 considered as an emergency fund, $12,000 of IRA funds for Wendy, $35,000 in other investments, and $50,000 in Frank's employer 401(k) plan.

## Questions

1. Using the needs approach, estimate the amount of additional life insurance, if any, that the Kampes should purchase to protect Wendy if Frank should die.

2. Should Wendy purchase an insurance policy? Why or why not? If so, what type of policy would you recommend for Wendy?

3. What type of life insurance policy would you recommend that Frank purchase?

4. What would happen to Frank's group life insurance if he leaves his present job?

5. What could happen to the Kampes' children if Frank or Wendy should die without adequate life insurance coverage?

6. Should the Kampes name the children as life insurance beneficiaries?

7. Which life insurance riders might the Kampes select when purchasing a policy?

8. Since they will make a concerted effort to become informed about life insurance, should they also purchase life insurance on the children, rather than waiting until later when they would have to reeducate themselves for life insurance shopping?

Visit our Web site for additional case problems, interactive exercises, and practice quizzes for this chapter—**www.prenhall.com/keown**.

# 10 Property and Liability Insurance

## Learning Objectives

**Understand,** buy, and maintain homeowner's insurance in a cost-effective way.

**Recover** on a liability or a loss to your property.

**Buy** the automobile insurance policy that's right for you.

**File** a claim on your automobile insurance.

There are very few places as beautiful as Malibu, California. It's home to famous surf and even more famous stars, including Steven Spielberg, Bruce Willis, Demi Moore, Nick Nolte, Mel Brooks, Tom Hanks, and Sylvester Stallone. In 1993, however, it was home to fire. Fed by the seasonal Santa Ana winds, fire roared through Malibu, destroying some homes yet miraculously leaving others untouched. While it was reported that Bruce Willis and Demi Moore lost their home, this later proved to be untrue, and they owed thanks to the firefighters who worked around the clock to control the blaze. However, for the less fortunate—for those who lost their homes—it was their insurance agents who were owed the thanks.

Barbara and John Lane, who lived just a few hills away, lost their entire house and all that was in it. However, before the ashes stopped smoldering, a State Farm representative was on the scene with a check for $5,000 temporary living expenses. Although the Lanes were in shock, they certainly would have been in worse shape without some help from their insurance. State Farm agent Jim Lawler was on the scene at 5:45 in the morning, taking care of his clients and his friends. "These [clients] are my friends," said Lawler. "I've been an agent here since 1963, and I know these people. I raised four kids with them through parochial schools and high schools."

For the Lanes, seeing Jim Lawler had special meaning. It was at his gentle prodding that they'd recently purchased a more expensive home insurance policy that allowed them to replace their home using materials that are up to today's stricter fire and earthquake codes. For others, the worth of their insurance policy was sorely tested: "I know our home was destroyed," were the words of Zari Shalchi upon seeing her burned-out home for the first time. "I knew it, but I had to see it. . . . Insurance? I don't know the company's name. My husband does, I think."

People don't like to think about their homes burning down or being destroyed by an earthquake or hurricane, nor do they like to think about what might happen if they were in an automobile accident. It's like having a cavity filled—you don't want to think about it, you'd rather just deal with it if and when it happens. That was certainly the case with the Shalchis. Unfortunately, when it comes to your home burning or having an automobile accident, if you haven't prepared for it ahead of time with insurance, the experience becomes much worse.

As with health and life insurance, the logic behind property insurance is drawn from **Principle 3: Diversification Reduces Risk.** Property insurance allows individuals to pool the financial risks associated with property losses—a fire, burglary, or auto accident—to eliminate catastrophic losses. Everyone shares in everyone else's property losses by paying the average cost. As a result, no one experiences a catastrophic loss.

Principle
P 3 Diversification
Reduces Risk

The purpose of homeowner's and automobile insurance and the other types of insurance is also the same: to guard

**Principle 10** Protect Yourself Against Major Catastrophes —The Case for Insurance

against financial catastrophe. The need for property insurance rises from **Principle 10: Protect Yourself Against Major Catastrophes.** In the case of property insurance, our philosophy continues to be to provide protection against major catastrophes while ignoring the small stuff. It's not the $60 broken window that you should be concerned about—it's the $60,000 damage from a fire that could wipe out your entire savings if you don't have homeowner's insurance.

The insurance discussed in this chapter protects you against the financial risks of loss of or damage to your home or automobile and the legal liabilities associated with injuries or property damage to others. Unfortunately, homeowner's and automobile insurance policies, just like life and health policies, are filled with their own jargon. Deciding how much and exactly what kind of insurance to buy is confusing and difficult. Don't worry, though. This chapter teaches you what you need to know to manage your homeowner's and automobile insurance like a pro.

**1** Understand, buy, and maintain homeowner's insurance in a cost-effective way.

**Peril**
An event or happening, whether natural or man-made, that causes a financial loss.

## Protecting Your Home

In the United States, the first type of homeowner's insurance was fire insurance, offered in 1735 by a small company in Charleston, South Carolina. It wasn't until 1958 that the first modern "homeowner's" policy was sold.

Before homeowner's insurance, separate insurance policies were needed for every **peril**—that is, there was an insurance policy to cover fire, theft, windstorm damage, and so forth. Homeowner's insurance simplified the process by offering protection against multiple perils in one overarching policy. This new type of policy gave families peace of mind. It also helped them keep better track of their coverage by consolidating what would have previously been numerous different policies, probably with numerous different companies.

Today's homeowner's policies are sold in only six basic versions. Of course, you can add extra forms of coverage and individualize your insurance, but standardization makes comparison shopping easy—much easier than shopping for any other type of insurance. Unfortunately, standardization has actually stifled competition a bit. As a result, the homeowner's insurance industry is dominated by the five largest insurers, which insure about half of all homes. Let's take a look at these six standardized policies.

### Packaged Policies: HO's

**HO's**
The six standardized "homeowner's" insurance policies available to homeowners and renters.

Today's six basic homeowner's policies are known as **HO's,** which stands for homeowner's. Although they're called homeowner's insurance, they cover more than the home. They also provide liability insurance and cover renters. Three of them, HO-1, HO-2, and HO-3, provide basic, broad policies specifically for homeowners. Policy HO-4 is actually renter's insurance, HO-6 is for condominium owners, and HO-8 is for older homes. Here's a brief look at typical HO policies:

▌ **HO-1: Basic form homeowner's insurance.** This form of homeowner's insurance provides very narrow coverage. As a result, it isn't available in most states.

- **HO-2: Broad form homeowner's insurance.** Although this form of homeowner's insurance provides broad coverage, it's a **named perils** form of insurance. That is, it covers a set of named perils, such as fire, lightning, windstorm, hail, explosions, and so on. If a peril isn't specifically named in this policy, it isn't covered. If that particular unnamed peril just so happens to turn your house into a pile of broken boards, you're stuck. This type of coverage generally costs 5 to 10 percent more than HO-1 coverage.

- **HO-3: Special form homeowner's insurance.** The only difference between HO-2 and HO-3 is the way they cover perils. HO-3 is more comprehensive because it covers all direct physical losses to your home. It offers **open perils** protection, meaning it covers all perils except those specifically excluded. Excluded perils might include flood, earthquake, war, and nuclear accident. Typically, this type of coverage costs 10 to 15 percent more than an HO-1 policy.

- **HO-4: Renter's or tenant's insurance.** This insurance is the same as HO-2, but is instead aimed at renters or tenants. Do you think you're covered by your landlord's insurance? You aren't! Let's say your neighbor's barbecue gets out of hand and your apartment is destroyed by fire. Renter's insurance would allow you to replace whatever equipment, furnishings, and personal stuff you lost. Renter's insurance covers your possessions but doesn't protect the actual dwelling. Your landlord's insurance policy should cover damage to the dwelling. After all, the building is the landlord's property, not yours. However, renter's insurance does provide liability coverage, so if you're the one who barbecued the building, you're covered.

- **HO-6: Condominium owner's insurance.** This insurance covers the personal property of co-op or condominium owners much like HO-4 coverage for the property of renters. In addition, it covers any structural improvements or alterations you may have made to your unit.

- **HO-8: Modified coverage—older homes homeowner's insurance.** This insurance is designed for older homes, insuring them for repair costs or actual cash value rather than replacement cost. Some older homes, because of their materials and details, have outrageously expensive replacement costs. In fact, with some older homes the replacement cost could easily be two or three times their market value.

Table 10.1 summarizes the basic coverage provided under each of these policies. Although each packaged policy provides a different type and level of insurance, all six HO's are divided into two sections. Section I addresses **property insurance**, which protects you against the loss of your property or possessions due to various perils. Section II provides for **personal liability insurance**, which protects you from the financial losses incurred if someone is injured on your property or as a result of your actions.

**Section I: Property Coverage** Property covered under homeowner's insurance is covered for a certain dollar amount. This is the maximum amount the insurance company will pay out for a given claim. If an item is insured for $100,000, the insurance company will pay out claims of up to $100,000.

Within Section I of all HO policies except HO-4, there are four basic coverages:

- Coverage A: Dwelling
- Coverage B: Other structures
- Coverage C: Personal property
- Coverage D: Loss of use

**Named Perils**
A type of insurance that covers a specific set of named perils. If a peril isn't specifically named, it isn't covered.

**Open Perils**
A type of insurance that covers all perils except those specifically noted as excluded.

**Property Insurance**
Insurance that protects you against the loss of your property or possessions.

**Personal Liability Insurance**
Insurance covering all liabilities other than those resulting from the negligent operation of an automobile or those associated with business or professional causes.

## Table 10.1    Comparing Homeowner's Insurance Policies

**HO-1 (Basic Form)**

| | |
|---|---|
| A. Dwelling: | Based on structure's replacement value, minimum $15,000 |
| B. Other structures: | 10% of insurance on house |
| C. Personal property: | 50% of insurance on house |
| D. Loss of use: | 10% of insurance on house |

*Covered Perils:*

| | | |
|---|---|---|
| ▪ Fire or lightning | ▪ Smoke | ▪ Windstorm or hail |
| ▪ Vandalism or malicious mischief | ▪ Explosion | ▪ Theft |
| ▪ Riot or civil commotion | ▪ Glass breakage | ▪ Aircraft |
| ▪ Volcanic eruption | ▪ Vehicles | |

| | |
|---|---|
| E. Personal liability: | $100,000 |
| F. Medical payments to others: | $1,000 per person |

**HO-2 (Broad Form)**

Coverage A, B, C, E, and F same as HO-1

| | |
|---|---|
| D. Loss of use: | 20% of insurance on house |

*Covered Perils: Same as HO-1, plus:*

| | |
|---|---|
| ▪ Falling objects | ▪ Freezing of plumbing, heating, air-conditioning, fire sprinkler, or appliance |
| ▪ Weight of ice, snow, or sleet | |
| ▪ Accidental discharge of water or steam | ▪ Accidental damage from electrical current |
| ▪ Accidental tearing apart or cracking of heating system, air-conditioning, fire sprinkler, or appliance | |

**HO-3 (Special Form)**

Coverage B, C, D, E, and F same as HO-2

| | |
|---|---|
| A. Dwelling: | Based on structure's replacement value, minimum $20,000 |

*Covered Perils: Same perils for personal property as HO-2*

▪ Dwelling and other structures are covered against risk of direct loss to property. All losses are covered except those losses specifically excluded.

**HO-4 (Contents Broad Form)**

Coverage E and F same as HO-1 and HO-2

| | |
|---|---|
| A. Dwelling: | Not applicable |
| B. Other structures: | Not applicable |
| C. Personal property: | Minimum varies by company |
| D. Loss of use: | 20% of insurance on personal property |

*Covered Perils: Same perils for personal property as HO-2*

**HO-6 (Joint Owner's Form)**

Coverage E and F same as HO-1 and HO-2

| | |
|---|---|
| A. Dwelling: | $1,000 minimum on the unit |
| B. Other structures: | Included in Coverage A |
| C. Personal property: | Minimum varies by company |
| D. Loss of use: | 40% of insurance on personal property |

*Covered Perils: Same perils for personal property as HO-2*

(table continues)

(table continued)

## HO-8 (Modified Coverage Form)

Coverage E and F same as HO-1 and HO-2

| | |
|---|---|
| A. Dwelling: | Based on structure's market value |
| B. Other structures: | 10% of insurance on house |
| C. Personal property: | 50% of insurance on house |
| D. Loss of use: | 10% of insurance on house |

*Covered Perils: Same as HO-1*

Coverage A protects the house and any attachments to it—for example, an attached garage. However, if the land surrounding the house is destroyed by an explosion, this coverage won't pay to repair or restore it.

Coverage B protects other structures on the premises that aren't attached to the house—for example, your landscaping, a detached garage, or an outhouse. The level of this coverage is limited to 10 percent of the home's coverage. For example, if the home carries $200,000 of insurance, the other structures would carry $20,000 insurance. Still, at $20,000, that's one valuable outhouse! Again, the land isn't covered, and if the additional structure is used for business purposes, it's not covered.

Coverage C protects any personal property that's owned or used by the policy-holder, regardless of the location of this property. In other words, if you're on a vacation in Hawaii and someone hits you with a pineapple and steals your suitcase, your personal property is still covered. In addition, the personal property of your guests is covered while that property is in your home. So, if your home burns down during a party, any personal property losses of guests would be covered.

The amount of this coverage is equal to 50 percent of the home's coverage. Thus, if the home carries $200,000 of insurance, the personal property insurance would be $100,000. Within this coverage there are limits on some types of losses. For example, there's a $200 limit on money, bank notes, gold, and silver. There's also a $1,000 limit on securities, valuable papers, manuscripts, tickets, and stamps, and a $2,500 limit on the theft of silverware, goldware, and pewterware. In addition, certain property is excluded from coverage—for example, animals, birds, and fish. Before buying any policy, you should be aware of all of its limitations.

Coverage D provides benefits if your home can't be used because of an insured loss. The amount of loss of use coverage is limited to 20 percent of the amount of insurance on the house. Under this coverage, three benefits are provided: additional living expenses, fair rental value, and prohibited use. The additional living expenses benefits reimburse you for the cost of living in a temporary location until your home is repaired. The fair rental value benefit covers any rental losses you might experience. For example, if you rent a room in your home for $300 per month, and because of a fire it's uninhabitable for 2 months, you'd receive $600 for the loss of rent. Prohibited use coverage provides living expenses for up to 2 weeks if a civil authority declares your home to be uninhabitable, perhaps because of a gas leak in a neighbor's home.

**STOP & THINK** When you consider buying a house, keep in mind how much the insurance will cost. The cost may affect your choice of an older versus a new home, because insurance may offer discounts of from 8 to 15 percent on a new house. Why? The electrical, heating, and plumbing systems, in addition to the overall structure, are likely to be in better shape in a newer home, reducing the risk that a fire or some other peril might occur.

## Section II: Personal Liability Coverage

Section II of a homeowner's insurance policy covers personal liability. It protects the policyholder and his or her family members from financial loss if someone is injured on their property or as a result of their actions. The minimum level of liability coverage per accident is $100,000. In addition, the medical expenses of anyone injured by the policyholder or his or her family or by an animal they might own are also covered in Section II.

Although this portion of the homeowner's insurance policy is often overlooked, it's extremely important because of the protection it provides against potentially catastrophic losses from liability suits. This protection covers liabilities from everything other than business and professional liability and liabilities resulting from the negligent operation of an automobile.

These days, when everyone wants to sue everyone else for outrageous settlements, it's good to have your liabilities covered. You never know when your close friends or dear Aunt Edith might slip on your stairs, scrape a shin, and sue you for several million dollars in damages.

The portion of Section II that covers the actual medical insurance to others is really a small medical insurance policy. It covers payments up to $1,000 for medical expenses to those non–family members who are injured in your home. For example, if someone falls down your stairs and breaks a leg, this coverage would take care of up to $1,000 worth of medical expenses per person.

## Supplemental Coverage

Coverage C of Section I of an HO provides protection for your personal property, but what if that protection isn't enough? Depending on the type and dollar value of your assets, or the perils that you face, you might want to consider supplemental coverage.

There are dozens of types of supplemental coverage to choose from. Some of the more common types include personal articles floaters, earthquake protection, flood protection, inflation guard, and replacement cost. In general, the additional coverage can be added through an **endorsement**, which is simply a written attachment to an insurance policy to add or subtract coverage.

**Endorsement**
A written attachment to an insurance policy to add or subtract coverage.

**Personal Articles Floater**
An extension to a homeowner's insurance policy that provides coverage for all personal property regardless of where it's located. This coverage applies to the policyholder and all household residents except children away at school.

**Personal Articles Floaters** **Personal articles floaters** provide extended coverage for all personal property, regardless of where the property is located, for the policyholder and all household residents except children away at school. This coverage is generally sold as an extension to the homeowner's policy on an "all-risk" basis; it covers losses of any kind other than specifically excluded perils, which generally include war, wear and tear, mechanical breakdown, vermin, and nuclear disaster.

There are a number of variations of the personal articles floater, such as scheduled floaters or scheduled endorsements and blanket floaters, but they all perform the same task: They provide extended coverage to personal property. Recall the limit on personal property coverage is set at 50 percent of the dwelling coverage, but within this coverage there are also limits on some specific types of losses. For example, there's a $2,500 limit on the theft of silverware, goldware, and pewterware. If the value of your silverware is $25,000, you might want a personal articles floater to cover your silverware to its market value.

**Earthquake Coverage** Because damage from earthquakes is specifically excluded from coverage in the standardized packaged HO policies, supplemental earthquake coverage is an important addition in high-risk areas. In fact, in California, insurers are required to offer earthquake coverage as an add-on. Of course, not all Californians elect to buy such coverage, but they should be able to get it easily if they want it. Actually, only about 20 percent of those affected by the 1989 San Francisco earthquake had earthquake coverage. The rates on this coverage vary depending on the earthquake risk. Rates near the San Andreas fault cost up to $4 per $1,000 of coverage, which means coverage on a $200,000 home would run $800 per year.

**Flood Protection**   Flood protection includes coverage from more than flood. It includes water damage from hurricanes, mudslides, and unusual erosion along the Great Lakes and the Great Salt Lake. It's also a bit different from other coverage in that it's generally administered and subsidized by the federal government through the Department of Housing and Urban Development (HUD).

To be eligible for flood insurance, your community must comply with HUD requirements, which involve floodplain studies and planning. Once a community receives approval from HUD, you can purchase up to $185,000 of coverage on your dwelling and an additional $60,000 on its contents.

**Inflation Guard**   An **inflation guard** endorsement automatically updates your property coverage based on an index of replacement costs that continually updates the cost of building a home. In effect, the coverage—along with the premiums—automatically increase each year.

This endorsement makes sure that inflation doesn't silently eat away at the level of real coverage you have on your home and your property. For example, if the cost of building a home increases by 5 percent per year, in just over 14 years the cost of building a home will double. If your coverage stays the same over that time, you'd have enough insurance to buy only half a house.

Note that the adjustment generally reflects increases in average costs nationally, not locally. Because construction costs don't necessarily rise at an equal pace throughout the nation, it's a good idea to periodically review your level of coverage.

**Personal Property Replacement Cost Coverage**   Homeowner's insurance is set up to pay the policyholder the actual cash value of the loss. Unfortunately, when you're talking about personal property, the **actual cash value**, which is the replacement cost minus estimated depreciation (wear-and-tear costs), can be well below the cost of replacing the asset. For example, if the property could be replaced for $500, and it's been used for half its expected life, it would have an actual cash value of $250. Moreover, under the actual cash value, you're responsible for maintaining detailed records of the date of purchase, purchase price, and estimated depreciation of all your property.

As an alternative, most homeowner's policies come with optional **replacement cost coverage**, which provides for the actual replacement cost of a stolen or destroyed item as opposed to the actual cash value. Replacement cost coverage can generally be added for an additional 5 to 15 percent over the cost of the homeowner's insurance without this option. Although replacement cost coverage doesn't mean that you no longer have to keep track of your possessions, it does mean that you'll be able to replace them in the event of a loss.

**Added Liability Insurance**   Basic policies generally provide $100,000 of liability coverage. Although this figure may sound like a lot, it's no longer uncommon for court judgments to climb well above this figure. Also, if you've accumulated a relatively sizable net worth, you need increased liability insurance to protect your assets. Fortunately, for a relatively small fee, most insurance companies will allow you to raise your level of liability coverage to $300,000 or $500,000.

Alternatively, you might want to buy a **personal umbrella policy**, which, for a reasonable cost, provides protection ranging from $1 million to $10 million against

**Inflation Guard**
An endorsement that automatically updates the level of property coverage based on an index of replacement costs that continually updates the cost of building a home.

**Actual Cash Value**
The replacement value of the house less accumulated depreciation (which is the decline in value over time due to wear and tear).

**Replacement Cost Coverage**
Additional homeowner's coverage that provides for the actual replacement cost of a stolen or destroyed item as opposed to the actual cash value.

**Personal Umbrella Policy**
A homeowner's policy that provides excess liability insurance with protection against lawsuits and judgments generally ranging from $1 million to $10 million.

lawsuits and judgments. An umbrella policy provides excess liability insurance over basic underlying contracts. It doesn't go into effect until you've exhausted your automobile or homeowner's liability coverage.

It's also quite broad in coverage, generally covering most losses. However, it does exclude acts committed with intent to cause injury, activities associated with aircraft and some watercraft, and most business and professional activities. Business owner and professional policies must be purchased separately.

**Understand, buy, and maintain homeowner's insurance in a cost-effective way.**

## How Much Insurance Do You Need?

Answering this question is easy. In fact, we've already started answering it. We've discussed both the need for inflation guard coverage to make sure inflation doesn't negate insurance coverage and the need for replacement cost coverage on possessions.

What about replacement cost coverage on our houses? This coverage actually provides us with the final answer to our question: You need enough insurance to allow for full replacement in the event of a loss—a total loss.

### Coinsurance and the "80-Percent Rule"

**Coinsurance Provision**
A provision or requirement of homeowner's insurance requiring the insured to pay a portion of the claim if he or she purchased an inadequate amount of insurance (in this case, less than 80 percent of the replacement cost).

Insurance companies have a way of encouraging you to be covered for a total loss. It's called a **coinsurance provision**, and it requires that you pay a portion of your own losses if you don't purchase what they consider an adequate level of insurance. Many companies follow the **80-percent rule** and require you to carry at least 80 percent of your home's full replacement cost. This 80-percent rule relates to losses on your dwelling only—not those on your personal property.

There are some restrictions to this coverage, though. First, the amount paid is limited to the limits of the policy—that is, a $100,000 insurance policy will pay only up to its $100,000 limit. Second, you usually have to rebuild your home on the same location. Third, if you don't rebuild your home, the insurer is liable only for the actual cash-value loss, which is generally quite a bit less than the replacement cost.

**80-Percent Rule**
A homeowner's insurance rule stating that the replacement cost coverage is in effect only if the home is insured for at least 80 percent of its replacement cost. This rule is intended to discourage homeowners from insuring for less than the replacement cost of their homes.

Finally, the replacement cost coverage is in effect only if your home is insured for at least 80 percent of its replacement cost.

This 80-percent rule makes insuring your home for less than at least 80 percent of its replacement cost seem unattractive. If your home currently has a replacement value of $100,000 and is insured for $80,000 and a fire causes damages of $50,000, you would be paid the full $50,000 with no deduction for depreciation (wear and tear). However, if the fire destroyed your home, you would collect only $80,000, the face value of your policy.

If the 80-percent rule isn't met, the homeowner must pay for part of any losses. This is commonly referred to as the coinsurance provision. If your house is insured for less than 80 percent of its replacement value, in the event of a loss you'll receive the greater of the following:

▮ the actual cash value of the portion of your house that was destroyed (remember that the actual cash value is the replacement cost minus depreciation)

*or*

▮ the amount of insurance purchased/80% of replacement cost × the amount of loss

What does all this mean? It means that it would be a grave mistake not to insure your home for at least 80 percent of its replacement cost. If you satisfy the 80-percent rule and your house is destroyed or damaged, your policy will pay to fully repair or replace your home up to the amount of insurance purchased. If you don't satisfy the 80-percent rule, you probably won't get enough to replace it. You may want more insurance, but certainly not less.

## The Bottom Line

Unfortunately, there's no neat, tidy formula to tell you exactly how much home-owner's insurance you need. Determining the amount of coverage you need is a procedure that requires some thought and foresight on your part. Because the amount of assets and possessions you've managed to pick up is always changing, so are your insurance needs. As has been the case for just about every personal finance matter we've examined so far, you need to revisit your insurance needs from time to time, just to make sure those needs are being met.

When determining how much homeowner's insurance you need, you should consider the following:

▌ You need enough insurance to cover the replacement of your home in the event of a complete loss. This coverage will need to reflect any changes in increased costs due to changing building codes.

▌ You should have protection against inflation eroding your coverage.

▌ If you're in a flood or earthquake area, you need special protection against these disasters.

▌ If you have detached structures or elaborate landscaping, you should determine whether or not they're adequately covered under a standard policy.

▌ If you have a home office, you should consider additional coverage. Remember, your homeowner's policy doesn't provide business liability coverage.

▌ You need adequate coverage for personal property. For most people, replacement cost property insurance is a good idea.

▌ If you have possessions that need special protection—for example, a valuable coin collection or jewelry—you should consider a floater policy.

▌ If your assets are much greater than the liability limits on your homeowner's policy, you should consider additional liability coverage.

▌ If you're renting, you need adequate insurance for your personal property.

## Keeping Your Costs Down

What determines the cost of your homeowner's policy? Three basic factors: (1) the location of your home, (2) the type of structure, and (3) your level of coverage and policy type. Location affects coverage because of differences in crime levels and regional perils (such as earthquakes in California and tornadoes in the Midwest). Older and less sound structures cost more to insure because they're more likely to have problems. In addition, the greater the coverage and more comprehensive the policy, the more it costs.

Still, there are some ways that the cost of homeowner's insurance can be kept down. Start by selecting a financially sound insurer with low comparative costs. Then take advantage of as many discounts as possible. Here are some potential discounts and savings methods:

▌ **High deductible discounts. Deductibles**, which are what you agree to pay before insurance coverage kicks in, can be thought of as coinsurance. The larger the deductible you are willing to accept, the less you pay for insurance coverage. Typically, insurance companies require a $250 deductible and provide discounts if you're willing to accept a higher deductible.

Understand, buy, and maintain homeowner's insurance in a cost-effective way.

**Deductible**
The amount that you are responsible for paying before insurance coverage kicks in.

# In The News

Kiplinger's Personal Finance Magazine June 1999

## "Getting a Second Opinion"

Tremors left cracks in the walls and foundation and leaks in the roof of Leon Robbins's home in south central Los Angeles, even though it was miles from the epicenter of the Northridge earthquake in January 1994. The estimated cost to repair the damage? Only $7,200 (just $400 short of the deductible), according to Robbins's insurer, Western Home Insurance Co. At least $22,300, according to a contractor that Robbins consulted. Or $40,000, according to another contractor, hired by Robbins's attorney after Western Home rejected the previous estimate.

*After hearing from 11 more Western Home policyholders with similar stories, a jury in Los Angeles County Superior Court in 1997 found the insurance company guilty of bad faith and awarded Robbins $7.7 million, including punitive damages. "We disagreed with the findings," says Western Home president Don Preusser. On appeal, the case was settled confidentially.* (☛A)

Western Home also settled with the other 11 policyholders for an undisclosed amount. "Almost everyone had been told that the damage was just under the deductible," says Brian Kabateck, a partner with Quisenberry & Barbanel, the law firm that handled the case.

What should you do if you think your insurer is lowballing your homeowner's claim? The first line of defense is to call one or more contractors to estimate the cost of repairs. The estimate may be free, or you may pay a fee if the estimate is clearly for insurance purposes.

*If you want more firepower on your side, consider hiring an independent adjuster to estimate damages and to go to bat for you with your insurer. While a contractor's estimate can help when your dispute is over the cost of repairs, an adjuster can be your advocate when you disagree with your insurer over what your policy actually covers or about reimbursements for possessions. An adjuster can also help you submit and document claims and can represent you in negotiations.* (☛B)

### THE BOTTOM LINE . . .

**A** One way to check a company's record is to look at the level of complaints it has generated. To do this contact your state insurance department (the location should be available at **www.naic.org**) and ask for the complaint ratio for all the insurers licensed in your state.

**B** Adjusters aren't cheap. You should expect to pay 10 percent of the amount recovered, or 25 to 45 percent of the difference between what your insurer offers and the amount you eventually receive. If you're interested in finding one, referrals are available through the National Association of Public Insurance Adjusters (**www.napia.com**).

Source: What If the Company Won't Pay?" *Kiplinger's Personal Finance Magazine*, June 1999: 70–78. Reprinted by permission of Kiplinger. © 1999 The Kiplinger Washington Editors, Inc.

---

**STOP & THINK** Typically the deductible on a homeowner's policy starts at $250. By increasing your deductible to $500, you could save up to 12 percent; $1,000, up to 24 percent; up to $2,500, up to 30 percent; and $5,000, up to 37 percent.

---

**W32 WORKSHEET**

Keep in mind that the purpose of insurance is not to offset all costs, only catastrophic ones. To keep the costs of homeowner's insurance under control, you'll have to share some of the risks with the insurance company. In other words, you should be responsible for all minor expenses, and the insurance company should cover all large expenses. Give serious consideration to taking as large a deductible as you can afford.

▮ **Security system/smoke detector discounts.** Many insurance companies also offer discounts of from 2 to 5 percent if you install security and smoke detector systems. Larger discounts are available if you install in-home sprinkler systems.

▮ **Multiple policy discounts.** Insurance companies often provide discounts to customers who have more than one policy—for example, their automobile *and* homeowner's coverage—with them.

▮ **Pay your insurance premiums annually.** If you pay your insurance premiums annually in one lump sum rather than quarterly, or extended over several months, most insurance companies will offer you a discount.

▮ **Other discounts.** Some companies offer a discount for homes made with fire-resistant materials, for homeowners over the age of 55, and for individuals who've had homeowner's insurance with a single company for an extended number of years.

# Checklist 10.1 ■ A Checklist for Homeowner's Insurance

Determine the amount and type of homeowner's insurance you need.

Put together a listing of top-quality (as listed in *A.M. Best's Key Rating Guide on Property and Casualty Insurers* also located at their Web site at **www.ambest.com**) insurance agents with a good local reputation who carry these insurers.

Consult with agents, letting them know what you are looking for. Give consideration to any recommendations or modifications they might suggest.

Get several bids on the total package, including all modifications, floaters, and extensions.

Conduct an annual review of your homeowner's insurance coverage.

■ **Consider a direct writer.** A **direct writer** is an insurance company that distributes its products to customers without the use of agents. Companies that don't use agents don't have to pay salaries or commissions, so they can afford to offer lower prices.

■ **Shop around.** Compare costs among high-quality insurers. Premiums for similar coverage can vary by as much as 25 percent. Checklist 10.1 reviews the process of shopping for homeowner's insurance.

■ **Double-check your policy.** Make sure the policy you receive is what you ordered. Check the type and level of coverage, and any endorsements that you requested. It'll be too late to correct any errors once you file a claim.

**Direct Writer**
An insurance company that distributes its products directly to customers, without the use of agents.

> **STOP & THINK** One healthy way to reduce your insurance premiums is to quit smoking. Smoking accounts for about 23,000 residential fires a year. As a result, many insurance companies offer discounts to nonsmoking families.

## Making Your Coverage Work

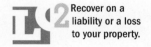

Recover on a liability or a loss to your property.

By now you should be able to go out and buy the policy that's just right for you. However, is that policy enough to protect you from losing your possessions and assets? Nope. How can your insurance company make good on your policy and pay you for a loss if it doesn't know what possessions you've lost or what they were worth?

For your homeowner's insurance to provide effective protection against loss, you need to establish proof of ownership and value your assets using a detailed inventory of everything you own. Unfortunately, putting together such a list is a tedious job. Still, if you can't prove that you owned a stereo worth $2,000, your insurance company isn't going to reimburse you for it if it gets stolen.

Fortunately, the inventory process isn't all that difficult. Begin by putting together a list of household items. To aid you in this process, most insurance agents should be able to provide you with an inventory worksheet. If not, you can get one from the Insurance Information Institute by calling 800-331-9146 or you can get one off the State Farm's Web page (**www.statefarm.com/educate/ brochure.htm**). Ideally, your inventory should be as detailed as possible and include the date of purchase, the cost, the model and serial number, and the brand name for each item.

Most people simply never get around to compiling a complete written inventory. However, you should at least make sure you keep written documentation of any valuable items you own, along with any appraisals you may have had.

As a time-saving measure, the Insurance Information Institute recommends that you also videotape your household inventory. Walk through each room in your home and videotape the contents, giving a running description of what you're taping as you go. Note the original cost and date of purchase of major items whenever possible. In

# Checklist 10.2 ■ What To Do in the Event of a Loss

Report your loss immediately. In the case of a burglary or theft, report the incident immediately to the police. If a credit or ATM card has been stolen, you should also notify the issuing company. In addition, you should notify your insurance agent.

Make temporary repairs to protect your property. If your house has sustained damage and your insurance agent hasn't had time to inspect it, don't let the damage sit untouched. Board up broken windows and holes in the roof or walls to prevent any further damage and to protect your home against burglary.

Make a detailed list of everything lost or damaged. Using your inventory—now you'll be glad you made one—put together a detailed list describing the items that were lost or damaged and their value. Present this list to your insurance agent and the police.

Maintain records of the insurance settlement process. Keep records of all your expenses.

Confirm the adjuster's estimate. Your insurance company will send an adjuster to evaluate the claim and recommend to the insurance company a dollar amount for the settlement. Before settling, get an estimate from a local contractor as to how much the repairs will cost. Don't agree to anything less than a fair settlement.

addition, make sure each room is taped from a number of different angles, with all closet doors open. Be sure to videotape the contents of drawers and cabinets. When taping valuables such as jewelry and silverware, take a careful shot of them.

Try to make your recording as comprehensive as possible. For example, include curtains, lamps, CDs, records, books, kitchenware, sporting equipment, and items in the attic and basement. You should also videotape the outside of your home, including your landscaping. If you don't have a video camera, many camera stores and independent claim services will tape your house for you.

Once you've finished your video or your inventory, you should keep it in a safety deposit box, with a family member living elsewhere, or with your insurance agent. Why not keep it yourself? Well, if your house burns down, your video or inventory would burn, too, and all your efforts would quickly go up in smoke.

OK, now you've got a good insurance policy and a video inventory of your house. Now you're effectively covered, right? Not exactly. To collect on a loss, you must follow a few basic steps outlined in Checklist 10.2.

Buy the automobile insurance policy that's right for you.

## Automobile Insurance

At this point, you should be pretty safe at home, thanks to your homeowner's insurance and your newfound knowledge of how to manage it and file claims. You need to leave home at least every now and again, though. What happens when you get in your car? Are you safe there, too? Not unless you have automobile insurance. Of course, if you drive, you have to have some form of automobile insurance—it's the law in most states.

Automobile insurance requirements are good to have as law, because there are an awful lot of car accidents each year. In fact, there are around 30 million accidents each year in the United States alone. That works out to about one accident for every five licensed drivers. In reality, though, some drivers have at least one accident per year, and others never have an accident in their lives.

Because you're going to need it if you drive, you're going to need to know how to buy automobile insurance. Let's start our discussion by taking a look at the standardized personal automobile policy.

# Personal Automobile Policy

Fortunately, automobile insurance is relatively standard, with all policies following a similar package format called the **personal automobile policy (PAP)**. Each policy contains both liability and property damage coverage, and each package of insurance includes four basic parts:

- **Part A: Liability coverage.** This coverage provides protection for you if you're legally liable for bodily injury and property damage caused by your automobile. It includes payment for any judgment awarded, court costs, and legal defense fees.
- **Part B: Medical expense coverage.** This coverage pays medical bills and funeral expenses, with limits per person for you and your passengers.
- **Part C: Uninsured motorist's protection coverage.** This coverage is required in many states and protects you by covering bodily injury (and property damage in a few states) caused by drivers without liability insurance.
- **Part D: Damage to your automobile coverage.** This coverage is also known as collision or comprehensive insurance, and provides coverage for theft of your auto or for damage from almost any peril other than collision.

Figure 10.1 illustrates the typical policy parts as they relate to the liability and property coverage. Now let's look at each coverage part in greater detail.

**PAP Part A: Liability Coverage**   Part A of a personal automobile policy involves liability coverage, which provides protection from loss resulting from lawsuits that might arise because of an auto accident.

Liability coverage can be presented as a **combined single limit**, meaning that the coverage applies to a combination of both bodily injury and property damage liability, without a separate limit for each person. For example, if you had total liability coverage of $100,000, then the total liability insurance—both bodily injury and property damage—in an accident, regardless of how many individuals were involved, would be $100,000.

Some insurers also issue **split-limit coverage**, which allows for either separate coverage limits for bodily injury and property damage, split-coverage limits per

**Combined Single Limit**
Auto insurance liability coverage that combines both bodily injury and property damage liability.

**Split-Limit Coverage**
Auto insurance liability coverage that allows for either separate coverage limits for bodily injury and property damage, split coverage limits per person, or both.

## Figure 10.1 Personal Automobile Insurance Coverage

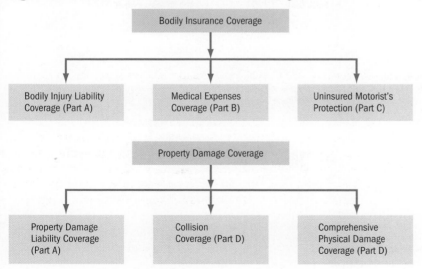

person, or both. For example, split-limit coverage limits of $200,000/$600,000/ $100,000 would mean you have $200,000 of bodily injury liability coverage for each person and $600,000 for each accident, in addition to $100,000 of property damage liability coverage. Figure 10.2 shows these limits graphically.

Considering the absurd sums of money judges are handing out in settlements of lawsuits over automobile accidents, it's a good idea to carry adequate liability insurance. Although most states require minimum levels of coverage, this is generally well below what is needed by most people. In fact, most professional financial planners recommend that you carry at least $100,000 of bodily injury liability coverage per person and $300,000 of bodily injury liability coverage for all persons. Also, they recommend that you carry at least $50,000 of property damage liability insurance coverage.

Of course, these are general recommendations and what you carry should reflect your net worth and annual income—the greater your assets, the more coverage you should carry.

**Figure 10.2** Reading Automobile Liability Split-Coverage Insurance Limits Quoted as Split Coverage

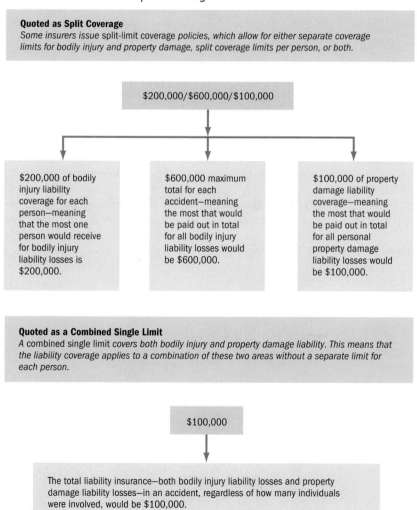

**Quoted as Split Coverage**
*Some insurers issue* split-limit coverage *policies, which allow for either separate coverage limits for bodily injury and property damage, split coverage limits per person, or both.*

$200,000/$600,000/$100,000

$200,000 of bodily injury liability coverage for each person—meaning that the most one person would receive for bodily injury liability losses is $200,000.

$600,000 maximum total for each accident—meaning the most that would be paid out in total for all bodily injury liability losses would be $600,000.

$100,000 of property damage liability coverage—meaning the most that would be paid out in total for all personal property damage liability losses would be $100,000.

**Quoted as a Combined Single Limit**
*A combined single limit* covers both bodily injury and property damage liability. This means that the liability coverage applies to a combination of these two areas without a separate limit for each person.

$100,000

The total liability insurance—both bodily injury liability losses and property damage liability losses—in an accident, regardless of how many individuals were involved, would be $100,000.

In addition to paying the policy limits for the damages you caused, the insurer also agrees under Part A to defend you in any civil cases arising from the accident and to pay all legal costs. These legal costs are paid *in addition* to your policy limits. However, the insurance company won't defend you against any criminal charges brought against you as a result of a charge such as drunk driving.

**PAP Part B: Medical Expenses Coverage**   Your medical expenses coverage pays all reasonable medical and funeral expenses incurred within 3 years by the policyholder, his or her family members, and other persons injured in an accident involving your covered automobile. In fact, it covers the policyholder and his or her family regardless of whether they're in an automobile or walking along the street, just as long as they're not injured by a vehicle that wasn't designed for use on public roads, such as a snowmobile or farm tractor.

If you're driving a car you don't own, your medical expenses will be covered, but not those of other passengers in the car or pedestrians who are injured—the owner of the car would be responsible for that insurance. In addition, your PAP medical expense coverage doesn't specify fault. That is, you're not insured based upon who is at fault in an accident. As a result, you receive payment for any medical expenses faster because the insurance company doesn't need to waste time establishing fault.

Typically, policy limits run anywhere from $1,000 per person up to $10,000 or more per person, with no limit on the number of individuals that can be covered in an accident. Generally, you should maintain at least $50,000 of coverage per person. Even if you have adequate medical insurance of your own, you should still carry a relatively high level of automobile coverage, because you can never be sure of the level of coverage your passengers have.

**PAP Part C: Uninsured Motorist's Protection Coverage**   **Uninsured motorist's protection coverage** provides coverage for injuries caused by an uninsured motorist, a negligent driver whose insurance company is insolvent, or a hit-and-run driver. To collect on a claim, not only must the other driver not have available insurance, but it must be shown that the other driver was at fault.

**Uninsured Motorist's Protection Coverage**
Coverage against injuries caused by a hit-and-run driver or by an uninsured motorist or a negligent driver whose insurance company is insolvent.

It's important to carry uninsured motorist's protection, because roughly as many as 15 percent of all drivers don't carry any insurance at all, and you never know when one might slam into your car. Most financial planners recommend that you carry at least $250,000 per person and $500,000 per accident.

You can also add underinsured motorist's coverage to your policy to provide protection against negligent drivers who don't carry adequate liability insurance. If you purchase $150,000 of underinsured motorist's coverage, you'll be protected for up to $150,000 regardless of how much insurance the negligent driver carried. For example, if the negligent driver carried $50,000 of coverage and your injuries amounted to $125,000, you'd receive $50,000 from the negligent driver's insurance policy and $75,000 from your underinsured motorist's policy, for a total of $125,000.

**Collision Loss**
The portion of auto insurance coverage that provides benefits to cover damages resulting from an accident with another vehicle or object.

**PAP Part D: Coverage for Damage to Your Automobile**   Part D coverage includes both **collision loss** and **other than collision loss**, generally called **comprehensive physical damage coverage**. The collision loss portion of the coverage provides benefits to cover damages resulting from an accident with another vehicle or object. Your automobile would be covered if it were in an accident with another automobile or hit a telephone pole. Likewise, your car would be covered if it were hit in a parking lot or if its door were damaged because the person who parked next to you dented it with his or her door and then drove off. Comprehensive physical damage coverage covers damage from fire, theft or larceny, windstorm, falling objects, earthquakes, and similar causes.

**Other Than Collision Loss or Comprehensive Physical Damage Coverage**
Auto insurance coverage for noncollision losses. For example, it would cover damage if the car were hit in a parking lot or if the door were damaged as a result of banging it into a parked car next to it.

With collision insurance, losses are covered regardless of whose fault the accident was. You should keep in mind that if the other driver was at fault and has liability insurance, you should be able to recover your losses regardless of whether or not you have collision coverage. Collision coverage assures you that you'll be able to pay for any damage to your car regardless of who was at fault. Collision coverage used to cover damage suffered to rental cars used for business purposes. Many insurers have stopped this practice, so if you commonly rent automobiles for business purposes, you might want to check your coverage.

The recommended limit on both collision and comprehensive physical damage coverage is the cash value of your automobile, and both coverages generally have deductibles associated with them. Usually, the deductible associated with collision coverage is larger than that for comprehensive physical damage coverage. Also, premiums decline sharply as deductibles are raised.

For example, one major insurance company charges an annual premium of $488 on comprehensive insurance on a new Pontiac Vibe for a youthful operator based on a deductible of $50. If the deductible is raised to $100, the premium drops to $420. By raising the deductible by $50, you can save $68 in annual premiums. In effect, a premium of $68 is being charged for $50 of additional coverage. If you have less than one accident per year, you're better off with the $100 deductible. If you have more than one accident per year, you should probably pay some attention to improving your driving skills. Table 10.2 provides a summary of the different parts of the PAP.

## Table 10.2 The Personal Automobile Policy (PAP)

| Coverage Description | Individuals Covered | Recommended Policy Limits |
|---|---|---|
| *Liability Coverage—Part A* | | |
| Part A of a personal automobile policy involves liability coverage and provides coverage against lawsuits that might arise from negligent ownership or operation of an automobile. | Nonexcluded relatives who live with the insured regardless of whether the automobile is owned or not. | $100,000 bodily injury liability coverage per person and $300,000 of bodily injury coverage for all persons. $50,000 of property damage liability coverage. |
| *Medical Expenses Coverage—Part B* | | |
| Your medical expenses coverage covers all reasonable medical and funeral expenses incurred by the policyholder and family members in addition to other persons injured while occupying a covered automobile. | The policyholder and his or her family regardless of whether they are in an automobile or walking, as long as they are injured by a vehicle that was designed for use on public roads. | $50,000 of coverage per person. |
| *Uninsured Motorist's Protection Coverage—Part C* | | |
| Uninsured motorist's protection coverage provides coverage for injuries caused by an uninsured motorist, a negligent driver whose insurance company is insolvent, or a hit-and-run driver. | Insured family members driving nonowned automobile with permission, and anyone driving an insured car with permission. | $250,000 of coverage per person and $500,000 of coverage per accident. |
| *Coverage for Damage to Your Automobile—Part D* | | |
| Protection against damage to or theft of your automobile is provided in Part D coverage. This coverage includes both collision loss and loss resulting from other than collision loss, generally called comprehensive physical damage coverage. | Anyone driving an insured automobile with permission. | Actual cash value. |

**Exclusions**   The PAP provides broad coverage, but there are a number of standard exceptions. Although there may be others, standard exclusions generally include the following:

- You're not covered in the case of intentional injury or damage.
- You're not covered if you're using a vehicle without permission of the owner.
- You're not covered if you're using a vehicle with fewer than four wheels.
- You're not covered if you're driving another person's car that is provided for you on a regular basis.
- You're not covered if you own the automobile but don't have it listed on your insurance policy.
- You're not covered if you're carrying passengers for a fee.
- You're not covered while driving in a race or speed contest.

## No-Fault Insurance

In an attempt to keep insurance costs down—in particular, those costs associated with settling claims—many states have turned to the concept of **no-fault insurance**. Today over half of all states have some variation of a no-fault system.

**No-Fault Insurance**
A type of auto insurance in which your insurance company protects you in the case of an accident regardless of who is at fault.

No-fault insurance is based on the idea that your insurance company should pay for your losses, regardless of who's at fault. All the legal expenses associated with attaching blame would then be lifted, and insurance coverage should prove to be less costly.

Under no-fault insurance, if you were in an accident, your insurance company would pay for your losses and the losses suffered by your passengers, and the other driver's insurance company would pay for his or her losses. Sounds like a good idea, right? Well, no-fault insurance has its problems. The biggest problem is that no-fault insurance imposes limits on medical expenses and other claims. In some states, the limited coverage simply may not be enough to cover all legitimate medical expenses.

Although many states have instituted some form of no-fault insurance, many others haven't. It's a good idea to know what kind of insurance your state requires. If you live in a "fault" state and are in an accident that was the other driver's fault, you collect from his or her insurance company—provided the other driver has insurance. If it's your fault, it'll be tough to collect on your own injuries beyond your part B coverage and you can expect your premiums to rise. If it's not all your fault and not all the other driver's fault, state law will determine what happens

**STOP & THINK**   Just having home and auto insurance may not be enough. Too often things happen that are unrelated to your home or car. What if you're riding your bike and you bump into an elderly man who falls and fractures his spine? Also, keep in mind that the liability coverage on your homeowner's insurance generally runs about $100,000 to $300,000, while the liability coverage on your auto insurance often is only $100,000. In a lawsuit today, that's peanuts. Don't take the risk: Consider an umbrella liability insurance policy—they aren't that expensive.

next. With no-fault insurance, you collect—up to a limit—regardless of who was at fault. You can still sue for "pain and suffering," but only if the other driver was at fault.

## Buying Automobile Insurance

Now that you know about the basic types of coverage in automobile insurance, you can make an informed choice in buying some. How much will you need to spend? Well, that depends on how good a comparison shopper you are. It also depends on some factors that are pretty much beyond your control. Let's take a look at these factors, and then at what you can do to get the best possible deal.

**Determinants of the Cost of Automobile Insurance**   The following are the major determinants of the cost of automobile insurance:

- **The type of automobile.** The sportier and more high-powered your car is, the more your insurance will cost. In fact, in buying an automobile, the cost of insurance should be factored into the purchase decision.
- **The use of your automobile.** The less you use your car, the less you'll have to pay in insurance premiums.
- **The driver's personal characteristics.** Young unmarried males generally pay the most for their insurance, because they have a statistically greater chance of having an accident. Age, sex, and marital status all go into determining how much you pay for insurance.
- **The driver's driving record.** If you've received traffic tickets or had traffic accidents, you'll probably have to pay more for your insurance. Exactly how much your premiums go up depends on the nature of your violations. If you receive a driving-under-the-influence-of-alcohol citation, you can expect a hearty increase in your premiums.
- **Where you live.** In general, because of a higher incidence of accidents and theft, insurance is more expensive for those who live in urban areas.
- **Discounts that you qualify for.** A wide variety of discounts are available for cars that have certain safety features and for individuals who have characteristics identified with safe drivers. Table 10.3 lists some of the most common automobile insurance discounts.

**Keeping Your Costs Down** There are several general ways you can keep your automobile insurance rates down while ensuring complete coverage. They include the following:

- **Shop comparatively.** Different insurers don't charge identical prices for identical coverage. In fact, rates can vary by as much as 100 percent from carrier to carrier, and that's why you'll want to get a minimum of three different quotes on your automobile insurance. In addition, make sure you get quotes with different size deductibles.
- **Consider only high-quality insurers.** You should check both *A. M. Best Reports* (**www.ambest.com**), considering only insurers earning one of Best's two highest

---

**Table 10.3** Common Automobile Insurance Discounts

*You can reduce your auto insurance premiums significantly by taking advantage of discounts. Listed below are the most common automobile insurance discounts.*

**Accident Free.** Ten-percent discounts on most coverage after 3 years without a chargeable accident. After 6 years, the discount rises to 15%.

**Multiple Automobiles.** Fifteen-percent discount for insuring more than one car with the same company.

**Low Annual Mileage.** Fifteen-percent discount if you drive fewer than 7,500 miles per year.

**Automobile and Homeowner's** together. Five to fifteen percent off both policies if with the same company.

**Low "Damageability."** Ten to thirty percent off collision and comprehensive premiums if the car is statistically less likely to result in an expensive claim because it is cheaper to repair or less appealing to thieves.

**Good Student.** Up to 25% discount for unmarried drivers under 25 who rank in the top 20% of their class, have a B average, or are on the honor roll.

**Over 50.** Ten-percent discount off the usual adult rate if you are over 50.

**Defensive Driving Course.** Five-percent discount if you complete a defensive driving course (many times only applies to drivers 55 or older).

**Passive Restraints.** Up to 40% discount on some coverages if you have airbags or automatic seatbelts. Antilock brakes also add a 5% discount.

**Noncommuter or Carpooler.** Fifteen-percent discount if you drive less than 30 miles to and from work each day.

**Antitheft Devices.** Fifteen-percent discount depending on where you live and the type of device.

# In The News

Kiplinger's Personal Finance Magazine June 1999

## *"When You Have a Claim"*

Ivan Culbertson's Jeep Cherokee was totaled when he was hit head-on in late October 1998 not long after the start of his final year at Willamette University College of Law. Rescuers pried him out of his car and rushed him to the hospital, where he had surgery on his face and shattered knee. The medical bills exceeded $16,000.

*The police found the other car's driver at fault, but that person's insurer, a small, high-risk company, denied Culbertson's claim. "Their excuse was that their insured said I was at fault," says Culbertson. He tracked down a copy of the police report and sent a copy to the company. It still denied the claim.* (☛A)

Having gathered his own evidence and kept track of every conversation and letter related to the case, Culbertson enlisted the help of the Oregon Insurance Division. An investigator agreed Culbertson wasn't at fault and sent a letter asking the insurance company to pay his claim. That worked. In March he received a check for the full amount of his claim, although the company still didn't admit its customer was at fault.

*Even if you choose an insurer with a good record, you can't guarantee trouble-free claims.*

*And as Culbertson's case illustrates, you may even have to deal with an insurer you've never heard of or would not have chosen yourself. So whenever you have a significant claim, be prepared for the possibility that you may have to battle for a fair settlement. Here are some tips:* (☛B)

- Report a claim quickly and try not to alter the scene until you contact your company—each one has different rules for presenting evidence. Save receipts for major items and living expenses, police reports, and anything else that supports your claim.
- Document all phone calls and letters (certified receipts always help). "Get in writing from the company why they're denying a claim," says Robert Hunter of the Consumer Federation of America. "Once they've told you the reason, they can't come up with a new reason."
- Do some research to build your case. If you and the company disagree on your car's value, for example, check a used-car pricing guide (visit Kelley Blue Book on the Web) or call a couple of dealers and report your findings to the adjuster.

- Try to avoid signing anything that releases the insurance company from further obligation to pay you. For example, it might take months before you realize that an earthquake has damaged your house's foundation.

### THE BOTTOM LINE . . .

**A** Fighting an insurance company is not something that you can put off forever. In fact in many states you only have a 1-year period after the claim is filed to sue. Make sure you keep an eye on the time deadlines.

**B** If you're not satisfied, don't let things simply run their course. Be a pain, pester the insurance company if things don't appear to be moving smoothly. The place to start is with the claims adjuster, then work up to the president, if necessary. Some shady insurance companies intentionally drag their feet hoping the insured takes whatever is offered.

Source: "What If the Company Won't Pay?" *Kiplinger's Personal Finance Magazine*, June 1999: 70–78. Reprinted by permission of Kiplinger. © 1999 The Kiplinger Washington Editors, Inc.

rankings, and *Consumer Reports* (**www.consumerinsure.org**) to assess the quality of the insurer before purchasing insurance.

- **Take advantage of discounts.** You can lower your premiums considerably by taking available discounts. Those in driver's education courses, over 50, graduates of defensive-driving courses, students with good grades, and car-pool participants all have the potential for discounts.
- **Buy a car that's relatively inexpensive to insure.** In making your purchase decision, factor in the cost of insurance on your new car.
- **Improve your driving record.** You have control over your driving record, and it goes a long way toward determining your premiums.
- **Raise your deductibles.** As with homeowner's insurance, raising your deductibles can significantly lower your premiums.
- **Keep adequate liability insurance.** With increasing medical and hospital expenses, damage awards have increased dramatically in recent years.

## Filing a Claim

There are a number of steps that you should take if you're involved in an automobile accident. After an accident, you might be too shaken up to remember them. Therefore, it's a good idea to keep in your glove compartment a list of what to do in case of an accident. Your "to do" list should include the following actions:

File a claim on your automobile insurance.

**35** WORKSHEET

1. Get help for anyone injured. Because it's a felony to leave the scene of an accident, you should have someone call the police and an ambulance.
2. Move your car to a safe place or put up flares to prevent further accidents.
3. Get the names and addresses of any witnesses. Get their license plate numbers if you can't get their names. Also get the names of those in the other car (or cars) involved in the accident.
4. Cooperate with the police.
5. If you think the other driver may have been driving under the influence, insist that you both take a test for alcohol.
6. Write down your recollection of what happened. If you have a camera, take pictures of the scene.
7. Don't sign anything, don't admit guilt, and don't comment on how much insurance you have.
8. Get a copy of the police report and make sure it's accurate.
9. Call your insurance agent as soon as possible.
10. Cooperate with your insurer. Remember, if there is a lawsuit, your insurer will defend you.
11. Keep records of all your expenditures associated with the accident.
12. In the case of a serious accident, meet with a lawyer so that you know what your rights are and what you can do to protect them.

## SUMMARY

There are six standardized packaged policies, each with a different type and level of insurance, available to homeowners and renters. All policies are identified as HO's. Three of them, HO-1, HO-2, and HO-3, are basic, broad policies specifically for homeowners. Policy HO-4 is renter's insurance, HO-6 is for condominium owners, and HO-8 is for older homes. Each of these HO policies is divided into sections that provide property insurance (Section I), and liability coverage (Section II).

Because there are some gaps in coverage, many homeowners purchase supplemental coverage. Some of the more common types of added coverage include personal articles floaters, earthquake protection, flood protection, inflation guard, and replacement cost.

You need enough insurance to cover the replacement of your home in the event of a complete loss. This coverage needs to reflect any changes in increased costs due to changing building codes. As your assets grow in value, it's important that you continuously review your homeowner's coverage to make sure that it reflects these changes.

How do you keep costs down? There are several ways, including taking a high deductible, installing a security system and smoke detector, having multiple policies with the same company, paying premiums annually, not smoking, considering a direct writer, and shopping around.

For your homeowner's insurance to provide effective protection, you must be able to verify your loss by establishing proof of ownership and value of your assets with a detailed asset inventory.

In the event of a loss, you should: report your loss immediately, make temporary repairs to protect your property, make a detailed list of everything lost or damaged, maintain records of the settlement process, and confirm the adjuster's estimate.

With automobile insurance, the various sections of the policy are divided up into "parts." There are two primary areas of automobile protection, which are detailed in the first four parts of your policy. First, there's protection against bodily injury, which includes bodily injury liability coverage (Part A), medical expenses coverage (Part B), and uninsured motorist's protection (Part C). Second, there's protection against property damage, which includes property damage liability coverage (Part A), collision coverage (Part D), and comprehensive physical damage coverage (Part D).

The four major determinants of the cost of automobile insurance are (1) the type of automobile and its use; (2) the drivers and their age, sex, marital status, and driving record characteristics; (3) where the policyholder lives; and (4) the discounts the policyholder qualifies for.

There are several general ways you can keep your automobile insurance rates down while ensuring complete coverage. They include comparison shopping, considering only high-quality insurers, taking advantage of discounts, improving your driving record, raising your deductibles, and keeping adequate liability insurance.

## REVIEW QUESTIONS

1. Describe the differences between the six basic types of standardized homeowner's policies.
2. List and describe the four parts of Section I and the two parts of Section II of a homeowner's insurance policy.
3. List and describe at least five examples of supplemental coverage available as an addition to homeowner's policies.
4. Should homeowners consider purchasing an umbrella policy? Why or why not? What exclusions apply?
5. What is meant by the 80-percent rule as it applies to the purchase of homeowner's insurance to protect the dwelling?
6. Develop a list of guidelines that homeowners should consider when purchasing a homeowner's policy.
7. Describe at least five ways to reduce the cost of homeowner's insurance.
8. Why is establishing proof of ownership a policyholder's responsibility? Describe the methods available.
9. List the steps that a homeowner should take in the event of a loss to make an insurance claim.

10. Describe the four parts of a standardized personal auto policy (PAP).
11. Explain the difference between split-limit auto liability coverage and single-limit liability coverage.
12. What is the difference between collison loss and comprehensive physical damage coverage? What common recommendations apply to the purchase of this coverage?
13. What is the difference between uninsured motorist's coverage and underinsured motorist's coverage?
14. Explain the fundamental concept of no-fault auto insurance. What problems exist with this system? Can you sue for damages?
15. List and describe the different types of auto insurance discounts that are commonly available.
16. Describe the factors that are major determinants of the cost of auto insurance.
17. List and briefly describe the ways a consumer can reduce the cost of auto insurance premiums.
18. Name several broad exclusions that would limit the amount of coverage available in a personal automobile policy.

## PROBLEMS AND ACTIVITIES

1. Jody Solan currently insures her home for 100 percent of its replacement value with an HO-2 policy. For Jody this works out to $140,000 in dwelling (A) coverage. What are the maximum dollar coverage amounts for Parts B, C, and D of her homeowner's policy?
2. Keith and Nancy Diem have personal property coverage with a $250 limit on currency, a $1,000 limit on jewelry, and a $2,500 limit on gold, silver, and pewter. They do not have a personal property floater. If $500 cash, $2,400 of jewelry, and $1,500 of pewterware were stolen from their home, what amount of loss would be covered by their homeowner's policy? If the Diems' deductible is $250, how much will they receive on their claim?

3. How much would a homeowner receive with actual cash-value coverage and replacement cost coverage for a three-year old sofa destroyed by a fire? The sofa would cost $1,000 to replace today, cost $850 three years ago, and has an estimated life of six years.
4. Carmella Estevez has a homeowner's insurance policy with $100,000 of liability insurance. She is concerned about the risk of lawsuits because her property borders a neighborhood park. What can she do to increase her liability coverage? How much will Carmella's yearly premiums change as a result of increasing her liability coverage?
5. Jerry Carter's home is currently valued, on a replacement cost basis, at $170,000. The last time

he checked he noticed that his home was insured for $130,000. If he has a $12,000 claim due to a kitchen fire, how much will his homeowner's insurance policy pay? How much would be paid if his home were totally destroyed? In order to obtain full replacement coverage how much insurance should Jerry carry on his house?

6. Carmen Viers called her insurance agent to learn how to reduce her $700 annual homeowner's insurance premium. The agent suggested increasing her current $250 deductible on her policy to $500. This would result in a 10-percent premium savings. Her agent also indicated that she could increase her deductible to $1,000 with an 18-percent savings, or $2,500 with a 25-percent savings. How much will Carmen save per year in premiums by choosing these new deductibles? Discuss the advantages and disadvantages of increasing her policy deductible.

7. Larry Simmons has split-limit 100/300/50 automobile liability insurance. Several months ago Larry was in an accident in which he was found to be at fault. Four passengers injured in the accident were seriously injured and were awarded $100,000 each because of Larry's negligence. How much of this judgment will Larry's insurance policy cover? What amount will Larry have to pay out of pocket?

8. Bill Buckely has split-limit 25/50/10 auto insurance coverage on his 1999 Subaru. Driving home from work in a snowstorm, he hit a Mercedes, slid into a guardrail, and knocked down a telephone pole. Damage to the Mercedes, the guardrail, and the telephone pole were $8,500, $2,000, and $4,500, respectively. How much will Bill's insurance company pay? How much will Bill be required to pay directly?

9. Jessica Railes is about to buy a condo and is shopping for an HO-6 policy. Her auto insurer quoted her an annual rate of $550. However, if she were to insure both the condo and her car with the same insurance company, the insurer would give her an 8-percent discount on her auto policy. By how much will this reduce Jessica's premium? In addition to the discount, what are other advantages of purchasing both auto and homeowner's insurance with the same company?

10. The Superior Insurance Company of Maine recently advertised the following discounts for qualified drivers:

   ▪ 10-percent discount to drivers who have not had an accident in the past 7 years.
   ▪ 15-percent discount for those with two or more cars.
   ▪ 10-percent discount for those who drive less than 10,000 miles a year.
   ▪ 5-percent discount for those who insure both their residence and car together.
   ▪ 20-percent discount if driver is a good student (student with a B average).
   ▪ 10-percent discount for someone aged 50 or older.
   ▪ 5-percent discount for someone aged 24 to 49.
   ▪ 5-percent discount for someone who has taken a defensive driving course.
   ▪ 10-percent discount for noncommuters.
   ▪ 5-percent discount for cars with antitheft devices.

   Jana, 25 years old, currently pays $1,200 for a PAP a year for her 2001 Buick Regal. She uses her car to commute roundtrip to and from work and her biannual cross-country trips to visit relatives. Last year she received a speeding ticket but took a defensive driving course in order to remove the ticket from her record; she has never had an accident. When she purchased her car she had an alarm installed. Jana is sure that she qualifies for at least one or more discounts. Calculate her new premium if she transfers to the Superior Insurance Company.

## SUGGESTED PROJECTS

1. Search the Internet for insurance-related Web sites, such as the following:

   ▪ Insurance News Network: **www.insure.com**
   ▪ A. M. Best: **www.ambest.com**

   Choose an insurance topic from one or more sites and prepare a one-page summary of the information provided and your review of the Internet site.

2. Prepare a detailed inventory of your personal property. Take photographs or make a videotape to provide additional evidence of property ownership. List the brand, model number, and serial number of valuable items such as appliances, stereo equipment, and computers.

3. Interview an insurance agent about the differences in cost on a homeowner's or auto insurance policy based on changes in the amount of the deductible that is selected. Write a one-page report of your findings.

4. Interview 25 to 30 persons and ask the following questions:

   ▪ What are your liability split-coverage auto insurance limits?

   ▪ If you own your own home, do you have an all-risk or covered perils coverage on the structure?

   ▪ If you own your own home, do you have replacement cost or actual cash-value coverage on the contents?

   ▪ If you are a renter, do you have a renter's insurance policy?

   ▪ Do you have an umbrella policy?

   Report the findings from your interviews. Did you find that the majority of respondents knew a little or a great deal about their current insurance coverages? Did many of the renters whom you interviewed have insurance? Why or why not? How many respondents knew what an umbrella policy was? Based on your interviews, what conclusions can you draw about the public's level of insurance knowledge?

5. Pick three different types of cars and compare the premiums (by interviewing an agent, visiting a Web site, or calling a toll-free information line) for a given amount of coverage (e.g., 100/300/50) for each vehicle, holding other factors such as driver, location, and annual mileage constant. Write a one-page report of your findings.

6. Compare the rates for a given amount of auto insurance (by interviewing an agent, visiting a Web site, or calling a toll-free information line) for:

   a. an unmarried male and an unmarried female of the same age

   b. a driver under age 25 and a driver over 25

   c. a city dweller and a driver living in a suburban/rural area

   d. a married driver and an unmarried driver of the same age

7. Obtain two or three quotes on the costs of renter's insurance in your area. Report on the price differences among different insurance carriers and differences in coverages. Also obtain price quotes for insuring both a car and a rental with the same insurance company. Describe any pricing differences that you might have found.

8. Interview a property and casualty insurance agent to find out what type of homeowner's and auto insurance policies are most commonly purchased in your area and which policy features are most often recommended to clients. Why do you think coverages and recommendations might be different in your area of the country versus other areas?

# Discussion Case 1

Graham and Eustacia Leyland are planning to buy a $185,000 home. The home is located three miles from a river that occasionally overflows its banks after a heavy rain. They estimate that their personal property is worth $75,000 but they really aren't sure. This includes the office and computer equipment that Eustacia uses as a freelance writer and a $5,000 coin collection inherited from Graham's father. The Leylands' net worth, including their current $120,000 home, is $400,000. The Leylands asked their insurance agent to find them the best coverage, taking advantage of all possible cost-saving measures. They do not want a lot of out-of-pocket expenses if their home or personal property is destroyed and they want their insurance to keep pace with increasing building costs.

## Questions

1. What type of homeowner's insurance policy is best for the Leylands?

2. What is the minimum amount of coverage that the Leylands should purchase on their new home? What risks do they face if they purchase only the minimum required coverage? How much insurance should they purchase in order to reduce their financial risks?

3. Should the Leylands buy flood insurance? How do they go about purchasing it?

4. In addition to supplemental flood insurance, what other coverages would you recommend that the Leylands purchase? Document your recommendations both in terms of protection offered and the cost of coverage.

5. Should the Leylands consider purchasing an umbrella policy? Why or why not?

6. What other advice would you give to the Leylands regarding their homeowner's insurance?

*Tips from Marcy Furney, ChFC, Certified Financial Planner™*

# Money Matters

## GOTCHA COVERED

*Adopt the mind-set that insurance* is to protect you from the major losses, it isn't a maintenance plan. Understand that the basis of insurance is pooling of risk. If all policyholders pay $100, and all make a $5,000 claim, the system won't work. Fraudulent and frivolous claims result in costs going up for everyone.

*If you must lower the bill for auto or home insurance,* consider increasing the deductible, not decreasing the amount of coverage. Also, make sure you're taking advantage of any discounts.

*Keep the deductible on property* insurance high enough to help avoid the temptation to file claims for small losses. A history of multiple claims may result in your policy being canceled or your coverage being moved to a higher-risk, higher-cost company. Claims experience may also prevent you from shopping around for lower rates.

*Check with your insurance* company regarding requirements to insure valuables such as furs, jewelry, antiques, or collections. Most require fairly recent appraisals (2 years old or less). Appraisals can be expensive, so do it right the first time. Don't assume that all items you own are fully covered by your homeowner's or renter's policy.

*Don't be lulled into a sense of security* with the basic limits on your auto and home policies.

Protect your assets with a personal umbrella policy, which increases your coverage to a million dollars or more.

*If you're a professional,* be sure to obtain liability insurance to cover your particular activities. Doctors are not the only practitioners subject to malpractice claims.

*When obtaining car insurance,* disclose all information regarding the use of your auto. If you drive your vehicle in the course of doing business, you may need business-class coverage on your personal auto policy or a special commercial policy. Driving under the wrong class of coverage could subject you to denial of any claims.

*Many discounts are governed by the type of car you drive,* how many cars you have, your age, or features of your home. In the states that allow defensive-driving course discounts without age restrictions, almost anyone can get a 5- to 10-percent reduction on many parts of a policy. Normally the discount will not apply to Parts C or D. One course can qualify you for up to 3 years of rate reduction and would probably pay for itself in 6 months to 1 year. Some states will allow you to take defensive driving for the insurance discount and then take it again in the same year to remove a ticket from your driving record.

# Discussion Case 2

Bronwyn Lipper recently graduated from college with a degree in biochemistry. She has a promising career ahead of her. Already her employer has offered to pay for graduate school, and in the past two years she has been promoted three times. Two years ago she purchased a townhouse for $130,000; today, her townhouse is valued at over $160,000. Last year Bronwyn purchased a new Chevy Suburban 4 × 4. She loves the feeling of power that she gets and the safety such a big SUV gives her on her 45-mile round-trip commute. Over all, Bronwyn feels economically secure. When she last checked, she had over $35,000 in savings and a growing retirement account. On her drive home from work last night she heard a report on the radio of a person who lost everything when he caused an auto accident and found out that he was

underinsured. Bronwyn certainly does not want this to happen to her. Help her think through the following questions and issues.

## Questions

1. After reviewing her personal automobile policy, Bronwyn noted that she had $40,000 in Part A coverage, $15,000 in Part B coverage, $40,000 in Part C coverage, and full Part D coverage. Is Bronwyn adequately insured? Explain your answer.

2. Bronwyn was quoted $1,400 a year for a split-coverage policy with the following limits: $50,000/$100,000/ $25,000, assuming a $100 deductible. Are these limits sufficiently high given Bronwyn's financial situation and

potential liability? What would you recommend as a minimum split-coverage limit? What will be the impact of your recommendation on her policy premium?

3. If she decides not to boost her liability limits, how will others be compensated for their losses if she is involved in a serious accident and found liable for expenses that exceed her policy limits?

4. Should Bronwyn maintain her Part D, Collision and Comprehensive, coverage? When should she consider reducing or canceling this part of her PAP?

5. The insurance company that quoted her a split-coverage policy also indicated that she could choose a $50, $100, $250, $500, or $1,000 deductible. If Bronwyn wants to reduce her premium costs what deductible should she choose? Why?

6. Should Bronwyn purchase uninsured motorist's coverage? Why or why not?

7. What type of discounts might be available for Bronwyn that will help reduce her annual insurance premium?

8. She has heard something about an umbrella policy but is unsure if it is appropriate in her case. Would you recommend that she purchase such a policy? Explain your answer. Approximately how much will such a policy cost, assuming that she insures her townhouse and car with the same insurance company?

9. If Bronwyn were to get in an accident in her daily commute, why should she never admit guilt, sign anything, or comment on how much insurance she has?

 Visit our Web site for additional case problems, interactive exercises, and practice quizzes for this chapter—**www.prenhall.com/keown**.

# CONTINUING CASE: Cory and Tisha Dumont

Cory and Tisha read a recent newspaper article that stated that personal bankruptcy and other financial problems often result from uninsured losses. This made them curious about their own insurance coverage. Cory and Tisha have come back to you for assistance in reviewing their insurance coverage. Because they want to buy their home very soon, they also are interested in homeowner's insurance. They compiled the following information for you to review.

## Life Insurance

|  | Cory | Tisha |
|---|---|---|
| Group life insurance | 2 times gross income | 1.50 times gross income |
| Whole life insurance | none | $50,000 |
| Cash value |  | $1,800 |
| Annual life insurance premiums | $0; employer paid | $0 for employer provided $720 for whole life (due next month) |
| Beneficiary | Tisha | Cory |
| Contingent beneficiary | Tisha's parents | Tisha's parents |

## Health Insurance

Tisha's employer provides a comprehensive major medical insurance policy that covers all members of the Dumont family to a lifetime cap of $1,000,000. The policy provides an 80/20-coinsurance provision with a $3,000 stop-loss provision. The Dumonts are subject to a $300 annual family deductible. Tisha's employer deducts a monthly premium of $239 per month; her employer pays the remainder of the premium. Because Tisha's company offered the better coverage, Cory chose to "opt out" of his coverage and receives a monthly "opt out fee" of $85 per month.

## Automobile Insurance (Both Cars)

| Type | Personal auto policy |
|---|---|
| Coverages | 25/50/25 split limit liability |
| Uninsured motorist | 25/50/25 split limit liability |
| Medical expense coverage | $20,000 |
| Collision | $200 deductible |
| Comprehensive | $200 deductible |
| Annual premium car 1 | $1,150 |
| Annual premium car 2 | $950 |
| Annual premium total | $2,100 |

## Umbrella Liability Insurance

None

## Disability Insurance

Tisha: $2,000 per month up to 6 months; premium paid by employer

Cory: None

## Homeowner's/Renter's Insurance

HO-4 renter's insurance policy with $25,000 of actual cash value coverage on personal property with an annual premium of $150.

## Questions

1. After reviewing the earnings multiple approach and the needs approach, Cory and Tisha opt for the simpler earnings multiple approach to estimate their life insurance needs. Explains Cory, "there are just too many unknowns in that needs approach formula. Years of income to be replaced I can understand. If I die tomorrow, I want to know that Tisha can buy a home and the kids can finish college. Chad is four and Haley is two. With 20 years of my income, they should be able to do that." Tisha agrees, although she cautions that before purchasing insurance she would like to confirm their estimates by completing the needs formula. They agree that they could earn a 5-percent after-tax, after-inflation return on the insurance benefit. Do Tisha and Cory have adequate life insurance? If not, how much should each consider purchasing? (Hint: Remember that expenses drop by 22 percent for a surviving family of three. Be sure to consult Table 9.2, "Earnings Multiples for Life Insurance.")

2. All of Cory's life insurance and half of Tisha's is provided through their employers. Is this a good idea?

3. Cory's been on the Web again, this time to read about universal life and variable life insurance. He has asked your opinion about purchasing one of these policies to provide additional insurance coverage for his family. What would you advise him to do? Defend your answer.

4. The Dumonts have asked you to review their life insurance policies and explain them "in plain English." What life insurance policy features would you look for?

5. An insurance agent recently suggested purchasing whole life policies for Chad and Haley. Costs would be cheap and Cory and Tisha could rest assured that the kids would always be insurable. Is this a good idea? Defend your answer.

6. Do Tisha and Cory have adequate health insurance? If not, what improvements would you suggest and why?

7. Assume Tisha is injured in a car accident and incurs $5,000 of medical bills. What are the options for paying this bill? How would your answer change if the $5,000 bill resulted from an emergency appendectomy? Assuming that no one else in her family has made a claim this year, how much of the bill would her insurance company pay?

8. Next month is the "annual open enrollment period" for health insurance benefits through Tisha's employer. It is the only time of the year when she can make changes to her policy. Tisha is considering switching to a different HMO or PPO plan. What are the advantages and disadvantages of each form of managed care?

9. Tisha is concerned about a possible layoff due to mergers among several accounting firms. What are some health insurance options available to the Dumonts if Tisha voluntarily leaves her job or is "downsized"? What are the advantages and disadvantages of Cory "opting out" in this situation?

10. Both Tisha and Cory are considering the purchase of disability insurance because Cory has none and Tisha's employer-provided policy is very short term. What policy features would you recommend they include?

11. Do Tisha and Cory have adequate renter's insurance? What recommendation would you make? Why?

12. Evaluate the Dumonts' auto insurance. What recommendations for changes, if any, would you make? Why?

13. How much would the Dumonts' policy pay if Cory or Tisha were at fault for an accident that resulted in $65,000 of bodily injury losses? How would the claim be paid?

14. What policy options could the Dumonts select to reduce the cost of their property and liability insurance?

15. What type of homeowner's policy should the Dumonts select when they purchase their first home? Should they consider adding an umbrella policy at this time? Explain your answer.

# 11 Investment Basics

## Learning Objectives

1. **Set** your goals and be ready to invest.

2. **Understand** how taxes affect your investments.

3. **Calculate** interest rates and real rates of return.

4. **Manage** risk in your investments.

5. **Allocate** your assets in the manner that is best for you.

A few years ago, Ki-Jana Carter didn't know anything about investing. How could he? Money had been tight in the two-bedroom apartment where he'd been raised outside of Columbus, Ohio. Carter's father had left when young Ki-Jana was just a baby, and his mom had to work 12- to 15-hour days just to make ends meet. Ki-Jana Carter didn't know about investing. He knew about football.

In 1995, Carter, a running back out of Penn State, became the first pick in the NFL draft. It was a dream come true for the 22-year-old—a career playing in the pros. During the preseason, Carter's mind wasn't on money or investments. It was on learning the playbook for the Cincinnati Bengals, his new team. However, a season-ending knee injury in his first preseason game served to teach him a more important lesson, one that many NFL players don't learn until too late: An NFL career—and the pay that comes with it—can vanish in an instant.

When Carter signed with the Bengals, he received a $19.2-million, 7-year contract, which included a $7.125-million signing bonus. Needless to say, he thought that the days of money being tight and living in a two-bedroom apartment were over. "I came out of college and felt invincible," says Carter. "After the injury it was like, 'Wow, I may not be making more money.'"

Worried that he really might not make any more money, Carter decided to protect the money he already had. To help him handle his money, he interviewed 14 different financial planners and chose Mark Griege, a fee-only planner who was paid a percentage of Carter's investments. Griege and Carter agreed it was time for Carter to learn about investing, so part of Griege's job was teaching Carter about investing. In other words, Griege not only told Carter what to do with his money, but also told him why.

Carter's investing goal is not only to protect his wealth and make money, but to understand investing from a commonsense perspective. "I see a lot of guys come into the league and want to go out and spend to show they have a lot of money," says Carter. "That's good now, but I'm trying to live like this when I'm 50, 60, 70." His new understanding of investing will allow him to achieve his financial goals.

An understanding of investing basics can go a long way toward helping you reach your financial goals, too. For example, understanding why interest rates fluctuate can mean the difference between getting in on an investment at the right time to make a nice profit and getting in at the wrong time to take a loss. A wise investment may wind up providing you with that down payment on a house or new car.

Not only will an understanding of investments help you achieve your goals, but it will also keep you from losing a bundle. Let's face it, the world of investing is littered with debt notices and red ink from all the people who went in unprepared and lost their shirts, and the rest of their clothes, in a bad investment.

Principle

**9** The Best
Protection Is
Knowledge

Set your goals
**1** and be ready to
invest.

Understanding investments means understanding how to get around the challenges while grabbing as many rewards as you can. Remember **Principle 9: The Best Protection Is Knowledge**—understanding the basics and logic of investing will protect you from potential pitfalls. It's worked for Carter and it can work for you. In 1999, after two major knee injuries and a broken wrist over five seasons with the Bengals, the oft-wounded Carter was cut in a salary cap move. After sitting out the 2000 season, he signed a one-year deal for the minimum base salary of $477,000 with the Redskins. And in 2001 Carter had his best year in the pros averaging 4.9 yards per carry and finally breaking over the 1,000 yards gained mark for his career. Thus, as of the 2002 season his football career is finally looking up, but it is far from certain. Fortunately, his financial future is set.

## Before You Invest

In personal financial planning, everything begins and ends with your goals, and investments are no exception. Before investing you must first decide what your goals are and how much you can set aside to meet those goals. Then you can develop an investment plan.

### Investing Versus Speculating

This chapter's about investing, not about speculating. What's the difference? Well, both involve risk. When you buy an **investment**, you put your money in an asset that *generates* a return. That is, part of its return comes in the form of an **income return**. Real estate pays rent, stocks pay dividends, and bonds pay interest. Even if the stock (such as Microsoft) or bond isn't paying interest now, it will sometime—so buying these assets is considered investing. It's the return that the asset generates now and will generate in the future that determines its value.

Some assets don't generate a return. Gold coins and baseball cards, for example, are worth more in the future only if someone is willing to pay more for them. Their value depends *entirely* on supply and demand. As a result, an asset of this type is considered **speculation**. Other examples of speculation include comic books, autographs, nonincome-producing real estate, and gems.

You can make a pretty penny speculating. The first issue of the X-Men appeared in September 1963 and cost 12¢. About 39 years later it was worth $6,400—that's an appreciation rate of over 32 percent per year. Why has it grown so in value? Supply and demand—someone's willing to pay $6,400 for it, so that's its value. It could have just as easily gone down and be worth nothing today.

That's the case with many baseball cards, "collector's POGs," and Pokemon cards purchased in the early 1990s. As the baseball card market crashed in those years, speculators who'd put their entire savings into this market after the spectacular increases in the value of cards during the 1970s and 1980s took heavy losses. Why did the value of these cards drop so? No one wanted to buy them.

People have speculated for centuries. In fact, in the sixteenth century, it was tulip bulbs. Shortly before the tulip bulb market crashed, one recorded trade had a single bulb being exchanged for the following: 17 bushels of wheat, 34 bushels of rye, 4 fat oxen, 8 fat swine, 12 fat sheep, 2 goat's-heads of wine, 4 kegs of beer, 2 tons of butter, 1,000 pounds of cheese, a complete bed, a suit of clothes, and a silver drinking cup!

**Investment**
An asset that generates a return. For example, stocks pay dividends and bonds pay interest, so they're considered investments.

**Income Return**
Investment return received directly from the company or organization in which you've invested, usually in the form of dividends or interest payments.

**Speculation**
An asset whose value depends solely on supply and demand, as opposed to being based on the return that it generates. For example, gold coins and baseball cards are worth more in the future only if someone is willing to pay more for them.

Today's new variation of speculative securities is derivatives. **Derivative securities** are those whose value is derived from the value of other assets. These securities are extremely risky and, for the beginning investor, should be considered speculative in nature. They allow you to invest with a small amount of cash in such commodities as gold, orange juice futures, and stock indices. Granted, they have appeal to those with nerves of steel and to those who don't realize the risks they're taking. However, they're extremely dangerous. In effect, you're betting on short-term movements in these underlying assets. In short, they're not something to rely on to achieve your financial goals.

With *investing*, as opposed to speculating, the value of an asset is determined by what return it earns, not merely by whether that asset is fashionable to own. In other words, investments have intrinsic value because they produce income, and although in the short term their price may wander a bit from their intrinsic value, in the long run the price approaches the intrinsic value. Investments are less risky, and their value is simply an extension of how much income they're producing now along with what they're expected to produce in the future. Certainly, investment is quite a bit duller than speculation, but when you're dealing with your financial security, dull and certain aren't bad things.

**STOP & THINK** If an asset doesn't generate a return, its value is determined by supply and demand. Putting money in it is speculating. Gold is a good example. Although financial gurus periodically proclaim gold as "the place for your savings," it's simply a form of speculation. In 1977 gold began to rise, going from under $200 per ounce to more than $850 per ounce by early 1980. Since 1980, gold has dropped in value to about $280 per ounce in early 2002. Stocks, conversely, increased at an average annual rate of 15.0 percent from 1980 through 2001. The bottom line is **invest,** don't speculate.

## Setting Investment Goals

You probably have goals or at least dreams—perhaps you'd like to buy a house, or maybe you'd like to retire early—but to reach those goals, you've got to formalize them. That's the point of **Principle 8: Nothing Happens Without a Plan**. That means you've got to (1) write your goals down and prioritize them, (2) attach costs to them, (3) figure out when the money for those goals will be needed, and (4) periodically reevaluate your goals. Fortunately, it's not that difficult, but if you never set goals, you'll never reach them.

Principle **8** Nothing Happens Without a Plan

In setting your goals it's important to be as specific as possible. Start with what you're saving for, then add in the cost and when you want to reach that goal. For example, rather than list "saving money" as a goal, state the purpose of your efforts, such as buying a car, and exactly how much you want saved by what time.

As we said in Chapter 1, in formalizing your goals it's easiest to think about them in terms of short-term, intermediate-term, and long-term time horizons. Short-term goals are any financial goals that can be accomplished within a 1-year period, such as buying a television or taking a vacation. An intermediate-term goal is one that would take between 1 and 10 years to accomplish—perhaps paying for college for an older child or accumulating enough money for a down payment on a new house. A long-term goal is one for which it takes more than 10 years to accumulate the money— retirement, for example.

In setting these goals, the key is to be realistic, which means your goals should reflect your financial and life situation. The following questions might help you focus in on what goals are important to you:

- If I don't accomplish this goal, what are the consequences?
- Am I willing to make the financial sacrifices necessary to meet this goal?
- How much money do I need to accomplish this goal?
- When do I need this money?

If you don't formally set goals, you never have to think about what's going to happen 10, 20, or 30 years from now. You also don't have any control over what will happen in the future. Once you've set your goals, you then have to use your time value of money skills to translate them into action. For example, if you'd like to retire in 40 years with $500,000 and you believe you can earn 8 percent on your investments, you'd need to invest $1,930.11 at the end of each year.

$$FV = PMT(PVIFA)$$
$$\$500{,}000 = PMT(259.052)$$
$$\$1{,}930.11 = PMT$$

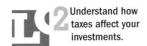

Understand how taxes affect your investments.

## Fitting Taxes into Investing

When we compare investment returns we want to make our comparison on an after-tax basis—that is, what we pay to Uncle Sam doesn't count. As we examine the different investment alternatives we'll look more closely at taxes, but several points hold true regardless of what we invest in.

WORKSHEET

- You should keep in mind that the tax rate you're concerned with is your marginal tax rate, because that's the rate you pay on the next dollar of earnings.
- Tax-free investment alternatives should be compared only on an after-tax basis. Of course, the higher your marginal tax bracket, the more attractive tax-free investments become.
- You can make investments on a *tax-deferred* basis, which means that not only does your investment grow free of taxes, but the money you invest isn't taxed until you liquidate your investment.
- When it comes to taxes, capital gains are better than income return. Recall from Chapter 4 that under the Taxpayers Relief Act of 1997, the maximum tax rate paid on long-term capital gains dropped from 28 to 20 percent, for those in the 15-percent tax bracket, it dropped to 10 percent. In addition, in 2001, these rates dropped to 18 and 8 percent on long-term capital gains on assets purchased beginning in the year 2001 and held for at least 5 years.

If you were in the 39.6-percent marginal tax bracket and had $50,000 of additional ordinary income, your tax bill would come to ($50,000 × 36.9%) = $18,450. If this $50,000 of additional income came in the form of long-term capital gains, your taxes would be only ($50,000 × 20%) = $10,000. Just as valuable as the tax break on capital gains income is the fact that you don't have to claim it—and, therefore, pay taxes on it—until you sell the asset. That is, you can time when you want to claim your capital gains.

Taxes make some investments better than they would otherwise be and others worse—it all gets back to **Principle 6: Taxes Bias Personal Finance Decisions**.

Principle

Taxes Bias Personal Finance Decisions

## Financial Reality Check

Before you put your investment program into place, you should make sure you have a grip on your financial affairs. We're talking about such things as making sure you're living within your means, have adequate insurance, keep emergency funds—in effect, making sure your financial house is in order.

**Balance Your Budget** If you don't live within your means, you'll never be able to save, invest, or achieve any of your financial goals—it's that simple! Control is crucial. It means keeping your credit card under control, using restraint, and commonsense buying. It means acting your wage.

If these are problems for you, consider trying the envelope system introduced in Chapter 2. Under that system, you begin each month with the dollar amount allocated to each major expenditure category put into a separate envelope. Each time you spend in that area, you simply take the money out of the envelope. When the envelope is empty, you're done spending in that area.

**Put a Safety Net in Place**   Insurance seems awfully dull until you need it, but there's no question, you need it. The need for insurance rises from **Principle 10: Protect Yourself Against Major Catastrophes**. The key concepts here are *planning* and *control*. After all, this whole book, and all of personal finance, is based on controlling your financial situation through careful planning. Insurance provides you with some degree of control over the unexpected. Your insurance coverage—life, property and liability, and medical—should be in place before you begin an investment program.

Principle **10** Protect Yourself Against Major Catastrophes

**Maintain Adequate Emergency Funds**   It doesn't take much experience with a budget to realize that no budget is set in stone. As **Principle 7** says, **Stuff Happens**. You never know when your car will have an unexpected meeting with a tree—you may walk away unharmed, but without some emergency funds, walking may be your only means of transportation for quite some time. How about being a victim of downsizing or getting hit with a big medical bill? It can happen to anyone.

Principle **7** Stuff Happens

Your emergency funds should be immediately available to you. Most financial planners recommend that you set aside an equivalent of 3 to 6 months' take-home pay. However, exactly what you need depends on whether you have access to other sources of emergency cash—for example, credit cards or lines of credit.

Saving up an emergency reserve can be painfully dull, especially if you see the stock market climbing or would like to buy a new car. If you don't have liquid funds to cover the unexpected, you might have to compromise your long-term investments. Such actions might ruin your plans and cause you to miss opportunities.

Principle **2** The Time Value of Money

## Starting Your Investment Program

There's no easy way to start an investment program. In fact, the first step—making the commitment to get started—may be the most difficult. The longer you postpone investing, though, the longer you do without the help of your biggest investment ally—*time*. See **Principle 2: The Time Value of Money**: The sooner you invest, the more you earn. As you should know by now, there's no substitute for time when it comes to investments—the earlier you begin planning for the future, the easier it is to achieve your goals. That's why **Principle 15: Just Do It!** is so important. Regardless of your level of income, you can make room for investing.

Principle **15** Just Do It!

How do you go about starting an investment program? The first step is to revisit the first two questions you asked when setting up your goals: If I don't accomplish this goal, what are the conse-

> **STOP & THINK**   You can reach your financial goals! In fact, if you have time on your side, it may be easier to reach them than you think. A small change in your spending and investment habits could produce big returns later on. For example, if you're 20 now and you save $15 per month—that works out to about 50 cents per day—at 12 percent, 50 years later your savings will have grown to over $585,000. The key is to start early.

quences? and Am I willing to make the financial sacrifices necessary to meet this goal? Once you have the commitment, the next step is to come up with the money.

**Principle 13** Pay Yourself First

**Pay Yourself First** This concept is so important that it became one of the axioms we introduced in Chapter 1—**Principle 13: Pay Yourself First**. That is, you first set aside your savings, and what's left becomes the amount you can spend.

When you pay yourself first, you're acknowledging the fact that your long-term goals are paramount. In effect, paying yourself first sets up a behavior pattern in which saving for long-term goals becomes automatic, and excuses for why this month's savings can be passed up no longer work.

**Make Investing Automatic** The most important step is the first one, making a start, even if it's only $50 a month. When you can increase your monthly investments, do it—and make it automatic. If your employer allows automatic withholding, take advantage of it. Your employer will automatically withhold money, which you can then direct to a bank, savings and loan, or credit union for investing. You can also have an amount automatically deducted from your checking account and sent to a brokerage firm or mutual fund.

**Take Advantage of Uncle Sam and Your Employer** If your employer offers matching investments, don't pass them by. Matching investments are about as close to something for nothing as you'll ever get. Also, keep an eye out for investments that are tax favored, such as traditional IRAs and Roth IRAs.

**Windfalls** Once in a while you're going to receive a bit of a windfall—perhaps an inheritance, a salary bonus, a gift, a tax refund, or maybe even something from the lottery. Don't fritter away this windfall: Invest some or all of it. It's a painless way of building up your investments.

**Make Two Months a Year Investment Months** Some financial advisors suggest that if you're having trouble starting your investment program, pick 2 months per year to cut back on your spending and make those your investment months. If you know that your "life of poverty" is over at the end of the month, it may be easier to stick to your savings.

## Investment Choices

Today there are more investment alternatives than ever. As a result, deciding on the right investment seems so bewildering that some people give up responsibility and blindly pass that duty on to an advisor. That doesn't mean the help of a financial advisor isn't right for some people. But just like Ki-Jana Carter, you should understand what you're doing with your money.

Fortunately, investments aren't as confusing as they seem from the outside. Actually, there are only two basic categories of investments:

- **Lending investments.** Savings accounts and bonds, which are debt instruments issued by corporations and by the government, are examples of lending investments.
- **Ownership investments.** Preferred stocks and common stocks, which represent an ownership position in a corporation, along with income-producing real estate, are examples of ownership investments.

Let's take a closer look.

**Lending Investments** Whenever you put money in a savings account or buy a bond, you're actually lending someone your money. The amount you've lent them is your investment. A savings account pays you interest on the balance you hold in your account. With a bond, your return is generally fixed and known ahead of time. It has a set **maturity date**, at which time the bond is terminated and the investor is returned the money that has been lent. The face value of the bond, which is the amount you receive when the bond matures, is referred to as the **par value** or **principal**.

Most bonds issued by corporations trade in units of $1,000, although bonds issued by federal, state, or local governments may trade in units of $5,000 or $10,000. Over the life of the bond, you receive semiannual interest payments, which are set when the bond is issued. The **coupon interest rate** refers to the actual rate of interest the bond pays. Most bonds have fixed interest rates, but some have variable or floating rates, meaning that the interest rate changes periodically to reflect current interest rates.[1]

Let's assume, for example, that you've bought a 20-year bond issued by the government, with a par value of $1,000 and an interest rate of 8 percent. You'll receive $80 per year in interest payments (0.08 × $1,000). Then, at maturity, which in this case is in 20 years, you'll be returned the par value, which is $1,000.

With lending investments, you usually know ahead of time exactly what your return will be, which isn't always a good thing. For example, because you've locked in an 8-percent return on your bond, if inflation suddenly climbs to 16 percent, your return won't even keep up with inflation. However, if inflation drops, your 8 percent may look even better than it did when you purchased the bond.

The biggest potential problem with lending investments arises when the lender experiences financial difficulties and can't pay the interest on the bond, or can't pay off the bond at maturity. If the firm that issued the bond goes bankrupt, the bondholders most likely lose their entire investment. Unfortunately, even though lending investments let you share a lender's financial pain, they don't let you share any of the pleasure. If the lender suddenly makes a ton of money, you don't.

With lending investments, the best-case scenario is that the issuer pays you all the interest that's owed and at maturity gives you back your principal. Actually, this best-case scenario is much better than it at first seems. If you carefully choose whom you lend money to, whose bonds you buy, or where you open a savings account, there can be much less risk with lending investments than with ownership investments. In addition, the returns can be quite respectable.

**Ownership Investments**   The two major forms of ownership investment are real estate and stocks. Real estate investments include such things as rental apartments and investments in income-producing property, such as shopping malls and office buildings. In each case, you're investing in something that generates a return: rent. Your home could also be considered a real estate investment. In a sense it generates income because it eliminates rent payments that you would otherwise have to make.

The major disadvantage of real estate investments is that they tend to be quite illiquid. That is, when it comes time to sell off your investment, you may have a hard time getting a fair price for it or even finding someone interested in buying it.

The most popular ownership investment is stocks, but the actual "ownership" isn't of an asset you can hold in your hand or live in. When you purchase 50 shares of General Electric **stock**, you've purchased a small portion of the General Electric Corporation. Although you own only a tiny fraction of GE, buying stock does make you an owner or equity holder, with "equity" being another term for ownership.

**Maturity Date**
The date at which the borrower must repay the loan or borrowed funds.

**Par Value or Principal**
The stated amount on the face of a bond, which the firm is to repay at the maturity date.

**Coupon Interest Rate**
The interest to be paid annually on a bond as a percentage of par value, which is specified in the contractual agreement.

**Stock**
A fractional ownership in a corporation.

---

[1]Zero-coupon bonds make no interest payments to the bondholder. We talk about these in Chapter 14.

**Dividend**
A payment by a corporation to its shareholders.

What do you get as an owner of GE? Don't count on any free lightbulbs. In the case of common stock ownership, you get a chance to vote for the board of directors, which oversees GE's operations. If GE earns a profit, you'll most likely receive a portion of those profits in the form of **dividends**, which are generally paid out quarterly.

As profits and dividends continue to increase, investors see the stock as more valuable and are willing to pay more to purchase it. Thus, the price goes up. There's no limit as to how high a stock's price can rise. Look at 1995 through 1999 when the average U.S. stock went up by over 37 percent, 23 percent, 33 percent, 28 percent, 21 percent, and 20 percent, respectively. Then, in 2000 and 2001, stock prices went down by 9 percent and 13 percent, respectively. One winner in 2001 was Network Associates, the antivirus software maker. Its stock went up 517 percent. Stock prices can also fall, and the fall can be huge. For example, on the downside in 2001, Enron went from something to almost nothing—taking many investors with it—as its stock price dropped by over 99 percent.

In the case of preferred stock, the dividend is generally fixed, with the preferred stockholder receiving a constant annual dividend as long as the firm has the cash to pay. You get a chance to vote for the board of directors if you own GE preferred stock, unless GE has suffered some financial problems and omitted some preferred stock dividends.

Of course, companies must pay the interest to debt holders before they can distribute dividends to stockholders. Thus, if debt, such as bonds, eat up a company's profits, stockholders get no dividends. Moreover, preferred stockholders take a "preferred" position to common stockholders—that is, they receive their dividends first. Common stockholders receive their dividends from whatever's left over.

## The Returns from Investing

**Capital Gain or Loss**
The gain (or loss) on the sale of a capital asset. For example, any return (or loss) from the appreciation (or drop in value) in value of a share of stock would be considered a capital gain (or loss).

When you invest your money, you can receive your return in one of two ways. First, an investment can go up or down in value—in the language of investments, this is referred to as a **capital gain** or **loss**. Although most people associate capital gains and losses with real estate and common stock, these gains and losses also come with bonds. In fact, most of the time when you buy a bond, you buy it for something other than its par value. That means if you hold it to maturity, you'll experience some capital gains or losses.

The second component of the return on your investment is the income return. Income return consists of any payments you receive directly from the company or organization in which you've invested. In the case of bonds, your income return is the interest you receive. In the case of common and preferred stocks, your income return comes in the form of dividends. The rate of return can be calculated as follows:

$$\text{rate of return} = \frac{(\text{ending value} - \text{beginning value}) + \text{income return}}{\text{beginning value}}$$

Thus, if a stock climbs from $45 to $55 per share over 1 year while paying $3 in dividends, its rate of return over that year would be

$$\text{rate of return} = \frac{(\$55 - \$45) + \$3}{\$45} = \frac{\$10 + \$3}{\$45} = \frac{\$13}{\$45} = 28.89\%$$

If you're calculating the rate of return over a number of years, you may want to break this down into the annual rate of return. You need only multiply the rate of return by $1/N$, where $N$ is the number of years for which the investment is held. Thus, the annualized rate of return can be calculated as follows:

$$\text{annualized rate of return} = \frac{(\text{ending value} - \text{beginning value}) + \text{income return}}{\text{beginning value}} \times \frac{1}{N}$$

If over a 3-year period a stock climbs from \$45 to \$68 per share and pays a total of \$7 in dividends, its annualized rate of return would be

$$\text{annualized rate of return} = \frac{(\$68 - \$45) + \$7}{\$45} \times \frac{1}{3} = \frac{\$23 + \$7}{\$45} \times \frac{1}{3} =$$

$$= \frac{\$30}{\$45} \times \frac{1}{3} = 0.667 \times 0.333 = 0.222, \text{ or } 22.2\%$$

## A Brief Introduction to Market Interest Rates

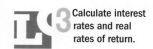

Calculate interest rates and real rates of return.

Interest rates play an extremely important role in determining the value of a share of stock, a bond, or a real estate investment. Interest rates also determine what we earn on savings and are closely tied to the rate of inflation. Therefore, you need to understand interest rates—how they're determined and what affects them—before making any investments. Let's start off by taking a look at what a real interest rate is.

### Nominal and Real Rates of Return

The **nominal** (or **quoted**) **rate of return** is the rate of return earned on an investment without any adjustment for inflation. It's the rate that's quoted in the *Wall Street Journal* for specific bonds or the rate your bank advertises for its savings accounts, and it determines how much interest you earn when you lend money to someone. How much have you *really* earned? The **real rate of return**, which is simply the nominal rate of return minus the inflation rate, tells you how much you've really earned after adjusting for inflation. If you earn 12 percent on an investment while the inflation rate is 4 percent, the nominal rate of return is 12 percent, and the real rate of return is 8 percent (12% − 4%).

**Nominal (or Quoted) Rate of Return**
The rate of return earned on an investment, unadjusted for lost purchasing power.

**Real Rate of Return**
The current or nominal rate of return minus the inflation rate.

### Historical Interest Rates

The nominal interest rates for high-quality bonds issued by corporations (corporate Aaa bonds), bonds with 30-year maturities issued by the federal government (30-year Treasury bonds), and bonds with 3-month maturities issued by the federal government (3-month Treasury bonds) over the recent past are shown in Figure 11.1. Notice that nominal interest rates have dropped considerably over the past 20 years. Today, the high rates experienced in 1981 seem almost too high to believe. In effect, as inflation slowed down, investors demanded a lower return on money they lent, which resulted in a drop in nominal interest rates. This link between inflation and nominal interest rates has its roots in **Principle 1: The Risk–Return Trade-Off**.

Although it's not shown in Figure 11.1, the real rate of interest can be calculated by simply subtracting the inflation rate from the nominal interest rate. In early 2002, as a result of the Federal Reserve's efforts to cut short-term rates, the real rate of return on 3-month Treasury bills was only 0.03 percent (the nominal rate of 1.63 percent minus the inflation rate at that time of 1.6 percent). However, looking back at the real rate of return on 3-month Treasury bills in 1998, we find that it stood at 3.21 (the nominal rate of 4.81 percent minus the inflation rate

**Principle**
The Risk–Return Trade-Off

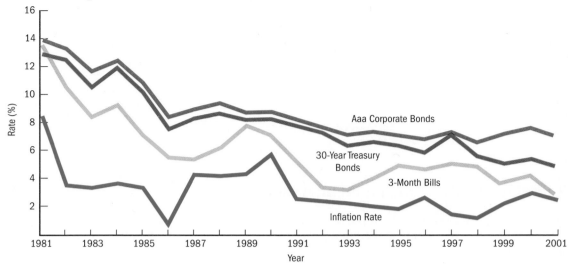

Figure 11.1 Interest and Inflation Rates, 1981–2001

Aaa Corporate Bonds

30-Year Treasury Bonds

3-Month Bills

Inflation Rate

Year

Rate (%)

**Real Risk-Free Rate of Interest k\***

The hypothetical interest rate existing on a security with no risk in a world with no inflation. It's generally thought of as the interest rate that would exist on very short-term Treasury bills in a world of no inflation.

**Inflation Risk Premium IRP**

The premium rate above the real rate of return that investors demand to compensate for anticipated inflation over the life of a security. This premium goes up and down as the level of anticipated inflation rises and falls.

**Default**

The failure of a debtor to make interest or principal payments when they are due.

**Default Risk Premium DRP**

An additional investment return to compensate investors for risking that the issuer may not pay the interest or principal on a security. The default risk premium should reflect the riskiness of the issuer.

for 1998 of 1.6 percent). You'll notice that the real rate of interest is different for long-term corporate bonds and 3-month Treasury bills. Why? The real rate of interest includes a compensation for risk, and corporate bonds have more risk than Treasury bills. Once again, that's **Principle 1: The Risk–Return Trade-Off** at work.

## What Makes Up Interest Rate Risk?

From Principle 1 we know that investors receive a return for delaying consumption. We call this return for delaying consumption $k^*$, the **real risk-free rate of interest**. You can think of it as the interest rate on a bond with no risk in a world with no inflation. Because very short-term Treasury bills are virtually risk free, the interest rate on them can be thought of as the real risk-free rate. We also know from Principle 1 that bond investors receive an additional return for taking on risk. The question we want to answer now is, "What makes up interest rate risk?"

Interest rate risk has many components. One is the possibility of changes in inflation. Increased inflation snatches up a portion of return on investments. As Principle 1 points out, investors will demand a return above the real rate of return to compensate for the anticipated inflation over the life of the investment. This additional return is referred to as the **inflation risk premium IRP**. The size of this premium goes up and down based on changes in the level of anticipated inflation.

In looking at Figure 11.1, it's interesting to note that the three debt instruments all carry different interest rate levels. Much of the difference between the high rates on long-term corporate bonds and the lower rates on 30-year Treasury bonds can be explained by the fact that corporate bonds may someday fail to make, or **default** on, their interest payments, whereas Treasury bonds won't. Remember, the government can just print more money.

In effect, corporate bonds, regardless of how highly rated they are, carry more risk than do Treasury bonds. As a result, they also have a higher return attached to them to compensate investors for taking on the risk of default. This additional return is referred to as the **default risk premium DRP**.

The default risk premium explains the difference between the interest rate levels on Treasury bonds and long-term corporate bonds, but it doesn't explain the rate differences between 3-month Treasury bills and 30-year Treasury bonds. After all, neither has any default risk, because they're both issued by the government. Instead, this difference is a result of the **maturity risk premium MRP**. This premium is an additional return demanded by investors on longer-term bonds to compensate for the fact that the value of bonds with longer maturities tends to fluctuate more when interest rates change. The longer the time to maturity, the greater the bond's price will fluctuate when interest rates change.

If you think about savings accounts, there's no maturity risk associated with them, because they don't really have a maturity date—you can withdraw your money at any time. This lack of a maturity risk premium explains why they have a lower interest rate than bonds.

Although it's not evident from the information presented in Table 11.1 and Figure 11.1, there's one final risk factor affecting interest rates—the **liquidity risk premium LRP**. It reflects the risk that some bonds can't be converted into cash quickly at a fair market price. These bonds, particularly bonds issued by small municipalities, are very infrequently traded. As a result, if you're forced to sell in a hurry, you may not find any buyers. To attract a buyer, you might have to sell these bonds for less than they're actually worth, or you might get stuck holding on to them. Investors therefore tack on a liquidity risk premium if they think a bond won't be able to be converted to cash quickly and at a fair price.

**Maturity Risk Premium MRP**
An additional return demanded by investors in longer-term securities to compensate for the fact that the value of securities with longer maturities tends to fluctuate more when interest rates change.

**Liquidity Risk Premium LRP**
An additional return for compensation for the risk that a security cannot be converted into cash quickly at a fair market price. It's close to zero for Treasury securities, which are easy to sell, and larger for securities issued by very small firms.

## Table 11.1 Interest and Inflation Rates, 1981–2001

| Year | 3-Month Treasury Bills | 30-Year Treasury Bonds | Aaa Rated Corporate Bonds | Inflation Rate |
|------|------------------------|------------------------|---------------------------|----------------|
| 1981 | 14.08% | 13.44% | 14.17% | 8.9% |
| 1982 | 10.69 | 12.76 | 13.79 | 3.9 |
| 1983 | 8.63 | 11.18 | 12.04 | 3.8 |
| 1984 | 9.52 | 12.39 | 12.71 | 4.0 |
| 1985 | 7.49 | 10.79 | 11.37 | 3.8 |
| 1986 | 5.98 | 7.80 | 9.02 | 1.1 |
| 1987 | 5.82 | 8.58 | 9.38 | 4.4 |
| 1988 | 6.68 | 8.96 | 9.71 | 4.4 |
| 1989 | 8.12 | 8.45 | 9.26 | 4.6 |
| 1990 | 7.51 | 8.61 | 9.32 | 6.1 |
| 1991 | 5.42 | 8.14 | 8.77 | 3.1 |
| 1992 | 3.45 | 7.67 | 8.14 | 2.9 |
| 1993 | 3.02 | 6.59 | 7.22 | 2.7 |
| 1994 | 4.29 | 7.37 | 7.97 | 2.7 |
| 1995 | 5.51 | 6.88 | 7.59 | 2.5 |
| 1996 | 5.02 | 6.71 | 7.37 | 3.3 |
| 1997 | 5.07 | 6.61 | 7.26 | 1.7 |
| 1998 | 4.81 | 5.58 | 6.53 | 1.6 |
| 1999 | 4.66 | 5.87 | 7.05 | 2.2 |
| 2000 | 5.66 | 5.94 | 7.62 | 3.4 |
| 2001 | 3.48 | 5.49 | 7.08 | 2.8 |
| Mean | 6.43 | 8.38 | 9.20 | 3.52 |

Source: *Federal Reserve Bulletin*, various issues, and *Federal Reserve Statistical Releases*, H.15 (519), G.13 (415), various issues.

## Determinants of the Quoted, or Nominal, Interest Rate

What do we get when we put all these premiums and required returns together? Quite simply, we get the quoted or nominal interest rate.

$$\text{nominal (or quoted) interest rate} = k^* + IRP + DRP + MRP + LRP$$

where

$k^*$ = the real risk-free rate of interest

$IRP$ = the inflation risk premium

$DRP$ = the default risk premium

$MRP$ = the maturity risk premium

$LRP$ = the liquidity risk premium

This equation is simply an in-depth explanation of **Principle 1: The Risk–Return Trade-Off** as applied to bonds. The return bondholders demand for delaying consumption is $k^* + IRP$, and the return they demand for taking on added risk is $DRP + MRP + LRP$. As long as you remember Principle 1, this equation will make more sense.

### How Interest Rates Affect Returns on Other Investments

The relationship between returns on all the different investment alternatives is extremely tangled. For example, common stocks tend to be riskier than bonds, so you won't invest in common stocks unless they have a higher expected return. That means that if bonds are returning 6 percent, you may be satisfied with a 9-percent return on stocks. However, if bonds were returning 12 percent, you wouldn't invest in stocks if the expected return were only 9 percent. You might demand a 15-percent return on your common stock investment.

In effect, the expected returns on all the investments are related—what you can earn on one investment determines what you demand on another. Interest rates can be thought of as a kind of a "base" return. When interest rates go up, investors demand a higher return on all other investments. When interest rates go down, the return investors demand on other investments goes down.

## A Look at Risk–Return Trade-Offs

From Principle 1 you know that risk goes hand in hand with potential return. The more risk you are willing to take on, the greater the potential return—but also, the greater the possibility that you will lose money. What does all this mean? It means you must take steps to eliminate risk without affecting potential return.

There's no question that you must accept some risk to meet your long-term financial goals, so you must balance the amount of risk you're willing to take on with the amount of return you need. Before we examine the sources of risk in investments, let's take a look at the historical levels of risk and return in the investment markets.

### Historical Levels of Risk and Return

Because a historical perspective in investments is a healthy thing, let's look at the historical levels of risk and return for the past 76 years.[2] If you look at these

---

[2]Roger G. Ibbotson and Rex A. Sinquefield, *Stocks, Bonds, Bills, & Inflation 2002 Yearbook* (Chicago: Ibbotson Associates, 2002).

## Figure 11.2 Risk–Return Relationship

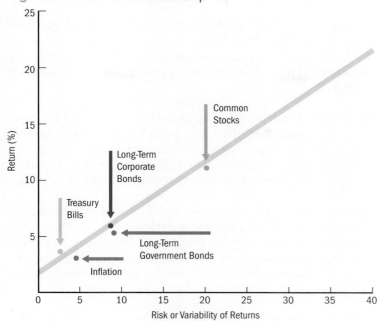

returns graphically, plotting average annual return against risk or variability of returns as our measure of risk, you get the graph in Figure 11.2. As you can see, it bears a strong resemblance to the risk–return trade-off graph presented in Chapter 1 (Figure 1.4).

Remember, when we presented the risk–return relationship described in Principle 1, we talked about expected return. Here you see that what was predicted by Principle 1 in fact holds. Investments that produce higher returns have higher levels of risk associated with them.

## Sources of Risk in the Risk–Return Trade-Off

The compensation that investors demand for taking on added risk differs for every investment because every investment has a different level of risk. The purpose behind presenting these "sources of risk" is to give you an intuitive understanding of what causes fluctuations in the prices and values of different investments.

Keep in mind that these sources are not mutually exclusive—that is, there's a good deal of overlap between some of them. It's very difficult to look at price fluctuation in an investment and try to attribute it solely to one or another "source" of risk. However, some investments are more vulnerable to one source of risk, while some are to another, so understanding these sources can tell you a lot about many investments.

**Interest Rate Risk** One source of risk to investors finds its roots in changes in interest rates. Regardless of their source, interest rate changes can be bad news for investors. For example, when market interest rates rise, the price of outstanding bonds declines, because new bonds with higher interest rates are now available. No one will want to buy your $1,000, 6.5-percent, 10-year bond when $1,000, 8-percent,

10-year bonds are available. The higher the interest rate climbs, the less your bond will be worth.

The same basic relationship holds for common stock. When market interest rates rise, the price of common stock drops. This fluctuation in security prices due to changes in the market interest rate is a result of **interest rate risk**. Unfortunately, because increases in interest rates affect all securities in the same way, it's impossible to eliminate interest rate risk.

**Interest Rate Risk**
The risk of fluctuations in security prices due to changes in the market interest rate.

**Inflation Risk**
The risk that rising prices will eat away the purchasing power of your money, and that changes in the anticipated level of inflation will result in interest rate changes, which will in turn cause security price fluctuations.

**Inflation Risk**  **Inflation risk** reflects the likelihood that rising prices will eat away the purchasing power of your money, and that changes in the anticipated level of inflation will result in interest rate changes, which will in turn cause security price fluctuations. Inflation risk is closely linked to interest rate risk, but it is important enough in the valuation and investment processes that it's generally treated as a totally separate source of risk.

Unexpected increases in inflation may cause a financial plan that appears to be solid to fall short in achieving its goals. You need to reevaluate your financial plan periodically to make sure it is adequate to meet your goals. Fortunately for those of you with stocks, over long periods of time common stocks have produced a return well above the rate of inflation, thereby preserving the purchasing power of your money.

**Business Risk**
The risk of fluctuations in security prices resulting from good or bad management decisions, or how well or poorly the firm's products are doing in the marketplace.

**Business Risk**  Most stocks and bonds are influenced by how well or poorly the company that issued them is performing. **Business risk** deals with fluctuations in investment value that are caused by good or bad management decisions, or how well or poorly the firm's products are doing in the marketplace. Businesses can go bankrupt, and management does make poor decisions. Look at Kmart, the nation's second largest discount retailer and the third largest general merchandise retailer. It fell from $13.55 in August 2001 to $0.85 in January 2002 as it filed for bankruptcy.

Business risk is different for different companies. Some companies seem to post even profits year in and year out, regardless of what's happening in the economy, while the profits levels of other firms tend to swing wildly.

**Financial Risk**
The risk associated with a company's use of debt. As a firm takes on more debt, it also takes on interest and principal payments that must be made regardless of how well the firm does. If a company takes on too much debt and can't meet its obligations, investors risk the company defaulting or dropping in stock value.

**Financial Risk**  **Financial risk** is risk associated with the use of debt by the firm. As a firm takes on more debt, it also takes on interest and principal payments that must be made regardless of how well the firm does. If the firm can't make the payments, it could go bankrupt. Thus, how the firm raises money affects its level of risk.

**Liquidity Risk**
Risk associated with the inability to liquidate a security quickly and at a fair market price. For securities that are thinly traded—that is, there's relatively little trading in them—liquidity risk can be substantial.

**Liquidity Risk**  **Liquidity risk** deals with the inability to liquidate a security quickly and at a fair market price. For investments that are infrequently traded, it can be hard to find a buyer. Sometimes it's impossible to find a buyer at a fair market price, and you wind up having to sell for less than an asset's worth— sometimes even for a loss.

Buying a piece of your favorite sports team has long been a popular investment for the super-rich, but there's a good deal of liquidity risk in such a venture. Harvey Lighton, owner of 3.1237 percent of the New York Yankees, learned this lesson in 1995 when he took out a newspaper ad offering a 1-percent stake in the Yankees for $2.95 million. There were no takers. He then considered a plan to take a 2-percent stake in the Yankees and divide it into 20,000 pieces, each representing one millionth of the team, and sell them for $500 each. That didn't work either. For investors who need money fast, liquidity risk is an important consideration.

**Market Risk**   **Market risk** is risk associated with overall market movements. There tend to be periods of bull markets—that is, times when all stocks seem to move upward—and times of bear markets, when all stocks tend to decline in price. The same tends to be true in the bond markets. These periods may be a result of changes in the economy, changes in the mood of investors, or changes in interest rates. Market risk and interest rate risk are examples of overlap in "sources" of risk.

**Market Risk**
Risk associated with overall market movements. There tend to be periods of bull markets, when all stocks seem to move upward, and times of bear markets, when all stocks tend to decline in price.

**Political and Regulatory Risk**   **Political** and **regulatory risk** results from unanticipated changes in the tax or legal environments that have been imposed by the government. Changes in the capital gains tax rate, or in the tax deductibility of interest on municipal bonds, or the passage of any new regulatory reform laws affect investment values and are examples of political and regulatory risk.

**Political and Regulatory Risk**
Risk resulting from unanticipated changes in the tax or legal environment.

**Exchange Rate Risk**   **Exchange rate risk** refers to the variability in earnings resulting from changes in exchange rates. For example, if you invest in a German bond, you first convert your dollars into German marks. When you liquidate that investment, you sell your bond for German marks and convert those marks into dollars. What you earn on your investment depends on how well the investment performed and what happened to the exchange rate. For the international investor, exchange rate risk is simply another layer of risk.

**Exchange Rate Risk**
The risk of fluctuations in security prices from the variability in earnings resulting from changes in exchange rates.

**Call Risk**   **Call risk** is the risk to bondholders that a bond may be called away from them before maturity. **Calling a bond** refers to redeeming the bond early, and many bonds are callable. When a bond is called, the bondholder generally receives the face value of the bond plus 1 year of interest payments. This risk applies only to investments in callable bonds.

**Call Risk**
The risk to bondholders that a bond may be called away from them before maturity.

**Calling a Bond**
The redeeming of a bond before its scheduled maturity. Many bonds are callable.

## Diversification

Diversification is a simple concept that most investors understand: Don't put all your eggs in one basket. **Diversification** works by allowing the extreme good and bad returns to cancel each other out, resulting in a reduction of the total variability or risk without affecting expected return.

It's important to understand the process of diversification. It not only eliminates a lot of risk, but also helps us understand what risk is relevant to us as investors. It's also important to understand that diversification reduces risk without affecting the expected return. That's what we saw when we introduced Principle 3 in Chapter 1. It works by allowing the good and bad observations to cancel each other out. As a result, variability, or risk, is reduced.

**Diversification**
The elimination of risk by investing in different assets. It works by allowing the extreme good and bad returns to cancel each other out. The result is that total variability or risk is reduced without affecting expected return.

**Systematic and Unsystematic Risk**   As you diversify your investments, the variability or risk of the combined holdings of your investments, which is called your **portfolio**, should decline. This reduction occurs because the stock returns in your portfolio don't fluctuate in the same way over time. For example, if you increase the number of stocks, the amount of variability in your portfolio declines, as shown in Figure 11.3.

However, you'll also notice in Figure 11.3 that not all risk is eliminated through diversification. The variability in returns common to all stocks, perhaps associated with movements in interest rates or in the economy, isn't eliminated through

**Portfolio**
A group of investments held by an individual.

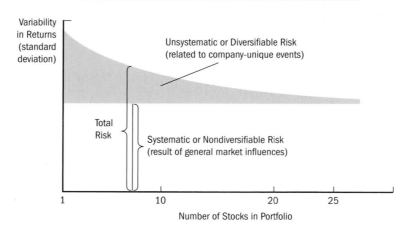

**Variability of Returns Compared with Size of Portfolio**

diversification. However, variability in one stock's returns unique to that stock tends to be countered and canceled out by the unique variability of another stock in the portfolio. For example, maybe in 2001 one of the stocks in your portfolio was McLoedUSA (a phone service provider that lost 97.3 percent of its value), but another stock in your portfolio was eBay (which had a great year and rose in price by 102.74 percent). The end result of holding these two very different stocks is that the bad year for McLoedUSA was canceled out by the really good year that eBay had. In a diversified portfolio the variability unique to individual stocks is canceled out or diversified away, but the variability common to all stocks remains.

What does the ability of diversification to eliminate only certain types of risk mean? It means that there are two basic types of risk: systematic and unsystematic. **Systematic risk**, which is sometimes called **market-related** or **nondiversifiable risk**, is that portion of a stock's risk or variability that *can't be eliminated* through diversification. It results from factors that affect all stocks. In fact, the term "systematic" comes from the fact that this type of risk systematically affects all stocks.

**Unsystematic risk**, which is also called **firm-specific** or **company-unique risk** or **diversifiable risk**, is risk or variability that *can be eliminated* through diversification. It results from factors unique to a particular stock. All risk has to be either systematic or unsystematic.

Keep in mind that these are *types* of risk, which is different from the *sources* of risk or variability we examined earlier. Figure 11.4 shows the relationship between these two types of risk.

As an example of unsystematic risk, think of what might happen to stocks of an oil producer and to those of a chemical firm as a result of an increase in oil prices. The oil producer would benefit from the increase in oil prices, which would in turn push its stock price up. The chemical firm may rely on oil as a primary factor in production and face increased costs. These costs would in turn push the price of the chemical firm's stock down. If these two stocks were in the same portfolio, these price changes would've canceled each other out.

Relating this back to **Principle 1: The Risk–Return Trade-Off**, we find that the only risk we're compensated for taking on is systematic risk, because unsystematic risk can be eliminated through diversification. In effect, unsystematic risk doesn't

**Systematic or Market-Related or Nondiversifiable Risk**
That portion of a security's risk or variability that *can't be eliminated* through investor diversification. This type of variability or risk results from factors that affect all securities.

**Unsystematic or Firm-Specific or Company-Unique Risk or Diversifiable Risk**
Risk or variability that *can be eliminated* through investor diversification. Unsystematic risk results from factors that are unique to a particular firm.

Principle

The Risk–Return Trade-Off

**Figure 11.4** The Relationship Between Total Risk, Systematic Risk, and Unsystematic Risk

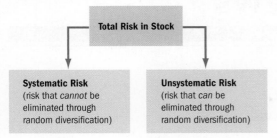

exist for diversified investors, and the market doesn't compensate investors for taking on risk they can eliminate for free. We can now see that investors demand a return for delaying consumption, and a return for taking on added *systematic* risk.

## Understanding Your Tolerance for Risk

Not everyone has the same tolerance for risk. Some individuals are continuously checking their investments' results. Others can take on risk without breaking a sweat or looking at a financial page in the newspaper. Which is better? That's a judgment call.

It doesn't matter whether you freak out at the slightest sign of risk or you act like a complete daredevil. What's important is recognizing your tolerance for risk, and acting—and investing—accordingly.

One way of developing an understanding of your tolerance for risk is to take one of the many risk-tolerance tests offered in magazines and personal finance self-help books. The answers are weighted, and according to the number of points you accumulate, you're labeled "more conservative," "less conservative," and so on.

Generally, the questions go something like this: You have a lottery ticket that has a one-in-five chance of winning a $100,000 prize. The minimum you would sell that lottery ticket for before the drawing is

1. $10,000
2. $15,000
3. $20,000
4. $30,000
5. $40,000

These tests can be helpful, but only if you answer honestly. When used by a financial planner, it's the discussions they generate that tend to reveal the most about risk tolerance.

Another way of determining your level of risk tolerance is to review your past actions. Are you willing to switch to a less secure job if it has opportunities your present job doesn't have? Do you worry about losing your job even if it's secure? Are you conservative or aggressive with your investments? Do you keep a very large emergency fund in liquid assets?

If you're willing to take on risks elsewhere but not in your investments, your aversion to this type of risk might be caused by a lack of knowledge. That is, your present investment strategy may be decidedly conservative simply because you do not understand investments and risk.

As you learn more about risk–return trade-offs and the effect of diversification on risk and the time dimension of risk, you'll better realize the investment

# In The News

Wall Street Journal Sunday September 24, 2000

## Investors' Worst Enemy: Themselves

### by Jonathan Clements

Forget about investment risk. What I worry about is investor risk.

The fact is that we can't control the markets. Like it or not, they will keep soaring and sinking, surprising us constantly. We can, however, control ourselves. Many investors could vastly improve their investment performance simply by displaying greater discipline and avoiding foolish mistakes.

Here are just three ways that we shoot ourselves in the foot:

1. *Saving Too Little.* Unfortunately, too many investors save far too little. Yet saving a hefty sum is the surest strategy for making our portfolios grow.

*Indeed, a prodigious savings rate can salve almost any investment wound. If we sock away a decent amount every month, we will have a good shot at reaching our investment goals, even if our portfolio performance disappoints.* (☞A)

2. *Investing Too Cautiously.* Even after the spectacular stock market gains of the 1980s and 1990s, my sense is that stocks remain a fleeting fancy for many rather than a long-term commitment.

To truly benefit from stock market investing, we need to allocate at least half of our portfolios to a diversified mix of stocks and then hang on for a bare minimum of five years, and preferably much longer. If investors stick with their stocks for just a few months or years, there is a fair chance they will come away poorer.

3. *Panicking During Declines.* Investors make many missteps. But few mistakes can do more damage more quickly than panic selling during a stock market tumble. If investors dump shares during a decline, they can lock in losses from which their portfolios may never recover.

*Short-term stock market losses are frequent and frequently terrifying, so we need to prepare ourselves mentally. According to Ibbotson, the stock market has lost money in 20 of the past 74 years, including 4 years when the market tumbled more than 20 percent. Folks who don't think they could sit tight through that sort of decline should probably lighten up on stocks now, before the market really does take a substantial dive.* (☞B)

## THE BOTTOM LINE . . .

A It is impossible to oversell the importance of living below your means. It is also important that you don't procrastinate with respect to investing—that just stops things cold. Remember **Principle 8: Nothing Happens Without a Plan**.

B Another thing you can do to improve your odds at no cost is to minimize trading. This not only keeps your trading costs down (also make sure you avoid any money management costs) but also puts off taxes.

challenges you actually face. You'll also better understand how important it is not to let your aversion to risk stop you from making lucrative investments to meet your goals.

**5** Allocate your risk assets in the manner that is best for you.

**Principle 11** The Time Dimension of Investing

## The Time Dimension of Investing and Asset Allocation

In Chapter 1 we introduced **Principle 11: The Time Dimension of Investing**. The essence of this principle is that as the length of the investment horizon increases, you can afford to invest in riskier assets. Thus, whenever someone asks what they should invest in, the proper response is a question: What is your investment horizon? This is because the returns on those risky assets—stocks—tend to dominate those of less risky assets—CDs and bonds—as the investment horizon lengthens. So even in the worst case scenario, you'll probably do quite a bit better with stocks than you would do with the more conservative alternative. It doesn't mean that there isn't any risk to investing in common stock. Clearly, there's still a lot of uncertainty as to how much you'll finally end up with. But if your investment horizon is long, you'll probably end up with a lot more if you invest in some risky assets.

Take stocks versus bonds. Without question, common stocks have provided the greatest return over the past 76 years, with large-company stocks earning on average

10.7 percent per year over this period. However, it hasn't been a smooth rise. Common stocks have also had the greatest risk or variability over that same period. In fact, on October 19, 1987, the stock market dropped by 23 percent, on October 27, 1997, it dropped by 7.2 percent and on September 17, 2001 (the first day the market was open for trading following the tragic events of September 11, 2001), it dropped by 7.1 percent. The problem with stocks is that "on average" may not be what you actually get. You may, for whatever reason, put your money in the stock market on the wrong day.

## How to Measure the Ultimate Risk on Your Portfolio

There are really three ways of looking at the risk associated with your investment returns: (1) looking at the variability of the average annual return on your investment, (2) looking at the uncertainty associated with the ultimate dollar value of the investment, and (3) looking at the distribution of ultimate dollar returns from one investment versus another. Let's begin by looking at the variability of the average annual return on your investment. Fortunately, this variability declines as the holding period increases. In fact, with any investment, you can almost guarantee that there'll be some bad years along with the good years. As a result, when you invest for a longer period, the exceptionally good and exceptionally bad years cancel each other out.

For common stocks, this is shown in Figure 11.5. Although the worst single year for large-company stocks, 1931, resulted in a 43.3-percent loss, the worst 5-year

**Figure 11.5** Reduction of Risk over Time

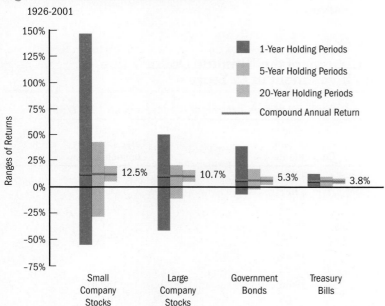

*Each bar shows the range of compound annual total returns for each asset class over the period 1926-2001.

period involved an average loss of 12.5 percent annually—the period from December 31, 1927, through December 31, 1932. But as we increase the investment horizon, the amount of the loss declines further: If we look at the range of average returns for 20-year investment horizons, we find that the best average return was 17.7 percent, and the worst was a positive 3.1 percent.

Unfortunately, this isn't the whole story. While the variability of the average annual rate of return declines as the investment horizon lengthens, the range of ultimate dollar value of the investment gets bigger. Look at what would happen if the large-company stocks perform in the future as they have over the past 50 years. First, let's assume you are just starting out and have 45 years until retirement and are trying to decide whether you should invest in stocks or bonds. Over the past 50 years, from 1952 through 2001, the average return on large-company stocks was 12.0 percent. That means that if large-company stocks act as they have for the past 50 years, a dollar invested today should grow to $163.99 in 45 years.

But that's only part of the story. As you can see in Table 11.2, there's a very big range with respect to the ultimate dollar value of the investment. In fact, while there's a 5-percent chance that your investment will grow to $1,525.74, there's also a 5-percent chance that it will only make it to $63.78. If we look at long-term corporate bonds over this same period, we would expect our $1 investment to grow to $14.78 with a 5-percent chance of hitting $41.79 if things go really well, and a 5-percent chance of only growing to $5.21 if things don't go well. In effect, the fifth percentile return on stocks beats the ninety-fifth percentile return on bonds!

What does all this tell us? It tells us two things: First, if your investment time horizon is long and you invest in something risky like common stocks, there's still a lot of uncertainty about what the ultimate dollar value of your investment will be. It also shows you that if your investment time horizon is long, you can afford to take on additional risk because even in the worst case, you'll probably be better off than if you took a conservative approach. This is an extremely important concept, because it means that our investment horizon plays an extremely important role in determining how we should invest our savings.

## Table 11.2 Distribution of the Ultimate Dollar Value of an Investment in 45 Years

| | Dollar Value of Your Investment ($1 invested on 12/31/99) | |
| --- | --- | --- |
| Percentile | Invested in Long-Term Corporate Bonds | Invested in Large-Company Common Stocks |
| 95th | $41.79 | $1,525.74 |
| 90th | 33.21 | 1,074.46 |
| 85th | 28.43 | 848.14 |
| 80th | 25.14 | 702.80 |
| 75th | 22.62 | 598.13 |
| 50th | 14.76 | 311.95 |
| 25th | 9.63 | 162.70 |
| 20th | 8.66 | 138.47 |
| 15th | 7.66 | 114.74 |
| 10th | 6.56 | 90.57 |
| 5th | 5.21 | 63.78 |

There are still other reasons why investors can afford to take more risk as their investment time horizon lengthens. One reason is that they have more opportunities to adjust consumption and work habits over longer time periods. If they are investing with a short time horizon, there isn't much they can do—either save more or spend less—to change their final level of wealth. However, if an investment performs poorly at the beginning of a long investment time horizon, the investor can make an adjustment by saving more, working harder, or spending less.

Another reason often given for investing in stocks when you have a long time horizon comes from the notion that whatever might cause stocks to crash might also cause bonds to crash. In effect, if stocks crash, there may be no place to hide. That is, if our economic system collapses or the world gets hit by a giant meteor, both stocks and bonds will take a big hit. As a result, investing in less risky assets (bonds) really doesn't help you if a crash ever comes.

## Asset Allocation

**Asset allocation** is an investments term that deals with how your money should be divided among stocks, bonds, and other investments. The investor should be well diversified, generally with holdings in several different classes of investments, such as domestic common stocks, international common stocks, and bonds. The objective is to increase your return on those investments while decreasing your risk.

The concept of asset allocation incorporates the concept of the time dimension of investing by recognizing that investing in common stocks is more appropriate the longer the investment horizon. That is investors with more time to reach their goals should have a larger proportion of common stocks in their portfolios. The closer you get to retirement, the smaller the proportion of your retirement funds that should be invested in common stocks.

The logic behind the asset allocation process is surprisingly simple, and finds its roots in three axioms: **Principle 3: Diversification Reduces Risk**; **Principle 4: Diversification and Risk—All Risk Is Not Equal**; and **Principle 11: The Time Dimension of Investing**. First, you should diversify to reduce risk. In addition, your ideal mix of stocks and other investments changes as your investment horizon changes. This is because stocks tend to dominate other investments over longer time horizons. As a result, the longer your investment horizon, the more money you should invest in common stocks.

No two investors should allocate in the same way. You don't want to do what your Uncle Bill does, nor will you want to follow your neighbor's plan, because your age, income, family situation, personal financial goals, and tolerance for risk will certainly vary. These factors will lead you in your own direction. Asset allocation is clearly the most important task you'll undertake in your investing career. How you go about your asset allocation will have far greater impact on your return than will choosing each individual stock or bond you hold.

Let's look at what asset allocation might mean for a typical investor who is saving for retirement. Keep in mind that saving for different goals implies different investment horizons. To simplify the presentation somewhat, let's also divide this investor's retirement savings life into the three financial life cycle stages: (1) the early years—a time of wealth accumulation (through age 54), (2) approaching retirement—the golden years (ages 55 to 64), and (3) the retirement years (over age 65).

**Asset Allocation**
An attempt to ensure that the investor's strategy reflects his or her investment time horizon and is well diversified, generally with investments in several different classes of investments, such as domestic common stocks, international common stocks, and bonds.

Principle
**3** Diversification Reduces Risk

Principle
**4** Diversification and Risk—All Risk Is Not Equal

Principle
**11** The Time Dimension of Investing

# In The News

Wall Street Journal Sunday June 10, 2001

## Five Reasons Diversification Works

by Jonathan Clements

Gamblers bet on stocks. Investors control risk. As the past year has made abundantly clear, you can't build a decent portfolio out of a hodgepodge of heavily touted stocks. Instead, to have a good shot at clocking healthy long-run gains, you have to control risk. And that means diversifying across a broad array of large, small, and foreign shares. Not convinced? Consider these arguments for diversification:

1. *Free Lunch.* Diversification is often described as Wall Street's only free lunch. How come? By spreading your bets across a host of stocks and stock market sectors, you can end up with a portfolio that is less risky than its component parts.

*For instance, foreign shares are undoubtedly more dicey than U.S. stocks, because there is the added risk that the dollar will rally, depressing the value of foreign stocks for U.S. holders. But if you add foreign shares to a U.S. stock portfolio, you can reduce the portfolio's overall volatility. The foreign shares won't move in sync with U.S. stocks and, thus, they may provide offsetting gains when the rest of your portfolio is suffering.* (☛A)

"People don't understand risk," says San Francisco investment advisor Robert Bingham. "What they fail to realize is that diversification, properly done, gives you the same return, but with much less risk, or greater return with the same risk."

2. *Limiting Losses.* Diversification doesn't just reduce volatility and ensure that your portfolio keeps up with the market average. It also helps you avoid the big investment hits that are so tough to recover from.

*For proof, look no further than the recent performance of the technology-heavy Nasdaq Composite Index and the more diversified Standard & Poor's 500 stock index. From last year's high to the recent low, the Nasdaq tumbled 68 percent, while the S&P 500 fell 28 percent.* (☛B)

If you hold an undiversified portfolio that looks like the Nasdaq Composite, you will have to earn 213 percent to recoup your full loss. But if your portfolio is comparable to the S&P 500, you will need only a 39 percent gain to get back to even.

## THE BOTTOM LINE . . .

**A** The reason foreign stocks add so much is that their movements don't necessarily mimic the movements of U.S. stocks. As a result, they tend to cancel out wide swings in stock movements and lessen your overall portfolio risk. That's the idea behind **Principle 3: Diversification Reduces Risk,** and **Principle 4: All Risk Is Not Equal.**

**B** One way to keep your portfolio diversified is to periodically rebalance your portfolio's allocation between Nasdaq and NYSE stocks in addition to stocks and bonds. That way you're always buying low and selling high in addition to keeping your portfolio well diversified.

Source: Jonathan Clements, "Five Reasons Diversification Works," *Wall Street Journal Sunday*, June 10, 2001: 3. Copyright (c) 2001, Dow Jones & Company, Inc. Reproduced with permission of DOW JONES & CO INC in the format Textbook via Copyright Clearance Center.

Asset allocation is not a one-time decision. Adjustments will need to be made as your life circumstances change. As you keep an eye on your portfolio, you may occasionally need to rebalance your mix to keep the percentage of each investment category in line with your current personal financial goals.

**Asset Allocation and the Early Years—A Time of Wealth Accumulation (Through Age 54)** Because the investment horizon is quite long, investors in this stage should place the majority of their savings into common stocks. These have the highest return associated with them; they also have the highest risk. However, because of the time dimension of investing and the long investment horizon, investing heavily in common stocks makes much more sense.

For investors who are just beginning this investment stage, a strategy of investing only in common stocks can be justified. However, most financial planners recommend that a portion of the investment funds be maintained in bonds. A mix of 80-percent common stocks and 20-percent bonds is relatively common. Although this can be used as a benchmark asset allocation breakdown, remember that your personal situation ultimately determines the appropriate breakdown for you.

## Figure 11.6 Return and Risk to Benchmark Asset Allocation Breakdown During the Early Years

| 1926-2001 | | 1967-2001 | |
|---|---|---|---|
| Stock/bond mix | 80/20 | Stock/bond mix | 80/20 |
| Annual compound return | 9.72% | Annual compound return | 11.0% |
| Years with losses (out of 76) | 21 | Years with losses (out of 35) | 9 |
| Worst annual loss (1931) | -35.73% | Worst annual loss (1974) | -20.30% |
| Bear market (1973-1974) | -32.25% | | |

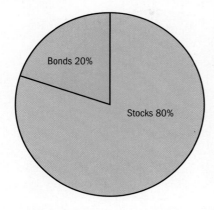

Source: *Stocks, Bonds, Bills & Inflation 2002 Yearbook,* © 2002 Ibbotson Associates, Inc. Based on copyrighted works by Ibbotson and Sinquefield. All rights reserved. Used with permission.

Looking at the performance of such an asset allocation breakdown since 1926, we find that the annual compound total return would have been 9.72 percent (Figure 11.6). The risk associated with such an asset allocation can be seen by examining the fact that in 21 out of 76 years since 1926, it would have earned losses. The worst annual loss over this period would have occurred in 1931, when such an allocation would have resulted in a 35.73-percent loss. In addition, over the 1973–1974 bear market, there would have been a 32.25-percent loss.

**Asset Allocation and Approaching Retirement—The Golden Years (Ages 55 to 64)**
For an individual approaching retirement, the goal becomes preserving the level of wealth already accumulated and allowing this wealth to continue to grow. As the investment horizon shortens, the investor should move some of his or her retirement portfolio into bonds.

In addition, the investor should maintain a diversified portfolio. For individuals approaching retirement, a mix of 60-percent common stocks and 40-percent bonds is a relatively common recommendation from financial planners. Again, depending on the investor's degree of risk tolerance, the proportion invested in common stocks may either increase or decrease.

Looking at the performance of a 60/40 asset allocation between stocks and bonds since 1926, we find that the annual compound total return would have been 8.74 percent (see Figure 11.7). For this asset allocation, losses were experienced in only 18 out of 76 years since 1926. The worst annual loss would have occurred in 1931, when such an asset allocation would have resulted in a 28.13-percent

Figure 11.7 Return and Risk to Benchmark Asset Allocation Breakdown
Approaching Retirement—The Golden Years

| **1926-2001** | | **1967-2001** | |
|---|---|---|---|
| Stock/bond mix | 60/40 | Stock/bond mix | 60/40 |
| Average annual return | 8.74% | Average annual return | 10.3% |
| Years with losses (out of 76) | 18 | Years with losses (out of 35) | 8 |
| Worst annual loss (1931) | -28.13% | Worst annual loss (1974) | -14.14% |
| Bear market (1973-1974) | -23.38% | | |

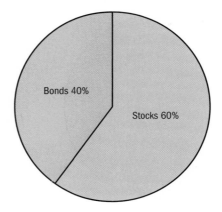

loss. In addition, over the 1973–1974 bear market, there would have been a 23.38-percent loss.

**Asset Allocation and the Retirement Years (Over Age 65)**  During your retirement years, you're no longer saving, you're spending. However, it's still necessary to allow for some growth in your investments simply to keep inflation from eating away your wealth. Income is now of importance, with capital appreciation a secondary goal. Safety is provided by diversification among various investment categories and movement out of common stocks.

As we saw in Figure 11.5, the volatility of common stocks increases as the holding period declines, making common stocks riskier for the investor with a short investment horizon. For individuals in their retirement years, a mix of 40-percent common stocks, 40-percent bonds, and 20-percent short-term Treasury bills is a relatively common recommendation from financial planners.

Looking at the performance of a 40/40/20 asset allocation between stocks, bonds, and Treasury bills since 1926, we find that the annual compound total return would have been 7.36 percent (Figure 11.8). For this asset allocation, losses were experienced in only 14 out of 76 years since 1926. The worst annual loss over this period would have been a 19.24-percent loss in 1931, and over the 1973–1974 bear market there would have been only a 12.17-percent loss.

In the late retirement years, safety and income are paramount. For this reason, the portion of the portfolio invested in common stocks declines further. For individuals in their late retirement years, a mix of 20-percent common stocks, 60-percent bonds,

**Figure 11.8** Return and Risk to Benchmark Asset Allocation Breakdown During the Retirement Years

| 1926-2001 | | 1967-2001 | |
|---|---|---|---|
| Stock/bond/Treasury bill mix | 40/40/20 | Stock/bond/Treasury bill mix | 40/40/20 |
| Average annual return | 7.36% | Average annual return | 9.26% |
| Years with losses (out of 76) | 14 | Years with losses (out of 35) | 5 |
| Worst annual loss (1931) | -19.24% | Worst annual loss (1974) | -7.25% |
| Bear market (1973-1974) | -12.17% | | |

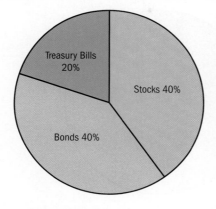

Source:   *Stocks, Bonds, Bills & Inflation 2002 Yearbook,* © 2002 Ibbotson Associates, Inc. Based on copyrighted works by Ibbotson and Sinquefield. All rights reserved. Used with permission.

and 20-percent short-term Treasury bills is a relatively common recommendation from financial planners.

Looking at the performance of a 20/60/20 asset allocation between stocks, bonds, and Treasury bills since 1926, we find that the average annual total return would have been 6.38 percent (Figure 11.9). Here, only 12 out of 76 years since 1926 experienced losses, with the worst annual loss being 11.64 percent in 1931. Over the 1973–1974 bear market, there would have been only a 3.29-percent loss.

## What You Should Know About Efficient Markets

The concept of **efficient markets** concerns the speed at which new information is reflected in security prices. The more efficient the market is, the faster prices react to new information. In a perfectly efficient market, security prices always equal their true value at all times—in other words, you can't systematically "beat the market." With efficient markets you're just as likely to pick winners as losers.

**Efficient Market**
A market in which all relevant information about the stock is reflected in the stock price.

## Is the Stock Market Efficient?

As you can imagine, the question of whether the stock market is efficient is a very emotional one for many investment advisors and analysts on Wall Street. If the

**Figure 11.9** Return and Risk to Benchmark Asset Allocation Breakdown During the Late Retirement Years

| **1926-2001** | | **1967-2001** | |
|---|---|---|---|
| Stock/bond/Treasury bill mix | 20/60/20 | Stock/bond/Treasury bill mix | 20/60/20 |
| Average annual return | 6.38% | Average annual return | 8.65% |
| Years with losses (out of 76) | 12 | Years with losses (out of 35) | 4 |
| Worst annual loss (1931) | -11.64% | Worst annual loss (1994) | -3.62% |
| Bear market (1973-1974) | -3.29% | | |

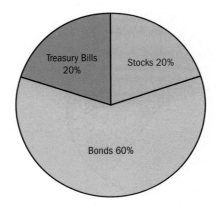

Treasury Bills 20%

Stocks 20%

Bonds 60%

Source: *Stocks, Bonds, Bills & Inflation 2002 Yearbook,* © 2002 Ibbotson Associates, Inc. Based on copyrighted works by Ibbotson and Sinquefield. All rights reserved. Used with permission.

stock market is truly efficient, then there's no benefit to much of what's done by stock analysts.

But before dealing with the question of how efficient the stock market is, it's important to understand why there can't be a definitive answer to this question. First of all, there's a question of the degree of efficiency. That is, although historical information may not help small investors earn abnormal profits, it has value to large investors. Improving your performance by 0.01 percent may be irrelevant for you, but for a manager with a $4-billion portfolio, it means an increase in profits of $400,000 (0.0001 × $4 billion = $400,000). In addition, if someone uncovers a new technique for predicting prices, he or she would be much better off using it rather than publishing it. As a result, we may only see results that indicate that the market is efficient.

However, reports of beating the market don't indicate that the market is inefficient. On average we would expect, just by chance, that half the investors will outperform the market and half will underperform the market. In general, you usually hear about those who beat the market. Not surprisingly, those who underperform the market tend not to publicize their results. The bottom line is that while we can't present a definite answer as to whether you can beat the market, we can give you enough understanding of the difficulties to help you define an investment strategy that makes sense.

## How Tough Is It to Consistently Beat the Market?

Very tough! On average, half the time you should outperform the market, and half the time you should underperform the market. Let's look at the performance of the "superstars" of investing. Every year *Barron's* offers a roundtable of Wall Street superstars' predictions for the upcoming year.

Looking at their predictions from 1967 through 1991, an investor who bought each one of the "picks" the day after the publication and held it for 1 year would have earned 0.021 percent above what was expected. If these picks were held for 2 or 3 years, they actually would have done worse than average.

Actually, the "superstar" picks were not as bleak as they appear. If the stocks were purchased on the day that the picks were made, not on the day they were published in *Barron's*, investors could have earned a return of just over 2 percent above the norm. What does this mean for the average investor? It means it's very difficult to pick underpriced stocks.

If it's so difficult to pick underpriced stocks, should we focus on timing the market—that is, buying stocks before the market rises? To get some perspective on how difficult it is to time the market, let's look at what the experts said about 1995—a great year, one in which the stock market went up by over 30 percent. The weekly Standard and Poor's advisory publication, *Outlook*, predicted the market would go up by 8.5 percent. Prudential Securities predicted no change in the stock market in 1995, saying that it was "fully valued."

**STOP & THINK** Just because a "system" has worked in the past doesn't mean it will in the future. A good example of how misleading good historical results are can be seen by looking at the "Super Bowl effect." The market tends to go up when a team from the premerger NFL wins the Super Bowl and tends to go down when a premerger AFL team wins. Through 1997 there have been 30 Super Bowls, and in 27 of those years this "system" correctly predicted the stock market. Statistically, the predictive power of this system appears to shoot right off the scale. Is this a technique that you should let guide your investment strategy? Heavens no! Although there's a strong statistical relationship, there's no cause and effect and no reason to believe that this relationship should hold in the future. Just look at 1998 and 1999 when the Broncos won the Super Bowl. The market should have dropped, but instead it rose by 28.6 percent and 21.0 percent respectively. Then, in 2000, the Rams won the Super Bowl, meaning the market should have gone up—instead, it dropped by about 9 percent. Finally, in 2001, the "system" worked again, as the AFC Baltimore Ravens won and the market dropped by about 12 percent.

# Checklist 11.1 ▪ What To Do

What does our understanding of efficient markets tell us about investing? It tells us several things.

Systems don't beat the market. It's long-term investing that works. There simply is no foolproof method for beating the market. Beware of "hot tips" and cold calls from stockbrokers. Remember the lessons of **Principle 12: The Agency Problem in Personal Finance.** There's an old saying on Wall Street: "Those that know don't tell, and those that tell don't know." If it sounds too good to be true, it probably is. The good news in all this is that if you can do as well as the market, you have done quite well indeed.

Keep to the plan. Don't try to time the market. Keep in mind that stock prices and interest rates go up and go down, but it's almost impossible to buy only when stock prices are low and sell only when they are high. You should invest regularly and view stocks in accordance with your investment horizon.

Focus on the asset allocation process. You should spend your energy on the appropriate asset allocation given your goals, your plan, and where you are in your financial life cycle. Recognize the time dimension of investing. Your asset allocation strategy should reflect your investment horizon.

Keep the commissions down. Because it's difficult to beat the market, make sure you don't give away too much of your return in the way of commissions. Be aware of what the commissions are and shop around.

Diversify, diversify, diversify. The benefits of diversification are still unchallenged.

If you don't feel comfortable, seek help! Don't let the fear of investing keep you out of the game. If you feel uncomfortable, seek the help of a qualified financial advisor.

The *Wall Street Journal* didn't get it right either. Its first-quarter prediction was for "A Grim First Quarter"—the market rose by 8 percent. More of the same was predicted for the second quarter—the market rose by 9.6 percent. The third quarter opened with the headline "Wall Street Still Has Jitters Despite First Half's Surge"—the market rose by 5 percent more. In the last quarter the *Wall Street Journal* cautioned that analysts "Expect Decline"—the market continued to climb, rising 6.8 percent in the final quarter.

The experts have also gotten it wrong in the other direction. At the beginning of 2001, 13 investment strategists who were surveyed by *Bloomberg News* predicted that the Standard & Poor's 500 Index would climb 21 percent in 2001 to a level of 1,593. Instead, the index dropped 12 percent to 1,148.

The bottom line is that you should keep to your plan and invest for the long term. If you try to time the market, you're just as likely to miss an upswing as you are to avoid a downswing.

Checklist 11.1 provides you with the implications of our understanding of efficient markets.

## SUMMARY

In personal financial planning, everything begins and ends with your goals. You must first decide what your goals are and how much you can set aside to meet those goals. Once you've done this, you can develop an investment plan.

It's important to know the difference between investments and speculation. Investing involves buying an asset that generates a return. Speculation occurs when an asset's value depends solely on supply and demand. Buying gold coins and baseball cards is considered speculation because they're worth more in the future only if someone is willing to pay more for them.

There are two basic categories of investments: (1) lending investments—for example, bonds, which are debt instruments issued by corporations and by the government; and (2) ownership investments—for example, preferred stock and common stock, which represent an ownership position in a corporation.

When you invest your money, you can receive your return as a capital gain or in the form of interest or dividends.

Interest rates play an extremely important role in determining the value of an investment. They are also closely tied to the rate of inflation. The nominal rate of return is the rate of return earned on an investment without any adjustment for lost purchasing power. The real rate of return is simply the current or nominal rate of return minus the inflation rate. It tells you how much you have earned after you've adjusted for inflation.

There are a number of different sources of risk associated with investments, including interest rate risk, inflation risk, business risk, liquidity risk, market risk, political and regulatory risk, exchange rate risk, and call risk.

As your investment horizon lengthens, you can afford to invest more in riskier assets. This is because the returns of risky assets tend to dominate those of less risky assets as the investment horizon lengthens.

Diversification works by allowing the extreme good and bad returns to cancel each other out. The ability to eliminate a portion of a portfolio's risk through diversification has led to the segmentation of risk into two types: systematic risk and unsystematic risk.

Asset allocation attempts to ensure that the investor is well diversified, generally with investments in several different classes of investments, such as domestic common stocks, international common stocks, and bonds. It also incorporates the concept of the time dimension of investing into the allocation process.

Efficient markets are concerned with the speed in which information is reflected in security prices. The more efficient the market is, the faster prices react to new information.

## REVIEW QUESTIONS

1. Explain the difference between investing and speculating. Give an example of each.

2. Briefly distinguish among short-, intermediate-, and long-term goals. Provide an example of each.

3. Why should you look for tax-favored investment strategies? How can these strategies help you attain your goals?

4. Why is it important to maintain an adequate emergency fund before creating and implementing an investment program? Approximately how much should you set aside in an emergency fund?

5. How might someone go about finding money from his or her daily living expenses to start an investment program?

6. Name and briefly describe the two basic categories of investments. Provide two examples of each.

7. When it comes to taxes, why are capital gains better than dividends or interest?

8. What is the basic difference between the nominal rate of return and the real rate of return? Which is a better measure of how well an investment has performed?

9. Nominal or quoted returns are given to bonds. How is the nominal rate of interest calculated? What types of investor risks does it reflect?

10. Investors need to be aware of nine sources of risk when calculating the risk–return trade-off. List and briefly describe these nine sources of risk.

11. Differentiate between systematic and nonsystematic risk. Which of these is more important to the average investor?

12. Why might investors not be willing to take risks with their investment portfolios even though they take risks elsewhere? What investment concepts might help them be more willing to take an appropriate amount of risk?

13. Name and describe the three ways to measure the risks associated with investment returns.

14. What is the long-term relationship between risk and time? Why is this an important concept to remember when developing and implementing an investment program?

15. What is meant by the term "asset allocation?" What makes asset allocation such a simple and powerful concept?

16. When should an investor change his or her asset allocation mix?

17. What is the purpose for adjusting your asset allocation as you age? Why wouldn't "the best" or highest returning portfolio always be prudent?

18. What is the relationship between market efficiency and the success of market timing? Does market timing work consistently? What six concepts should the average investor keep in mind in order to increase investment rates of return?

## PROBLEMS AND ACTIVITIES

1. Using the tables in Appendix D, calculate how much will you need to save at the end of each year assuming the following:

   a. You have 30 years until retirement.

   b. You will need $1 million in savings.

   c. You feel you can earn a 9-percent return on your investment.

2. Everyone needs an emergency fund. Assume your best friend asks you to evaluate a list of investments for an emergency savings fund. Comment on the appropriateness of each of the following:

   a. Certificate of deposit

   b. Three-month Treasury bills

   c. Gold and silver coins

   d. Portfolio of technology stocks

   e. Money market mutual fund

3. Jana just found out that she is going to receive an end-of-year bonus of $40,000. She is in the 35 percent marginal tax bracket. Calculate her tax on this bonus. Now assume that instead of receiving a bonus, Jana receives the $40,000 as a long-term capital gain. What will be her tax? Which form of compensation offers Jana the best after-tax return? Would your calculation be

different if the gain was short term rather than long term?

4. As a savvy student of personal finance, you've just learned that a company in your hometown made so much money last year that they are going to distribute a huge cash distribution this quarter. In order to get in on the deal you've got to make a quick decision. Which security should you buy in order to receive the cash payment— stock in the company or a bond offered by the company? Explain your answer.

5. After reading this chapter, it isn't surprising that you're becoming an investment wizard. Last year you purchased 100 shares of KSU Corporation for $37 per share. Over the past 12 months KSU's price has gone up to $45 per share, and you received a dividend of $1 per share. What was your total rate of return on your investment in the KSU stock?

6. Your investment in KSU stock was so successful that you decided to hold it for 5 more years. Remember, you purchased 100 shares for $37 per share. Unfortunately, the price of KSU stock hasn't done much; the price is back to where you purchased it. The good news is that you earned $1 per share for five years. Calculate your annualized total rate of return. Compared to a bank account, earning 2-percent interest, how did your stock investment do?

7. You just learned that a blue chip company will issue a bond with a maturity of 100 years. The bond appears to be a good deal because it yields 8.50 percent. Assuming that the inflation rate stays at 4 percent, what is the bond's real rate of return today? If you were looking for a bond to purchase and hold for several years, would you buy this bond? Explain your answer in terms of future inflation projections and the length of the bond's maturity.

8. Calculate the nominal rate of interest for a new bond that will mature in 10 years assuming the following bond characteristics and market risks:

   a. 3-month T-bill rate of 4 percent
   b. Anticipated yearly inflation of 3 percent
   c. Low or no chance of default
   d. A premium of 0.25 percent for every year until maturity
   e. No liquidity premium

9. Tim recently purchased a bond with a 10-year maturity for $1,000. The bond pays annual interest of $100. What interest rate is Tim receiving on his investment? Today Tim learned that market interest rates for 10-year bonds are 6 percent. How much could Tim sell his bond for today? How much could he sell the bond for tomorrow if interest rates move up to 15 percent? Based on your calculations, what is the relationship between interest rates and the value of bonds?

10. Outline the typical investment goals associated with each of the following life-cycle events. Provide a recommended asset allocation for each stage.

   a. the early years
   b. the golden years
   c. the retirement years
   d. the late retirement years

## SUGGESTED PROJECTS

1. Before you can develop an investment plan, you must identify your investment goals. List five short-term and five long-term investment goals for yourself. Ask your spouse or other members of your family if they have identified investment goals. If so, how are your goals similar?

2. For a group project, identify several no-load mutual funds. Find information about the automatic investment program for a particular no-load mutual fund. Specifically, determine minimum monthly deductions, time commitments, and any other relevant information. Summarize the information in a group report.

3. You've learned that interest rates can be used as a base return to compare all investments. Using a current edition of either the *Wall Street Journal*, *USA Today*, or your local newspaper, find the current yield of a long-term U.S. government bond (10- or 30-year maturity). What is the minimal return that you would require before purchasing the following investments?

a. high-quality corporate bond

b. speculative technology stock

c. baseball card collectible

4. It is commonly assumed that the older a person gets, the less risk tolerant he or she becomes. Do you believe this assumption? Interview several retired persons about their risk tolerance, and how it has affected their asset allocation. Did their changes, if any, follow the recommendations found in this chapter? What do your results tell you?

5. Given the information collected in project 4, analyze each person's risk tolerance. Were they taking more or less risk with their portfolio than recommended? Why might this be the case? Explain your answers in a one- to two-page report.

6. Most mutual fund and brokerage house Internet sites offer free asset allocation and risk-tolerance assessment services. Visit three or four Internet sites and respond to the questions for the asset allocation programs. Print out the results and write a brief summary of your findings, paying close attention to how accurately the programs assessed your risk tolerance. Were the asset allocation recommendations consistent across the programs?

7. Explain why "your asset allocation mix will have a far greater impact on your return than will the choosing of each individual stock or bond that you hold."

8. Finance professors often assert that the stock market is efficient. Explain market efficiency and provide an example of a contradiction to the theory. Explain why the average investor often has a hard time taking advantage of "market inefficiencies."

9. Search the Internet for investment sites and look for stories about day traders—individual investors who trade stocks on a daily basis. Write a brief report on your findings. Did you find that most day traders are investors or speculators? How many day traders really beat the market over an extended period of time?

10. Complete an online search for articles on company earnings or earnings forecasts for three to five companies. Determine how the announcement affected the share prices. What type and source of risk influenced the individual performance of these companies? Give a brief description of your findings.

# Discussion Case 1

John, age 28, and Emily, age 27, have just had their first child, Lindsey. They have a combined income of $45,000 and rent a two-bedroom apartment. For the past several years John and Emily have taken financial responsibilities one day at a time, but it has finally dawned on them that they now must start thinking about their financial future. For the last several months John has noticed the stock market begin to move higher, and he is convinced that they should be investing in stocks. Emily is more interested in investing in collectibles like sports memorabilia, because she's been reading reports of baseball trading card speculators making huge profits. When asked what their goals are John replies that he'd like to save for retirement, and Emily mentions her top priority as saving for Lindsey's college expenses. They both agreed that they'd like to buy a house and pay off their credit card bills, which amount to $4,000. When asked to list their investments, all they could come up with was a savings account worth $650.

## Questions

1. What should be John and Emily's first priority before investing or making any investment plans?

2. Before investing in stocks, bonds, or collectibles, what type of account should John and Emily establish? What would be an appropriate "investment" for this type of account? How much should they accumulate before investing in other assets?

3. Supposing that John and Emily asked you to prioritize their goals, how would you rank their investment objectives?

4. Match investment alternatives to the objectives ranked in question 3.

5. Should John and Emily invest all their money in one investment strategy (stocks or collectibles)? Explain your answer in terms of diversification and the asset allocation process.

# Money Matters

## KNOW THYSELF

The typical question at every social gathering is "So, what's good to invest in these days?" My answer is, "It all depends!" The best advice I can give anyone is to invest based on your own personal profile, not on a hot tip from the media, a party, or coffee break conversation. To establish your profile, ask yourself the following questions:

**What am I investing for? Is it retirement, a new home, college for the children,** and so forth? For some lucky people the goal may just be to make some extra money grow.

**When will I need the money? In other words, what is your time horizon?** Will you need all the funds at some definite date, or will it be used to provide an income? For example: Many people think they must have all their money accessible on the day they retire. In reality, they need to continue to have their "nest egg" invested so that it will provide for them over many years. Short time limits (a year or two) normally do not allow you to work around the inherent volatility of the market.

**How much will I be investing?** If you have a large sum, the options are quite different from those open to you with a small monthly amount. In the latter case, you may need to choose among mutual funds that allow as little as $50 monthly purchases rather than attempting to buy 1 or 2 shares of stock each time. The dollar amount will also control the level of diversification you can achieve in individual stocks and bonds versus mutual funds.

**What is my volatility or risk tolerance?** If you anticipate a panic attack the first time your account statement shows a current balance much lower than what you contributed, you have some decisions to make. Can you learn to cope with it, will you settle for small returns from "safe" investments, or do you need an advisor to help you over the humps?

**How knowledgeable am I about the different investment vehicles available?** Are you willing to do a lot of "homework," or would you rather pay an advisor for his or her expertise? Your answer to these questions will determine how you go about actually investing-full-service broker, financial planner, investment advisor, discount broker, or directly with mutual fund companies.

So now that you know yourself, "just do it." If fear, lack of time, or inadequate information is holding you up, "Get thee to an advisor!"

## Discussion Case 2

Last year Marcel graduated from high school and received several thousand dollars from an uncle as a graduation gift. Marcel is now in his first year of college. He just heard of a guy in his dorm who invested in an Internet company and made a huge profit in a few months. Marcel likes the idea of making some money fast and is considering investing his graduation gift money in an Internet stock. Marcel's roommate, Luc, just finished a personal finance course and is concerned that Marcel may be getting himself into trouble. Luc learned that Marcel has run up a fairly large credit card bill and has trouble balancing his budget on a monthly basis, because Marcel tends to spend his entire paycheck each week. In addition, Marcel really doesn't know much about investing or how people actually "make money investing." Luc has asked you to help him work through the following questions so that he can talk to Marcel about his investment plans.

### Questions

1. Before investing any money what five things should Marcel do first?

2. Is Marcel's strategy of investing in an Internet stock to make quick profits investing or speculating? Support your answer.

3. Luc started talking to Marcel about market efficiency and market timing. Based on what you now know, how likely is that Marcel can pick one stock that will "beat the market?"

4. Calculate the annualized rate of return Marcel will receive if he purchases shares in an Internet stock at $50 per share, holds the shares for three years, and sells them at $90.

What is his after-tax rate of return if he is in the 15-percent marginal tax bracket?

5. What potentially significant disadvantage does Marcel face if he sells his Internet stock after only 10 months, for $65 per share, and incurs a short-term capital gain?

6. Should Marcel be concerned about interest rates if he is going to invest in a speculative security? Why or why not?

7. What other financial risks does Marcel face if he invests in an Internet stock?

8. By investing in one stock has Marcel increased or decreased his systematic risk? What about unsystematic risk?

9. Luc has urged Marcel to invest for the long term using a diversified approach. Marcel is skeptical. Explain why Luc is probably correct.

10. How should Marcel allocate his assets, given his stage in the life cycle?

Visit our Web site for additional case problems, interactive exercises, and practice quizzes for this chapter—**www.prenhall.com/keown**.

# 12 Securities Markets

**Learning Objectives**

**1** Identify and describe the primary and secondary securities markets.

**2** Trade securities using a broker.

**3** Locate and use several different sources of investment information to trade securities.

**M**ost parents don't buy stocks on the recommendation of their children, but that's what Mary and Tom Sanchez did. In March 1986, their 15-year-old daughter, Jennifer, a self-proclaimed "computer geek," convinced them to invest $10,000, which was about 15 percent of their total savings, into a stock that was going public at the time—Microsoft. In fact, Jennifer also invested her entire savings (paper route and baby sitting money, along with some money from her grandparents) of $750.

Back then, Microsoft was a small firm in Seattle with an unknown future run by a young, untested computer genius, Bill Gates. In fact, Microsoft was so small and unknown that it was difficult finding a stockbroker who had access to Microsoft shares at its initial price of $21 per share. The Sanchezes did, though, and they're glad of it. They even convinced Mary's brother Jim to invest $5,000 in Microsoft. He wasn't fortunate enough to be able to buy in at $21, but he was able to buy the stock later that month at $26. By early 2002, the Sanchezes' $10,000 investment had grown to over $4.1 million, and Mary's brother Jim's investment of $5,000 had grown to $1.5 million. It may well be worth considerably more today. As for Jennifer, her $750 would have been worth about $304,000, but instead it took the form of a new Porsche 911 convertible, along with about $230,000 in savings.

It wasn't until about 11 years later that Jennifer made another recommendation. Jennifer, an avid Star Wars memorabilia collector, had come across an online auction service that she believed "the world can't live without"—eBay. On Jennifer's recommendation, both she and her parents invested $50,000 each. When they bought their eBay stock in September 1998, it was selling for $18 per share. Nine months later, in June 1999, when they sold their eBay stock, both Jennifer and her parents received $5 million each. Their investment had grown tenfold! Two years later, in April 2001, Jennifer locked on to another winner, investing $100,000 in Network Associates Inc., an antivirus software maker. In February 2002, when Jennifer sold her shares, they had climbed to over $500,000. Needless to say, Jennifer is now known as an "investment wizard" rather than a "computer geek." Not everyone does as well with their investments as the Sanchezes did. However, one way to greatly improve your chances for success is to understand the rules of the investment game—in this case, how the securities markets work. Very few people feel comfortable, or should feel comfortable, playing a game without knowing the rules. That's the purpose of this chapter—to introduce you to the rules of the securities markets. This chapter is actually a continuation of the previous chapter. Now we look at how the investments markets operate and prepare you to go out and make your own investments.

It would be nice if we could all have the same success as the Sanchezes. Unfortunately, that kind of success can't be guaranteed. However, one thing is certain: The first step to becoming rich through a great investment is learning how to make that investment.

**Identify and describe the primary and secondary securities markets.**

# Security Markets

Both stocks and bonds are first bought when they are issued by corporations as a means of raising money. After the initial issue, stocks and bonds are traded—bought and sold—among investors. These trades occur in the securities markets. Just as retail goods are bought and sold at markets, such as Kmart or Sears, securities are bought and sold at appropriate markets.

A **securities market** is simply a place where you can buy or sell securities. These markets can take the form of anything from an actual building on Wall Street in New York to an electronic hookup between security dealers all over the world. Securities markets are divided into primary and secondary markets. Let's take a look at what these terms mean.

## The Primary Markets

A **primary market** is a market in which new, as opposed to previously issued, securities are traded. For example, if Nike issues a new batch of stock, this issue would be considered a primary market transaction. Actually, there are two different types of offerings in the primary markets: initial public offerings and seasoned new issues.

An **initial public offering (IPO)** is the first time the company's stock is traded publicly. The initial offering of Microsoft stock was an IPO. IPOs draw a good deal of attention in the press because they show how much a company is worth in the public's eye, and they tend to be great opportunities for huge financial gains or losses.

It's hard to determine how much people will be willing to pay for a share of a newly traded company's stock. As a result, some IPO prices are set way too low, resulting in huge profits for anyone lucky enough to buy shares at the IPO price. A good example of a company whose low IPO price resulted in huge profits is Verisity, which first went public in March 2001. By the end of the year the company's stock had risen 170 percent.

Of course, some IPO prices are set too high, resulting in horrible losses for those unlucky enough to buy. Briazz "went public" (the term used when companies make their initial public offering) in May 2001. By the end of the year, the company's stock had lost almost 89 percent of its value.

IPOs are enticing, because they give the investor the chance to get in on the ground floor of a company. It's always nice when you then wind up riding the investment elevator all the way to the penthouse, but you do run the risk that the ground floor will cave in and your investment will wind up in the basement, buried under rubble. Table 12.1 provides a listing of the big winners and losers in the IPO market in 2001.

IPOs are particularly tough on the small investor, because the most promising ones tend to be "bought up" by large investors before the smaller investor has a chance to buy in. In effect, there may not be enough stock to go around. This brings us back to **Principle 5: The Curse of Competitive Investment Markets**. The result with IPOs is that bigger accounts and more-favored clients might get first pick—certainly that was the case when Netscape went public—and the smaller investor may be left out.

**Seasoned new issues** refer to stock offerings by companies that already have common stock traded in the marketplace. For example, a sale of new shares of stock by Reebok would be considered a seasoned new issue.

Stocks and bonds are generally sold in the primary markets with the help of an **investment banker** serving as the **underwriter**. An underwriter is simply a middleman

---

**Securities Markets**
A term used to describe where financial securities or instruments—for example, common stocks and bonds—are traded.

**Primary Market**
A market in which newly issued, as opposed to previously issued, securities are traded.

**Initial Public Offering (IPO)**
The first time a company's stock is traded publicly.

**Principle 5**
The Curse of Competitive Investment Markets

**Seasoned New Issue**
A stock offering by companies that already have common stocks traded in the marketplace.

**Investment Banker**
The "middleman" between the firm issuing securities and the buying public. This term describes both the firms that specialize in selling securities to the public and the individuals who work for investment banking firms.

**Underwriter**
An investment banker who purchases and subsequently resells a new security issue. The issuing company sells its securities directly to the underwriter, who then sells the issue to the public and assumes the risk of selling the new issue at a satisfactory price.

## Table 12.1  Best and Worst IPOs of 2001 Performers

**Five Best Performers**

| Issuer | Issue Date | Offer Price | % Change from Offer | |
| | | | In 1st-Day Trading | Through Dec. 31 |
| --- | --- | --- | --- | --- |
| **Verisity** Electronic-system technology, software | March 21 | $7.00 | +14.3% | +170.7% |
| **Magma Design Automation** Chip-design and implementation software | Nov. 19 | 13.00 | +46.1 | +129.2 |
| **Monolithic System Technology** Maker of memory chips | June 27 | 10.00 | +12.2 | +108.0 |
| **Williams Energy Partners** Storage, transportation of petroleum products | Feb. 5 | 21.50 | +11.6 | +91.2 |
| **Nassda** Chip-design software | Dec. 12 | 11.00 | +40.5 | +85.6 |

**Five Worst Performers**

| Issuer | Issue Date | Offer Price | % Change from Offer | |
| | | | In 1st-Day Trading | Through Dec. 31 |
| --- | --- | --- | --- | --- |
| **Briazz** Cafe operator | May 2 | $8.00 | +0.4% | −88.9% |
| **ATP Oil & Gas** Gas and oil exploration | Feb. 5 | 14.00 | 0.0 | −79.9 |
| **Investors Capital Holdings** Financial advisor | Feb. 8 | 8.00 | −6.1 | −64.9 |
| **Align Technology** Orthodontic appliances | Jan. 25 | 13.00 | +33.2 | −64.6 |
| **Torch Offshore** Provides infrastructure for oil exploration | June 7 | 16.00 | +0.4 | −62.8 |

Source:   Standard & Poor's.

who buys the entire stock or bond issue from the issuing company and then resells it to the general public in individual shares. Merrill Lynch, Goldman Sachs, Credit Suisse First Boston, and Citigroup/Solomon Smith Barney all specialize in investment banking. Actually, we use the term "investment banker" to refer to both the overall firm and the individuals who work for it.

Single investment banking companies rarely underwrite securities issues by themselves. Usually, there is one managing investment banking company handling the issue—advising and working with the issuing company on pricing and timing concerns—that then forms a syndicate of other investment banking companies. This syndicate will underwrite the IPO or seasoned new issue.

Most security issues are announced using **tombstone advertisements**, which are merely ads placed in a newspaper, magazine, or online service, providing details on the offering and the names of the underwriting syndicate. Figure 12.1 shows a tombstone advertisement for a new issue of homestore.com common stock. If a tombstone

**Tombstone Advertisement**
An advertisement that provides a listing of the underwriting syndicate involved in the new offering in addition to basic information on the offering.

Figure 12.1 A Tombstone Advertisement for a New Issue of Stock by homestore.com.

*This announcement is neither an offer to sell nor a solicitation of an offer to buy any of these Securities.*
*The offer is made only by the Prospectus.*

# 8,050,000 Shares

## Common Stock

---

## Price $20 a Share

---

*Copies of the Prospectus may be obtained in any State from only such*
*of the undersigned as may legally offer these Securities in*
*compliance with the securities laws of such State.*

**MORGAN STANLEY DEAN WITTER**

**DONALDSON, LUFKIN & JENRETTE**

**MERRILL LYNCH & CO.**

**BANCBOSTON ROBERTSON STEPHENS**

**WARBURG DILLON READ LLC**                        **DAIN RAUSCHER WESSELS**
                                                   *a division of Dain Rauscher Incorporated*

**FIRST UNION CAPITAL MARKETS CORP.**              **JANNEY MONTGOMERY SCOTT INC.**

**EDWARD D. JONES & CO., L.P.**                    **VOLPE BROWN WHELAN & COMPANY**

**THOMAS WEISEL PARTNERS LLC**

*September 16, 1999*

ad interests investors, they can simply contact a member of the underwriting syndicate to request a **prospectus**, which describes the issue and the issuing company's financial prospects. Unfortunately, by the time most tombstone ads appear, all the stock is already sold.

**Prospectus**
A legal document that describes a securities issue and that is made available to potential investors.

## Secondary Markets—Stocks

Securities that have previously been issued and bought are traded in the **secondary markets**. In other words, if you bought 100 shares of stock in an IPO and then wanted to resell them, you'd have to sell the shares in the secondary market. Only issuing companies (and their underwriters) can sell securities in the primary markets. The proceeds from the sale of a share of IBM stock on the secondary market go to the previous owner of the stock, not to IBM. In fact, the only time IBM ever receives money from the sale of one of its securities is on the primary market.

**Secondary Markets**
The markets in which previously issued securities are traded.

The secondary markets can take the form of either an organized exchange or an over-the-counter market. An **organized exchange** occupies a physical location where trading occurs. In other words, an organized exchange is actually a building in which stocks are traded. In an **over-the-counter market**, transactions are conducted over the telephone or via a computer hookup. How is it determined where a security will trade? Larger, more frequently traded securities, such as GM, IBM, General Electric, and Exxon, are traded on organized exchanges. Those that are less frequently traded, along with many new and high-tech stocks, are relegated to the over-the-counter markets. In either case, the secondary markets make it much easier for sellers to find buyers and vice versa.

**Organized Exchange**
An exchange that occupies a physical location where trading occurs, such as the New York Stock Exchange.

**Over-the-Counter Market**
A market in which transactions are conducted over the telephone or via a computer hookup rather than in an organized exchange.

**Organized Exchanges**   There are nine major organized exchanges in the United States: (1) the New York Stock Exchange (NYSE), (2) the American Stock Exchange (AMEX), (3) the Pacific Stock Exchange (Los Angeles and San Francisco), (4) the Chicago Stock Exchange, (5) the Philadelphia Exchange (Philadelphia and Miami), (6) the Cincinnati Stock Exchange, (7) Intermountain Stock Exchange (Salt Lake City), (8) Spokane Stock Exchange, and (9) the Boston Stock Exchange.

The New York Stock Exchange and the American Stock Exchange are considered national stock exchanges, and the others are generally termed **regional stock exchanges**. If a firm's stock trades on a particular exchange, it is said to be *listed* on that exchange. Securities can be listed on more than one exchange. Without question, the NYSE is the big player, with over 80 percent of the typical trading volume.

**Regional Stock Exchanges**
Organized stock exchanges located outside New York City and registered with the Securities and Exchange Commission.

***The New York Stock Exchange (NYSE)***   The New York Stock Exchange, also called the "Big Board," is the oldest of all the organized exchanges. It began in 1792 when 24 traders signed the Buttonwood Agreement, a pact named after the tree under which traders gathered, obligating them to "give preference" to each other in security trading. When winter came, the 24 traders moved to the back room of Wall Street's Tontine Coffee House, leaving the other traders out in the cold.

The members of the Exchange occupy "seats." A seat is a membership card, and the number of seats on the New York Stock Exchange is limited to 1,366, a number that hasn't changed since 1953. The only way to acquire a seat is to buy one from a current owner for whatever the market price is. The highest price a seat has ever sold for is $2.6 million. Large brokerage firms such as Merrill Lynch might own over 20 seats.

## Table 12.2   Initial Listing Requirements for the NYSE, 1999

*Profitability*

Earnings before taxes (EBT) for the most recent year must be at least $2.5 million.

For the 2 years preceding that, EBT must be at least $2.0 million

*Size*

Net tangible must be at least $40.0 million.

*Market Value*

The market value of publicly held stock must be at least $100.0 million.

*Public Ownership*

There must be at least 1.1 million publicly held common shares.

There must be at least 2,000 holders of 100 shares or more.

To be listed on the NYSE, a firm must meet strict requirements. Table 12.2 lists the current requirements for the NYSE and demonstrates how restrictive those requirements really are. If a firm fails to maintain the minimum requirements, it's delisted and no longer traded on the NYSE.

In early 2001 there were over 2,800 NYSE-listed companies from all over the world, with more than 310 billion shares worth $12.3 trillion available for trading. The NYSE is the largest organized securities exchange in the world. Included among NYSE-listed stocks are companies such as PepsiCo, AT&T, Wal-Mart, Coca-Cola, and Circuit City.

**The American Stock Exchange (AMEX)**   The American Stock Exchange is the second most important of the organized exchanges and generally lists stocks of firms that are somewhat smaller than those listed on the NYSE. Although the AMEX operates in a manner similar to the NYSE, it has only 660 seats and lists just over 800 firms. Its trading volume is only 3 percent of that on the NYSE. It may rank as number two in terms of the number of companies it lists, but when it comes to the dollar volume of daily trades, it's actually smaller than some regional exchanges.

**Regional Stock Exchanges**   Regional exchanges trade in securities of local or regional firms. Requirements for listing are much more relaxed (e.g., net assets of $1 million as compared to $100 million for the NYSE). Many regional exchanges also list stocks found on the NYSE and AMEX to encourage more trading. Some stocks trade on both the NYSE or AMEX and also on a regional exchange. Actually, the West Coast exchanges have the advantage of operating in a different time zone, allowing customers to trade well after the NYSE closes.

**Over-the-Counter (OTC) Market**   The over-the-counter market is simply a linkup of dealers, with no listing or membership requirements. For the most part, the over-the-counter market is highly automated. A nationwide computer network allows brokers to see up-to-the-minute price quotes on roughly 35,000 securities.

OTC listings are often made up of companies that are too new or too small to be listed on a major exchange. These companies also often have fewer shares available. As a result, in some cases small amounts of buying or selling may have a significant impact on the price of these companies' stocks.

Depending on the frequency of trading activity, trading information is passed among dealers in one of several ways. Information on stocks that trade very infrequently is mailed daily to member dealers on what are called "pink sheets," which are named for the color of paper on which they're printed. For example, if you wanted to buy or sell shares of a local Blacksburg, Virginia, bank, information for that bank would most likely be mailed to dealers by the National Quote Bureau. Unfortunately, the quote on the "pink sheet" may not be current, making trading in these securities a bit more difficult.

An OTC stock that's more frequently traded would be handled by the NASDAQ. In 1971 the National Association of Securities Dealers Automated Quotations system (NASDAQ) was set up to allow dealers to post bid and ask prices for OTC stocks over a computer linkup. A **bid price** is the price at which an individual is willing to purchase a security, and an **ask price** is the price at which an individual is willing to sell a security.

If a security is traded more frequently, it might be listed on the National Market System (NMS), which is just a sophisticated version of the NASDAQ. In total, about 10,000 of the 35,000 OTC securities are listed on the NASDAQ/NMS. These include companies like Dell, Microsoft, eBay, AOL, Intel, and Oracle. Although there are approximately twice as many securities listed on the NASDAQ/NMS as there are listed on the NYSE, the dollar volume of trading on the NASDAQ/NMS is substantially less than it is on the NYSE.

Still, the NASDAQ/NMS has grown to the point where it's the second largest secondary securities market in the United States, as measured by dollar trading volume. Many large high-tech companies have chosen not to seek listing on the NYSE, but instead remain traded on the NASDAQ/NMS. As a result, you see firms such as Intel and Microsoft traded on the NASDAQ/NMS alongside smaller companies such as Noodle Kid.

## Secondary Markets—Bonds

Although some bonds are actually traded at the NYSE, most of the buying and selling of bonds doesn't occur on the organized exchanges. Instead, bond dealers buy and sell bonds out of their holdings. Generally, bond dealers deal directly only with large financial institutions; the smaller investor can gain access to them only through a broker acting as an intermediary. Your broker will buy or sell the bond from the bond dealer and then pass it on to you, charging you a commission for the service.

Secondary markets tend to be for smaller, individual investors, and there just aren't all that many small, individual investors interested in corporate bonds. However, volume of trading in the secondary market for government bonds is enormous. In fact, trading volume in government bonds runs in the billions of dollars each month. Government bond trading is dominated by the Federal Reserve, commercial banks, and other financial institutions.

## International Markets

International security markets have been around for centuries. In fact, around 2000 B.C. the Babylonians introduced debt financing, and by 400 B.C. the Greeks had developed a security market of sorts. Today, it's possible to invest internationally, with huge investment markets across the globe. The world bond market today is valued at over $25 trillion. In terms of this market, the United States dominates. However, Japan, Germany, the United Kingdom, and France are all major players.

How do you buy a Japanese stock? There are three ways. First, some foreign shares are traded on exchanges in the United States. For example, just over 300 foreign companies are traded on the NYSE and over 60 are traded on the AMEX. In

**Bid Price**
The price at which an individual is willing to purchase a security.

**Ask Price**
The price at which an individual is willing to sell a security.

addition, over 400 are traded on the NASDAQ. However, many of these companies are Canadian.

Another way international stocks can be traded is through **American Depository Receipts (ADRs)**. With ADRs, shares of stock aren't traded directly. Instead, the foreign firm's stock is held on deposit in a bank in the foreign firm's country. The foreign bank issues an ADR, which represents direct ownership over those shares. The ADR then trades internationally just like a normal share of stock. Examples of foreign firms with ADRs include Sony and Toyota. Finally, you can go online and invest directly in international stocks through **www.intltrader.com**. It allows you access to multinational giants like Nestlè, BASF, Foster's Brewing, Quantas, Porsche, Toshiba—plus thousands of other international companies. The cost is also quite reasonable, with the purchase of up to 8,000 foreign shares.

Today, many investment advisors recommend that their clients increase their international investments. They cite relatively low-priced stocks coupled with strong economies. Certainly, there are real opportunities abroad. In fact, since 1980, U.S. foreign holdings have increased more than 100-fold. Foreign equity investments now account for 10 percent of U.S. investors' holdings. However, there are also risks.

For example, the Japanese stock market started plummeting in January 1990 and didn't stop until it lost 63 percent of its value by August 1992. From then until early 2001, it continued to slowly slide—missing the great stock market surges that took place in the United States in the late 1990s. By early 2001, it still stood about 75 percent below its high 11 years previously.

## Regulation of the Securities Markets

Securities market regulation is aimed at protecting the investor and providing a level playing field so that all investors have a fair chance of making money. There are actually two levels of regulation: general regulation by the Securities and Exchange Commission (SEC, a federal agency) and self-regulation directly by the exchanges (or, in the case of the OTC market, by the National Association of Securities Dealers, NASD).

**SEC Regulation**  The great stock market crash of 1929 inspired much of the legislation that governs the securities markets today. In the period following the crash, the Securities Act of 1933 and the Securities Exchange Act of 1934 were enacted. The Securities Act of 1933 required disclosure of relevant information on initial public offerings and registration with the Federal Trade Commission. Firms issuing securities must provide a registration statement with detailed financial information to the SEC at least 20 days before the offering date. If found to be factual, this information must then be provided to all potential investors in the form of a prospectus.

The Securities Exchange Act of 1934 spoke directly to the secondary market and created the Securities and Exchange Commission to enforce the trading laws. Keeping with the principle of disclosure, publicly traded companies were required to provide periodic financial statements to the SEC and to provide shareholders with annual reports. This act also required all exchanges to register with the SEC.

The cornerstone of both pieces of legislation is disclosure of relevant information relating to the offering of the security. Many other acts and laws have been passed to regulate the securities markets. For example, the Investment Advisers Act of 1940

# In The News

**Wall Street Journal February 12, 2002**

## *Don't Be Shy: Emerging Markets Are OK*

### by Jonathan Clements

Strap yourself in, close your eyes, and clench your teeth. It's time to invest in emerging markets. Here's why a smidgen of emerging-markets exposure could be a great addition to your portfolio:

*Bargain Hunting*: Once markets have momentum, they often keep barreling along. But for the gains to be sustained, you need rock-bottom valuations.

*Emerging markets score on that criterion. "In September of last year, emerging markets were at a 16-year low relative to the Standard & Poor's 500, based on price-to-book value and price-to-earnings ratios," says Chris Alderson, lead manager of the T. Rowe Price Emerging Markets Stock Fund. "We had a pretty sharp rally in the fourth quarter, but we're still at a multiyear low."* (☛A)

Mr. Alderson continues: "Historically, emerging markets have outperformed when the global economy is recovering, and that seems to be happening right now."

*Reducing Risk*: Lately, investors have lamented the way foreign stock markets have increasingly moved in sync with U.S. shares, thus trimming the risk-reduction benefits that come with international diversification. But the story is more complicated than that, according to a study by William Goetzmann, Lingfeng Li, and K. Geert Rouwenhorst.

The three authors found that the correlation among major markets has indeed increased in recent decades. But at the same time there has been a rapid rise in the number of countries with active stock markets, and these markets have proved to be good diversifiers for U.S. stock investors.

"The good news is you can still get the diversification benefit," says Mr. Goetzmann, a finance professor at Yale University's School of Management. "The bad news is you have to risk your money in these fringe markets."

*In other words, emerging markets—as erratic as they are—could help to temper your stock portfolio's overall volatility. But don't go overboard. Consider putting maybe a quarter of your foreign-stock exposure in emerging markets, suggests David Booth, co-chairman of Dimensional Fund Advisors in Santa Monica, California.* (☛B)

### THE BOTTOM LINE ...

**A** There is no question about the risk associated with emerging markets. While they went up by 79.6 percent in 1993, they went down in 5 out of the 8 following years.

**B** It doesn't seem right that you can reduce risk by adding a risky component to your portfolio, but as long as that new component counters and cancels out the movements in your existing portfolio—and that's exactly what emerging markets do—you'll end up with less total variability. That's the logic in **Principle 3: Diversification Reduces Risk** and **Principle 4: All Risk Is Not Equal.**

---

provides investor protection against unethical investment advisors and requires advisors to register with the SEC and provide the SEC with semiannual reports. Under the Investor Protection Act of 1970, the Securities Investor Protection Corporation (SIPC) was established to provide up to $500,000 of insurance to cover investors' account balances in the event that their brokerage firm goes bankrupt.

**STOP & THINK** What is the purpose of market regulation? It's to give everyone an equal chance of making money in the stock market. The disclosure principle allows all investors to view the same information at the same time and thereby have an equal chance of making trading profits. That's what guides the majority of the laws governing the securities markets—giving everyone a fair chance at making money.

**Self-Regulation** Much of the day-to-day regulation of the markets is left to the securities industry and is performed by the exchanges and the NASD. The willingness and zeal with which the exchanges approach self-regulation is inspired by the fear that if self-regulation doesn't work, government regulation will be imposed.

After the October 1987 market crash, the NYSE self-regulated like mad and imposed a number of "circuit breakers" to head off or slow potential future market crashes. The idea behind these "circuit breakers" is that by closing the market in the event of sharp declines, investors will be given a chance to step back and assess the price decline rather than reacting on instinct.

**Insider Trading and Market Abuses**   Much of the logic behind regulation of the market stems from the desire to level the playing field with respect to the securities markets. The Insider Trading Sanctions Act of 1984 and the Insider Trading and Securities Fraud Enforcement Act of 1988 made it illegal to trade while in the possession of inside information, or "material" nonpublic information held by officers, directors, major stockholders, or anyone with special insider knowledge.

Has insider trading disappeared? Certainly not. In fact, *Business Week*, after analyzing the largest 100 mergers and takeovers of 1994, came to the conclusion that one out of three of those deals was preceded by stock price run-ups or abnormal volume that could not be explained by the publicly available information at the time.

Another potential abuse involves **churning**, or excessive trading on a client's account. Although churning is illegal, it's also practically impossible to prove. Churning can easily take place if the client has relinquished trading control to the broker, but it also takes place on traditional accounts. That's why it's so important to select an honest broker whom you can trust.

**Churning**
Excessive trading in a security account that is inappropriate for the customer and serves only to generate commissions.

**2** Trade securities using a broker.

## How Securities Are Traded

Trading securities is like so many other important things in life: You can't really do it unless you know how. This section will teach you how to do it and explain the different types of trades and trading mechanisms. You'll notice that when we discuss the different trading mechanisms, we refer to all securities as stocks. We're not favoring stocks or saying that these trading mechanisms apply only to stocks. We're just being lazy, and stocks are the most frequently traded of the different securities.

### The Role of the Specialist

**Continuous Markets**
Markets in which trading can occur at any time, with prices free to fluctuate as trading occurs.

The NYSE and the AMEX both are considered **continuous markets**, which means that trading can occur on them whenever the exchanges are open. Unfortunately, buyers and sellers don't necessarily come to the market at the same time. For example, a large order to buy stock in Guidant, a producer of medical products, may arrive at the market at 11:07 A.M. If there isn't much in the way of Guidant stock for sale at that time, the price of that stock might rise considerably. At 11:10 A.M., a large order to sell Guidant stock may reach the market. This time, if there isn't much demand for the stock, its price may drop by quite a bit.

**Specialist**
An exchange member who oversees the trading in one or more stocks and is responsible for maintaining a "fair and orderly" market in those stocks by buying or selling for his or her own account.

This bouncing up and down of stock prices is caused when supply and demand don't meet in the market at the same time. It's the role of the **specialist** to take care of this potential problem and to "maintain a fair and orderly market."

Exchanges assign specialists to each stock, for which they act as both broker and dealer. If you'd like to buy a stock at a particular price, the specialist keeps track of your order, and when the stock price drops to the level you specified, the specialist executes your order. The specialist acts as a facilitator, keeping track of all the buy and sell offers and matching trades when appropriate.

The specialist also buys and sells stock from inventory to relieve the price changes that result when buy and sell orders randomly reach the market at different times. Specialists not only maintain an inventory of stock, but also are required to maintain bid and ask prices at which they're willing to buy or sell additional inventory. When someone wants to sell a bunch of stock and there's no one to buy, the specialist will buy it. If someone wants to buy some stock and there's no one to buy it from, the specialist is there to supply the stock.

At times specialists absorb excess supply and at other times they provide stock out of inventory for excess demand. In that way they keep the market from fluctuating more than it would otherwise. But don't think specialists can always prevent market problems.

They certainly didn't manage to prevent the big market crash on October 17, 1987, when stock prices fell by about 25 percent. On that day, in a desperate attempt to stabilize the market, specialists bought $486 million of stock. Still, the market fell dramatically. In attempting to keep prices from bouncing around too much, NYSE specialists generally act as either the buyer or the seller in almost 20 percent of the share volume traded. The remaining shares traded involve individuals' orders meeting directly in the market without the help of the specialist.

## Order Characteristics

When you place an order to buy or sell stock, you need to be clear about the size of the order and the length of time the order is to be outstanding.

**Order Size**   Common stock is sold in lots or groups of 100 shares on the New York Stock Exchange. These lots are referred to as **round lots**. Orders involving between 1 and 99 shares of stock are referred to as **odd lots** and are processed by "odd lot dealers" who buy and sell out of their inventory.

**Round Lot**
A group or lot of 100 shares of common stock. Stocks are traded in round lots on the New York Stock Exchange.

**Time Period for Which the Order Will Remain Outstanding**   When you order a hamburger at Burger King, you want your order filled right away, not in a week. Well, when you order stock, you better specify when you want your order filled, or you just might have to wait a week and pay more than you bargained for. Ordering alternatives include **day orders**, which expire at the end of the trading day during which they were made; **open orders**, also called **good-till-canceled (GTC) orders**, which remain effective until filled or canceled; and fill-or-kill orders, which, if not filled immediately, expire.

**Odd Lot**
An order involving between 1 and 99 shares of stock.

**Day Order**
A trading order that expires at the end of the trading day during which it was made.

Your broker can be given the power to make trades for you if you open a **discretionary account**. Because a discretionary account gives your broker power over your money, you should consider it only if you've worked with your broker for years, and only under unusual circumstances. There's no question that problems do occur with discretionary accounts, and the easiest way to avoid the problems is to avoid discretionary accounts.

**Open or Good-Till-Canceled (GTC) Order**
A trading order that remains effective until filled or canceled.

**Discretionary Account**
An account that gives your broker the power to make trades for you.

## Types of Orders

**Market Orders**   Whenever you place an order, you want to make sure that it is carried out in exactly the way you intended. A number of different types of orders act as instructions for how you would like your order to be executed.

A **market order** is simply an order to buy or sell a set number of securities immediately at the best price available. These orders can generally be executed within minutes of being placed. Once your order is placed with your broker, it's teletyped to the floor of the NYSE, where it's either executed electronically or received by a floor broker. The floor broker takes the order to the location on the exchange floor where that stock trades and executes the trade. As a result, when you place a market order, you can be relatively certain that the order will be executed quickly. However, you can't be certain of the price at which it'll be executed.

**Market Order**
An order to buy or sell a set number of securities immediately at the best price available.

**Limit Orders**   A **limit order** specifies that the trade is to be made only at a certain price or better. In other words, if a limit order to sell stock is made, the stock will be sold only at a certain price or above. If a limit order to buy is made, the stock is bought only at a certain price or below. Limit orders allow you to limit your bid or ask price to what you feel is an acceptable level. If the specified price isn't available, your trade isn't made. Your order is given to the specialist, who'll execute the limit order if the price moves to your acceptable level.

**Stop Orders**   A **stop** or **stop-loss order** is an order to sell if the price drops *below* a specified level or to buy if the price climbs *above* a specified level. Stop-loss orders are used to protect your profits. They allow you to bail out of the stock if the market starts to tumble, or to buy in if the price starts to rise.

For example, say you'd purchased Circuit City in September 2001 at $10.00 per share and by late January 2002 it was selling at $29.84 per share. Of course, you never know when Circuit City might have some problems or when the market might fall. Circuit City's price could dive, killing part or all of your $19.84 per share gain. If you wanted to lock in some of the gains you'd already made, you could do so by using a stop-loss order to sell Circuit City at $25.

You wouldn't want to use a stop-loss order for the full $29.84 current price, because your stock would then be sold immediately while the price remained $29.84. You also wouldn't want to use a stop-loss order for an amount very close to $29.84, say $29.50 or so, because market prices commonly fluctuate up and down. You wouldn't want your stop-loss order to be executed on a routine fluctuation just before an uncommon rise up to, say, $40 per share.

You want to set the stop-loss order price just right so that you safeguard against only a major fluctuation. Thus, if the price of Circuit City tumbled to $25, your stop-loss order would activate and sell your Circuit City stock at the best price possible, which may end up being less than $25. In this way you can "lock in" some of the paper profits.

---

**STOP & THINK**   Limit orders and stop-loss orders are aimed at taking some risk out of investing. The limit order allows you to buy into a stock at what you feel is a good price. Its downside is that if the stock's price continues to rise, your order may never be executed. A stop-loss order allows you to sell the stock quickly if the price falls. Remember, however, that a stop-loss order doesn't guarantee you will sell the stock at the price you set; a stop-loss order becomes a market order when the set price is reached. That means the stock could continue to fall before someone is willing to buy your shares.

---

## Short Selling

Although it's obvious that you can make money in the stock market when stocks rise in price, you can also make money when prices decline. With **short selling** you're wishing for bad news: The more the stock drops in price, the more money you make. Short selling involves borrowing stock from your broker, selling it, and replacing the stock later. Then, if the stock price goes down, you buy it back and return it to your broker. You make a profit by buying it for less than you sold it.

If the price of the stock goes up, you have to buy it back at a higher price. You lose! In effect, selling short lets you reverse the order of buying and selling. That is, when you invest in stock, the goal is to buy low and later to sell high. With short selling, the goal is to sell high and later to buy low.

Short selling isn't necessarily free, or even cheap. Because you've borrowed someone's stock and sold it, you not only have to replace it later, you also have to repay any dividends that were paid during the period for which the broker was without the stock. Also, to protect itself from short sellers who might lose the money, the broker keeps the proceeds from the short sale until it gets its stock back.

**Figure 12.2** Profits from Purchasing Versus Selling Short

Profit from Purchasing Stock and Later Selling It

Profit = (Ending Price + Dividends) – Initial Price – Total Commissions Paid

vs.

Profit from Selling Stock Short

Profit = Initial Price – (Ending Price + Dividends) – Total Commissions Paid

To provide the brokerage firm with further protection that the short seller will be able to repurchase the stock in the future, the short seller must put up some collateral—referred to as a **margin requirement**—during the period of the short sale.

Let's suppose that you feel strongly that McDonald's stock price is about to fall from its present level of $70 per share, and you want to make money off McDonald's misfortune. First, you call your broker and sell 1,000 shares of McDonald's short. The proceeds of $70,000 are credited to your account, although you can't withdraw those funds. Your broker also has a 50-percent margin requirement, which means you must have an additional $35,000 in cash or securities in your account to serve as collateral. Most short sellers keep Treasury bills or notes in their account for this purpose.

Now let's assume that McDonald's drops to $50 per share, and you decide it's time to buy. You call your broker to purchase 1,000 shares of McDonald's for a total cost of $50,000. Thus, you've made $20,000 on your short sale by selling high ($70 per share) and later buying low ($50 per share). Remember, though, that when you sell short, you also have to cover any dividends that occurred during the period the broker was without the stock. Thus, your profits are actually equal to the initial price less the total of the ending price and the dividends, as shown in Figure 12.2.

Of course, if McDonald's price went up, you'd lose money, because you'd have to buy back the stock. Thus, if McDonald's stock went up to $90 per share, you'd lose $20,000 on your short sale, in addition to having to cover any dividends that occurred during the period the stock was sold short. You'd also have to listen to your broker laugh when you gave back the more expensive stock. In this case, you'd have sold low ($70 per share) and later bought high ($90 per share). Given the fact that the long-term trend of the stock market is upward, selling short is extremely risky and isn't something you should become involved in.

> **Margin Requirement**
> The percentage that an investor must have on deposit with a broker when selling short.

## Dealing with Brokers

Trade securities using a broker.

Although you can purchase securities through most financial planners, the most common means of purchasing common stock directly is through a stockbroker. A stockbroker is simply someone licensed to buy or sell stocks for others. In fact, most financial planners are, among other things, stockbrokers.

There are three general categories of brokers: full-service brokers, discount brokers, and deep discount brokers. In addition, you can also deal directly, that is over the phone or in person, with your broker, or you can do your trading online, without ever interacting directly with a broker. The differences between them center on advice and cost. As we'll see later when we examine the cost of trading, the difference in cost can be substantial.

## Brokerage Accounts

Just as a bank account represents money you have on deposit at a bank, a brokerage account represents money or investments you have at a brokerage firm. For most investors, this account includes securities and possibly some cash. It can also include other investments. If there are enough different investments, combining these different accounts into an all-in-one account, called an asset management account, might be best.

When we first introduced **asset management accounts** in Chapter 5, we defined such an account as a comprehensive financial services package offered by a brokerage firm that can include a checking account; a credit card; a money market mutual fund; loans; automatic payment on any fixed debt (such as mortgages); brokerage services (buying and selling stocks or bonds); and a system for the direct payment of interest, dividends, and proceeds from security sales into the money market mutual fund.

The major advantage of such an account is that it automatically coordinates the flow of funds into and out of your money market mutual fund. For example, interest and dividends received from securities owned are automatically "swept" into the money market mutual fund. If you write a check for an amount greater than what is held in your money market mutual fund, securities from the investment portion of your asset management account are automatically sold, and the proceeds "swept" into the money market fund to cover the check.

## Types of Brokers

**Full-Service Brokers**   A **full service broker** or **account executive** is paid on commission, based on the sales volume generated. With a full-service broker, each investor is assigned a broker who oversees his or her account. That broker gives advice and direction to the client, and then executes the trades. The more frequently trades are made, the more the broker earns.

**Discount Service Brokers**   A **discount service broker** simply executes trades without giving any advice. Because discount brokerage firms don't provide advice, they're able to operate more efficiently, and as a result their commissions are generally between 50 and 70 percent lower than commissions charged by full-service brokers.

**Deep Discount Brokers**   In 1994, some of the discount brokers cut prices even further, undercutting the dominant discount brokers, such as Charles Schwab and Fidelity Investments. These **deep discount brokers** execute some trades for up to 90 percent off the price of what a full-service broker might charge.

**Online Discount and Deep Discount Brokers**   Most **online brokers** are also discount or deep discount brokers. An online broker allows you to execute trades electronically over the Internet. In fact, you can set up your account and execute trades without ever speaking to another human. If you do need help, it's generally available over the phone.

The advantages of trading through an online broker are that the costs are generally extremely low, in some cases dropping below $7 per trade. In addition, you can execute the trade immediately, with the confirmation coming back within seconds or a minute at most. Also, most online brokers provide customers with a wealth of information, including analyst's recommendations and reports along with earning estimates. This kind of information was formerly available only through your broker.

---

**Asset Management Account**
Comprehensive financial services packages offered by a brokerage firm that can include a checking account; credit and debit cards; a money market mutual fund; loans; automatic payment of fixed payments, such as mortgages or other debt; brokerage services (buying and selling stocks or bonds); and a system for the direct payment of interest, dividends, and proceeds from security sales into the money market mutual fund.

**Full-Service Broker or Account Executive**
A broker who gives advice and is paid on commission, where that commission is based on the sales volume generated.

**Discount Service Broker**
A "no-frills" broker who executes trades without giving any advice and thus charges much lower commission than a full-service broker.

**Deep Discount Service Broker**
A very low cost, no-frills discount broker with prices that undercut traditional discount brokers.

**Online Broker**
A broker that allows you to execute your trades electronically over the Internet.

# Checklist 12.1 ▌ Picking a Brokerage Firm

Are you willing to pay a higher commission for investment advice? If so, a full-service broker may be right for you.

Does the brokerage firm provide both safekeeping and recordkeeping services?

Are the accounts insured up to $500,000 by the Securities Investor Protection Corporation (SIPC) against the event that the brokerage firm faces financial difficulties?

Does the brokerage firm provide an 800 number for transactions and quotes?

Do you receive interest on idle cash in your account?

Now, because you don't have a broker when you trade online, you gain access to all the resources your broker has.

In deciding which type of broker to use, regardless of whether you're considering a full-service, discount, deep discount, or online broker, you need to answer several questions provided on Checklist 12.1. Remember, not all brokerage firms provide the same services at the same cost, so it's a good idea to investigate the alternatives before choosing one to work with.

## Cash Versus Margin Accounts

Investors with **cash accounts** pay in full for their security purchases, with the payment due within 3 business days of the transaction. Investors with **margin accounts** borrow a portion of the purchase price from the broker. In other words, with a margin account, both you and your broker put in $500 to purchase $1,000 worth of stock. The broker comes up with this money by borrowing the funds from a bank and paying what's referred to as the "broker's call money rate," which is generally the prime rate. The broker then charges you this rate plus a 1- to 2-percent service fee.

There's a limit on the percentage of the purchase price that you must initially pay, called the **margin** or **initial margin**, which is set by the Federal Reserve. For the past 20 years it's been 50 percent. Keep in mind that 50 percent is the minimum margin required by the Federal Reserve and that the broker you work with may require more.

The only time purchasing on margin is to the advantage of the investor is when the return on the stocks is greater than the cost of the borrowing. To demonstrate, let's assume that the margin is 50 percent and that you purchase 200 shares of DaimlerChrysler stock at $50 per share. In this case, the stock would cost a total of $10,000 (200 × $50), and you'd pay $5,000 and borrow the remaining $5,000 from your broker:

| | |
|---|---|
| Total cost: 200 shares at $50 per share | $10,000 |
| Amount borrowed: total cost (1 – margin %) | −5,000 |
| Margin: investor's contribution | $ 5,000 |

When you purchase securities on margin, they remain in the brokerage firm's name because the shares are used as collateral for the margin loan. What drives investors to make margin purchases is the desire to leverage their profits as those securities go up in price. Let's look at what would happen to your investment if the price of DaimlerChrysler's stock rose 40 percent to $70 per share.

**Cash Accounts**
Securities trading accounts in which the traders pay in full for their security purchases, with the payment due within 3 business days of the transaction.

**Margin Accounts**
Securities trading accounts in which the traders borrow a portion of the purchase price from their broker.

**Margin or Initial Margin**
A maximum limit set on the percentage of the purchase price of a security that must initially be paid for by the investor, which is set by the Federal Reserve.

| | |
|---|---|
| Total value of 200 shares at $70 per share | $14,000 |
| Margin loan | −5,000 |
| Margin (the net value of your investment) | $ 9,000 |

Your initial contribution of $5,000 is now worth $9,000, meaning you made $4,000 on an investment of $5,000—an 80-percent gain on your investment despite a stock price increase of only 40 percent. Actually, your return would be a bit less because you'd also have been paying interest on the portion of the purchase that was financed with borrowed funds, not to mention the commissions you pay when you buy and sell the stock.

Don't get too excited about margin purchases. Although the leverage that margin purchases provide can amplify stock price gains in a positive way, it can also amplify stock price losses in a negative way. Let's assume that the value of the DaimlerChrysler stock drops to $30 per share.

| | |
|---|---|
| Total value of 200 shares at $30 per share | $6,000 |
| Margin loan | −5,000 |
| Margin (the net value of your investment) | $1,000 |

Your initial investment of $5,000 is now worth $1,000, meaning you lost $4,000—an 80-percent loss despite only a 40-percent drop in DaimlerChrysler's stock price. Thus, the leverage that margin purchases produce is often referred to as a "double-edged sword," because it amplifies both gains and losses.

Margin accounts are set up in such a way that when stock prices fall, only the amount you've put in suffers the loss in value. To protect your broker, a maintenance margin is in place. The **maintenance margin** specifies a minimum percentage margin of collateral that you must maintain—which is often the same as the initial margin. If the margin falls below this percentage, the broker issues a margin call. A **margin call** requires you to replenish the margin account by adding additional cash or securities to bring the margin back up to a minimum level. Alternatively, the broker can sell securities from your margin account to bring the margin percentage up to an acceptable level. Again, you take the loss.

Margin accounts aren't for the novice. To protect yourself from the increased risk, you should use a cash account when you purchase securities. The biggest hurdle with a cash account is the short settlement period—3 days—which often isn't enough time to mail a check to your broker. Of course, overnight mail solves this problem, but it'll cost you.

A less expensive alternative is to link your bank electronically with your brokerage firm, which you can do through the **Automated Clearing House (ACH) Network**. The ACH Network is an electronic payment system that links 14,000 banks, credit unions, and savings and loan institutions. In fact, you may already rely on it if you have your paycheck directly deposited or if you have your checking account automatically debited for utility or cable TV payments.

The big advantage to using the ACH Network is speed and cost. To set up such a payment system, you generally need only sign a form authorizing your brokerage firm to access your bank account. After the agreement goes into effect, which generally takes about 2 weeks, all you need do to transfer funds is dial an automated service or call your brokerage firm directly.

**Maintenance Margin**
The minimum percentage margin of collateral that you must maintain.

**Margin Call**
A requirement that you replenish your margin account by adding cash or securities to bring it back to a minimum level.

**Automated Clearing House (ACH) Network**
An electronic payments system that links 14,000 banks, credit unions, and savings and loan institutions.

## Registration: Street Name or Your Name

Another choice you have when buying securities is whether you'd like the securities registered in the street name or in your name. Securities registered in the "street name" remain in the broker's custody and appear in the broker's computers as a computer entry in your name. You still own the securities and you'll receive any dividends or interest payments just as if the securities were registered in your name, but these securities are, in fact, more convenient to sell because the actual stock certificates or bonds don't have to be delivered to your broker.

The only disadvantage to leaving your securities in the broker's "street name" comes with brokerage firms that impose a charge called a "maintenance fee" against accounts that don't trade within a certain time frame. In this case, you may accrue charges if you don't make additional trades within a set time period. Before opening an account with a broker, you should ask if maintenance charges are imposed against dormant accounts. If so, try another broker.

## Joint Accounts

If you're buying securities along with your spouse, there are several alternative forms of joint accounts, each with different estate planning implications. You should have a strong understanding of how they work or confer with your lawyer before setting up your account.

Under an account with **joint tenancy with the right of survivorship**, when one of the individual owners dies, the other receives full ownership of the assets in the account. The assets bypass the lengthy court process called probate where the assets are transferred according to the instructions left in the deceased's will. However, they may be subject to estate taxes. With a **tenancy-in-common account**, the deceased's portion of the account goes to the heirs of the deceased rather than to the surviving account holder.

**Joint Tenancy with the Right of Survivorship**
A type of joint ownership in which the surviving owner receives full ownership of the assets in the account when the joint owner dies.

**Tenancy-in-Common Account**
A type of joint ownership in which the deceased's portion of the account goes to the heirs of the deceased rather than to the surviving account holder.

## Brokers and the Individual Investor

To understand the advice you typically receive from a broker, you need to understand that although you may consider your broker a friend, when talking investments, he or she is a salesperson. Moreover, your broker isn't a security analyst and most likely lacks the time or background to evaluate the recommendations he or she receives from analysts. When you get advice to buy or sell a security, you should realize that this may simply be someone else's recommendation that your broker is passing on, and that the only way your broker makes money is by having you trade as often as possible.

In fact, the dialogue your broker uses in convincing you to invest may have been carefully scripted by the marketing wizards back at the brokerage firm's main office. Keep in mind that a typical broker with 3 years or more of experience is expected to bring in between $40,000 and $120,000 in trades every working day. That doesn't mean you shouldn't take advice. Rather, you should take that advice and investigate it.

This relates back to **Principle 12: The Agency Problem in Personal Finance**. As we have said so often throughout this text, you bear all the consequences of bad decisions, so you *must* take responsibility for your own financial affairs. This is also why it's so important to do your homework when selecting a broker.

Principle
**12** The Agency Problem in Personal Finance

You must also realize where you fit into the scheme of things at a brokerage firm: at the bottom of the totem pole. Brokerage firms make a lot less money from helping you than they do from helping institutional investors, such as managers of pension funds or mutual funds. As a result, it's the institutional investors that talk directly with the analysts, and it's the institutional investors that are first in line to receive the analysts' reports. Although you'll get phone calls and research reports from your broker, you must remember that they're coming from a salesperson, and that, although convincingly written, they may not be overly valuable. Again, you must take responsibility for your own financial affairs.

There's one thing that you *can* do to increase the performance of your investments, and that is to keep the transaction costs—that is, commissions and fees—down to a minimum. Unfortunately, that's becoming more and more difficult with a full-service broker, because over the past decade institutional investors have placed increasing pressure on brokerage firms to cut costs. To please institutional investors, many brokerage firms have transferred costs to the individual investor—you—by charging for such services as initiating accounts, maintaining dormant accounts, and closing them down. So much for being low man on the totem pole.

If you have a portfolio worth over $100,000, you should probably use a discount broker. Although you might not have an account executive to hold your hand, you'll have a greater return on your investments. However, remember that not all discount brokers are the same—services and costs can vary dramatically from one to another. If you're a smaller investor, you might not want to deal with a broker at all and instead put your money directly in a mutual fund.

When purchasing bonds, there's no advantage to using a discount broker. In general, the commissions charged by a full-service versus a discount broker for bonds will pretty much be the same, especially for larger purchases. If you're going to buy bonds through a broker, you might as well use a full-service broker, because it doesn't cost more. If you're buying Treasury bonds, there's no reason to go through a broker at all. Treasury bonds can be purchased directly through the Treasury Department or through any of the Federal Reserve Banks, and no commission will be charged.

### Choosing a Broker

As with choosing a financial advisor, choosing a broker should be done with great care. It's a serious decision, one that can have a major impact on your financial future. First, you must decide whether you want a full-service, discount, or deep discount broker. If you decide on a discount broker, you should look for one with a reputation for honesty and efficiency in servicing clients. If you do decide on a full-service broker, take a look at Checklist 12.2.

## Checklist 12.2 ■ Choosing a Broker

Look for a broker with a reputation for integrity, intelligence, and efficiency in servicing clients.

Ask business colleagues, your banker, and your friends who are successful investors for recommendations.

Look for a broker with experience and with a record of proven advice. If you work with someone who's been in the business since 1987, that broker will have experienced at least one market downturn.

Look for a broker who understands your investment philosophy and is willing to work within your investment boundaries to achieve your goals.

Interview prospective brokers to find out about background, training, and experience.

Be up-front about your financial circumstances and how much you will invest. Ask for a general recommendation for a person in your situation, and listen.

Ask for a sample portfolio. Be sure to interview several candidates and compare notes to find a good fit.

Look for a broker who has a reputation for allowing customers to say no without undue pressure. Ask for names of clients whose financial situation is similar to yours whose accounts he or she has handled for at least 3 years, and call them.

Look for a broker who is up-front with you regarding costs—both maintenance costs on your account and commissions—and what research recommendations are based on.

# In The News

Wall Street Journal December 4, 2001

## How the Stock Drop Has Schooled Me

### by Jonathan Clements

Every 25 years or so, stocks post back-to-back losing years. Heard old-timers talk about the scars left by the 1973–74 stock market crash? Now, you and I also have our scars.

Make no mistake: The recent bear market has been brutal. It has certainly affected my views on the market. How so? Here are two lessons I have learned from the grueling share-price decline:

*Spending and Saving*: Suppose you invested $500 in stocks every month, beginning at the March 2000 market peak, for a total investment of $10,000. From then through Nov. 28, the Standard & Poor's 500 stock index nosedived 23.5 percent. But according to Baltimore's T. Rowe Price Associates, your $10,000 would have shrunk to only $8,600, or 14 percent less than your cost.

Now, imagine the same scenario, except this time you start with $100,000 and withdraw $500 at the end of each month. Retirees who followed that spending strategy would have pulled out $10,000—and seen their portfolio shrink by more than 33 percent, to $66,500.

What's the lesson here? Clearly, tumbling share prices can wreak havoc. But the amount of damage done depends on where you are in the cycle of spending and saving. That's a notion I have only recently come to appreciate.

*The market decline has been roughest on those who just retired. Even if these folks enjoy generous returns through the rest of their retirement, they may not benefit much, because their portfolios have been so depleted by a combination of falling share prices and their own spending.* (☛A)

*Staying on Target*: I have long argued that investors should reduce risk by spreading their money across a broad array of stocks. *But as the bear market has unfolded, I have come to realize that diversification alone isn't enough. Instead, to get diversification's full benefit, you need to combine broad market exposure with rebalancing.* (☛B)

The idea is to establish target portfolio percentages for large stocks, smaller companies, real estate investment trusts, and foreign markets. Then, every year or so, you rejigger your investment mix to get back to these targets.

### THE BOTTOM LINE . . .

**A** However, those who still have a long way to go until retirement may actually benefit from downturns in the sense that they have the opportunity to buy more shares at cheaper prices and position themselves for the next rally.

**B** Portfolio rebalancing allows you to remain true to your goals. If you would have rebalanced your portfolio after the spectacular Nasdaq gains in the late 1990s, you would have locked in some of those profits while reducing your exposure to Nasdaq stock price fluctuations.

## The Cost of Trading

Trade securities using a broker.

We've already touched briefly on the cost of trading in our discussion of full-service, discount, and deep discount brokers. We'll now look at what the costs are. Interestingly, the savings can be dramatic. Commissions associated with the purchase of 500 shares of stock at $20 per share—a total purchase of $10,000 of common stock—can range from a high of $253 with a full-service broker down to about $7 with a deep discount broker. In percentage terms, that's 2.53 percent versus 0.0995 percent. Keep in mind that this sales commission is to buy the stock. The broker charges a similar commission to sell the stock. Thus, your stock would have to rise by 5.06 percent before you'd break even and cover your commissions if the stock were purchased from the more expensive full-service broker.

Many brokers also charge a transaction fee, which in general is quite small. What's not quite small is the inactive account annual fee, which is imposed by most full-service brokers at a rate of $50 per year. If you don't make a security transaction during the year, your account is debited $50, which can be a sizable cost for smaller accounts. Moreover, this fee has the effect of encouraging trading when the trade may not be in your best interest. You should try to avoid firms that charge annual fees on inactive accounts.

With smaller transactions, the savings from using a discount broker are less noticeable. For a $3,000 purchase (100 shares of stock at $30 per share) the costs might range from a high of $91 with a full-service broker to $7 with a discount broker. In percentage form, that's a cost of 3.03 percent versus 0.23 percent. Again, you should keep in mind that these costs are doubled with a "round trip"—that is, buying the stock and later selling it.

With respect to the purchase of Treasury bills, there's no cost advantage to using a discount broker. In fact, when the amounts purchased go above $10,000, the cost advantage many times swings to the full-service broker.

So what's the bottom line on the cost of trading? In a nutshell, discount brokers are less expensive than full-service brokers, and for larger purchases, this cost difference is even more dramatic. If you make large purchases, you should definitely consider a discount broker. If you're a smaller investor, you should and can avoid the potentially costly inactive account fee regardless of whether you choose a full-service, discount, or deep discount broker.

If you're purchasing Treasury securities through a broker, you should do so with a full-service broker that doesn't charge an inactive account fee. However, if you're buying Treasury securities, you can totally avoid any fee by purchasing them directly from the Treasury or a Federal Reserve Bank.

### Online Trading

**Online Trading**
Making trades on the Internet.

The two basic ways you can execute your trades are dealing directly with a broker or **online trading**. Although many investors are more comfortable going through a broker, it tends to be less expensive to make the trades yourself online. Just a few years ago, online trading simply didn't exist. But every day more and more investors are investing through the Internet. In fact, by 2000, about 30–40 percent of all trades by individual investors were made with the click of a mouse.

## Checklist 12.3 ■ Tips for Online Investing

Online trading is quick and easy, online investing takes time. With a click of a mouse, you can buy and sell stocks from more than 100 online brokers offering executions as low as $5 per transaction. Although online trading saves investors time and money, it does not take the homework out of making investment decisions. You may be able to make a trade in a nanosecond, but making wise investment decisions takes time. Before you trade, know why you are buying or selling and the risk of your investment.

Set your price limits on fast-moving stocks: market orders versus limit orders. To avoid buying or selling a stock at a price higher or lower than you wanted, you need to place a limit order rather than a market order. For example, if you want to buy the stock of a "hot" IPO that was initially offered at $9, but don't want to end up paying more than $20 for the stock, you can place a limit order to buy the stock at any price up to $20. By entering a limit order rather than a market order, you will not be caught buying the stock at $90 and then suffering immediate losses as the stock drops later in the day or the weeks ahead.

If you cancel an order, make sure the cancellation worked before placing another trade. Although you may receive an electronic receipt for the cancellation, don't assume that means the trade was canceled. Orders can only be canceled if they have not been executed. Ask your firm about how you should check to see if a cancellation order actually worked.

If you trade on margin, your broker can sell your securities without giving you a margin call. Now is the time to reread your margin agreement and pay attention to the fine print. If your account has fallen below the firm's maintenance margin requirement, your broker has the legal right to sell your securities at any time without consulting you first.

No regulations require a trade to be executed within a certain time. There are no Securities and Exchange Commission regulations that require a trade to be executed within a set period of time.

*Source:* "Tips for Investing Online." The Securities and Exchange Commission, 2002.

Despite the fact that the manner in which orders are executed is changing, the principles that guide investing remain the same. However, because of the fast pace of online trading—that is, the instant access to your account and nearly instantaneous execution of your trades—it is important to protect yourself. As with everything else in investing or personal finance, this all goes back to **Principle 9: The Best Protection Is Knowledge**. Checklist 12.3 provides a number of tips for online investing—that is, things you need to know if you're considering trading online.

While many of these trades are executed by investors with a buy and hold philosophy, many are also executed by **day traders**. A day trader is an individual who trades with a very short-term investment horizon. Typically they station themselves at the computer and look for stocks that are moving up or down in value. Their goal is to ride the momentum of the stock and get out before it changes direction. To say the least, this is a risky course of action.

If you are considering day trading, keep a few facts in mind:

**Principle**

**9** The Best Protection Is Knowledge

**Day Traders**
Individuals who trade, generally over the Internet, with a very short time horizon, generally less than 1 day.

- **Be prepared to suffer severe financial losses**. It is typical for day traders to suffer severe financial losses in their first months, and many never make a penny. That means you should never consider day trading with money you can't afford to lose.

- **Don't confuse day trading with investing—they aren't the same**. Day traders aren't interested in value, just in what the stock might do in the next few hours or day.

- **Don't believe claims of easy profits**. People have a tendency to talk more when they make money, but not when they lose it. In fact, day trading has been called "a trading method for transferring wealth from unsophisticated investors to sophisticated investors."

- **Watch out for "hot tips" and "expert advice" from newsletters and Web sites catering to day traders**. There's no question that someone makes money from these; unfortunately, it isn't the investor. The same is true for those "educational" seminars, classes, and books about day trading— they may not be objective. Many times the seminar speaker, instructor teaching a class, or author of a publication about day trading stands to profit if you start day trading.

**STOP & THINK** Keep in mind the difference between trading online and day trading. Any time you start clicking your mouse with the intention of making some money by investing for a day or two at a time, think twice—you're not investing, you're speculating. There's no question someone will make money, but it probably won't be you. Big money from day trading only happens on TV commercials.

The bottom line is, avoid day trading. It's speculating, not investing.

## Sources of Investment Information

**3** Locate and use several different sources of investment information to trade securities.

To say the least, there's a wealth of investment information available. An awful lot of planning and many decisions have to be made before you're at the point of selecting specific securities in which to invest. And once you're ready to invest, you'll want to gather as much information as you can.

If you're going to make informed decisions, you have to seek out information, read it, and interpret it. Fortunately, you don't have to do your own research.

That's already done for you, and it's available from the companies themselves, from brokerage firms, from the press—magazines, newspapers, and investment advisory services, and, of course, on the Web.

## Corporate Sources

Annual reports are a great source of information. Most annual reports are available for free directly from the company itself. In reading an annual report, the first thing to keep in mind is that although the report is factual, those facts are interpreted in as favorable a light as possible. For example, annual reports generally begin with a letter from the president that highlights the year and gives prospects for the upcoming year. It does so with real attention to public relations. If the president says, "It was a challenging and troublesome year," he or she may really be trying to say, "We lost a lot of money last year."

In looking at an annual report, you should concern yourself with the trends in sales, profits, and dividends, looking for upward movement in all three. You should also pay attention to the explanation of how well the firm performed during the year and what management projects for the future. Finally, give close attention to the positives and negatives outlined in the annual report. Are profits up or down? Are new products being introduced? How are the sales on those new products? Are sales climbing or falling? Are new plants being opened or closed?

You look at these items because most changes a firm experiences are gradual—things tend to get worse or better over time. By looking at an annual report, you may be able to judge the direction of the changes that are taking place today and that will affect the company's stock price tomorrow.

## Brokerage Firm Reports

Most full-service and some discount brokers provide customers access to research reports prepared by the brokerage firm's security analysts. These reports cover the direction of the economy as a whole. They also look directly at individual companies, analyzing the companies' prospects and concluding with recommendations of buy, hold, or sell. "Buy" indicates a positive recommendation, "sell" a negative recommendation, and "hold" a neutral recommendation.

These reports provide you with the logic behind the recommendation. Even if you don't buy the recommended stocks, the reports are of value to read because they show you the logic that leads an analyst to recommend that a stock be bought or sold. If you're interested in a research report on a specific company, simply call up your broker and request it—it's as simple as that.

## The Press

To begin with, every investor should read the *Wall Street Journal*. It contains insights, data, and financial news that are essential for any investor. A number of other excellent financial magazines are worth a look, including *Forbes*, *Fortune*, and *Barron's*, along with a number of personal finance magazines, such as *Money*, *Smart Money*, and *Kiplinger's Personal Finance*. The place to start is on the Web, and the first place to look is at the Personal Finance Navigator (**www.prenhall.com/keown**). There you'll find links to lots of excellent sites.

Another place to look is at the financial periodicals in the public library. If you're just starting out, some of the personal finance magazines are the easiest to digest. At whatever level you're comfortable, dig in, because the only way to really learn about investments is to jump in. The more you read, the more sense it'll all make, and, more important, the more comfortable you'll feel.

Once you're ready to move beyond the magazines and the *Wall Street Journal*, the major sources of information on the market and individual stocks are Moody's Investors Service, Standard & Poor's, and Value Line. These are all investment advisory services and are available at many libraries.

Moody's, which is published by Dun and Bradstreet, puts out a number of different investment publications, including the weekly *Bond Survey*, which highlights the week's activity in the bond market, and *Moody's Handbook of Common Stock*, which is published quarterly and includes background and a brief description of over 1,000 companies. *Moody's Manuals* present historical financial data in addition to management information on both listed and OTC firms.

Standard & Poor's also provides comprehensive financial information on large listed and OTC firms in *Standard & Poor's Corporate Records*. Equally interesting is *Corporation Reports*, which contains a brief summary of the firm's current outlook, any important developments, and a business summary. To keep the information current, it's updated quarterly.

Of the investment advisory services, the *Value Line Investment Survey* is perhaps the most useful for investors. This publication follows approximately 1,700 companies and provides a one-page summary of each firm's outlook, updating the forecast four times a year. What makes Value Line unique is that it rates every stock on a scale of 1 to 5, with 1 being the most favorable rating on timeliness and safety. Figure 12.3 provides an example of a Value Line company summary for Disney.

In addition to evaluating individual stocks, Value Line examines and ranks different industries, picking out those it feels have the highest investment potential. Value Line also gives weekly evaluations of the economy, as well as the stock and bond markets, advising investors where they should put money, which direction interest rates are headed, and whether or not the stock and bond markets are headed up or down.

## Internet Sources

There is an incredible amount of corporate information, including news groups, free software, and discussion groups, on the Web, with new sites being added almost daily. For example, the Securities and Exchange Commission filings for corporations and mutual funds that file electronically can be accessed via the Edgar project (**www.edgar-online.com/**) at no charge. Corporate information is also available from investment companies and commercial online services. In addition, economic, monetary, and stock data are available from the Federal Reserve, the University of Michigan Web server, and other data providers on the World Wide Web.

This provides you, regardless of how small an investor you are, with the same opportunities as any other investor. Still, you've got to be careful of where you get your information. Remember, there are no controls on who can post information on the Internet. As a result, you may end up with a market analysis written by a 12-year-old. You've also got to keep in mind that the Agency Problem abounds on the Internet. Much of what appears is self-serving in nature. It is either placed there by stockbrokers trying to push stocks on their own Web home pages or by companies trying to improve their stock prices. Look out for those get-rich-quick schemes on the Internet. Someone may get rich, but it's not you.

# Figure 12.3 The Value Line Investment Survey

Source: Copyright 2002 by Value Line Publishing, Inc. Reprinted by Permission. All Rights Reserved.

**DISNEY (WALT)** NYSE-DIS | RECENT PRICE **23.87** | P/E RATIO **41.2** (Trailing: 29.1 / Median: 28.0) | RELATIVE P/E RATIO **2.05** | DIV'D YLD **0.9%** | **VALUE LINE**

| | |
|---|---|
| TIMELINESS **4** | Raised 2/8/02 |
| SAFETY **2** | Raised 2/25/00 |
| TECHNICAL **4** | Lowered 2/8/02 |
| BETA 1.05 | (1.00 = Market) |

LEGENDS: 20.0 x "Cash Flow" p sh — Relative Price Strength — 4-for-1 split 5/92 — 3-for-1 split 7/98 — Options: Yes — Shaded area indicates recession

**2004-06 PROJECTIONS**

| | Price | Gain | Ann'l Total Return |
|---|---|---|---|
| High | 45 | (+90%) | 18% |
| Low | 30 | (+25%) | 7% |

**Insider Decisions**

| | M | A | M | J | J | A | S | O | N |
|---|---|---|---|---|---|---|---|---|---|
| to Buy | 0 | 0 | 0 | 0 | 0 | 0 | 0 | 0 | 0 |
| Options | 0 | 0 | 1 | 0 | 0 | 0 | 0 | 0 | 0 |
| to Sell | 0 | 0 | 1 | 0 | 0 | 0 | 0 | 0 | 1 |

**Institutional Decisions**

| | 1Q2001 | 2Q2001 | 3Q2001 |
|---|---|---|---|
| to Buy | 383 | 381 | 446 |
| to Sell | 479 | 462 | 441 |
| Hld's(000) | 1052868 | 1078327 | 1161680 |

Percent shares traded: 18.0 / 12.0 / 6.0

Target Price Range 2004 | 2005 | 2006

**% TOT. RETURN 1/02**

| | THIS STOCK | VL ARITH. INDEX |
|---|---|---|
| 1 yr. | -30.2 | 0.2 |
| 3 yr. | -34.2 | 31.2 |
| 5 yr. | -9.4 | 72.0 |

High/Low annual price range: High 11.4 / 10.8 / 15.1 / 16.0 / 16.2 / 21.4 / 25.8 / 33.4 / 42.8 / 38.7 / 43.9 / 34.8; Low 7.2 / 7.8 / 9.5 / 12.0 / 12.6 / 15.0 / 17.8 / 22.1 / 22.5 / 23.4 / 26.0 / 15.5

| | 1985 | 1986 | 1987 | 1988 | 1989 | 1990 | 1991 | 1992 | 1993 | 1994 | 1995 | 1996 | 1997 | 1998 | 1999 | 2000 | 2001 | 2002 | © VALUE LINE PUB., INC. 04-06 |
|---|---|---|---|---|---|---|---|---|---|---|---|---|---|---|---|---|---|---|---|
| Revenues per sh A | 1.30 | 1.58 | 1.82 | 2.15 | 2.83 | 3.70 | 3.96 | 4.77 | 5.31 | 6.40 | 7.70 | 10.10 | 11.21 | 11.34 | 12.09 | 12.52 | 11.70 | | 15.25 |
| "Cash Flow" per sh | .18 | .24 | .34 | .42 | .55 | .65 | .58 | .72 | .78 | .97 | 1.15 | 1.32 | 1.51 | 1.52 | 1.30 | 1.58 | 1.40 | 1.45 | 2.10 |
| Earnings per sh A B | .11 | .15 | .24 | .32 | .43 | .50 | .40 | .51 | .54 | .68 | .84 | .74 | .92 | .90 | .66 | .90 | .98 | .60 | 1.25 |
| Div'ds Decl'd per sh C | .03 | .03 | .03 | .04 | .05 | .06 | .07 | .08 | .10 | .12 | .14 | .17 | .20 | .21 | .21 | .21 | .21 | .21 | .25 |
| Cap'l Spending per sh | .12 | .11 | .18 | .37 | .46 | .45 | .59 | .35 | .49 | .65 | .57 | .86 | .95 | 1.13 | 1.03 | 1.02 | .89 | 1.00 | 1.05 |
| Book Value per sh D | .76 | .90 | 1.17 | 1.48 | 1.87 | 2.21 | 2.48 | 2.99 | 3.13 | 3.50 | 4.23 | 8.54 | 9.46 | 10.16 | 11.65 | 11.25 | 11.25 | | 13.35 |
| Common Shs Outst'g E | 1552.5 | 1568.4 | 1580.4 | 1598.4 | 1623.6 | 1581.6 | 1562.4 | 1573.2 | 1606.5 | 1572.3 | 1573.2 | 2022.0 | 2025.0 | 2050.0 | 2064.0 | 2069.0 | 2089.0 | 2090.0 | 2130.0 |
| Avg Ann'l P/E Ratio | 14.7 | 20.3 | 21.1 | 15.8 | 16.6 | 19.3 | 23.3 | 22.4 | 25.3 | 21.1 | 20.4 | 27.2 | 27.4 | 37.6 | 46.0 | 39.5 | 30.4 | | 30.0 |
| Relative P/E Ratio | 1.19 | 1.38 | 1.41 | 1.31 | 1.26 | 1.43 | 1.49 | 1.36 | 1.49 | 1.38 | 1.37 | 1.70 | 1.58 | 1.96 | 2.62 | 2.57 | 1.54 | | 2.00 |
| Avg Ann'l Div'd Yield | 1.6% | .9% | .5% | .6% | .5% | .5% | .6% | .6% | .6% | .7% | .7% | .7% | .7% | .6% | .7% | .6% | .7% | | .7% |

**CAPITAL STRUCTURE as of 9/30/01**

Total Debt $9769 mill. Due in 5 Yrs $6613 mill.
LT Debt $8940 mill. LT Interest $650 mill.
(Total interest coverage: 2.8x) (22% of Cap'l)

Pension Liability None
Pfd Stock None
Common Stock 2,038,612,034 shs. (78% of Cap'l) as of 11/30/02

MARKET CAP: $48.7 billion (Large Cap)

| | 1991 | 1992 | 1993 | 1994 | 1995 | 1996 | 1997 | 1998 | 1999 | 2000 | 2001 | 2002 | 04-06 |
|---|---|---|---|---|---|---|---|---|---|---|---|---|---|
| Revenues ($mill) A | 6182.0 | 7504.0 | 8529.0 | 10055 | 12112 | 21288 | 22473 | 22976 | 23402 | 25020 | 25269 | 24500 | 32500 |
| Operating Margin | 20.5% | 21.4% | 22.6% | 22.0% | 22.6% | 21.4% | 22.8% | 22.0% | 18.6% | 21.3% | 12.0% | 12.0% | 20.0% |
| Depreciation ($mill) | 263.5 | 317.3 | 364.2 | 409.7 | 470.2 | 1134.0 | 1177.0 | 1240.0 | 1307.0 | 1370.0 | 1754.0 | 1755 | 1800 |
| Net Profit ($mill) | 636.6 | 816.7 | 889.1 | 1110.4 | 1343.6 | 1533.0 | 1890.0 | 1870.8 | 1383.0 | 1891.7 | 2058.0 | 1265 | 2685 |
| Income Tax Rate | 37.5% | 37.3% | 37.6% | 34.8% | 34.8% | 43.6% | 41.9% | 41.5% | 42.9% | 41.1% | 44.8% | 39.0% | 39.0% |
| Net Profit Margin | 10.3% | 10.9% | 10.4% | 11.0% | 11.1% | 7.2% | 8.4% | 8.1% | 5.9% | 7.6% | 5.2% | 5.2% | 8.3% |
| Working Cap'l ($mill) | 1323.3 | 1813.8 | 1690.8 | 1662.2 | 2294.3 | d252.0 | 603.0 | 1850.0 | 2493.0 | 1605.0 | 810.0 | 400 | 1000 |
| Long-Term Debt ($mill) | 2074.3 | 2207.0 | 2088.0 | 2773.8 | 2855.6 | 12223 | 10224 | 9562.0 | 9278.0 | 6959.0 | 8940.0 | 10200 | 9500 |
| Shr. Equity ($mill) | 3871.3 | 4704.6 | 5030.5 | 5508.3 | 6650.8 | 16086 | 17285 | 19388 | 20975 | 24100 | 22672 | 23490 | 28440 |
| Return on Total Cap'l | 11.9% | 13.0% | 13.5% | 14.4% | 15.3% | 6.8% | 8.2% | 7.5% | 5.5% | 6.8% | 7.0% | 4.5% | 8.0% |
| Return on Shr. Equity | 16.4% | 14.4% | 17.7% | 20.2% | 20.2% | 9.5% | 10.9% | 9.6% | 6.6% | 7.8% | 9.1% | 5.5% | 9.5% |
| Retained to Com Eq | 14.2% | 15.1% | 15.1% | 17.4% | 17.5% | 7.8% | 9.0% | 7.5% | 6.6% | 6.0% | 7.1% | 3.5% | 7.5% |
| All Div'ds to Net Prof | 14% | 13% | 14% | 14% | 13% | 18% | 18% | 22% | 32% | 23% | 21% | 35% | 20% |

**CURRENT POSITION ($MILL.)**

| | 1999 | 2000 | 9/30/01 |
|---|---|---|---|
| Cash Assets | 414 | 842 | 618 |
| Receivables | 3633 | 3599 | 3343 |
| Inventory (Avg Cst) | 4867 | 4308 | 671 |
| Other | 1286 | 1258 | 2397 |
| Current Assets | 10200 | 10007 | 7029 |
| Accts Payable | 4588 | 5115 | 4603 |
| Debt Due | 2415 | 2502 | 829 |
| Other | 704 | 739 | 787 |
| Current Liab. | 7707 | 8402 | 6219 |

**ANNUAL RATES** of change (per sh)

| | Past 10 Yrs. | Past 5 Yrs. | Est'd '99-'01 to '04-'06 |
|---|---|---|---|
| Revenues | 13.0% | 8.0% | 5.0% |
| "Cash Flow" | 9.0% | 4.5% | 5.5% |
| Earnings | 6.5% | 2.5% | 8.0% |
| Dividends | 11.5% | 3.5% | 12.5% |
| Book Value | 17.5% | 16.0% | 4.0% |

**QUARTERLY REVENUES ($ mill.) A**

| Fiscal Year Ends | Dec.31 | Mar.31 | Jun.30 | Sep.30 | Full Fiscal Year |
|---|---|---|---|---|---|
| 1998 | 6339 | 5242 | 5248 | 6147 | 22976 |
| 1999 | 6589 | 5510 | 5522 | 5781 | 23402 |
| 2000 | 6816 | 6206 | 5964 | 6034 | 25020 |
| 2001 | 7433 | 6049 | 5975 | 5812 | 25269 |
| 2002 | 7048 | 5650 | 5800 | 6002 | 24500 |

**EARNINGS PER SHARE A B**

| Fiscal Year Ends | Dec.31 | Mar.31 | Jun.30 | Sep.30 | Full Fiscal Year |
|---|---|---|---|---|---|
| 1998 | .37 | .17 | .20 | .16 | .90 |
| 1999 | .23 | .13 | .20 | .10 | .66 |
| 2000 | .25 | .18 | .28 | .19 | .90 |
| 2001 | .31 | .25 | .29 | .13 | .98 |
| 2002 | .15 | .10 | .20 | .15 | .60 |

**QUARTERLY DIVIDENDS PAID C**

| Calendar | Mar.31 | Jun.30 | Sep.30 | Dec.31 | Full Year |
|---|---|---|---|---|---|
| 1998 | .037 | .044 | .044 | .044 | .17 |
| 1999 | .044 | .053 | .053 | .053 | .20 |
| 2000 | -- | -- | -- | .21 | .21 |
| 2001 | -- | -- | -- | .21 | .21 |
| 2002 | -- | -- | -- | | |

**BUSINESS:** The Walt Disney Company operates Disneyland, Walt Disney World (Magic Kingdom, Epcot Center, Disney-MGM Studios, Animal Kingdom), ABC TV & radio networks, and a cruise line. Supplies filmed entertainment, publishes books, records music. Sells via Disney Stores. Owns The Disney Channel, ESPN, A&E, and Lifetime TV. Earns Tokyo Disneyland royalties; owns 39% of Disneyland Paris. Acquired Capital Cities/ABC 2/96, Infoseek Cp. 11/99. Foreign sales: 17% of revenues. '01 depreciation rate: 6.9%. Has about 116,000 employees. Officers/directors own 2.2% of stock (1/02 proxy). Chairman & CEO: M.D. Eisner. Inc.: Delaware. Address: 500 South Buena Vista St., Burbank, CA 91521-7320. Telephone: 818-560-1000. Internet: www.disney.com.

**Disney's results are showing sensitivity to current conditions.** Year-over-year operating income from its two largest segments, Media Networks and Theme Parks & Resorts, were down 58% and 51%, respectively, during the December quarter. (Fiscal year ends September 30, 2002.) Its Media unit has been struggling as a result of lower ratings at the ABC network and a weak advertising market. Meanwhile, economic softness and the war on terrorism continue to dampen attendance, spending, and hotel occupancy at the Walt Disney World Resort. Attendance was up slightly at the Disneyland Resort in California, but this was because of promotions to local residents, who tend to spend less at the resort than visitors from other areas. **The March quarter is likely to be another challenging one for the company.** The economic environment remains subdued, and the advertising market has yet to show signs of a recovery. Also, viewership at ABC and Disney's ESPN cable network will probably be down this quarter as a result of the Winter Olympics being aired on NBC. Too, operating margins should continue to be squeezed at the theme parks, given the reduction in travelers and high fixed costs.

**Disney does have some bright spots.** Its cable business, within its Media unit, has been performing well. Income from cable operations actually rose 6% during the difficult December quarter, due to an increase in fees and subscriber growth. Elsewhere, Disney has been taking cost-cutting measures at the Disney World Resort to compensate for lower attendance. Finally, we are expecting a turnaround in the economy sometime in the second half of 2002, which would help improve Disney's bottom line.

**These shares remain untimely for the year ahead.** The company's near-term earnings prospects remain unattractive, though its share price has begun to recover from its September lows. We believe that economic issues will weigh on these shares in the months ahead. But longer term, the potential for an earnings rebound leaves Disney stock with appealing 3- to 5-year capital gains potential, considering its risk profile (Safety rank: 2). *Michael P. Maloney* February 22, 2002

(A) Fiscal year ends Sept. 30th. (B) Diluted earnings. Excludes nonrec. items: '87, (3¢); '93, (36¢); '95, 2¢; '96, (9¢); '97, 4¢; '98, 1¢; '99, (4¢); '00, 2¢; '01 ($1.00). Excl. loss from retained interest in Disney Internet Group: '00, 35¢. Next egs. report due early May. (C) Policy to pay single annual div'd. adopted in fiscal '99. Div'd payment date: about Dec. 22nd. Next div'd meeting about Nov. 1, '02. Goes ex about Nov. 10, '02. (D) Incl. intang. In '01: $14.5 billion, $0.72/sh. (E) In mill., adj. for stock splits.

| Company's Financial Strength | A |
|---|---|
| Stock's Price Stability | 70 |
| Price Growth Persistence | 85 |
| Earnings Predictability | 70 |

The best place to start is the Web site dedicated to this book, the Personal Finance Navigator at **www.prenhall.com/keown**. Click on "Contents" then go to Chapter 12 and look at the section titled "Sources of Investment Information." You'll find some great sites. These sites are also continuously monitored and updated, so that links are provided to the best and most useful sources.

## Investment Clubs

Another excellent source of information is "investment clubs." In recent years, investment clubs have become increasingly popular for their social, educational, and investment value. Every club works a bit differently, but most clubs have required dues (of, say, $10 per month), with the dues then being pooled and invested in the club's name.

The real value of these clubs is not from what you might earn on your investment, but from the knowledge and experience you gain from going through the investment process. With a club, you're often able to gain access to financial planners and investment advisors that you wouldn't be able to access as an individual. Once again, the more you know, the better off you are.

## SUMMARY

The primary securities market is where new securities are sold. A new issue of IBM stock would be considered a primary market transaction. Actually, the primary markets can be divided into two other markets: those for initial public offerings (IPOs) and those for seasoned new issues. An initial public offering is the first time the company's stock is traded publicly. Seasoned new issues are stock offerings by companies that already have common stock traded in the market.

Securities that have previously been issued are traded in the secondary markets. Many securities in secondary markets are traded on organized exchanges, which actually occupy a physical location. The New York Stock Exchange is the oldest of all the organized exchanges, dating back over 200 years. The American Stock Exchange is the second most important of the organized exchanges. The OTC market, in which transactions are conducted over telephone or via a computer hookup, is a highly automated nationwide computer network that allows brokers to see up-to-the-minute price quotes on roughly 35,000 securities and execute trades on those securities.

Securities market regulation is aimed at protecting the investor and providing a level playing field so that all investors have a fair chance of making money. There are actually two levels of regulation: the Securities and Exchange Commission, and self-

regulation directly by the exchanges or, in the case of the OTC, by the National Association of Securities Dealers (NASD).

Common stocks are sold in lots or groups of 100 shares on the New York Stock Exchange—this is referred to as a round lot. Orders involving between 1 and 99 shares of stock are referred to as odd lots, and are processed by "odd lot dealers" who buy and sell out of their inventory.

An investor must specify a time period for which the order will remain outstanding. Alternatives include day orders, which expire at the end of the trading day during which they were made; open orders, also called good-till-canceled (GTC) orders, which remain effective until filled; and fill-or-kill orders, which, if not filled immediately, expire.

Other types of orders can specify the price you want to trade on. A market order is simply an order to buy or sell a set number of securities immediately at the best price available. A limit order specifies that the trade is to be made only at a certain price or better. A stop-loss order is an order to sell if the price drops below a specified level or to buy if the price climbs above a specified level.

Investors have a choice of whether to pay cash or borrow from their broker. Investors with cash accounts pay in full for their security purchases, with the payment due within 3 business days of the transaction. Investors with margin accounts borrow a portion of the purchase price from their broker. Short selling involves borrowing stocks from your broker and selling them with an obligation to replace the stocks later. Then, if the price goes down, you buy them back, make a profit, and return the stocks to your broker.

A full-service broker gives investment advice and is paid on commission, where that commission is based on the sales volume generated. A discount service broker simply executes trades without giving any advice and charges less for transactions. In general, discount brokers are less expensive than full-service brokers, and for larger purchases, this cost difference is quite dramatic.

If you're going to make informed investment decisions, you have to seek investment information, read it, and interpret it. Fortunately, you don't have to do your own research. That's already done for you, and it's available from the companies themselves, from brokerage firms, and from the press—magazines, newspapers, investment advisory services, and the Web. The Web is the first place you'll want to look, with new investment sites being added almost daily. This provides all investors with the same opportunities. Still, because there are no controls on who can post on the Web, you've got to be careful on where you get your information. You've also got to keep in mind that the Agency Problem abounds on the Internet. Much of what appears is self-serving in nature or may not be accurate. In addition, joining an investments club can also be a real learning experience and can provide you with access to investment research that you might not otherwise find.

## REVIEW QUESTIONS

1. What is a securities market? Does a market have to take the form of an actual building? Give an example to support your response.

2. What are the differences between the primary and secondary markets? Which market sells IPOs and seasoned new issues?

3. How does the performance of Align Technology, from Table 12.1, support the idea that "investing" in IPOs may be a form of speculation?

4. The OTC market is significantly different from organized exchanges. Briefly explain listing and membership requirements in the OTC, and how a market is determined.

5. Differentiate between the "bid price" and "ask price."

6. Brokers recommend international investments because they help diversify one's portfolio. Name another advantage and risk associated with international investments.

7. Name three ways that a U.S. investor can purchase international equities.

8. Name the two securities regulation organizations. What is their primary purpose for securities market regulation?

9. What are the purpose and the limits of Security Investors Protection Corporation?

10. Much has been written about "insider-trading abuses." What is meant by this term? What two pieces of legislation have been enacted to curb insider-trading abuses?

11. What is "churning?" Why is this of concern to individual investors?

12. What is a continuous market? What is the primary reason stock prices move up and down in a continuous market? Who stabilizes the price in this type of market and how do they accomplish it?

13. What is a discretionary account? Who can make buy and sell decisions in such an account? Should individual investors open discretionary accounts?

14. The timing of a securities transaction is very important. Differentiate among day orders, open orders, GTC orders, and fill-or-kill orders. In addition to timing of orders, pricing instructions are also important. Differentiate among the following:

   a. Market order

   b. Limit order

   c. Stop-loss order

   Why would someone consider using a limit or stop-loss order?

15. Should the average investor consider using short-selling techniques? Why or why not?

16. What is the primary benefit of an asset management account?

17. How do the services and costs vary with the different types of full-service, discount service, deep discount, and online brokerage accounts?

18. What happens if an investor receives a margin call? How would this relate to the margin requirement or the maintenance margin?

19. What are the primary ownership differences between tenancy-in-common and joint tenancy with the right of survivorship?

20. The typical broker is required to bring in between $40,000 and $120,000 in trades every working day. Does this cause an agency problem?

21. What are the two primary methods of executing trades?

22. List five publications and three Web sites that can be used to gather financial news or research.

23. What are the major benefits of joining an investment club?

## PROBLEMS AND ACTIVITIES

1. After studying the fundamental trends from CDX Company's annual report, you have decided to purchase one round lot of the firm's stock on the open market. On Monday morning you call a stockbroker and ask for a price of CDX stock. The broker indicates that the bid price is 45.125 and the ask price is 45.625. Assuming you wanted to place a market order to purchase shares, how much would you pay?

2. Which securities market regulations deals with each of the following:
   a. Disclosure of relevant information on initial public offerings and registration with the FTC.
   b. Created the Securities and Exchange Commission (SEC).
   c. Protects investors against unethical investment advisors by requiring advisors to register with the SEC.
   d. Established disclosure and regulation of the mutual fund industry.
   e. Established up to $500,000 of insurance to cover investors' account balances in the event that their brokerage firm goes bankrupt.
   f. Made it illegal to trade securities while in the possession of inside information.

3. Julie Braten, an active investor, recently recorded the following transactions in her brokerage account:

   | | |
   |---|---|
   | November 1 | Bought 274 shares of OPP |
   | November 7 | Bought 50 shares of RSVP |
   | November 11 | Sold 150 shares of OPP |
   | November 22 | Bought 100 shares of TXBI |
   | November 27 | Sold 100 shares of OPP |

   Which of the transactions would be considered a round lot? Which were odd-lot transactions?

4. Josephine just made another fantastic investment: She purchased 350 shares in Great Gains Corporation for $21.50 per share. Yesterday the stock closed at $43.75 per share. In order to lock in her gains she has decided to employ a stop-loss order. Assuming she set the order at $43, what is likely to happen? Why might this not be a wise decision? At what price would you recommend setting the stop-loss order? Why?

5. Uncle John and Aunt Martha own 1,000 shares of AI Inc. in a brokerage account that is titled "John and Martha, Tenancy-in-Common." Explain how the assets would be handled if John passed away. What if both passed away simultaneously? Would these scenarios be different if the account was titled "John or Martha, Joint Tenancy with the Right of Survivorship?"

6. Assume you just purchased 300 shares of Kmart at $9 per share, and 50 percent of this was purchased "on the margin." Fill in the blanks to determine your contribution to this transaction:

   Total cost              $_____
   Amount borrowed        −_____
   Contribution           =====

   What would happen to your investment if the price of Kmart stock rose to $18 per share (ignoring any possible dividends)?

   Total value             $_____
   Loan                   −_____
   Margin                 =====

   What was your profit?

   What would happen to your investment if the price of Kmart stock fell to $6 per share (ignoring any possible dividends)?

   Total value             $_____
   Load                   −_____
   Margin                 =====

   What was your loss?

7. Consider the following transaction timeline for XYZ Corp:

   November 12—placed an open order for 500 shares

   November 13—order filled at $25.25 per share

   January 4—current market price $61.50 per share

   January 5—placed stop-loss order at $50.00 per share

   March 29—current market price $52.00 per share

   April 2—short sold 300 shares XYZ Corp. at $55.00 per share

   April 28—current market price $49.75 per share

   May 30—covered short sell at $27.25 per share

   Calculate the total amount earned or lost excluding trading costs.

8. Determine which of the following two companies would be eligible for listing on the NYSE:

|  | Firm 1 | Firm 2 |
|---|---|---|
| Earnings before taxes for the year | $5 million | $2.7 million |
| Value of publicly held stock | $105 million | $80 million |
| Number of common shares | 3 million | 1 million |
| Number of holder of 100 shares | 3,000 | 2,500 |

9. Last year you sold short 400 shares of stock selling at $90 per share. Six months later the stock had fallen to $45 per share. Over the 6-month period the company paid out two dividends of $1.50 per share. Your total commission cost for buying and selling the shares came to $125. Determine your profit or loss from this transaction.

## SUGGESTED PROJECTS

1. Make a list of 10 products and services that you use on a daily basis. Examples might include soft drinks, detergents, utilities, and textbooks. Next to the list of products and services make a note of which company produced the good or service. Check Moody's, Standard & Poor's, or Value Line to determine the stock exchange on which the companies are traded and a recent closing stock price. Further review at least a two-year price history. Did you notice any relevant trends that might lead to the recommended purchase or sale of stock? Explain your recommendations in a brief written or oral report.

2. Visit your library's business reference section and identify companies listed on the "pink sheets." Why are these companies listed here rather than on the NASDAQ or NYSE? Using the information presented in this chapter, would you consider investing in a security listed in the pink sheets? Would you recommend a pink sheet listed company to a close friend or relative?

3. Obtain one week's worth of the *Wall Street Journal*. Read through each issue and either photocopy or clip all examples of tombstone advertising. Which firms consistently show up as underwriters and syndicate participants? Based on your sample of tombstone advertisements, what types of security issues are being offered? As an investor, do you find tombstone advertisements very useful?

4. Using the information from project 3 and information found on the Internet, write a one-page paper on why these types of advertisements are used. Support your answer with information provided in the Securities Act of 1933.

5. Using your local phone book, obtain a listing of stockbrokers, financial planners, and investment advisors in your area (check the Yellow Pages using the foregoing titles). Call three different investment firms and ask them how they are compensated for their services. Also ask them to send this information to you via mail. Do you think that there will be a difference in how the three are compensated? Do you see any potential agency problems in the way these firms or individuals are compensated?

6. Obtain the phone number of a deep discount broker. You can usually obtain a phone number of a firm in a personal finance magazine or through an Internet search. Using the five questions presented in Checklist 12.1, "Picking a Brokerage Firm," as a basis for questioning, interview the discount brokerage firm's representative. Based on the information provided in the interview, does the firm appeal to you? Why or why not?

7. This chapter has pointed out that small investors fit very "low on the totem pole" within the scheme of things at most brokerage firms. Why do you think this is? In terms of receiving timely and unique investment advice, what do you think being "low man on the totem pole" means for you? How might you be able to compensate and "level the playing field?"

8. Some investors continue to hold stock certificates as proof of ownership, but most investors hold their securities in street name. Ask a relative or friend who owns stocks if they hold the certificates directly or if the certificates are held in street name, and determine why your friend or relative made this choice. This chapter describes one possible disadvantage of leaving securities in street name. Do you think this was a consideration in the person's choice?

9. Did you know that every publicly owned and traded company in the United States is required by law to provide quarterly and annual reports to anyone who asks for one? Based on this knowledge, obtain the phone number for a company where you purchase goods or services (use Moody's, Value Line, Standard & Poor's, or phone numbers from a product's package). Call the company and request an annual report. In looking at the annual report, do you see any noticeable trends in sales, profits, and dividends?

10. In this chapter you learned about "churning." However, this is not the only market abuse. Get online at the NASD Regulation homepage (www.nasdr.com) to research other abuses that the NASD regulates. Write a short report of your findings.

11. To learn more about online brokerage services and fees, visit www.fool.com. Select the "choose a broker" page and then visit the Discount Broker Center. Use the information found to make an informed decision about online brokerages. Which brokerage most closely fits your needs? Which one offers the widest range of services? Which one has the lowest cost structure? Do any of the services not offer mutual funds? Is this a deterrent from using that site? Why? Report on your findings in a small group discussion.

## Discussion Case 1

Miles heard about a fantastic restaurant chain that is issuing an initial public offering, so he took Dollie to try one of the nearby restaurants. To say the least, they loved it. The restaurant specializes in Thai food and Turkish coffee. According to the tombstone advertisement, the underwriting syndicate appears very reputable. Miles thinks that this opportunity may be the next "*Jet Blue*" and thinks that buying stock in the IPO is almost a sure thing. Dollie isn't quite so convinced, because she reasons that if the investment was such a sure thing, why would she and Miles get a shot at the deal? Miles and Dollie have a brokerage account worth $20,000. They are thinking of investing at least $5,000 in the IPO. What advice would you give Miles and Dollie?

### Questions

1. Is Miles correct in thinking that an IPO will dramatically increase in value?

2. What risks might Miles be overlooking when he envisions huge profits?

3. How easy is it for small investors to invest in an IPO? Why might this be the case?

4. Given the lack of information available to small investors about most IPOs and the information you learned in Chapter 11, would you consider IPOs investing or speculating? How would you explain this to Dollie and Miles?

5. Based on your perception of risk and return in relation to IPOs, what would you recommend to Miles and Dollie?

# Money Matters

## TERMS OF ENRICHMENT

A recent study by a well-known brokerage firm showed that almost 95 percent of individual investors lose money or just break even on stock trades. Primarily this is true because they didn't enter into the process armed to make logical, informed decisions. Be prepared to avoid some of the pitfalls, such as these:

**"Falling in love" with a stock**. Just because you inherited a stock from your favorite Grandmother doesn't mean it must always be a viable part of your portfolio. One that has made money for you for several years may become a loser over time. Emotion does not belong in the decision-making process, and there is no "rate of return" for loyalty to a particular investment. Know when to let go.

**Investing too heavily in your employer**. Many people purchase large amounts of their employer's stock because they feel that they work for a good company. If the company goes away, not only have they lost their job, they may have lost a fair amount of their assets. The value of stock in the secondary market may have little to do with how good an employer the company is. (This is not to say that you shouldn't take advantage of some of the excellent company-sponsored stock purchase plans.)

**Selling low and buying high**. Stock is the one thing in America that people don't seem to want when its "on sale" (when prices are down). Professional money managers normally do not sell just because the price falls or buy because everyone else is. In fact, they more often do the opposite. Their decisions are based on detailed analysis of the stock and how it fits with their portfolio objectives. The key is to be able to evaluate what may be driving the movement of the price, and avoid making decisions based on panic, fear, or rumors or "hot tips."

**The hog factor**. Don't be a "hog" and hold on to stocks when they are way up in hopes of them going up further. The saying is "Bears make money. Bulls make money, and Hogs get slaughtered" or something like that. Not "selling high" in hopes of "selling higher" can have disappointing results. You may want to sell part of the holdings and keep the rest for potential continued rise. Alternatively, you could buy the same stock again later and "ride another wave."

**Failing to realize the commitment involved**. If you are not willing or able to invest the time necessary to do good research and actively tend to your portfolio, perhaps you should seek professional assistance via a mutual fund or other managed account.

**Excessive trading costs and taxes**. The phrase "playing the market" is sadly appropriate for the actions of some people. They perceive that success in investing lies in moving things around a lot. Consequently, even if they are lucky enough to make some good choices, trading costs and taxes on short-term gains eat up most of what they made.

# Discussion Case 2

Wally and Bonnie are in their early 40s and until now they have always kept their savings in the bank. They liked the idea that a deposit in a bank was insured and guaranteed and that, regardless of what happened in the economy or to the bank, they could always get their money. Wally and Bonnie recently talked with a stockbroker about funding their retirement. The stockbroker pointed out that in terms of reaching their retirement goals, a bank account did not pay enough interest. The broker recommended that Wally and Bonnie invest in a combination of stocks, bonds, mutual funds, and money market accounts. Wally and Bonnie are skeptical about the ultimate safety of their investments. Specifically, Wally is worried about what would happen to their securities and cash if the brokerage firm went bankrupt, and Bonnie is concerned that the markets are rigged and that only those with inside information ever make any money. Both are equally concerned that the markets are unregulated gambles and that there is no way to regulate the ethics of brokers. They've come to you for some advice on what to do.

## Questions

1. Does Wally need to be concerned about the lack of insurance in his brokerage account? Is there a specific securities act you could sight to back up your answer?

2. Bonnie is concerned about insider trading. Do you agree with Bonnie? Why or why not?

3. Name two securities acts that protect investors in terms of regulation. Also name two organizations that oversee the securities markets and the actions of investors.

4. In working with a broker, what should Wally and Bonnie watch for that might lead them to conclude that the broker is not working for their best interest?

5. Provide Wally and Bonnie a list of questions to ask potential brokers to assure them of receiving the best service at the lowest costs.

6. Wally and Bonnie are considering bypassing the broker and going directly online to trade. What cautions would you share with them? What is the difference between online investing and day trading?

7. Would you recommend that Wally and Bonnie own their securities in a tenancy-in-common account or a joint tenancy with rights of survivorship account?

---

Visit our Web site for additional case problems, interactive exercises, and practice quizzes for this chapter—**www.prenhall.com/keown**.

# 13 Investing in Stocks

**Learning Objectives**

**1**
**Invest** in stocks.

**2**
**Read** stock quotes in the newspaper or in financial periodicals.

**3**
**Classify** common stock according to basic market terminology.

**4**
**Value** stocks.

**5**
**Understand** the risks associated with investing in common stock.

While Anne Scheiber was alive, no one paid much attention to her. After all, she was just a quiet woman living alone in a studio apartment in Manhattan. She never took vacations or traveled; she never bought furniture; she never ate out; she didn't spend money on new clothes. In fact, neighbors claimed that when they saw her outside her apartment, which was rare, she always wore the same black coat and hat.

It wasn't until her death in 1995 at 101 that she received much notice. In her will, Anne Scheiber revealed that she had a $22 million fortune, almost all of which she bequeathed to Yeshiva University, a small New York school. This gift came as a huge surprise, not only because Scheiber had seemed poor for most of her life, but also because she hadn't attended Yeshiva and, in fact, was totally unknown at the university.

Although the idea of a seemingly poor person leaving a fortune to an institution she'd never even visited is fascinating, how Anne Scheiber amassed her fortune is even more interesting. She started out plainly enough, working as an auditor for the IRS, earning $3,150 per year. As an auditor, though, she had the opportunity to scrutinize the investment habits of many of the wealthy people she audited.

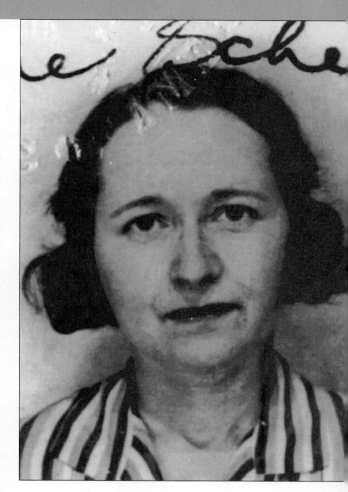

Over time, Scheiber noticed that most of the fortunes of the wealthy were based on common stock investments. She decided that if it worked for the wealthy, it could work for her, too. When she retired in 1943, Scheiber invested her $5,000 nest egg entirely in common stocks.

At first she stuck to companies she knew, beginning with the popular movie studios Universal and Paramount. She went in for the then small soft drink companies Coca-Cola and PepsiCo, as well as a number of drug companies, including Bristol-Myers Squibb and Schering-Plough, also small companies at the time.

Her stock dabblings continued throughout her life. On the rare occasions when Scheiber ventured out of her apartment in her later years, she usually went to see her stockbroker or to read the *Wall Street Journal* at the local library (in keeping with what appeared to be a miserly existence, she never actually bought the paper). In the 42 years up to her death in early 1995, Anne Scheiber's stock holdings increased in value over 4,000-fold, making her a multimillionaire, even though she never lived like one. One of her best investments was the 1,000 shares of Schering-Plough she bought for $10,000 in 1950 and sold in 1994 for over $4 million.

Anne Scheiber may not have lived like a millionaire, but she certainly invested like one. Even if you didn't have her investing skill, it would've been hard not to make money in the stock market any time over the past 76 years. In fact, even with the ups and downs and all the risks of investing in the stock market (such as the crash on October 19, 1987, when the value of a typical stock fell by over 20 percent in one day), if you'd invested a dollar in the common stock of a typical large company on the last day of 1925, it would've grown to $2,279.13 by the end of 2001. Moreover, if you'd invested your dollar in a typical small-company stock, it would've grown to $7,860.05 over the period 1926–2001.

Now you're probably thinking that you don't want to wait 76 years to see some serious returns on your investments. That's fine—you don't have to. The cumulative return on the stock of a typical large company from 1995 through 1999 was a cool 351 percent. Five years isn't that long to wait to almost triple your money, is it? Unfortunately, over the next 2 years about 20 percent of this total amount was lost. Thus, when we talk about common stock, we're talking about risk and return. It's an investment that fits with a longer investment horizon. We're also talking about the place where fortunes—such as Anne Scheiber's—are made.

 Invest in stocks.

## Why Consider Stocks?

Now you know that the possible returns on stock investments are high and that the accompanying risks are also high. But you may be wondering just how stocks generate returns. Simply, they generate returns the same way owning your own business does. When you buy common stock, you purchase a small part of the company. When the company does well, you do well and receive a small part of the profits. If the company does poorly, so do you, and you either get nothing or even lose money.

Returns from common stocks come in the form of dividends and capital appreciation. A **dividend** is simply a company's distribution of profits to its stockholders. It can be in the form of cash or more company stock, but it's always a liquid asset you can use right away. Capital appreciation refers to an increase in the selling price of your shares of stock, perhaps as the company's earning prospects improve. You can't really appreciate or benefit from capital appreciation until you actually sell your stock.

**Dividends**
A company's distribution of its profits in the form of cash or stock to its shareholders.

Unfortunately, neither dividends nor capital appreciation is guaranteed with common stocks. You never know when a seemingly healthy company's going to have a lousy year and not have any profits to distribute—Apple Computer is a good example. Even when companies do have good years and plenty of profits, they're not required to distribute dividends. For example, in 2002 Microsoft still hadn't issued any dividends.

Capital appreciation on stock prices is even less certain. Look, for example, at what happened in 2001 to the common stock of IasiaWorks, the data center services provider: It fell by 97.3 percent. At the same time, the common stock of Ameristar Casinos, the riverboat casino operator, rose by 388.8 percent. Stock prices can jump up and down for the strangest reasons or for no reason at all.

Now you're probably wondering why you should bother investing in stocks if they don't guarantee return. Here's why:

▌ **Over time, common stocks outperform all other investments**. Although stocks aren't guaranteed to give you any return at all, they usually give you a great return anyway. Figure 13.1 compares the returns on various investments over the period 1926–2001. Common stock clearly blows away the alternatives and exceeds the inflation rate by a wide margin.

- **Stocks reduce risk through diversification**. When you include different types of investments that don't move (experience changes in returns) perfectly together over time in your portfolio, you're able to reduce the risk in your portfolio. Stocks move differently than other investments—such as bonds—and different stocks move in different ways. Holding several types of stock can greatly reduce your risk.
- **Stocks are liquid**. You can't be assured of what you'll get when you want to sell your stock, but you won't have a difficult time selling it. The secondary markets for common stock are extremely well developed, and, as such, you will be able to sell your stock whenever you want with minimum transaction costs.
- **The growth in your investment is determined by more than just interest rates**. With some investments, the potential for price appreciation is largely a function of interest rates going down. With common stock, you're not a slave to interest rates. Sure, a change in interest rates can and often will affect your stock prices. However, the earning prospects and performance of the firm will also affect stock prices. If you hitch your star to a company that performs well, you can make money even when interest rates jump.

Once you've made the plunge, you'll want to watch over your investment. Checklist 13.1 provides a number of questions you'll want to consider as your investment progresses.

Now that you know why common stocks make good investments, you should know a thing or two about them in general. Let's take a look at some stock basics.

**Figure 13.1** Returns on Different Investments, 1926–2001

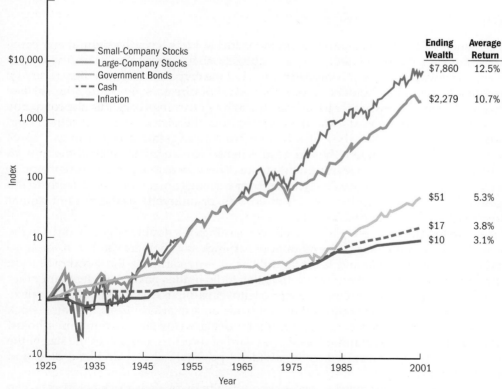

*Hypothetical value of $1 invested at year-end 1925. Assumes reinvestment of income and no transaction costs or taxes.

Source: Computed using data from *Stocks, Bonds, Bills, & Inflation 2002 Yearbook*™, © 2002 Ibbotson Associates Inc. Based on copyrighted works by Ibbotson and Sinquefield. All rights reserved. Used with permission.

# Checklist 13.1 ■ Investment Progress Checklist

Is the return on my investment meeting my expectations and goals? Is this investment
    performing as I was led to believe it would?
Is the company making money? How is it doing compared to its competitors?
How much money will I get back if I sell my investment today?
How much am I paying in commission or fees?
Have my goals changed? If so, are my investments still suitable?
What criteria will I use to decide when to sell?

**Invest in stocks.**

## The Language of Common Stocks

If you're going to invest in common stock, you certainly ought to know a bit about common stock and your rights as a common stockholder. You shouldn't invest in common stock if you can't talk the language of common stock.

### Limited Liability

Although as a common shareholder you're considered one of the many actual owners of the corporation, your liability in the case of bankruptcy is limited to the amount of your investment. The most you can lose, if the company goes broke, is what you invest.

### Claim on Income

As owners of the corporation, the common stockholders have the right to any earnings that are left after all debt and other obligations have been paid. The dividend is the typical way to distribute these earnings, but the corporation isn't obligated to pay dividends to its shareholders. Instead, the board of directors gets to decide whether to pay dividends or whether to reinvest the leftover earnings back into the company.

Obviously, common stockholders benefit from the distribution of income in the form of dividends. But they also benefit from reinvestment of earnings. How? Plowing earnings back into the firm results in an increase in the value of the firm, in its earning power, and in its future dividends. These increases in turn cause the price of the common stock to rise. In effect, leftover earnings are distributed directly to the common stockholder in the form of dividends, or indirectly in the form of capital appreciation on the common stock.

Common stockholders' claim on leftover earnings is a double-edged sword. On the one side, there's no limit to the amount of earnings stockholders can get. If the company has a banner year and takes in millions in extra earnings, the stockholders are entitled to the whole kaboodle. On the other side, if after paying off debt and other monetary obligations the company has no leftover earnings, the stockholders get zilch.

Although most corporations pay dividends on a quarterly basis, common stock dividends aren't automatic. They must be declared by the corporation's board of directors. On the **declaration date**, the board of directors announces the size of the dividend, which is expressed as the dividend per share, the ex-dividend date, and the payment date.

Because companies need to know who actually owns their stock before they can pay a dividend, they set a cutoff date known as the **ex-dividend date**. On the ex-dividend date, the stock begins trading "without dividend"—that is, if you buy it after the ex-dividend date, you don't get the dividend for that year. Of course, if you

**Declaration Date**
The date on which the board of directors announces the size of the dividend, the ex-dividend date, and the payment date.

**Ex-Dividend Date**
The date on which the stock "goes ex," meaning it begins trading in the secondary market "without dividend." In other words, if you buy the stock after its ex-dividend date, you don't get the dividend.

buy the stock before the ex-dividend date, you get the dividend. On the payment date, the corporation sends out dividend checks to shareholders.

## Claims on Assets

When a company does well and has a lot of earnings to distribute, common stockholders receive their share only after creditors are paid. What happens when a company does so poorly that it goes bankrupt? Well, common stockholders are stuck waiting in line again. The creditors have the right to sell off the remaining company assets to regain their money. Only after the claims of the creditors have been paid off do stockholders get to sort through the rubble and try to extract the money they'd invested. Unfortunately, when companies do go bankrupt, the stockholders are usually plain out of luck.

## Voting Rights

Common stockholders are entitled to elect the company's board of directors. Usually, one share of stock equals one vote, although some, but not many, companies issue different "classes" of stock with greater or less voting power. Common stockholders not only have the right to elect the board but also must approve any changes in the rules that govern the corporation.

Voting for directors and charter changes occurs at the corporation's annual meeting. Stockholders may attend the meeting and vote in person, but most vote by proxy. A **proxy** is a legal agreement to allow a designated party to vote for a stockholder at the corporation's annual meeting. A proxy vote isn't the same as asking your buddy to hand in something for you that's already filled out. It gives your "buddy" the right to make decisions for you.

Usually the firm's management goes after and gets most of the proxy votes. However, in times of financial distress or when management takeovers are threatened, *proxy fights*—battles for proxy votes between rival groups of shareholders who want to take control of the company or aim it in a new direction—occur.

**Proxy**
A legal agreement a stockholder signs to allow someone else to vote for him or her at the corporation's annual meeting.

## Stock Splits

Occasionally a firm may decide that its stock price is getting too high for the smaller investor to consider purchasing. To keep the price down and thereby encourage more investors to buy, the company "splits the stock." A **stock split** involves substituting more shares for the existing shares of stock. In effect, the number of shares of stock outstanding increases without there being any increase in the market value of the firm. As a result, each share of stock is worth less.

For example, let's assume you own 100 shares of Coca-Cola common stock and that it's just reached $120 per share. Your investment is worth $12,000. The management of Coca-Cola believes that $120 per share is more than the normal small investor can afford and wants the price lowered. Coca-Cola's managers decide to split the stock three for one. Thus, investors receive three shares of new Coca-Cola stock for every share of "old" Coca-Cola common stock that they own. There's no gain in wealth to the stockholder, so each new share of stock would be worth $40 ($120/3). You now own 300 shares of Coca-Cola stock, which is selling at $40 per share, but your total investment is still worth $12,000.

**Stock Split**
Increasing the number of stock shares outstanding by replacing the existing shares of stock with a given number of shares. For example, in a two-for-one split for every share of existing stock you hold, you would receive two shares of new stock.

## Stock Repurchases

Sometimes companies buy back their own issued shares of common stock in what's called a **stock repurchase**. As a result, there are fewer shares outstanding, so each

**Stock Repurchase**
A company's repurchasing, or buying back, of its own common stock.

remaining stockholder owns a larger proportion of the firm. Stock repurchases are extremely common, with well over 1,000 of these plans announced during most years. For example, in February 2002, Kimberly-Clark announced it would buy back 3 percent of its outstanding common stock.

## Book Value

The book value of a company is calculated by subtracting the value of all the firm's liabilities from the value of its assets, as given on the balance sheet. To relate book value more easily to the price of the stock, divide the company's book value by the number of shares it has outstanding to get the book value per share.

Book value is a historical number. That is, it reflects the value of the firm's assets when they were purchased, which may be vastly different from their value today. For a firm whose assets were purchased a number of years ago, book value has little or no meaning. Still, this measure of value is often talked about and used in valuing stock.

## Earnings Per Share

Earnings per share reflects the level of earnings achieved for every share of stock. Because it focuses on the return earned by the common stockholder, it looks at earnings after preferred stock dividends have been paid.

Preferred stock dividends are subtracted from net income because, as we see in the next chapter, they're paid before common stock dividends are paid. Net income less preferred stock dividends is available to the common shareholders.

This figure tells investors how much they've earned on each share of stock they own—but not necessarily how much the company will pass along in dividends. This figure is available in the daily stock price listings in most newspapers and can be used to compare the financial performance of different companies. Earnings per share is calculated as follows:

$$\text{earnings per share} = \frac{\text{net income} - \text{preferred stock dividends}}{\text{number of shares of common stock outstanding}}$$

## Dividend Yield

**Dividend Yield**
The ratio of the annual dividends to the market price of the stock.

The **dividend yield** on a share of common stock is the amount of annual dividends divided by the market price of the stock. The dividend yield tells investors how much in the way of a return they would receive if the stock price and dividend level remain constant. For example, if the price of the stock is $50 and it pays $4 per share in dividends, the dividend yield would be 8 percent ($4/$50 = 8%).

Many companies that have tremendous growth possibilities choose to reinvest their earnings rather than pay them out in dividends. As a result, many growth companies simply don't pay dividends. For example, Microsoft pays no dividends now, but someday will either pay large dividends or buy back its own stock at hefty prices.

## Market-to-Book or Price-to-Book Ratio

The market-to-book or price-to-book ratio is a measure of how highly valued the firm is. When interpreting this ratio, remember that book value reflects historical costs and, as such, may not be overly meaningful. This ratio is calculated as follows:

$$\text{market-to-book ratio} = \frac{\text{stock price}}{\text{book value per share}}$$

Most stocks have market-to-book ratios above 1.0, and they commonly range up to about 2.5.

## Stock Indexes: Measuring the Movements in the Market

Everyday you hear financial reports on television or the radio in which someone says: "The market was up today as the Dow rose 27 points." Did you ever wonder just what that person was talking about? "The Dow" is simply a **stock market index** that measures the performance of various stock prices. A stock index won't tell you exactly how each one of your investments performed. Instead, indexes provide a simple way of measuring stock performance in general. To understand stock listings and stock performance, you need to be familiar with the Dow and other market indexes.

**Stock Market Index**
A measure of the performance of a group of stocks that represent the market or a sector of the market.

### The Dow

The oldest and most widely quoted of the stock indexes or averages is the **Dow Jones Industrial Average (DJIA)**, or **Dow**, started by Charles Dow in 1896. The DJIA's original purpose was to gauge the sense or well-being of the market based on the performance of 12 major companies. The Dow is currently comprised of the prices of 30 large industrial firms, only one of which—General Electric—was in the original group of 12.

Because the DJIA is based on the movement of only 30 large, well-established stocks, many investors believe it reflects price movements for large firms rather than for the general market. Actually, these 30 stocks represent over 25 percent of the market value of the NYSE, making this average more representative than one might think at first glance.

Another criticism of the DJIA is that it weights stocks based on their relative prices. As a result, when a high-priced stock moves a small amount, it has an inordinately large impact on the index. Still, with all its faults, the DJIA does a relatively good job of reflecting market movements. As you can see in Figure 13.2, the DJIA has had its share of ups and down since 1960.

**Dow Jones Industrial Average (DJIA), or Dow**
A commonly used stock index or indicator of how well stocks have done. This index is comprised of the stock prices of 30 large industrial firms.

### The S&P 500 and Other Indexes

In addition to the Dow, there are a number of other stock indexes. The most well known of these is the **Standard & Poor's 500 Stock Index** or **S&P 500**. The S&P 500 is a much broader index than the DJIA, because it's based on the movements of 500 stocks, primarily from the NYSE, but also including some stocks from the AMEX and the OTC market. Because the S&P 500 is a broader index, it probably better represents movements in the overall market than does the Dow.

In addition, there is the Russell 2000, which is made up of companies that rank in size from the 1,001st through the 3,000th largest companies, and the Wilshire 5000, which is a very broad-based index made up of stocks from the NYSE, the American Stock Exchange, and the NASDAQ. Also, the NYSE, the AMEX, and the NASDAQ all have indexes that chronicle the movements of their listed stocks, and Standard & Poor's calculates six other general indexes. Still, when investors talk about movements in the market, they generally refer to the Dow.

**Standard & Poor's 500 Stock Index or S&P 500**
Another commonly used stock index or indicator of how well stocks have done based on the movements of 500 stocks, primarily from the NYSE.

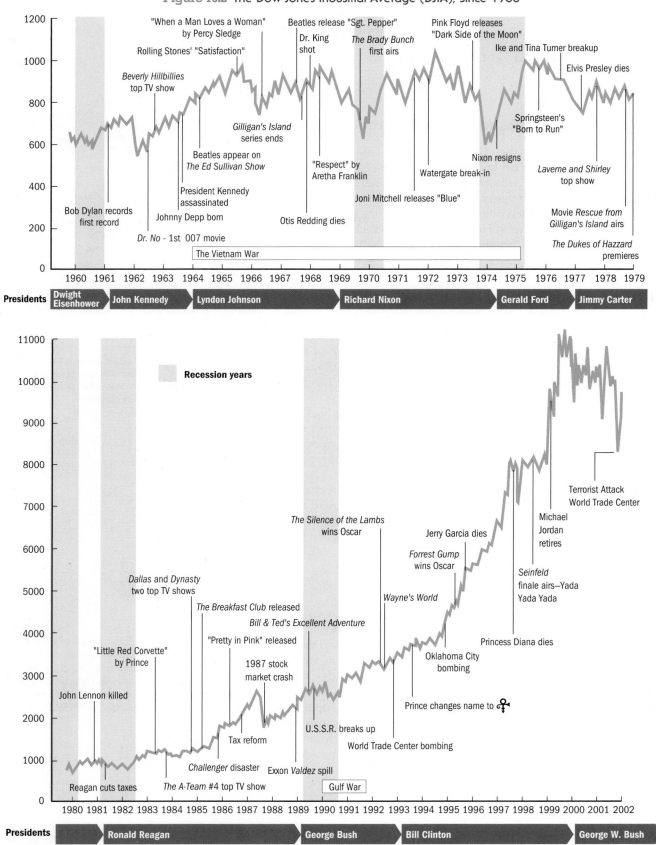

**Figure 13.2** The Dow Jones Industrial Average (DJIA), Since 1960

## Market Movements

So what do all these indexes tell us? Basically they tell us whether stock prices in general are rising or falling. A **bear market** is simply a stock market characterized by falling prices. The term "bear" comes from the fact that bears swipe downward when they attack. A **bull market** is one characterized by rising prices. The term "bull" comes from the fact that bulls fling their horns upward when they attack.

## Reading Stock Quotes in the Newspaper

Figure 13.3 provides a visual summary of how to read NYSE listings. Actually, most newspapers use the same format for stocks listed on the NYSE, the AMEX, and the OTC market. The price and volume listings for stocks traded on the NYSE are

**Figure 13.3** How to Read Stock Listings in the *Wall Street Journal*

The Money and Investing Section of the *Wall Street Journal* contains the composite results of the previous day's trading of NYSE-listed firms on the NYSE and on the five regional exchanges in addition to results for stocks traded on the American Stock Exchange and on the NASDAQ.

**52 Weeks Hi and Lo:** The highest price and lowest price paid for the stock over the past 52 weeks excluding the latest day's trading. As you can see, Disney's stock has traded between 34.80 and 15.50 over the past 52 weeks.

**Sym:** Each stock's ticker symbol appears to the right of the name. For example, the symbol DIS identifies the Disney Corporation. A *pf* next to the stock's name indicates that it is preferred stock.

**Ytd % Chg:** Reflects the stock price percentage change for the calendar year to date, adjusted for stock splits and dividends over 10%.

**PE:** The P/E ratio is used as a measure of relative stock performance. It is calculated by dividing the stock's closing price by its earnings per share for the most recent four quarters. A high P/E ratio suggests that investors are optimistic about the stock's prospects. Some of the reasons for high and low P/E ratios include the firm's growth prospects, the riskiness of the firm, its industry, and the accounting procedures the firm uses.

**Yld%:** The percentage yield is calculated by dividing the cash dividend by the closing price of the stock.

**Vol 100s:** The number of shares traded during the previous day is given under Vol 100s. Shares are generally traded in units of 100 shares. Thus, the number 65518 under Disney indicates that 6,551,800 shares traded during the previous day.

**Last & Net Chg:** Last refers to the price at which the last trade of the day took place, while Net Change refers to the change from the previous day's close, so, for example, Disney's stock closed $0.33 lower than it did the previous day.

**Div:** The stock's annual cash dividend, if any, is given in dollars and cents. For example, Donnelly's annual dividend is estimated to be $0.40.

Underlined quotations are those stocks with large changes in volume, per exchange, compared with the issue's average volume.
**Boldfaced quotations** highlight those issues whose price changed by 5% or more if their previous close was $2 or higher.

### NEW YORK STOCK EXCHANGE COMPOSITE TRANSACTIONS

Quotations as of 4 p.m. Eastern Time
Tuesday, February 26, 2002

| YTD % CHG | 52 WEEKS HI | LO | STOCK (SYM) | DIV | YLD % | PE | VOL 100S | LAST | NET CHG |
|---|---|---|---|---|---|---|---|---|---|
| − 3.6 | 45.65 | 22.83 | DmndOffshr DO | .50 | 1.7 | 22 | 7262 | 29.30 | ... |
| − 8.9 | 43.55 | 25.91 | Diebold DBD | .66f | 1.8 | 39 | 2433 | 36.85 | + 0.29 |
| + 6.3 | 21.79 | 16.51 | DiilrdCapTr DDT | 1.88 | 9.6 | ... | 98 | 19.55 | − 0.24 |
| + 25.8 | 22.50 | 12.06 | Dillards DDS | .16 | .8 | 75 | 15368 | 20.12 | + 1.27 |
| + 3.5 | 11.61 | 5.35 | Dimon DMN | .20 | 2.7 | 12 | 340 | 7.45 | + 0.05 |
| + 15.3 | 34.80 | 15.50 | Disney DIS | .21 | .9 | cc | 65518 | 23.89 | − 0.33 |
| − 3.8 | 16.20 | 10.10 | Dist&Srv ADS DYS | .25e | 2.0 | ... | 302 | 12.60 | − 0.05 |
| − 22.3 | 17.24 | 9.75 | djOrthopedics DJO n | ... | ... | ... | 1373 | 10.33 | + 0.33 |
| + 9.0 | 30.49 | 14.60 | DoleFood DOL | .60f | 2.1 | 11 | 2159 | 29.25 | + 0.38 |
| − 2.6 | 24.05 | 10.50 | DirGenl DG | .13 | .9 | 27 | 9475 | 14.51 | + 0.14 |
| + 6.4 | 25.78 | 8.40 | DirThrfty DTG | ... | ... | 29 | 455 | 16.49 | + 0.37 |
| + 1.0 | 25.40 | 24.56 | DominionCNG Trl DMGA n | .53e | 2.1 | ... | 490 | 25.20 | + 0.05 |
| + 6.9 | 25.05 | 15.70 | DominResVA DOM | 3.16e | 14.9 | ... | 511 | 21.16 | + 0.26 |
| − 3.0 | 69.99 | 55.13 | DominRes D | 2.58 | 4.4 | ... | 17736 | 58.30 | − 0.40 |
| − 5.3 | 66.56 | 55.50 | DominRes PIES | 4.75 | 8.4 | ... | 164 | 56.55 | − 0.15 |
| + 7.2 | 10.92 | 6.80 | Domtar g DTC | .14g | ... | ... | 227 | 10.81 | + 0.21 |
| − 8.7 | 40.35 | 24.45 | Donaldson DCI | .32f | .9 | 20 | 3777 | 35.45 | − 0.47 |
| − 4.1 | 31.90 | 24.30 | DonelleyRR DNY | .96 | 3.4 | cc | 1903 | 28.46 | − 0.24 |
| + 14.1 | 16.20 | 12.75 | Donnelly A DON | .40 | 2.7 | 41 | 69 | 15 | + 0.60 |
| − 0.6 | 5.45 | 1.06 | DotHillSys HIL | ... | dd | ... | 92 | 1.67 | − 0.07 |
| + 7.3 | 43.55 | 26.40 | DoverCp DOV x | .54 | 1.4 | 33 | 7942 | 39.76 | + 0.27 |
| + 1.3 | 17 | ... | 10.90 | DoverDowns DVD | .18 | 1.2 | ... | 827 | 15.50 | − 0.38 |
| − 10.0 | 39.67 | 23.66 | DowChem DOW | 1.34 | 4.4 | dd | 23747 | 30.39 | + 0.08 |
| − 1.7 | 64.30 | 43.05 | DowJones DJ | 1.00 | 1.8 | 70 | 1476 | 55.64 | + 0.04 |
| + 2.7 | 27.47 | 24.87 | DowneyFnlCap DFT x | 2.50 | 9.4 | ... | 44 | 26.50 | + 0.27 |
| + 14.9 | 60.10 | 32.62 | DowneyFnl DSL | .36 | .8 | 11 | 422 | 47.40 | + 0.04 |
| + 25.6 | 26 | 10.04 | DrReddyLab ADR RDY n | .10e | .4 | ... | 5818 | 23.80 | + 1.40 |
| − 2.9 | 34.85 | 13.40 | DrilQuip DRQ | ... | ... | 34 | 130 | 23.41 | − 0.99 |
| − 0.6 | 25.18 | 24.80 | DTE EnergyTrl DTEA n | ... | ... | ... | 236 | 25 | − 0.04 |
| + 10.7 | 49.88 | 32.64 | DuPont DD | 1.40 | 3.0 | 11 | 40535 | 47.04 | + 0.09 |

actually a combination of all trades of NYSE-listed firms, regardless of where the trade occurred—whether on the NYSE or on one of the regional exchanges.

By looking at the stock quote in the paper, investors can see how much a stock's price jumped up or down by examining its highest and lowest prices during the previous day, which are listed along with the closing price. Finally, the change from the previous day's closing price is listed, which, along with the stock's high and low over the past 52 weeks, gives you a sense of the direction the stock price is taking.

For example, according to the listing in Figure 13.3, what was the last price Disney sold for? How many shares traded yesterday? What is Disney's ticker symbol? What is the price earnings ratio for Disney? How about for Dole Food? The last price Disney sold for was $23.89, and 65,518 lots of 100 shares traded for a total of 6,551,800 shares! The ticker symbol for Disney is *DIS*. The price earnings ratio for Disney was listed as "cc," which means the price earnings ratio was over 100; for Dole Food, the price earnings ratio was 11.

<table>
<tr><td>L<br>3</td><td>Classify common stock according to basic market terminology.</td></tr>
</table>

## General Classifications of Common Stock

Analysts just love to use such terms as "blue chip," "speculative," and "growth" to describe common stocks. These aren't formal classifications, but they're terms you should be familiar with. We'll introduce several of the most prevalent "classifications," noting that different analysts may view the same stock as falling into different classifications.

**Blue-Chip Stocks**

Common stocks issued by large, nationally known companies with sound financial histories of solid dividend and growth records.

**Growth Stocks**

Common stocks issued by companies that have exhibited sales and earnings growth well above their industry average. Generally, these are smaller stocks, and many times they are newly formed.

**Income Stocks**

Common stocks issued by mature firms that pay relatively high dividends, with little increase in earnings.

**Speculative Stocks**

Common stocks that carry considerably more risk and variability than a typical stock. A stock's classification can change over time.

**Cyclical Stocks**

Common stocks issued by companies whose earnings tend to move with the economy. A stock's classification can change over time.

- **Blue-chip stocks. Blue-chip stocks** are common stocks issued by large, nationally known companies with sound financial histories of solid dividend and growth records. Some examples of companies whose common stock is considered blue chip are General Electric, Texaco, and Procter & Gamble.
- **Growth stocks. Growth stocks** issued by companies that have exhibited sales and earnings growth well above their industry average. Generally, these are smaller companies, and many times they are newly formed. These companies often pay very low or no dividends; instead they retain earnings and plow those funds back into the company. An example of a company whose common stock is considered a growth stock is Microsoft, which has posted huge increases in earnings while not paying dividends.
- **Income stocks. Income stocks** are generally associated with more mature firms that pay relatively high dividends, with little increase in earnings. The stocks of most utilities are considered income stocks, because utilities generally pay relatively high dividends and don't experience much growth in earnings.
- **Speculative stocks. Speculative stocks** carry considerably more risk and variability. Moreover, with speculative stocks it's generally difficult to forecast with precision the direction of the issuing company's future profits. These stocks are usually traded on the OTC market. Ciena, which produces optical networking equipment, was riding high during 2001—climbing by 182.6 percent—but saw its stock price drop by 82.4 percent in 2001. It is an example of a company whose stock is considered speculative.
- **Cyclical stocks. Cyclical stocks** are those issued by companies whose earnings tend to move with the economy. When the economy slumps, earnings drop. When the economy recovers, so do earnings. Stocks issued by firms in the auto, steel, and housing industries are generally considered cyclical.

- **Defensive stocks. Defensive stocks** aren't nearly as affected by swings in the economy, and in some cases, they actually perform better during downturns. Why? Because companies behind defensive stocks tend not to be hurt by downturns. The insurance industry, for example, is largely unaffected by swings in the economy, and some auto parts suppliers, such as Midas and Monroe, actually see increased sales during downturns as consumers avoid purchasing new cars and instead repair their present cars.

- **Large caps, mid caps, and small caps. Large-, mid-,** and **small-cap stocks** refer to the size of the firm issuing the stock—more specifically, to the level of its capitalization, or market value. For example, Ford would be considered a large-cap stock because its total market value is $27,706 million. Sanmina, a manufacturer of custom-designed circuit boards used in sophisticated electronics equipment, is considered a mid-cap stock because its market value is $5,595 million. On the other hand, Bridgeford Foods Corporation would be considered a small-cap stock because its total market value is only about $113 million. Over the period 1926–2001, small-cap stocks outperformed large-cap stocks, registering an annual average return of 12.5 percent as opposed to 10.7 percent for large-cap stocks.

## Valuation of Common Stock

What's the value of any investment? A number of different methods can be used to determine what an investment is worth. All can be more than a bit tricky. These methods can also help us understand why an investment's price moves one way or the other. Let's take a look at three of the most popular valuation methods.

### The Technical Analysis Approach

**Technical analysis** focuses on supply and demand, using charts and computer programs to identify and project price trends for a stock or for the market as a whole. The logic behind technical analysis is that although economic factors are of great importance in determining stock prices, so are psychological factors, such as *greed* and *fear*.

Technical analysts believe that these two factors, greed and fear, reinforce trends in the market. Greed pushes investors to put their money in the market when the market is rising, and fear has them pull their money out if a downturn appears. In effect, no one wants to be the last aboard a market upturn, and no one wants to be the last out if the market is falling.

Technical analysis takes a number of forms, including the interpretation of charts and graphs and mathematical calculations of trading patterns, all aimed at spotting some trend or direction for stocks. Technical analysts might look into the past for trends or patterns that give some clue as to where investors might be heading. In addition, they might look for price levels where stock prices might get stuck. These price levels are referred to as resistance or support levels.

Unfortunately, although technical analysis may appeal to the novice investor, it's been found to be of little value. Although there appear to be distinct trends in past movements of the market, the problem comes in identifying these trends before they surface. Moreover, some of these patterns may have been useful in the past, but without any economic logic behind them, what's to say they'll continue to act as good predictors?

**Defensive Stocks**
Common stocks issued by companies whose earnings tend not to be affected by swings in the economy and in some cases actually perform better during downturns. A stock's classification can change over time.

**Large Caps, Mid Caps, and Small Caps**
Classifications of common stock that refer to the size of the issuing firm—more specifically, to the level of the firm's capitalization, or its market value. A stock's classification can change over time.

Value stocks.

**Technical Analysis**
A method of stock analysis that focuses on supply and demand, using charts and computer programs to identify and project price trends for a stock or for the market as a whole.

In short, technical analysis should be viewed as something to avoid because it encourages moving in and out of the market, which is dangerous, as opposed to simply buying and holding stocks.

## The Price/Earnings Ratio Approach

**Price/Earning Ratio**
The price per share divided by the earnings per share. Also called the earnings multiple.

The **price/earnings ratio** is used regularly by security analysts as a measure of a stock's relative value. This price-earnings ratio (P/E ratio), or earnings multiplier, is simply the price per share divided by the earnings per share. It's an indication of how much investors are willing to pay for a dollar of the company's earnings. The more positive investors feel about a stock's future prospects, or the less risk they feel the stock has, the higher the stock's P/E ratio.

For example, a stock with estimated earnings per share next year of $6.50, which is currently selling for $104, would have a P/E ratio of 16 ($104/$6.50). If the prospects for this stock improved—perhaps the company introduces a new product that in a few years should greatly increase profits—the stock price might rise to $130, which would be a new P/E ratio of 20 ($130/$6.50). A stock with a P/E ratio of 20 would be referred to as "selling at 20 times earnings." How do we use P/E ratios to value stocks? By deciding whether or not the stock's P/E ratio is too high or too low.

How do you determine an appropriate P/E ratio for a specific stock? First, you determine a justified P/E ratio for the market as a whole by looking at past market P/E ratios, taking into consideration the strength of the economy, interest rates, the deficit, and the inflation rate. Then you simply make a judgment call. In effect, it's a bit arbitrary. This overall market P/E ratio is then adjusted depending on the specific prospects for the individual stock. For example, if the growth potential is above average, it is adjusted upward—but how much higher is the real question. Although determining an appropriate or justified P/E ratio for a given stock is difficult, we can at least point to some of the factors that drive P/E ratios up and down:

**Fundamental Analysis**
Determining the value of a share of stock by focusing on such determinants as future earnings and dividends, expected levels of interest rates, and the firm's risk.

▌ **The higher the firm's earnings growth rate, the higher the firm's P/E ratio.** In effect, the market values a dollar of earnings more if those earnings are expected to grow more in the future.

▌ **The higher the investor's required rate of return, the lower the P/E ratio.** If interest rates rise, or if the firm becomes more risky, the P/E ratio will fall. Likewise, if interest rates drop, or the firm becomes less risky, the P/E ratio should rise.

**STOP & THINK** Many analysts and investors use the market's P/E ratio as a measure of whether the market is overpriced or underpriced. In recent years they've viewed the average market P/E ratio as being in the 15 to 35 range. If the market's P/E ratio is much above this level, the market is overpriced, and if it's much below this level, the market is underpriced. However, keep in mind that anticipated inflation and the health of the economy and future corporate earnings play a major role in determining the market's P/E ratio.

Figure 13.4 shows the average P/E ratio since 1943, which should give you an idea of a typical P/E ratio. These ratios seem to vary from 7 on up. In recent years, the average has been in the 15 to 35 range. The P/E ratio for growth stocks is much higher—generally beginning at 40 and going on up.

As you can see, since 1980 the average P/E ratio has risen. One reason for this rise is the drop in inflation over this period. Because this valuation method focuses on such fundamental determinants as future earnings, expected levels of interest rates, and the firm's risk, it's considered to be a type of **fundamental analysis**.

**Figure 13.4** The Average Price/Earnings Ratio on the S&P 500, Since 1943

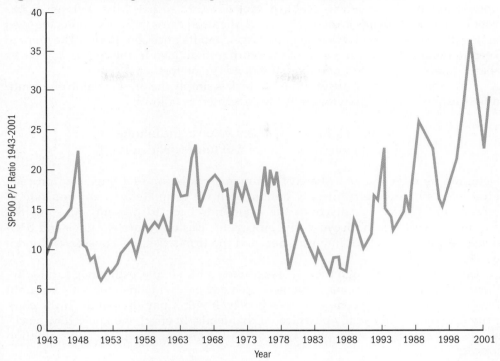

## The Discounted Dividends Valuation Model

If we take the returns that result from owning an investment and bring them back to the present, all we need do is add them up to determine the value of that investment. In effect, *the value of any investment is the present value of the benefits or returns that you receive from that investment.* We're simply taking what we learned in Chapter 3, in which we moved money through time, and applying it. This simple valuation principle—bring the returns back to the present and add them up—serves as the foundation for valuing all securities and assets.

When you purchase a share of common stock, you get dividend payments whenever they're declared, and then at some future point in time you generally sell the stock. Hopefully, you sell it for more than you purchased it for, thus receiving capital gains (the difference between what you purchased the stock for and what you sold it for).

Where does that price you're going to get when you sell your common stock come from? Well, it's based on the future dividend payments the buyer expects while the stock is held plus some capital gains. What that buyer eventually gets for the stock when it's sold is again based on future dividend payments plus capital gains. This little exercise can be carried on ad nauseam. And what it illustrates is that the value of a share of stock should be the present value of its future dividends. That's all that the firm pays out, and that's what the value of a share of stock should be based on.

Moreover, companies can pay out those dividends forever, because common stock has no termination date. Of course, you'll be hoping for capital gains, but how much the stock rises in price will be based on what investors feel is going to happen to dividends in the future.

This is an important concept, but it's also one that's difficult for many students to understand, especially when you have stock in a firm such as Microsoft, which has yet to pay any dividends at all. However, as Microsoft earns more and more, the level of its future dividends grows larger and larger, and its price should rise. The point to keep in mind is that earnings eventually turn into dividends, the company pays its shareholders in dividends, and those dividends go on forever.

Thus, the value of a share of common stock is simply the present value of the infinite stream of dividend payments. It can be written as follows:

$$\frac{\text{value of a share}}{\text{of common stock}} = \frac{\text{present value of the infinite}}{\text{stream of future dividends}}$$

Determining the value of a share of common stock becomes a three-step process. First, we estimate the future dividends, then we estimate our required rate of return, and finally, we discount the dividends back to present values at the required rate of return. Because this process focuses on future earnings and dividends, expected levels of interest rates, and the firm's risk, it's considered fundamental analysis.

Unfortunately, although this process sounds quite simple, estimating future dividends is an almost unmanageable task. Remember, dividends aren't known until they're declared. If the company does poorly, it won't pay dividends. If the company does well, it'll usually pay nice fat dividends. In effect, we know how stocks *should* be valued, but we have a very difficult time implementing this valuation process.

To use this method, we must predict what will happen to dividends in the future. Unfortunately, this means that the answers we get from our valuation formula won't be overly reliable. That is, because the assumption we make might not be accurate, our conclusions might not be accurate. However, this method is still valuable for the insights and implications it yields as to what determines and affects stock prices.

To simplify the calculations, we must assume that *dividends will grow at a constant rate forever*. Making this assumption, the value of a share of stock can be written as follows:

$$\text{value of common stock} = \frac{\text{dividends next year}}{\text{required rate of return} - \text{growth rate}}$$

Rewriting this using the notation from Chapter 3, we get

$$\frac{\text{value of}}{\text{common stock}} = \frac{D_1}{k - g}$$

where

$D_1$ = the dividend next year

$k$ = appropriate required rate of return given the risk level of the common stock

$g$ = the constant annual growth rate in dividends

Let's look at an example of a share of common stock expected to pay $5 in dividends next year ($D_1$ = $5). In addition, let's assume dividends are expected to grow at a rate of 4 percent per year forever ($g$ = 0.04), and that given the risk level of this common stock, the investor's required rate of return is 12 percent ($k$ = 0.12). Plugging this information into our stock valuation formula, we can calculate the value of the common stock as follows:

$$\begin{aligned}
\text{value of common stock} &= \frac{D_1}{k - g} \\
&= \frac{\$5}{0.12 - 0.04} \\
&= \frac{\$5}{0.08} = \$62.50
\end{aligned}$$

Thus, the value of this stock is $62.50. If the stock is selling for less than its value, we should buy it. If it's selling for more than its value, we shouldn't buy it.

Although we now have a value for the share of stock, the formula we used to get it is very limited. In fact, if we try to take this formula and apply it to a company which hasn't paid any dividends in the past, it simply doesn't make sense.

Of course, we used a very simple and basic assumption about dividend values. In the real world, this "discounted dividends valuation model" is used by most major brokerage firms to estimate the value of common stock. However, when analysts use this approach, their calculations are much more complicated than ours. But both calculations are based on the same principles. For our purposes, though, even more important than the exact calculations are this model's principles and implications about stock valuation.

## Why Stocks Fluctuate in Value

Although the assumptions we made with our discounted dividend valuation model limit its use as an accurate tool for valuing stocks, the model does help us understand the underlying factors that affect the price of a share of common stock. Let's examine these factors now.

**Interest Rates and Stock Valuation**   There's an inverse relationship between interest rates and the value of a share of common stock. As interest rates rise, investors demand a higher return on their common stock. As the required return rises, the present value of the future dividends declines. If you look at the common stock valuation equation, you can easily see that when $k$ increases, the value of the stock decreases, and when $k$ decreases, the value of the stock increases.

For example, in 1995 declining inflation resulted in a 2-percent drop in interest rates. Keep in mind that as anticipated inflation declines, investors demand less in the way of a return for delaying consumption (remember **Principle 1: The Risk–Return Trade-Off**), and as a result, interest rates also drop. The bottom line was that declining inflation caused interest rates to drop by 2 percent in 1995 and the result was that stocks surged by 37 percent!

Principle 1
The Risk–Return Trade-Off

**Risk and Stock Valuation**   As the stock's risk increases, so does the investor's required rate of return. Again, we have to remember **Principle 1: The Risk–Return Trade-Off**. Investors demand additional return for taking on added risk. At Apple Computer in early 1996, as its prospects became more uncertain, investors began to view Apple as a more risky investment than they had previously. To compensate for this added risk, investors increased their required rate of return on Apple's stock, resulting in a decline in its market value. Then, when Apple's fortunes changed with the introduction of the iMac, its price rose in 1998 and 1999, climbing from about $6 per share to over $50 per share, as it became less risky. Then in late September 2000, Apple Computer admitted that its prospects were exaggerated, and that the risk

# In The News

Wall Street Journal September 9, 2000

## Don't Ignore Luck's Role in Stock Picks

### by Jonathan Clements

When stock market investors take a hit, they rail at their stupidity and question their investment strategy. But there is a fair chance that the real culprits are bad luck and skewed expectations. Here are two examples of when that is the case.

*All Over the Map:* Just as your portfolio likely will include a fair number of losing stocks, so you may have exposure to stock market sectors that post lackluster returns for long periods. Were you wrong to invest in those sectors? Probably not.

*"In the 1990s, U.S. stocks beat international stocks,"* notes William Reichenstein, an investments professor at Baylor University in Waco, Texas. *"That doesn't mean international diversification isn't needed or doesn't work. International diversification is about reducing risk before the fact. In 1990, no one knew that the United States would be the hottest market for the decade. Similarly, today no one knows which region will be the hottest market. That's why we diversify internationally."* (☞**A**)

*Timing Patterns:* Did you load up on stocks, only to see the market tank? Don't

feel bad. Short-run market activity is utterly unpredictable. That is why investors who buy stocks need a long time horizon.

"When people buy and the market goes down, that is when regret hits the most, because they can easily imagine postponing the purchase," Meir Statman, a finance professor at Santa Clara University in California, says. "People feel that the market is picking on them personally." But in truth, buying stocks ahead of a market decline is just bad luck.

Similarly, folks can also draw the wrong lesson from their successes. For instance, if you made a brilliantly timed switch between stocks and cash, that may bolster your self-confidence and make you think you are smarter than you really are.

*"People tend to pat themselves on the back because of one or two good market calls,"* says Minneapolis financial planner Ross Levin. *"The danger is, you think that you can accurately predict the direction of the market. If you're not careful, you'll end up being*

*out of stocks during a big market rally. People should decide what portion of their portfolio they want in stocks and then stick with it."* (☞**B**)

## THE BOTTOM LINE . . .

**A** The same thing goes for sectors—since you don't know which will be the next "hot" sector, the key is to diversify your portfolio and make sure you don't miss out entirely.

**B** It makes it a lot easier to deal with wild market fluctuations once you admit that your gains and losses may be a result of bad luck rather than bad brains. That's what's behind **Principle 5: The Curse of Competitive Investment Markets.**

Source: Jonathan Clements, "Don't Ignore Luck's Role in Stock Picks," *Wall Street Journal*, September 9, 2000: C1. Copyright (c) 2000, Dow Jones & Company, Inc. Reproduced with permission of DOW JONES & CO INC in the format Textbook via Copyright Clearance Center.

---

level faced by technology companies in general was much greater than most people perceived. In effect, Apple admitted that it is in a ruthlessly competitive market for desktop and portable PCs. The result was a drop in the stock price of Apple Computer to about one-third of its price just days earlier.

**Earnings (and Dividend) Growth and Stock Valuation** Although the stock valuation equation uses dividend growth to determine value, most analysts think about value in terms of earnings. As earnings grow, so does the company's capacity to pay dividends. In effect, the more earnings a company has, the more it can give out in the way of dividends. As a result, earnings growth is generally viewed as the *cause* of any increase in dividends.

We generally talk about a positive relationship between the expected growth rate for earnings and stock prices, which makes sense. As the firm earns more and is able to return more to its shareholders, the stock price should rise. Looking at our valuation equation, you can see that as *g* increases, the denominator decreases, and thus, the value of the stock should increase.

> **STOP & THINK** It's a bit intimidating to think about all the analysis that you can do in selecting a stock. Fortunately, much of it's already done for you and it's available online. Take a look at Quicken's Investing Web site at **www.quicken.com:80/investments**.

## Stock Investment Strategies

There are several investment strategies you can follow when purchasing stock. As we take a look at a few of them, keep in mind that you can use more than one of these approaches at once. Still, you've got to be alert, especially when your money is on the line. Checklist 13.2 provides a number of things you should look out for.

### Dollar Cost Averaging

**Dollar cost averaging** is the practice of purchasing a fixed dollar amount of stock at specified intervals. The logic behind dollar cost averaging is that by investing the same dollar amount each period instead of buying in one lump sum, you'll be averaging out price fluctuations by buying more shares of common stock when the price is lowest, and fewer shares when the price is highest.

Table 13.1 presents an example of dollar cost averaging, where the investor buys $500 worth of stock each quarter for 2 years instead of investing everything all at once. The reason the investor in this example did better with dollar cost averaging is that the market price bounced from $40 to $55, allowing the investor to buy more shares for the same amount of money when prices dipped.

Lucky people buy stocks when the price is low, and unlucky people buy when the price is high. The problem is that no one knows if a given price is going to be a high or a low, because you never know what stocks will do in the future. Dollar cost averaging's intent is to even out your luck by letting the highs and lows cancel each other out.

Recently, dollar cost averaging has come under some criticism as an inefficient way to invest a lump sum in the market. This criticism centers on the fact that over time, stocks generally tend to rise in price. So if you have a lump sum of money to invest, it's better to get it into the market as soon as possible to get in on those rising prices. For example, look at the stock market from 1995 through the first half of 1999:

**L1** Invest in stocks.

**Dollar Cost Averaging**
A strategy for purchasing common stock in which the investor purchases a fixed dollar amount of stock at specified intervals, for example, quarterly.

# Checklist 13.2 ■ Be Alert

**Look out for:**

Recommendations from a sales representative based on "inside" or "confidential information," an "upcoming favorable research report," a "prospective merger or acquisition," or the announcement of a "dynamic new product."

Telephone sales pitches; NEVER send money to purchase a stock (or other investment) based simply on a telephone sales pitch.

Representations of spectacular profit, such as, "Your money will double in 6 months." Remember, if it sounds too good to be true, it probably is!

"Guarantees" that you will not lose money on a particular securities transaction, or agreements by a sales representative to share in any losses in your account.

An excessive number of transactions in your account. Such activity generates additional commissions for your sales representative, but may provide no better investment opportunities for you.

A recommendation from your sales representative that you make a dramatic change in your investment strategy, such as moving from low-risk investments to speculative securities, or concentrating your investments exclusively in a single product.

Pressure to trade the account in a manner that is inconsistent with your investment goals and the risk you want or can afford to take.

## Table 13.1  Dollar Cost Averaging

| Date | Dollar Cost Averaging, Investing $500 per Quarter | | | | | Lump-Sum Investment Buying 80 Shares at $50/Share |
|---|---|---|---|---|---|---|
| | Money Invested | Price | Shares Purchased | Total Shares Owned | Market Value | Market Value |
| Year 1, quarter 1 | $  500 | $50 | 10.0 | 10.0 | $  500 | $4,000 |
| Year 1, quarter 2 | 500 | 46 | 10.9 | 20.9 | 961 | |
| Year 1, quarter 3 | 500 | 40 | 12.5 | 33.4 | 1,336 | |
| Year 1, quarter 4 | 500 | 50 | 10.0 | 43.4 | 2,170 | |
| Year 2, quarter 1 | 500 | 55 | 9.1 | 52.5 | 2,888 | |
| Year 2, quarter 2 | 500 | 45 | 11.1 | 63.6 | 2,862 | |
| Year 2, quarter 3 | 500 | 50 | 10.0 | 73.6 | 3,680 | |
| Year 2, quarter 4 | 500 | 52 | 9.6 | 83.2 | 4,327 | |
| **Total** | $4,000 | $48.50 | 83.2 | 83.2 | $4,327 | $4,160 |

it went no place but up. That means that the sooner investors got their money in the stock market, the more they made. In fact, history shows that over all the 12-month periods from 1926 through 1991, you would be better off investing in a lump sum 64.5 percent of the time. But with the bouncing around of stock prices in 2000, 2001, and 2002, this approach has regained much of its lost popularity.

In spite of all this, dollar cost averaging has merit. First, it's good if you want to avoid being killed rather than make a killing in the market. That is, if you buy stock over an extended period, it's less likely that all your money will be invested right before a market crash. Second, dollar cost averaging keeps you from trying to time the market.

"Timing the market" is attempting to wait for the lowest possible price before buying. It's virtually impossible to do. Unfortunately, it's awfully tempting to try. Moreover, in timing the market, an investor can wait and wait for the market to come down and miss a major upturn. That's pretty much the case from 1995 through the first half of 1999—if you were looking for a low point in the market to invest, you never would have entered the market. In effect, market timing is like an antigravity machine—a great idea, but making it work is the problem. Third, and most important, dollar cost averaging forces investing discipline. You are investing in stocks regularly, and investing becomes part of your budgeting and planning process.

## Buy-and-Hold Strategy

**Buy-and-Hold**
An investment strategy that involves simply buying stock and holding it for a period of years.

As you might guess, a **buy-and-hold** investment strategy involves buying stock and holding it for a period of years. There are four reasons why such a strategy is worth considering. First, it aims at avoiding timing the market. By buying and holding the stock, the ups and downs that occur over shorter periods become irrelevant. Second, the buy-and-hold strategy minimizes brokerage fees and other transaction costs. Constant buying and selling really racks up the charges, but buying and holding has only the charge of buying. By keeping these costs down, the investor retains more of the stock's returns. Third, holding and not selling the stock postpones any capital gains taxes. The longer you can go without paying taxes, the longer you hold your money, and the longer you have to reinvest and earn returns on your returns. Finally, a buy-and-hold strategy means your gains will be taxed as long-term capital gains.

## Dividend Reinvestment Plans (DRIPs)

If you want to use common stock to accumulate wealth, you must reinvest rather than spend your dividends. Without reinvesting, your accumulation of wealth will be limited to the stock's capital gains. Unfortunately, many dividends may be small enough that you figure you might as well spend them on a pack of Juicy Fruit rather than reinvest them. Hey, you don't need to pay a brokerage fee to buy Juicy Fruit.

One way to avoid buying too much gum and not enough stock is through a **dividend reinvestment plan**, or **DRIP**. Under a dividend reinvestment plan, you're allowed to reinvest the dividend in the company's stock automatically without paying any brokerage fees. Most large companies offer such plans, and many stockholders take advantage of them. For example, nearly 40 percent of all PepsiCo stockholders participate in dividend reinvestment plans.

**STOP & THINK** If you employ a buy-and-hold strategy while buying stock using the dollar cost averaging method, a downturn in the market isn't necessarily bad. It simply means that when you're buying, you're getting more shares of stocks. Dollar cost averaging is best served by a market that doesn't climb steadily but bounces up and down.

**Dividend Reinvestment Plan (DRIP)**
An investment plan that allows the investor to automatically reinvest stock dividends in the same company's stock without paying any brokerage fees.

# In The News

## Wall Street Journal July 10, 2001

### Analysts' Reports: Don't Believe the Hype

by Jeff D. Opdyke

#### BUY, SELL, OR HOLD?

It is the most basic question of investing and the one to which investors seek a clear answer when turning to Wall Street for stock market advice. Yet more often than not, the answer is cloaked in semantic mystery, where a buy isn't always a buy and a hold often means sell. What is an investor to do?

*To start with, don't blindly heed buy recommendations. Kent Womack, a finance professor at Dartmouth College, in Hanover, New Hampshire, found in a study published in 1996 that "new buy recommendations are only marginally valuable." The ensuing price rise of about 3 percent in the 6 months after the call, he says, "would probably cover your commission cost." (☛A)*

What Mr. Womack did find is that analysts are at their best when they are critical. His research showed that "investors should really listen when an analyst turns negative on a stock." Following a downgrade, shares often slip about 7 percent over the next several months. With outright sell recommendations, he found, shares typically fall about 10 percent.

Bearish signals, he says, "are incredibly valuable." Currently, 66 percent of all stock recommendations are buy or strong buy, according to First Call; 32 percent are neutral.

The irony: While analysts often put a hold on a stock as way of warning professional investors away from the shares, few have the nerve to call a stock a sell, a plainspoken indication to individual investors to dump or avoid a stock.

*As a rule, analysts typically loathe the S-word for fear of antagonizing the company and, in turn, losing investment-banking business, which bolsters the firm's bottom line and often helps fuel an analyst's pay. Thus, analysts rely on word games to communicate with the Street, putting out recommendations such as market perform when they really mean sell. (☛B)*

So, it is high time to get hip, and start giving haircuts to those research calls. First Call's Mr. Hill says investors should ratchet down every recommendation one notch: A strong buy means buy; a buy means hold; and a hold or neutral means sell. "That's the only way to make sense of these things," he says.

#### THE BOTTOM LINE . . .

A Make sure you don't take these one-word evaluations at face value—keep in mind the fact that only about 1 percent of all research recommendations are sells. Once again, keep in mind **Principle 9: The Best Protection Is Knowledge.** Keep your eye on information provided in the research report rather than that one-word evaluation.

B Analysts may also feel uncomfortable giving a firm a poor evaluation if their firm is doing investment banking business with that firm—this information should be provided in the report. This gets back to **Principle 12: The Agency Problem—Beware of the Sales Pitch.**

Source: Jeff D. Opdyke, "Analysts' Reports: Don't Believe the Hype," *Wall Street Journal*, July 10, 2001: C1. Copyright (c) 2001, Dow Jones & Company, Inc. Reproduced with permission of DOW JONES & CO INC in the format Textbook via Copyright Clearance Center.

A dividend reinvestment plan is a great way to let your savings grow, but it's not without drawbacks. The major drawback is that when you sell your stock, you'll have to figure out your income taxes—and that can be overwhelming. Each time you reinvest dividends, you're effectively buying additional shares of stock at a different price. Moreover, even though you don't receive any cash when your dividends are reinvested, you still have to pay income tax as if you actually received those dividends.

A final drawback is the fact that you can't choose what to do with your own dividend. What if the company you've invested in is performing moderately well, and you just heard about another company whose stock price is rising faster than the blood pressure of a fat man with a love of salt? You're stuck reinvesting instead of trying something new.

Despite these drawbacks, dividend reinvestment plans appeal to many investors. Two sources of companies offering DRIPs are Standard & Poor's *Directory of Dividend Reinvestment Plans* and Evergreen Enterprises' *Directory of Companies Offering Dividend Reinvestment Plans*, both of which may be available at your library.

Understand the risks associated with investing in common stock.

## Risks Associated with Common Stocks

In Chapter 11 we examined several different sources of risk associated with investing in all securities. Stocks have more risk than other investments, but they also have more potential return. You should already know quite a bit about risk and return from our list of principles. Let's use some of those principles to explore the relationship between stocks and risk and to see if we can't lower our risk while still maintaining our return.

Principle 1 The Risk–Return Trade-Off

### Principle 1: The Risk–Return Trade-Off

We can view stocks as being at the upper end of the risk–return line as shown in Figure 13.5. Watching the S&P 500 drop by 10.54 percent and NASDAQ drop by

**Figure 13.5 The Risk–Return Relationship**

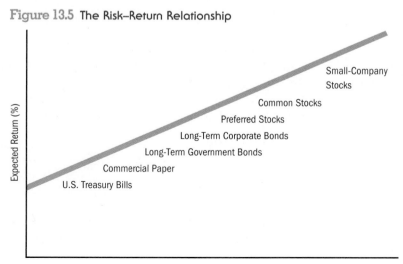

25.30 percent during the week of April 10, 2000, reminds us of the risk associated with common stock. Without those risks, you wouldn't expect the high returns that common stocks provide. Thus, there's a great deal of potential risk if the firm does poorly, and a great deal of potential return if the firm does well.

## Principle 3: Diversification Reduces Risk

Fortunately, you can eliminate much of the risk associated with common stock simply by diversifying your investments. In this way, when one of your stocks goes bust, another investment soars, making up for the loss. Basically, diversification lets you iron out the ups and downs of investing. You don't experience the great returns, but you don't experience great losses either.

What you're looking for to help diversification along is investments that don't move in like patterns. For example, you might invest in stocks from a wide variety of industries and also include international stocks. In addition, you might make sure that you invest in more than just stocks.

Principle

Diversification Reduces Risk

## Principle 4: Diversification and Risk—All Risk Is Not Equal

As you saw in Chapter 11, the ability to eliminate a portion of a portfolio's risk through diversification has led to the segmentation of risk into two types: systematic or nondiversifiable risk, and unsystematic or diversifiable risk. Principle 4 deals with the fact that in a well-diversified portfolio, only systematic risk remains. In fact, as your stock portfolio increases in size to 10 or 20 stocks, approximately 60 percent of the total risk is eliminated, and almost all of the remaining risk is systematic risk. As a result, we're very concerned with how much systematic risk an investment has.

To measure systematic risk, we use **beta**, which can be found in Value Line and other investment publications. The beta for the market is 1.0—that's the benchmark against which specific stock betas are measured. A stock with above-average systematic risk would have a beta greater than 1.0, and a stock with below-average systematic risk would have a beta less than 1.0. The vast majority of betas are positive because most stocks move with the market.

The easiest way to interpret beta is to think of it as a measure of relative responsiveness of a stock. For example, if the market goes up by 20 percent and a stock has a beta of 1.5, then that stock would go up by 30 percent (20% × 1.5 = 30%). Conversely, if the market went down by 20 percent, that same stock would go down by 30 percent (−20% × 1.5 = −30%). In other words, a stock with a beta greater than 1.0 tends to amplify both the up and the down movements in the market. By the same token, a stock with a beta of less than 1.0 tends to mute the movements in the market. Thus, beta is a measure of the relative responsiveness of stock to market movements, with a stock that's 30 percent more volatile than the market having a beta of 1.3, and one that's 50 percent more volatile than the market having a beta of 1.5.

What does all this mean to you as an investor? First, once your stock portfolio is diversified, it tends to move closely with all the other stocks in the marketplace. That is to say, the returns to a diversified portfolio are more a function of major changes in anticipated inflation, interest rates, or the general economy rather than of events unique to any specific company in the portfolio. Second, it means that the only way to fully diversify is to make sure that you invest in more than one type of investment—include domestic and international stocks along with bonds in your portfolio. Finally, if your portfolio is well diversified, you should keep an eye on its beta.

Principle

Diversification and Risk—All Risk Is Not Equal

**Beta**

The measure of systematic risk. It is a measure of how responsive a stock or portfolio is to changes in the *market portfolio*, such as the S&P 500 Index or the New York Stock Exchange index.

## Principle 11: The Time Dimension of Investing

We know how to reduce or even eliminate unsystematic risk, but wouldn't it be nice if we could also tolerate a little more risk? Well, we can—as long as we're patient. In the short run, market fluctuations are a killer. Nothing is more painful than experiencing a big fat market downturn and then needing your money. However, the longer your investment time horizon, the more you can afford to invest in riskier assets—that is, stocks.

When you invest in stocks, you're almost certain to experience a bad year or two. Holding on to stock for only a year is very risky, because the year you choose to hold it just might be one of those bad years. Figure 13.6 lists the average yearly return for large- and small-cap stocks and shows how bad a bad year can really be. For example, if you'd chosen to make a 1-year investment in small company stocks in 1973, you'd have been one unhappy camper by year's end. Of course, if you'd made that same investment a mere 2 or 3 years later, you'd have made a hefty return—more than enough to go out and buy a new pair of bell-bottoms and the latest disco records.

As you can see, 1-year returns are amazingly variable, making short-term investments in stocks very risky. However, as the length of the investment horizon increases, you can afford to invest in riskier assets. This is because, as you saw in Chapter 11, the returns on those risky assets tend to dominate those of less risky assets as the investment horizon increases. This means that even in the worst case scenario, you'll probably do quite a bit better with stocks than you would do with the more conservative alternative. It doesn't mean there isn't any risk to investing in common stock. Clearly, there's still a lot of uncertainty as to how much you'll finally end up with. If your investment horizon is long, you'll probably end up with a lot more if you invest in some risky assets.

The longer you hold on to stocks, the more likely you are to hit a very good year, such as 1995, 1996, 1997, 1998, or 1999. Of course, you're also more likely to hit a bad year like 2000 or 2001, but the very good will cancel out the very bad. Does all this mean a reduction in profits? Not at all. Figure 13.7 shows how holding stocks for longer periods reduces the variability of the average annual return on your investment. The truth is, it's hard to beat the long-term return from common stock investments. Look at Figure 13.8: You'll see that common stocks far outpaced corporate bonds and Treasury bills over the 10-year period 1992–2001. Now you can see why so many investors favor the buy-and-hold strategy for investing in stocks.

In addition, investors can afford to take on more risk as their investment time horizon increases because they have more opportunities to adjust consumption and work habits over longer time periods if a risky investment doesn't pan out. If they are investing with a short time horizon, there isn't much they can do to meet their goals. However, if an investment performs poorly at the beginning of a long investment time horizon, the investor can make an adjustment by saving more, working harder, or spending less.

If you can understand Principle 11, you can understand the concepts behind all the "asset allocation" talk of brokers and financial planners. Understanding Principle 11 can also provide you with an understanding of why you can't answer the question, Which investment is the best one for me? until you first answer another question, How long is my investment time horizon? That is, when do I need my money back? If you're investing for the long run, it's hard to beat stocks.

## Figure 13.6 A Histogram of Annual Percentage Returns, 1960–2001

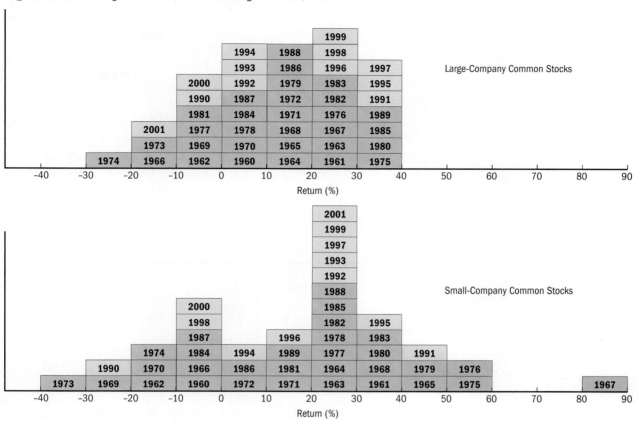

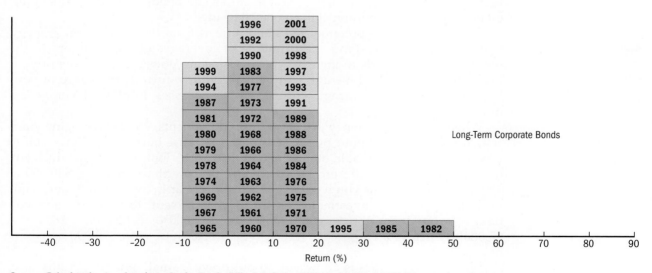

Source: Calculated using data from *Stocks, Bonds, Bills, & Inflation 2002 Yearbook*™, © 2002 Ibbotson Associates Inc. Based on copyrighted works by Ibbotson and Sinquefield. All rights reserved. Used with permission.

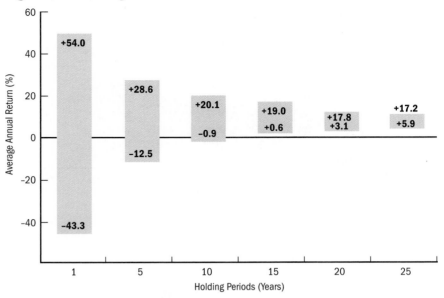

Figure 13.7 The Range of Returns on Common Stocks, 1926–2001

Source: Calculated using data from *Stocks, Bonds, Bills, & Inflation 2002 Yearbook™*, © 2002 Ibbotson Associates Inc. Based on copyrighted works by Ibbotson and Sinquefield. All rights reserved. Used with permission.

## Understanding the Concept of Leverage

**Leverage**
Using borrowed funds to increase your purchasing power.

Another factor that can affect your investment return is borrowing some of the money you invest. Is this a common practice? Yes. In fact, although some investors borrow some of the money they invest in stocks and bonds, most investors in real estate borrow a large portion of the money they invest.

To understand the potential risks and returns from this investment strategy, you must first understand the principle of leverage. **Leverage** refers to the use of borrowed funds to increase your purchasing power. If the value of your investment increases, leverage will increase your return. If the value of your investment declines, leverage will magnify your losses. In effect, leverage is a double-edged sword.

When you borrow money to pay for your investments, you're leveraging yourself. You've increased your purchasing power because borrowing allows you to invest more than you would otherwise be able to. Let's look at a case in which you invest $100,000 with 20 percent down, and borrow the remaining $80,000 at 10 percent. This means you would pay $8,000 per year in interest to finance your investment. If your investment went up by 20 percent, to $120,000, and you paid off your loan, you would be left with $32,000 or ($120,000 − $80,000 − $8,000), which is a 60-percent return (you started out with $20,000 and now have $32,000).

What leverage does is allow you to put down a small amount (in this case, $20,000) and benefit from the capital gains on a much larger amount (in this case, $100,000 made up of your $20,000 and $80,000 of borrowed money). If your investment drops by 20 percent, you'd not only lose the $20,000 you invested, but also be out the $8,000 interest you paid—in effect, you'd lose even more than you invested.

**Figure 13.8** Investment Performance Over the 10-Year Period Ending December 31, 2001

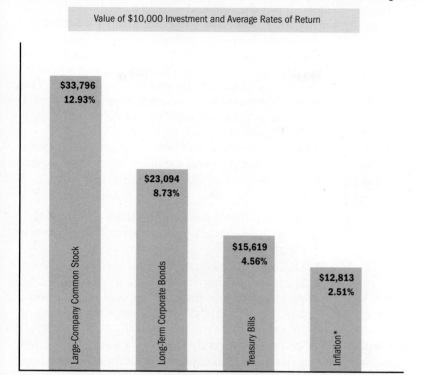

Value of $10,000 Investment and Average Rates of Return

- Large-Company Common Stock: **$33,796 / 12.93%**
- Long-Term Corporate Bonds: **$23,094 / 8.73%**
- Treasury Bills: **$15,619 / 4.56%**
- Inflation*: **$12,813 / 2.51%**

*This means that, given the 2.51% average inflation over this 10-year period, the purchasing power of $10,000 at the beginning of 1992 would be equivalent to that of $12,813 at the end of 2001.

Source: Calculated using data from *Stocks, Bonds, Bills, & Inflation 2002 Yearbook*™, © 2002 Ibbotson Associates Inc. Based on copyrighted works by Ibbotson and Sinquefield. All rights reserved. Used with permission.

## SUMMARY

Stock is a solid investment because over time common stocks outperform all other investments; stocks reduce risk through diversification; stocks are liquid; and the growth in your investment is determined by more than just interest rates.

The health of the stock market is measured by stock indexes. The oldest and most widely quoted of the stock indexes is the Dow Jones Industrial Average (DJIA) or Dow. Other useful indexes include the Standard & Poor's 500, the Russell 2000, and the Wilshire 5000.

Stocks can be classified according to the traits of the company issuing the stock. Common classifications include blue-chip, growth, income, speculative, cyclical, defensive, and large-, mid-, and small-cap stocks.

A number of methods can be used to determine what a share of stock is worth. One approach is technical analysis. An alternative approach is the price/earnings ratio approach. Under this approach, a justified price/earnings ratio is estimated for each stock. This price/earnings ratio (P/E ratio), or earnings multiplier, is simply the price per share divided by the earnings per share.

A final approach is the discounted dividend model. We know that the value of any investment is simply the present value of all the returns we receive from that investment. Thus, the value of a share of common stock is simply the present value of the infinite stream of dividend payments. Three factors—interest rates, risk, and expected future growth—combine to determine the value of common stock.

When purchasing stock there are several investment strategies you can follow, including dollar cost averaging, buy-and-hold, and dividend reinvestment plans. Dollar cost averaging involves investing over time rather than jumping into the market all at once. Buy-and-hold involves investing and leaving your money invested for a number of years. Dividend reinvestment plans involve having your dividends automatically reinvested in the stock.

Four principles play an important role when we invest in stocks. Using the idea of a risk–return trade-off as described in Principle 1, we can view stocks as being at the upper end of the risk–return line.

Principle 3 describes how diversification works to smooth out the ups and downs in stock returns and in so doing, eliminates risk. Principle 4 leads us to a distinction between systematic and unsystematic risk, using the beta to measure systematic risk. Principle 11 shows that you can afford to take on more risk if your investment horizon is long. This concept is important because it means that the investment horizon plays a large role in determining how we should invest our savings.

Leverage or the use of borrowed funds to increase your purchasing power can also affect your investment return.

## REVIEW QUESTIONS

1. Explain how stocks generate returns.
2. List and describe four reasons why someone should consider investing in stocks.
3. Name the six questions an investor should ask periodically to check the progress of stock investments.
4. What is meant by the term "limited liability," and why is this concept important to common stock investors?
5. In terms of a common shareholder's claim on assets, when will a stockholder receive payment if a company declares bankruptcy?
6. What is a stock split? Why might a stock split occur?
7. How are stocks weighted in the Dow Jones Industrial Average (DJIA)? How does this differ from the Standard & Poor's 500 Stock Index? Which of these two indexes better represents movements in the overall market? Why?
8. What is the difference in a bear market and a bull market? How can you easily remember the stock price trends when you hear these terms?
9. Describe the following stock classifications: (a) blue-chip stock, (b) growth stock, (c) income stock, (d) speculative stock, (e) cyclical stock, and (f) defensive stock. Identify a stock as an example of each.

10. How is a firm's market capitalization calculated? How does market capitalization help investors classify stocks?
11. Describe the basic differences between technical analysis and fundamental analysis. List examples of different tools a technical analyst and a fundamental analyst might use when valuing an investment.
12. The discounted dividends valuation of a stock price is based on what investors expect to happen to dividends in the future. Explain why this rule applies even when a company is not currently paying dividends.
13. In terms of the risk–return tradeoff (Principle 1), why is there an inverse relationship between interest rates and the value of a share of common stock?
14. What advantages does dollar cost averaging offer over a buy-and-hold strategy? When is a buy-and-hold approach a better investment strategy?
15. Summarize the advantages and disadvantages of DRIPs.
16. Explain two ways an investor can reduce risk when purchasing stocks.
17. What does beta measure? How can this measurement help you assemble an appropriate portfolio?
18. Describe the advantage of using leverage when purchasing stock. What is the primary risk associated with using leverage?

   a. How much was your investment worth prior to the split?

   b. Assuming GE's management decides to split the stock three-for-one, how many shares would you own after the split?

## PROBLEMS AND ACTIVITIES

1. Assume that you own 200 shares of GE selling at $39 per share. In order to make the stock more affordable for the average investor, GE's management has decided to split the stock.

c. What is the new price per share immediately after the split?

d. How much would your investment be worth after the three-for-one split?

2. The Haley Corporation has just announced year-end results as follows:

| | |
|---|---|
| Value of company assets | $12,500,000 |
| Net income | $1,600,000 |
| Common stock dividends | $500,000 |
| Preferred stock dividends | $400,000 |
| Number of shares of common stock outstanding | 2,000,000 |
| Closing price of Haley Corporation's stock | $75.00 per share |

a. Calculate the book value per share

b. Calculate earnings per share

c. Calculate Haley Corporation's dividend yield

d. Calculate the market-to-book ratio

3. The Wildcat Corporation recently announced that its year-end estimated earnings per share next year would be $3.25. Wildcat stock is currently selling for $43 per share.

a. What is the P/E ratio for the Wildcat Corporation?

b. Assume prospects for the Wildcat Corporation deteriorate and the company now estimates next year's earnings to be $2.00 per share. What would be the new P/E ratio?

4. You've just learned that Graham Records has purchased the lifetime distribution rights to the music of a new band called the French Fries. Based on this good news you've estimated that Graham Records should pay $4 in dividends next year. You also think that the dividends paid out should increase by 5 percent a year indefinitely. As a knowledgeable investor you've determined your required rate of return is 9 percent.

a. What is your estimate of the value of Graham Records common stock?

b. What would the value of the stock be if you did not anticipate any increase in the dividend over time?

c. If the required rate of return increased to 12 percent, what would happen to the stock price?

5. An investor is considering investing in one of the following three stocks. Stock X has a market capitalization of $7 billion, pays a relatively high dividend, with little increase in earnings, and a P/E ratio of 11. Stock Y has a market capitalization of $62 billion but does not currently pay a dividend. Stock Y has a P/E ratio of 39. Stock Z, a housing industry company, has a market capitalization of $800 million and a P/E of 18.

a. Classify these stocks according to their market capitalizations.

b. Which of the three would you classify as a growth stock? Why?

c. Which stock would be most appropriate for an aggressive investor?

d. Which stock would be most appropriate for someone seeking a combination of safety and earnings?

6. Use the following data to answer the questions that follow.

| Company | Beta |
|---|---|
| Savoy Corp. | 0.70 |
| Hokie Industries | 1.35 |
| Graham Records | 2.05 |
| Expo Enterprises | −0.45 |
| S&P 500 | 1.00 |

a. If the S&P 500 goes up by 35 percent, how much should the stocks of Savoy, Hokie, Graham, and Expo change in value?

b. If the stock market drops by 10 percent, which of the foregoing stocks should outperform the others? Why?

7. Use the information in Table Q7. to answer the questions that follow.

a. What is the current dividend yield for Philip Morris (MO) based on the stock's recent closing price?

b. What is your estimate of Philip Morris's earnings for the year based on the recent closing price?

**Q7. Table**

| 52 Weeks | | | | | | Vol. | | | | Net |
|---|---|---|---|---|---|---|---|---|---|---|
| Hi | Lo | Stock | Sym | Div | PE | 100s | Hi | Lo | Close | Chg |
| 55.20 | 43.00 | PhlMorris | MO | 2.32 | 13 | 5232 | 55.20 | 54.74 | 54.78 | −0.17 |

c. Based on the net change, at what price did Philip Morris close yesterday?

8. Assume an investor made the purchases listed in Q8. Table below on the first day of every quarter for a year. Use the information provided to fill in the missing blanks.

9. Using the calculations from question 8, assume that instead of investing $200 every quarter, the investor decided to make a lump-sum purchase on the first day of the year with $800. If at year-end the price of the stock closed at $35 per share, which investment strategy, dollar cost averaging or lump-sum investing, produced the greater return?

10. Paula is considering purchasing stock using leverage. She wants to buy $50,000 in stock, with 30 percent down, borrowing the remaining $35,000 at 12 percent interest.

a. Is Paula allowed to borrow 70 percent for this transaction? Why or why not? (*Hint:* See "Margin Accounts" in Chapter 12.)

b. What is the maximum percentage and dollar amount Paula can borrow?

c. If her investment loses value, must Paula continue to maintain the initial minimum requirement?

11. Using the information from problem 10, and assuming Paula borrows the maximum allowable amount, answer the following two questions.

a. If Paula's investment appreciates by 50 percent after one year, and she pays off her loan, how much will she make in dollars? What percent rate of return does this represent?

b. If Paula's investment depreciates by 20 percent, how much will she lose in dollars? In terms of a percentage loss, how much will she lose?

## SUGGESTED PROJECTS

1. Visit **www.quote.yahoo.com**, **www.morningstar.com**, or similar Web site. Use these sources to obtain the book value, earnings per share, dividend yield, price-to-book ratio, and P/E ratio on six to eight companies of your choice. Based on your knowledge of these companies and the information obtained, categorize each stock using the six general common stock classifications.

2. Using Checklist 13.1, "Investment Progress Checklist," interview a friend or relative who makes investments about one or more of their stock holdings. Write a brief report based on your findings. Be sure to include in your discussion how your friend or relative feels about commissions and whether or not he or she has a strategy for deciding when to sell.

3. Some of the stocks that make up the Dow Jones Industrial Average were changed in 1997 and in 1999. Using the *Wall Street Journal, Barron's*, on the Web at **www.dogsofthedow.com/thedow.htm**, or another source, make a list of the firms that currently make up the DJIA and record the dividend yields of each stock. Considering that each of these stocks is considered a blue-chip firm, why would the dividend yields be so different?

4. Using the Internet, visit the NASDAQ homepage (**www.nasdaq.com**) each day for one week. Track the performance of the NASDAQ composite index for the week. Did you notice any significant trend during that time? Do you think that investors were bullish or bearish for the week?

5. Review the general classifications of common stock. Based on your personal comfort level (risk tolerance), which type of stock would most interest you? Why?

**Q8. Table**

| Quarter | Price | Money Invested | Shares Purchased | Total Shares Owned | Market Value |
|---------|-------|----------------|------------------|--------------------|--------------|
| 1 | $30 | $200 | ____ | ____ | ____ |
| 2 | $50 | $200 | ____ | ____ | ____ |
| 3 | $60 | $200 | ____ | ____ | ____ |
| 4 | $35 | $200 | ____ | ____ | ____ |
| Total | | $800 | | | |

6. Every evening the major news networks report that "the market" is up, down, or unchanged. Ask at least 10 people what they think is meant by "the market." Report your findings in a one-page summary, and then answer the following questions:

a. How did most individuals define the market?

b. Do you agree, after reading this chapter, with those you asked? How would you define the market? Why?

c. Is it possible to have multiple markets within a single market? Why or why not?

7. The publication *Value Line Investment Service* or *Mutual Funds* magazine provides investors information on most major U.S. industries, also known as "sectors." Using this information, choose a sector that interests you (e.g., technology or transportation), and find the average P/E ratio for the sector. Next, choose a stock within that sector and compare the P/E for the stock to the sector average. Are the ratios different? What factors do you think influence the stock's P/E ratio? Based on your findings, would you consider the stock to be overvalued or undervalued as compared to other stocks in the industry?

8. Many people believe that the risks and returns associated with investing in stocks are equivalent to those with gambling. Take a poll of classmates, friends, relatives, and others to determine how many associate stock investing with gambling. What is your opinion on the issue? Report the

findings from your poll to your class. Use your findings and the following questions as part of a class discussion: "Can you think of situations when purchasing a stock is the same as gambling in a casino?" "What historical data can you use to argue against the notion that investing in stocks is gambling?" "If you were able to participate in an IPO, would you consider it an investment or a gamble?" Why?

9. As a group project, using the following stocks, develop a portfolio that has an average beta equal to 1. You must include all stocks, but the weighting is yours to develop.

| Stock Name | Sector | Beta |
|---|---|---|
| SAS Corp. | Financial | .75 |
| Dipper Group | Industrial | .90 |
| Startech Inc. | Technology | 1.60 |
| Robust Corp. | Consumer Goods | .45 |
| Sunlight Inc. | Energy | 1.05 |
| Medi-serve Group | Health Care | 1.10 |

Given what you have learned about beta as a measure of volatility, have each member of the group individually adjust the allocation of the portfolio in response to an anticipated market decline. Was each member's adjustment appropriate? What was the rationale behind the adjustments? Give a brief presentation on how your group allocated their original portfolio and then defend each member's adjustments in their revised portfolios.

# Discussion Case 1

Although saddened by the death of her favorite aunt, Sunny was extremely surprised to learn that she was named the only heir. A personal note in the will said, "for your own shop." Sunny and her aunt often visited antique shops and Sunny's dream was to own such a shop. Sunny is expecting to receive approximately $50,000. She hopes to invest this money for her future shop, but she knows very little about stocks or investment strategies. After discussing financial planning topics with Sunny, the following issues became clear. First, the $50,000 is all the money Sunny has saved for her goal. Second, Sunny is very cautious financially and is fearful of investing all her money at once because she has heard conflicting reports concerning stock valuation. Use your

knowledge of common stock classifications and investment strategies to answer the following questions.

## Questions

1. Which type of stock or combination of stocks would be appropriate for Sunny? Develop your answer in terms of Sunny's risk tolerance, time frame, and goal.

2. What role should cyclical and defensive stocks play in Sunny's portfolio?

3. Would you recommend small capitalization stocks to Sunny? Why or why not?

*Tips from Marcy Furney, ChFC, Certified Financial Planner™*

# Money Matters

## A FOOL AND HIS MONEY

If you are a beginning investor and subject to the adrenaline rush of success, you may fall victim to some of the more complicated and even questionable investment vehicles and strategies. More and more companies are buying prime television time to tell you how you can quickly multiply your money. Remember the caution, "If it looks too good to be true, it probably is," especially when considering the following:

**Options (also known as puts and calls).** Brokers may tell you that options can multiply the returns on a stock you own (a long position) with only moderate risk. Maybe, maybe not. Options are simply opportunities to buy/sell stocks at a future date for a particular price. You are essentially betting on a move in the price of the stock. Amateurs should stay away. On some options, you stand to lose only the price you paid for them. On others, the loss ceiling is almost unlimited.

**Commodities.** Fuel oil, cocoa, wheat, the infamous pork bellies, and many other items are staples in the commodity market. Brokers must have special securities licenses to sell them, and the risks are huge. This is not the place for your kids' college money. Again you gamble on moves in prices.

**Limited Partnerships.** Though there may be a few good ones, many people still hold the remnants of limited partnerships at values far below what they paid. Such "investments" were sold at one time as tax breaks with big losses in the early years. Now some investors are paying extra taxes and penalties for disallowed deductions. The general partner and the underlying property

or objective drive the success of the partnership. There is a very limited secondary market for these holdings.

**Gold and Precious Metals.** Besides being offered as an inflation hedge, gold is being sold as the only viable means of exchange in the case of full economic collapse. If you believe that is true, buy it for that purpose, but don't buy simply out of fear. Investigate the assaying and storage costs before taking possession of gold bullion, and remember that the pricing of gold coinage is based on more than just the value of the metal.

**Investment Systems.** According to the infomercials, you can become wealthy in no time with real estate, commodities, currency hedges, day trading, and other stock speculation strategies. All you have to do is buy the right system. These are usually costly, time consuming, and have very low success rates. The traditional methods of investing may not be very exotic or offer such splendid outcomes, but they have served millions of people well for many years. Though history is no guarantee of future performance, you can put heavy odds on the old tried and true when it comes to the future of your money.

4. Given Sunny's fear about current stock valuations, what investment strategy would you recommend for her? Why?

5. Why might Sunny consider enrolling in an automatic investment plan?

6. Provide Sunny with four reasons she should consider using a buy-and-hold strategy.

7. Explain a dividend reinvestment plan to Sunny. Would you recommend that she participate in DRIPs with a portion of her portfolio? If so, how much and why?

# Discussion Case 2

Pete and Jessica, on the advice of their next-door neighbor, recently purchased 500 shares of a small capitalization Internet stock, trading at $80 per share. Their neighbor told them that the stock was a "real money maker" because it recently had a two-for-one stock split and would probably split again soon. Even better, according to

the neighbor, the company was expected to earn $1 per share and pay a $0.25 dividend next year. Pete and Jessica have so far been less than impressed with the stock's performance—the stock has underperformed the S&P 500 index this year. Pete and Jessica have come to you for some independent advice.

## Questions

1. Assuming that the stock actually splits two for one, how many shares will Pete and Jessica own? What will be the market value of their stock after the split? How will the split affect the value of their holdings? Was their next-door neighbor correct in thinking that the stock split made the stock a "real money maker"?

2. Pete and Jessica aren't sure if they overpaid for their stock. Calculate the value of the stock using the discounted dividends valuation model, assuming a 10 percent required rate of return and a 2 percent growth in dividends. Based on your calculation, did they overpay? How accurate is this valuation model for this type of stock?

3. Using the information provided, calculate the stock's P/E ratio. Would you classify this investment as a growth or value stock?

4. Since Pete, in particular, is worried about the price of the stock, explain to him how and why corporate earnings are so important in the valuation of common stocks.

5. Should Pete and Jessica be using the S&P 500 index as a benchmark for this stock? Why or why not? What benchmark recommendation would you make?

6. Yesterday they received a cold call from a stockbroker wanting to sell them an initial public offering in a cable television company. Jessica was worried because the broker promised a "no lose guarantee." Should they invest with this type of broker?

7. Name at least five things Pete and Jessica need to look out for when making stock investments.

8. Pete, the worrier in the family, is concerned about the risk of owning one stock. Should he be? How many stocks should be held in a portfolio in order to reduce systematic risk by at least 60 percent?

---

 Visit our Web site for additional case problems, interactive exercises, and practice quizzes for this chapter—**www.prenhall.com/keown**.

# 14 Investing in Bonds and Other Alternatives

## Learning Objectives

1 **Invest** in the bond market.

2 **Understand** basic bond terminology and compare the various types of bonds.

3 **Calculate** the value of a bond and understand the factors that cause bond value to change.

4 **Compare** preferred stock to bonds as an investment option.

5 **Understand** the risks associated with investing in real estate.

6 **Know** why you shouldn't *invest* in gold, silver, gems, or collectibles.

For Marvin Lee Aday, the road to riches has been a strange and bumpy one. After graduating from high school, he started his career as the lead vocalist for the rock group Popcorn Blizzard. Unfortunately, the Popcorn Blizzard wasn't much of a money maker, so Aday took a job as a parking-lot attendant at the Aquarius Theatre in Los Angeles. It was there that he met an actor appearing in the musical *Hair*, who suggested he try out for a part in the play. And so began his career in theater, cast in the role of Ulysses S. Grant, in which he continued when *Hair* moved to Broadway.

For the next several years, Aday was a Broadway regular, even appearing as Buddha in the musical *Rainbow*, but his big break came when he was cast in the dual role of Eddie and Dr. Scott in one of the strangest musicals ever to hit New York—*The Rocky Horror Show*. He also played Eddie in the film version, *The Rocky Horror Picture Show*.

Finally, in 1977, Aday, who was by now going by his nickname, Meatloaf, hit the big time financially when he released his first album, *Bat Out of Hell*, with the hit songs "Paradise By the Dashboard Lights" and "Two Out of Three Ain't Bad."

From there, however, his career just seemed to take a wrong turn. Bad management, bad lawyers, bad advice, contract problems with his record company, and problems with the IRS all seemed to hit at once. He lost his condo and house in Connecticut, his Mercedes-Benz, and his grand piano.

Faced with financial ruin, Meatloaf regrouped and began touring small clubs, with his wife serving as the tour manager just to cut costs. Finally, in 1989, he took on Bernie Gilhuly as his business manager. After straightening out Meatloaf's tax problems, Gilhuly set up an investment strategy aimed at insuring Meatloaf's financial future. Given Meatloaf's rocky road to riches, he was a bit shy when it came to taking risks. As a result, Gilhuly put most of Meatloaf's investment money into bonds.

For Meatloaf, things kept getting better in the nineties. He staged one of the biggest rock music comebacks of all time, releasing the album *Bat Out of Hell II: Back Into Hell* in 1993, which featured the song "I'll Do Anything for Love (But I Won't Do That)." Today, the money keeps pouring in as his rock and movie careers continue to flourish, and he keeps about half his investment portfolio in bonds. "I don't need to take big risks with my investments," says Meatloaf. "I take a risk with what I do as a performer, where the odds of success are ridiculously low."

Like a lot of investors, Meatloaf chose bonds because they carry less risk than stocks. Many investors are drawn to bonds because of the steady income they provide. However, merely because they offer a steady income doesn't mean that you can't earn spectacular returns. This is something

Meatloaf certainly knows. In fact, in 1995, long-term Treasury bonds went up in value by almost 32 percent! In 1997 they returned another 15.9 percent, followed by 13.1 percent in 1998. Unfortunately, 1999 was tough on bonds: They dropped by about 9.0 percent. But in 2000 they rose by 21.5 percent, while stocks dropped by 9.1 percent, then in 2001 they rose by 3.7 percent while stocks dropped by 11.9 percent! Bonds are a great source of income and a great source of diversity for your investment portfolio. Now let's jump ("to the left, and a step to the") right in and explore the world of bonds.

Invest in the bond market.

## Why Consider Bonds?

To begin with, a bond is simply a loan or an IOU. When you buy a bond, you become a lender. The bond issuer—generally a corporation, the federal government and its agencies, a city, or a state—gets the use of your money and in return pays you interest, generally every 6 months, for the life of the bond. At maturity, the issuer returns your money, or actually returns the face value of the bond, which may be more or less than what you originally paid for it.

How exactly do bonds fit into your investment portfolio?

▌ **Bonds reduce risk through diversification.** As you learned earlier, when you put together investments whose returns don't move together over time, you're able to reduce the risk in your portfolio. Remember the week of April 10–14, 2000, when the S&P 500 went down by 10.54 percent and Nasdaq went down 25.30 percent, and that same week bond prices rose. The same thing happened in the days following the terrorist attack on the World Trade Center and the Pentagon—stock prices fell while bond prices climbed. And, for the year 2000, while stocks dropped by 9.1 percent, long-term government bonds rose by 21.5 percent! The same thing happened in 2001, stocks dropped by 11.9 percent while long-term government bonds rose by 3.7 percent.

▌ **Bonds produce steady current income.** For those needing some income to achieve their financial goals, bonds are a good choice. For example, you may be retired and desire additional income from your investment portfolio to supplement your pension income. With bonds, provided they don't default on their interest payments, you'll receive steady interest income annually.

▌ **Bonds can be a safe investment if held to maturity.** Interest on bonds must be paid, or the firm can be forced into bankruptcy. So bond interest payments will be made at all costs—unlike dividend payments on common stocks. As a result, bonds are a relatively safe investment. In addition, bond rating services provide reliable information on the riskiness of bonds. If the bond doesn't default and you hold it to maturity, you know exactly what your return will be. In the world of personal finance, it's unusual to find an investment that's so low in risk that it actually returns exactly what it promises.

Now that you know why bonds make good investments, you should know a thing or two about bonds in general. Let's take a look at bond basics.

## Basic Bond Terminology and Features

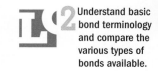

**L 2** Understand basic bond terminology and compare the various types of bonds available.

Bonds are like just about everything else we've seen so far in this book: If you can't talk the talk, you're going to fall flat on your face when you try to walk the walk. This section should get you fairly conversant in the language of bonds.

### Par Value

The **par value** of a bond is its face value, or the amount returned to the bondholder at **maturity**, the date when the bond comes due. For bonds issued by corporations, the par value is generally $1,000. A bond's market price, which is its selling price, is generally expressed as a percentage of the bond's par value. For example, a bond that matures or comes due in the year 2010 that has a $1,000 par value may be quoted in the *Wall Street Journal* as selling for $95\frac{1}{8}$.

That doesn't mean you can buy the bond for $95.125. It means that the bond is selling in the secondary market for $95\frac{1}{8}$ percent of its par value, which is actually $951.25 ($1,000 × $95\frac{1}{8}$%). At maturity in the year 2010, the bondholder will receive the par value of $1,000 and the bond will be terminated (but not by Arnold Schwarzenegger).

**Par Value**
The face value of a bond, or the amount that's returned to the bondholder at maturity. It's also referred to as the bond's denomination.

**Maturity**
The length of time until the bond issuer returns the par value to the bondholder and terminates the bond.

### Coupon Interest Rate

The **coupon interest rate** on a bond indicates what percentage of the par value of the bond will be paid out annually in the form of interest. An 8-percent coupon interest rate and a $1,000 par value will pay out $80 (8% × $1,000) annually in interest until maturity, generally in semiannual installments.

Keep in mind that when you purchase a bond and hold it to maturity, your entire return is based on the return of the par value or principal and the payment of interest at the coupon interest rate. The only real risk involved is that the bond issuer won't have the funds to make these payments and will default.

**Coupon Interest Rate**
The annual rate of interest to be paid out on a bond, calculated as a percentage of the par value.

### Indenture

An **indenture** is the legal document that provides the specific terms of the loan agreement, including a description of the bond, the rights of the bondholders, the rights of the issuing firm, and the responsibilities of the bond trustees. A bond trustee, usually a banking institution or trust company, is assigned the task of overseeing the relationship between the bondholder and the issuing firm. A bond indenture may run 100 pages or more in length, with the majority of it devoted to defining protective provisions for the bondholder.

**Indenture**
A legal agreement between the firm issuing a bond and the bond trustee who represents the bondholders.

### Call Provision

A **call provision** entitles the bond issuer to repurchase, or "call," the bonds from their holders at stated prices over specified periods. If interest rates go down, the issuer will call the bonds and replace them with lower-cost debt. The terms of the call provision are provided in the indenture and generally set the call provision at approximately the par value plus 1 year's worth of interest.

Obviously, a call provision works to the disadvantage of the investor. However, bonds with call provisions generally pay higher returns as compensation. Still, if you

**Call Provision**
A bond provision that gives the issuer the right to repurchase, or "call," the bonds from their holders at stated prices over specified periods.

own high-paying long-term bonds and you're counting on receiving those semiannual interest payments for the next 10 years or so, having them called away from you could rain on your parade.

To make callable bonds more attractive, the issuer many times includes in the indenture some protection against calls. Generally, that call protection comes in the form of a **deferred call**. With a deferred call, the bond can't be called until a set number of years have passed since the bond was issued. Although not as safe as a noncallable bond, a bond with a deferred call at least provides protection against an immediate call.

**Deferred Call**
A bond provision stating that the bond can't be called until a set number of years have passed since it was issued.

## Sinking Fund

No one likes to have to pay off debts all at once, and that goes for bond issuers, too. Most set up a **sinking fund** to set aside money on a regular basis to pay off the bonds at maturity. With a sinking fund, the firm either calls, using the bond's call provision, or repurchases in the open market a fraction of the outstanding bonds annually. In this way, the issuer spreads out the large payment that would have otherwise occurred at maturity.

**Sinking Fund**
A fund to which the bond issuer deposits money to pay off a bond issue.

The advantage of a sinking fund for the investor is that the probability that the debt will be successfully paid off at maturity increases, thereby reducing risk. Without a sinking fund, the issuer faces a major payment at maturity. If the issuer were to experience financial problems when the debt matures, repayment could be jeopardized. The big disadvantage of a sinking fund for investors is the fact that it may result in the bond being called away from you.

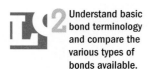
**2** Understand basic bond terminology and compare the various types of bonds available.

## Types of Bonds

There's an old science joke that says there are four different types of bonds: ionic, covalent, metallic, and James. Well, in the world of finance there are more types of bonds than that (but James is the only one with a license to kill). There are thousands of outstanding bonds floating around the securities markets, and more are probably on the way as you read this.

It's a vast understatement to say that these bonds aren't all alike. The easiest way to explain the differences is to break them down into bonds issued by corporations, by the U.S. government and its agencies, and by states and localities, and examine each group separately. As you'll see, each type of bond has unique advantages and disadvantages to the investor.

## Corporate Bonds

Borrowing money by issuing bonds is a major source of funding for corporations. In fact, **corporate bonds** account for about half of the bonds outstanding. Generally these bonds are issued in denominations of $1,000 in order to appeal to smaller investors. There are several different types of corporate bonds from which you can choose, with one major difference being whether or not the bond is secured.

**Corporate Bonds**
Bonds issued by corporations.

**Secured Corporate Debt**   A **secured bond** is one that's backed by collateral, which, as you should remember, is a real asset that can be seized and sold if a debtor doesn't pay off his or her debt. A **mortgage bond** is secured by a lien on real property. Typically, the value of the real property is greater than that of the mortgage bonds issued, providing the investor with a margin of safety in case the market value of the secured property declines.

**Secured Bond**
Any bond that is backed by the pledge of collateral.

**Mortgage Bond**
A bond secured by a lien or real property.

In the event of bankruptcy, the bond trustees have the power to sell the secured property and use the proceeds to pay the bondholders. If the proceeds from this sale don't cover the bonds, the bondholders fall in line with the others who are owed money.

**Unsecured Corporate Debt**   The term **debenture** applies to any unsecured long-term bond. When bonds are unsecured, the earning ability of the issuing corporation is of great concern to the investor. Debentures are also viewed as being more risky than secured bonds and, as a result, have a higher yield associated with them.

**Debenture**
Any unsecured long-term bond.

Firms with more than one issue of debentures outstanding often specify a hierarchy by which some debentures get paid back before others if the firm goes bankrupt. The claims of the subordinated debentures—bonds lower down in the hierarchy—are honored only after the claims of secured bonds and unsubordinated debentures have been satisfied. As you might imagine, subordinated debentures are riskier than "normal" or unsubordinated debentures and have a higher return associated with them to compensate for the added risk.

## Treasury and Agency Bonds

Without question, the biggest single player—and payer—in the bond market is the U.S. government. Given the constant talk on the news about our national debt and the balanced budget, it should come as no surprise that our government spends more than it takes in. The alternatives to financing an unbalanced budget are to sell some assets (anybody want to buy Nebraska?), raise taxes, or borrow more money. The latter choice has been found to be the most acceptable approach and has led to the issuance of huge sums of debt by our government. Given the enormous amount of debt financing that goes on, it's not surprising that there are a number of different types of government debt to choose from.

These securities are generally viewed as being risk free, given the government's ability to tax and print more money. When corporations run out of money, they can't just print more, but the government can. Hey, it owns the mints! In addition to there being no default risk on Treasury bonds, there's no risk that government bonds will be called, because the government no longer issues callable bonds.

Because there's no default or call risk associated with government bonds, they generally pay a lower rate of interest than other bonds. In addition, most interest payments received on federal debt are exempt from state and local taxation.[1]

Treasury-issued debt has maturities that range from 3 months to 30 years. Today approximately 70 percent of that debt has a maturity of 5 years or less, but the Treasury has a good deal of latitude in its choice of maturities. When investors speak of Treasury debt with different maturities, they speak of *bills, notes,* and *bonds.* The only difference between these is the maturity and the denomination.

If the Treasury debt has a maturity of 3, 6, or 12 months, it's referred to as Treasury *bills*. If, when issued, it has a maturity of 2, 3, 5, or 10 years, it's referred to as Treasury *notes*. Treasury *bonds* have maturities of more than 10 years and are issued today with 20-year maturities. In terms of denomination, Treasury bills have a minimum denomination of $1,000, Treasury notes with maturities of less than 5 years have a minimum denomination of $1,000, and securities that mature in 5 or more years also have denominations of $1,000.

---

[1]Federal debt issued by FNMA, the Federal National Mortgage Association, is not exempt from state and local taxation.

One advantage of purchasing Treasury securities is that you can do it yourself through a program called Treasury Direct, thereby avoiding brokerage fees, which range upward from $25 per transaction. You need only set up an account with the Federal Reserve and Treasury Direct. Then you can make trades and keep track of all your transactions electronically. You can also sell your security before maturity through the Fed for a $34 fee. For instructions, contact the Bureau of Public Debt at **www.publicdebt.treas.gov**.

**Agency Bonds**
Bonds issued by government agencies other than the Treasury.

In addition to the Treasury, a number of other government agencies, such as the Federal National Mortgage Association (FNMA) and the Federal Home Loan Banks (FHLB), issue debt called **agency bonds**. Although these aren't directly issued through the Treasury, they're issued by federal agencies and authorized by Congress. They're still viewed as being virtually risk free and carry an interest rate slightly higher than that carried on Treasury securities. In general their minimum denomination is $25,000, with maturities that vary from 1 to 40 years, although the average maturity is approximately 15 years.

**Pass-Through Certificate**
A certificate that represents a portion of ownership in a pool of federally insured mortgages.

**Pass-Through Certificates**  Of the agency securities, the most interesting to investors are those issued by the Government National Mortgage Association (GNMA), or "Ginnie Mae," called **pass-through certificates**. A GNMA pass-through certificate represents an interest in a pool of federally insured mortgages. What GNMA has done is package a group of mortgages worth $1 million or more, guarantee those mortgages, and sell "certificates" with minimum denominations of $25,000, called pass-through certificates, to finance the mortgages. In effect, pass-through certificates can put an average homeowner with $25,000 to invest on the other side—the lending side—of a mortgage.

Because all the payments from the mortgages financed by the pass-through certificates (less a processing fee and a GNMA insurance fee) go to the certificate holders, the size of the monthly check depends on how fast the mortgages are paid off. In addition, the monthly check the investor receives represents both principal and interest. At maturity there's no return of principal as there is with a bond. With the last payment, the pass-through security is completely paid off, just as your home mortgage would be.

**Inflation-Indexed Bond**
A bond that pay investors an interest rate that's allowed to vary and is set at approximately 3 percent above the rate of inflation.

**Treasury Inflation-Indexed Bonds**  The newest and most exciting Treasury bond for investors is the **inflation-indexed bond**. These bonds have a maturity of 10 years and a minimum par value of $1,000. They initially carried a coupon interest rate of 3.375 percent, meaning they paid $33.75 in interest a year, and more recently carried an interest rate of 3.8 percent. When there are changes in the consumer price index (the government's measure of the effect of inflation on prices), there's a corresponding change in the par value of the bond.

For example, if there's a 3 percent increase in the consumer price index, the par value of these bonds will go up by 3 percent, from $1,000 to $1,030. That means you get a little more interest each year, and at maturity you also get a little more. That's because interest payments are then determined using this new par value. So if the par value of the bond rises to $1,030 and the interest rate on the bond is set at 3.8 percent, the bondholder now gets 3.8 percent of $1,030, or $39.14 (3.8% × $1,030) per year, and at maturity this bond now pays $1,030.

The big headache with respect to these bonds comes in determining taxes. The IRS considers the upward adjustment in the par value of the bonds as interest income, and you have to pay taxes on it during the year the adjustment was made, even though you don't receive this money until the bond matures.

The advantage of these bonds is that investors will be guaranteed a real return—that is, a return above inflation. In addition, the effects of inflation on interest rates will be equalized as the interest payments and the bond's par value rise to reflect inflation. In effect, you win if there's inflation.

**U.S. Series EE Bonds**   The government also issues savings bonds directly aimed at the small investor. U.S. Series EE bonds are issued by the Treasury with variable interest rates and denominations so low they can be purchased for as little as $25 each. When a Series EE bond is purchased, its price is one-half its face value, with face values going from $50 to $10,000. In other words, you buy a bond, wait a specified amount of time, and get double your money back.

Series EE bonds are liquid in the sense that they can be cashed at any time, although cashing them before they mature may result in a reduced yield. Making them more attractive is that they earn 85 percent of the average 6-month Treasury security notes for bonds sold during the first 5 years and 85 percent of the average 5-year Treasury security rate thereafter. Although this minimum return can be changed at any time by the Treasury, the new minimum applies only to newly issued Series EE bonds, not to outstanding ones. The actual rate earned on Series EE bonds varies with the market interest rate, but it's currently quite competitive.

**I Bonds**   In addition to Series EE savings bonds, the U.S. Treasury also issues I bonds. An I bond is an accrual-type bond, meaning the interest is added to the value of the bond and paid when the bond is cashed in. These bonds are sold at face value and grow with inflation-indexed earnings for up to 30 years. The return on an I bond is a combination of two separate rates: a fixed rate of return and a semiannual inflation rate. That means you get a fixed rate plus an additional return based on changes in the rate of inflation (as measured by the Consumer Price Index for all Urban consumers [CPI-U]).

With an I bond, you can invest as little as $50 or as much as $30,000 per year. In addition, I bonds also have tax advantages. They allow you to defer federal taxes on earnings for up to 30 years and are exempt from state and local income taxes. In addition, these bonds are very liquid and can be turned into cash any time after 6 months.

## Municipal Bonds

**Municipal bonds,** or **"munis,"** are bonds issued by states, counties, and cities, in addition to other public agencies, such as school districts and highway authorities, to fund public projects. There are thousands of different issues of municipal bonds, with over $1 trillion in outstanding value. Their popularity stems from the fact that they're tax exempt—interest payments aren't taxed by the federal government or, in general, by the state as long as you live in the state in which the bonds were issued.

In fact, if you live in a city and buy a municipal bond issued by that city, your income from that bond would be exempt from city, state, and federal taxes. For example, if you live in New York, which has an income tax, and purchase a municipal bond issued by that city, you'll be exempt from paying taxes on the interest you receive at the federal, state, and city levels. Capital gains from selling municipal bonds before maturity, though, are taxed.

There are two basic types of municipal bonds: general obligation bonds and revenue bonds. A **general obligation bond** is backed by the full faith and credit—that is,

**Municipal Bonds, or "Munis"**
Bonds issued by states, counties, and cities, as well as other public agencies, such as school districts and highway authorities, to fund public projects.

**General Obligation Bond**
A state or municipal bond backed by the full faith and credit—that is, the taxing power—of the issuer.

# In The News

Wall Street Journal December 12, 2000

## Need a Lift? Inflation Bonds Are Handy

### by Jonathan Clements

Inflation-indexed Treasury bonds don't quite rival the Swiss Army knife. But it's amazing what you can do with them.

Need income? Worried about stocks? Want a place to park some cash? Inflation bonds can come in handy. Here's how:

*Portfolio Protection:* If inflation takes off or the economy tumbles into recession, stocks will get whacked. Want to cushion that blow? Traditionally, stock investors have added a dollop of regular bonds to their portfolios.

That works well in a recession, when interest rates tend to fall, driving up the price of regular bonds, whose fixed-interest payouts now seem more attractive. But when inflation takes off, interest rates climb. Result: Both stocks and regular bonds get crushed.

*That is where inflation bonds come in. They won't do as well as regular bonds in a recession. But during periods of rising consumer prices, inflation bonds will sparkle, thus helping to offset your stock market losses.* (☞**A**)

If you want to complement a stock portfolio, "you can substitute inflation bonds for nominal bonds and get more return for the same amount of risk or the same return for less risk," Mr. Hammond says. "They have about a third of the volatility of nominal bonds if you compare bonds of comparable maturity."

*Parking Place:* Because inflation bonds don't perform as erratically as regular bonds, they can be a good place to stash your emergency money.

*You never know when you will need this emergency money. Maybe you will have to call on your reserve next month—or maybe the money will sit untouched for the next decade.* (☞**B**)

Because your time horizon is uncertain, you want the money to be readily available, but you also want it to earn healthy returns. Inflation bonds look good on both counts. Mr. Volpert figures your chances of losing money in any given year are slim. "You might even have better downside protection than

you would with a short-term bond fund," he says.

## THE BOTTOM LINE . . .

**A** With normal bonds, when interest rates rise, generally as inflation increases, bond prices go down. As a result, your investment in bonds loses money. That's not the case with inflation-indexed bonds. With them your bond principal increases at a rate that matches the inflation rate.

**B** The primary complaint with inflation-indexed bonds is that each year you have to pay taxes on both the interest you earn plus the step-up or increase in the bond's principal.

---

**Revenue Bonds**
State or municipal bonds that have interest and par value paid for with funds from a designated project or specific tax.

**Serial Maturities**
Bonds, generally municipals, with various maturity dates, usually at set intervals.

the taxing power—of the issuer. **Revenue bonds** derive the funds to pay interest and repay the bonds from a designated project or specific tax and can pay only if a sufficient amount of revenue is generated. If a revenue bond derives its funding from a toll road and traffic isn't very heavy, the bond might go unpaid.

Municipal bonds also come with many different maturities. In fact, most municipal bond offerings have **serial maturities**. That is, a portion of the debt comes due, or matures, each year until the issue is exhausted. In effect, it works like a sinking fund. It's important that you choose the maturity date you want so you get the principal back when you need and expect it.

Although municipal bonds are issued by a "government," they're not risk free. In fact, in the past there have been several cases in which local governments have failed to pay on municipal bonds. Cleveland defaulted on some debt in the late 1970s, and then in the mid-1990s, Orange County, California, defaulted on $800 million of its short-term debt. The primary revenue source for most general obligation municipal bonds is real estate taxes. If local governments overestimate future tax intakes—say, the government thinks more people will move in when instead a bunch of people move out—they get stuck holding a lot of debt they can't handle.

Remember, unlike the federal government, state and local governments can't print more money when they run short. As you might expect, it's very difficult for an investor to judge the quality of a municipal bond offering. Fortunately, the rating agencies that we discuss shortly in conjunction with corporate bonds also rate municipal bonds.

One of the disadvantages of municipal bonds is that if you have to sell them before they mature, it can be difficult to find a buyer. This is especially true for many smaller issues for which there simply is not a secondary market.

## Special Situation Bonds

We've already seen the main classification of bonds, but before moving on there are two special types of bonds that deserve mention. They are zero coupon bonds and junk bonds.

**Zero Coupon Bonds**   **Zero coupon bonds** are simply bonds that don't pay interest. Instead, these bonds are sold at a discount from their face or par value, and at maturity they return the entire par value. As a result, the entire return is made up by the bond's appreciation in value from its discount purchase price to its price at maturity.

A zero coupon bond can be thought of as something like a savings bond. The obvious appeal of zero coupon bonds is to those investors who need a lump sum of money at some future date but don't want to be concerned about reinvesting interest payments. Zero coupon bonds are issued by corporations and municipals, and there are even mortgage-backed zeros, but without question the dominant player in this market is the U.S. government. The government's zero coupon bonds are called STRIPS.

The major disadvantage of these bonds is that while you don't receive any income annually, you're taxed as though you do. The IRS considers any annual appreciation in value (or as the IRS calls it, the undistributed interest) as subject to tax. Another disadvantage of zero coupon bonds is that they tend to fluctuate in value with changes in the interest rate more than traditional bonds do. For example, in 1994, 30-year zero coupon Treasury bonds dropped 18.7 percent, then in 1995 they rose in price by 63.1 percent. Zero coupon bonds aren't a good investment if you may have to sell the bond before it matures. Zero coupon bonds are best suited for tax-deferred retirement accounts such as IRAs or Keogh plans, where the tax disadvantage disappears.

**Junk Bonds**   **Junk bonds**, or low-rated bonds, also called high-yield bonds, are bonds rated BB or below. (We explain bond ratings in the next section.) Originally, the term applied to bonds issued by firms with previously sound financial histories that were currently facing severe financial problems and suffering from poor credit ratings. Today, junk bonds refer to any bond with a low rating. The major issuers of junk bonds are new firms that haven't yet established a performance record.

Because junk bonds carry a much greater risk of default, they also carry an interest rate 3 to 5 percent above AAA grade long-term bonds. The problem with junk bonds is that they haven't been around long enough for us to really know what will happen in a major recession.

In investing, it's never a good idea to volunteer to be a guinea pig. With junk bonds that's what you'd be doing. Moreover, most junk bonds are callable. That means that if the firm does do well and recovers from its difficulties, then the bond will be called. If the firm doesn't do well, the bond could default. Neither alternative is a good one. Junk bonds are probably something the prudent investor should avoid. Hey, they're not called junk for nothing!

**Zero Coupon Bonds**
Bonds that don't pay interest and are sold at a deep discount from their par value.

**Junk Bonds**
Very risky, low-rated bonds, also called high-yield bonds. These bonds are rated BB or below.

# In The News

**Wall Street Journal July 24, 2001**

## Bond Fans: Try a New Chicken Dance

### by Jonathan Clements

DON'T PUT ALL YOUR eggs in one basket, especially if you're a little chicken.

In the 15 years through year-end 2000, intermediate-term U.S. government bonds gained an average 8.1 percent a year, according to Chicago's Ibbotson Associates. The journey wasn't always smooth, with intermediate bonds losing money in two years, 1994 and 1999.

Over the same stretch, junk bonds had an even rougher time, suffering three calendar-year losses, while foreign bonds got slapped with four losing years. Still, if you had combined an 80 percent stake in intermediate governments with 10 percent positions in junk and foreign bonds, you would have been pleasantly surprised.

*That three-sector portfolio, like intermediate-term government bonds, lost money in 1994 and 1999, but its losses were smaller, calculates Baltimore's T. Rowe Price Associates. The reason: While the three sectors each had their rough moments, those moments didn't always coincide and, thus, the diversification tended to smooth out*

*performance. Moreover, despite the reduced volatility, the portfolio had a slightly higher return, gaining 8.4 percent a year.* (☛A)

"Investors don't perceive the need to diversify with bonds," says T. Rowe Price Vice President Steven Norwitz. "But, in fact, diversification may be more worthwhile in the bond area. The correlation between high-quality bonds and junk bonds tends to be lower than the correlation between different sectors of the U.S. stock market."

The correlation between U.S. and foreign bonds is also low. *Much of this comes from currency swings and, thus, you will likely get more diversification benefit from funds that rarely or never hedge (eliminate their currency risk).* But Chris Cordaro, a financial planner in Chatham, New Jersey, prefers funds that limit their currency exposure. (☛B)

"If you leave your foreign bonds unhedged (don't eliminate their currency risk), you get greater diversification benefit, but you also get greater volatility in the individual fund," he says. "People view bonds as a safety net. From a

behavioral standpoint, you're probably better off with a hedged fund, because you'll be happier and stick with it for longer."

### THE BOTTOM LINE . . .

**A** Diversification is just as important when investing in bonds as it is when investing in stocks. The principle is the same and it all boils down to **Principle 3: Diversification Reduces Risk.**

**B** Hedging away currency risk involves making investments that rise in value when a foreign currency, say, for example, the Mexican peso, drops in value relative to the dollar. In effect, they offset foreign currency exchange risk.

---

**L·3** Calculate the value of a bond and understand the factors that cause bond value to change.

## Evaluating Bonds

Not only do you need to know bond terms and what kind of bonds there are, you also need to know how to evaluate them. That means understanding what a bond yield and a rating are, and knowing how to read a bond quote in the newspaper.

### Bond Yield

The bond's yield is simply the return on investment. Note that yield isn't the same as coupon interest rate. The coupon interest rate tells you what your interest payments are as a percentage of the bond's par value. The bond's yield tells you what your return is as a percentage of the price of the bond.

There are two ways of measuring yield. The first, called the current yield, simply looks at the return from interest payments on the bond. The second, called the yield to maturity, takes into account total return, including interest and allowing for the fact that you may have purchased the bond for either more or less than it returns at maturity.

**Current Yield**
The ratio of the annual interest payment to the bond's market price.

**Current Yield** The **current yield** on a bond refers to the ratio of the annual interest payment to the bond's market price. If, for example, you're considering a bond with an 8-percent coupon interest rate, a par value of $1,000, and a market price of $700, it would have a current yield of

$$\text{current yield} = \frac{\text{annual interest payments}}{\text{market price of the bond}}$$

$$= \frac{0.08 \times \$1,000}{\$700} = \frac{\$80}{\$700} = 11.4 \text{ percent}$$

**Yield to Maturity**   The **yield to maturity** is the true yield or return you receive if you hold a bond to maturity. Basically, it's the measure of expected return. In effect, calculating the yield to maturity is the same as solving for the annual interest rate, $i$, in Chapter 3, where we discussed the time value of money. This measure of return considers the annual interest payments the bondholder receives as well as the difference between the bond's current market price and its value at maturity.

Remember, regardless of whether you bought your bond at a price above or below its par value, at maturity you get exactly its par value. If you paid less than $1,000 for your bond, the bond will appreciate over its lifetime, climbing up to $1,000 at maturity. Conversely, if you paid more than $1,000 for your bond, it'll slowly drop in value over its lifetime, falling to $1,000 at maturity when it's redeemed.

If you have a financial calculator, solving for the yield to maturity, or $i$, is quite easy. If you don't have a financial calculator, you can use a formula to calculate the approximate yield to maturity (you need a calculator to calculate the actual yield to maturity). This formula first determines the average annual return by adding the annual interest payments to the average amount that the bond increases or decreases in price each year. The annual change in bond price is based on the notion that at maturity the bond will be worth its par value—because it'll be redeemed at this price—and simply calculates the amount the bond must increase or decrease to get to its par value and divides this by the number of years left to maturity.

This average annual return is then divided by the average value of the bond—the average of its par value and current market price. Thus, the *approximate yield to maturity* is calculated as follows:

$$\frac{\text{approximate}}{\text{yield to maturity}} = \frac{\text{annual interest payments} + \dfrac{\text{par value} - \text{current price}}{\text{number of years to maturity}}}{\dfrac{\text{par value} + \text{current price}}{2}}$$

Let's look at an example of a bond that has 10 years left to maturity, has a par value of $1,000, a current price of $880, and a coupon interest rate of 10 percent. It pays $100 annually in interest to the bondholder (coupon interest rate × par value = annual interest payment, or 0.10 × $1,000 = $100). Plugging these numbers into the approximate yield to maturity formula, you get

$$\frac{\text{approximate}}{\text{yield to maturity}} = \frac{\$100 + \dfrac{\$1,000 - \$880}{10}}{\dfrac{\$1,000 + \$880}{2}}$$

$$\frac{\text{approximate}}{\text{yield to maturity}} = \frac{\$100 + \dfrac{\$120}{10}}{\$1,880/2}$$

$$= \$112/\$940 = 11.91 \text{ percent}$$

As we noted earlier, you'd need a financial calculator to get the true yield to maturity. If you did calculate the true yield to maturity, you would find it to be 12.14 percent, a difference of only 0.23 percent.

The approximate yield to maturity formula also works for bonds that are selling above their par or maturity value. Changing the current market price to $1,100 in our example, we can recalculate the approximate yield to maturity as follows:

$$\frac{\text{approximate}}{\text{yield to maturity}} = \frac{\$100 + \dfrac{\$1,000 - \$1,100}{10}}{\dfrac{\$1,000 + \$1,100}{2}}$$

$$\frac{\text{approximate}}{\text{yield to maturity}} = \frac{\$100 - \dfrac{\$100}{10}}{\$2,100/2}$$

$$= \$90/\$1,050 = 8.57 \text{ percent}$$

**Equivalent Taxable Yield on Municipal Bonds**   The appeal of municipal bonds (munis) is their tax-exempt status. Thus, in comparing municipal bonds to other taxable bonds, the comparison must be between equivalent taxable yield—that is, the yield a taxable bond must offer to match the equivalent taxable yield on the municipal bond. The equivalent taxable yield on a municipal bond is calculated as follows:

$$\frac{\text{equivalent}}{\text{taxable yield}} = \frac{\text{tax-free yield on the municipal bond}}{(1 - \text{ investor's marginal tax bracket})}$$

Keep in mind that the tax bracket referred to includes all taxes avoided by the muni. This bracket could include federal, state, and local taxes. Thus, if the municipal bond were yielding 7 percent and the investor were in the 38-percent marginal tax bracket, the equivalent taxable yield on a municipal bond would be

$$\frac{\text{equivalent}}{\text{taxable yield}} = \frac{0.07}{(1 - 0.38)} = \frac{0.07}{0.62} = 0.1129, \text{ or } 11.29\%$$

The higher the individual's tax bracket, the more attractive municipal bonds are.

## Bond Ratings—A Measure of Riskiness

**Principle**

**1** The Risk–Return Trade-Off

John Moody first began to rate bonds in 1909. Since that time, two major rating agencies—Moody's and Standard & Poor's—have provided ratings on thousands of corporate, city, and state bonds. These ratings involve a judgment about the future risk potential of a bond—specifically its default risk or the chance that it may not be able to meet its obligations of interest or repayment of principal sometime in the future.

The poorer the bond rating, the higher the rate of return demanded by investors. That's exactly what you'd expect, given **Principle 1: The Risk–Return Trade-Off**. Generally, these bond ratings run from AAA for the safest bonds to D for extremely risky bonds. Interestingly, a bond with an A rating is considered only a medium-grade bond rather than a high-grade bond. Table 14.1 provides a description of the different bond ratings.

**STOP &THINK**   While AAA is the highest corporate bond rating, you might not want to demand a AAA rating on your bond investments. That's because AAA ratings are relatively rare. Even Ford doesn't have a AAA rating. In fact, only about 21 or so of the *Fortune* 500 firms are rated AAA. On the other hand, there are plenty of B-rated bonds around; however, although a B may be a good grade in a class, it's only a speculative grade when it comes to bond ratings.

## Table 14.1   Interpreting Bond Ratings

| Bond Rating Category | Standard & Poor's | Moody's | Description |
|---|---|---|---|
| Prime | AAA | Aaa | Highest quality, extremely strong |
| Very strong | AA | Aa | Very strong capacity to pay |
| Strong | A | A | Strong capacity to pay |
| Medium | BBB | Baa | Changing circumstances could impact the firm's ability to pay |
| Speculative | BB, B | Ba, B | Has speculative elements |
| Very speculative | CCC, CC | Caa, C | Extremely speculative |
| Default | C | C | An income bond that doesn't pay interest |
| Default | D | D | Has not been paying interest or repaying principal |

As an investor, you should be aware of a bond's rating and its risk. Unfortunately, because bonds are so expensive—selling for around $1,000 each—diversification can be difficult unless you have a great deal of money invested in bonds. So if you buy bonds, avoid the risky ones. Check their ratings, which are available at most local libraries, or ask your broker.

### Reading Corporate Bond Quotes in the *Wall Street Journal*

Figure 14.1 provides a visual summary of how to read corporate bond listings. Recall that although corporate bonds generally have a par or face value of $1,000, their selling price is quoted as a percentage of par. Even though a bond may appear to be selling at 101, it's actually selling at 101 percent of its par value, which is $1,000. Thus, a bond listed as selling at 101 is actually selling for $1,010.

What's listed in the paper isn't exactly what you'd pay if you purchased the bond. You're also expected to pay for any **accrued interest** on the bond. Remember, interest is generally paid only every 6 months. Thus, if it's been 5 months since interest was last paid, the bond has accrued 5 months' worth of interest. This accrued interest isn't reflected in the listed price of the bond, but you still need to pay the seller for the accrued interest that's already been earned.

If this bond pays $48 in interest every 6 months, then 5 months' worth of accrued interest would be $\frac{5}{6} \times \$48 = \$40$. That means that although the bond is listed as selling for $1,010, if you purchased it you'd actually pay $1,010 + $40 = $1,050. This sum of both the quoted or stated price and the accrued interest is often referred to as the **invoice price**.

### Reading Treasury Quotes in the *Wall Street Journal*

Figure 14.2 provides a visual summary of how to read Treasury securities listings. When reading Treasury and agency securities listings, you'll notice quotes for both a bid price and an ask price, with the bid price representing what another investor was willing to pay for the security and the ask price representing what another investor was willing to sell the security for. In addition, Treasury and agency securities trade in thirty-seconds ($\frac{1}{32}$). Thus, if a security is listed at 102:31, that translates to $102\frac{31}{32}$ percent of the security's par value. If the par value of this bond is $10,000, then it would sell for $10,296.88 ($10,000 \times 102\frac{31}{32}\%$).

**Accrued Interest**
Interest that has been earned on the bond but has not yet been paid out to the bondholder.

**Invoice Price**
The sum of both the quoted or stated price of a bond and the bond's accrued interest. It's the price you pay if you buy the bond in the secondary market.

**Figure 14.1** How to Read Corporate Bond Listings in the *Wall Street Journal*

The Money and Investing Section of the *Wall Street Journal* contains daily trading details for corporate bonds traded on the New York Stock Exchange. This actually represents only a small portion of bond trading, with most bond trading taking place in the over-the-counter market among securities dealers.

**Bonds:** The name of the issuer is given in the first column, followed by the original interest rate, and the year the bond matures in, with an occasional *s* added as a break between numbers. For example, the 6s09 is referred to as a "six of oh-nine," meaning it is a 6% bond due in 2009.

**Vol:** Volume provides the volume of trading during the previous day in thousands of dollars. For example, 251 ATT 8⅛ 24 bonds traded during the previous day.

**Net Chg:** Net change refers to the change in the closing price from the prior day's close. Again, a ¼ change reflects a change of $2.50. That is, ¼% of the bond's par value which is $1,000.

THE WALL STREET JOURNAL THURSDAY, JANUARY 28, 2002

**NEW YORK EXCHANGE BONDS**

Quotations as of 4 p.m. Eastern Time

Wednesday, January 27, 2002

**NEW YORK BONDS**

**Corporation Bonds**

| BONDS | CUR YLD. | VOL. | CLOSE | NET CHG. |
|---|---|---|---|---|
| AES Cp 4½05 | cv | 89 | 46 | − ½ |
| AES Cp 8s8 | 12.1 | 254 | 66 | + 1 |
| AMR 9s16 | 9.3 | 144 | 96½ | − ⅛ |
| ATT 6¾04 | 6.6 | 19 | 101⅝ | − 1¼ |
| ATT 5⅝04 | 5.6 | 1253 | 100½ | + ⅛ |
| ATT 7s05 | 6.9 | 21 | 102⅛ | + ¼ |
| ATT 7¾07 | 7.5 | 320 | 103⅞ | − ¼ |
| ATT 6s09 | 6.4 | 330 | 94½ | + ⅛ |
| ATT 8⅛22 | 8.1 | 162 | 100⅜ | + ⅝ |
| ATT 8⅛24 | 8.1 | 251 | 100¼ | + ¾ |
| ATT 8.35s25 | 8.2 | 125 | 101⅞ | + ⅞ |
| ATT 6½29 | 7.7 | 285 | 84½ | + ⅜ |
| ATT 8⅝31 | 8.5 | 194 | 101⅛ | − ⅜ |
| AmFnGp 7⅛07 | 7.8 | 40 | 92 | + 2 |
| ARetire 5¾02 | cv | 43 | 60 11/32 | + 3 11/32 |
| Anixter zr20 | ... | 11 | 27 | ... |
| ARch 10⅞05 | 9.3 | 20 | 117 | + 1 |
| ARch 9⅛11 | 7.8 | 10 | 117⅛ | + 1 |
| Bevrly 9s06 | 9.0 | 5 | 100 | + ½ |
| Bluegrn 8¼12 | cv | 44 | 84 | + 1⅛ |
| BosCelts 6s38 | 9.1 | 2 | 65⅞ | − ¼ |
| CallonP 11s05 | 12.4 | 5 | 89 | ... |
| Case 7¼16 | 10.7 | 20 | 67½ | + 1½ |
| Caterplnc 6s07 | 5.9 | 15 | 101⅛ | ... |
| ChespkE 7⅞04 | 7.8 | 20 | 101 | + ½ |
| vjChiq 10s09f | ... | 25 | 86 | + 1 |
| ClrkOil 9½04 | 9.5 | 22 | 100 | ... |
| Coeur 13⅜03 | cv | 25 | 105 | + 2¾ |
| Coeur 6⅜04 | cv | 36 | 50 | + 2½ |
| Consec 8⅛03 | 9.0 | 206 | 90¾ | + ¾ |
| Conseco 10½04 | 11.9 | 120 | 88¼ | − ¼ |
| Conseco 10¼02 | 10.3 | 86 | 100 | − ½ |
| CrownC 7⅛02 | 8.7 | 146 | 82 9/32 | + 1 1/32 |
| CrwnCF 7s06 | 10.1 | 12 | 69 | + 10 |
| DevonE 4.9s08 | cv | 18 | 99½ | ... |
| DevonE 4.95s08 | cv | 15 | 98¾ | − ½ |
| Dole 7s03 | 6.9 | 91 | 101¾ | − ⅜ |
| Dole 7⅞13 | 7.6 | 46 | 103½ | + ½ |

**Cur Yld:** The current yield gives the annual interest divided by the most recent price. In effect it tells you how much you would earn on this bond over the next year if the bond's price remained the same. A *cv* indicates a convertible bond.

**Close:** The closing price from the prior day is shown in this column. You must keep in mind that bond prices are traditionally quoted as a percent of par, with the typical par value of a corporate bond being $1,000. Thus, the closing price on the ATT 6s09 bond of 94½ means that this bond's last trade during the prior day was at $945.00. In effect, each ⅛ reflects $1.25. Thus, a bond quoted at 101⅝ would be selling for $1,016.25.

Source: Reprinted by permission of the *Wall Street Journal*, © 2002 Dow Jones & Company, Inc. All rights reserved worldwide.

LO 3 Calculate the value of a bond and understand the risks and factors that cause bond value to change.

## Valuation Principles

The valuation of bonds has its roots in Principles 1 and 2. **Principle 2: The Time Value of Money** allows us to bring the investment returns back to present, while **Principle 1: The Risk–Return Trade-Off** tells us what discount rate to use in bringing those returns back to present.

# Figure 14.2 How to Read Treasury and Agency Securities Listings in the *Wall Street Journal*

The Money and Investing section of the *Wall Street Journal* contains daily trading details for U.S. Treasury offerings. Treasury bills are issued with maturities of 3 or 6 months every Monday in minimum denominations of $10,000, and with 1-year maturities on a monthly basis. Treasury issues maturing in between 1 and 10 years are referred to as notes, while those with maturities greater than 10 years are called bonds.

**How They Work:** The interest rate on inflation-indexed Treasuries remains the same for the life of the bond. But every six months, your principal is adjusted for inflation. Future interest payments are based on the adjusted principal. Suppose you invested $1,000 in a 30-year inflation-indexed bond with a yield of 3.95%, which won't change. But if inflation rises 4%, the value of your principal will grow to $1,040 and you'll earn 3.95% on that amount.

**Maturity Mo/Yr:** The year and month of maturity are given in this column. An *n* to the right of the year of maturity denotes a note. A *p* identifies bonds that are exempt from withholding tax if held by nonresident aliens.

**Ask Yld.:** This refers to the yield or effective return on the investment. If you bought the bond today and held it to maturity, this would be your return.

**Days to Maturity:** Because of their short maturity, Treasury bills also list the number of days to maturity.

**Rate:** Rate refers to the original interest rate on the bond.

## TREASURY BONDS, NOTES & BILLS

Wednesday, January 27, 2002

Representative and Indicative-Over-the-Counter quotations based on $1 million or more.

### GOVT. BOND & NOTES

| RATE | MATURITY MO/YR | BID | ASKED | CHG. | ASKED YLD. |
|---|---|---|---|---|---|
| 6¼ | Mar 02n | 100:12 | 100:13 | − 1 | 1.50 |
| 6⅝ | Mar 02n | 100:12 | 100:13 | − 1 | 1.62 |
| 6⅜ | Apr 02n | 100:24 | 100:25 | − 1 | 1.60 |
| 6⅝ | Apr 02n | 100:26 | 100:27 | .... | 1.57 |
| 7½ | May 02n | 101:05 | 101:06 | − 1 | 1.71 |
| 6½ | May 02n | 101:06 | 101:07 | .... | 1.63 |
| 6⅝ | May 02n | 101:06 | 101:07 | − 1 | 1.69 |
| 9⅛ | May 18 | 138:23 | 138:24 | + 32 | 5.49 |
| 9 | Nov 18 | 137:26 | 137:27 | + 31 | 5.50 |
| 8⅞ | Feb 19 | 136:22 | 136:23 | + 32 | 5.51 |
| 8⅛ | Aug 19 | 128:23 | 128:24 | + 30 | 5.54 |
| 8½ | Feb 20 | 133:12 | 133:13 | + 32 | 5.54 |
| 8¾ | May 20 | 136:17 | 136:18 | + 33 | 5.54 |
| 8¾ | Aug 20 | 136:24 | 136:25 | + 33 | 5.54 |
| 7⅞ | Feb 21 | 126:29 | 126:30 | + 31 | 5.56 |
| 8⅛ | May 21 | 130:00 | 130:01 | + 30 | 5.56 |

### U.S. TREASURY STRIPS

| MATURITY | TYPE | BID | ASKED | CHG. | ASKED YLD. |
|---|---|---|---|---|---|
| May 02 | ci | 99:23 | 99:23 | ... | 1.37 |
| May 02 | np | 99:21 | 99:21 | .... | 1.70 |
| Aug 02 | ci | 99:09 | 99:10 | .... | 1.53 |
| Aug 02 | np | 99:05 | 99:06 | .... | 1.79 |
| Nov 02 | ci | 98:29 | 98:29 | + 1 | 1.55 |
| Feb 03 | ci | 98:02 | 98:03 | + 3 | 2.01 |
| Feb 03 | np | 97:31 | 98:00 | + 3 | 2.13 |
| May 03 | ci | 97:13 | 97:14 | + 4 | 2.16 |
| Jul 03 | ci | 96:25 | 96:26 | + 4 | 2.37 |
| Aug 03 | ci | 96:17 | 96:18 | + 5 | 2.41 |
| Aug 03 | np | 96:11 | 96:12 | + 5 | 2.54 |
| Nov 03 | ci | 96:01 | 96:02 | + 5 | 2.37 |
| Nov 03 | np | 95:14 | 95:15 | + 5 | 2.74 |
| Jan 04 | ci | 94:26 | 94:27 | + 6 | 2.85 |
| Feb 04 | ci | 94:15 | 94:16 | + 6 | 2.90 |
| Feb 04 | np | 94:13 | 94:15 | + 6 | 2.93 |
| May 04 | ci | 93:13 | 93:14 | + 7 | 3.10 |

### TREASURY BILLS

| MATURITY | DAYS TO MAT. | BID | ASKED | CHG. | ASKED YLD. |
|---|---|---|---|---|---|
| Mar 07 '02 | 7 | 1.71 | 1.70 | − 0.01 | 1.72 |
| Mar 14 '02 | 14 | 1.72 | 1.71 | − 0.01 | 1.73 |
| Mar 21 '02 | 21 | 1.75 | 1.74 | + 0.01 | 1.77 |
| Mar 28 '02 | 28 | 1.76 | 1.75 | + 0.02 | 1.78 |
| Apr 04 '02 | 35 | 1.72 | 1.71 | + 0.01 | 1.74 |
| Apr 11 '02 | 42 | 1.71 | 1.70 | − 0.02 | 1.73 |
| Apr 18 '02 | 49 | 1.71 | 1.70 | − 0.01 | 1.73 |
| Apr 25 '02 | 56 | 1.71 | 1.70 | − 0.01 | 1.73 |
| May 02 '02 | 63 | 1.74 | 1.73 | + 0.01 | 1.76 |
| May 09 '02 | 70 | 1.73 | 1.72 | − 0.01 | 1.75 |
| May 16 '02 | 77 | 1.72 | 1.71 | − 0.02 | 1.74 |
| May 23 '02 | 84 | 1.73 | 1.72 | − 0.01 | 1.75 |
| May 30 '02 | 91 | 1.73 | 1.72 | − 0.01 | 1.75 |
| Jun 13 '02 | 105 | 1.73 | 1.72 | − 0.01 | 1.75 |
| Jun 13 '02 | 105 | 1.73 | 1.72 | − 0.01 | 1.75 |
| Jun 20 '02 | 112 | 1.72 | 1.71 | − 0.02 | 1.74 |
| Jun 27 '02 | 119 | 1.73 | 1.72 | .... | 1.75 |
| 05 '02 | 127 | 1.72 | 1.71 | − 0.03 | 1.74 |

### INFLATION-INDEXED TREASURY SECURITIES

| RATE | MAT. | BID/ASKED | CHG. | *YLD. | ACCR. PRIN. |
|---|---|---|---|---|---|
| 3.625 | 07/02 | 101-12/13 | .... | 1.250 | 1104 |
| 3.375 | 01/07 | 102-17/18 | + 1 | 2.809 | 1116 |
| 3.625 | 01/08 | 103-11/12 | + 6 | 2.994 | 1094 |
| 3.875 | 01/09 | 104-12/13 | + 7 | 3.157 | 1078 |
| 4.250 | 01/10 | 107-01/02 | + 5 | 3.227 | 1050 |
| 3.500 | 01/11 | 102-01/02 | + 6 | 3.230 | 1016 |
| 3.375 | 01/12 | 101-08/09 | + 9 | 3.222 | .995 |
| 3.625 | 04/28 | 104-05/06 | + 9 | 3.382 | 1093 |
| 3.875 | 04/29 | 108-22/23 | + 9 | 3.381 | 1075 |
| 3.375 | 04/32 | 101-20/21 | + 11 | 3.288 | 996 |

*-Yld. to maturity on accrued principal.

**Bid:** Bid refers to the previous day's midafternoon bid price that Treasury dealers were willing to buy the issue for. In the bond market, prices are quoted at a percent of par and each one-hundredth of par is referred to as a point. Treasury bond prices generally trade in 32nds of a point. To keep things simple and avoid repeating the figure 32 all the time, all numbers after a colon in a price represent 32nds. Thus, the price of 136:17 means 136 $^{17}/_{32}$ of the bond's par value. If the bond's par is $10,000, you could sell it for $13,653.125.

**Chg.:** Change reflects the change in the ask price from the previous day.

**Asked:** Asked refers to the asking or selling price dealers were willing to sell the issue for at midafternoon during the previous day.

**U.S. Treasury STRIPS:** This is a zero coupon bond issued by the Treasury; that is, it does not pay any interest. At maturity you receive the par value of the bond. You will notice that STRIPS that mature in the more distant future are sold at a deeper discount. That is because the only return the investor receives is in appreciation of the bond's value.

**Treasury Bills: Bid and Asked:** You will also note that Treasury bills are quoted in hundredths. Thus, a yield of 1.73 is 1.73%.

**\*Yld. & Accr. Prin.:** These refer to the inflation adjusted yield to maturity and the current accrued principal including all cumulative inflation adjustments.

From the previous chapter, you already know that the value of any investment is simply the present value of all the returns that you receive from that investment. This is how you value stocks, and it's also how you value bonds. In effect, we'll simply bring the returns or benefits back to the present and add them up. With bonds, the process is quite simple—you merely find out the value in today's dollars of the interest and principal payments, and add them together.

## Bond Valuation

When you purchase a bond, you get interest payments for a number of years, and then at maturity the bond is redeemed and you receive the par value of the bond back. Thus, *the value of a bond is simply the present value of the interest payments plus the present value of the repayment of the bond's par value at maturity*. In general, the value of a bond should be approximately the same as its price, because that's what you and other investors would be willing to pay for the bond. Thus, by understanding how bonds are valued, we can also understand what causes bond prices to rise and fall.

Now, let's bring the interest payments and the repayment of the bond's par value at maturity back to present. The interest payments come in the form of an annuity—that is, the investor receives the same dollar amount each year. The repayment of par comes in the form of a single cash flow.[2] Thus, the value of the bond can be written as

$$\text{value of the bond} = \frac{\text{present value of the}}{\text{interest payments}} + \frac{\text{present value of repayment}}{\text{of par at maturity}}$$

Rewriting this using the notation from Chapter 3, we get

$$\text{value of the bond} = \$I(PVIFA_{k\%,\,n\,\text{yr}}) + \$\text{par}(PVIF_{k\%,\,n\,\text{yr}})$$

where

$\$I$ = the annual interest payments

$\$\text{par}$ = the par value, or what the bond will be redeemed for at maturity

$n$ = the number of years to maturity

$k$ = the appropriate discount rate or required rate of return given the risk level of the bond

Let's look at an example. We're considering buying a bond that matures in 20 years with a coupon interest rate of 10 percent and a par value of $1,000. How much should we pay for it? Well, first we need to decide what return we require on that bond. Let's assume that given the current interest rates and risk level of this bond, our required rate of return is also 10 percent per year. To determine the value of the bond, we need only bring the interest payments and repayment of par back to present using our required rate of return as the discount rate.

---

[2]Actually, the calculation of the value of a bond is slightly more complicated because most bonds pay interest semiannually rather than annually. Although accommodating this complication is relatively simple, the principles behind bond valuation don't change. Moreover, the effect on the value of the bond is only slight. Because our presentation is meant to illustrate how the value of a bond is determined in the marketplace and how changes in interest rates are reflected in bond prices, we won't deal with semiannual interest payments.

The annual interest payments we'll receive if we buy this bond are equal to the bond's coupon interest rate of 10 percent times the par value of the bond, which is $1,000. Thus, the annual interest payments are $100. Recall that the *PVIFA* can be determined using a financial calculator or looked up directly in Appendix D, and the *PVIF* can also be determined using a financial calculator or looked up in Appendix B. The value of the bond can now be calculated as follows:

$$\begin{aligned} \frac{\text{value of}}{\text{the bond}} &= \frac{\text{present value of the}}{\text{interest payments}} + \frac{\text{present value of repayment}}{\text{of par at maturity}} \\ &= \$100(PVIFA_{10\%,\ 20\ yr}) + \$1,000(PVIF_{10\%,\ 20\ yr}) \\ &= \$100(8.514) + \$1,000(0.1486) \\ &= \$851.40 + \$148.60 \\ &= \$1,000 \end{aligned}$$

Thus, the value of this bond would be $1,000. If we purchased it for $1,000, we'd be paying exactly its par value. The reason we'd buy at par is that we'd be earning our entire required rate of return from the interest payments—we required a 10-percent return and we receive a 10-percent return in the form of interest.

Now let's look at the same bond and assume that the current level of interest rates has gone up and, as a result, so has our required rate of return—to 12 percent. How much should we pay for this bond now? In this case, the only change is in the value of $k$, the discount rate or required rate of return. Recalculating the value of the bond, we find it to be

$$\begin{aligned} \frac{\text{value of}}{\text{the bond}} &= \frac{\text{present value of the}}{\text{interest payments}} + \frac{\text{present value of repayment}}{\text{of par at maturity}} \\ &= \$100(PVIFA_{12\%,\ 20\ yr}) + \$1,000(PVIF_{12\%,\ 20\ yr}) \\ &= \$100(7.469) + \$1,000(0.104) \\ &= \$746.90 + \$104.00 \\ &= \$850.90 \end{aligned}$$

When we raise our required rate of return to 12 percent, the value of the bond falls to $850.90. As a result, we would want to buy this bond *at a discount*, that is, below its par value. We're requiring a 12-percent return on this bond, but its interest rate is only 10 percent. We'd need to receive the remaining return from the appreciation of the bond in value. As a result, we'd buy it for $850.90 and at maturity receive $1,000 for it.

Let's see what happens to the value of this bond when our required rate of return goes down. Assume that the current level of interest rates has gone down and, as a result, so has our required rate of return, this time to 8 percent. Again, the only change is in the value of $k$, the discount rate or required rate of return. Recalculating the value of the bond, we find it to be

$$\begin{aligned} \frac{\text{value of}}{\text{the bond}} &= \frac{\text{present value of the}}{\text{interest payments}} + \frac{\text{present value of repayment}}{\text{of par at maturity}} \\ &= \$100(PVIFA_{8\%,\ 20\ yr}) + \$1,000(PVIF_{8\%,\ 20\ yr}) \\ &= \$100(9.818) + \$1,000(0.215) \\ &= \$981.80 + \$215.00 \\ &= \$1,196.80 \end{aligned}$$

Thus, when the required rate of return drops to 8 percent, the value of the bond climbs to $1,196.80. As a result, we would be willing to buy this bond *at a premium*, that is, above its par value. Again, this makes sense, because if the bond pays 10 percent in interest and we require an 8-percent return, we'd be willing to pay more than $1,000 for it.

In reflecting on this example, notice that as your required rate of return goes up, the value of the bond drops, and when your required rate of return goes down, the value of the bond increases. What can cause your required rate of return to change?

First, if the firm that issued the bond becomes riskier, your required rate of return should rise. The result of this would be a drop in the value of the bond—that certainly makes intuitive sense. A second factor that can cause you to alter your required rate of return on a bond is a change in general interest rates in the market. Perhaps there is an increase in expected inflation and, as a result, you demand a higher return for delaying consumption, pushing interest rates up. That means you can now earn a higher return on alternative investments. You won't buy this bond unless its return is adjusted upward to meet the competition.

Thus, when interest rates in general rise, the value of outstanding bonds falls. Because the value of these bonds falls, so does their price. Alternatively, when interest rates fall, the value and price of outstanding bonds rise. As we'll see, this inverse relationship between bond values or prices and interest rates is extremely important.

Principle 5
The Curse of Competitive Investment Markets

## Why Bonds Fluctuate in Value

Obviously, if you invest in bonds, it's important to know what makes them move up and down in value, and therefore in price. Let's begin by summarizing the key relationship that underlies bond valuation. *There's an inverse relationship between interest rates and bond values in the secondary market: When interest rates rise, bond values drop, and when interest rates drop, bond values rise.*

As interest rates rise, investors demand a higher return on bonds. If a bond has a fixed coupon interest rate, the only way the bond can increase its return to investors is to drop in value and sell for less. Thus, we have an inverse relationship between interest rates and bond values (and prices).

The importance of this relationship can't be overstated. Bond prices fluctuate dramatically, and this relationship explains much of the fluctuation. For example, in 1994 interest rates went up, and as a result long-term Treasury bonds posted average losses of 7.8 percent. Then, in 1995, interest rates dropped, and those same bonds returned 31.7 percent. Interest rates turned the other way in 1996, and Treasury bonds then returned −0.9 percent in 1996. In 1997 and 1998, interest rates dropped again, resulting in returns of 15.9 percent and 13.1 percent, respectively. Then, in 1999 interest rates rose and long-term Treasury bonds lost 9.0 percent, but in 2000 interest rates fell and Treasury bonds returned 21.5 percent! Figure 14.3 shows the relationship between bond prices and interest rates since the end of 1925 and illustrates the inverse relationship that exists between them.

Not only do bond values change when interest rates change, but *longer-term bonds fluctuate in price more than shorter-term bonds*. Remember from Chapter 3 that the further in the future a cash flow is, the more its present value will fluctuate as

---

**STOP &THINK**

Your immediate reaction to learning of this inverse relationship between interest rates and bond prices may be to try to use it to make money. Before you forecast interest rates and invest in bonds, let's think back to **Principle 5: The Curse of Competitive Investment Markets.** Beating the market is extremely difficult. To use this inverse relationship between interest rates and bond prices, you not only have to forecast interest rates, but you have to outforecast the experts. Knowing which way interest rates are going will not be enough if other investors know the same thing: You need to know which way interest rates are going when no one else knows.

---

**Figure 14.3** The Relationship Between Bond Prices and Changes in Interest Rates
When yields (interest rates) increase, bond prices decrease.

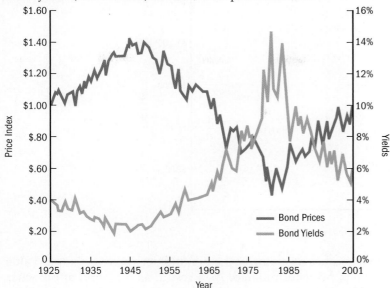

a result of a change in the interest or discount rate. Thus, when interest rates change, longer-term bonds fluctuate in price more than shorter-term bonds. Figure 14.4 shows how between 1970 and 2001, long-term bonds bounced up and down much more dramatically in response to interest rate changes than short-term bonds.

In addition, *as a bond approaches its maturity date, its market value approaches its par or maturity value.* Without question, a bond will sell for its par or maturity value at

**Figure 14.4** The Relationship Between Length of a Bond's Maturity and Amount of Price Fluctuation When Interest Rates Change

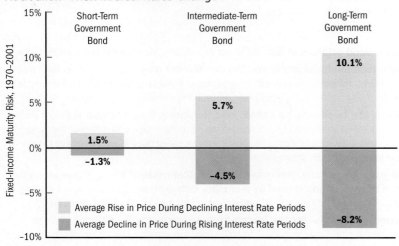

**Figure 14.5** The Price Path of a 12% Coupon Bond over Its Life

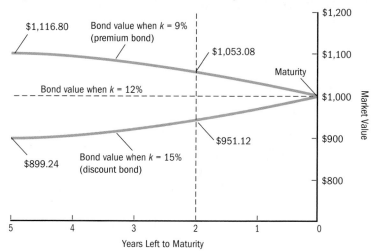

maturity. We know this because at maturity the bondholder receives the par value from the issuer, and the bond is terminated. As a result, as the bond approaches maturity, the market price of the bond approaches its par value. Figure 14.5 illustrates this point.

Finally, *when interest rates go down, bond prices go up, but the upward price movement on bonds with a call provision is limited by the call price.* In effect, investors simply won't

## Table 14.2   The Pros and Cons of Investing in Bonds

**Benefits of Bonds**

- **If interest rates drop, bond prices will rise.** If interest rates drop, that inverse relationship between interest rates and bond prices will work in your favor. In that case, you'll want a long-term, noncallable bond.
- **Bonds reduce risk through diversification.** Any time you add a new investment to your portfolio that doesn't move in tandem with the other investments in your portfolio, you reduce your portfolio risk.
- **Bonds produce steady current income.** What more need we say?
- **Bonds can be a safe investment if held to maturity.** If you hold the bond to maturity and it doesn't default, it'll return exactly what it promises.

**Dangers of Bonds**

- **If interest rates rise, bond prices will fall.** The longer the maturity, the more the bond will fluctuate.
- **If the issuer experiences financial problems, the bondholder may pay.** If an issuer can't make interest or principal payments, the bond will plummet in value. Minor financial problems can also cause the bond to drop in value. Of course, any time the bond rating drops, bond values drop like a stone.
- **If interest rates drop, the bond may be called.** Most corporate bonds are callable. In theory, when interest rates drop, the value of a bond should rise. However, the issuer may decide to refinance the bond offering with bonds that have a lower interest rate. The bonds may be called away, leaving investors to reinvest the proceeds from the called bonds at lower interest rates.
- **If you need to sell your bonds early, you may have a problem selling them at a reasonable price, particularly If they're bonds issued by a smaller corporation.** There simply isn't a strong secondary market for the bonds of smaller corporations. In short, bonds aren't a very liquid investment.
- **Finding a good investment outlet for the interest you receive may be difficult.** If you're using bonds to accumulate wealth, it may be difficult to find a good investment outlet for the interest you receive. Without reinvesting the interest payments, there'll be no accumulation of wealth from investing in bonds unless you're investing in zero or very low coupon bonds.

# Checklist 14.1 ▮ Picking a Good Bond

**Think about taxes.** Make sure you consider the effect of taxes. Consider municipals, particularly if you're in a high tax bracket.

**Keep that inverse relationship between interest rates and bond prices in mind.** If interest rates are very low, the only way they can go is up (which would cause bond prices to drop), so you might want to invest in shorter-term bonds.

**Avoid losers and don't worry about picking winners.** This advice applies if you're buying a corporate bond rather than a government bond. First, you must keep in mind that with corporate bonds you get the same return unless the firm defaults. Look for and avoid firms that might experience major financial problems. All other firms are pretty much the same.

**Consider only high-quality bonds.** Limit yourself to bonds rated AA or above. In this way you minimize any worry regarding a possible default by the issuer.

**Buy your bond when it's first issued, rather than in the secondary market.** The price is generally fair, and the sales commission on newly issued bonds is paid by the issuer.

**Avoid bonds that might get called.** Before you buy a bond, ask your broker or financial planner if the bond is likely to be called. If so, pick another one.

**Match your bond's maturity to your investment time horizon.** In this way you can hold the bond to maturity and avoid having to sell in the secondary market, where you don't always get a fair price.

**Stick to large issues.** If you think you might have to sell before maturity and are buying a corporate bond, make sure you buy a bond issued by a large corporation—the secondary market is generally more active for them.

**When in doubt, go Treasury!** If you're still unsure, it's better to be safe than sorry—buy a Treasury bond.

---

pay more than the call price for a bond, because they know it could be called away from them for that price at anytime. Before moving on, let's make sure you understand the pros and cons of bonds. Table 14.2 lists the benefits and dangers of bonds, while Checklist 14.1 looks at picking a good bond.

## What Bond Valuation Relationships Mean to the Investor

Several important points can be gleaned from the discussion of bond valuation relationships. You know that bond prices can fluctuate dramatically and that interest rates drive these changes. In addition, you know that there's an inverse relationship between interest rates and bond prices: When interest rates go up, bond prices go down. Conversely, when interest rates go down, bond prices go up. Given this inverse relationship between interest rates and bond prices:

> **STOP & THINK** If you're looking for a safe bond, it's hard to beat a Treasury. Sure, they fluctuate when interest rates go up and down just like any other bond, but there is no question about the interest and principal payments being made on time. Treasury bonds are noncallable (at least for the first 25 years), won't be downgraded or default, and are liquid. On top of that, you can buy them directly from the Federal Reserve and avoid brokerage commissions.

▮ If you expect interest rates to go up (and, therefore, bond prices to fall), you'd want to mute the inverse relationship by purchasing very short-term bonds. Although there still may be some price fluctuation, it'll be minor.

▮ If you expect interest rates to go down, and therefore bond prices to rise, you'd want to amplify this relationship as much as possible by purchasing bonds with very long maturities that aren't callable. In this case, the bonds will fluctuate as much as possible, and if interest rates go down, the price of the bonds will rise.

## Preferred Stock—An Alternative to Bonds

**Preferred stock** is often referred to as a hybrid security because it has many of the characteristics of both common stock and bonds. From the investor's point of view,

**Preferred Stock**
Stock that offers no ownership or voting rights and generally pays fixed dividends. The dividends on preferred stock are paid out before dividends on common stock can be issued.

**4** Compare preferred stock to bonds as an investment option.

preferred stock is probably closer to bonds. On the one hand, preferred stock is similar to common stock in that it has no fixed maturity date and not paying its dividends won't bring on bankruptcy. On the other hand, preferred stock is similar to bonds in that its dividends are of a fixed size and are paid before common stock dividends are paid. A share of preferred stock is also similar to a bond in that it doesn't carry voting rights.

The size of the preferred stock dividend is generally fixed as a dollar amount or as a percentage of the stock's par value. Because these dividends are fixed, preferred stockholders don't share in profits but are limited to their stated annual dividend. Just as with a bond, if the firm has a great year and earns lots of money, the preferred stock dividend doesn't change.

## Features and Characteristics of Preferred Stock

To gain a better understanding of preferred stock, let's take a moment to look at some of its features and characteristics.

**Multiple Issues**   A firm can issue more than one issue of preferred stock, each with a different set dividend. In fact, some firms have well over 10 different issues of preferred stock outstanding.

**Cumulative Feature**
A feature of preferred stock that requires all past unpaid preferred stock dividends to have been paid before any common stock dividends can be declared.

**Cumulative Feature**   Most preferred stock carries a **cumulative feature**, which requires that all past unpaid preferred stock dividends be paid before any common stock dividends are declared. This feature provides the preferred stock investor with some degree of protection, because otherwise there'd be no reason why preferred stock dividends wouldn't be omitted or passed when common stock dividends are passed.

**Adjustable-Rate Preferred Stock**
Preferred stock on which the quarterly dividends fluctuate with the market interest rate.

**Adjustable Rate**   In the early 1980s, **adjustable-rate preferred stock** was introduced to provide investors with some protection against wide swings in the value of preferred stock that resulted from interest rate swings. With adjustable-rate preferred stock, the amount of quarterly dividends fluctuates with interest rates under a formula that ties the dividend payment to a market interest rate. As a result, when interest rates rise, rather than the value of the preferred stock dropping, the preferred stock's dividend rises and the value of the preferred stock stays relatively constant.

**Convertible Preferred Stock**
Preferred stock that the holder can exchange for a predetermined number of shares of common stock.

**Convertibility**   Some preferred stock is also **convertible preferred stock**, which means that its holder can, at any time, exchange it for a predetermined number of shares of common stock. The trade-off associated with convertible preferred stock is that the convertibility feature may allow the preferred stockholder to participate in the company's capital gains, but the preferred stock has a lower dividend associated with it than regular preferred stock.

**Callability**   Much of the preferred stock outstanding is callable. Just as with bonds, if interest rates drop, there's a good chance that the preferred stock will be called away by the issuing firm.

## Valuation of Preferred Stock

When you buy a share of preferred stock, you get a steady stream of dividends that go on forever, because preferred stock never matures. Thus, *the value of a share of preferred stock is simply the present value of the perpetual stream of constant dividends that the pre-ferred stockholder receives.* As such, the value of a share of preferred stock can be written as follows:

$$\frac{\text{value of}}{\text{preferred stock}} = \frac{\text{present value of the perpetual}}{\text{stream of constant dividends}}$$

Because preferred stock dividends go on forever, they constitute a perpetuity (remember this term from Chapter 3). The calculation of their present value can be reduced to

$$\frac{\text{value of}}{\text{preferred stock}} = \frac{\text{annual preferred stock dividend}}{\text{required rate of return}}$$

When interest rates rise (causing your required rate of return to rise), the value of a share of preferred stock declines. Conversely, when interest rates decline (causing your required rate of return to drop), the value of a share of preferred stock rises. This is the primary valuation relationship in valuing preferred stock and, as we just saw, in valuing bonds.

Let's look at an example. If the Gap has an issue of preferred stock outstanding with an annual dividend of $4, and given the level of risk on this issue, investors demand a required rate of return of 10 percent on this preferred stock, its value would be

$$\frac{\text{value of}}{\text{preferred stock}} = \frac{\$4}{0.10} = \$40$$

As you can see, if the required rate of return on this preferred stock dropped to 8 per-cent, its value would climb to $4/0.08, or $50. Thus, as market interest rates rise and fall (causing investors' required rates of return to rise and fall), the value of preferred stock moves in an opposite manner.

## Risks Associated with Preferred Stock

We've said that preferred stock is a hybrid between bonds and common stock. Unfortunately, when it comes to advantages and disadvantages for the investor, it's also a hybrid, taking disadvantages from both common stock and bonds but advan-tages from neither. The problems with preferred stock for the individual investor include the following:

▌ If interest rates rise, the value of the preferred stock drops.
▌ If interest rates drop, the value of the preferred stock rises and the preferred stock is called away from the investor (remember, most preferred stock is callable).
▌ The investor doesn't participate in the capital gains that common stockholders receive.
▌ The investor doesn't have the safety of bond interest payments, because preferred stock dividends can be passed without the risk of bankruptcy.

Given all these drawbacks and very few advantages, you may be wondering who buys preferred stock. The answer is, other corporations, because corporations receive a tax break on the dividend income from preferred stock.

If you do decide to invest in preferred stock, you'll want to pay attention to the preferred stock's rating. Just like bonds, preferred stocks are rated by Moody's and Standard and Poor's. The majority of preferred stock falls into the medium-grade levels. Just as you'd expect from **Principle 1: The Risk–Return Trade-Off**, the lower the preferred stock's rating and, therefore, the riskier the preferred stock, the higher the expected return.

## Investing in Real Estate

Since the end of World War II, real estate investments have created more fortunes than almost any other investment. Unfortunately, since the late 1980s, those same real estate investments have also destroyed quite a few fortunes. Still, real estate remains a popular investment, particularly for the very wealthy.

Most American households—in fact, about two-thirds—own their own homes, and for them, it's the biggest investment they're likely to make. In fact, as we saw in Chapter 8, housing costs take up over 26 percent of after-tax income. The question now becomes, Do you want to go beyond this personal investment and make an additional investment in real estate?

First, let's discuss what types of investments in real estate you might consider. They can be categorized as direct or indirect. With a direct investment, you directly own the property. This type of investment might include a vacation home or commercial property—an apartment building or undeveloped land. With an indirect investment, you're an investor in a group that owns the property and has hired a professional to manage it. Indirect investments include partnerships that buy and manage property, called real estate syndicates, and investment companies that pool the money of many investors and invest in real estate, called real estate investment trusts, or REITs.

### Direct Investments

Vacation homes are the most popular of all the direct real estate investments. However, since 1987 their investment appeal has suffered severely because of a change in the tax laws that now views a vacation home as a second home only if you don't rent it out for more than 14 days per year. The significance of this change is that only if your vacation home is viewed as a second home can you deduct your mortgage interest and taxes when you compute your income taxes.

If you rent your vacation home for more than 14 days per year, which many investors do, it's considered rental property, and your deductions are determined by how the property is managed and your income. In the best case, your income will cover your expenses, providing you with a home rent-free during vacations, but this generally isn't the case. Because of the complexity surrounding the tax benefits of a vacation home, you really need the help of a tax accountant or financial planner to analyze a vacation home before you invest. Even then, you should realize that much of your return is likely to depend on future price appreciation. The bottom line is that if you buy a vacation home, it should be bought for pleasure, not investment.

Commercial property, such as apartment buildings, duplexes, and office buildings, are also best left to professionals who specialize in the management of such investments. It's simply too active an investment for most individuals. Not only does management take a good deal of sophistication, but evaluating a price for commercial property is complicated. This is another area the individual investor should avoid. Fortunately, there are enough good investment opportunities in stocks and bonds to make passing on real estate relatively painless.

Investing in undeveloped land, although popular among very rich and sophisticated investors, is risky, and because the land is undeveloped, it doesn't produce any cash flow. In fact, because you have to pay taxes on the undeveloped land, it produces a cash outflow while you're holding it. Obviously, the purpose of buying undeveloped land is to have it rise in value and then sell it. However, developing the land to the point where it climbs in price can cost a lot of money. Moreover, there's no guarantee that the land will rise in price. As a result, this investment too is better left to the experts.

## Indirect Investments

Indirect investments in real estate, because you're working directly with professional managers, are better suited for the individual investor. Unfortunately, the appeal of real estate syndicates was severely dampened as a result of tax reform in the late 1980s. Again, evaluating how attractive an investment a real estate syndicate actually is can be quite difficult. So this is another investment alternative that should be left to the experts.

The most attractive real estate alternative is the real estate investment trust, or REIT. Because this type of investment is akin to a mutual fund that specializes in real estate investments, we'll hold off discussion until mutual funds are presented in Chapter 15.

## Investing in Real Estate: The Bottom Line

Without question, the major draw for investing in real estate is the income the property can generate coupled with the opportunity for capital gains. Unfortunately, the tax advantages that helped produce real estate fortunes in the past are largely gone or are on the way out. In addition, direct investments in real estate are very active forms of investing, in which time, energy, and knowledge are all important ingredients. Why work that hard when you don't have to?

Other drawbacks to investing in real estate include illiquidity. That is, if you do have to sell your property holdings, it may take months to find a buyer, and there's no guarantee that you'll actually get what you feel is a fair price. In addition, overbuilding in some areas has actually resulted in a decline of property prices. For example, Southern California has seen dramatic drops in property values in recent years. The bottom line is that real estate investment is not well suited to the novice investor.

## Investing (Speculating) in Gold, Silver, Gems, and Collectibles

Know why you shouldn't *invest* in gold, silver, gems, or collectibles.

Don't do it! Putting your money in gold, silver, platinum, precious stones, and the like is speculation. When we differentiated between investing and speculating in Chapter 11, we said that with investing, the value of your asset is determined by what return it earns, not merely by whether that asset is a fashionable one to own or not. If an asset doesn't generate a return, its value is determined by supply and demand, and putting money in it is speculating.

Gold, silver, platinum, diamonds, rubies, and collectibles are perfect examples of speculation. Look at gold. Since 1982 it's been selling for between $270 and $500— most recently (mid-2002) at the low end of this price range. Still, on late-night infomercials across the nation you'll still see hucksters proclaiming gold as "the place for your savings." Don't buy into their sales pitch—it's simply another form of speculation.

Collectibles deserve a bit more discussion because as entertainment, they're a perfectly fine purchase, but they shouldn't be confused with investments. Again, they involve speculation, not investment. Stamps, coins, comic books, and baseball cards, for example, are worth more in the future only if someone's willing to pay more for them. Their value depends entirely on supply and demand, and it doesn't always go up, as the baseball card "crash" in the early 1990s demonstrates.

Does this mean you should avoid collectibles? Yes, if you're looking to them as an investment. Remember, investment is quite a bit duller and more certain than speculation, but when you're dealing with your future financial security, dull and certain aren't bad things. If you want to spend your money on collectibles for entertainment purposes, go ahead. They can be fun, but don't expect them to provide for your financial future. I (the author), for example, collect old *Mad* magazines. There's no question that their price may go down, but to me, that's not a concern ("What, me worry?"), because they aren't an investment and aren't intended to be sold.

## SUMMARY

Why might you consider investing in bonds? There are several reasons. Bonds reduce risk through diversification, produce steady current income, and if held to maturity, can be a safe investment.

When you invest in a bond and hold it until it matures, your return is based on two things: (1) semiannual or annual interest payments and (2) the return of the par value or principal. The danger is that the bond issuer will not have the funds to make these payments. There are two measures of return on a bond: current yield and yield to maturity. The current yield on a bond refers to the ratio of the annual interest payment to the bond's market price. The yield to maturity is the true yield or return the bondholder receives if the bond is held to maturity.

Thousands of bonds outstanding have been issued by corporations, the U.S. government and its agencies, states, and localities. There are also a number of special situation bonds, including zero coupon bonds and junk bonds.

The value of a bond is simply the present value of the stream of interest payments plus the present value of the repayment of the bond's par value at maturity. There's an inverse relationship between the value of a bond and the investors' required rate of return. Thus, when the required rate of return goes up, the value of the bond drops, and when the investor's required rate of return goes down, the value of the bond increases.

Preferred stock is a security with no fixed maturity date and with dividends that are generally set in amount and don't fluctuate. Just as with bonds, a firm can issue more than one series or class of preferred stock, each with unique characteristics. In addition, most preferred stock carries a cumulative feature, which requires that all past unpaid preferred stock dividends be paid before any common stock dividends are declared.

Real estate investments can be categorized as either direct or indirect. With a direct investment, you directly own the property. With an indirect investment, you're an investor in a group that owns the property and has hired a professional to manage it. These are probably investments best left to the professional.

Gold, silver, platinum, diamonds, rubies, and collectibles are perfect examples of speculation, and should be avoided. As such, you should only consider purchasing them if you aren't concerned about what might happen to their price in the future, because they aren't an investment.

# REVIEW QUESTIONS

1. What are three reasons investors should consider adding bonds to their portfolios?

2. Compared to stocks, why are bonds generally considered to be relatively safe investments?

3. What is an indenture and why is it an important document for bond investors?

4. Why do firms issue bonds with call provisions? How do firms make callable bonds more attractive to investors? How does the issuer pay for called bonds?

5. Why are government bonds considered risk free? Describe the possibility of default risk associated with Treasury bonds.

6. Compare Treasury bills, notes, and bonds in terms of maturity and yield.

7. What is a pass-through certificate, and how is a pass-through both similar to and different from a Treasury security? Give an example of an agency that issues pass-throughs.

8. Describe a Treasury inflation-indexed bond. Who should consider these bonds for an investment portfolio?

9. What advantages do I bonds offer investors? At purchase, how do I bonds differ from EE bonds?

10. What types of entities issue municipal bonds? What significant feature of municipal bonds attracts investors? Given this feature, who should consider investing in municipal bonds?

11. Of the two types of municipal bonds, which type has the greater default risk? Why?

12. What is a zero coupon bond? Give an example of when the use of zero coupon bonds might be appropriate in an investment portfolio. Do you think these types of bonds should be owned in taxable or tax-deferred accounts?

13. What potential risks do investors face when they invest in junk bonds? How are investors compensated for these risks? What rating would you expect to see a junk bond carry?

14. Explain the difference between current yield and yield to maturity. Which is a more accurate measure of the return an investor will receive?

15. An investor's required rate of return is important when valuing a bond. What two factors can cause an investor's required rate of return to change?

16. Describe the relationship between interest rates and bond values. If investors' required rate of return decreases, what should happen to the value of bonds? Would this bond be purchased at a premium or discount? How did you make this determination?

17. What features do preferred stock shares offer investors? What feature, similar to a bond, should cause investors to demand a higher dividend yield?

18. Describe the differences between direct and indirect real estate investments.

19. Provide five examples of speculation. What distinguishes these "investments" from stocks, bonds, and real estate?

# PROBLEMS AND ACTIVITIES

1. Suppose that you are interested in purchasing a bond issued by the VPI Corporation. The bond is quoted in the *Wall Street Journal* as selling for 88.375. How much will you pay for the bond if you purchase it at the quoted price? Assuming you hold the bond until maturity, how much will you receive at that time?

2. Inflation-indexed bonds pay investors a fixed interest rate; however, the principal is adjusted based on the consumer price index. The semiannual interest payments are based on the inflation-adjusted principal. Answer the following questions assuming that an inflation-indexed bond, currently selling for $1,000, carries a coupon interest rate of 4 percent:

   a. How much will you receive for your first interest payment, if you buy this bond, assuming no interest adjustment to principal during this time period?

   b. If there's a 1-percent increase in inflation, what will be the new par value of the bond?

   c. What is your new semiannual interest payment?

   d. What is the principal worth, at maturity, assuming a 2.5-percent annual inflation rate and 10-year duration?

3. How much will a $500 EE savings bond cost when you initially purchase it? Assuming the bond earns 4.10 percent annually, approximately how long will it take for the bond to reach its stated face value?

4. An investor is considering purchasing a bond with a 5.50-percent coupon interest rate, a par value of $1,000, and a market price of $927.50. The bond will mature in 9 years. Based on this information, answer the following questions:

   a. What is the bond's current yield?

   b. Calculate the bond's approximate yield to maturity using the formula.

   c. What is the bond's yield to maturity using a financial calculator?

5. Three friends, Jodie, Natalie, and Neil, have asked you to determine the equivalent taxable yield on a municipal bond. The bond's current yield is 3.75 percent with 5 years left until maturity. Jodie is in the 15-percent marginal tax bracket, Natalie is in the 27-percent bracket, and Neil is in the 35-percent bracket. Calculate the equivalent taxable yield for your three friends. Assuming a similar AAA corporate bond yields 4 percent, which of your friends should purchase the municipal bond?

6. A highly rated corporate bond with 5 years left until maturity was recently quoted as selling for $103\frac{1}{2}$. The bond's par value is $1,000, and its initial interest rate was 6.5 percent. If this bond pays interest every 6 months, and it has been 4 months since interest was last paid, how much would you be required to pay for the bond?

7. An XYZ $5\frac{1}{2}$ 12 bond with a par value of $1,000 recently had an asked price of $95\frac{5}{8}$ and bid price of $95\frac{3}{8}$. Calculate the following:

   a. When will the bond mature?

   b. How much would you have to pay to purchase this bond?

   c. If you owned the bond, how much would someone have to pay to buy it from you?

   d. What is the current yield, assuming a closing price of $95\frac{1}{2}$?

8. If the par value of a Treasury bond you're interested in purchasing is $10,000, how much would you pay if the ask price on the bond was 99:31?

9. Using Appendices E and C, calculate the value of the following bonds:

| Par Value | Interest Rate | Required Rate of Return | Years to Maturity |
|---|---|---|---|
| $1,000 | 8% | 8% | 10 |
| $1,000 | 8% | 12% | 10 |
| $1,000 | 8% | 7% | 10 |

10. What is the value of a preferred stock that pays an annual dividend of $3.50 when the required rate of return is 8.5 percent? What is the value when the required rate of return changes to 6 percent and 11.5 percent, respectively?

## SUGGESTED PROJECTS

1. Connect to the Federal Reserve through the Internet (**www.federalreserve.gov**) and locate information about the government's Treasury Direct program. Pay particular attention to the procedures for buying and selling inflation-indexed bonds. Write a brief report explaining how often inflation-indexed bonds are sold and what the minimum investment is for individuals. In your report discuss the advantages and disadvantages of using Treasury Direct rather than a brokerage firm.

2. Think about the advantages offered by municipal bonds. In terms of marginal tax rates, what type of investor should consider investing in municipal bonds? Is there an advantage to purchasing municipal bonds issued by the state in which you live? If yes, what is that advantage?

3. Your wealthy uncle has asked you to help him value the bonds in his portfolio. Through the years he has observed that some bonds sell well below or well above stated par values. He has asked your assistance in clarifying how to value a bond. What does your uncle need to provide you before you can begin to value a bond using the formulas provided in the text? If your uncle is worried about losing money in bonds, what rules can he use to reduce his risks? (Hint: Think about bond maturities and the relationship between interest rates and bond prices.)

4. Over the years you may have received U.S. savings bonds as gifts. If you don't know if you have

bonds in your own name ask your relatives if you have been given any EE savings bonds. Once you've accumulated your bonds, visit the Bureau of the Public Debt on the Web at **www.publicdebt. treas.gov/sav/sav.htm**. Use the information provided to find out how much your bonds are worth, how much interest you are earning, and when your bonds will mature.

5. After reading this chapter, a classmate has come to you confidentially after class to discuss making some money trading bonds based on an interest rate projection formula she learned in economics class. She tells you that it is easy to make money whenever interest rates fall because bond prices always move in the opposite direction of interest rates. Do you think that your classmate is correct in her thinking? Using Principle 5 discuss why it's hard to find exceptionally profitable trading opportunities.

6. Until recently, investors purchased bonds almost entirely for income. Over the past 20 years investors have witnessed increased bond price volatility and the advent of junk bonds. Assume that you were going to advise a favorite relative about picking a good bond. Use as many of this chapter's concepts to put together a

discussion list to share with your relative. (List at least five points.)

7. Take a poll of friends, family, and work colleagues using the following three questions:

a. Do you think that real estate is a safer investment than bonds?

b. Do you think of your house as an investment?

c. Do you think of your jewelry as an investment?

Write a brief summary of your findings, paying close attention to gender and age differences in the way people responded.

8. Provide three or four examples of collectibles. For each tell whether you agree with the rule that "collectibles are a form of speculation and should be avoided." Explain your answer. Under what circumstances should someone consider purchasing speculative investments?

9. Applying what you have learned about future value, write a short essay explaining why the current market value (CMV) of a long-term bond is more volatile than the CMV of a shorter duration bond. To illustrate your point, present a hypothetical example of each valuation showing a 2-percent increase and decrease in current interest rates.

# Discussion Case 1

While waiting for a plane recently you had the opportunity to meet Miguel, a recent college graduate. Once Miguel heard that you knew something about investing he immediately began to ask you questions about bonds. Miguel indicated that from what he had heard from his friends, the stock market was overvalued and that bonds were a safer place to invest. Miguel admitted that he really didn't know much about either stocks or bonds but that he hoped to start saving so that he could purchase a house in the next five years. Miguel also mentioned that he had heard about preferred stock and real estate as alternatives to bonds. His roommate recommended that he buy a preferred stock that paid a $4.50 annual dividend or purchase farmland 13 miles out of town. Answer the following questions in a way that will help Miguel learn about investment concepts.

## Questions

1. Make a list of at least four advantages of investing in bonds.

2. Make a list of at least five dangers involved with investing in bonds.

3. If Miguel thought that interest rates were going to increase, what type of bond should he purchase? Why?

4. Assuming that Miguel wanted to take the greatest amount of risk in betting against a rise in interest rates, what investment strategy should he use?

5. Develop a checklist of rules that Miguel should use when purchasing a bond.

6. Explain to Miguel why he might want to consider investing in preferred stock rather than bonds.

7. What is the fair market value of the preferred stock that Miguel is considering purchasing if his required rate of return is 8 percent?

8. If Miguel really wanted to purchase real estate to meet his objective, would a direct or indirect real estate investment be more appropriate for him? Explain your answer.

9. Describe for Miguel how liquidity issues can impact the value of a real estate investment.

10. Should Miguel consider investing in gold to meet his objectives? Why or why not?

# Money Matters

## A BONDING EXPERIENCE

**Because you don't have to pay tax on the earnings of Series EE Savings Bonds until you cash them, they can serve as a tax-deferred account for any funds that you need to keep liquid.** *Consider them an alternative to bank savings accounts for money you don't wish to expose to any risk of loss of principal.*

**Be aware of the potential downside of pass-through certificates.** *Because they are a pool of mortgages, homeowners' reactions to interest rates determine their outcome. If interest rates fall, a number of mortgages will be refinanced, and you will start getting your principal back in large chunks. Normally the older the mortgage pool, the greater the principal return. This means you must deal with some reinvestment risk throughout the life of the pool rather than just at a future maturity date. In other words, where will you put the return of principal in a falling interest rate environment?*

**The tax-free nature of municipal bonds may not be truly beneficial to everyone.** *Compute the equivalent taxable return for your tax bracket before you choose them. If you are in a low bracket, you may find that you can make enough with taxable alternatives to pay the taxes and still come out ahead. If you are attempting to avoid state income tax, buy municipals for your state of residence. Keep in mind that although dividends are income tax free, capital gains are not.*

**If you are relying on a steady income flow from bonds, make sure they are not callable and that you hold them to maturity.** *Laddering the maturity of bonds will help stabilize income and reduce the amount of funds exposed to reinvestment risk at any one time. Liquid funds are available at each maturity, so selling a bond to get money for other needs is seldom necessary.*

**Even if you are an aggressive investor, don't discount the value of holding some bonds for diversification.** *They may be boring when the market is riding high, but you'll appreciate them when they slow the downward spiral of your portfolio.*

**Owning a bond mutual fund is not the same as holding individual bonds.** *In a fund, the average maturity and manager's trading activity determine the impact of price volatility when interest rates change. If you hold individual bonds to maturity, price volatility is not a factor you must deal with.*

# Discussion Case 2

About six months ago, Jinnie inherited a portfolio that included a number of bonds. Jinnie knows very little about investing in general and practically nothing about bonds specifically. She put together the following chart for your review. All Jinnie knows for sure is that she now owns seven bonds, ranging in maturity from 3 to 20 years. The following chart indicates the bond, its Standard & Poor's rating, its maturity, and current yield.

**Bond Rating Chart**

| Bond | Standard & Poor's Rating | Years to Maturity | Current Yield |
|---|---|---|---|
| ABC Corp. | AAA | 3 | 9.00% |
| XYX Industries | AA | 5 | 8.25% |
| INTL Limited | A | 7 | 7.00% |
| MED Corp. | BBB | 10 | 9.00% |
| SPEC Inc. | BBB | 12 | 7.00% |
| LAM Corp. | CCC, CC | 15 | 10.00% |
| BAD Inc. | C | 20 | 11.00% |

## Questions

1. After a cursory review of the yields, does anything stand out that should cause Jinnie to worry?

2. In terms of bond maturity dates, what should an investor expect? What is happening in this example?

3. In terms of Standard & Poor's ratings, are the differences in yields reasonable?

4. Using your responses from questions 2 and 3, is Jinnie being adequately compensated for the risk she is taking?

5. What is the minimum interest rate differential that Jinnie should expect between an AAA-rated bond and a BBB-rated bond? Is this the case in the example?

6. If interest rates were to increase by 1 percent or 2 percent, which of the bonds would be least affected? Why?

7. If Jinnie asked for a recommendation on which bonds to sell and which to buy more of what would you recommend? If you purchase more of one particular issue, even if it offers the best risk and duration adjusted return, what other types of risks could you expose Jinnie to? (Hint: Review the types of risks found in Chapter 11.)

8. Since Jinnie does not plan to use these funds for many years, would Series EE savings bonds or I bonds offer any advantage as an investment alternative?

---

Visit our Web site for additional case problems, interactive exercises, and practice quizzes for this chapter—**www.prenhall.com/keown**.

# 15 Mutual Funds: An Easy Way to Diversify

## Learning Objectives

**Weigh** the advantages and disadvantages of investing in mutual funds.

*1*

**Differentiate** between types of mutual funds and investment trusts.

*2*

**Classify** mutual funds according to objectives.

*3*

**Select** a mutual fund that's right for you.

*4*

**Calculate** mutual fund returns.

*5*

I t's been a long and unusual road to the top for Scott Adams. He worked at Crocker Bank in San Francisco from 1979 to 1986 before moving on to Pacific Bell. At Pacific Bell he was earning about $70,000 and working in cubicle 4S700R when he was fired on June 30, 1995—"budget constraints" was the reason given. For most people, getting laid off from a high-paying job would have been devastating. But for Adams, creator of the Dilbert comic strip, his job had become a social release and more a source of material than of income.

He began drawing his comic strip about Dilbert, a mouthless engineer with a perpetually bent necktie, and company back in 1989. Today, *Dilbert* appears in more than 1,200 newspapers in 29 countries. Adams's Dilbert books ride the top of the best-sellers list, and his speaking fee is now up to $10,000 a speech (he gives about 35 per year). In short, he's doing a lot better than he was at Pacific Bell, although he won't reveal his actual earnings because, as he says, "my family might expect better gifts from me."

What does Adams do with all his money? He invests it in mutual funds. That might not be what you'd expect from a guy who's used his cartoon to make fun of mutual funds. In one comic strip, he had Dilbert consulting with a financial advisor who was pushing his firm's "churn 'n' burn" family of mutual funds. "We'll turn your worthless equity into valuable broker-age fees in just three days!" the advisor raved.

In another strip, he had Dogbert, Dilbert's potato-shaped dog and companion, set himself up as a financial consultant and announce that "I'll tell all my clients to invest in the 'Dogbert Deferred Earnings Fund.'" "Isn't that a conflict of interests?" Dilbert asks. "Only if I show interest in the client," replies Dogbert.

Adams tried picking his own stocks for a while, but decided to hand his money over to the professionals. "My years of dabbling versus the experts just showed me that they were better than me." Today he primarily invests in index funds.

Scott Adams, like so many novice investors, has found mutual funds to be an ideal way of entering and maintaining a presence in the market. There's an awful lot of comfort in let-ting a professional manager do all the work for you. As more and more investors have taken advantage of this comfort, mutual funds have seen a dramatic surge in popularity.

In fact, there are approximately 8,200 mutual funds to choose from today—up from a mere 161 in 1960. Not only has the number of mutual funds skyrocketed, but their total assets have also—to over $6.97 trillion by year-end 2000. As Figure 15.1 shows, this is an annual growth rate of 20 per-cent over the past 10 years.

**Mutual funds** aren't another category of investments. Instead, they're simply a way of holding investments like stocks and bonds. They pool your money with that of other

**Mutual Fund**
An investment fund that raises funds from investors, pools the money, and invests it in stocks, bonds, and other investments. Each investor owns a share of the fund proportionate to the amount of his or her investment.

## Figure 15.1 Mutual Fund Growth

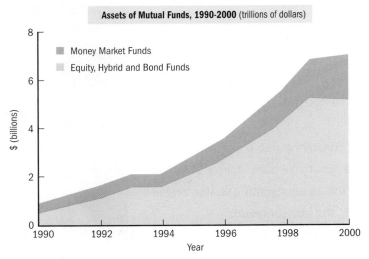

**Assets of Mutual Funds, 1990-2000** (trillions of dollars)

Source: Investment Company Institute, *2001 Fact Book*, 39th ed. (Washington, DC, 2001).

investors and invest it in stocks, bonds, and various short-term securities. Professional managers then tend this investment, making sure it grows nicely. Mutual funds let you diversify even with small investment amounts. In fact, your investment may be only $1,000 or even less, and with that investment you may own a fraction (a very small fraction) of up to 1,000 different stocks.

It's this instant diversification that makes mutual funds so popular with many investors. Remember, as **Principle 3** tells us, **Diversification Reduces Risk,** and mutual funds give smaller investors the same ability to diversify and reduce risk as big investors with lots of money have. Still, not all mutual funds are created equally—at least from the investor's perspective. This chapter will help you be careful in choosing right and avoiding the "churn 'n' burn" family of funds.

Principle
**3** Diversification
Reduces Risk

Weigh the advantages and disadvantages of investing in mutual funds.

## Why Invest in Mutual Funds?

Investing in mutual funds provides you with a bevy of benefits, especially if you're a small investor. Mutual funds level the investments playing field between large and small investors. Unfortunately, there are also drawbacks to investing in mutual funds. These disadvantages don't offset the advantages of mutual funds, particularly for small investors, but it's good to know what they are. After all, forewarned is forearmed. Let's take a look at first the advantages and then the disadvantages of investing in mutual funds.

### Advantages of Mutual Fund Investing

▌ **Diversification.** Mutual funds are an inexpensive way to diversify. For the small investor, this is an extremely important benefit. If you have only $10,000 to invest, it'd be difficult to diversify your holdings without paying exorbitant

**Table 15.1** A Listing of Sector Diversification and the 10 Largest Holdings of Vanguard's Windsor II Fund Investments, January 31, 2002

**Sector Diversification (% of Common Stocks)**

| Effective Date | 01/31/2002 Windsor II Fund Inv | 01/31/2002 S&P 500 Index | | 10 Largest Holdings as of 01/31/2002 |
|---|---|---|---|---|
| Autos and Transportation | 0.8% | 1.9% | 1 | Philip Morris Cos., Inc. |
| Consumer Discretionary and Services | 14.5% | 13.1% | 2 | Sears, Roebuck & Co. |
| Consumer Staples | 10.8% | 7.6% | 3 | Entergy Corp. |
| Financial Services | 26.2% | 19.2% | 4 | Citigroup, Inc. |
| Health Care | 4.3% | 14.3% | 5 | Bank of America Corp. |
| Integrated Oils | 8.1% | 5.2% | 6 | Allstate Corp. |
| Materials and Processing | 2.4% | 3.0% | 7 | American Electric Power Co., Inc. |
| Other Energy | 3.8% | 1.4% | 8 | J.P. Morgan Chase & Co. |
| Producer Durables | 4.3% | 3.2% | 9 | Occidental Petroleum Corp. |
| Technology | 3.4% | 17.5% | 10 | Cendant Corp. |
| Utilities | 16.1% | 8.0% | | |
| Other | 5.3% | 5.6% | | |

Source: Vanguard's Windsor II Fund, **www.vanguard.com.**

commissions. But, when you invest in a mutual fund, you're purchasing a small fraction of the mutual fund's already diversified holdings. Table 15.1 provides a description of the sector diversification along with a listing of the 10 largest holdings out of the 329 securities held by Vanguard's Windsor II Fund. As you can see, that degree of diversification simply couldn't be obtained by an individual investor with limited funds.

▌ **Professional management.** A mutual fund is an inexpensive way to gain access to professional management. Because fund managers control millions and sometimes even billions of dollars in assets and make huge securities transactions, they have access to all the best research from several brokerage houses. As a result, professional managers are in a much better position to evaluate investments, especially alternative investments. For the small or novice investor, having a professional to lead the way may be essential in taking that first step into the market.

▌ **Minimal transaction costs.** Because mutual funds trade in such large quantities, they pay far less in terms of commissions. For example, if you were trading stocks valued at less than $1,000, the brokerage fees might run up to 50 cents per share. For a mutual fund, those fees might be only 2 cents per share, because volume traders (investors who make a ton of trades) often have the power to negotiate lower fees. Over the long run, these lower transaction costs should translate into higher returns.

▌ **Liquidity.** Mutual funds are easy to buy and sell—just pick up the phone. Although many securities can be hard to trade, mutual funds never keep your money tied up while you're waiting for a transaction to take place. In effect, mutual funds are liquid enough to provide easy access to your money.

▌ **Flexibility.** Given that there are over 8,200 different mutual funds to choose from, it should come as no surprise that they cover many objectives and risk levels. As an individual investor, you should be able to spell out your desired objectives and risk level, and from that find a fund that fits your needs.

▌ **Service.** Mutual funds provide you with a number of services that just wouldn't be available if you invested individually. For example, they provide bookkeeping services, checking accounts, automatic systems to add to or withdraw from your account, and the ability to buy or sell with a single phone call. With a mutual fund, you can also automatically reinvest your dividends and capital gains.

▌ **Avoidance of bad brokers.** With a mutual fund you avoid the potentially bad advice, high sales commissions, and churning that can come with a bad broker. Remember, a broker's job is trading—brokers don't make money unless you trade. A mutual fund manager's job is to make you money.

## Disadvantages of Mutual Fund Investing

▌ **Lower-than-market performance.** Not only is there no guarantee that mutual funds will outperform the market, but also on average they underperform the market. In fact, during the 15 years to the end of 2000, 84.5 percent of U.S. actively managed mutual funds underperformed the S&P 500 index, with 77.5 percent underperforming in the past 10 years and 81.6 percent in the past 5. Simply because they have some expenses to pay—administrative and brokerage costs—whereas "the market" has no transaction costs at all—it's just a measure of how much stocks go up or down. Still, if your goal in investing is to make money, mutual funds do quite well.

▌ **Costs.** The costs associated with investing in mutual funds can vary dramatically from fund to fund; you should investigate their costs before investing. Some funds charge a sales fee that can run as high as 8.5 percent, in addition to an annual expense fee that can run up to 3 percent. You have to pick your funds wisely, or you might wind up spending your money foolishly.

▌ **Risks.** Not all mutual funds are truly safe. In an attempt to beat the competition, many funds have become specialized or segmented. When mutual funds focus on small sectors of the market, such as "health/biotechnology stocks," "Latin America," or "Asian markets: Russia," they tend not to be very well diversified. As a result, their returns are subject to unsystematic risk.

For example, over the 12-month period ending in March 2002, the "science and technology" sector funds lost on average 44.08 percent as the high-tech markets crumbled. Over the same period, the "gold-oriented fund" category climbed by 33.12 percent. A more diversified fund would have been able to smooth out these losses with gains in other industries. Remember, diversification is a huge advantage of mutual funds, but choosing a nondiversified, segmented fund turns that advantage into a disadvantage.

Principle **4** All Risk Is Not Equal

▌ **Systematic risk.** Many investors view the diversification of mutual funds as eliminating all risk. You should know better. Remember, as **Principle 4: All Risk Is Not Equal** says, you can't diversify away systematic or market risk (risk resulting from factors that affect all stocks). Thus, if there's a market crash, investing in mutual funds isn't going to protect you.

▌ **Taxes.** When you invest using a buy-and-hold strategy, you can assure yourself of long-term capital gains, and you don't pay taxes on your capital gains until you sell your stock. Mutual funds, though, tend to trade relatively frequently, and when they sell a security for a profit, you have to pay taxes on your capital gains. Mutual funds don't let you defer your taxes—they make you pay as you go.

Differentiate between types of mutual funds and investment trusts.

## Mutual Fund-Amentals

A mutual fund pools money from investors with similar financial goals. When you invest in a mutual fund, you receive shares in that fund. You're really investing in a diversified portfolio that's professionally managed according to set goals or financial

**Figure 15.2** Pooled Investments

Investors pool their funds, give them to a professional investment manager, and the professional invests those funds in a diversified portfolio.

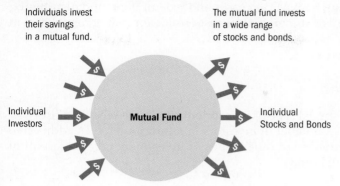

Individuals invest their savings in a mutual fund.

The mutual fund invests in a wide range of stocks and bonds.

Individual Investors

Mutual Fund

Individual Stocks and Bonds

objectives—for example, investing only in international stocks or only in high-yield bonds. These investment objectives are clearly stated by the mutual fund and then used by the fund investment advisor in deciding where to invest.

Your shares in the mutual fund give you an ownership claim to a proportion of the mutual fund's portfolio. In effect, individual investors buy mutual fund shares, the mutual fund managers take this money and buy securities, and the mutual fund shareholders then own a portion of this portfolio. This concept is illustrated in Figure 15.2. It's important to note that mutual fund shareholders don't directly own the fund's securities. Rather, they own a proportion of the overall value of the fund itself.

When you own shares in a mutual fund, you make money in three ways. First, as the value of all the securities held by the mutual fund increases, the value of each mutual fund share also goes up. Second, most mutual funds pay dividends to shareholders. If a fund receives interest or dividends from its holdings, this income is passed on to shareholders in the form of dividends.

If the fund sells a security for more than it originally paid for it, the shareholders receive this gain in the form of a capital gains distribution, generally paid annually. The shareholder, of course, can elect to have these dividends and capital gains reinvested back into the fund or receive these earnings in the form of a check from the fund.

Before looking at the different types of mutual funds, let's look at how a mutual fund is organized. The fund itself is generally set up as a corporation or trust and is owned by the fund shareholders, who elect a board of directors. The fund is then run by a management company, generally the group that initially organized the fund. Often a management company will run many different mutual funds. In fact, Fidelity and Vanguard, two of the largest management companies, each have a mutual fund for almost every goal.

Each individual fund then hires an investment advisor, generally from the management company, to oversee that particular fund. The advisor then supervises the buying and selling of securities. For this service, the advisor is generally paid a percentage of the total value of the fund on an annual basis. This management fee usually runs about one-half of 1 percent, although it can vary considerably from fund to fund. In addition to the management fee, other operating expenses bring the average total cost of operations to about 1 percent of the fund's total assets per year.

In addition to the investment advisor, the fund generally contracts with a custodian, a transfer agent, and an underwriter. The custodian acts as a third party safeguarding the fund's assets, in addition to making payments for the fund's securities and receiving money when securities are sold. Generally, the custodian is a bank not affiliated with the fund's management company. In this way the fund shareholders get an independent watchdog to safeguard their investment. The transfer agent is really a record keeper, keeping track of purchases and redemptions, and distributing dividends and capital gains. The underwriter is responsible for selling new shares in the mutual fund.

## Investment Companies

**Investment Company**
A firm that invests the pooled money of a number of investors in return for a fee.

Actually, a mutual fund is a special type of **investment company**—that is, a firm that invests the pooled money of a number of investors in return for a fee. In addition to mutual funds, there are a number of other types of investment companies, all of which closely resemble mutual funds.

### Open-End Investment Companies or Mutual Funds

**Open-End Investment Company or Mutual Fund**
A mutual fund that has the ability to issue as many shares as investors want. As investors buy more shares, the fund grows, and when they sell shares, the fund shrinks. The value of all the investments that the fund holds determines how much each share in the mutual fund is worth.

By far the most popular form of investment companies are **open-end investment companies** or **mutual funds**. These account for over 95 percent of all the money put into the various investment companies. The term "open-end" simply means that this type of investment company can issue an unlimited number of ownership shares. That is, as many people who want to invest in the fund can, simply by buying ownership shares.

A share in an open-end mutual fund is not really like a share of stock. It doesn't trade in the secondary market. In addition, you can buy ownership shares in the mutual fund only directly from the mutual fund itself. When you want out, the mutual fund will simply buy back your shares. No questions asked. There's never a worry about finding a buyer.

**Net Asset Value (NAV)**
The dollar value of a share in a mutual fund. It's the value of the fund's holdings (minus any debt) divided by the number of shares outstanding.

The price that you pay when you buy your ownership shares and the price you receive when you sell your shares is based on the **net asset value (NAV)** of the mutual fund. The net asset value is determined by taking the total market value of all securities held by the mutual fund, subtracting out any liabilities, and dividing this result by the number of shares outstanding.

$$\text{net asset value (NAV)} = \frac{\text{total market value of all securities} - \text{liabilities}}{\text{total shares outstanding}}$$

For example, if the value of all the fund's holdings is determined to be $850 million, the liabilities are $50 million, and there are 40 million shares outstanding, the net asset value would be

$$\text{net asset value (NAV)} = \frac{\$850 \text{ million} - \$50 \text{ million}}{40 \text{ million shares}} = \$20 \text{ per share}$$

**Closed-End Investment Company or Mutual Fund**
A mutual fund that can't issue new shares. These funds raise money only once by issuing a fixed number of shares, and thereafter the shares can be traded between investors. The value of each share is determined both by the value of the investments the fund holds and investor demand for shares in the fund.

In effect, one share, which represents a one-forty-millionth ownership of the fund, can be bought or sold for $20. Thus, the value of the portfolio that the mutual fund holds determines the value of each share in the mutual fund.

### Closed-End Investment Companies or Mutual Funds

A **closed-end investment company** or **mutual fund** can't issue new shares in response to investor demand. In fact, a closed-end fund has a fixed number of shares. Those shares are initially sold by the investment company at its inception, and after that they trade between investors at whatever price supply and demand dictate. In effect, a closed-end fund trades more like common stock than like a mutual fund.

Just as with common stock, there are a limited number of closed-end fund shares outstanding. When you want to buy (or sell) ownership shares in a closed-end fund that's already in operation, you have to buy (or sell) them from (to) another investor in the secondary market. Unlike open-end mutual funds, closed-end funds don't sell directly to you and certainly won't buy back your shares when you want to sell them. Because the price of ownership shares in a closed-end fund is determined by supply and demand for those shares, not by their net asset value, shares in some closed-end funds actually sell above, while others sell below, their net asset value.

In recent years closed-end funds have enjoyed a good deal of popularity, because they are the only means by which investors can participate in some markets. For example, the South Korean government holds a tight reign on the common stock of Korean companies. As a result, the only means of investing in South Korean companies is through a closed-end fund such as the Korea Fund.

## Unit Investment Trusts

A **unit investment trust** is simply a fixed pool of securities, generally municipal bonds, with each unit representing a proportionate ownership in that pool. Although very similar to a mutual fund, a unit investment trust is actually an entirely different beast. For example, unit investment trusts aren't managed. Also, instead of actively trading securities (as mutual funds), unit investment trusts have passive investments. That is, the trust purchases a fixed amount of bonds and then holds those bonds until maturity, at which time the trust is dissolved.

A unit investment trust generally works something like this: First, the investment company announces the formation of the trust, advertises, and sells the ownership shares through brokers. Generally, there's a minimum required investment of around $1,000, from which a sales commission of 3.5 to 4.9 percent is subtracted. The remaining funds are then invested in municipal bonds. The investment company's role is then collecting and passing on the interest and principal payments accruing from the bond portfolio to the investors.

The advantage of unit investment trusts comes from the diversification that they offer. Many municipal bonds are relatively risky, and as a result, diversification holds real value. Unfortunately, because most municipal bonds sell with a minimum price of $1,000, many smaller investors simply don't have the funds to allow for sufficient diversification. A unit investment trust solves this problem handily.

Although most investors hold unit investment trusts until maturity, there's a secondary market for some of the larger units. In addition, most brokers stand ready to repurchase and then resell units, although when units are sold to brokers, they generally are sold at a discount. Unit investment trusts are really aimed at the long-term investor. If your time horizon is less than 10 years, you should avoid unit investment trusts and stick with mutual funds.

## Real Estate Investment Trusts (REITs)

A **real estate investment trust**, or **REIT**, is similar to a mutual fund in that a professional manager uses the pooled funds of a number of investors to buy and sell a diversified portfolio. In this case, though, all the holdings in the portfolio deal with real estate. Shares in REITs are traded on the major exchanges, and most REITs have no predetermined life span.

From the investor's perspective, a REIT looks just like a mutual fund that specializes in real estate rather than securities. There are some technical differences, though.

**Unit Investment Trust**
A fixed pool of securities, generally municipal bonds, in which each share represents a proportionate ownership interest in that pool. The primary difference between a unit investment trust and a mutual fund is that with a unit investment trust the investments are passive. That is, the bonds are purchased and then held until maturity, at which time the trust is dissolved.

**Real Estate Investment Trust or REIT**
An investment vehicle similar to a mutual fund that specializes in real estate investments, such as shopping centers or rental property, or makes real estate loans.

For example, a REIT must collect at least 75 percent of its income from real estate and must distribute at least 95 percent of that income in the form of dividends. In addition, most REITs also are actively involved in the management of the real estate that they own.

You should note that not all REITs are the same. There are actually three different types: equity, mortgage, and a hybrid of the two. An equity REIT is one that buys property directly and, in general, also manages that property. When investors buy into an equity REIT, they're hoping that the real estate will appreciate in value. With a mortgage REIT, the investment is limited to mortgages. Investors receive interest payments only, with little chance for capital appreciation. A hybrid REIT invests in both property and mortgages, resulting in some interest and capital appreciation.

Do REITs make sense? They certainly have some diversification value in that they don't move closely with the general stock market. They're also reasonable alternatives for investors who want to invest in real estate, but don't know enough to do it alone. Moreover, although some REITs aren't that liquid, they do tend to be much more liquid than direct investments in real estate.

If you're serious about investing in a REIT, you should make sure that it's actively traded. (The more heavily traded a security is, the more liquid it is.) However, you should keep in mind that there are real risks in real estate. As you probably already know, the real estate market is highly volatile, as the crash in housing prices in California in the late 1980s and early 1990s demonstrates.

## The Costs of Mutual Funds

Although some mutual funds have no sales commission, others impose a commission when you buy into the fund or when you liquidate your holdings, some require a hefty annual management fee, and still others pass on marketing expenses to shareholders. To say the least, the costs associated with mutual funds are complicated.

### Load Versus No-Load Funds

**Load**
A sales commission charged on a mutual fund.

**Load Fund**
A mutual fund on which a load or sales commission is charged.

Mutual funds are classified as either being load or no-load funds. A **load** is simply a sales commission on your ownership shares; thus, a **load fund** is one that charges a sales commission. Load funds are actually mutual funds that are sold through brokers, financial advisors, and financial planners, who tack on the sales commissions/loads for themselves. These commissions can be quite large, typically in the 4-percent to 6-percent range, but in some cases they can run all the way up to 8.5 percent.

In general, the commission is charged when you purchase ownership shares in the fund. However, some funds charge the commission when you liquidate your holdings and sell your ownership shares back to the fund. This type of liquidation charge is referred to as a **back-end load**. With a back-end load, the up-front sales commission is eliminated and replaced with an annual charge of 1 percent, in addition to a liquidation fee of up to about 5 percent of your initial investment or the market value of your investments, whichever is smaller.

**Back-End Load**
A commission that's charged only when the investor liquidates his or her holdings.

This liquidation fee is generally set up on a sliding scale, though. For example, you might pay 5 percent if you sell the fund in the first year, 4 percent if you sell the fund in the second year, 3 percent if you sell the fund in the third year, and so forth until the fee just disappears.

**No-Load Fund**
A mutual fund that doesn't charge a commission.

A mutual fund that doesn't charge a commission on your ownership shares is referred to as a **no-load fund**. When you purchase a no-load mutual fund, you generally don't deal with a broker or advisor. Instead you deal directly with the mutual fund investment company via direct mail or through an 800 telephone number. There's no salesperson to pay, and as a result, no load.

Keeping costs down is always an excellent idea, which makes no-load funds seem the obvious choice. It's a fact that no-load funds perform just as well as load funds—they just don't have salespeople on commission. Without question, you're better off with a no-load fund.

## Management Fees and Expenses

Managing a mutual fund costs money—a lot of it. Funds run up big expenses paying the investment advisor, the custodian, the transfer agent, and the underwriter, in addition to the sales commissions on securities trades, operating expenses, legal fees, and so on. You'd be wise to keep an eye on these expenses. Be sure to check out a fund's **expense ratio**, which compares the fund's expenses to its total assets (expense ratio = expenses/assets). Typically, this ratio ranges from 0.25 to 2.0 percent, although some funds have expense ratios that run in excess of 4 percent.

You want to be sure to invest in a fund with a nice, low expense ratio. Why? Because the funds themselves don't pay the cost of their expenses—you do. Mutual funds are quick to pass their expenses on to you, with these expenses paid for by selling some of the fund's securities and thereby lowering the net asset value. The trading costs make up a good-sized portion of a typical fund's expenses and are closely related to the fund's **turnover rate**, which provides a measure of the level of the fund's trading activity. In general, the higher the turnover rate, the higher the fund's expenses. In addition, the larger the turnover, the greater will be the short- and/or long-term capital gains taxes. Remember, you pay capital gains taxes only when you sell the stock.

**Expense Ratio**
The ratio of a mutual fund's expenses to its total assets.

**Turnover Rate**
A measure of the level of a fund's trading activity, indicating what percentage of the fund's investments are turned over during the year.

## 12b-1 Fees

Mutual funds have to make themselves known to investors, so they tend to have some marketing expenses. Marketing expenses, including advertising and promotional fees, are passed on to the fund shareholders through **12b-1 fees**. These fees can run up to 1 percent annually, and they don't benefit the shareholders in the least. They serve only to allow the fund manager to pass on some of the fund's expenses. In fact, studies have found that funds that charge these fees have higher expense ratios but don't exhibit better performance. In effect, a 12b-1 fee is a hidden (you have to read through the fund's literature or ask to find it) and continuous load, as every year you pay out a portion of your investment to cover the fund's marketing costs.

Is there any value to you from the 12b-1 fee? No, no, and no. If your fund earns 10 percent before a 1 percent 12b-1 fee, after the fee it earns only 9 percent. If you invested $10,000 in this fund and left it in for 20 years, earning 10 percent you'd end up with $67,275, but earning 9 percent you'd end up with only $56,044. The 12b-1 fee just cost you $11,231. Where's the advantage to that?

**12b-1 Fee**
An annual fee, generally ranging from 0.25 to 1.00 percent of a fund's assets, that the mutual fund charges its shareholders for marketing costs.

**STOP & THINK** It's impossible to overemphasize how important a fund's expenses ratio is in determining a fund's eventual return. Of course, you shouldn't pick your fund based on the expense ratio alone, but you should eliminate all load funds and those with above-average expense ratios from consideration. Let's face it, there are enough funds to pick from so that you can be choosy.

## Types and Objectives of Mutual Funds

To make choosing mutual funds a little easier, funds are categorized according to objective. You should note that these classifications aren't always completely reliable. Fund managers get to classify their own funds. A fund manager might classify a

**L3** Classify mutual funds according to objectives.

fund as a stock fund, only to have major holdings in bonds. Hey, you don't have to believe everything you read.

When choosing a mutual fund, you'll need to first figure out what your objectives are. What do you want a mutual fund to do for you? Once you've figured that out, you have but to look, and chances are one of the many mutual funds will suit your needs perfectly—or at least claim to. Before investing, be sure that a given mutual fund actually lives up to its classification.

## Money Market Mutual Funds

**Money market mutual funds** invest in Treasury bills and other very short-term notes, usually those with maturities of under 30 days. Because these investments are of such short maturity, they're generally regarded as practically risk-free. Most require massive investments—ranging from $10,000 upward, making them out of the reach of the common investor. Money market mutual funds use the pooling principle to make these short-term investments available to the smaller investor.

You may have even seen money market funds offered at your local bank, and, in fact, many of these funds work much like interest-bearing checking accounts. For a minimum investment of usually $1,000, you tend to get interest rates that are tied to short-term interest rates and are, thus, higher than you can earn on a basic savings account, as well as limited check-writing privileges. One of the limits on this privilege is that you can't write checks for less than anywhere between $250 and $500. Money market mutual funds have proved immensely popular because they carry no loads, trade at a constant NAV of $1, and charge very minimal annual maintenance fees.

The extreme popularity of money market mutual funds has spawned several specialized variations. One is the **tax-exempt money market mutual fund**, which invests only in very short-term municipal debt. The returns on the funds are exempt from federal taxes, making them popular investments among people in higher tax brackets.

There are also money market mutual funds that invest solely in U.S. government securities in order to avoid any risk whatsoever. These funds are commonly called **government securities money market mutual funds**. They pay a rate slightly lower than traditional money market mutual funds, but in theory are safer. However, because of the very short maturities of their holdings and the extreme diversification associated with money market mutual funds, there's virtually no risk in them anyway. Thus, you don't really need to bother with government securities money market mutual funds.

## Stock Mutual Funds

Of the different types of mutual funds, **stock funds** are by far the most popular. In fact, as Figure 15.3 shows, stock funds now account for over half of all mutual funds. Don't think that these funds hold *nothing* but stocks, though. They do have some limited holdings in cash, bonds, and short-term investments (such as those in money market mutual funds). But their main emphasis is indeed firmly on stock.

Because the stock market is so varied and wide-ranging, as we've seen in earlier chapters, there are of course many different types of stock funds to choose from. When reading the following discussion of some of the more popular types of stock funds, think about which ones might be best suited for your investment needs.

**Aggressive Growth Funds**   An aggressive growth fund is one that tries to maximize capital appreciation while ignoring income. In other words, these funds tend to go for stocks whose prices could rise dramatically, even though these stocks

## Figure 15.3 How Mutual Fund Assets Are Invested (Year-End 2000)

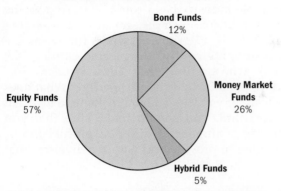

**How Mutual Fund Assets Are Invested**

Bond Funds
12%

Money Market
Funds
26%

Equity Funds
57%

Hybrid Funds
5%

*Hybrid funds include balanced asset allocation and other similar funds.

Source: Investment Company Institute, *2001 Fact Book,* 39th ed. (Washington, DC, 2001).

tend to pay very small dividends. Thus, the dividend yield on stocks in funds of this type tends to be quite low. Stocks with high P/E ratios and those of young companies that primarily trade on the OTC market are perfect for aggressive growth funds. Unfortunately, these stocks can not only gain big, but can lose big, too. As a result, the ownership shares of aggressive growth funds tend to experience wider price swings, both up and down, than do the share prices on other funds.

**Small-Company Growth Funds**  Small-company growth funds are similar to aggressive growth funds except they limit their investments to small companies that trade on the OTC market. The purpose of small-company growth funds is to uncover and invest in undiscovered companies with unlimited future growth. Again, these are very risky funds with a good deal of price volatility.

**Growth Funds**  The differences between aggressive growth funds and growth funds are pretty small, but growth funds generally pay more attention to strong firms that pay dividends. Still, these funds are looking for the potential big gainers. Growth funds are less risky than their aggressive growth cousins, though. Because of the stable dividends, their shares tend to bounce around less in price.

**Growth-and-Income Funds**  This general category of funds tries to invest in a portfolio that will provide the investor with a steady stream of income in addition to having the potential for increasing value. These funds focus on everything from well-established blue-chip companies with strong stable dividends and growth opportunities to stocks with low price-earnings ratios and above-average dividends. Because of the steady income these funds provide, the shares tend to fluctuate in price less than the market as a whole.

**Sector Funds**  A sector fund is a specialized mutual fund that generally invests at least 65 percent of its assets in securities from specific industries. For example, there are sector funds dealing with the chemicals, computer, financial services, health/biotechnology, automobile, environmental, utilities, and natural resources industries, to name just a few. Although investing in these funds is much less risky than investing in a single stock, sector funds are riskier than traditional mutual funds because they're less diversified. In fact, the idea behind a sector fund is to *limit* the degree of diversification by limiting investment to a specific industry.

**STOP &THINK** When you see a listing of which mutual funds did best last year, invariably a sector fund will appear at the top of the list. Of course, a sector fund will also appear at the bottom of the list. Their lack of diversity makes sector funds highly volatile and not for the weak of heart. If you'd rather not risk putting all your marbles—and dollars—on a single industry, sector funds aren't for you.

If that industry does well, the sector fund does well. If that industry has a rough year, so does the sector fund. For example, for the year ending March 1, 2002, Pilgrim's Russia A fund was the best-performing equity mutual fund earning 74.9 percent, whereas ProFunds Ultra Wireless Svc. Fund dropped in value by 75.9 percent. What does this mean for you? Well, if you're going to invest in a sector fund, you should make sure that you diversify your holdings, perhaps among a number of different mutual funds. Investing in a single sector fund isn't going to provide you with the diversity that makes mutual funds so advantageous.

**Index Funds** An index fund is one that simply tries to track a market index, such as the S&P 500. It does so by buying the stocks that make up the S&P 500. Much of the value of an index fund comes from its low expense ratio, which can be anywhere from 0.25 to 1.25 percent lower than those of other funds. These funds are great for those who don't want to try to "beat the market" and want the diversification of a mutual fund with costs as low as possible.

**International Funds** An international fund concentrates its investments in securities from another country. In fact, two-thirds of the fund's assets must be invested outside the United States. Some international funds focus on general world regions—the Pacific Basin, Latin America, or emerging nations. Some focus on specific countries—Japan or Canada—in an attempt to capture abnormal growth in that specific area of the world. Other international funds look for companies outside the United States that have the potential for abnormal growth, and invest directly in them regardless of location.

As with sector funds, international funds don't offer the level of diversification that traditional mutual funds offer, so putting all your money in an international fund wouldn't be wise. However, these funds are good in small doses, because they tend not to move with the U.S. stock market and thus can serve to reduce the variability of returns for all your holdings combined.

Unfortunately, these funds open you up to political and currency risks you'd never have to consider with domestic stocks. As a result, you need to understand the political and economic climate of all the countries represented in an international fund. Otherwise, you won't know what kind of risky situation you could be getting into.

## Balanced Mutual Funds

**Balanced Mutual Fund**
A mutual fund that tries to "balance" the objectives of long-term growth, income, and stability. To do this, these funds invest in a mix of common stock and bonds, as well as preferred stock in some cases.

A **balanced mutual fund** is one that holds both common stock and bonds, and in many cases, also preferred stock. The objective of these funds is to earn steady income plus some capital gains. In general, these funds are aimed at those who need steady income to live on, moderate growth in capital, and moderate stability in their investment.

As you might expect, the ratio of bonds to stocks can vary dramatically between balanced funds. Not all balanced funds are equally balanced. In fact, some balanced mutual funds specialize in international securities, hoping to cash in on high returns elsewhere around the world. Still, on the whole, balanced funds tend to be less volatile than stock mutual funds.

# In The News

Wall Street Journal Sunday July 15, 2001

## Why Indexing Is a Winning Strategy

### by Jonathan Clements

*The more I learned, the less I knew. When I first started writing about mutual funds in the late 1980s, I confidently assumed it was possible to pick market-beating stock funds. That confidence has evaporated.* (☞A)

Sure, you might be able to stack the odds in your favor by sticking with low-cost stock funds run by managers with decent track records. To do better, you need a little luck.

But who wants to rely on luck, especially when there is a surefire alternative? That alternative is market-tracking index funds. With these funds, you may give up all chance of beating the market. But you will fare far better than most other investors. Here's why:

The case for indexing rests on a piece of unassailable logic. Investors, as a group, cannot outperform the stock market, because together they are the market. In fact, once costs are figured in, investors collectively are destined to lag behind the market average.

That's where index funds get their edge. They aim to match a market average, while charging far lower expenses. Index funds don't incur hefty trading costs and they don't use the pricey services of professional stock pickers. Indeed, as disdainful Wall Streeters like to quip, any monkey can run an index fund.

"Before fees, it appears that active managers do about as well as the orangutans," says David Booth, co-chairman of Dimensional Fund Advisors in Santa Monica, California. "Once fees are considered, it appears the orangutans do better. After all, they work for bananas."

Suppose you owned an index fund that matched the Wilshire 5000's performance.

*Over the past 15 years, you would never have ranked among the top 20 percent of funds in any year. But cumulatively, your results would have been dynamite, outperforming 56 percent of diversified U.S. stock funds over the past five calendar years, 60 percent over 10 years, and 67 percent over 15 years. (In truth, you would have done even better than these*

*numbers suggest. Rotten actively managed funds tend to get liquidated or merged out of existence and, thus, these numbers reflect what statisticians call "survivorship bias.")* (☞B)

### THE BOTTOM LINE . . .

**A** The reason it's so hard to "beat the market" goes back to **Principle 5: The Curse of Competitive Investments Markets.**

**B** Indexing works equally well in the bond market. For example, over the past five calendar years, Vanguard's Total Bond Market Index Fund outperformed 95 percent of all high-quality taxable U.S. bond funds, according to Morningstar.

## Asset Allocation Funds

An **asset allocation fund** is quite similar to a balanced fund in that it invests in a mix of stocks, bonds, and money market securities. In fact, these funds have been described as balanced funds with an attitude. Asset allocation funds differ from balanced funds in that they move money between stocks and bonds in an attempt to outperform the market. That is, when the fund manager feels stocks are on the rise, a higher proportion of the fund's assets are allocated to stocks.

Asset allocation funds can be viewed as balanced funds that practice market timing. Unfortunately, the track record for market timers is less than impressive. In fact, market-timing attempts are more likely to produce additional transaction costs rather than additional returns. You should think carefully before investing in such a fund.

**Asset Allocation Fund**
A mutual fund that invests in a mix of stocks, bonds, and money market securities. Asset allocation funds differ from balanced funds in that they aggressively move money between stocks and bonds in an attempt to outperform the market. That is, when the fund manager feels stocks are on the rise, a higher proportion of the fund's assets are allocated to stocks.

## Life Cycle Funds

**Life cycle funds** are the newest type of mutual fund to hit the market. They're basically asset allocation funds that try to tailor their holdings to the investor's individual characteristics, such as age and risk tolerance. Life cycle funds go beyond the traditional strategies of growth and income and instead focus on where you are in your financial life cycle. For example, in 2002, Vanguard had four LifeStrategy funds,

**Life Cycle Funds**
Mutual funds that try to tailor their holdings to the investor's individual characteristics, such as age and risk tolerance.

each one aimed at satisfying the objectives of the four different stages of the financial life cycle we discussed in Chapter 1.

## Bond Funds

**Bond funds** appeal to investors who want to invest in bonds but don't have enough money to diversify adequately. In general, bond funds emphasize income over growth. Although they tend to be less volatile than stock funds, bond funds fluctuate in value as market interest rates move up and down.

Bond funds involve a number of differences from individual bond purchases.

▌ With an investment of as little as $1,000 you can buy into a diversified bond portfolio. Then you can add to your investment with smaller amounts whenever you wish.

▌ Bonds funds offer more liquidity than individual bonds. As we noted in Chapter 14, one of the disadvantages of investing in bonds is that they can be difficult to sell before maturity. With a bond fund, you can both buy and sell at whatever the fund's NAV is, and you don't have to worry about getting a bad price when forced to sell an individual bond at the "wrong time."

▌ With a bond fund, you're getting professional management.

▌ Like an individual bond, a bond fund produces regular income. However, with a bond fund, you can choose to receive a monthly check to help your cash flow, or you can have your money automatically reinvested in the fund to buy more bonds.

▌ If you buy bonds directly rather than through a bond fund, you won't have any mutual fund expenses to deal with.

▌ The bond fund doesn't mature, whereas individual bonds do. When bonds within the bond fund mature, they're replaced with new bonds. As a result, you're never guaranteed to receive a lump-sum payment.

If you're looking for income, a logical place to look is to bonds or to a bond fund. Whether to buy a bond or a bond fund will depend on your individual goals and needs. You'll probably look closer at a bond fund if you want to invest small amounts of money, you need to keep your investments liquid, and you'll sleep better at night knowing a professional's choosing the securities and keeping them well diversified. Conversely, if you need to know with certainty that in a specific number of years you'll get the principal back, you have a large amount to invest, and you're disciplined enough to reinvest your interest payments, then you might want to stick with individual bonds.

**STOP & THINK** The expense ratios on bond mutual funds can vary dramatically. The average expense ratio in 2001 for bond funds was 1.1 percent. However, this ratio ranged between approximately 0.18 to over 2.0 percent. Given the fact that long-term government bonds averaged a return of only about 5.3 percent from 1926 to 2001, it's extremely important to keep expenses low if you're investing in bonds. If your expenses are 2 percent and your return is only 5.3 percent, over one-third of your return is already gone.

Bond funds can be differentiated both by the type of bond that they invest in—U.S. government, municipal, or corporate—and by maturity—short term, intermediate term, or long term.

**U.S. Government Bond Funds or GNMA Bond Funds** U.S. government bond funds invest in securities issued by the federal government or its agencies. For example, U.S. Treasury bond funds specialize in Treasury securities. Obviously, there's no default risk associated with these funds. However, they do fluctuate in value as interest rates move up and down. A number of funds specialize in mortgage-backed securities issued primarily by the Government National Mortgage Association, or GNMA.

These funds hold pools of individual residential mortgages that have been pack-aged by GNMA and resold to the bond fund. This type of fund also carries interest rate risk in addition to prepayment risk—that is, the risk that as interest rates drop, the mortgages will be refinanced and prepaid. As with other bond funds, a government bond fund is aimed at those who need steady current income.

**Municipal Bond Funds**   The advantage of municipal bond funds is that the interest is generally exempt from federal taxes. Moreover, if you invest in a municipal bond fund that invests only in bonds from your state, the income may also be exempt from state taxes. In fact, if you live in New York City and invest in a fund that limits its investments to municipal bonds issued by New York City, you avoid federal, state, and local income taxes on the interest payments. Obviously, for investors in higher tax brackets, avoiding taxes is a big deal.

**Corporate Bond Funds**   Unless you haven't been paying any attention at all, you've probably guessed that corporate bond funds invest in various corporate bonds. Some corporate bond funds focus mainly on high-quality, highly rated bonds, but others, usually called high-yield corporate bond funds, focus on the much lower rated and much riskier junk bonds. As you know from **Principle 1: The Risk–Return Trade-Off**, when you take on more risk, as you do when you invest in junk bonds, your expected return is higher.

Because corporate bonds have the potential for defaulting, it's essential that you diversify if you're going to invest in them. That's where a corporate bond mutual fund comes in—it does the diversifying for you. Of course, you'll want to carry this diversification a bit further by investing in more than just bonds.

When selecting a corporate bond fund, be sure to remember that approximately two-thirds of them carry loads in the 4 to 5 percent range. Although the loads are pretty constant, the returns aren't. As interest rates go up, corporate bond funds and their NAV go down in value. As interest rates drop, corporate bond fund values rise, along with their NAV.

**Bond Funds and Their Maturities**   Different bond funds also specialize in different length maturities, with short-term (1 to 5 years in maturity), intermediate-term (5 to 10 years in maturity), and long-term (10 to 30 years in maturity) funds. We know from bond valuation relationships presented in Chapter 14 that there's an inverse relationship between interest rates and bond prices. That is, when interest rates rise, bond prices drop, and when interest rates drop, bond prices rise. We also know that when interest rates change, longer-term bonds fluctuate in price more than shorter-term bonds. As a result, the longer the bond fund's maturity, the higher its expected return, but also the greater the fluctuation in its NAV if interest rates change.

## Mutual Funds Services

Aside from the fact that you can probably find a mutual fund with objectives that almost perfectly match your investment goals, what's so special about mutual funds? A lot, actually. Diversification is probably the biggest advantage, but convenience may well be a close second. Mutual funds offer the convenience of being able to buy and sell securities at will, with reduced commissions and professional advice.

That's really just the tip of the convenience iceberg, though. Mutual funds offer myriad services for investors—services that make investing easy and even fun. Let's take a look at a few of the more popular services. As we do, think about which services would be most helpful and appealing to you.

**Automatic Investment and Withdrawal Plans**  An automatic investment plan allows you to make regular deposits directly from your bank account. For example, if you want to invest $100 on the fifteenth of each month, an automatic investment plan lets you do so without lifting a finger. Basically, all you need do is check a box on the mutual fund's account registration form and *voilà*—your $100 will find its way from your savings account to your fund account each and every month. An automatic investment plan is a way of dollar cost averaging when investing in a mutual fund. You should recall from Chapter 13 that the logic behind dollar cost averaging is that by investing the same dollar amount on a regular basis, you'll be buying more common stock when the price is lowest and less when the price is highest.

The automatic investment plan is also a good way of moving excess funds from a money market account into the stock market. For example, if you have more money than you feel you need invested in a money market account but are worried about transferring it all at once into the stock market, an automatic investment plan will let you move the funds into the market smoothly over a longer period of time.

Conversely, an automatic or systematic withdrawal plan allows you to withdraw a dollar amount or a percentage of your mutual fund account on a monthly basis. For example, if you were retired and wanted to supplement your income, you might elect to have $250 paid out to you automatically on a monthly basis. Many funds require a minimum fund balance of between $5,000 and $10,000 to participate in an automatic withdrawal plan, with a minimum withdrawal of $50 per month.

**Automatic Reinvestment of Interest, Dividends, and Capital Gains**  With a mutual fund, you have your choice of receiving interest, dividends, and capital gains payments or having them reinvested by purchasing more shares in the fund. If you're using the mutual fund as a long-term investment, you should have the distributions automatically reinvested. Reinvestment in the securities markets produces the same growth effects as compound interest—that is, you'll start earning money on your past earnings.

If you're investing in a bond and income fund, you'll get little or no capital appreciation on your holdings. Instead, most of your return will be from dividends, which are distributed back to you each year. If you don't reinvest these distributions, you won't accumulate much wealth. You'll be spending your earnings instead. Over 70 percent of all mutual fund shareholders choose to reinvest their dividends and capital gains.

**Wiring and Funds Express Options**  If you anticipate needing your funds or your returns fast, you can choose a wiring and funds express option. This option allows you to have your returns/money wired directly to your bank account. It also works the other way and allows you to invest money in the fund immediately by wiring money directly to the fund. In this way you can have your money sent and invested in the fund in the same day. This option is a bit like the automatic investment and withdrawal plan, except the transactions don't happen automatically/monthly.

**Phone Switching**  Phone switching allows you to move money from one fund to another simply by making a phone request. If you want to move some of your money from your domestic stock fund to an international stock fund, you can do it easily and, generally, cost free with just one phone call.

**Easy Establishment of Retirement Plans**  Most mutual funds provide for the easy establishment of IRS-approved tax-deferred retirement accounts, including IRA, 401(k), and Keogh plans. The fund will provide you with everything you need to establish such a plan and then handle the administrative duties. In addition, most

# In The News

Wall Street Journal Sunday July 29, 2001

## *Why Investors Cling to Managed Funds*

### by Jonathan Clements

*Index funds may have won the performance battle. But they clearly haven't won the hearts of investors.* (☞A)

Before costs, stock market investors collectively match the market average. After costs, most folks lag behind and, thus, would be better off with market-tracking index funds. Yet, if you listen to Wall Street and the business media, you would think that beating the market was commonplace.

"There's a general perception that the goal of investing is to beat the market," says Terrance Odean, a finance professor at the University of California at Davis. "If you're new to the market, what you hear about is how to pick individual stocks and how to pick actively managed funds. You don't hear a lot of people talking about index funds."

And when indexing is discussed by brokers, fund-company executives, and others on Wall Street, it is often in scathing terms. Make no mistake: These derogatory comments are entirely self-serving.

The fact is, the harder folks try to beat the market, the more Wall Street earns, as performance-hungry investors rack up hefty trading costs and pay fat mutual fund management fees. But the Street's gain is our loss. Those steep investment costs make it even less likely that we will beat the market.

Wall Street wants investors to believe they can beat the market. But let's be honest: It is an easy sales job.

"Wall Street is playing to the prejudices of investors," says Meir Statman, a finance professor at Santa Clara University in California. "It feeds into our sense of how the world works. We see the market as a game of skill rather than a game of luck. We want to believe that people who choose stocks carefully do better."

*But no matter how carefully we pick stocks and funds, most of us will still rank among the market's losers. Who will win? We all like to think we are unusually perceptive, smarter than average, and destined for success. This self-confidence infects our investment decisions. We believe that we can succeed, even as most others fail.* (☞B)

### THE BOTTOM LINE . . .

**A** Only about 12 percent of stock mutual fund assets are in index funds—that's up only 2 percent from 10 years ago.

**B** Actually, things are worse than they seem. When a mutual fund does poorly, it usually changes its name, is taken over by another fund, or just disbands. That means only the good ones survive, and the survivors have a hard time beating index funds. That's **Principle 5: The Curse of Competitive Investment Markets** at work again.

Source: Jonathan Clements, "The Case for Index Funds—Making the Market Work for You: Why Investors Cling to Managed Funds," *Wall Street Journal Sunday*, July 29, 2001: 3. Copyright (c) 2001, Dow Jones & Company, Inc. Reproduced with permission of DOW JONES & CO INC in the format Textbook via Copyright Clearance Center.

---

funds have representatives available to answer questions you might have when setting the plan up. Retirement plans are a key part of any sound personal financial plan, and getting someone else to set one up and manage it for you is a huge advantage.

**Check Writing**   Check-writing privileges associated with money market mutual funds can prove very handy when you need to use money from your investments directly for making purchases or in an emergency. As we mentioned before, there are minimum levels, generally in the $250 to $500 range, for which the checks can be written.

**Bookkeeping and Help with Taxes**   Some of the larger investment companies provide a "tax cost" service that actually calculates your taxable gains or losses when you sell shares. Because the calculation of taxes associated with buying and selling shares in a mutual fund can be enough to drive you crazy, this is a service well worth having. Unfortunately, it's also a service not offered by all mutual funds.

## Buying a Mutual Fund

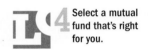
Select a mutual fund that's right for you.

Now that you know something about mutual funds, you may well be wondering how you go out and buy one. The process of buying a mutual fund involves determining your investment goals, identifying funds that meet your objectives, and evaluating those funds. Your local library and the Internet (e.g., Morningstar at **www.morningstar.com**) should hold a wealth of information to help your evaluation. Brush up on your math, though, because much of the evaluation process is going to focus on cost. As you'll see, mutual fund expenses can vary dramatically from one fund to another.

## Step 1: Determining Your Goals

The first step in buying a mutual fund involves determining exactly what your investment goals and time horizon are. In Chapters 1 and 2 we discussed identifying your goals and putting together an investment plan. We described the budgeting and planning procedure as a five-step process. Investing in mutual funds conforms to step 4. However, before you make it to step 4, you must have a clear understanding of why you're investing. Is it to provide additional income to supplement your retirement income, or is it to save for your children's education or for your own retirement 30 years from now? Do you want your investments to be tax deferred? How much risk are you comfortable with? Once you've answered these questions, you're ready to go out and find a fund.

## Step 2: Meeting Your Objectives

To identify a fund's objectives, the first place to look is in one of the mutual fund advisory publications. For example, *Morningstar Mutual Funds* (**www.morningstar.com**) provides fund analysis and classifies funds by objective and management style. The objective classification uses the categories of funds we examined earlier and is based on the wording the fund uses in its prospectus. Figure 15.4 presents an example of a Morningstar fund analysis for the Vanguard's Windsor II Fund. As you can see, the objective here is "growth and income."

It's not always safe to assume the fund's name reflects its investment strategy or objectives. What's in a name, right? In truth, the fund's name may imply an objective, but that objective may not bear much resemblance to that fund's actual investment strategy. Morningstar will usually adjust its objective classifications to reflect the fund's actual investment practices, not just its name.

Unfortunately, just knowing the fund's stated objective isn't always very helpful. As the mutual fund industry has grown, so have the number of objectives, and with growth comes confusion. For example, three funds, all investing in identical portfolios made up of high-technology, small-cap firms, could end up with three different objective categories—small company, aggressive growth, and specialty or sector (technology), depending on how they market themselves. Moreover, the different objective categories are open to misinterpretation. For example, the term "growth" can be interpreted to mean growth in capital, growth in earnings, or an investment style.

To help with this problem, Morningstar provides an investment style box, which serves as a visual tool for better understanding the fund's true investment style. Figure 15.5 shows the setup for investment style boxes for stock and bond funds. For stock funds, the horizontal axis of the investment style box covers a value-oriented style to a growth-oriented style. A value-oriented style would reflect investments in stocks that are currently undervalued in terms of price, while a growth-oriented style would indicate investments in stocks that have the potential to grow at an above average rate. A blend investment style is somewhere between. The vertical axis categorizes funds by the size of the companies in which the fund invests, from small to large.

For bond funds, the investment style categorization groups funds by maturity—short, intermediate, and long—and by credit quality or risk—high, medium, and

# Figure 15.4 Morningstar Analysis for Vanguard's Windsor II Fund

**Investment Objective:** This section contains a brief description of the fund's objective. The objective assigned to this fund by Morningstar is given in the upper right-hand corner of the report.

**Manager's History:** Identifies who is running the fund and for how long.

**Historical Performance:** Here you find historical performance for a number of periods in addition to how different indexes performed over those same periods.

**Analyst's Review:** This section presents Morningstar's analysis of the fund's prospects and performance.

**Category Rating:** The category rating is based on the fund's relative performance in one of 44 categories according to investment styles, for example, big-company growth funds, utility funds, Europe funds, and so on.

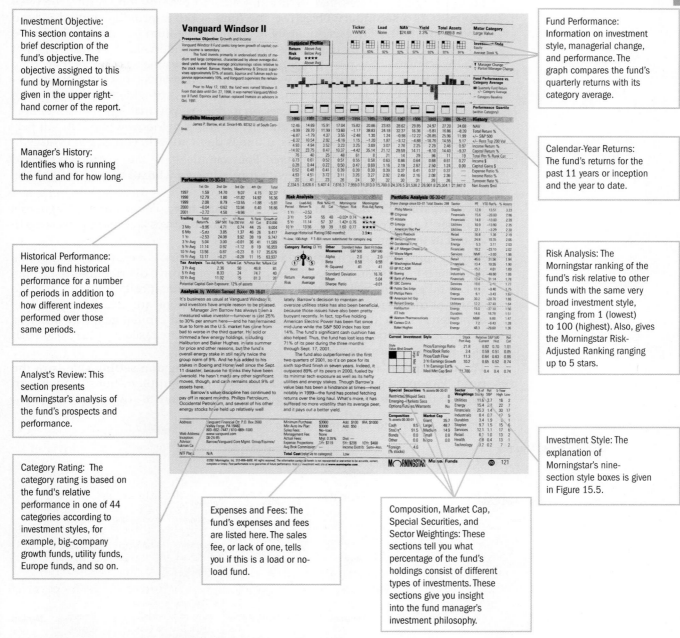

**Fund Performance:** Information on investment style, managerial change, and performance. The graph compares the fund's quarterly returns with its category average.

**Calendar-Year Returns:** The fund's returns for the past 11 years or inception and the year to date.

**Risk Analysis:** The Morningstar ranking of the fund's risk relative to other funds with the same very broad investment style, ranging from 1 (lowest) to 100 (highest). Also, gives the Morningstar Risk-Adjusted Ranking ranging up to 5 stars.

**Investment Style:** The explanation of Morningstar's nine-section style boxes is given in Figure 15.5.

**Expenses and Fees:** The fund's expenses and fees are listed here. The sales fee, or lack of one, tells you if this is a load or no-load fund.

**Composition, Market Cap, Special Securities, and Sector Weightings:** These sections tell you what percentage of the fund's holdings consist of different types of investments. These sections give you insight into the fund manager's investment philosophy.

Source: *Morningstar Mutual Funds*, 2002. Morningstar, Inc., Chicago, IL 2002. Used by permission.

low. With this information you don't need to be concerned about what a fund's objective actually means. The investment style classification should be more helpful.

Of course, you should also go directly to the source and examine the **mutual fund prospectus**, which you can get simply by calling the mutual fund and asking. Let's look at the prospectus for Vanguard's Windsor II Fund, portions of which are highlighted in the Morningstar analysis in Figure 15.4. Investment companies are required by law to offer a prospectus, which contains the following information:

**Mutual Fund Prospectus**
A description of the mutual fund, including the fund's objectives and risks, its historical performance, its expenses, the manager's history, and other information.

- **The fund's goal and investment strategy.** For example, Vanguard's Windsor II Fund prospectus states that the fund seeks "to provide long-term growth of capital." As a secondary objective, the fund seeks to provide some dividend income and that it "invests primarily in large and medium-size companies whose stocks are considered by the Fund's advisors to be undervalued." It also says that this investment strategy will most likely lead to investment in stocks that "may be below average in comparison with such fundamental factors as earnings, revenue, and book value. In addition, value stocks often provide an above-average dividend yield." The prospectus goes on to remind you that "the Fund's performance—whether before taxes or after taxes—does not indicate how it will perform in the future." In other words, if things don't go well, you've been warned.

- **The fund manager's past experience.** For example, Vanguard's Windsor II Fund follows a multiadvisor approach with four advisors who all have been with the fund since at least 1991.

- **Any investment's limitation that the fund may have.** For example, Vanguard's Windsor II Fund prospectus states that the fund "reserves the right to invest up to 20% of its assets in foreign securities."

- **Any tax considerations of importance to the investors.** For example, Vanguard's Windsor II Fund's prospectus states that "you can receive distributions of income or capital gains in cash, or you can have them automatically invested in more shares of the Fund." In either case, these distributions are taxable to you. It is important to note that distributions of dividends and capital gains are declared in December—if paid to you by the end of January—are taxed as if they had been paid to you in December."

- **The redemption and investment process for buying and selling shares in the fund.** Vanguard's Windsor II Fund has four distribution options: (1) you can reinvest the entire distribution, (2) you can reinvest only the capital gains portion

**Figure 15.5** Morningstar's Investment Style Boxes

| Equity (or Stock) Style Box | | | | |
|---|---|---|---|---|
| **Risk** | **Investment Style** | | | **Median Market Capitalization** |
| | Value | Blend | Growth | |
| Low | Large-Cap Value | Large-Cap Blend | Large-Cap Growth | Large |
| Moderate | Mid-Cap Value | Mid-Cap Blend | Mid-Cap Growth | Medium |
| High | Small-Cap Value | Small-Cap Blend | Small-Cap Growth | Small |

| Bond Style Box | | | | |
|---|---|---|---|---|
| **Risk** | **Duration** | | | **Quality** |
| | Short | Intermediate | Long | |
| Low | Short-Term High Quality | Interm-Term High Quality | Long-Term High Quality | High |
| Moderate | Short-Term Medium Quality | Interm-Term Medium Quality | Long-Term Medium Quality | Medium |
| High | Short-Term Low Quality | Interm-Term Low Quality | Long-Term Low Quality | Low |

Within the equity style box grid, nine possible combinations exist, ranging from large-cap value for the safest funds to small-cap growth for the riskiest.

Within the bond box grid, nine possible combinations exist, ranging from short duration or maturity/high quality for the safest funds to long duration or maturity/low quality for the riskiest.

Source: *Morningstar Mutual Funds*, 2002. Morningstar, Inc., Chicago, IL 2002. Used with permission.

and receive a check for the dividend distribution or vice versa, (3) you can receive a check for both the dividend and capital gains distribution, or (4) you can electronically direct them into a bank.

▮ **Services provided investors.** The prospectus should explain the services provided. For example, Vanguard's Windsor II Fund provides telephone representatives 24 hours a day, 365 days a year.

▮ **Performance over the past 10 years or since the fund has been in existence.** Most funds generally show this by demonstrating what would have happened if you had put $10,000 in the fund 10 years earlier or when the fund was formed.

▮ **Fund fees and expenses.** Information on the fund's sales and redemption charges is given. In addition, information on the management fee and fees for marketing expenses, called 12b-1 fees, are included.

▮ **The fund's annual turnover ratio.** Information is provided on how frequently the fund's investment portfolio changes or turns over. For 2001, Vanguard's Windsor II Fund turnover ratio was 33 percent.

There's also a part B to the prospectus, which can be obtained separately and contains a listing of the fund's holdings, as well as additional information on the fund management.

In assessing a fund's objective, you should pay close attention to past performance. If it's intended as a long-term investment, how has it done over the past 10 years? If it's intended to produce current income, what's it paying out in terms of its current yield?

## Step 3: Evaluating the Fund

Once you've found some funds with objectives that match your own, it's time to get picky and start evaluating them. Evaluation centers on looking closely at past performance and scrutinizing the costs associated with the funds. Although past performance doesn't necessarily predict future results, it can give you further insights into the investment philosophy and style of the fund.

In evaluating performance, be sure not to compare apples to oranges. Just as it would be inappropriate to compare a fund that has an objective of income with one that has an objective of growth, it's also inappropriate to compare any single fund to an average for all mutual funds of all categories combined. Be sure to limit comparisons to those between funds with the same objectives.

It's also important to look at longer periods of performance to see how the fund does in both market upturns and downturns. Looking at only short-term performance won't help you gauge whether the fund's overall performance is improving or deteriorating.

It's not necessarily true that funds that do well in one year will do well in the following year. For example, in 1999 ProFunds UltraOTC Svc fund rose by 229.73 percent. However, in 2000 the fund fell by 73.96 percent, and in 2001, it fell by another 23.62 percent. In picking a mutual fund, you should first focus on objectives, diversification, and keeping expenses to a minimum. After that, look at what the fund has done in the past. A fund's past volatility and investment approach tend to continue into the future. There's even some (weak) evidence of consistency in performance—winners stay winners and losers stay losers—but as ProFunds UltraOTC Svc fund shows, that's not always the case.

## Sources of Information

"So," you may be thinking, "I have a hard time finding my socks. How am I supposed to find all this stuff about mutual funds?" Start by trucking over to the library or check out what's available on the Web. There's a wealth of information available to aid you in evaluating mutual funds, and just about all of it can be found in the average library. The *Wall Street Journal* provides daily mutual fund listings and quotes. In addition, in a monthly review, the *Wall Street Journal* expands its coverage of mutual funds and presents data prepared by Lipper Analytical Services.

These data include the fund's objective, its year-to-date return, and its return over the past month, year, 3 years, 5 years, and 10 years. These returns are also ranked relative to other funds with similar objectives. In addition, the data include the maximum initial sales commission and the annual expenses for each fund. Figure 15.6 provides an example of the monthly fund listings from the *Wall Street Journal*, along with an explanation of how to read the tables.

Another good source of information is *Forbes*, which publishes an annual mutual fund survey each August. In this survey, funds are ranked for their performance in both up and down markets, and on the average P/E ratios and the average size of the stocks that they invest in. *Forbes* also provides mailing addresses and telephone numbers for all the major funds. Other special issues on mutual funds are offered by such magazines as *Consumer Reports, Business Week, Kiplinger's Personal Finance* magazine (**www.kiplinger.com/investments/funds**) and *Smart Money* (**www.smartmoney.com/intro/funds**).

Two other excellent sources of information that are available at many libraries are *Wiesenberger Investment Companies Service* and *Morningstar Mutual Funds* (**www.morningstar.com**). An example of the Morningstar listing for a stock fund was presented earlier in Figure 15.4. You'll note that the Morningstar listing contains a ton of information. Among other things, it provides information on the fund's potential capital gains exposure, which gives the investor an idea of the fund's vulnerability to taxation. It also provides information on the fund's expense ratio, turnover ratio, and performance relative to the S&P 500 and the Russell 2000, a broader-based stock index.

You'll also find a historical profile of the fund's performance, including an evaluation of its return, risk, and ranking. Morningstar awards stars to the best performers in four large fund groups—U.S. equity, international equity, taxable bond, and municipal bond—as well as a "category rating" to the top performers in 44 categories according to investment style—for example, big-company growth funds, utility funds, Europe funds, and so on. A fund can be awarded as many as five stars or a category rating of up to five, but only the top 10 percent of the funds in each group receive a top rating. For example, Vanguard's Windsor II Fund presented in Figure 15.4 received a historical rating of four stars and a category rating of three out of five.

There's an awful lot of mutual fund material available on the Web. The first place to look is the Personal Finance Navigator, which is maintained by the author of this book. It is continuously updated with new links. Perhaps the best site dedicated to mutual funds is the Morningstar site (**www.morningstar.com**). It includes a fund screener that is easy to use and covers almost all mutual funds. If you like you can pay an additional $10 per month and get access to more in-depth material—this investment provides you with much of what is available in the hard-copy guide along with search abilities. Without question, this is the place to start. Another excellent site is PersonalFund.com (**www.personalfund.com**). This site helps you calculate the impact of taxes and expenses on your investment. FundAlarm (**www.fundalarm.com**) is another excellent site. It provides commentary and insight along with help in deciding when you might consider selling a fund. Two other Web sites that focus on mutual funds and provide guidance along with insights are MaxFunds.com (**www.maxfunds.com**) and Forbes Funds (**www.forbes.com/funds**)—both are worth a visit. Finally, if you've decided to go for an index fund, the first place to visit is IndexFunds.com (**www.indexfunds.com**). Among other things,

**How to Read These Tables**

Data come from two sources. The daily Net Asset Value (NAV) and Net Change calculations are supplied by the National Association of Securities Dealers (NASD). Performance and cost data come from **Lipper Analytical Services Inc.**

Though verified, the data cannot be guaranteed by Lipper or its data sources. Double-check with funds before investing.

Performance calculations assume reinvestment of all distributions and are after subtracting annual expenses. But figures don't reflect sales charges ("loads") or redemption fees.

These expanded tables appear monthly. Other days, you'll find net asset value and the daily change and year-to-date performance.

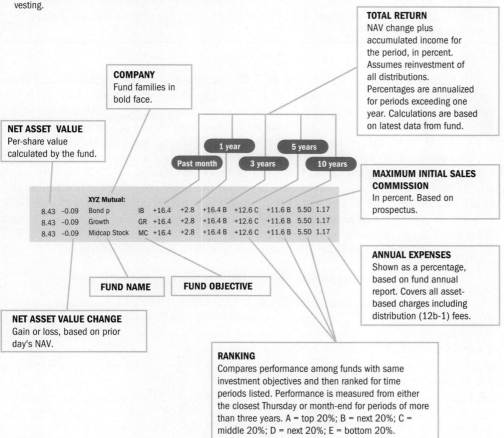

**TOTAL RETURN**
NAV change plus accumulated income for the period, in percent. Assumes reinvestment of all distributions. Percentages are annualized for periods exceeding one year. Calculations are based on latest data from fund.

**COMPANY**
Fund families in bold face.

**NET ASSET VALUE**
Per-share value calculated by the fund.

**MAXIMUM INITIAL SALES COMMISSION**
In percent. Based on prospectus.

**ANNUAL EXPENSES**
Shown as a percentage, based on fund annual report. Covers all asset-based charges including distribution (12b-1) fees.

**FUND NAME**    **FUND OBJECTIVE**

**NET ASSET VALUE CHANGE**
Gain or loss, based on prior day's NAV.

**RANKING**
Compares performance among funds with same investment objectives and then ranked for time periods listed. Performance is measured from either the closest Thursday or month-end for periods of more than three years. A = top 20%; B = next 20%; C = middle 20%; D = next 20%; E = bottom 20%.

| | | | | Past month | 1 year | 3 years | 5 years | 10 years | | |
|---|---|---|---|---|---|---|---|---|---|---|
| | | | XYZ Mutual: | | | | | | | |
| 8.43 | -0.09 | Bond p | IB | +16.4 | +2.8 | +16.4 B | +12.6 C | +11.6 B | 5.50 | 1.17 |
| 8.43 | -0.09 | Growth | GR | +16.4 | +2.8 | +16.4 B | +12.6 C | +11.6 B | 5.50 | 1.17 |
| 8.43 | -0.09 | Midcap Stock | MC | +16.4 | +2.8 | +16.4 B | +12.6 C | +11.6 B | 5.50 | 1.17 |

this site helps you track the movements of some of the alternative indexes that index funds are based on.

## Calculating Fund Returns

You've set your goals, found some mutual funds that share those goals, and narrowed down your list of funds by reading through several helpful sources of information. Now what do you do? Well, as when making any investment, you want to pick the one that's going to cost the least and return the most (see Checklist 15.1).

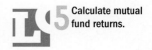

Calculate mutual fund returns.

# Checklist 15.1 ▌ Buying a Mutual Fund

In terms of costs, we've already seen the various loads, management, and other fees that can be charged to mutual funds. All we need to say is, avoid as many as you can. Morningstar and the other sources of information will help you figure out which funds charge which expenses and thus which funds to skip. Let's now take a look at returns and how you can figure out how much a mutual fund will make for you.

The return from investing in a mutual fund can be in the form of distributions of dividends, capital gains, or a change in NAV of the shares held. To qualify as an investment company and avoid being taxed on the fund's earnings, a fund must distribute a minimum of 97 percent of the interest and dividends earned and at least 90 percent of capital gains income. (Capital gains result from selling securities for more than what they were originally bought for.)

Thus, the total return from a mutual fund can be calculated as follows:

$$\text{total return} = \frac{\text{dividends distributed} + \text{capital gains distributed} + (\text{ending NAV} - \text{beginning NAV})}{\text{beginning NAV}}$$

For example, let's assume we have a fund with

| | |
|---|---|
| beginning NAV | = $19.45 |
| ending NAV | = $23.59 |
| dividends distributed | = $ 0.60 |
| capital gains distributed | = $ 0.47 |

Our return can be calculated as follows:

$$\text{total return} = \frac{\$0.60 + \$0.47 + (\$23.59 - \$19.45)}{\$19.45}$$

$$= \frac{\$0.60 + \$0.47 + \$4.14}{\$19.45}$$

$$= \frac{\$5.21}{\$19.45} = 26.79\%$$

Thus, the return was 26.79 percent.

If you automatically reinvest any distributions, your return results from both the increase in the NAV of the shares and the increased number of shares you hold. As you automatically reinvest any distributions, the number of shares that you hold increases. As a result, your return can be calculated by taking the value of your ending holdings minus your initial investment and dividing this by the value of your initial investment.

$$\text{total return} = \frac{(\text{number of ending shares} \times \text{ending price}) - (\text{number of beginning shares} \times \text{beginning price})}{(\text{number of beginning shares} \times \text{beginning price})}$$

Thus, if you initially purchase 500 shares at an NAV of $19.45 and, as a result of automatically reinvesting any distributions, you end up with 585 shares with an NAV of $23.59, your return would be

$$
\begin{aligned}
\text{total return} &= \frac{(585 \times \$23.59) - (500 \times \$19.45)}{(500 \times \$19.45)} \\
&= \frac{\$13,800.15 - \$9,725.00}{\$9,725.00} \\
&= \frac{\$4,075.15}{\$9,725.00} \\
&= 41.90\%
\end{aligned}
$$

Thus, the return would be 41.9 percent. Keep in mind, though, that these formulas don't take taxes into account.

Calculating a fund's return should help you spot funds that have been consistent winners over time and avoid those that have performed poorly. Once you've found a fund that fits your objectives and keeps expenses to a minimum, you might as well go for past winners and avoid losers. That's the message from Yale's Roger Ibbotson, who's found some evidence of strong performers over the past 3 years remaining strong performers for the following 3 years. It's also the message of New York University's Edwin Elton and Martin Gruber, who find that poor performers tend to continue to lag for the following 3 years.

**STOP & THINK** Look closely at the expenses and fees charged for managing a mutual fund before investing—their impact can be significant. Look, for example, at a mutual fund with an expense ratio of 1.3 percent (the average expense ratio for equity funds is 1.35 percent) versus one with an expense ratio of 0.2 percent. If you put $25,000 in both of these funds, each returning 10 percent compounded over the next 25 years, you'd end up with a not so insignificant $58,000 more in the lower expense fund.

## Making the Purchase

After all of your figuring, matching, picking, evaluating, and calculating, you should know exactly what fund you want. Now it's time to do some buying. Load funds are generally sold through salespeople—perhaps a broker or a financial advisor. No-load funds, though, tend to be sold directly by the investment company. If you decide to keep costs down and go for a no-load fund, you have two choices. You can deal directly with the investment company that runs the fund, or you can purchase the no-load fund through a "mutual fund supermarket."

**Buying Direct: Dialing 1-800 . . .** The easiest way to buy a mutual fund is to pick up the phone. Vanguard and Fidelity, the two largest mutual fund families, both have 800 numbers you can use to set up an account, to move money into and out of your funds, to switch funds, and to request educational material. However, unless you want to transfer money electronically, you'll still have to send your money to Vanguard or Fidelity through the mail, and when you sell your holdings, you'll generally receive a check in the mail. Otherwise, most everything can be done over the phone. Again, it's not having salespeople that allows these families of funds to keep their costs down.

**Buying Through a "Mutual Fund Supermarket"**   The downside of buying directly from the mutual fund is that if you have money in eight different mutual fund families, you'll have eight different statements to deal with. If you decide you want to move money from one family to another, you're in for a real headache. Luckily, in 1992 Charles Schwab & Co. introduced the concept of the "mutual fund supermarket," where you could pick from among 600 mutual funds that make up 70 different mutual fund families and buy them through Schwab.

The question most people ask is, Why does Schwab do it? If Schwab makes a commission, don't these no-load funds now become load funds? The answer is that Schwab convinced the mutual fund companies to give up a portion of their management fees—initially about $2.50 per year for every $1,000 in assets invested—for any mutual funds purchased through Schwab. Both parties seemed to benefit—Schwab got some commissions it wouldn't otherwise have received, and the mutual funds got some new investors.

Today there are eight major players in the "mutual funds supermarket" arena. How do you go about choosing from them? Begin by looking at the lineup of no-transaction-fee funds available. The biggest two, Fidelity Funds Network and Schwab, have signed up key mutual fund families. However, not all funds are available on a no-transaction-fee basis from each "supermarket." For example, mutual funds from the Twentieth Century mutual fund family are only available from Charles Schwab.

You should also be aware of differences in minimum balances necessary to open an account. In addition, Fidelity and Schwab have different transaction fees for funds not available on a no-fee basis. Each of these "supermarkets" charges a relatively small transaction fee when purchasing any no-load mutual funds from the T. Rowe Price, USAA, or Vanguard mutual fund families. You can avoid these transaction fees altogether by simply purchasing these funds directly from their mutual fund families. Many banks also sell mutual funds. Unfortunately, investors often don't realize that mutual funds sold by banks aren't insured by the federal government, as are most bank accounts. Moreover, most mutual funds sold by banks are also load funds.

## SUMMARY

When you invest in a mutual fund, you're buying a fraction of a very large portfolio. This portfolio may include stocks, bonds, short-term securities, and even cash. Your money is pooled with that of other investors to purchase the fund's holdings. The shareholders then own a proportionate share of the overall portfolio. The value of mutual fund shares goes up and down as the value of the mutual fund's investments goes up and down.

Investment companies invest the pooled money in return for a fee. An open-end investment company is actually an open-end mutual fund. It has the ability to issue and redeem shares on a daily basis, and the value of the portfolio that it holds determines the value of each ownership share in the mutual fund. The price paid for an open-end mutual fund share or received when the share is sold is the net asset value (NAV).

A closed-end fund has a fixed number of shares. Those shares are initially sold by the fund at its inception, and after that they trade between investors at whatever price supply and demand dictate. A unit investment trust is a pool of securities, generally municipal bonds, with each share representing a proportionate ownership in that pool. A real estate investment trust, or REIT, is similar to a mutual fund, with the funds going either directly into real estate or for real estate loans.

Although some mutual funds have no sales commission, others impose a sales commission, and still others require a hefty annual management fee. A load is simply a sales commission; thus, a load fund is one that charges a sales commission. A mutual fund that doesn't charge a commission is referred to as a no-load fund.

To allow you to more easily choose from the approximately 8,200 mutual funds available, funds are categorized according to objective. The process of selecting a mutual fund involves determining your investment goals, identifying funds that meet your objectives, and evaluating those funds. There's a wealth of information available to aid you in evaluating mutual funds. The *Wall Street Journal* provides daily mutual fund listings and quotes. Two other excellent sources of information are *Wiesenberger Investment Companies Service* and *Morningstar Mutual Funds*.

You should be very aware of any and all mutual fund expenses and try to avoid them. The return from investing in a mutual fund can be in the form of dividends or capital gains distributions, or a change in the NAV of the shares held. Capital gains result from selling securities for more than what they were originally bought for.

## REVIEW QUESTIONS

1. List and explain the seven advantages associated with owning a mutual fund. Which of these advantages relates to Principle 3? How?

2. List and explain the five disadvantages of mutual funds.

3. Diversification for small investors is a primary advantage of mutual funds. Why can't a mutual fund diversify away systematic risk?

4. What is a mutual fund? What makes a mutual fund different from owning a stock or bond directly?

5. Mutual fund investors make money in three ways. Name and briefly describe each. How are these reflected in the formula for calculating total return?

6. Describe the organization of a mutual fund. What is the role of the investment manager or advisor? How are they typically compensated?

7. Describe the four most common types of investment companies.

8. What is an REIT and how is one similar to and different from a mutual fund?

9. What is the primary difference between a load fund and a no-load fund? What is a back-end load? A 12b-1 fee?

10. What kinds of mutual fund costs are reflected in the expense ratio? How can these affect long-term earnings?

11. List the six major categories of mutual funds. What is the fundamental difference among these categories? What two categories are most alike? Why?

12. Why are money market mutual funds considered practically risk free?

13. What is an index fund and why should most investors consider purchasing shares in an index fund versus another type of stock fund?

14. What are the three main categories of bond funds? What is the primary advantage of each category?

15. List the seven special services offered to investors by most mutual fund companies. For each, explain its benefit to a specific type of investor.

16. How does an automatic investment plan facilitate Principle 13?

17. Summarize the three steps involved in the mutual fund selection process.

18. What is a "mutual fund supermarket"? What are the advantages and disadvantages of buying funds this way versus buying direct?

## PROBLEMS AND ACTIVITIES

1. Calculate the net asset value (NAV) for a mutual fund with the following values:

   Market Value of Securities Held in the
     Portfolio = $1.2 billion
   Liabilities of the Fund = $37 million
   Shares Outstanding = 60 million

2. The following information pertains to the Big Returns Fund:

   Front-end load: 5.50 percent
   Back-end load: 3 percent declining for 3 years

   Management fee: 0.90 percent
   12b-1 fee: 0.50 percent

   Assume that you wanted to purchase $2,500 worth of shares in this fund. How much would you pay in initial commissions? If you sold your shares two years after your initial purchase, how much would you pay in commissions? How much in annual expenses would you pay to own this fund?

3. Match the following types of stock funds to the appropriate stocks that would typically be found in each portfolio.

| | | | |
|---|---|---|---|
| Growth Funds | a) | foreign stocks | |
| U.S. Government Bond Funds | b) | moves money from stocks to bonds to maximize return | |
| Growth and Income Funds | c) | market basket that represents the S&P 500 | |
| Life Cycle Funds | d) | mix of stocks, bonds, and money market securities | |
| Sector Funds | e) | 65 percent of stocks from the technology industry | |
| Index Funds | f) | dividend-paying blue-chip stocks | |
| Balanced Funds | g) | tailored to investor characteristics | |
| International Funds | h) | high growth and high P/E companies | |
| Small-Company Funds | i) | companies with strong earnings and some dividends | |
| Asset Allocation Funds | j) | federal agency securities | |
| Aggressive Growth Funds | k) | small companies that trade on the OTC | |

4. Zap Fund is the mainstay of your portfolio. The investment company just announced its year-end distributions. The long-term capital gain per share is $4.60 and the dividend per share is $2.10. Assuming the NAV increased from $39.10 to $46.21, calculate your total annual return.

5. At the beginning of last year Thomas purchased 200 shares of the Web.com Fund at an NAV of $26.00 and automatically reinvested all distributions. As a result of reinvesting Thomas ended the year with 265 shares of the fund with an NAV of $32.20. What was his total return for the year on this investment?

6. Which of the funds in Q.6. Table below in terms of costs, would be the better investment for someone who initially invests $5,000 and knows the fund will be sold at the end of five years? (Assume that each fund's total return is 12 percent before expenses a year.)

7. Use the information in Q.7. Table below to answer the questions that follow:

   a. How much would you pay for one share of each fund?

   b. Calculate tomorrow's NAV assuming each fund loses 5 percent.

8. Melanie is considering purchasing shares in an international bond fund. She has limited her search to one open-ended and one close-ended fund. Information on the funds follows:

| | Open-Ended | Closed-Ended |
|---|---|---|
| NAV | $12.00 | $24.45 |
| Sales Price | no-load | $26.00 |
| Annual Expenses | 1.45% | 1.15% |
| YTD Return | 12.00% | 12.50% |

   a. How much would Melanie pay for the open-ended fund? How much would she pay for the closed-ended fund?

   b. Is the closed-ended fund selling at a discount or a premium to its NAV?

   c. Given both fund's similar returns and expense ratios, would you recommend that Melanie purchase the closed-ended fund? Why or why not?

**Q. 6. Table**

| | Fund 1 | Fund 2 | Fund 3 |
|---|---|---|---|
| Front-end load | 8.50% | 4.50% | 0.00% |
| Back-end load | 0.00% | 3.00% within 3 years | 0.00% |
| Management fee | 0.55% | 0.95% | 1.00% |
| 12b-1 fee | 0.00% | 0.25% | 1.00% |

**Q. 7. Table**

| Fund Name | NAV | YTD % Ret | Front-End Load | EXP Ratio |
|---|---|---|---|---|
| Biggers Better | 131.23 | −2.4 | 5.50 | 1.35 |
| JPEG Bold | 12.24 | +16.3 | 0.00 | 0.95 |
| Snazzy Growth | 14.56 | +7.3 | 0.00 | 2.05 |

9. The reinvestment of capital gains and dividends can make a significant difference in your total return. Consider the following problems to determine the difference reinvestment can make over a five-year period.

| | |
|---|---|
| Initial purchase amount | $10,000 |
| Initial purchase date | January 1 |
| Initial purchase price | $19.30 per share |
| Annual capital gains distribution rate | 1.5% |
| Annual dividend distribution rate | 0.6% |
| Annual price appreciation rate | 7.4% |

Assume all distributions are received or reinvested at the end of each year at the closing net asset value (NAV) for that day. Ignore tax consequences for both scenarios.

a. Determine your ending investment value plus the total of distributions received assuming no reinvestment.

b. Determine your ending investment value assuming all distributions are reinvested.

c. Calculate and explain the difference.

## SUGGESTED PROJECTS

1. For the 15-year period ending December 2000 almost 85 percent of actively managed mutual funds lagged the S&P 500 Index. Why don't actively managed mutual funds beat the market? Using the Web or another source (e.g., mutual fund newsletter, magazine, or professionals), identify three to five funds that have beat the market for the past year or longer period. Using the Web sites **www.morningstar.com** or **www.smartmoney.com**, research the individual stocks or sectors of the economy that comprise the fund. Can you explain why these funds are beating the market? Is the S&P 500 Index always the appropriate "yardstick" with which to measure? Why or why not?

2. Review the most recent copy of *Morningstar Mutual Funds, Value Line Mutual Funds*, or *Weisenberger Investment Companies Service*. Which service offers the most useful information in the easiest to read and understand format? Compare the ratings from each service for a single mutual fund. Were the ratings significantly different from each other? Why might this happen?

3. Repeat the exercise described in question 2, but instead of using print information sources visit different Web sites and compare the information. Which Web site offers the most useful information in the easiest to read and understand format? Compare the ratings from each service for a single mutual fund. Were the ratings significantly different from each other? Why might this happen?

4. Consult a recent copy of *Value Line* to obtain phone numbers for REITs representing the equity, mortgage, and hybrid REIT sectors. Call the firms and request an annual report. Review the reports to determine if the fund focus is clearly explained. Compile a list of the kinds of information included in the fund annual reports.

5. Check out the Web site offered by the Mutual Fund Education Alliance at **www.mfea.com**. Use this Web site to sort the funds listed according to their expense ratios. Is there a correlation between low expense ratios and better performance? If all other areas of comparison are equal, why are mutual funds with low expense ratios always a good recommendation?

6. Consult a magazine, such as *Kiplinger's Personal Finance, Money*, or *Mutual Fund Magazine*, or a mutual fund Web site for the toll-free number for a mutual fund. Call the fund and request a prospectus, or request it from the Web site. Review the prospectus to locate the key pieces of information as outlined in this chapter. In general, did you find the information provided easy to read and understand? Was the mutual fund's purpose and investment strategy stated in a clear and concise manner? Compare the information to that provided on any of the mutual fund comparison Web sites. Was the information provided from the different sources consistent?

7. Call or visit the Internet site for one of the two largest brokerage firms that offer a "mutual fund supermarket" (Charles Schwab at 1-800-435-4000; or Fidelity at 1-800-544-9697). Obtain a list of funds available through the supermarket. According to the information provided, what are some of the advantages of purchasing funds through a supermarket? Does the information describe how the brokerage firms selling the

funds get paid? How do you think they are compensated for offering this service?

8. As a group project identify mutual funds that you think fit into each of the Morningstar investment style boxes described in the chapter. Use your knowledge of mutual fund classifications and other references to generate the list. (To help find the ticker symbols of the funds selected, visit the Yahoo Mutual Fund Families Web site at **quote.yahoo.com**.) Once you have identified the mutual funds and their respective ticker symbols, visit **www.morningstar.com** to identify the style of each fund. Pick three funds from each style box and record the P/E ratio and median market capitalization. Does the P/E and market capitalization match the given style box? Why or why not?

What conclusions can you draw about the validity and usefulness of the Morningstar style box?

9. Repeat the project described in item 8 but record the risk rating information for the three funds in each style box. Compare your findings to the risk ratings associated with the boxes as given in the text. What conclusions can you draw about the validity and usefulness of the Morningstar style box?

10. Use the three-step process offered in the text to select a mutual fund based on your current circumstances. What classification of fund(s) would be appropriate given (a) the amount of money available to open an account, (b) your time horizon for using the money, (c) your goal or investment objective for the money, and (d) your risk tolerance?

## Discussion Case 1

Rick Phillips recently received $15,000 for the movie rights to his new book. He has always been interested in investing, but until now lacked sufficient resources. Rick has followed several telecom stocks over the past year. The share prices have fluctuated dramatically, but Rick is definitely interested in this type of stock. He feels that wireless telecommunication companies offer great possibilities. When you asked Rick if he was comfortable with the risk associated with such an investment, he indicated that he was if superior returns could be obtained.

### Questions

1. Given the fact that Rick only has $15,000 to invest, explain why he should consider investing in mutual funds rather than individual stocks.

2. In what type(s) of stock mutual fund(s) would you recommend Rick invest? Why?

3. In helping Rick make an investment choice, what factors would you tell him are most important when choosing a mutual fund?

4. Although most mutual funds will provide Rick with some level of diversification, what type of risk will Rick still be exposed to if he purchases a single mutual fund?

5. To assure Rick of the liquidity and marketability of his investment, would you recommend that he invest in an open-end or closed-end mutual fund? Why?

6. In terms of costs, would you recommend load or no-load funds to Rick? Why?

7. Develop a model portfolio of three mutual fund types (e.g., index, growth, bond, etc.) to help Rick understand the benefits of diversification. Explain your choices. Be sure to consider issues of risk and volatility.

## Discussion Case 2

Mahalia has decided that she needs to invest her savings somewhere else besides a bank account where she is only earning 1.25 percent annually. She has heard that money market mutual funds and short-term bond funds may provide higher yields than bank accounts and offer stability of principal similar to the bank. Mahalia's primary investment goal is to keep her savings (about $15,000 when she last checked) secure and accessible so that she can make a down payment on a house within the next three

years. She has several questions regarding investing in mutual funds and has come to you for help.

### Questions

1. Identify the types of mutual funds that would be appropriate in meeting Mahalia's objective.

2. What sources could Mahalia use to obtain specific information and ratings on different funds?

*Tips from Marcy Furney, ChFC, Certified Financial Planner™*

# Money Matters

## THE FEELING IS MUTUAL

**When deciding how and where to invest, many people fail to take into account their particular tax situation.** *Consequently, income taxes eat up a large part of their return. Understanding some of the tax implications may allow more of the earnings to end up in your pocket.*

**Mutual funds pass along to shareholders the taxable income from their investments in the form of dividends and capital gains.** *Even if all distributions are automatically reinvested, the tax liability is your responsibility. The percent of total return that these taxable elements comprise could be of great concern to anyone attempting to lower their income taxes.*

**When funds pay out capital gains (normally at the end of the year), the price per share decreases by the amount paid out.** *If you buy just before a capital gain distribution is made, you pay the higher share price and part of your original investment is immediately returned to you in the form of a taxable capital gain. In other words, don't buy a tax liability by investing right before a distribution date.*

**Consider tax implications when moving money from one fund to another.** *Even if you "transfer" within the same fund family, the IRS deems the transaction a sale and purchase and you are taxed on any gain from the sale.*

**Unlike individual stocks on which you control when gains will be taken, mutual funds have capital gains when the manager decides to sell appreciated assets.** *Morningstar and other analyses give an estimate of the percent of the fund's assets with such exposure. This information may sway your choice when selecting from a group of similar funds. Some have extremely large unrealized capital gains, which could become the shareholders' tax liability at any time.*

**Fund companies that provide cost-basis information for shareholders may not do so if you make several partial redemptions.** *It is important to keep records of all purchases, distributions, and withdrawals so that you can determine the gain or loss from any sale. When selling part of your shares, you may be able to choose an average cost per share figure or designate specific shares to sell. It all depends on whether you are trying to reduce or increase your taxable gain at that time. Beware: Once you choose a method of determining cost basis, you normally cannot change it for the life of that particular fund.*

**You may wish to consult your financial planner or tax advisor before any purchases or redemptions are made.** *Ownership of the fund (e.g., parent versus child), taxability of the income, and use of gains and losses are important aspects of your overall financial picture.*

3. When reviewing a fund's prospectus or an analysis provided by Morningstar, what specific type of information should Mahalia look for?

4. When evaluating a fund, how much importance should Mahalia place on a fund's past performance?

5. Given Mahalia's goal and your response to question 1, how important are loads, fees, and expenses in her search for a good mutual fund?

6. Provide Mahalia with six reasons she should consider purchasing shares in a bond fund.

7. What type of bond fund would you recommend? Why?

8. In terms of the risk–return trade-off, what length of maturity for a bond fund would be appropriate for Mahalia?

9. Name and describe at least four services provided by mutual funds that should appeal to Mahalia.

Visit our Web site for additional case problems, interactive exercises, and practice quizzes for this chapter—**www.prenhall.com/keown**.

# CONTINUING CASE: Cory and Tisha Dumont

As Cory and Tisha Dumont have reviewed your answers to the first three sections of this case they have come to realize that their need for financial planning assistance was far greater than they realized. They have taken your advice to heart and consistently reduced expenses. To their great surprise they have already accumulated $1,500 for an emergency fund. They feel that they are getting a handle on their basic money management skills and are more confident in their insurance knowledge and product selection. Now they have decided to focus on developing an investment plan.

Recall that Cory and Tisha still have $13,000 invested in a market index mutual fund for a house down payment. They also have $2,500 in a bank account earning 3 percent interest and average $1,800 in their checking account earning 1.75 percent interest. (Their $1,500 in emergency funds is in addition to these savings amounts.) The shares of Great Basin Balanced Mutual Fund, given to Tisha by her father, are worth $2,300. After completing a risk tolerance questionnaire on an investment Web site, Tisha and Cory confirmed that their attitudes toward risk were very different. Tisha is much more comfortable with "gambling" higher risks for higher returns, whereas Cory wants a "safe bet." Help the Dumonts answer the following questions regarding the management of their investments.

## Questions

1. What investment risks should be of primary concern to the Dumonts when choosing a savings or investment account for their emergency fund? What account would be most appropriate? Why?

2. Based on the Dumonts' stage in the life cycle, what type of investment asset allocation would be appropriate, assuming they want to establish a retirement savings fund? What types of stocks or mutual funds should they consider for the equity portion of their asset allocation plan? Should they consider international common stocks or mutual funds? Why or why not? What types of bonds or bond funds would be appropriate for the fixed-income portion of their asset allocation plan? (Hint: Be sure to consider the bond maturity, rating, and type of issuer.)

3. Briefly explain the concept of efficient markets for Cory and Tisha. But, more importantly, based on that understanding, what six strategies should they use to guide their investment management?

4. Cory and Tisha invested in a market index mutual fund to save for their future "dream house." Tisha would like to purchase a house in 2 to 3 years. Would you recommend that they maintain, increase, or decrease their holdings in this type of fund given their objective? Explain your answer. What type of fund or other investment would you recommend?

5. When Cory and Tisha do purchase a house, should they consider this an investment? Explain your answer in terms of (a) liquidity and (b) how market values for real estate are determined.

6. What sources of investment information can Cory and Tisha use to learn more about potential stock, bond, and mutual fund investments?

7. If Cory and Tisha had the funds to create a portfolio of common stocks, approximately how many stocks would they need to include in their portfolio to achieve adequate diversification? Explain to the Dumonts how owning a combination of securities can reduce risks as addressed by Principles 3 and 4. What combination might be the most effective for risk reduction, as measured by beta?

8. The Dumonts, in the 27.5-percent marginal tax bracket, are concerned about the federal taxes paid on investment earnings. Show the calculations to answer the following questions.

   a. A tax-free money market mutual fund is currently yielding 2.40 percent. Should Cory and Tisha move their savings into this fund or keep their money in the bank earning 3.00 percent?

   b. If a U.S. Treasury note is currently yielding 8 percent, what is the minimum interest rate that the Dumonts must receive in order to purchase an equivalent municipal bond?

9. Calculate the amount of money the Dumonts will have in their savings account if they add no other funds and keep it invested at 3 percent over the next 25 years. Calculate how much they can accumulate over 25 years if they move the money into a money market mutual fund earning 5 percent. Based on your calculations, should the Dumonts reallocate their savings into a money

market mutual fund? What advantages and disadvantages should be considered?

10. Cory's parents recently gave the Dumonts $40,000 to start education funds for Chad and Haley. A stockbroker has recommended that Cory and Tisha include a 10-year corporate bond in the portfolio. The bond currently yields 8 percent and sells for $1,000. If interest rates increase 2 percentage points and the bond is sold, how much will the bond sell for at that time? Calculate the bond price if rates fall 1 percent. What investing rule has this proved?

11. The same stockbroker who recommended a bond for Chad's college savings also recommended that Haley's college savings portfolio include a preferred stock paying a $5 dividend, currently selling for $53, to help fund Haley's college expenses. If the Dumonts' required rate of return is 10 percent, how much should the preferred stock sell for?

12. Should the Dumonts take the stockbroker's advice and buy the bond for Chad and the preferred stock for Haley to meet college savings needs? Defend your answer and provide other investment alternatives that the Dumonts should consider.

13. Explain to Cory and Tisha why mutual funds may be a good alternative for meeting their investment objectives. What specific types of mutual funds would be appropriate for meeting the following investment objectives, given their time horizon and risk tolerance? (*Hint:* Feel free to develop an asset allocation strategy by suggesting percentages for each fund type(s) included.)

   a. emergency fund
   b. house down payment savings
   c. college fund for Chad
   d. college fund for Haley
   e. retirement fund for Cory
   f. retirement fund for Tisha

14. Recall that when Tisha turned 21 years old her father gave her shares in the Great Basin Balanced Mutual Fund. Today the fund is worth $2,300. Assuming that Tisha will use this fund as a long-term investment (maybe for retirement), and given her risk tolerance and age, does this type of fund match her objective? What investment risk is most important when thinking about investments for a college fund and retirement? Would this be a good fund if she decided to use it to save for college expenses for Chad and Haley? Defend your answers.

15. What mutual fund services would you recommend that the Dumonts use to systematically save for their goals? Why? How might these services be integrated with a portfolio accumulation strategy?

16. Would you recommend no-load or load funds to the Dumonts? Why? What other factors are important to consider when comparing different mutual funds with the same objective?

17. Should the Dumonts consider using a mutual fund supermarket? What are the advantages and disadvantages of using this investment strategy?

18. Give Cory and Tisha a simple explanation of brokerage accounts, asset management accounts, and margin accounts. Help the Dumonts consider each of these alternatives, noting advantages and disadvantages.

19. Explain to Cory and Tisha the advantages and disadvantages associated with managing an investment portfolio through (a) a discount brokerage firm, (b) a traditional brokerage firm, and (c) an Internet brokerage. If they choose a broker, what type of agency problems should they consider?

20. Online investing, not day trading, seems like the simplest and cheapest approach. If the Dumonts choose to use an online brokerage, what strategies would you recommend regarding orders, trades, margins, and other account activity?

# 16 Retirement Planning

PART 5: LIFE CYCLE ISSUES

**Learning Objectives**

**1** **Understand** the changing nature of retirement planning.

**2** **Set up** a retirement plan.

**3** **Contribute** to a tax-favored retirement plan to help fund your retirement.

**4** **Choose** how your retirement benefits are paid out to you.

**5** **Put together** a retirement plan and effectively monitor it.

**M**ost people assume that if you make it big early in life, retirement planning should be a breeze. You live off your plenty and put a little away and let time and compounding work their magic. For Tina Turner, though, making it big early in life didn't make anything a breeze. Born in 1939 to cotton plantation workers in Brownsville, Tennessee, Turner moved to St. Louis to live with relatives when she was in her teens. It was there she met Ike Turner, her future husband and singing partner.

Together they hit the big time, becoming huge stars by the time the seventies arrived, with such hits as "River Deep, Mountain Wide," and an R&B-style version of Creedence Clearwater Revival's "Proud Mary." Unfortunately, the big time isn't all that Ike hit. After being beaten bloody in July 1976, Tina Turner finally walked out of her 20-year abusive marriage to Ike. When she left, she had no recording contract, no savings, no fancy cars or homes—just 36 cents and a Mobil gas card.

For a while, Turner and her four children lived on food stamps. Although facing poverty, she couldn't bring herself to take any money when she finally divorced Ike in 1978. Instead, she managed to support herself and her family by playing Holiday Inns and any other minor clubs that would book her. By 1979, she found herself $500,000 in debt, with no prospects and no one to lend a helping hand. It looked as if Tina Turner had retired to a life of poverty and obscurity.

Fortunately, along came Roger Davies, a young Australian promoter, who signed on as her manager. With his help, Turner paid off her bills, put together a new backup band, and got a fresh start. Despite record company skepticism, she managed to get a new recording contract, and by 1984 she had a number-one hit with "What's Love Got to Do With It." Today Turner continues to be a major star, and you'd better believe that she's planned for her next retirement to be a life of comfort and ease.

You may think you're too young or not wealthy enough to worry about retirement. Think again. Regardless of your age, you need to start thinking about retirement. Actually, you need to do more than think—you need to start saving. By saving for retirement, you're really focusing on a specific financial goal. Of course, as you learned in Chapters 1 and 2, you're going to have a lot of financial goals in your life. Retirement, though, is a biggie. After all, how well you do in achieving your retirement goal is probably going to determine how much you enjoy the last 20 or more years of your life.

Unfortunately, for most people, today looms larger than tomorrow. That car loan or mortgage you're trying to pay off this year will no doubt seem to be far more important than your financial situation 30 to 40 years from now. It's hard to worry about retiring when you're young. Just think how worried you'll be when you're 65 and you don't have a dime to retire on. Big money in a second career may have worked for Tina Turner, but it probably won't work for you. Fortunately,

with a sound plan and a little discipline, you can retire to a life of relative ease without ever having to fret or fear.

Time was when retirement planning wasn't necessary—retirement meant taking a pension from your employer and letting Social Security pick up any slack. Not anymore. Thanks to the recent drive to cut spending, employers tend not to pay pensions, and those that still do have reduced them to as little as possible. That leaves a lot of slack for Social Security, but thanks to the government's drive to cut its own spending, there might not be such a thing as Social Security by the time you retire.

Nowadays, you've got to come up with the funds for your retirement all by yourself. Sound scary? Well, it's actually not. We'll explain exactly how to make a good retirement plan. But first we should explain how Social Security and employer-funded pensions work. No, we're not trying to rub it in and show you what you're missing. You simply need to know about past retirement plans before you can dive into the present ones.

Understand the changing nature of retirement planning.

## Social Security

For many senior citizens, Social Security is their primary source of retirement income. For younger workers who won't face retirement for 40 years, the Social Security system may seem more like a mirage—they can see it now, but when they get there it may disappear. Still, for many of the millions of individuals receiving benefits, Social Security is the difference between living in poverty and modest comfort. Let's take a look at how the Social Security system currently functions.

### Financing Social Security

To begin with, Social Security isn't an investment. When you pay money into Social Security, you're purchasing mandatory insurance that provides for you and your family in the event of death, disability, health problems, or retirement. Moreover, the benefits paid by Social Security aren't intended to allow you to live in comfort after you retire. They're intended to provide a base level of protection.

Whether you want to or not, you fund Social Security during your working years by paying taxes directly to the Social Security system. If you're not self-employed, both you and your employer pay into the system—each pays 7.65 percent of your gross salary up to $84,900 in 2002. This deduction appears on your pay slip as "FICA," which stands for the Federal Insurance Contributions Act.

These funds actually go to both Social Security and to Medicare (the government's health insurance program for the elderly, which we discussed in Chapter 9). Medicare also keeps on taxing after the Social Security cap has been reached, taking an additional 1.45 percent from both you and your employer.

If your salary were $84,900 in 2002, your FICA contribution would be $6,494.85. If you're self-employed, you have to pay both the employer and employee portions of FICA, at a rate of 15.3 percent up to the $84,900 limit, paying a total of $12,989.70. In addition, you pay Medicare 2.9 percent on all net earnings above $84,900.

These funds cover the payments currently being made to retirees by Social Security, while allowing for a "built-in surplus" for payouts in the future. In other words, the FICA taxes being paid by today's workers are providing the money for benefit payments for today's retirees. The money you pay to FICA isn't saved up and invested just for you. Instead it gets pooled with the money all other current workers are paying to FICA and goes into a senior citizen's Social Security benefits check.

The idea is that when you get old and retire, the FICA taxes paid by people working then will go into your benefits check. Unfortunately, the proportion of current workers to current Social Security recipients is shrinking rapidly. Whereas 40 years ago there were 16 workers for every Social Security recipient, today the ratio is down to 3 workers to every recipient. And the problem won't go away. In fact, it will only get worse when in 40 years the ratio of working contributors to recipients will be down to 2-to-1.

## Eligibility

Roughly 95 percent of all Americans are covered by Social Security. The major groups outside the system include police officers and workers continuously employed by the government since 1984, both of whom are covered by alternative retirement systems.

To become eligible for Social Security, all you have to do is pay money into the system. As you do, you receive Social Security credits. In 2002, you earned one credit for each $870 in earnings, up to a maximum of four credits per year. To qualify for benefits, you need 40 credits.

Once you've met this requirement, you become eligible for retirement, disability, and survivor benefits. Earning beyond 40 credits won't increase your benefits. If you die, some of your family members may also be eligible for Social Security benefits, even if they never paid into the system.

## Retirement Benefits

The size of your Social Security benefits is determined by (1) your number of years of earnings, (2) your average level of earning, and (3) an adjustment for inflation. The formula attempts to provide benefits that would replace 42 percent of your average earnings over your working years, adjusted upward somewhat for those in lower income brackets and downward for those in higher income brackets. Thus, the benefits are slightly weighted toward individuals in lower income brackets because they, in general, have less savings to rely on at retirement.

To be eligible for full retirement benefits, you need to be at least 65 years old if you were born in 1937 or earlier. The retirement age to receive full benefits gradually rises for those born in 1938 until it hits 67 for those born in 1960 or later. Reduced benefits can be received by those who retire as early as age 62. However, those benefits are *permanently* reduced by five-ninths of 1 percent for the first 36 months and five-twelfths of 1 percent for subsequent months before the "full" retirement age. That means people scheduled to receive full benefits at age 67 and who retire at age 62 will receive only 70 percent of their full benefits, and this reduced level of benefits is permanent.

If you delay retirement, you can increase your Social Security benefits. The longer you work, the higher the average earnings base on which your benefits are calculated. In addition, those who delay retirement also have a percentage added to their benefits. For those turning 65 in 2000, the rate is 6.5 percent per year. That rate gradually increases in future years, until it reaches 8 percent per year for people turning 65 in 2008 or later. Table 16.1 provides an estimate of the size of the Social Security benefits at retirement for someone who was 22 in 2002 and retired at the Social Security retirement age.

### Table 16.1  Estimated Monthly Benefit Amount in Year-2002 Dollars

| Your Age in 2002 | Retirement Age | Your Earnings in 2002 | | | |
|---|---|---|---|---|---|
| | | $20,000 | $40,000 | $60,000 | $100,000 |
| 22 | 62 in 2042 | $613 | $986 | $1,189 | $1,407 |
| | 67 in 2047 | $876 | $1,409 | $1,699 | $2,011 |
| | 70 in 2050 | $1,086 | $1,748 | $2,107 | $2,493 |

Source: Social Security Administration, 2002. **www.ssa.gov/cgi-bin/benefit.cgi.**

Keep in mind that, depending on the level of your income and how you file your tax return, your Social Security benefits may be taxed. The amount of your benefits that can be taxed is based on your "combined income," which is determined by combining these factors: the sum of you and your spouse's adjusted gross income as reported to the IRS on your 1040 tax form plus nontaxable interest, plus one-half of your Social Security benefits.

In 2002, for those retirees filing joint returns with "combined income" between $32,000 and $44,000, 50 percent of their benefits was taxable. For those retirees with "combined income" greater than $44,000, 85 percent of their benefits was taxable. If you're retired, file an individual return, and have a "combined income" between $25,000 and $34,000, you'd have to pay taxes on 50 percent of your Social Security benefits. If your income is above $34,000, you'd pay taxes on 85 percent of your benefits. With the passage of the Senior Citizens' Freedom to Work Act of 2000, the Social Security retirement earnings limit was eliminated meaning that starting with the month you reach full retirement age (currently age 65 but rising to age 67), you will get your benefits with no limit on your earnings.

You should also be aware of the fact that the government won't automatically start sending you your Social Security check just because you're officially retired. You must notify your Social Security office and file an application 3 months before you want your first check to arrive. You are then strongly encouraged to have your monthly benefits directly deposited in a checking or savings account at your bank.

**STOP & THINK**   There's no question that there may be significant changes in the Social Security system by the time you retire. A Haeworth Robertson, former chief actuary for Social Security, has warned that "it will be virtually impossible to increase taxes enough to fulfill the benefit promises being made to Baby Boomers." The bottom line is that you bear the responsibility for your own financial affairs, and you can't rely on Social Security alone for your retirement.

How important is Social Security? Take a look at Figure 16.1. As you can see, many low-income retirees depend on Social Security benefits to get by. The poverty rate for retirees, if they did not receive Social Security, would be about 50 percent, as shown in Figure 16.1.

### Disability and Survivor Benefits

Although retirement benefits are the focus of our attention in this chapter, Social Security is actually a mandatory insurance program. Insurance against poverty at retirement is only one portion of its coverage. Social Security also provides disability and survivor benefits.

Disability benefits provide protection for those who experience a physical or mental impairment that is expected to result in death or keep them from doing any

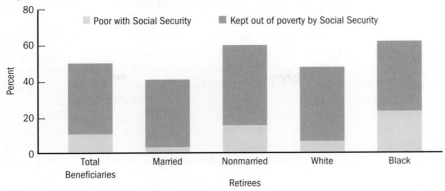

Figure 16.1 Over Half of Retirees Would Be Below Poverty Without Social Security

Source: Social Security Administration, 1999.

substantial work for at least a year. "Substantial work" is generally defined as anything that generates monthly earnings of $500 or more.

Social Security also provides survivor benefits to families when the breadwinner dies. These payments include a small, automatic one-time payment at the time of death to help defray funeral costs, as well as continued monthly payments to the spouse if he or she is over 60, over 50 if disabled, or any age and caring for a child either under 16 or disabled and receiving Social Security benefits. Continued monthly payments are also available to your children if they're under 18 or under 19 but still in elementary or secondary school, or if they're disabled. Your parents can also qualify for survivor benefits if you die and they're dependent on you for at least half of their support.

## Employer-Funded Pensions

Twenty years ago, a "guaranteed" pension provided by your employer was the norm. You'd work for one company for most or all of your working life, and that company would reward your loyalty and hard work by taking care of you during retirement. In today's job scene, where companies aren't quite so generous any more and where employees change jobs as often as they change clothes, pension plans are rare. However, some companies do still offer pensions, but most call them "defined-benefit plans," not "pensions."

### Defined-Benefit Plans

Under a **defined-benefit plan**, you receive a promised or "defined" payout at retirement. These plans are generally **noncontributory retirement plans**, which means you don't have to pay anything into them. (With a **contributory retirement plan**, you, and usually your employer, do pay into the plan.) The payout, which you receive as taxable income, is generally based on a formula that takes into account your age at retirement, salary level, and years of service.

The formulas can vary dramatically from company to company. Some focus only on salary during the final few years of service, which is better for you, while others use an average of all your years' salary as a base to calculate pension benefits. One commonly used formula is to pay out 1.5 percent of the average of your final 3 to 5 years' worth of salary times your number of years of service.

**Defined-Benefit Plan**
A traditional pension plan in which you receive a promised or "defined" pension payout at retirement. The payout is based on a formula that takes into account your age at retirement, salary level, and years of service.

**Noncontributory Retirement Plan**
A retirement plan in which the employer provides all the funds and the employee need not contribute.

**Contributory Retirement Plan**
A retirement plan in which the employee, possibly with the help of the employer, provides the funds for the plan.

$$\text{monthly benefit} = \frac{\text{average salary}}{\text{over "final years"}} \times \text{years of service} \times 0.015$$

Thus, if you retired after 25 years of service with an average salary of $70,000 over the final years, you'd receive $26,250 ($70,000 × 25 × 0.015 = $26,250), which would be 37.5 percent of your final average salary. In general, the most that employees, even those who've spent their entire careers with the same company, ever receive from a defined-benefit pension is 40 to 45 percent of their before-retirement income.

One nice thing about a defined-benefit plan is that the employer bears the investment risk associated with the plan. That is, regardless of what the stock and bond markets do, you're still promised the same amount. You also have the option of extending pension coverage to your spouse. When you die, your spouse will continue to receive payments.

Unfortunately, companies can change their pension policies with little notice. One additional problem with defined-benefits programs is that they lack **portability**—that is, if you leave the company, your pension doesn't go with you. If you're **vested**, meaning you've worked long enough for the company to have the right to receive pension benefits, you'll eventually get a pension. However, it'll likely be small because pensions are generally based on years of service and salary levels. If you're not yet vested and you leave, you can kiss your pension good-bye.

Another problem with defined-benefit plans is that few of them—in fact only 1 in 10—adjust for inflation once the benefits begin. The benefit level stays constant over your retirement while inflation reduces the spending power of each dollar.

A final problem with defined-benefit plans is that they're not all **funded pension plans**, in which the employer makes regular pension contributions to a trustee who collects and invests the retirement funds. In other words, the employer sets up a separate account to guarantee the payment of pension benefits.

In an **unfunded pension plan**, pension expenses are paid out of current company earnings. These are pay-as-you-go pension plans. Needless to say, a funded plan is much safer than an unfunded plan, which would disappear if the company went under. Fortunately, the law requires employers to notify employees if their pension fund is less than 90 percent funded.

## Cash-Balance Plans: The Latest Twist in Defined-Benefit Plans

In recent years over 500 companies, including Eastman Kodak, CBS, Citigroup, and IBM, have switched from traditional defined-benefit plans to **cash-balance plans**. Cash-balance plans use a different formula for accumulation of benefits, one in which workers are credited with a percentage of their pay each year, plus a predetermined rate of investment earning or interest. Typically, this account earns interest at close to the long-term Treasury bond rate.

This sounds an awful lot like a defined-contribution plan, but it's not. That's because the accounts grow at this set rate, regardless of how much is actually earned. In addition, workers don't get to make investment decisions and they generally get lower returns on their cash balances than they would have been able to earn.

Let's look a bit closer at how they work. Under a cash-balance plan, employers contribute a percentage of your salary each year into your account. This generally ranges between 4 and 7 percent. The contribution then grows, generally at the 30-year Treasury bond rate, although some companies will allow its growth to be tied to the S&P 500 index. Then, if you leave the company, you can generally roll the balance into an IRA (i.e., an individual retirement account, explained later in this chapter).

**Portability**
A pension fund provision that allows employees to retain and transfer any pension benefits already earned to another pension plan if they leave the company.

**Vest**
To gain the right to the retirement contributions made by your employer in your name. In the case of a pension plan, employees become vested when they've worked for a specified period of time and, thus, gained the right to pension benefits.

**Funded Pension Plan**
A pension plan in which the employer makes pension contributions directly to a trustee who holds and invests the employees' retirement funds.

**Unfunded Pension Plan**
A pension fund in which the benefits are paid out of current earnings on a pay-as-you-go basis.

**Cash-Balance Plan**
A retirement plan where workers are credited with a percentage of their pay, plus a predetermined rate of interest.

What's the good news? First, your retirement benefits are much easier to track. It is also better for young employees, because they start to build up benefits much earlier. In addition, if you leave the company, you can take your cash balance with you. Why have 17 of the *Fortune* 100 converted to cash-balance plans? It's not because these companies are trying to shower their employees with money; it's because they save money with them as a result of reduced future benefits for older workers. Just look at IBM, which switched in 1999: It will save about $200 million a year in pension contributions.

## Plan Now, Retire Later

LO2 Set up a retirement plan.

Principle 8 Nothing Happens Without a Plan

It's incredibly easy to avoid thinking about retirement. This brings us back to **Principle 8: Nothing Happens Without a Plan**. Saving isn't a natural event—it must be planned. Unfortunately, planning isn't natural either. Although an elaborate, complicated plan might be ideal, you might be better off with a modest, uncomplicated retirement plan.

Once the plan becomes part of your financial routine, you can modify and expand it. The bottom line is that a retirement plan can't be postponed. The longer it's put off, the more difficult accomplishing your goals becomes. Figure 16.2 shows the seven steps of the retirement planning process. Let's take a look at each step in depth.

### Step 1: Set Goals

The first step in planning for your retirement is figuring out just what you want to do when you retire. Naturally, you'll want to be able to support yourself and pay any

**Figure 16.2** The Seven Steps to Funding Your Retirement Needs

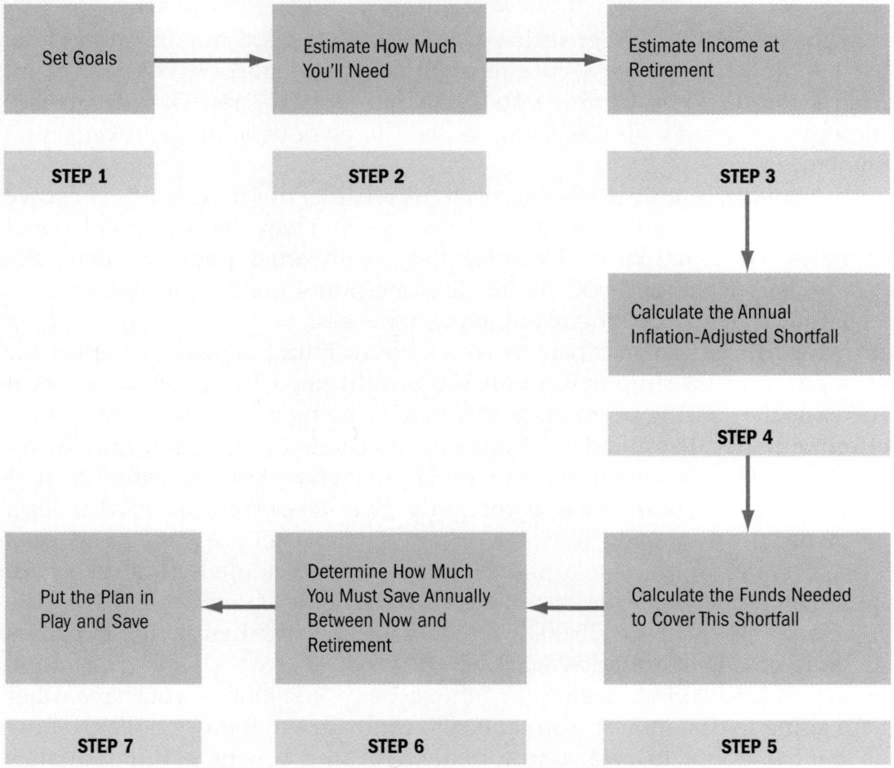

medical bills, but that could cost a little or it could cost a whole lot. Therefore, you need to start by asking yourself some basic questions: How costly a lifestyle do you want to lead? Do you want to live like a king or more economically, perhaps like a minor duke or nobleman? Do you currently have any medical conditions that you know are going to be costly later in life?

Once you've answered these questions, you can pretty much set your basic goal of being able to support yourself and pay your medical expenses. Then it's time to think about other goals. Do you want to stay in your current house, or will you want to move to Florida and eat early-bird specials? Do you want to live in a retirement community or your own residence? Do you want to travel? Do you want to be able to buy that Dodge Viper and hit the open road? Do you want to have money set aside for your family? It might be hard to sit down and consider everything you might want to do when you retire, but you'll need to be as exhaustive as possible when thinking about and setting your goals.

As you learned in Chapter 1, goals aren't entirely useful unless you include the element of time and decide when you hope to achieve them. In the case of retirement, you need to figure out exactly when you'd like to retire. The typical retirement age is 65, but more and more people are putting off retirement until 70 or even later.

The time frame for achieving your goals is more important than you might think. For example, if you want to retire at age 60, you'll need to save up a lot of money to be able to pay for a lengthy retirement. If you really love your job and don't want to retire until you're 70, though, you won't need to save as much because your period of retirement should be shorter, and you'll be giving yourself an extra 10 years to prepare for it.

## Step 2: Estimate How Much You'll Need

Once you've got your retirement goals in place, it's time to start thinking about how to achieve them and turn into a secure retirement. The second step of retirement planning helps you do so by turning your goals into dollar. These figures are estimates of how much money you're going to need to achieve your goals once you reach retirement.

Of course, estimates aren't always accurate or reliable, but, hey, it's the best we can do. It'd be nice if we could all see into the future—that way we wouldn't have to rely on estimates. We'd just know. Unfortunately, we're stuck guessing about the future. If you're smart, though, you can make some pretty good educated guesses. All you need do is start with your current living expenses.

Why do your future needs start with your current living expenses? Well, your main goal is going to be supporting yourself. You'll need to use the amount it currently takes as the starting point for how much it's going to cost to support yourself in retirement. Because elderly people have usually paid off their houses and consume less than younger people, most financial planners estimate that supporting yourself in retirement will cost only 70 to 80 percent of what it costs before retirement.

When you first began to make a financial plan, you calculated what it costs to support yourself when you calculated your personal income statement. Let's say the number you came up with was $35,000. Well, your basic retirement living expenses would then be somewhere around $28,000 ($35,000 × 0.8).

Of course, this $28,000 is just the tip of the iceberg. Remember, you have other goals that are going to cost money. You'll need to estimate—in today's dollars—how much each goal is going to cost you annually. Adding up the estimated costs

## Table 16.2    The Average Tax Rate

To estimate your anticipated average tax rate at retirement, you can use the following tables based on current tax rates. If you anticipate a change in future tax rates—for example, a flat tax—use that number.

| Retirement Income | Average Tax Rate | |
| --- | --- | --- |
| | Couples Filing Jointly | Individuals |
| $ 20,000 | 7% | 10% |
| 30,000 | 10 | 14 |
| 40,000 | 12 | 17 |
| 50,000 | 14 | 20 |
| 60,000 | 17 | 22 |
| 70,000 | 19 | 23 |
| 80,000 | 21 | 24 |
| 90,000 | 22 | 25 |
| 100,000 | 23 | 26 |
| 150,000 | 28 | 30 |

of achieving all your goals, including the base amount for your living expenses, will give you, in today's dollars, the income amount you'll need each year to fund your retirement.

However, you're not done yet. Don't forget the government. Yes, you need to factor in the effect of taxes. Table 16.2 gives you a rough idea of the average tax rate you'll pay on your required retirement income. All you need do is divide the amount of retirement income you'll need by (1 − your tax rate). This figure will tell you exactly how much pretax income, in today's dollars, you'll need each year to fund your retirement.

Take a look at Larry and Louise Tate, introduced in Chapter 2. They calculated their annual living expenditures to be $52,234. To obtain an estimate of their annual living expenses at retirement in today's dollars, they'd multiply this amount by 0.8, which would come to $41,787. They'd then need to adjust this amount for any additional expenditures to meet their other goals. For example, the Tates may wish to move to a more expensive area of the country, or they may wish to travel more after retirement.

Let's assume that the Tates wish to take two additional vacation trips annually at $2,000 per trip, measured in today's dollars, for an increase of $4,000 per year. They would thus need a total of $45,787 for their annual living expenditures at retirement in today's dollars, as calculated on line D of Figure 16.3.

The Tates now must adjust this number for taxes. Using Table 16.2, we see that the average tax rate for retirement income between $40,000 and $50,000 is approximately 12 percent. However, since the Tates intend to retire in a state with a relatively high state income tax, they have decided to use 14 percent rather than 12 percent as their estimated tax rate. The Tates must simply divide their annual living expenditures by (1 − 0.14), or 0.86, resulting in $53,241. In effect, of this $53,241, 14 percent, or $7,454, will go to pay taxes, leaving $45,787 to cover living expenditures.

W37 WORKSHEET

## Step 3: Estimate Income at Retirement

As you've probably guessed, once you know how much income you're going to need when you retire, the logical next step is figuring out just how much income you're going to have. First, estimate your Social Security benefits. The Social Security

**Figure 16.3** Worksheet for Funding Retirement Needs

| | The Tates Example | Your Numbers |
|---|---|---|
| **STEP 1: Set Your Goals.** | | |
| **STEP 2: Estimate Your Annual Needs at Retirement.** | | |
| A. Present level of living expenditures on an after-tax basis | $52,234 | _____ |
| B. Times 0.80 equals: Base retirement expenditure level in today's dollars | × 0.80 = $41,787 | _____ |
| C. Plus or minus: Anticipated increases or decreases in living expenditures after retirement | + $4,000 | _____ |
| D. Equals: Annual living expenditures at retirement in today's dollars on an after-tax basis | = $45,787 | _____ |
| E. Before-tax adjustment factor, based on an average tax rate of 14% (If the average tax rate is not known, it can be estimated using Table 16.2, "The Average Tax Rate.") This is used to calculate the before-tax income necessary to cover the annual living expenses in line D. In this case, assume an average tax rate of 14%. Thus, line F, the before tax income = line D/line E, where line E = (I − Average Tax Rate) | ÷ 0.86 | _____ |
| F. Equals: The before-tax income necessary to cover the annual living expenses in line D | line D divided by line E = $53,241 | _____ |
| | | |
| **STEP 3: Estimate Your Income Available at Retirement.** | | |
| G. Income from Social Security in today's dollars | $18,000 | _____ |
| H. Plus: Projected pension benefits in today's dollars | + $25,000 | _____ |
| I. Plus: Other income in today's dollars | + $0 | _____ |
| J. Equals (lines G + H + I): Anticipated retirement income, in today's dollars | = $43,000 | _____ |
| | | |
| **STEP 4: Calculate the (Annual) Inflation-Adjusted Shortfall.** | | |
| K. Anticipated shortfall in today's dollars (line F minus line J) | = $10,241 | _____ |
| L. Inflation adjustment factor, based on an anticipated inflation rate of 4% between now and retirement with 30 years to retirement (FVIFs are found in Appendix A): $FVIF_{\text{inflation rate \%, no. years to retirement}}$ | × 3.243 | _____ |
| M. Equals: Inflation-adjusted shortfall (line K × line L) | = $33,212 | _____ |

**STEP 5: Calculate the Total Funds Needed at Retirement to Cover This Shortfall over the Number of Years You Expect to Be Retired (assuming an inflation-adjusted return of 5% [return (9%) minus the inflation rate (4%)] during your retirement period, with retirement anticipated to last for 30 years).**

| | | |
|---|---|---|
| N. Calculate the funds needed at retirement to cover the inflation-adjusted shortfall over the entire retirement period, assuming that these funds can be invested at 9% and that the inflation rate over this period is 4%. Thus, determining the present value of a 30-year annuity assuming a 5% inflation-adjusted return (PVIFAs are found in Appendix D). $PVIFA_{\text{inflation-adjusted return, no. years in retirement}}$ | = 15.373 | _____ |
| O. Equals: Funds needed at retirement to finance the shortfall (line M × line N) | × line M = $510,568 | _____ |

**STEP 6: Determine How Much You Must Save Annually Between Now and Retirement. (30 years until retirement and earning a 9% return) to Cover the Shortfall.**

| | | |
|---|---|---|
| P. Future value interest factor for an annuity for 30 years, given a 9% expected annual return: $FVIFA_{\text{expected rate of return, no. years to retirement}}$ (FVIFAs are found in Appendix C) | = 136.305 | _____ |
| Q. Equals: PMT, or the amount that must be saved annually for 30 years and invested at 9% in order to accumulate the line O amount at the end of 30 years | line O divided by line P = $3,746 | _____ |

Administration mails out annual earnings and benefit statements to all workers age 25 and older (about 125 million) who are not already receiving monthly Social Security benefits. The statement provides estimates of the Social Security retirement, disability, and survivors benefits they and their family could be eligible to receive now and in the future. (If you didn't save your Social Security statement, call or visit a local Social Security office; call 1-800-772-1213 or visit the Web site, **www.ssa.gov**.) You can also get an estimate of social security benefits from the Social Security benefits calculator located at **www.ssa.gov/retire2/calculator.htm**. To the Social Security benefits, you add any projected pension benefits in today's dollars plus any other retirement income available.

To determine how much your pension will pay, stop at your company's employee benefits office. Get a copy of your individual benefit statement, which describes your pension plan and estimates how much your plan is worth today and the level of benefits you'll receive when you retire. There are a number of basic questions included in Checklist 16.1 that you should be able to answer about your company's pension fund.

The Tates estimate their Social Security income to be $18,000 and their pension benefits to be $25,000, giving them a total level of retirement income of $43,000 in today's dollars.

## Step 4: Calculate the Inflation-Adjusted Shortfall

Now it's time to compare the amounts from steps 2 and 3. For most people, there's a big difference between the retirement income they need and the retirement income they'll have. As pensions are phased out and Social Security becomes less certain, that difference is going to get bigger and bigger. For the Tates, the before-tax income level they need is $53,241 (line F of Figure 16.3), whereas their available income is only $43,000 (line J), leaving a shortfall of $10,241 (line K).

## Checklist 16.1 ■ Questions You Should Be Able to Answer About Your Company's Pension Plan

Is this a noncontributory or contributory plan?
What are the pension requirements in terms of age and years of service?
Is there an early retirement age, and if so, what are the benefits?
What is the full benefits retirement age?
How does the vesting process work?
If I retire at age 65, how much will I receive in the way of pension payments?
If I die, what benefits will my spouse and family receive?
What is the present size of my pension credit today?
If I am disabled, will I receive pension benefits?
Can I withdraw money from my retirement fund before retirement?
Can I borrow on my retirement fund, and if so, what are the terms?
If my company is taken over or goes bankrupt, what happens to the pension fund?
Is the plan funded? If not, what portion of the benefits could the company pay today?
Is my pension plan a defined contribution plan or a defined benefit plan?
What are the choices available to me regarding ways that the pension might be paid out?

Of course, this shortfall is in today's dollars, as are all our calculations so far. To determine what the shortfall will be in retirement dollars, 30 years from now, the Tates must project $10,241 into the future. This is simply a problem involving the future value of a single cash flow.

As you should recall, we need an inflation rate to work a future value problem. Let's assume that the inflation rate over the next 30 years will be 4 percent annually. To move money forward in time 30 years, assuming a 4-percent rate of inflation, multiply it by the $FVIF_{4\%, 30 \text{ yr}}$, which is 3.243 (as found in Appendix A), yielding an inflation-adjusted shortfall of $33,212.

$$FV = PV(FVIF_{i\%, n \text{ yr}})$$
$$FV = \$10,241(FVIF_{4\%, 30 \text{ yr}})$$
$$FV = \$10,241(3.243)$$
$$FV = \$33,212$$

## Step 5: Calculate the Funds Needed to Cover This Shortfall

By now you should know how much of an annual shortfall you'll have in your retirement funding. That is, you'll know how much additional money you'll need to come up with each year to support yourself in retirement. The question then becomes, How much must you have saved by retirement to fund this annual shortfall?

Let's return to our example of the Tates. We know they have an annual shortfall of $33,212 in retirement (future) dollars. They don't want inflation to erode the value of their savings. That means they'll want their retirement savings to grow by 4 percent each year just to cover inflation. In addition, assume they can earn a 9-percent return on their retirement funds. That is to say, whereas the shortfall payout will increase by 4 percent per year to compensate for inflation, they earn 9 percent per year on their investment. In effect, they earn an inflation-adjusted rate of 5 percent (that is, $9\% - 4\%$) per year.

Thus, in determining how much the Tates need to have saved if they wish to withdraw $33,212 per year while earning a 5-percent inflation-adjusted return, you're really determining the present value of an annuity. In this case, it's a 30-year annuity, because the Tates want this retirement supplement to continue for 30 years, and it's discounted back to the present at 5 percent as follows:

$$PV = PMT(PVIFA_{i\%, n \text{ yr}})$$
$$PV = \$33,212(PVIFA_{5\%, 30 \text{ yr}})$$
$$PV = \$33,212(15.373)$$
$$PV = \$510,568$$

Thus, we multiply the inflation-adjusted shortfall of $33,212 by the $PVIFA_{5\%, 30 \text{ yr}}$ of 15.373 (found in Appendix D), which shows that $510,568 is the amount that the Tates need to accumulate by retirement.

## Step 6: Determine How Much You Must Save Annually Between Now and Retirement

Now you know the total amount you'll need to have saved by the time you retire, but you're not about to put it all away at once. Instead, you'll need to put money away little by little, year by year. The question you'll need to answer in this step is, How much do you need to put away each year?

The Tates know they need to accumulate $510,568 by the time they retire in 30 years. To determine how much they need to put away each year to achieve this amount, they need to know how much they can earn on their investments between now and when they retire. Let's assume they can earn 9 percent. This then becomes a simple future value of an annuity problem, solving for $PMT$ in the formula.

$$FV = PMT(FVIFA_{i\%,\, n\,\mathrm{yr}})$$
$$\$510{,}568 = PMT(FVIFA_{9\%,\, 30\,\mathrm{yr}})$$
$$\$510{,}568 = PMT(136.305)$$
$$PMT = \$3{,}746$$

Therefore, the Tates must save $3,746 each year for the next 30 years at 9 percent to meet their retirement goals.

## Step 7: Put the Plan in Play and Save

OK, you've finally figured out exactly how much you need to save each year to achieve your retirement goals. Now all you need do is save. This last step should be the easiest, right? Wrong. It's actually one of the hardest. There are countless ways to save for retirement, and choosing the one that's best for you requires knowing something about what's available out there.

In the next few sections, we'll walk you through the various types of retirement savings plans, and we'll give you plenty of good advice to get you on your way. Whatever you decide to do, be sure not to take saving too lightly in the retirement planning process. Watch out for that last step—it's a doozie!

## What Plan Is Best For You?

What's the best way to save for retirement? Well, that really depends on your circumstances. There are so many options available, some of them very job or occupation specific, that it's hard to make general statements about what plans are right for everyone. However, it's safe to say that you should certainly try to use a tax-favored retirement plan.

Most of these plans are tax deferred and work by allowing investment earnings to go untaxed until you remove these earnings at retirement. In essence, they allow you to put off paying taxes so that money that would have gone to the IRS can be invested by you. In addition, some plans allow for the contributions to be made on either a fully or partially tax-deductible basis. In retirement planning, **Principle 6: Taxes Affect Personal Finance Decisions** can't be overstressed.

There are several advantages to tax-deferred plans. First, because the contributions may not be taxed, you can contribute more. You can contribute funds that would otherwise go to the IRS. Second, because the investment earnings aren't taxed until they're withdrawn at retirement, you can earn money on earnings

**STOP & THINK** Personal savings rates have fallen over the past 20 years. A poll conducted by Fidelity Investments/Public Agenda in 1997 found that nearly half of Americans had saved less than $10,000 for retirement. This figure includes all savings: savings accounts, bonds and mutual funds. Keep in mind, the more you save, the higher your retirement income will be.

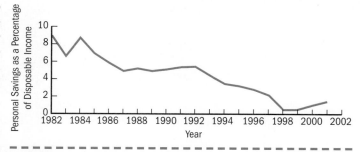

Principle 6 Taxes Affect Personal Finance Decisions

that also would have otherwise gone to the IRS. In other words, you can earn compound interest on money that would normally have gone to the IRS.

Figure 16.4 shows just how dramatic this compounding can be. Let's assume you wish to invest $2,000 of before-tax income on an annual basis in a retirement account. Let's also assume you can earn 9 percent compounded annually on this investment and your marginal state and federal tax rate is 31 percent.

If you invest in a tax-deferred retirement account to which the contributions are fully tax-deductible, you'll start off and end up with more money. You'll start with more money because, after taxes, you'll still have your full $2,000 to invest. You'll end up with more money because you'll be able to compound more of your earnings instead of paying them to the IRS.

Investing in a fully taxable retirement account is a different story. To begin with, you won't be able to invest the entire $2,000 because 31 percent of this amount will go toward taxes, leaving you with only $1,380 to invest. In addition, the investment earnings will also be taxed annually, at a rate of 31 percent.

Figure 16.4 compares these retirement plans with annual investments of $2,000 of before-tax income for 30 years. After 10 years you'd have accumulated $33,121 in the tax-deferred account but only $19,511 in the taxable account. After 20 years the tax-deferred account would have grown to $111,529, whereas the taxable account would be at $55,150. Finally, after 30 years the tax-deferred account would have grown to $297,150, whereas the taxable account would have accumulated only $120,250.

Of course, Uncle Sam does catch up eventually. When you withdraw your retirement funds, the interest earned on them over the years is taxed, but at least you had the chance to earn plenty of extra interest.

Obviously, there are major advantages to saving on a tax-deferred basis. It's pure and simple, smart investing. Before you look into any other types of retirement investments, check out the ones that are tax favored. There are plenty of these plans currently available. Some are employer-sponsored, and others are aimed at the self-employed. Let's take a look.

**Figure 16.4** Saving in a Tax-Deferred Retirement Account Versus Saving on a Nontax-Deferred Basis

Assuming an investment of $2,000 of before-tax income on an annual basis in a retirement account where those contributions are fully tax deductible versus investing $2,000 of before-tax income on a nontax-deferred basis. A 9% annual return is assumed on these investments, with investment earnings in the tax-deferred account being tax deferred, and earnings in the other account being taxed annually. A marginal state and federal tax rate of 31% is also assumed.

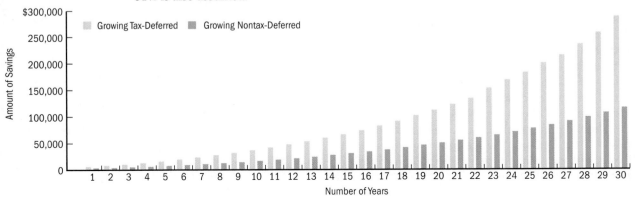

# Employer-Sponsored Retirement Plans

## Defined-Contributions Plans

Under a **defined-contribution plan**, your employer alone or you and your employer together contribute directly to an individual account set aside specifically for you. In effect, a defined-contribution plan can be thought of as a personal savings account for retirement. Your eventual payments aren't guaranteed. Instead, what you eventually receive depends on how well your retirement account performs. Many defined-contribution plans allow you to choose how your account is invested.

In recent years the popularity of such programs has skyrocketed because they involve no risk for the employer. The employer's job involves a bit of bookkeeping and making a financial contribution. Employers don't really care what you eventually receive; their responsibility ends with their contribution. In effect, defined-contribution plans pass the responsibility for retirement from employer to employee. They also pass the risk, because they aren't insured and payments aren't guaranteed.

Defined-contribution plans generally take one of several basic forms, including profit-sharing plans, money purchase plans, thrift and savings plans, or employee stock ownership plans.

**Profit-Sharing Plans**   Under a **profit-sharing plan**, employer contributions can vary from year to year depending on the firm's performance. The exact size of the company's contribution to each employee depends on the employee's salary level. Although many firms set a minimum and a maximum contribution—for example, between 2 and 12 percent of each employee's salary annually—not all firms do. A contribution is not necessarily guaranteed under this type of plan. If the firm has a poor year, it may pass on making a contribution to the plan.

**Money Purchase Plans**   Under a **money purchase plan**, the employer contributes a set percentage of employees' salaries to their retirement plans annually. For the employer, such a plan offers less flexibility, because contributions are required regardless of how well the firm does. For the employee, these plans are preferable to profit-sharing because of the guaranteed contribution.

**Thrift and Savings Plans**   Under a **thrift and savings plan**, the employer matches a percentage of employees' contributions to their retirement accounts. For example, Viacom (the company that owns MTV, Blockbuster, VH1, Showtime, and Nickelodeon, among others) matches employee contributions to their retirement plans at a rate of 50 cents for every dollar contributed, up to 6 percent of salary for employees earning under $65,000. For those employees making more than $65,000 Viacom matches at the same rate, but only up to 5 percent of salary. Above this amount, contributions aren't matched, but employees can continue to contribute up to 15 percent of their salary.

**Employee Stock Ownership Plan**   Under an **employee stock ownership plan (ESOP)** the company's contribution is made in the form of company stock. Of all the retirement plans, this is the riskiest, because your return at retirement depends on how well the company does. If the company goes bankrupt, you might lose not only your job, but also all your retirement benefits. Of course, if the company's stock price soars, you could do extremely well. However, an ESOP doesn't allow for the degree of diversification that you need with your retirement savings. In short, an ESOP isn't something you can safely rely on.

## Defined-Contribution Plan
A pension plan in which you and your employer or your employer alone contributes directly to a retirement account set aside specifically for you. In effect, a defined-contribution plan can be thought of as a savings account for retirement.

## Profit-Sharing Plan
A pension plan in which the company's contributions vary from year to year depending on the firm's performance. The amount of money contributed to each employee depends on the employee's salary level.

## Money Purchase Plan
A pension plan in which the employer contributes a set percentage of employees' salaries to their retirement plans annually.

## Thrift and Savings Plan
A pension plan in which the employer matches a percentage of the employees' contributions to their retirement accounts.

## Employee Stock Ownership Plan or ESOP
A retirement plan in which the retirement funds are invested directly in the company's stock.

# 401(k) Plans

**401(k) Plan**

A tax-deferred retirement savings plan in which employees of private corporations may contribute a portion of their wages up to a maximum amount set by law ($11,000 for tax year 2002 and rising by $1,000 per year until it reaches $15,000 in 2006). Employers may contribute a full or partially matching amount, and may limit the proportion of the annual salary contributed (typically to 15 percent).

A **401(k) plan** is really a do-it-yourself variation of a profit-sharing/thrift plan. These can be set up as part of an employer-sponsored defined-contribution plan, with both the employer and the employee contributing to the plan, or with only the employee making a contribution. Over the past 20 years these plans have exploded in terms of popularity. In fact, about 9 out of 10 large employers—that is, companies employing over 500 workers—provide 401(k) plans for their workers. Corporations love them because they allow the retirement program to be handed over entirely to the employee.

A 401(k) plan is simply a tax-deferred retirement plan in which both the employee's contributions to the plan and the earnings on those contributions are tax-deductible, with all taxes being deferred until retirement withdrawals are made.[1] In essence, a 401(k) is equivalent to the tax-deferred retirement plan presented earlier in Figure 16.4.

The advantages to such an account are twofold. First, you don't pay taxes on money contributed to 401(k) plans, which means you can contribute into your retirement account money that would have otherwise been paid out as taxes. Second, your earnings on your retirement account are tax-deferred. Thus, you can earn a return on money that would otherwise have been paid out in taxes.

The end result, as shown in Figure 16.4, is that you can accumulate a much larger retirement nest egg using a 401(k) account than you otherwise could. So you should invest the maximum allowable amount in your 401(k) account. You should do this before you consider any other taxed investment alternatives. Moreover, this should be automatic—that is, *your 401(k) should be paid* before you receive anything. Only after you have maxed out on your 401(k) contributions should you consider other investments.

Many 401(k) plans are set up as thrift and savings plans, in which the employer matches a percentage of the employee's contribution. For example, Coca-Cola matches dollar for dollar the first 3 percent of employees' earnings contributed to the 401(k) plan. This matching program has resulted in an 87-percent participation rate, and an average savings balance per worker of over $100,000. At rival PepsiCo, the 401(k) benefits aren't nearly as attractive. PepsiCo doesn't match employee contributions. As a result, only 45 percent of PepsiCo's employees participate in their 401(k) plan, and their average savings balance per worker is less than one-fifth that of Coke's. So much for the choice of a new generation.

Needless to say, a matching 401(k) program increases participation. In addition, a matching plan is an offer too good to refuse. It's free money, and you should take advantage of any matching the company is willing to do.

**Guaranteed Investment Contracts or GICs**

A contract with an insurance company that guarantees a specified return on all investments in the pension plan. These are similar to CDs.

Also, 401(k) plans offer a wide variety of investment options. In fact, over half of all 401(k) plans offer five or more investment choices. These options range from conservative guaranteed investment contracts (GICs) to aggressive stock funds.

**Guaranteed investment contracts (GICs)** are just relatively conservative investments that look much like certificates of deposit. They're issued by insurance companies and generally pay a fixed rate of interest one-half to 1 percent above the Treasury rates. In spite of their name, GICs aren't guaranteed. You should be aware of the issuer's rating—they could be quite risky. In most cases, you're much better

**403(b) Plan**

A tax-deferred retirement plan that's essentially the same as a 401(k) plan except that it's aimed at employees of schools and charitable organizations.

---

[1]A **403(b) plan** is essentially the same as a 401(k) plan except that it's aimed at employees of schools and charitable organizations. Although our discussion will focus on 401(k) plans, it also holds true for 403(b) plans.

off with the aggressive stock funds, especially if you have a long time to go before you retire.

Keep in mind what we learned in **Principle 11: The Time Dimension of Investing**. If you're going to be retiring shortly, perhaps you're better off investing in a solid GIC. However, if you have a while before retirement, holding stocks will reduce their risk while not reducing their return. A conservative investment such as a GIC will allow you to keep pace with inflation but not much more. Stocks will have more ups and downs, but over time your results will be better. Despite this fact, almost half of all participants choose GICs when they're available. Unfortunately, most people simply don't have the knowledge of investments or personal finance to protect themselves. After taking this course, you shouldn't have that problem.

Principle

**11** The Time Dimension of Investing

---

**STOP & THINK** According to a 1999 survey by Hewitt Associates, 21 percent of workers eligible for 401(k) plans don't put a penny in them. Even worse, this figure has remained the same over the previous five years. That means that an awful lot of people are assuming away the future. Make sure you aren't one of them; fund your 401(k) to the max.

---

**How Much Can You Contribute?**   The Tax Relief Act of 2001 included a number of provisions that both reduce the complexity and increase the savings limits. Specifically, it increased the limits on contributions to qualified retirement plans and allowed greater flexibility with respect to withdrawals, rollovers, and continuation of plans.

In addition, the act increased the limits on employee contributions to 401(k) and 403(b) plans (also SEP-IRAs plans, which will be covered shortly) to $11,000 in 2002 rising by $1,000 per year to $15,000 in 2006 and on with indexing for inflation in $500 increments. The act also, effective 2002, provided increased contribution levels for taxpayers over 50 to allow them to "catch up" with where they needed to be. For example, the act allows an additional "catch-up" of $1,000 beginning in 2002 and rising to $5,000 by 2006.

## Retirement Plans for the Self-Employed and Small Business Employees

Contribute to a tax-favored retirement plan to help fund your retirement.

Fully tax-deductible retirement plans for the self-employed or small business employee—which includes anyone who has his or her own business, works for a small business, or does freelance work on a part-time basis—hold the same basic advantages as employer-sponsored plans available in large corporations. You qualify for such a plan if you do any work for yourself (even if you work full-time for an employer and are covered by another retirement plan there).

It's surprising how many individuals qualify for these plans and either don't realize it or do nothing to take advantage of another tax-deferred retirement tool. Examples of those who are eligible are lawyers, doctors, dentists, carpenters, plumbers, artists, freelance writers, and consultants. Basically, if you're at all self-employed, either full-time or part-time, or work for a small business, you can contribute to a Keogh or self-employed retirement plan, a simplified employee pension plan (SEP-IRA), or the new savings incentive match plan for employees (SIMPLE) plan.

## Keogh Plan or Self-Employed Retirement Plan

The **Keogh plan** was introduced in 1962 in an effort to provide self-employed individuals and employees of unincorporated businesses an opportunity to make large

**Keogh Plan**
A tax-sheltered retirement plan for the self-employed.

tax-deductible payments to a retirement plan. Today, Keogh plans are quite similar to corporate pension or profit-sharing plans. The establishment of a Keogh plan is relatively easy. You simply select a bank, mutual fund, or other financial institution and approach it. In general, the institution will have the paperwork needed to establish the plan already completed. It will provide you with a prototype plan, and you simply fill in the blanks.

When you set up the Keogh plan, you'll be asked to choose a defined-contribution and/or a defined-benefit Keogh plan. These options are not mutually exclusive—your Keogh plan can contain both. Under a defined-contribution plan, you choose the level of your contribution to the plan. There's no guarantee of the retirement payout, because the benefit will depend solely on the income earned on what went in. If you don't put anything in, you can't get anything out.

There are a number of ways to set up defined-contribution Keogh plans. With some you must annually contribute a fixed percentage of profits. Others give you a good deal of flexibility in terms of varying your level of annual contributions and may even let you skip a year with no penalty. The total amount that can be contributed in one employee's name for 2002 is the lesser of $40,000 ($35,000 for 2001) or 100 percent of the employee's annual earnings (25 percent for 2001).

Under a defined-benefit Keogh plan, rather than contribute a percentage of your earnings, you're allowed to contribute whatever amount you deem necessary to meet your retirement payout schedule, which is determined by an IRS formula along with some actuarial assumptions. In the extreme case, you could actually contribute 100 percent of your self-employed earnings. The big drawback with the defined-benefit Keogh plan is that it's both costly and complicated to administer, requiring a professional actuary to oversee the plan. As a result, it's generally used as a catch-up plan by those who've neglected to set up a pension plan in the past.

Regardless of which type of Keogh plan you end up with, they're all self-directed, meaning you decide what securities to buy and sell and when. As with 401(k)s, the payment to the plan comes out before you determine your taxes, so any contributions reduce your bill to Uncle Sam. Withdrawals can begin as early as age $59\frac{1}{2}$ and must begin by age $70\frac{1}{2}$. If you need your money early, you'll have to pay a 10-percent penalty except in cases of serious illness, disability, or death.

## Simplified Employee Pension Plan

A **simplified employee pension plan (SEP-IRA)** works like a defined-contribution Keogh plan funded by the employer. SEP-IRAs are used primarily by small business owners with no or very few employees. Each employee sets up his or her own individual retirement account and the employer makes annual contributions to that account. For 2002, the deduction limit was increased to 25 percent of the employee's salary or $30,000, whichever is less, with additional "catch-up" contributions for individuals who are 50 years old or older.

In addition, there's flexibility in making contributions. For example, they can be made one year and not the next, and when they are made, they're immediately vested. The advantage of a SEP-IRA program is that it works about the same as a Keogh plan but is easier to set up. It simply means filling out a one-page form. In addition, a SEP-IRA doesn't have the reporting requirements of a Keogh.

## Savings Incentive Match Plan for Employees

Small employers can establish a **savings incentive match plan for employees** or **SIMPLE plan**—SIMPLE IRAs and SIMPLE 401(k)s. These new SIMPLE plans may

**Simplified Pension Plan or SEP-IRA**
A tax-sheltered (you don't pay taxes on any earnings while they remain in the plan) retirement plan aimed at small businesses or at the self-employed. It works like a 401(k) plan, allowing employers to contribute up to the lesser of $40,000 or 100 percent of the employee's earnings in 2002, with the employer contribution going directly into the employee's IRA.

**Savings Incentive Match Plan for Employees or SIMPLE Plan**
A tax-sheltered retirement plan aimed at small businesses or the self-employed that provides for some matching funds by the employer to be deposited in your retirement account.

# In The News

Wall Street Journal Sunday June 4, 2000

## A Must-Do Checklist for Retirement

### by Jonathan Clements

Here are two items that should be on your preretirement checklist:

1. Get a Handle on Expenses. "I don't believe any living-expense number my clients give me," says Richard Van Der Noord, a financial planner in Macon, Georgia. "The number they give me off the cuff is very different from the number we get if they go through an expense worksheet."

Conventional wisdom suggests you need 70 percent or 80 percent of your preretirement income to live comfortably in retirement. But this rule of thumb can be highly misleading.

Sure, after you quit the workforce, you will no longer have commuting costs, need work clothes, or pay Medicare and Social Security payroll taxes. But other expenses don't go away and some will increase, like medical and travel costs.

*"Before anyone retires, they should take a look at the dark side," says Henry "Bud" Hebeler, a retired engineer who runs a Web site devoted to retirement issues* (**www.analyzenow.com**).

*"Think about uninsured medical, dental and drug bills. Consider how many times you may have to replace your automobile. Estimate costly home-maintenance items such as replacing your roof."* (☞**A**)

2. Review Your Debts. By the time you quit the workforce, "you'd like to be in a situation where the only debt you have is your mortgage," says Kenneth Klegon, a financial planner in Lansing, Michigan. That means paying off car loans and credit card balances.

Mr. Klegon, however, doesn't advocate paying off your mortgage. "It's a myth that you need to have your house paid off before you retire," he says. "Yes, it's one less bill every month. But the question is, what could you earn if you invested that money instead? Remember, a mortgage is the cheapest loan you'll ever get."

*Before you leave the workforce, set up a home-equity line of credit, which you can draw on if you need a hunk of cash at short notice. Why the rush? You may find it difficult to qualify for a credit line once* *you retire and no longer have a regular income.* (☞**B**)

### THE BOTTOM LINE . . .

**A** The place to start is to analyze your current spending—to do this go back through your checkbook and credit card receipts. Also, don't be too certain that your expenses will drop too much when you retire. After all, you'll be on a 52-week vacation.

**B** If you still need money, you might consider moving into a smaller house. If that's the case, you might consider doing it sooner as opposed to later. That way you can invest the freed-up capital sooner.

---

be set up by employers with fewer than 100 employees earning $5,000 or more, covering all their employees, including themselves, as part of a 401(k). Employee contributions are excluded from income, and the earnings in the retirement plan are tax deferred. In addition to employee contributions, there are some matching funds provided by the employer—although the employer does have some flexibility in determining how much to contribute. The maximum contribution to a SIMPLE plan is $7,000 in 2002, and in 2003 and thereafter the limit is increased in $1,000 increments until it reaches $10,000 in 2005. For those age 50 or older that limit is increased by an additional $500 in 2002, $1,000 in 2003, $1,500 in 2004, $2,000 in 2005, and $2,500 in 2005.

Why did Congress decide to establish one more type of retirement plan? Because many smaller businesses were put off by complex and expensive alternative plans and, thus, didn't provide retirement plans for their employees. That's where the SIMPLE plans fit in, because the rules governing them are, as the name implies, simple.

## Individual Retirement Accounts (IRAs)

With the passage of the Taxpayer Relief Act of 1997, there are now three types of IRAs to choose from: the traditional IRA, the Roth IRA, and the Education IRA.

**3** Contribute to a tax-favored retirement plan to help fund your retirement.

# Traditional IRAs

**Individual Retirement Account or IRA**

A retirement account to which an individual can contribute up to $3,000 annually in 2002 through 2004, $4,000 annually in 2005 through 2007, and $5,000 annually in 2008. This contribution may or may not be tax-deductible, depending on the individual's income level and whether he or she or his or her spouse is covered by a company retirement plan.

**Individual retirement accounts (IRAs)** were established in 1981, and for the first 5 years were relatively simple. They let you deposit up to $2,000 of before-tax income in your IRA. With the Tax Reform Act of 1986, simplicity was stripped from the program. Today, this contribution can be fully tax deductible, partially tax deductible, or not tax deductible, depending on the level of your earnings and whether you or your spouse has a company retirement plan.

**An Increase in the IRA Contribution Limit**   The Tax Relief Act of 2001 further complicated IRAs by gradually increasing the maximum contribution. In addition, as we pointed out when we looked at taxes, the new law also allowed for a tax credit to certain low-income taxpayers who make contributions to qualified retirement plans or IRA accounts.

For the first 20 years the maximum annual IRA contribution was set at $2,000. Under the Tax Relief Act, the maximum amount that could be contributed to a traditional IRA account and a Roth IRA account rose to $3,000 for the years 2002 through 2004, $4,000 for years 2005 through 2007, and in 2008 it increases to $5,000 and thereafter it is adjusted for inflation in $500 increments. In addition, individuals age 50 and over are permitted to make additional annual contributions of $500 in 2002 through 2005 and $1,000 in 2006 and thereafter.

The act also allows for a tax credit to low-income taxpayers for certain retirement savings contributions. Effective for years 2002 through 2006, a nonrefundable tax credit would be available for certain taxpayers who make contributions to qualified retirement plans or IRA accounts. This Saver's Tax Credit is a nonrefundable income tax credit that can run up to $2,000 per year for certain taxpayers with adjusted gross income that does not exceed $50,000. It is equal to a percentage of certain employee contributions to an IRA for tax years 2002 through 2006. To be eligible you must be 18 or over by the end of the taxable year, and not be a full-time student or be claimed as a dependent on someone else's tax return. The credit rate is based on the taxpayer's adjusted gross income for the taxable year. For example, for those with a "married filing joint" status and adjusted gross income (AGI) between $0 and $30,000, the saver's credit rate is 50%; for those with AGI between $30,001 and $32,500 the saver's credit rate is 20%; and for those with AGI between $32,500 and $50,000 the saver's credit rate is 10%. Needless to say, this is a credit that you'll want to take advantage of if you qualify.

If both you and your spouse are employed and aren't covered by a company retirement plan, you can contribute up to the maximum, which was $3,000 in 2002, annually on a tax-deferred basis to your IRA. A married couple with only one spouse working outside the home may both contribute to an IRA, provided the "working spouse" has at least earned income up to the amount contributed. If neither of you is an "active participant" in a retirement plan at work, or if your joint adjusted gross income is below the IRS cutoff, your IRA contributions are entirely tax deductible.

What's an "active participant"? If you have a defined-benefit retirement plan, you're considered an "active participant." In addition, if you have a defined-contribution plan and either you or your employer contributed to it during the year, you're considered an "active participant." However, if neither you nor your employer contributed to your defined-contribution plan during the year or your income is below the cutoff level, you can make a fully deductible contribution to your IRA.

There's also a provision that allows a nonworking spouse to make a deductible contribution to an IRA even if the working spouse is covered by a qualified retirement plan or their income is high. Under this provision, a nonworking spouse can make a fully deductible contribution to an IRA as long as their "modified" adjusted gross income (AGI) is below $150,000, even if the other spouse is covered by a qualified retirement plan, where "modified" AGI is adjusted gross income before subtracting IRA deductions. In addition, a partial deduction is allowed until income hits $160,000. Partial tax deductions are also available for IRA contributions, again depending on income level.

For the tax year 2002 the trigger point for full deductibility of IRA contributions is $34,000 of "modified" AGI for those filing single returns and $54,000 for those filing jointly. Once "modified" AGI reaches $44,000 for single returns and $64,000 for those filing a joint return, deductibility is totally phased out.

These phaseout zones continue to rise through 2007, as follows:

| Year | Filing Single Returns | Filing Joint Returns |
|------|----------------------|---------------------|
| 2002 | $34,000–44,000 | $54,000–64,000 |
| 2003 | 40,000–50,000 | 60,000–70,000 |
| 2004 | 45,000–55,000 | 65,000–75,000 |
| 2005 | 50,000–60,000 | 70,000–80,000 |
| 2006 | 50,000–60,000 | 75,000–85,000 |
| 2007 | 50,000–60,000 | 80,000–90,000 |

Above those dollar limits, IRA contributions are still allowed, but they're nondeductible for tax purposes if your spouse is in a qualified plan. However, even if you don't qualify for a tax deduction, an IRA may be a smart move. Nondeductible IRAs have the advantage that your investment grows free of income taxes until you withdraw money from the account.

If you do contribute to a nondeductible IRA, you must file IRS Form 8606 with your income taxes. You'll want to keep a copy of this form showing that your contribution was made on an after-tax basis to avoid paying taxes a second time when you finally withdraw your money. Also, don't mix deductible and nondeductible IRA contributions together; it will be hard to prove down the road what is not taxable.

If all contributions to your IRA are tax deductible, then all withdrawals from your IRA will be taxed, unless you're just moving your money into another IRA. There are also restrictions on the timing and amount of IRA withdrawals, as follows:

▌ Distributions before age $59\frac{1}{2}$ are subject to a 10-percent tax penalty with few exceptions.

▌ After you turn $70\frac{1}{2}$ you must start receiving annual distributions under a life expectancy calculation.

▌ You can make penalty-free withdrawals provided you (a) are making them to buy your first home, (b) are using them for college expenses, (c) you become disabled, (d) you need the money to pay medical expenses in excess of 7.5 percent of your AGI, or (e) you need the money to pay medical insurance payments if you've been unemployed for at least 12 consecutive weeks. There is, however, a limit of $10,000 on penalty-free withdrawals to buy a first home.

**STOP & THINK** Saving for retirement using an IRA can reap big benefits. If you're in the 30-percent tax bracket, putting $3,000 a year into an IRA equates to less than $8.22 per day, and only $5.75 per day of spendable, after-tax income. If you start your IRA when you're 22—putting it in an IRA that pays 10 percent at the beginning of each year—and continue that practice for 45 years, you'll end up with over $2.16 million.

If you tried to do this without an IRA, paying taxes on your $3,000 and then investing it at a before-tax rate of 10 percent, you'd end up with only $600,074. Granted the money in your IRA would be taxable income when you withdrew it, it's still a pretty sizable sum.

In addition to annual contributions to an IRA, you can roll over a distribution from a qualified employer plan or from another IRA into a new IRA. Why would you ever do this? If you get a new job or if you retire early, you may be faced with that 10-percent early distribution penalty. To get around this penalty, you can instead have your distributions "rolled over" into a new IRA. If you're going to "roll over" your distributions into a new IRA, make sure you see a financial advisor or tax accountant ahead of time because there are a number of rollover rules you need to follow to avoid taxes.

What are your investment choices with an IRA? You can go with stocks, bonds, mutual funds, real estate, CDs—almost anything. It's your call because IRAs are self-directed, and you can change your IRA funds from one investment to another at any time without paying taxes. The only things you can't invest in are life insurance or collectibles, other than gold or silver U.S. coins. You also can't borrow from your IRA, and you can't use it as collateral for a loan.

## The Roth and Education IRAs

The passage of the Taxpayer Relief Act of 1997 added two new IRAs to choose from—the Roth IRA and the Education IRA. Congress passed this legislation to encourage saving—both for retirement and for education. Also under the new law, more people qualify for the tax breaks from an IRA—particularly nonworking spouses and middle-income taxpayers covered by pension plans.

Under the **Roth IRA**, contributions are not tax deductible. That is, you'd make your contribution out of after-tax income. But once the money is in there, it grows tax free and when it is withdrawn, the withdrawals are tax free. Remember, with a traditional IRA, your contributions are made with before-tax income, but withdrawals are taxed. With the Roth IRA the taxation process is reversed: You put after-tax income into the IRA, but you don't pay taxes when the money is withdrawn. One similarity between the traditional IRA and the Roth IRA is that with both, you don't pay any taxes while your money is in the IRA.

Obviously, the big advantage of the Roth IRA is that you can avoid taxes when you finally withdraw your money. Of course, as with everything else in the tax code, there are some exceptions. First, to avoid taxes, you must keep your money in your Roth IRA for at least 5 years.

Who's eligible to put money into a Roth IRA? A lot of people! The income limits don't begin until $95,000 for single taxpayers and $150,000 for couples, and are totally phased out at $110,000 for individuals and $160,000 for couples. Keep in mind that even if you have a 401(k) account, you can also contribute to an IRA. You can have both a traditional IRA and a Roth IRA; however, your total contributions to both are limited to the maximum IRA contribution levels of $3,000 for the years 2002 through 2004, $4,000 for years 2005 through 2007, and in 2008 increasing to $5,000 and thereafter it is adjusted for inflation in $500 increments.

Another great feature of the Roth IRA is that, at any time, you can pull out an amount up to your original contribution without getting hit with a tax penalty. Also new with the Roth IRA, there is no requirement that distributions begin by age $70\frac{1}{2}$.

In addition to your annual contribution, if your income is less than $100,000 (either on a joint or individual return) you can also roll money from your existing IRA into your Roth IRA without incurring a 10-percent penalty. Granted, it would trigger taxes on your withdrawal, but you can spread the taxes by rolling over a portion of your traditional IRA to a Roth each year over as many years as you like. Then, when you make your future withdrawals at retirement, there would be no taxes to pay.

According to a study by T. Rowe Price a major mutual fund company, this switch is probably a good idea if you have enough money outside your IRA to pay taxes and you are under 55. However, this study was based on the assumption that you stay in

**Roth IRA**
An IRA in which contributions are not tax deductible. That is, you'd make your contribution to this IRA out of after-tax income. But once the money is in there, it grows tax free and when it is withdrawn, the withdrawals are tax free.

the same tax bracket after retirement. If you expect to drop to a lower tax bracket, the decision becomes more difficult.

## Traditional Versus Roth IRA: Which Is Best for You?

Mathematically, you end up with the same amount to spend at retirement if you use a traditional IRA or a Roth IRA, provided both are taxed at the same rate. So which one should you choose? If you can afford it, the answer is the Roth IRA. That's because you can take care of taxes ahead of time and end up with more money to spend at retirement. In effect, you're actually putting more money into the Roth IRA because the Roth IRA includes a $2,000 contribution *plus* the taxes you'd pay on that $2,000 contribution.

In terms of after-tax contributions, if you are in the 30-percent tax bracket a $2,000 contribution to a Roth IRA would cost you $2,857 of before-tax income—$2,000 for the contribution and $857 for taxes ($2,857 × 0.30 = $857). If you put $2,000 in a traditional IRA and let it grow at 10 percent for 40 years, you end up with $90,519 before you paid any taxes—after taxes, at 30 percent, you'd have $63,363. If you'd put $2,000 in a Roth IRA, you'd need a bit more money on the front end (as we just showed, $2,857), because you'd have to pay taxes, but you'd end up with $90,519 after 40 years and no taxes!

## Saving for College

Sure, college isn't retirement, but if you don't save properly for your children's college education, you may end up having to postpone retirement after dipping into your retirement savings. Fortunately, there are some tools out there meant to both help and inspire you to save for college. Let's first look at the **Coverdell Education Savings Account** or as it is commonly called, the **Education IRA.** It works just like the Roth IRA, except with respect to contributions. Contributions are limited to $2,000 annually per child for each child younger than 18 (and beyond for special needs beneficiaries), with income limits beginning at $95,000 for single taxpayers and $190,000 for couples. Again, the earnings are tax free and there is no tax on withdrawals to pay for education with the definition of what qualified education expenses are now including certain elementary and secondary school expenses.

Under the Tax Relief Act of 2001, individuals now have until April 15 of the following year to make contributions for the taxable year. In addition, the new act also allows taxpayers to claim a Hope credit or a Lifetime Learning credit in the same year as taking a distribution from an Education IRA provided that the same expenses aren't used for both purposes.

Savings must be withdrawn by the time the child reaches age 30, although any leftover amounts can be rolled over into accounts for younger siblings. If the money in the Education IRA isn't used for college, you may have to pay taxes plus a 10-percent penalty on its withdrawal.

How much can you save using an Education IRA? If you contribute $2,000 every year starting in 2002 and assume an 8 percent return on investment, you'd have just under $75,000 in 18 years—not bad, eh? Now let's add some reality to that number. Consider the fact that in 2002 the cost of four years at a public university is $51,618 (for tuition, room and board, and all other expenses) and $112,365 for a private college, according to The College Board. If those prices should increase by 5 percent each year, they would climb to $124,225 and $270,420 in 18 years. Now that $75,000 would be helpful, but you'd still be short, and that's if you contributed $2,000 per year for 18 years. If you got a late start, say you began investing with 12 years to go, you'd end up with just under $38,000, which wouldn't even cover one year at a private college.

**Coverdell Education Savings Account or Education IRA**
An IRA that works just like the Roth IRA, except with respect to contributions. Contributions are limited to $2,000 annually per child for each child younger than 18, with income limits beginning at $95,000 for single taxpayers and $190,000 for couples. The earnings are tax free and there is no tax on withdrawals to pay for education.

Although the Education IRA is a great way to save for your child's education, 529 plans hold several advantages over it. However, if you're so inclined, you can actually open both type of accounts. Let's now take a look at 529 plans.

The **529 plans** are tax-advantaged savings plans used only for college and graduate school, allowing you to contribute up to $250,000, which can then grow tax-free. These plans began in the 1990s out of the rule that doesn't allow the federal government to tax money that's given to a state. The result was that these accounts were tax deferred, a situation that was later made permanent by Congress. Thus, by 2002, more than 35 of these plans were established with at least 12 more in the works.

Although these plans are all sponsored by individual states, they are open to all applicants regardless of where you live. Thus, a resident of North Carolina can put money in a 529 plan in Michigan or in any state for that matter. You can also invest directly or you can invest through a financial advisor (and, of course, pay a commission). One of the appealing things about a 529 plan as opposed to an Education IRA is how much you can contribute. With a 529 plan, many state plans let you contribute more than $100,000 and some (like Wisconsin's Tomorrow's Scholar Fund) allow a maximum contribution of $250,000 that can then grow tax free.

As with any other investment, you've got some decisions to make. The first decision is what type of plan to choose. There are two basic types of 529 plans: "prepaid college tuition plans" and "college savings plans." The college savings plans offer you much more flexibility—both in terms of how they can be used and the investment alternative. One problem with college saving plans is that they generally guarantee that you will be covered only if your child chooses to go to a public in-state college or university. That loss of flexibility may not seem important when college is 10 years away, but when the day comes to pick a college, that loss of flexibility may become extremely important.

Next, you've got to decide whether to go it alone or pay a commission for it and ask an advisor. There are some quality no-commission programs offered by fund families like Fidelity and T. Rowe Price that would make selecting a plan relatively easy. However, given the fact that this is an area of constant change, there may be some advantages to having an advisor. In any case, that decision shouldn't keep you away from 529 plans. Given the constantly evolving nature of these products and the variety of them, an advisor might be a good idea. You'll also want to take a look at the investment alternatives within the plan, since they are generally limited. Also, check out how flexible the plan is. For example, find out if there are time limits on when the account must be used and what expenses can be covered by the plan. Finally, check the enrollment fee as well as any annual fees. Those things can mount up if you aren't careful.

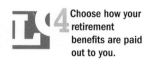
**4** Choose how your retirement benefits are paid out to you.

## Facing Retirement—The Payout

You might think that once you've saved enough for retirement, coming up with a plan for distributing those savings would be simple. Think again. Your distribution or payout decision affects how much you receive, how it's taxed, whether you're protected against inflation, whether you might outlive your retirement funds, and a host of other important concerns.

Some plans have more flexibility than others—for example, traditional (non-Roth) IRAs allow for withdrawals to begin at age $59\frac{1}{2}$, and at age $70\frac{1}{2}$ withdrawals become compulsory. Still, there are also several basic distribution choices that include receiving your payout as a lump sum, receiving it in the form of an annuity for a set number of years or for your lifetime, or some combination. Unfortunately, there isn't one best way to receive your retirement distribution. However, there are a number of important points to keep in mind when making this decision.

- Make sure you plan ahead before you decide how a payout is to be received. Make sure you understand the tax consequences of any move.
- In deciding how a payout is to be received, make sure you look at all your retirement plan payouts together. You may want to take some plan distributions in a lump sum and others as an annuity.
- Once you receive your retirement plan payout, make sure you use your understanding of investing, including diversification and the time dimension of risk, when deciding what to do with those funds.

Let's now take a look at some of the specifics behind these distribution options.

## An Annuity, or Lifetime Payments

An annuity provides you with an annual payout. This payout can go for a set number of years, it can be in the form of lifetime payments for either you or you and your spouse, or it can be in the form of lifetime payments with a minimum number of payments guaranteed. In short, just deciding on an annuity isn't enough—you must also decide among several variations of an annuity.

**Single Life Annuity**   Under a **single life annuity**, you receive a set monthly payment for your entire life. Think of this type of annuity as the Energizer bunny—it just keeps going and going, at least as long as you do. If you die after 1 year, the payments cease. Alternatively, if you live to be 100, so do your payments.

**Single Life Annuity**
An annuity in which you receive a set monthly payment for your entire life.

**An Annuity for Life or a "Certain Period"**   Under an **annuity for life or a "certain period,"** you receive annuity payments for life. However, if you die before the end of the "certain period," which is generally either 10 or 20 years, payments will continue to your beneficiary until the end of that period. Because a minimum number of payments must be made (payments must continue until the end of the certain period), an annuity for life or a "certain period" pays a smaller amount than a single life annuity. In addition, the longer the "certain period," the smaller the monthly amount.

**Annuity for Life or a "Certain Period"**
A single life annuity that allows you to receive your payments for a fixed period of time. Payments will be made to you for the remainder of your life, but if you die before the end of the time period (generally either 10 or 20 years), payments will continue to be made to your beneficiary until the end of the period.

**Joint and Survivor Annuity**   A **joint and survivor annuity** provides payments over the life of both you and your spouse. Under this choice, the two most common options are: (1) a 50-percent survivor benefit, which pays your spouse 50 percent of the original annuity after you die, or (2) a 100-percent survivor benefit, which continues benefits to your spouse at the same level after you die. Of course, the higher the survivor benefit, the lower the size of the annuity. Many firms provide medical benefits to pensioners and their spouses over their entire life when this type of annuity is chosen as the payout method.

**Joint and Survivor Annuity**
An annuity that provides payments over the life of both you and your spouse.

Most individuals who are married choose this option. In fact, if you're married and you choose another option, your spouse must sign a waiver giving you permission to accept that alternative payout.

The advantages of an annuity include the fact that it can be set up in such a way that you or you and your spouse will continue to receive benefits regardless of how long you live. In addition, some firms continue to pay for medical benefits while an annuity pension payout is being received.

The disadvantages include the fact that there's no inflation protection. Although you know for certain how much you'll receive each month, the spending power of this amount will be continuously eroded by inflation. In addition, such an annuity payout method doesn't allow for flexibility in payout patterns. For example, if there's a financial emergency, the pattern can't be altered to deal with it. In addition, under the annuity there is little flexibility to leave money to heirs.

Annuities are usually available with employer-sponsored retirement plans, but insurance companies also sell them. Depending on how attractive your employer's annuity options are, you may be better off taking a lump-sum distribution and purchasing an insurance company annuity on your own. The point here is that you aren't restricted to the annuity options offered by your employer. You should compare them with the other options available from the highest-rated insurance companies before making a decision.

### A Lump-Sum Payment

**Lump-Sum Option**
A payout arrangement in which you receive all your benefits in one single payment.

Under a **lump-sum option**, you receive your benefits in one single payment. If you're concerned about inflation protection, or if you're concerned about having access to emergency funds, a lump-sum distribution, or taking part of your money in a lump sum and putting the rest toward an annuity, may be best. If you do take your benefits in a lump sum, you'll be faced with the job of making your money last for your lifetime and for your loved ones after you're gone. That's not all bad—you get to invest the money wherever you choose, and you may end up earning a high return.

The big advantage to a lump-sum payout is the flexibility it provides. Unfortunately, you'll run the risk of making a bad investment and losing the money you so carefully saved. Table 16.3 provides a listing of some of the advantages and disadvantages of an annuity versus a lump-sum payout.

### Table 16.3 An Annuity or Lifetime Payments Versus a Lump-Sum Payout

| Annuity or Lifetime Payments | Lump Sum Payout |
|---|---|
| *Advantages* | *Advantages* |
| Payments continue as long as you live. | Flexibility to allow for emergency withdrawals. |
| Employer health benefits may continue with the annuity. | Allows for big-ticket purchases—for example, a retirement home if desired. |
| *Disadvantages* | Potential for inflation protection. |
| In general, no inflation protection. | Allows for money to be passed on to heirs. |
| No flexibility to make withdrawals in the event of a financial emergency. | Control over how the money is invested. |
| Doesn't allow for money to be passed on to heirs—payments stop when you die. | *Disadvantages* |
| | You could run out of money. |
| | You might not have the discipline to keep from spending the money. |
| | Complicates the financial planning process because you're responsible for your own retirement funding. |

## Tax Treatment of Distributions

If you receive your payout in the form of an annuity, those payments will generally be taxed as normal income. If you were born before 1936 and receive a lump-sum payout, you can use a 10-year averaging technique, which allows taxes to be calculated as if the payout were received in smaller amounts over a 10-year period. In this way you can ease your tax burden slightly. But you must pay the taxes all at once—not over 10 years.

An alternative to paying taxes on a lump-sum payout is to have the distribution "rolled over" into an IRA or qualified plan. This rollover makes a lot of sense if you've taken a new job or retired early and don't need the money now. You avoid paying taxes on the distribution while the funds continue to grow on a tax-deferred basis.

## Putting a Plan Together and Monitoring It

For most individuals, there won't be a single source of retirement income: Most people rely on retirement savings from a combination of different plans. What works best for you depends on where you work and what your retirement benefits are. However, the place to start is with the seven steps outlined at the beginning of this chapter. In addition, you should make sure you invest the maximum allowable amount in tax-sheltered retirement plans because they both reduce your taxes and allow your retirement funds to grow on a tax-deferred basis.

Your investment strategy should also reflect your investment time horizon. Think back to **Principle 11: The Time Dimension of Investing**. Early on you should be willing to take on more risk—going with a strong dose of stocks in your retirement portfolio. As retirement draws near, you should gradually switch over to less risky investments. If you're uncertain about putting together your plan, or if you'd like another opinion, don't hesitate to see a professional financial planner. Figure 16.5 illustrates the typical sources of retirement income for a retired couple.

Monitoring your retirement planning, both before and after you retire, is an ongoing process in which adjustments are constantly made for new and unexpected changes in your financial and personal life. Although it's impossible to point out all the complications that might occur, a number of things that should be kept in mind are provided in Checklist 16.2.

**Figure 16.5** Where Your Retirement Income Comes From

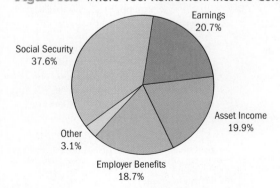

Earnings
20.7%

Social Security
37.6%

Asset Income
19.9%

Other
3.1%

Employer Benefits
18.7%

Source: U.S. Department of Labor, 2002.

# Checklist 16.2 ■ Possible Complications

Changes in inflation can have a drastic effect on your retirement. Not only do changes in anticipated inflation affect the value of any stocks and bonds that you own, they also affect the amount of money that you'll need for a comfortable retirement.

Once you retire, you may live for a long time. Your investment strategy should include a dose of stocks that reflect your investment time horizon. The strategy of investing in bonds and CDs after retirement, while widely advised, probably doesn't match most retirees' time horizons. Remember, you want to earn enough on your retirement savings to cover inflation and allow your money to grow conservatively, but grow just the same.

Monitor your progress and monitor your company. Don't be afraid to adjust your goals along with what's necessary to meet those goals. Make sure you track the performance of your retirement investments. In addition, monitor your company's health, especially if you participate in an ESOP. If your company's financial future is questionable, try to move your investments into something other than company stock.

Don't neglect insurance coverage. There's no quicker way to get in financial trouble than to experience a disaster that should have been covered by insurance but wasn't. Make sure your coverage is both up to date and at an adequate level.

An investment planning program may make things easier. There are a number of very good Internet sites that will help. For example, Fidelity has a retirement investing center at **personal300.fidelity.com/retirement/** and Vanguard has a Retirement Resource Center at **majestic.vanguard.com/RRC/DA**. In addition, *Smart Money*, *Kiplinger's*, and *Money* all have retirement sections in their Web sites.

# In The News

**Wall Street Journal August 24, 1999**

## Golden Years Carry a Hefty Price Tag

It is a rule of thumb that could cause a fistful of trouble.

*For years, financial advisors have suggested that retirees can live comfortably on 70 percent or 80 percent of their preretirement incomes. Seem like a reasonable target, as you sock away money for retirement? In truth, even with that sum, you may be a lot less comfortable than you imagine.* (☛A)

True, once you quit the workforce, there are no more 401(k) contributions, and you don't have to pay Medicare and Social Security payroll taxes anymore. You also don't have to buy work clothes, fork over union dues, and pay commuting costs.

But a lot of other expenses stay the same or rise, and a bunch of new ones appear. Result? You may want to save a tad more each year or work a little longer, so your retirement portfolio is larger and, thus, can generate more income. Here's why that extra money could come in handy:

**Uncle Sam, M.D.:** *"Many people assume that once they're on Medicare, everything will be taken care of," says John Rother, director of* legislation and public policy for AARP, the seniors' organization based in Washington. "Nothing could be further from the truth." (☛B)

Medicare expects you to pay part of the cost for many medical services, and it usually doesn't cover prescription drugs, nursing homes, dental costs, hearing aids and glasses, among other items.

***Hitting the road:*** Many folks plan to travel more when they retire. It isn't cheap.

***Lend me a hand:*** Maybe you used to cut the lawn every week, clean the gutters every fall, and paint rooms when needed. Eventually, however, you may feel compelled to hire somebody to do these chores.

***Family calls:*** *"If you're an early retiree, your parents may still be living," Mr. Hebeler notes. "They get into trouble, and you want to help them. I have a friend who just had to buy his father a new car. Most often, people have to put their parents in some sort of assisted-care facility. That happened to both my wife's mother and to my father."* (☛C)

### THE BOTTOM LINE . . .

**A** Although many financial planners use a 70 percent of preretirement income as a general rule of thumb, you'll want to make that decision for yourself. If you think you'd like to travel or go out regularly, you might want to raise that figure. Your family situation will also affect this decision.

**B** Future medical advances will be accompanied by increased costs. For that reason, you might see medical costs in the future far exceed their present level. In addition, as your life expectancy climbs, there's a good chance so will your medical bills.

**C** It's very difficult to say no when your kids come calling for financial help. If you want to be in a position to say yes if the need ever arises, you'll have to plan ahead.

## SUMMARY

For many individuals, Social Security is the primary source of retirement income. About 95 percent of all Americans are covered by Social Security. The size of your Social Security benefits is determined by (1) the number of years of earnings, (2) the average level of earning, and (3) an adjustment for inflation.

Funding your retirement needs can be thought of as a seven-step process: Set goals, estimate how much you'll need to meet your goals, estimate your income at retirement, calculate the inflation-adjusted shortfall, calculate the funds needed to cover this shortfall, determine how much you must save annually between now and retirement, and put the plan in play and save.

One way in which you can earn more on your investments is through tax-deferred retirement plans. Some of these are employer-sponsored plans, whereas others are aimed at the self-employed individual. In either case, the advantages are essentially the same. First, because the contributions may not be taxed, you can contribute more. In essence, you can contribute funds that would otherwise go to the IRS. Second, because the investment earnings aren't taxed, you can earn money on earnings that also would have otherwise gone to the IRS.

A 401(k) plan is really a do-it-yourself tax-deferred retirement plan. Over the past 20 years 401(k)s have exploded in terms of popularity. A 403(b) plan is essentially the same as a 401(k) plan except that it is aimed at employees of schools and charitable organizations. These are excellent investment vehicles.

The three basic types of plans for the self-employed are SEP-IRAs, SIMPLE plans, and Keogh plans. Another method to fund retirement is via an individual retirement account, or IRA. There are three types of IRAs: traditional IRAs, Roth IRAs, and Education IRAs.

Another important retirement decision is the distribution or payout decision, which affects how much you receive, how it is taxed, whether you are protected against inflation, whether you might outlive your retirement funds, and a host of other important concerns. Your basic distribution choices are to receive your payout as a lump sum, to receive it in the form of an annuity or lifetime payments, or some combination of the two.

You must monitor your progress toward your retirement goal, both before and after you retire, constantly allowing for new and unexpected changes that occur in your financial and personal life.

## REVIEW QUESTIONS

1. What are you purchasing with your payroll deduction to Social Security?

2. How many credits do you need to qualify for Social Security benefits? How is a credit earned? How many can you earn each year?

3. How is the amount of someone's Social Security benefit determined? What percentage of income does Social Security typically replace? What percentage of full benefits do those retiring at age 62 receive?

4. What is meant by the term "disability and survivor benefits"? How does the Social Security Administration define "substantial work"?

5. Describe one type of noncontributory retirement plan. What are the advantages and disadvantages of this plan?

6. What is vesting? What does it mean for an employee? An employer? Why is it important when initially considering a job offer? When thinking about changing jobs?

7. Describe a cash-balance retirement plan. What are the advantages and disadvantages for the employee? What advantages, if any, does this plan offer an employer?

8. List and briefly explain the seven steps involved in retirement planning.

9. Describe a tax-deferred retirement plan. Discuss two advantages of this plan.

10. Compare and contrast a defined-contribution plan and a defined-benefit plan. Who is responsible for the investment of funds for each plan? How are benefits determined? How are these plans advantageous to an employer?

11. List the five most common examples of a defined-contribution plan. For each, cite a unique advantage or disadvantage for the employee.

12. What is a 401(k) plan and how does it differ from a 403(b) plan? Describe two advantages associated with contributing to such plans.

13. What is a guaranteed investment contract (GIC)? A GIC might appeal to what type of investor?

14. What is a "catch-up" provision? Who can use it? Why?

15. Briefly describe a Keogh, SEP-IRA, and SIMPLE plan, noting how each is funded. Generally,

what advantages do these plans share with other tax-deferred plans?

16. Who manages the investments in a Keogh, SEP-IRA, or SIMPLE plan? Generally, if withdrawals are made prior to age $59\frac{1}{2}$, will the IRS impose a penalty? When might the penalty be waived?

17. How does the Roth IRA differ from the traditional IRA? What characteristics are common to both?

18. Describe the Coverdell Education Savings Account. How does it differ from the 529 plans?

19. What is an annuity? Describe the different annuity variations for retirement distributions.

20. What is meant by the term "rollover?" Why is this important?

## PROBLEMS AND ACTIVITIES

1. Kristen earned $51,250 last year. Calculate her total FICA contribution for the year. How much did her employer pay toward FICA?

2. Last year Ruth earned $10,350 in Social Security benefits. For the entire year, she had a combined income of $28,900. How much of, if any, of her Social Security benefit is taxable?

3. Porter is 65 years old. He is a part-time carriage driver in Central Park in New York City. This year he anticipates earning $19,750 from his job. How will his earnings affect his Social Security benefits?

4. Anne-Marie and Yancy calculate their current living expenditures to be $47,000 a year. During retirement they plan to take one cruise a year that will cost $3,000 in today's dollars. Anne-Marie estimated that their average tax rate in retirement would be 6 percent. Yancy estimated their Social Security income to be about $17,000 and their pension benefits are approximately $20,000. Use this information to answer the following questions.

   a. How much income will Anne-Marie and Yancy need in retirement assuming 70 percent replacement and an additional $3,000 for the cruise?

   b. Calculate their projected annual income shortfall in today's dollars.

   c. Determine, in dollars, the future value of the shortfall 20 years from now, assuming an inflation rate of 5 percent.

   d. Calculate their necessary annual investment to reach their retire goals.

5. Russell and Charmin have current living expenses of $57,000 a year. Estimate the amount of income they will need to maintain their level of living in retirement. Assume their average tax rate will be 13 percent.

6. Anita currently has 25 years of service and a final average annual salary of $37,000 over her last 5 years of employment. She was looking forward to retirement but has been offered a promotion. If she continues to work for 5 more years and increases her average annual salary to $47,000, how will her monthly pension benefit change?

7. Reece is comparing retirement plans with prospective employers. ABC, Inc., offering a salary of $38,000, will match 75 percent of his contributions up to 10 percent of his salary, his maximum contribution. XYZ Company will match 100 percent of his contribution up to 6 percent of salary, but he can contribute up to 15 percent of his income. XZY Company is offering a $35,000 salary. If Reece assumes that he will contribute the maximum amount allowed and keep these first year retirement funds invested for 30 years with 9 percent return, how much will his account be worth? How can he use this information in his career choice?

8. Peter and Blair recently reviewed their future retirement income and expense projections. They hope to retire in 25 years. They determined that they would have a retirement income equal to $67,000 in today's dollars. They also calculated that they would actually need $86,000 in retirement income to meet all of their objectives. Calculate the total amount that Peter and Blair must save if they wish to meet their income projection (assume a 3 percent inflation rate).

9. Current tax laws allow grandparents to gift, with restrictions, $110,000 to a 529 plan for the benefit of a grandchild. If done shortly after the birth of the child, with a 7 percent annual return and no other contributions, what will the account be worth when the child is 18 and ready to enter college?

10. Using the same scenario with a Coverdell Education Savings Account, how much would the $2,000 annual contributions be worth when the child is 18 and ready to enter college?

## SUGGESTED PROJECTS

1. Take a survey of friends, relatives, and classmates to determine if they think Social Security is a funded or unfunded plan. Were you surprised at the responses? Do your respondents consider Social Security as a part of their retirement plan? Report your results.

2. Visit the Web sites for several mutual funds to determine the minimum initial investment to open a regular account and an IRA account. Are the amounts different? Why? Review the account application (available on the Web or by calling the toll-free number) to determine if there are questions applicable only to the regular or IRA account. Report your findings.

3. Make a list of factors that you would want to consider before establishing your own retirement goals. How would these factors change if you were assisting a close older relative in setting retirement goals?

4. Contact your current employer, or an employer you would like to work for, and request a pension benefits package summary. Specifically, what types of plans does the organization offer? A defined-benefit plan? A defined-contribution plan? A cash-balance plan? Rank the plans offered, noting advantages and disadvantages of each. Which plan would you choose?

5. "Pay yourself first" is a fundamental strategy when planning for retirement. Interview a group of young professionals to determine if they are implementing this strategy. Are they eligible to participate in their company retirement plan(s)? If not, what other retirement planning products are available to them? How did they decide the amount to save for retirement? Are they taking advantage of the company match, if applicable? Prepare a report of your findings.

6. Some people argue that you should never invest in a traditional IRA if the contribution is nondeductible. Ask a benefits administrator, a human resource specialist, or financial planner if they agree with this assertion. Discuss the short- and long-term tax advantages of a Roth and traditional IRA. What criteria do these professionals consider when asked to recommend an IRA? Would their answer change if either a 401(k) or 403(b) plan were available in addition to an IRA? Why or why not?

7. Ideally, retirement preparation spans most of your lifetime. Ask a relative or friend who appears to be enjoying retirement about retirement planning. Consider both financial and personal implications. Review the principles listed in Chapter 1 and ask how those strategies, in retrospect, impacted their retirement planning.

8. Talk with someone who is currently retired about his or her sources of retirement income. Is current income sufficient to meet needs? What unexpected expenses (e.g., appliance replacements, home maintenance, recreation, or medical care) have had a major impact on their retirement level of living? Do you think they are putting enough effort into monitoring the plan? Together develop a list of recommendations to keep in mind with monitoring a retirement plan.

9. Talk with an employee assistance professional or benefits administrator about common mistakes employees make when planning for retirement. Organize your questions around the time frames of (a) the early to middle years of employment, (b) the latter years of employment, (c) the retirement decision and distribution options, and (d) the early and later years of retirement. Report your findings.

## Discussion Case 1

Bill (age 42) and Molly Hickok (age 39), residents of Anchorage, Alaska, have become increasingly worried about their retirement. Bill, a public school teacher, dreams of retiring at 62 so they can travel and visit family. Molly, a self-employed travel consultant, is unsure that their current retirement plan will achieve that goal. She is concerned that the cost of living in Alaska along with their lifestyle has them spending at a level they could not maintain.

Although they have a nice income of more than $100,000 per year, they got a late start planning for retirement, which is now just 20 years away. Bill has tried to plan for the future by contributing to his 403(b) plan, but he is only investing 6 percent of his income where he could be investing 10 percent. Use what they told you along with the information below to help them prepare for a prosperous retirement.

# Money Matters

## RETIRE RIGHT

***Don't consider your retirement funds as a source of dollars for emergencies.*** *Withdrawal from qualified retirement accounts can result in taxes, penalties, and even investment company charges. Money in employer-sponsored plans is normally not even accessible as long as you're employed by the company, unless the plan allows for loans or special IRS-defined hardship withdrawals.*

***Include medical insurance costs in your calculation of retirement needs,*** *especially if you are planning to retire before you are eligible for Medicare. Many employers are paring down or eliminating postretirement medical coverage. Even with Medicare, you may need a supplement plan, which could cost several hundred dollars a month for you and your spouse.*

***Get information on the shortfalls of Medicare coverage for nursing home and custodial care and on the eligibility requirements for Medicaid.*** *You may find that you need long-term care insurance before retirement and must include its cost in your calculation of annual financial needs. If you anticipate having to care for elderly family members, it could be advantageous to assist them in purchasing such coverage.*

***If you plan to "roll over" money from a company retirement plan to an IRA,*** *get assistance from your financial advisor or IRA investment company in executing a "trustee-to-trustee transfer."*

*Through this process the money flows directly to the IRA account or comes to you via a check made payable to the IRA. If you take possession of the funds at any time or even receive a check made out to you, 20 percent withholding applies to the distribution.*

***If you are in a low income-tax bracket and meet the requirements to fund a Roth IRA or a regular deductible IRA,*** *give the potential outcome great consideration when deciding which to use. Foregoing a small tax deduction now (doing the Roth IRA) could result in a sizable source of tax-free money at retirement.*

***Investigate joint and survivor annuity payment options from qualified retirement plans carefully.*** *Once you make a decision, it is usually irrevocable. You will receive a lower monthly payment while you are living so that income can go to your spouse when you die. If your spouse dies before you, your monthly amount probably won't go up. You may find that you can take the larger single life payment, use some of the money to pay for life insurance to provide your spouse an income when you die, and still net more income than the joint and survivor arrangement would provide. This "pension maximization" process also provides potential funds to beneficiaries if the annuitant and spouse die before all equivalent retirement assets are spent.*

| | |
|---|---|
| Molly's income | $78,000 |
| Bill's income | $42,000 |
| Projected Social Security benefit | $2,600/mo |
| Current annual expenditures | $70,000 |
| Bill's Roth IRA | $20,000 |
| Bill's 403(b) plan | $47,800 |
| Marginal tax bracket | 27% |

## Questions

1. Do they qualify for any other tax-advantaged saving vehicles? If so, what? To what extent?

2. Since Bill does not receive a company match, should he invest the maximum amount in his Roth IRA annually or just invest more in his 403(b)? Defend your answer.

3. Assuming Bill and Molly can reduce expenses, how do their retirement savings limits differ before and after age 50?

4. Calculate their after retirement income need assuming a 3 percent inflation rate.

5. Calculate their projected after retirement income assuming an 8 percent rate of return and a 20-year retirement period.

6. How much will Bill and Molly need to invest annually to make up their shortfall? Into what account(s) would you suggest the investments be made?

7. What Social Security survivor benefits are currently available to Molly and Bill?

# Discussion Case 2

Timur and Marguerite recently met with the benefits administrator at Timur's employer to establish a retirement date and to discuss payout options for his pension. Timur just turned 67, while Marguerite, a self-employed artist, will be 62 in 6 months. The benefits administrator was helpful in outlining potential sources of income that they can expect in retirement. Annual estimates are as follows:

| | |
|---|---|
| Social Security | $9,000 |
| Defined benefit | $12,000 (single life annuity) |
| Marguerite's work | $5,000 |
| Defined contribution | $10,000 (single life annuity) |
| Other | $4,000 |

The defined-contribution payout was calculated based on a 401(k) balance of $250,000 earning approximately 8 percent. The benefits administrator indicated that a 100-percent joint and survivor annuity would decrease yearly benefits by about $2,000 in the defined benefit plan and $1,500 in the defined contribution plan. Timur's company does not offer an annuity for life option.

## Questions

1. In order to receive a single life annuity, what would Timur need to do?

2. What are the advantages associated with taking the pension payouts in the form of an annuity? What are the disadvantages?

3. Based on the information provided, which type of annuity would you recommend that Timur and Marguerite choose?

4. Would you recommend that Timur and Marguerite take the annuity offered in the defined-contribution plan, or would you counsel them to take a lump-sum payment? Why? What are the disadvantages associated with your recommendation?

5. Assuming they decided to take the 401(k) in a lump-sum payment, what two methods could they employ to reduce taxes?

6. What recommendations would you make to Timur and Marguerite to help them monitor expenses and safeguard their retirement lifestyle?

7. Timur has considered part-time employment in addition to receiving his retirement and Social Security benefits. Are there restrictions on his earnings or his benefits if he finds a part-time job?

 Visit our Web site for additional case problems, interactive exercises, and practice quizzes for this chapter—**www.prenhall.com/keown**.

# 17 Estate Planning: Saving Your Heirs Money and Headaches

There was something in the way he moved us. On the album cover of his 1970 album "All Things Must Pass," his first solo album after the breakup of the Beatles, George Harrison sits peacefully in a chair in a field, his beard long, his clothes rustic—almost Hobbit-like—looking more like a character from the *Lord of the Rings* than a rock star. It is a wonderful way to remember him.

At age 58, on November 29, 2001, Harrison, "the quiet Beatle," creator of the rock benefit concert, film producer, and composer of "Something," "Here Comes the Sun," and "While My Guitar Gently Weeps," died after a lengthy battle with cancer.

As his family prepared to scatter his ashes on the Ganges, a hand-written message from the former Beatle was placed on his official Web site. The words were the opening lines to his 1970 song "All Things Must Pass." They read:

"A sunshine doesn't last all morning, a cloudburst doesn't last all day; seems my love is up and has left you with no warning, but it's not always been that grey, and all things must pass, all things must pass away."

Harrison had planned for his death, and left the bulk of his $300 million fortune to his wife Olivia and son Dhani.

He also donated 10 percent of his fortune to the International Society of Krishna Consciousness. He realized something most of us try to avoid—that we will not live forever.

Most people cringe at the thought of estate planning, mostly because it involves death. Many individuals avoid it, ignoring the inevitable or assuming that only the rich need to deal with it. However, there's value in estate planning for practically everyone. Once you're dead, there might not be anyone to provide or look out for your spouse or kids. With estate planning, you ensure that you preserve as much as possible of your wealth—no matter how little that may be— for your heirs. It also ensures that the guardianship of your children will fall to whomever you name.

Estate planning finds much of its logic in **Principle 10: Protect Yourself Against Major Catastrophes**—in this case, the catastrophe is your death. Much of what happens in estate planning is done to keep taxes to a minimum, which brings us back to **Principle 6: Taxes Affect Personal Finance Decisions**. As you'll see, the basic choices available to you with respect to minimizing taxes and passing on your estate are the use of a will, gifts, and trusts.

You'll also see that estate planning can be an extremely complicated process. Our purpose here isn't to make you an expert in estate planning but to alert you to its benefits and challenges. Hopefully, after studying this chapter you'll have a better understanding of the concepts, terminology, process, techniques, and tools of estate planning. And you'll be better able to plan for the disposition of whatever you have accumulated.

Principle **10** Protect Yourself Against Major Catastrophes

Principle **6** Taxes Affect Personal Finance Decisions

**Estate Planning**
The process of planning for what happens to your accumulated wealth and your dependents after you die.

**Estate planning** is simply planning for what happens to your wealth and your dependents after you die. Regardless of how large your estate is, the basic objectives remain the same. First, you want to make sure your property is distributed according to your wishes and your dependents are provided for. Providing for your dependents will, among other things, involve selecting a guardian for your children if they're under 18. Second, you want to pass on as much of your estate as possible, which means you'll want to minimize estate and inheritance taxes. Finally, you'll want to keep settlement costs, including legal and accounting fees, to a minimum. In essence, you'll be developing a strategy to give away and distribute your assets while paying the minimum in taxes and fees. Estate planning may seem a bit gloomy because it forces you to think about your own demise. Fortunately, there's one aspect of estate planning that doesn't deal with your own death. Unfortunately, it deals with your incapacitation. Yes, the final objective of estate planning is determining who is to have decision-making authority in the event that you become unable to care for yourself as a result of physical or mental impairment.

Understand the importance and the process of estate planning.

## The Estate Planning Process

Once you recognize these basic objectives, you'll want to fine-tune them to meet your specific needs and goals. For example, you might want to protect your current spouse from claims on your assets by your ex-spouse. You might also want to induce your kids to go to college by leaving all of your money to them in a fund that they can access only after they graduate. No matter how you choose to fine-tune the basic objectives of estate planning, the financial planning process remains the same for everyone. Let's take a look at that process.

The estate planning process has four steps.

### Step 1: Determine What Your Estate Is Worth

Estate planning starts with determining the value of your assets. After all, you can't really think about distributing what you've got until you *know* what you've got. The easiest way to figure out what you've got and what it's worth is by looking at your personal balance sheet (see Chapter 2). It should list all of your assets and their respective values, as well as your net worth.

Your net worth was calculated by determining what you own and subtracting from that what you owe.

$$\text{your estate's net worth} = \text{value of your estate's assets} - \text{level of estate's liabilities}$$

In this case, your estate's net worth should be recalculated with several changes. First, you must keep in mind that when you die, your life insurance will pay off. In calculating the value of your life insurance, you should use the death benefit as its value rather than its cash or surrender value. In addition, you should include any death benefits associated with an employer-sponsored retirement plan.

It's important to get a sense of your wealth, not only because you'll need to know what you have to distribute, but also because its level will determine how much tax planning you'll need. For example, in 2002 and 2003 the first $1 million of your estate can be passed on tax free, with this limit climbing gradually until

**STOP &THINK** Most people are surprised to see how much their estate is worth. Once you start adding a home plus furnishings to a couple automobiles, savings, and investments, things add up. The only way to determine what your estate is worth is to go through the numbers.

the tax is repealed in 2010, only to reappear in 2011 unless Congress acts to kill it for good. You'd approach estate planning differently if your estate were worth $500,000 than you would if it were worth $3 million.

## Step 2: Choose Your Heirs and Decide What They Receive

Once you know just what you've got, you can figure out who's going to get it when you go. Most married people will just leave everything to their spouse, and others might just get a little silly and leave everything to their faithful pet horse.

If all you own is a bunch of oats, maybe leaving your assets to a horse isn't such a bad idea. However, most of us have more complicated estates, and we need to put a great deal of thought into dividing them up among our heirs. You'll want to consider the relationships you have with various people and the relationships those people have with your assets. You also have to consider the needs of your dependents and potential heirs.

If you have a child with special needs, such as a handicapped child needing special schooling or a child who's an exceptionally talented artist in need of a special art program, you may want to make sure those needs are taken care of first. Alternatively, some of your children may have already completed college, and you may want to earmark college funds to those children who haven't yet finished or even started college.

## Step 3: Determine the Cash Needs of the Estate

Once you know what you've got and who's going to get it, your estate planning is done, right? Nope. Before your property can be distributed to your heirs, all legal fees, outstanding debt, and estate and inheritance taxes must be paid. It's a good idea to have enough funds in the form of liquid assets—Treasury bills, stocks, and bonds—to cover your estate tax needs, or to provide tax-free income to your heirs from a life insurance policy that will cover your estate taxes.

## Step 4: Select and Implement Your Estate Planning Techniques

The final step is determining which estate planning tools are most appropriate to achieve your goals. In general, you'll need a combination of several planning techniques. Some of the most commonly used include a will, a durable power of attorney, joint ownership, trusts, life insurance, and gifts.

These tools can be a little tricky to use, and once you've figured out how to use them, implementing your estate plan can be amazingly complex. As a result, you should consult a legal specialist in estate planning to help you with the tools and to handle the details of implementing your plan.

But just because you'll need a professional to help you use them doesn't mean you don't need to understand the tools of estate planning. After all, you'll need to be able to speak the same language as the professional so you can fully understand his or her advice. Remember **Principle 9: The Best Protection Is Knowledge**. We examine and explain all the major tools of estate planning that you need to understand. First, however, we need to discuss taxes, because the use of most estate planning tools is based on tax consequences.

Principle **9** The Best Protection Is Knowledge

## Understanding and Avoiding Estate Taxes

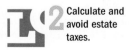
Calculate and avoid estate taxes.

Estate taxes are central to estate planning because of the high tax rate imposed on estates. Earlier we mentioned that in 2002 and 2003 the first $1 million of an estate can be passed on tax free. This $1 million tax-free transfer will be gradually raised until the tax is totally eliminated in 2010. Of course, the IRS likes to make everything as complicated as possible, so we'd better explain how this tax-free transfer works.

Instead of simply charging no taxes at all on the first $1,000,000 of an estate, the IRS actually charges a hefty 18-percent tax rate on the first $10,000 of an estate and keeps raising this rate all the way up to 39 percent by the time the amount hits $1,000,000. The IRS then issues an estate tax credit, called a **unified tax credit**, to everyone which in 2002 was $345,800, which effectively nullifies the taxes on the first $1,000,000 of an estate. Above this tax-free threshold, $1,000,000, rates kick in at an effective rate of 41 percent, which then quickly climbs to 50 percent. Table 17.1 presents the 2002 and 2003 rate schedule. Let's take a look at how estate taxes have changed as a result of the Tax Relief Act of 2001.

The centerpiece of the Economic Growth and Tax Relief Reconciliation Act of 2001, or Tax Relief Act of 2001 as it is commonly called, was the eventual repeal of estate taxes. But just like a classic western movie, the Tax Relief Act of 2001 disposes of estate taxes, sending them into the sunset, and just like a classic western movie, there may be a sequel with estate taxes returning. Beginning in 2002, estate taxes begin to disappear, and in 2010, estate taxes are gone. However, in 2011, if lawmakers do nothing, the federal estate tax returns to 55 percent and estates of over $1 million would be taxed at the top rate. In effect, the much talked about repeal of estate taxes in 2010 is actually a one-year suspension of estate taxes. If there are problems balancing the budget, you can bet on estate taxes returning if they ever actually disappear, but you can also count on the exemption being larger than it was.

Beginning in 2002, estate and gift taxes are reduced. The estate taxes would be phased out over 9 years, and the unified tax credit would be increased. Under the act, the top estate and gift tax rates gradually drop from 55 percent to 45 percent in 2007. Over the phase-in period through 2009, the unified credit exemption amount for estate tax purposes increases from $675,000 (its 2001 level) to $3.5 million. Then in 2010 the estate tax is completely repealed, while the gift tax remains in place, but with the maximum rate of 35 percent and an exemption of $1 million. The following summarizes these changes:

| Year | Estate and Tax-Free Transfer Exemption | Highest Estate and Gift Tax Rates |
|------|----------------------------------------|-----------------------------------|
| 2002 | $1 million | 50% |
| 2003 | $1 million | 49% |
| 2004 | $1.5 million | 48% |
| 2005 | $1.5 million | 47% |
| 2006 | $2 million | 46% |
| 2007 | $2 million | 45% |
| 2008 | $2 million | 45% |
| 2009 | $3.5 million | 45% |
| 2010 | Tax repealed | Estate tax repealed; gift tax top rate will equal the top individual rate |

An awful lot of wills have to be rewritten to make sure that full advantage of the new exemption is taken. It also means there's a moving target as to how big an estate can be passed on tax free. As a result, sometimes we'll refer to this amount as the "estate-tax-free transfer threshold" and not even mention the dollar amount because it changes each year.

**Table 17.1**    Federal Estate and Gift Tax Rates for Tax Years 2002 and 2003

| Value of Taxable Estate Plus Taxable Gifts | Your Tax Liability Is |
| --- | --- |
| Less than $1,000,000 | $0 |
| $1,000,000 to $1,250,000 | 41% of amount over $1,000,000 |
| $1,250,000 to $1,500,000 | $102,500 plus 43% of amount over $1,250,000 |
| $1,500,000 to $2,000,000 | $210,000 plus 45% of amount over $1,500,000 |
| $2,000,000 to $2,500,000 | $435,000 plus 49% of amount over $2,000,000 |
| over $2,500,000 | $680,000 plus 50% of amount over $2,500,000 |

Given the high estate tax rates imposed, your personal tax strategy should shift toward estate tax planning once your net worth climbs above the tax-free transfer threshold. Individuals with a net worth below the tax-free transfer threshold should focus on income tax strategies and on nontax estate planning concerns.

To deal with your estate taxes properly, you'll need to calculate what those taxes will be. However, before you can calculate these taxes, there are a couple other taxes—gift and generation skipping—as well as a deduction that we need to consider.

## Gift Taxes

Gifts are an excellent way of transferring wealth before you die. They reduce the taxable value of your estate and allow you to help out your heirs while you're still alive—*and the recipient of the gift isn't taxed*. Under the present law, you're permitted to give $11,000 per year tax free to as many different people as you like.

Let's look at a couple with four children and eight grandchildren and an estate valued at $5.3 million. Over a 5-year period, the couple could transfer to each of their children and grandchildren a total of $22,000 per year tax free—$11,000 from the husband and $11,000 from the wife for a total of $110,000 to each child and grandchild. These gifts would reduce the couple's taxable estate from $5.3 million to $3.98 million and result in significantly lower estate taxes. Remember that the exclusion for annual gifts applies to each spouse. That is, a husband and wife can give up to $22,000 jointly to each of their children or to whomever they wish without paying any taxes.

> **STOP & THINK** Keep in mind that because gift giving is an annual exclusion, it's renewable. That means every year you get another gift exclusion that allows you to give $11,000 tax free to as many different people as you like.

If you'd like to give more than that, you can. However, the gift tax and the estate tax *work together with a total lifetime tax-exempt limit (which is $1 million in 2002 and 2003) on gifts over and above the yearly tax-free limit of $11,000 per recipient*. Therefore, in 2002 the first $1,000,000 of your estate *minus* total lifetime non-tax-exempt gifts (that portion of gifts in excess of $11,000 per year per person) can be transferred tax free. If your lifetime non-tax-exempt gifts total $100,000, in 2002 the first $900,000 rather than the first $1,000,000 of your estate would not be taxed.

However, there is a limit as to how much of the tax-free transfer exclusion can be used. The Tax Relief Act of 2001 created a $1 million lifetime gift tax exclusion, which began in 2002, with the top gift tax rate gradually declining. Thus, if you go over the $1 million lifetime gift exclusion, the gift and estate tax systems are no longer "unified." This gift tax was retained largely to limit the amount of income tax that taxpayers can avoid by gifting income-producing and/or appreciated assets to family members in lower income tax brackets. After increasing to $1 million in 2002, the gift tax exemption remains constant with no indexation.

The reason gifts and estates are taxed together at the same rate up to the $1 million lifetime gift limit is to avoid presenting an incentive, beyond the annual $11,000 gift exclusion, for individuals to give away as gifts the assets in their estates before they die, instead of as bequests after they die. Once you get beyond the annual $11,000 exclusion, without going over the $1 million lifetime gift limit, you'll pay exactly the same amount in taxes whether you pass on your estate as a gift while you are alive or pass it on at death.

The $11,000-per-year tax-free gift is indexed to inflation in $1,000 increments. In fact, it started out as a $10,000 per-year level in 1997 and, as a result of inflation, increased to $11,000 in 2002. If the consumer price index rises by 11 percent over 4 years, the tax free-tax exclusion would then rise by $1,000 to $12,000. While 11 percent of $11,000 is actually $1,210, the tax-free gift exemption only increases by $1,000, because changes have to be in $1,000 increments. However, that extra $210 wouldn't be lost—it would carry over and count toward the next $1,000 adjustment.

## Unlimited Marital Deduction

The U.S. tax code allows for an unlimited marital deduction for gift and estate tax purposes, which means that there's no limit to the size of transfers between spouses that can be made on a tax-free basis. In other words, when a husband or wife dies, the estate, regardless of size, can be transferred to the survivor totally tax free. Whereas an estate valued at up to the tax-free transfer threshold (which was $1 million in 2002 and 2003) can be transferred tax free to any beneficiary, there's no limit on the value of an estate that can be transferred to a spouse. All federal estate taxes can be avoided through the use of the unlimited marital deduction.

The unlimited marital deduction doesn't apply to spouses who aren't U.S. citizens. The logic behind this law is to prevent non-U.S. spouses from returning to their home countries with an untaxed estate. Once they left the United States, Uncle Sam would never get any more tax dollars from the estate, and the IRS isn't about to let that happen.

For tax year 2003, if you're married to a non-U.S. citizen and your estate is less than $1 million, there's no need to be concerned, because you can pass on $1,000,000 tax free to anyone, regardless of citizenship. However, to offset the limited marital deduction for noncitizens, the annual gift tax exclusion of $11,000 is raised to $106,000 (in tax year 2001) per year adjusted annually for inflation for non-U.S. citizen spouses. That is, if you are married to a non-U.S. citizen, you can make an annual $106,000 tax-free gift to your spouse.

## The Generation-Skipping Transfer Tax

There's an additional tax imposed on gifts and bequests that skip a generation—for example, gifts or bequests that pass assets from a grandparent to a grandchild. The purpose of such a tax is to wring potentially lost tax dollars from the intervening generation. In effect, the assets are taxed as if they moved from the grandparents to their own children, and then from their children to the grandchildren. In 2002, the **generation-skipping tax** is a flat 50 percent and is imposed *in addition to* any estate and gift taxes. Beginning in 2002, the generation-skipping transfer (GST) tax is reduced and will be phased out over 9 years. Under the Tax Relief Act of 2001, the GST tax rate gradually drops to 45 percent in 2007. Then in 2010 the GST tax is

**Generation-Skipping Tax**
A tax on wealth and property transfers to a person two or more generations younger than the donor.

repealed for the year 2010 only and will reappear as it was under the prior law in 2011 unless Congress acts to permanently repeal it.

Obviously, this is a tax you want to avoid. There are two ways around it. First, if you have the resources, you should make effective use of the $11,000 gift tax exclusion in addition to the education and medical expense gift tax exclusions provided in the law. Second, there is a $1,060,000 exemption (indexed for inflation) from the generation-skipping transfer tax for lifetime gifts and bequests at death. For a couple, this would mean a total of just over $2 million can be passed on to grandchildren without triggering the generation-skipping tax. So unless you're very rich, you don't need to worry about the generation-skipping tax. If you are very rich, you can afford to hire a professional to help you attempt to work around this tax.

## Calculating Estate Taxes

The calculation of estate taxes can be viewed as a four-step process, as outlined in Figure 17.1. To walk you through this process, we use the example with the 2002 and 2003 tax-free transfer threshold of $1,000,000 presented in Figure 17.2.

The process of calculating your estate taxes starts by calculating the value of the gross estate, which is simply the value of all your assets and property at the time of your death. Remember, you'll have to include the death benefits of any insurance policy or retirement plan you have. The example in Figure 17.2 assumes you have a gross estate of $1.4 million.

In step 2, you calculate your taxable estate by subtracting the funeral and estate administrative expenses, along with any debts and taxes you owe, from the gross estate calculated in step 1. Keep in mind that in step 2 you need to subtract any and all liabilities or mortgages existing at the time of death. In addition, you subtract any allowable deductions, such as the unlimited marriage deduction and any charitable deductions you have coming. Remember, gifts to charity are tax-deductible, and there's no limit on the size of charitable gifts. Our example in Figure 17.2 assumes that your expenses, debt, and income and other taxes owed totaled $100,000.

To calculate the gift-adjusted taxable estate in step 3, the step 2 value must be adjusted for any taxable lifetime gifts that you've made. Remember that the annual gift tax exclusion allows for only one $11,000 (in 2002) gift per year per individual. Let's

Figure 17.1 Calculation of Estate Taxes

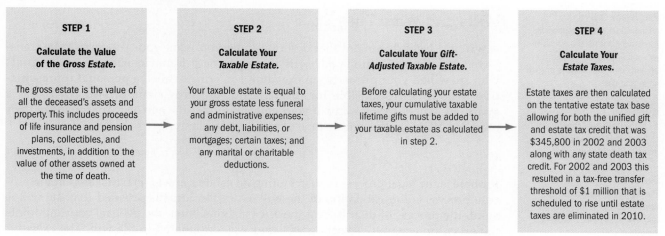

| STEP 1 | STEP 2 | STEP 3 | STEP 4 |
|---|---|---|---|
| **Calculate the Value of the *Gross Estate*.** | **Calculate Your *Taxable Estate*.** | **Calculate Your *Gift-Adjusted Taxable Estate*.** | **Calculate Your *Estate Taxes*.** |
| The gross estate is the value of all the deceased's assets and property. This includes proceeds of life insurance and pension plans, collectibles, and investments, in addition to the value of other assets owned at the time of death. | Your taxable estate is equal to your gross estate less funeral and administrative expenses; any debt, liabilities, or mortgages; certain taxes; and any marital or charitable deductions. | Before calculating your estate taxes, your cumulative taxable lifetime gifts must be added to your taxable estate as calculated in step 2. | Estate taxes are then calculated on the tentative estate tax base allowing for both the unified gift and estate tax credit that was $345,800 in 2002 and 2003 along with any state death tax credit. For 2002 and 2003 this resulted in a tax-free transfer threshold of $1 million that is scheduled to rise until estate taxes are eliminated in 2010. |

**Figure 17.2** Calculation of Estate Taxes for the 2002 or 2003 Tax Year

| | Amount | Total Amount |
|---|---|---|
| **STEP 1: Calculate the value of the *gross estate*.** | | |
| A. Value of gross estate | | $1,400,000 |
| **STEP 2: Calculate your *taxable estate*.** | | |
| Less: | | |
| Funeral expenses | $10,000 | |
| Estate administrative expenses | 40,000 | |
| Debt | 0 | |
| Taxes | 0 | |
| Marital deduction | 0 | |
| Charitable deduction | 50,000 | |
| Total | | − $100,000 |
| Equals: | | |
| B. Taxable estate | | = $1,300,000 |
| **STEP 3: Calculate your *gift-adjusted taxable estate*.** | | |
| Plus: | | |
| Cumulative taxable lifetime gifts (in excess of annual tax-free gift allowance per person) | | + $200,000 |
| Equals: | | |
| C. Gift-adjusted taxable estate | | = $1,500,000 |
| **STEP 4: Calculate your *estate taxes*.** | | |
| Calculation of taxes on the value in line C (from Table 17.1): | | $210,000 |

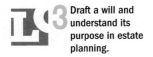
Draft a will and understand its purpose in estate planning.

**Will**

A legal document that describes how you want your property to be transferred to others after your death.

**Beneficiary**

An individual who is willed your property.

**Executor or Personal Representative**

An individual who is responsible for carrying out the provisions of your will and managing your property until the estate is passed on to your heirs.

**Guardian**

An individual who'll care for any children under the age of 18 and manage their property.

**Probate**

The legal procedure that establishes the validity of a will and then distributes the estate's assets.

assume over your life you have given heavily to your children, and one of your gifts exceeded the allowable gift tax exclusion by $200,000. Thus, the gift-adjusted taxable estate is $1.5 million, which results in taxes of $210,000 (calculated from Table 17.1).

How about state death taxes? The federal government provides a maximum credit for state taxes that are paid, allowing you to receive credit toward your federal estate taxes for the amount you pay in state estate taxes. About half of the states use this maximum credit level as their estate tax rate. You may have to pay state estate taxes, but in general, these taxes have no impact on the total amount of estate taxes, both state and federal, that you pay. The only difference is to whom the money is paid. However, under the Tax Relief Act of 2001, the state death tax credit is reduced by 25 percent each year and totally eliminated in 2005. The credit is replaced with an unlimited state death tax deduction. The end result here is that many states are going to see a reduction in revenues, which may in turn lead those states to consider legislative changes to make up for those losses.

## Wills and What They Do

A **will** is a legal document that describes how you want your property to be transferred to others. Within your will you designate **beneficiaries**, or individuals who are willed your property; an **executor**, sometimes called a **personal representative**, who'll be responsible for carrying out the provisions of your will; and a **guardian**, who'll care for any of your children under the age of 18 and manage their property. Wills are the cornerstone of solid estate planning.

### Wills and Probate

**Probate** is the legal process of distributing an estate's assets. The first step in the probate process is the validation of the will. Once the court is satisfied that the will is valid, the process of distributing the assets begins. First, the probate court appoints the executor, generally selecting whoever was designated in the will. The executor

# In The News

Wall Street Journal Sunday December 16, 2001

## Ways to Leave a Good Impression

### by Jonathan Clements

Whether it is the result of denial or sloth, it seems many people's most immediate legacy is a morass of disorderly documents and unintended consequences.

Want your heirs to remember you fondly? Try these four steps:

1. *Make a List.* Grab a piece of paper and *write down everything you own, including stocks, bonds, mutual funds, bank accounts, real estate, and anything else of more than modest value.* (☛A)

"If you draw up a list of all your assets, you'll solve 90 percent of the problems that come up with administering an estate," says Ed Slott, an accountant in Rockville Centre, New York. "In administering estates, the biggest problem is finding out what assets there are and who gets what."

2. *Keep It Simple.* Look at the list you just drew up. Do you have more than one savings account? Does your portfolio read like a who's who of yesterday's hottest funds? Do you own parcels of land you will never develop? Maybe it is time to simplify your finances, both for your own sake and for the sake of your heirs.

3. *Prepare for the Worst. Like your estate, your death may also be messy. Consider drawing up a living will and a health care power of attorney, so that your family knows your wishes concerning life-prolonging medical procedures and so somebody can make medical decisions for you. While you're at it, have a durable power of attorney drafted that allows somebody to make financial decisions on your behalf, should you become incapacitated.* (☛B)

4. *Take Stock.* Many older investors don't hold their shares in a brokerage account, instead hanging onto the stock certificates. Result? After their death, their children often can't find the certificates. And once the kids do locate them, they are in for a headache.

"Holding stock certificates is a no-no," says Jonathan Forster, an estate-planning lawyer in Tysons Corner, Virginia. "After your death, your beneficiaries have to deal with the transfer agent and that's a huge hassle. It's much better if you have the stocks in a brokerage account."

## THE BOTTOM LINE . . .

A Not only write down everything you own, but also make sure your heirs know where your key papers and documents are located.

B Along with your will, a living will, health care power of attorney, and durable power of attorney are three things that you should make sure you look into while you're in good shape. Once you need them, it's generally too late to get them.

Source: Jonathan Clements, "Nine Ways to Leave a Good Impression," *Wall Street Journal Sunday*, December 16, 2001: 3. Copyright (c) 2001, Dow Jones & Company, Inc. Reproduced with permission of DOW JONES & CO INC in the format Textbook via Copyright Clearance Center.

---

usually receives a fee ranging from 2 to 5 percent or more of the value of the estate for overseeing the distribution of the estate's assets and managing those assets during the probate process. Once the assets have been distributed and the taxes have been paid, a report is filed with the court and the estate is closed.

The advantage, and really the only purpose, of going through the probate process is to validate the will—to allow for challenges and make sure that this is in fact the last will and testament of the deceased. In the case of a challenge to the will, probate allows for the challenge or dispute to be settled. Probate also allows for an orderly distribution of the assets of an individual who dies intestate, or without a valid will.

The disadvantages associated with probate center on its cost and speed. There are numerous expenses—legal fees, executor fees, court costs—that make the probate process expensive. In fact, probate can run from 1 to 8 percent of the value of the estate, depending on the laws of the state in which the deceased lived. In addition, the probate process can also be quite slow, especially if there are challenges to the will or tax problems.

## Wills and Estate Planning

Because all wills must go through the potentially slow and costly probate process, wills aren't the preferred way to pass on your property. However, wills still play an extremely important role in the estate planning process. There are a number of reasons why you need to have a will, including the following:

- If you don't have a will, the court will likely choose a relative as the guardian to your children under the age of 18 and their property. This relative may be your choice for guardian anyway, but you may feel more comfortable naming a friend as their legal guardian.
- In the case of children with special needs, a will may be the most appropriate way of seeing that those needs are taken care of.
- Property that isn't co-owned or in trusts is transferred according to your wishes as expressed in your will.
- If you wish to make special gifts or bequests, they can be easily made through a will. Even the future care of your pets can be handled through a will.
- If you don't have a will, the court will appoint an administrator to distribute your assets. Not only might this distribution conflict with your desires, but the costs of an administrator to your estate will be more than the cost of having a will drawn up, leaving less for your heirs.

In short, if you don't have a will, your assets will be distributed according to state law, which may very well be different from your wishes.

If you die without a valid will, state laws dictate the distribution of your assets. These laws will determine who gains custody of your children and how your property is dispersed. Thus, regardless of the size of your estate, a will is a good idea, especially if you have kids. Just take a look at Howard Hughes, who died in 1976, seemingly without a will and with an estate valued at $42 billion. Within 5 months, over 30 different wills appeared, all of which were eventually declared invalid. After 11 years, the estate was finally settled, with lawyers claiming about $8 million, Uncle Sam taking half, and the rest going to his 22 cousins.

## Writing a Will

Although it's possible to write your own will, it's not a particularly good idea. Handwritten wills, and even oral wills, are accepted in some states, but they're a lot riskier than a formally prepared legal will. You're taking the chance that the probate court might disallow your will on the grounds of some overlooked technicality.

You should have a lawyer either draw up or review your will. Fortunately, a simple will should cost only around $250. Of course, the more complicated the will is, the more expensive its preparation will be.

Once your will has been drawn up, it needs to be signed, and the signing needs to be witnessed by two or more people. It then must be stored in a safe place and periodically reviewed and updated. The most common storage place is with your lawyer. If you change lawyers, you need to remember to retrieve and relocate your will. An alternative is to store it at home in a safe fireproof place. Of course, you should make sure that others know exactly where it can be found.

Many people store their wills in safety deposit boxes. However, after you die your safety deposit box may be sealed until it can be examined and inventoried for tax purposes. Thus, storing your will there isn't a particularly good idea. In some states your will can be stored with the clerk of probate court.

A will should contain several basic features or clauses, including the following:

- **Introductory statement.** The introductory statement identifies whose will it is and revokes any prior wills. Revoking prior wills is important so that there aren't conflicting wills circulating. Multiple wills can really make a mess out of the probate process and slow things down terribly (to the point that your heirs might drop dead from old age before your estate is settled).

- **Payment of debt and taxes clause.** This clause directs the payment of any debts, dying and funeral expenses, and taxes.
- **Disposition of property clause.** This clause allows for the distribution of money and property. It states who is to receive what, and what happens to the remainder of the estate after all the bequests have been honored.
- **Appointment clause.** This clause names the executor of the estate and the guardian if there are children under 18.
- **Common disaster clause.** This clause identifies which spouse is assumed to have died first in the event that both die simultaneously.
- **Attestation and witness clause.** This clause dates and validates the will with a signing before two or more witnesses.

Approximately one in three wills is challenged. For that reason, it's important that you understand the requirements for a valid will. First, you must be mentally competent when the will is written. Second, you can't be under undue influence of another person. For example, if you're physically threatened or forced to sign the will, it will be invalidated. Finally, the will must conform to the laws of the state.

## Updating or Changing a Will—The Codicil

You should periodically review your will to make sure it conforms to your present situation. If your family expands or if you get married or divorced, you should alter your will appropriately. If the changes are substantial, it's best to write a new will and expressly revoke all prior wills. If the changes are minor, they can be effected through the use of an attachment called a **codicil**. A codicil is simply a document that alters or amends a portion of the will. A codicil should be drawn up by a lawyer, witnessed, and attached to the will.

**Codicil**
An attachment to a will that alters or amends a portion of the will.

## Letter of Last Instructions

A **letter of last instructions** isn't a legally binding document. It's a letter, generally to the surviving spouse, that provides information and directions with respect to the execution of the will. Much of what's contained in the letter of last instructions is simply information—information on the location of the will, who should be notified of your death, and the location of legal documents such as birth certificates, Social Security numbers, and tax returns. It also has information as to the location of financial assets, including insurance policies, bank accounts, safety deposit boxes, stocks, and bonds.

A letter of last instructions often includes a listing of personal property and valuables as well. Finally, the letter contains funeral and burial instructions, along with your wishes regarding organ donation. The purpose of such a listing is simply to make dealing with your estate easier on your survivors. Generally, if you have an attorney prepare your will, he or she will also prepare a letter of last instructions. Although it doesn't carry the same legal weight as a will, it's honored in most states.

**Letter of Last Instructions**
A letter, generally to your surviving spouse, that provides information and directions with respect to the execution of the will.

## Selecting an Executor

An executor takes on the dual role of (1) making sure that your wishes are carried out and (2) managing your property until the estate is passed on to your heirs. To say the least, this is both an important and a time-consuming task. You should take care in naming your executor. For smaller estates it may be a family member, but for larger estates, it should be a lawyer or a bank trust officer with experience as an executor. Generally, executors are paid for their services, but on smaller estates, family members many times accept money only to cover expenses.

Not only does the executor deal with personal matters such as sending copies of the will to all the beneficiaries and publishing death notices, but he or she is also responsible for paying any necessary taxes, paying off the debts of the estate, managing the financial matters of the estate, distributing the assets remaining after bequests have been honored as specified in the will, and reporting a final accounting of the distribution to the court.

## Other Estate Planning Documents

A **durable power of attorney** provides for someone to act in your place in the event that you become mentally incapacitated. In effect, it empowers someone to act as your legal representative. The durable power of attorney is, of course, separate from your will, and it goes into effect while you're alive but unable to act on your own. You can set up the power of attorney so that any degree of legal power is transferred. It should be very specific as to which aspects of your affairs it covers and does not cover, and should mention specific accounts.

A **living will** allows you to state your wishes regarding medical treatment in the event of a terminal illness or injury. Included with the living will should be a health care proxy, which designates someone to make health care decisions should you become unable to make those decisions for yourself. A health care proxy would allow you to designate a trusted friend to make life support decisions for you if you lose the capacity to decide.

## Avoiding Probate

Unless you really want to tie up the time and money of your heirs, it's a good idea to avoid probate. Think of probate as a necessary evil. It's essential to validate your will and ensure that its provisions are carried out, but it can be a time- and money-eating hassle. The three simplest ways of avoiding probate are through joint ownership, gifts, and trusts.

### Joint Ownership

When assets are owned jointly, they're transferred to the surviving owner(s) without going through probate. In effect, the surviving owner(s) immediately assumes your ownership share of the property. There are three different forms of joint ownership: tenancy by the entirety, joint tenancy, and tenancy in common. **Tenancy by the entirety** ownership exists only between married couples. Property held by a married couple under tenancy by the entirety can be transferred only if both husband and wife agree. In addition, upon the death of one, the property automatically passes directly to the survivor.

Under **joint tenancy with the right of survivorship**, two or more individuals share the ownership of assets, which many times are held in a joint account at a bank or a brokerage firm. When one joint owner dies, the ownership passes directly on to the surviving owner or owners, bypassing the will.

With **tenancy in common**, two or more individuals share ownership of the assets. When one of the owners dies, that owner's share becomes part of the deceased's estate and is distributed according to the deceased's will. The other joint owner or

**Durable Power of Attorney**
A document that provides for someone to act in your place in the event that you become mentally incapacitated.

**Living Will**
A directive to a physician that allows you to state your wishes regarding medical treatment in the event of an illness or injury that renders you unable to make decisions regarding life support or other measures to extend your life.

 Avoid probate.

**Tenancy by the Entirety**
A type of ownership limited to married couples. Property held this way can be transferred only if both the husband and wife agree. In addition, upon the death of one, the property automatically passes directly to the survivor.

**Joint Tenancy with the Right of Survivorship**
A type of ownership in which two or more individuals share the ownership of assets, usually in a joint account at a bank or a brokerage firm. When one joint owner dies, the ownership passes directly on to the surviving owners, bypassing the will.

**Tenancy in Common**
A type of ownership in which two or more individuals share ownership of assets. When one of the owners dies, that owner's share isn't passed on to the other owners. It becomes part of the deceased's estate and is distributed according to the deceased's will.

owners don't receive the deceased's ownership shares unless the deceased's will states so expressly.

Although joint ownership—particularly tenancy by the entirety and joint tenancy—is probably the simplest way of avoiding probate, it does have some drawbacks. If a husband and wife have an estate valued at $2.0 million that they would like to pass on to their children and own it jointly, when one dies, the estate is left in total to the surviving spouse. In 2002 and 2003 that spouse would then only be able to pass on $1.0 million of the $2.0 million estate before estate taxes kick in. Of course, this estate tax-free threshold climbs until it is eliminated in 2010. If the property weren't owned jointly, the first spouse could pass on $1.0 million tax free to his or her children, and then, when the surviving spouse dies, the remaining $1.0 million could be passed on tax free.

Another disadvantage of joint ownership is that all owners have the right to use the jointly owned asset, and if the relationship between those involved deteriorates, one of the joint owners could use the asset up. For example, if a bank account is jointly owned, one of the joint owners could "take the money and run." This nasty kind of rip-off is illegal, but it's also difficult to stop.

In addition, because joint ownership takes mutual agreement or a divorce settlement to dissolve, there can be problems if the relationship between the parties deteriorates. For example, one individual may wish to sell some jointly owned property for a great profit, but another joint owner might block the sale just out of spite. Without cooperation between the parties, joint ownership can seem like a prison.

Still, there are situations in which joint ownership is an excellent idea. For example, a jointly owned bank account allows survivors to access funds immediately, which can help pay for funeral expenses. In addition, joint property is also valuable in a divorce because it gives both parties some bargaining power, thereby forcing compromises that might not otherwise occur.

The concept of **community property** represents another form of joint ownership. Community property is simply any property acquired during a marriage, assuming both husband and wife share equally in the ownership of any assets acquired during the marriage. It doesn't include assets each spouse owned individually before the marriage or gifts and inheritances acquired during marriage that have been kept separate.

**Community Property**
Property acquired during marriage (depends on state law).

Upon the death of either the husband or the wife, the surviving spouse automatically receives one-half of the community property. The remaining portion of the property is disposed of according to the will, or in the absence of a will, according to state law. Currently only a few states, located primarily in the West, recognize community property.

## Gifts

Not only can you give away $11,000 per year tax free to as many people as you want, but also anything you have given away is no longer yours and doesn't go through probate. Gifts avoid probate, reduce the taxable value of your estate, and allow you to help out your heirs while you're still alive. And the recipient doesn't pay taxes on the gift.

Gifts are also a good way of transferring property that grows in value, such as stocks or real estate. If, for example, you hold on to a stock investment that continues to grow in value, your estate will continue to grow in value, and the more your estate is worth over the estate tax-free transfer threshold, the more your heirs will lose to estate taxes. If you can afford to part with the stock investment and you know you want to pass it on to someone else anyway, you might consider giving it as a gift.

One major exception to the annual gift exclusion rule deals with life insurance policies. If a life insurance policy is given away within 3 years of the owner's death, it is included in the estate for tax purposes. Here's how it works. Let's assume that you gave your daughter a $500,000 policy that had a cash value of $11,000. First, there'd be no gift tax on the gift because its cash value would fall into the $11,000 or less category. Then let's assume that 3 years and 1 day later you die.

In this case, the $500,000 insurance policy payout wouldn't be included in your estate for tax purposes. If, however, you'd died one day before 3 years was up since you gave the policy to your daughter, the entire $500,000 would be included in your estate for tax purposes. The bottom line is that if you're intending to give away a life insurance policy, it's much better to do it sooner rather than later.

In addition to the $11,000 gift tax exclusion, there is an *unlimited gift tax exclusion on payments made for medical or educational expenses*. You can make this type of gift to anyone regardless of whether the person is related to you or not. The only requirement is that you make the payment directly to the school, in the case of education expenses, or to the institution providing the service, in the case of medical expenses. In fact, the unlimited gift tax exclusion for medical expenses can even cover health insurance payments. You can give someone $11,000 and then pay for his or her health insurance, medical, and educational expenses!

The primary disadvantage to gifts is that once you've given your assets away, you might find that you need them. In addition, because you no longer have control over the assets you give, they may be squandered. Wouldn't it just stink to give your son $11,000 to go buy a car and watch him squander it on a full-body tattoo? Still, a lifetime gift-giving program should be given serious consideration.

Up to this point we've been talking about avoiding probate by giving gifts to your family and other individuals. You can also avoid probate by giving gifts to charity, in which case you don't have to worry about any limits on what can be given tax free, because there aren't any. If you have a specific charity in mind, or if you're just an incredibly nice person, you can give an unlimited amount of your estate away to federally recognized charities on a tax-free basis. In fact, your charitable gifts are even tax deductible, so you not only reduce your estate taxes by giving to charity, you also reduce your yearly income tax. See, it pays to be charitable!

## Naming Beneficiaries in Contracts

Insurance contracts and employee retirement plans can also be used to transfer wealth while avoiding probate. Insurance policies, either term or cash-value, can be set up so that someone other than the insured owns the policy. For example, a wife could own an insurance policy on the life of her husband, or a child could own an insurance policy on the life of a parent. One of the major advantages of life insurance is that the proceeds don't go through probate.

Many employee retirement plans pay benefits to spouses upon the death of the employee. These benefits don't go through probate and begin immediately upon the death of the worker. In addition, Social Security benefits go directly to the surviving spouse and dependent children.

## Trusts

**Trust**
A legal entity in which some of your property is held for the benefit of another person.

A **trust** is a legal entity that holds and manages an asset for another person. A trust is created when an individual, called a grantor, transfers property to a trustee—which can be an individual, an investments firm, or a bank—for the benefit of one or more people, the beneficiaries. Virtually any asset can be put in a trust—money, securities, life insurance policies, and property.

Why do people use trusts? Here are some of the more common reasons:

- **Trusts avoid probate.** Trusts bypass the costly and time-consuming process of probate.
- **Trusts are much more difficult to challenge in court than are wills.** If there are concerns that a will may be challenged, placing the property in a trust can minimize the problem. Challenges to the will don't affect a trust unless the challenge is that the deceased was incompetent or was under undue influence when the trust was formed.
- **Trusts can reduce estate taxes.** Trusts can be used to shelter assets from estate taxes.
- **Trusts allow for professional management.** If a spouse doesn't have the understanding or desire to manage money effectively, a trust can provide the desired professional management.
- **Trusts provide for confidentiality.** Whereas a will becomes a matter of public record, a trust does not. Thus, if you want privacy, perhaps to keep from offending a relative who doesn't receive all he or she may expect, a trust may be just the thing for you.
- **Trusts can be used to provide for a child with special needs.** A trust can be set up to provide the necessary funds for a child with special needs. For example, if you have a handicapped child in need of special care or schooling, or a gifted child who may benefit from summer enrichment programs, trusts can be set up to provide the necessary funding. A special needs trust can provide funds for disabled children of majority age without eliminating government benefit programs like Medicaid.
- **Trusts can be used to hold money until a child reaches maturity.** Because most children don't have the maturity or understanding necessary to handle large sums of money, a trust can be used to hold those funds until the children reach a designated age. The funds don't have to be immediately dispersed. Instead, they can be distributed over any period of time that is desired.
- **Trusts can ensure that children from a previous marriage will receive some inheritance.** If you leave your estate to a second spouse, children from your previous marriage may never receive any inheritance. A trust can ensure that they receive what you wish.

Because there are so many different types of trusts, many people find them confusing. However, all trusts can be classified as being either living trusts or testamentary trusts.

## Living Trusts

A **living trust** is one in which you place your assets while you're living. There are two types of living trusts, revocable and irrevocable.

**Revocable Living Trusts**   With a **revocable living trust** you place the assets into the trust while you're alive, and you can withdraw the funds from the trust later if you wish. It's simply an alternative way of holding your assets. While your assets—for example, your house—are in a revocable living trust, you have access to them, can receive income from them, and can use them. In addition, you pay taxes on whatever income your assets earn.

In other words, there doesn't appear to be much difference between assets in a revocable living trust and assets owned outright until you die or become incompetent,

**Living Trust**
A trust created during your life.

**Revocable Living Trust**
A trust in which you control the assets in the trust and can receive income from the trust without removing assets from the estate.

# In The News

Wall Street Journal Sunday July 9, 2000

## Estate-Planning Pitfalls to Avoid

### by Jonathan Clements

Whether it's picking up the pieces after a parent or spouse's death or deciding what to do with our own estate, the financial issues involved are charged with emotion—and that can lead us to make big mistakes. Here are two common pitfalls:

1. *Putting Things Off.* Many folks die without a will. Some do so out of ignorance. But for many, it is a refusal to confront the inevitable.

"It's very difficult for people to acknowledge that time is limited," says Kathleen Gurney, founder of Financial Psychology Corp. in Sonoma, California. (☛A)

Richard Van Der Noord, a financial planner in Macon, Georgia, says this procrastination also reflects "a superstition that as long as you don't deal with getting your estate plan in order, you won't die."

2. *Don't Ask, Don't Tell.* Tensions are highest between adjacent generations, notes Jerrold Lee Shapiro, a professor of counseling psychology at Santa Clara University. Because of these tensions, children find it tough to talk to their parents about the parents' estate, and often these important discussions never happen.

*"It's one of the hardest conversations you'll ever have," Jerrold Lee Shapiro, a professor of counseling psychology at Santa Clara University, says. "I've been doing couples therapy for over 30 years. And the last thing they'll talk about is money issues. That's the big taboo."* (☛B)

Mr. Shapiro notes that, as the parents grow older, they feel they are losing control. When prodded by their children to draw up a will or put money in a trust, the parents feel like they are being asked to cede even more control.

"To the parents, it's like you're trying to throw them in the ground," Mr. Shapiro says. "The loss of control is very frightening and brings up all those visions of dying."

### THE BOTTOM LINE . . .

**A** This becomes even more important in the case of blended families with children from earlier marriages. You can save your family a lot of pain if you plan ahead.

**B** Talking to an elderly parent about estate planning is both painful and difficult. Try one of these lines: "Can we talk?"— the direct approach—they may be willing, "We're thinking about rewriting our will and we'd like your advice," or "Where do you keep the important papers, so we can get access to them if there is an emergency?"

---

at which point the trust beneficiary takes control of the assets in the trust. It's important to remember that there are no tax advantages to a revocable living trust—they don't reduce your estate taxes. However, when you die, assets held in a living trust go directly to your beneficiary. It is the high costs of probate and the privacy attained by avoiding probate that explain much of the use of revocable living trusts. Table 17.2 summarizes the advantages and disadvantages of a revocable living trust.

**Irrevocable Living Trust**
A trust in which you relinquish title and control of the assets when they are placed in the trust.

**Irrevocable Living Trusts** An **irrevocable living trust**, as the name suggests, is permanent. It can't be changed or altered once it's been established, because you no longer hold title to the assets in the trust. The trust becomes a separate legal entity. It pays taxes on the income and capital gains that its assets produce. This fact takes on major importance when you die, because assets in an irrevocable living trust aren't considered part of your estate, and any appreciation of assets would not be subject to estate tax. This type of trust also bypasses probate.

Obviously, the major difference between a revocable and an irrevocable living trust centers on the fact that with a revocable trust, you retain title to and have control of the assets in the trust. Table 17.3 summarizes the advantages and disadvantages of an irrevocable living trust.

## Testamentary Trusts

**Testamentary Trust**
A trust created by your will, which becomes active after you die.

A **testamentary trust** is one created by a will: It doesn't exist until probate has been completed. There are a number of different purposes for testamentary trusts,

## Table 17.2   Advantages and Disadvantages of Revocable Living Trusts

*Advantages of Revocable Living Trusts*

- The assets in the trust avoid probate upon your death.
- You maintain the power to alter or cancel the trust.
- If you become incompetent, your assets will continue to be professionally managed by the trustee.
- You can replace the trustee if you do not have confidence in his or her skills.

*Disadvantages of Revocable Living Trusts*

- There are no tax advantages—you pay taxes on any income and capital gains on the assets in the trust.
- The assets in the revocable living trust are considered part of your estate for estate tax purposes.
- The assets in the revocable living trust cannot be used as collateral for a loan.

including reducing estate taxes, providing professional investment management, and making sure your estate ends up in the right hands. Let's look at some of the more common types of testamentary trusts.

**Standard Family Trusts (also Known as A-B Trusts, Credit-Shelter Trusts, and Unified Credit Trusts)**   Standard **family trusts** can be used to reduce estate taxes when one spouse dies before the other. Look, for example, at a husband whose estate is valued at $1,000,000 with a wife whose estate is valued at $1,000,000 in 2002 or 2003. Eventually, the couple would like their estate to pass to their children rather than to the government in the form of taxes. Figure 17.3 shows how this couple would pass their estates on to their children using a simple will, and Figure 17.4 shows how they do it using a trust instead.

Using a simple will, the husband would pass his estate to his wife tax-free (remember, in 2002 and 2003 there are no estate tax on estates of $1 million and less). His wife's estate then becomes worth $2.0 million. If his wife uses a simple will to leave her estate to the children, the government will impose estate taxes of $435,000. However, using a standard family trust, when the husband dies his assets go directly into the trust for their children. There are no taxes imposed on this transfer, because the estate would not be valued at more than $1,000,000.

**Family Trust**
A trust established to transfer assets to your children, while allowing the surviving spouse access to funds in the trust if necessary. Upon the death of the surviving spouse, the remaining funds in the trust are distributed to the children tax free.

## Table 17.3   Advantages and Disadvantages of Irrevocable Living Trusts

*Advantages of Irrevocable Living Trusts*

- The assets in the trust avoid probate upon your death.
- Any price appreciation on assets in the trust is not considered part of your estate, and no estate taxes are imposed on it when you die.
- Income earned on assets in the trust can be directed to the beneficiary, which can result in tax savings if the beneficiary is in a lower tax bracket.

*Disadvantages of Irrevocable Living Trusts*

- You no longer maintain control over the assets in the trust.
- The assets in the trust cannot be used as collateral for a loan.
- It may be more expensive to set up than the probate costs you are trying to avoid.
- Setting up the trust can involve a lot of paperwork.

**Figure 17.3** Using Trusts to Reduce Estate Taxes: A Simple Will and a $2.0 Million Estate in 2002 or 2003

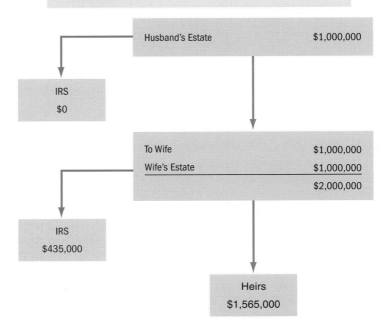

**Simple Will ($2.0 Million Estate):** Assume it's the tax year 2003 and that you and your spouse each own assets valued at $1.0 million. There will be a substantial estate tax liability if a simple will is used to transfer all the assets to the surviving spouse. Assume that in 2003 the husband dies first. His $1.0 million will automatically transfer to his wife and no tax will be imposed due to the unlimited marital deduction. This will result in the wife's estate increasing in value by $1,000,000. When she dies later in 2003, her estate will be valued at $2.0 million. Estate taxes on an estate valued at $2.0 million are $435,000. This tax will be due within 9 months of her death.

| | |
|---|---|
| Husband's Estate | $1,000,000 |

IRS
$0

| | |
|---|---|
| To Wife | $1,000,000 |
| Wife's Estate | $1,000,000 |
| | $2,000,000 |

IRS
$435,000

Heirs
$1,565,000

Such a trust allows the wife to get income from the children's trust for as long as she lives, and even to take funds directly from the principal if necessary. Although the trustee must agree to allow her access to the funds in the trust, the selection of an understanding trustee by the husband can ensure her all the access she needs. Because she doesn't technically own the funds in the trust, her estate is still valued at $1,000,000, which she can leave to the children tax free. Upon the death of the wife, the funds in the trust are automatically distributed to the children as well, all tax free. Using a trust saved the family in our example $435,000.

**Qualified Terminable Interest Property Trust (Q-TIP)**

A trust that gives the individual establishing the trust the ability to direct income from the trust to his or her spouse over the spouse's life, and then, at the spouse's death, to choose to whom the assets go.

**Qualified Terminable Interest Property Trust (Q-TIP)** A **qualified terminable interest property trust**, or **Q-TIP**, gives the individual establishing the trust the ability to direct income from the trust to his or her spouse over the spouse's life, and then, at the spouse's death, to choose to whom the assets go. The primary reason for using a Q-TIP trust is to keep your estate from ending up in the hands of your spouse's future husband or wife rather than your children after you die. Q-TIP trusts are generally set up so that your spouse receives the income on your estate while he or she is alive, and after your spouse's death, the assets in the trust are passed on to your children.

**Figure 17.4** Using Trusts to Reduce Estate Taxes: A Family Trust and a $2.0 Million Estate in 2002 or 2003

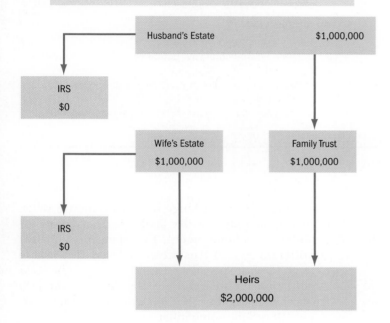

**Optimum Marital Will Plan ($2.0 Million Estate):** Assume it's the tax year 2003 and that you and your spouse each own assets valued at $1,000,000. At death, your assets can be directed into a trust rather than have them passed directly to the surviving spouse. Assume that in 2003 the husband dies first. Up to $1,000,000 can automatically pass into a trust—known as a standard family trust. This trust allows his estate to shelter his unified credit equivalent (his $1,000,000 tax-free transfer), plus appreciation, from estate taxes when his wife eventually dies. At her death, her $1,000,000 will pass tax free to family members or heirs.

Husband's Estate — $1,000,000

IRS — $0

Wife's Estate — $1,000,000

Family Trust — $1,000,000

IRS — $0

Heirs — $2,000,000

**Sprinkling Trusts**   A **sprinkling trust** is simply a trust that distributes income according to need rather than to some preset formula or your whims. The trustee is given discretion to determine who needs what among a designated group of beneficiaries, and then "sprinkles" the income among them according to need.

**Sprinkling Trusts**
A trust that distributes income according to need rather than to some preset formula. The trustee is given discretion to determine who needs what among the designated beneficiaries and then "sprinkles" the income among them according to need.

## A Last Word on Estate Planning

After viewing the complexities associated with estate planning, it is a natural reaction to say to yourself, "It's a great idea to look at some day." Today should be that some day. Estate planning begins with a will. From there, what happens next depends on the value of your estate and whether or not you have loved ones with special needs.

Once you have a basic understanding of the process, objectives, and tools of estate planning, you should approach a professional. By no means should you attempt your own estate planning. Finally, you should make sure your family knows where your estate planning documents are. Checklist 17.1 will help you organize your affairs.

Understand the importance and the process of estate planning.

**40** WORKSHEET

**41** WORKSHEET

# Checklist 17.1 ■ Estate Planning

**Do you and the members of your family know the location of . . .**

Your will, durable power of attorney, and living will (with the name of the attorney who drafted them)?

The name of your attorney?

Your letter of last instructions, including burial requests and organ donor information?

Your Social Security number?

Your safety deposit box and the key to it?

A record of what is in your safety deposit box?

Your birth certificate?

Your marriage certificate?

Any military discharge papers?

Insurance policies (life, health, and property/liability) along with the name of your insurance agent?

Deeds and titles to property (both real estate and real, for example, automobiles)?

Your stocks, bonds, and other securities, and who your broker is?

Any business agreements, including any debts owed you?

All checking, savings, and brokerage account numbers, along with the location of those accounts?

The name of your accountant?

Your last year's income tax return?

The name of past employers, along with any pension or retirement benefits information?

**You should also:**

1. Calculate the size of your estate.
2. Estimate how much of your estate would be lost to taxes if you died.
3. Know who the executor of your will is and who your beneficiaries are.
4. Select a guardian for your children if they are under 18.

## SUMMARY

Estate planning involves planning for what happens to your accumulated wealth and your dependents after you die. Estate planning can be viewed as a four-step process: Determine what your estate is worth; choose your heirs, determine their needs, and decide what they receive; determine the cash needs of the estate; select and implement your estate planning techniques.

The purpose of going through the probate process is to allow for validation of the will—to allow for challenges and make sure this is in fact the last will and testament of the deceased. A will is a legal document that describes how you want your property to be transferred to others.

Within your will, you designate beneficiaries or individuals who are willed your property. You also designate an executor who'll be responsible for carrying out the provisions of your will. In addition, you can also designate a guardian who'll care for any children under the age of 18 and manage their property. You should periodically review your will to make sure that it conforms to your present situation.

Trusts are legal entities that hold money or assets. Some of the more common reasons for trusts are (1) trusts avoid probate, (2) trusts are much more difficult to challenge in court than are wills, (3) trusts can reduce estate taxes, (4) trusts allow for professional management, (5) trusts provide for confidentiality, (6) trusts can be used to provide for a child with special needs, (7) trusts can be used to hold money until a child reaches maturity, and (8) trusts can ensure that children from a previous marriage will receive some inheritance.

With a revocable living trust, you place the assets into the trust while you are alive, and you can withdraw the funds from the trust later if you wish. An irrevocable living trust, as the name suggests, is permanent. A testamentary trust is one that is created by a will. Because these trusts are established by a will, they aren't created until probate has been completed. Here are some guidelines based on the 2002 and 2003 estate tax-free transfer threshold of $1 million. Keep in mind that this threshold will gradually rise with the estate tax being totally eliminated in 2010.

*If your estate's valued at less than $1 million (in 2003):* Other than a will, which is especially important if you have children, there's no need for estate planning because you can pass on up to $1 million free of taxes. The only exception is if you have children with special needs that require a trust set up to manage their investments.

*If you're married and have an estate valued between $1 million and $2 million (in 2002 or 2003):* With an estate valued above $1 million but below $2.0 million, you should make sure that the $1 million tax-free estate transfer for both you and your spouse is taken advantage of. If your estate is valued at $2.0 million and your assets are owned jointly, when either one of you dies, the entire estate is passed on to the survivor, leaving an estate valued at $2.0 million and tax problems when your spouse dies. These problems could be avoided with a standard family trust.

*If you're single and have an estate valued at over $1.0 million or are married and have an estate valued at over $2.0 million (in 2002 or 2003):* For estates valued at more than $1.0 million for individuals or $2.0 million for couples, the only way to avoid taxes is to reduce the value of the estate. Three effective ways of reducing your estate are by spending, giving money away, and giving away your life insurance policy. Take advantage of the $11,000 annual gift exclusion—give the money directly or have it build up in a trust.

## REVIEW QUESTIONS

1. Define estate planning. List five objectives to be accomplished through estate planning.
2. Describe the four steps in the estate planning process.
3. What is the estate-tax-free transfer threshold for the years 2002 and 2003, and how does this relate to the unified tax credit?
4. How did the Tax Relief Act of 2001 change estate and gift taxes for the years before and after 2010? What happens in 2010?
5. Explain the annual gift tax exclusion. How is it used as an estate planning tool?
6. Explain the $1,000,000 lifetime gift exclusion created by the Tax Relief Act of 2001. Why are the gift and estate tax systems no longer "unified" once this exclusion is exceeded?
7. What is the gift tax rate projected to be in 2010?
8. Describe the unlimited marital deduction. How does this change if the spouse is a non-U.S. citizen?
9. What is the generation-skipping tax and how can it be avoided?
10. List and briefly describe the four steps involved in the process of calculating estate taxes.
11. How will changes under the Tax Relief Act of 2001 affect state death taxes?

12. What is probate and why is it often prudent to take steps to avoid probate?
13. List five reasons why having a will is important.
14. Describe the basic clauses in a will.
15. List three characteristics of a valid will.
16. Describe the following estate planning documents: (a) codicil, (b) letter of last instructions, (c) durable power of attorney, (d) living will, and (e) health care proxy.
17. What are the roles and duties of an executor?
18. List four strategies for transferring property that will avoid probate.
19. List and briefly describe (a) the ways to title jointly owned property and (b) the advantages and disadvantages of these approaches of owning property with other people.
20. Briefly explain the gifting exceptions that apply to (a) life insurance, (b) medical and educational expense, and (c) charitable gifts.
21. What is a trust? Name five possible advantages of using trusts in estate planning.
22. What are fundamental differences between a living and testamentary trust? Categorize each of the following as living or testamentary and briefly describe each of the following trusts: irrevocable trust, qualified terminable interest property (Q-TIP) trust, revocable trust, sprinkling trust, and standard family trust.

## PROBLEMS AND ACTIVITIES

1. As the first gift from their estate, Lilly and Tom Phillips plan to give $20,000 to their son, Raul, for a down payment on a house.

   a. How much gift tax will be owed by Lilly and Tom?

   b. How much income tax will be owed by Raul?

   c. List three advantages of making this gift.

2. What is your estate tax liability if the value of your estate plus taxable gifts is $2,200,000 at the time of your death in 2003? Show your calculations. How would the estate tax liability change if $1,200,000 of the estate were held in an irrevocable trust?

3. Millie Gustafson is a widow with a taxable estate of $1,250,000. She has made no taxable lifetime gifts prior to her death in 2002.
   a. Calculate the federal estate tax due before the unified credit.
   b. What is the amount of the unified credit?
   c. Calculate the estate tax due.

4. Following his death in 2002, Zane Wulster's gross taxable estate was valued at $1,800,000. He has made a total of $200,000 of gifts that exceeded the annual gift tax exclusion.
   a. Calculate the federal estate tax due before the unified credit.
   b. What is the amount of the unified credit?
   c. Calculate the estate tax due.

5. Morgan, a single widow, recently passed away. The value of her assets at the time of death was $1,100,000. She also owned an insurance policy with a face value of $100,000. The cost of her funeral was $18,000, while estate administrative costs totaled $52,000. As stipulated in her will, she left $100,000 to charities. Based on this information, answer the following questions:
   a. Determine the value of Morgan's gross estate.
   b. Calculate the value of her taxable estate.
   c. What is her gift-adjusted taxable estate value?
   d. How much is her year 2003 estate tax?

6. May Yee had a $950,000 net worth at the time of her death in 2002. In addition, she had a $250,000 whole life policy with $40,000 of accumulated cash value; her niece was designated as the beneficiary. She also had a $150,000 pension plan benefit, also payable to her niece.
   a. What was the value of May Yee's gross estate?
   b. How much of her estate is taxable?
   c. How much estate tax will need to be paid?
   d. How much of her estate must pass through probate?

7. About four years ago Joy began to worry about estate taxes. Her estate at the time was valued at $1,500,000. For years 1999, 2000, and 2001 she gave $10,000 to each of her five nieces and nephews. In 2002 she increased the gifts to $11,000 per the increased annual gift tax exclusion. She has also paid tuition totaling $35,000 for her uncle's son while he pursued a graduate degree. In addition, she has paid for her sister's repeated hospital stays during the past two years, which cost in excess of $55,000. Explain to Joy how her generosity has impacted her estate tax liability. Specifically, calculate the value of her taxable estate had she died prior to making her gifts, and the value of her taxable estate if she passed away in 2002.

8. Assuming a taxable estate of $4 million, how much of the estate would be taxable in years 2009, 2010, and 2011 given the current law? What is the highest estate tax rate for each year?

9. Answer the following questions based on the assumption that you and your spouse each own assets valued at $750,000.
   a. If you die first and leave your assets to your spouse without establishing a trust, calculate the estate taxes due on your spouse's estate assuming no change in estate value. How much is passed on to heirs?
   b. Calculate the estate tax on your spouse's estate if you use a standard family trust and pass the estate-tax-free transfer threshold for the year 2003 to the trust and the remainder to your spouse. How much is passed on to heirs assuming no change in estate value?
   c. Which method produces the least amount of estate tax?

10. Daisy and Onslo Bucket have $3.8 million of assets: $1,400,000 in Onslo's name, $1,400,000 in Daisy's, and $1 million of jointly owned property. Their jointly owned property is titled using joint tenancy with right of survivorship. Daisy also co-owns a $300,000 beach house with her sister, Hyacinth, as tenants in common.
   a. What is the maximum amount of estate value that can be transferred by the Buckets free of estate tax in 2003? In 2005? In 2010?
   b. What do the Buckets need to do to reduce their expected estate tax liability?
   c. Who would receive Daisy's half-share in the beach house if she were to die?

## SUGGESTED PROJECTS

1. Locate three to five articles about problems experienced by individuals or families who failed to develop estate plans or to identify responsible parties in the event of physical or mental impairment. Summarize your findings. In your opinion, is the

cost of "failing to plan" worth the price of avoiding the issue(s)?

2. Conduct a literature search for three to five current articles on estate planning. What recommendations are suggested to capitalize on current and future changes in estate taxation? Do the articles offer any projections on how the law will change for year 2010 or subsequent years?

3. Ask friends and family if they have written a will or living will, created a trust, or designated a health care proxy. Based on your interviews, what would you say is the number-one reason most people avoid estate planning? Write a brief summary and present your findings to the class.

4. Prepare a brief summary of the techniques most commonly used in estate planning. Follow this summary with a short description of the reasons why most individuals should consult with a legal specialist before creating and implementing an estate planning technique or strategy.

5. Confidentiality is a primary reason to avoid probate. Research the probate court procedures in your state and observe the court proceedings. Summarize the findings.

6. Make a list of criteria that you would use in selecting the executor of your estate and heirs named to inherit your assets. How would these criteria change if you were selecting a guardian for children?

7. Contact three law firms to determine the cost of preparing a simple will and the kinds of information needed by the attorney. Prepare a report of your findings.

8. Prepare a letter of last instructions. Discuss it with one or more family members. Have they prepared a letter of last instruction or implemented other estate planning strategies?

9. Locate a list of medical treatments generally included in living wills prepared in your state of residence. Research the meaning of these procedures. Write a report describing your feelings regarding medical treatment in the event of a terminal illness or incapacitation. Whom would you select as a health care proxy?

10. Discuss with a close adult friend or relative his or her estate plans including the use of a will, trusts, lifetime gifting, a living will, and/or a durable power of attorney. Write a one-page report of your findings.

# Discussion Case 1

Lee and Marta Howard are in their early seventies. Recently they have grown concerned about probate and estate taxes. They calculated that this year they will have a combined net worth of $900,000. In addition to this amount, Lee owns a $200,000 whole life insurance policy on his life. They are also considering giving their recently divorced son $100,000 to start a financial counseling practice. Although a bit ashamed to admit as much, they recently indicated that they do not have a will or any other type of estate planning instrument.

## Questions

1. Should Lee and Marta be concerned about probate? Why or why not?

2. Would you recommend that Lee and Marta move ahead in drafting their own will or should they hire an outside expert? Explain your answer.

3. What should they look for when choosing an executor or personal representative?

4. Once they have a completed and signed will where should they keep it? Where should they definitely not keep the will?

5. What should Lee and Marta include in a letter of last instructions?

6. Help the Howards understand the differences between revocable and irrevocable living trusts by listing the advantages and disadvantages of both.

7. Assuming that the Howards give their son $100,000 next month, how much tax must their son pay on this gift?

8. What options does Lee have for gifting his whole life insurance policy, either to an individual or a charity? What are the consequences for his estate tax planning?

9. Assume that Lee and Marta (a) own all assets jointly, except for the life insurance policy that Lee owns, and (b) do not give their son the $100,000 gift. If Lee were to die in 2002 and leave his assets to Marta through a marital transfer, how much in estate taxes will be due if Marta dies in 2003? How much is passed on to heirs?

10. Now calculate the estate tax on Marta's estate if the Howards use a standard family trust and pass Lee's assets, up to the estate-tax-free transfer threshold limit for the year 2002, to the trust and the remainder to Marta. How much is passed on to heirs if Marta dies in 2003? (Assume any increase in estate value between 2002 and 2003 is spent for Marta's care.)

# Money Matters

## ALL IN THE FAMILY

***If you have any assets, a spouse, and/or children—GET A WILL!*** *If you die without one, your state will "write one for you" based on intestacy laws. Often those laws are directly opposed to your intent. For example, part of your estate may go to your parents when you would have wanted your spouse to inherit everything, or the guardian appointed for your children may be someone you always detested.*

***Beware of do-it-yourself will packages or computer software.*** *Although many are good, some leave out very important sections of a viable will or are not valid in your state. Also, such tools may not provide any coaching on how bequests should be worded to avoid confusion at probate. One error could run your beneficiaries more in probate costs than the attorney's fee to do it right the first time.*

***Although living trusts are excellent tools for certain people, do your homework before deciding if one is right for you.*** *Unfortunately, they are often "sold" by persons quoting highly exaggerated probate costs and using other scare tactics. Be sure your situation warrants the time and expense. Probate costs vary greatly from state to state and you may find the expense of such a trust is much more than your estate would pay for probate. If you do choose a living trust, use a qualified attorney to set it up.*

***One of the biggest erosions of large estates with business or real estate holdings is forced sale of assets at "fire sale" prices to pay taxes.*** *If your assets are primarily illiquid, you may want life insurance to provide the funds necessary to preserve those valuable holdings.*

***Consider using an irrevocable life insurance trust as a source of money for estate taxes.*** *If structured properly, the trust may use annual exclusion gifts ($11,000 in 2002) to beneficiaries to pay insurance premiums. Proceeds from the policy are not your assets, and you are able to reduce the size of your estate with the annual gifts. By purchasing the life insurance through the trust initially, rather than using a policy you may already have, you avoid the chance of proceeds reverting to your estate if you die within 3 years.*

***Business owners who do not wish to burden their beneficiaries with trying to run a company after their death should investigate a "buy-sell agreement."*** *There are several types of such plans that provide for another shareholder, partner, or even key employee to purchase the business from the estate. Funding is often provided through life insurance. In such a win-win situation, forced sale of the company is avoided and the deceased owner's family receives the liquidity they may need.*

# Discussion Case 2

Cindy and Ned Lipman were recently married, each for the second time. Both are concerned about leaving assets to the adult children from their previous marriages and are reluctant to comingle their individual assets. Together, they have an estate valued at $1.25 million, of which $750,000 is in Cindy's name. They live in Cindy's $200,000 home that she received in her divorce settlement.

Planning for incapacitation is another estate planning concern. Cindy's 86-year-old mother and 84-year-old uncle both have Alzheimer's disease and she is concerned that it may be hereditary. Ned recently lost his father to a long-term illness and has vowed never to become a "vegetable" lying in a hospital bed. Cindy, on the other hand, believes all steps should be taken to prolong a person's life. Neither Cindy nor Ned has revised their wills since their marriage. The wills still name their previous spouses as executor and beneficiary of their respective estates.

## Questions

1. What type of trust is appropriate for remarried couples such as the Lipmans? How might your answer change if the individuals have sufficient assets to independently provide for themselves following the death of either spouse?

**2.** How much estate tax would Cindy and Ned owe on their respective estates?

**3.** What can Cindy and Ned do to address their concerns about estate planning in the event of incapacitation?

**4.** Would Cindy and Ned make good health care proxies for one another? Why or why not?

**5.** Since Cindy and Ned both have valid wills, are revisions necessary? If so, what changes should be made?

Visit our Web site for additional case problems, interactive exercises, and practice quizzes for this chapter—**www.prenhall.com/keown**.

# CONTINUING CASE: Cory and Tisha Dumont

After seeing a newspaper clip about the Web site death-clock.com, Cory talked Tisha into checking out their life expectancy. From the "pessimistic" view, Cory would die at age 53. Cory jokingly commented, "Forget the life insurance premiums and saving for retirement, I'm living it up *now*!" The "normal" perspective projected Cory to live to age 73, whereas Tisha was projected to die at the age of 79. Her reply to Cory, "You may live it up now, but I've got 6 years to live it up without you! And, if I inherit all our assets, I could be a wealthy old lady! We need to save and invest even more. Wonder how much fun a wealthy old lady could have?" Although Cory and Tisha could joke about their death-clock.com experience, it did raise some important financial issues for them to consider. They don't plan to retire or to transfer their estate until sometime far in the future, but their concerns are clearly a part of the financial planning process.

With your assistance they have reviewed their spending, credit usage, insurance needs, and investment plans. In short, by developing a financial plan and changing a few spending habits, they are building an estate for the future. They are concerned about financial independence during their "golden years"—however long they might be—and want to make the most of their retirement options. They are also concerned about preserving their estate for the benefit of the children, regardless of the timing of their death.

## Questions

1. Assuming the "deathclock" projection is accurate, Cory is concerned about getting back as much as possible of his Social Security taxes. At what age can he retire and receive full Social Security benefits? If he delays retirement, he can expect what percentage increase in his benefits? What is the earliest age that Cory can retire and receive Social Security? How will early retirement affect his benefits?

2. Assuming Cory and Tisha were old enough to retire today and receive Social Security, what percentage of their Social Security benefit would be taxable?

3. If Cory or Tisha were to die tomorrow, what kind of Social Security benefits, if any, would the surviving spouse, Chad, and Haley receive? For how long?

4. Both Cory and Tisha are eligible for a "qualified" or tax-favored retirement plan at work.
   a. What are two unique benefits of such a plan?
   b. Why are these benefits, and time value of money, particularly important in retirement planning?
   c. What must the Dumonts do to be "active participants"?
   d. What are "catch-up" provisions? Why and how are they used?

5. Cory and Tisha are interested in other retirement saving strategies. What is the maximum amount they could contribute to an IRA? If they decided to contribute to a traditional IRA, would they receive a full or partial tax deduction? Why? What are the advantages and disadvantages of opening a Roth IRA instead of a traditional IRA? What advantages are common to both plans?

6. Cory's company is planning to convert all employees to a cash-balance retirement plan. Explain this plan, noting advantages and disadvantages for Cory.

7. The Dumonts estimate their current living expenses at approximately $60,000—which they joke could be very comfortable living during retirement *without the kids*.
   a. How much income, before and after taxes, will they need to retire, assuming an average tax rate of 17 percent during retirement?
   b. Assume that through a combination of savings, Social Security, and pension plan distributions Cory and Tisha are able to earn $45,000 annually in retirement. Determine their retirement income shortfall. Assuming a 4 percent inflation rate and 35 years until retirement, calculate their inflation-adjusted shortfall.
   c. If Cory and Tisha can earn a 5 percent inflation-adjusted return, determine how much they must accumulate in savings over the 35 years to fund the annual inflation-adjusted shortfall as calculated earlier.
   d. How much do the Dumonts need to start saving each year for the next 35 years at 10 percent to meet their saving accumulation goal as calculated in part c?

8. If, for 30 years, Cory and Tisha invested $2,000 at the end of every year in a tax-free account, what would be the future value of the account if they earned 9 percent annually? If instead they first paid taxes (marginal tax rate of 27.5 percent) and then made the investment, how much would the account be worth at the end of 30 years? Based on these calculations, what advice would you give to Cory and Tisha regarding their retirement savings? What principle of saving in an IRS tax-deferred plan does this example demonstrate?

9. Recall that Cory has $2,500 in a pension account with a former employer. When Cory resigned, the account value was almost $4,000 but only $2,500 is available to him. Explain the difference. What options and tax implications should Cory compare to claim his retirement benefits? He has considered a surprise vacation for the family, an IRA account, or another mutual fund account to fund a 25-year anniversary trip with Tisha.

10. Tisha has considered offering accounting services to small businesses. She has obtained a business license and plans to work out of her home. Would she qualify for a small business/self-employed retirement plan? If so, what plan should she consider?

11. Tisha has indicated that she thinks a single life annuity will be her choice when she begins to receive retirement pension benefits. She thinks this is the best payout structure because (a) she has earned the entire benefit, (b) she can control the investment of the funds, and (c) Cory will receive his own pension. Will Tisha automatically be able to choose a single life annuity payout option? Assuming that Cory does not want Tisha to have a single life annuity, what type of joint and survivor annuity will provide the greatest immediate payout and provide Cory a guaranteed income should he outlive Tisha?

12. After retirement, what expected and unexpected changes should the Dumonts monitor to safeguard their future?

13. At this stage of the life cycle, which of the five objectives of estate planning are most important to the Dumont household? Preparation of what two estate planning documents would enable them to accomplish these objectives? Where should the documents be kept?

14. Recall that Cory's parents recently gave each of the children a $20,000 gift to be invested for college. How much federal income tax and gift tax are due on this transfer? Will there be any generation-skipping transfer tax due? The senior Dumonts planned to give Chad $30,000 instead of $20,000 but were advised not to. Why?

15. Cory and Tisha want to develop other saving strategies to fund education costs. What are the advantages or disadvantages of opening a Coverdell Education Savings Account or a 529 plan for each of the children? Could they establish both types of accounts?

16. The Dumonts are curious as to why someone would want to avoid probate. Having the court oversee the will and the distribution of assets sounds like a good thing. Explain why avoiding probate may be an important issue in estate planning. What four steps could the Dumonts take to avoid probate?

17. Recently, Cory reluctantly agreed to be named as executor for his older sister Emily's estate. Does serving as executor include acting as guardian for her child, who is younger than Chad and Haley? What are the duties that Cory would be expected to perform as executor?

18. The Dumonts recently noticed on their bank statement that their $3,000 savings account is owned jointly with right of survivorship. Provide a simple explanation of this term.

19. The Dumonts have always considered a trust a financial tool of the wealthy. But they do want to learn more about estate planning. Provide a simple explanation of how both living and testamentary trusts, which by definition are quite different, can accomplish the same purpose of reducing estate taxes.

20. Cory's parents joked that they planned to die in 2010 to handle all their estate tax problems. What did they mean? How might relying on the unlimited marital deduction be an equally ineffective strategy?

# 18 Fitting the Pieces Together

## Learning Objectives

**Understand** the importance of beginning your financial planning early.

**Understand** that achieving financial security is more difficult for women.

**Discuss** how major life events—marriage and children—affect your financial plan.

**Understand** and manage the keys to financial success.

**Deal** with all kinds of debt in the real world.

Movies imitate life—and sometimes we see things we just don't like to acknowledge. For example, the fact that money is more important than it should be. Just look at Robby, in the movie *The Wedding Singer,* played by Adam Sandler. Remember when he was left at the altar? "Geeze, you know that information might have been a little more useful to me yesterday." Why did he get dumped? It all boiled down to money.

It takes the rest of the movie, along with a little help from Billy Idol, for things to work out for Robby. Along the way, Robby falls in love with Julia, played by Drew Barrymore, who is already engaged to Glenn, a Wall Street bond broker.

"Hey, you know why she's marrying him, don't you?" Julia's roommate asks Robby.

"The money thing, the security, the nice house, I guess. That's important to some people," is Robby's reply.

"No, it's not important to some people. It's important to all people."

"Hey, then I guess I'm in big trouble."

In the end, true love conquers all, and it turns out that money doesn't really matter after all. That may not be the case for you, or perhaps Billy Idol might not be there to save the day.

Let's face it, in movies as well as in real life, money not only determines whether you meet your goals, but how people relate to you. In fact, money problems are the number one cause of divorce. The bottom line is that you're going to find that money matters affect your life in ways you could never have imagined. You're also going to find that what happens in your financial future is your choice.

What's most amazing about all this is that we know money is important, but most of us never learn how to handle it. This is where you're ahead of the game: You've been introduced to the basics of financial planning. In this chapter, we recap much of what you've already learned, but we put it together in the form of an action plan. We also look at some of the special problems you may face in the near future—we focus on the life events that could throw a monkey wrench into your financial plan. We examine the keys to financial success and ruin. We take a final look at debt, a topic we've covered in bits and pieces throughout the book. Finally, we talk about getting started—that is, putting your financial plan into action. Following the advice in this chapter should set the stage for a sound financial future.

The key in all this is to remember that your financial future starts now. You'll find challenges with student loans and credit card debt; with budgeting, spending and saving; with the financial shocks of marriage and children. Remember the words of Robby: "I'm a big fan of money. I like it. I keep it in a jar on top of my refrigerator. I'd like to put more in that jar." Right now, the time is yours. Make a choice: You can take control, or you can let things just happen and make your job a heck of a lot tougher in the future. Let's get at it. Choose wealth, and see if we can't fill up your jar.

## The Ingredients of Success

Without question, the term "only as strong as the weakest link" applies to personal finance. It is simply impossible to succeed financially unless you:

- evaluate your financial health, set your goals, and develop an action plan
- plan and budget
- manage your cash and credit
- control your debt
- make knowledgeable consumer decisions
- have adequate health, life, property, and liability insurance
- understand investing principles
- make investment decisions that reflect your goals
- plan for retirement
- plan for what happens to your accumulated wealth and your dependents after you die

Everything in personal finance starts with the budgeting and planning process first outlined in Chapter 1 and presented in Figure 1.1. You've got to periodically review your financial progress and reexamine your financial plan. In other words, personal finance is an ongoing process, with no financial plan being fixed for life. But, even though financial plans don't last forever, without them, goals are a mere fantasy.

There isn't a topic covered in this book that is not essential to your personal financial health. As such, you'll want to keep revisiting all these topics to make sure that your financial plan reflects your current financial health and what's going on in your life.

Let's now try to put all this together. First, let's take a look at your place in the financial life cycle. Then let's add some reality to the discussion and look at some of the unique personal finance problems faced by women. We'll follow that with a discussion of some of the major life events that you may be facing in the near future—marriage and children. Then we will look at the 12 decisions that you will be making that will determine whether you succeed financially. Finally, we will take an in-depth look at debt—because it is something that you'll have to make some big decisions on in the very near future. Finally, we will end with a call to action—to begin your financial plan today.

**Understand the importance of beginning your financial planning early.**

## What Now? A Look Back at the Financial Life Cycle

In Chapter 1 we examined the financial life cycle. Most of you are at the front end of that life cycle—just learning the ropes—and along the way realizing that it's harder than it looks. Making it tougher is the fact that up until this course, you probably didn't discuss personal finance with anyone. Talk about sex is everywhere, but talk about money just doesn't happen. Sure we talk about how big the Powerball lottery has grown, or how much money Bill Gates is worth. But we don't talk about our savings, budget, or investments. In fact, if you think about it, your parents probably never discussed their finances with you, and you've probably been through at least 12 years of schooling and never, until now, taken a course in personal finance.

It's time to change all that. Let's take personal finance out of the closet and begin by looking at your place in the financial life cycle. Next time you're out with some friends, ask them if they have an IRA or if they've begun saving for retirement—you now know enough to hold your own.

Because your financial decisions are going to affect your lifestyle, make sure that these decisions reflect not only your financial goals, but also your values. Remember, you can't separate your personal and financial lives. No matter how much money you have, you won't be happy if your lifestyle violates your values. Financial success is judged not only by whether you're spending less than you earn, but also by whether you've found a balance between your goals and values, your personal life and your finances.

Now let's look at where the typical college grad is in the financial life cycle. A lot will be going on in the next 10 years. You'll be buying a car and perhaps a house, establishing credit, getting married, buying insurance, paying taxes, and perhaps having a baby or two. That's a lot, but it's not all. You'll also want to set up an emergency fund, start saving for your goals, and begin putting money in an IRA and a retirement account. These are 10 years you can never get back, and 10 years when you clearly have the choice of choosing wealth.

Unfortunately, personal finance is the last thing most young singles think of. They're too busy living life to the fullest. As for personal finance, well, there's plenty of time for that, after all they just got out of college. Young singles also tend to view everything as temporary. After all, how can you plan for the future until you're married? By now you should know that this attitude squanders your strongest ally on the road to financial success—time. You'll never be able to recapture your early years. Remember Selma and Patty Bouvier from Chapter 3, page 67?

If beginning when you turn 19 you put away $2,000 at the end of each year for 7 years in a IRA that earns 11 percent per year, and then nothing thereafter, you'd end up at 65 with about $1.272 million! If you waited until you were 25 to start that IRA and made payments every year for 40 years, you still wouldn't catch up—you'd only end up with $1.164 million. Moreover, if you wait until you're 30 to start that IRA and make 35 payments, you'll end up with $683,179! There's simply no substitute for starting early. It's without doubt the simplest strategy: to recognize your financial future starts now and just do it.

Now let's add some realism to our discussion and see why it's even more important for women to take control of their finances. We'll also look at two life events that can have a major impact on your financial future: marriage and children.

## Women and Personal Finance: Why It's Important

**L(2** Understand that achieving financial security is more difficult for women.

The basic principles of personal finance don't change whether you're a man or woman, nor does the desire for financial security. However, the effort needed to achieve your financial goals does change: It's much tougher to achieve financial security if you're a woman. The bottom line is that it doesn't really matter if a woman has a partner in life or not. It is essential that women take responsibility for their financial future; there is just too much at stake. Moreover, the idea that someone will take care of you is a dangerous myth. Even if you have a partner who is willing and knowledgeable, you've still got to take responsibility for your own financial future.

Consider these facts:

▌ Over 90 percent of all women will take sole responsibility for their financial decisions at some point in their lives.

▌ Twenty percent of all women never marry.

- Forty-seven percent of first marriages and 49 percent of second marriages end in divorce.
- Seventy-five percent of women do not know how much they need to save for retirement.
- Women tend to be more conservative with their investments, which means their investments tend to earn less.
- At age 65, women outnumber men by 3 to 2, and at 85 they outnumber them 5 to 2.
- Seventy-five percent of married women eventually end up widowed, and the average age of widowhood is 56.
- Although only about 12 percent of all elderly people live in poverty, about three-fourths of them are women.
- Eighty percent of all widows who are now living in poverty were not living in poverty when their husbands died.
- In 2000, the median personal income for women 65 and older was $10,899. For men in the same age group, it was $19,168.
- More single young women ages 21–34 (53 percent) said they were living from paycheck to paycheck than did single young men (42 percent).

Depressing, eh?

Because women generally earn less, are less likely to have pensions, qualify for less income from Social Security, and live longer than men, planning for their financial independence, in particular during their retirement years, is more difficult than it is for men. In addition, women must dispel the myth that someone will take care of them—the odds are it's not going to happen. What does all this mean? It means that women have to take charge of their money and their financial future. Where does a woman start?

**Principle 9**
The Best Protection Is Knowledge

The first step is to acquire knowledge. As you learned in **Principle 9: The Best Protection Is Knowledge**. We'll assume that since you're reading this book you're taking a class in personal finance. That's a great start, but just like everything else in life, things change. As a woman, you'll want to keep as current as you can with respect to personal finance.

If you're married, make sure you're involved in family investment decisions. Try subscribing to one of the personal finance magazines like *Kiplinger's Personal Finance Magazine*, *Smart Money*, or *Money*. Also make sure you keep visiting the Personal Finance Navigator Web site that accompanies this text—use it as a free financial advisor. You might also want to join an investment club, which is a great way to learn more about investments and get some hands-on experience. If you do decide to join a club, look for one whose members are all women. Remember, over 90 percent of all women take sole responsibility for their financial decisions at some point in their lives. When that time comes for you, you'll want to know what you're doing.

**Principle 8**
Nothing Happens Without a Plan

The next step is to make things happen. That means you need a plan. As we know from **Principle 8: Nothing Happens Without a Plan**. In fact, there isn't anything special or different that needs to be done if you're a woman—the principles in this text apply to either gender. However, you've got to realize that women face bigger obstacles when planning for their financial futures, and that it's up to each one of us—male or female—to make sure our financial future is secure.

Although the principles are gender neutral, there are some essential actions you should consider if you're a woman. You want to make sure your plan recognizes that women live longer than men and that half of all marriages end in divorce. Make sure you're involved in your husband's pension decisions, and make sure you fund any employer-sponsored retirement plans and spousal IRAs to the fullest. Finally, if you aren't confident, see a financial planner about your specific concerns as a woman. An advisor may be able to aim you in some directions you might not have considered. Just as important, a financial advisor can serve as a great motivator.

## Life Events

L3 Discuss how major life events—marriage and children— affect your financial plan.

Financial planning is not a one-time activity; it changes as you react to different life events. Although you don't know what the future will bring, you can anticipate problems and prepare yourself to take advantage of opportunities. To help in preparing you for the future, we now look at the financial aspects of several major life events. Each of these events will have a profound financial impact on you. But as with much of life, just knowing what's ahead gives you an advantage.

### Marriage

Most married couples plan their wedding down to the smallest detail but spend little time talking about money and planning their financial lives together. That's probably not a great idea, given the fact that money problems are one of the top reasons people get divorced. Managing your money when you're single is tough enough. But when you're married, you not only have to plan for your own expenses, but also those of your partner.

Your partner may bring student loans, credit card debt, a past bankruptcy, or other financial problems to the marriage. And let's face it, you're marrying this person's money, too. On top of all this is the fact that opposites tend to attract. That means if you're a saver, you might end up married to a spender, and if you're a spender, there might be a saver in your future. In either case, if you don't do some financial planning from the beginning, there'll also be some arguments in your future.

The place to start is with a discussion about money. The goal is to find out your partner's financial history, habits, and goals. Take a look at Checklist 18.1.

Once you have an understanding of each other's views on money, it's time to see how this translates into spending habits. You'll want to track your expenses carefully for a month. When you do this, it's important to keep track of *all* your expenses, including money spent on candy and soda. This should provide fuel for more discussion as you see how financial views translate into action. You will now have enough background to make a budget. Set out your goals and make plans to attain

## Checklist 18.1 ▪ Marriage and Money

**In talking with your future partner, ask these questions:**

How did your family handle money? Did they have debt problems? Did they use credit cards?

How much income is enough? How do you feel about both spouses working after you have children?

How much do you earn? Do you have other sources of income? What do you own?

How do you feel about debt? Do you have debt? Do you have other financial commitments—for example, aging parents who may need financial support or children from a previous marriage?

Once you're married, will you invest separately? Who will pay for what? Will you have one or two checking accounts?

Do you or your partner need life insurance, and if so how much? How about health insurance? What do your employee benefits include?

them using what you've learned in this book. Just as important as setting up a budget, identify expenses that you can eliminate. Tracking your spending will also let you plan savings, which you'll want to make automatic: Remember **Principle 13: Pay Yourself First**.

Once you're married, review and revise your plan annually, or whenever there is a significant change in your life—for example, the arrival of a child. If you can't get your financial plans settled by yourself, be sure to contact a financial planner. A planner will help you set up a plan that works and guide you through any conflicts you might have. If you're still having problems, you can seek the help of a financial counselor, a financial planner who specializes in counseling couples about money.

Given that a typical wedding now costs in excess of $15,000 and a divorce can cost even more, it doesn't make sense to let financial problems bring it down. The real key here is talk, talk, and more talk—all about money.

Two other financial decisions you face when you get married are whether to have joint or separate checking accounts and credit cards. Clearly, one checking account is easiest for most couples, but if you have incompatible money management styles, consider two accounts. That's kind of the financial equivalent of two bathrooms. It makes record keeping more tedious, and you may not get as good a deal on your checking account from the bank, but if your money management styles are dramatically different, it may be the best choice.

With respect to credit cards, you want not only to control credit card spending but also to use your credit card to establish a strong credit history. If you've ever heard stories of a divorced, widowed, or separated stay-at-home spouse unable to get credit, you know how difficult this can be. The way to avoid this potential problem is for each spouse to have his or her own credit card.

## Children: The Ultimate Financial Surprise

In Chapter 1 we discussed the cost of raising a child. But who thinks of children in such cold terms as cost? After all, they're little bundles of joy . . . with serious price tags attached. As we saw, the cost of raising a child from birth to age 18 runs about $165,630 and rising. Even worse, when you add in the cost of a college education and lost wages resulting from child-rearing duties, *U.S. News and World Reports* estimates that for a medium income family, a child requires an investment in excess of $1.45 million over 22 years. Yikes! Keep in mind, a medium income family is just over $42,000 per year. This is all pretty scary, given the fact that conceiving a child is virtually cost free, and in many cases, thought free.

What this all means is that there are serious financial implications to having a child, implications that will have a serious effect on your financial plans. Certainly, there is more to life than money, and you just can't quantify the joys and satisfaction of child raising. But you want to make sure you take the financial pain out of having children by planning ahead. First, make sure your health insurance is up to date and complete, and once you have your child, make sure you notify your insurance company. In addition to health insurance, review your life and disability insurance, and make sure you have enough coverage. If you have a tax-free flexible spending account, make sure it's ready for your new addi-

**STOP &THINK** It's generally considered bad taste to look at the decision to have children in economic terms—after all, children are their parents' hope for the future, and the continuation of their bloodlines. Let's look at what you might have done with some of that money if you decided to pass on parenthood, and here we've only accounted for $80,052 of the $165,630 spent over the first 18 years of life according to Table 1.2. In fact, according to the *U.S. News and World Report*, if you add in things like lost income, lost career opportunities, and college, the figure climbs to $1.45 million for a middle-income family to raise a typical child for the first 22 years of life.

| Some of What You Spent on Your Child | | | How You Might Have Spent That Money on Yourself | | |
|---|---|---|---|---|---|
| Age | Spent per year at age | Cost | Age | Spent per year at age | Cost |
| 0 | Average cost of delivery | $6,400 | 0 | 7-day safari for two in Kenya | $6,400 |
| 1 | An au pair (live-in nanny) | $20,000 | 1 | New 2003 VW Beetle | $20,000 |
| 3 | Montessori preschool | $4,000 | 3 | Set of Ping ISI golf clubs | $4,000 |
| 5 | The "must-have" toy: the (very rare) original 8-inch "Buttercup" PowerPuff Girl | $1,800 | 5 | Mint copy of Beatles "Butcher Block" cover to "Yesterday and Today" signed by all the Beatles | $1,800 |
| 7 | After school program for the gifted | $3,564 | 7 | 2 Box seat season tickets to the Baltimore Orioles | $3,564 |
| 8–9 | Private school | $18,770 | | | |
| 10 | Violin and lessons (3 times per week) | $4,150 | 8–9 | A 2003 Mazda Miata | $18,770 |
| 11 | Self-defense lessons (3 times per week) after being beaten up when going to violin lessons after school | $3,750 | 10 | Membership in a health club with personal trainer (3 times per week) | $4,150 |
| | | | 11 | One more year of a personal trainer (3 times per week) | $3,750 |
| 12 | Therapy to improve self-esteem (once a week) | $5,000 | 12 | Another year of personal training plus a week in Cancun (to show off) | $5,000 |
| 13 | Clothes from Abercrombie and Fitch (to help with self-image) | $3,500 | 13 | 60" Sony home theatre with home theatre surround sound | $3,500 |
| 14 | Transportation to and from community sentencing for using fake ID | $199 | 14 | Sony MP3 player | $199 |
| 15 | Bill from Mystic Tattoos | $189 | 15 | Navy SEALs watch from the Sharper Image catalog | $189 |
| 16 | Laser tattoo removal | $2,796 | | | |
| 16 | Increased automobile insurance premiums | $1,345 | 16 | Executive massage chair from Sharper Image and 3 nights at the Plaza | $2,796 |
| 16.5 | Increase in auto insurance after two tickets and one accident (including lawyer fees) | $2,250 | 16 | Orvis 2-day fly-fishing course and basic gear | $1,345 |
| | | | 16.5 | DVD player, Dolby receiver, Bose AM15 speakers, and 35" TV | $2,250 |
| 17 | SAT prep course | $600 | 17 | CD-stereo system for your car | $600 |
| **Total (not including college)** | | **$80,052** | **Total (not including college savings)** | | **$80,052** |

**Now add in 5 years of college for your child or a Mercedes-Benz S600 at $132,800 for you!**

tion. You'll want to make sure you've saved up enough to cover the new baby costs. This is also a time to update your will and make sure you've named a guardian for your child. Finally, you'll want to review your financial plan, and start saving for Junior's college education.

## Making Financial Success Happen

Understand and manage the keys to financial success.

Although nothing in life is guaranteed, you do have choices. You can choose wealth in your future. Certainly, wealth is easier for some than for others. No doubt where we start from in life is important. But you're going to make a lot of decisions over your lifetime, many of them with financial implications, and if you pay attention to those decisions, you can choose wealth. As we said before, we all know that money doesn't mean happiness, but we also know that money problems can make you miserable.

What is important is that you understand that *building wealth is part of a satisfying life*. It doesn't necessarily bring happiness, but it does provide a means to achieve your goals—and it's satisfying to achieve your goals. Before we look at some of the most important decisions you'll be making when you choose wealth, let's take a look at how the rich get rich. You'll notice that for the most part their lifestyles are a reflection of the decision to choose wealth.

## How the Rich Become Rich

Before we look at how people become rich, we must first differentiate between income and wealth. The fact that someone earns $250,000 per year doesn't necessarily make that person wealthy; it just means he or she has a large income. If he or she spends the $250,000 on expensive cars, exclusive clothes, rare wine, and travel to exotic places, that person won't end up with much in the way of wealth. That's because wealth is net worth, which is calculated as your assets minus your liabilities. In order to create wealth you've got to bring in more than you spend—it's that simple. In fact, this section could have easily been titled "A Penny Saved Is a Penny Earned."

In their classic book, *The Millionaire Next Door: The Surprising Secrets of America's Wealthy*, Stanley and Danko surveyed the habits of wealthy Americans and found a good deal of commonality. The average net worth of those surveyed was somewhere between $1 and $5 million, and this was not inherited wealth. In fact, this level of wealth wasn't even created on a huge salary—most millionaires have incomes of less than $100,000. They own a home, valued at $278,000 (which is not extravagant); are self-employed; own a business or are a partner in a business; are still on their first marriage; and have, on average, three kids. In terms of personal traits, frugality is the key. They clip coupons, they buy on sale, they practice financial discipline and self-denial. For example, although such people could afford a Mercedes, their typical car is American made, 3 years old, and used, with the most common being a Ford F-150 pick-up. In short, for them it's not a "material world," and they aren't "material girls" (or guys).

The practice of frugality is extremely important and empowering for several reasons. Frugality sets the stage for success in personal finance. Once you start building wealth, that success will breed more success, and everyone feeds on success. It allows you to live below your means, that is, to spend less than you bring in. It also allows you to stretch your money so that you can spend less and have more. And it takes the emphasis off some of the manipulative traps marketers have set for you—the need for $150 sneakers, $40 designer T-shirts, $100 bottles of wine, and that $4.50 "to die for" Cafe Latte from Starbucks. It helps you recognize that money is not happiness, and you don't need everything to be happy. It's a lot easier to be happy if your happiness doesn't depend on money. The state of mind that frugality brings makes that a lot easier.

## The Keys to Success: A Dozen Decisions

In choosing wealth you'll face a number of different hurdles and decisions—some of them financial and some of them lifestyle. Even worse, you'll make some of these decisions without even knowing it. What we'll do now is take a look at them and try to understand their ramifications.

**Number 1: Become Knowledgeable**   Armed with an understanding of the basics of personal finance, it becomes much easier to avoid financial pitfalls and bad advice—remember **Principle 9: The Best Protection Is Knowledge**. In fact, you'll find the ability to evaluate financial advice and make good financial decisions invaluable. Unfortunately, managing their personal finances is one of the few things people seem willing to do without an understanding of what they're doing. Certainly, no

Principle

**9** The Best Protection Is Knowledge

one would attempt a heart by-pass if they didn't know what they were facing, but when it comes to personal finance and investing, too many people are willing to take a stab at it even though they don't have the slightest idea what they're doing. The results are generally sad: Often that lack of knowledge attracts the unethical and incompetent characters who loiter around wherever money is present.

Knowledge will keep you from falling prey to those who are always willing to help you with (or help themselves to) your money. In addition, knowledge will spur on your commitment to personal finance. When you understand the concepts of the time value of money and stock valuation, you gain an appreciation for starting your financial plan early in life, and that appreciation leads to action. An understanding of personal finance also gives you the ability to handle those unwanted financial surprises that are all too frequent in life. In short, knowledge will keep you out of financial trouble because, as we all know, it's a lot easier to do things right if you understand what you're doing.

**Number 2: Don't Procrastinate** The biggest threat to your financial future comes from within. Although bad advice can slow your financial progress, procrastination stops it. Unfortunately, very few things are more natural than procrastination. In fact, you're probably pretty good at it already. Postponing that term paper really didn't hurt you; after all, as long as you handed it in on time, it doesn't matter. As you should know by now, it's not the same with personal finance: There's a big difference whether you invest $2,000 for retirement now or the day before you retire.

Still, it's awfully easy to put off facing your financial future. If you aren't married, you may be keeping your life on hold, waiting for that special person to make financial sacrifices with. Or when you graduate you may think you deserve a break from "student poverty." Or you may just think there's no sense saving now, when in the future you'll earn a lot more and saving will be a lot easier.

Unfortunately, there's always a reason to put it off. But while you may feel you aren't earning enough money right now, wait until you get married and have kids. How about adding those home mortgage payments into the mix? Just when you think you've made it out of the woods, paying for college will be staring you in the face.

The bottom line is that your financial future starts now. You know enough about the time value of money to realize that procrastination will only make your future work a lot harder. As the Rolling Stones sang, "Time is on my side." With personal finance, there is hardly a truer statement. But unfortunately, as time goes by it becomes a lost advantage that can't be recaptured. Remember **Principle 15: Just Do It!**

Principle **15** Just Do It!

**Number 3: Live Below Your Means** You always hear people saying, "We don't spend money on anything extravagant, but we just can't seem to get ahead." The answer to their problem is uncomfortably simple: *You can't save money unless you spend less than you earn.* The problem is that people tend to spend to their level of earning, and in many cases, beyond. Unfortunately, our culture makes that natural. For many people, "you are what you buy." Their image comes from the car they drive, the labels on their clothes, and the wine they drink. It seems many people think if they earn a certain amount of money, they should live and look a certain way. Even worse, shopping has gone from a chore, to a hobby for some, and to a lifestyle for others. The result is regardless of how much you make, it all goes toward the necessities of life—the more you make, the more necessities there are.

How do you get out of this trap? The answer is you've got to change your attitude toward spending. You've got to be realistic with respect to what you can really afford. This all flows from that somewhat depressing truth: You can't have it all.

# In The News

## Four Ways to Get Your Finances in Shape

### by Jonathan Clements

Looking to get your finances on track after the shellacking of the past two years? As you reassess your finances, follow these four investment principles:

1. Aim Before Firing. *Investing isn't about getting rich, beating the market, or enjoying the thrills of Vegas in the comfort of your own home. Instead, investing is about amassing the money necessary to pay for your financial goals.* (☞A)

Need a fatter retirement nest egg? Maybe you should postpone quitting the workforce. Already saved enough for your kids' college? Rather than continuing to pursue high returns, maybe you should take less risk.

2. *Play the Angles.* When picking investments, there are three key attributes to consider: risk, return, and cost. You have a lot of control over risk and investment costs. Meanwhile, trying to pick winning investments is a bit of a crap shoot. So what do most investors do? You guessed it: They focus relentlessly on returns, while ignoring risk and costs.

3. Discount History. *Index funds? Many investors loathe the idea of simply mimicking the stock market's results. Instead, they go hunting for winning investment strategies, often starting their search by studying market history.*

*But history doesn't offer a reliable guide to the future. Past share-price patterns may not persist, historically successful stock-picking strategies often lose their luster, and funds with great performance records frequently falter.* (☞B)

4. *Doubt Yourself.* True, history may not be much help. But bolstered by irrepressible self-confidence, we all like to think we can buck the odds and beat the market. Maybe, however, we would be better served by a little humility.

Every day, millions of investors pore over the market, all trying to find winning investments. If there are screaming bargains to be had, they don't stay that way for long. Indeed, at any given moment, the safest assumption is that stocks and bonds are fairly valued.

The bottom line: All our market-beating efforts may prove self-defeating. After all, the more we strive to beat the market, the

higher our investment costs—thus, making it harder to earn superior returns.

## THE BOTTOM LINE . . .

A The place to start is with goals and a plan. After all, remember **Principle 8: Nothing Happens Without a Plan.**

B The logic behind index funds comes from **Principle 5: The Curse of Competitive Investments Markets.** While it is tough to beat the market over a long period of time, it isn't tough to lower costs, and after all, $10,000 invested for 40 years at 11 percent grows to just over $650,000, but if there were 2 percent annual expenses on that investment, it would only grow to about $314,000.

---

You've got to make choices. The place to start is to track your spending. Once you see what you're spending, you'll also see what you can cut. For example, that morning *USA Today*, cinnamon scone, and a cup of Cafe Suisse that you pick up on the way to work may cost you $6.75 a day. If there are 22 work days in a month, say goodbye to $148.50 each month and $1,782.00 over the year. And even worse, before you spent it, there were taxes. If you're in the 27 percent marginal tax bracket, that means you needed to earn $2,441 (that is, $1,782/[1 − .27]) to cover your morning fix on the way to work. Cutting out the nonnecessities will allow you to follow **Principle 13: Pay Yourself First.** That is, make savings automatic.

---

**STOP & THINK** If you ever saw the movie *Willie Wonka and the Chocolate Factory*, or read the book *Charlie and the Chocolate Factory*, on which the movie is based, you'll remember a little girl named Veruca Salt. She was a nasty piece of work. She constantly demanded things, screaming **"I WANT IT NOW!"** Her desires and the way she acted were clearly out of control. She didn't make it through the story—but if she had, with that attitude her financial future would not have been very bright. There's no easier way to foil a financial plan than with a lack of control and impulse buying. Control is crucial.

---

**Principle 13 — Pay Yourself First**

**Number 4: Realize You Aren't Indestructible** You're young, you're healthy, and the mere fact you can eat dorm food and live means you're indestructible. That doesn't mean your TV might not fail you, or your car might not meet an untimely death. So make sure you have an emergency fund.

Now let's look at insurance. If you're single and don't have any dependents, you probably don't need any life insurance. In fact, you can take a look at Table 9.1 to see whether or not you need any. If you need it, keep your costs down by shopping for term insurance on the Internet, and when there's a major change in your life, such as the birth of children, review your coverage. As for health insurance, let's face it, you need it, and let's face it, it's expensive. Hopefully, your job will provide you with adequate coverage. In fact, when you're job hunting, make sure you look very closely at the health care benefits.

OK, you've got your life and health insurance, are you ready for action? The answer is no. Consider this fact: If you're under 35, there is a 65-percent chance that an accident or long-term illness will keep you out of work for a minimum of 6 months. Moreover, about half of all mortgage foreclosures come as a result of insufficient disability insurance. That's because while you're down, your bills won't stop, and Social Security won't kick in unless the illness is terminal or you're disabled for at least a year. In fact, the Social Security rules are so restrictive that you might not get any help from it. That means you've got to protect yourself. Where do you start? Check your company's disability coverage. If your company provides it, make sure it's enough. If not, find a personal policy and get covered.

Is that it? Heck no! The most important thing you can do is recognize that *you* aren't indestructible. Lead a healthy lifestyle. That means have regular checkups, don't smoke, exercise regularly, eat healthy, keep your stress level down, become a defensive driver, and avoid excessive alcohol consumption. The bottom line is that a healthy lifestyle will save you a good deal of money.

**Number 5: Protect Your Stuff (and Look Out for Lawyers)**   Having home and auto insurance is something of a no-brainer: You need it, assuming you have a home and a car. Fortunately, there are ways to keep the cost down. The key is to keep your deductibles as high as you can afford. After that, go for as many discounts as you can. Keep in mind, insurance isn't a maintenance plan, it's protection against major financial disasters.

As you look at your auto insurance policy, take a good look at the level of liability insurance. Given the level of jury awards given to auto fatalities, you're probably underinsured. If you're driving and someone is injured, you could be facing financial ruin. Remember, the liability coverage on your auto liability insurance generally is only $50,000, while the median jury award for traffic fatalities runs above $500,000.

What happens if you're driving and your cute little dog Pooksie jumps on your lap and you lose control of your car and hit someone? Your insurance company will pay the cost to defend you and Pooksie in court and pay damage awards, but only up to the policy limit. All this means that going for "the minimum I need" may set you up for a financial disaster. You need more than the minimum level of coverage, and one way to afford it is to raise your deductible. That also means you may need a larger emergency fund in the case of an accident. An alternative approach is to give some serious thought to a personal umbrella policy. The bottom line here is to make sure your insurance actually protects you from financial ruin.

**Number 6: Embrace the "B" Word (Budget)**   When most people think of a budget they think of a financial strait jacket, something that takes all the spontaneity out of life. After all, your "20-something" years are supposed to be a "live for the moment" time. In reality, a budget is a means to reach your goals. If it makes you feel too much like your folks to think about sticking to a budget, think of it as a "cash flow plan."

What does a budget (or cash flow plan) do for you? It forces you to use restraint, to think about what you spend money on, to live below your means, and (yes) to be frugal. For example, if you've already spent this month's budgeted amount on restaurants, you'll be eating at home the rest of the month or you'll have to save up money, perhaps from passing on that new Smash Mouth CD, if you want to eat out. Unfortunately, self-restraint is tough, especially with all those advertisers with their sights on your money bombarding you from TV, the Internet, the radio, newspapers, and magazines.

Without a budget, your financial future is bleak at best. With a budget, you'll avoid the nightmares financial chaos brings and be able to save.

Before you can put a budget or cash flow plan in place, you've got to find out where you're money is going. To do that, you'll want to track your expenses carefully for a month. To help you with this, take a look at Worksheet 4, "The Budget Tracker." You'll also want to go back to Chapter 2 and review the sections titled "Developing a Cash Budget" and "Implementing the Cash Budget." You'll find that while you're setting up your budget, you'll be able to identify expenses you can eliminate. Also keep in mind **Principle 13: Pay Yourself First**. Make sure your savings are automatically deposited in a mutual fund or other investment so you don't have a chance to get to that money.

Principle

**13** Pay Yourself First

**Number 7: Reinvent and Upgrade Your Skills**   There was a time when the first job you took would be your job for life. You'd stick with that company for 30 or 40 years, collect a gold watch, and retire. Welcome to the new world—the world of downsizing, restructuring, reorganizing—all words that mean you're gone. In today's world it doesn't matter that you've been a loyal employee for 20 years and it doesn't matter that you come in early and leave late. What matters are your skills: Are they needed? What do they bring to the company? Your history with the company is irrelevant; the real question is, what do you add to the company today? Sounds pretty cold, doesn't it? Well, it is, but that's how the business world works today. Nothing is long term. If a company needs your skills and talents, you're in good shape. If not, you're out.

The question is, how do you prepare for this kind of job insecurity? The answer is to make sure your skills and talents are needed. That means you'll want skills that are both valuable and that can't be acquired with little or no effort. You'll also want to take some care in picking a career. You want to have a skill businesses are willing to pay for. Maybe that skill is having a CPA, a unique computer skill, or more advanced building construction skills. How do you keep your skill level both valuable and unique? The answer is to continuously reinvent and upgrade your skills through education. The education you're getting right now will prepare you for a job when you graduate, but it won't be enough to keep that job for life. Given the pace of innovation, no one can stand still and expect to survive. Let there be no doubt, education is the best investment you'll ever make.

**Number 8: Hide Your Plastic**   There probably isn't a more dangerous threat to your financial well-being than credit cards. The real problem is that there's no real problem with credit cards, just with credit card debt. Unfortunately, for most people these two go hand in hand, especially if you're a student with lots of needs but no real income. It would seem that college students would be the last people credit card issuers would want to tap—after all, given their income they can't be great credit risks.

But that is far from the case. They set up tables on campus and bribe students into filling out an application with offers of free Frisbees, calling cards, and other goodies. And it works. In fact, one-fifth of all college students have four or more cards. With credit cards in hand, it simply becomes too easy to spend money—that pizza late at night, or those "must-have" tickets to the Rolling Stones 50th Anniversary Tour. People simply spend more with credit cards—about 30 percent more—than they do with cash. For students, it's particularly tempting to use credit cards. After all, you'll be earning the big bucks in a few years, so paying them off shouldn't be any problem . . . should it? The average undergraduate has about $1,843 in credit card debt, and 9 percent of undergraduates have credit card debt between $3,000 and $7,000.

The only real answer is restraint. Don't use credit cards except for emergencies, and then use them with the utmost restraint. Your goal should be to make it into the next stage of your financial life (that stage where you make money) with as little debt as possible. When you get there, credit cards are great, but make sure you pay them off every month. If not, take the scissors to them.

**Number 9: Stocks Are Risky, But Not as Risky as Not Investing in Them**   Stocks are risky. If you didn't learn that in Chapter 14, you probably learned it by listening to stories on the nightly news describing the wild market gyrations. For example, Network Associates, a Santa Clara, California, computer security software maker, took an 84 percent dive in 2000 and followed that by climbing 517 percent in 2001. On the other hand, OSI Pharmaceuticals Inc., a biotechnology firm, climbed by over 909

# In The News

Wall Street Journal Sunday February 13, 2001

*Some Insights to Keep You Afloat*

by Jonathan Clements

Forget the confident predictions of television gurus and Internet bulletin-board pundits. These are—at best—nothing more than informed guesses. Put too much faith in them and you could repeat the blunder of the late 1990s, when folks thought technology stocks were a "sure thing."

The brutal reality is that there are very few sure things. In fact, here are some investment insights that I consider undeniably true.

*Victory Isn't Assured:* The stock and bond markets may not be perfectly efficient. But they are efficient enough that there are no guaranteed ways of scoring market-beating returns.

*"We all look back now and say we should have bought Dell or we should have bought Amazon,"* says Sheldon Jacobs, editor of No-Load Fund Investor, a newsletter in Ardsley, New York. *"But what should we buy today? Somewhere out there, there's a future Dell or a future Amazon. But it's hard to pick them."* (☞A)

*High Costs Hurt Returns:* When you pick a stock or fund, you can't be sure you have yourself a winner. But if you use a discount broker, stick with low-cost funds, and minimize your portfolio's tax bill, you will definitely keep more of whatever you make.

*Risk Can Be Reduced:* If you take an undiversified stock portfolio and spread the money across more stocks, you cut risk by ensuring your fortunes aren't hitched to any one company. Such diversification also smooths out returns, as the sting of losing stocks is diluted by gains elsewhere in the portfolio.

*Time Creates Money: Every so often, you read stories about ordinary folks who die and leave behind millions, much to the surprise of family and neighbors. Typically, these millionaires were avid savers and stock market investors. But almost always, these folks share another trait: They lived to a ripe old age.* (☞B)

*Savings Generate Wealth:* It sounds trite, and it isn't the sort of thing folks like to hear. But I'll say it anyway: If you want to make your portfolio grow faster, the surest strategy is to save more money.

## THE BOTTOM LINE . . .

**A** The logic here comes from **Principle 5: The Curse of Competitive Investments Markets**. What makes things worse is that with hindsight we can always see the winners, and that leads us to believe that we might actually be able to systematically pick winners.

**B** Right now your biggest investment advantage is that you have a long time horizon until you retire. That means whatever you invest now will have a long time to compound. The bottom line is that you best not blow your advantage—that means start investing today, and take advantage of those tax-advantaged investments first, the 401(k)s and the IRAs.

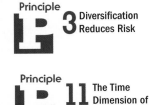

**Principle** **3** Diversification Reduces Risk

**Principle** **11** The Time Dimension of Investing

percent in 2000, and followed that in 2001 by tumbling by 42.9 percent. With those kind of ups and downs, it's no wonder stocks are considered to be risky—and in fact, they are. Should you put your money in these risky investments? If your investment horizon is long, the answer is yes, but you'll want to eliminate as much risk as you can through diversification. One easy way to do this is through a stock index mutual fund. You'll also want to review **Principle 3: Diversification Reduces Risk** and **Principle 11: The Time Dimension of Investing**, and let your asset allocation decisions be guided by your time horizon. If all this talk of investing in stocks gives you heart palpitations, go back to Chapter 11 and take another look at the section called "The Time Dimension of Investing and Asset Allocation." As long as your investment time horizon is long, stocks are prudent.

If the risk of stock price fluctuations is not your biggest fear, what is? The fear of not keeping up with inflation and taxes. In effect, it is the fear that you won't earn enough on your investments to meet your goals. Just look at a 3-percent rate of inflation. After 23 years you've lost half your purchasing power, and if the inflation rate is 4 percent, it will take less than 18 years. In fact, as shown in Figure 18.1, over the period from 1926 through 2001, stocks returned an average of 10.7 percent. But when you look at these returns adjusted for inflation, they fall to 7.4 percent. For bonds, the average return over that same period was 5.3 percent and after inflation 2.2 percent. For short-term investments (Treasury bills) the return was 3.8 percent before inflation and 0.7 percent after. Throw in taxes and things get even worse. What does all this mean? If you don't take some prudent risks, you don't have a chance of meeting your goals.

**Number 10: Exploit Tax-Favored Retirement Plans to the Fullest**  If you're lucky, you'll get a chance to participate in the best investment (aside from education) around. What is it? It's a tax-deductible contribution to an employer's retirement saving plan with a matching contribution from the employer. Why is it so great? Because your contributions aren't taxed, that means you can contribute money that would have otherwise gone to the IRS. In addition, because the investment earnings aren't taxed until they're withdrawn, you earn money on earnings that the IRS

**Figure 18.1** Returns Before and After Inflation, 1926–2001*

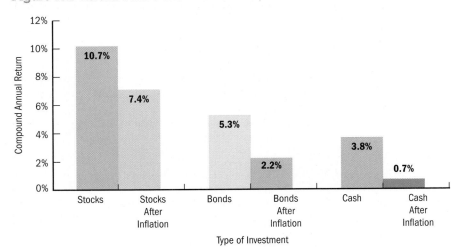

*Assumes reinvestment of income and no transaction costs or taxes.
Source: Ibbotson SalesBuilder™ Presentations, © 2002 Ibbotson Associates, Inc. All rights reserved. Used with permission.

would have collected. While you're doing all this, don't forget to take full advantage of a Roth or traditional IRA.

What should be your strategy? When you get out in the real world, max out on these tax-favored retirement plans. If you aren't sure this is the right approach, go back to Chapter 16 and reread the section called "What Plan Is Best for You?" If that doesn't convince you, read it again until you are convinced.

**Number 11: How Many Children You Have**  There's not much to say. Children can be wonderful, but they are expensive. At one time, children were money in the bank. When they were young, they worked the farms or in the family business, and when you got old, your children were there to take care of you. In short, a great deal. Times have changed, to say the least. This doesn't mean you shouldn't have as many children as you want, but you should be aware of the costs involved.

**Number 12: Stay Married**  Divorce is expensive, really expensive. An amicable divorce runs in excess of $1,000 while an unfriendly one can easily hit $10,000 and up with no limit. But it isn't just the cost of divorce that makes it in your best financial interests to stay married, it's also the fact that married people tend to earn more money and accumulate more wealth than single people living separately or together. The statistics are convincing: Married men earn 26 percent more than unmarried men, and married couples earn 61 percent more than families headed by single men. For divorced women with children, the tale is the saddest: Their income is only about 40 percent of that of a married couple. Clearly, for women with children, divorce opens the doors to poverty.

Why do married couples do better financially? One reason is that the cooperation learned in a successful marriage can translate into a career advantage. In addition, a successful marriage requires money management and budgeting. Unnecessary expenditures are eliminated, and you now have someone to answer to when you spend $900 for an autographed picture of the Three Stooges on eBay. On top of all this, being single is expensive. Most people spend a lot of time and money searching for that right person. What does all this mean? You should take real care in picking a spouse, and once you're married, put serious effort into making your marriage work. It also means you shouldn't have children if you aren't married—no two ways about it. Things don't always turn out as planned, but if you don't plan, they never turn out.

## Tying Things Together: Debt and the Real World

Deal with all kinds of debt in the real world.

We've talked about debt a number of times in this book. We talked about credit card debt, consumer loans, home mortgages, home equity loans, auto loans, and student loans. It's now time to bring all of this together.

As you enter the real world, you take with you some college education, unlimited hope and potential, and lots of debt. In fact, the typical college student has three credit cards and owes $2,700, according to a study of undergraduates by Nellie Mae, a subsidiary of Sallie Mae, a leading provider of federal loans to students. Moreover, it's been estimated that the typical grad with loans—and that's about half of all college students—will leave college with both a diploma and about $17,500 in debts. Some of that debt will be from credit cards and some—on average, about $13,000 of it—will be from student loans.

There was once a time when you had to go out and find a lender if you wanted to borrow some money. Today, you just go to your mailbox. You'll find credit cards giving you frequent flier miles along with low teaser rates of 0.0 percent; coupons for loans that look like checks for $10,000 or more; or "preapproved" home equity loans for up to a quarter of a million dollars. If you're worried about having too much debt, just turn on the television and you'll find Jim Palmer and others hawking consolidation loans that will give you "one low monthly payment."

## The Trap of Too Much Debt

What's happened is that debt is being marketed to adults the same way toys are marketed to children—and for many, it's just too hard to resist. Here are some of the results.

▌ *Students and those with little capacity to repay are being given the opportunity to ring up debts at will.* Look at Cal Duncan, 24, of Blacksburg, Virginia. He got his first credit card (along with a free Frisbee) as a sophomore at Virginia Tech. As Cal says, "All I needed to get that credit card was my college ID and a pulse." After 4 years at Virginia Tech, Cal graduated with a degree in business and 8 credit cards. These cards came with all kinds of free goodies, including phone calling cards, a savings bond, thermos coffee cups for the car, and meals at Burger King and Taco Bell. "It was like getting something for nothing. All I had to do was sign my name and I'd get a free gift along with a credit card. And, once I had the cards, it was hard not to use them."

Most of Cal's charging during his college days came in his senior year. "I figured I'd be earning the big bucks next year, so there was no reason to deprive myself of that pizza, or CD, or that night out." That same attitude stayed with Cal during his first year on the job. When reality finally set in, Cal had amassed credit card debt which, along with his outstanding student loans, more than equals his annual salary. As Cal says, "It was all too easy. It just didn't seem like I was spending real money. I remember heading to Krogers to buy a box of macaroni and cheese and part way there thinking of all the money I was going to make the next year. I turned around and headed home where I called Papa John's Pizza because they take Visa and MasterCard—why suffer when I was planning on making the big bucks in the future? Never did I imagine that it would be anything but easy to pay it off."

▌ *People are encouraged to borrow more than they should; in fact, borrowing is becoming part of our culture.* As long as you make your credit card payments, regardless of how painful those payments are, you'll be tempted by increased borrowing limits and you'll receive more credit card offers. Now that Cal is in the real world, working to pay off his debts, he still receives "a weekly offer" of a new credit card. It's the youngest group of consumers who are most at risk here. They're the ones who grew up on plastic and seem to have the biggest problem controlling its usage. In fact, according to a recent survey, of those aged 30 and under, almost 60 percent do not pay off their credit card bills every month—for those 60 or older, this number falls to less than 15 percent.

▌ *Bankruptcies have reached an all-time high.* As a result of the ease of borrowing, the typical American is taking on much more debt than ever before. In fact, debt as a percent of annual disposable income has nearly doubled over the past 40 years. Unfortunately, that's more debt than many of us can accommodate. The result in 2001 was that almost 1.4 million Americans filed for bankruptcy topping the record set in 1998.

With all this bad debt and low teaser rates, it would seem that banks wouldn't be making any money, but that's not the case. Today, banks make mortgage, credit card, and auto loans; package them; and sell them as "collateralized securities." That means that an investor, rather than the bank that issued your credit card, may be holding your credit card debt. What this does is makes it easier for banks to make more credit card loans, and if you don't pay, it's not their problem. It's now the problem of whoever bought the credit card loans from your bank. The result: a never-ending stream of credit card debt offers, regardless of the borrower's ability to repay.

## Successful Debt Management

After hearing all the stories of doom associated with people taking on too much debt, you should keep in mind that debt isn't all bad. In fact, without it, it would be impossible for most people to ever buy a home. The bottom line is that debt and borrowing are pretty complicated, and as a result, you'll want to understand the keys to successful debt management.

**Key #1: The Obvious: Spend Less Than You Earn and Budget Your Money**   The key to controlling debt is both obvious and simple: spend less than you earn, and if you can't afford it, don't charge it. This all goes back to "Choosing Wealth Number 3: Live Below Your Means." Of course, that may mean some changes in your lifestyle, but no matter what else you do with your financial plan, its success depends on your ability to spend less than you earn.

This also means that you've got to have an active budget, and you've got to stick to it. Of course, the budget has to be flexible enough to work, but it also means you can't borrow to make spending match up with money that comes in. Even more important, it means control. That is, not letting lenders decide where and when you're going to borrow. A budget simply doesn't make sense if it relies on borrowing to pay for day-to-day expenditures. A budget also doesn't make sense if it doesn't have any savings built into it. Let's face it, apart from saving for retirement and your children's education, you're going to run into some emergencies along the way—perhaps medical needs, unemployment, or divorce—that will force you to dip into your reserves.

**Key #2: Know the Costs**   Perhaps the best deterrent against unnecessary borrowing is to know the costs. You should know your credit card interest rate, your statement due date, and your credit limit. You should also know that if you don't pay your bill in full, you'll also be paying interest.

When economists talk about borrowing, they talk about "forgoing future consumption opportunities in lieu of present consumption." That is, spending money that you haven't yet earned and paying it back with future earnings. In fact, there's an old saying that "spending money you haven't earned yet is like using up years you haven't lived yet." What all this means, of course, is that you won't be able to spend as much in the future—most people understand that—but they don't understand how *much* future consumption they have given up when they put that pizza on their credit card. If you put that pizza on a credit card that charges 18 percent and you don't pay off your balance each month, you bought one expensive pizza. Moreover, as shown in Table 6.4 in Chapter 6, if you only pay off the minimum, you may be paying interest on that pizza for 93 months! Things are even worse with "payday" loans, as we saw in Chapter 7. The annual interest rate can get up in the 400 percent range. Just knowing what you're paying may be enough to control that need to spend.

If you do end up borrowing money, make sure you do it from a quality lender. Checklist 18.2 provides some early warning signs on lenders to avoid.

# Checklist 18.2 ▮ Lenders: Early Warning Signs

**Avoid any lender who**

Tells you to falsify information on the loan application. For example, the lender tells you to say your loan is primarily for business purposes when it's not.

Pressures you into applying for a loan or applying for more money than you need.

Pressures you into accepting monthly payments you can't make.

Fails to provide required loan disclosures or tells you not to read them.

Misrepresents the kind of credit you're getting. For example, calling a one-time loan a line of credit.

Promises one set of terms when you apply, and gives you another set of terms to sign—with no legitimate explanation for the change.

Tells you to sign blank forms—the lender says they'll fill them in later.

Says you can't have copies of documents that you've signed.

Source: "Need a Loan?" Federal Trade Commission, July 1999.

**Key #3: Understand the Difference Between Good and Bad Debt** Not all borrowing is a bad idea. When does borrowing make sense? Whenever the item fulfills one of your goals. It should outlive the financing, and it should provide a return that is greater than the cost. For example, borrowing to finance your education makes sense because you will use that education long after you've paid off your student loans, and your education should more than pay for itself in terms of employment opportunities. The same is true for a home mortgage. Your house should be standing long after you've paid off your mortgage. In addition, you'll no longer have to pay rent, and hopefully, your home will appreciate in value. An auto loan may also fit this definition of good debt because your car should still be running when your loan is paid off.

But auto loans aren't always good debt. In order for them to qualify as good debt, you must have a sufficient down payment and make sure the payments are large enough to pay the car off as opposed to rolling unpaid debt from this car to the next one. With 6-year auto loans now available, you may really be "renting" your car, because it may not be worth anything by the time it's paid off. If that's the case, try a less expensive car or consider the used car market.

How about that big screen TV? It should last longer than the payments. Having a big screen TV may be one of your goals, but it won't provide a return greater than the cost. Once that TV is in your home, its value is only a fraction of what it was originally. Try saving up to pay for this type of expenditure and not letting the seller decide how you're going to finance it. What about normal day-to-day operating expenses—food, rent, clothes? Borrowing to finance these expenses will set you up for future problems that only winning the lottery can solve.

Unfortunately, sometimes there isn't a real choice. An emergency may come up and you may not have any choice. If that happens you should know that you are going to have to adjust your lifestyle so you can undo the financial damage that you've done as soon as possible.

**Key #4: Make Sure You Can Repay What You Borrow—Set Your Own Standards** Just because someone is willing to lend you money is no reason to accept the loan. For example, as you learned in Chapters 7 and 8, most mortgage lenders generally like to see the ratio of your PITI (principal, interest, taxes, and insurance) plus other debt payments to your monthly gross income at 36 percent or less. What if you find a lender who is willing to lend you up to the point where your PITI is 40 percent of your gross monthly income? Should you go with that loan and buy a bigger house? The answer is you have to determine your own borrowing capacity and stick to it. A few years ago this wasn't a problem, but today lenders have become extremely competitive and are now willing to lend more on less income. The result is that it's much easier to get in debt over your head today than it was just a few years ago.

One way to avoid it is to apply the standards a bank would to yourself. Don't let the ratio of your PITI plus other debt payments climb above 36 percent of your monthly gross income. In fact, if you think this obligates too much of your monthly income, lower that to 33 percent or even less. The problem many people run into is that once they get the home mortgage, they take on even more debt. They buy furniture, appliances, and electronics to fill the house, and a car to fill the garage. Also look to the debt limit ratio, which is the percentage of your take-home pay or income that is taken up by nonmortgage debt payments:

$$\text{debt limit ratio} = \frac{\text{total monthly nonmortgage debt payments}}{\text{total monthly take-home pay}}$$

We looked at this in Chapter 7 and discussed a limit of 20 percent. Also, look at the debt resolution rule in Chapter 7. The bottom line is that regardless of how you decide to do it, you have to manage your own debt. You have to limit it to an acceptable level, because with all the competition in the lending industry, you may get the opportunity to borrow more than you can afford.

**Key #5: Keep a Clean Credit Record—It's a Source of Emergency Money**  A poor credit history can hurt you in getting a car loan, an apartment, and even a job. That, by itself, should be enough inspiration to keep your credit record clean. However, one thing many people don't realize is that your credit record also determines what rate you're going to pay when you borrow. Those who have the greatest need for low borrowing rates end up paying the highest rates. This holds true for the interest rate on credit cards all the way to the rate on home mortgages. Is the rate differential significant? You bet. In fact, the interest rate on mortgage home loans can be up to 6 percent more for individuals with poor credit ratings— that's almost twice as high.

You can also look at your borrowing capacity as an emergency account. If and when an emergency comes, having untapped borrowing capacity will allow you to borrow money when you most need it. A habit of borrowing up to your limit only sets up problems in the future. It also forces you to keep a larger emergency fund than you would otherwise have to. And because less liquid investments generally have a higher return than do highly liquid investments, you will be able to earn more on your investments.

The way to avoid these problems is to avoid borrowing up to your full capacity, to pay your bills on time, and to make sure no errors pop up in your credit reports. You'll want to review your credit report every 2 to 3 years. If you look back to Table 6.2, you'll find the location of the major credit bureaus. If you find an error, make sure it gets corrected.

**STOP & THINK** In an emergency, the best asset you have is good credit.

**Key #6: Don't Live With Bad (And Expensive) Debt**  In 2001, according to CardWeb.com, average credit card debt per household with at least one credit card was $8,562, up from $2,985 in 1990. Unless it's paid off every month, that's a lot of what we have called "bad" debt. It's debt that often is a result of buying without forethought. Because the average interest rate on a credit card then was around 18.3 percent, that's expensive borrowing.

The strategy many credit card borrowers use is to jump to a teaser rate—that is a low rate that lasts, in general, for 6 months. After the 6-month period is over, the rate jumps to the postpromotional level, generally somewhere around 20 percent. The idea is to then jump again. Unfortunately, credit card companies have strategies to counter this ploy. On some cards, a balance cannot be transferred for an entire year, or on the new card, the low rate may only apply to new purchases. One alternative is to try to negotiate down your rate on your current card. A better alternative is to get rid of your bad debt entirely.

If you want to rid yourself of bad debt, the first thing that must be done is to eliminate the lifestyle pattern that led to the debt in the first place—you've got to start living below your means. Once you've made the necessary lifestyle adjustments, you've got to attack your debt with dogged determination. First, you've got to pay much more than the minimum. Table 6.4 will give you an idea of how long it will take to eliminate your debt. This is no fun, but the alternative is no hope.

If you're paying 18 percent on your debt and it doesn't look like an end is in sight, you might consider liquidating some investments that pay less than that. For example, if you have money in a savings account that pays 6 percent, you'd be much better off using your savings account to pay off your debt. In fact, you'll save more than the differential of 12 percent (eliminating 18 percent debt payments but losing 6 percent income from your savings account), because you'd have to pay taxes on that 6 percent return from your savings.

If you don't have an investment to liquidate, you might consider borrowing at a lower rate to pay off your 18 percent debt. For example, you might want to get a home equity loan. One advantage of such a loan is that the interest you pay is tax deductible. You could also consider borrowing against your life insurance if it has cash value, or borrowing from friends and family. Of course, these are desperate measures, and they can be taken only once. That means you've got to make a serious lifestyle change if you're going to take this path. This should also make clear the crippling effect bad debt can have on your financial future.

## Getting Started: Just Do It

It's now time to put things together and begin to build your financial future. You should now know enough to try it yourself, without the help of a financial advisor. Let's put some of the concepts we've examined in the previous chapters to work. And if all this has made your head spin, this section will give you enough direction to get going. If you're having second thoughts about starting, just look back a bit in this chapter at the section titled "Number 2: Don't Procrastinate." Starting your plan today may be the most important financial decision you'll ever make.

Begin with budgeting and planning. Figure 1.1 gives an outline of this process. Find out where you stand, define your goals, develop a plan, and revise the plan as your life changes. This means putting together a balance sheet, income statement, ratio analysis, record-keeping system, and a budget. You'll want to rely heavily on Chapter 2 for this.

You'll also want to pay close attention to managing your cash—things like controlling banking fees and ATM charges. It also means making sure you have the necessary emergency funds. Chapter 5 should help here.

You should rid yourself of "bad" debt. We've talked about "bad" debt in this chapter and how it can cripple your financial future. If you've got it, get rid of it. If you don't have it, avoid it. You might want to review the section on "Debt and the Real World" in this chapter, along with the material in Chapters 6 and 7.

Your safety net—your life, health, disability, property and liability insurance—should be in order. Chapters 9 and 10 should help you with this.

It's also time to start investing. Try stocks and mutual funds. You'll find that success breeds an enthusiasm for investing (and saving) that simply cannot be explained in a text. You'll want to keep your attention focused on taxes—take advantage of any tax-favored plans like IRAs and 401(k)s available to you. You'll want to begin thinking about, and planning for, retirement—it simply is never too soon, at least if you want to enjoy retirement. You'll find help with this in Chapters 3 and 4 and 11 through the end of the book. You don't have to know everything about investing to get started. In fact, right now, if you've gotten this far in this class, you're well ahead of most people when they begin investing.

Still, nothing in this book will be of help to you if you procrastinate. That means follow **Principle 15: Just Do It**!

Principle **15** Just Do It!

## SUMMARY

Without question, it's much tougher to achieve financial security if you're a woman. That's because women generally earn less, are less likely to have pensions, qualify for less income from Social Security, and live longer than men. As a result, it is of the *utmost importance* that women take responsibility for their financial future.

Marriage and children further complicate planning for your financial future. The key to controlling financial problems when you marry is an open and frank discussion about money with your partner. The goal is to find out your partner's financial history, habits, and goals. You can also take the financial pain out of children by planning ahead of time.

As for becoming rich, the one common trait seems to be frugality. Several key decisions in life will determine how your financial future turns out. You'll want to gain an understanding of personal finance; avoid procrastination; live below your means; have adequate life, health, property and liability insurance; become an active budgeter; keep your skills fresh; avoid credit card debt; take some prudent risks with your long-term investments; max out on tax-favored retirement plans; understand that children are expensive and plan accordingly, and stay married.

Controlling debt is another financial challenge. One key to doing this is to spend less than you earn and budget your money. You should also know the costs. In fact, this may be the best deterrent against unnecessary debt. You should understand the difference between good and bad debt. Borrowing makes sense whenever the item purchased fulfills one of your goals, outlives the financing, and provides a return greater than the cost. Also, just because someone is willing to lend you money is no reason to accept the loan. In addition, you should keep a clean credit record, and if you have any bad (and expensive) debt, get rid of it. Begin by eliminating the lifestyle pattern that led to the bad debt in the first place—start living below your means.

## REVIEW QUESTIONS

1. Name 10 critical strategies for personal finance success.
2. List at least five reasons why women tend to have a tougher time than men achieving financial security.
3. Name four unique obstacles that women face in relation to their financial independence, particularly when planning for retirement.
4. Summarize two strategies that women should implement to compensate for the unique financial challenges they face.
5. List the three steps a couple should follow to prepare for the financial realities of their marriage.
6. When should a married couple maintain a single checking account, and when should each partner have his or her own account?
7. Why should women maintain a credit card in their own name, even after getting married?
8. List and describe five financial planning issues that should be addressed when children are born.
9. Describe the difference between income and wealth. Are all high-income earners wealthy?

10. How can the practice of frugality set the stage for personal finance success?

11. List and briefly describe the basic decisions you must make in order to achieve real wealth.

12. Name five strategies to help you compensate for one reality of life—"no one is indestructible."

13. Identify four ways a simple budget, or cash flow plan, can help you achieve wealth.

14. Why are equities a prudent investment strategy for accomplishing future goals? Be sure to consider the effects of taxes and inflation.

15. What might be described as the "best" investment (aside from education)? Explain why you should take full advantage of any tax-favored investment alternatives available to you.

16. Name three social trends that reflect the role of debt in American society. What factors contribute to these trends?

17. What are the keys to debt management? How do you differentiate good and bad debt?

18. In addition to negotiating a lower interest rate on your credit card(s), what other strategies can be used to eliminate bad debt?

19. Why does financial planning require a "call to action"?

## PROBLEMS AND ACTIVITIES

1. Calculate the future value of an account after you've contributed $1,000 at the end of each year for 40 years if you can earn 9 percent compounded annually, assuming that you don't take a withdrawal during the 40-year period. Now calculate the value of the same account if you stop making contributions after 30 years. What does this tell you about the power of time when trying to accumulate wealth?

2. Explain why insurance products play such a critical role when attempting to accumulate long-term wealth. What insurance products do you consider essential for yourself after graduation? What coverage might your employer provide? What products will you need to purchase?

3. Why should you continue to upgrade your skills even after graduation? Name a few methods for upgrading and reinventing your skills in your career field. Estimate the costs associated with these strategies. Will you, or your employer, likely be responsible for the cost of these investments in yourself? Have these issues come up in job interviews?

4. Adam anticipates bimonthly take-home pay of $920. His payments include $110 for school loan payment and $150 for credit card debt accumulated during his "senior year—who cares, just charge it" debacle. He is determined *not* to reduce the credit card repayment and estimates he can pay off the debt in another 10 months. In the meantime, he would really like to buy a new sofa so he would not be embarrassed to bring a date to his apartment. Calculate and interpret his debt limit ratio. Assuming he can take on more debt, what is the maximum payment he can add to his budget? What suggestions on frugal living might he consider to avoid or postpone the sofa debt?

5. This chapter asserts that "building wealth is part of a satisfying life" that is built on a balance between (a) a personal life that reflects your values and goals and (b) financial decisions that reflect your spending. React to this statement by reflecting on your values and goals and their implications for your future.

6. Todd and Katie have a combined gross annual income of $85,000. Calculate their projected PITI payment using the ratios of 28 percent and 36 percent. Assume they lose 35 percent of gross income to pay for taxes, benefits, and retirement. Calculate the projected payments as a percentage of take-home pay. Interpret your results. What advice would you give Todd and Katie about determining their own borrowing capacity?

7. Review the keys to financial success noting how many mention "financial restraint." How can an understanding of frugality and financial planning give you the freedom to spend while practicing financial restraint?

8. Tax-favored retirement plans with a matching contribution from the employer have been described as three sources of "free money." What are those three sources of savings that result in the advice to "max out tax-favored retirement plans"?

9. As inflation and taxes increase, why is it more important for investors to take prudent risks with equity investments? How is this principle affected by the investment time horizon?

## SUGGESTED PROJECTS

1. Because women tend to be more conservative in their investments, they tend to earn less. As a group project, visit an investment Web site (e.g., **www.mfea.com**, **www.moolera.com**, or **moneycentral.msn.com**) to assess your risk tolerance. Compare your results. Are there gender differences within the group? Could learning about the principles (e.g., 3, 9, and 11) change your results? Prepare a report of your findings and discussion.

2. Develop a detailed budget for yourself using the Budget Tracker Worksheet. Next month record all expenditures, regardless of how small, that you make. Calculate the variances between the budgeted and actual amounts. Write a brief narrative of your budgeting experience.

3. Visit the U.S. Department of Education Web site **www.ed.gov/index.jsp** to learn more about student loan repayment. See the Financial Aid page. Review the repayment calculators and determine the monthly repayment for your loans, if applicable, or a hypothetical loan amount. Calculate the debt limit ratio using your projected take-home pay. Assuming you can take on more consumer debt, what is the maximum repayment you can safely add?

4. As a group project, ask everyone in your class (or other classes) to estimate how much total debt they will have upon graduation. How much of their total debt is for (a) student loans, (b) credit cards, and (c) other consumer debt (e.g., auto or electronics loans)? Ask everyone to record their information, without names, and submit to your group. Summarize your findings, noting trends and averages. Are members of your sample in danger of

financial troubles after graduation due to their debt levels? If so, what intervention strategies can your group recommend?

5. Make a list of typical items paid for through borrowing. Share your list with friends and relatives and ask them to quickly categorize the debts as good or bad. Record their reactions. Then explain the characteristics of good and bad debt and ask them to review the list again. Did their classifications change? How does the average person view debt? Had your respondents considered the characteristics of good and bad debt when making borrowing decisions? Summarize your results.

6. To learn about the services offered to households experiencing debt problems, visit the Internet sites for the National Foundation for Credit Counseling at **www.nfcc.org/**, Genus Credit Management at **www.genus.org/**, or Myvesta, the Financial Health Center at **myvesta.org/home.htm**. Check the telephone or other community directory for other national or local services. What educational or debt counseling services are available? What is the profile of the typical client served? What strategies are typically used to assist clients? What are the expectations of clients seeking assistance? What costs, if any, are charged?

7. "The more you make, the more necessities there are." Discuss this quote with a sample of friends or relatives representing different stages of the life cycle and income levels. Can they recall specific goods or services that became necessities as their income increased? For those in the stages of increasing incomes, what goods or services do they aspire to have become necessities?

# Discussion Case 1

Your sister Chris and her boyfriend Doug recently announced plans to be married after graduation in May. Although you are extremely fond of both of them and want their relationship to succeed, you are concerned about their financial future. Neither Chris nor Doug completed a personal finance course while in college. Chris is a spender who has known few limits on her wants since she was a teenager. Doug, on the other hand, has worked, saved, and invested since a teenager to help provide for college costs. He will complete college with approximately $12,600 in student loans. But their income in their first year out

of college will total $90,000, due in large part to Doug's choice of major and practical work experience during college. Chris, who admits having no financial skill or interest, is content to let Doug handle all those matters, since he seems to be good at it and will always earn more than she does.

## Questions

1. Make a list of questions that Chris and Doug should discuss before they get married.

# Money Matters

## TAKE MY ADVICE

I have borrowed some advice from *The Parenting Handbook* (there must be one because all parents say the same thing), which surprisingly may be applicable to our financial world. Though we may wish to consider personal finance a deep and intricate subject, handling money may be as simple as living life like a kid who actually listened to his or her parents.

**"Here's your allowance. When it's gone, you will have to live without until next week."** *Because it's pretty hard to get a loan or credit card as a kid, "learning to live without" is a brutal reality. Identifying needs versus wants, prioritizing them, and living below your means are the keys.*

**"I guess if Patty jumped off a cliff, you would too."** *Following the pack can lead to disastrous investment decisions, tremendous debt, low self-esteem, and generally poor financial health. Making informed decisions and focusing on personal goals, rather than trying to buy status and happiness or conform to the ideal of the hour, are the ingredients of good personal finance.*

**"Do your homework before you go out to play."** *You should investigate and be informed before you make any major financial decision. Also, you've got to do the things without a lot of glamour, like saving for that distant retirement or "doing homework," before you spend time and money on the things that bring immediate gratification.*

**"If you keep crossing your eyes, they'll stay that way."** *Successful money management is a habit. If you develop a habit of using credit as a safety net for overspending, there is no quick fix. Just proclaiming your goals won't make them happen. The continuous positive movement toward them with tried and proven methods results in accomplishment.*

**"Wear clean underwear in case you have a wreck."** *Though I could never exactly reconcile this one, I take poetic license here to interpret it as a warning to be prepared. A financially sound lifestyle includes purchasing insurance to handle those catastrophes you can't just cover with savings. Of course, Mom didn't say to "wear your best underwear," so I'll stretch it even further to mean you shouldn't waste money by overinsuring or covering things you can handle on your own.*

**"Do it by yourself."** *Especially with women, the development of financial autonomy is important. If you are married, knowledge and input from both parties are essential. If you are single, cut the apron strings, and learn to make decisions on your own. Depending on a parent or spouse to handle your finances can result in you being without a resource at the very time you need it most—at the death of a parent or departure of a spouse.*

2. The discussion of money issues considered in question 1 is the first of a four-step process to help couples successfully manage their finances. The process might be summarized as (a) talk, (b) track, (c) plan and act, and (d) review and revise. Describe the steps and the objective of each.

3. Explain to Chris why it is important that she become informed and involved in her financial future—regardless of how well Doug fulfills the role of husband and provider.

4. Why is it a dangerous myth for Chris to assume that Doug will always be there to take care of her?

5. Identify three essential actions that Chris should take to ensure her financial future.

6. Help Chris and Doug consider the issues of joint or separate checking accounts and credit cards. Why are these important issues to resolve prior to marriage?

7. What financial issues should Chris and Doug review, and perhaps take action on, prior to the birth of a child?

8. Aside from the obvious pain and emotional turmoil to Chris, Doug, and their extended family, why is it financially sound advice to stay married?

9. Doug is anxious to quickly repay his student loan debt, but he also wants to take advantage of the matching contribution on his employer-provided retirement account. Advise Doug on the priorities of these expenses within the budget. Assuming he has a choice of equity and fixed-income investment products, which category would you recommend for his retirement savings? Defend your answers.

10. Why should insurance protection be a critical component of the financial plan developed by Chris and Doug? What strategies can help keep insurance costs down?

# Discussion Case 2

Jena has been so excited about what she has learned in her personal finance management class that she has been telling everyone, "You should take this class." Now her dormitory hall monitor has asked her to prepare a talk on "credit and the young professional." She has decided to use a question-and-answer format. Help her answer the following questions.

## Questions

1. Why is it easy for college students to get and use credit cards? Aside from the obvious impact of "forgoing future consumption" to repay the debt, how can student credit practices affect your financial future?

2. Name three debt and credit trends that suggest that few people are practicing frugality.

3. What does it mean to determine your own borrowing capacity and stick to it? Why is this strategy necessary when "choosing wealth"?

4. What is the relationship between borrowing capacity and an emergency account? What is the advantage or disadvantage of using less liquid accounts for emergency savings and, in the event of an emergency, immediately relying on credit?

5. What financial ratios are useful in monitoring your borrowing capacity? How are these ratios calculated and interpreted?

6. What are the five keys to successful debt management?

7. What steps might be utilized to eliminate bad debt?

8. Review the 10 "ingredients to success." Which strategies could be utilized to avoid bad debt?

 Visit our Web site for additional case problems, interactive exercises, and practice quizzes for this chapter—**www.prenhall.com/keown**.

# Appendix A

## Compound Sum of $1

| n | 1% | 2% | 3% | 4% | 5% | 6% | 7% | 8% | 9% | 10% |
|---|------|------|------|------|------|------|------|------|------|------|
| 1 | 1.010 | 1.020 | 1.030 | 1.040 | 1.050 | 1.060 | 1.070 | 1.080 | 1.090 | 1.100 |
| 2 | 1.020 | 1.040 | 1.061 | 1.082 | 1.102 | 1.124 | 1.145 | 1.166 | 1.188 | 1.210 |
| 3 | 1.030 | 1.061 | 1.093 | 1.125 | 1.158 | 1.191 | 1.225 | 1.260 | 1.295 | 1.331 |
| 4 | 1.041 | 1.082 | 1.126 | 1.170 | 1.216 | 1.262 | 1.311 | 1.360 | 1.412 | 1.464 |
| 5 | 1.051 | 1.104 | 1.159 | 1.217 | 1.276 | 1.338 | 1.403 | 1.469 | 1.539 | 1.611 |
| 6 | 1.062 | 1.126 | 1.194 | 1.265 | 1.340 | 1.419 | 1.501 | 1.587 | 1.677 | 1.772 |
| 7 | 1.072 | 1.149 | 1.230 | 1.316 | 1.407 | 1.504 | 1.606 | 1.714 | 1.828 | 1.949 |
| 8 | 1.083 | 1.172 | 1.267 | 1.369 | 1.477 | 1.594 | 1.718 | 1.851 | 1.993 | 2.144 |
| 9 | 1.094 | 1.195 | 1.305 | 1.423 | 1.551 | 1.689 | 1.838 | 1.999 | 2.172 | 2.358 |
| 10 | 1.105 | 1.219 | 1.344 | 1.480 | 1.629 | 1.791 | 1.967 | 2.159 | 2.367 | 2.594 |
| 11 | 1.116 | 1.243 | 1.384 | 1.539 | 1.710 | 1.898 | 2.105 | 2.332 | 2.580 | 2.853 |
| 12 | 1.127 | 1.268 | 1.426 | 1.601 | 1.796 | 2.012 | 2.252 | 2.518 | 2.813 | 3.138 |
| 13 | 1.138 | 1.294 | 1.469 | 1.665 | 1.886 | 2.133 | 2.410 | 2.720 | 3.066 | 3.452 |
| 14 | 1.149 | 1.319 | 1.513 | 1.732 | 1.980 | 2.261 | 2.579 | 2.937 | 3.342 | 3.797 |
| 15 | 1.161 | 1.346 | 1.558 | 1.801 | 2.079 | 2.397 | 2.759 | 3.172 | 3.642 | 4.177 |
| 16 | 1.173 | 1.373 | 1.605 | 1.873 | 2.183 | 2.540 | 2.952 | 3.426 | 3.970 | 4.595 |
| 17 | 1.184 | 1.400 | 1.653 | 1.948 | 2.292 | 2.693 | 3.159 | 3.700 | 4.328 | 5.054 |
| 18 | 1.196 | 1.428 | 1.702 | 2.026 | 2.407 | 2.854 | 3.380 | 3.996 | 4.717 | 5.560 |
| 19 | 1.208 | 1.457 | 1.753 | 2.107 | 2.527 | 3.026 | 3.616 | 4.316 | 5.142 | 6.116 |
| 20 | 1.220 | 1.486 | 1.806 | 2.191 | 2.653 | 3.207 | 3.870 | 4.661 | 5.604 | 6.727 |
| 21 | 1.232 | 1.516 | 1.860 | 2.279 | 2.786 | 3.399 | 4.140 | 5.034 | 6.109 | 7.400 |
| 22 | 1.245 | 1.546 | 1.916 | 2.370 | 2.925 | 3.603 | 4.430 | 5.436 | 6.658 | 8.140 |
| 23 | 1.257 | 1.577 | 1.974 | 2.465 | 3.071 | 3.820 | 4.740 | 5.871 | 7.258 | 8.954 |
| 24 | 1.270 | 1.608 | 2.033 | 2.563 | 3.225 | 4.049 | 5.072 | 6.341 | 7.911 | 9.850 |
| 25 | 1.282 | 1.641 | 2.094 | 2.666 | 3.386 | 4.292 | 5.427 | 6.848 | 8.623 | 10.834 |
| 30 | 1.348 | 1.811 | 2.427 | 3.243 | 4.322 | 5.743 | 7.612 | 10.062 | 13.267 | 17.449 |
| 40 | 1.489 | 2.208 | 3.262 | 4.801 | 7.040 | 10.285 | 14.974 | 21.724 | 31.408 | 45.258 |
| 50 | 1.645 | 2.691 | 4.384 | 7.106 | 11.467 | 18.419 | 29.456 | 46.900 | 74.354 | 117.386 |

| n | 11% | 12% | 13% | 14% | 15% | 16% | 17% | 18% | 19% | 20% |
|---|------|------|------|------|------|------|------|------|------|------|
| 1 | 1.110 | 1.120 | 1.130 | 1.140 | 1.150 | 1.160 | 1.170 | 1.180 | 1.190 | 1.200 |
| 2 | 1.232 | 1.254 | 1.277 | 1.300 | 1.322 | 1.346 | 1.369 | 1.392 | 1.416 | 1.440 |
| 3 | 1.368 | 1.405 | 1.443 | 1.482 | 1.521 | 1.561 | 1.602 | 1.643 | 1.685 | 1.728 |
| 4 | 1.518 | 1.574 | 1.630 | 1.689 | 1.749 | 1.811 | 1.874 | 1.939 | 2.005 | 2.074 |
| 5 | 1.685 | 1.762 | 1.842 | 1.925 | 2.011 | 2.100 | 2.192 | 2.288 | 2.386 | 2.488 |
| 6 | 1.870 | 1.974 | 2.082 | 2.195 | 2.313 | 2.436 | 2.565 | 2.700 | 2.840 | 2.986 |
| 7 | 2.076 | 2.211 | 2.353 | 2.502 | 2.660 | 2.826 | 3.001 | 3.185 | 3.379 | 3.583 |
| 8 | 2.305 | 2.476 | 2.658 | 2.853 | 3.059 | 3.278 | 3.511 | 3.759 | 4.021 | 4.300 |
| 9 | 2.558 | 2.773 | 3.004 | 3.252 | 3.518 | 3.803 | 4.108 | 4.435 | 4.785 | 5.160 |
| 10 | 2.839 | 3.106 | 3.395 | 3.707 | 4.046 | 4.411 | 4.807 | 5.234 | 5.695 | 6.192 |
| 11 | 3.152 | 3.479 | 3.836 | 4.226 | 4.652 | 5.117 | 5.624 | 6.176 | 6.777 | 7.430 |
| 12 | 3.498 | 3.896 | 4.334 | 4.818 | 5.350 | 5.936 | 6.580 | 7.288 | 8.064 | 8.916 |
| 13 | 3.883 | 4.363 | 4.898 | 5.492 | 6.153 | 6.886 | 7.699 | 8.599 | 9.596 | 10.699 |
| 14 | 4.310 | 4.887 | 5.535 | 6.261 | 7.076 | 7.987 | 9.007 | 10.147 | 11.420 | 12.839 |
| 15 | 4.785 | 5.474 | 6.254 | 7.138 | 8.137 | 9.265 | 10.539 | 11.974 | 13.589 | 15.407 |
| 16 | 5.311 | 6.130 | 7.067 | 8.137 | 9.358 | 10.748 | 12.330 | 14.129 | 16.171 | 18.488 |
| 17 | 5.895 | 6.866 | 7.986 | 9.276 | 10.761 | 12.468 | 14.426 | 16.672 | 19.244 | 22.186 |
| 18 | 6.543 | 7.690 | 9.024 | 10.575 | 12.375 | 14.462 | 16.879 | 19.673 | 22.900 | 26.623 |
| 19 | 7.263 | 8.613 | 10.197 | 12.055 | 14.232 | 16.776 | 19.748 | 23.214 | 27.251 | 31.948 |
| 20 | 8.062 | 9.646 | 11.523 | 13.743 | 16.366 | 19.461 | 23.105 | 27.393 | 32.429 | 38.337 |
| 21 | 8.949 | 10.804 | 13.021 | 15.667 | 18.821 | 22.574 | 27.033 | 32.323 | 38.591 | 46.005 |
| 22 | 9.933 | 12.100 | 14.713 | 17.861 | 21.644 | 26.186 | 31.629 | 38.141 | 45.923 | 55.205 |
| 23 | 11.026 | 13.552 | 16.626 | 20.361 | 24.891 | 30.376 | 37.005 | 45.007 | 54.648 | 66.247 |
| 24 | 12.239 | 15.178 | 18.788 | 23.212 | 28.625 | 35.236 | 43.296 | 53.108 | 65.031 | 79.496 |
| 25 | 13.585 | 17.000 | 21.230 | 26.461 | 32.918 | 40.874 | 50.656 | 62.667 | 77.387 | 95.395 |
| 30 | 22.892 | 29.960 | 39.115 | 50.949 | 66.210 | 85.849 | 111.061 | 143.367 | 184.672 | 237.373 |
| 40 | 64.999 | 93.049 | 132.776 | 188.876 | 267.856 | 378.715 | 533.846 | 750.353 | 1051.642 | 1469.740 |
| 50 | 184.559 | 288.996 | 450.711 | 700.197 | 1083.619 | 1670.669 | 2566.080 | 3927.189 | 5988.730 | 9100.191 |

| n | 21% | 22% | 23% | 24% | 25% | 26% | 27% | 28% | 29% | 30% |
|---|---|---|---|---|---|---|---|---|---|---|
| 1 | 1.210 | 1.220 | 1.230 | 1.240 | 1.250 | 1.260 | 1.270 | 1.280 | 1.290 | 1.300 |
| 2 | 1.464 | 1.488 | 1.513 | 1.538 | 1.562 | 1.588 | 1.613 | 1.638 | 1.664 | 1.690 |
| 3 | 1.772 | 1.816 | 1.861 | 1.907 | 1.953 | 2.000 | 2.048 | 2.097 | 2.147 | 2.197 |
| 4 | 2.144 | 2.215 | 2.289 | 2.364 | 2.441 | 2.520 | 2.601 | 2.684 | 2.769 | 2.856 |
| 5 | 2.594 | 2.703 | 2.815 | 2.932 | 3.052 | 3.176 | 3.304 | 4.436 | 3.572 | 3.713 |
| 6 | 3.138 | 3.297 | 3.463 | 3.635 | 3.815 | 4.001 | 3.196 | 4.398 | 4.608 | 4.827 |
| 7 | 3.797 | 4.023 | 4.259 | 4.508 | 4.768 | 5.042 | 5.329 | 5.629 | 5.945 | 6.275 |
| 8 | 4.595 | 4.908 | 5.239 | 5.589 | 5.960 | 6.353 | 6.767 | 7.206 | 7.669 | 8.157 |
| 9 | 5.560 | 5.987 | 6.444 | 6.931 | 7.451 | 8.004 | 8.595 | 9.223 | 9.893 | 10.604 |
| 10 | 6.727 | 7.305 | 7.926 | 8.594 | 9.313 | 10.086 | 10.915 | 11.806 | 12.761 | 13.786 |
| 11 | 8.140 | 8.912 | 9.749 | 10.657 | 11.642 | 12.708 | 13.862 | 15.112 | 16.462 | 17.921 |
| 12 | 9.850 | 10.872 | 11.991 | 13.215 | 14.552 | 16.012 | 17.605 | 19.343 | 21.236 | 23.298 |
| 13 | 11.918 | 13.264 | 14.749 | 16.386 | 18.190 | 20.175 | 22.359 | 24.759 | 27.395 | 30.287 |
| 14 | 14.421 | 16.182 | 18.141 | 20.319 | 22.737 | 25.420 | 28.395 | 31.691 | 35.339 | 39.373 |
| 15 | 17.449 | 19.742 | 22.314 | 25.195 | 28.422 | 32.030 | 36.062 | 40.565 | 45.587 | 51.185 |
| 16 | 21.113 | 24.085 | 27.446 | 31.242 | 35.527 | 40.357 | 45.799 | 51.923 | 58.808 | 66.541 |
| 17 | 25.547 | 29.384 | 33.758 | 38.740 | 44.409 | 50.850 | 58.165 | 66.461 | 75.862 | 86.503 |
| 18 | 30.912 | 35.848 | 41.523 | 48.038 | 55.511 | 64.071 | 73.869 | 85.070 | 97.862 | 112.454 |
| 19 | 37.404 | 43.735 | 51.073 | 59.567 | 69.389 | 80.730 | 93.813 | 108.890 | 126.242 | 146.190 |
| 20 | 45.258 | 53.357 | 62.820 | 73.863 | 86.736 | 101.720 | 119.143 | 139.379 | 162.852 | 190.047 |
| 21 | 54.762 | 65.095 | 77.268 | 91.591 | 108.420 | 128.167 | 151.312 | 178.405 | 210.079 | 247.061 |
| 22 | 66.262 | 79.416 | 95.040 | 113.572 | 135.525 | 161.490 | 192.165 | 228.358 | 271.002 | 321.178 |
| 23 | 80.178 | 96.887 | 116.899 | 140.829 | 169.407 | 203.477 | 244.050 | 292.298 | 349.592 | 417.431 |
| 24 | 97.015 | 118.203 | 143.786 | 174.628 | 211.758 | 256.381 | 309.943 | 374.141 | 450.974 | 542.791 |
| 25 | 117.388 | 144.207 | 176.857 | 216.539 | 264.698 | 323.040 | 393.628 | 478.901 | 581.756 | 705.627 |
| 30 | 304.471 | 389.748 | 497.904 | 634.810 | 807.793 | 1025.904 | 1300.477 | 1645.488 | 2078.208 | 2619.936 |
| 40 | 2048.309 | 2846.941 | 3946.340 | 5455.797 | 7523.156 | 10346.879 | 14195.051 | 19426.418 | 26520.723 | 36117.754 |
| 50 | 13779.844 | 20795.680 | 31278.301 | 46889.207 | 70064.812 | 104354.562 | 154942.687 | 229345.875 | 338440.000 | 497910.125 |

| n | 31% | 32% | 33% | 34% | 35% | 36% | 37% | 38% | 39% | 40% |
|---|---|---|---|---|---|---|---|---|---|---|
| 1 | 1.310 | 1.320 | 1.330 | 1.340 | 1.350 | 1.360 | 1.370 | 1.380 | 1.390 | 1.400 |
| 2 | 1.716 | 1.742 | 1.769 | 1.796 | 1.822 | 1.850 | 1.877 | 1.904 | 1.932 | 1.960 |
| 3 | 2.248 | 2.300 | 2.353 | 2.406 | 2.460 | 2.515 | 2.571 | 2.628 | 2.686 | 2.744 |
| 4 | 2.945 | 3.036 | 3.129 | 3.224 | 3.321 | 3.421 | 3.523 | 3.627 | 3.733 | 3.842 |
| 5 | 3.858 | 4.007 | 4.162 | 4.320 | 4.484 | 4.653 | 4.826 | 5.005 | 5.189 | 5.378 |
| 6 | 5.054 | 5.290 | 5.535 | 5.789 | 6.053 | 6.328 | 6.612 | 6.907 | 7.213 | 7.530 |
| 7 | 6.621 | 6.983 | 7.361 | 7.758 | 8.172 | 8.605 | 9.058 | 9.531 | 10.025 | 10.541 |
| 8 | 8.673 | 9.217 | 9.791 | 10.395 | 11.032 | 11.703 | 12.410 | 13.153 | 13.935 | 14.758 |
| 9 | 11.362 | 12.166 | 13.022 | 13.930 | 14.894 | 15.917 | 17.001 | 18.151 | 19.370 | 20.661 |
| 10 | 14.884 | 16.060 | 17.319 | 18.666 | 20.106 | 21.646 | 23.292 | 25.049 | 26.924 | 28.925 |
| 11 | 19.498 | 21.199 | 23.034 | 25.012 | 27.144 | 29.439 | 31.910 | 34.567 | 37.425 | 40.495 |
| 12 | 25.542 | 27.982 | 30.635 | 33.516 | 36.644 | 40.037 | 43.716 | 47.703 | 52.020 | 56.694 |
| 13 | 33.460 | 36.937 | 40.745 | 44.912 | 49.469 | 54.451 | 59.892 | 65.830 | 72.308 | 79.371 |
| 14 | 43.832 | 49.756 | 54.190 | 60.181 | 66.784 | 74.053 | 82.051 | 90.845 | 100.509 | 111.120 |
| 15 | 57.420 | 64.358 | 72.073 | 80.643 | 90.158 | 100.712 | 112.410 | 125.366 | 139.707 | 155.567 |
| 16 | 75.220 | 84.953 | 95.857 | 108.061 | 121.713 | 136.968 | 154.002 | 173.005 | 194.192 | 217.793 |
| 17 | 98.539 | 112.138 | 127.490 | 144.802 | 164.312 | 186.277 | 210.983 | 238.747 | 269.927 | 304.911 |
| 18 | 129.086 | 148.022 | 169.561 | 194.035 | 221.822 | 253.337 | 289.046 | 329.471 | 375.198 | 426.875 |
| 19 | 169.102 | 195.389 | 225.517 | 260.006 | 299.459 | 344.537 | 395.993 | 454.669 | 521.525 | 597.625 |
| 20 | 221.523 | 257.913 | 299.937 | 348.408 | 404.270 | 468.571 | 542.511 | 627.443 | 724.919 | 836.674 |
| 21 | 290.196 | 340.446 | 398.916 | 466.867 | 545.764 | 637.256 | 743.240 | 865.871 | 1007.637 | 1171.343 |
| 22 | 380.156 | 449.388 | 530.558 | 625.601 | 736.781 | 865.668 | 1018.238 | 1194.900 | 1400.615 | 1639.878 |
| 23 | 498.004 | 593.192 | 705.642 | 838.305 | 994.653 | 1178.668 | 1394.986 | 1648.961 | 1946.854 | 2295.829 |
| 24 | 652.385 | 783.013 | 938.504 | 1123.328 | 1342.781 | 1602.988 | 1911.129 | 2275.564 | 2706.125 | 3214.158 |
| 25 | 854.623 | 1033.577 | 1248.210 | 1505.258 | 1812.754 | 2180.063 | 2618.245 | 3140.275 | 3761.511 | 4499.816 |
| 30 | 3297.081 | 4142.008 | 5194.516 | 6503.285 | 8128.426 | 10142.914 | 12636.086 | 15716.703 | 19517.969 | 24201.043 |
| 40 | 49072.621 | 66519.313 | 89962.188 | 121388.437 | 163433.875 | 219558.625 | 294317.937 | 393684.687 | 525508.312 | 700022.688 |

# Appendix B

## Present Value of $1

| n | 1% | 2% | 3% | 4% | 5% | 6% | 7% | 8% | 9% | 10% |
|---|------|------|------|------|------|------|------|------|------|------|
| 1 | .990 | .980 | .971 | .962 | .952 | .943 | .935 | .926 | .917 | .909 |
| 2 | .980 | .961 | .943 | .925 | .907 | .890 | .873 | .857 | .842 | .826 |
| 3 | .971 | .942 | .915 | .889 | .864 | .840 | .816 | .794 | .772 | .751 |
| 4 | .961 | .924 | .888 | .855 | .823 | .792 | .763 | .735 | .708 | .683 |
| 5 | .951 | .906 | .863 | .822 | .784 | .747 | .713 | .681 | .650 | .621 |
| 6 | .942 | .888 | .837 | .790 | .746 | .705 | .666 | .630 | .596 | .564 |
| 7 | .933 | .871 | .813 | .760 | .711 | .665 | .623 | .583 | .547 | .513 |
| 8 | .923 | .853 | .789 | .731 | .677 | .627 | .582 | .540 | .502 | .467 |
| 9 | .914 | .837 | .766 | .703 | .645 | .592 | .544 | .500 | .460 | .424 |
| 10 | .905 | .820 | .744 | .676 | .614 | .558 | .508 | .463 | .422 | .386 |
| 11 | .896 | .804 | .722 | .650 | .585 | .527 | .475 | .429 | .388 | .350 |
| 12 | .887 | .789 | .701 | .625 | .557 | .497 | .444 | .397 | .356 | .319 |
| 13 | .879 | .773 | .681 | .601 | .530 | .469 | .415 | .368 | .326 | .290 |
| 14 | .870 | .758 | .661 | .577 | .505 | .442 | .388 | .340 | .299 | .263 |
| 15 | .861 | .743 | .642 | .555 | .481 | .417 | .362 | .315 | .275 | .239 |
| 16 | .853 | .728 | .623 | .534 | .458 | .394 | .339 | .292 | .252 | .218 |
| 17 | .844 | .714 | .605 | .513 | .436 | .371 | .317 | .270 | .231 | .198 |
| 18 | .836 | .700 | .587 | .494 | .416 | .350 | .296 | .250 | .212 | .180 |
| 19 | .828 | .686 | .570 | .475 | .396 | .331 | .277 | .232 | .194 | .164 |
| 20 | .820 | .673 | .554 | .456 | .377 | .312 | .258 | .215 | .178 | .149 |
| 21 | .811 | .660 | .538 | .439 | .359 | .294 | .242 | .199 | .164 | .135 |
| 22 | .803 | .647 | .522 | .422 | .342 | .278 | .226 | .184 | .150 | .123 |
| 23 | .795 | .634 | .507 | .406 | .326 | .262 | .211 | .170 | .138 | .112 |
| 24 | .788 | .622 | .492 | .390 | .310 | .247 | .197 | .158 | .126 | .102 |
| 25 | .780 | .610 | .478 | .375 | .295 | .233 | .184 | .146 | .116 | .092 |
| 30 | .742 | .552 | .412 | .308 | .231 | .174 | .131 | .099 | .075 | .057 |
| 40 | .672 | .453 | .307 | .208 | .142 | .097 | .067 | .046 | .032 | .022 |
| 50 | .608 | .372 | .228 | .141 | .087 | .054 | .034 | .021 | .013 | .009 |

| n | 11% | 12% | 13% | 14% | 15% | 16% | 17% | 18% | 19% | 20% |
|---|------|------|------|------|------|------|------|------|------|------|
| 1 | .901 | .893 | .885 | .877 | .870 | .862 | .855 | .847 | .840 | .833 |
| 2 | .812 | .797 | .783 | .769 | .756 | .743 | .731 | .718 | .706 | .694 |
| 3 | .731 | .712 | .693 | .675 | .658 | .641 | .624 | .609 | .593 | .579 |
| 4 | .659 | .636 | .613 | .592 | .572 | .552 | .534 | .516 | .499 | .482 |
| 5 | .593 | .567 | .543 | .519 | .497 | .476 | .456 | .437 | .419 | .402 |
| 6 | .535 | .507 | .480 | .456 | .432 | .410 | .390 | .370 | .352 | .335 |
| 7 | .482 | .452 | .425 | .400 | .376 | .354 | .333 | .314 | .296 | .279 |
| 8 | .434 | .404 | .376 | .351 | .327 | .305 | .285 | .266 | .249 | .233 |
| 9 | .391 | .361 | .333 | .308 | .284 | .263 | .243 | .225 | .209 | .194 |
| 10 | .352 | .322 | .295 | .270 | .247 | .227 | .208 | .191 | .176 | .162 |
| 11 | .317 | .287 | .261 | .237 | .215 | .195 | .178 | .162 | .148 | .135 |
| 12 | .286 | .257 | .231 | .208 | .187 | .168 | .152 | .137 | .124 | .112 |
| 13 | .258 | .229 | .204 | .182 | .163 | .145 | .130 | .116 | .104 | .093 |
| 14 | .232 | .205 | .181 | .160 | .141 | .125 | .111 | .099 | .088 | .078 |
| 15 | .209 | .183 | .160 | .140 | .123 | .108 | .095 | .084 | .074 | .065 |
| 16 | .188 | .163 | .141 | .123 | .107 | .093 | .081 | .071 | .062 | .054 |
| 17 | .170 | .146 | .125 | .108 | .093 | .080 | .069 | .060 | .052 | .045 |
| 18 | .153 | .130 | .111 | .095 | .081 | .069 | .059 | .051 | .044 | .038 |
| 19 | .138 | .116 | .098 | .083 | .070 | .060 | .051 | .043 | .037 | .031 |
| 20 | .124 | .104 | .087 | .073 | .061 | .051 | .043 | .037 | .031 | .026 |
| 21 | .112 | .093 | .077 | .064 | .053 | .044 | .037 | .031 | .026 | .022 |
| 22 | .101 | .083 | .068 | .056 | .046 | .038 | .032 | .026 | .022 | .018 |
| 23 | .091 | .074 | .060 | .049 | .040 | .033 | .027 | .022 | .018 | .015 |
| 24 | .082 | .066 | .053 | .043 | .035 | .028 | .023 | .019 | .015 | .013 |
| 25 | .074 | .059 | .047 | .038 | .030 | .024 | .020 | .016 | .013 | .010 |
| 30 | .044 | .033 | .026 | .020 | .015 | .012 | .009 | .007 | .005 | .004 |
| 40 | .015 | .011 | .008 | .005 | .004 | .003 | .002 | .001 | .001 | .001 |
| 50 | .005 | .003 | .002 | .001 | .001 | .001 | .000 | .000 | .000 | .000 |

| n | 21% | 22% | 23% | 24% | 25% | 26% | 27% | 28% | 29% | 30% |
|---|-----|-----|-----|-----|-----|-----|-----|-----|-----|-----|
| 1 | .826 | .820 | .813 | .806 | .800 | .794 | .787 | .781 | .775 | .769 |
| 2 | .683 | .672 | .661 | .650 | .640 | .630 | .620 | .610 | .601 | .592 |
| 3 | .564 | .551 | .537 | .524 | .512 | .500 | .488 | .477 | .466 | .455 |
| 4 | .467 | .451 | .437 | .423 | .410 | .397 | .384 | .373 | .361 | .350 |
| 5 | .386 | .370 | .355 | .341 | .328 | .315 | .303 | .291 | .280 | .269 |
| 6 | .319 | .303 | .289 | .275 | .262 | .250 | .238 | .227 | .217 | .207 |
| 7 | .263 | .249 | .235 | .222 | .210 | .198 | .188 | .178 | .168 | .159 |
| 8 | .218 | .204 | .191 | .179 | .168 | .157 | .148 | .139 | .130 | .123 |
| 9 | .180 | .167 | .155 | .144 | .134 | .125 | .116 | .108 | .101 | .094 |
| 10 | .149 | .137 | .126 | .116 | .107 | .099 | .092 | .085 | .078 | .073 |
| 11 | .123 | .112 | .103 | .094 | .086 | .079 | .072 | .066 | .061 | .056 |
| 12 | .102 | .092 | .083 | .076 | .069 | .062 | .057 | .052 | .047 | .043 |
| 13 | .084 | .075 | .068 | .061 | .055 | .050 | .045 | .040 | .037 | .033 |
| 14 | .069 | .062 | .055 | .049 | .044 | .039 | .035 | .032 | .028 | .025 |
| 15 | .057 | .051 | .045 | .040 | .035 | .031 | .028 | .025 | .022 | .020 |
| 16 | .047 | .042 | .036 | .032 | .028 | .025 | .022 | .019 | .017 | .015 |
| 17 | .039 | .034 | .030 | .026 | .023 | .020 | .017 | .015 | .013 | .012 |
| 18 | .032 | .028 | .024 | .021 | .018 | .016 | .014 | .012 | .010 | .009 |
| 19 | .027 | .023 | .020 | .017 | .014 | .012 | .011 | .009 | .008 | .007 |
| 20 | .022 | .019 | .016 | .014 | .012 | .010 | .008 | .007 | .006 | .005 |
| 21 | .018 | .015 | .013 | .011 | .009 | .008 | .007 | .006 | .005 | .004 |
| 22 | .015 | .013 | .011 | .009 | .007 | .006 | .005 | .004 | .004 | .003 |
| 23 | .012 | .010 | .009 | .007 | .006 | .005 | .004 | .003 | .003 | .002 |
| 24 | .010 | .008 | .007 | .006 | .005 | .004 | .003 | .003 | .002 | .002 |
| 25 | .009 | .007 | .006 | .005 | .004 | .003 | .003 | .002 | .002 | .001 |
| 30 | .003 | .003 | .002 | .002 | .001 | .001 | .001 | .001 | .000 | .000 |
| 40 | .000 | .000 | .000 | .000 | .000 | .000 | .000 | .000 | .000 | .000 |
| 50 | .000 | .000 | .000 | .000 | .000 | .000 | .000 | .000 | .000 | .000 |

| n | 31% | 32% | 33% | 34% | 35% | 36% | 37% | 38% | 39% | 40% |
|---|-----|-----|-----|-----|-----|-----|-----|-----|-----|-----|
| 1 | .763 | .758 | .752 | .746 | .741 | .735 | .730 | .725 | .719 | .714 |
| 2 | .583 | .574 | .565 | .557 | .549 | .541 | .533 | .525 | .518 | .510 |
| 3 | .445 | .435 | .425 | .416 | .406 | .398 | .389 | .381 | .372 | .364 |
| 4 | .340 | .329 | .320 | .310 | .301 | .292 | .284 | .276 | .268 | .260 |
| 5 | .259 | .250 | .240 | .231 | .223 | .215 | .207 | .200 | .193 | .186 |
| 6 | .198 | .189 | .181 | .173 | .165 | .158 | .151 | .145 | .139 | .133 |
| 7 | .151 | .143 | .136 | .129 | .122 | .116 | .110 | .105 | .100 | .095 |
| 8 | .115 | .108 | .102 | .096 | .091 | .085 | .081 | .076 | .072 | .068 |
| 9 | .088 | .082 | .077 | .072 | .067 | .063 | .059 | .055 | .052 | .048 |
| 10 | .067 | .062 | .058 | .054 | .050 | .046 | .043 | .040 | .037 | .035 |
| 11 | .051 | .047 | .043 | .040 | .037 | .034 | .031 | .029 | .027 | .025 |
| 12 | .039 | .036 | .033 | .030 | .027 | .025 | .023 | .021 | .019 | .018 |
| 13 | .030 | .027 | .025 | .022 | .020 | .018 | .017 | .015 | .014 | .013 |
| 14 | .023 | .021 | .018 | .017 | .015 | .014 | .012 | .011 | .010 | .009 |
| 15 | .017 | .016 | .014 | .012 | .011 | .010 | .009 | .008 | .007 | .006 |
| 16 | .013 | .012 | .010 | .009 | .008 | .007 | .006 | .006 | .005 | .005 |
| 17 | .010 | .009 | .008 | .007 | .006 | .005 | .005 | .004 | .004 | .003 |
| 18 | .008 | .007 | .006 | .005 | .005 | .004 | .003 | .003 | .003 | .002 |
| 19 | .006 | .005 | .004 | .004 | .003 | .003 | .003 | .002 | .002 | .002 |
| 20 | .005 | .004 | .003 | .003 | .002 | .002 | .002 | .002 | .001 | .001 |
| 21 | .003 | .003 | .003 | .002 | .002 | .002 | .001 | .001 | .001 | .001 |
| 22 | .003 | .002 | .002 | .002 | .001 | .001 | .001 | .001 | .001 | .001 |
| 23 | .002 | .002 | .001 | .001 | .001 | .001 | .001 | .001 | .001 | .000 |
| 24 | .002 | .001 | .001 | .001 | .001 | .001 | .001 | .000 | .000 | .000 |
| 25 | .001 | .001 | .001 | .001 | .001 | .000 | .000 | .000 | .000 | .000 |
| 30 | .000 | .000 | .000 | .000 | .000 | .000 | .000 | .000 | .000 | .000 |
| 40 | .000 | .000 | .000 | .000 | .000 | .000 | .000 | .000 | .000 | .000 |

# Appendix C

## Compound Sum of an Annuity of $1 for *n* Periods

| n | 1% | 2% | 3% | 4% | 5% | 6% | 7% | 8% | 9% | 10% |
|---|---|---|---|---|---|---|---|---|---|---|
| 1 | 1.000 | 1.000 | 1.000 | 1.000 | 1.000 | 1.000 | 1.000 | 1.000 | 1.000 | 1.000 |
| 2 | 2.010 | 2.020 | 2.030 | 2.040 | 2.050 | 2.060 | 2.070 | 2.080 | 2.090 | 2.100 |
| 3 | 3.030 | 3.060 | 3.091 | 3.122 | 3.152 | 3.184 | 3.215 | 3.246 | 3.278 | 3.310 |
| 4 | 4.060 | 4.122 | 4.184 | 4.246 | 4.310 | 4.375 | 4.440 | 4.506 | 4.573 | 4.641 |
| 5 | 5.101 | 5.204 | 5.309 | 5.416 | 5.526 | 5.637 | 5.751 | 5.867 | 5.985 | 6.105 |
| 6 | 6.152 | 6.308 | 6.468 | 6.633 | 6.802 | 6.975 | 7.153 | 7.336 | 7.523 | 7.716 |
| 7 | 7.214 | 7.434 | 7.662 | 7.898 | 8.142 | 8.394 | 8.654 | 8.923 | 9.200 | 9.487 |
| 8 | 8.286 | 8.583 | 8.892 | 9.214 | 9.549 | 9.897 | 10.260 | 10.637 | 11.028 | 11.436 |
| 9 | 9.368 | 9.755 | 10.159 | 10.583 | 11.027 | 11.491 | 11.978 | 12.488 | 13.021 | 13.579 |
| 10 | 10.462 | 10.950 | 11.464 | 12.006 | 12.578 | 13.181 | 13.816 | 14.487 | 15.193 | 15.937 |
| 11 | 11.567 | 12.169 | 12.808 | 13.486 | 14.207 | 14.972 | 15.784 | 16.645 | 17.560 | 18.531 |
| 12 | 12.682 | 13.412 | 14.192 | 15.026 | 15.917 | 16.870 | 17.888 | 18.977 | 20.141 | 21.384 |
| 13 | 13.809 | 14.680 | 15.618 | 16.627 | 17.713 | 18.882 | 20.141 | 21.495 | 22.953 | 24.523 |
| 14 | 14.947 | 15.974 | 17.086 | 18.292 | 19.598 | 21.015 | 22.550 | 24.215 | 26.019 | 27.975 |
| 15 | 16.097 | 17.293 | 18.599 | 20.023 | 21.578 | 23.276 | 25.129 | 27.152 | 29.361 | 31.772 |
| 16 | 17.258 | 18.639 | 20.157 | 21.824 | 23.657 | 25.672 | 27.888 | 30.324 | 33.003 | 35.949 |
| 17 | 18.430 | 20.012 | 21.761 | 23.697 | 25.840 | 28.213 | 30.840 | 33.750 | 36.973 | 40.544 |
| 18 | 19.614 | 21.412 | 23.414 | 25.645 | 28.132 | 30.905 | 33.999 | 37.450 | 41.301 | 45.599 |
| 19 | 20.811 | 22.840 | 25.117 | 27.671 | 30.539 | 33.760 | 37.379 | 41.446 | 46.018 | 51.158 |
| 20 | 22.019 | 24.297 | 26.870 | 29.778 | 33.066 | 36.785 | 40.995 | 45.762 | 51.159 | 57.274 |
| 21 | 23.239 | 25.783 | 28.676 | 31.969 | 35.719 | 39.992 | 44.865 | 50.422 | 56.764 | 64.002 |
| 22 | 24.471 | 27.299 | 30.536 | 34.248 | 38.505 | 43.392 | 49.005 | 55.456 | 62.872 | 71.402 |
| 23 | 25.716 | 28.845 | 32.452 | 36.618 | 41.430 | 46.995 | 53.435 | 60.893 | 69.531 | 79.542 |
| 24 | 26.973 | 30.421 | 34.426 | 39.082 | 44.501 | 50.815 | 58.176 | 66.764 | 76.789 | 88.496 |
| 25 | 28.243 | 32.030 | 36.459 | 41.645 | 47.726 | 54.864 | 63.248 | 73.105 | 84.699 | 98.346 |
| 30 | 34.784 | 40.567 | 47.575 | 56.084 | 66.438 | 79.957 | 94.459 | 113.282 | 136.305 | 164.491 |
| 40 | 48.885 | 60.401 | 75.400 | 95.024 | 120.797 | 154.758 | 199.630 | 295.052 | 337.872 | 442.580 |
| 50 | 64.461 | 84.577 | 112.794 | 152.664 | 209.341 | 290.325 | 406.516 | 573.756 | 815.051 | 1163.865 |

| n | 11% | 12% | 13% | 14% | 15% | 16% | 17% | 18% | 19% | 20% |
|---|---|---|---|---|---|---|---|---|---|---|
| 1 | 1.000 | 1.000 | 1.000 | 1.000 | 1.000 | 1.000 | 1.000 | 1.000 | 1.000 | 1.000 |
| 2 | 2.110 | 2.120 | 2.130 | 2.140 | 2.150 | 2.160 | 2.170 | 2.180 | 2.190 | 2.200 |
| 3 | 3.342 | 3.374 | 3.407 | 3.440 | 3.472 | 3.506 | 3.539 | 3.572 | 3.606 | 3.640 |
| 4 | 4.710 | 4.779 | 4.850 | 4.921 | 4.993 | 5.066 | 5.141 | 5.215 | 5.291 | 5.368 |
| 5 | 6.228 | 6.353 | 6.480 | 6.610 | 6.742 | 6.877 | 7.014 | 7.154 | 7.297 | 7.442 |
| 6 | 7.913 | 8.115 | 8.323 | 8.535 | 8.754 | 8.977 | 9.207 | 9.442 | 9.683 | 9.930 |
| 7 | 9.783 | 10.089 | 10.405 | 10.730 | 11.067 | 11.414 | 11.772 | 12.141 | 12.523 | 12.916 |
| 8 | 11.859 | 12.300 | 12.757 | 13.233 | 13.727 | 14.240 | 14.773 | 15.327 | 15.902 | 16.499 |
| 9 | 14.164 | 14.776 | 15.416 | 16.085 | 16.786 | 17.518 | 18.285 | 19.086 | 19.923 | 20.799 |
| 10 | 16.722 | 17.549 | 18.420 | 19.337 | 20.304 | 21.321 | 22.393 | 23.521 | 24.709 | 25.959 |
| 11 | 19.561 | 20.655 | 21.814 | 23.044 | 24.349 | 25.733 | 27.200 | 28.755 | 30.403 | 32.150 |
| 12 | 22.713 | 24.133 | 25.650 | 27.271 | 29.001 | 30.850 | 32.824 | 34.931 | 37.180 | 39.580 |
| 13 | 26.211 | 28.029 | 29.984 | 32.088 | 34.352 | 36.786 | 39.404 | 42.218 | 45.244 | 48.496 |
| 14 | 30.095 | 32.392 | 34.882 | 37.581 | 40.504 | 43.672 | 47.102 | 50.818 | 54.841 | 59.196 |
| 15 | 34.405 | 37.280 | 40.417 | 43.842 | 47.580 | 51.659 | 56.109 | 60.965 | 66.260 | 72.035 |
| 16 | 39.190 | 42.753 | 46.671 | 50.980 | 55.717 | 60.925 | 66.648 | 72.938 | 79.850 | 87.442 |
| 17 | 44.500 | 48.883 | 53.738 | 59.117 | 65.075 | 71.673 | 78.978 | 87.067 | 96.021 | 105.930 |
| 18 | 50.396 | 55.749 | 61.724 | 68.393 | 75.836 | 84.140 | 93.404 | 103.739 | 115.265 | 128.116 |
| 19 | 56.939 | 63.439 | 70.748 | 78.968 | 88.211 | 98.603 | 110.283 | 123.412 | 138.165 | 154.739 |
| 20 | 64.202 | 72.052 | 80.946 | 91.024 | 102.443 | 115.379 | 130.031 | 146.626 | 165.417 | 186.687 |
| 21 | 72.264 | 81.698 | 92.468 | 104.767 | 118.809 | 134.840 | 153.136 | 174.019 | 197.846 | 225.024 |
| 22 | 81.213 | 92.502 | 105.489 | 120.434 | 137.630 | 157.414 | 180.169 | 206.342 | 236.436 | 271.028 |
| 23 | 91.147 | 104.602 | 120.203 | 138.295 | 159.274 | 183.600 | 211.798 | 244.483 | 282.359 | 326.234 |
| 24 | 102.173 | 118.154 | 136.829 | 158.656 | 184.166 | 213.976 | 248.803 | 289.490 | 337.007 | 392.480 |
| 25 | 114.412 | 133.333 | 115.616 | 181.867 | 212.790 | 249.212 | 292.099 | 342.598 | 402.038 | 471.976 |
| 30 | 199.018 | 241.330 | 293.192 | 356.778 | 434.738 | 530.306 | 647.423 | 790.932 | 966.698 | 1181.865 |
| 40 | 581.812 | 767.080 | 1013.667 | 1341.979 | 1779.048 | 2360.724 | 3134.412 | 4163.094 | 5529.711 | 7343.715 |
| 50 | 1668.723 | 2399.975 | 3459.344 | 4994.301 | 7217.488 | 10435.449 | 15088.805 | 21812.273 | 31514.492 | 45496.094 |

| n | 21% | 22% | 23% | 24% | 25% | 26% | 27% | 28% | 29% | 30% |
|---|------|------|------|------|------|------|------|------|------|------|
| 1 | 1.000 | 1.000 | 1.000 | 1.000 | 1.000 | 1.000 | 1.000 | 1.000 | 1.000 | 1.000 |
| 2 | 2.210 | 2.220 | 2.230 | 2.240 | 2.250 | 2.260 | 2.270 | 2.280 | 2.290 | 2.300 |
| 3 | 3.674 | 3.708 | 3.743 | 3.778 | 3.813 | 3.848 | 3.883 | 3.918 | 3.954 | 3.990 |
| 4 | 5.446 | 5.524 | 5.604 | 5.684 | 5.766 | 5.848 | 5.931 | 6.016 | 6.101 | 6.187 |
| 5 | 7.589 | 7.740 | 7.893 | 8.048 | 8.207 | 8.368 | 8.533 | 8.700 | 8.870 | 9.043 |
| 6 | 10.183 | 10.442 | 10.708 | 10.980 | 11.259 | 11.544 | 11.837 | 12.136 | 12.442 | 12.756 |
| 7 | 13.321 | 13.740 | 14.171 | 14.615 | 15.073 | 15.546 | 16.032 | 16.534 | 17.051 | 17.583 |
| 8 | 17.119 | 17.762 | 18.430 | 19.123 | 19.842 | 20.588 | 21.361 | 22.163 | 22.995 | 23.858 |
| 9 | 21.714 | 22.670 | 23.669 | 24.712 | 25.802 | 26.940 | 28.129 | 29.369 | 30.664 | 32.015 |
| 10 | 27.274 | 28.657 | 20.113 | 31.643 | 33.253 | 34.945 | 36.723 | 38.592 | 40.556 | 42.619 |
| 11 | 34.001 | 35.962 | 38.039 | 40.238 | 42.566 | 45.030 | 47.639 | 50.398 | 53.318 | 56.405 |
| 12 | 42.141 | 44.873 | 47.787 | 50.895 | 54.208 | 57.730 | 61.501 | 65.510 | 69.780 | 74.326 |
| 13 | 51.991 | 45.745 | 59.778 | 64.109 | 68.760 | 73.750 | 79.106 | 84.853 | 91.016 | 97.624 |
| 14 | 63.909 | 69.009 | 74.528 | 80.496 | 86.949 | 93.925 | 101.465 | 109.611 | 118.411 | 127.912 |
| 15 | 78.330 | 65.191 | 92.669 | 100.815 | 109.687 | 119.346 | 129.860 | 141.302 | 153.750 | 167.285 |
| 16 | 95.779 | 104.933 | 114.983 | 126.010 | 138.109 | 151.375 | 165.922 | 181.867 | 199.337 | 218.470 |
| 17 | 116.892 | 129.019 | 142.428 | 157.252 | 173.636 | 191.733 | 211.721 | 233.790 | 258.145 | 285.011 |
| 18 | 142.439 | 158.403 | 176.187 | 195.993 | 218.045 | 242.583 | 269.885 | 300.250 | 334.006 | 371.514 |
| 19 | 173.351 | 194.251 | 217.710 | 244.031 | 273.556 | 306.654 | 343.754 | 385.321 | 431.868 | 483.968 |
| 20 | 210.755 | 237.986 | 268.783 | 303.598 | 342.945 | 387.384 | 437.568 | 494.210 | 558.110 | 630.157 |
| 21 | 256.013 | 291.343 | 331.603 | 377.461 | 429.681 | 489.104 | 556.710 | 633.589 | 720.962 | 820.204 |
| 22 | 310.775 | 356.438 | 408.871 | 469.052 | 538.101 | 617.270 | 708.022 | 811.993 | 931.040 | 1067.265 |
| 23 | 377.038 | 435.854 | 503.911 | 582.624 | 673.626 | 778.760 | 900.187 | 1040.351 | 1202.042 | 1388.443 |
| 24 | 457.215 | 532.741 | 620.810 | 723.453 | 843.032 | 982.237 | 1144.237 | 1332.649 | 1551.634 | 1805.975 |
| 25 | 554.230 | 650.944 | 764.596 | 898.082 | 1054.791 | 1238.617 | 1454.180 | 1706.790 | 2002.608 | 2348.765 |
| 30 | 1445.111 | 1767.044 | 2160.459 | 2640.881 | 3227.172 | 3941.953 | 4812.891 | 5873.172 | 7162.785 | 8729.805 |
| 40 | 9749.141 | 12936.141 | 17153.691 | 22728.367 | 30088.621 | 39791.957 | 52570.707 | 69376.562 | 91447.375 | 120389.375 |

| n | 31% | 32% | 33% | 34% | 35% | 36% | 37% | 38% | 39% | 40% |
|---|------|------|------|------|------|------|------|------|------|------|
| 1 | 1.000 | 1.000 | 1.000 | 1.000 | 1.000 | 1.000 | 1.000 | 1.000 | 1.000 | 1.000 |
| 2 | 2.310 | 2.320 | 2.330 | 2.340 | 2.350 | 2.360 | 2.370 | 2.380 | 2.390 | 2.400 |
| 3 | 4.026 | 4.062 | 4.099 | 4.136 | 4.172 | 4.210 | 4.247 | 4.284 | 4.322 | 4.360 |
| 4 | 6.274 | 6.363 | 6.452 | 6.542 | 6.633 | 6.725 | 6.818 | 6.912 | 7.008 | 7.104 |
| 5 | 9.219 | 9.398 | 9.581 | 9.766 | 9.954 | 10.146 | 10.341 | 10.539 | 10.741 | 10.946 |
| 6 | 13.077 | 13.406 | 13.742 | 14.086 | 14.438 | 14.799 | 15.167 | 15.544 | 15.930 | 16.324 |
| 7 | 18.131 | 18.696 | 19.277 | 19.876 | 20.492 | 21.126 | 21.779 | 22.451 | 23.142 | 23.853 |
| 8 | 24.752 | 25.678 | 26.638 | 27.633 | 28.664 | 29.732 | 30.837 | 31.982 | 33.167 | 34.395 |
| 9 | 33.425 | 34.895 | 36.429 | 38.028 | 39.696 | 41.435 | 43.247 | 45.135 | 47.103 | 49.152 |
| 10 | 44.786 | 47.062 | 49.451 | 51.958 | 54.590 | 57.351 | 60.248 | 63.287 | 66.473 | 69.813 |
| 11 | 59.670 | 63.121 | 66.769 | 70.624 | 74.696 | 78.998 | 83.540 | 88.335 | 93.397 | 98.739 |
| 12 | 79.167 | 84.320 | 89.803 | 95.636 | 101.840 | 108.437 | 115.450 | 122.903 | 130.822 | 139.234 |
| 13 | 104.709 | 112.302 | 120.438 | 129.152 | 138.484 | 148.474 | 159.166 | 170.606 | 182.842 | 195.928 |
| 14 | 138.169 | 149.239 | 161.183 | 174.063 | 187.953 | 202.925 | 219.058 | 236.435 | 255.151 | 275.299 |
| 15 | 182.001 | 197.996 | 215.373 | 234.245 | 254.737 | 276.978 | 301.109 | 327.281 | 355.659 | 386.418 |
| 16 | 239.421 | 262.354 | 287.446 | 314.888 | 344.895 | 377.690 | 413.520 | 542.647 | 495.366 | 541.985 |
| 17 | 314.642 | 347.307 | 383.303 | 422.949 | 466.608 | 514.658 | 567.521 | 625.652 | 689.558 | 759.778 |
| 18 | 413.180 | 459.445 | 510.792 | 567.751 | 630.920 | 700.935 | 778.504 | 864.399 | 959.485 | 1064.689 |
| 19 | 542.266 | 607.467 | 680.354 | 761.786 | 852.741 | 954.271 | 1067.551 | 1193.870 | 1334.683 | 1491.563 |
| 20 | 711.368 | 802.856 | 905.870 | 1021.792 | 1152.200 | 1298.809 | 1463.544 | 1648.539 | 1856.208 | 2089.188 |
| 21 | 932.891 | 1060.769 | 1205.807 | 1370.201 | 1556.470 | 1767.380 | 2006.055 | 2275.982 | 2581.128 | 2925.862 |
| 22 | 1223.087 | 1401.215 | 1604.724 | 1837.068 | 2102.234 | 2404.636 | 2749.294 | 3141.852 | 3588.765 | 4097.203 |
| 23 | 1603.243 | 1850.603 | 2135.282 | 2462.669 | 2839.014 | 3271.304 | 3767.532 | 4336.750 | 4989.379 | 5737.078 |
| 24 | 2101.247 | 2443.795 | 2840.924 | 3300.974 | 3833.667 | 4449.969 | 5162.516 | 5985.711 | 6936.230 | 8032.906 |
| 25 | 2753.631 | 3226.808 | 3779.428 | 4424.301 | 5176.445 | 6052.957 | 7073.645 | 8261.273 | 9642.352 | 11247.062 |
| 30 | 10632.543 | 12940.672 | 15737.945 | 19124.434 | 23221.258 | 28172.016 | 34148.906 | 41357.227 | 50043.625 | 60500.207 |

# Appendix D

## Present Value of an Annuity of $1 for n Periods

| n | 1% | 2% | 3% | 4% | 5% | 6% | 7% | 8% | 9% | 10% |
|---|----|----|----|----|----|----|----|----|----|-----|
| 1 | .990 | .980 | .971 | .962 | .952 | .943 | .935 | .926 | .917 | .909 |
| 2 | 1.970 | 1.942 | 1.913 | 1.886 | 1.859 | 1.833 | 1.808 | 1.783 | 1.759 | 1.736 |
| 3 | 2.941 | 2.884 | 2.829 | 2.775 | 2.723 | 2.673 | 2.624 | 2.577 | 2.531 | 2.487 |
| 4 | 3.902 | 3.808 | 3.717 | 3.630 | 3.546 | 3.465 | 3.387 | 3.312 | 3.240 | 3.170 |
| 5 | 4.853 | 4.713 | 4.580 | 4.452 | 4.329 | 4.212 | 4.100 | 3.993 | 3.890 | 3.791 |
| 6 | 5.795 | 5.601 | 5.417 | 5.242 | 5.076 | 4.917 | 4.767 | 4.623 | 4.486 | 4.355 |
| 7 | 6.728 | 6.472 | 6.230 | 6.002 | 5.786 | 5.582 | 5.389 | 5.206 | 5.033 | 4.868 |
| 8 | 7.652 | 7.326 | 7.020 | 6.733 | 6.463 | 6.210 | 5.971 | 5.747 | 5.535 | 5.335 |
| 9 | 8.566 | 8.162 | 7.786 | 7.435 | 7.108 | 6.802 | 6.515 | 6.247 | 5.995 | 5.759 |
| 10 | 9.471 | 8.983 | 8.530 | 8.111 | 7.722 | 7.360 | 7.024 | 6.710 | 6.418 | 6.145 |
| 11 | 10.368 | 9.787 | 9.253 | 8.760 | 8.306 | 7.887 | 7.499 | 7.139 | 6.805 | 6.495 |
| 12 | 11.255 | 10.575 | 9.954 | 9.385 | 8.863 | 8.384 | 7.943 | 7.536 | 7.161 | 6.814 |
| 13 | 12.134 | 11.348 | 10.635 | 9.986 | 9.394 | 8.853 | 8.358 | 7.904 | 7.487 | 7.103 |
| 14 | 13.004 | 12.106 | 11.296 | 10.563 | 9.899 | 9.295 | 8.746 | 8.244 | 7.786 | 7.367 |
| 15 | 13.865 | 12.849 | 11.938 | 11.118 | 10.380 | 9.712 | 9.108 | 8.560 | 8.061 | 7.606 |
| 16 | 14.718 | 13.578 | 12.561 | 11.652 | 10.838 | 10.106 | 9.447 | 8.851 | 8.313 | 7.824 |
| 17 | 15.562 | 14.292 | 13.166 | 12.166 | 11.274 | 10.477 | 9.763 | 9.122 | 8.544 | 8.022 |
| 18 | 16.398 | 14.992 | 13.754 | 12.659 | 11.690 | 10.828 | 10.059 | 9.372 | 8.756 | 8.201 |
| 19 | 17.226 | 15.679 | 14.324 | 13.134 | 12.085 | 11.158 | 10.336 | 9.604 | 8.950 | 8.365 |
| 20 | 18.046 | 16.352 | 14.878 | 13.590 | 12.462 *11.966* | 11.470 | 10.594 | 9.818 | 9.129 | 8.514 |
| 21 | 18.857 | 17.011 | 15.415 | 14.029 | 12.821 | 11.764 | 10.836 | 10.017 | 9.292 | 8.649 |
| 22 | 19.661 | 17.658 | 15.937 | 14.451 | 13.163 | 12.042 | 11.061 | 10.201 | 9.442 | 8.772 |
| 23 | 20.456 | 18.292 | 16.444 | 14.857 | 13.489 | 12.303 | 11.272 | 10.371 | 9.580 | 8.883 |
| 24 | 21.244 | 18.914 | 16.936 | 15.247 | 13.799 | 12.550 | 11.469 | 10.529 | 9.707 | 8.985 |
| 25 | 22.023 | 19.524 | 17.413 | 15.622 | 14.094 | 12.783 | 11.654 | 10.675 | 9.823 | 9.077 |
| 30 | 25.808 | 22.397 | 19.601 | 17.292 | 15.373 | 13.765 | 12.409 | 11.258 | 10.274 | 9.427 |
| 40 | 32.835 | 27.356 | 23.115 | 19.793 | 17.159 | 15.046 | 13.332 | 11.925 | 10.757 | 9.779 |
| 50 | 39.197 | 31.424 | 25.730 | 21.482 | 18.256 | 15.762 | 13.801 | 12.234 | 10.962 | 9.915 |

| n | 11% | 12% | 13% | 14% | 15% | 16% | 17% | 18% | 19% | 20% |
|---|-----|-----|-----|-----|-----|-----|-----|-----|-----|-----|
| 1 | .901 | .893 | .885 | .877 | .870 | .862 | .855 | .847 | .840 | .833 |
| 2 | 1.713 | 1.690 | 1.668 | 1.647 | 1.626 | 1.605 | 1.585 | 1.566 | 1.547 | 1.528 |
| 3 | 2.444 | 2.402 | 2.361 | 2.322 | 2.283 | 2.246 | 2.210 | 2.174 | 2.140 | 2.106 |
| 4 | 3.102 | 3.037 | 2.974 | 2.914 | 2.855 | 2.798 | 2.743 | 2.690 | 2.639 | 2.589 |
| 5 | 3.696 | 3.605 | 3.517 | 3.433 | 3.352 | 3.274 | 3.199 | 3.127 | 3.058 | 2.991 |
| 6 | 4.231 | 4.111 | 3.998 | 3.889 | 3.784 | 3.685 | 3.589 | 3.498 | 3.410 | 3.326 |
| 7 | 4.712 | 4.564 | 4.423 | 4.288 | 4.160 | 4.039 | 3.922 | 3.812 | 3.706 | 3.605 |
| 8 | 5.146 | 4.968 | 4.799 | 4.639 | 4.487 | 4.344 | 4.207 | 4.078 | 3.954 | 3.837 |
| 9 | 5.537 | 5.328 | 5.132 | 4.946 | 4.772 | 4.607 | 4.451 | 4.303 | 4.163 | 4.031 |
| 10 | 5.889 | 5.650 | 5.426 | 5.216 | 5.019 | 4.833 | 4.659 | 4.494 | 4.339 | 4.192 |
| 11 | 6.207 | 5.938 | 5.687 | 5.453 | 5.234 | 5.029 | 4.836 | 4.656 | 4.487 | 4.327 |
| 12 | 6.492 | 6.194 | 5.918 | 5.660 | 5.421 | 5.197 | 4.988 | 4.793 | 4.611 | 4.439 |
| 13 | 6.750 | 6.424 | 6.122 | 5.842 | 5.583 | 5.342 | 5.118 | 4.910 | 4.715 | 4.533 |
| 14 | 6.982 | 6.628 | 6.303 | 6.002 | 5.724 | 5.468 | 5.229 | 5.008 | 4.802 | 4.611 |
| 15 | 7.191 | 6.811 | 6.462 | 6.142 | 5.847 | 5.575 | 5.324 | 5.092 | 4.876 | 4.675 |
| 16 | 7.379 | 6.974 | 6.604 | 6.265 | 5.954 | 5.669 | 5.405 | 5.162 | 4.938 | 4.730 |
| 17 | 7.549 | 7.120 | 6.729 | 6.373 | 6.047 | 5.749 | 5.475 | 5.222 | 4.990 | 4.775 |
| 18 | 7.702 | 7.250 | 6.840 | 6.467 | 6.128 | 5.818 | 5.534 | 5.273 | 5.033 | 4.812 |
| 19 | 7.839 | 7.366 | 6.938 | 6.550 | 6.198 | 5.877 | 5.585 | 5.316 | 5.070 | 4.843 |
| 20 | 7.963 | 7.469 | 7.025 | 6.623 | 6.259 | 5.929 | 5.628 | 5.353 | 5.101 | 4.870 |
| 21 | 8.075 | 7.562 | 7.102 | 6.687 | 6.312 | 5.973 | 5.665 | 5.384 | 5.127 | 4.891 |
| 21 | 8.176 | 7.645 | 7.170 | 6.743 | 6.359 | 6.011 | 5.696 | 5.410 | 5.149 | 4.909 |
| 23 | 8.266 | 7.718 | 7.230 | 6.792 | 6.399 | 6.044 | 5.723 | 5.432 | 5.167 | 4.925 |
| 24 | 8.348 | 7.784 | 7.283 | 6.835 | 6.434 | 6.073 | 5.747 | 5.451 | 5.182 | 4.937 |
| 25 | 8.442 | 7.843 | 7.330 | 6.873 | 6.464 | 6.097 | 5.766 | 5.467 | 5.195 | 4.948 |
| 30 | 8.694 | 8.055 | 7.496 | 7.003 | 6.566 | 6.177 | 5.829 | 5.517 | 5.235 | 4.979 |
| 40 | 8.951 | 8.244 | 7.634 | 7.105 | 6.642 | 6.233 | 5.871 | 5.548 | 5.258 | 4.997 |
| 50 | 9.042 | 8.305 | 7.675 | 7.133 | 6.661 | 6.246 | 5.880 | 5.554 | 5.262 | 4.999 |

| n | 21% | 22% | 23% | 24% | 25% | 26% | 27% | 28% | 29% | 30% |
|---|---|---|---|---|---|---|---|---|---|---|
| 1 | .826 | .820 | .813 | .806 | .800 | .794 | .787 | .781 | .775 | .769 |
| 2 | 1.509 | 1.492 | 1.474 | 1.457 | 1.440 | 1.424 | 1.407 | 1.392 | 1.376 | 1.361 |
| 3 | 2.074 | 2.042 | 2.011 | 1.981 | 1.952 | 1.923 | 1.896 | 1.868 | 1.842 | 1.816 |
| 4 | 2.540 | 2.494 | 2.448 | 2.404 | 2.362 | 2.320 | 2.280 | 2.241 | 2.203 | 2.166 |
| 5 | 2.926 | 2.864 | 2.803 | 2.745 | 2.689 | 2.635 | 2.583 | 2.532 | 2.483 | 2.436 |
| 6 | 3.245 | 3.167 | 3.092 | 3.020 | 2.951 | 2.885 | 2.821 | 2.759 | 2.700 | 2.643 |
| 7 | 3.508 | 3.416 | 3.327 | 3.242 | 3.161 | 3.083 | 3.009 | 2.937 | 2.868 | 2.802 |
| 8 | 3.726 | 3.619 | 3.518 | 3.421 | 3.329 | 3.241 | 3.156 | 3.076 | 2.999 | 2.925 |
| 9 | 3.905 | 3.786 | 3.673 | 3.566 | 3.463 | 3.366 | 3.273 | 3.184 | 3.100 | 3.019 |
| 10 | 4.054 | 3.923 | 3.799 | 3.682 | 3.570 | 3.465 | 3.364 | 3.269 | 3.178 | 3.092 |
| 11 | 4.177 | 4.035 | 3.902 | 3.776 | 3.656 | 3.544 | 3.437 | 3.335 | 3.239 | 3.147 |
| 12 | 4.278 | 4.127 | 3.985 | 3.851 | 3.725 | 3.606 | 3.493 | 3.387 | 3.286 | 3.190 |
| 13 | 4.362 | 4.203 | 4.053 | 3.912 | 3.780 | 3.656 | 3.538 | 3.427 | 3.322 | 3.223 |
| 14 | 4.432 | 4.265 | 4.108 | 3.962 | 3.824 | 3.695 | 3.573 | 3.459 | 3.351 | 3.249 |
| 15 | 4.489 | 4.315 | 4.153 | 4.001 | 3.859 | 3.726 | 3.601 | 3.483 | 3.373 | 3.268 |
| 16 | 4.536 | 4.357 | 4.189 | 4.033 | 3.887 | 3.751 | 3.623 | 3.503 | 3.390 | 3.283 |
| 17 | 4.576 | 4.391 | 4.219 | 4.059 | 3.910 | 3.771 | 3.640 | 3.518 | 3.403 | 3.295 |
| 18 | 4.608 | 4.419 | 4.243 | 4.080 | 3.928 | 3.786 | 3.654 | 3.529 | 3.413 | 3.304 |
| 19 | 4.635 | 4.442 | 4.263 | 4.097 | 3.942 | 3.799 | 3.664 | 3.539 | 3.421 | 3.311 |
| 20 | 4.657 | 4.460 | 4.279 | 4.110 | 3.954 | 3.808 | 3.673 | 3.546 | 3.427 | 3.316 |
| 21 | 4.675 | 4.476 | 4.292 | 4.121 | 3.963 | 3.816 | 3.679 | 3.551 | 3.432 | 3.320 |
| 22 | 4.690 | 4.488 | 4.302 | 4.130 | 3.970 | 3.822 | 3.684 | 3.556 | 3.436 | 3.323 |
| 23 | 4.703 | 4.499 | 4.311 | 4.137 | 3.976 | 3.827 | 3.689 | 3.559 | 3.438 | 3.325 |
| 24 | 4.713 | 4.507 | 4.318 | 4.143 | 3.981 | 3.831 | 3.692 | 3.562 | 3.441 | 3.327 |
| 25 | 4.721 | 4.514 | 4.323 | 4.147 | 3.985 | 3.834 | 3.694 | 3.564 | 3.442 | 3.329 |
| 30 | 4.746 | 4.534 | 4.339 | 4.160 | 3.995 | 3.842 | 3.701 | 3.569 | 3.447 | 3.332 |
| 40 | 4.760 | 4.544 | 4.347 | 4.166 | 3.999 | 3.846 | 3.703 | 3.571 | 3.448 | 3.333 |
| 50 | 4.762 | 4.545 | 4.348 | 4.167 | 4.000 | 3.846 | 3.704 | 3.571 | 3.448 | 3.333 |

| n | 31% | 32% | 33% | 34% | 35% | 36% | 37% | 38% | 39% | 40% |
|---|---|---|---|---|---|---|---|---|---|---|
| 1 | .763 | .758 | .752 | .746 | .741 | .735 | .730 | .725 | .719 | .714 |
| 2 | 1.346 | 1.331 | 1.317 | 1.303 | 1.289 | 1.276 | 1.263 | 1.250 | 1.237 | 1.224 |
| 3 | 1.791 | 1.766 | 1.742 | 1.719 | 1.696 | 1.673 | 1.652 | 1.630 | 1.609 | 1.589 |
| 4 | 2.130 | 2.096 | 2.062 | 2.029 | 1.997 | 1.966 | 1.935 | 1.906 | 1.877 | 1.849 |
| 5 | 2.390 | 2.345 | 2.302 | 2.260 | 2.220 | 2.181 | 2.143 | 2.106 | 2.070 | 2.035 |
| 6 | 2.588 | 2.534 | 2.483 | 2.433 | 2.385 | 2.339 | 2.294 | 2.251 | 2.209 | 2.168 |
| 7 | 2.739 | 2.677 | 2.619 | 2.562 | 2.508 | 2.455 | 2.404 | 2.355 | 2.308 | 2.263 |
| 8 | 2.854 | 2.786 | 2.721 | 2.658 | 2.598 | 2.540 | 2.485 | 2.432 | 2.380 | 2.331 |
| 9 | 2.942 | 2.868 | 2.798 | 2.730 | 2.665 | 2.603 | 2.544 | 2.487 | 2.432 | 2.379 |
| 10 | 3.009 | 2.930 | 2.855 | 2.784 | 2.715 | 2.649 | 2.587 | 2.527 | 2.469 | 2.414 |
| 11 | 3.060 | 2.978 | 2.899 | 2.824 | 2.752 | 2.683 | 2.618 | 2.555 | 2.496 | 2.438 |
| 12 | 3.100 | 3.013 | 2.931 | 2.853 | 2.779 | 2.708 | 2.641 | 2.576 | 2.515 | 2.456 |
| 13 | 3.129 | 3.040 | 2.956 | 2.876 | 2.799 | 2.727 | 2.658 | 2.592 | 2.529 | 2.469 |
| 14 | 3.152 | 3.061 | 2.974 | 2.892 | 2.814 | 2.740 | 2.670 | 2.603 | 2.539 | 2.477 |
| 15 | 3.170 | 3.076 | 2.988 | 2.905 | 2.825 | 2.750 | 2.679 | 2.611 | 2.546 | 2.484 |
| 16 | 3.183 | 3.088 | 2.999 | 2.914 | 2.834 | 2.757 | 2.685 | 2.616 | 2.551 | 2.489 |
| 17 | 3.193 | 3.097 | 3.007 | 2.921 | 2.840 | 2.763 | 2.690 | 2.621 | 2.555 | 2.492 |
| 18 | 3.201 | 3.104 | 3.012 | 2.926 | 2.844 | 2.767 | 2.693 | 2.624 | 2.557 | 2.494 |
| 19 | 3.207 | 3.109 | 3.017 | 2.930 | 2.848 | 2.770 | 2.696 | 2.626 | 2.559 | 2.496 |
| 20 | 3.211 | 3.113 | 3.020 | 2.933 | 2.850 | 2.772 | 2.698 | 2.627 | 2.561 | 2.497 |
| 21 | 3.215 | 3.116 | 3.023 | 2.935 | 2.852 | 2.773 | 2.699 | 2.629 | 2.562 | 2.498 |
| 22 | 3.217 | 3.118 | 3.025 | 2.936 | 2.853 | 2.775 | 2.700 | 2.629 | 2.562 | 2.498 |
| 23 | 3.219 | 3.120 | 3.026 | 2.938 | 2.854 | 2.775 | 2.701 | 2.630 | 2.563 | 2.499 |
| 24 | 3.221 | 3.121 | 3.027 | 2.939 | 2.855 | 2.776 | 2.701 | 2.630 | 2.563 | 2.499 |
| 25 | 3.222 | 3.122 | 3.028 | 2.939 | 2.856 | 2.776 | 2.702 | 2.631 | 2.563 | 2.499 |
| 30 | 3.225 | 2.124 | 3.030 | 2.941 | 2.857 | 2.777 | 2.702 | 2.631 | 2.564 | 2.500 |
| 40 | 3.226 | 3.125 | 3.030 | 2.941 | 2.857 | 2.778 | 2.703 | 2.632 | 2.564 | 2.500 |
| 50 | 3.226 | 3.125 | 3.030 | 2.941 | 2.857 | 2.778 | 2.703 | 2.632 | 2.564 | 2.500 |

# Appendix E

## Monthly Installment Loan Tables ($1,000 loan with interest payments compounded monthly)

**Loan Maturity (in months)**

| Interest | 6 | 12 | 18 | 24 | 30 | 36 | 48 | 60 | 72 | 84 | 96 |
|---|---|---|---|---|---|---|---|---|---|---|---|
| 4.00% | 168.62 | 85.15 | 57.33 | 43.42 | 35.08 | 29.52 | 22.58 | 18.42 | 15.65 | 13.67 | 12.19 |
| 4.25% | 168.74 | 85.26 | 57.44 | 43.54 | 35.19 | 29.64 | 22.69 | 18.53 | 15.76 | 13.78 | 12.31 |
| 4.50% | 168.86 | 85.38 | 57.56 | 43.65 | 35.31 | 29.75 | 22.80 | 18.64 | 15.87 | 13.90 | 12.42 |
| 4.75% | 168.98 | 85.49 | 57.67 | 43.76 | 35.42 | 29.86 | 22.92 | 18.76 | 15.99 | 14.02 | 12.54 |
| 5.00% | 169.11 | 85.61 | 57.78 | 43.87 | 35.53 | 29.97 | 23.03 | 18.87 | 16.10 | 14.13 | 12.66 |
| 5.25% | 169.23 | 85.72 | 57.89 | 43.98 | 35.64 | 30.08 | 23.14 | 18.99 | 16.22 | 14.25 | 12.78 |
| 5.50% | 169.35 | 85.84 | 58.01 | 44.10 | 35.75 | 30.20 | 23.26 | 19.10 | 16.34 | 14.37 | 12.90 |
| 5.75% | 169.47 | 85.95 | 58.12 | 44.21 | 35.87 | 30.31 | 23.37 | 19.22 | 16.46 | 14.49 | 13.02 |
| 6.00% | 169.60 | 86.07 | 58.23 | 44.32 | 35.98 | 30.42 | 23.49 | 19.33 | 16.57 | 14.61 | 13.14 |
| 6.25% | 169.72 | 86.18 | 58.34 | 44.43 | 36.09 | 30.54 | 23.60 | 19.45 | 16.69 | 14.73 | 13.26 |
| 6.50% | 169.84 | 86.30 | 58.46 | 44.55 | 36.20 | 30.65 | 23.71 | 19.57 | 16.81 | 14.85 | 13.39 |
| 6.75% | 169.96 | 86.41 | 58.57 | 44.66 | 36.32 | 30.76 | 23.83 | 19.68 | 16.93 | 14.97 | 13.51 |
| 7.00% | 170.09 | 86.53 | 58.68 | 44.77 | 36.43 | 30.88 | 23.95 | 19.80 | 17.05 | 15.09 | 13.63 |
| 7.25% | 170.21 | 86.64 | 58.80 | 44.89 | 36.55 | 30.99 | 24.06 | 19.92 | 17.17 | 15.22 | 13.76 |
| 7.50% | 170.33 | 86.76 | 58.91 | 45.00 | 36.66 | 31.11 | 24.18 | 20.04 | 17.29 | 15.34 | 13.88 |
| 7.75% | 170.45 | 86.87 | 59.03 | 45.11 | 36.77 | 31.22 | 24.30 | 20.16 | 17.41 | 15.46 | 14.01 |
| 8.00% | 170.58 | 86.99 | 59.14 | 45.23 | 36.89 | 31.34 | 24.41 | 20.28 | 17.53 | 15.59 | 14.14 |
| 8.25% | 170.70 | 87.10 | 59.25 | 45.34 | 37.00 | 31.45 | 24.53 | 20.40 | 17.66 | 15.71 | 14.26 |
| 8.50% | 170.82 | 87.22 | 59.37 | 45.46 | 37.12 | 31.57 | 24.65 | 20.52 | 17.78 | 15.84 | 14.39 |
| 8.75% | 170.95 | 87.34 | 59.48 | 45.57 | 37.23 | 31.68 | 24.77 | 20.64 | 17.90 | 15.96 | 14.52 |
| 9.00% | 171.07 | 87.45 | 59.60 | 45.68 | 37.35 | 31.80 | 24.89 | 20.76 | 18.03 | 16.09 | 14.65 |
| 9.25% | 171.19 | 87.57 | 59.71 | 45.80 | 37.46 | 31.92 | 25.00 | 20.88 | 18.15 | 16.22 | 14.78 |
| 9.50% | 171.32 | 87.68 | 59.83 | 45.91 | 37.58 | 32.03 | 25.12 | 21.00 | 18.27 | 16.34 | 14.91 |
| 9.75% | 171.44 | 87.80 | 59.94 | 46.03 | 37.70 | 32.15 | 25.24 | 21.12 | 18.40 | 16.47 | 15.04 |
| 10.00% | 171.56 | 87.92 | 60.06 | 46.14 | 37.81 | 32.27 | 25.36 | 21.25 | 18.53 | 16.60 | 15.17 |
| 10.25% | 171.68 | 88.03 | 60.17 | 46.26 | 37.93 | 32.38 | 25.48 | 21.37 | 18.65 | 16.73 | 15.31 |
| 10.50% | 171.81 | 88.15 | 60.29 | 46.38 | 38.04 | 32.50 | 25.60 | 21.49 | 18.78 | 16.86 | 15.44 |
| 10.75% | 171.93 | 88.27 | 60.40 | 46.49 | 38.16 | 32.62 | 25.72 | 21.62 | 18.91 | 16.99 | 15.57 |
| 11.00% | 172.05 | 88.38 | 60.52 | 46.61 | 38.28 | 32.74 | 25.85 | 21.74 | 19.03 | 17.12 | 15.71 |
| 11.25% | 172.18 | 88.50 | 60.63 | 46.72 | 38.40 | 32.86 | 25.97 | 21.87 | 19.16 | 17.25 | 15.84 |
| 11.50% | 172.30 | 88.62 | 60.75 | 46.84 | 38.51 | 32.98 | 26.09 | 21.99 | 19.29 | 17.39 | 15.98 |
| 11.75% | 172.42 | 88.73 | 60.87 | 46.96 | 38.63 | 33.10 | 26.21 | 22.12 | 19.42 | 17.52 | 16.12 |
| 12.00% | 172.55 | 88.85 | 60.98 | 47.07 | 38.75 | 33.21 | 26.33 | 22.24 | 19.55 | 17.65 | 16.25 |
| 12.25% | 172.67 | 88.97 | 61.10 | 47.19 | 38.87 | 33.33 | 26.46 | 22.37 | 19.68 | 17.79 | 16.39 |
| 12.50% | 172.80 | 89.08 | 61.21 | 47.31 | 38.98 | 33.45 | 26.58 | 22.50 | 19.81 | 17.92 | 16.53 |
| 12.75% | 172.92 | 89.20 | 61.33 | 47.42 | 39.10 | 33.57 | 26.70 | 22.63 | 19.94 | 18.06 | 16.67 |
| 13.00% | 173.04 | 89.32 | 61.45 | 47.54 | 39.22 | 33.69 | 26.83 | 22.75 | 20.07 | 18.19 | 16.81 |
| 13.25% | 173.17 | 89.43 | 61.56 | 47.66 | 39.34 | 33.81 | 26.95 | 22.88 | 20.21 | 18.33 | 16.95 |
| 13.50% | 173.29 | 89.55 | 61.68 | 47.78 | 39.46 | 33.94 | 27.08 | 23.01 | 20.34 | 18.46 | 17.09 |
| 13.75% | 173.41 | 89.67 | 61.80 | 47.89 | 39.58 | 34.06 | 27.20 | 23.14 | 20.47 | 18.60 | 17.23 |
| 14.00% | 173.54 | 89.79 | 61.92 | 48.01 | 39.70 | 34.18 | 27.33 | 23.27 | 20.61 | 18.74 | 17.37 |
| 14.25% | 173.66 | 89.90 | 62.03 | 48.13 | 39.82 | 34.30 | 27.45 | 23.40 | 20.74 | 18.88 | 17.51 |
| 14.50% | 173.79 | 90.02 | 62.15 | 48.25 | 39.94 | 34.42 | 27.58 | 23.53 | 20.87 | 19.02 | 17.66 |

| Interest | 6 | 12 | 18 | 24 | 30 | 36 | 48 | 60 | 72 | 84 | 96 |
|----------|-----|-----|-----|-----|-----|-----|-----|-----|-----|-----|-----|
| 14.75% | 173.91 | 90.14 | 62.27 | 48.37 | 40.06 | 34.54 | 27.70 | 23.66 | 21.01 | 19.16 | 17.80 |
| 15.00% | 174.03 | 90.26 | 62.38 | 48.49 | 40.18 | 34.67 | 27.83 | 23.79 | 21.15 | 19.30 | 17.95 |
| 15.25% | 174.16 | 90.38 | 62.50 | 48.61 | 40.30 | 34.79 | 27.96 | 23.92 | 21.28 | 19.44 | 18.09 |
| 15.50% | 174.28 | 90.49 | 62.62 | 48.72 | 40.42 | 34.91 | 28.08 | 24.05 | 21.42 | 19.58 | 18.24 |
| 15.75% | 174.41 | 90.61 | 62.74 | 48.84 | 40.54 | 35.03 | 28.21 | 24.19 | 21.55 | 19.72 | 18.38 |
| 16.00% | 174.53 | 90.73 | 62.86 | 48.96 | 40.66 | 35.16 | 28.34 | 24.32 | 21.69 | 19.86 | 18.53 |
| 16.25% | 174.65 | 90.85 | 62.97 | 49.08 | 40.78 | 35.28 | 28.47 | 24.45 | 21.83 | 20.00 | 18.68 |
| 16.50% | 174.78 | 90.97 | 63.09 | 49.20 | 40.91 | 35.40 | 28.60 | 24.58 | 21.97 | 20.15 | 18.82 |
| 16.75% | 174.90 | 91.09 | 63.21 | 49.32 | 41.03 | 35.53 | 28.73 | 24.72 | 22.11 | 20.29 | 18.97 |
| 17.00% | 175.03 | 91.20 | 63.33 | 49.44 | 41.15 | 35.65 | 28.86 | 24.85 | 22.25 | 20.24 | 19.12 |
| 17.25% | 175.15 | 91.32 | 63.45 | 49.56 | 41.27 | 35.78 | 28.98 | 24.99 | 22.39 | 20.58 | 19.27 |
| 17.50% | 175.28 | 91.44 | 63.57 | 49.68 | 41.39 | 35.90 | 29.11 | 25.12 | 22.53 | 20.73 | 19.42 |
| 17.75% | 175.40 | 91.56 | 63.69 | 49.80 | 41.52 | 36.03 | 29.24 | 25.26 | 22.67 | 20.87 | 19.57 |
| 18.00% | 175.53 | 91.68 | 63.81 | 49.92 | 41.64 | 36.15 | 29.37 | 25.39 | 22.81 | 21.02 | 19.72 |
| 18.25% | 175.65 | 91.80 | 63.93 | 50.04 | 41.76 | 36.28 | 29.51 | 25.53 | 22.95 | 21.16 | 19.88 |
| 18.50% | 175.77 | 91.92 | 64.04 | 50.17 | 41.89 | 36.40 | 29.64 | 25.67 | 23.09 | 21.31 | 20.03 |
| 18.75% | 175.90 | 92.04 | 64.16 | 50.29 | 42.01 | 36.53 | 29.77 | 25.80 | 23.23 | 21.46 | 20.18 |
| 19.00% | 176.02 | 92.16 | 64.28 | 50.41 | 42.13 | 36.66 | 29.90 | 25.94 | 23.38 | 21.61 | 20.33 |
| 19.25% | 176.15 | 92.28 | 64.40 | 50.53 | 42.26 | 36.78 | 30.03 | 26.08 | 23.52 | 21.76 | 20.49 |
| 19.50% | 176.27 | 92.40 | 64.52 | 50.65 | 42.38 | 36.91 | 30.16 | 26.22 | 23.66 | 21.91 | 20.64 |
| 19.75% | 176.40 | 92.51 | 64.64 | 50.77 | 42.51 | 37.04 | 30.30 | 26.35 | 23.81 | 22.06 | 20.80 |
| 20.00% | 176.52 | 92.63 | 64.76 | 50.90 | 42.63 | 37.16 | 30.43 | 26.49 | 23.95 | 22.21 | 20.95 |
| 20.25% | 176.65 | 92.75 | 64.88 | 51.02 | 42.75 | 37.29 | 30.56 | 26.63 | 24.10 | 22.36 | 21.11 |
| 20.50% | 176.77 | 92.87 | 65.00 | 51.14 | 42.88 | 37.42 | 30.70 | 26.77 | 24.24 | 22.51 | 21.27 |
| 20.75% | 176.90 | 92.99 | 65.12 | 51.26 | 43.00 | 37.55 | 30.83 | 26.91 | 24.39 | 22.66 | 21.42 |
| 21.00% | 177.02 | 93.11 | 65.24 | 51.39 | 43.13 | 37.68 | 30.97 | 27.05 | 24.54 | 22.81 | 21.58 |
| 21.25% | 177.15 | 93.23 | 65.37 | 51.51 | 43.26 | 37.80 | 31.10 | 27.19 | 24.68 | 22.96 | 21.74 |
| 21.50% | 177.27 | 93.35 | 65.49 | 51.63 | 43.38 | 37.93 | 31.24 | 27.34 | 24.83 | 23.12 | 21.90 |
| 21.75% | 177.40 | 93.47 | 65.61 | 51.75 | 43.51 | 38.06 | 31.37 | 27.48 | 24.98 | 23.27 | 22.06 |
| 22.00% | 177.52 | 93.59 | 65.73 | 51.88 | 43.63 | 38.19 | 31.51 | 27.62 | 25.13 | 23.43 | 22.22 |
| 22.25% | 177.65 | 93.71 | 65.85 | 52.00 | 43.76 | 38.32 | 31.64 | 27.76 | 25.27 | 23.58 | 22.38 |
| 22.50% | 177.77 | 93.84 | 65.97 | 52.13 | 43.89 | 38.45 | 31.78 | 27.90 | 25.42 | 23.74 | 22.54 |
| 22.75% | 177.90 | 93.96 | 66.09 | 52.25 | 44.01 | 38.58 | 31.91 | 28.05 | 25.57 | 23.89 | 22.70 |
| 23.00% | 178.02 | 94.08 | 66.21 | 52.37 | 44.14 | 38.71 | 32.05 | 28.19 | 25.72 | 24.05 | 22.86 |
| 23.25% | 178.15 | 94.20 | 66.34 | 52.50 | 44.27 | 38.84 | 32.19 | 28.33 | 25.87 | 24.20 | 23.02 |
| 23.50% | 178.27 | 94.32 | 66.46 | 52.62 | 44.39 | 38.97 | 32.33 | 28.48 | 26.02 | 24.36 | 23.19 |
| 23.75% | 178.40 | 94.44 | 66.58 | 52.75 | 44.52 | 39.10 | 32.46 | 28.62 | 26.18 | 24.52 | 23.35 |
| 24.00% | 178.53 | 94.56 | 66.70 | 52.87 | 44.65 | 39.23 | 32.60 | 28.77 | 26.33 | 24.68 | 23.51 |
| 24.25% | 178.65 | 94.68 | 66.82 | 53.00 | 44.78 | 39.36 | 32.74 | 28.91 | 26.48 | 24.83 | 23.68 |
| 24.50% | 178.78 | 94.80 | 66.95 | 53.12 | 44.91 | 39.50 | 32.88 | 29.06 | 26.63 | 24.99 | 23.84 |
| 24.75% | 178.90 | 94.92 | 67.07 | 53.25 | 45.03 | 39.63 | 33.02 | 29.20 | 26.78 | 25.15 | 24.01 |
| 25.00% | 179.03 | 95.04 | 67.19 | 53.37 | 45.16 | 39.76 | 33.16 | 29.35 | 26.94 | 25.31 | 24.17 |

# Index

*Note: Boldface page numbers indicate first use of key terms.*